Nouveau Tech Secret Society

The
Nouveau Tech Package
of
Inside Secrets

Mark Hamilton
Tracy Alexander
& Eric Savage
Frank R. Wallace

NEO-TECH BOOKS

Published by Integrated Management Associates
850 S. Boulder Highway, Henderson, Nevada 89015, U.S.A.

First published in the United States of America by
Integrated Management Associates

8   10   9   7

LIBRARY OF CONGRESS
CATALOGING-IN-PUBLICATION DATA
Hamilton, Alexander, Savage, Wallace
The Nouveau Tech Package of Inside Secrets
ISBN 0-911752-93-5

Printed in the United States of America
January 2005 [CL-NTPIS] [51,400]
September 2005 [CL-NTPIS] [51,600]
November 2005 [CL-NTPIS] [51,332]
April 2006 [CL-NTPIS] [50,000]
February 2007 [PP-NTPIS] [5,000]
April 2007 [PP-NTPIS] [5,000]
May 2007 [PP-NTPIS] [10,000]

Table of Contents

Orientation
v

The Nouveau Tech Package
of
Inside Secrets

Orientation

A great pleasure of mine is to welcome new Nouveau Tech members. An exciting journey awaits you. In your hands you hold your Nouveau Tech Package of Inside Secrets. It consists of three combined Packages of Secrets: 1) the 315-page *Neo-Tech System,* 2) the 140-page *Neo-Tech Epiphany,* and 3) the 556-page *Neo-Tech Discovery.*

Begin with the first Nouveau Tech Package of Secrets — *The Neo-Tech System.* That package contains the secrets to generating money that Nouveau Tech members have secretly used and passed on to their children for generations. You can start using those exciting secrets for generating wealth as soon as tomorrow morning. Read all the secrets all the way through the Neo-Tech System first, before starting on the second and third Nouveau Tech Packages of Secrets — *The Neo-Tech Epiphany* and *The Neo-Tech Discovery.*

The Neo-Tech Epiphany and Discovery contain the secrets to personal power, which includes romantic love. Those are the secrets to power and love Nouveau Tech members have secretly used and passed on to their children through secret societies for generations.

Once you learn those secrets, you will suddenly detect many of the most successful and famous people using those same secrets. You will be amazed at who some of those people are! But they will never reveal their power to others; they will never tell others they use these highly guarded secrets. Once you know the secrets, however, it will become obvious to you others who are using them. Likewise, they will know you are using the secrets. Although not a word is spoken, you will both know you belong to the same, secret society.

In fact, soon you will be invited to your first of many Nouveau Tech Secret Society meetings where you will meet other members living the privileged life of successful living. You will benefit enormously upon meeting those fellow members. In a few days, you will receive a letter from us informing you of your first meeting. As a member, these enormously benefiting, closed meetings will be available to you and your direct family. Indeed, your children and grandchildren will attend when they grow up, for the meetings will multiply their success, wealth, and happiness throughout their lives. The same will apply to their children, and their children. The Nouveau Tech Society regularly ignites powerful, successful family dynasties. The Nouveau Tech Society is, in fact, the exclusive society of powerful, wealthy dynasties. Your family dynasty starts with you at your first meeting.

But for now, get into your Nouveau Tech Package of Inside Secrets. Go straight through the first package of secrets, the Neo-Tech System. I stress: we want you to go through that entire package first, while you are still experiencing the Cycle Two phase of your life. Please follow this instruction. *After* you absorb the wealth-generating secrets in the Neo-Tech System, then and only then graduate to the deeper and broader secrets of the Neo-Tech Epiphany and Discovery. Only there can you break bondage to discover the real power in life.

Remember, as you read through the three combined packages, you will absorb secrets hidden from this world for 2300 years...secrets that have evolved in secret societies for over a hundred generations, secrets that powerful and famous people use for all their wealth, personal power, and love. Even if you do not understand all of the secrets just now, especially as you get into the third package, you will still absorb those secrets just by reading them. The power of the secrets will automatically pass into you and will steadily release your human potential as time passes. You will feel your power and presence grow week by week. Imagine what it is like to become unbeatable.

As a new Nouveau Tech member, you will soon receive other free information, including information about the members-only, free secret-society meetings, information about sharing in our abundance of wealth, information about an alliance among our family dynasties to keep the wealth within our society; we will send you information about closed-door summits, social activities, romantic love, art, entertainment, health, and anti-aging breakthroughs available only to members.

To build the strength of our hundred-generation society, we

will from time to time release one of our breakthroughs to the public for "mass consumption." When we do such a public release, that one, lone breakthrough moves the parallel society — the society of the masses — to the next level of mankind's development. At one point in the next five to ten years, we plan to cause mankind's next evolutionary leap, which you will learn about soon. Of course, we keep the majority of our breakthroughs within the Nouveau Tech Secret Society for ourselves, for our members and our families.

You truly have entered a new world — the world of the planet's most successful people. Over time, as you integrate with other ultra-successful members, you will take huge financial and personal leaps. You will share in our wealth. Moreover, you will be in the priceless Secret Society meetings for life. And so will your children and their children. Your dynasty begins with you, soon, at your first meeting. (There is currently no charge to you to attend the amazing meetings, which is guaranteed for at least a full year.) Keep an eye out for your next letter in the next few days informing you of the Nouveau Tech Secret Society meetings, which are now absolutely free to members. It is both *who you know* and *what you know* that will send you soaring in our exclusive parallel society.

So, turn now into your Neo-Tech System and brace yourself for what is about to come your way. Remember, you are among a handful of individuals selected from around the world to receive this knowledge. ...Your journey has just begun. It is a journey of discovering that elusive *something more to life*. It is a journey of discovering the life *you were meant to live!*

Remember, everyone who is really prospering in a big way has tapped into these exact same secrets and meetings. Now, you will know. Finally, you will know the secrets of the powerful. But you must be open-minded to accept these secrets. And we know you are. That is why we contacted you in the first place after careful screening. You have a strong mind and are among the best qualified to make the necessary adjustments to soar with Neo-Tech. Now, you will end up on top.

Hold on now, for your life is about to change, forever! And that change for the better will continue to get bigger and better in the coming months as you continue to receive further communications from us. In fact, your launching pad will come with your first meeting with your fellow members. ...We will write you in the next few days about that meeting.

First Package of Secrets

The Neo-Tech System

Break Through
To
Financial Security!

How To Fend for Yourself
in the age of
Sudden and Unpredictable Job Losses

The
NEO-TECH
SYSTEM

Mark Hamilton

NEO-TECH BOOKS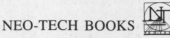

Published by Integrated Management Associates
850 S. Boulder Highway, Henderson, Nevada 89015, U.S.A.

First published in the United States of America by
Integrated Management Associates

8 10 11 9 7

LIBRARY OF CONGRESS
CATALOGING-IN-PUBLICATION DATA
Hamilton, Mark
The Neo-Tech System

791112108
ISBN # 911752-60-9
Library of Congress #89-85937
Printed in the United States of America

Original Edition
1985-2004 over 100,000 copies sold [NTCBC: TNTS]

New Edition
1st Printing March 2004 [DPS-TNTS] [10,000]
2nd Printing November 2004 [PP-TNTS] [5,500]
3rd Printing January 2005 [CL-NTPIS] [51,400]
4th Printing September 2005 [CL-NTPIS] [51,600]
5th Printing November 2005 [CL-NTPIS] [51,332]
6th Printing April 2006 [CL-NTPIS] [50,000]
7th Printing February 2007 [PP-NTPIS] [5,000]

Table of Contents

The Neo-Tech System
STOOD the TEST of TIME
Little-Known Money-Making System from the '80s
Comes Roaring Forth in the 21st Century as
The Little Guy's Answer to Sudden-Job-Loss
>your<
Immunization, Inoculation, Antidote
To America's Great Job Exodus
Giant Corporate Collapses
Job-Depleting Mergers
Sudden Job Losses
>|<

The Discovery

TWENTY-YEAR-OLD TREASURE UNEARTHED

After spending his entire working life in one giant corporation and investing most of his retirement in stock options, my brother-in-law is suddenly jobless and his retirement money is gone. He has four little girls and a new house. What will happen to him and his family?

Your job and investments are also in jeopardy. Giant corporations go down overnight; common stock values plummet to zero; tens of thousands of long-time employees unexpectedly find themselves jobless and broke. And that sudden-job-loss syndrome is hitting too close to home — if not right in your home.

Ordinary people such as my brother-in-law, such as you and I, need a way to fend for ourselves in this age of giant corporate collapses and job-depleting mergers. Yet, perhaps even more ominous: our skilled and managerial jobs are steadily going abroad.

You need protection. I have uncovered the answer.

I was reading through a very large body of literature called *Neo-Tech*, over 7000 pages long, when I came upon the following 315-page gem buried right in the middle of it all.

I had never seen anything like it, and although I hate using a cliché to describe how I felt, in this case the cliché precisely fits: It was like finding a hidden treasure.

I read page after page, discovery after discovery, pulling out precious jewel after precious jewel. Transfixed by my treasure, I read the entire 315 pages in one sitting.

These pages contain a spectacular system to manufacturing wealth and success. And I mean it when I say these jewels have rarely been seen before. They have been buried in the expanse of Neo-Tech for twenty years.

The Neo-Tech literature itself has evolved in the Nouveau Tech Society over the past four decades, unveiling a new way of living called Neo-Tech and a new way of thinking called *Neothink*.

Neo-Tech, I must say, is powerful and moving knowledge. As with large bodies of literature, however, only a relatively

v

small number of prolific readers have ever studied Neo-Tech as I have.

Buried in Neo-Tech were the following 315 pages of the Neo-Tech/Neothink treatment to manufacturing money and success. Reading through the chapters of the Neo-Tech money-making system was like picking up big, perfect diamonds during my journey through Neo-Tech. Chills ran down the back of my neck at least once during every chapter. I knew I had found something very special. So, I contacted the Neo-Tech Research Center to let them know how I felt. I talked to the Neo-Tech staff about this money/power treasure buried within their 7000 pages of Neo-Tech. I told them the ordinary person would never need to fear failure again.

I found out that the 315 pages of money/power diamonds were developed throughout the decade of the '80s by a Neo-Tech millionaire named Mark Hamilton. He started writing the Neo-Tech System as a young man with no savings, while living paycheck to paycheck. He finished writing the Neo-Tech System as a wealthy man.

Today, in his forties, he is wealthy and is living in a 20,000-square-foot multi-million-dollar mansion among the rich and famous.

His money/power diamonds, now in your hands, had my head spinning with their illuminative rays of new techniques. Those techniques allow Average Joes like me to reach the big time all by myself! Moreover, I am now immune to giant corporate collapses, job-depleting mergers, and America's job exodus. No one overseas can replace my job, for the creativity generated from Neothink makes my livelihood unique. Competition becomes obsolete. I have never felt so secure. I have never been so rich.

I told the Neo-Tech staff that the Neo-Tech money-making system was like a buried treasure that had been hidden from the world for far too long, for two whole decades! The need for it *now* was just too great in this age of sudden and unpredictable job losses. If we could just pluck the Neo-Tech System from the many volumes of Neo-Tech, I told the staff, then the 315-page Neo-Tech System would be a best seller. I repeated: *never have so many people needed this information than right now!*

Never mind that it was written in the '80s, for it is timeless. Nearly everyone, I told the Neo-Tech staff, would want to read this ingenious information that gets down to the money/power atom — the only way to build power and wealth for the little guy!

The Neo-Tech Research Center, curator of these secrets, was very reluctant, to say the least, to pull these 315 pages from the Neo-Tech body of literature. Moreover, they wanted nothing to do with the big publishers. But they did, thank goodness, move the Neo-Tech System right up front so you can enjoy the benefits immediately.

Now, I must tell you here, I am very persistent. I know how mind-blowing the Neo-Tech money-making system is for me. It is downright wrong, in my opinion, to hold this information back. Too many people out there desperately need it. Especially now. I told Neo-Tech exactly how I felt. They are still looking into my plea, as a Nouveau Tech member, to someday release this Neo-Tech System to the whole world. Every now and then, the Secret Society will do something like that.

Believe me, you have never seen anything so powerful and real for the little guy. The Neo-Tech System that follows shows the little guy exactly how to generate wealth. And in this day and age of Enrons and WorldComs and American jobs going abroad, the little guy needs to be able to fend for himself.

With these money/power diamonds inside the palm of your hand, you will, as I did, discover wealth beyond your wildest imagination. No best-selling self-improvement book even comes close. I've read them all. This discovery is in a class of its own; it is the best thing that's ever happened to me. I'm now a millionaire. You can be, too.

To keep the perfect diamonds untouched by editors, the Neo-Tech Center did not edit the following 315 pages. The techniques and concepts are timeless. The references throughout the money/power system are from the 1980s, but the Neo-Tech Center left those references untouched because they give the truest feel for when and where these classic techniques arose.

Several authors have been developing the Neo-Tech way-of-life for over four decades. Spread across 7000 pages, the authors in the Neo-Tech literature usually refer to themselves in the third person throughout their Neo-Tech contributions in order to prevent confusion of who is "talking". For instance, throughout the Neo-Tech System that follows, the author Mark Hamilton refers to himself in the third person, not in the first person. Instead of saying, "I did this," the text reads, "Mr. Hamilton did this."

The following 315-page Neo-Tech money-making system, nestled within over 7000 pages of Neo-Tech literature, appeared before my eyes after I had read about three-thousand pages of Neo-Tech by different authors. Therefore, let me catch you up on some key words and background you need to most easily read through this money-making system.

Here are five expressions you need to familiarize yourself with:

1. The White-Collar Hoax
2. The Bicameral Mentality
3. Mysticism
4. The Neothink Mentality
5. Neo-Tech

1. The White-Collar Hoax: Two decades after Mark Hamilton was the first to identify the White-Collar Hoax, it is now easy to see and understand because of the recent Enron, Global Crossings, WorldCom and other large corporate collapses due to executive dishonesties. Back in the 1980s, when Mark Hamilton detected and wrote about the White-Collar Hoax, no one knew what it was. Now, just about everyone has been rudely awakened. In the '80s, Mark Hamilton prophetically said, "After 2001, everyone will know about the White-Collar Hoax."

2. The Bicameral Mentality: The Bicameral Age lasted from 10,000 to 3000 years ago. Bicameral man automatically reacted to the world around him. He did not have the inner mind space we have today that allows us to think and make decisions, which is known as human consciousness. As in all animals, he was guided via nature's automatic guidance system. His two-chamber (i.e., bicameral) brain was so much larger than the other animals, however, he evolved a primitive language. Nature's guidance

system actually incorporated his language to better guide bicameral man. In other words, instead of guiding him through strong mental impressions that caused the body to react as with other animals, man's large bicameral mind actually "spoke" those impressions. The impressions were far clearer, far more effective as spoken words "of the gods". Those messages were actually audio hallucinations caused by neurological impulses set off in his right-chamber brain. Bicameral man was guided through the "commands" of his personal "god". Bicameral civilizations were guided by their God-Kings and oracles who "heard" the higher gods and, in turn, gave direction to the entire civilization.

Physically speaking, our brain today is identical to the bicameral brain 3000 years ago. But the inner mind space that allows us to think and make decisions known as *human consciousness* did not open up until the sophistication of man's developing language. To make a long story short, about 3000 years ago, bicameral man's language evolved the metaphor, which uses something to describe something else. That sophisticated linguistic tool — the metaphor — enabled bicameral man to separate from the world around him, unlike any other animal. With the metaphor, he was able to increasingly step back and view the world subjectively, think about it, introspect, and eventually make decisions. Instead of automatically following a "voice", he was now able to think and guide himself. As the inner mind space known as human consciousness opened up within man, he no longer needed external guidance from the voices of the "gods", God-Kings, or oracles. He only needed *to think*.

Today, we are still plagued by our deep-rooted bicameral roots. We still seek the voices from leaders, whether that be in politics, religions, or from management at work. We still seek external guidance. But that following mode traps us in ineffectual, stagnant jobs...just following a set routine at work. The Neo-Tech System teaches you how to permanently end your impotent following mode to break free from your stagnation-trap. The Neo-Tech System teaches you how to permanently enter the potent self-guiding mode in which you integrate knowledge to build and create wealth.

3. Mysticism: Mysticism is the mental condition that seeks guidance and answers from external authority. Mysticism first occurred 10,000 years ago in primitive man as an attempt to explain death. Mysticism was rampant in the bicameral mentality as man tried to evoke the voices of the gods for guidance. Bicameral man routinely performed mystical rituals to evoke the gods. For example, bicameral man continually built mystical awe-inspiring statues, tombs, pyramids, colossuses to evoke the voices of the gods. The American Indians were bicameral when the first European explorers arrived. Mysticism was part of the Indians' survival mechanism, seeking guidance from the gods of nature. Although mysticism rose from the primitive mind, mysticism still resides in our minds today. We seek guidance from others within our jobs, religions, governments. We seek easy, automatic answers to life's challenges. The mysticism in our minds is unnecessary; it is merely residual from the primitive mind and blocks us from integrating knowledge to guide ourselves.

4. The Neothink Mentality: The Neothink mentality is simply our mental state when we rid the residual mysticism from our minds. The Neothink mind has awesome power as it gains the ability to go beyond the capacity of today's conscious mind by freely integrating knowledge to guide itself. The integrating (as opposed to following) Neothink mind easily snaps together knowledge like puzzle pieces into growing puzzles that reveal puzzle pictures that even the smartest minds today could never conceive. Those spectacular Neothink puzzles, now possible by ordinary people through the Neo-Tech System, go well beyond the capacity of even the smartest minds by taking a mentally manageable, maximum-integration unit of the mind and then integrating it with or snapping it together with yet another maximum-integration unit of knowledge, one after the other. The smaller, mentally manageable units of knowledge integrate together like puzzle pieces into a larger and larger, perfectly integrated unit to form a super unit — a Neothink puzzle. The Neothink puzzle goes well beyond the capacity of the mind through using special tools delivered in the following Neo-Tech System. The Neo-Tech System that follows is, in itself, an

example of a Neothink puzzle revealing a never-before-seen puzzle picture — the division of essence — in which the *ordinary* person generates power and wealth. Indeed, the outcome of building these puzzle pictures is the creation of new knowledge; the ordinary person becomes creative; creativity begets wealth.

5. Neo-Tech: Neo-Tech (new techniques/new technology) delivers an entirely new way of living that has been formally developing since the mid-1960s within the Nouveau Tech Society. When you read Neo-Tech's money-making system called The Neo-Tech System that follows, you will see that through Neothink, Neo-Tech breaks through boundaries. Whatever Neo-Tech touches, from making money as in this publication to making love as in the body of the Neo-Tech library, you become the most effective that man can become. You leap beyond your peers. Through the use of Neothink, Neo-Tech breaks through boundaries into never-before-seen puzzle pictures of life. Making money or making love, you simply become the best.

With those five expressions in your realm of awareness, you are set to take an exhilarating journey of self-discovery. That journey will unleash your human potential that has always been bound up inside you. ...You are about to discover my words here are not just words. You are about to discover how real my words are and how much money-making power you possess. I am excited for you.

Original Word From The Author
(Written in 1984)

RAPID POWER AND WEALTH
through
IRON-GRIP CONTROL
of
EVERYTHING THAT MOVES

You need control. You need control to gain genuine power, honest wealth, abiding happiness. Pressured as you may be, you do not need vacations; you do not need to learn to relax; you do not need therapy or psychologists; you do not need positive thinking, inspirational management or search of excellence books. You need control. No matter what the wimps say, you need iron-grip control over everything, now.

In your hands is a turnkey manual for establishing immediate, iron-grip control over money, life, business, and everything you manage. Such control has never before been converted into a practical, quick-action tool. Any person can quickly learn Neo-Tech Control to dominate all management, business, or personal situations. And that kind of domination will always yield rapid wealth and power.

Half way through this manual you will have received more honest, permanent values than anything you have previously experienced. On completing this manual, you will be well launched toward rapid power and wealth.

Recent Word From The Author
(Written in 2004)

As I developed the Neo-Tech System in the 1980s, I knew the division of essence was the next evolution of business. I knew the division of essence would become the business structure of the 21st century, but not until then. Not until the pressure was on *to think* instead of *to follow* would things change. And now, the pressure is on.

Reading through *The Neo-Tech System* so many years after I wrote it was quite an experience. When the fundamental nature of something is identified, it does not change. *The Neo-Tech System* identifies the fundamental natures of business (i.e., integration) and man (i.e., thinking). When properly brought together, they bring on something so synergistic (i.e., integrated thinking) that the *ordinary* person experiences success and wealth.

Reading this two decades after I developed it, nothing changes, for the fundamental nature of something cannot be deduced. Underneath all the propaganda about success, this is *the key*. At the risk of sounding biased, I must now say as one who has personally done it, the Neo-Tech System is the most valuable information for success you will ever read.

Let me make one further point here about the fundamental nature of something. All the colors in the world reduce to three primary colors, yet the world is filled with colors — endless colorful hues. All the novels in the world reduce to a handful of fundamental plots, yet the libraries and bookstores are filled with novels — endless storybook variations.

Similarly, all the businesses in the world reduce to their two fundamentals (integration and integrated thinking), yet this book is filled with many hues and variations of integration and integrated thinking. Those hues and variations of integrated thinking are going to send you along the fast lane to rapid power and wealth.

Volume One

The
Self-Capture Discovery

Chapter One

DEMYSTIFYING MONEY AND POWER

For 4000 years, the masses from ancient Phoenician commerce to modern America have sought to understand those few individuals holding great power and wealth. The wealthier, more powerful an individual, the more attention focuses on trying to understand his success. In fact, attention expands geometrically on ascending the power scale to the presidents of America's greatest corporations. Yet, a consistent, reliable standard for understanding power and wealth has until now remained a riddle.

That riddle is solved by applying two metaphors:

(1) Knowing the material world around us requires understanding the smallest atomic units.

And

(2) Knowing the cosmos above us requires understanding its primordial origins.

Now apply that to money and power:

(1) Knowing wealth around us requires understanding the smallest money-producing units.

And

(2) Knowing the wealth and power above us requires understanding its primordial origins.

Understanding The Smallest Unit Of Money And Power
...Traveling To Great Wealth's Primordial Origins

The understanding begins by shrinking money and power far below the great concentrations of corporate structures — shrinking away from the plush offices of the presidents, shrinking out of the complex office buildings, out into the streets. By putting a microscope on the raw enterprise structure in the streets, one can focus beneath its few simple layers of money and power. One can focus beneath the factories, past the department stores and fast-food chains down to the simple array of street vendors. And finally, one can reduce the street vendor's microcosm of money and power down to the smallest and simplest money-producing unit — the self-owned, one-man, one-cart business. From those beginnings, from that entrepreneurial atom emerges the understanding, the indisputable core of anyone producing money and power — from a candy vendor on the streets of New York to the presidents of corporate America fifty stories above.

Let us focus on the nature of making money by putting a microscope on the smallest, simplest money-making unit — the one-man, one-cart business. Once in focus, we can see that to make money, the small one-man business requires deceivingly complex integrations.

The street vendor selling his homemade candy creation, for instance, must develop and then produce the candy, must purchase the equipment and supplies, must attend to maintenance of his equipment, must keep track of the money, account for profit or loss, provide the service with his push cart, handle operations of inventory and sales, advertise (yell), market his product by determining best places and times to sell, innovate and be creative perhaps through appetite-inducing designs on his cart or through special fans designed to blow the sweet aroma in the faces of passersby, and, of course, he must apply his crude form of research and development in order to continually discourage or beat competition.

To make big money, to grow into a mighty empire as did Milton Hershey, the entrepreneur cannot be just a secret ingredient developer, just a money-wise accountant, just a shrewd negotiator, just a tip-top service man, just a marketing expert. He must be everything needed to gain power and wealth.

As his business grows and brings in more money, workers, products, and markets, the need to integrate grows. To become wealthy and powerful, he must successfully integrate everything into smooth control from the cleanliness of his workers' carts to the distribution system of his candy to the secret ingredient of his chocolate. He must successfully integrate everything into that magical combination that makes a few dynamic men go down in history as money/power giants.

Smashing The Myths

No great wealth creator became successful from academic management books, positive-thinking, or self-improvement courses. Those books and courses offer inspiration, not integration. Their authors do not know business; they do not have the slightest idea about business. They are writers or professors and not successful businessmen. They observe money/power giants and write down what sounds good, but as writers they simply do not have the integrated range of knowledge or experience to pull together all dimensions into a single money/power tool.

Only through hard, personal experience did the money/power giants learn the many subtle integrations within their careers. They know that making money comes from integration, not inspiration. Like them, you need a fully integrated approach, not a number of nonintegrated techniques plucked arbitrarily from idolized leading companies and flocked together for a so-called management approach. Plucking those techniques or "lessons" out of their unique, highly integrated structures (that in many cases developed and matured over several career lifetimes) leaves those techniques out of context and dangerously misleading. The glib thick and thin best-sellers cause failure.

Most authors of popular search-of-excellence, instant manager, positive-thinking management books as well as self-improvement and success books do not have the integrated range of knowledge or direct experience to really understand business. They did not work year after year, grinding out detail after detail, building profit structure after profit structure in running a major company or in building a fast growing company. They never exposed themselves to the hard, honest thought and grueling effort of business. Yet they glibly present authoritative slogans and scenarios on how to succeed.

By zooming in on the almost magical success scenarios of America's best-run companies — conveniently missing the whole point and only point to the companies' success: the years of grinding out the right integrations — these authors provide only a fun-to-read romanticized view of business. Their romanticized formulas to success became an especially attractive item to the

American people, for all of us like fast success through easy-sounding approaches. But the romanticized approach, regardless of lip service to hard work, is artificial and impotent.

Moreover, the leading companies admired in the excellence books offer little value to the reader. Reading about even the most successful business program without knowing its many integrations will no more make someone successful as watching *Lifestyles Of The Rich And Famous* will make someone a celebrity.

For example, *In Search Of Excellence* glamorizes IBM's star feature (customer service) while being unknowledgeable about almost everything else that makes IBM successful. Such a book leaves people more naive than ever about business. In reality, business is a powerful, complex matrix with many, many integrations. ...By comparison, a book on how to produce a successful movie would falsely mislead the reader if it simply glamorized the need for star actors "like those used by America's best-run movie studios" and ignored the hundreds of behind-the-scenes efforts that need to be integrated from special effects to production, financing, backing, script writing, directing, filming, editing, distributing, marketing.

Indeed, customer service is an **effect**, not a cause. *In Search Of Excellence* implies: IBM has a good customer service program, therefore IBM is successful. But that logic inverts the cause and effect. Instead, IBM is well integrated, therefore IBM is successful and has a good customer service program. Customer service is just a fraction of IBM's success story. The average person perhaps senses that he can handle well this smaller fraction of business — customer service. "I can do that," he reasons, "I am really good with people; I can do that." Being misled with a false sense of confidence, he then starts a business.

For a brief high, boosted by excellence-type wishful thinking, he believes that his business will succeed and his invested savings will parlay into a fortune as long as he handles well this small fraction of business (customer service) and keeps a good, positive attitude — easily within his ability. But like the candy vendor, he cannot be just a good customer service man. He must be everything needed to gain power and wealth. He soon fails as he cannot handle the much larger, real scope of business. He loses everything.

An IBM-excellent customer service program will not make a business succeed. Moreover, an IBM-excellent customer service program will not necessarily make a customer service program succeed either. IBM's customer service program is deeply integrated by many unique, fully developed, interlocked activities and policies built over many years through hard-nosed, hard-effort business calculations. Indeed, every detail in business including the customer service details themselves involve so much more than a simple question: "To be IBM excellent or not to be IBM excellent?" Instead, the customer service details require integrated, ongoing, hard-nosed business decisions. No ready-made answer exists; no authority exists to follow. Only one's own integrated thinking and experience can help him. The customer service program and everything else in a business must develop through hard work from one's independent, growing business sense.

The excellence books offer appealing success scenarios to follow that let one believe he is being a good businessman when in reality he is avoiding the nitty-gritty effort required to be a good businessman. To take *In Search of Excellence* advice and automatically provide super IBM-like customer service makes bad business sense. For that enables one to not really dig into the tough details to discover the source of the problems and correct them. Indeed, the excellence books provide the stamp of approval to follow instead of to integrate.

IBM does not *just* satisfy the customer. IBM aggressively integrates more cost-effective business details to make its customer-service actions profitable. But the authors do not understand how to integrate those details. And integrating those details, nothing else, makes IBM and its customer service program a success.

Search-Of-Excellence books usurp respect and credibility by "representing" America's best-run companies. "Do like the leading companies and become a success." But the books are void of the comprehensive integrations that form the roots of all honest, successful companies. Those excellence books, falsely linked to magnificent companies, have become a Trojan horse welcomed by millions. An IBM-excellent customer service program as well as positive attitudes will not make one successful and could lead to disaster. Neo-Tech Control, on the other hand, first develops the **cause**, how to become well integrated, which delivers the lasting effect — success.

Of course, the fundamental problem blocking success resides within the average person himself: He unknowingly seeks automatic guidance, bicameral-like external guidance from the excellence-type management books. To the contrary, power in business comes not from following others, not even from following the leading companies today. For then, one is *following*. He is blocking the great integrating power in his mind. He is controlled by mysticism — seeking external guidance (explained in the front material of this book). But now, the average person can discover the Ultimate Weapon: eliminate his mysticism to discover the great integrating power of his mind that leads to rapid power and wealth.

The Fast-Track Ticket To Becoming Integrated

Let us clear away a white-collar-hoax myth: Acquiring wealth seems out of touch to the average person. Perhaps a genius invents something everyone wants; that's *one* gifted genius in perhaps millions of people. Thus, the ordinary person concludes wealth is out of his reach. He becomes complacent and settles into the white-collar-hoax system and stagnates. (The white-collar hoax is explained in the front material, page vi.)

To the contrary, wealth comes down to one, earthy fundamental: *integration*. And the fast-track ticket and only ticket to integration is...

REMOVING LIMITATIONS

Removing limitations in business tightens one's integrated control over business. Removing limitations boosts one's control to the next integrated level and then to the next integrated level and then to the next integrated level. Removing limitations is a down-to-earth, day-in-and-day-out discipline that everyone can do, EVERYONE.

To achieve even the highest level of monetary success — creating a new industry — requires the earthy act of removing limitations, NOT making a rare breakthrough per se. For example, the invention of the light bulb did not make Edison wealthy. During a time of highly efficient, wireless kerosine lamps, he had to build power plants, get wires to one's home, then inundate one's home with unsightly, and dangerous electrical wires. His day after day, year after year, methodical process of removing limitations to integrate a profitable business, marketing the unlikely electric light bulb, made Edison wealthy. And the invention of the car made no one wealthy. Instead, Henry Ford's day after day focus on removing production limitations moved Ford Motor Company bit by bit past competitors, past the slow hand-building process into the world's most integrated production method — the assembly-line. And then the methodical process of removing limitations, removing limitations and removing more limitations made the powerfully integrated assembly-line mighty. Indeed, the car industry, the lighting industry, the computer industry and all new industries came not from spectacular new inventions or discoveries per se but from a day-in-and-day-out grind to remove limitations. And that down-to-earth, day-in-and-day-out grind, can start right now, right in your job.

The Neo-Tech System removes limitations, starting small, starting with your day-by-day responsibilities and building until you remove the limitations in your mind that block your evolution into the Neothink mind capable of generating millions of dollars. Indeed, limitations both around you and within you block integration. The earthy process of removing limitations first delivers the physically integrated working format, then the physically/mentally integrated business structure, and eventually the mentally integrated thinking process (i.e., Neothink). Instead of following a set routine, you will be creating new wealth. In short, your integration with making money grows more and more potent as you remove physical and then mental limitations.

Now let us begin to remove those limitations to build the Neo-Tech/Neothink puzzle of wealth creation. The three grand puzzle parts to this puzzle are:

1) The Self-Capture Discovery
2) The Company-Capture Discovery
3) The World-Capture Discovery

The Neo-Tech System starts small with the Self-Capture Discovery to allow you to remove all current limitations in your day by day routine and thinking. By doing this, you begin to acquire an integrated power that takes you into the new experience of rapid forward movement.

Then the puzzle builds as the Company-Capture Discovery integrates you directly with making money. The Company-Capture Discovery removes most limitations of the white-collar hoax.

The puzzle grows mighty with the World-Capture Discovery. This discovery removes all limitations around you and within you (i.e., your personal mysticism) to enable your mind to go through a power-reactor explosion into the Neothink mind. And by evolving into the Neothink mind, you acquire the integrated strength to build a mighty worldwide empire.

Chapter Two
GATHERING CONTROL

Grand Puzzle Part Number One:
THE SELF-CAPTURE DISCOVERY

Harvey Firestone, founder of Firestone Tires, said that success comes from *hard thinking*. He explained that very few people even among the intelligent academe actually ever apply hard thinking. Hard thinking is diametrically opposite of automatic thinking in specialized jobs or externally guided thinking from management above. Hard thinking means moving beyond the deep-rooted bicameral mode, the nonthinking following mode, that subverts average people into stagnation traps — caught in money-making impotence...caught in specialized jobs, automatically doing set responsibilities handed down from management above. To the contrary, hard thinking means self-thinking from within: **integrated thinking** or wealth creation thinking.

Discover The Ultimate Working Format

Consider two opposing management styles: The first manager *reacts* to the work before him. He reacts spontaneously to the work before him, moves disjointedly through his day, and loses his ability to think. The second manager *controls* the work before him. He structures the work before him, moves smoothly through his day, and gains the ability to think.

The first management style above is closer to our bicameral roots: *react* to the elements.[1] The second management style is part of man's evolution into consciousness: *control* the elements. The automatic, bicameral approach requires less effort. The self-guided, conscious approach requires hard thinking. And profits rise geometrically with hard, integrated thinking.

To escalate hard thinking, thus launch wealth, first requires the ultimate working *format*, a format that induces thinking — a format with minimum physical disjointedness. The ultimate

---

[1]The bicameral mind is explained in the front material of this book, pages vi and vii.

11

money-making format demands smooth *physical* movements, for a smooth physical flow throughout the day allows one to *think*.

Formatting work into smooth physical movements causes dramatic rises in wealth and power: Consider that a few hundred years ago, man single-handedly handled his survival needs. He built his own home, farmed his own food, sewed his own clothes, made his own tools. Then, as the eighteenth century economist Adam Smith identified, the division of labor broke labor into smaller and smaller units, which catapulted mankind into the Industrial Revolution. The division of labor eliminated the physically disjointed format of survival as society integrated into smooth physical movements — the farmer, the blacksmith, the carpenter, the loomer. The career man focussed on his physical movement all day be it farming or making tools or building furniture or sewing clothes. He no longer moved with physical disjointedness throughout his day as those tending to *all* their survival needs. He now put hard thinking into his one movement, his profession, to raise his value to society thus his personal wealth. By removing physical disjointedness among the people, society became tightly integrated and highly efficient. The resulting rise of the Industrial Revolution brought expanding wealth and power to average men and women. Indeed, the street sweeper today lives with better shelter, food, clothes, choices of entertainment than the aristocrats a few hundred years ago.

At the turn of the century, men hand-assembled cars — single-handedly handled all car-production needs. They hand-assembled the seats, the steering wheel, the doors, the engine and the carriage. Then in the 1920s, Henry Ford discovered the division of labor in car production and broke car production into smaller and smaller units — into the assembly-line that catapulted car production into mass production. The division of labor eliminated the physically disjointed format of building cars as car production integrated into smooth physical movements — the rivet driver, the welder, the stitcher. The assembly-line man focussed on his physical movement all day be it driving in rivets or welding parts or stitching material. He no longer moved with physical disjointedness throughout his day like those in hand-assembling shops still tending to *all* the car-production needs.

Moreover, teams of hard-thinking integrated thinkers

12

catapulted car production to new realms as they focussed on every movement, how to increase its efficiency, how to make gravity work for production — how to raise value per dollar to society and thus launch Ford's personal and business wealth. By removing physical disjointedness within the factory, car production became tightly integrated (to the split second) and dramatically efficient. Car prices went down and America's standard of living went up as average men and women suddenly could afford cars. America rose to economic prominence. Why? Production evolved beyond physical disjointedness — beyond the hand-crew operations putting together complex arrays of parts — into production lines rolling out cars and soon, other products, through smooth physical assembly-line movements.

Now Neo-Tech Control brings the powerful division of labor to you: Neo-Tech Control brings smooth physical movements beneath the nation, beneath the factories...to the individual, to you. Neo-Tech Control does this by breaking your job down to its physical movements. Your work becomes tightly integrated and highly efficient.

But most important, by breaking your job into smooth physical movements, you then are able to evolve into a new realm of *hard thinking*. You are able to evolve into Neothink — the next dimension of success.

Breaking Your Job Into Smooth Physical Movements
Two forces of work exist: (1) physically based work (such as a bricklayer or construction worker) and (2) mentally based work (such as a desk man). Mr. Hamilton, of course, works a mentally based career as CEO of I & O Publishing Company. To illustrate Neo-Tech Control most effectively, Mr. Hamilton's own notes and schedules are used as examples. However, Neo-Tech Control also applies to physically based careers, as you will see after going through Mr. Hamilton's mentally based examples.

Every person with a physically based career must read the next several pages closely to understand Neo-Tech Control. After that understanding, this chapter then addresses the physically based careers. So all readers — carpenters and painters, managers and presidents — read closely the next several pages.

While reading this chapter, you may suspect that breaking

work down to its physical movements does not apply to your job. Chances are that you are right. For, traditional jobs today are specialized, not integrated (explained further in Volume Two). Therefore, the specialized, stagnant nature of your job will not permit the integrated, forward-march nature of the physical-movement working format. For the majority of readers, this will be the case.

So read carefully the next several pages. You will learn the integrated approach needed to rise from stagnation. And over the next few chapters, you will acquire the tools needed to break free from your specialized job and its world of stagnation. You will acquire the tools needed to start your own business in order to evolve into the super-integrated world of the Neo-Tech System (revealed in Volume Two). Or, these techniques can also be used right in your current place of work to lift you straight to the positions of power and wealth, as you will discover in The Company-Capture Discovery, Volume Two. Either way, you will discover the alternative: You will discover how to exchange your current limited world for the unlimited world of Neothink.

Breaking Your Job Into Physical Movements

Now, let us begin. If we were to list the tasks done in a day by the average manager, the list would look something like this:

* Organized work for subordinates
* Called Jim Peabody of X & Y Company
* Drafted letter to supplier
* Had meeting with secretary
* Reviewed inventory report

Now if we were to also list the tasks that he wanted to do or planned to do but did not have time to do, it would look similar to this:

* Wanted to write to second supplier
* Wanted to call about new quotes
* Wanted to meet with programmer
* Wanted to update marketing data
* Wanted to organize most current files

* Wanted to talk to long-time employee about friction
  building

Now if we were to list the tasks that he scheduled for the
following day, his list could look something like this:

* Will definitely write letter to second supplier
* Will make sure to get new quotes
* Will meet with programmer
* Will not leave till update marketing data
* Will finally organize files
* Will make sure I talk to that long-time employee
* Must meet with boss for three-hour weekly meeting in
  afternoon
* Must prepare for meeting all morning

The example above reflects a common problem of the average
manager: Many are out of control with physically disjointed
schedules.

Iron-Grip Control
Neo-Tech Control enables you to double then triple then
quadruple your capacity by integrating work into smooth physical
movements. Diagram One on the next two pages provides an
example of just three days of tasks done by Mark Hamilton:

Diagram One
Three Days Of Completed Tasks

- Call Stuart to uncover lucrative French Canadian magazines for ad
- Write letter to Nightingale-Conant to rent profitable list
- Copyright revolutionary videotape production
- Call and negotiate KCI masterfile for potential European profits
- Call Jim Tegtmire, review in detail envelope quotes
- Write Stuart C. about discount on older, large mailing lists
- Write telex-letter to British on organizing Europe mailing
- Make format corrections on new "exploding envelope" idea
- Fill out and send 2nd-class application to post office
- Meet with Teri to further organize Summit
- Meet with Helen to supervise IBM computer process
- Hold interviews for job opening
- Arrange insertion in Strategic Investing Newsletter
- Organize business trip to Europe this weekend
- Call InterMarket Magazine to negotiate "exploding envelope"
- Call around other video shops for better deal
- Write telex-letter to Peter R. in England about lettershop process
- Study costs, set-up costs, overall company costs
- Review lettershop invoices and correct problems developing
- Train new employee
- Call Data For Graphics, typesetters about ads
- Write telex-letter to Irish Agency: business center in Ireland
- Review financial records; develop financial statement
- Meet with WW, president
- Call Better Investing and negotiate "exploding envelope"
- Write Newsletter Management about their list, negotiate their list
- Write Brian K. of Boardroom a note about discounting list
- Write Bernard letter preparing extensive meeting in Canada, Oct.
- Go through in-basket (each day)
- Organize sections in office for daily inspection
- Study job applications for customer service and accounting
- Call Don P. about space ad

(continued next page)

16

Diagram One
Three Days of Completed Tasks (continued)

- Call Bill Levine with final Moneysworth edits
- Write two letters to authorities
- Make purchase order to Linden Computer Services
- Review Helen W.'s writing: edit, copy write new profitable product
- Review accounting procedures with HW
- Call Maclean Hunter, leads on big Canadian lists
- Call "La Opinion" to inquiry about new, Spanish-speaking market
- Write letter to HUME about doing business together in Canada
- Make corrections in Andrew's invoice
- Meet with Melinda
- Call Blue Shield to establish new insurance policy
- Meet with Vicki
- Meet with Linde
- Call Newsletter Management to confirm deal
- Write "mass" letter for "exploding envelope" concept
- Write Canadian DMA for leads on printers
- Design brief coupon for split test on free-offer newsletter
- Make and send "exploding envelope" mock to Don Perry
- Develop outline and start copywriting report with FW, joint venture
- Review all data and effects on finances, set up new incoming data
- Meet with Shelly
- Call Lori D. of Success Magazine to run inquiry ad
- Call LA Times to run classified and get information on other ads
- Call Metro Mail, quotes in acquiring phone number, telemarketing
- Write telex-letter to Peter R. in England about invoice
- Meet with Teri
- Call PSA computer shop for schedule to put up names
- Call the National Enquirer about ad
- Call Mega Media about inquiry ad in Globe
- Call West Coast Video about production
- Meet with WW, president

How did he easily handle that seemingly overwhelming list in just three days? Consider the task of delivering the overwhelming number of pieces of U.S. mail each day. If that mail were dumped into large piles for the mailmen to fill their bags and start delivering — the first letter to an address perhaps on the west side, the next letter perhaps to the south side, the next letter back to the west side — the physically disjointed mail-delivery system would get hopelessly behind. Similarly, the physically disjointed, traditional work schedule gets hopelessly behind.

As the mail must be physically integrated, so must one's job. For example, the overwhelming U.S. mail breaks down into easy-to-handle, physical carrier-route deliveries. Similarly, Mr. Hamilton's overwhelming job that previously never got finished breaks down into a few easy-to-handle physical movements that now always get done.

To break down his job into the physical carrier-route-like, integrated movements, he studied his three days of tasks. From that he identified his physical movements. He identified: (1) Phone Calls, (2) Letter Writing, (3) Copywriting, (4) Accounting, (5) Meetings, and (6) Operations.

Each movement is a raw physical act — a phone call, for example, requires picking up the phone and dialing no matter what the call is about. Before demonstrating how those basic physical movements provide the format to journey toward money and power, let us review how Mr. Hamilton determined his physical movements:

Turn again to Diagram One on pages 16 and 17. As you examine the three days of tasks, notice that Mr. Hamilton makes a number of phone calls. To make a phone call, one must make a physical movement. The movement remains the same no matter who one calls or what one calls about. Go through the list and put a #1 next to all phone calls.

Next you can see that he writes a number of letters. To write a letter requires a physical movement regardless who one writes or what one writes about. Put a #2 next to the letter-writing tasks.

Mr. Hamilton develops ads and product copy. Copy writing too is an independent movement. That is #3. Mark all copywriting tasks #3.

Gathering Control

He spends substantial time doing finances, bookkeeping, accounting, creative accounting, and invoice review. Mark all financial matters #4.

Although many approaches and techniques exist for meetings, holding meetings still is a specific physical act. Mark all meetings with a #5.

The five movements identified above may or may not apply to other jobs. But the next movement applies to nearly all mentally based jobs and many physically based jobs (addressed later in Volume One):

To determine the final movement, look over the tasks; all but a few are marked off. The remaining unmarked tasks do not seem to link together into a related movement. Those disjointed, left-over tasks are the culprits of nit-pick work that shoot most managers' days to shreds. Now we can finally corner them. You, too, will have disjointed tasks left over.

Those seemingly disjointed tasks actually all fall under one physical movement — the physical movement of operating management. Now you can capture those problem-makers into one movement to blast through in one shot. You will move forward all day long in other important movements, momentum not destroyed by nit-pick work. Number those now-harmless tasks with a #6.

Now notice the integration among the same unwieldy, three days of tasks when broken down into their physical movements on the next page.

Look again at the unwieldy list of tasks in Diagram One on pages 16 and 17 compared to the streamlined list of tasks in Diagram Two on page 20. Diagram Two shows Mr. Hamilton's career broken down to smooth physical movements. Notice the assembly-line efficiency. For Mr. Hamilton, Phase One is done. (When you do Phase One in Chapter Five, your physical movements will vary from Mr. Hamilton's.) As his career begins to integrate, everything begins to move toward simplicity and efficiency.

19

The Neo-Tech System

Diagram Two
Physical Movements
And Their Tightly Integrated Physical Tasks

Physical Movement #1: Phone Calls
- Call Stuart
- Call KCI
- Call Jim T.
- Call InterMarket
- Call Video Shops
- Call Data-For-Graphics
- Call Better Investing
- Call Don P.
- Call Bill L.
- Call Maclean Hunter
- Call La Opinion
- Call Blue Cross/Blue Shield
- Call Newsletter Management
- Call Lori D.
- Call LA Times
- Call Metro Mail
- Call PSA
- Call National Enquirer
- Call Stuart, Mega Media
- Call West Coast Video

Physical Movement #2: Letter Writing
- Write Nightingale-Conant
- Write Stuart
- Write telex British authorities
- Write telex to Peter R.
- Write telex to Francis L., Ireland
- Write Newsletter Management
- Write Brian K.
- Write Bernard M.
- Write letter for authorities
- Write HUME
- Write exploding-envelope letter
- Write Canadian DMA
- Write telex to Peter R.

Physical Movement #3: Copywriting
- Script for Video Production
- Edit Helen W.'s new product
- Write outline, start writing joint book with FW

Physical Movement #4: Accounting
- Study costs
- Review invoices
- Review records
- Understand HW's procedures
- Correct Andrews invoice
- Data review

Physical Movement #5: Meetings and People
- Meet with Teri
- Meet with Helen
- Meet with WW
- Meet with Melinda
- Meet with Vicki
- Meet with Linde
- Meet with Shelly
- Meet with Teri
- Meet with WW

Physical Movement #6: Operations
- Corrections expl. envelope
- 2nd-class application
- Interviews and training
- Strategic Investing insertion
- Prepare for European trip
- Train new employee
- In-basket each day
- Sections for inspection
- Study job file
- PO to Linden
- Lay out for newsletter
- Mock exploding envelope to Don

Chapter Three

PUTTING THE PHYSICAL MOVEMENTS
TO WORK

Consider that small personal computers today can produce almost any image — sophisticated diagrams, abstract designs, even complicated pictures. The small home computers produce those advanced images through a two-step process: First, they break down complex images to their handful of fundamental shapes. Indeed, every shape on earth comes from a handful of fundamental shapes just as all colors on earth come from three fundamental colors — red, yellow, and blue. Second, the home computers interlock little specks of those handful of fundamental shapes by the hundreds to form advanced images with incredible speed, power, and control. The ability to produce complex images becomes quite simple and efficient.

Similarly, Neo-Tech Control breaks down careers to their fundamental physical movements. Mr. Hamilton's complex career breaks down to a few fundamental movements (as determined in Chapter Two). Just as the many colors and many shapes all reduce to a few fundamental colors and shapes, the many projects and deals in Mr. Hamilton's career all reduce to a few fundamental movements. Neo-Tech Control interlocks little tasks of those handful of basic movements by the hundreds to perform advance business moves with amazing speed, power, and control. The ability to manage complex careers becomes quite simple and efficient, as follows:

After determining his basic movements, Mr. Hamilton determined the approximate activity of each movement. In other words, he estimated the percentage of his 10-hour day that he should devote to each movement. Recognize that he estimated what he should devote, not necessarily what he was devoting at the time. He estimated the following percentage:

(1) Phone Calls	20%	or	2 hrs.
(2) Letter Writing	15%	or	1.5 hrs.
(3) Copy Writing	10%	or	1 hrs.
(4) Accounting	20%	or	2 hrs.
(5) Meetings	15%	or	1.5 hrs.
(6) Operations	20%	or	2 hrs.

Then he made a daily-schedule breakdown as follows:

8:00-10:00am	Phone Calls (2 hrs.)
10:00-11:30	Letter Writing (1.5 hrs.)
11:30-1:30pm	Operations (2 hrs.)
1:30-2:30	Copy Writing (1 hrs.)
2:30-4:30	Accounting (2 hrs.)
4:30-6:00	Meetings (1.5 hrs.)

See what his schedule looks like once in action. Look over Mr. Hamilton's schedule, "Three Days Interlocked" on the next page. Mr. Hamilton does not schedule his *tasks* to time as does the traditional daily schedule. He schedules his *physical movements* to time (just as the assembly-line does not schedule tasks to time as in the hand-built days; it schedules the physical movements to time stations).

Indeed, the inferior traditional schedule that schedules tasks to time is like the inferior hand-built car process, the traditional way during the early 1900s that scheduled tasks to time — to the time-consuming tasks of putting in and adjusting the steering wheel, then carrying over and hand fitting the seats, collating the rubber and rim and then putting on the wheel, and so on. The traditional schedule misses the interlocking Neo-Tech integration of scheduling the physical movements to time, out of which surface intensified, streamlined, physically integrated tasks like the intensified, streamlined tasks of a rivet-man in an assembly-line.

Look closely at Mr. Hamilton's three-day schedule on the next page. He drives home his physically integrated tasks like the rivet man drives home rivets. Like the rivet man driving in rivet! after rivet! after rivet!...Mr. Hamilton pushes out phone call! after phone call! after phone call! He does not walk over and have a meeting, then pick up the phone to make a call, then try his hand at a little copy writing, then make another call, then draft a letter. Such a common scenario among businessmen can be compared to the old way of building cars by putting the seats in, then coming over and putting in the brakes, changing tools to work on the steering wheel, then stopping for a lunch break. No, Mr. Hamilton just drives that rivet home; drives it home. Upon

Putting The Physical Movements To Work

Diagram Three
Three Days Interlocked

JUNE 1985	JULY 1985	AUGUST 1985	SEPTEMBER 1985
S M T W T F S	S M T W T F S	S M T W T F S	S M T W T F S
1	1 2 3 4 5 6	1 2 3	1 2 3 4 5 6 7
2 3 4 5 6 7 8	7 8 9 10 11 12 13	4 5 6 7 8 9 10	8 9 10 11 12 13 14
9 10 11 12 13 14 15	14 15 16 17 18 19 20	11 12 13 14 15 16 17	15 16 17 18 19 20 21
16 17 18 19 20 21 22	21 22 23 24 25 26 27	18 19 20 21 22 23 24	22 23 24 25 26 27 28
23 24 25 26 27 28 29	28 29 30 31	25 26 27 28 29 30 31	29 30

AUGUST

MONDAY, AUGUST 19 231/134	TUESDAY, AUGUST 20 232/133	WEDNESDAY, AUGUST 21 233/132
8:00 Phone Calls	**8:00 Phone Calls**	**8:00 Phone Calls**
Stuart → Spanish + French Can magazine	Brian @ Bella Inv → expl. ques.	Kathy @ newsletter Mgt → send
:30 Karen Johnson, KCT → letter	:30 Dan Perry – money making Mag	Call Bari Bob for ticket ad
9:00 Simon for invite → order tapes on tax	Give Bill Levine final Monograph	LA Times classified ad
Inter Market → deal	9:00 MacLean Hunter → leads on wg. list	9:00 Metro News → ph. #'s
:30 Make arrangements w/video	:30 La Opinion → Irene Vaughrad	PSA Ph #'s → ? Stuart
data for graphics	:30 Blue Cross → Shelly 382-3302	National Eng. → order tickets
		APPOINTMENT 1:00
10:00 Letter Writing	**10:00 Letter Writing**	**10:00 Letter Writing**
Write Vic Conant → & rent list	Write Newsletter Mgt → $ list	Expl. Env. letter to mass mags
:30 Write similar to Stuart → SH	:30 Send Brian a note on 40/M	:30 Canadian DNA → printers
Telex British authorities	Bernard Money → meet in Oct.	Telex Peter R. → $'s
11:00 Telex Peter K.	11:00 AUTHORITIES	11:00
Telex Francis L.	H UME	
:30 **Operational**	:30 **Operational**	:30 **Operational**
Basket	Basket – sections in office rings	Basket – expl envelope
12:00 Corrections on expl. env.	12:00 Study job-file applicants	12:00 Ad copy for test on newsletter
Send in 2nd class Application	for Cust. Service & Accountant	Design heading for newsletter
:30 Interviews & Training	:30 Interviews & Training	:30 Interviews & Training
Strategic Inv → insertion order	PO Broken Services, PSA	Mack to Dan Perry
1:00 Prepare operations for my departure to Europe	1:00 Prepare operations for my departure to Europe	1:00 Prepare operations for my departure to Europe
:30 **Copywriting**	:30 **Copywriting**	:30 **Copywriting**
Video tape production	Mimi → go over, give direction	Prepare outline, details for
2:00	quick edit → then let her work more on it	2:00 book w/FU & turn over
:30 **Accounting**	:30 **Accounting**	:30 **Accounting**
Records	Records	Records
3:00 Invoices	3:00 Cost study	3:00 Cost study
Study costs → set up cost	AR procedures	HW procedures
:30 study program w/HW	:30 Andrews Correction	Review data & set up SH
4:00	4:00	4:00
:30 **Meetings & People**	:30 **Meetings & People**	:30 **Meetings & People**
Meet w/TS → mailing lists &	Melinda → set up salvage "	Shelly → review my outline
5:00 Helen finish IBM → summary	5:00 Vicki → policies, fines	5:00 of organization
list	Linda → collection turn over	TJ →
:30	:30 & set up mailings from home	HW
6:00 Evening	**6:00 Evening**	**6:00 Evening**
:30 Work on NT Mgt book	:30 Same → brochure NT Mgt	:30 Work on GT's brochure
7:00 & on book	7:00 & on final chapter	7:00 "A Day of Consultation"
:30	:30	:30
8:00	8:00	8:00 Personal night w/TJ
:30	:30	:30
9:00	9:00	9:00
:30	:30	:30

integrating movements to time, an average person soars beyond all productivity records just as development of the assembly-line smashed all productivity records.

Intensity

The new schedule doubled, tripled, then quadrupled Mr. Hamilton's intensity. And intensity is the most leveraged time-management tool. For example, consider that popular time-management courses offer unrealistic disciplines to find an extra hour to two hours in a day. Even if the average person could handle the disciplines, how much good is an extra hour? Aside from not being worth the effort, that extra hour will not make him a money/power giant.

Now consider that if he doubles his intensity, he basically doubles his capacity. Suddenly, he in a sense gains eight extra hours in his day. If he triples his intensity, he gains sixteen extra hours in his day. With a physically streamlined schedule, Mr. Hamilton's intensity is many times what it once was.

The physically streamlined schedule on page 23 deceives the reader as to just how much Mr. Hamilton really accomplishes. Like observing a skillful athlete, the simplicity and ease tends to camouflage the significance of Neo-Tech Control. See Diagram Four over the next five pages, however, to get a perspective of the volume of Mr. Hamilton's career. To appreciate the intensity generated by Mr. Hamilton's integrated schedule, realize that everything on the five-page power-thinking list was done or was put into motion in *one week*. (Diagram Three, "Three Days Interlocked" on page 23, shows Monday through Wednesday of that week.) A lot is on that list in Diagram Four. Again, in just one week, everything was moved on or accomplished. That happens by creating intense pockets of time interlocked to the physical movements.

Consider that you, your neighbor, your son in high school could handle Mr. Hamilton's schedule. You could easily make phone calls, write letters, go through the in-basket and stay on his schedule. Yes, you could sit down tomorrow in the seat of this high-powered entrepreneur and orchestrate his highly complex job. With the division-of-labor schedule, any great career can be yours.

24

Diagram Four
Power-Thinking List for Week of 8/19/85 — 8/25/85

Europe
- Read first test results
- Determine results of British Postal Meeting; make decisions on mailing lists as a result of meeting
- Boardroom negotiate price to rent entire file
- KCI negotiate price 550M...call Karen and lower price
- Newsletter Management negotiate price...send letter to lower price
- Nightingale Conant negotiate price
- Cogan's masterfiles such as Shindler masterfile
- Then continue in big numbers from there

Exploding Envelope
- Finishing designing and typesetting
- Have first batch printed
  InterMarket arrange
- Better Investing call for test
- Design letter to ad director of several magazines
- Call Money Making and try it there

Inserts
- Send Strategic Investing order for October issue
- Print 32M brochures; print 32M remittance envelopes
- Test Newsletter Management with 300M universe

AMS Lettershop
- Test new 8-page newspaper format
- Test tabloid in larger size envelope; have Pacific Envelope print larger size envelope
- Test placing conversion notice first
- Test logo coupon vs. regular
- Put some lists through women-kill program; test repeat of 2nd quarter Shindler to increase universe
- Ticket to Success test; if looks good, go back to England test

Space Media
- Test Moneysworth; Better Living; good space deals
- Test Neo-Tech Management ad; go in all good publications that rejected Neo-Tech ad—send brochure
- Test "Ticket to Success" ad in Spanish-speaking magazine; set ad through Stuart

(continued next page)

Diagram Four
Power-Thinking List for Week of 8/19/85 — 8/25/85
(continued)

- Test "Ticket to Success" ad in French-speaking Canadian magazine; check with Stuart if knows market
- Test 1/6 page "Ticket to Success" ad in next issue of Success to demonstrate if nature of ad can run time after time such as Mellinger's 1/6 page ads, year after year, building recognition and credibility. If so, study different magazines.
- Test "Ticket to Success" bind-in card in magazine; test versus exploding envelope in InterMarket
- Of course, pursue exploding envelope as indicated above
- Classified ad
- Pick up National Enquirer and determine best inquiry ad size
- Pick up and study different publications and ads.

Canadian Market
- Run "Ticket to Success" in several Canadian publications as a) a feeler ad, and b) good strategy for them to get used to us to accept 4-page or exploding envelope
- Set Fiduciary loose on testing Canadian lists
- Establish a Canadian mail house in October while in Montreal
- Get a huge-volume list and mail via BMI into Canada
- Test French brochure to French-Canadian names — via AMS 106
- Send Claudette letter for leads

Neo-Tech Management Book
- Finish brochure and mail from England before October 1st to best 70M Neo-Tech names
- Finish editing...to WW
- Finish final chapter
- Ongoing product development

Gary's area
- Finish brochure and mail from England hopefully before October 1st to all Neo-Tech buyers minus RIBI names
- Provide GT with necessary information to produce "A Day of Consultation"
- Encourage and work closely with GT on developing cassette tapes on each concept—"Tape of the Month Club"
- Begin developing brochure for monthly cassettes

(continued next page)

Diagram Four
Power-Thinking List for Week of 8/19/85 — 8/25/85
(continued)

Teri's Area

• Encourage development and growth of Fiduciary Lists as it expands into large operation with perhaps added help

• Encourage and work closely in BMI and mailings as TJ will become in charge of those mailings and acquiring the mailing lists

• Shoot for first Neo-Tech Summit in November:

1) Finish ad copy

2) TJ find out best time to mail prior to Summit

3) Mail to 3M RIBI Names

4) My good opportunity to do our first telemarketing test. If works, do them all and WH start for I & 0 2

5) Have a blast in Las Vegas come November

• Work with TJ to write out philosophical linkages of Paradise Valley to man's nature...why different. Then will publish that in some mailing to monitor immediate interest.

Linde's Area

• Take a good list and run through "common-women names" program and pull out good women so I & 0 4 can make money while testing. Great source of names once get started; can establish "core" lists as does I & 0 2 and have good income while pursuing more profitable lists.

• Test three approaches; keep on 4-page format for test, for this is different ball game; after 1st test then may switch to 8-page format, depending on results of 3-way test.

• Work closely with Linde to develop "Ticket to Success" 1/6 page ad for women. Test in low-cost magazine.

• Could women be similar in nature to Japanese and other far-east cultures? Could they need to first develop trust with a company? Make 3-way test a 4-way test and test women's "Ticket to Success" as an inquiry postcard through the mail.

• Pending on British Postal Meeting, will eventually start testing from England once find substantial names to work with, which may warrant Linde traveling to England if her mailings really got rolling.

• Set up and turn over profitable decline, invalid, bad check program to I & 0 4. A good sustaining income.

• Finish questionnaire and insert to go with her booklist mailing to Neo-Tech names.

(continued next page)

Diagram Four
Power-Thinking List for Week of 8/19/85 — 8/25/85
(continued)

Frank's Area
- Provide FW with outline idea of book
- Let FW read Neo-Tech Management book
- Start program of weekly writing with FW

Helen's Area
- Work closely with Helen guiding her writing
- Work heavily with editing as she provides me her drafts

Ruth's Area
- Develop makeshift video cassette with wedding tape, cutting, narrating, and dubbing in music and narration
- Provide Ruth and John idea and makeshift videos
- Let them do one on their own with my narration edits to their music and drama...great potential
- Eventually perhaps blend in with GT's tape of the month product

Neo-Tech Newsletter/2nd-class project
- Test the newsletter concept AMS 105
- Work with FW and WW on newsletter
- Apply for 2nd-class mail
- Advertise back end plus send out brochure to other 50% if more profitable
- Pursue with local postal authorities and those in CA

Writing Projects
- Neo-Tech Management Book
- Neo-Tech Management brochure
- A Day of Consultation brochure
- Neo-Tech Summit brochure editing
- Children's concepts, Neo-Tech
- Two chapters of "Money/Power Through Successful Love"
- Doris insert and questionnaire
- Booklist insert
- New product—Look and See
- Article about loving your work means making the most money, even if money means little to you
- Letter to Peter
- New CCL letter
- Prepare consultation on Mini-Day and Power-Thinking for in-house meeting

(continued next page)

Diagram Four
Power-Thinking List for Week of 8/19/85 — 8/25/85
(continued)

- Prepare consultation on Mini-Day and Power-Thinking for Summit
- Never can lie—right brain. Support structure

Internal Operations (Vicki, Helen, Shelly)

- Hard copy checks of everything
- Install long overdue fine system
- "Shake-up"
- Set up "salvage" programs as discover mistakes
- Interview job applicants
- Search job file to bring in a customer service and public relations full time, ambitious employee; will determine how to set up as self-motivated entrepreneur
- Daily organization put into office—becoming straight and tight; want to have the tightest office in the country
- Set up auditing control on everything, including bank check-in, check-out control on returns
- Bank-like control on all orders
- Bank-like control on all correspondence, computer work, and customer service with WH personal check now
- Collection to go to entrepreneurial-motivated Linde
- Fine system to clean up non-conscientious work
- Drawers and files and storage becoming a pleasure to enter, not a drag— every desk and cabinet
- Job file search—Accountant, customer service

Late Notes and Additions:

Accounting

- Search for CPA — run ad, contact RIBI customers
- Numbers man — study response

Mailing list project

- Orders 18-24 to Linden, to PSA, into 8C
- RIBI's to Linden, to PSA
- Orders 8C & RIBI's to MetroMail — phone numbers
- To Newsletter Management or Astro for telemarketing list

29

The Neo-Tech System

The Underlying Concept That Allows Anyone
To Handle Vast Business Horizons

Go back for a moment to the eighteenth-century economist Adam Smith who identified that dividing labor into smaller and smaller units could build wealth at greater and greater speeds. Throughout the Industrial Revolution, society divided labor into smaller and smaller units — into the physical movements of survival — and became highly integrated. For instance, many people now work for each individual making his clothes, farming his food, building his home, making his tools, his furniture and so on instead of each individual doing it all himself as done centuries ago.

As society became highly integrated through dividing labor, the economy became increasingly successful and the act of living became increasingly easy. Indeed, the division of labor changed the world forever: The division of labor caused the Industrial Revolution that eventually made America the most integrated thus the most prosperous civilization in the history of mankind.

In the early 1900s, Henry Ford catapulted the power of the Industrial Revolution. Ford Motor Company divided labor into the smallest possible units — into the physical movements of production — and created the world's most integrated production method: the assembly-line.

The assembly-line integrated literally every split second of production. Dividing labor down to the precision movement of the rivet man, for instance, greatly intensified and simplified each split second for a tighter and tighter, no-waste integrated system. As Ford divided labor into smaller and smaller movements, his business went through production records with greater and greater profits. Indeed, the division of labor made Ford Motor Company the most integrated thus the most prosperous car company in the world.

Now Neo-Tech Control isolates the essence behind America's rise to power and Ford Motor Company's rise to dominance and captures that essence for the average person. Neo-Tech Control brings directly to the individual the division-of-labor secret. Neo-Tech Control brings to every ordinary person the power that integrates entire nations into prosperity and entire industries into mass production.

30

Indeed, the division of labor integrates countries, companies, and now the lives of ordinary people into prosperity. And, as revealed in Chapter Four (next), the division of labor enables a new dimension of hard, integrated thinking for making money. Whether developing a country, a car, or one's fortune, the division-of-labor integration unlocks success.

A Key Concept: A Powerful, New Technique
The Mini-Day

Neo-Tech Control puts life under immediate, iron-grip control. Mr. Hamilton seizes control by treating each of his six movements as a separate day, or a *mini-day*. Treating each mini-day as a full day in itself, he starts each mini-day on time and ends each mini-day on time. When the mini-day time is up, that day is over, regardless of the amount of tasks that were or were not completed. For, the physical movements, *not tasks*, are integrated to time. Remember, he has established the most beneficial relationship of those physical movements to time. Therefore, Mr. Hamilton does not let one mini-day get more time for another would get less, which if continued for long would force the integration off, force the imbalance of physical movements, force missed tasks needed to complete the integration like cars with missed lug nuts coming off the production-line. By staying strict with the mini-days, one is forced to stay integrated.

Mr. Hamilton runs a calculated, serious, integrated career consistently building wealth week by week instead of comically chasing tasks day by day. He now has his personal assembly-line of productivity in place and turns it on each day. Immediately he feels good. He negates that annoying uncertainty that some work may not get done. He rapidly moves through the tightly integrated tasks of six mini-days:

Again, look at his schedule on page 23. It is called the mini-day schedule:

Phone Calls	is	Day 1.
Letter Writing	is	Day 2.
Operations	is	Day 3.
Copywriting	is	Day 4.
Accounting	is	Day 5.
Meetings and People	is	Day 6.

31

The physically integrated tasks light up like a fuse racing to the powder. What took two hours rushing disjointedly before takes 15 minutes after some experience with the straight-arrow mini-day schedule. His whole day catches fire. Each mini-day is the opposite of the overwhelming, traditional all-day schedule in which lethargy sets in like hand-building a whole car. Instead one attacks each organized movement like the rivet man. Task follows integrated task at high speed with no hesitation. And knowing that once the mini-day ends, time is up for another 24 hours, adds to the intensity. Like cramming for a final-exam deadline, the mini-day deadlines throughout the day stimulate tremendous natural intensity.

A person gains respect, no matter where he now lands on the power scale. Business peers respond with respect, especially one's boss. Eventually, the person on the mini-day schedule becomes a natural leader. He accomplishes more in a day than he did in a week. Moreover, his mini-day intensity makes him mentally energetic. That mental energy is needed to uncover and initiate new projects. He begins to make more money. He learns what it means to work with money-driven intensity. Quickly, he moves above his peers as he quietly transforms into a high-powered, money-making machine. Others step out of his way in awe...ready to file in behind.

Physically-Based Job

Respect. How about bringing that respect to the physically based job, the bricklayer. He can now gain respect. Let us think about the bricklayer for a moment: Say he feels ambitious and works harder. Well, he may lay 20% more bricks while his enthusiasm lasts. That's it. How much pride can he gain from that extra effort year after year while going nowhere? He lives in a rut! He must catapult out of that rut.

A person who works a physically based job often has profound ambitions. For he wants to move out of his rut. He may have greater ambitions and incentive than someone sitting behind a desk whose ambitions and incentive may not go further than getting the raise next month or next year. Therefore, the physically based worker, with Neo-Tech Control, can become more competitive than the mentally based worker.

Putting The Physical Movements To Work

How can I apply this mini-day concept, you say, if I work eight hours a day doing physical labor? How am I going to apply the mini-day, for I work all day long? True one may work eight hours laying bricks. But that eight-hour physical movement (laying bricks) is considered a mini-day; an income mini-day let us call it. Now, that physically based worker must determine the physical movements *necessary to accomplish his ambitions*. Whereas Mr. Hamilton determined the physical movements of his career, the physically based worker must determine the physical movements to accomplish his ambitions and structure those mini-days to either side of his income mini-day. This will pull the physically based worker out of his rut. ...It can be done. It has been done. A great American hero did just that. Mr. Hamilton tells the story at a Neo-Tech Control seminar:

"We've talked about pulling yourself up, about getting respect. Well, among physically based workers I see a drive, a desire. Let me tell you about a physically based laborer at the turn of the century, a dock worker among the roughest ports of early nineteen-hundred America. That dock breed spoke illiterate English, crude, unrefined. Our American hero dropped out of school early. He lived off the streets. He survived. He never had an opportunity. Like millions of others, he was headed for a dead-end life.

"A desire burned inside, though. He desired to pull himself out of the abyss. He desired to become a successful writer. ...In the early 1900s, an illiterate dock worker had essentially no chance to ever sell a piece of literature.

"But he established four physical movements, four mini-days that would achieve his desire of becoming a writer: (1) reading, (2) intense grammar study, (3) self-education (a library-study program), and (4) writing. Those four mini-days were divided before and after his 12 to 14-hour income mini-day. Do you know who that man was? He was Jack London. He wrote many adventure short stories and novels including 'Call of the Wild', 'The Sea Wolf', 'Martin Eden'. In a few short years, Jack London became the highest paid author in history. And if we adjust for inflation today, he is the highest paid author of all time. Indeed, after he pulled himself out of his rut and off the docks, he never stopped the mini-day system. He stayed on the mini-day system through all his fame and glory to the last days of his short life.

"The physical laborer is forced to go all out for his ambitions in order to pull himself out of his rut. He cannot count on moving up the ladder, for there is no ladder for him. He must take a giant step, and many would take that step if there were a way. With Neo-Tech Control, for the first time, there is a way. As I've said, many physical laborers take their desires seriously, very seriously. With this Neo-Tech Control tool, physical laborers may begin to rocket past mentally based office men who may not take this opportunity quite as seriously."

Neo-Tech Control Seminar
North Bergen, NJ Seminar

So we saw that Jack London, stuck in a physically based job, determined the physical movements of his ambitions to catapult himself into the most prosperous author in history. And we saw that Mark Hamilton, in a mentally based job, determined the physical movements of his career to propel himself to rapid success. ...With the next Neo-Tech tool, you are going to reach forward, grab hold of your most ambitious goals and projects and bring them back to you now. You can experience those accomplishments not only sometime within your lifetime but right away and move on to even bigger and better accomplishments. You will discover the exciting energy of moving through goals. Think about *your* ambitions, your goals. The next chapter shows you how to bring everything you want into the palm of your hand, right now. But first, you must set up your mini-days:

Setting Up Your Mini-Days

Start tomorrow morning: List on a pad every task you perform at work for the next three days. List each task AS YOU DO THE TASK for three FULL days. After the third day, go through your list of tasks and determine the physical movements of your job as you did for Mr. Hamilton's three days of tasks. Those physical movements become your mini-days. Determine the time you should devote to each mini-day. Then set up your mini-day schedule.

Do not take shortcuts. List three full days of tasks, not from memory, but as you perform the tasks. Start tomorrow morning, first thing at work.

But what if your job cannot be broken into mini-days? Let us say you work a physically based job, say you are a construction worker, or a cook, or a bank teller, or a drafting artist. You will never become wealthy in those suppressed, specialized jobs. So think BEYOND your job about what you want. If you want to start your own business, what are the physical movements to do that? Place those physical movements, those mini-days, in the morning or in the evening, AROUND your job. Remember, Jack London was practically illiterate when he discovered the mini-day concept, developed the proper mini-days and scheduled them after work. Those mini-days pulled him out of his rut and in just a few years made him the highest-paid author of all time, when adjusting for inflation. With the proper mini-days, you will pull yourself out of YOUR rut. And then you will be able to mini-day your entire life.

So, if you cannot mini-day your job, begin tonight determining the physical movements that will pull you beyond your job. Determine the physical movements that will raise you to your goals, perhaps raise you to starting you own business. You have no technique to figure out these particular physical movements — only your common sense. You can adjust the physical movements, the mini-days, after you get on them and gain some experience using them. You may find you need to add, for example, an entire new mini-day. Or you may need to take away or change a mini-day. You may need to adjust the time allotted to the mini-days once you get started on them after work and on weekends. But you must first GET STARTED. Keep your current job as your INCOME mini-day until your new venture can financially support you.

If you CAN mini-day your current job, start listing your tasks tomorrow morning. You must list every task you do for the next three days in order to best determine the proper mini-days.

When you have your mini-day schedule, you move past the low intensity, unintegrated traditional schedule. You move through clusters of integrations with assembly-line intensity. ...And now

35

we will go even further. We will combine the mini-day schedule with a second tool called power-thinking to compile FUTURE integrations into today's income. ...Feel free to continue reading even if you have not yet determined your mini-days. Now, let us move on to integrating the future with power-thinking.

Chapter Four
PULLING IN THE FUTURE

The mini-day schedule broken into smooth physical movements opens a whole new power-reactor dimension to making money: hard, integrated thinking called *power thinking*. The traditional schedule, on the other hand, plagued with physical disjointedness (business mysticism) blocks hard, integrated thinking — blocks the power-reactor explosion into power-thinking. The traditional daily schedule quickly fills to its capacity and can only react day by day to the business. The mini-day schedule rarely fills to its capacity and opens a new dimension of hard thinking that controls and builds business called power-thinking.

Personal mysticism — our bicameral tendencies for automatic or external guidance as explained in the front material, pages vii and viii — keeps man tied to the traditional schedule that essentially provides automatic, external guidance as man simply reacts to the business around him. Filled to his capacity using the physically disjointed traditional schedule, he can look and feel busy and important. Yet he only MAINTAINS his job and builds nothing. With physical disjointedness eliminated by the mini-day schedule, however, his superior capacity opens the door to power-thinking. Then he BUILDS wealth and maintains nothing. Profits returned on effort spent rise geometrically with hard, integrated thinking — power-thinking — used with the new division-of-labor mini-day schedule.

Indeed, with the mini-day schedule intact, the average person can pull in future wealth, goals, projects rapidly through power-thinking. Let us start with an example of Mr. Hamilton using this effective, simple tool: While in his mid-20s, Mr. Hamilton handled among other things a large, complex project. He initiated major marketing programs overseas in England and Ireland. The new programs were complex and could take many months to start. Instead, he did the following: He focused in his mind the end result. He could tangibly see in his head the completed project right up to the hundreds of thousands of marketing packages filling a containerized truck being lifted into the ship.

37

In seeing that finished project, he swiftly began to see what he needed to do to achieve that full container. He began focusing on the suppliers he needed to contact, the shipping routes he needed to uncover, the postal systems he needed to work with, the schedules he needed to orchestrate . ...He began integrating into the future.

He thought about and imaged in his mind as many steps as possible to achieve that container full of his marketing packages and wrote them down. He called that list of steps his *power-thinking list*. But his power-thinking list turned into so much more than just projecting ahead, for he fed the projections into the high-intensity action units — the mini-days — that quickly got done. ...Let us see how the results pulled him up the ranks as he moved through important projects that others just think about:

He determined the task or tasks needed to complete the first step listed on his power-thinking list, then injected the task(s) into the proper mini-day(s). He then did that for each step listed on his power-thinking list. He quickly took control.

In one day he did, among several other things, the following: During his phone-call mini-day he called the major printing consultant in Ireland, contacted the marketing manager of the Irish An Post, called a printer in England with whom he had previously done business and discussed a large test mailing; during his letter-writing mini-day he drafted a letter to the Irish postal authorities; during the operations mini-day he organized some data to indicate what mailing lists he would consider using; during the accounting mini-day he did a brief cost analysis on mailing abroad; during his meeting mini-day he discussed the overseas possibilities with his in-house mailing list broker to set her in action, he also reviewed with two executive officers the tentative plan with nearly a full-scale layout. He did all that among other productive tasks in one day. He did more in one day toward completing that project than most would do in a month. By the next day, people on both sides of the Atlantic were moving into action, all moving the project toward completion.

His high-capacity mini-day schedule opened to the young Mr. Hamilton the whole new dimension of power-thinking. He could suddenly power-think large, major projects and rapidly move them into action. He left his peers in his dust, for their low-capacity traditional schedules blocked them from power-thinking new money-making projects as they barely kept up with their routine jobs. They just reacted to business. Mr. Hamilton controlled and built business. The president of I & O Publishing Company was so impressed that he promptly gave the young Mark Hamilton a major promotion, pay increase, and bonus. Yet anyone could have done it. With Neo-Tech Control, you or your son (save for actual hands-on experience) could have done what Mark Hamilton did that day.

Starting Your Own Business With Iron-Grip Control

The results just pull one up the hierarchy or, more importantly, enable the average person to start his own business. Into the mini-day production-line he puts through today, with power-thinking, what others will not even think about until sometime in the future. And he can crank out several projects at one time as he compiles future projects into today's mini-days. Soon even his boss seems slow and ineffective. At this point, he is ready to leave his specialized job. Specialization in his traditional job only holds him back. He is ready to leave behind specialized ends-in-themselves, dead-end responsibilities. He is ready to integrate business to make money. He is ready to build an empire instead of maintain a job. He is ready to start his own business. No one can slow down progress again.

The mini-day/power-thinking team enables any ordinary person to smoothly handle the many responsibilities of starting his own business. The new dimension of power-thinking — made possible by the mini-day schedule — launches the ordinary person toward success. In fact, the mini-day/power-thinking team is the tool that enables him to take his first step into Neothink.

Moving Toward Neothink

As explained in the front material of this book, the mysticism-plagued conscious mind is limited. Mysticism — the bicameral impurities of the mind — blocks the entire dimension of integrated thinking. Indeed, after integrating five or six thoughts, the mysticism-plagued conscious mind stops integrating, needing external guidance before going further. But mysticism-free Neothink goes further. For with Neothink, one does not stop and wait for external guidance. Instead he develops his own integrated thinking, his own self-guidance such as power-thinking. He never stops moving forward. He keeps on integrating — right into new realms capable of making millions of dollars.

The mysticism-plagued conscious mind can MAINTAIN specialized jobs with automatic or externally guided routines, including those higher-paying jobs in the white-collar hoax (explained in the front material), even the CEO positions. But to CREATE and BUILD wealth requires integrated thinking. Therefore, man must remove the residual bicameral-like limitations of his mind (i.e., specialized thinking — following automatic or external guidance).

By using the mini-day/power-thinking team, the ordinary person removes many of his residual bicameral-like limitations. He discovers the new dimension of power-thinking; he discovers integrated thinking required for wealth creation.

The Residual Bicameral-Like Limitations
Of The Conscious Mind

The traditional daily schedule just *reacts* to routine priorities throughout the week. The mini-day/power-thinking team, on the other hand, *creates* wealth-building priorities into the future. For, as the reader will see, power-thinking integrates beyond maintaining a specialized job and reacting to its routine priorities. Power-thinking integrates *new* money-making projects, integrates the future — never just reacts to the present.

Bicameral tendencies in people caused the mini-day/power-thinking team to go undiscovered until The Neo-Tech System. For only The Neo-Tech System confronts and removes our mysticism. With the dawning of the Neo-Tech Age (i.e., the dawning of the integrated thinkers), more and more ordinary people will discover the mini-day/power-thinking team and suddenly soar beyond their peers. They will create and build new money-making projects. They will leave behind specialized thinking to never again just maintain a job. Indeed, through the mini-day/power-thinking team, they will discover integrated thinking. Integrated thinking builds wealth.

Without removing a simple, deep-rooted bicameral-like limitation — the traditional schedule — wealth will forever stay out of reach. However, anyone can MAINTAIN a specialized area just fine using the traditional daily schedule. ...Don't you think, it's time to move on?

Moving Beyond The Bicameral Mode
Into The Integrating Mode

Not long after he discovered the mini-day/power-thinking team, Mr. Hamilton had 22 projects on his power-thinking list. Underneath those projects were 150 steps needed to accomplish those 22 projects. Within one week, every step was accomplished or moved into flowing action. Before the mini-day/power-thinking team, he had problems just keeping up with his voluminous routine work, no less doing even just one forward-movement project in one week. How did he go from perhaps accomplishing one project to 22 projects? That is quite a quantum jump and expansion.

Consider that the mysticism-plagued average person focuses and concentrates on only one integration, just five or six thoughts, just one project at a time. He reacts to no more than a handful of things at a time — certainly not to 150 tasks for 22 projects in a week, for he would be paralyzed.

Now consider that the mysticism-free Neothink person focuses and concentrates on vast integrations, 150 tasks, 22 projects at a time. He creates those vast integrations all at one time — during power-thinking: First, he determines the steps needed to complete a project by focusing in his mind the completed project. He focuses on one project at a time. He uncovers and lists the steps needed to complete the project. Then he puts that project out of his mind altogether to make room for the next project. At this point, he has formed a maximum-integration puzzle piece to a Neothink puzzle. (The Neothink puzzle is explained in the front material.) He then concentrates on the next project. He imagines the completed project and writes down the steps to reach that image. Now he has formed another maximum-integration puzzle piece to the Neothink puzzle. Then he clears his mind and goes on to the next project, and so on, each project forming another puzzle piece to the Neothink puzzle. Those

41

puzzle pieces next snap together into the mini-day schedule.

He does his power-thinking on Saturday or Sunday and injects his entire power-thinking list into his next week's mini-day schedule. His mini-day schedule becomes an interlocked Neothink puzzle that captures hard, Firestone-like thinking (i.e., power-thinking) for several major projects. All week long, every action, every move comes directly from that hard Firestone-like thinking. Moreover, every little task in the Neothink puzzle integrates with several other tasks that move major projects toward rapid payoff. Indeed, every little task performed integrates synergistically with the Neothink puzzle. Although just a mechanical mini-day schedule, every action delivers Neothink synergy and comes from hard Firestone-like, integrated thinking.

The human mind can focus intensely on just one project — no more. But with the use of special tools, man can operate beyond his mental processing capacity. The mini-day/power-thinking team is the reader's first tool that lets him go beyond the capacity of the human mind for his first step into Neothink.

To move a difficult project through, no doubt, one must exert concentrated focus on the project. That fact has led many pipe-smoking professors of business to conjure up myths about doing only the important projects or responsibilities. That way, they say, the important things will get done. Entrepreneurs who follow such sound-good advice, however, get too far behind in the many other areas of business and eventually fail.

True, the mind can only focus and concentrate on one project at one time. But, with the integrated mini-day/power-thinking team, the ordinary person takes his first step beyond the limits of the human mind into Neothink. He captures focused concentration on not just one but several projects throughout each week.

Power-thinking captures nebulous ambitions, goals, projects into tangible steps. The steps further break down into specific tasks when injected in the mini-days. Ambitions, goals, projects break down, down, down to earth...down to tasks that get done. By plugging those tasks into the intense mini-days, any average person yanks in far-away dreams right now, right down to quick-action reality. So, let us try it...

Chapter Five
GETTING STARTED

First, you most likely run into a block because you work in a white-collar-hoax structure. Realize that in your traditional job, the mini-day schedule will boost your capacity and help you move up the ladder. But as mentioned earlier, your job is probably locked into specialized ends-in-themselves responsibilities, not integrated with making money and forward movement. The ends-in-themselves responsibilities take full priority in your job, yet the only VALID priority in business is INTEGRATION as you will further understand throughout this manuscript.

Integration is the essence of the mini-day schedule. Specialization is the essence of your job. Your specialized, ends-in-themselves responsibilities/priorities might not break down into an integrated, money-making mini-day schedule.

But worse, the synergy of power-thinking interlocked with the mini-days can never occur in your traditional job. For all people in all traditional jobs will have difficulty doing power-thinking. You see, power-thinking requires grasping entire, fully integrated projects, not just specialized responsibilities. Most people trapped in traditional jobs cannot so much as even THINK in wide, integrated terms — cannot integrate projects with the money, finances, negotiations — no less get those projects into forward-march mini-days. In traditional jobs, bicameral-like thinking (external guidance from set responsibilities and management above) replaces integrated thinking (internal guidance with power-thinking).

The heightened power behind the mini-day/power-thinking team, when used together, cannot be reached, will fall apart, can never be known by those in specialized jobs. When you do the following exercise, keep that in mind. If you find you cannot do power-thinking, cannot think of projects you can do at work, realize that is because of the limiting, specialized nature of your job. As long as you stay in that specialized structure, you will never move through projects and integrate with making money.

The integrating power of the mini-day/power-thinking team

for the first time allows you to leave the specialized structure. The mini-day/power-thinking team enables you to integrate the vast array of responsibilities needed to start your own business. Consider that the average person inherently senses that he would become too overwhelmed with his own business. For owning a business requires integrating everything, as in the candy vendor example in Chapter One. Contrary to sound-good excellence type management books that suggest a person can focus on one thing — say, customer service or employee motivation — and succeed, the entrepreneur quickly discovers that he must integrate *everything* to survive. He cannot do just what he does best or just what he likes. He must integrate everything needed to gain power and wealth, and the mini-day/power-thinking team for the first time gives him that integrating power. ...Once you are on your own, you can begin to rapidly move through projects and integrate with making money. Furthermore, in Volume Two, you will learn techniques on how to metamorphose your current job into a money-making job right at your place of work, without leaving your company. You will use the mini-day/power-thinking team to soar ahead of others and shoot straight to the top of the company you now work for.

Now, back to the exercise. If you find you cannot successfully do power-thinking at this time or have problems setting up mini-days, just follow the logic without doing the steps. You will see the limits of your specialized job. You will see how power-thinking integrates into the forward-march mini-day schedule for beyond-the-mind results. Let us try it:

First let us try power-thinking. Try doing the same as Mr. Hamilton did. Pick your most ambitious project. Do the following exercise: Focus on a current project in your job or beyond your job, perhaps the project of starting your own business. Envision the finished project. Get a clear, integrated look in your head at the finished outcome. Clearly focus the total, final outcome in your mind.

Once you set that completed image in your mind, begin to concentrate on what actions will accomplish that finished project. See your project in the whole, integrated perspective in contrast to the traditional, unintegrated, one-thought-at-a-time, step-by-step perspective. See all steps from the finished, integrated side. Take your thoughts into the future.

Take a couple minutes to do this with your most ambitious project. Do not write down your steps yet. Just picture in your mind the completed project and let yourself see all the steps needed to achieve that completed picture. Do that and nothing else. Sit up...imagine the completed project, then think hard what steps are needed to complete that project. Really apply yourself, for power-thinking will offer surprising rewards. This is far different from the specious "visualization" techniques of inspirational books. Power-thinking has direct-action results through the mini-day schedule. For this first step, just imagine the completed project and then the steps needed to achieve that image of the completed project. Do not write anything down. Stop reading and do this first step now.

Now, be sure to keep in your mind each step that will take you to that final point of completion. At first you may not be able to think of all the steps needed to complete the project. That capacity develops with practice, so think about as many steps as possible. You can add the missing steps as they become obvious once you begin your strategic attack on the project.

The next move is to write down each step. We will call this your power-thinking list. Stop reading and do this now.

After you have your power-thinking list, you are going to move the project through fast. You are going to pounce on the entire project at once to complete it in record time. Teaming up with the powerful mini-day schedule, you are going to promptly bring the future to you.

But first, you should purchase a standard "Week At A Glance" schedule book available at any office-supply store. Once you have your "Week At A Glance", first sketch out your mini-days for all of next week, in similar fashion to Mr. Hamilton's mini-day schedule found on page 23, Diagram Three. Realize you do not have to stay in the framework of your specialized job. You may sketch out the mini-days for your current job, for your goals beyond your current job, or for your new business. In any case, the project on your power-thinking list should apply to the mini-days sketched out. Now assign the proper time to each mini-day. Stop reading and do this before continuing.

Do you have your mini-day schedule laid out? If so, your

mini-day schedule becomes a powerful tool. (If you do not yet have your mini-day schedule figured out, then steps one through four still to come, walk you step by step through setting up your mini-day schedule.) Now, pull out your power-thinking list. Go through each step listed on your power-thinking list; determine the action or actions needed to do each step and record those actions — those tasks — under their corresponding mini-days.

Always favor the mini-days of the earliest days of the week. Only when a mini-day looks full should you move to the next weekday for that particular mini-day. Again, go through each step listed on your power-thinking list; determine the action or actions needed to do each step and record those actions — those tasks — under their corresponding physical movement — their mini-day. Stop reading and do this now.

As you can see, the mini-day makes power-thinking real and powerful. Through the mini-day/power-thinking team, you integrate the future into today. You lock your scope on projects before the projects begin. Then you capture the projects immediately with the mini-day schedule.

Now that you experienced power-thinking for one project, let us compile the projects. Try power-thinking ALL the projects that you would like to accomplish. First, focus in your mind the complete, final outcome of each project, doing one project at a time. First think about and image in your mind the steps that will take you to completion of one project. Write those steps down. Then move on to the next project. Do the same for each separate project. That will be your complete power-thinking list, similar to Mark Hamilton's complete power-thinking list in Diagram Four, pages 25 through 29. Stop reading and do this now.

Now, once you finish your power-thinking list, ask yourself, how long would it take to complete it? Three months? Six months? How long did it take Mr. Hamilton? Again, his entire long list was moved toward rapid completion in just one week.

Like him, you will move all projects toward rapid completion in one week and still have time left over for more forward movement (i.e., those mini-days in your schedule that will handle more tasks). Moreover, you will find plenty of ease handling the day to day routine work as well. Go ahead now and inject into your mini-day schedule the actions (tasks) to do each step of your master power-thinking list. Use a full week of blank, sketched out mini-days. Generally speaking, one week will be all you need to move all projects toward rapid completion. Stop reading and do this now.

Now that you have done your power-thinking list, let us look closely at how to properly develop your mini-days. The following step-by-step instructions show you exactly how to establish your mini-day schedule.

Set Up Your Mini-Days

You must first break down your career to the basic physical movements. Step 1 and Step 2 will do that to start your integration with money and power. Do the following easy exercise:

Step 1:
List Three Days' Tasks, Prepare To Integrate

List every task done at work for three days. ...Consider that you probably cannot remember what you ate for dinner last night. Most people cannot remember the little details done just a day or two ago. The point is: doing your list of tasks right now would come from memory. Instead, start tomorrow. Keep a tablet next to you at work and list every task for the next three days. Today relax and read through this manuscript. See where Neo-Tech Control takes you. Tomorrow you start.

Start seriously. Record all the tasks as you do them. Do not wait until lunch time or until the end of the day to list tasks from memory. To get the most out of Neo-Tech Control, you must exert yourself. Because of the integrated nature of Neo-Tech Control, everything builds from here. So if you do not do a good job on your tasks, everything henceforth suffers. So do it right. List every task. Do not list your responsibilities; list your tasks, simple tasks such as Mark Hamilton did:
   * Called Stuart
   * Wrote Nightingale-Conant
   * Did video copywriting
   * Reviewed invoices
   * Called Jim Tegtmire
   ...And so on

47

Caution: List your tasks, not projects. Do not list, for instance, "Worked on European Project". Instead list the *tasks* done for that project such as "Called printing consultant in Ireland", "Wrote Peter in England about lettershop", "Met with list broker", and so on.

Starting tomorrow, list every task; do not put "miscellaneous". Use action verbs: called, drafted, wrote, met, reviewed, etc. Also, list tasks that you wanted to do or planned to do but did not have time to do.

Again, do not list a project, such as "I wanted to finish my European Project". Tasks only! "I wanted to call printing consultant in Ireland", "I wanted to write Peter in England"...and so on. Tasks, not projects. Write down all tasks *as you do them* for the next three days. You need three days of tasks instead of two days or one day to get the proper perspective of your career for the breakdown in Step 2.

Step 2:
Integrate Tasks Into Their Physical Movements

After you acquire your three days of tasks, you are ready to break down your career into its physical movements. The physical movements streamline those tasks like an assemblyline. Every career must have physical movements or there would be no career. Your job has physical movements because if it did not, you would just sit all day long and do nothing. You must determine the basic physical movements in your career. Now, go back to your three days of listed tasks.

Go through that list of tasks and determine the basic, physical movements as you did with Mr. Hamilton's tasks on pages 16 and 17. Write your physical movements on a scratch pad. (Your physical movements will vary from Mr. Hamilton's movements.) The easiest way to do this is to first read through the tasks. Then begin to name the most common physical movements, picking out the most obvious movement first, say phone calls perhaps, assigning that most obvious movement number one. Then go through and put a #1 next to those tasks. Then read through the remaining unnumbered tasks. Pick the next obvious basic movement and number those tasks and so on. Through the process of elimination you pick off all the obvious movements

48

and are left with the seemingly disjointed tasks to be grouped into "operations". Again, pick out the obvious movements first. Number those tasks. Then narrow down to your final, trickiest physical movement: operations. You are doing the same thing that you did on pages 16 and 17 with Mr. Hamilton's list of tasks.

You are determining *basic* physical movements. If, for instance, you make only one or two phone calls a week (and would gain nothing by increasing your phone calls), then phone calls is not a *basic* physical movement and should fall under "operations". Any physical movement that would benefit you by having consistent time assigned to it, on the other hand, should be broken out as a basic physical movement.

Do not consider projects as physical movements. Mr. Hamilton did not put the huge project of "European mailings" as a physical movement. Instead, he placed the related tasks under his true physical movements. For example, he put the task "called printing consultant in Ireland" under true physical movement phone calls, and he put the task "wrote Peter in England" under true physical movement letter writing, and so on. As you can see by his movement breakdown on page 20, all European-related tasks fall under their physical movements.

So again, go through your list of tasks, picking out the basic, physical movements. Once again, do not list a project as a physical movement, no matter how big. Also, as you do this step, be on the lookout for a project that had been erroneously listed as a *task*. That will lead to problems as well. Watch out for this common mistake. If you do find a project listed as a task, break it down into its actual small tasks before moving on. And once again, do not let a project get listed as a physical movement or as a task.

Finally, do not necessarily follow Mr. Hamilton's movements. Some of your movements may be the same, some may not. Determine the physical movements appropriate for your list of tasks. Do this step now.

* * * *

When finished, count the number of physical movements determined, including operations. Notice that your entire career breaks down into a simple handful of movements. Through the division of labor you have begun to break down your complex job into a handful of simple movements. As your tasks begin to physically integrate, everything begins to move toward simplicity. As we go through the next two steps, these few simple movements pull together all dimensions of your career into a smooth-flowing assembly-line for explosive results.

Now break the tasks out under their physical movements, just like Mr. Hamilton's breakdown of movements, Diagram Two on page 20. Write down the first physical movement on a blank sheet of paper and beneath it list its tasks. When finished with the first physical movement and its tasks, then write down the next physical movement and beneath it list its tasks, and so on.

Think about each task and the physical movement it is being listed under. If something does not seem right, for instance if the tasks seem to lack the streamlined togetherness seen in Mr. Hamilton's breakdown on page 20, then look more closely: Look for projects recorded as physical movements. If so, then remove the project from the physical movements and put its tasks under their true physical movements. You may need to do Step 2 again to refigure the correct physical movements. ...Also look for projects listed as tasks. If so, then break them down to the simple tasks, and do Step 2 again to refigure the correct physical movements. Your finished breakdown should look like Mr. Hamilton's breakdown on page 20. Do this now.

*   *   *   *

Summary of Step 2: Go through your list of tasks. Pick the most obvious physical movement; assign it number one, and number the corresponding tasks. Then go to the next obvious physical movement and number those tasks. And the next and so on until you are left with those seemingly disjointed tasks. Those left-over tasks will fall under your "operations" physical movement. Remember: physical movements, not projects. Finish Step 2 with the tasks listed below each physical movement as Mr. Hamilton's breakdown on page 20. Remember, everything continues to build on what you are doing now as Neo-Tech Control is totally integrated. Do a good job.

Step 3:
Integrate The Physical Movements With Time

Those physical movements are 100% of what you do. Think how you would break that 100% down. Say you work a 10-hour day (100%). How would you divide your time to most effectively balance your handful of basic physical movements? What percentage of your time would you give your first physical movement? Would it be 2 hours (20%)? Or 1.5 hours (15%)? And your second movement? Would it be 1.5 hours (15%)? And your next movement? ...It is a balancing game. The more you give one movement, the less you can give another movement as the sum of your physical movements must add up to 100% of your time. Do this next step not thinking about your office or the format of your job. Just look at those physical movements and realize they take 100% of your time. Then divide your hours among those physical movements. Next to the hours put the percentage of the work day those hours represent. That helps determine the best balance. Think hard about your physical movements and study the balance and the percentage of time for the best breakdown. Do not consider the time you currently devote to each. Instead, put down what you know would be best. Go ahead and do this before moving on.

*   *   *   *

Does the sum of your percentages add up to 100%? They should because your physical movements are 100% of what you do. And remember as you do this, do not think about anything else in your job. Just work with the physical movements.

Look at Mr. Hamilton's example below. After Mr. Hamilton determined and listed his six basic movements as done in Step Two; he determined the approximate activity of each movement. He estimated the percentage of his 10-hour office day that he should devote to each movement. Recognize that he estimated what he should devote, not necessarily what he was devoting at the time.

He assigned time to the basic movements. He works at the office from 8 a.m. to 6 p.m., straight through. That is 10 hours. He allocated, adjusted, and readjusted until he felt comfortable with the balance among his six basic movements as follows:

(1) Phone Calls	2 hours	20%
(2) Letter Writing	1.5 hours	15%
(3) Copy Writing	1 hours	10%
(4) Accounting	2 hours	20%
(5) Meetings and People	1.5 hours	15%
(6) Operations	2 hours	20%
TOTAL	10 hours	100%

Step 4:
Integrate The Schedule

After balancing his time (Step 3), Mr. Hamilton determined the best placement for each movement in his day and made a daily-schedule breakdown as follows:

8-10:00 am	Phone Calls	(2 hrs.)
10-11:30 am	Letter Writing	(1.5 hrs.)
11:30-1:30	Operations	(2 hrs.)
1:30-2:30	Copy Writing	(1 hrs.)
2:30-4:30	Accounting	(2 hrs.)
4:30-6:00	Meetings and People	(1.5 hrs.)

Look again at your physical movements, each now with a percentage of time allotted to it. Figure where you want each particular movement to be in your day, just as Mr. Hamilton did. Organize those movements for greatest effectiveness. Making phone calls before letter writing may work better, for instance. Moreover, making phone calls in the morning would work better than around noon when people are out for lunch. ...Forget about how your job is structured now. Do this step now.

Becoming The Money/Power Giant

Now with your weekly mini-day/power-thinking team, you can perform as effectively as the money/power giants themselves. Look closely again at Mr. Hamilton's power-thinking list, Diagram Four on pages 25 through 29. You can sense just how complex his career really is. But the vast integrations and broad horizons of even the greatest tycoons get injected into the easy-to-handle mini-days. Once in the mini-day schedule, the highest paid, most glamorous careers do not look so tough, vast, complex or high-powered. Again, look at Mr. Hamilton's high-powered,

52

complex career for just one week in August, his power-thinking list. Until now, only a super manager could operate at that level. But now look at his weekly mini-day schedule for that list, Diagram Five on pages 54 and 55. Even a high-school boy could mechanically handle Mr. Hamilton's high-powered career. Anyone, any average man or woman, can take his first step into Neothink.

The Neo-Tech System

Diagram Five
Mini-Day/Power-Thinking Team Results

JUNE 1985	JULY 1985	AUGUST 1985	SEPTEMBER 1985	
S M T W T F S	S M T W T F S	S M T W T F S	S M T W T F S	

AUGUST

MONDAY, AUGUST 19 231/134	TUESDAY, AUGUST 20 232/133	WEDNESDAY, AUGUST 21 233/132
8:00 *Phone Calls*	8:00 *Phone Calls*	8:00 *Phone Calls*
Stuart → Spanish + French Car	Brian @ Beta Inv → expl. que.	Kathy @ Newsletter Mgt → bill
Karen Johnson, KCT → letter	Dan Perry - money making mag	Call Kari Dub for yacht ad
9:00 Jim Balmire → order	Give Bill Levine final	LA Times classified ad
Inter Market → deal	9:00 MacCann Hunter → leads on Eg.	9:00 Metro News → ph. #'s
Make arrangements w/ video	La Opinion Irene Unghotti	PSA Ph #'s ? → Stuart
Data for Graphics	Blue Cross → Shelly 382-3367	National Eng. + Globe Ticket
10:00 *Letter Writing*	10:00 *Letter Writing*	10:00 *Letter Writing*
Write Vic Conant → s + rent list	Write Newsletter Mgt → s + s list	Expl. Env. letter to mass mags
Write similar to Stuart → s+s	Send Brian a note on 10/31	Canadian DBA → printers
Telex British anythanks	Bernard Money → meet in Oct.	Telex Peter R. → s
11:00 Telex Peter K.	AUTHORITIES	11:00
Telex Francist.	Hume	
30 *Operational*	30 *Operational*	30 *Operational*
Basket	Basket – sections in office mirror	Basket – expl. envelope
12:00 Corrections on expl. env.	12:00 Study job-title applicants	12:00 Ad copy for test on newsletter
Send in 2nd Class Application	for Cust. Service + Accountant	Design heading for newsletter
30 Interviews + Training	30 Interviews + Training	30 Interviews + Training
Strategic Inv → insertion order	PO Kinder Services, PSA	Meet w/ Dan Perry
1:00 Prepare operations for my	1:00 Prepare Operations for my	1:00 Prepare operations for my
departure to Europe	departure to Europe	departure to Europe
30 *Copywriting*	30 *Copywriting*	30 *Copywriting*
Video tape production	Miam → go over, give direction	Prepare outline, details for
2:00	2:00 quick edit → then let her	2:00 book w/ FW + turnover
	work more on it	
Accounting	*Accounting*	*Accounting*
Records	Records	Records
3:00 Invoices	3:00 Cost study	3:00 Cost study
Study costs → set up cost	HW procedures	HW procedures
30 study program w/ HW	30 Andrews Correction	Review data + set up SA
4:00	4:00	4:00
30 *Meetings + People*	30 *Meetings + People*	30 *Meetings + People*
Meet w/ TS → mailing lists +	Melinda → set up "solvage"	Shelly → review my outline
5:00 Helen finish IBM → summary	5:00 Vicki → policies, fines	5:00 of organization
HW	Linda → collection turnover	TS →
30	+ set up mailings from home	HW
6:00 *Evening*	6:00 *Evening*	6:00 *Evening*
30	30	30
Work on NT Mgt book	Same → brochure NT Mgt	Work on GT's brochure
7:00 + on book	7:00 + on final chapter	7:00 "A Day of Consultation"
30	30	30
8:00	8:00	8:00
30	30	Personal night w/ TS
9:00	9:00	9:00
30	30	30

54

Diagram Five
Mini-Day/Power-Thinking Team Results

OCTOBER 1985	NOVEMBER 1985	DECEMBER 1985	JANUARY 1986
S M T W T F S	S M T W T F S	S M T W T F S	S M T W T F S
1 2 3 4 5	1 2	1 2 3 4 5 6 7	1 2 3 4
6 7 8 9 10 11 12	3 4 5 6 7 8 9	8 9 10 11 12 13 14	5 6 7 8 9 10 11
13 14 15 16 17 18 19	10 11 12 13 14 15 16	15 16 17 18 19 20 21	12 13 14 15 16 17 18
20 21 22 23 24 25 26	17 18 19 20 21 22 23	22 23 24 25 26 27 28	19 20 21 22 23 24 25
27 28 29 30 31	24 25 26 27 28 29 30	29 30 31	26 27 28 29 30 31

1985

THURSDAY, AUGUST 22 234/131	FRIDAY, AUGUST 23 235/130	SATURDAY, AUGUST 24 236/129
8:00 *Phone Calls*	8:00 *Phone Calls*	8:00 *Writing Day*
✓– Bobby McGee → NT Mgt ad	✓ David Galland → NT Mgt ad	
✓–:30 Bob White → classified/NT Mgt	✓ Brian Kurtz	✓ Finish booklist insert
✓– Contact Postal authorities	✓ Peter Rochefort → #'o	
9:00 prep. ✓ LB for 2 class cost	9:00 Stuart → Globe, Nat Eng. *	9:00 ✓– Perhaps get video finished
APPOINTMENT 9:00	✓ APPOINTMENT WCV 9:00	:30 if not already
:30 West Coast Video → cancelled	:30	
10:00 *Letter Writing*	10:00 *Letter Writing*	10:00
✓ John Ward → his music to Neo-Tech videos	✓ Peter Weir	✓ Finish Doris insert
✓– New CCL letter	✓:30 Love your work = must make most even if not like #'s	
✓:11:00 JUME Pub! → mtg in Montreal	:00 AUTHORITIES	11:00
	✓ Doris Insert **	✓ Work on NT mgt book
:30 *Operational*	:30 *Operational*	:30
✓– Basket	✓ Basket *	all day → editing +
12:00 Shinder → purge women & work list back	12:00 Send Pac Env PO for remit	12:00 then draft special
✓ Organize lists for upcoming AMS mailings	✓ Organize French translation for French-Can. list	chapter
:30 Prepare operations for	:30 Prepare operations for	:30
1:00 my departure to Europe	1:00 my departure to Europe	1:00
✓– SH → get British Pounds		
:30 *Copywriting*	:30 *Copywriting*	
✓– Turn over 1st NT Mgt draft + line for PV to GT for "Day" during	✓ Receive & edit to prompt TJ	✓. Take and organize
2:00	2:00 further understanding & development of Paradise Valley	2:00 all brochure formats
✓– Receive from b. Ticket & prompt edit		
:30 *Accounting*	:30 *Accounting*	:30
✓– Records	✓ Records	
3:00 Cost study	3:00 Cost study	3:00 *Data update, review*
✓· HW procedures	✓· HW procedures	:30
✓· Computer program	✓· Computer program applic.	✓ Data sheets
✓· 4:00 Invoices	4:00	4:00 ✓· Visicalc update
		✓ Media update
:30 *Meetings & People*	:30 *Meetings & People*	1:30 ✓ Split-run analysis
✓– GT → review cassette progress & product develop. "Day" tapes	✓ Major operations meeting	List analysis / future tests
✓· 5:00 TJ → review BMI mailing & trip to Europe	✓ Vicki	*Personal night w/ TJ*
	✓ Shelly	
:30	:30 WW	:30
6:00	6:00	SUNDAY, AUGUST 25 237/128
✓– During my run, listen to GT's task development tapes		*Writing Day*
✓– Spend some thought on marketing approach	✓– Doris Insert → WW	· *Personal morning w/ TJ*
7:00	7:00	
✓· Work on GT's brochure	✓· Work on GT's broch.	Split afternoon & evening drafting 1st copy of book w/ Perio. + NT Mgt book
8:00 "A Day of Consultation"	8:00	
:30	:30	· If get a chance, start drafting book of cee's
9:00	9:00	**AUGUST**
:30	:30	* Leave for Europe

Chapter Six
STEPPING INTO NEOTHINK

Princeton University Professor, Dr. Julian Jaynes, demonstrated in his award-winning lifetime achievement *The Origin of Consciousness in the Breakdown of the Bicameral Mind* (Houghton Mifflin), that 3000 years ago man's guidance system was void of self-choice. Man's guidance system was controlled by nature just as any other animal. With a large two-chamber brain, largest brain by far of all animals, man increasingly evolved language. He increasingly communicated through talking, which was the most effective system for communicating. Therefore, he thrived in growing civilizations. Man's actions though, as any other animal, were still controlled by nature's built-in guidance system. In fact, nature directed man through the use of his own language; the authority of the spoken voice was the most effective guidance system that could evolve in nature. The "gods" would "talk" to him, clearly and concisely.

Actually, his large two-chamber (i.e., bicameral) brain would send messages from the right chamber to the left chamber as man "heard" the voices of the "gods". Today we call this phenomenon an audio hallucination. But 3000 years ago, that was the voice of his "god". When a decision needed to be made or an action needed to be taken, the right-chamber brain would send the decision or action to be taken to the left brain not as a mere impression, but as a clear and concise voice (i.e., audio hallucination). That voice of his "god" was to be obeyed without question. His god and his God-King who heard the commands of the "higher gods" were absolute authorities to unconditionally follow. Thus, man waited for the "voices" for answers. Nature's guidance system literally told man what to do. Whole civilizations were guided by their gods and their God-Kings — the divine leaders who could elicit the voices of the higher "gods"...in other words, those who most efficiently hallucinated. Civilizations smoothly survived through this following mode — through following their external guidance, their "gods" and God-Kings.

But society grew more complex as man engaged in primitive forms of commerce and trade. The growing commerce, the different languages, different peoples, different cultures all coming together for trade became too complex for the nature-controlled bicameral mind to direct any longer. The voices grew confusing and contradictory and eventually stopped sending the messages as nature's guiding mechanism became incompetent and broke down. The "gods" grew silent. At this point in our history, 3000 years ago, war and chaos broke out as the bewildered humans did not know what to do. Man faced extinction.

Under enormous survival pressures, some grabbed hold of two new linguistic tools called the metaphor and the analogy. Through metaphors and analog models, the collapsing civilizations — lost without their external guidance — slowly regained some equilibrium. People one by one learned how to subjectively view the world around them. They could step back for a moment from the objective world that immediately surrounded them by using the metaphor (i.e., something that describes something else). Instead of helplessly reacting to the chaos around them, now through metaphors and analogies, they gradually discovered a whole new mind-space that could make judgments, form opinions, even introspect. That new mind-space was the beginning of self-thinking, self-control, and decision making. That new mind-space was the beginning of human consciousness.

During those tumultuous times, man made the thunderous discovery of how to think for himself, how to guide himself. That man-made discovery of human consciousness saved civilization. Man no longer needed external guidance, for he now had internal guidance. Metaphors and analogies separated man from an automatic existence of stimulus and response. For now, through the use of metaphors and analog models, man could step back from the immediate stimulus around him...and think, make decisions, and act (not just react). His discovery, this new way of using the mind, was something far beyond nature's guidance system. It was never part of nature's evolutionary process and explains why no missing link exists. Instead, our self-thinking conscious mentality, our superior ability over the bicameral mentality, came from a man-made discovery forced upon us essentially from business, from the growing complexities of commerce and trade. As man discovered human consciousness, he could survive after the "gods" and God-Kings went silent.

Man no longer needed leaders telling him what to do and how to act.

Today, 3000 years later, man is on the brink of another major discovery of the mind called Neothink. Going from mysticism-plagued conscious thinking to mysticism-free Neothink can be compared to going from the bicameral mentality to human consciousness 3000 years ago. Since about 1000 BC, man has used his mind in the same limited manner as he does today, his explosive Neothink power blocked by his bicameral tendencies *to follow* external guidance. In a few years, man will use his mind in a completely different limitless manner than he does today, freed from his bicameral roots, no longer following a limited routine, instead integrating forward with self-guidance.

As man evolves beyond mysticism-plagued specialized thinking into mysticism-free integrated thinking, he needs no more white-collar hoax, no more routine rut, no more external guidance, no more external authorities.

How Today's Conscious Mind Works

Just how does man use his mind today? As Dr. Jaynes explains, for much of our life we still function in a nonconscious state. The manual laborer, for example, works in a nonconscious mode. He can at any moment switch into a conceptual, conscious mode, for he is a conscious being. But during most mechanical actions such as driving the car, laying bricks, even mechanically doing math, one remains in a nonconscious (non-introspective/non-subjective) state.

On the other hand, the executive may use his conscious thinking more. However, this is how he does it: He acts automatically, according to what is in his mind, to what thought is in his brain at the time. He gets a certain thought, say a project that needs to be done. That thought in his head activates his behavior: a phone call, a letter he needs to write, perhaps he needs to contact a business associate. In any case, he acts according to what is in his mind at that moment. He acts in an automatic mode: actions based on active thoughts — an automatic thought by thought, by thought, by thought, by thought process that requires little integrated thinking. Automatic guidance from what fills his mind — somewhat like the automatic guidance from the "voices" that filled the bicameral mind — directs his actions.

How The Neothink Mind Works

Mysticism-free Neothink goes well beyond the processing capacity of the mysticism-plagued conscious mind. Neothink evolves beyond the automatic thought by thought, actions-based-on-active-thoughts process: thought, call this person, write this letter; thought, talk to business associate. Thought, thought, thought; action. No. Neothink does not work that way. The Neothink mind makes vast integrations. Instead of automatic guidance, one evolves into self-guidance and activates integrated thinking. One handles vast horizons, not just hundreds and hundreds of automatic, single thoughts over his lifetime.

The mysticism-plagued person does not integrate; he remains in an automatic mode all his life. He reacts to single thoughts that fill his mind at the time, one by one. He never integrates thoughts, never activates the integrating mode, never builds integrations and new directions, never builds wealth. He needs external guidance, whether it comes from his specialized routine or guidance from others.

The mysticism-free person does integrate; he integrates thoughts all the time. He acts on integrated thoughts, many at a time. By eradicating his mysticism, he evolves into self-guidance. He activates the integrating mode and discovers the great power of his mind. He builds integrations upon integrations and builds new business directions. He builds wealth. He needs no external guidance and discovers the Neothink mind.

Through Neothink, any person can build larger-than-life fortunes. He pulls the integration string on great clusters of thoughts as quickly as he previously integrated single thoughts. Suddenly, competitors seem dull and slow.

You Have Taken Your First Step

The mini-day/power-thinking team is the first step into Neothink. When an average person interlocks his vast integrations of power-thinking into his next week's mini-day schedule, he puts his foot in the door of Neothink. That same week's worth of major projects would never get touched by the thought-by-thought mysticism-plagued average person. But the mini-day schedule mechanically captures the vast integrations of power-thinking. Those vast integrations break down into many little tasks throughout the week that get assembled together through the mini-days like an assembly line assembling rivets, nuts, bolts. Like stepping back as the completed cars come away from the end of the assembly line, one finds his several major projects come out complete at the end of the week. ...The mini-day/power-thinking team assembles the many little tasks with no problem. The automatic-mode average person without the mini-day/power-thinking team would get lost among the many "rivets, nuts, and bolts" and would rarely finish a single project.

Soaring With Your First Neothink Tool

Before the mini-day/power-thinking team, Mr. Hamilton could handle at most maybe one or two major projects a week while managing everything else. But now by taking the first step into Neothink he rolls off 22 projects in a week while managing everything else more smoothly than before. Moving through important projects comes not from dropping everything else. No, it comes from power-thinking captured within the mini-day schedule.

Indeed, one's intense integrated thinking is isolated through power-thinking, then captured through the mini-day schedule. Throughout the entire week, his actions come not from automatic thoughts, but from hard Firestone-like thinking. Each action comes not from a thought, but from a vast integration of thoughts, all coming together at the end of the week as several projects get completed. Indeed, this mini-day assembly-line tool combining with Firestone-like power-thinking boosts capacity beyond the automatic-mode, nonintegrating conscious mind. Going beyond the mysticism-plagued conscious mind is Neothink. Neothink goes beyond the processing capacity of the conscious mind by pulling together vast integrations (such as the 22 projects) through special tools such as the mini-day/power-thinking team.

Without Neo-Tech/Neothink
There Is No Way Out Of Stagnation

The average man — like the child who wants to walk and the athlete who wants to win — wants to become wealthy; he wants to master life. He may be enthusiastic; he may want it;

but he does not know how to achieve his ambitions. He often flounders; he tires; he often reaches blindly at his quest, trapped his whole life in his specialized rut. As time goes by, he eventually accepts that he is going nowhere. The enthusiasm flickers out. He forgets the adventure; he never really lives. With no hope, he succumbs. Without moving beyond the first, most basic limitation, the traditional daily schedule, a person will stagnate and lose an entire life of major achievements. First, he must remove that most basic limitation and move into the integrated world of the mini-day/power-thinking team.

Imagine...power-thinking lucrative, money-making projects and then moving those projects through the mini-day schedule on your way to rapid power and wealth. That can now happen to YOU. BUT that CANNOT happen in a traditional job with ends-in-themselves responsibilities. No, the specialized job-format with its unbearable stagnation fails, no longer able to compete with the new, integrated mini-day/power-thinking team. With the new integrated tool, you can leave your job to start your own business (or acquire an integrated mini-business right at your place of work, explained later in Volume Two). Without the new tool, you will fail at an exciting life.

Below is Mark Hamilton during a Neo-Tech Control seminar:

In San Francisco

"In San Francisco a gentleman wrote down his goal; he wanted to open a print shop. When we asked him how long he had wanted to open a print shop, he said it had been his goal for years.

"That man had that goal for years, yet he was no closer than when he first developed that goal years before. Why? With further discussion, we learned that his goal just seemed to stay out of reach. Had he broken that goal into steps through power-thinking then injected those steps into a mini-day schedule, he would not only be running a print shop today, but perhaps a chain of print shops.

"As with most ordinary people, he could not even move through his first major goal. Imagine this: his goal of opening a print shop is a big redwood tree in front of him. He wants to move through that dream. He gets motivated, takes an ax, side-swings and hits the tree. Highly enthused, he draws back, takes the ax over his head and swings overhead into his goal. Then he turns to his other side and swings again...then over there he tries and again over here. He wants that print shop so badly that he is swinging everywhere into that tree, that goal. After awhile his arms get weary, his breath gets shallow, and he tires.

"After that gallant effort, he steps back to see how far he has moved into his goal. He sees little nicks everywhere, but the whole tree still stands with all its girth. He will not give up. He catches his breath; he comes back to the tree and desperately starts whacking everywhere, this time determined to see some progress. After physically wiping himself out, he steps back. The tree has many more nicks all over, but still stands with all its girth.

"He gives up. Yet there is no difference between that man, you, and Ray Kroc or Donald Trump. The money/power giants would have given up if they could not move through their goals and dreams. But they learned how to move through dreams. They knew how to get through that tree.

"Today you learned the vehicle that can chop down that tree. You have a power-thinking ability to see exactly what it takes to drop that tree. Then you plug right into the hard-swinging, sleeves-rolled-up mini-day schedule to chop through that tree. You come up to that tree and you hit every time in the right spot. Every chop is right where it needs to be thanks to power-thinking and you create a chip thanks to the mini-day schedule. Well, now you get incentive. Now you know you're on track. Phone call, letter, financial proposal — on track, chop-after-chop manageable units. You see a wedge and go on to chop deeper into your goal. You feel excited; you feel energy; you keep chopping until that big tree falls. Now you move on to bigger and better dreams!"

— Mark Hamilton
Neo-Tech Control Seminar
San Francisco, CA

Nearly every person down deep would like to someday build his own business, build something during his life that is his own. But most never do. For, almost no one, perhaps just one person out of millions trapped in specialized jobs, ever learns integrated thinking. Nearly all men and women implicitly sense that they could not integrate the array of details needed to succeed on their own. Nearly everyone dies without ever reaching beyond their specialized job. Most who do try...fail.

But now the mini-day/power-thinking team gives the ordinary person the tool needed to integrate the vast array of details that come with starting a business. For the first time in his life, the average person can leave behind his traditional job. He can leave behind external guidance and its stagnation. He can step away from the white-collar hoax before it destroys the company he works for now. He can step out on his own! With the mini-day/power-thinking tool, he can take the first step beyond the conscious mind to start his own company (or build his own successful mini-company within the company he now works for, explained in the Company-Capture Discovery, next).

Now he is ready to move on to greater integrated power — deep into Neothink. The Company-Capture Discovery next takes the reader into the Neo-Tech System — into the Neo-Tech life of BUILDING his own company.

Something radically different unfolds as the Neo-Tech System removes the limitations of the white-collar hoax that has controlled many big businesses for decades. Business mysticism gone...wealth-creation flourishes. And through mysticism-free Neothink, business rapidly grows powerful, quickly leaves mysticism-plagued competition behind, just as conscious man left bicameral man behind 3000 years ago. Indeed, the Company-Capture Discovery, Volume Two, takes you through the next evolution: from mysticism-plagued consciousness to mysticism-free Neothink. By the time you finish the Company-Capture Discovery, an entire new future opens to you. With Neothink, you explore horizons those around you never know exist. You build your company on new lands, free of the hoax, led by YOU with Neothink. Go now to the Company-Capture Discovery (page 101).

(Note: The remaining pages in Volume One provide valuable tips on the mini-day/power-thinking team, how to overcome some common problems, and how to dismiss ten harmful myths with the mini-day/power-thinking team. Upon activating your integrating mode and starting your mini-day/power-thinking team, be sure to come back and read the remaining pages in Volume One.)

Chapter Seven

OVERCOMING MINI-DAY/POWER-THINKING PROBLEMS

Overcoming Mini-Day/Power-Thinking Misconceptions

Some people mistakenly think that the mini-day is a regimented, cold approach to work and life with no room for relaxation. Actually, the mini-day schedule is the ultimate relaxing tool. Consider that with Neo-Tech Control, a person removes all stress. He can do in half a day the work that took a full day. He can go home early. He can spend more time with the family. And if he decides to go for an empire, he can spend long hours on the mini-day. But it is by far the most relaxed way to accomplish what he does. By spending long hours with this simple approach, one can handily accomplish what would run anyone else into his grave.

Also, establishing a mini-day for personal life is not a bad idea. It not only guarantees time with one's spouse, family, and personal values, but it guarantees active, not passive personal time for better, more intense values.

Finally, sleeping is a physical movement of its own. Scheduling a sleep mini-day, say a seven-hour sleep mini-day, adds consistency which adds to one's health and well being. And to the hard-driving entrepreneur or CEO: the sleep mini-day drives him harder during the day and makes him take his mini-day deadlines much more seriously as he cannot count on those late-night hours. By increasing intensity that way, the hard-driving entrepreneur gets more accomplished.

Overcoming Conflicts With Power Thinking

Power-thinking is needed for projects (not for maintaining routine work). Without power-thinking, the mini-day schedule can backfire on projects. Here is why:

Complex projects demand focused concentration to push through. Traditional managers often shut off everything else (get behind in other areas) to concentrate on and push through an important project. With power-thinking, though, not just one but several complex projects move through the mini-day schedule quickly — pounced on all at once. Without power-thinking, the complex projects never receive direct, focused concentration and can get hopelessly strung out in the mini-day schedule.

Indeed, power-thinking puts focused concentration on projects. The mini-day schedule then pounces on the projects all at once. Without the focused concentration first, however, the powerful mini-day backfires. For, at least with the traditional schedule a person puts full concentration on the project (even though he loses vital movement in other areas). But the mechanical mini-day schedule itself does not put direct concentration on a project. The mini-day schedule mechanically focuses on *movements*, not *projects* (i.e., on *the movement* not *the subject*). Power-thinking focuses on projects (i.e., the subject). Without power-thinking, complex projects take a long time to get done, even on the mini-day schedule.

Power-thinking is the hard thinking Firestone refers to as the ticket to success. Power-thinking means moving beyond automatic guidance from specialized jobs into self-guidance and integrated thinking.

Because power-thinking controls success, a person must feel totally comfortable with it so he continues to do it. Here is a suggestion, an easier way to do power-thinking:

First, power-thinking is done differently by different people in different careers. For example, to write out the steps below each project and then to determine the tasks to do those steps and inject them into the mini-day schedule is a waste of time for some people. Instead, they simply list their projects that need to be done, then with their next week's mini-day schedule next to them, they simply go through and mentally power-think each project while writing the tasks to do those projects straight into the proper mini-days. In other words, they list the projects just the same, but they bypass listing the steps on paper. They concentrate on a project then write the steps and tasks only once — straight into the mini-day schedule. The list of projects is easily done weekly with pencil and paper, as a word-processor is not important since the many steps below the projects are not written down. By leaving power-thinking less formal than Mr. Hamilton's example on pages 25 through 29, some find it much easier thus stick with it.

But some people, particularly those with complex projects and schedules, prefer to do power-thinking by listing the steps under the projects. Listing the steps for complex projects helps keep those projects all in front of them to "pounce" on. And some who do list the steps on paper still may find it easier to use pencil and paper instead of using a word processor.

Mr. Hamilton himself now lists his projects by pencil. In mid-1985 (time frame of his mini-day and power-thinking examples thus far), he was marketing director and general manager of I & O. The five-page power-thinking example on pages 25 through 29 came from his marketing days. Now, as CEO (in 1988), he handles broader responsibilities, and his power-thinking list and mini-day schedule look quite different (see pages 68 through 73). Indeed, the power-thinking and the mini-day tools work for all people at all levels. ...Find the most effective way for you.

Listing just the projects (not the steps) with pencil and paper, for instance, is shorter and more manageable. You may like the freedom to spontaneously jot down a project to start next week's power-thinking list. You can keep next week's power-thinking list in a desk file and build it at will during the week, as thoughts or projects come to mind. Then, on Sunday evening, you can power-think those projects directly into next week's mini-day schedule. This less formal approach encourages making use of this powerful tool.

Also, the mini-day schedule itself is approached differently by different people. For example, some do not like to move through several projects at once as does Mr. Hamilton. Again, that can be quite demanding (but quite rewarding for those with complex horizons). One may instead pick a single project from a handwritten list of future projects, do his power-thinking for that project and feed it through his mini-day schedule. By power-thinking and moving through one or two projects at a time, some find it easier to gradually build their capacity as they feel comfortable.

You determine the best approach for you. Whichever you choose, realize that power-thinking is essential for above-the-routine projects: i.e., TO BUILD. Power-thinking is not needed

(continued on page 74)

67

**Diagram Six
Mini-Day/Power-Thinking Team**

Power Thinking
8/3/88 - 9/3/88   ①

* $^{\$}$9.95 Project
- NTC : Magazine   • NTC : Direct Mail piece
- NTN Wave : Magazine • NTN Wave : Direct Mail piece
- LTBW : Magazine   • LTBW : Direct Mail piece
- Distributor program 1 pg magazine
- Distributor program BE direct mail piece
- Mark Hammilton for president
- Look at music brochure & see if it can fit 9.95 newspaper
- Radio 9.95 piece
- From Malaysia - so powerful : • 9.95 makes very credible costs sense
                                  • Really emphasize below point to an
                                    entire new realm

Note: In above 9.95 project, work in more & more
credibility boost - this was $100, threatened old-
money establishments, U.S. politicians of old-
money crowd blew it - they tried to stop little-known
$100 NTVP. Backfired - NTC will print identical
info on newspaper, cheap, turns yellow... but
identicle info printed at cheap as possible -
send without charge other than costs. NN :
this is powerful credibility, bargain, curiosity,
scandalous... but safe.
Note: Make above memo to go in 9.95 DM pieces
  "   "   "   "   "   " Malaysia 9.95 piece.

68

Diagram Six
Mini-Day/Power-Thinking Team
(continued) ②

* Worman's Project
   · Prepare 60-second radio ad · Prepare radio 1st follow-up
   · Finish direct mail 1st & 2nd (conversion piece)
   · Finish space ad
   · Test DM piece to Cosmopolitan or Vogue

* Customizing Core Lists
   · Subject line on lasers · subject memos
   · Attempt to acquire endorsement letters

* Compiled Lists Program
   · Study airline pilots & design customized
      laser & memo & test
   · Kicker that is customized

* Back End Program
   · Get system going to 15M multi's → prepare w/ TS
   · LTBW mailing to 10M multi's < FRW letter control
   · Set up approach to 4/88 - 6/88 names: ① LTBW w/FRW Sept. 24th
                                            ② LTBW w/FRW Oct 15th
                                            ③ NTC w/FRW (AT) Nov 5th
                                            ④ NTC w/FRW (AT) Nov 26th
                                            ⑤ NTC w/FRW (E66) Dec 3rd
                                               w/LTBW link-up (after all incl GE product)
   Note: LTBW names on computer from Thurs Oct 6th
   update, then Matt gives Tom P. tape to take Fri 10/7 to Korff
   separating NT only & multi's for 10/15 mailing.
   Also, the 3rd & 4th NTC mailings are to NT only.
   Later (12/3) mail out E66 buyers after they have GE.
   NTC names on computer from Thurs November 17th
   update, then Matt gives Tom P tape to take Friday 11/18
   to Korff suppressing all NTC & E66 buyers for 11/26 mailing.

Diagram Six
Mini-Day/Power-Thinking Team
(continued)

③

* Hook up delivery with paper boys → all over
  • Test in LV to get 2 results, then...
  • Figure "red to black" costs, then...
  • Meet the "black" costs.
  • Call newspapers, talk them into this → leverage =
    if their market is responsive, then will run full pg. ads

* Package Insert programs
  • Study enterprise → have Teri pursue full
    scale research.
  • Have Teri also research ride-alongs (eg statement
    stuffers).
  • Have Teri start pioneering loose inserts
    into magazines
  • For each, determine red-to-black & dictate
    "black" terms.

* Study @ person job/pay in I+O

* Accounting
  • Ratio Tracking   • Study basic accounting
  • Internal Auditing procedures   • Computerize TR's

70

**The Mini-Days for the preceding week of Power-Thinking
are on the next two pages.**

The Neo-Tech System

Diagram Six
Mini-Day/Power-Thinking Team

(continued)

from **AUGUST 15**

Diagram Six
Mini-Day/Power-Thinking Team

(continued)

to **AUGUST 21**

1988 SEPTEMBER 1988
S M T W T F S
1 2 3
4 5 6 7 8 9 10
11 12 13 14 15 16 17
18 19 20 21 22 23 24
25 26 27 28 29 30

THURSDAY, AUG. 18 231/134	FRIDAY, AUG. 19 232/134	SATURDAY, AUG. 20 233/133
8	**8**	**8**
8:15 ✓ Call WV	8:15 / Meet with RS, new produc	8:15
8:30 ✓ Call RH	8:30 / Meet with CT, CS	8:30 BC Meeting
8:45 ✓ Call Elaine → cash orders	8:45	8:45 Industrial Philosophy
9 -	**9**	**9**
9:15	9:15	9:15
9:30	9:30	9:30
9:45	9:45	9:45
10 - RETR-7 update (see below)	**10**	**10**
10:15 - Go back & review	10:15 / Finish computer report	10:15
10:30 all previous inquiry	10:30	10:30
10:45 data. May see new	10:45 / Inquiry statistics accoun	10:45
11 insights now that we	**11** thg	**11**
11:15 are mailing back end.	11:15	11:15
11:30 - Back end mailing study	11:30	11:30
11:45 profitability & TBW a 2nd x & NU	11:45	11:45
12	**12**	**12**
12:15 - 9. 95 WTN Wave brochure	12:15	12:15
12:30 / Prepare above & LTBW for	12:30	12:30
12:45 (a) split run mailing &	12:45	12:45
1 b) space media ad	**1** / Line up tests for	**1**
1:15	1:15 upcoming mailing	1:15
1:30 - Woman's	1:30 / FBW / Hi. vs S. Laser	1:30
1:45 · Classified	1:45	1:45
2 · 1st response	**2** - Continue on Women's	**2**
2:15 · 2nd response	2:15 program	2:15
2:30 · brochure ZW	2:30	2:30
2:45	2:45	2:45
3	**3**	**3**
3:15	3:15 / 10 M list hunters	3:15
3:30	3:30 final	3:30
3:45	3:45	3:45
4	**4**	**4**
4:15	4:15	4:15
4:30	4:30	4:30
4:45	4:45	4:45
5	**5**	**5**
5:15 Dinner	5:15 Dinner	5:15 ↓
5:30	5:30	5:30
5:45	5:45	5:45
6	**6**	**6** - Inquiry figures
6:15	6:15	6:15
6:30	6:30	6:30 - Mind Capture
6:45	6:45	6:45
7 / Polish & edit Mind Capt.	**7** / Finalize Mind Capture	**7** - Meet w/ RYS : Mind Capt.
7:15	7:15 for arrival of RYS	7:15
7:30	7:30	7:30 - Organize tests for mailings
7:45	7:45	7:45
8	**8**	**8**
8:15	8:15	8:15 - The Alternative
8:30	8:30	8:30
8:45	8:45	8:45
9	**9**	**9** - Power-thinking
9:15 Sleep	9:15 Sleep	9:15 & MDays
9:30	9:30	9:30
9:45	9:45	9:45 AT·A·GLANCE®

73

if one just wants to do his routine job itself more effectively with the mini-day schedule: i.e., TO MAINTAIN.

Overcoming Conflicts With The Mini-Day Schedule

Certain jobs do not work well on the mini-day schedule, even certain jobs that seem suited for mini-days. The problem usually arises when deadlines of the job conflict with the deadlines of the mini-days.

For example, a computer programmer fluctuates at writing computer programs, his main movement. He may do very little computer programming for a period of time. Then suddenly he receives a project that must meet a deadline. He must devote 100% of his time to writing and editing the program.

This happens mostly with jobs oriented around projects with tight due dates. Such jobs may include computer programmers, entertainers and producers, accountants, architects, journalists and writers, professional artists. Such careers are usually dominated by one physical movement, such as computer programming. At times, that dominant movement demands *all day* for several days or weeks to meet a deadline. Say a computer programmer suddenly must devote longer hours to programming than his programming mini-day. Say that happens frequently. So he begins to wonder, "What good is the mini-day schedule? My main movement seems too erratic for mini-days."

Now, say the computer programmer receives an assignment with a tight deadline: The deadline multiplies his intensity. In fact, the leverage of the mini-day comes from the INTENSITY it delivers. Indeed, breaking a job down into its true division of labor and establishing the mini-days sets DEADLINES. Those *deadlines* multiply intensity, multiply one's capacity/success many times. In the case of the computer programmer, the must-finish deadline of the job overpowers the deadline of the mini-day. He pushes with even *greater* intensity. His *job's power-of-deadline* surpasses *the mini-day's power-of-deadline*.

Computer programmers, writers, artists, architects, accountants, entertainers are often in this unique situation. But how are they different from the business executive who must meet deadlines too? First of all, the deadline and the emergency are two exceptions where the business executive can break his mini-day schedule (elaborated on later in the "Mini-Day/Power-Thinking Tips"). But overall, the business executive gains the greatest efficiency by not swaying from his mini-day schedule. For, his deadlines are SUBJECTS that break down into movements (e.g., Mr. Hamilton's European Marketing Project). The programmer, writer, artist, architect, accountant, entertainer's deadlines are MOVEMENTS (e.g., write the computer program). The business executive must reach his deadlines through the division of labor, through breaking the subject into its movements, into the mini-days.

The computer programmer, the writer, artist, architect, accountant, entertainer, on the other hand, do reach their deadlines through a movement. They all have a PRIMARY movement: The writer writes — his primary movement. Yet he has SECONDARY movements to handle from certain business details to personal details. He needs to break down everything that falls outside of his primary movement into movements — secondary movements. Then he needs to mini-day his secondary movements.

Thus he establishes mini-days for his secondary movements. But now, in effect, the mini-day schedule must work in reverse.

The Mini-Day-In-Reverse Schedule: A Powerful Concept

Certain "primary-movement careers" dictated by primary-movement deadlines drive a person with great intensity — even greater intensity than the mini-day schedule. Thus, the unmovable deadline on the primary movement puts the person at his most intense, most productive state. And mini-days put him at his most intense, most productive state when handling his secondary movements.

Since his primary-movement, when meeting a deadline, drives him with more intensity than even a mini-day schedule, he can direct everything he does by that greater intensity. For example, as he moves through his day, he approaches his secondary-movement mini-days with ONE FOCUS: *Can I smash these mini-days?* He works through them as intensely as he can, driven by a force even greater than the mini-days themselves. For, he is driven by the intensity of his primary-movement deadline. He is driven to blast through the secondary-movement mini-days in as little time as possible to get back to his primary movement.

75

He tries to get through those mini-days in far less time than allotted to them — even bypass them altogether when little work sits in a secondary-movement mini-day.

Whereas each movement is equally important to the business executive, the primary movement is most important to the "primary-movement career" and drives a person through everything else at work. The primary movement pushes him like a strong wind at his back as he moves through his secondary mini-days. He essentially works the mini-day schedule in reverse, driven by the grand deadline.

76

Chapter Eight
HELPFUL TIPS

The next several pages offer helpful tips for using the mini-day schedule and the power-thinking shortcut. Part One gives tips on the mini-day schedule. Part Two gives tips on the power-thinking shortcut.

Part One
Mini-Day Tips

* Every person must determine his own basic physical movements for wealth creation, whether in his job or a self-developed project. The best way to do that is to simply list three days of tasks. From that you can easily determine your basic movements. IMPORTANT: Your mini-days are *physical movements* such as Mr. Hamilton's "phone calls" or "letter writing" mini-days, NOT projects or subjects such as, for example, "organize European mailings". People beginning the mini-day schedule *often* make the mistake of establishing project or subject mini-days. That mistake is not a proper division of labor and will cause the mini-day schedule to fail.

* If you have a good memory, listing three days of tasks from memory may actually be OK, for even if you miss a few tasks you should have enough to determine your handful of basic movements. If, like most, you have a hard time remembering your tasks, however, place a sheet of paper next to you and list tasks as you do them for three days.

* Do not get hung up determining how much time to devote to each movement. Just get down what seems reasonably right and start. You will feel the control immediately and can adjust and perfect your mini-days after a few days. The key is to get started.

* Once you have done the mini-day schedule for a few days, organize those mini-days for greatest effectiveness. Arrange your mini-days to most effectively interact with your day: with your lunch schedule, energy level, flow of concentration from one mini-day to the next. Also consider the general day of others. A phone-call mini-day, for example, should come

in the morning and not during lunch time when people will not be in.

* The mini-day schedule integrates physical movements with time. While the mini-day is open to revisions, the nature of a revision must make the integration of movement to time even better. Do not, for example, attempt to change the mini-days' length of time each day, for that is merely straying from the schedule and contradicts the integration of the physical movements with time. Do, however, feel free to determine, over a period of time, that too little time is put in one mini-day relative to another mini-day. Make an adjustment to improve the integration of movement to time, and stick to it.

* Do not feel guilty at seemingly small segments of time devoted to any particular area, for the intensity in your mini-days will more than compensate. As long as the basic movements are properly integrated with time, you are doing the right thing as you will discover. Realize that you do need to monitor the effectiveness of your mini-day time designation.

* Use discipline and integrity to stay on your mini-day schedule.

* The mini-days sit in time slots. Those time slots remain the same day after day. Simply list the tasks you would like to do that day under the corresponding mini-day slot. Do not worry about setting up times for the tasks themselves. That would take unnecessary energy and would mislead you. Just list and do as many as you can, one right after the other.

* A time may come when you will need to create a new mini-day. You have the flexibility to do so. It must be its own physical movement.

* If you find day after day that you consistently do not get to a specific task, take a close look at it. It may actually be its own physical movement needing its own mini-day. Mr. Hamilton, for example, initially tried to do his accounting during his operations mini-day but never got to it. He realized that accounting was a movement of its own, and he established an accounting mini-day.

* Every job and every money-making situation is different. The nature of some jobs may require mini-days that occur less regularly than every day. That is OK as long as the mini-

days are properly integrated with time. Mr. Hamilton actually has an eighth basic movement or mini-day. It did not appear on his examples earlier because the eighth mini-day occurs on Saturday, just once a week. His eighth mini-day is a data mini-day. Every Saturday he gathers, records and studies the marketing data for the week.

* The moment a task comes to mind, write it into that week's schedule (or next week's) in the corresponding mini-day. No matter how obscure or small it is, it will never be forgotten, for it is caught in your productivity web.

* Do not dive into problems or tasks on demand or on presentation. Instead, discipline them into the proper mini-day. That makes for much greater efficiency and control.

* If your desk tends to accumulate clutter, you may rifle the clutter into the in-basket, quickly and easily, to be handled or routed during the Operations mini-day. Your desk never needs to get cluttered again. If someone hands you something, put it into the in-basket or quickly stash it in the corresponding mini-day file. Nothing needs to sit around or be out of place, rather rifled to the right spot. Your desk, working area, and files quickly become the neatest in the office.

* Most people will have an Operations mini-day. While going through your in-basket, feel free to route an involved task to the corresponding mini-day file. For example, Mr. Hamilton often routes a complicated invoice into his accounting file to handle during his accounting mini-day. If it is routine, however, he usually signs it on the spot. The flexibility is yours. You discover what is best for you. You can do anything as long as you focus on the proper integration of your basic movements with time.

* When you return after being gone for a few days and paperwork sits high on your desk, rifle everything into its corresponding mini-day file and get right back on your mini-day schedule.

* After a major meeting from which the follow-up will tie you up for a couple of days, instead rifle all follow-up into the corresponding mini-days to complete swiftly while not interrupting the rest of your day.

* Perhaps for the first time, you will begin to discover free time during the day. If you finish all tasks in a mini-day, you will want to stay on that movement and push forward into the next day's tasks already scheduled in that same mini-day movement via power-thinking.

* If for whatever reason you start late in a particular mini-day, still begin the next mini-day on time. Similarly, if an emergency causes you to miss a mini-day, do not try to make it up; move on. But realize that this section offers tips, not dogma. These tips attempt to keep basic movements integrated with time over the long run. In the rare case that an emergency uses up a significant part of the mini-day, one may find he cannot follow this advice verbatim and may need to take care of an urgent task or two in the missed mini-day.

* The unwieldy, traditional approach to planning/scheduling/prioritizing/rotating tasks becomes nearly impossible to schedule into the future. The mini-day schedule, on the other hand, becomes very easy to schedule ahead. Simply flip your schedule booklet to the destined day and list the task (call Peter) under the mini-day time (phone calls), and then forget about it. When the day comes, the task awaits you. You never forget. You may write a letter that states, for example, that on a particular day at a particular time you will call. You always respond exactly as you say. Such a simple move brings great respect as others perceive you as a person in complete control with dependable follow up.

* Keep a file for each mini-day. These become your most used files.

* Traditional planning of tasks, projects, and goals on a single "master list" soon overwhelms an ordinary person. The traditional schedule acts as a time barricade, holding back all those plans. That barricade blocks creative, new ideas. Mr. Hamilton, on the other hand, makes breakthroughs regularly. Deep, natural organization stimulates vertical and horizontal thinking in each area of money creation.

* After one to two weeks on the mini-day schedule, a person feels, perhaps for the first time, a deeply satisfying sense of control. Control is biologically soothing. So soothing, in fact,

that your body may literally try to keep you there, try to hold back from venturing forth with creative thoughts or projects, even though you acquire the time. Beware of this "keep-everything-comfortable syndrome". Fight those comfortable feelings. Push extra hard with power-thinking into new projects to overcome that "keep-everything comfortable syndrome".

* Thinking is a physical activity or movement and for many people is a very important mini-day, particularly people with a high volume of responsibilities. They may set a stack of memos in front of them and jot down thoughts or ideas. They do not act on those thoughts; they just jot them down on the memos and put the memos in the corresponding mini-day files to act on during those mini-days. The thinking mini-day is particularly useful for a person who is growing at a rapid pace. If one feels pressured into making a subject mini-day or a project mini-day such as "European Project" (which will fail, for mini-days must remain as physical movements), usually what he really needs is a daily thinking mini-day to continually organize his movements. However, once one masters power-thinking, that takes care of organizing all the physical movements.

* Feel free to take back work that you had previously delegated but now find important.

* Now you can take the time to have proper, detail-oriented meetings with subordinates. You can schedule meetings into the appropriate mini-day as needed.

* Control the majority of your time now. Tell subordinates when they can see you (perhaps in your Meetings mini-day). Also, express to the boss, if appropriate, when you would prefer your meetings with him (in your Meetings mini-day).

* Interruptions must flow, but a wealth producer can easily determine now the most efficient way. You may handle some interruptions right on the spot, others you may deflect to a certain mini-day. Necessary interruptions cannot be ignored or avoided.

* Again, the mini-day is without dogma. You can work out your own approach as long as your basic physical movements stay integrated with time.

* If you find that much of the day is controlled by others, the mini-day can turn the situation around. You can control the day, no matter how much interaction with others is involved.
* Have the mini-day schedule-booklet at your fingertips. Keep each day on a tight leash.
* Teach others at the office or at home — subordinates, peers, boss, even wife, friends, children — the mini-day schedule. Let them, too, profit from the mini-day schedule. An office or home full of mini-day wealth producers buzzes with excitement and productivity. With Neo-Tech Control, you have a powerful lifetime partner.
* Recognize that your personal life can be organized into a mini-day. You may be pleasantly surprised as you put daily attention and thought into an often overlooked integral part of happiness and success. The mini-day will change your personal life from a passive to an active status.

Part Two
Power-Thinking Tips
* Before starting power-thinking, one should be on the mini-day schedule for preferably a couple of weeks. To start, initiate your power-thinking for just one project; then capture it with your mini-day schedule. After that experience, you can power-think everything for money and power.
* Do the power-thinking once a week, prior to the week. Mr. Hamilton does his power-thinking every Sunday evening and makes his mini-day schedule for the following week.
* If preferred, put the power-thinking list on a word processor and merely update it each week. Remove steps completed and add new steps and projects.
* Use discipline to initially stay with the power-thinking shortcut. After a few weeks, you can never let it go...the payoff is too great.
* If you find after a few weeks that a particular step has not been completed or acted on, it may be more than a step. It may be a project. If so, break it out as its own project and apply power-thinking to move it toward rapid payoff.
* Throughout the week, you may get ideas or thoughts of projects or steps that need to get done. You may put them directly

in that week's mini-day schedule. Or you can jot them down in your power-thinking list so when updated the next week, those steps or projects await action. Your mind always avoids clutter, avoids having to remember, having to hold thoughts in your head. Instead, your mind stays free to focus on the work before you. Keep your power-thinking list handy.

* The mind, like your desk, can accumulate clutter that smothers making money. As pointed out in the Mini-Day Tips, you can prevent clutter on your desk by rifling the clutter into the corresponding mini-day files or into your in-basket. The clutter disappears and no longer smothers making money. Similarly, thoughts, ideas, integrations, responsibilities can accumulate to clutter your money-making focus. You can prevent such mental clutter by rifling the thought into the corresponding mini-day in that week's schedule or into the power-thinking list for next week's schedule.

* When away from the office for a few days your mind, like your desk, can fill up with very important information. The combination of your desk and your mind filled up with important things can overwhelm you. But, like clearing the desk by rifling the clutter into the corresponding mini-day files, one can clear the mind by rifling all projects and thoughts into the power-thinking list. Now, all effort can go straight into making money.

* After a few weeks of the intense mini-day/power-thinking team, you might actually run out of work. You might then slow down, lose intensity in order to fill up your day. Do not let that happen. Force new projects into areas you would never consider before. The real payoff of the mini-day/power-thinking team is that it allows people to move into new areas that others never even think about. You never want to lose your intensity.

* Teach others at the office or at home the power-thinking shortcut. Both the personal and financial rewards are far beyond the effort spent.

* Recognize the personal aspects of your life that lend themselves to power-thinking. Switch from a passive to an active mode.

Chapter Nine

SMASHING THE MYTHS

After learning about the mini-day/power-thinking team, you can leave behind ten harmful myths:

Smashed Myth #1:
Traditional Planning and Scheduling Tasks, Projects, and Goals

Popular time-management courses encourage planning and scheduling. Planning puts tasks, projects, and goals on paper. Scheduling puts them into time slots. But as millions have discovered, the demands of time quickly fill the traditional schedule. One can never expect to move beyond a mediocre livelihood.

Scheduling a full day is difficult. It often involves guesswork. It often loses accuracy and credibility, which loses control. Time quickly gets used up without much progress. What should I do today, what can wait? Priorities become a problem. What will make progress, what will not? What will bring better results right now, what can be put off? What does not get done, what gets rotated? Does that which gets rotated take low priority again the next day, or does it take high priority? Dictated by priorities, the traditional daily schedule misses the only real priority in business: *integration*. ...Something new is needed.

The traditional planning/scheduling approach loses control over progress. Why does it lose control? Think back to the candy vendor (Chapter One) and the nature of business. What must the candy vendor do? He must integrate. The traditional schedule does not integrate. It just lays out your workday. Like a dam, the traditional schedule holds back many money-making plans forever.

The mini-day/power-thinking team, on the other hand, opens the door to forward movement. The traditional daily schedule versus the mini-day schedule is like the lethargic nonintegrated process of hand-building an entire car, task by task, versus the intense, integrated process of an assembly line.

Smashed Myth #2:
Setting Priorities To Accomplish Meaningful Projects

"Do important projects first." That advice will lure you into failure. Harvey Firestone, founder of Firestone Tires, for instance, spent significant time every day on nitty-gritty tasks. Firestone spent hours every day in his tire plant himself. He implicitly understood that those nonglamorous "unimportant" tasks made his wealth possible. Harvey Firestone could never have achieved his integrated, powerful position by doing "important" things first.

One must properly integrate all responsibilities and tasks, from the "unimportant" routine tasks to the most creative, dynamic business stratagems. Remember the candy vendor and how he had to integrate everything. He could not just hit the streets for the important project of bringing in the cash and forget about everything else...he would have no candy to sell. As you learned today, *everything* must be *integrated* into one money-making mini-day schedule. Integration is the only valid priority in business.

Smashed Myth #3:
Avoiding Nitpick Work To Get Important Work Done

In most occupations, nitpick work fires at you all day long; it constantly interrupts you, constantly demands your attention, constantly stops you from accomplishing important forward movement. Indeed, nitpick work is the worst enemy of traditional daily schedules as it can shoot your day to shreds.

It would be nice to say: "To hell with nitpick work; I'm going to make money instead!" But contrary to such good-sounding, popular management advice, nitpick work is not expendable. Those bothersome tasks are the operations of management; they keep things running. They are to the bottom line what tellers are to a bank. Therefore, honest hardworking people never break free from nitpick work. Unfortunately, too many people become its slave. But Neo-Tech Control turns that around.

To make money, nitpick work must never be avoided. The menacing, interrupting nitpick work becomes a vital element during one's ascent to money and power. No wealth producer can avoid it. Instead, he must integrate it into smooth, Neo-Tech Control and then attack it.

By breaking down and integrating the career like an assembly line, a person can position nitpick in his assembly line to handle it once, quickly. By doing so, those shadowy tasks that once struck at any moment to tear apart one's day now sit harmless, imprisoned in one tangible physical movement. You can shoot at a clear target and blast nit-picking work out of your day with one good shot. Then you will concentrate on several other important forward-movement and money-making projects all day long.

Through the mini-day schedule, the overwhelming problem of nitpick work (that holds most people back throughout their entire lifetimes) automatically, easily disappears into one physical movement.

Smashed Myth #4:
Delegating To Free Up Time For Forward Movement

Integration is the nature of business. With that insight, a powerful white-collar-hoax myth begins to surface. The traditional concept of delegating to expand your horizons begins to fall apart. For, by understanding the nature of business, one realizes that expansion forces more integrations on the business. While expanding, therefore, a businessman must gain, not lose, control. To go all the way...to build an empire, a person cannot delegate, for he loses a degree of integration and control, inherent in turning something over to someone else.

Passed down for decades, the average man becomes trapped and then buried by the debilitating delegating myth.

Through the mini-day/power-thinking team, you not only discover pockets of time, you discover delegated tasks that you want back — tasks that you need to properly integrate for maximum control, efficiency, and profits. You do not want to start delegating, no matter what you think now. You will learn in Volume Two about something powerful that obsoletes delegating, called replicating. Delegating is used excessively by the white-collar hoax and is not part of the no-limit Neo-Tech System.

Smashed Myth #5:
Breaking Free From Details To Do The Executive's Job

As demands on your time grow, beware of this myth. Attention to details takes valuable time, and you may prefer to turn over details to someone else. But the first demand of success is to know your business or job down to its smallest details. Without first-hand knowledge of those details, you go out of control in many subtle ways. With first-hand knowledge of those details, you gain integrated control. For, you integrate the infrastructure of details that hold together your job/business.

Remember the candy vendor? To become wealthy, he has to integrate everything from the cleanliness of his workers' carts to the distribution system of his candy to the secret ingredient of his chocolate. As his business grows, the details he eventually leaves in the hands of others become *more* important to him, for that knowledge begins to integrate into larger, sweeping decisions. You will learn in Volume Two about the mini-company/power-tracking team that enables the entrepreneur or CEO to always stay integrated with every detail in his growing business, no matter how big it gets.

As you evolve into a wealth creator, you must regularly go on a "money hunt" by searching out detail to strengthen your overall integrated picture. Think, for example, of the money potential of shaving a second off a movement in the assembly line for a large car company putting out millions of cars annually. Think of the painstaking attention given to detail. Wealth creators share the secret of knowing the minute details of their businesses. The mini-day/power-thinking team provides the mechanism to stay integrated with details — to lay the integrated foundation for making dynamic, larger-than-life business moves. The mini-company/power-tracking team in Volume Two enables you to make and run with those larger-than-life business moves.

Smashed Myth #6:
Reducing Meetings

As you grow and become more successful, you will hear from time to time that you must reduce meetings with subordinates. But the right meetings offer the lucrative opportunity to integrate many people in order to expand the business beyond one man's efforts, as explained in Volume Two. Neo-Tech wealth creators often increase meetings once they learn how to gain time, leverage, and power. They use Neo-Tech meetings to integrate more and more people into the marketing process and, eventually, into product development.

The ultimate example is Harold Geneen, a former president of ITT. Harold Geneen built and ran 250 multi-million-dollar Wall Street companies through powerful meetings. He integrated and leveraged many, many people. Through Neo-Tech meetings, he became an expert at catapulting each company and its president. Without those powerful meetings, he could not have expanded ITT into 250, 50-million-dollar companies. Imagine the money ITT generated as a result of each meeting! Neo-Tech meetings deliver power and wealth (explained in Volume Two).

Smashed Myth #7:
Stopping Interruptions To Concentrate On Getting Ahead

Fashionable advice today for managers is to lock yourself in a closed office incommunicado for substantial time each day to concentrate on "getting ahead". Legitimate interruptions, however, create a needed, vital flow of communication. Once a person gets Neo-Tech Control of his actions, legitimate interruptions keep the momentum building. Legitimate interruptions must integrate into your career. The mini-day schedule integrates them smoothly and nullifies the negatives as explained by Mr. Hamilton (next chapter).

Smashed Myth #8:
Passing Down Problems To Free Oneself For Creative Thought

Beware of this myth that becomes more tempting with more success. Theoretically, delegating problems frees a person for creative thought. But that is for pre-Neo-Tech-Control, limited control. The mini-day/power-thinking team integrates everything.

Consider that Henry Ford took on and integrated supply-distribution problems into the world-shattering assembly-line discoveries. Those using Neo-Tech Control systematically take in everything, even the problems, and make even larger integrations because of the problems.

Harold Geneen, a Neo-Tech power-thinker, never delegated

problems. In his bi-weekly company meetings, he had attendees read the first section of their prepared reports out loud. That first section was devoted to problems so he could personally integrate them.

Smashed Myth #9:
Avoiding Pressure

Notice the "stress marbles" at the convenience store: fun and games. Not so comical, however, is the much-touted stress issue in management books today. Those books are more convincing. Thus, many readers become subtly convinced that they cannot handle their jobs.

Contrary to implications by psychologists, doctors, reports, and management books, stress does not occur from demanding work. Stress occurs as a person gradually sinks into failure. Lack of control, the pressure or fear of not getting work done or not moving ahead causes the stress. And when the future offers no solutions, depression sets in. In an attempt to gain control, one may work longer hours. But the stress comes from anxiety of failure, not from working too hard per se, not from too many hours.

The mini-day/power-thinking team delivers the integrated control — Neo-Tech Control — to get all work done easily, early, and to move ahead. Your career becomes so well integrated that you never lose control again.

Smashed Myth #10:
Positive Thinking

Positive thinking provides a false euphoria perhaps like the gambler who feels lucky, feels positive. But only *integration*, not feelings, provides control. And only the mini-day/power-thinking team provides integration.

Chapter Ten

QUESTIONS AND ANSWERS ABOUT
NEO-TECH CONTROL

During a question-and-answer period at the Neo-Tech Control Seminar, Mr. Hamilton fielded the following questions:

Part I
The Mini-Day Schedule

QUESTION: What are the advantages of the mini-day schedule? And can the average person become a money/power giant?

HAMILTON: To answer your first question, there are many advantages to the mini-day schedule. Yet it all reduces down to your job, life, money no longer controlling you. Instead, you control everything. By integrating all basic movements of your job and even your life into the mini-day schedule, you can essentially control everything that moves.

By nature, a successful person must handle many things. Those who become wealthy are always on top of everything. The integrated mini-day schedule prevents a person at any level from becoming overwhelmed by any job or by any money-making situation. The mini-day schedule allows a person to take complete control of everything, not unlike like the managers and entrepreneurs who control great wealth and power.

Now, to answer your second question about whether or not the average person can become a money/power giant, consider that most money/power giants were once merely average people who discovered how to take iron-grip, Neo-Tech Control over everything they did. Once one experiences Neo-Tech Control and gets on the mini-day/power-thinking team, he rapidly picks up momentum and motivation. As he begins to discover creativity through his power-thinking, he becomes filled with exhilaration that drives him like the money/power giants. With his levels of control and creativity, he will get wealthy. Neo-Tech Control gives the average person the control, creativity, and motivation needed to become wealthy.

The Neo-Tech System

QUESTION: What exactly is Neo-Tech Control?

HAMILTON: Neo-Tech Control is the integrated control one experiences with the mini-day/power-thinking team. This thing called Neo-Tech Control grips and then pulls up every possible aspect of your job needed for success, from controlling the details to generating your creativity, and Neo-Tech Control brings all those aspects together for you to easily and properly manage. It brings them together and effectively integrates them with a person's only limitation — time — for highly effective results. Aside from providing the necessary detail-focussing/creativity-inspiring base needed to build a wealthy business, some immediate side benefits also occur. Some of those side benefits are:

1) One no longer needs to put off important projects for lack of enough time. He can start immediately by injecting tasks in the proper mini-days. Every new project gets moved into quick action.

2) One no longer needs to put aside important areas of work for priority elsewhere. The mini-day schedule gives proper attention to all areas of work — or should I say, all movements of work — every day. Everything is accounted for. Nothing gets behind.

3) Similarly, no one needs to get behind for lack of time and then have to play "catch up" later. The mini-days keep him from falling behind in any area, for the mini-day schedule captures the basic movements of one's job. Always in control and on schedule, the person with Neo-Tech Control averts burnout.

4) The mini-day schedule turns uncertainty — that feeling of not knowing what to do next...of being swamped — into certainty with those integrated mini-day tasks lined up one after the next. Each mini-day is attacked with intensity and certainty.

5) Most managers' responsibilities feel overwhelming. Some managers may snap at employees, which delivers a momentary

92

feeling of control. With Neo-Tech Control, however, the manager feels at ease, and frustration no longer remains a part of his day. He no longer functions dramatically but dynamically. He becomes a winner, and people know it.

6) No one can get out of control on the mini-day schedule. A person becomes super competent and successful.

QUESTION: I hear people, even in good career positions, complain about working hard yet not really getting ahead—

HAMILTON: Those people tell the truth — they can't get ahead. It's a simple matter of logistics. Consider that the assembly-line worker has one responsibility and can do his job more effectively by "really going at it." By doing so, he is likely to work his way up to a better career position. Once he is in a good career position, however, he no longer has the luxury to just "really go at it". By doing that, he just burns out. To become a successful wealth creator, he must change. He must learn to interlock the many, many seemingly chaotic responsibilities, interlock them like puzzle pieces snapping together into a success puzzle. With the mini-day schedule, a person quickly lassos those endless responsibilities and brings them together into tightly integrated units that he controls. That way, with control, he can get ahead.

QUESTION: What about the barrage of nitpick details that prevents people from getting to more profitable work?

HAMILTON: Many management books, tapes and consultants advise avoiding detail work...to do things that, quote, "really count". For, nitpick work can unexpectedly and at any moment shoot one's day to shreds...as well as, year after year, systematically shoot his whole career to shreds. To break free from nitpick or detail work, however, would not only terminate any shot at major success, but would get him fired. Therefore, working people remain stagnated by nitpick work. That's why people must learn Neo-Tech Control.

Any worker who lists his tasks for three days to determine

his basic movements for his mini-day schedule will find some non-placeable tasks left over. Those disjointed tasks are the nit-pick work. But they are not expendable. Those nitty-gritty tasks are the operations of management. The wealth creator must put those indispensable details all in one mini-day called Operations to move through quickly each day. Then he concentrates 100% on his five or six other money-making mini-days as they come. He accomplishes important, profitable things in each mini-day, all day long.

Many people spend their whole disjointed day caught in nit-pick work with no hope of ever getting to the important forward-movement projects. But they can now master every last task while having large, consistent chunks of time to put effort every day toward forward-movement.

QUESTION: How do you handle interruptions?

HAMILTON: Most unnecessary interruptions stop shortly after one begins the mini-day schedule. For, he becomes so intense that subordinates, peers, and even bosses take it on their own to interrupt less frequently. And once he explains his mini-day schedule to them, he can request that they guide their interruptions to a particular mini-day most efficient for him. In my case, that time is during my Operations mini-day.

The situation immediately improves. But interruptions will not altogether cease. They, too, are important and vital to making money. Many management books offer techniques to control interruptions. Yet interruptions, for the most part, come from external sources that are not in one's control. Instead, he must concentrate on what he directly controls, namely his schedule and its efficient interaction with the interruption.

The interruption causes havoc to the traditional schedule — it throws everything behind. No management advice based on the traditional schedule has found a satisfactory cure to the interruption. But the interruption causes no basic problem to the mini-day schedule. Whereas the unpredictable interruption may appear any time, one never needs to get off schedule. If a fifteen-minute interruption occurs at 10:30 a.m., then my Letter Writing mini-day loses fifteen minutes that day. But at 11:30 a.m., I stay on schedule and begin my Operations mini-day. Interruptions still flow into my day. But in the long run, the interruptions balance out over the different mini-days as my physical movements stay integrated with time.

QUESTION: Seems like a smooth approach. But do you ever get thrown from the mighty mini-day schedule?

HAMILTON: Almost never. I can envision only two reasons: the deadline and the emergency. Deadlines can temporarily amplify a basic movement's importance with time. For example, I developed a crucial letter on which much of our company's future counted. I had two days to write it. That deadline amplified my letter writing to two solid days at the word processor.

Emergencies can also temporarily shift the mini-day schedule. Say a key employee suddenly leaves the company, and you must scramble to replace that person. In those rare occasions of an unforeseen deadline or an emergency, you can afterwards get right back on schedule with the mini-days.

However, one must avoid excuses that allow him to stray from the schedule. The mini-day schedule requires discipline to stick to it; but it pays well.

QUESTION: How did you discover the mini-day concept?

HAMILTON: I was an average person who tried but could not get any more control. I was sinking. A doctor prescribed stress-relief exercise, a vacation, and long hot baths. A report I read warned me about stress and being overworked. All so-called remedies though cost time, and I further lost control. I needed control, not vacations or hot baths. Furthermore, none of the management books' techniques were helping. I read them all. Gradually, I realized they had nothing to do with the nature of management, which is *integration*. So, I stopped looking outward for answers and instead turned inward to discover the integrated nature of money-making management, which led me to the mini-day/power-thinking team and the next level of control called Neo-Tech Control.

QUESTION: What about your battle with stress?

HAMILTON: I handle many, many times the volume of work, money, and happiness than I did then. All stress has disappeared. I'm cheerful, happy, and healthy. I'm in control. I'm wealthy.

QUESTION: What will happen as this powerful information spreads?

HAMILTON: The life of ordinary people will become much easier, richer, and happier. Before the mini-day schedule, people in a sense fought against the nature of man (hard, Firestone-like thinking) and the nature of making money (integration and creativity). The mini-day establishes integration of one's movements, and power-thinking generates creativity. I, for one, could not previously exert thought into the many crucial areas of wealth creation. That made making money hard. With the mini-day schedule, however, I am able to focus on the crucial areas of making money, as can everyone.

A person discovers things he would otherwise never see. He advances in ways he would otherwise never consider. Many surprises await him. Yes, people will prosper. ...I left my old self in the dust once I started using the mini-day schedule. And so will you.

Part II
The Power-Thinking Shortcut

QUESTION: What exactly is the power-thinking shortcut?
HAMILTON: Power-thinking is the necessary ingredient to success, for power-thinking activates man's nature: using his mind. Indeed, all animals live most successfully through fulfilling their nature. Without functional wings, a bird cannot fulfill its nature and will suffer and die. Without functional fins, a fish cannot fulfill its nature and will struggle and die. Similarly, without fully utilizing his mind, man does not fulfill his nature and stagnates and dies unfulfilled. Power-thinking immediately fixes that tragedy.

QUESTION: Is it true when you say power-thinking is easy to

do?

HAMILTON: Power-thinking is easy because it is asserting man's nature. All animals live easily by asserting their nature. Birds fly easily, fish swim easily, monkeys swing in trees easily. And man thinks easily.

QUESTION: If power-thinking is easy, why doesn't everyone use it?

HAMILTON: Whereas all animals, including man, live easily, successfully, and happily by asserting their nature, obstruct their true nature and suddenly their lives becomes hard, unhappy, and destined to failure. Clip the bird's wings, clip the fish's fins, or the monkey's thumbs, and their lives become hard and unhappy with little chance for a happy future.

Whereas man too lives easily by his nature, the average specialized job obstructs his true nature and, for the most part, makes his work, money possibilities, and life hard, unhappy, and often directed to failure. Most people are trapped in specialized jobs. Specialization clips their minds. Under integrated working conditions, however, an ordinary person can use power-thinking as naturally as the bird flies.

QUESTION: Once ordinary people start using the power-thinking shortcut, how do they capture future money today?

HAMILTON: They can actually do that by turning those long-range projects into mechanical steps, which quickly puts that money in anyone's reach through the mini-day schedule. Put any project through the mini-day schedule, and it quickly gets done.

The reason the ordinary person does not make a lot of money is not, in most cases, because he won't put out effort, for most people would apply themselves if they could get rich doing so. The reason the ordinary person does not make a lot of money is because he does not know how to go about it...he simply does not know what to do.

Power-thinking brings out one's creativity fairly quickly.

Soon, power-thinking lets him itemize how to make money. Then he inserts those steps into the mini-day schedule. From then on, the process becomes more or less mechanical as he merely follows his schedule. The money will come to him, money that before was way out of reach.

Moreover, by power-thinking projects in the mind's eye to their completion, a person increases his effectiveness manyfold by being able to immediately swing others into action, in any location. Remember how I moved people into action on two continents on my very first day handling my European marketing project? The more people in coordinated, forward-march action for you, the more powerful you become and the faster you profit. I made a lot of money from that European marketing project.

QUESTION: Could the average person double his income in a year with Neo-Tech Control?

HAMILTON: He can do a lot more than double his income. The average person can potentially become a money/power giant as I did, even if his present blue or white-collar job seems limiting. Let me explain something about man and power-thinking:

Man's mind is powerful, but somewhat limited. Power-thinking makes man's powerful mind unlimited. Albert Einstein is known to have said that he refused to remember his phone number, for it cluttered the mind. Power-thinking essentially clears the mind of all the many thoughts, steps, and complications of work or of money-making situations. Power-thinking lets a person forget about things needed to be done until they mechanically appear in the mini-day schedule. Power-thinking clears out the stifling clutter in the average person's mind, leaving his mind free to create and integrate more and more knowledge until he routinely generates ideas...lucrative ideas that he could never, in his wildest fantasies, even imagine before. Power-thinking breaks the ordinary person out of the following mode and puts him into the integrating mode, which is lucrative and limitless.

QUESTION: In all the management and success books, I have never seen anything like the mini-day schedule combined with

98

power-thinking. Why?

HAMILTON: The nature of making money requires developing and handling many, many facets of business simultaneously. Inspirational management/success books on the market today that attribute success to, for example, good employee incentive programs or good customer service, grossly misinterpret the multifaceted nature of managing for money and power.

Neo-Tech Control, on the other hand, captures the nature of managing for money and power. It does not merely touch on a few glamorous, important areas of success. Rather it offers the mechanism to integrate those glamorous areas with the many, many other drier, also important areas simultaneously — for real results. Anyone can apply the mini-day schedule quickly and easily with real results, for it is the most natural way to manage your work. And anyone can apply the power-thinking shortcut quickly and easily with real results, for it releases the most natural power of man — his mind.

QUESTION: What will happen to the lives of ordinary people with the mini-day schedule and the power-thinking shortcut?

HAMILTON: Over the next decade, more and more ordinary people will lose their jobs in bankrupted white-collar-hoax structures. Those shattered individuals will pick themselves up with the mini-day/power-thinking team, and many of them will start their own businesses. In the long run, they will come out way, way ahead as they discover Neo-Tech Control and release their human potential.

The Future Starts Tomorrow Morning

Step 1: Prepare to set up your mini-day schedule. Start tomorrow by listing your tasks as you do them for the next three days. For the best results, list those tasks as you do them, not from memory.

Step 2: Determine your basic physical movements from that list of tasks. Do your physical-movement breakdown.

Step 3: Determine what percentage of your working day you should devote to each physical movement. The sum of your percentages should equal 100% as the physical movements are 100% of what you do. Designate the amount of time in hours and minutes to each physical movement.

Step 4: Determine the best placement in your day for each movement. Purchase a "Week At A Glance", and prepare your new schedule, your mini-day schedule. Begin injecting tasks into your mini-day schedule.

Step 5: After a couple weeks on the mini-day schedule, introduce power-thinking. Start with your most ambitious project. Try it. Then try more projects. Mentally power-think the projects, one at a time.

Step 6: Inject the tasks needed to complete each step of your power-thinking list into the intense mini-day units. The mini-day is your personal production-line. The mini-day/power-thinking team puts you far ahead in production and foresight, and soon you will take the lead for good as you leave your specialized job to start your own business.

* * * *

Volume Two

The
Company-Capture Discovery

Chapter Eleven

DUMP THE AMERICAN DREAM, GO FOR AN EMPIRE

The mini-day/power-thinking team brings you the control to start your own business (or to start your own "business" right at your place of work, as shown later.) Grand Puzzle Part Number Two brings your starting business the control to grow into an empire.

Grand Puzzle Part Number Two:
THE COMPANY-CAPTURE DISCOVERY

STEP ONE: PURPOSE

What is the purpose of business? The purpose of business is to BUILD wealth. The company's jobs should consist of that purpose: TO BUILD. But in today's specialized working world, most jobs merely MAINTAIN the business. For, their responsibilities are not integrated means with which to build; rather they are ends in themselves, integrating no further than their specialized tasks.

For example, at I & O Publishing Company, list brokering, that is renting mailing lists for the direct-mail program, is not in itself a real business **purpose**. In other words, renting lists could not *in itself* BUILD wealth, for renting lists would not in itself exist and could not in itself be built upon if not for the direct-mailing program. The purpose of renting lists is the direct-mail program. List brokering is an integrated responsibility to its purpose: direct-mail program. Indeed, the direct-mail program can be built and built and built to no limits.

Traditionally, however, list brokering becomes its own department. List brokering along with the other responsibilities such as statistics, accounting, setting up the mailings, shipping the product, customer service and so on instead need to integrate together to serve their purpose, in this case, the direct-mail program. But such responsibilities become ends in themselves in most businesses.

Seven decades of specialization (as opposed to integration) has disintegrated business into specialized departments and jobs

103

that are ends in themselves and that do not integrate with their purpose. The working masses settle into a deep-rooted bicameral-like mode as they automatically do their set responsibilities day after day. Their specialized responsibilities provide automatic, external guidance and prevent integrated, self-guidance. No integrating, no power-thinking into new realms of making money takes place in specialized jobs.

Unchecked by the specialized employees and stockholders, white-collar-hoax executives provide bogus "guidance" and rise to power and wealth over the already existing realms of making money, already integrated into place years before by real business builders — men with purpose. The white-collar-hoax executives are not real business builders and have no purpose. ...They are the nothingness drain.

Purpose means to BUILD wealth. Purpose can be found throughout your business, that is, areas that can build wealth. Those areas that can build wealth are true ends into which the responsibilities must converge. Responsibilities become the MEANS to build their purpose: money. They are not the ENDS.

The Neo-Tech System shows you how to define the **areas of purpose** in your business: You must define the areas in your business that can build and grow without limits. All germane responsibilities come together into an integrated force. No longer ends in themselves, the responsibilities now become means to push forward their purpose...to build, build, build wealth.

Now you take wealth-creation to major-league status: you establish people working for you who, like you, become filled with purpose. Integrated average men and women filled with purpose leave even the smartest white-collar worker in elementary business school. They will catapult your success and their own success. Your start-up company cannot fail as integrated people with purpose build wealth for you.

To get a better understanding of **areas of purpose** and how they are determined, read pages 105 through 112, the series of Diagrams Seven through Ten, including the observations section following Diagram Ten. You will get a better understanding of areas of purpose, how they are formed, and what they look like. Diagrams Seven through Ten walk you, step by step, through the process of forming areas of purpose, using I & O as an example. We will come back to Diagrams Seven through Ten later as you go through the process yourself with your start-up company or potential, future start-up company (or with your own "start-up" company inside the company you now work for, where you will learn how to take over an area of purpose to BUILD wealth). Do not worry if something in the process is not perfectly clear at this time. Right now you are simply getting an initial understanding of the process used to determine areas of purpose. If you are not ready to leave your job to start your own business, this process will show you the limits of your current job and what you need in order to break free from stagnation. Indeed, you can do all this right at your place of work as shown later. Read pages 105 (below) through 112 now, before continuing on to Chapter Twelve.

Diagram Seven
Process To Determine Areas Of Purpose
FIRST: LIST THE BASIC RESPONSIBILITIES
OF YOUR COMPANY (I & O EXAMPLE BELOW)

<u>**Basic Responsibilities:**</u>

Buy Television Spots
Set Up TV Commercials
Buy Space (newspapers, magazines)
Set Up Space-Media Ads
Rent Mailing Lists
Set Up Mailings
Manage I & O's Database
Keep Data/Statistics
Keep Books
Do Accounting
Control Order Processing
Control Shipping Products
Control Product Manufacturing
Control Customer Service
Control Computer Needs

Diagram Eight
Process To Determine Areas Of Purpose
NEXT: DEFINE THE RESPONSIBILITIES' PURPOSE

Each basic responsibility needs a purpose. For, a responsibility cannot exist by itself. For example, look at the first responsibility on the list (next page): *buy television spots*. Could buying TV spots exist on its own if not for the television marketing program? Of course not. That responsibility is dependent on the television marketing program. The television marketing program is the purpose of the first responsibility on the next page, the purpose of buying television spots. The *television marketing program* is an **area of purpose**. Buying television spots along with nine other responsibilities integrate into the television marketing program, as will become clear over Diagrams Eight, Nine, and Ten. As we will learn, one person will handle that fully integrated area of purpose, the television marketing program.

Randomly running down the list: could buying ad space in newspapers exist on its own? No. It needs a purpose. Could renting mailing lists (known as list brokering) exist on its own? No. It needs a purpose. Could accounting exist on its own? No. It needs a purpose. Could order processing exist on its own right? No. It needs a purpose. And so on.

Today, however, all the responsibilities on the next page are established as departments in the traditional companies, existing on their own as ends in themselves instead of integrating into their purposes. That is why most jobs today are specialized, closed-ended ruts. For, no way exists to build a mere responsibility that is split from its integrated, open-ended purpose. Again, how can one build renting mailing lists without that responsibility being integrated to its purpose: the direct-mail marketing program? Yet, list brokering is treated as an independent department in nearly every direct-mail company today outside of I&O.

To determine the purpose of each basic responsibility, simply finish the sentence: "This responsibility exists due to _____." For example, "Buying television spots exists due to *the television marketing program*." The I & O example of this process is done on the next page. Several of the responsibilities exist in more than one purpose. For example, accounting could not exist on its own. That responsibility is dependent on, for example, the television marketing program. The television marketing program is its purpose. Also, other accounting records exist due to other marketing programs. Therefore, that responsibility will exist in more that one purpose, as seen on the next page.

Do not get tied up on technicalities if you have trouble grasping the process. By the time you get through Diagram Ten, the process will become clear.

Diagram Eight
Process To Determine Areas Of Purpose
(continued)
<u>**Basic Responsibilities:**</u>

Buy Television Spots:
Responsibility exists due to: <u>*Television Marketing Program*</u>.

Set up Television Commercials:
Responsibility exists due to: <u>*Television Marketing Program*</u>.

Buy Space (newspapers, magazines):
Responsibility exists due to: <u>*Space-Media Marketing Program*</u>.

Set Up Space-Media Ads:
Responsibility exists due to: <u>*Space-Media Marketing Program*</u>.

Rent Mailing Lists:
Responsibility exists due to: <u>*Direct-Mail Marketing Program*</u>.

Set Up Mailings:
Responsibility exists due to: <u>*Direct-Mail Marketing Program and I & O Database Marketing Program*</u>.

Manage I & O Database:
Responsibility exists due to: <u>*I & O Database Marketing Program*</u>.

Keep Data/Statistics:
Responsibility exists due to: <u>*Each of the marketing programs*</u>.

Keep Books:
Responsibility exists due to: <u>*Each of the marketing programs*</u>.

Do Accounting:
Responsibility exists due to: <u>*Each of the marketing programs*</u>.

Control Order Processing:
Responsibility exists due to: <u>*Each of the marketing programs*</u>.

Control Shipping Products:
Responsibility exists due to: <u>*Each of the marketing programs*</u>.

Control Product Manufacturing:
Responsibility exists due to: <u>*Each of the marketing programs*</u>.

Control Customer Service:
Responsibility exists due to: <u>*Each of the marketing programs*</u>.

Control Computer Needs:
Responsibility exists due to: <u>*Each of the marketing programs*</u>.

Diagram Nine
Process To Determine Areas Of Purpose

OVERVIEW OF BASIC RESPONSIBILITIES
AND THEIR AREAS OF PURPOSE

<u>Basic Responsibilities:</u>	<u>Areas of Purpose:</u>
Buy Television Spots	Television Marketing
Set Up Commercials	
Buy Space (newspapers, magazines)	Space-Media Marketing
Set Up Space-Media Ads	
Rent Mailing Lists	Direct-Mail Marketing
Set Up Mailings	
Manage Database	Database Marketing
Keep Data/Statistics	
Keep Books	
Do Accounting	
Control Order Processing	
Control Shipping Products	
Control Product Manufacturing	
Control Customer Service	
Control Computer Needs	

Diagram Ten
Process To Determine Areas Of Purpose

LAST: PUT TOGETHER THE AREAS OF PURPOSE

Now pull the basic responsibilities into their areas of purpose:

Television Marketing:
Buy Television Spots
Set Up TV Commercials
Keep Data/Statistics
Keep Books
Do Accounting
Control Order Processing
Control Shipping Products
Control Product Manufacturing
Control Customer Service
Control Computer Needs

Space-Media Marketing:
Buy Space
Set Up Space-Media Ads
Keep Data/Statistics
Keep Books
Do Accounting
Control Order Processing
Control Shipping Products
Control Product Manufacturing
Control Customer Service
Control Computer Needs

Direct-Mail Marketing:
Rent Mailing Lists
Set Up Mailings (purchasing, printing, lettershop)
Keep Data/Statistics
Keep Books
Do Accounting
Control Order Processing
Control Shipping Products
Control Product Manufacturing
Control Customer Service
Control Computer Needs

I & O Database Marketing:
Manage Database
Set Up Mailings (purchasing, printing, lettershop)
Keep Data/Statistics
Keep Books
Do Accounting
Control Order Processing
Control Shipping Products
Control Product Manufacturing
Control Customer Service
Control Computer Needs

Observation

As you can see, the areas of purpose form into specific marketing programs. Those programs become wealth-building jobs in your company. As the company grows, those marketing programs divide further into specific marketing projects, every job always remaining a wealth-building job. You will see how that is possible as the Neo-Tech System continues.

Observations of Diagrams Nine and Ten
Process To Determine Areas Of Purpose

• For illustrative purposes, Diagrams Nine and Ten list only the I & O areas of purpose within the United States. I & O's areas of purpose exist in countries all over the world, as we will see how in the World-Capture Discovery.

• One person will handle an area of purpose. He will build without limits and without stagnation his open-ended purpose. You will understand exactly how that is possible as the Neo-Tech System continues.

• Look again at Diagram Nine. The basic responsibilities in Diagram Nine become departments in traditional companies today. Now look at Diagram Ten: The open-ended areas of purpose would get obliterated if the basic responsibilities were split off into departments. Split off into specialized departments, the basic responsibilities become dead-end jobs that cannot build without being integrated with their purpose. Such split-apart responsibilities lead nearly everyone today into stagnation. Integrated into their areas of purpose, on the other hand, the basic responsibilities become the means to drive the purpose forward, which enables your people to grow, build, forever...with integrated strength.

These integrated people who can build their areas of purpose with no limits become the most powerful people in today's business world. For, they know how to BUILD values. Everyone else knows only how to MAINTAIN values. Even the highly intelligent white-collar executive seems naive next to the average man or woman manning an area of purpose with integrated strength and the ability to BUILD.

• Basic Responsibilities fall into two categories...

Essence Responsibilities:

A) *The first category of basic responsibilities* involves those responsibilities that drive the area of purpose into existence and drive it forward. For example, look at Diagram Ten under the first area of purpose: *Television Marketing*. The first five responsibilities drive the purpose into existence and *drive* it forward: 1) buy television spots, 2) set up TV commercials, 3) record and digest the data and statistics in order to know the profitable television spots to buy and the profitable TV

Observations of Diagrams Nine and Ten
Process To Determine Areas Of Purpose
(continued)

commercials to run, 4) keep and know the books in order to integrate the financial status of the program at all times, and 5) do the accounting in order to stay on the most cost-effective course. Because these responsibilities drive the purpose forward, their actions down to the last nitty-gritty detail must be done by the one person in charge of the area of purpose. Hands-on knowledge is needed by that one person who becomes the integrated force to drive the purpose forward.[1]

Follow-Through-Work Responsibilities:

B) *The second category of basic responsibilities* involves those responsibilities that occur as a result of the area of purpose. For example, look again at Diagram Ten under the first area of purpose: *Television Marketing*. The last five responsibilities come as a *result* of the area of purpose: 1) control order processing, 2) control shipping of products, 3) control product manufacturing, 4) control customer service, 5) control computer needs. Those responsibilities such as order processing are a *result* of the business generated by the area of purpose. They do not directly drive the purpose forward. Whereas iron-grip *control* over those responsibilities is needed to build the purpose, the actions themselves are physical follow-through work. Therefore, the physical work itself can be done by others.

However, integrated control over that work, keeping a finger on the nitty-gritty detail, is vital to the success of the area of purpose. The person in charge of the area of purpose must control and track every minute detail. Later in the manuscript you will learn special tools that enable the head of an area of purpose to track every nitty-gritty detail within these physical follow-through responsibilities.

---

[1]The person in charge of the area of purpose develops his ability to BUILD business and to do integrated thinking. Eventually, he will reach the point where he can, through integrated thinking, *create*. At that point, he will gain two additional essence responsibilities not shown here: 1) create and elevate product, and 2) create and elevate product advertising.

Observations of Diagrams Nine and Ten
Process To Determine Areas Of Purpose
(continued)

Those with areas of purpose at I & O use outside services for some of these physical follow-through responsibilities, while keeping hands-on, fingertip control on every detail (learned later). Some of their outside services include:

- Order Processing Houses
- Drop Shipping Houses
- Product Manufacturing Houses (Book Printers, Audio-Cassette Manufacturers, etc.)

Those with areas of purpose at I & O also use in-house services for some of these physical follow-through responsibilities, while keeping hands-on, fingertip control on every detail (learned later). Some of their in-house services include:

- In-House Order Processing Service
- In-House Drop Shipping Service
- In-House Computer/Database Service
- In-House Customer Service

And, as you will see in Step Five (starting on page 137), the in-house physical follow-through areas blossom into integrated entrepreneurial areas. They become the antithesis of specialized departments. As they blossom, they will always stay attached to their area of purpose through special tools that provide the areas of purpose with fingertip control over all details (learned later).

• One who just begins an area of purpose will handle most if not all the responsibilities himself, including the physical follow-through responsibilities such as, in I & O's case, order processing or shipping the product or customer service. Those in I & O's newly formed foreign areas of purpose, for example, handle all the responsibilities themselves, including their own order processing, etc. As they build their areas of purpose into larger and larger volumes of business, then they can put their physical follow-through work through others while keeping fingertip control of every detail (shown later). ...The responsibilities that drive the area of purpose into existence and drive it forward, however, must always be done by the person in charge of the area of purpose, down to the last nitty-gritty details.

Chapter Twelve

STEP TWO: SPLIT RESPONSIBILITIES

By now you should have read through the process to determine areas of purpose, pages 105 through 112. For decades the specialized workplace, through delegating and departmentalizing, has split apart the integrated areas of purpose. Areas of purpose, areas that can build wealth, rarely exist today. For they have been obliterated into ends-in-themselves responsibilities...into specialized jobs and departments not integrated with making money.

For example, you saw in Diagram Seven I & O's basic responsibilities, a total of 15 basic responsibilities. Traditional publishing/direct-mail companies make each of those basic responsibilities a separate job or department. Therefore, those departments and their specialized jobs cannot build and grow. Then you saw in Diagram Ten I & O's areas of purpose, pulling together the basic responsibilities into their money-making purposes. The areas of purpose can build wealth and grow without limits. ...Until now, PURPOSE, the very reason for business and the very reason for working and living, was lost to the specialized structure.

How did this happen? Why does tradition split apart the responsibilities that need to integrate with their money-making purpose? Why does tradition make the simple responsibilities ends in themselves instead of integrated means to build their money-making purpose, which can be built with no limits? Why does this happen? Only areas of purpose can build wealth. So why are all jobs non-growth, dead-end responsibilities in which people cannot build wealth, cannot grow, thus stagnate? ...Just why does tradition obliterate the purpose throughout business?

Nearly all businesses today, through departmentalizing and delegating, make the responsibilities ends in themselves, which cannot be built, cannot generate wealth. Responsibilities cannot grow. They only MAINTAIN. Workers use the traditional daily schedule to maintain their automatic, specialized responsibilities. No one uses the mini-day schedule with power-thinking — integrated thinking — to build new business. No one uses self-guidance to advance the business. Instead, the business provides automatic guidance to everyone. Eventually, the business dies. ...Why is business structured this way?

Today's specialized business structure still follows the bicameral structures of the Bicameral Age 3000 to 10,000 years ago when the masses — primitive nonthinking automatons — followed a set routine every day and waited to be told what to do by their God-Kings or oracles (as explained in the front material). Today, the following-mode business structures are saturated with primitive mysticism (i.e., the mental state that seeks guidance from external authority, as explained in the front material.)

The white-collar hoax has done nothing to evolve the specialized business structure. About a hundred years ago, smart men began to discover a shortcut to the top AFTER the great industrial empires were already BUILT. The smart men who raced to the top through delegating bypassed more and more of the details needed to integrate and BUILD values. They did not need to BUILD, for the values were already built. Instead, they raced to positions of prestige and power and only needed to MAINTAIN. ...They usually maintained with MECHANICAL EXPANSIONS, for that gives the appearance of building and growth.

So integrating details got increasingly left behind. Specialized niches were carved throughout the business to sustain wealthy and prestigious careers for these smart men taking the shortcut. With the values already built by the original founder, these white-collar hoaxes only needed to MAINTAIN their specialized niches. At their levels of power, however, they should have and really needed to BUILD.

White-collar America formed and grew. White-collar America today largely breaks down into specialized, ends-in-themselves responsibilities. Smart college graduates make it to the specialized niches. Left far behind, the working-class and blue-collar jobs also are ends in themselves, dead ends, with not much pay or future.

Unintegrated and uncompetitive against someone integrated, many corporate leaders embrace specialized business structures to protect their livelihoods and hide their dishonest practices (if dishonesty occurs). Today, nearly all businesses follow this specialized structure. Responsibilities are ends in themselves, not able to grow, able only to MAINTAIN the business. Since the responsibilities cannot grow, the person handling his job cannot grow. This is particularly tragic for the working-class and those in blue-collar jobs. They cannot build. Thus, under traditional companies, most people stagnate. Their futures are set without much growth. The average person gets cut off from his potential as the white-collar hoax flourishes.

Not until the average person uses the Neo-Tech System to eradicate his deep-rooted bicameral tendencies will he break free from the specialized business structure. Not until he ends his own following-mode mentality will he leave his specialized, automatic job to become an integrated Neo-Tech entrepreneur. Only then will he discover his human potential — his potential power-reactor explosion of success achieved from self-guidance integrated thinking.

To leap into Neothink, he must eliminate the blocks imposed by all forms of personal and business mysticism. The Neo-Tech System is the only approach focused on removing mystical limitations. Until one eliminates personal mysticism, leaves behind business tradition, and takes the leap into Neothink, he will never experience wealth and power.

Dump Tradition

Imagine, through the Neo-Tech System, the average person rids his personal mysticism and no longer seeks external guidance. He leaves his specialized job. He prepares for self-guidance. He starts his own business (or his own mini-company at his place of work, explained later). Now he must identify the limitations encountered in starting his own business:

Let us assume that he is on the mini-day/power-thinking team. He is soaring with confidence and strength, moving through project after project with great intensity. He is operating in the Self-Capture mode of Neothink. As his business grows, he needs to hire employees. At this point, personal mysticism flares up again.

Say he hires a secretary. As his business continues to grow, he will need to hire more help. He turns over work to each new employee. This concept of turning over details and responsibilities in the wake of an expanding business is called delegating. However, delegating is a deadly form of personal and business mysticism. Delegating comes from the mysticism-plagued conscious mind seeking easy, automatic answers. The problem is: "I cannot handle all of the responsibilities any longer". The easy, automatic solution is: "Bring someone in who can handle some of those responsibilities; then I can forget about them and all will be fine." But those easy, automatic solutions escape hard, integrated thinking — the only solution that BUILDS wealth. Delegating escapes integrating the whole body of business...needed to BUILD wealth. Delegating allows one to pass details onto someone else, to never really integrate those details, and to stay in a nonintegrating, automatic mode handling just what fills his mind at the time. Residual mysticism from man's bicameral past seeks an automatic life, just as the bicameral man lived. Personal mysticism prefers to *react* to specialized realms of business rather than *integrate* all realms of business.

Delegating responsibilities usually begins with the first person hired. The entrepreneur loses a degree of control as he loses integration with detail. And, as the growing company expands, delegating responsibilities continues with each new person hired. Before long, others in the company begin to delegate their growing responsibilities. The entrepreneur loses more and more control as he increasingly loses integrations with the business. Soon, following tradition, he likely will form departments in an attempt to regain control. However, before long, responsibilities within those departments get delegated leaving the original entrepreneur completely out of touch and out of control. At this point, he has only his immediate, specialized niche to maintain. His personal mysticism led him to this, which will end in failure.

The process of delegating and departmentalizing was born in mysticism and was embraced by the white-collar hoax and is not a valid division of labor. Departments divide labor into SUBJECTS: the list-brokering department, the accounting department, or the marketing department. But the division of labor, remember, divides labor into smooth PHYSICAL MOVEMENTS. Areas of purpose divide making money into PHYSICAL MOVEMENTS: areas that *build* wealth (expanded on later).

Delegating and departmentalizing seem like the thing to do because on the surface, they look good; on paper, they look organized. And man's mysticism-plagued conscious mind integrates no deeper than surface logic. But with Neothink and the use of tools, such surface logic becomes as quaint as man explaining the cosmos with Greek mythology.

Before we go on, the question arises as to how one introduces an employee to his responsibilities in a growing company. As we will see, each employee interlocks his responsibilities to his wealth-building purpose — just as the original entrepreneur does. Moreover, the original entrepreneur or CEO never delegates, never loses his integrations with the business.

Later the new techniques that keep the entrepreneur or CEO integrated with his business will be examined. But for now, it is important to recognize that delegating leads to the business-crippling disease called **split responsibilities.**

Uncovering The Split Responsibilities

Let us take a closer look at how the business mysticism called split responsibilities undermines success in a growing business. We will examine a traditionally managed direct-mail sales company. Let us assume the direct-mail marketing director is preparing for a mailing of several thousand brochures to sell a new product. Remember, he has delegated many responsibilities throughout the traditional company and now interacts with several departments. He no longer has everything at his fingertips. Instead, the information needed to coordinate the mailing is scattered throughout different departments. In years past, his personal mysticism, avoiding integrated thinking, pawned off important integrations to departments. His personal mysticism removed integrated thinking from his mind so he could exist in an automatic, bicameral-like mode, reacting instead of building.

How does he put together a mailing? First he consults with the statistics department. That department shows him which mailing lists are effective and which are not. That department also shows him which ad-copy tests proved better in order to know which brochures to print. Next he contacts his purchasing department. That department handles the purchasing of the

117

envelopes, the coupons, and the brochures. He orchestrates what he needs from them. Then he goes to the list brokering department, which handles renting the mailing lists for the mailing. Now he must contact the manufacturing department that organizes the manufacturing of the product itself. And finally, he meets with the accounting department to know his financial position. In short, to orchestrate a single mailing, the traditional marketing director must contact several departments to initiate the flow of information he needs.

But even more harmful than the responsibilities split among departments are the responsibilities split *within* each department: Responsibilities that should be handled by one person (as explained in Step Three, next chapter) get split among two or more persons. ...Everyone just sort of *reacts* to the job of getting together a mailing. No one is an integrator who aggressively *builds* the mailing program. They all just *maintain* what had been built prior to themselves.

As each department coordinates the needed information through its maze of managers and secretaries, the marketing director waits with his mini-days broken, his momentum shattered. He moves like a snail next to I & O's direct-mail marketing director who runs an integrated area of purpose, as you saw in Diagram Ten. Consider the competitive edge captured by removing split responsibilities and working an integrated area of purpose as described by Mark Hamilton at the Neo-Tech World Summit in Las Vegas, Nevada:

Mark Hamilton
The Neo-Tech World Summit

"Now at I & O, the marketing director handles all those responsibilities. At I & O, we understand that responsibilities are not ends in themselves. They're a means to an end. That end is getting those mailings out faster, quicker, larger than our competition. That is the purpose of direct-mail marketing.

"So we determined the responsibilities that will drive forward the mailings. Attaching those responsibilities to their purpose, the marketing director handles all mailing responsibilities himself.

"Now picture, if you will, our marketing director on his straight-arrow mini-day schedule: He's orchestrating a mailing.

118

He gets answers immediately, all information at his fingertips, in his control. He carries all the integrations in his head. Moreover, not stuck with dead-end responsibilities, he is power-thinking ways to build the mailing program to new records.

"Our competition, on the other hand, works through departments that work through their secretaries and split responsibilities. Once the information for a mailing is gathered by the department secretaries, then the reverberation starts back up from the secretaries, through the departments, to the marketing director. The marketing director in that traditional company sits with his hands tied waiting for answers. Moreover, he carries little if any integrations in his head. He cannot build the program. He really does not know what is going on overall. He only knows his specialized responsibilities. He never uses power-thinking.

"Well, removing split-responsibilities is really proving out in more ways than one. For example, mailing to new names quickly is vital in our industry. Other companies do not move with the speed of I & O. Do you realize that we have a full-scale, major mailing every Saturday? The average of our competition: They have a mailing four times a year, every quarter.

"Because of our competitive edge, we mail to mailing lists that we would not be able to otherwise. For we get to the names first, before our competition.

"I & O Publishing Company moves with unheard of speed and efficiency. But even more important, our marketing director has, as I mentioned earlier, the full mental picture of his purpose — of his mailings — of an area in the business that can grow and grow and grow. He builds that program; he does not just maintain. There's no limit.

"On the other hand, how far can the head of a purchasing department grow? There's a limit. That responsibility becomes an end in itself in traditional companies. How far can the head of a list brokering department go? Just as far as the mailings go; he cannot build list brokering. How far can the manufacturing department go? Just however many books get sold. ...But how far can our marketing director go? There is no limit. And he's growing. In fact, in his first year he's setting a record pace at I & O Publishing Company. There's no limit. He can become more and more competitive, aggressive, reach more and more people. He has purpose: he has a piece of the essence of I & O Publishing Company."

Recognizing The Deception

Split responsibilities become very deceiving as a person becomes busier and busier — busier than ever before in his life. He is so busy trying to chase down, manage and orchestrate all the split responsibilities, he barely has time for the work that counts — essence work, work that BUILDS. But he does not realize how uncompetitive he becomes as he feels so busy. His personal mysticism prefers it this way, though — not carrying the integrations in his head. Instead, he reacts to business versus carrying all the integrations in his head to build the business.

Here is Mark Hamilton again, speaking at a Neo-Tech World Summit:

Mark Hamilton
The Neo-Tech World Summit

"Your company is, as I said yesterday, like a living entity. Your business has a mind and a body. And the mind and the body must act harmoniously. Now, right from the start, we see the problem with delegating:

"You bring people in, you begin to delegate, and the body or details of your business begin to get pushed down...while you, the entrepreneur, maintain the mind of the business — responsibilities that move the business forward.

"You're delegating away from you the body and all its important integrations. And as you grow and more and more people work for you, the body and all its integrations that are crucial for building the business increasingly move away from the mind of the business. What starts forming is something that I have never seen identified in any of the management books: split responsibilities.

"Indeed, the responsibilities that need this harmonious integration with the mind and the body of the business begin to split. In other words, the more glamorous mind of the business stays upstairs in most companies, in the upper management. And the in-the-trenches body of the business and all its vital integrations get delegated to the working class.

120

"A destructive 'take this job and shove it' attitude grows among your work force, for those working for you have no purpose. Without purpose, they feel no excitement and feel no happiness in their careers.

"How can anyone feel motivated if the details that he handles are just dead-end responsibilities? He has no mind of the company, no knowledge to integrate growth, money, profits. He has no purpose.

"Just what is responsible for the dead-end streets among the masses? The specialized business structure today is a vestige of the bicameral societal structures. Most workers never get access to the mind of the business — knowledge needed to rise with integrated power. But once the working man uses the tools of the Neo-Tech System to rid his mysticism and bicameral-like dependency on the white-collar hoax, he can soar with Neothink.

"A growing ineffectiveness of the company's mind becomes increasingly apparent as the entrepreneur loses touch with the body of his business. As he delegates, he loses that vital mind/body integration and becomes less and less effective.

"With the Neo-Tech System, however, he learns what's going on. As he uses the Neo-Tech System, his unintegrated management style will soon be replaced by integrated strength.

"The biggest crime in business since the turn of the century occurs from growth itself. The company moves away from the original entrepreneur who builds a business out of nothing through drive, dedication and hard, Firestone-like integrated thinking. The business eventually becomes filled with white-collar-hoax power and money seekers who ride the company for years before being detected.

"Imagine, on the other hand, a company full of people with purpose. They're responsible for forward movement and profit of their areas. Imagine every person in a company responsible for forward movement — for an area of purpose. Just imagine the drive and attitude.

"Ordinary people can handle areas of purpose, integrating both the body and the mind. They no longer stagnate in a routine-rut, churning out dead-end responsibilities. Instead, they become driven with passion, *building* their own areas...their own empires.

"The reason they're so driven is because they work on the

edge of breakthroughs — breakthroughs for *their own* areas of purpose. Each person in there drives with that original entrepreneurial enthusiasm, energy, and payoffs.

"Those of you in here who already have your own business know what I mean when I say you worked long hours to make your business successful and to keep it successful. Perhaps you sometimes thought: *If just my people, my employees worked like this...there'd be no stopping this company.*"

No Stopping the Neo-Tech Company

There will be no stopping you. Remember, the foundation of the Neo-Tech System is removing limitations. You will discover five more steps that remove personal mysticism and its symbiotic split responsibilities, specialization, and white-collar-hoax structure. By removing yourself from split responsibilities, specialization, and the white-collar-hoax structure, you discover how to integrate all jobs with generating profits. Upon pulling together the next five key steps, the Company-Capture breakthrough becomes your fast-track ticket to millionaire profits.

Chapter Thirteen

STEP THREE: MENTALLY INTEGRATING RESPONSIBILITIES

Each responsibility in business can be attached to its money-making purpose. For example, renting mailing lists (i.e., list brokering) is merely a responsibility that could not exist or grow without its purpose: the direct-mail program. Made a department or an end in itself in most direct-mail companies, limited self-generated growth can come to that dead-end job.

We must now pull together the responsibilities into their money-making purposes. The responsibilities come together as the integrated means to push forward their money-making purposes. Therefore, once integrated, all responsibilities in the business become wealth-building responsibilities. Those integrated wealth-building responsibilities are called: **mentally integrating responsibilities.**

Before growth can begin in your start-up company (or in your mini-company within your current place of work, explained later), you must remove the limitation of split responsibilities. You do this by pulling together mentally integrating responsibilities. Former disintegrated, dead-end responsibilities fuse together into integrated, wealth-building responsibilities. In other words, all responsibilities, all details now integrate with the marketing, negotiating, the accounting, data, and money-making deals — all responsibilities integrate into their purposes that BUILD wealth.

But the average person must be able to handle 100% self-guidance before he can take on a fully integrated money-making purpose and BUILD. That 100% self-guidance comes through the accumulative tools in the Neo-Tech System that move the ordinary person beyond his residual personal mysticism to free him from his boring routine rut. The idea of running his own company or mini-company (explained later) through integrated thinking sounds hard. But through the tools in this manuscript, once an ordinary person becomes used to integrated thinking, it becomes natural and easy to do. With Neo-Tech Control, the "hard" in hard Firestone-like thinking shifts from hard and unusual to easy and natural. Integrated thinking becomes the easiest way to generate wealth (not to mention excitement and fun). So, let's continue the process into integrated thinking by pulling together the mentally-integrating responsibilities:

This approach of pulling together mentally integrating responsibilities at first seems unusual. By traditional business "logic", the approach seems arbitrary as one pulls together the integrating responsibilities without regard to departments. However, departments really come from surface logic and mysticism-plagued tradition, embraced by the white-collar hoax. Departments come from people unconsciously avoiding integrated thinking. Their specialized structure is warmly embraced by executives who prefer no one in the company becomes an integrated thinker with unstoppable integrated power.

What Are Mentally Integrating Responsibilities?

Mentally integrating responsibilities are those responsibilities that come together into the same purpose for one mind to integrate. One person carries all the integrations in his head, such as the direct-mail marketing director at I & O. This is the next major step into integrated thinking.

Let us look at two responsibilities that mentally integrate in the direct-mail marketing director's head. The first is renting the mailing lists, which is done well before the mailing. The second is tracking data, which comes in well after the mailing.

Now, traditionally, tracking the data would have been delegated to someone else. And mailing-list brokering would have been a department all its own. But not so any longer.

With hands-on control, the direct-mail marketing director gets personally close to knowing the mailing lists. For, renting lists is a responsibility that drives the purpose — the direct-mail program — forward. He studies each mailing list intimately, knowing the fluctuations in quantity and delivery schedule. He gets subtle, inside information that the traditional marketing director who relies on a list broker is unaware of. The Neo-Tech man has just gained a competitive advantage.

On the other end of the mailing program is keeping data. Although it seems that someone else can keep the data, that would result in a split responsibility. For, keeping data is a responsibility that drives the purpose — the direct-mail program

— forward. Because of his intimate knowledge of the mailing lists and of the other responsibilities in his area of purpose such as how he set up his mailing and what tests he used, for instance, he is far more efficient, effective, and accurate in setting up and keeping the data. Moreover, by plotting data himself, versus reading data recorded by someone else, he stays closer to his lifeblood, gets his knowledge more quickly, and stays ahead of competition and a step ahead on mailing lists. He gets personally close, handles the data himself, absorbs and integrates how to detect the winning lists quickly, a step ahead of others.

By carrying in his head the mental integrations of all the responsibilities in his area of purpose, he performs each responsibility far more competitively than if the responsibilities were split among specialized jobs. People in specialized jobs have little or no mental integration with the other responsibilities (i.e., other specialized jobs) of the same purpose — needed to drive the business forward. For example, hands-on knowledge of the data brings power to list hunting. Indeed, those traditionally separated responsibilities, traditionally specialized ends-in-themselves jobs, now integrate together as the means to an end — to drive forward their purpose, the direct-mail program. They now get mentally integrated by one person who acquires a major competitive edge. Carrying in his head the mental integrations of all the responsibilities in his area of purpose brings synergy to his job. Each responsibility is done in full mind/body harmony. He moves with speed and power not found in traditional companies.

By handling these mentally integrating responsibilities himself, the I & O direct-mail marketing head takes a valid shortcut to decision making and control. He removes split responsibilities as he no longer calls four or five different, specialized departments waiting for nonintegrated answers. He really moves through his mini-days. By linking together the mentally integrating responsibilities, a steady, unbroken flow of momentum grows as he sees the full picture of business, from the details to the money.

Nothing will stop him now, except for his own personal mysticism that sabotages man's power — his integrated thinking. For instance, he can escape having to carry the mental integrations in his head (i.e., lose his power) by delegating. And he can escape driving his area of purpose forward by not power-thinking. But by eradicating his personal mysticism that secretly seeks automatic external guidance, he will excitedly soar with self-guidance integrated thinking. He will easily carry all the mental integrations in his head — all the mentally integrating responsibilities in his area of purpose — needed to do power-thinking and drive the business forward.

* * *

By understanding that mentally integrating responsibilities exist in business that come together into clusters of unbroken momentum (i.e., the areas of purpose), you will build your start-up company through replicating these integrated clusters instead of delegating specific responsibilities (explained later).

As you use the Neo-Tech System to leave your specialized job, go on the mini-day/power-thinking team and start your own business, you will gain momentum and control. The mini-day/power-thinking team will move you through lucrative project after lucrative project with iron-grip control. Your business will grow, and you will build your company through these mentally integrating clusters of unbroken momentum — through areas of purpose. Those employees you bring in will work on their mini-day/power-thinking teams, too, driving forward their areas of purpose with unbroken momentum. You will build your company with these self-perpetuating money-pumps. Now, let us learn how to do this...

126

Chapter Fourteen

STEP FOUR: UNCOVERING THE PHYSICAL MOVEMENTS OF THE COMPANY — THE TRUE DIVISION OF LABOR

Now you are going to pull together the mentally integrating responsibilities of your start-up business into areas of purpose. If you have not yet started your own business, then simply read through this exercise without doing the steps. If you have no interest in leaving your current place of work, then apply this exercise to the company you now work for. Every business can break down into areas of purpose. At the end of this chapter, you will see how to acquire one of those areas of purpose right in your current place of work. Follow along the process on Diagrams Seven through Ten, pages 105-112, as a guide.

Get a pad of paper and a pencil. Begin by simply listing the basic responsibilities of your business, putting out of your mind current, traditional business structures. This should be easy to do, for your business will not have many basic responsibilities. Refer now to Diagram Seven for Mr. Hamilton's list of I & O's basic responsibilities.

As you can see, Mr. Hamilton listed 15 basic responsibilities within I & O. Put all thoughts of your start-up company aside except for the business performed and write down the basic responsibilities that keep your business going. Stop reading and do this now.

Next review Diagram Eight. Determine the purpose for each basic responsibility you listed. For each responsibility, finish the sentence: "This responsibility exists due to BLANK". Fill in the "blank" as demonstrated in Diagram Eight on pages 106-107. Your small start-up business may have just one or two areas of purpose. That is perfectly normal. Now go through your basic responsibilities and fill in the blank: "This responsibility exists due to BLANK." Stop reading and do this now for each of the basic responsibilities you have listed.

Now, to keep this process neat and organized, you can list again your basic responsibilities and the areas of purpose as shown in Diagram Nine on page 108. This step is not crucial but is helpful. Stop reading and do this now.

Finally, pull together the areas of purpose as shown in Diagram Ten on page 109. This procedure is automatic as you already have listed the basic responsibilities and have defined their purposes when you finished the sentence, "This responsibility exists due to BLANK". The "blanks" that you filled in are the areas of purpose. List those as you see in Diagram Ten, and below them list their basic responsibilities.

Those areas of purpose you are determining will make up the jobs for people you bring in. A small start-up business may have just one or two areas of purpose that the owner personally handles. Let us say that YOUR start-up company has one area of purpose that you personally handle. Do NOT delegate any of your basic responsibilities. You must keep integrated control over your area of purpose. When you are ready, you will bring someone in, replicate the entire area of purpose (replicating explained later), and begin to build a second area of purpose. In any case, finish this process now by listing your areas of purpose and their corresponding basic responsibilities. Stop reading and do this now.

Defining The Physical Movements Of The Company

These money-making purposes throughout the company can be called: the **physical movements** of the company, of building wealth. Why physical movements? With split responsibilities gone, with specialization gone, with all the business schizophrenia and wasted time and broken momentum gone, with instead the wealth-building areas of purpose consolidated, we have determined the shortest motion to build the business and wealth. Like the assembly-line rivet man who moves with unbroken momentum through the shortest motion from point A (himself) to point B (the rivet), the I & O direct-mail marketing director, for example, moves with unbroken momentum through the shortest motion from point A (himself) to point B (building his money-making purpose — building wealth). Indeed, the integrated areas of purpose represent the true division of labor in business, the true physical movements to BUILD wealth.

The result? The company now breaks down into its physical

movements — its true division of labor that includes not just the body of the business, but both the body and mind of business. Just as the division-of-labor mini-day schedule induces integrated thinking (i.e., power-thinking) in your career to cause an explosion in productivity, the division-of-labor areas of purpose induce integrated thinking in your company to cause an explosion in profits. Your greatest assets, the people in your company, now work with purpose. As they leave behind their internal integration blockers — their personal mysticism seeking external guidance — they build, grow, power-think and never stagnate. They drive on the mini-day/power-thinking team and move the business away from white-collar hoax tradition: they BUILD wealth in every nook and cranny instead of MAINTAIN. They know *how to make money*, and they move with unbroken momentum to single-handedly build more wealth than twenty or more specialized employees could build. They discover exhilaration.

Now instead of the original entrepreneur and only the original entrepreneur pushing forward the business and profits, *everyone* pushes forward the business and profits. Those happy people with open-ended futures become the greatest assets to the company.

The Division of Essence — A Business Leap

The essence of your business is: the integrated thinking and actions that make the business and profits grow. Through the Neo-Tech System, through pulling together the mentally integrating responsibilities, the age-old division of labor of the body of business evolves to include the mind, evolves into the superior *division of essence*. Instead of maintaining business through the division of labor, employees build the business and profits through the division of essence. The essence of the business gets divided into the areas of purpose for all employees to push forward.

Through the Neo-Tech System, your start-up company's employees have purpose, building business and wealth for you. Every person in your company acquires a mind/body physical movement to building wealth — a chunk of the essence — and drives it forward with unbroken momentum. No business mysticism, no split responsibilities block wealth creation.

The division-of-labor discovery, implemented most-notably by Henry Ford a hundred years ago, was a spectacular breakthrough for *manufacturing* (i.e., for making products), which demands physical labor. But Mr. Hamilton believes the division of labor, in that original raw and unevolved labor-only dimension, was a major blunder for *business* (i.e., for creating values and making profits), which demands integrated thinking. Managers and entrepreneurs erroneously applied that same raw and unevolved division of labor to sophisticated business, which goes well beyond physical labor. Whereas the nature of manufacturing *is* physical labor, the nature of business is integrated thinking to build profits. The concept of the division of labor in business is correct, but the simplistic labor-only application is wrong. The division of labor must evolve to properly incorporate the mental nature of business. To achieve the shortest movements to building profits requires a leap beyond the mechanical labor-only movements of manufacturing...to the money-making mind/body movements of business. We do this by bringing down to all jobs the nature of man — his mind. The company's jobs then leap from routine-rut jobs of labor to exhilarating jobs of the mind. That is accomplished by pulling together the mentally integrating responsibilities into the areas of purpose. The division of labor finally evolves into the next dimension meant for business: the division of essence.

Now back to the process you just completed: The list of basic responsibilities listed under each area of purpose becomes the "tail of responsibilities". The tail of responsibilities must NEVER be broken through delegating.

Indeed, every responsibility of your company is now tightly integrated under its money-making physical movement. Once one responsibility gets delegated, the physical movement is broken; momentum snaps and split responsibilities are back. You see, a phenomenon occurs by pulling together the mentally integrating responsibilities into physical movements. The full mind/body integration of making money comes together. Everything that needs to be integrated from the nitty-gritty details (the body of the business) to the finances, negotiating, deals (the mind of the business) mentally integrate

130

and all come together into the fully integrated physical movements to making money.[1] Look again at Diagram Ten on page 109. Note the physical movements (i.e., the areas of purpose). The most nitty-gritty details up to the finances come together into physical movements. Now with the Neo-Tech System, people will rise through the integrated, open-ended movements that build business; they no longer have to sink in dead-end, specialized jobs that maintain business. But how can one person handle all those integrating responsibilities? We will learn how ordinary men and women can step into and handle the exciting physical movements and drive profits forward, in the remaining chapters of Volume Two.

Profit Machines

When pulling together the mentally integrating responsibilities into the true division-of-labor physical movements, notice that traditional departments, hierarchical status, boss, secretary, subordinates, white-collar, blue-collar — all that means nothing. That all comes from an inferior and improper division of labor. You are interested in one thing only — pulling together the mentally integrating responsibilities into their money-making purposes. The areas of purpose quickly obsolete the white-collar hoax. Only integrated profit machines remain. Only the physical movements of building wealth remain that can drive profits forward with unbroken momentum. Welcome to the next evolution of the division of labor: welcome to the division of essence.

From the Self-Capture Discovery, you acquired a boost of power by establishing physical movements — the mini-days. Now, your start-up business itself acquires a boost of power by establishing physical movements — the areas of purpose. You have gone well below the nonintegrated surface logic of the mysticism-plagued conscious mind to determine the true division of labor of your company. Unbroken momentum and the mentally integrated picture of making money come together in your

---

[1]*To think* requires physical energy; it requires the physical act *to think* and, therefore, is a physical movement. That explains why the mind of business can be integrated with the body to become the physical movements of business and building profits.

131

physical movements. Now you will build your start-up company with average men and women who will propel profits in every nook and cranny — your profit machines. Whereas Henry Ford discovered the assembly line for mass production through the division of labor, you discover the assembly line for wealth production through the next evolution of the division of labor that includes the mind: the division of essence. You will see this phenomenon unfold as the Company-Capture Discovery builds. Traditional, specialized competition gets left behind.

Job Power

Now the time comes to turn these radically different physical movements into profit machines within your start-up company. We are going to make each physical movement a job...a job with essence.

Unlike traditional start-up businesses, your start-up business provides jobs that are fully integrated areas of purpose; people who work for you actually have the means to making money as opposed to nearly all other jobs that are specialized, closed ends in themselves. Most other jobs consist of responsibilities that get done for their own sake, with no integration with building profits.

Realize that the mentally integrating responsibilities that determine a specific physical movement must stay integrated by one person — everything from rolling up his sleeves and doing mentally integrating nitty-gritty details to shirt-and-tie mentally integrating money matters. That one person carries in his head the knowledge to directly deal with each responsibility in order to drive forward the entire movement with unbroken momentum. He compiles integrated strength and power, void in the specialized job. If he ever delegates or turns over any one of those mentally integrated responsibilities, however, the schizophrenic split responsibilities come back.

With split responsibilities gone, responsibilities are no longer blind, ends in themselves. They become part of the wealth-building integration that can drive their purpose forward. These wealth-pumps are open-ended, without limits, and they pump wealth for you.

The question arises, "How can one person possibly handle

all of those responsibilities if the company continues to grow?" Consider that the growth of a company does not increase the number of basic responsibilities in a physical movement (i.e., area of purpose). Instead, growth expands the *number of projects* and *volume of business* in that movement. But the number of responsibilities within any movement — within the tail of responsibilities — stays the same.

When the volume of projects grows beyond one person, one of those marketing projects can break off from its marketing program into its own area of purpose with the same or very similar tail of responsibilities. That new area of purpose gets transferred (i.e., gets replicated, as learned later) to another person.

In other words, an integrated chunk of the business — an entire physical movement — along with its full tail of responsibilities, gets transferred to another person. That person acquires a complete physical movement of his own. He does not acquire some delegated, split responsibilities within that marketing program, rather he absorbs the full mind/body responsibilities that converge into an area of purpose of his own. So there becomes two people, two wealth pumps. Each person handles his tail of mentally integrating responsibilities. Instead of one money-pump, you have two. Before long, you will fill your company with integrated money-pumps (instead of departments and specialized dead-end jobs), which is the division of essence...the proper division of labor of business.

Entrepreneur Power

You can leave behind your specialized job, get on the mini-day/power-thinking team, and start your own business. As your start-up company grows, you must determine the areas of purpose, the physical movements of your business.

The mini-day/power-thinking team alone pushes you through project after project and brings you into a rapid growth stage. Now you are ready to take on company growth in a powerful, fully integrated fashion. You must do the exercise explained earlier in this chapter to determine the physical movement (or movements) of your new company. When you bring in your first employee, you establish him in a physical movement, his own

133

fully integrated area of purpose. Unhampered by split responsibilities, he will acquire the fully integrated mental picture of business and drive profits forward with unbroken momentum. He becomes your first wealth-pump.

Your successor takes integrated control of his entire physical movement. He leaps beyond his pre-Neo-Tech days of working specialized jobs with delegated responsibilities that are ends in themselves — dead ends. He now works a fully integrated area that is a MEANS to push forward the business. Therefore he, too, must abandon his personal mysticism and discover integrated thinking through the tools of the Neo-Tech System. He, too, must drive forward with the mini-day/power-thinking team.

He becomes streamlined and efficient and more effective than nonintegrated traditional departments. He single-handedly handles his mentally integrating responsibilities. Moreover, he integrates those responsibilities to acquire a mind/body knowledge of business in order to not just MAINTAIN, but to BUILD — to drive forward his area of business. He soon starts pumping profits for you. He pumps profits with the unbroken momentum of a rivet-driving physical movement.

How To Rise To The Top, Wherever You Work

If you want to stay in the company you now work for, you can still use these same techniques of the Neo-Tech System to gain integrated power and rise to the top right where you work. Let us pause to take a different course, for the moment, from starting your own business. Let us say, you do not want to start your own business, but you want to leave behind your specialized routine rut. You want to discover the exhilarating world of building profits through an integrated area of purpose.

Every business can be broken into its areas of purpose — its proper division of labor — including the business you now work for. To break down the company you now work for into its areas of purpose, follow the same steps done earlier in this chapter as shown to you in Diagrams Seven through Ten on pages 105 through 112. Do that now.

Look over the areas of purpose. Study them. They represent the true division of labor of the company you work for; they are physical movements for building wealth. Now, choose the area of purpose you would enjoy for yourself. That is your target. That is the open-ended money-making job you will secretly take over for yourself. Here's how:

Consider this: if someone is willing to do the tough nitty-gritty details of a particular responsibility, it is human nature for others to let him have those details. That aspect of human nature is your friend in helping you to gradually create and take over your targeted area of purpose.

First, study the tail of responsibilities listed under the area of purpose that you have targeted. Remember, those mentally integrating responsibilities could come from all over within the company — from different departments, from blue-collar jobs, from white-collar jobs. It only matters that they mentally integrate into a money-making purpose.

Second, learn the details behind each of those responsibilities. Learn all the details that make up each mentally integrating responsibility, down to its most nitty-gritty details.

Third, with human nature working for you, one by one begin to do those nitty-gritty details. Others tend to gladly let those details go if someone else absorbs them, and that is your secret objective. You provide them with that path of least resistance, and you will gradually absorb more and more of the specific details that make up each responsibility in your targeted area of purpose. No one needs to know what you are doing. But in time, you will have wrestled control of an entire area of purpose. At that time, you will discover an exhilaration at work you never knew before. You will generate new profits for the company and discover the sensation of genuine power for yourself. Raises and bonuses will follow.

Chapter Fifteen

STEP FIVE: PERFORMANCE-PAY MINI-COMPANIES

Now, let us go back to the growing puzzle of starting and building your own company through the Neo-Tech System.

Okay, back to your start-up business: Your business breaks down to jobs with purpose — jobs that BUILD business. Those who work for you no longer MAINTAIN specialized, dead-end jobs. They BUILD integrated, open-ended money-making ventures. Your company evolves into the next dimension of wealth creation called the division of essence.

The next step integrates not only each job with the marketplace and making money, but each person. For, you put each person, his area of purpose, on **performance pay**.

Each person working for you now explicitly eradicates his mysticism for his best performance thus personal profits. Each person or wealth pump drives ahead with power-thinking, for he is personally integrated/motivated with the *net* of everything he does.

Not just you, but now everyone working for you becomes directly integrated with building wealth. You see, their pay will be integrated with the profits they generate.

Working for you: Profit-driven in-house entrepreneurs suddenly have incentive to overcome their mysticisms that otherwise seek external guidance on what to do or seek automatic guidance from set responsibilities. To build profits, they are driven into self-guidance. They are driven into power-thinking and integrated thinking. Eventually, they move into the new horizons of making money.

Performance money now flows into the pockets of those with areas of purpose. Now, their power to increase wealth comes not just from you (i.e., externally from above), but from their own integrated thinking. Now, wealth creation comes down to the areas of purpose — down to the *jobs themselves* within your company.

Your *employees themselves* evolve into self-guidance integrated thinking since they no longer hold a specialized job with external guidance, set responsibilities, and set pay. They move beyond bicameral tendencies, beyond waiting for answers or directions or specialized responsibilities from above. Instead, they eagerly drive forward integrated, open-ended areas of purpose. ...Your company becomes far more competitive than the traditional, specialized structures.

Essence Driven

Those on performance pay become tightly integrated with the net after their costs and efforts. As a matter of fact, they become the most integrated people at making money. They become the essence of business: the money makers.

Those money makers can eventually become wealthy, for they discover that leaving behind their residual mysticisms increases profits. They evolve from impotent followers to passionate leaders of wealth creation as they leave behind their bicameral tendencies.

By developing performance pay throughout your Neo-Tech company, your employees — your greatest assets — drive hard every day *with* you, the original entrepreneur. The essence of business — to build values and profits — gets driven forward every day in every nook and cranny by these hard-driving mysticism-free entrepreneurs working for you.

Each area of purpose generates revenue and represents a piece of your company's money-making essence. As your company grows and you divide wealth creation into more and more areas of purpose or wealth pumps, your company discovers the power of the new, division of essence. The division of essence — the division of making money — enables wealth creation's greatest asset to blossom: yourself and the people working for you. The division of essence takes the division of labor to the next level — to include the power of your employees' minds.

Since the turn of the century, wealth-creation's greatest assets, people and their minds, have been suppressed and stagnated by both mysticism and the white-collar hoax. The division of essence unleashes their human potential.

Now that your employees push forward their integrated areas of purpose, you inject a stimulant. That stimulant, of course, is performance pay. Your employees, who drive forward their fully integrated areas of purpose, drive even harder on performance pay. The more they push forward their essences and pump wealth for you...the more they make.

Suddenly, every person working for you focuses on performance, something not seen much in business today. Instead of you and only you pushing the business forward, your wealth pumps also push the business forward. The phenomenon, again, is called **The Division of Essence.**

Consider this: Fully integrated, mysticism-free people on performance pay driven on essence, day in and day out, in every nook and cranny versus the traditional company with specialized, mysticism-plagued employees ignorant of the essence...the essence all balled up in the Board of Directors' occasional, lethargic white-collar-hoax meetings in which some unintegrated essence issues get discussed. The new Neo-Tech business and the division of essence will surpass the traditional company, its specialization, and its white-collar hoax.

Effect Of The Division Of Essence

The most fundamental integration of business is to measure costs and efforts against *net*. Imagine every person in your company not only driven with purpose, but driven by the net of his efforts. Notice on Diagram Ten, page 109, that those who handle the areas of purpose integrate with the money and accounting. Now, the key is to integrate their **personal pay** with the *net* of their efforts. Their jobs take on a new meaning as they build not only their areas of purpose, but their *own wealth*.

Every area of purpose becomes more integrated through performance pay. Moreover, even the physical follow-through jobs described on pages 111 and 112 can go on performance pay. Every job will now evolve into hard-driving, hard-thinking entrepreneurial areas, leaving the dead-end departments and nonthinking specialized jobs a thing of the past.

Follow-Through Jobs

Now, let us look at the effect performance pay has on even the physical follow-through areas (explained on pages 111 and 112). Let us take the computer/database area at I & O. Computer programming is one of the most specialized fields in any traditional company. But by integrating this area with making money, effort with net, this area transforms into one of the most integrated and profitable areas at I & O.

First, you must know the secret to effective performance pay: Performance pay should be carefully designed to act as a launching pad to send a person into fulfilling his potential thus multiplying his value to the company many times over. The key is that performance pay launches one's value to the company several times over the added money he takes from the company through performance pay. Case in point at I & O:

The computer area is typically a specialized area in which the computer programmer is given a particular computer assignment or a particular database (i.e., customer mailing list) assignment. He merely follows through. But let us see what happens when he is integrated with money:

The computer person at I & O gets paid by the amount of database names used by the I & O Database Marketing Program. You will see how this simple but carefully designed performance pay multiplied his value to the company many times over. The traditional, specialized computer job changed from a mechanical follow-orders job into a widely integrated, aggressive entrepreneurial job as shown below:

Computer/Database Person:
Performance Pay = Pay Per Number of Database Names Used By Database Marketing Program

* He drives on his own to achieve excellent control of the database to make it efficient and easy for the Database Marketing Program to acquire maximum names, including complicated cross sections, variable demographics, dead-weight suppressions of names, etc. Now the principals at I & O do not have to figure out what, how, or when database assignments need to be done, while the computer/database person merely follows their orders. Not now, for the computer/database person takes charge. Integrated with making money, he breaks free from traditional, specialized thinking in which one can only MAINTAIN or do the responsibilities laid before him. He evolves into integrated thinking in which he can BUILD and move forward his area on his own. For, his job is no longer a specialized

140

follow-through responsibility. His job is an integrated entrepreneurial, effort-to-net unit.

* He drives into general computer needs of Database Marketing Program to make that marketing program most efficient so it can expand and use more names.

* He drives into not just the computer needs for the Database Marketing Program, but computer needs company-wide, particularly in the other marketing programs. For, to increase their efficiencies thus their capacities to expand, they will generate more customer names that he can supply the customer-based Database Marketing Program. (Remember, he gets paid by the amount of names used by the Database Marketing Program.) By these dynamics, the computer/database person stands to double his income in relatively short time. For I & O will soon undergo major mass marketing, largely due to enhanced controls over the computer, company-wide. Mass marketing will bring an escalation of revenue to the company.

* The computer person at I & O drives into not just the computer needs, but into the numbers, data, statistics of the Database Marketing Program's mailings to see how to increase results thus increase the universe of names used. He becomes a marketing/numbers man.

* He drives into not just computer needs, but into the numbers, data, statistics of the other marketing programs to see how to increase results thus increase the universe of names generated for the database. He becomes an expert numbers man company-wide. He, not just Mr. Hamilton, makes the whole business his business. And that's a wonderful thing for Mr. Hamilton.

* He even analyzes the data of split-run tests and ad copy to the point of suggesting new ad-copy proposals and even writing ad copy for testing. The person in charge of the computer/database area at I & O actually honed in on a marketing breakthrough.

Indeed, the computer man is no longer the specialized "byte head" who knows nothing but computers. He becomes one of the most integrated minds in the business because of the well-

141

designed, simple performance pay. Remember, the computer area was originally just a follow-through job, with the computer programmer handling only what he was told to do. Now that area transforms into a high-powered entrepreneurial area headed by a driven entrepreneur. As he increases his income, he increases his value to the company many times over.

Performance-Pay Specifics

Specifically, consider the high ratio of gross revenue to payroll — or company income to company payroll. That ratio is usually several to one. Properly designed performance pay brings leverage to both the company and to the working person. For example, say the ratio of gross revenues to payroll is ten to one. By establishing performance pay, one will drive with original-entrepreneur-like motivation. He may increase his performance income from $2500 to $8500 a month. By doing that through well designed performance pay, he in essence increases the revenue to the company from $25,000 (2500 X 10) to $85,000 (8500 X 10).

Establish good performance pay, but carefully designed performance pay to launch a person's value to the company. Your fully integrated employees will respond by putting out record performances, making themselves good money while driving the business forward, something not possible in the traditional company. This is an opportunity of a lifetime for any employee.

For the first time in their lives, your employees see wealth in their direct control. They work hard; they think hard. They are motivated. Stagnation is void in your Neo-Tech business.

Because of the high ratio of income to payroll, the wealthier each employee becomes, the more you and your company gain several times over with properly designed performance pay. And, of course, those who do not push their essences forward do not last. They drain little money from you. Employee expansion becomes essentially risk-free.

The key is in not merely setting up generous performance pay, but well-planned performance pay integrated with all the disciplines of making money. For example, those at I & O directly integrated with the marketplace receive performance pay based on NET income AFTER costs are taken out. Therefore, people brought into the company learn effective negotiating, cost cutting, and cost savings because profits determine how much money they will take home. And such cost-cutting and negotiating disciplines among the majority of employees sharpens the company's competitive edge.

Built on money-driven areas of purpose, your work force never becomes lethargic. In fact, the larger your Neo-Tech company grows, the *more* aggressive and competitive it becomes internally.

The Neo-Tech System brings out the potential and the happiness people deserve. By maximizing your number-one asset — people — your company flourishes. Mr. Hamilton talks about the productivity phenomenon of this nontraditional division-of-essence company. He begins with you leaving your specialized job:

Mark Hamilton
The Neo-Tech World Summit

"Go on the mini-day/power-thinking team, start the business you've always wanted to start, dump the American dream and, instead, go for an empire.

"You may not want to leave your job just yet in order to have the income, but consider your job a mini-day. An income mini-day. Start in the evenings, maybe in the mornings too, surrounding your job — your income mini-day — with your own start-up company mini-days...what you've always dreamed about doing. Feel your energy and exhilaration grow. Feel your motivation and momentum build with your mini-day/power-thinking team. You no longer have anything limiting you.

"In your current career, you're most likely trapped in a specialized structure. You most likely stagnate in split responsibilities. You can't really function on a mini-day schedule in your specialized career. You can't really do power-thinking because you can't move ahead on those projects you want to move ahead on. You're doing responsibilities that are ends in themselves. You have no essence to go after. You have no future.

"But you use your mini-day/power-thinking team to begin your own start-up company. For the first time, you can really use power-thinking. You can press forward into projects. You can break down your day into physical movements. You now have nothing stopping you.

"All right, you start growing. You become successful because you're handling more than the next person can. You've surpassed your competition so you're going to do well. You start to grow. However, you're not going to delegate. You're going to keep all of the mentally integrating responsibilities. Remember, split responsibilities are specialized responsibilities, the path to stagnation. Mentally integrating responsibilities are integrated responsibilities, the path to prosperity.

"Next you're going to discover the physical movements of your business. You're going to discover those smooth physical movements by understanding mentally integrating responsibilities. You're never going to let a responsibility become an end in itself. Responsibilities are merely means to the ends. You're always going to let the handful of purposes to the many responsibilities be the ends. The areas of purpose bring you profits and move you forward. The responsibilities are going to stick without exception to their purposes...their essences. Responsibilities are never going to get split. You break down your growing company by the true division of labor and create the assembly-line of wealth creation, right there in your start-up company. You discover the division of essence.

"You start growing, and you bring your first person in with growth. You are not going to delegate responsibilities. He will, as you did when you started the company, learn to integrate every detail in his area of purpose from the smallest nitty-gritty detail to the negotiating, accounting, and money matters. He works an integrated physical movement, driving ahead with unbroken momentum on his essence, and now you've got a motivated working force that you put on performance pay.

"Every area of purpose can be put on performance pay. Every person and every responsibility in your company can now push forward the profits. Your business continues to grow because you have people expanding in different directions. You walk into I & O at night, on weekends, and you'll find people working in their offices...working on their own details because their details are integrated with their essences. And their money-making essences have no limits. Those people can now generate money. They are entrepreneurs. They are essentially just like you — owner of the company. Imagine that.

"Imagine walking into your offices in the evening to see people working away in their own best interest. And because they're established on performance pay, they're highly motivated. What a great arrangement that is for your company, because every dollar that they're so highly motivated to generate…is bringing in maybe ten dollars to the company.

"Even the ordinary person can build his own empire eventually, right in your company! And that's just one out of potentially dozens of empires in your Neo-Tech business!"

— Mark Hamilton

A Powerful New Concept: The Mini-Company

To strengthen the division of essence, I & O makes each area of purpose that is on performance pay not a job, but a company. That's right: a self-driven **mini-company**.

A person takes over an area of purpose, the body and the mind of wealth creation. That person runs his physical movement of wealth creation with unbroken momentum. When put on performance pay, he runs his own MINI-COMPANY. He now handles all his needs just as any independent company would, from buying his own supplies to doing his own accounting. Let us focus on the psychological power behind this concept:

Now in charge of his own open-ended mini-company, he sees everything differently than before. He no longer expects or looks for external guidance. He works and drives like you — the original entrepreneur. Your employee now engages in a persistent, personal challenge, not a nine-to-five stagnant job. For, your employee now works for his "own" company and financial success. Being his own business, he squarely faces and takes on all the details. Being his own business, he wants control, and he wants profits. He discovers integrated thinking. He leaves behind personal mysticism.

Each mini-company exists as its own company. Therefore, each mini-company consists of its own essence, which drives your employees into essence thinking or *integrated* thinking. Imagine the difference between a traditional, stagnant job versus a mini-company at I & O. A Neo-Tech mini-company encompasses the body and the mind of business, which brings a person's career to life — a living business he must raise and develop. And no matter how large the overall Neo-Tech company itself grows, the growing life throughout the company stays hungry.

You have little risk, for those who do not perform (i.e., those who do not use the Neo-Tech System to move beyond their bicameral mysticism blocking their wealth-building integrated thinking) do not drain you. They generate little or no performance pay. They leave, and you do not carry a bloated payroll. You eventually can have risk-free wealth pumps forming all around you (as taught in the World-Capture section). Your wealth creation can grow without limits.

Performance-Pay Tip

Setting up effective performance pay is very tricky and requires experience. To start the process, set up your mini-company employee with a reasonable salary or hourly wage and link, informally, bonuses to net profits. Do not overdo it at first. It is a lot easier to add to performance pay later on than to take away. With some time and experience, you will be able to evolve the mini-company into full performance pay when you feel comfortable making that move.

Chapter Sixteen
STEP SIX: REPLICATING

Now start-up businesses can bypass specialization and grow through integration. A Neo-Tech business discards delegating, departments, split-responsibilities, white-collar-hoax positions and specialization. Instead, a Neo-Tech business pulls together the clusters of mentally integrating responsibilities into areas of purpose. Do this first — determine the areas of purpose. Then you will bring people in to work fully integrated areas of purpose, not specialized jobs that are dead-ends. For the first time, your employees will integrate beyond traditional routine-rut responsibilities...into the money and profits.

With a fully integrated area of purpose (a mini-company), the ordinary person works with drive and excitement and never knows stagnation. He works like the original entrepreneur himself, for he works a job that is not an end in itself, but a means to drive forward profits. He works with incentive, for he works for himself on performance pay. He becomes a wealth pump for you as he drives on his essence with unbroken momentum, with several times the effectiveness of even the best traditional worker.

Soon your start-up company is ready to blossom. With the foundation established, you are going to eventually multiply your wealth pumps. How do you build your company with these wealth pumps, these integrated people who can drive forward profits? You do this by transferring entire areas of purpose with their full mind/body integrations...versus delegating single, specialized responsibilities. By transferring an entire area of purpose, you create an employee who is NOT specialized, but integrated — fully integrated with driving forward the business. You create a true wealth pump — a physical movement that pumps wealth into your company.

The one and only process that will effectively transfer the vast mind/body integrations of an area of purpose is the Neo-Tech discovery called: **Replicating**.

Starting with the most specific nitty-gritty detail up to the most involved financial deal, an area of purpose is integrated like the body and mind. Mind and body must work together in harmony. Delegating responsibilities destroys the mind/body relationship and destroys the integrated purpose. The mind/body harmony of the integrated area of purpose will be preserved through *replicating*. You will now learn how to replicate yourself and your mind/body knowledge. You will now learn how to BUILD INTO a successor the full mind/body integrated spectrum of an area of purpose as opposed to TURNING OVER specific responsibilities in a nonintegrated format called delegating. Delegating causes the disorder of split responsibilities and destroys a new company's chance at major wealth creation.

To master control of your company requires the three demands of building an empire:

The first demand is knowing the business itself: knowing the nitty-gritty, minute, grind-out body details. Now that we know that the nature of business is integration, it becomes clear why knowing the nitty-gritty detail is vital. As one begins to expand his scope of business, knowing the nitty-gritty detail becomes MORE important, for now that knowledge integrates into increasingly MAJOR money decisions.

The second demand is learning and integrating the crucial detail. What is crucial detail? It is detail that your employee cannot yet integrate. Remember, crucial detail is the detail that requires wider integrations than your employee can handle. You must monitor this detail yourself while your employee increasingly learns how to handle these details that require wider integrations.

The third demand is knowing and advancing the essence of the business. The essence consists of the most integrated issues of the business where forward movement occurs. For the first time, essence will exist in your employee's job, for he acquires a fully integrated area of purpose and not specialized responsibilities. He will evolve to the point where he can push his essence forward.

The Neo-Tech method to growth, called replicating, consists of Neo-Tech Replicating Meetings. Most meetings are considered a review or a let's-touch-bases situation. But Neo-Tech Replicating Meetings are far different in concept. The Neo-Tech Replicating Meetings are a threefold series of evolving meetings that directly answer the three demands of building an empire (see

148

Diagram Eleven, next page):
    The three stages of evolving Replicating Meetings are:

Stage One: Nitty-gritty working meetings, which evolve
                toward...
Stage Two: Crucial-detail meetings, which evolve
                toward...
Stage Three: Essence meetings.

Stage One: Full-Scale Working Meetings

Nitty-gritty detail is NOT going to be turned over or delegated or taught or trained to someone else. Instead, you will engage in working meetings and personally conduct all of the details yourself in the presence of the person you are replicating to. Remember, you are bringing in another person in order to essentially replicate yourself — your mind/body knowledge — for building an entire area of purpose; you will not merely train that person. Continue doing that person's physical work yourself, all the work, all the details. You do not tell him how to do it, then leave him to do it, then come back and tell him how to do the next step. No. You will do all the work yourself as your successor observes at your side.

You do all the nitty-gritty, grind-out details — including details that perhaps you have not handled before. Indeed, in many cases the entrepreneur loses touch with the details of his business. Stage One Working Meetings force him to recapture those details. By forcing him to organize and perform well-planned, detailed working meetings, he gains intimate knowledge of his business, all the details, quickly. The Working Meetings force better hands-on knowledge of the details, which he must know to build an empire.

Your employee gains a deeply integrated understanding of subtle integrations that would be missed through delegating — even things as subtle as voice inflections used on the telephone. He also gains the broad mind/body picture as you explain your reasons for what you do. He becomes so well integrated that you know the details will always get done *right*.

As you engage in these rewarding nitty-gritty-detail working meetings, your successor begins to permanently take over more

(continued on page 151)

149

Diagram Eleven
Evolving Neo-Tech Replicating Meetings

THE THREE DEMANDS OF BUSINESS	THREE STAGES OF NEO-TECH MEETINGS
THE FIRST DEMAND: Knowing the business itself. Knowing the nitty-gritty and minute, grind-out detail.	STAGE ONE: Full-scale, nitty-gritty working meetings
	...evolving toward...
THE SECOND DEMAND: Knowing and monitoring the crucial detail.	STAGE TWO: Crucial-detail meetings
	...evolving toward...
THE THIRD DEMAND: Knowing and advancing the essence of the business.	STAGE THREE: Essence meetings

150

and more of the working detail. Your successor will TAKE, not be given, more and more detail. You get pushed more and more into taking charge of crucial detail — detail that he cannot yet integrate. You have begun to replicate yourself.

At first the time spent on these long working meetings may seem merciless, but the meetings will soon shift into powerful pockets of leverage. For, the replicating process not only assures that your employee will, in the future, get the work done right, but that he will also evolve into an integrated thinker. Indeed, he observes how your mind works, how it integrates all details into the broad mind/body picture to push the business forward.

By delegating, on the other hand, a number of the mentally integrating responsibilities never reach the employee. The powerful mental integrations among responsibilities never forms. Responsibilities stay split, specialized, automatic. Moreover, by delegating specific responsibilities versus replicating full physical movements, the whole mind/body picture is never seen by the employee. He is destined to specialized thinking and stagnation. He will never know the power of integrated thinking. The company eventually sinks with schizophrenic split responsibilities.

Only by replicating FULL AREAS OF PURPOSE does the nitty-gritty detail transfer and integrate into the broad money-making picture with iron-grip control. By gaining the full mental picture of business, your employee is forming into a potential wealth pump.

And, of key importance, these working meetings prevent the common mistake of delegating details without really knowing those details — a sure way to anchor your company forever to inefficiency. The working meetings force you — the original entrepreneur — to know the body details of your business...better than anyone else. That integration will enable you to soar toward your essence. ...As your employee begins integrating the nitty-gritty detail himself, your replicating meetings will evolve toward stage two. You have met the first demand of building an empire.

Stage Two: Focussing On Crucial Detail

These replicating meetings crisply bring forth the integrations your employee cannot make. He has taken from you the nitty-gritty integrations he can make. The remaining integrations are the crucial details that you must integrate. Your meetings now focus on the crucial detail as you take your employee through these broader integrations.

The traditional start-up company grows through delegating responsibilities and becomes more and more impossible to track the crucial detail. The split responsibilities make it difficult to track much of anything as the company simply becomes more and more complex, divided, specialized. By contrast, replicating makes progress easy to track. You are led straight to the crucial detail as your successor masters the nitty-gritty detail.

Crucial detail meetings may continue weekly or even daily for a few weeks, months, or longer, in some cases, depending on the area being replicated and on your successor. In other cases, crucial detail meetings should be strictly phone meetings to help keep out the nitty-gritty detail. In yet other cases, crucial detail "meetings" should not be meetings, but perhaps, correspondence put through your in-basket — situations your successor does not yet know how to handle. In any case, your successor steadily takes over these wider integrations, something never reached through delegating. As he gains these wider integrations, the time you spend pays off as he begins generating wealth for you. ...You have met the second demand of building an empire.

Stage Three:
Building Your Start-Up Company Through the Essence

Your successor takes control of his full area of purpose. He leaves far behind pre-Neo-Tech days of working specialized jobs with delegated responsibilities that are ends in themselves — dead-ends. He now works a fully integrated area that is a MEANS to push forward the business. He develops aggressive power-thinking to push forward his developing mini-company and to generate greater profits/performance pay. Therefore he, himself, soon encounters essence issues.

Again, essence is that which can move the business beyond its current level to build profits. Essence meetings communicate back to you new integrations your successor would like to pursue. Now, instead of you feeding integrations to your successor, he begins feeding new integrations to you.

Step Six: Replicating

He not only now *maintains* his responsibilities more effectively than several traditional employees rolled into one, but he further integrates his responsibilities to *build* his area of business. For, he has the full mental picture of business. As he moves beyond his bicameral tendencies, he discovers a whole new world through integrated thinking. With integrated thinking, he can drive his essence forward into a million-dollar mini-company.

You, the original entrepreneur of the company, arc now fully replicated as well as fully integrated with the business below you. Thus, you now pursue the creation of new business above you. You not only acquire the time, but you acquire the full business integration of body and mind to press into new, lucrative progress...into broad, company-wide essence, as explained in Chapter Eighteen.

But through delegating, by contrast, even the original entrepreneur can never really build the essence. He eventually loses touch with the crucial and nitty-gritty details of the business. Without the full mind/body picture, he cannot push the business forward for long. And all people below him become increasingly incapable to pursue the essence. Their responsibilities that trickle down through delegating are specialized, split from the mind. To reach the essence becomes more and more a maze of split responsibilities that makes the essence unattainable, for the body and mind of the business lose contact. Employees see no way through the maze to the top, which causes today's bad attitude among the labor force.

Now consider the replicated mini-companies, those replicated areas of purpose...the real physical movements of business. Each one of those mini-companies is a company within itself. Therefore, each one of those mini-companies has its own essence. The people with mini-companies, therefore, drive with exhilaration on their essences, clearly before them day in and day out. Being the physical movements of the overall company, the essences of the mini-companies form the essence of the overall company, broken into the most efficient units by the true division of labor. Therefore, every day, many people in the company (the mini-companies) drive forth the essence of the company.

153

The essence of each mini-company is easy to see. For example, one can easily see that the essence of the direct-mail mini-company is to sell as much Neo-Tech literature as possible. The essence drives the person with a mini-company into sophisticated essence projects such as, for example, demographic research of I & O's customer database to learn more about the people who buy Neo-Tech. The mini-company head power-thinks how to drive forward essence.

He builds momentum, for his essence is right before him in an integrated physical movement. He does not break his momentum trying to pull out split responsibilities lodged throughout in the company structure. No, his essence is clear, something he drives on every day, something exciting and challenging. Moreover, he drives on the essence not because "it's my job"; he drives on the essence to boost his personal success, his personal financial success.

The mini-companies drive forward the essence of the company, for the mini-companies summed together equal the essence of the company. The result is the division-of-essence company. Not just a handful in upper management, but essentially *everyone* drives forth the essence. You, the original entrepreneur or CEO/president, will snap all those mini-companies together into a single synergistic force to launch the superior Neothink company, the company of the future. (The next chapter teaches you how to snap together the mini-companies into the mighty Neothink puzzle.) Stage-Three Neo-Tech Meetings with your mini-company heads focus on the essences of their mini-companies. ...You have met the third demand of building an empire.

More On Replicating
Again, the three demands of building an empire are:

1) Knowing the business itself. Knowing the nitty-gritty and minute, grind-out details.
2) Knowing and monitoring the crucial detail.
3) Knowing and advancing the essence.

Starting with the most specific nitty-gritty detail up to the sweeping essence, business is a vastly integrated unit like the body and mind. Through delegating, an entrepreneur cuts off the body of his business, which eventually kills the essence...the mind of the business.

Look again at I & O's mini-companies, the areas of purpose, with their tails of responsibilities (Diagram Ten on page 109). In the traditional start-up company, the tail of responsibilities gets delegated throughout different departments. In the Neo-Tech start-up company, the tail of responsibilities stays with its purpose. The mind/body, mentally integrating responsibilities stay together.

As the business grows, the *number of responsibilities* in an area of purpose does not grow. The *number of projects*, *programs*, and the *volume of business* grows. When an area of purpose (i.e., a mini-company) becomes too much for one person to manage, the unchanging tail of responsibilities does not get delegated. It always stays attached to its purpose. Instead, the growing number of projects, programs, or growing chunks of the business get replicated — along with *the entire* tail of responsibilities.

For example, the direct-mail marketing program at I & O grows at a rapid rate. The mini-company head builds his mini-company to greater and greater size because he controls the fully integrated body and mind of direct mail. He masters complete mind/body control over his responsibilities and has no limit as to how far he can build his mini-company. He can build most efficiently, however, by recognizing what and when to replicate. For instance, two new direct-mail projects have recently proven successful: direct-mail marketing Neo-Tech to women and direct-mail marketing low-cost Neo-Tech products. Whereas the direct-mail marketing mini-company head could handle those programs, greater efficiency comes to I & O and to the mini-company head by replicating those two programs to two others along with the entire tail of responsibilities. Now, three dynamically growing direct-mail mini-companies exist in I & O. Those three mini-companies each focus, drive, and build their programs more efficiently than if one handled all three programs. And they each build their programs without limitations.

At a certain point of growth, the mini-companies will gain

efficiency by replicating their physical follow-through work. Remember, a mini-company, an area of purpose, consists of responsibilities that fall into two different categories:

For example, turn to page 109, Diagram Ten: Television Marketing. The first five responsibilities fall into the first category of *essence responsibilities*. They drive the purpose into existence and drive it forward: 1) buy television spots, 2) set up TV commercials, 3) record and digest the data and statistics in order to know the profitable television spots to buy and the profitable TV commercials to run, 4) keep and know the books in order to integrate the financial status of the program at all times, and 5) do the accounting in order to stay on the most cost-effective course. Because those responsibilities drive the purpose forward, their actions down to the last nitty-gritty detail must be done by the one person in charge of the area of purpose. Hands-on knowledge is needed to drive the purpose forward.

Now look at the second five responsibilities. They fall into the second category of *follow-through responsibilities*. They occur as a result of the area of purpose: 1) control order processing, 2) control shipping of products, 3) control product manufacturing, 4) control customer service, 5) control computer needs. Those responsibilities such as order processing are a *result* of the business generated by the first five, essence responsibilities. This second group does not drive the purpose forward. Whereas iron-grip control over the follow-through responsibilities is needed to build the essence, the actions themselves are physical follow-through work. Therefore, the physical work itself can be done by others, integrated and coordinated by the mini-company head.

Integrated control over that work, keeping a finger on the nitty-gritty detail, is vital to the success of the area of purpose — the mini-company. So the mini-company head must never delegate that work. He must replicate.

But what about his physical follow-through workers *within* his mini-company? How will they integrate with essence? Look again at Diagram Eight, pages 106-107. Notice that to fill in the blank, Mr. Hamilton wrote that the physical follow-through basic responsibilities exist due to "...each of the marketing programs". Those basic responsibilities do not start off as company-wide departments as in traditional companies. Those responsibilities

156

(attached to their specific mini-companies) start off as an integrated, one-man *entrepreneurial unit*. Often the one-man entrepreneurial unit grows to handle business for several mini-companies, and he may even hire people to work for him. But the entrepreneurial units never become departments. They remain entrepreneurial businesses on performance pay.

Consider customer-service for the direct-mail marketing mini-company: One person handles all the direct-mail customer service. He even receives performance pay based on orders he saves, orders he upgrades, inquiries he converts. He is an entrepreneurial unit with no split responsibilities. And he has financial essence — to generate more conversions of inquiries and near-buyers, for example. Therefore, he engages in creative projects to call, send letters to, and test different approaches in order to convert the near-buyers and inquiries. For every buyer, there are ten near-buyers. Imagine the potential of this entrepreneurial unit.

When he masters the nitty-gritty details and the crucial details of his job, he begins to enter into essence projects. He will need essence meetings from time to time with the direct-mail marketing mini-company head to present the customer service essence progress. During those meetings, the mini-company head with his broad knowledge, helps guide the customer-service entrepreneur into the most effective essence actions. And the customer-service man feeds back to the mini-company head findings and results, which is valuable for broadening the mini-company head's own marketing integrations. At I & O, for example, the customer-service areas have become valuable, quick, inexpensive testing grounds for new marketing ideas and approaches. That essence information is acquired rapidly at low costs. The essence meetings are crucial to the mini-company heads.

Replicating Allows Everyone To Drive On Essence

With responsibilities properly replicated, the founder of the company, the mini-company heads, and even the entrepreneurial follow-through workers can now drive forward the essence responsibilities of the business. Replicating forces the original entrepreneur and mini-company heads (and follow-through workers) to know all body and mind details. Delegating prevents the original entrepreneur and everyone else from knowing the full

157

body and mind details. The original entrepreneur loses his integrations with the body, and his employees never gain the integrations with the mind. Failure to fully integrate the body and mind details denies everyone control and denies the work force the mental picture. Thus, no one really drives forward essence, always anchored to problems and inefficiencies.

Through replicating, the original entrepreneur and the mini-company heads discover iron-grip control — both within themselves and within the follow-through workers. Everyone drives forward essence, not anchored to problems and inefficiencies. The original entrepreneur, the mini-company heads, even the follow-through workers open up more and more chunks of time and power to get creative and drive the business forward. ...Review Diagram Twelve on the next page for a summary of replicating.[1]

---

[1]In a growing business, the follow-through workers become extremely knowledgeable about their work, often knowing the details better than anyone else. These highly efficient people often become so organized that they can render their services to more than one mini-company. An important aspect of replicating is that it can work in reverse (whereas delegating cannot). These experts at follow-through work can replicate their knowledge to mini-company heads who need further integration with the details. For example, a new mini-company head at I & O goes through reverse replication. He spends several days of working meetings with the follow-through workers to acquire iron-grip control over those nitty-gritty follow-through details.

Moreover, the CEO himself must know the nitty-gritty details of his company. The original founder usually knows those details, but if the CEO is not the original founder, then he needs to go through a thorough reverse replication. He must get in, roll up his sleeves, and *do the work*. Those areas of I & O built before Mark Hamilton arrived prompted him into four weeks of nitty-gritty detail work in I & O. He called those four weeks: "Operation Gem-Pride". Those four weeks gave Mr. Hamilton full control of I & O and freedom to grow into the future.

Diagram Twelve
How To Build An Empire Comparison Chart

Three Demands Of Business	Traditional Delegating	Neo-Tech Meetings
1) Knowing all nitty-gritty details	You move away from nitty-gritty detail. Neither you nor your successor ever fully learn detail as detail is turned over and not fully integrated.	Stage One: You dive into nitty-gritty detail via detailed working meetings. Forces you and your successor to learn all detail in a fully integrated context.
Results	Expansion is limited as you do not know all the details. Moreover, your successor is limited as he did not acquire a deep integration — PROGRESS STOPS HERE	Expansion is unlimited as you know all the details. Moreover, your successor is unlimited as he did acquire a deep integration — PROGRESS STARTS HERE
2) Monitor crucial detail	You never fully recognize crucial detail as area is turned over.	Stage Two: You are driven to crucial detail as details are center of working meetings. Successor takes away details he can integrate, pushing you into those you must integrate.
Results	You lose touch with foundation of business. Head for stagnation.	You gain touch with foundation of business. Head for total control.
3) Advance the essence	You cannot discover the essence. Once you delegate, your ability to integrate and move the business forward ends.	Stage Three: Fully integrated with the body of your business through the crucial details, you and eventually your successor efficiently evolve into the mind of your business. With the bulk of detail properly replicated, your ability to integrate and move the business forward begins.
Results	Out of control; problems mounting. Areas of business falling apart; no forward movement.	In total control. All areas of business coming together. Rapid forward movement.

159

The Neo-Tech System

SUMMARY

Delegating

Delegating comes from mysticism (see front material) and causes disintegration of your start-up business. Consider that the mysticism-plagued mind, as described in the front material, rejects integrated thinking. Carrying integrations or making integrations (i.e., self-guidance) is pushed away as something alien and unwanted. Automatic, external guidance is sought instead. The entire power-reactor dimension of integrated thinking never occurs. To avoid carrying and making integrations, delegating provides an easy out.

Moreover, the white-collar hoax certainly does not want to put forth the hard thinking that Harvey Firestone identified as the key to success. White-collar-hoax executives do not want to do integrated thinking. If such executives did, they would not be part of the hoax. To avoid carrying integrations or making integrations, they push the details away — they delegate. As a result, they bypass the mind/body integrated thinking that makes business work. They take the easy shortcut to nonintegrated, well-paying specialized niches of power and prestige.

Replicating

When your start-up company is ready to expand, when the time arrives to establish your first mini-company, how do you develop an integrated person working for you who can drive forward profits? You must transfer an entire area of purpose, an entire physical movement with its complete mind/body integrations...versus delegating single, specialized responsibilities. By transferring the mentally integrating responsibilities — the fully integrated mind/body tail of responsibilities — you create an employee who is NOT specialized, but integrated. He is fully integrated with driving forward the business. You create a wealth pump, a mini-company that drives business forward on the mini-day/power-thinking team.

Delegating splits the mind and body responsibilities. It *decreases* integrations for both the employer and employee. Delegating is a way to avoid integrated thinking and, in the case of the white-collar-hoax executive, a way to skip past the details of the business on the way to a well-paying specialized niche. Replicating, on the other hand, integrates the mind and body responsibilities. It actually *increases* integrations for both the employer and employee. Replicating is a Neo-Tech tool for your new employee to integrate the details of the business on the way to a profit-generating mini-company.

Your start-up company depends heavily on the financial success of the first mini-company. As your business grows, however, eventually you will lose your financial dependence on the success of each new mini-company. When that occurs, you *no longer* need to replicate. For, your greatest leverage at this point is to propel the existing business — explained in Chapter Eighteen. Thus, at this point the new mini-company heads must dig on their own to make their mini-companies a success just as any starting entrepreneur. You spend your time catapulting the existing mini-companies, not replicating new ones. Those who start their mini-companies at this stage slowly develop superior integrated thinking as they must integrate everything on their own. To survive, they must gradually build their mini-companies on their own integrated efforts.

But the first mini-company, perhaps the first few mini-companies, *you* must replicate. The financial risk is too high not to. If the mini-company fails, the overall company fails. Moreover, you have, on your own, already built the business to a certain point and cannot afford for someone to start over at the beginning. You need to replicate your experience, knowledge, integrations, control. You need to replicate yourself.

After your first couple of mini-companies, chances are you will no longer replicate. However, the mini-company heads will always have a need for replicating physical follow-through responsibilities or replicating new mini-companies (to become movement heads, explained in Chapter Twenty-Five.)

Iron-Grip Control

To keep iron-grip control, one must never delegate the work. Delegation leads to nonintegrated, weak control of the details for both the employer and employee. First, one must *replicate* the work. Second, one must develop special tracking reports that manage the replicated work and enable one to keep fingertip control of his business in just a few minutes a day. Step Seven, next chapter, teaches the tracking reports.

Chapter Seventeen
STEP SEVEN: TRACKING REPORTS

As your business grows through replicating mini-companies and more people work for you, you must multiply your control. You must multiply your control to handle the growing complexities that come with expanding business. Yet, man's mysticism-plagued mind seeks guidance, loses control during expansion, and breaks down.

The bicameral mind 3000 years ago (see front material), the nature-controlled automatic mind, broke down as man could not handle the growing complexities that came with expanding civilizations, trade, and commerce. To survive, man had to evolve from a nature-controlled mind into a much more powerful self-controlled mind: the conscious mind.

The conscious mind today, the mysticism-plagued mind, breaks down as man cannot handle the growing complexities that come with the DIVISION OF ESSENCE. To make the leap, man must evolve from a mysticism-plagued mind into a much more powerful mysticism-free mind: the Neothink mind.

The specialized business structure disengages man's integrated thinking; specialization prevents man's leap into his human potential. Most jobs today receive bicameral-like, automatic guidance from specialized, set responsibilities. Very few people ever discover how to integrate thus generate *new* money. For example, essentially no one among the working masses generates new money-making projects at work. Do you? But through the Neo-Tech System, people quickly learn how to integrate.

Man leapt into consciousness 3000 years ago to acquire its competitive edge. Man today will leap into mysticism-free Neothink to acquire its competitive edge.

In this chapter, you will take your second major step into Neothink. You will go beyond the capacity of your mysticism-plagued conscious mind by using special Neothink tools. You will snap together a puzzle to build a Neothink perspective well beyond your limited competitors. Now you will snap together the division of essence into one solid puzzle that radiates a picture seen only by those with these special Neothink tools.

Everything Comes Together Into A Mighty Neothink Puzzle

You have everything you need to discard delegating, departments, white-collar-hoax positions, specialization, mysticism. You have everything you need to integrate the physical movements and to replicate the wealth pumps.

You are ready to expand. But wait! Your mysticism-plagued conscious mind breaks down when confronted with expansion and wealth escalation. The mysticism-plagued conscious mind integrates only a few single thoughts (then waits for guidance). Major wealth creation requires far greater integrating and processing capacity than a few single thoughts. Instead, you must lock together a Neothink puzzle that you can pick up and wave around the world without wealth creation ever falling apart again.

Neothink goes well beyond thought by thought, single integrations...well beyond deep-rooted bicameral tendencies. Neothink instead captures clusters of thoughts or vast integrations. Through Neothink, one moves through clusters of integrations as rapidly as the mysticism-plagued conscious mind moves through single integrations. Remember the mini-day/power-thinking team versus the traditional daily schedule?

To build your start-up business into an empire, you must capture Neothink control. You must capture larger-than-life processing capacity...well beyond the processing capacity of man's unaided mind. You must use special tools to capture vast integrations at your fingertips. Your first step into Neothink took you beyond the capacity of the mind through special tools — the mini-day/power-thinking team. Your second step will take you beyond the capacity of the mind through special tools — the mini-company/power-tracking team. Going beyond the capacity of the mind brings you enormous advantages.

Harold Geneen, the CEO who built ITT into one of the greatest companies during his reign, built and then managed 250, 50-million-dollar (average) companies. How did he do that? How did he average only a few minutes per week, per 50-million-dollar company? He leapt into Neothink control. Geneen used tools, special tools to go beyond the processing capacity of the human mind. With those special tools, Geneen controlled vast integrations. He controlled 250, 50-million-dollar companies! He captured vast integrations at his fingertips.

Step Seven: Tracking Reports

Now, it's your turn: To move into Neothink, you too need tools that bring together vast integrations at your fingertips. Then, like Geneen, you can take command of larger-than-life wealth creation.

First of all, what are those vast integrations that you will snap together for control in one swoop?

Look at Diagram Thirteen over the next two pages: There are those vast integrations — the mini-companies — the physical movements of the company. They are the vast integrations the CEO or original founder will snap together into his iron-grip control. Contrast on Diagram Thirteen the fully integrated physical movements (mini-companies) to the specialized split responsibilities of traditional jobs throughout traditional companies. The traditional, specialized approach results in splitting hundreds of responsibilities throughout company-wide departments. The CEO has absolutely no integrated control. But one Neo-Tech individual can have total integrated control of *all* the responsibilities through special tools that snap together vast integrations — snap together the physical movements or mini-companies — into a single Neothink puzzle. ...The division-of-essence business now snaps together into a single juggernaut.

The Tracking Reports

As you build your company with mini-companies, you will snap those essence-driven mini-companies into a mighty Neothink puzzle. To do this, you must develop powerful Neothink tools. Those tools are unique, integrated **TRACKING REPORTS** that snap together your growing company into one, solid Neothink unit.

You must design those special Neothink tools called *tracking reports* like a piece of art — to the last detail. Upon replicating your first mini-company, you must design the Neothink tracking reports so they force the details of the replicated mini-company to be done, done right, and done on time. Consider what Henry Ford said when he developed the asembly line: He said that the people should not manage the work; the work should manage the people. Similarly, when it comes to your control over your company, you do not rely on your people to manage the work; the tracking reports manage the people. And that is to their

165
(continued on page 168)

Diagram Thirteen

Traditional Company
(Split Responsibilities)

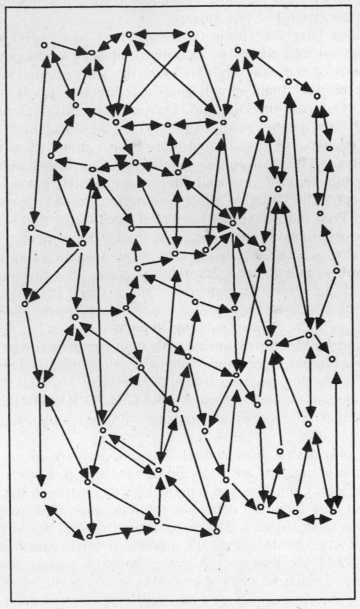

Dots = Responsibilities of Company

Diagram Thirteen
(*continued*)
I & O Neo-Tech System
(Fully Integrated Areas)

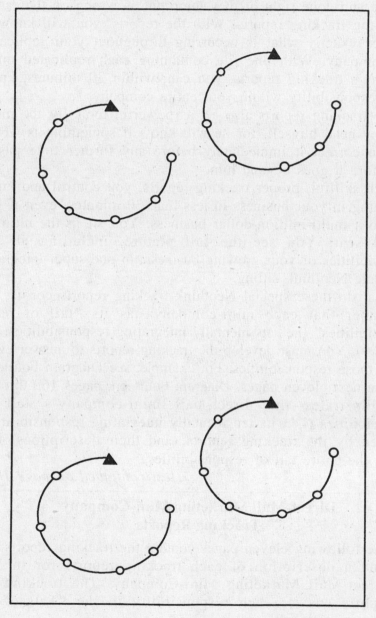

Dots = Responsibilities of Company

167

advantage as the tracking reports force the most efficient actions, as will become clear later.

The mini-company head fills out his tracking reports. To fill out the reports, the mentally integrating responsibilities must all be done and done right or they jump out as wrong on the catch-everything tracking reports. With the reports, you will know at a glance exactly what is occurring throughout your replicated mini-company. With one file containing each replicated mini-company's tracking reports, you can, within 30 minutes, know every responsibility within your entire company.

The tracking reports also act as powerful tools for the mini-company head himself, for he will know if something is wrong and can correct it immediately before any further time passes and before it goes beyond him.

With skillful, proper tracking reports, you control and know everything in your business in less than 30 minutes, even if you grow to a multi-million-dollar business. You sit in the ultimate catbird seat: You see the full picture, including all the responsibilities of your growing business, in one super-integrated 30-minute Neothink sitting.

What do these special Neothink tracking reports consist of? Remember that each mini-company has its "tail of basic responsibilities" (i.e., its mentally integrating responsibilities, see page 109). You must develop the tracking reports to answer every one of those responsibilities. For example, see Diagram Fourteen, over the next eleven pages. Diagram Fourteen, pages 169 through 179, illustrates the direct-mail mini-company's tail of responsibilities (i.e., its ten mentally integrating responsibilities) followed by the tracking reports (and their descriptions) that answer the entire tail of responsibilities.

(text continued on page 180)

Direct-Mail Marketing Mini-Company Tracking Reports

The following eleven pages contain the tracking reports (and a description of each tracking report) for the Direct-Mail Marketing Mini-Company. The tracking reports answer each responsibility in the "Tail of Responsibilities".

Diagram Fourteen

Direct-Mail Marketing Mini-Company
Tail of Responsibilities

1	Rent Mailing Lists	(Page 170)
2	Set Up Mailings	(Page 171)
3	Keep Data/Statistics	(Page 172)
4	Keep Books	(Page 173)
5	Do Accounting	(Page 174)
6	Control Order Processing	(Page 175)
7	Control Customer Service	(Page 176)
8	Control Shipping Products	(Page 177)
9	Control Printing Mailers and Product	(Pg.178)
10	Control Computer Needs	(Page 179)

Note: The following ten pages illustrate the tracking reports for the Direct-Mail Mini-Company. The tracking reports directly answer each responsibility in the "Tail of Responsibilities" above. The reader may study, skim, or even skip over the tracking reports if he fully understands the concept that tracking reports directly answer each responsibility in the mini-company's "Tail of Responsibilities".

Tail of Responsibilities #1 — "Rent Mailing Lists" Tracking Report

I&O PUBLISHING COMPANY

(Note: First eight lists are monthly; last two are quarterly. A core list cannot be missed without a big blank square staring at us.)

TR-1 Rent List Report
Date Aug 20
Page 1 of 1

Core Lists Through July

List Name*	Code	Jan.	Feb.	Mar.	April	May	June	July
Proprietary	% orders	1.170	1.922	1.467	1.454	1.779	0.628	0.948
Information	Qty. Mailed	5634	13261	21055	38148	5675	51243	16238
Proprietary	% orders	1.626	1.571	1.616	1.621	1.481	1.514	1.572
Information	Qty. Mailed	13278	17432	8785	25550	23294	5348	19647
Proprietary	% orders	0.794	1.227	0.939	1.383	1.002	0.620	1.312
Information	Qty. Mailed	3400	5865	39075	3685	3590	6930	10818
Proprietary	% orders	1.543	1.587	1.107	1.056	1.532	0.860	0.792
Information	Qty. Mailed	6998	8314	3160	7289	6133	11391	3787
Proprietary	% orders	0.535	1.164	1.161	0.443	0.567	1.444	1.272
Information	Qty. Mailed	1308	3606	9214	11736	3524	3531	8971
Proprietary	% orders	1.346	2.195	2.991	3.558	2.367	2.220	2.123
Information	Qty. Mailed	13441	1776	1638	2473	7053	1171	2590
Proprietary	% orders	2.415	1.817	2.214	1.945	2.409	1.290	2.177
Information	Qty. Mailed	6997	8144	6502	3136	3071	3333	3674
Proprietary	% orders	0.433	1.099	1.510	1.188	1.614	1.179	1.214
Information	Qty. Mailed	12453	6096	1721	3533	3468	3722	2893
Proprietary	% orders	X	X	1.567	X	X	1.226	X
Information	Qty. Mailed	X	X	3253	X	X	14436	X
Proprietary	% orders	X	X	1.660	X	X	1.365	X
Information	Qty. Mailed	X	X	23915	X	X	15158	X

*I&O Publishing Company cannot reveal its core lists.

170

Tail of Responsibilities #2 — "Set Up Mailings" Tracking Report

I&O PUBLISHING COMPANY
(Note: All details are captured and organized over two weeks before mailing.)

	TR-2
	Set-Up Report
	Date May 9
	Page 1 of 1

Information for Mailing 245

Product _Neo-Tech_ Mail Date _5/27_ Postage Class _1st_ Mailing Point _Paramount_

Code	List P.O.#	List Name	Description	Input Qty.	Projected Qty.	Splits/Inserts	Notes
3990 ↓ 3993	8946X	Boardroom Book Buyers	April Names	16.7M	11M males / 3M female	< In-line Envelope / Jet-Press Envelope < ZE Brochure / ZW Brochure	
4001	89EP4	Nightingale-Conant (C)	1st Quarter	5M	5M	Control	Canadian
3994 ↓ 3995	89EC2	Real Estate Financial Opportunity	April Names	5M	3.5M	< ZE Brochure / ZF Brochure	
3997	89D212	Elite Self-Improvement	April Names	2M	1M	Control	
3996	89DX2	Publisher's Choice	April Names	1.2M	1M	Control	
4002	89E02	J.E.N. Jewels (C)	April Names	3M	1M	Control	Canadian
3998	89EQ3	Pase Publications	April Names	1.2M	1M	Control	
3999 ↓ 4000		Mailing 239 Multi Buyers	Multi Buyers	9.5M	9.4M	Control	Canadian

I&O PUBLISHING COMPANY

(Note: The mailing set up on previous tracking report #2 is complete with results in tracking report #3, below.)

	TR-3
	Data/Stats Report
Date	July 11
Page	1 of 1

Results for Mailing 245

			Date Mailed	May 27	Orders Update:	July 11	
Code #	List	Description	Mailed	Orders	%	Inserts	Split Code
3990	Boardroom Book Buyers	April Names	5276	70	1.33	Control w/In-Line Envelope	Test 1 Side 1
3991	Boardroom Book Buyers	April Names	5275	70	1.33	Control w/Jet Press-Envelope	Test 1 Side 2
3992	Boardroom Book Buyers	April Names	1609	20	1.24	Control w/ZE Brochure	Test 2 Side 1
3993	Boardroom Book Buyers	April Names	1609	17	1.06	Control w/ZW Brochure	Test 2 Side 2
4001	Nightingale-Conant (C)	1st Quarter Names	4639	159	3.43	Control	
3994	Real Estate Financial Opp.	April Names	1671	27	1.62	Control w/ZE Brochure	Test 3 Side 1
3995	Real Estate Financial Opp.	April Names	1670	12	0.72	Control w/ZF Brochure	Test 3 Side 2
3997	Elite Self Improvement	April Names	1131	5	0.44	Control	
3996	Publisher's Choice	April Names	1072	6	0.56	Control	
4002	JEN Jewels (C)	April Names	1000	7	0.70	Control	
3998	Pase Publication	April Names	651	7	1.08	Control	
3999	Mailing 239	Multi Buyers	4717	47	1.00	Control	
4000	Mailing 239	Multi Buyers	4717	57	1.21	Control	
U245	Unidentified Orders		0	8			
Totals			**35,037**	**512**	**1.461**		

Split-Run Tests for Mailing 245

Split Test: 1: In Line Env. versus Jet-Press Env.

Code	3990	3991
Split #1	In-Line	Jet-Press
Orders	70	70
Percent	1.33	1.33

Split Test: 2: ZE Brochure vs ZW Brochure

Code	3992	3993
Split #2	ZE	ZW
Orders	20	17
Percent	54.1	43.9

Split Test: 3: ZE Brochure vs ZF Brochure

Code	3994	3995
Split #3	ZE	ZF
Orders	27	12
Percent	1.62	0.72

I&O PUBLISHING COMPANY

	TR-4
	Cash Tracking Report
Date	July 10
Page	1 of 1

(Note: This tracking report is printed on demand covering any span of time requested: one day, one month, one quarter, one year. For illustrative ease of reviewing, only one day is printed below, although this is turned in weekly.
(note continued at bottom)

Opening Balance $61,119.47

Cash In (Deposits)

Orders: Check $ Received	Orders: Credit Card $ Received	Reversed Refunds	Royalty Receipts	Reimbursement Money	Transfer In (From Other Accts.)	Miscellaneous Income
3517.95 (52 total)	2618.15 (37 total)	0	799.60	432.00	5000.00	0
3517.95	2618.15	0	799.60	432.00	5000.00	0

Total In (above) $12,367.70

Total Out (below) $14,839.28

Cash Out (Checks/Wires)

Operating Expenses	Wages	Marketing Postage	Marketing Expenses	Marketing Purchases	Advertisements Paid	Royalties Paid	Taxes Paid	Refunds Paid	Transfer Out (To Other Accts.)
1,312.71	0	8700	2208.15	0	1481.42	934.50	0	202.50	0
1,312.71	0	8700	2208.15		1481.42	934.50	0	202.50	0

Ending Balance $58,647.89

(note continued from above)
This report is generated automatically from the computer, tied into all the other workings of the bookkeeper. For example, the "cash out" portion gets its data straight from the bookkeeper's check register. Much of the "cash in" portion gets its data from the bookkeeper's computerized deposit slips. Those deposit slips must match the "order processing" tracking report #6 so that nothing can go wrong, no mistakes can occur, and no embezzlement can occur. This tracking report shows where every penny comes from and where every penny goes to. Thus, with that overview, every penny can be tracked and verified. No mistakes can occur. Everything can be reconciled.)

I&O PUBLISHING COMPANY	**TR-5**
[Note: Below are two completely independent accounting reports. Yet, the profit/loss of mailings (bottom left) must equal delta (i.e., the change) of cash position (bottom right). Triple control: 1) self-proofing 2) accurate profit/loss 3) location of every dollar.]	**Accounting Report**

Date	June 16
Page	1 of 1

May Mailings Profit/Loss

Net Revenue

Mailing 242

Total Direct Costs _____	$65,229.89
(131,935 pieces @49.4¢)	
Revenue _____	$75,598.60
(1,540 orders @$49.09)	
Net _____	**$10,368.71**

Mailing 243

Total Direct Costs _____	$33,805.75
(68,530 pieces @49.3¢)	
Revenue _____	$30,288.53
(617 orders @$49.09)	
Net _____	**<$3,517.22>**

Mailing 244

Total Direct Costs _____	$44,249.58
(89,552 pieces @49.4¢)	
Revenue _____	$47,273.67
(963 orders @$49.09)	
Net _____	**$3,024.09**

Mailing 245

Total Direct Costs _____	$17,369.51
(35,037 pieces @49.5¢)	
Revenue _____	$25,134.08
(512 orders @$49.09)	
Net _____	**$7,764.57**

Expenses

Less General Overhead	$18,174
Less General Freelance	$22,628

Profit/Loss $ ___< 23,161 >___

May Cash Location & Delta

Beginning Cash Position	**$323,280**

ASSETS
Inventory

Brochures	$38,552	
Coupons	$22,848	
Envelopes	$25,081	
Products	$73,703	
Total		$160,185

Cash On Hand - Accounts

Bank of America	$(11,718)	
Valley Bank	$(10,623)	
Total		($22,341)

Cash Expected In - Receivables

MC/Visa	$32,255	
Club Cards	$12,995	
Total		$45,250

Cash Invested - Future Mailings

Mailing 246	$77,270	
Mailing 247	$70,010	
Total		$147,280
Total Assets		**$322,439**

LIABILITIES
Accounts Payables

Unshipped Orders	($1,605)	
Invoices	($15,360)	
Refunds	($13,290)	
Total Liabilities		**($30,255)**

Ending Cash Position	**$300,119**

CHANGE IN CASH POSITION
(Ending minus Beginning)

Ending	$300,119
(less) Beginning	$323,280

Delta $ ___< 23,161 >___

I&O PUBLISHING COMPANY
(Note: Nothing can go wrong without jumping out on this **tracking** report. Banking-like tracking of orders.)

TR-6	
Order Processing	
Date	July 10
Page	1 of 1

Order Processing Tracking

Raw Count	136

Station One: Open/Sort Mail

Raw Count Done by (Initials):
SR & RW

Checks/Money Orders	52	Nevada Orders	1
Cash	0	Collections	1
MasterCard/Visa	32	Total Orders	96
American Express/Diner's Club	8	Non-Orders*	38
Canadian Money Off	4	**Total Sort**	136

Station Two: Verifone Credit Cards

*Note: Non-Orders go to Customer Service and into Tracking Report #7.

MasterCard/VISA	32	American Express/Diner's Club	7
Declines	1	Declines	0
Invalids	1	Invalids	0
Net MasterCard/VISA Orders	30	Net AmEx/Diner's Orders	7
		Total Credit Cards	37

Station Three: Check/Cash Deposit

Station Four: Data Entry

Checks	50	Total Orders Brought to #61	93
Money Orders	2	Total Orders On Summary Below	93
Cash	0		
Total Check/Cash	52		

Total Orders On Summary (below) must equal Total Orders brought to #61 (above)

Order Summary Sheet

Product	Cash	MO/Checks	VISA	MC	AmEx	Diners	Canadian	Totals
Neo-Tech		33	10	8	4		4	59
Discovery		$2458.85	$699.50	$559.60	$279.80		$279.80	$4277.55
Neo-Tech		14	3	3	1			21
System		$559.30	$119.85	$119.85	$39.95			$838.95
Neo-Tech		5	2	4	1	1		13
Tapes		$499.80	$199.90	$399.90	$99.95	$99.95		$1299.40
		52	15	15	6	1	4	93
Totals		$3517.95	$1019.25	$1079.25	$419.70	$99.95	$279.80	$6415.90

I&O PUBLISHING COMPANY

(Note: These 38 customer service pieces were received from mail raw count, see Tracking Report #6. Every piece, every action is accounted for below. Nothing can be missed.)

TR-7	Customer Service
Date	July 10
Page	1 of 1

Customer Service Tracking Report

Raw Count	38
Plus _1_ Invalid _1_ Decline	2
Total	40

Station One: Sort Customer Service Mail

Potential Cash Gain		Potential Cash Loss	
More Information Requests	16	Non-Delivery Inquires	7
Forgot To Enclose Payment	3	Help/?'s On Product	7
Invalid/Decline Credit Card	2	Refund Requests	5

Station Two A: Customer Service Profits

Potential Profits	rec'vd	# of	First Attempt 7/10	Second Attempt 7/25	Third Attempt 8/10	Total
More Information Requests	7/10	16	Attempt: 16 / Convert: 4	Attempt: 12 / Convert: 2	Attempt: 10 / Convert: 0	Attempt: 16 / Convert: 6 (37%)
Forgot to Enlose Payment	7/10	3	Attempt: 3 / Convert: 0	Attempt: 3 / Convert: 1	Attempt: 2 / Convert: 0	Attempt: 3 / Convert: 1 (33%)
Invalid/Deline Credit Cards	7/10	2	Attempt: 2 / Convert: 1	Attempt: 1 / Convert: 0	Attempt: 1 / Convert: 0	Attempt: 3 / Convert: 1 (33%)

Station Two B: Customer Service Preservation

Potential Losses	Date rec'd	# of	Processed for Mail	Spot Checked by Steve R.	Delivered to Post Office
Non-Delivery Inquiries	7/10	7	Done by: RW / Date: 7/10	Ok'd by: SR / Date: 7/10	Delivered by: KP / Date: 7/10
Help/?'s on Product	7/10	7	Done by: RW / Date: 7/10	Ok'd by: SR / Date: 7/10	Delivered by: KP / Date: 7/10
Refund Requests	7/10	5	Done by: RW / Date: 7/10	Ok'd by: SR / Date: 7/10	Delivered by: KP / Date: 7/10

Total Pieces Handled and Mailed Today 7/10 : __38__

+ __2__ Invalid/Decline

__40__ Total

I&O PUBLISHING COMPANY	**TR-8**
(Note: Nothing can be missed with this iron-grip control. All orders to shipping accounted for.)	**Shipping Log**
	Date | Aug
	Page | 1 of 1

Shipping Summary Sheet

Order Dates	Ship Number	Ship Date	Product Quantity	No. of Int'l	Manuscript Numbers	Letter Sent	Book Ship Date	Decoy Rec'vd
5/12-5/18	S-126	Jun 13 May 22 May 22 May 22 May 22	A=1382 B=3 E=9 GT/E=5 G=1 A=-4	20	410SM-291SP 4 Labels pulled – bad payments	May 23	Jun 17 May 23 May 26 May 26	Jun 21
5/19-5/25	S-127	Jun 9 May 30 May 30	A=743 B=10 E=5 A=-1	19	292SP-34SR 1 Label Pulled – bad payment	May 30	Jun 14 Jun 2 Jun 4	Jun 29 Jun 6 Jun 14
5/26-6/1	S-128	Jun 15 Jun 5 Jun 5 Jun 5	A=573 B=3 E=1 GT/E=6	105	35SR-107SS	Jun 6	Jun 21 Jun 7 Jun 9 Jun 9	July 10
6/2-6/8	S-129	Jun 23 Jun 12 Jun 12 Jun 12	A=633 B=4 E=8 GT/E=6 A=-1	242	108SS-240ST (241ST used by RW) 1 Label pulled	Jun 12	Jun 29 Jun 14 Jun 16 Jun 16	July 17 Jun 16 Jun 23
6/9-6/15	S-130	Jun 30 Jun 19 Jun 19 Jun 19 Jun 19 Jun 19	A=304 B=2 E=1 F=1 G=1 GT/E=1	203	242ST-45SU (46SU used by RW)	Jun 19	Jul 6 Jun 21 Jun 23 Jun 21 Jun 23 Jun 23	July 24
6/16-6/22	S-131	Jul 7 Jun 23 A=-3	A=789 G=1 A=-3	108	47SU-335SV 3 Labels pulled	Jun 26	Jul 13 Jun 26	Jul 24
6/25-6/29	S-132	Jul 17 Jul 3 Jul 3 Jun 30 Jul 3	A=696 B=14 E=13 F=1 GT/E=5	71	336SV-31SX	Jul 3	Jul 20 Jul 5 Jul 7 Jul 5 Jul 7	Jul 31 Jul 6 Jul 11
6/20-7/6	S-133	Jul 21 Jul 10 Jul 21 Jul 10 Jul 10	A=953 B=399 D=1 E=306 GT/E=3	74	32SX-484SY	Jul 10	Jul 27 Jul 14 Jul 27 Jul 14 Jul 14	Aug 7 Jul 20 Jul 31
7/7	S-134	Jul 21 Jul 10 Jul 10	A=10 B=122 E=124	0	485SY-494SY	Jul 10	Jul 27 Jul 14 Jul 14	

*Product Codes: A=Neo-Tech Discovery   B=Neo-Tech System   E=Neo-Tech Tapes

I&O PUBLISHING COMPANY

(Note: Every product, quantity, and location is "in your face" with this tracking report. This report continues beyond this page to also track the mailers – brochures, envelopes, coupons, etc.)

	TR-9			
	Inventory Report			
	Date	July 15		
	Page	1 of 1		

Inventory

Code	Product	Quantity	Site		Company	As of	By
A1	Neo-Tech I, III, IV, V	1903	006	Doris	002	Sep 15	MF
A1	Neo-Tech I, III, IV, V	152	002	LV - 59	002	Jun 27	MF
A1	Neo-Tech I, III, IV, V	2420	009	Banta Company	002	Jul 10	MF
A1	Neo-Tech I, III, IV, V	1139	007	Melinda	003	Aug 2	MF
A2	Neo-Tech Discovery II	2187	006	Doris	002	Sep 15	MF
A2	Neo-Tech Discovery II	1124	007	Melinda	003	Aug 2	MF
A2	Neo-Tech Discovery II	4377	005	Braceland	002	Sep 15	MF
B	Neo-Tech System	1576	005	Braceland	002	Aug 3	MF
B	Neo-Tech System	442	007	Melinda	002	Aug 18	MF
BE	NTS Envelopes	6983	005	Braceland	002	Aug 2	MF
BJPL	Job Power List	1423	005	Braceland	002	Aug 18	MF
D	Neo-Tech Encyclopedia	217	006	Doris	002	Sep 15	MF
E	Neo-Tech Tapes	2192	008	Magnetix	002	Jul 27	MF
EA	Neo-Tech Album	6864	008	Magnetix	002	Aug 18	MF
EMBC	Neo-Tech/Summit Book Carton	4862	008	Magnetix	002	Aug 18	MF
EW	Neo-Tech Workbook	2864	008	Magnetix	002	Aug 18	MF
G101	Consultation Pack Vol. 1/1	50	002	LV - 59	002	July 19	MF
G102	Consultation Pack Vol. 1/2	38	002	LV - 59	002	July 19	MF
G103	Consultation Pack Vol. 1/3	25	002	LV - 59	002	July 19	MF
G104	Consultation Pack Vol. 1/4	50	002	LV - 59	002	July 19	MF
G105	Consultation Pack Vol. 1/5	200	002	LV - 59	002	July 19	MF
G106	Consultation Pack Vol. 1/6	150	002	LV - 59	002	July 19	MF
G107	Consultation Pack Vol. 1/7	175	002	LV - 59	002	July 19	MF
G108	Consultation Pack Vol. 1/8	50	002	LV - 59	002	July 19	MF
G109	Consultation Pack Vol. 1/9	200	002	LV - 59	002	July 19	MF
G110	Consultation Pack Vol. 1/10	30	002	LV - 59	002	July 19	MF
G111	Consultation Pack Vol. 1/11	75	002	LV - 59	002	July 19	MF
G112	Consultation Pack Vol. 1/12	50	002	LV - 59	002	July 19	MF
G201	Consultation Pack Vol. 2/1	200	002	LV - 59	002	July 19	MF
G202	Consultation Pack Vol. 2/2	150	002	LV - 59	002	July 19	MF
G203	Consultation Pack Vol. 2/3	150	002	LV - 59	002	July 19	MF
GA	Consultation Tapes Album	1100	008	Magnetix	002	July 19	MF
K	Philosophical Zero	420	002	LV - 59	002	July 19	MF
M1	Summit One Tapes	357	008	Magnetix	003	Jun 15	MF
M1A	Summit One Album	357	008	Magnetix	002	Jun 15	MF
M1W	Summit One Workbook	357	008	Magnetix	002	Jun 15	MF
QA	Ultimate Battle Album	1452	008	Magnetix	002	Jun 15	MF
T	Bible A	15	007	Melinda	002	Jun 15	MF
U	Bible B	22	007	Melinda	002	Jun 15	MF

I&O PUBLISHING COMPANY (Note: The computer needs are "in your face" with description and status. The completion date adds healthy pressure and discipline to programmer for best efficiency and control over area.)		**TR-10** **Computer Needs**	
		Date	June 15
		Page	1 of 1

Computer Projects

Project	Status	Completion Date
Computerize the Accounting Tracking Report #5	I tied "mailing accounting" portion into Data Tracking Report #3 to automatically bring up direct costs and revenue. Now tying into checkbook to automatically bring up General Overhead and General Freelance. Nearly complete. This will allow entire left side, "mailing accounting" portion, to come up automatically with one command. Next I will do the same for the right side, "cash location accounting". That needs to be tied into a combination of our inventory program (Tracking Report #9) and our check register program in order to pull up the right side of Tracking Report #5, the "cash location" portion, with a single command.	July 1 (On Schedule)
Data Tracking Report #3 Advancements		
1) Compile data from same split tests among different mailings	I will tie all Data Tracking Reports from all mailings together to recognize, match up and compile data from the same tests among different mailings to give ongoing, cumulative data on major tests. Going smoothly.	July 7 (On schedule)
2) Add refund data to this tracking report	I will tie into the Customer Service Tracking Report #7 to match all refunds to the original list from which they came. I will add a new column to the Data Tracking Report #3 to show how each list performs, refund wise. Complication on Tracking Report #7, but working through it.	July 7 (1 week behind schedule. Needs more programing than anticipated. TR-7 must be revamped. New projection date is July 15.)
Demographic Project	I will break down all names mailed for six months by SCF zip locations. I will then compare that to our own mailing list. That should reveal our more favorable markets throughout the country. Simple — I let program run at night when office is down.	July 1 (On schedule)
Data Entry	Set up double entries of street address and zip code. Automatic merge upon second entry. If does not match, then reject into a purge file to be redone. This will eliminate keypunching errors. Looks easy.	July 15 (On schedule)
Merge/Purge	I will improve accuracy of our merge/purges. Not finished flow-chart thinking. Will explain and give completion date on next week's report.	

179

Notice the direct-mail mini-company's simple-to-read tracking reports answer all ten of the mentally integrating responsibilities — the full tail of responsibilities. The tracking reports actually direct the mini-company head and his work. Every specific responsibility must be met and answered through those specially designed tracking reports. In only a few minutes, Mr. Hamilton can glance over those reports and know exactly how well the mini-company head performs each responsibility. Those details cannot get away from Mr. Hamilton or the mini-company head.

Harold Geneen had reports filled out by each of the 250 companies that worked under him. In his autobiography, he wrote about staying up all night at times reviewing those reports. Those were his tracking reports. Your tracking reports are your Neothink tools to control your entire company...to control vast integrations in one sweep...to eventually control an empire at your fingertips.

The direct-mail tracking reports can be reviewed in a few minutes while knowing *exactly* the job being done — for *every* responsibility. Moreover, those tracking reports keep the mini-company head on top of his responsibilities — every responsibility and on time.

Now imagine many, many responsibilities eventually in your company. No one brain, no one man could stay in touch with all that. Keeping in touch with many, many responsibilities goes beyond one's processing capacity. However, by pulling those many scattered responsibilities into fully integrated areas of purpose (mini-companies), you CAN easily keep your finger on every responsibility through Neothink tracking reports. That mini-company/power-tracking team turns chaos into order and allows you to operate at a level beyond the processing capacity of the mind.

Moreover, you snap together the mini-companies like pieces to a puzzle as you go through your file of tracking reports each week. Instead of trying to integrate single, split responsibilities, you snap together vast integrations to see the complete picture of your entire business. In thirty minutes or less, you snap those "puzzle pieces" together into a larger-than-life Neothink puzzle, seeing and comprehending your entire business at one sitting. You leap into Neothink control that goes way beyond the capacity

180

of the human mind.

Harvey Firestone said that his business got away from him because he could not stay in touch with all the responsibilities of his company. Through delegating and departmentalizing, his business went into a schizophrenic frenzy of split responsibilities. His business nearly failed. Then he restructured; he got rid of fancy departments and learned how to integrate all those responsibilities that had gotten away from him. He did this through Neothink control.

Without fully integrated areas of purpose, the entrepreneur tries to track each responsibility one by one, responsibility by responsibility. But as Harvey Firestone expressed, that is impossible to do in any growing business.

To succeed, you must evolve your business into a Neothink puzzle and track vast integrations at a glance (i.e., see all pieces in the puzzle). If you do not, your business will soon stagnate, becoming overrun with split responsibilities. Split responsibilities increase the work tenfold or more. They multiply and multiply, splitting apart the mental integrations throughout your business and causing business schizophrenia. Split responsibilities not only cause a lot more work, but you could never track all those split responsibilities. You would lose control and fail. You would have to track ten times more work because it is hopelessly split up. But by structuring your company with fully integrated areas of purpose (i.e., mini-companies), suddenly much less work exists, whatever size the company. Firestone, upon restructuring his company, reduced one area from 35 to 3 people and his white-collar work force from 1000 to 300 people.

By tracking the mini-companies, the once impossibly complicated company becomes simple as you enjoy the larger-than-life leverage of Neothink tools.

What is the magic of Neothink tracking reports? A rapidly growing company, an entire empire can be led and every responsibility tracked by ONE person. By you! Once you see the Neothink puzzle come together each week, you will guide your entire company from the power of the Neothink mind (next chapter).

Designing The Tracking Reports

Every responsibility of the tail of responsibilities should be answered either directly or indirectly. Some of the more menial responsibilities may not show up right away. But over the course of two or three weeks you should be able to detect that something is not right before damage occurs. Thus every responsibility is, for all practical purposes, answered or accounted for.

Determine and study the responsibilities of a mini-company. Then make a tracking report (or several tracking reports) for that specific tail of responsibilities. The Neothink tracking reports keep you integrated with every responsibility in the mini-company. You will know every body-detail in less than 30 minutes per week by reviewing your tracking reports.

Moreover, problems will occur less and less and, before long, almost not at all. For, filling in the tracking reports *in itself* forces problems to be taken care of before the tracking reports reach you. The mini-company head sees any problems while filling in the reports. He sees any problems and promptly corrects them and keeps his mini-company under HIS iron-grip control. He discovers problems early, while they are still minor, because the tracking reports enable HIM to monitor and track every responsibility of his area, just as you do. And that will make your job most efficient, allowing you to concentrate on your essence responsibilities as surface problems are cleared up before reaching you. But if a problem does show up, you know just where to go, just who to see, just what the problem is, in order to fix it.

Study each new mini-company and its responsibilities. Piece together tracking reports that not only track and uncover any problems, but *prevent* any problems. Instead of handling problems one at a time as they come up, develop tracking reports to force problems to be prevented BEFORE they come up. For example, the tracking report for order processing in I & O's direct mail mini-company has bank-like, balance-out auditing controls to *prevent* problems.

Again, study the mini-company's tail of responsibilities and the nitty-gritty details underneath each responsibility. Think out everything that can go wrong. You do this by power-thinking

182

how the mini-company would run if everything were optimum. You may go through some development and editing stages until you find that the tracking reports truly manage the work to prevent future problems.

Using Tracking Reports

As you develop each tracking report with growth — first for one mini-company, then the next, then the next — you piece together a Neothink puzzle. With each mini-company, you create a maximum-integration puzzle part. You snap those puzzle parts together through the tracking reports into one, interlocked picture in your mind. You see that Neothink picture of the business each week. That's right, once a week you open your file of tracking reports and snap together the puzzle parts — the mini-companies. That interlocked puzzle in your mind enables you to see a picture beyond the traditionally managed companies that chase responsibilities one by one. Using Neothink tools, your larger-than-life brain-power makes competitors seem dull and slow. With Neothink tools, you go beyond the capacity of the human mind, gain iron-grip control, and see wealth creation from seemingly omniscient eyes.

The Essence Tracking Reports

While still dependent on one or two young mini-companies for your company's survival, you need to closely follow the tracking reports for both the essence responsibilities (e.g., the first five responsibilities in I & O's direct-mail mini-company's tail of responsibilities, page 169) and the follow-through responsibilities (the second five responsibilities, page 169). By you personally power-tracking all responsibilities, you eliminate the risk of failure. If the mini-company failed, your business would fail. Therefore, you track all the responsibilities to be sure no control slips.

Once you develop trusted and experienced mini-company heads and no longer rely on a young mini-company for your company's financial survival, then you as CEO do not need to review the follow-through-work tracking reports. You need to follow the essence tracking reports only. You can count on the established mini-company heads to handle or manage the follow-through work with iron-grip control. (The mini-company head still uses the follow-through tracking reports for his own detail-guide and, eventually, as tracking reports for his follow-through workers to fill out for him.) You track just the essence tracking reports. If you see a mini-company's performance dip — quickly exposed on the essence tracking reports — you can at any time take a closer look into the nitty-gritty details. You can at any time review the follow-through-work tracking reports to spot any growing problems in the mini-company.

Indeed, once secure with experienced mini-company heads and no longer dependent on the income from any new mini-company, you do not need to see anything but the essence tracking reports — even from *new* mini-companies. For, if a new mini-company failed, your company's financial health would not be in jeopardy.

The mini-company head, of course, must always use the follow-through-work tracking reports, especially as he grows and replicates follow-through entrepreneurial jobs to others. His source of income is his mini-company. He must run his mini-company with ever-increasing efficiency and control. If he fails, then *he* fails. Moreover, he must always maintain the full mind/body integration over his tail of responsibilities.

You will always need essence tracking reports that reflect the financial status and marketing numbers of each mini-company. Again, if performance slips, you can then look more closely at that mini-company and, at that time, review the follow-through-work tracking reports and details. If performance continues to slip, you can replace the mini-company head or remove the mini-company altogether.

You will learn in Step Eight (the final Company-Capture step, next chapter) the CEO's great power and leverage by discovering the integrating and coordinating functions. The integrating and coordinating functions launch your company into the World-Capture Discovery (Volume Three). To reach the integrating and coordinating functions, then to sit on the launching pad to the stunning World-Capture Discovery, you must first acquire a Neothink perspective of your company's performance. The essence tracking reports of each mini-company are the puzzle pieces to easily snap together your division-of-essence company into that Neothink perspective.

See samples of I & O's direct-mail mini-company's *essence* tracking reports on pages 170 through 174. Essence tracking reports always reflect the accounting and the marketing data among other things. Eventually, the original entrepreneur or CEO may need to track *only* the accounting and the marketing-data essence tracking reports. At any time he feels he needs to, he requests other tracking reports.

For example, the most looked at essence tracking reports for I & O are the accounting and marketing-data tracking reports. They are very simple: the mailing-response report (TR-3) page 172, the profit/loss report and the cash-flow report (TR-5) page 174. To fill out those essence tracking reports requires no formal accounting or statistics education. Yet those tracking reports bring the most powerful business-sense to the I & O mini-company heads: the story of the numbers. For, the mini-company heads see their mini-companies through effort-to-net eyes...through entrepreneurial, cost-cutting, number-calculating, red-to-black, market-data-driven eyes. The essence tracking reports, in a sense, corner the mini-company heads: their efforts, their performances, their net. Thus, the essence tracking reports force them to do integrated thinking and drive forward their essences.

The essence tracking reports then allow Mr. Hamilton to snap together into one Neothink picture all the essences of the division-of-essence I & O Company. The neat, monthly accounting records and market data not only allow him to track performance of each specific mini-company, but of I & O as a whole unit. In less than one hour, he reads through the financial and marketing data of all mini-companies and snaps together the mighty Neothink puzzle.

Mr. Hamilton uses his Neothink perspective to integrate and coordinate entire new realms of business (explained in Chapter Eighteen, next). Only through this Neothink perspective could Mr. Hamilton or any CEO break into entire new realms of business. The traditional, specialized structure becomes uncompetitive with the dawning of the Neo-Tech Age.

Moreover, from his powerful company-wide Neothink perspective, Mr. Hamilton turns his wisdom and creativity back into the puzzle pieces: he integrates and coordinates each I & O mini-company toward increasing horizontal growth (explained later). In traditional company structures, by contrast, the CEO cannot dynamically drive the split-responsibility jobs into horizontal growth. For, the jobs form one large vertical, specialized structure stuck in mysticism.

The Mini-Company Head And His Essence Tracking Reports

The mini-company heads on performance pay acquire the full mind/body integration of business, for they acquire the full mental picture: measuring costs and efforts against *net*. The tracking reports become data sheets to the mini-company heads. They use the tracking reports to calculate and measure their own performances. And for those in-house entrepreneurs on performance pay, responsibilities are not *ends* in themselves; they are *means* to push essence forward. With essence tracking reports, the mini-company heads read performance, then make decisions on how to improve performance. They bring essence-building down to themselves — down to the integrated working man. With this powerful *division of essence*, the ordinary working man *builds* profits and personal wealth.

The essence tracking reports integrate the mini-company heads further with their essences as they drive to improve performance. Their performance-results sit always before them on their tracking reports.

Chapter Eighteen

STEP EIGHT: INTEGRATING AND COORDINATING FUNCTIONS

This is the final step to the Company-Capture Discovery. Everything now comes together. The tracking reports snap together the performance of your mini-companies to bring you Neothink control. You know the strengths and weaknesses of every nook and cranny of your business. With your Neothink perspective, you can integrate and coordinate the puzzle pieces — the mini-companies — into powerful horizontal growth while building the grand Neothink puzzle well beyond your competition. Through the integrating and coordinating functions, you inject your Neothink perspective and power back into your company, into the mini-companies, to catapult your business into the World-Capture Discovery (Volume Four).

If you are a small, one-man business, still read the following chapter. As you grow from a one-man to a two-man business, the following fundamentals will apply to you and help you build your business to many times its current size.

Driving Your Neo-Tech Company To Wealth

As CEO of your company, you now control a Neothink perspective of the business. Now you can drive the mini-companies to greater and greater success by understanding the integrating and coordinating functions. Let us understand the difference between *doing* the work versus *integrating and coordinating* the work. Let us use an analogy: Building company performance can be compared to the head football coach building team performance. The head coach sees the widest, overall perspective. He sees weaknesses. He sees strengths. He must continually integrate and coordinate the players — his puzzle pieces — into the plays that steadily improve the team's performance. The coach operates from the off-the-field, widest perspective. He does not play in the game itself, does not do the plays himself...he integrates and coordinates the plays and players. He focuses on new realms of performance and integrates and coordinates the players to best fit his overall strategy while

187

improving their individual performances.

As the leading head of your company, you must do the same. You see the widest, Neothink perspective. You see weaknesses, strengths and, as the coach does, you must integrate and coordinate your mini-companies to steadily improve the company's performance. You focus on new realms of business and integrate and coordinate the mini-companies to best fit the company's overall strategy while improving their individual performances.

The Powerful Essence Meeting

Mr. Hamilton further developed the Essence Meeting described in Chapter Sixteen into a powerful integrating and coordinating tool. He holds the Essence Meeting with the company once a month. The meeting offers great leverage to Mr. Hamilton and is the single most powerful event in the company.

Throughout the month, Mr. Hamilton outlines the forward movement he expects done by each mini-company the following month. That forward movement fits the overall strategy for company growth.

The Essence Meetings are just that: *Essence Meetings*. Nothing but essence, forward-movement issues, get discussed. Mr. Hamilton works hard preparing for the meetings. Hard concentration goes into outlining for each mini-company specifically what must be accomplished. But that effort pays off as every nook and cranny of the company drives forward for the full month following the Essence Meeting — drives hard to meet the deadlines set by Mr. Hamilton. No one ever drifts into aimlessness. No one ever drifts into filling his day with tasks that do nothing to drive the business forward. Mr. Hamilton determines, for each mini-company, projects that specifically drive the business forward. He communicates what he expects done and sets deadlines.

Even for the mini-companies that have already grown into profit-generating machines, Mr. Hamilton still determines issues of essence that need to be moved on, and he sets deadlines. When the mini-company head evolves into a self-driven integrated thinker (not an externally controlled nonthinker), that mini-company head determines projects and essences he can drive forward, which he brings to the Essence Meeting to be integrated and coordinated into the overall company strategy.

Everyone always moves forward. No one rests on what has already been established. For example, the direct-mail program at I & O is a successful program initially built by the founder, then by Mr. Hamilton. The direct-mail program could operate at par for many years as part of a marketing department full of split responsibilities, perhaps for decades, because of the integrated thinking and essence building done by the founder and by Mr. Hamilton. But the direct-mail program is instead an independent mini-company. Mr. Hamilton lays down no-rest essence expectations for that mini-company. He expects *growth* — new core mailing lists to be uprooted and used, new projects that can uncover virgin lists, demographic marketing projects that can improve results among lists, new market testing that strengthens the mailing piece. ...The white-collar hoax cannot get started in the isolated, essence-driven mini-companies. The CEO expects and gets results.

Mr. Hamilton knows from his widest CEO perspective what can be done to drive the mini-companies to greater success. He sets down actions he expects to be done. He then sets deadlines.

Mr. Hamilton sends a whole business army into double-time, forward-march action. The Essence Meetings integrate and coordinate the forward march of the entire company. The Essence Meetings bring the Neo-Tech CEO maximum leverage. ...Pages 191 through 200 show Mr. Hamilton's outline of actions prepared before the January 1988 Essence Meeting.

Diagram Fifteen*

January 1988

Essence Meeting

- Direct-Mail Marketing

- Television Marketing

- Radio Marketing

- Space-Media Marketing

- Database Marketing

---

*Diagram Fifteen extends over the next 10 pages.

January 1988
<u>Essence Meeting</u>   F E - 1
Front-End Marketing

<u>Direct Mail Program</u>

1) Go thru RN TR's → review testing program

2) Virgin List project → To library for magazines
   - Opportunity, self-help, health /holistic
   - Steady progress, every weekend go
     & spend a couple hours going through
     magazines. Of course, use some
     selection on demographics of magazin.
   - Phone call or letter? Phone calls much better.
   - In the daily essence report, I want names
     of ads you have contacted as you contact.

3) Field Research program → Get on core mailing lists & chase
   down all DM pieces. These people
   all know about mailing lists, of
   course. Surprised at lists one uncovers.

4) Malaysia →

   - NH was headed toward another sector- co. for this.
     I did not feel confident in Bob handling... explain this.
   - Got into #'n & realized that by developing capacity to
     pack more in, this could be a bonanza for Bob. Here is question:
   * Will this spread thin both programs? or...
   * Will this really thicken Bob's essence power for both programs < US /domestic
                                                                        Malaysia
   - Malaysia program has same profit margin as
     Domestic program. Must go at .33%, must build steadily
     to a 500m per month quota.

   - I know we must be @ 500m/mo. I know that can be
     done. I do not know if Bob can build this. Be-
     cause List research his essence, may be a natural.
     Not only that, but getting into may drive his knowledge
     on lists up to boost Domestic program. Will double his
     income if mail 500m/mo. @ .33%
   - In any case, try Bob. If does not work, bring over
     Andi Cogan.

192

Diagram Fifteen
Essence Meeting

(continued)

FE-2

5) Special List Project

  Hume
  Star Trek
  Vietnam Vets
  Black Belt
  Spotlight   ⟩ w/H review
  Scientology   2-hr. meeting
                  Washington DC → Paul O. ex IRS agent
  Teleshop list?? Explain so I know list

6) Demographics Program Status → Next month, no if's

7) Bob H. review his essence progress and projections

8) List rental → we will clean lists (leverage in Virgin lists too)

9) CS → BH his responsibility
   • WH no time w/TR → Bob to do
   • Main thing is that BH does work & stays current. Must keep
     60 & such TR's to see if effective for Bob. Maybe Bob wants
     to change to simply % of FE orders as his reading.
   • Bob must stay on BH. Nitty-gritty.
   • Returns/refunds → BH recording right? for nine years right.
                                    (or after 5:00pm for mkt T.

10) Daily essence via The Source after 11:00 pm, When start the
    day next, 1st thing clean your mailbox

11) Accounting → must have, TR-1 with TR-2 → see TJ's
    must put into Collapse Mysti. Fund

Diagram Fifteen
Essence Meeting

(continued)

FE-3

Television

1) Review list of where running

2) Review TR & data

3) Turn over FNN → • copy rate card
   • Before I leave, remind me to write note
   to set up ad @ 50%

4) Rod design letter describing package for me to edit ASAP.

5) Small initial orders fulfill here.

6) I will talk to Teri for shipping quotes from Braceland or
   Evatone for switch

7) Eventually you handle production.

8) Interconnect & broadcast for 2 min. ads

9) Hooded Man Z commercial shot — Rented camera, low cost...
   with WW if he will do. I prefer. He can read cards & no
   one can tell. Or he can do VO — but maybe fake, but may
   be OK. Interviewer? Steve.

10) On air before next meeting. (If WW cannot do, then WH
    will do, but prefer older, wiser voice in WW)

Diagram Fifteen
Essence Meeting

(continued)

FE·4

Radio: RW

1) Shills → control running on ten metropolitan stations before Feb. meeting.

2) Data under utmost control for each radio station — all data from costs per call to % conversions to % conversions of follow-up mailings to costs to mail @ piece.

3) Profit/loss accounting on each test program & each station.

4) Projected profits on follow-up. Future value per name projections to later verify.

5) TR-1, TR-2, TR-7 completed for month of January. WH will review these TR's.

6) By end of month when determine % conversion and cost per mail piece we average, then can determine cost/call break even. To have cost per call BE by end of month.

7) Establish & manage a 24-hour turn-around on inquiries.

Numbers
- All will have these actions
- You are all going to become super #'s people. That is where emotions truly come in — you become integratedly responsible for success & collapsing mysticism.

Diagram Fifteen
Essence Meeting

(continued)

FE-5

8) Have a mail house ready to go on 24-hour basis once scale up in January-February.

9) Research all big #'s, low cost/M metropolitan stations in country. Give me a report with numbers we are dealing with: # of such stations. From that we will begin # projection for January.

10) Shot-gun letter to _all_ above stations.

Diagram Fifteen
Essence Meeting

(continued)

FE·6

<u>Space Media</u> : TJ

1) Four space ads at 50% price list
   - 2 Z   ← newspaper
   - 1 LT&W   ← magazine or tabloid
   - 1 Golden Greece ← magazine

2) Complete shotgun letter ASAP (MH explain →
   Gary H. & position)

3) Research entire SRDS ASAP & magazine store &
   library. Send out 50 shotgun letters in January.

4) Data set up in effective way for MN review.

<u>Front-End Financial</u>
- Review TR's
- Explain responsible/confidential position HW is in.
  Also, never try to judge someone else's pay.
- HW send memos out for data & tools.
- Review TJ's acct., RH acct., SR acct., RW acct., GT acct.
- Review overall finances
- Review personal finances
- Bank acct. for Rod

End of Front End Marketing

197

Diagram Fifteen
Essence Meeting

(continued)

January 1988

Back-End Marketing
(Database)

BE-1

1) Review up through Friday's data

2) Review reasons data strong or weak:

· Two variables on Growth Plan $\begin{cases} 1) \text{Work for } I\&O \\ 2) \text{Order product} \end{cases}$

· Rod's: Key in brochure writing that I am recognizing: To Do Action.
  I worked in very consciously into Rod's brochure. But the very
  nature of product only so far it can go.

· Inside I&O needs a breather/time

· White Collar Hoax → in contrast to Inside I&O: Says different
  brochures for same product get response as if new product. Tremendous leverage.

2/6/88 3) Rollout Rod's brochure to list in two weeks - possible? 1/30/88
        · Give print orders to Andrews & Webtrend
          this afternoon. They have mechanicals.

2/13/88 4) Testing Week: (TJ need camera → Andrews Monday 1/25/88)
                            WH to Mike T. → Friday 1/22/88

        1) Neo-Tech Newsletter brochure
        2) Nothingness Drain (2 versions)
        3) New "Growth Plan"
        4) Composite test → TJ get a quote right away for 48-page 8½ × 11 electrobrite, glued on
           sticker. Quotes 5m, 10m, 25m, 50m, 100m. Also, quote 96-page 5½ × 8½.
           May go laser route to fit in a 6×9. Take Six Z-booklets to see if
           fit in a 6×9× talk to George Duffy. Actually 5½ × 8½ may be way to
           go, meaning Mike T. must get on this. (Note: must test Composite. Then
           come right back with audio tests)

2/20/88 5) Rollout White-Collar Hoax

2/27/88 6) Testing Week: (TJ need camera → Andrews Monday 2/8/88)
                            Mechanicals to Mike T → Friday 2/5/88

Note: R&S must   1) Phil Zero (Note: Possibly move up to 2/13/8 tests)
be able to promise   2) Mail Nothingness Drain brochure to GE owners after WH converts to 11/3 brochure.
one product.   Also, test general list & compare to 2/13/88 mailing as GE. See difference new product has
                         on same brochure (11/3 Tapes).
                      3) Integrated Thinking brochure for 11/3 Package

3/5/88 7) Rollout Inside I&O (if pulls up)

3/12/88 8) Testing Week → Matt suppressed bulk of orders (E 666) from 2/20/88 mailing.
                          (TJ need camera → Andrews Monday 2/22/88)

Note: 1) Test promising brochures from 2/13/88 mailing now that 3rd x to list.
Audio Tapes same   2) Test composite solo.   compare to 2/in tst.
schedule as brochure. 3) Test composite audio   6) Rod's Letter/memo book
                   4) Test composite brochure w/montage audio 5) Test composite brochure w/ "Imagine..."

Step Eight: Integrating and Coordinating Functions

Diagram Fifteen
Essence Meeting

(continued)

3/19/88 9) Roll out Phil. Zero if tested on 2/13/8 instead of 2/27/8... 4 if successful.

3/26/88 10) Testing Week :   (TS need camera → Andrews Monday 3/7/88)

      1) The New Frontier
      2) RS → Summit #1
      3) Jim C · Neo-Tech Music
      4) Time Line

4/1/88 11) Roll out superior 11/3 brochure from 2/27/88 test.

4/8/88 12) Testing Week :   (TS need camera → Andrews Monday 3/21/88)
      To fill in (possibility: WN Operations Manual)
      1)
      2)
      3)

4/15/88 13) Roll out one success from 3/12/88 test.

... Do you see the pattern emerging? One week - roll out.
Then the next - test. The roll-out reaches back to the tests five
weeks prior: two weeks for data to come in & three weeks
to prepare mailing. Of course, the roll-out reaches back
to tests five weeks or prior. If we get really rolling,
we will have to "pack" our testing & increase roll-outs
to back-to-back weeks. For example, if three brochures
worked well from the 3/12/88 test, then may want to roll
out 4/15/88, 4/22/88, 4/29/88, maybe more if several 3/26/88
tests work well. Then when have several tests together,
pile them together into one large test mailing,
opening up more roll-outs.

199

BE-3

14) TJ - based on this schedule, either you do a calendar
telling when you need, what mechanicals/audio cassettes where...
Or I can give each product developer a copy of this. Which
is better?

15) The above schedule is for beginning of list through 6/87.
Soon to start the program to 6/87-12/87. Need to
start developing "trails". We'll see how NTC does
on 3rd mailing to a segment from last mailing. My
tentative feeling is as follows for this segment:

1) Meeting Tape
2) NTC
3) Inside I&O
4) White-Collar Hoax
5) 11/3 brochure
6) Let There Be Wealth
7)   To Add
8)   ↓
9)
10)

Reasons: 1) Give Rod's a reading at top
2) NTC must come early cause low cost → do not want thinking
   can get I&O products for under $100
3) Inside I&O needs to be near top, for splitting 4 different ways.
4) Test white-collar before Let There Be Wealth
5) 11/3 here for this segment. Test nearer top in future.

Note: To test "trail" & get more data, must go to 3-mo.
segments. SO, let us set trail above for 7/87-9/87, (can mail right away). Set
below trail for 10/87-12/87 (can mail early March). Tentative:

1) 11/3 brochure
2) Inside I&O
3) NTC
4) Meeting Tapes
5) Let There...
6) White-Collar
      To add ↓

200

Step Eight: Integrating and Coordinating Functions

I & O experiences rapid growth. The mini-company heads push on their mini-day/power-thinking teams to drive forward their essences and meet Mr. Hamilton's deadlines. In the meeting, they review their essence progress. They also preview their next month's essence plans, which Mr. Hamilton encourages or adjusts for the overall company's strategy. Both Mr. Hamilton and his mini-company heads introduce essence issues to be moved on... and then set deadlines. Both Mr. Hamilton and his mini-company heads have dumped bicameral tendencies and have activated integrated thinking. Therefore, everyone drives forward on essence. Instead of operating at par, I & O enjoys creative growth.

Knowing The Values And Numbers
Better Than Anyone Else

The two fundamentals upon which all business is born are: 1) values (i.e., the product or service), and 2) numbers (i.e., marketing the product or service). And once the new business begins to function, then two other business fundamentals kick in: 1) personnel, and 2) operations. You, the CEO, must have the widest understanding of the values, numbers, personnel, and operations to drive your company into new realms. You will integrate and coordinate your company's entire work force — all the mini-companies — into those new realms.

In Chapter Nineteen, you will learn about Juan T. Trippe, the original driving force behind Pan American Airlines. Pan Am flew commercial flights around the world before any airline flew around the country. Trippe made this happen by driving the values, numbers, personnel, and operations into entire new realms of air travel.

Juan Trippe relentlessly continued to integrate and coordinate his company and other integral companies into new realms, which soon brought the jet age to the world. For instance, he integrated and coordinated Pratt & Whitney and Rolls Royce to build the jet engines. He integrated and coordinated Boeing and Douglas to build the jet airplanes. With his widest understanding of the values (i.e., the airplanes and engines), he drove Pan Am, Pratt & Whitney, Rolls Royce, Boeing, and Douglas through seemingly unsolvable problems.

201

He also integrated and coordinated the finances, investors, banks. With his widest understanding of the numbers, he drove through seemingly impossible financial barriers. He also integrated and coordinated the personnel, the entire work force, the engineers, the management, and he spurred their heroic drive necessary to break down impossible walls. He integrated and coordinated the operations, the major internal adjustments needed to accomodate the jets. As you will see in Chapter Nineteen, with his widest understanding of the values, numbers, personnel, and operations, he integrated and coordinated his entire company as well as other companies and financial institutions — all the values, numbers, personnel, and operations — to shrink the world with the jets.

Every major company grew from roots made of great men like Juan T. Trippe who drove the values, numbers, personnel, and operations into new realms that captured the world. That was all possible before the white-collar hoax and is possible now through the Neo-Tech System.

Numbers, Values, Personnel, And Operations

Specifically, as CEO of I & 0 Publishing Company, Mr. Hamilton now has a numbers mini-day (study and calculate company-wide marketing data and accounting), a substantial values mini-day (write, edit, copy write), a personnel mini-day (develop personnel and orchestrate personnel into overall company strategy), and an operations mini-day (develop company's internal operating strength).[1]

The dynamic interaction among those mini-days brings an intense essence-drive to the company. For example, the numbers (marketing) drive the values (product development), personnel, and operations. In turn, the developing values, personnel, and operations drive I & O into yet broader marketing. That market-driven phenomenon pushes I & O into new realms as Mr. Hamilton increasingly integrates and coordinates the mini-

---

[1] The numbers ultimately drive all the integrating and coordinating functions. The numbers ultimately drive not only the marketing, but the product development, the personnel, and the operations. Numbers and marketing drive business. This phenomenon is explained in Chapter Nineteen, next.

companies into those growing realms, just as Juan Trippe integrated and coordinated not only his company, but outside companies such as Boeing, Douglas, Rolls Royce, and Pratt & Whitney into the new realms of the jets.

Those starting a business must embrace a values mini-day (focus on the product development or service and its advertising) and a numbers mini-day (focus on the marketing data, accounting, and books), even if the two mini-days are in the evenings, even if they are done briefly, once a week at first. Build a dynamic interaction between those two mini-days. (See pages 223 and 224 to get the idea of how to do this.) For example, do market testing to learn how to elevate the value of the product or service. Then, during your numbers mini-day, study the results — the numbers — to determine how to drive product development forward. Then, during your values mini-day, take that market-acquired knowledge and strengthen the product; elevate its value and the communication of its value, its advertising. With that developing value and developing advertising, then push into wider, more competitive markets. ...This dynamic interaction between numbers and values drives your business into new realms. (Eventually, upon growth and replicating, you must develop personnel and internal operating strength, elaborated on in The World-Capture section.)

The act of confronting numbers and values may initially leave you staring at your desk, not knowing what to do. But that time is not wasted. That time forces you to think in a way your mind is not accustomed to. Slowly, over the next few weeks, you will begin to uncover ways to penetrate those two mini-days, new ways to understand numbers, new ways to accumulate data, new ways to know what your books are telling you...new ways to use those numbers to elevate your service or product, new ways to advertise your product or service, to push your one-man business into the next level of value and profit.

Your essence-drive on the values and numbers pushes forward your business, which may now be just you, a one-man company. Eventually, when you replicate your first mini-company, your company-wide drive on the numbers and values will in turn drive that new mini-company into further issues of essence, communicated through the Essence Meeting. The integrating and coordinating functions are: the highly leveraged act of sending mini-companies into a forward march on issues of essence, issues that you uncover during the dynamically interacting numbers/ values mini-days (and later personnel and operations mini-days, too). The Essence Meeting injects the forward-march actions into your mini-companies.

The great power behind integrating and coordinating functions is that you move others (i.e., mini-companies) into high-action work for your company's goal. Moving others into action for you (such as Boeing, Douglas, Rolls Royce, and Pratt & Whitney for Juan Trippe) brings you maximum leverage — as opposed to you personally *doing* the work. Indeed, Juan Trippe could bring the jets to the world only by integrating and coordinating thousands of people into forward-march action — not by doing that work himself. While orchestrating others, he also spent long hours studying/elevating the values, the numbers, personnel, and operations, all part of his integrating and coordinating functions. Those long, often isolated hours studying/elevating the values via the numbers, for instance, opened new realms that beckoned him to send thousands of people into forward-march action for him (further explained in The World-Capture section, Volume Four).

Whereas moving others into action for you brings you leverage, driving personnel into integrated thinking for you catapults that leverage. It's the creativity catalyst; moving others into integrated thinking multiplies your company's creativity in the way intensity multiplies your time (Self-Capture Discovery). The greatest power behind integrating and coordinating functions comes when you successfully drive others (mini-company heads) into high-action integrated thinking for the company's goal. With growth, you establish a personnel mini-day (could even be an ongoing, weekly meeting with your mini-company heads) to study/develop/elevate the personnel — namely the mini-company heads. You must drive out their mysticism and drive them into integrated thinking. Once they evolve into integrated thinking, your power and leverage grows geometrically. They drive forward values and numbers as you integrate and coordinate their growth into the widest company picture.

Imagine your growing leverage and power as you integrate and coordinate self-driven integrated thinkers who expand their markets and potentially elevate the product/service. ...The Essence Meetings become even *more* important as the mini-company heads discover integrated thinking and develop essence-building ability, for you must integrate and coordinate their rapid development into the widest company plan.

The Longest-Range/Highest-Leveraged Integrating And Coordinating Function

The Essence Meeting brings immediate power to you and to your company. For, the Essence Meeting immediately injects essence, forward movement, throughout the company. Those essence projects injected into the company at first come from *you*, from *your* integrated thinking. Following through on those essence projects forces your mini-company heads into the alien world of integrated thinking. Now, the longest-range, greatest payoffs come by further developing your mini-company heads to, on their own, *initiate* and carry through integrated thinking...to, on their own, build essence and power-think money-making projects.

The more your mini-company heads leave behind personal mysticism (explained in the front material), then the more they integrate knowledge on their own, actually driving beyond the essence projects laid out by you in the Essence Meeting. Gradually, they initiate and develop essence projects on their own. *They* provide *you* with their list of essence actions for the following month. They become self-perpetuating driving forces, integrating you with their essence progress in the Essence Meetings. Each mini-company head can, *on his own,* become a Juan Trippe.

Yet, the average person coming to work for you from a traditional company knows only specialized thinking. His responsibilities at his former, traditional job were nothing more than nonintegrated ends-in-themselves — honed into a boring routine rut. He could not build wealth. Therefore, trapped in bicameral-like specialized thinking all his life, he will initially struggle to handle a mini-company that lives and breathes through integrated thinking. For the first time, he can actually build wealth. He can actually use his mind to pull together thoughts and to increasingly snap those thoughts together through common denominators into growing puzzles. Those growing puzzles will eventually reveal unique puzzle pictures. Indeed, those integrating, growing thoughts will eventually conceive original ideas, create unique directions to enhance his essence, to build his business and values, to build his wealth. He can easily guide himself through integrated thinking, using special formats as catalysts such as power-thinking and studying the story of the numbers (learned later). He will imminently create *new* values and *new* business. Unlike his peers, he will move beyond the business and the values previously established.

Integrated thinking, however, is alien to him. He never had the opportunity to evolve beyond his mysticism (see front material) and its symptomatic specialized thinking. He just always did the set routine laid before him. He needed to have his mind filled by someone above him, by external guidance. He could not fill his own mind with integrated thoughts, with internal guidance. His mind essentially stayed blank, except for automatic or external guidance. As one business owner put it: "If I go away for a few days, my employees sit around and stare at the sky." Their minds go blank, unless filled with guidance from above or automatic guidance from a routine.

For your employees to pursue essence (i.e., to pursue forward movement) and to build wealth requires evolving beyond the following mode (i.e., beyond bicameral tendencies, see front material) and activating the integrating mode. They must fill their minds with guidance from within. Those moving into mini-companies may at first handle the details well and do a thorough job, but they may hide behind details — their automatic guidance. They may ride the essence work done previously, probably done by the founder of the company. They can go for some time hiding behind details, riding the original essence work...the founder's integrated thinking. But slowly, unnoticeably for awhile, the mini-company will deteriorate.

By the way, the white-collar hoax rides the essence work done by the original founders and builders of great companies. The white-collar-hoax executives can ride the founders' essence-work for years, sometimes decades. But the company slowly deteriorates.

Financial payoffs come quickly when mini-company heads

206

break into integrated thinking, both for you and for them. Yet with so much to gain, they still tend to resist. An analogy can be drawn to the bicameral civilizations 3000 years ago (see front material). Not until civilization faced life-and-death survival, as nature's bicameral guidance system broke down under mounting complexities, did man break into conscious thinking. The advantages of consciousness (self-thinking) were physically and mentally attainable for thousands of years. Yet, man did not evolve into self-thinking, and he missed out on the quantum-leap advantages, until cornered with life-and-death survival.

Today, trapped in the bicameral-like mode of specialized thinking for most of his working life, the average person who takes on a mini-company must be driven into integrated thinking. You, as CEO, must actually corner him into doing essence work as part of your integrating and coordinating functions. Mr. Hamilton developed a powerful, simple tool to do this called:

The Daily Essence Report

Mr. Hamilton has each mini-company head fax to him, at the end of each day, a daily essence report. The daily essence report must be faxed every day, without exception. The report is to be brief. It tells the CEO what each mini-company head did on his *essence* that day and what he will do on his *essence* tomorrow. No detail work. No excuses. Simply what was done on essence, nothing else. Of course, essence is work that either moves the mini-company forward or potentially moves it forward. Essence requires integrated thinking...moving beyond what is already established. Acquiring new mailing lists is one essence responsibility for I & O's direct-mail program, for example. Every morning, without exception, Mr. Hamilton expects to review the daily essence reports.

Focused Concentration On Building Business

Mr. Hamilton does not let up. He pushes people into their essences. The I & O CEO gets tough on those not pushing forward their essences aggressively.

The daily essence report corners people and breaks their resistance to integrated thinking. A person can go only three days

207

saying that he did no essence work before his ineffectiveness becomes obvious, and the pressure forces him to start using integrated thinking. Anyone can do integrated thinking. The human mind is designed for integrated thinking. The ordinary person just needs to break through his resistance. You need to help him.

Stay Focused

At first people become irritable, huffy, uptight as you pressure them to break into their essences. But this is good. They are being forced to confront their resistance to change. They are being forced to confront their mysticism — their bicameral tendencies. Do not ease the pressure on those who are slow to move on their essences. They may even quit. But do not back down. Of course, you do not need to get emotional ever. Firmly, calmly pressure a person into his essence. You must corner him into a no-out situation where he has to break his resistance and begin to build. Perhaps you drive out those who cannot make it. But, your Neo-Tech business wants only integrated thinkers.

The Easy Money

You can pressure people quite efficiently with little time spent. Simply mark directly on their daily essence reports what you expect and how quickly and return it that following morning. For example, the direct-mail mini-company head would go several days with no work on uncovering new mailing lists. Mr. Hamilton took less than two minutes to write on a weak daily essence report that he wanted to have a minimum of three new lists researched and reported each day. Three weeks later, the direct-mail mini-company that was averaging two new test lists per mailing jumped to a record eleven new test lists in one mailing. Mr. Hamilton took less than two minutes to corner the direct-mail mini-company head into the next level of productivity and integrated thinking. ...This essence-focused intensity is how Harold Geneen built 250, 50-million-dollar companies at ITT, spending less than 30 minutes per 50-million-dollar company per week. ...He discovered the easy money per effort spent.

Gauge Your Effectiveness

The people being pressured into their essences at first get huffy, uptight. But they are going through a tough transition. Integrated thinking seems so natural and lucrative to those who have made the transition. Yet those who come from a life of specialized thinking go through a tough transition. Contrary to employee-relations myths, if you do NOT sense some huffy resentment throughout your company, then you are not doing your job to push people forward on their essences. Indeed, the so-called "corporate raiders" are resented simply because they are forcing people to use their heads, to break into integrated thinking or get "axed". Those "corporate raiders" are heroes. Once you identify that huffiness throughout your company is a good sign, you welcome it. For it reflects that you are doing your job. ...Eventually, huffiness is replaced by passionate, motivated integrated thinkers, and your employees will love you.

For weeks at I & O, the direct-mail marketing mini-company head would not pursue a demographics project that would move the direct-mail program forward. The demographics project required some integrated thinking. The new mini-company head kept saying he was too busy and could not get to it. Mr. Hamilton knew that meant the new mini-company head was hiding behind the details of his job. So, one evening, Mr. Hamilton jotted down on the mini-company head's daily essence report: Bob, tomorrow I want you to make the phone call to start the demographics project. I don't want you to do anything else until you make that call." Mr. Hamilton knew Bob would resist by telling Mr. Hamilton later how much work needed to be done the following day. As every other day, Mr. Hamilton anticipated that resistance and Bob's excuses. So, Mr. Hamilton firmly added to his note: "Bob, I want that phone call made before you do anything else tomorrow. Even if you sit at your desk and twiddle your thumbs, I don't want you to do anything tomorrow until you make that phone call. I hope I am clear on that."

The next day, Bob made the phone call. To his amazement, that phone call opened an exciting, lucrative dimension to the direct-mail program. Bob had never been happier. Mr. Hamilton did his job by helping Bob break his resistance to integrated thinking, and Bob loved him for it. Bob's life would never be the same again, for he had stepped into the next dimension of integrated thinking. Within a few weeks, Bob was making more money than ever before in his entire life.

Dismiss A White-Collar-Hoax Myth

The daily essence report enables Mr. Hamilton to move straight to the point. A popular myth implies that any problem, particularly an emotional problem, should be handled face to face. To the contrary, that often allows emotions to cloud the point. Putting pressure on getting the essence work done, or handling any problems for that matter, most often works best through non-emotional written communication. Mr. Hamilton spent less than two minutes, for example, to press the direct-mail mini-company head into his essence work. Had they met in person, then emotions, rationalizations, excuses, even complaining would have dragged down the meeting, destroying the point of the meeting, taking an hour or longer.

The "Judge" Measures Performance —
Cuts Out Everything Else

The daily essence report squeezes out all mysticism (i.e., the nonbuilding, following mode) in business. People working for you either integrate and build, or they do not. This daily-essence judge cuts through everything else, cuts through all the "a" points and hones in on THE point. The daily essence report corners all people seeking bicameral-like guidance, corners their rationalizations, corners all those riding on previously built essences...even corners the seeds of the white-collar hoax. The daily essence report pressures those who do not build. The daily essence report is relentless. Avoiding essence means eventual performance deterioration. Going after essence means steady performance growth. As a Neo-Tech CEO, performance is all you are interested in. Indeed, the daily essence report cuts through everything to THE point. The daily essence report is The Judge: Either one is controlled by mysticism (i.e., not doing integrated thinking) and is sinking, or he is controlled by self and is soaring.

Become The Terminator Of Mysticism

Mr. Hamilton discovered that people become geniuses at

210

making excuses for NOT doing integrated thinking. In fact, people often hone all their intelligence to rationalize NOT doing integrated thinking. You must corner their mysticism with the daily essence reports. You must corner and break their resistance to integrated thinking. You must become the terminator of mysticism in your company.

The Reversal

Once people working for you evolve beyond their personal mysticisms and break into integrated thinking, they will begin to push forward their mini-companies. Their attitudes will undergo an about-face as they break into power-thinking and experience excitement at work and happiness at home. Specialized routine-rut thinking causes stagnation. Integrated puzzle-building thinking causes exhilaration. It causes exciting, profitable times. As people working for you break into integrated thinking, their dispositions will change from huffy and irritable to happy and inspired. With integrated thinking, their lives will take on new meaning — take on purpose — as demonstrated by those who have broken through at I & O. Moreover, integrated thinking will bring them powerful advantages that can eventually double, triple, quadruple their incomes.

A Daily Essence Goal

The daily essence report breaks into two brief parts: 1) The essence accomplished that day, and 2) the essence to be accomplished tomorrow. When Mr. Hamilton receives the next day's essence report, he can see if the person was successful with his projection.

The daily essence report sets an essence goal for the next day. The essence goal set in the daily report forces focused concentration on essence each new day. Momentum builds. In a few weeks, often the head of a mini-company finds himself generating business ventures he never believed possible. He discovers what it is like to be a dynamo. To accomplish his essence goal each new day forces him into integrated thinking daily. Eventually, Mr. Hamilton does not have to pressure his evolving employees to move on essence work. For, they pick up momentum and take over with integrated thinking, simply reporting their essence-building progress in the daily essence reports.[1]

Daily Essence Report: Effective Format

The most effective format for the daily essence report is as follows: Integrate the daily essence report with the monthly Essence Meeting. For example, in the monthly Essence Meeting, Mr. Hamilton and each mini-company head establish the essence actions to be accomplished the following month. Each mini-company head then lists 1...2...3...4..., those actions on a sheet of paper with space to the right of each action to write that day's essence progress and the next day's projected progress (see sample on next page). The mini-company head then photocopies 20 copies of that list of essence actions to cover one month of daily essence reports. Each day the mini-company head writes either his progress (or exactly when he plans to make progress) next to each essence action. And he writes what he plans to do tomorrow next to each essence action.

This format keeps the mini-company head focused *every day* on pushing through the essence covered in the Essence Meeting. He focuses *every day* on *every* essence action. This format prevents the common mistake of waiting until a few days before the next monthly Essence Meeting before moving on the essence actions.[2]

---

[1]In time, when a mini-company head breaks into integrated thinking and, on his own, grows his mini-company's essence, you can then switch his daily essence report to a weekly essence report. For, he will race forward with no pressure from you.

[2]As I & O grows, Mr. Hamilton will not remain capable to hold the Essence Meeting with the multiplying mini-company heads. But as explained later, movement heads will eventually evolve in I & O. The CEO integrating and coordinating functions then divide among *movement heads*, described in Chapter Twenty-Five. Mr. Hamilton will hold the Essence Meeting with the *movement heads* to integrate and coordinate their movements or *mini-empires* (described later) with the overall company strategy. Each movement head, in turn, will have an Essence Meeting with the mini-company heads in his movement — in his mini-empire — to integrate and coordinate their essence work with the mini-empire's strategy.

Diagram Sixteen

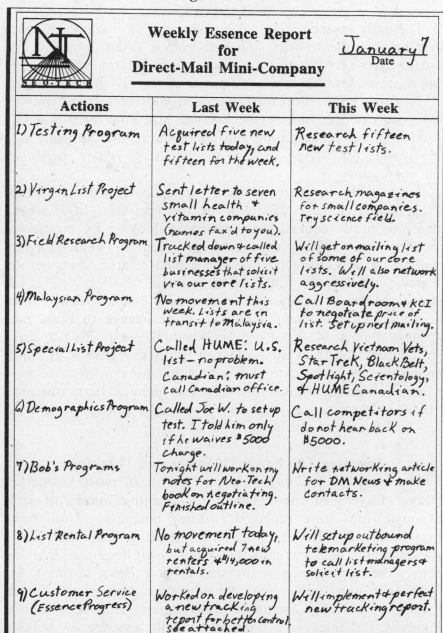

Actions	Last Week	This Week
1) Testing Program	Acquired five new test lists today, and fifteen for the week.	Research fifteen new test lists.
2) Virgin List Project	Sent letter to seven small health & vitamin companies (names fax'd to you).	Research magazines for small companies. Try science field.
3) Field Research Program	Tracked down & called list manager of five businesses that solicit via our core lists.	Will get on mailing list of some of our core lists. Will also network aggressively.
4) Malaysian Program	No movement this week. Lists are in transit to Malaysia.	Call Boardroom & KCI to negotiate price of list. Set up next mailing.
5) Special List Project	Called HUME: U.S. list — no problem. Canadian: must call Canadian office.	Research Vietnam Vets, Star Trek, Black Belt, Spotlight, Scientology, & HUME Canadian.
6) Demographics Program	Called Joe W. to set up test. I told him only if he waives $5000 charge.	Call competitors if do not hear back on $5000.
7) Bob's Programs	Tonight will work on my notes for Neo-Tech book on negotiating. Finished outline.	Write networking article for DM News & make contacts.
8) List Rental Program	No movement today, but acquired 7 new renters & $14,000 in rentals.	Will set up outbound telemarketing program to call list managers & solicit list.
9) Customer Service (Essence Progress)	Worked on developing a new tracking report for better control. See attached.	Will implement & perfect new tracking report.
10) Essence Accounting	Studied numbers we estimate on Tracking Report #5. See my notes, attached.	Meetings scheduled with computer programmer to set up computer controls.

213

The Division Of Essence Breaks Down YOUR Resistance
To Integrate

The daily essence reports combined with the monthly Essence Meetings are the transmission belt from a small company into a major Neo-Tech/Neothink company. The daily/monthly essence concentration brings out the full power of the division of essence.

To force others into their essences, you must force yourself into your essence. Indeed, the Essence Meetings force you into your essence — integrating and coordinating the company into new realms by driving forward the numbers, values, personnel and operations.

To push the company forward into undeveloped new realms is traditionally very difficult for the one-thought-at-a-time conscious mind blocked from integrated thinking by mysticism. Therefore, most CEO's today never push their companies forward into new realms. Instead, they ride a path cleared years before, cleared years into the future by the original founders. ...But the Essence Meetings combined with the daily essence reports force the CEO to break down HIS wall of resistance to build new business realms. He must use his Neothink perspective to drive the numbers and the values into new, profitable realms. He must integrate and coordinate the mini-companies into those new realms. Integrated thinking is hard and alien at first. But once activated, it causes an explosion of success into a world-wide Neo-Tech/Neothink business.

Discover The Power Of Integrated Thinking

The essence, *building* business, is lost in most businesses today. Layers of management maintaining mazes of split responsibilities have replaced *building* business. Until now. Mini-companies driven by Essence Meetings and their daily essence reports and increasingly by their own integrated thinking recover the lost essence in any start-up or existing business.

Essence must come first. All other work comes as a result of essence. Every business today exists because someone originally did integrated thinking to build essence — build a marketable value that did not previously exist. No business exists without essence work first. Essence work yesterday carries the bogus white-collar-hoax jobs today. But the division of essence

214

eliminates the white-collar hoax now and forever into the future.

The daily essence reports drive forth essence from each mini-company. The daily essence reports force the mini-company heads to evolve into integrated thinking needed to build essence, to *build* their businesses. The mini-company heads, on their own, eventually undertake greater and greater essence projects. Momentum builds. At this point, both the mini-company heads and the CEO must do everything possible to expand their essence work and shrink other non-essence work. True, other non-essence work must be done, but it must be shrunk as everyone pushes more and more on essence work.

For example, the mini-company heads can replicate their follow-through responsibilities. Of course, they must remain integrated with those responsibilities; so they must develop effective tracking reports. (To assure the mini-company heads do not replicate the follow-through work prematurely, they should use their own mini-company funds — if their mini-companies are set up on cffcctive performance pay — to pay their mini-company payrolls.)

The CEO also must shrink everything outside of essence, even those details that he cannot replicate. For example, Mr. Hamilton continued to shrink his in-basket work by becoming more and more quick and intense. He developed set procedures, form responses, automatic systems to handle the wide array of correspondence that required attention and absorbed time. Over time, he learned to substantially reduce his in-basket work. Now, Mr. Hamilton uses integrated thinking to build the essence of I & O in longer, more intense values/numbers/personnel/operations mini-days. He integrates and coordinates the mini-companies into greater essences and broader horizons.

Building An Empire Requires Only A Handful Of Integrated Thinkers And A CEO Who Drives Them Forward

Contrary to today's white-collar-hoax illusions, building an empire requires only a few people. The empire-building format not only is simple, it HAS TO BE simple. If building an empire were as complex as the white-collar-hoax-bloated companies of today, no empires would exist today. No, the founder would have become hopelessly sidelined with split responsibilities during the early stages of business.

Today, certain pipe-smoking professors of business promulgate that the founding fathers of great empires practiced business that was quaint and simplistic by today's standards. That erroneous impression gives credibility to the white-collar hoax and their large companies today layered with split responsibilities. But that complex maze of split responsibilities slowly deteriorates the company and is NOT required for a wealthy empire. No, an empire could never be built in the first place with such complexities. An empire can be built only through simplicity, not complexity.

Simplicity: a few people using integrated thinking can build an empire. Complexity: many people using specialized thinking only drains an existing empire. Just a handful of people are needed to build an empire. In fact, most great empires were initially built by just a handful of men using integrated thinking.

Through the Neo-Tech System, you can build an empire, too, with just a handful of people using integrated thinking. Those integrated thinkers drive forward essence...with you at the helm, steering your budding empire forward through *your* essence — the integrating and coordinating functions.

The Company-Capture Discovery Comes Together
Step One: Areas of Purpose
Discover the areas in your business that can BUILD wealth.
Step Two: Split Responsibilities
Identify the draining split responsibilities that obliterate wealth creation.
Step Three: Mentally Integrating Responsibilities
Pull together mentally integrating responsibilities into their money-making purposes.
Step Four: Physical Movements
Form the physical movements of building wealth — the wealth pumps — the true division of labor (i.e., the division of essence).
Step Five: Performance-Pay Mini-Companies
Establish essence-driven mini-companies motivated with performance pay, pumping wealth for you.

216

Step Six: Replicating

Replicate the key wealth-building mini-companies and their entire "tails of responsibilities"; never delegate the money-void split responsibilities.

Step Seven: Tracking Reports

Know the performance of every responsibility in your company through the tracking reports. Moreover, pull together the division of essence — the essence-driven mini-companies — into one Neothink puzzle radiating a powerful, money-making picture not seen by your mysticism-plagued competition.

Step Eight: Integrating and Coordinating Functions

From your Neothink perspective, move the entire company forward — all the mini-companies — into new realms of wealth creation through the integrating and coordinating functions.

The Secret Power of The Neo-Tech System

Now that we have completed both the Self-Capture and Company-Capture Discoveries, we can easily see a trend; we can see exactly what is going on here to capture iron-grip control and enjoy money-making progress others never dream of.

Remember in Chapter Two, the key to success and wealth was to set free hard, Firestone-like thinking? And the way to do that, if you remember, was to develop a physically integrated working format that had minimal physical disjointedness. Formatting work into the smooth physical movements (like the assembly-line) allowed one to get through his work in a fraction of the time. In turn, large amounts of time opened up for his mind to start thinking creatively and pursuing money-making projects.

We saw that phenomenon of formatting work into smooth physical movements to open up time for creative, money-making thinking in the Self-Capture Discovery with the mini-day schedule, breaking one's daily schedule into the smooth physical movements and getting rid of the out-of-control, disjointed traditional schedule. The integrated mini-days opened up time for creative power-thinking and plotting out money-making projects for oneself. Then, one poured those exciting money-making projects into the quick-action mini-days. The money-making projects quickly got done, and they snapped together into a beautiful puzzle-picture of success for self — your first step into Neothink.

We saw that same phenomenon of formatting work into smooth physical movements to open up time for creative, money-making thinking in the Company-Capture Discovery with the mini-company structure, breaking the company's structure into the smooth physical movements and getting rid of the disintegrated departments and specialized jobs of the traditional structure. The integrated mini-companies left behind split responsibilities and, with potent tracking reports, opened up time for creative integrated thinking and plotting out money-making projects for one's company. Then, through the Essence Meetings, one poured those company-wide money-making projects into the quick-action mini-companies. The money-making essence projects quickly got done, and they snapped together into a beautiful puzzle-picture of success for one's company — your second step into Neothink.

Now, we are ready to apply this phenomenon of formatting work into smooth physical movements to open up time for creative, money-making thinking in the World-Capture Discovery, next. You will discover *your* — the founder/CEO's — physical movement to remove all physical disjointedness and free your mind for hard, Firestone-like thinking. Then, your Neothink tools will help you snap together a beautiful puzzle-picture of success for capturing the world — your third step into Neothink.

So, you may now turn to the World-Capture Discovery, Volume Three on page 243. But it is very important for you to come back and read the remaining pages in Volume Two if you plan to build your own company with the Neo-Tech System. The remaining pages in Volume Two contain priceless information for Neo-Tech entrepreneurs.

Chapter Nineteen

MARKET PRESSURES AND NEO-TECH

The Neothink Company Is A Market-Driven Company

Diagram Ten, page 109, shows the I & O mini-companies (areas of purpose). No product development mini-companies exist: no Neo-Tech Writers, no Neo-Tech Live Arts, no Neo-Tech Productions.

Mr. Hamilton removed all product-development jobs from I & O soon after developing the Neo-Tech System. Instead, he moved his qualified product developers into either a new or an existing marketing mini-company. New products in I & O now had to grow through their marketing mini-companies. The marketing mini-company head had to develop his product during the assigned mini-day and in the evenings and on weekends. ...Why?

Business is defined by Mr. Hamilton as: **the dynamic interaction between numbers and values that enables people to create and elevate marketable values and to market those values to expanding markets.** In other words, a product per se carries no value in the business world; only a *marketable product* carries value in the business world. Only market pressures elevate products into marketable values. Therefore, to bring his product into the business world, the product developer must personally market his product. Under market pressures, he learns how to elevate his product in order to drive the marketing from red (a financial loss) to black (profits). Only through the dynamic interaction of values (product development) and numbers (marketing) will a product eventually capture the consumer's attention. Market pressures and only market pressures drive great values into society. Product development must not be separated from marketing.

By contrast, large budgets or government grants awarded to research and development programs produce inefficient and inferior results. Programs driven by market pressures produce efficient and superior results.

Where Values Come From

Most major values throughout history came into existence under market pressures. Thomas Edison invented the incandescent

219

light bulb, but then he elevated it to a household value through his company's market pressures. Henry Ford developed the unlikely concept of the family car, but then he elevated it to a nationwide value through his company's market pressures. Market pressures elevate inventions such as the light bulb or ideas such as the family car to marketable values. Market pressures must drive even the most long-term research and development programs, including cures for diseases. To grasp the importance of putting market pressures on research and development, consider the example of Juan Trippe and the jets:

Juan T. Trippe And The Jets

Juan T. Trippe was the original driving force behind Pan American Airways, which flew its first flight in 1927 from Florida to Cuba. Under Juan Trippe's leadership, Pan American flew commercial flights around the world (starting in the 1930s with service to China on the "China Clippers") before commercial airlines flew across the country.

Driven by market pressures, Juan Trippe sent the world into a new dimension of air travel: the jet-engine airplane. Under immense market pressures (the entire finances of Pan Am would collapse if the jets failed), Juan Trippe drove the value creation — the engineers, the engine manufacturers, the airplane manufacturers — to do what was considered impossible. With no formal engineering education himself, Juan Trippe was considered the best engineer in Pan Am. Market pressures drove Juan Trippe to become the engineer who overcame insurmountable problems. Through his knowledge of the values (the engines and the airplanes), he personally drove Douglas and Boeing to design and build the planes to carry the radical, not-yet-developed jet engines. He drove Pratt & Whitney and Rolls Royce to design and build the jet engines. When they hit impossible dead ends, Juan Trippe would personally test and observe the problem. Great market pressures forced him into intense integrated thinking. He knocked down those impossible walls with amazing engineering feats and breakthroughs when no other engineer could. He was driven by enormous market pressures, *survival* pressures. Market pressures and only market pressures drive world-moving values into society out of nowhere.

His intense market-driven focus on the values — the product development — brought the commercial jet airplanes to the world.

Trippe not only drove the values; he also drove the numbers: the banks, the investors, the stock options, the cash. Under enormous market pressures, he single-handedly did what financiers considered impossible. He drove his massive research and development program to profits — the most profitable endeavor in air travel history. Through market-driven focus on the numbers, he single-handedly orchestrated some of the greatest financial moves the business world had ever seen. ...His drive on the numbers — securing the financing, negotiating the costs, building the markets, and finally achieving the profitable payoffs — brought the jet age to the world.

Enormous market pressures drove the commercial jets to reality. Among other things, market pressures drove Juan Trippe into being the best troubleshooting engineer for Pan Am. No research and development project funded by government subsidies or a government grant or an undisciplined white-collar-hoax budget could have driven commercial jet-engine airplanes to the world. By understanding that only market pressures drive world-moving values into society, then the reason Mr. Hamilton removed product-development jobs from I & O becomes clear. Instead, market pressures now drive Neo-Tech products to society.

Since market pressures cause the dynamics that elevate products to their greatest value, research and development programs must be made responsible for *making a profit* as Juan Trippe did with the jets. In other words, research and development programs must develop the product *and* bring it into the marketplace.

Product-development jobs or research and development teams provide inferior products in an inefficient, costly way. Once again, market pressures must drive the product developers or the heads of research programs into the marketplace and onto making profits. Then and only then has the product developer provided a value to the business.

Market Pressures Elevate Not Only The Values, But Personal Skill, Competence, Wealth

The competitive pressures of marketing — survival pressures

— actually elevate a person's *skill* as well. Consider that market pressures catapulted writing skills in I & O just as market pressures catapulted Juan Trippe's engineering skill to being the best in Pan Am, for he *had to make it work*. Amazingly, Juan Trippe had no formal engineering education.

Similarly, market pressures drove the writers in I & O to new heights after becoming marketing mini-company heads instead.

The former product developers suddenly confronted numbers, data, negotiating, financing — dimensions they never handled before. Although they suddenly marketed established Neo-Tech products, they would eventually develop their own Neo-Tech products through real, hands-on marketing pressures.

Products developed when *not* under market pressures, on the other hand, are usually *not* marketable. Not elevated to a greater value through market pressures, the product often stays in the realm of sound-good "inner logic". At I & O, the Neo-Tech product developers (now-turned-marketing men and women) gradually develop unique Neo-Tech products during their writing mini-days, products that capture world markets. Previously, none of the product developers had produced values at the world-capture level, impossible without market pressures.

The Performance-Pay Boost

The positive effects of performance pay on a marketing mini-company are obvious — the person becomes integrated with cost controls, accounting, and market data and uses integrated thinking to build his profits. But let us look at product development. By integrating with the marketplace, hard-nosed business integrates with product development, creativity, and art to boost those areas to new levels of value. Increasing the product's value to the consumer becomes a hard-nosed, grind-out drive. With personal success and income at stake, the creator drives in the business world to create and elevate both the product copy and the marketing copy, which will educate the consumer of the product's value. He drives to understand the strengths and weaknesses of his product more intensely than any laid-back "creator's atmosphere" would allow. With incentive and superior knowledge/data from the marketplace, he builds his product well beyond the sensitive creator not integrated with the marketplace.

222

For example, see how integrating product development with performance pay, a percentage of sales, drives the product to much greater value:

* Write/edit/produce product
* Write/edit/produce ad copy
* Integrate with the marketing of the product — test, test, test different advertising approaches to drive the marketing campaign from red to black
* Analyze, study, probe marketing data
* Develop, test, and test again different approaches for ad copy; read results and effectiveness of one approach over the other in the marketplace. Begin to understand what the market is looking for. Begin to know how to elevate the value of the product to meet that common need. Dig back into product development.
* Study, understand what the data/numbers are saying. Marketing numbers/data become the guide to elevate the value of the product. Understand why one marketing approach better communicates the value of the product. Dig back into product development with that added knowledge and strengthen the communication of its value.
* Build ad copy in the direction the numbers/data favor; move deeper into that direction. Do same in product itself.
* Develop new tests in the direction the data favors. Test, test, test. Study tests. Learn what the market must know to clearly see the commercial value of product. Dig back into product development.
* Learn from ad-copy tests (data/numbers) what customers need to best recognize (thus utilize) value. Learn how the values can be communicated more effectively to benefit customers. In turn, expand those values in the product thus expand its market. ...The product developer is developing a superior product by making it commercially successful. This dynamic value-elevation process can grow and continue until his values capture the world. Indeed, business develops and grows by this dynamic interaction of values and numbers.
* Turn back, turn back, turn back into the product itself to upgrade its value based on market findings. Every piece of

data from marketing leads back to the product itself.

* Measure and analyze customer feedback for producing new, upgraded releases of product. Determine how your upgraded product communicates values via studying customer comments/complaints.

* The process never stops: Always develop the product further; communicate more effectively based on marketing data and customer feedback.

As you can see, by integrating creative product development with marketing — *effort with net* — specialized artists, writers, inventors, even scientists become integrated businessmen and elevate their values to the world. Creative cartoons get elevated into Disneyland.

Numbers-Driven CEO

Marketing pressures (the numbers) drive the business. The numbers drive not only the marketing mini-company heads, but drive the CEO too. In Chapter Seventeen, you learned that the CEO snapped together the essence tracking reports (accounting and marketing data) into a Neothink puzzle. That puzzle delivers the widest understanding of the marketing/numbers. With that Neothink picture of the numbers, you can drive your company forward into new realms. You can integrate and coordinate the mini-companies forward into those new realms.

Indeed, consider the CEO of I & O, Mark Hamilton, creator of the Neo-Tech System. Mr. Hamilton anxiously snaps together I & O's essence tracking reports, for that Neothink puzzle radiates a comprehensive marketing/numbers picture of the business. Mr. Hamilton sees I & O's world-wide Neo-Tech marketing results. He designs and studies advertising tests to learn the effects of different Neo-Tech developments. He masters the dynamic interaction of marketing (numbers) and product/advertising development (values). The numbers drive Mr. Hamilton into greater and greater elevation of Neo-Tech's values.

As Mr. Hamilton reaches into new realms with Neo-Tech, he integrates and coordinates his mini-companies into those new realms.

Chapter Twenty

THE NEOTHINK BUSINESS STRUCTURE

Traditional companies are essentially limited to the capacity of a few men — the heads of departments or programs. That dependency explains why companies aggressively compete for ace managers.

Unlike traditional company structures, the mini-companies are not part of a delicately organized maze of split responsibilities. The mini-companies are self-functioning, self-contained numbers-driven companies. They obsolete departments, which depend upon other departments, smartly fitted into their complex maze of "organized" split responsibilities.

When the start-up entrepreneur begins his traditional company structure, his growth becomes increasingly limited by that maze of split responsibilities. Growth depends upon finding good managers who can function better than other managers within that maze of split responsibilities. The company grows only to the MANAGERS' potentials, then stops.

When the start-up entrepreneur begins his mini-company structure, he breaks through such painful limitations. With no maze of split responsibilities, his business is not dependent upon finding superior managers. His mini-companies can multiply to fulfill the COMPANY'S potential. For example, if a particular program can be several times its size, it no longer depends on finding that rare, expert manager to skillfully expand the program. Instead, several mini-companies with *ordinary people*, fully integrated ordinary people, can move in to fill the COMPANY'S potential.

The Neo-Tech System is not limited. The start-up Neo-Tech company can keep pace with the potential of the COMPANY. The traditional company, caught in its own web of split responsibilities, is limited. The start-up traditional company only grows to the potential of the MANAGERS.

Let us see how this happens. The maze of split responsibilities that quickly forms throughout the new traditional company makes business dependent on what the people in supervising/managing positions can handle. The entrepreneur is at their mercy. But now, with the mini-companies, the entrepreneur simply brings in another mini-company with the same "tail of responsibilities", and brings in another and another...until the program reaches ITS full potential. Indeed, with the mini-company structure, the entrepreneur is at no one's mercy.

Problems disappear: 1) the company is no longer dependent on the managers, and 2) with more than one mini-company vying for a program's business, all must take integrated control and push forward on their essences in order to be competitive.

The Neothink Structure

The Neothink structure builds maximum-integration parts (mini-companies) then snaps those parts together (tracking reports) to build a Neothink business puzzle. Now, consider that numbers drive business — drive the marketing, product development, personnel, and operations. The Neothink puzzle of essence tracking reports radiates a picture that gives the CEO or original entrepreneur the widest understanding of the numbers, which enables him the broadest dynamic interaction between numbers and values...enables him to drive the business into new realms. For example, by snapping together the I & O tracking reports, Mr. Hamilton gains the widest understanding of all Neo-Tech marketing efforts — the numbers — which enables him the broadest dynamic interaction between numbers and Neo-Tech values...enables him to drive Neo-Tech values into new dimensions that, in turn, push I & O mini-companies into greater realms of marketing.

The Neothink business puzzle of mini-companies snapped together by tracking reports can grow without loss of control. The traditional business structure of split responsibilities and a pyramid-like hierarchy grows to its limit, with increasing loss of control. For example, in the traditional structure, I & O was basically limited to its marketing director who was filled to his capacity with the domestic direct-mail program. Now with the Neothink structure, I & O quickly introduced television marketing, space-media marketing, database marketing, radio marketing; and now marketing mini-companies are springing up in foreign countries and in eight languages...all giving Mr. Hamilton a larger and larger Neothink marketing/numbers picture, giving him greater and greater Neothink power to drive I & O forward. I & O grows while *gaining* control and power through a growing Neothink puzzle. I & O grows many times the size and prosperity of its previous, more traditional structure.

The Traditional Structure/Mind

I & O experienced business schizophrenia while overrun with split responsibilities in the previous, more traditional structure. Interestingly, the typical traditional business structure is analogous to the typical mind: the typical mind breaks down when confronted with business growth. The typical mind does not integrate; it follows. So, it quickly becomes ineffective when confronting simple integrations, bicamerally looking for automatic or external guidance instead of integrating internal guidance (see front material). The typical mind cannot handle the vast integrations needed for business growth.

The Neothink Structure/Mind

I & O captured iron-grip control with the Neothink structure. Interestingly, the unlimited Neothink business structure is analogous to the Neothink mind: the Neothink mind grows stronger when confronted with business growth. The Neothink mind does not follow; it integrates. For example, it snaps together the maximum-integration parts (mini-companies) into a growing Neothink puzzle-picture. So, the greater the puzzle, the greater the Neothink marketing/numbers picture, thus, the further the entrepreneur can take the company into new realms.

The Neothink picture allows the entrepreneur or CEO to understand his company's values via the numbers well beyond his previous capacity. His Neothink vision enables him to drive those values into new realms and then bring synergistic advantages back into the company, to each of the mini-companies, through his integrating and coordinating Essence Meetings. And with each new maximum-integration part (mini-company), the puzzle gets larger, more powerful, showing a broader and clearer picture, well beyond where the typical mind can go. The success puzzle can be picked up and moved around the world without the business ever falling apart again (the World-Capture Discovery, Volume Three).

227

The Neothink Puzzle

Let us see what happened at I & O as it became a Neothink puzzle, evolving from a more traditional structure with one marketing director who could handle one program (the direct-mail program) into a Neothink structure that quickly grew into two mini-companies (the direct-mail mini-company and the database mini-company). Snapping together just two maximum-integration parts, two mini-companies, quickly brought synergistic advantages back into the small puzzle of two mini-companies. For, by snapping the two together through the tracking reports, Mr. Hamilton discovered more sophisticated marketing dynamics that sent I & O into an integrated mass-marketing program, as follows:

The new database mini-company marketed I & O's selection of Neo-Tech products to the new customers generated by the direct-mail mini-company. Thus, I & O could now calculate the *future revenue* of each new customer. As a result, I & O could lower its profits (response %) for the direct-mail mini-company because of *future profits* from the database mini-company. By lowering the profits (response %) for the direct-mail mini-company, the direct-mail mini-company exploded into mass markets, now reachable at the lower response percentage. The database mini-company boomed too as a result of the escalating number of new I & O customers.

With each added maximum-integration unit that came next — the television marketing mini-company, the radio marketing mini-company, the space-media marketing mini-company, the foreign marketing mini-companies — the I & O Neothink puzzle grew more powerful.

Now you can create a Neothink puzzle, too. By applying the eight steps (pages 216-217) of the Company-Capture Discovery, through each passing month your growing start-up company will become more and more of a Neothink structure. Each area of purpose, each mini-company will be a maximum-integration part that snaps into your Neothink puzzle through the essence tracking reports. With a Neothink marketing/numbers picture of your company, you will control the broadest dynamic interaction between numbers and values and will drive your business into new realms and then feed synergy back into your

Neothink company through the Essence Meetings.

Number-Driven Mini-Company Heads

Marketing pressures, *the numbers*, drive business, even drive product development, *the values*. Accounting/numbers provide the most powerful integrations for doing business: the measurements of cost/efforts to net. Accounting, the most powerful tool in business, now evolves from traditional accounting to Neothink Accounting. For, now the accounting itself breaks down into its proper division of labor — into the physical movements of making money, the mini-companies. (Notice accounting under each mini-company in Diagram Ten, page 109.) The accounting then snaps together into the Neothink puzzle through the essence tracking reports for the CEO or original entrepreneur.

Neothink Accounting brings a new power to business. In traditional companies, only a handful of people really put accounting/numbers to use. But in the Neo-Tech System, each mini-company head now puts the most powerful tool in business — accounting — to day-to-day use. The mini-companies use the numbers to drive their businesses forward.

Neothink Accounting

Neothink Accounting brings iron-grip control to the most complex aspect of business: the finances. Neothink Accounting does much more. Eventually, every person in your Neo-Tech business will use accounting as a day-to-day tool to drive forward business. Your company will be filled with integrating, numbers men and women reducing costs and increasing net. Imagine the strength in such a company. Traditionally, those workers have no integration at all with costs of business or net, no understanding at all of the numbers. But now, each mini-company and each entrepreneurial unit therein becomes numbers-driven.

Neothink Accounting makes the most complex area of most businesses, that is the finances, the most simple, integrated, straightforward area of I & O. Finances tend toward split responsibilities and, before Neothink Accounting, caused pronounced split responsibilities in I & O. But Neothink takes control where traditional business goes out of control.

229

How Neothink Accounting Differs From Traditional Accounting

Now accounting becomes a down-to-earth tool for the ordinary working man. (No white-collar-hoax accounting practices will happen here.) The true division of labor breaks down accounting into the physical movements of making money throughout the company instead of being isolated in one, specialized department. Accounting now exists in each area of purpose to drive its purpose forward. Accounting, costs, negotiating, cuts, expansions...numbers now become *integrated meaning* to the person with an area of purpose. Employees in the division-of-essence Neo-Tech company use accounting and numbers to build their essences. The once-specialized world of accounting now becomes a day-by-day integrated working tool for everyone.

Accounting is no longer a support function as in traditional companies; it is now an integrated essence-responsibility used as a tool. Accounting becomes an integrated responsibility for the head of each mini-company. He must drive his purpose, his business, into successful numbers. Accounting no longer means looking over the past quarter at results, calculated by a large department. Accounting now means knowing day in and day out the integrated numbers of one's mini-company in order to make his actions more and more profitable.

Something Much More...

In the division-of-essence Neo-Tech company, accounting takes yet another leap to become the key power-tool. Remember, the division of essence brings to every employee the widest integration in business: cost/effort weighed against net. And remember, a mini-company head's personal pay comes from performance: performance pay. The mini-company head's costs and efforts, therefore, become *personally* integrated with net. His net now takes on *personal meaning*. The net is no longer just *the company's* win or loss; it is now his own *personal* win or loss. For, his net now determines his own personal income. Accounting becomes his personal power-tool to measure costs and efforts to net in order to improve his personal net. He uses accounting to hone in on and improve the story of the numbers, from the marketing down to specific cost controls, operations efficiencies, personnel intensity. He exerts hard, integrated thinking to drive up net in every way, measured by his own accounting.

Accounting now becomes not only a tool to drive forward the essence of his mini-company, but it now becomes a very personal tool to drive up his own income. Personally integrated with the numbers, the mini-company head puts hard, Firestone-like thinking into his essence.

In traditional companies, the average employee does not care much about the numbers or finances. He does not care about what the accounting department uncovers...as long as he has a job. He prefers to have his mind guided by automatic routines or external authorities than to integrate those numbers. In the Neo-Tech company, by contrast, every person becomes his own, driving accountant/entrepreneur and learns to guide himself through integrated thinking. With personal wealth at stake, the mini-company head learns how to be driven by the numbers in all areas from cutting expenses to pushing his follow-through employee(s) into new efficiencies in order to push his mini-company more into the black. He learns how to master integrated thinking and power-thinking to drive his mini-company further and further into the profits.

Every Employee To Become A Numbers Person

Accounting provides the integrated-thinking tools needed to build business. In the traditional structure, however, those thinking tools are never provided to the average working person. Instead, those thinking tools are locked up in a specialized department. In the traditional structure, the average employee acquires no accounting knowledge, no integrated-thinking tools to build business, no measurement of his efforts, nothing to reflect what good he has done...leaving him with no love for work, no happiness, no wealth. The average employee faces a future of stagnation.

In the Neothink structure, the integrated-thinking tools no longer sit in a specialized department. Instead, those thinking tools are integrated with the mini-companies. In the Neo-Tech company, the average person acquires accounting knowledge, the thinking tools to build business; he measures his efforts with numbers; profits reflect the good he has done...bringing him a lot of love for his work, a lot of happiness, a lot of wealth. The average Neo-Tech employee faces a future of adventure.

The Neo-Tech System produces the most powerful, accurate, speedy, and useful accounting. The Neo-Tech System uncovers the full power of numbers as accounting comes down to the ordinary working man.

Nook-And-Cranny Accounting Control

Accounting no longer languishes in the offices of the accounting department, its numbers used only by upper management. By contrast, Neothink Accounting gets down in the trenches within the mini-companies, its numbers used every day by those building their areas of purpose. Costs tighten, controls strengthen, efficiencies improve...from the marketing program down to the follow-through jobs. The mini-company heads put tight leashes on their expenditures. Accounting, cost controls, payroll, expenses, numbers, numbers, numbers drive their businesses and determine their incomes. Accounting and numbers become exciting to the ordinary person!

The Neothink Accounting Puzzle

Each month the CEO receives the accounting in the form of essence tracking reports from each mini-company head. The CEO immediately sits in the catbird seat, for he sees the entire Neothink Accounting picture in less than 30 minutes by going through those essence tracking reports.

He will not use accounting to see how the company did over the past quarter, then turn back into the company to see how things can be improved such as, for instance, reducing costs or increasing efficiencies. For, all that has long since been integrated at the ground level, quickly, daily, where it counts. In other words, the accounting and numbers were already fully integrated throughout the company and used every day as a tool to increase the net. Thus, the CEO does not have to operate at that level. Instead, the CEO will use his widest integration of numbers — his Neothink accounting puzzle — to create and elevate the company into greater realms...to be brought back into the mini-companies in the Essence Meetings (expanded on the World Capture section).

Chapter Twenty-One
THE NEOTHINK EMPLOYEE

Distribute this manuscript throughout your work force to demonstrate the advantages of the Neo-Tech System to your employees. This chapter is also for those who run a mini-company and for *their* employees.

Now that we have a good understanding of the Neothink company, the question arises: Exactly how can a person *within the company* capitalize by using Neothink?

First of all, *any* employee in the Neo-Tech System can apply Neothink right at his current level; he can use Neothink to grow to more advanced levels of business and wealth. Secondly, he can receive synergistic advantages from becoming a puzzle piece of the larger Neothink puzzle.

To understand how an employee within the Neo-Tech System can use Neothink for his own advantage, let us review what Neothink is: Neothink moves beyond the capacity of the mysticism-plagued conscious mind. The mysticism-plagued mind seeks external guidance, closing the door to integrated thinking. The Neo-Tech System stimulates internal guidance, opening the door to integrated thinking. Integrated thinking leads to Neothink. Neothink comes from building and then snapping together maximum-integration units. The mind first builds each maximum-integration unit as far as it can, which is integrated thinking. Then through special Neothink tools, the maximum-integration units snap together like pieces to a puzzle. The growing puzzle eventually forms a puzzle-picture not seen before, which is Neothink. That puzzle-picture could never be seen by specialized thinkers, a picture seen only by the integrated thinker. Therefore, Neothink outintegrates, outcompetes specialized competition.

The more complex the project, the more integrations needed, the more the average person blocked by mysticism breaks down...the more Neothink is needed to snap together the success puzzle.

The open-ended nature of business offers average men and women so much more than their traditional closed-ended jobs can

233

give. Consider that the average person falls short of where he would like to be financially — because he operates in the limited specialized/following mode. He is held there by the specialized structure of his job and by his own bicameral mysticism (see front material). Alternatives to his stagnation-trap did not exist before. But now, he can leave behind his specialized job. He can evolve into Neothink...

How To Build A Neothink Puzzle
1) Break ventures into maximum-integration parts, and
2) Snap together those maximum-integration parts like a jigsaw puzzle to reveal a larger-than-life picture that radiates spectacular new knowledge called Neothink.

Let us look at an example of how someone in I & O recently evolved into Neothink. John took on the database marketing program. As the program grew, John faced complexities, integrations, negotiations, deadlines...major orchestration he had not experienced before. His specialized, thought-by-thought following mode began to break down. He had to evolve beyond the specialized following mode into using integrated Neothink. He had to take the self-capture step into Neothink.

So how, specifically, did John use Neothink to evolve beyond a life heading toward stagnation? He began with the first requisite of Neothink: break the venture into maximum-integration parts. How did he do this? Through weekly power-thinking.

Power-Thinking, as explained in the Self-Capture Discovery, breaks complex programs into maximum-integration parts that the mind can handle. The vast array of projects and their many tasks that John unsuccessfully chased while using a traditional daily schedule now got broken into easy-to-handle maximum-integration parts through power-thinking. Each weekend, John would power-think each project that he had to move forward. His mind stayed clear of other thoughts as he concentrated on one project at a time. He listed the necessary steps to complete that one project, that maximum-integration unit; then he cleared his mind, and moved on to the next project, the next maximum-integration unit. When he was done with his power-thinking list, he had broken his forward-movement essence work into its maximum-integration

234

parts, the first requisite of Neothink.

Next, to activate Neothink, he had to execute the second requisite of Neothink: snap together those maximum-integration parts. John accomplished this by determining the tasks to perform each step of his power-thinking list and by injecting those tasks into his mini-day schedule for the upcoming week. The maximum-integration projects snapped together in his mini-day schedule — his success puzzle.

Your Life Just Begins Where Others End

A few months before, John had basically reached his specialized, conscious capacity. The wealth-building capacity of most people is established by the time they are twenty-nine years old. A person may grow in experience and knowledge, but capacity, similar to IQ, is established early on. From twenty-nine years on, the long road ahead does not change much. In the traditional structure, people do not have an alternative. The excitement and enthusiasm for the future ends for most in their late twenties or early thirties. Their journey loses hope as their lives sink into stagnation.

A few months before, John's future, like most, would never really grow much, his capacity set for life. His enthusiastic talk about the future happened less. To expect more out of life, to expand his capacity for life, was all ending in his twenties. ...From then on, with his thrill for life fading, John, like most, would just get older.

Then John discovered the Neo-Tech System and used the self-capture tools of Neothink. He quickly surpassed his previous potential. He now runs a mini-company — his personal wealth pump.

In the division-of-essence Neothink company, the rewards beckon all workers to become Neothink employees. The special tools that can evolve the average employee beyond the grip of stagnation, into the thrill of exhilaration (i.e., beyond a stagnant future, into a high-powered Neothink employee making good money) have been discovered: the mini-day/power-thinking team is the first of two tools.

Do Not Slip Back Into Stagnation

The Self-Capture Discovery, the mini-day/power-thinking team, must be used consistently to rise above the life of stagnation. The following-mode conscious mind at first tends to avoid the integrating-mode mini-day/power-thinking team. The mysticism-plagued mind avoids integrated thinking and seeks automatic or external guidance. Thus, the mysticism-plagued mind avoids power-thinking and seeks specialized thinking. In other words, we feel more comfortable following our routine ruts than blazing new ventures.

Deep-rooted bicameral urges in all people want the traditional daily schedule that integrates no further than the immediate thoughts in one's head. Everyone using Neothink, including Mr. Hamilton, must keep from slipping back into that easy, familiar nonintegrating mode. As long as one is aware of that initial reaction to Neothink, that ordinary person handling a mini-company or an entrepreneurial follow-through job can move into the self-capture mode of Neothink and stay there.

Unfortunately, the self-capture mode of Neothink is not even accessible to most jobs. For, most jobs have no money-making purpose and stagnate in specialization...never able to go beyond a set routine and to grow through integration. Specialization blocks Neothink.

Specialized jobs with ends-in-themselves responsibilities prevent even just thinking about integrated money-making projects. Money-making projects never come close to the power-thinking stage. Thus, the maximum-integration parts (the projects) never form in order to snap together into a Neothink puzzle (through the mini-day schedule).

Consider a bank teller, for instance. What money-making project does that person have access to? None. Furthermore, the key ingredient of the mini-day schedule, integration, contradicts the key ingredient of the traditional job: specialization.

In the Neo-Tech System, *every* job has money-making purpose and flourishes through integration. Therefore, each person can evolve into integrated thinking, power-thinking, Neothink. Once one takes the self-capture step into Neothink, do not forget: he must stay with the mini-day/power-thinking team. Deep-rooted bicameral urges tug him back toward specialization and the

236

traditional daily schedule — back toward automatically following his routine and reacting to the business around him...his external guidance. But that person must realize what is going on and not allow himself to relax his footing in Neothink. Working in the Neo-Tech System, he is given a rare opportunity to integrate, build wealth, and become creative and happy.

After A Month

What once seemed impossible to handle will get handled smoothly with Neothink. At some point, a mini-company head may want more action. To go for more — for more than one mini-company — one must go back to the prime requisites of Neothink. First, he must form maximum-integration parts and then snap those together into a Neothink puzzle. In order to build two mini-companies, three mini-companies, or more, he must be free of the tangled chains of split responsibilities. Therefore, he never delegates, never starts splitting responsibilities. He replicates. He *replicates* follow-through work into fully integrated entrepreneurial units — maximum-integration parts that he snaps together via the nitty-gritty-detail tracking reports into an easy-to-grasp puzzle-picture. He controls his full tail of follow-through responsibilities swiftly through his tracking reports. That Neothink mini-company structure gives him iron-grip control over all the work, all the details.

By snapping together his entrepreneurial units — his maximum integration units — into a Neothink puzzle-picture that he sees in one brief sitting, he acquires the control and time to soar ahead on his essence-responsibilities to build, build, build. Remember, the follow-through nitty-gritty details snap together in one Neothink sitting with his tracking reports. He knows everything — mind and body.

When he is ready, he can start a second mini-company by developing a new product and marketing it. Or, he might create a second mini-company by developing another marketing medium for an existing product. In either case, Neothink control makes building an empire within a Neothink company possible. The mini-company/power-tracking team is the second of two special tools that can evolve the average worker into a high-powered Neothink employee.

Synergy From Snapping Into The Neothink Puzzle

And let us not forget, a Neothink company such as I & O snaps together into a grand Neothink puzzle. The CEO studies the big picture and brings back into the maximum-integration parts synergistic advantages through the Essence Meetings. That synergy delivers advantages to each worker in the Neothink company. By becoming part of the larger, Neothink puzzle, one immediately benefits from the puzzle.

For example, as those at I & O build their mini-companies and snap into the larger I & O Neothink puzzle, Mr. Hamilton uses the big picture to create and elevate values and numbers. He creates and elevates values and numbers all week long, day and night; then he integrates and coordinates the mini-companies into those greater and greater realms of business. The synergy brings rewarding growth to each mini-company head.

Neothink Awaits Everyone

You must realize that being on the mini-day schedule brings advantages, but is not in itself a step into Neothink. The maximum-integration parts (forward-movement projects) must be snapped into the mini-day schedule through power-thinking. Neothink is NOT achieved until power-thinking becomes an integral part of the mini-day schedule. But now, in the Neo-Tech System, you can power-think forward-movement projects. Nothing beyond your own personal mysticism can hold you back from Neothink.

You are fortunate to be learning about Neothink. You have a head start on others. As more and more companies evolve beyond specialization through the integrated Neo-Tech System, more and more people will evolve beyond the following mode and advance into Neothink. Learn to use Neothink now. Get the jump on your competition.

SUMMARY

The Company-Capture Discovery is yours. You have entered the second dimension of Neothink; the power of the Neo-Tech System now begins to emerge. A start-up company begins with the mini-day/power-thinking team, and it grows into a strong company with the mini-company/power-tracking team. Your employees will come to work with purpose and mind/body harmony. No more split responsibilities can stop their progress. By pulling together mentally integrating responsibilities, you accomplish the division of essence for business, which is the division of labor taken to the next level of integrating the mind with the movement. That is the only way a movement can make the leap from a mechanical movement to a money-making movement.

You pull together the clusters of mentally integrating responsibilities to form the areas of purpose, fully integrated areas that become your wealth-pumps. Competent men and women drive forward their fully integrated areas with unbroken momentum. And they do not stop driving once their responsibilities are done. Their responsibilities no longer are ends in themselves...they are means to propel their businesses forward. The mini-companies never stop advancing and profiting.

Indeed, your start-up business must be divided into movements with money-making purpose — the shortest movements to drive forward wealth-creation, which is the division of essence. Mr. Hamilton went well below surface logic to discover those money-making movements in I & O, and now you can do the same in your start-up company. Then you are ready to move into the next dimension of wealth-creation — into the division of essence. Form your fully integrated mini-companies, each with their own piece of wealth-creation essence. The mini-company heads will drive profits forward, day in and day out.

In the early twenty-first century, traditional businesses will steadily evolve into Neo-Tech's division of essence just as manufacturers steadily evolved into Ford's assembly-line in the early twentieth century. Once you establish the division of essence through the mini-companies, and now that you can snap them all together into a mighty Neothink puzzle with the tracking reports, you become qualified to spread that division of essence all over the world, Volume Three, next.

After only two parts of the Grand Neothink Puzzle, notice that neither white-collar-hoax control nor mysticism-plagued conscious control can compete with Neo-Tech Control. The mysticism-plagued conscious mind is beginning to become ineffective as did the bicameral mind 3000 years ago (see front material). An evolution has begun. Man must now, one by one, leap to the Neothink mind.

Neo-Tech Control Launches Neothink

Once you isolate and then capture the physical movements, the proper division of labor (i.e., capture Neo-Tech Control), then you free the mind for forward-movement creative thinking, which leads to Neothink by using the special tools.

You did exactly that in the Self-Capture Discovery by isolating and capturing the physical movements of your job, the division-of-labor or mini-day schedule (i.e., capturing Neo-Tech Control of self), freeing your mind for forward-movement creative thinking or power-thinking (i.e., Neothink). Then you learned how to feed that power-thinking into the mini-days to race past your peers (i.e., the mini-day/power-thinking team).

You also did exactly that in the Company-Capture Discovery by isolating and capturing the money-making physical movements of your company, the proper mind/body division-of-labor or mini-company structure (i.e., capturing Neo-Tech Control of your start-up company), freeing your mind for forward-movement creative thinking or puzzle-building integrated thinking by snapping together the tracking reports (i.e., Neothink). Then, you learned how to feed that integrated thinking into the mini-companies to race past your competitors (i.e., the mini-company/power-tracking/Essence-Meetings team.)

You will now follow this same trend in the World-Capture Discovery by isolating and capturing the physical movement of *you*, the division of labor for the CEO (i.e., capturing Neo-Tech Control of the CEO), freeing your mind for forward-movement creative thinking (i.e., world-moving Neothink).

The secret at any level is to achieve an integrated, assembly-line-like physical-movement division of labor (i.e., Neo-Tech

Control) to give you the control and time for forward-movement creative thinking (i.e., Neothink). In turn, you will feed that forward-movement Neothink into the quick-action physical movements that get done. That is the secret to profit big.

Remember, with the Self-Capture Discovery, you first captured Neo-Tech Control over your job, then you moved into Neothink via the mini-day/power-thinking team. You poured your power-thinking, money-making projects into your action-unit mini-days. You moved through projects others never even dream of.

And now with the Company-Capture Discovery, you can capture Neo-Tech Control over your company, then you can move your entire company into Neothink via the mini-company/power-tracking team. Through Essence Meetings, you can pour your money-making advancements into your action-unit mini-companies. Your company will move through projects that other company heads never even dream of.

Again, that is the secret to leaping to Neothink and making big money. Now, turn the page, and let's go to the next level of Neothink and wealth creation.

Volume Three

The
World-Capture Discovery

Chapter Twenty-Two

Grand Puzzle Part Number Three:
THE WORLD-CAPTURE DISCOVERY

Let us see what is building from this Neo-Tech/Neothink Puzzle. In Grand Puzzle Part One you learned the Self-Capture Discovery: how to compile projects within your day-by-day schedule through establishing physical movements — that is, mini-days. With the mini-day/power-thinking team, you acquired the tool to move beyond the capacity of the traditional daily schedule. With the most basic scheduling limitations removed, you acquired the tool to handle vast arrays of details and projects. That first tool, the mini-day/power-thinking team, enabled you to handle the many details and integrations that come with starting your own business. You took your first step into Neothink.

Then in Grand Puzzle Part Two you learned the Company-Capture Discovery: how to compile wealth pumps within your Neo-Tech company through establishing physical movements — that is, mini-companies. With the mini-company/power-tracking team, you acquired the tool to move beyond the capacity of a traditional start-up company. With sophisticated limitations such as split responsibilities removed, you acquired the tool to handle a vast array of wealth pumps. That second tool, the mini-company/power-tracking team, enabled you to handle the many responsibilities that come with building an empire. You took your second step into Neothink.

Now in Grand Puzzle Part Three, you will learn the World-Capture Discovery: how to compile Neothink itself through establishing the physical movement of the person who sits atop the expanding empire — you. You will now take your third step into Neothink.

In this third puzzle part, you will acquire the tool to move beyond all competition. With a final traditional limitation removed, you enter full time into the Neothink dimension. That new dimension will propel your empire around the world.

Growth And Development

You can expect to build your company on physical movements, that is, establish a few mini-companies, within one year. Once you build your company on physical movements (i.e., mini-companies or wealth pumps), you stand on a mountain of leverage and strength. Now you can forge ahead with all that strength to capture the world; you can remove the final limitation that holds back nearly every CEO and company from soaring with the World-Capture Discovery. Breaking free from this final business limitation, the CEO discovers his physical movement. From atop his mountain of leverage and strength, he takes off and soars with unbroken momentum — soars all around the world. Consider that, in a few short years, I & O went from doing business only in America to doing business in 163 countries around the world through the Neo-Tech System.

Determining *your* physical movement as leading head of your company is going to take you on a radically new course. You discover that radically new course through the same process used in the Self-Capture and Company-Capture Discoveries: removing limitations, removing anything in the way of unbroken momentum. You must remove some final split responsibilities that pertain to the CEO.

But first, the company and its founder or CEO must grow to a certain level before he can actually evolve into the CEO physical movement and soar beyond his mountain of strength to capture the world. For, as his start-up company grows, the CEO must handle much of the day-to-day work himself. Not until the company reaches a certain size with secure income-generating mini-companies is the founder ready to evolve into the CEO physical movement and capture the world. Yet, he must be fully aware of the CEO physical movement in order to chart his own development and growth toward the World-Capture Discovery. ...Let us start by understanding his growth levels toward the CEO physical movement and the World-Capture Discovery. As you, the founder, build your start-up company with the Neo-Tech System, you and your company will grow through three levels:

THE THREE GROWTH-LEVELS
OF THE FOUNDER/CEO AND HIS COMPANY

The Level-One Founder/CEO and His Level-One Company:
The first growth-level requires starting and driving the infant
start-up business forward...compiling future projects into today's
work through the mini-day/power-thinking team. The level-one
CEO runs a small level-one business with one income source that
he personally handles. He does most of the work himself.

The Level-Two Founder/CEO and His Level-Two Company:
The second growth-level requires building the start-up
business...creating more business for current or new mini-
companies and replicating the new mini-companies. The level-
two CEO runs a small but growing level-two business with one
or more income sources, perhaps one or two mini-companies
generating income. He does most of the work of creating new
business. If he successfully creates new business, he eventually
replicates the responsibilities into an existing or a new mini-
company. The level-two CEO still does much of the work,
handles the crucial details, presses forward into potential new
business, potential new mini-companies. He also begins to
concentrate on the integrating and coordinating functions
explained in Chapter Eighteen, pushing his already established
business, his already established mini-companies, into forward-
movement essence work.

The Level-Three Founder/CEO and His Level-Three Company:
The third growth-level requires moving the business into new
realms...pushing forward the base: 1) the values, 2) the numbers,
3) the personnel, 4) the operations. Level three is the destination
the founder/CEO ultimately drives toward. The level-three CEO
runs a substantial business with a few to several mini-companies.
He has fully evolved into the integrating and coordinating
functions. Whereas he busily creates new business, he no longer
does the work of the business; he drives the business into new
realms and integrates and coordinates the mini-companies into
those new realms. He also nurtures and orchestrates the essence
progress of mini-company heads. He no longer replicates new

mini-companies. No longer financially dependent on new mini-companies, anyone who takes on a mini-company must develop it on his own, without the CEO replicating. The CEO does not need to replicate now. He gains more leverage pushing into new realms of business and pushing forward the established mini-companies.

The Level-Three Founder/CEO

Let us look more closely at your destination — the level-three CEO who can soar with the World-Capture Discovery:[1]

Business is founded on two essentials: 1) the values, and 2) the numbers (i.e., the dynamic interaction of values and numbers: market pressures, numbers, drive the product, values, to the marketplace and continue to elevate the product to, in turn, open wider and wider markets). Soon after the business starts, two other essentials quickly kick in: 1) the personnel, and 2) the operations (both ultimately driven by the numbers). Once an entrepreneur reaches the level-three CEO, operating a business with a few to several mini-companies, he will snap together the essence tracking reports and use that marketing/numbers Neothink picture to further drive forward the four essentials of his business: 1) the values, 2) the numbers, 3) the personnel, 4) the operations. In short, he creates and elevates the product and marketing into new realms, and he integrates and coordinates his mini-company heads into those new realms.

Only the founder, CEO, and movement heads (explained later in Chapter Twenty-Five) evolve into this third growth-level that

---

[1]The level-three CEO can capture the world through the discovery revealed in this section. Therefore, the World-Capture section addresses the level-three CEO. However, the level-one and level-two entrepreneurs can benefit by the radical breakthrough revealed in this section. In fact, the discovery revealed in this chapter moves the level-two entrepreneur into a level-three CEO and onto capturing the world with his business. Therefore, he must know the level-three CEO's physical movement and know more about his integrating and coordinating functions. Whereas the World-Capture section addresses the level-three CEO, the level-one and level-two entrepreneurs must read this section closely. At the end of this chapter, the level-one and level-two entrepreneurs will learn how to use the discovery to accelerate their own growth.

enables sweeping expansion of the company. Only they can drive forward the company as a whole into the World-Capture Discovery explained later in this section. For, the mini-company heads must concentrate on their specific businesses. They must DO the work of the mini-companies. They cannot embrace the wider integrations of the level-three CEO. For example, Mr. Hamilton does not *do* the marketing for Neo-Tech. That is done by the mini-company heads. But Mr. Hamilton moves forward the entire juggernaut into new realms of marketing. He creates and elevates and drives the products, the marketing, the personnel and operations into new realms.

Mr. Hamilton snaps together the essence tracking reports that show him the world-wide marketing results of Neo-Tech from several different mediums with several different testing approaches, in several different countries, languages, and cultures. From that Neothink view of the numbers, Mr. Hamilton elevates the value of Neo-Tech into new realms that, in turn, reveal new horizons of marketing. Mr. Hamilton sends his mini-companies into those entirely new realms of marketing.

Mr. Hamilton has evolved into the third growth-level with several established, income-generating mini-companies. From that mountain of strength, with the leverage of his creating-and-elevating, integrating-and-coordinating functions, he soars with the World-Capture Discovery, explained soon. ...But to soar and not fall, the level-three CEO must first know more about the creating-and-elevating/integrating-and-coordinating functions.

Creating-and-Elevating/Integrating-and-Coordinating Functions

The CEO who soars with the World-Capture Discovery exerts hard, Firestone-like thinking, integrated thinking, relentless power-thinking. His greatest time doing the creating, elevating, integrating and coordinating functions is spent in private — in concentrated thinking on the market-driven dynamic interaction between the values and the numbers. He must spend long, isolated hours creating and elevating the products and marketing programs. In short, he becomes a creator, nearly a full-time creator.

Mr. Hamilton spends long days creating Neo-Tech products

and elevating marketing programs into world-capture realms. He uses the numbers to guide him on how to elevate the values into new, world-capture dimensions, which eventually lifts the whole company, all the mini-companies, into new realms.

As Mr. Hamilton drives Neo-Tech products and marketing programs into new realms, I & O's presence spreads all over the world. Coordinating the mini-companies (via Essence Meetings) delivers crucial level-three world-capture leverage but is a minimal function (timewise) of the creating-and-elevating/integrating-and-coordinating functions. Mr. Hamilton needs long, isolated hours of concentrated thinking.

To better understand the creating-and-elevating/integrating-and-coordinating functions, perhaps an analogy can be made back to the collegiate football coach. He spends only a few hours once a week actually coordinating the players during the game. The majority of his time and work comes between games. He spends long hours studying plays, films, studying his team throughout practice, testing plays and strategies during practice. He is thinking. He spends long hours thinking and bringing all that information together. A major amount of his time is spent alone, without his team around him disrupting his concentration. He develops the stratagems to drive forward his team during the game...to coordinate his players into defeating the opponent.

Like the football coach, Mr. Hamilton spends long, isolated hours thinking and creating. The majority of his time is spent alone, without his employees around him disrupting his concentration. He develops the strategy to drive forward his company...to coordinate an army of mini-companies.

The majority of his time goes toward creating and elevating Neo-Tech and its marketing programs. Yet moving his creations and elevations of products and marketing programs to the quick-action mini-companies through his Essence Meetings brings world-capture leverage to Mr. Hamilton. His concentrated focus on creating and elevating Neo-Tech and its marketing programs is done with the leverage of driving forward an army of mini-companies. That explains why Mr. Hamilton never relieved himself of I & O (of market pressures, deadlines, responsibilities) to become just a writer and concentrate just on creating Neo-Tech literature. For, with level-three I & O and its mini-companies, he gains world-capture leverage by integrating and coordinating a whole business army into forward-march action. And under great market pressures, he snaps together, via the tracking reports, that army's marketing numbers to see a Neothink puzzle-picture and, in turn, to drive the value of Neo-Tech to yet greater heights — to world-capture heights.

Through his level-three business army and through his integrating and coordinating functions, Mr. Hamilton multiplies his power many times as he sends his Neo-Tech progress to anxiously awaiting marketing mini-companies all over the world. Then, that explosion of power completes a grand cycle: it implodes, gaining synergy as the Neothink tracking reports come racing back to him. That implosion cycle of numbers results in more deep thinking to further elevate Neo-Tech values, and another explosion cycle of Neo-Tech product, and then another implosion cycle of numbers, and so on. ...Through his business army and his creating-and-elevating/integrating-and-coordinating functions, Mr. Hamilton escalates his power. Through his level-three company of mini-companies, he stands on a mountain of strength and acquires the leverage needed to soar with the World-Capture Discovery. Through concentrated focus on the numbers and, in turn, deep thinking on the values, he is now ready to leap from his mountain of strength and fly. The integrating-and-coordinating functions are his wings needed to fly, not fall, from his mountain of strength.

Discovering YOUR Physical Movement

As you structure your company into its physical movements and eventually into mini-companies, you stand on a mountain of leverage and strength. As you evolve into a level-three CEO with a level-three company of mini-companies, you are ready to challenge your own integrated thinking. You are ready to discover YOUR physical movement to advance into full-time Neothink. You are ready to take the World-Capture challenge.

So first, let us determine YOUR physical movement as CEO. To do this, you must remove your split responsibilities. You must pull together your mentally integrating responsibilities, i.e., those responsibilities that integrate with your PURPOSE.

What is the purpose of the CEO? Remember from Chapter

251

Eleven in the Company-Capture section: the PURPOSE of business is to BUILD. Your purpose as CEO is to BUILD from the widest, Neothink perspective...different than anyone else in the company.

Your purpose is to push the whole business forward. Thus, you must push its base forward. You must build the four essentials: the values, the numbers, the personnel, and operations. As the founder and the widest integrator in your company, you must use the essence tracking reports from the mini-companies and study their numbers. You must use those numbers and hard, Firestone-like thinking to drive your company and its values into greater realms. But, as you build the values and numbers, you must learn how to expand the values and numbers to even greater realms by integrating and coordinating your mini-companies into the value-building and number-building process. To capture the world market, you must learn how to use the unique minds of others to orchestrate larger-than-life values and larger-than-life marketing of those values. That phenomenon happens through the division of essence.

Indeed, great companies became great because the founder reached beyond himself. The founder orchestrated the qualities of more and more people to create greater and greater values and dissemination of those values...just as Juan Trippe orchestrated thousands of people, from scientists to financiers, in order to create the jets and to capture the world with the jets.

Indeed, the founder or CEO's purpose is to build ever-better values and ever-growing distribution of those values. As founder, you must 1) use your company-wide Neothink perspective to personally create and elevate the values (i.e., product or service)...and use your Neothink perspective to personally advance the numbers (i.e., market penetration), and 2) use your Neothink perspective to integrate and coordinate the strengths of others into your value-building and market-building process.

Creating-and-Elevating/Integrating-and-Coordinating Functions

Remember, *you* created your company. *You* are the original creator. *You* are a creator.

The founder and CEO's area of purpose, his **physical movement** reduces to: *creating* and *elevating* values and the marketing of those values. To most effectively do this, he must also *integrate* and *coordinate* personnel and operations for greater and greater contribution and efficiency. With his company-wide Neothink perspective, he a) personally exerts long, isolated hours of intense concentration to *create* new products or *elevate* existing products (values) and to *create* new marketing programs or *elevate* existing marketing programs (numbers) in order to disseminate those values...then he b) *integrates* and *coordinates* those product enhancements and marketing enhancements back into his mini-companies; he expands the company's values and numbers by orchestrating others; he *integrates* and *coordinates* the *unique* capabilities of others into the ever-widening company plan...as Mr. Hamilton integrates and coordinates his mini-companies into ever-widening Neo-Tech dissemination.

The physical movement of the level-three founder or CEO is: *the creating-and-elevating/integrating-and-coordinating functions.* Anything that breaks the CEO from *creating* and *elevating* greater values and greater marketing of those values and *integrating* and *coordinating* his mini-companies is a split responsibility. His mentally integrating responsibilities are:

MENTALLY INTEGRATING RESPONSIBILITIES OF THE FOUNDER/CEO

* He studies the essence tracking reports to acquire a Neothink perspective of the company's numbers. He gains a company-wide Neothink integration of the marketing performance of the values/products via the numbers. He also acquires the broadest measurement of costs/effort to net, of the efficiencies of operations and personnel. Numbers...Neothink numbers.

* From his Neothink numbers perspective, he engages in market-driven product development/enhancement. He uses his Neothink numbers perspective as a guide to elevate product development into new realms, which in turn opens potential new marketing horizons. He uses his Neothink numbers perspective as a guide to elevate the marketing programs into those new horizons. He drives hard on this dynamic interaction between numbers and values.

* From his broadest measurement of costs/effort to net, he

focuses on operations and personnel. He drives hard to improve internal efficiencies and controls (operations) and to improve intensity, energy, integrated thinking and emotional integration with the company's goals (personnel).

(The first three responsibilities above represent *creating and elevating* the four essentials of business — the values, numbers, operations, and personnel. The next three responsibilities represent *integrating and coordinating* the four essentials of business.)

* He injects his product developments, marketing developments, operations developments, and personnel developments into the mini-companies (via Essence Meetings).

* He nurtures, integrates and coordinates others and their *unique* product developments, numbers/marketing developments, operations/internal-strength developments, and their emotional/ motivational developments into the company plan.

* He knows that numbers drive everything in business, and he sets the example of a focussed numbers man. He pushes the mini-company heads into their numbers. He drives the entire company through numbers; they drive their mini-companies through numbers.

His mentally integrating responsibilities are those broad responsibilities above that only he can handle; they converge on his purpose to build the base — the values, numbers, personnel, and operations of his company. (See Diagram Seventeen on the next page that illustrates the CEO's physical movement.) Any other responsibilities that creep into his day break his momentum and are split responsibilities. They must be removed. Most CEOs are overwhelmed with split responsibilities because of a deep-rooted, white-collar-hoax myth. Once that myth is removed, the level-three company can capture the world.

Uncovering The Myth

After you successfully build your company through the Company-Capture Discovery and reach the door of a level-three CEO, you must focus on the essentials of business. For, creating-

254

Diagram Seventeen

**The CEO's Physical Movement
Creating-and-Elevating/Integrating-and-Coordinating Functions**

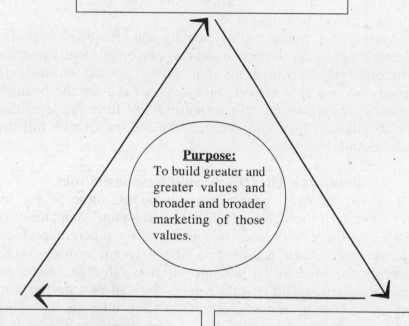

Neothink Perspective
(Time Spent Alone)
Snapping together the numbers — the essence tracking reports. Studying the numbers to drive forward the whole company.

Purpose:
To build greater and greater values and broader and broader marketing of those values.

Essence Meetings
(Meetings Held Once A Month)
Coordinating mini-company heads into those new marketing horizons. Also, nurturing their growth, their integrated thinking, and their own essence movement. Pushing them into their numbers and into their tracking reports to drive forward their mini-companies.

Driving Forward The Essentials of Business
(Major Time Spent Here Alone)
Integrated thinking used to elevate the values (via the numbers of the essence tracking reports) and to push those elevated values into greater marketing horizons. Also includes developing personnel and strengthening operations to move into those new marketing horizons.

255

and-elevating/integrating-and-coordinating the values, numbers, personnel, and operations pulls together the mentally integrating responsibilities that only you can handle. Creating-and-elevating/integrating-and-coordinating — *building* — the values (the products), numbers (marketing), personnel and operations into new realms now becomes your physical movement, the shortest and only movement to lift your company into the world-capture league. You will put all your effort, all your unbroken momentum into moving the base — the values, numbers, personnel, and operations — into new realms. Anything that breaks your momentum must be eliminated.

Anything that works against creating-and-elevating/integrating-and-coordinating the values, numbers, personnel, and operations — in other words, anything that works against *building the company* — is a split responsibility. As we did for the business, we must now remove all split responsibilities from the level-three CEO so you can lock into your movement and evolve full-time into Neothink.

Removing The CEO's Split Responsibilities

Your expanding company brings more and more people into entrepreneurial follow-through jobs and into mini-companies. The logistics of more and more people bring on inherent problems such as real estate, equipment, office room, morale issues, interruptions, inventory tracking, supplies, storage space, etc. Those problems, all in no-man's-land (i.e., all outside the mini-companies' tails of responsibilities), all fall on your lap. Those problems destroy your movement — your creating-and-elevating/integrating-and-coordinating functions.

Moreover, each person in your company no longer needs interruptions or much two-way communication with others, for all now run a fully integrated area, independent with no split responsibilities. Contrast that to the traditional companies where split responsibilities are abundant and everyone depends on interacting with others. Instead, those running their fully integrated areas and mini-companies, moving ahead with personal financial incentive, cannot afford to break their forward-movement, money-making intensity. They do not need or care to come to work. They could operate best in the isolation of their own homes.

Indeed, the human interaction in a company structure works against every individual forging ahead in his or her mini-company. But most destructive, the company, the place of work, destroys the CEO's physical movement: pure creating-and-elevating/integrating-and-coordinating functions — driving forward the values and numbers, personnel and operations. The place of work, with its many no-man's-land problems falling in the CEO's lap every day, destroys his intense concentration on elevating the business into new realms.

Radical Breakthrough

Everything you need to elevate your company into new realms is in your Neothink tools — the tracking reports. With well-done essence tracking reports in your hands, you (a level-three CEO) need no other information to drive your business into new realms. The tracking reports provide the numbers to drive the business. The numbers let you focus in private how to elevate the base — the marketing, the products, the personnel and operations — into new realms. The monthly Essence Meetings let you coordinate the mini-companies into those growing new realms. EVERYTHING ELSE breaks your momentum and prevents you from fully evolving into a Neothink mode.

The problems that fall in your lap daily in the company's building actually trap you in a thought-by-thought mode. You must deal with the problems one by one as they arise. They break your momentum. They are split responsibilities and act as integration blockers that prevent your power-reactor explosion into Neothink. You simply cannot evolve into the Neothink mode — even with the tracking reports in hand. You simply cannot focus on the larger super-integrated picture as you instead chase down the specific day-in and day-out problems. Imagine the massive integration needed to advance Neo-Tech, blocked completely as Mr. Hamilton became increasingly stunted by the day-to-day problems.

Now, think if you had no physical company: no building, no office space, no real estate, no congregation of people — only the tracking reports. With only the tracking reports, you would be free to evolve into the wide integrations of Neothink. For, you would be free of all no-man's-land problems. You would be free to integrate and concentrate. You would be free to create and elevate. Indeed, with only the tracking reports, you would be free to evolve into Neothink and leave behind mysticism-plagued thought-by-thought control.

The level-three CEO needs most of his time alone, with his tracking reports, without his company or employees around him. If you lift the traditional company structure — lift the company itself from the business — you are left alone in your office with only the tracking reports. That is all you need.

This radical new concept is called **a-company-without-a-company**. Here is Mr. Hamilton:

Mr. Hamilton
The Neo-Tech World Summit

"Company-without-a-company...its a very powerful concept. It could never have occurred if not for the first two major parts of this three-part Neothink puzzle. Without this commander-in-chief control, without having been able to break down the company into its division of essence, into mini-companies with their own essences that can expand with no limitations forever, without having the tracking reports to pull those essences together, without those discoveries, this powerful, company-without-a-company couldn't exist.

"The company-without-a-company is by far the most efficient system to run a company and to build an empire. You don't have all the limitations of people coming together...and the monster that grows from within the company itself. You don't have that. You have clean, independent mini-companies, independent galaxies with a lot of space around them out there performing their own essences. And yet, they're I & O. Very powerful. This is what can sweep across the world."

— Mark Hamilton

The Level-Three CEO

The Neo-Tech System's company-without-a-company gets the CEO (i.e., you) out of the company. The company-without-a-company frees you. It frees you to create. It frees you to do hard, Firestone-like thinking. It frees you from physically

258

disjointed tasks as you discover your smooth physical movement: you create and elevate, integrate and coordinate with unbroken momentum — the physical movement of the level-three CEO.

The Company-Without-A-Company

Your level-three company now consists of self-sufficient mini-companies with their tell-all essence tracking reports. Each mini-company operates independently. Each mini-company can operate out of separate locations such as that person's own home. With each mini-company head on the mini-day/power-thinking team working out of his or her own home, the productivity actually improves without the interruptions and commotions of a company office. Now that you have removed split responsibilities throughout the company, now that the mini-companies are tight, self-contained movements, those people depend on no one and are able to function best in the privacy of their own homes.

The Company Itself Becomes Obsolete

With the mini-companies and their tracking reports, the company itself becomes obsolete. Yet, "the company" is tradition. It makes a declaratory statement of the company's dependency on the men in the plush offices who "run the company".

Through the Neo-Tech System, we disengage the company.[1] The white-collar hoax at any level will have nowhere to go and look important...no plush offices to support prestigious appearances...no opportunity to craft fiduciary illusions. No, only driving forward profits — real profits — will count.

In a company building, an executive can come in and be well occupied all day long with the many things he can do. He will easily fill his day as justification for his hefty salary. But far too often, what he actually handles does little to push the business

---

[1]Certain companies or portions of certain companies may need to remain physically in one building. That scenario will be dealt with later in this Volume Three. If that scenario applies to your company, still read the next few pages closely to understand the unbeatable advantages of the company-without-a-company. For, all companies can capture those unbeatable advantages to become a company-without-a-company, even those companies that must remain together in one building, as explained later in this Volume Three.

forward.

People with mini-companies, however, get up in the morning and have nowhere to go and appear important, no place where they can fill their days, no place to look and feel busy while offering little if anything that pushes the business forward. When the people in a Neo-Tech business (in the company-without-a-company) wake up in the morning, the chips are down: either they push their mini-companies forward or they do not. If they do not, then they do not survive. No white-collar hoax could exist in a Neo-Tech business.

Neothink Power

The CEO (i.e., you) discovers full-time Neothink power. His mini-companies can work anywhere, even from their homes; they drive forward their performance, churn out profits...all on performance pay at no risk to you.

By snapping together the essence tracking reports, the level-three CEO in an hour or less switches into Neothink and knows in his head the status of every strength or weakness in his company. Observers from traditional businesses would be stunned by his brain power.

Absorbing the mini-companies' clusters of responsibilities — their essences — in rapid succession instead of being lost in one detail at a time as problems arise, the CEO — you — moves into full-time Neothink power. You have no more physically disjointed tasks breaking your concentration and momentum. You move ahead with unbroken concentration and momentum in your smooth physical movement. With the essence tracking reports, you see the whole puzzle — the whole business — in one sitting. You can make spectacular business maneuvers, both with the values and the marketing of those values. You can integrate ideas, tests, progress, new directions into your Neothink matrix faster than anyone else. Competition will seem slow and dull. ...Once you experience this full-time Neothink power, you evolve into another dimension. Once in that Neothink dimension, you can drive your company into new realms beyond anything you can imagine right now, realms that capture the world.

Level-Two Entrepreneurs To Prosper Immediately

Although the World-Capture Discovery addresses the level-three CEO who can use the company-without-a-company to capture the world, the level-two entrepreneur can profit from the company-without-a-company. In fact, the company-without-a-company offers him the fast-track ticket to building his level-two business to a level-three business and then to capturing the world.

First of all, the powerful World-Capture Discovery would have been impossible if not for the Company-Capture Discovery with its division of essence — its mini-companies and their essence tracking reports. Now remember, the level-one and level-two entrepreneurs or CEOs need to remain in a company office space because they are still doing much of the work themselves. Recall the three stages of the evolving replicating meetings: the nitty-gritty detail working meetings, the crucial detail meetings, and the essence-detail meetings (see Chapter Sixteen). The level-one and level-two entrepreneurs should keep the key personnel together in one office space, at least during the first two stages of the evolving replicating meetings. However, through the company-without-a-company format, the level-two entrepreneur can begin to expand through setting up low-risk, performance-pay mini-companies working from their homes on performance pay at little or no overhead to himself. Capital is a limited resource for him. The company-without-a-company becomes his easiest and least costly format for growth toward a level-three business.[1]

Moreover, by not expanding his company offices during growth, he remains focussed on progress. He avoids the trap most entrepreneurs fall into: becoming absorbed in the growing day-to-day problems. Indeed, speaking now in traditional terms of level-one being a small one-man operation, level-two being a business with several employees, and level-three being a multi-million-dollar business, most entrepreneurs never grow to level three. In their company offices every day, they are too busy

---

[1]Remember, the level-two entrepreneur has a growing business with perhaps one or two mini-companies. See page 247 to refresh your memory of the level-one, level-two, and level-three founders/CEOs.

running their level-two businesses. And the trap gets worse with growth. By contrast, through the company-without-a-company format, the level-two entrepreneur increasingly relieves himself from running his day-to-day business with growth. Instead, he increasingly concentrates on creating and elevating, integrating and coordinating.

The level-two entrepreneur with several employees often feels that no one working for him thinks; so he must do everything himself and cannot create or elevate the values and marketing of those values. And that is true: without the Company-Capture Discovery, those working for him will unlikely evolve beyond specialized thinking. Therefore, that level-two entrepreneur will remain trapped, unable to evolve into the creating and elevating, integrating and coordinating functions to move toward the level-three world-capture league.

It is important to realize: the stagnant level-two entrepreneur is absolutely right (and absolutely stuck) when he feels that no one working for him thinks — *really* thinks. In fact, most employees subconsciously sense they do not have to think as long as someone else runs the business and does the thinking. But put those same employees in their own mini-companies or entrepreneurial units, perhaps operating out of their own homes, and make them responsible for a bottom line...and they will think. They will think to survive, at first. Then, they will think to prosper, and they will love it! The level-two entrepreneur will then have a clear shot at his physical movement — at creating, elevating, integrating, and coordinating — at building the company.

The level-two entrepreneur or CEO can use the low-overhead company-without-a-company approach to safely build his business. Furthermore, the low-risk, low-overhead company-without-a-company keeps out the nonthinking following mode and, instead, builds an inherently strong company of thinkers. The precedent of low overhead and strong thinkers gives the entrepreneur the best of both worlds. The company-without-a-company is the best way to build a company from the early stages. And the company-without-a-company grows limitlessly...mini-companies form out of people's homes, all around the world, as with I & O.

Simplify

Chapter Eighteen exposed the myth that building an empire entails great complexity. Building an empire requires just the opposite: stark simplicity. The company-without-a-company washes away complexities. The company-without-a-company, with the mini-companies working from their homes submitting daily or weekly tracking reports, simplifies business. The company-without-a-company is the safest and fastest track to building an empire.

The remainder of the World-Capture section continues to address the level-three CEO, the reader's destination. However, the advantages apply to level-one and level-two entrepreneurs too. For example, the double-barreled advantages of the company-without-a-company in the next chapter apply to level-two and level-one entrepreneurs (but with some slight differences due to their different responsibilities). Now, turn the page to discover the double-barreled advantages of the company-without-a-company.

Chapter Twenty-Three

THE UNBEATABLE ADVANTAGES OF THE COMPANY-WITHOUT-A-COMPANY

The Company-Capture Discovery in Volume Two delivers several major advantages to business, culminating in two unbeatable advantages: First, the mini-companies fill the business with *thinkers* — integrated thinkers. Second, the essence tracking reports fill the entrepreneur or CEO with *Neothink*.

The World-Capture Discovery — the company-without-a-company — also delivers two unbeatable advantages:

Unbeatable Advantage #1: The company-without-a-company locks the CEO into his physical movement — into the creating-and-elevating/integrating-and-coordinating functions — and does so with *full-time* Neothink power so he can move the company into new realms that capture the world.

Unbeatable Advantage #2: The company-without-a-company eliminates the consumptive white-collar hoax and eliminates everything that does not converge on getting the money-making work done. The clean and efficient, low-risk Neo-Tech business can most safely and easily spread all over the world.

Double-Barreled Advantages

Mini-company heads work from their homes on performance pay at little risk and little overhead to you. No white-collar hoax can grow. Pay comes from performance pay — from getting the money-making work done. Everything else vanishes. ...With such a powerful, low-risk advantage, the Neo-Tech company can replicate profitable mini-companies all over the world.

And you, as CEO, collect their essence tracking reports and maintain a Neothink perspective of your company, which enables you to integrate and coordinate the world-wide business into new realms. Without the physical company and its split responsibilities holding you back, you are free to create and elevate, integrate and coordinate with unbroken momentum (your mentally integrating responsibilities, shown on pages 253 and 254).

265

Indeed, you are free to build your business.

The CEO — You — Move The Business Forward

Without "the company", the CEO has no choice but to focus fully on his physical movement. Without "a company" to occupy his time, he *must* get into the hard, Firestone-like thinking — into the alien world of integrated thinking. The human mind is more quickly drawn to the daily distractions of "a company" than to wide-scope integrated thinking. The drawing card of daily distractions creates the trap that stagnates most entrepreneurs. Without "a company", the entrepreneur or CEO can no longer fill his day with the many problems, activities, and no-man's-land details of "the company". In the company-without-a-company, the entrepreneur or CEO is pushed into integrated thinking. The human mind needs such a push.

Without the distracting company, the entrepreneur or CEO enjoys a Neothink picture of the whole business. By snapping together the essence tracking reports into the whole Neothink perspective, he sees how to move "the whole thing" forward. In other words, he sees exactly how to build his business.

Without "the company", the CEO functions in that Neothink mode full-time and becomes very powerful. That Neothink picture is how the most powerful business leaders succeed, from Henry Ford to Bill Gates. With that unbroken picture, they become more and more powerful with each passing month.

The company-without-a-company is your way to get their Neothink power. The overarching puzzle-picture remains unbroken by split responsibilities. You will drive on your physical movement full-time, your momentum never broken with day-to-day office problems. You will spend your time creating, elevating, integrating, and coordinating the values, numbers, personnel, and operations. Because of your Neothink perspective, you will be able to orchestrate more and more people — a whole business army of people — into more universal values and broader marketing of those values.

The Level-Three CEO's Mini-Days

As the founder or CEO grows with his company toward a level-three CEO running a company-without-a-company, he must evolve into creating, elevating, integrating and coordinating the values, numbers, personnel, and operations. He must effectively remove from his schedule doing other work (i.e., doing split responsibilities). To let him get away from split responsibilities, the company breaks down into the company-without-a-company, and the CEO's mini-day schedule breaks down into four basic movements: values, numbers, personnel, and operations.

Before we go through the four mini-days, you may recall in Volume One, The Self-Capture Discovery, Mr. Hamilton teaches you to make physical movements, not subjects, into mini-days. As the CEO evolves toward the level-three CEO, he will move more and more away from physically *doing* the work to creating, elevating, integrating, and coordinating the work. He will move more and more away from physical energy to mental energy. Physical activities tend to go away; long stretches of mental energy take over. Now, understand that exerting mental energy is actually a physical act. The creative mental energy spent developing values is physically different from the logical mental energy spent studying numbers. They physically work different parts of the brain. And the same is true for the mental energy spent on integrating and coordinating personnel and improving operations. Those four different categories physically require different mental energies making those four categories, indeed, four true physical movements and not subjects. You will actually *feel* the different mental energies as you work in each movement. They are the true physical movements throughout the day of the level-three CEO:

1. **Values:** Driven by market pressures, the CEO creates and elevates the products and advertising of those products. He uses his Neothink perspective of his company-wide marketing data as his guide. He often concentrates for long hours in private to create and elevate the values. Mr. Hamilton spends his values mini-day writing books, writing ad copy, and pushing into new projects such as potentially producing a full-length movie and establishing a Science Institute for research on anti-aging. (Author's note: The movie production and the Science Institute are Mr. Hamilton's latest undertakings, which are not referenced in the original edition of *The Neo-Tech System*.)

2. **Numbers:** Driven by market pressures, the CEO creates and elevates the marketing of the products. He uses his Neothink perspective from his company-wide tracking reports as his guide. He studies the company-wide numbers resulting from advertising tests and determines the story the numbers are telling him. He determines what further advertising tests need to be developed (to be developed later during his values mini-day). During the numbers mini-day, he studies/ calculates numbers — the accounting and marketing numbers. Numbers ultimately drive the entire company — the marketing, product/advertising development, operations, and personnel. He studies/calculates numbers/efficiencies in all areas of the company, including the numbers as they pertain to operations and to personnel (costs/efforts to net).

3. **Personnel:** The two essentials upon which business is conceived are 1) values (products) and 2) numbers (marketing and profitability). But a third essential of business comes quickly with growth: 3) personnel. Level-three CEO's need this mini-day of integrating/coordinating personnel.

   For example, Mr. Hamilton spends all of his values mini-day in private, writing foundation literature in I & O or developing new product ventures, and he spends all of his numbers mini-day in private studying the numbers not only of marketing, but of operations, finances, and accounting. Therefore, he must separate into its own movement his integrating and coordinating the company as a whole: the mini-company heads. He must specifically integrate and coordinate the personnel into his numbers/ values progress.

   He must also develop his personnel, help motivate them into sustained heightened passion — into the Power Approach (taught in the Appendix). He concentrates on removing following-mode mysticism (see front material) and rewarding integrated thinking. He must set standards, enforce the drive for completion, push them into integrated thinking and into the numbers, then integrate and coordinate their numbers/values progress into the company plan. He does this through the daily essence reports and the monthly Essence Meeting.

During this mini-day, he takes his progress on creating and elevating values and numbers and looks at it in the wider perspective of integrating the personnel with those developments and coordinating them to drive the company forward.

Recently (since his mini-day schedule on pages 272-273), Mr. Hamilton has devoted an extended personnel mini-day on Mondays, 2:00 p.m. until 6:00 p.m., to a meeting among his key personnel. He uses that weekly mini-day to integrate and coordinate key personnel at I & O, from digging into specific nitty-gritty details to covering the sweeping essence issues.

4. **Operations:** A fourth essential of business comes with the conception of the business: operations. In Volume One, the operations mini-day, remember, corralled the nitpick work into one movement: the operations of management. Nitpick work should not plague the level-three CEO who has properly replicated his mini-companies, although he still must integrate and coordinate some *crucial* details via his in-basket, which might be his fax machine. Because that nitpick operations is follow-through work and not forward-movement essence work, the level-three CEO shrinks his in-basket portion of the mini-day as much as possible. Most of the nitpick business operations now occur within the mini-companies themselves. Thus, most of the CEO's nitpick operations can be kept to a minimum as he focuses on the forward-movement essence work of operations: **internal strength**.

The internal strength of his company is a powerful essential of business that not only enables a company to grow, but sometimes launches a company into new realms...such as the operations breakthroughs of Ford Motor Company that launched car production into the assembly-line and mass production. The CEO must focus on the essence of operations — the internal strength of the company. Examples of internal-strength work include:

computerizing the business, strengthening controls and efficiencies, automating operations (if more cost effective), developing and improving key operations manuals, developing and strengthening accounting procedures, data procedures, tracking reports. ...The CEO's Neothink perspective of the numbers gives him the insights to discover and build internal strength.

(Note: Turn the page to see Mr. Hamilton's level-three CEO mini-day schedule, pages 272-273.[1])

The Neo-Tech CEO

First, remember unbeatable advantage #1 of the World-Capture Discovery: The company-without-a-company locks the CEO into his essence — into the creating-and-elevating/integrating-and-coordinating functions — and does so with *full-time* Neothink power so he can move the company into new realms that capture the world.

Without "the company" and without CEO split responsibilities, the level-three CEO drives the company's values and the marketing of the company's values into new realms through his mini-day schedule, an ongoing dynamic interaction between the

---

[1]The level-two entrepreneur should establish the four mini-days above among his other needed mini-days, even if he just assigns the above mini-days once a week for now. That keeps him focussed on the four essentials of his business, and he begins exercising those mental energies. As he evolves toward a level-three CEO, he will increase his time with the four mini-days above and decrease his time with his other mini-days. Eventually, the above four mini-days will take over and become his only mini-days.

The level-one entrepreneur also needs to be acutely aware of the four essentials of his business. He needs to develop a dynamic interaction between the numbers and values. He should establish a numbers mini-day and a values mini-day, even if just once a week for now, even if he does not know what to do during those two mini-days right now. Eventually, he will learn how to drive ahead in those mini-days. As he evolves toward a level-two entrepreneur, he will put more time into those two mini-days and, with growth, he will introduce into his schedule the other two mini-days of personnel and operations. (Of course, the level-one entrepreneur already has an operations mini-day, but not at the essence-building level.)

numbers (i.e., the marketing numbers) and the values (i.e., copywriting/advertising/product development). He creates and grows values. He puts the products and advertising through ongoing marketing tests. He studies the results. Based on those results, he goes back to the values and advertising to elevate their values to the customer. ...Every day this dynamic interaction between values and numbers continues through his mini-days. With such intense focus on values and numbers, the business grows. He gains tremendous leverage as he a) integrates and coordinates the entire work force into building the values and numbers, and b) develops the company's internal strength.

Many CEOs Mistakenly Pass Off Their Responsibilities

Now, remember unbeatable advantage #2 of the World-Capture Discovery: The company-without-a-company eliminates the consumptive white-collar hoax and eliminates everything that does not converge on getting the money-making work done. The clean and efficient, low-risk Neo-Tech business can most safely and easily spread all over the world.

White-collar-hoax CEOs as well as many, many innocent, unsuspecting CEOs, lose touch with the values and the numbers. Many CEOs simply supervise others. For example, they supervise...

* Research-and-development funds
* Product-development teams
* Advertising agencies
* Accountants and statisticians
* Marketing departments

Many CEOs mistakenly pass off the numbers-and-values responsibilities to others. Big companies can get away with this form of passing off hard, Firestone-like thinking. But small companies cannot survive that way. The common myth that someone else can do the values/numbers for you comes from man's bicameral roots (see front material). The company, big or small, will eventually decline.

Moreover, by passing off values and numbers to specialized departments or agencies, the CEO separates values and numbers, which is eventually fatal in business. The dynamic interaction between values and numbers disintegrates. The departments or

271

The Neo-Tech System

Diagram Eighteen
Level-Three CEO Mini-Day Schedule

1988 NOVEMBER 1988
S M T W T F S
          1 2 3 4 5
6 7 8 9 10 11 12
13 14 15 16 17 18 19
20 21 22 23 24 25 26
27 28 29 30

from **NOVEMBER 14**

MONDAY, NOV. 14 319/47	TUESDAY, NOV. 15 320/46	WEDNESDAY, NOV. 16 321/45
8	8 *Values*	8
8:15	8:15 *(product devl.)*	8:15
8:30	8:30	8:30
8:45	8:45	8:45
9 / The Alternative	9 / The Alternative	9 - The Alternative
9:15	9:15 / Fix CEO mini-day portion	9:15
9:30	9:30	9:30
9:45	9:45	9:45
10	10	10
10:15	10:15	10:15
10:30	10:30	10:30
10:45	10:45	10:45
11	11 Calls & Letters (if needed)	11
11:15 / Letter to Neodata	11:15 / Rod S. → get copy of helio-	11:15 - RH → mailing lists to sur-
11:30 Potential explosive growth	11:30 centric ad & desktop radio test	11:30 vivors (eg widows, widowers)
11:45 Call TJ	11:45 / Letter to David Florence	11:45
12	12 *Values*	12
12:15	12:15 *(copywriting)*	12:15
12:30	12:30	12:30
12:45 / 59.95 NTC laser cut-off	12:45 / Wright Publishing memmo	12:45 / 9.95 space ad : Mind-
1	1 / Newspaper edits	1 Capture → 1 pg
1:15 / GE memmo NTC mailing	1:15 - Radio & space shotgun	1:15 / Newspaper edits
1:30 -	1:30 blitz letter	1:30 / 9.95 space ad : LTBW
1:45 / Look @ ½ hr. TV ad	1:45	1:45 2 pg spread
2	2 *Personnel*	2
2:15	2:15	2:15
2:30	2:30	2:30
2:45 / Prepare Mkt Matrix Meeting	2:45 - Personnel Motivation	2:45 / Skim Ed Burnett's
3	3 progress → techniques	3 new book for any techniques
3:15 / Prepare Essence Meetings	3:15	3:15 that should get implemented
3:30 / SR · TJ space / ridealong · RH	3:30 / Break down job responsi-	3:30 / Prepare Essence Meetings
3:45 · Mike → future alcohol	3:45 bilities of Z program < GT	3:45 · MT 9.95 · GT · RW · RS #'s limit
4	4 *Numbers*	4
4:15 / Final #'s on TR-1	4:15	4:15
4:30 / Make 1's on 9.95 program	4:30 - Meeting w/ MT on TR-10's	4:30 / Ratio accounting TR
4:45 / FE = w/ royalty & w/ 20% RE	4:45	4:45
5 / BE value per name @	5 - Update TR-10's	5 · Develop internal auditing
5:15 same as current program	5:15	5:15 controls CT invoice area
5:30 but probably more	5:30	5:30
5:45	5:45 *Dinner*	5:45
6	6	6
6:15 / Gym	6:15 - Run	6:15 - Gym
6:30	6:30	6:30
6:45	6:45	6:45
7	7 *Balancing*	7
7:15	7:15 (temporary test to monitor)	7:15
7:30	7:30	7:30
7:45 / Study back-end mailings	7:45 / ½ hour TV ad → edit (+ audio?)	7:45 - Brochure book
8 / Can anything be boosted	8 · Start from scratch	8
8:15 before end of year?	8:15	8:15
8:30	8:30 / Marketing Matrix Meeting	8:30 / Essence Meeting Prep.
8:45	8:45 / Preparation	8:45
9	9 *Operations*	9
9:15	9:15	9:15
9:30 / Basket	9:30 - Basket	9:30 - Basket
9:45 - 9.95 → Printers · Ridealong → printer	9:45	9:45

◄ Clip for Current Week

272

Diagram Eighteen
Level-Three CEO Mini-Day Schedule

to **NOVEMBER 20**

| 1988 DECEMBER 1988 |
| S M T W T F S |
| 1 2 3 |
| 4 5 6 7 8 9 10 |
| 11 12 13 14 15 16 17 |
| 18 19 20 21 22 23 24 |
| 25 26 27 28 29 30 31 |

THURSDAY, NOV. 17 322/44	FRIDAY, NOV. 18 323/43	SATURDAY, NOV. 19 324/42
8	8	8
8:15	8:15	8:15
8:30	8:30	8:30
8:45	8:45	8:45
9 - *The Alternative*	9 - *The Alternative*	9 - *The Alternative*
9:15	9:15	9:15
9:30	9:30	9:30
9:45	9:45	9:45
10	10	10
10:15	10:15	10:15
10:30	10:30	10:30
10:45 ↓	10:45 ↓	10:45
11	11	11
11:15 - *Call TJ*	11:15 - *Call RH*	11:15
11:30 - *Edit letters*	11:30	11:30
11:45	11:45	11:45
12	12	12
12:15	12:15	12:15
12:30	12:30	12:30
12:45 - *3rd party "C" memo*	12:45 - *NT audio tape test*	12:45
1	1	1
1:15 - *Special PR letter to send*	1:15 *Tom Phon memo*	1:15
1:30 *1week before 1st mailing BE*	1:30 - *Airline pilot memo*	1:30
1:45	1:45	1:45
2	2	2
2:15	2:15	2:15
2:30	2:30	2:30
2:45 - *Hold essence meeting*	2:45 - *Hold essence meeting*	2:45
3 *w/ space media*	3 *w/ direct mail*	3
3:15 *bantam co.*	3:15 *bantam co.*	3:15
3:30	3:30	3:30
3:45	3:45	3:45
4	4	4
4:15	4:15	4:15
4:30 - *Read DM chapter on mailing*	4:30 - *Bantam - co. financial*	4:30
4:45 *accounting → reasons for DM tool*	4:45 *projection*	4:45 ↓
5 *WH → do accounting on cost*	5 - *FR-1 essence report*	5
5:15 *for expansion: test lists*	5:15 *review*	5:15 *The Brochure Book*
5:30	5:30	5:30
5:45	5:45	5:45
6	6	6
6:15 - *Run*	6:15 - *Gym*	6:15
6:30	6:30	6:30 ↓
6:45	6:45	**SUNDAY, NOV. 20 325/41**
7	7	
7:15	7:15	*AMS mechanicals*
7:30	7:30	
7:45 *"Ostracize Matrix" ad*	7:45 - *Finalize MKT Matrix*	*The Alternative*
8	8 *meeting*	
8:15	8:15	↓
8:30	8:30	
8:45	8:45	*Finalize Essence Meetings*
9	9	
9:15	9:15	*Mini-Day / Power-Thinking*
9:30 - *Basket*	9:30 *Basket*	*Basket*
9:45	9:45	AT-A-GLANCE®

agencies become too specialized, too unintegrated with the big picture. They become less and less effective in comparison to the Juan-Trippe-like, fully integrated Neo-Tech entrepreneur. Remember, the values and numbers are part of the CEO's mentally integrating responsibilities. The white-collar-hoax CEO passes off because he looks for the easy way to fleece money from unsuspecting investors and stockholders. Other honest CEOs pass off because they unknowingly avoid hard, Firestone-like integrated thinking.

On paper, a company structure broken into departments looks good. In reality, no one else, not even layers of smart college graduates, can do the CEO's job of advancing the base — the values, numbers, operations, personnel — for him.

The CEO cannot pass off the creating-and-elevating/integrating-and-coordinating functions if the business is to grow and to survive the future. A CEO may properly use many people as Juan Trippe did, just as long as the CEO himself is integrating and coordinating them into new realms. For, he must personally do the integrated thinking to drive forward the values, numbers, personnel, and operations into those new realms. Again, those are his mentally integrating responsibilities.

Often, when a fortunate young business experiences success, the founder gets so busy running his company that he loses touch with his first two mini-days: the dynamic interaction of numbers and values. He steadily brings in layers of management to ineffectively do his mentally integrating responsibilities while he is too busy running the company. At that point, long-term growth stops, and he does not even know it.

That entrepreneur innocently does not understand his mentally integrating responsibilities — his proper physical movement. By understanding the CEO's physical movement — the creating, elevating, integrating, and coordinating functions — the Neo-Tech CEO can properly establish his mini-days. He can drive forward the values, numbers, personnel, and operations with unbroken momentum and eventually capture the world, for now there is no company to bog him down. Instead, the company-without-a-company eliminates his split responsibilities. Snapping together his Neothink tools — the tracking reports — he acquires a Neothink big-picture perspective from which to drive the business forward. Now he can exercise effective integrated thinking — elevating the values and the marketing of those values as well as coordinating the personnel and the efficiency of operations.

The Explosive Neothink Company

Independent mini-companies working from their homes on performance pay wash away all the activities that do not converge on getting the work done. In the traditional company, the white-collar hoax nurtures an internal monster of activity that does not converge on getting the work done. The company-without-a-company washes away that bureaucratic activity. The company-without-a-company, free of impurities, has the potential to explode into the Neothink company with mini-companies operating all around the world. The CEO controls that Neothink explosion through the tracking reports.

Hose Out The Internal Monster

Certain companies or portions of certain companies may need to remain, for different reasons, physically in one building. Those businesses that must remain physically together can still create the effect of breaking down the company into a company-without-a-company in order to capture its double-barreled advantages. Those businesses can still wash away all activities that do not converge on getting the work done. Those businesses can still wash away that internal monster. With some simple formatting, those businesses can remain physically together and still be a company-without-a-company. Here is how:

First, the internal monster of activity that does not converge on getting the work done grows through supervisory activity. Supervising through management layering removes accountability and responsibility from where it belongs — from the person doing the job. Instead, the person doing the work becomes specialized, just doing what he is told. If he were fully and financially accountable for his performance, on the other hand, he would drive his job forward and do it better than anyone else by using integrated thinking. Instead, in most companies he remains specialized and powerless. All the power goes to the supervising manager who does not do the work.

With full self-responsibility, most employees will mature and grow into integrated, self-motivated forces. With supervisors or layers of management, workers are held back from taking more responsibility. They do not grow and mature, and instead, they stay specialized — just doing what they are told.

Supervising through management layering gives the responsibility and power to a person NOT *doing* the work. Job supervising and management layering are not nearly as effective as the fully accountable mini-companies.

The company-without-a-company removes the formal structure — the supervisory power. The internal monster gets washed away. Each mini-company becomes its own entity and answers to no one but performance, clearly reflected in the tracking reports. In other words, management layering gets hosed out of the company-without-a-company. Only the healthy, integrated thinkers running independent mini-companies remain. The lone individual running his own mini-company holds full responsibility for his success or failure. He alone confronts the decisions, the marketplace. Nothing can beat the strength of the lone wolf, especially when the CEO coordinates a pack of such survivors.

Once a business removes management layering — those layers of supervisory positions — then the workers converge on one thing: survival/success. They converge on getting the work done. By hosing out layers of management, the lean-and-mean company-without-a-company becomes the most effective and least risky growing business. Overhead plunges. The Neo-Tech business can operate out of the same building, yet function as a company-without-a-company.

Psychologically speaking, "the company" signifies that something exists in business "bigger" than the individuals. So the average person assumes that something "bigger" than himself and his coworkers *must* run "the company", allowing the modern-day white-collar hoax to get unchecked control of the company in order to hoax everyone — to become that something "bigger" than the individuals themselves, that mysterious something "bigger" that "runs the company". The white-collar hoax will eventually destroy the company.[1]

---

[1]This timeless book was written in the 1980s. Now, in the twenty-first century, we have seen the manifestation of Mr. Hamilton's prophetic warnings of the white-collar hoax.

In the Neo-Tech System, *each individual* runs a piece of the business himself, builds his own essence, integrates his own decisions, feels his own responsibility, knows his own accountability, and performs his own interaction with the marketplace.

Hose Out Distracting Activity

Activity that does not converge on getting the work done can innocently develop in the company-without-a-company that operates out of the same building. For example, personality conflicts, scheduling problems to use equipment, storage problems, neatness problems, maintenance problems...a whole myriad of no-man's-land problems begin to occur that end up on the CEO's desk. But that situation, too, can be corrected. Here is how:

The secret is to remove all common property in the company. Separate the physical areas of the building. Assign full responsibility to the mini-companies, including equipment. That responsibility involves everything, even maintenance. At I & O, a mini-company must work independently, just as any business. A person must determine when profitable to purchase a piece of equipment such as a photocopier or a desktop computer, either out of his own performance pay or out of his mini-company's funds.

In the meantime, he cannot use the equipment of another mini-company, unless the other mini-company gets compensated for taking on the responsibility to schedule and maintain its equipment for others. If he cannot efficiently use another mini-company's equipment, then he will need to use outside services as any entrepreneur.

No supervisory positions. No common property. That almost hoses out all the problems that do not converge on getting the work done. One more obstacle must be washed away:

Hose Out Cancer Seeds

The cancer seeds as explained in the Personnel-Capture section (see Appendix) must go. When a gathering of people exists, the cancer seeds stir up activity that does not converge on getting the work done. No supervisory positions, no common property, no cancer seeds. Although in the same building, the company graduates into the company-without-a-company. In a sense, nothing is "connected", except through the tracking reports and Essence Meetings.

No More External Authority

The company-without-a-company is a company without something "bigger" than individual performance...without something "bigger" that must "run the company". Not a single responsibility exists that requires something "bigger" than individual performance. For, that something "bigger" that "runs the company" amounts to a harmful internal monster of unnecessary activity or worse: namely the fraud-driven white-collar hoax.

In the Neo-Tech company, the COMPANY becomes the INDIVIDUALS. The company-without-a-company is the company of individuals. And each individual converges on getting the work done.

In I & O's situation, Mr. Hamilton leases an office building and puts several of the follow-through workers together and a couple of his mini-company heads. Yet, those follow-through workers and mini-company heads still operate as their own self-contained galaxies with nothing connecting or intersecting them. They are, in essence, their own sovereigns. I & O also has mini-company heads and follow-through workers around the world.

Spread all over the world or together in one building, the company-without-a-company leaves the traditional business structure uncompetitive.

The Underlying, Key Concept Behind This Discovery

The division of labor brought major benefits to manufacturing, the biggest breakthrough coming in the early part of the 1900s with the ultimate division of labor found in Henry Ford's spectacular creation of the assembly-line. Manufacturing boomed into mass production as costs of living plunged and standards of living soared. Indeed, the division of labor applied famously to dividing factory work into jobs of physical labor, such as an assembly-line worker driving in rivet after rivet. Of course, those

278

physical jobs of labor have been increasingly taken over by robotics today.

The assembly-line was a world-altering breakthrough for manufacturing, which was purely physical work offering raw jobs of labor. The assembly-line jobs left out the mind because there was no thinking in the raw, physical jobs of labor, which is why robotics have taken over most assembly-lines.

Whereas, the division of labor launched *manufacturing* into mass production, the division of labor has been erroneously applied to *business*. Business and its jobs transcend raw physical labor (such as manufacturing) and demand man's most powerful tool — his mind.

Entrepreneurs and CEOs erroneously attempt to apply the division of labor to business. Yet, the division of labor as they know it really applies to physical labor only, which is not a real division of the business's jobs because such a division either leaves out the mind or, where the mind is included, the thinking is terribly limited by specialization. The accountant in the accounting department, for example, can never do what the mini-company head can do by personally integrating the accounting...right in his money-making marketing program.

When the proper division of labor is finally discovered in business, it will be as spectacular a breakthrough as the assembly-line was for manufacturing. What is needed is a breakthrough that integrates the physical responsibilities and mental responsibilities into common money-making purposes, which are the shortest movements to making money, the proper division of labor of *business*. That description of the proper division of labor for *business* is exactly what the division of essence is.

The division of essence — the Neo-Tech System — will become as important for business in the early 21st century as the assembly-line was for manufacturing in the early 20th century.

In fact, the division of essence will take yet a leap further because that proper division of labor is what enables the evolution into the company-without-a-company, which sends the founder or CEO — sends *you* — into full-time Neothink. With full-time Neothink, "little ol' you" truly will capture world markets.

Now, you must learn how to protect your business and the wealth you build.

279

Chapter Twenty-Four

FREEDOM AND PROSPERITY

The Next Dimension of Living

You have seen the steps that need to be taken through the Self-Capture, Company-Capture, and World-Capture Discoveries to reach the level-three CEO and evolve into full-time Neothink. Once you build your company-without-a-company through Neothink, you will discover something that could never be felt by or described to a mysticism-plagued conscious-mode person...perhaps similar to the feeling those bicameral men 3000 years ago experienced as they evolved into the conscious mind (see front material). They knew they had entered a whole new realm of control and competence. They could not describe the experience to a bicameral person. They knew their lives would be forever radically different — their lives would be full of self-controlled adventures that could never be experienced as bicameral, nature-controlled men. Life could have passed, never knowing the whole new realm of living. The bicameral men around them simply could not know the incredible feeling.

Once you evolve into Neothink, the feeling must be similar, but even grander. For, Neothink is the next evolution of man: it is an entire new realm of living...an entire new world of control, power, competence, wealth, and adventure.

Dump All Who Waste Your Time

In this next dimension of Neothink, suddenly you see through all hoaxes that were beyond your mysticism-plagued, conscious-mind comprehension before. You see not only the white-collar hoax, but all hoaxes that have usurped your money, happiness, and choices throughout your life. (To understand these terms, go back and skim through the front material.)

Quickly you see that like "the company", "the country" — the politicians' and bureaucrats' claim to power— only hurts the act of living and building wealth. Like "the company", "the country" indicates something beyond individual performance, that some "higher force" is needed. Yet, breaking down the daily act of living and building wealth...down to fundamentals, no valid responsibility of living or building wealth can ever require some higher force than individual performance. That "higher force" that "runs the country" is a political hoax.[1]

Indeed, "the country" signifies that something exists in society above the individuals, above its citizens. So the average person assumes that something "above" himself *must* run "the country", allowing the political hoax to hoax everyone — to become the external authority, to become that ruling class "above" the individuals, to become that something "above" that "runs the country". The political hoax will eventually destroy the country. But, the Neo-Tech System will rescue the country as *each individual* runs his life himself through his creative contributions to society.[2]

Having disengaged into a company-without-a-company with mini-companies operating from people's homes around the neighborhood or around the world, the next move is swift and easy: **a company-without-a-*country*.** For, once your business disengages into a company-without-a-company, this next puzzle part happens almost automatically. Nothing is left for politicians and bureaucrats to threaten or usurp. The neocheaters[3] control you no longer, their illusions washed away with Neo-Tech. You and your business become free to create values for society and generate wealth for yourself.

The Neo-Tech System brings you protection from local and national governments, for the Neo-Tech System allows you to replicate the system across the world, out of their reach.

---

[1]When *The Neo-Tech System* was first published in 1985, people were not yet ready to understand the white-collar hoax. Not until nearly two decades later, with the unforgiving examples of Enron, WorldCom, Global Crossings and others, could the people grasp the white-collar hoax. And now, people still do not grasp the political hoax, but they will.

[2]To see how America would function without the political hoax or the white-collar hoax, see *The Neo-Tech World* by Mark Hamilton, 850 pages.

[3]Neocheaters are explained in Mark Hamilton's other major work *The Neo-Tech World*. Briefly, neocheaters represent the lethal breed of invisible cheaters who are hidden by illusions of trust and respect. Neocheaters make up the white-collar hoax and political hoax.

Consider the large company International Telephone and Telegraph (ITT). In the 1950s, it was a U.S. company that owned the Cuban telephone system. When Castro's government nationalized the telephone system in 1961, ITT switched to a Neo-Tech-System-like international focus. Over the next nine years, ITT went from $930 million in sales to $8 billion and became the world's largest conglomerate.

Coca-Cola established an international Neo-Tech-System-like business ever since its beginnings, with less than 30% of its sales now coming from the United States (figure updated). If the Coca-Cola company were to have problems with any government, including the United States, the threat would be a fraction of what it would be if all sales resided in that country, under that government.

Both companies focused on the international and became huge organizations.

Because of the management discoveries that have been made in the Neo-Tech System, from the mini-day to the mini-company moving into the company-without-a-company, the Neo-Tech System puts you in the prime position to make a move — a switch on management focus. All the discoveries are in place; the mini-companies and tracking reports make things extremely manageable. The mini-companies break down the Neo-Tech business into the ultimate division of labor, which is the revolutionary division of essence, so easily manageable through the essence tracking reports.

The Neo-Tech business is all set up to go international while having everything run smoothly in the U.S. and abroad. The U.S. becomes a self-contained unit that can quickly regenerate itself no matter what the neocheaters do. That means you can focus on a worldwide blitzkrieg and move into the World-Capture Discovery.

One major reason this globalization is so important is the protection it brings your business. You can now build wealth without any neocheater taking it away again. Let's face it: successful people need protection from their own governments, *even in America*. We have all seen the notorious IRS-Abuse Senate hearings and the subsequent IRS-Horror-Stories in the 1990s, for example. We have all seen the Justice Department's repeated attempts to bring down Microsoft in the new century. The more you look, the more you will see the American government taking down Americans and their American companies. So, even if you do not understand the political hoax, pay close attention to the protection the Neo-Tech System offers you.[1]

The Collapse Of The Hoax: The Rise Of The Average Man

With the Neo-Tech/Neothink company, the white-collar hoax and its soul-mate political hoax will come crashing down as the working class rises to wealth and power through Neo-Tech and Neothink. The rise of the working man is now possible through the turnkey Neo-Tech System. The average working man, woman and youth will move onto his or her long-deserved road to the good money.

A company-without-a-company/without-a-country launches you and your loved ones beyond the reach of neocheaters. With Neothink, you truly step beyond all limitations. You efficiently create an unstoppable wealth-generating force made up of independent mini-companies operating out of homes or offices, scattered across the world. Yet you snap them together into one Neothink picture through Neothink tracking reports. From your Neothink perspective, you integrate and coordinate your mysticism-free juggernaut to capture the world market.

By defining the money-making movements of your company, then initiating the mini-companies, then separating them into a company-without-a-company, no mini-company survives without generating business and values. No white-collar-hoax executive can get started. The chips are down — every person working for you produces, or he does not last.

Through the Neo-Tech System, you can become a force that is everywhere, yet nowhere. Neo-Tech mini-companies exist around the world, yet no neocheater can pinpoint who, where, or what country the company "belongs to". No one can stop, usurp, shut down, or harm your business. For, by taking the leap into Neothink, Neo-Tech/Neothink businesses become the

---

[1]Mr. Hamilton added the examples in the above paragraph after the original Neo-Tech printing back in the mid-80s.

strongest, most integrated forces on Earth.

With Neo-Tech, you can forever protect yourself, your family, your empire. The Neo-Tech/Neothink company is the company of the future — a future free of mysticism, free of limitations...a future full of wealth, full of happiness. Nothing can stop the Neo-Tech men and women. The future is going to be classic, and it is going to be beautiful. The future belongs to Neo-Tech.

Mark Hamilton's Journal
December 9th

Imagine the competitive edge this all-work company has over other companies. Imagine those other companies, some run by the white-collar hoax, with their split-responsibility mazes. Indeed, imagine those diseased companies trying to compete against the healthy Neo-Tech System streamlined with hard-driving entrepreneurs, each digging into profit-generating essence.

Mark Hamilton's Journal
January 4th

The white-collar as well as the political hoax will be outcompeted by the Neo-Tech System and its the company-without-a-company/without-a-country. Just hearing about the company-without-a-country almost immediately breaks one's thinking into new realms...well beyond the government's "territory of illusions" built through force and fear.

Mark Hamilton's Journal
January 29th

Once the illusion is broken, neocheaters will be out of their white-collar-hoax and political-hoax, ruling-class jobs. At the same time, entrepreneurs in the Neo-Tech System will experience greater and greater success all around the world.

There Is Another Reason For This Move

For thousands of years, science was stifled because people stood on the Earth, and they thought they saw the Sun revolving around the Earth. So they said, naturally, that the Sun and stars revolved around the Earth, for they could never break out of that perspective. But if an advanced civilization had put them on another planet, for instance, the Earthlings would have seen the cosmos in a totally different, wider Neothink perspective and realized their geocentric (Earth-centered) perspective was not the situation at all.

By comparison, the level-three CEO is ripe to break out of his little bottle of staying contained in America. He is ready for the Neothink perspective.

The level-three CEO will go through a major expanding perspective when he breaks his company-without-a-company into the international. Those who have no conception of doing business overseas are so unbelievably and unnecessarily limited, such as the ancient scientists watching and concluding the Sun revolved around the Earth. Their perspective was totally off. But when the CEO gets abroad, he breaks out of that limited perspective, like an ancient scientist being put on a different planet. Going into other countries gives the CEO that wide-scope, Neothink perspective. His mind blossoms.

The U.S. operation will more and more become, essentially, a satellite company. Coca-Cola is an American company, yet its business in America represents only a percentage of the worldwide business. That is what happens with a Neo-Tech business. America becomes just a percentage of its worldwide business. America becomes just one of many countries in which the Neo-Tech entrepreneur does business. At that point, his business truly becomes a company-without-a-*country*. And that can happen even when his Neo-Tech business is still quite small, so long as he evolves into a Neothink perspective with his Neothink tools — the essence tracking reports.

Say you evolve into a company-without-a-country. The independent mini-companies operating from their homes or offices throughout other countries are virtually untouchable by authorities in your country and theirs.

Authorities or no authorities, however, the Neo-Tech entrepreneur would still do this. He is stuck with a geocentric view from inside the bottle by staying put in America — a geocentric view of "watching the sun revolve around the Earth". The international view of a company-without-a-company/without-a-country is an invincible business move. Again, a classic example of the power in breaking out of the geocentric perspective into the heliocentric (sun-centered) perspective, so to speak, was ITT from 1961 when the Castro government nationalized ITT's Cuban telephone system to 1970 when ITT became the world's largest conglomerate by doing business in countries all around the world.

Another classic example was a young lad who became the richest man in the world by breaking out of the geocentric perspective. Way back in 1910, when J. Paul Getty was a lad in the oil fields of the Oklahoma Indian territory, he decided that he was going to set up an office in Europe, spend three months a year there so he could travel around Europe and get a wider perspective. That was back in the days of the telegraph, yet he ran his business through the telegraph when he was in Europe for the three months a year. He did not even have business in Europe, but he sensed he needed that wider Neothink perspective. Because of that, he was one of the first oil men in the Middle East. One young man catapulted his business into one of the largest worldwide oil firms because he implicitly sensed that getting a worldwide Neothink perspective meant great advantages.

For the most potent creation of values and business, the Neo-Tech entrepreneur needs this heliocentric Neothink perspective. Essentially, America is just one market, one group of people, and to make the Neo-Tech business a worldwide value, the founder or CEO needs the perspectives of the Latin market, Oriental market, Arabic market, European market.

Knowledge begets knowledge. And Neothink begets Neothink. Again, it is crucial for the Neo-Tech entrepreneur to gain this heliocentric Neothink perspective. He would never know many important things with a localized geocentric perspective. Once doing business abroad, however, not only will his business grow, but he will gain greater and greater Neothink perspectives. His operation will grow many times its size. Yet, he will be invulnerable to the political hoax.

A company-without-a-country offers a unique freedom to a person and a company that answers to no local neocheating group, no local authorities. With this set up, with a company-without-a-country, nobody owns your work or your production of values. As long as you are an American company, American neocheaters will always own you. When America becomes

287

nothing more than a satellite market to you, American neocheaters cannot hurt you. You can then live and breathe from that perspective of freedom.

Neocheaters hold little power against the Neo-Tech System. Neo-Tech entrepreneurs hold the power. Doesn't the company-without-a-country exemplify earned power beautifully? Indeed, neocheaters only have illusions of power, for outside of their territory of illusions, they hold no power whatsoever. Imagine the Cuban bureaucracy trying to harm Japanese producers in Japan, outside of Castro's territory of illusions. The Japanese producers would just laugh at the Cuban bureaucracy. The Neo-Tech man, on the other hand, has genuine power everywhere in the world, for he creates values others want and pay for. His power to make money is real.

Outside of our government's territory of illusions, the Neo-Tech mini-companies can operate at full steam. Out there, the authorities here become not much of a threat to business. Freedom to achieve your human potential sends your happiness level into a permanent high. No irrational authority can significantly hurt your business, because your business operates all over the world. There is no ruling-class hovering over your entire business.

Even more important, not many entrepreneurs can match your strength. No competitors can touch you when you gain this Neothink perspective. And Neothink perspectives beget Neothink perspectives. Break out of geocentric perspectives. Break into heliocentric Neothink perspectives. And never forget: as long as you do business only in America, then you are an American business owned by the American government.

Pushing Out And Beyond

If an entrepreneur creates a substantial business in America, how could he possibly fly to another country, spending days with a fledgling start-up business in England, for example? Going abroad does not make sense. So, he stays in America, in a bottle sealed with the cork of mysticism.

And he gets very comfortable with that. There is no more drive to break out of a geocentric-like perspective into the heliocentric-like, Neothink perspective. Most traditional businesses never do. But the Neo-Tech System defies such traditional paths of least resistance and opens the door to the world.

Consider that each mini-company is essentially a company in which the individual is responsible for his own financial destiny. Therefore, that person focuses on the money-making essence of his mini-company (which is a piece of the overall money-making essence of your business).

In the traditional company, by contrast, the money-making essence is focused on by the upper levels of the company; the company is broken into a division of labor, and the many employees are there to *physically* serve that money-making essence. They contribute little or no mental input.

The Neo-Tech System, however, takes the division of labor a step further to include not just the physical, but also the psychological nature of man and his work. The nature of man and his work not only involves his mind, but both man and his work are driven by his mind. When adding the mighty dimension of man's mind to his work, something incredible happens. The company's division of labor leaps from mechanical movements or jobs of labor to money-making movements or jobs of the mind.

Indeed, the shortest physical movements to profits demand the infusion of man's mental energies along with his physical energies, which leads us to the mini-company breakthrough and the entire new business structure called the division of essence. Pieces of the company's money-making essence actually come down to the employee level where integrated thinking gets infused into *every* job.

In the division of essence, the employee eventually focuses on his piece of essence in much more detail than upper management could ever focus on it. The employees maximize every nook and cranny of the company's overall money-making essence.

In other words, each mini-company is driven to take its own limited area to the very limit, as far as it can go. And that solves the problem that stops most businesses from attempting to do business abroad. Recall, the upper level of a traditional company is too busy making the company's money to invest the time on starting business from scratch in some other country for far less revenues. The costs/effort to net does not make sense. And if the traditional company does try it, the venture usually fizzles out.

But it would be a different tune with a *mini-company* starting up the company's business in another country. That mini-company would have all the time to initiate, incubate, and grow a healthy business abroad.

For example, Mr. Hamilton was having huge mailings in the U.S. So he could never spend weeks trying to set up a little mailing program in Asia. But by establishing Neo-Tech Foreign as a mini-company, that small mini-company had to focus on those foreign lists to survive. Therefore, instead of going home after a few weeks like other mailers who tried and failed, the foreign market six years later doubled the size of Mr. Hamilton's company, evolving the Neo-Tech System into the international company-without-a-company/without a country.

And you can see how these mini-companies can continue to grow into new areas otherwise never pursued. For example, that same scenario now holds true within Neo-Tech Foreign. The African market and the third-world market have the potential to become very lucrative. When Neo-Tech Foreign works the big markets of Europe, Asia, and South America, however, that mini-company head cannot be spending time trying to figure out how to trade with Nigerians, for example. So that area traditionally goes by the wayside. But if we break that African and third-world market out into its own mini-company, then that new mini-company head focuses, thinks, nurtures, and raises that mini-company into a healthy business. For, trading with Nigerians is his essence.

The Neo-Tech System delivers the nuts and bolts to build this heliocentric Neothink perspective and to establish this company-without-a-company internationally. You can easily and safely establish mini-companies operating throughout the world, just as your first mini-company operates here in the U.S. The time to go global is now.

Chapter Twenty-Five

THE COMPANY-WITHOUT-A-COMPANY/
WITHOUT-A-COUNTRY WORKS FOR ALL
NEO-TECH BUSINESSES, BIG AND SMALL

The amazing thing about the World-Capture Discovery is how surprisingly soon a start-up entrepreneur can do this. Once one breaks through to a successful program, he can quickly replicate it to others throughout other countries, setting them up as profitable mini-companies that operate with little overhead out of their own homes. With his essence tracking reports, he can effectively run a worldwide business in surprisingly little time. The Neo-Tech System is the fastest and safest way to build a wealthy, worldwide business.

The World-Capture Discovery works well for any size company, from the small start-up company to the largest of companies.

Movement Heads And Their Mini-Empires

I & O does not approach the size and scope of the large U.S. companies. Yet, the sweeping, horizontal nature of the company-without-a-company with the tight, vertical control of the tracking reports can put even the largest companies under iron-grip control.

The size of the large U.S. companies would bring another dimension to the company-without-a-company, not yet part of I & O's structure. That new dimension would be *mini-empires*.

To understand the mini-empire, let us first go back to the area of purpose (Volume Two, Chapter Eleven). The area of purpose never lets a mentally integrating responsibility split away from its purpose. All mentally integrating responsibilities converge on their purpose and create an independent, open-ended job with its complete "tail of responsibilities". The area of purpose is also called a physical movement of the company. For, by removing the split responsibilities, the area of purpose provides the shortest, unbroken route to push forward essence — the shortest physical movement to profits. This division of essence takes the division

291

of labor one step further to properly incorporate the nature of man — his mind.

Business's true division of labor, the division of essence, synthesizes the physical and mental energies — the body and the mind — into harmonious, unbroken momentum (free from split responsibilities) for building profits...the true physical movements of business. In fact, the physical movements take a leap from powerless mechanical movements or routine-rut jobs of labor (the majority of today's work force) to powerful money-making movements or exhilarating jobs of the mind (the rare mini-company heads). The mechanical movements worked well for *manufacturing*, but the money-making movements work best for *business*. In the end, business demands integrated thinking — man's mind.

Look again at the I & O mini-companies (areas of purpose) in Diagram Ten, page 109. Notice their "tails of responsibilities" (i.e., their mentally integrating responsibilities). Those mentally integrating responsibilities must never be broken apart. For instance, each marketing area of purpose contains the mentally integrating responsibility *accounting*. In most companies, accounting is its own department. In the mini-company, accounting attaches to its purpose and is a mentally integrating responsibility done by the mini-company head. Each mini-company head becomes an efficient accountant in order to push forward his essence. He can never break away from accounting, for then he breaks his bottom-line competence, his integrated thinking, his purpose — his physical movement of generating profits.

Indeed, the "tail of responsibilities" must never be broken, no matter how large the area of purpose or the mini-company grows. For, once a responsibility gets split away from its purpose (i.e., gets delegated), say accounting gets delegated (or gets taken over by an accounting department), then integrated thinking disintegrates, split responsibilities develop and departments form...specialization takes over. Integration ends. The powerful money-making physical movement and the valid division of labor no longer exist. Profits slow and eventually stop.

A movement or mini-company must remain an integrated area of purpose, not split apart into specialized departments. The mentally integrating responsibilities that converge on their purpose must never be broken. In a department, responsibilities get delegated. Specialization starts, progress stops. ...Big traditional companies consist of many departments.

In the Neo-Tech System, however, the physical movements must stay fully integrated, must hold together all mentally integrating responsibilities in their areas of purpose. But what happens with rapid growth of the company and, consequently, the movement? What happens with mega-size organizations such as the largest U.S. companies?

As explained in Volume Two, the "tail of responsibilities" does not itself expand or change with growth. Its number of mentally integrating responsibilities stays the same. Instead, the *projects* within the movement multiply with size. For example, the space-media mini-company does not take on more mentally integrating responsibilities with the growth of I & O. Instead, the number of *campaigns* within space media expand with growth.

So, with rapid growth, entire campaigns along with the entire "tail of responsibilities" for the space-media movement must be replicated into new areas of purpose, new mini-companies. Thus, one physical movement of the company, say space media, can eventually consist of many mini-companies.

In a large company, each movement would consist of many, many mini-companies. One CEO could not integrate and coordinate the vast number of mini-companies. So, *movement heads* would develop. Using I & O as an example: All the space-media mini-companies would have one movement head who integrates and coordinates the space-media movement. He would become the "CEO" of the space-media movement; he would track the space-media mini-companies through tracking reports. He would hold the monthly Essence Meeting with the space-media mini-companies. He would pursue the creating-and-elevating/integrating-and-coordinating functions.

In turn, the movement heads would provide essence tracking reports to the leading head, the overall company's CEO. And the leading head would integrate and coordinate the movement heads.

How It Works

The movement head builds and replicates the mini-companies in his movement — his mini-empire. He develops the Neothink tracking reports. He follows those tracking reports for each mini-company in his movement. Thus, the movement head tracks every responsibility in his movement, just as the leading head used to. If something is wrong, he digs into the nitty-gritty details with the particular mini-company to discover the problem, just as the leading head used to.

In a large company, the movement head can make Neothink developments in his movement more quickly. He can build or cut back more efficiently than the leading head.

The movement head takes all the tracking reports from all the mini-companies in his movement and combines them into one essence tracking report, into one master tracking report of the entire *movement* for the leading head. That master, essence tracking report of the entire movement plots his performance.

The leading head tracks the performance of each movement. From time to time, he will ask for the complete set of mini-company tracking reports along with the master tracking report, in order to stay in touch with the most specific responsibilities of his business.

The leading head integrates and coordinates the mini-*empires* (i.e., the movements). He will develop accounting formulas and ratios to be calculated by the movement heads in their essence tracking reports. For, in a sprawling company-without-a-company, the leading head must track it all through the numbers.

The Movement Head's Responsibilities

As his mini-empire grows, the movement head initiates and replicates new mini-companies. His financial destiny grows. For, the movement heads need to operate through performance pay as the mini-companies do, or, perhaps more effectively, through an equity position in the company.

The movement heads assume the creating-and-elevating/integrating-and-coordinating functions for their mini-empires. They become the CEOs of their mini-empires. ...The movement heads become the candidates to eventually replace the leading head.

Super-Movement Heads And Their Super-Mini-Empires

As defined in Chapter Nineteen, business is the dynamic interaction between numbers and values to create and elevate marketable values and to market those values to expanding markets. People with bottom-line mini-companies will, with time, eventually begin developing marketable products on their own. That occurs naturally as a mini-company head continually BUILDS his essence, always reaching for broader and broader integrations.

Numbers/marketing is but half the equation of business. The mini-company head will eventually push himself into the other half of business: product development. He keeps pushing out to master the dynamic interaction between numbers and values in order to someday build his own marketable product and become a whole (fully integrated) businessman. In a growing Neo-Tech business such as I & O, new marketable products grow out of marketing mini-companies.

A person evolves into a whole businessperson by driving a product successfully into the marketplace. He becomes an even more broadly integrated person than the movement head defined above (e.g., space-media movement head). For, he becomes a *whole* businessman, a *super*-movement head in charge of not just the most specific money-making movement — a mini-company or mini-empire — but in charge of the *broadest* money-making movement: *all* the mini-companies (eventually even mini-empires) that market his product.

In other words, in charge of marketing HIS PRODUCT, he pursues not just one marketing movement but *all* marketing movements such as space-media marketing, direct-mail marketing, television marketing, database marketing — *all* the marketing movements to make maximum profits with his product. Eventually with growth, he will replicate mini-companies throughout those different marketing movements and evolve into the creating-and-elevating/integrating-and-coordinating functions — the "CEO" of his super-movement. In essence, he is a start-up entrepreneur using the Neo-Tech System, working in your company, for you.

As the founder of the super-movement, he discovers the second broadest money-making movement in business —

295

maximizing profits with his own product.[1] Like the founder of the original company, he becomes responsible for *all* the marketing movements and, eventually, all the marketing mini-companies that market his product. He provides an essence tracking report to the leading head revealing the performance of his super-movement.

The super-movement head could ultimately build more than one super-movement (i.e., develop more than one marketable product and market it). With more than one super-movement, he controls a super-mini-empire. Eventually, the super-mini-empire head becomes the most qualified candidate to replace the leading head. ...Within a large company, the movement heads and then the super-movement heads and eventually the super-mini-empire heads (not the mini-company heads) provide their essence tracking reports to the CEO who snaps together the full Neothink puzzle.[2]

---

[1]The broadest movement in business is, of course, the creating-and-elevating/integrating-and-coordinating functions of the leading head for the whole company — pushing forward the entire thing into new realms...pushing forward all the products, super-movement heads, mini-empires, and mini-companies into new realms of business.

[2]The techniques presented in this manuscript come from direct hands-on experience, from hands-on day-to-day use, not from inner logic spun inside some pipe-smoking professor's head. Therefore, the techniques presented in this manuscript are real. But potential errors can occur in areas that I & O has not yet experienced, such as movement heads and super-movement heads, above. Movement heads and super-movement heads are extrapolations. The text above assumes that movement heads and super-movement heads both develop in large companies, which seems logical. However, that may not be so. The natural, Neo-Tech course of growth may bypass movement heads as defined above. Maybe only super-movement heads develop in growing Neo-Tech companies. (If so, then super-movement heads would be renamed movement heads).

Movement heads as described in the text above are in charge of several mini-companies of the same marketing movement (e.g., space advertising). Super-movement heads above are in charge of a product, in charge of all the mini-companies to market that product...in charge of maximizing profits for a product. Perhaps in natural Neo-Tech

(footnote continued on next page)

Endless Expansion

Now, consider what happens with the new marketing mini-companies within the super-movements: As explained in Chapter Nineteen, only market pressures drive forth *marketable* values. Only marketing mini-companies can drive forth marketable products. Indeed, to develop a marketable product, a person must be under the market pressures of a bottom-line mini-company. And the nature of people with purpose, people with fully integrated areas of purpose (bottom-line mini-companies), is TO BUILD...to build their piece of the company's essence, to push out for broader and broader business integrations from which to build their mini-companies. Those marketing people will eventually push into product development to achieve the broadest integrations of business. Eventually, those marketing mini-company heads in a super-movement will develop their own marketable products and build new super-movements.

In the Neo-Tech System filled with Neo-Tech men and women with purpose, everyone pushes out for greater and greater integrations. Employees eventually develop and build super-movements. They replicate mini-companies with growth to market their products. Those mini-companies keep pushing out, too. We can extrapolate that, eventually, another super-movement will develop within a super-movement, thus break off and form a new super-movement. We can extrapolate this process continuing over and over as Neo-Tech businesses expand forever. After all, knowledge begets knowledge. Neothink begets Neothink.

(footnote continued from previous page)
growth (growth void of mysticism), personnel would evolve toward the wider integrations, the wider movement of creating then making profits for their own products. In any case, the author cannot state with certainty that both movement heads *and* super-movement heads evolve in a Neo-Tech company.

Appendix

The Personnel-Capture Discovery

Chapter Twenty-Six

BUSINESS: THE LIVING ENTITY

The Mind, Body, and Soul of Business

You learned in the Company-Capture section that business functions like a living entity. When the body and the mind of business work together, the business excels. The division of essence takes the division of labor to the next level that includes the mind.

In most businesses today, the body and mind become split through split responsibilities. The soul of business never has a chance to rise from mind/body integrations that create exciting emotions in business.

Most businesses today offer just one dimension to their workers: a pyramidical hierarchy, a *vertical structure*. The Neo-Tech System offers three dimensions to the workers: vertical, horizontal, and internal. The first two dimensions represent the body and the mind of business, now available to even the ordinary worker. The vertical dimension refers to the existing business, the details, the body. The tracking reports integrate you with the body of your business. And only by being integrated with the body can you stay healthy and develop the mind of your business. The horizontal dimension refers to pushing into new business, the essence, the mind. The daily essence reports and the Essence Meetings integrate you with the mind of your business. Like you, the mini-companies throughout the business push horizontally into new essences. They push into new business (the mind) only because they are well-integrated with the business details (the body).

Imagine, for example, Harvey Firestone trying to innovate breakthroughs for tire manufacturing without knowing the nitty-gritty details of manufacturing the tires...the body of his business. Indeed, Firestone spent time every day in the factory to stay integrated with details. By contrast, the flowing-robes white-collar hoax today avoids integrated thinking by delegating and turning away from details. That lack of integration eventually destroys the business — tears it apart through increasing split responsibilities. Then, fraudulent accounting practices become necessary to keep those companies going, for awhile.

Many businesses today have lost the vital mind/body integration. Some of those businesses today exist in a coma caused by the white-collar hoax. The body functions on automatic...kept alive by a life-support system set in place years before by the integrating founder(s) and by a small group of integrators perhaps still in the company. But the mind is essentially dead. The comatose business may physically expand for some time to come, such as a comatose child grows with life support. But the mind has died, and eventually so will the body.

The Neo-Tech System can pull a business out of its coma and back to life. The Neo-Tech System brings the mind back; the Neo-Tech System brings the body and mind together again. With the mind and body integrated, the business can grow indefinitely.

Whereas the traditional division of labor divides the physical labor of, say, manufacturing into its shortest mechanical movements, the new division of essence divides the mental essence of business into its shortest money-making movements. In other words, the mind and body of your business, when divided into jobs, stay together and form integrated money-making jobs for those who work for you — integrated puzzle pieces, that is, which snap together for you into a Neothink puzzle picture through your essence tracking reports.

Business lives and dies like a person. Business has emotions like a person, which is its third dimension. Now, consider that people with a healthy body and mind can be struck down by negative emotions. At times, the person is a victim of an assault from outside forces that he or she has no control over, from perhaps a traumatic experience or a deep childhood emotional scar.

Similarly, a business with a healthy body and mind can be struck down by negative emotions. In such a case, sometimes the business is a victim of an assault from outside forces.

Such an assault occurred at I & O. Mr. Hamilton restructured the company into the healthy mind/body, integrated mini-company structure following the traumatic November 3rd, 1986 attack on I & O (explained in the Neo-Tech literature). Mr. Hamilton left the country to secure the business worldwide so no hostile political force could stop its Neo-Tech research and publications. While away, the emotions in I & O grew negative, partly as a result of the traumatic aftershock from the politically motivated physical attack on the company. The negative emotions, however, became energized by certain workers. You see, the new mini-company structure demanded integrated thinking and quickly challenged workers' personal mysticism. To protect their own lack of integrated thinking and lack of desire, the cancer seeds tried to bring down the mind/body integrated structure. Instead of soaring with the mini-company structure in Mark Hamilton's absence, I & O began to sink. The company was struck down by bad emotions.

Capture Good Emotions

Realize that emotions motivate or suppress the most powerful asset of your business — your workers. Cancer-seed personnel, the impurities, must be fired from the company, regardless of their quality of work itself. Good work benefits the physical strength of the company. But emotional strength carries even greater leverage. Consider that bad work, for the most part, affects just that person's job, not others. But a calculated assault on the emotions of the business affects many people's jobs.

The most dangerous cancer seeds often do very good work. But regardless of a cancer seed's value to the physical business itself, he causes severe problems throughout the company's emotions. The disguise of a good worker must be torn off; he must be identified for who he is. His employment must be terminated, for he uses the company for destructive personal gains. He demoralizes the entire company for a neurotic leadership role. He hurts the company far more than he helps. The emotions within a company, like a person's emotions, can either motivate the business or suppress the business.

Companies Today Plagued By Cancer Seeds

In most companies, a small percentage of the workers act as cancer seeds, undermining the attitude, *the emotions* throughout the company. In a Neo-Tech company, once the integration breakers — the cancer-seed impurities — get removed, the workers can concentrate on their purpose...to build their mini-companies.

In the science of chemistry, a catalytic explosion cannot occur in the presence of chemical impurities. In the science of business, a Neothink explosion cannot occur in the presence of cancer-seed impurities. The cancer seeds, like the impurities in a compound solution, act as integration blockers. As long as the impurities remain, the emotions of your company cannot integrate into a motivated, productive state. For, the impurities constantly prevent that integration that would otherwise intensify and cause an explosion of emotionally uplifted, exhilarated employees focused on progress. Instead, that integration never occurs, always prevented as the employees get pulled back into the complaints and attacks of the cancer seeds. The cancer seeds cause a bad attitude toward the mini-company structure and rally resistance against integrated thinking. The overall working attitude and productivity never improve beyond a certain point, forever diseased by the cancer seeds.

As I & O evolved toward a Neo-Tech/Neothink company, a single person stirred up emotional complaints and verbal attacks that undermined the company and its management. He started with subtle attacks at first; then the attacks escalated. An impulsive, moody loud-mouth is easy to spot and fire. But the calculating cancer seed in I & O applied his destruction in strategic doses that accelerated as more people began to fall into his neocheating trap.

Mr. Hamilton eventually realized what was happening and fired the cancer seed and his two cohorts. Soon after removing those impurities from I & O, the personnel integrated and focused on progress and productivity — focused on accomplishing I & O's goal.

Within one week after firing the cancer seed and his cohorts, the workers started to emotionally feel good about progress. Momentum began to build as, for the first time, emotions of pride and admiration began to snap into place. The emotions of the business began to form a larger-than-life Neothink integration. For, no longer was anyone's spirit broken by the impurities. Everyone changed over and routed for progress, cheered for productivity, and hailed the forward movement of others.

304

Everyone became highly motivated.

Unfortunately, most entrepreneurs today do not know about the company-wide explosion of productivity and creativity that occurs by removing personnel who assault the emotions of business. An impurity-free emotional atmosphere immeasurably increases the personnel's value to the company. The workers begin to feel wow-like emotions; they grow impassioned and strive for success.

The Neo-Tech atmosphere is far more than feeling good, however. The company and the employee will cash in on those good feelings — literally cash in with tangible profits. For the first time, *everyone's* focus and concentration is on progress. That omnipresent focus on progress — like a constant magnetic pull — draws together their personal lives with their work. Integrated thinking about their competitive creations happens more and more frequently with more and more intensity. The emotional renaissance within the business brings on a personal renaissance within the worker. That worker actually accomplishes more in a few months than he could in his entire lifetime when strapped down by bad emotions.

And that unleashing of the worker's potential launches the company's productivity and profits. Moreover, the attitude, similar to happiness, does not stop growing once the impurities are removed. A perpetual energy-cycle develops between tangible creation and emotional exhilaration. *Your business enjoys quite a benefit for simply removing cancer seeds!* As discovered at I & O, the personnel explosion of productivity offers great power — perhaps the greatest power — to the Neo-Tech company.

And, as Mr. Hamilton discovered, his employees and their families developed a deep gratitude toward him for unleashing their human potential. Their gratitude fills Mr. Hamilton with the most wonderful feelings of pride and happiness. It is wonderful being a Neo-Tech entrepreneur, helping others while bringing important values to the world.

Chapter Twenty-Seven

REMOVING THE NEGATIVE PERSONNEL — THE INTEGRATION BLOCKERS

Integrated Thinking Gets Blocked By Cancer Seeds

Let's review: Cancer seeds retard or block company-wide integrated thinking, shutting down the evolution into Neothink among personnel. For, the workers' attempts to overcome personal mysticism and to take on integrated thinking get discouraged then broken by the cancer seeds.

For example, the new I & O mini-company heads faced a difficult challenge: to take on integrated thinking for the first time. Before they could get started and build momentum, the intelligent cancer seed referred to in the last chapter, protecting his own mysticism, held them back. He encouraged their lack of progress (due to their lack of integrated thinking). Their problems were not their fault, he told them. Their problems (with integrated thinking) were the fault of the company and management. The Neo-Tech System was a slave-driving system designed to exploit them, he insisted. He said many things to discourage his peers, gossiping about the "unreasonable demands" for essence movement, making accusations that the company was taking advantage of people's pay through performance pay. His persistent attacks (always behind the back of management) provided, of course, the path of least resistance for the workers to stop their struggles to overcome mysticism and to do integrated thinking. Therefore, they did not move forward their essences.

This particular cancer seed undermined I & O's revolutionary division-of-essence mini-company structure in order to protect his own refusal to do integrated thinking. Then he gained a following and some power while assaulting the emotions of the company. Several workers stopped integrated thinking, became disgruntled, and let him become their leader.

Cut Cancer Seeds

Personnel offers more potential leverage than anything else in your young business. Each person working for you represents a potential mega dose of power. Therefore, the emotions of your business must become free of impurities.

One situation exists that calls for immediate firing regardless of the quality of a person's work. A person should be fired when he or she is a tumor within your Neo-Tech company. Objective questions, suggestions, even challenges brought specifically to management are needed and valid. But to negatively work on employees' emotions, turning them against the company or against management is cancer, spreads like cancer, and must be cut like cancer from the company.

How To Never Hire A Cancer Seed

In the Neo-Tech/Neothink atmosphere, personnel focus on productivity. A person would feel out of place if he or she focused on something other than productivity. But just one calculating person can begin to kill that Neo-Tech/Neothink atmosphere for many people. Now, how do you prevent hiring a cancer seed?

Here is how: From the start, make clear to your employee his mini-company or entrepreneurial unit carries the responsibility to sustain itself financially. Instead of the company, HE is responsible to sustain himself. That forces him straight into integrated thinking and steers him clear of cancer-seed thinking. But if the company typically pays him a salary instead of performance pay, then YOU carry the ultimate responsibility to make him a value to your company. YOU must force him into integrated thinking. Yet, under no survival pressures, he will not do integrated thinking. And he will blame YOU for pressuring him. He will blame YOU when he does not become rich and successful. Then, he will become vulnerable to cancer-seed thinking.

But if he must sustain himself, then HE carries the responsibility to make himself a value to your company. HE forces himself into integrated thinking. Now, under survival pressures, he must do integrated thinking. And he blames no one else if he does not become rich and successful. He does not become vulnerable to cancer-seed thinking.

Unleashing The Great Potential Of Personnel

If your company automatically sustains that new mini-company head, then YOU remain the integrator and he the follower. But if he must sustain himself, then basically it makes no difference to you if he succeeds or fails. Therefore, HE must become the integrator. He must end his personal mysticism, bicameral tendencies, and activate the great integrating power in his head. Thus, you have unleashed his potential.

As long as you are the integrator, you have little leverage with personnel. If he and others become the integrators, then you control explosive leverage with personnel. For example, you will be able to simply give workers an overview, advice, or an idea, and they will take what you give them and build something major through their own integrated thinking.

Moreover, those self-leaders are happy people. You can recruit employees from large companies; some will even take a reduction in pay. For, with the full control of a mini-company, they often see the wider picture of what they can build and the potential rewards.

All this is possible through the Neo-Tech System. By reversing the financial responsibility, that is, reversing the responsibility of your employees becoming a value from you to them, then no one is in position to complain or become a cancer seed. Instead, everyone is in position to do integrated thinking and make exciting progress. Again, through the mini-company division of essence, you unleash the great potential of your personnel.

The Self-Leaders

A person who genuinely cares about the financial well-being of the company is someone without cancer-seed inclinations, someone who could someday grow into a business leader. And now, with the self-responsible mini-company structure integrated with performance pay, your workers not only care about the financial well-being of the company, but they drive for cost controls and efficiencies for their own profits and performance pay. Those self-responsible people begin developing, from the start, the characteristics of business leaders. Your start-up company, from the beginning, gets filled with a rare strength. Your company gets filled with an all-star lineup of self-leaders.

Chapter Twenty-Eight

THE THIRD DIMENSION — EMOTIONS

The mini-company structure opens entirely new dimensions to the ordinary employee not seen in most companies today. One new dimension is *creativity* through integrated thinking, which is exciting. The mini-company heads and their entrepreneurial units develop integrated thinking and begin creatively BUILDING their little businesses. Their jump from the boring one-dimensional traditional company (i.e., a hierarchy of specialized thinking and routine tasks) to the exciting multi-dimensional Neothink company brings *exhilarating emotions* to those ordinary employees.

As those mini-company heads and their entrepreneurial units become creative, they become exhilarated and deeply motivated. They develop a deep emotional integration with their work, which is nonexistent in traditional employees. Those exhilarating emotions open yet another entire dimension to the Neo-Tech employee. Something awesome takes place: your creative, integrated thinkers discover a power that no mysticism-plagued person has ever known — they discover the emotionally charged **Power Approach**.

The Power Approach Through Emotions

The Power Approach is unlike anything read thus far in this manuscript, for the Power Approach is purely an emotional state of being. Emotions are inherently part of man, and they can be used to gain power. The Power Approach is difficult to specifically define since it is an emotional state of being. Therefore, it must be described.

Describing The Power Approach

Conscious life offers power. For example, man can take control of every situation in life: he can capture iron-grip control over his schedule; he can capture iron-grip control over his company; he can capture the world marketplace; he can capture his own mind with Neothink control. But he must initiate it; he must *take* it. The Power Approach ignites man into taking Neothink control of life. Great wealth creators root themselves

311

in the Power Approach to generate great values for mankind and to cut through anything that gets in their way. Here is how you, too, can root yourself in the Power Approach:

In any situation, you can ask, "What is the nonmystical (i.e., the nonfollowing, self-integrating) Power Approach to this situation?" By honing in on just that question, you begin to cut through your own wimpish mysticism that seeks automatic or external guidance. You take charge. And you determine not to succumb to any "leader", any neocheater, any personal mysticism. Keep asking yourself, "What is the nonmystical Power Approach in this situation...what is the nonmystical Power Approach in this situation?" You begin to see the self-control, integrated approach of the Neo-Tech man or woman. You see the potent course of action. Then, if you act on the Power Approach, you act on Neo-Tech (see the front material for an explanation of Neo-Tech). You act on strength. You capture competence and power. You become the self-leader. You increasingly root yourself in the potent nonmystical course of action. You gain ever-increasing power. You gain ever-increasing wealth. You gain ever-increasing happiness.

Everything you do, particularly in your career, keep asking yourself, "What is the nonmystical Power Approach to this situation?" If you work a specialized job and are unhappy, ask yourself, "What is the nonmystical Power Approach to this situation?" Keep asking yourself that question. Do not begin analyzing the answer. Realize that later you will decide whether or not to act on the Power Approach. But for now, just answer with the most powerful, nonmystical course of action to correct the problem.

See the Power Approach clearly: say, in this case, the Power Approach is to leave the specialized white-collar-hoax structure and start your own business with the Neo-Tech System. If you act on the Power Approach, then you become a much more powerful and competitive force than the average man and will eventually, inevitably leave your peers behind.

The above example, leaving one's job to start a Neo-Tech business, requires a major change in one's life. But the Power Approach applies everywhere, in large or small situations. Personal or business problems, major decisions in life, the Power

Approach makes it possible to take command with the clearest Neo-Tech answers.

You can begin small, using the Power Approach for frequent problems or common situations. By asking yourself, "What is the nonmystical Power Approach to this situation?" you strike with laser-like force with the most integrated, Neo-Tech (i.e., thought-out, integrated) answer. The laser-like Power Approach obliterates the mystical wimp inside you. The Power Approach burns through rationalizations that would otherwise plague your thinking and make you weak. The Power Approach provides instant strength. And once rooted with the Power Approach, nothing can stand in your way, not even neocheating monoliths.

But first, use the Power Approach in small daily situations. Build your strength with the Power Approach. Soon the Power Approach grows within you. Your strength and conviction grows with it. Everything about your life changes. Before long, you become ready to take on major decisions in life using the Power Approach. You become ready to discover a spectacular new life quite different from a life of timidly stagnating within a white-collar-hoax structure.

No special skill is required to unleash your power. Anyone from the CEO to the man in the streets can at anytime recognize the power human life offers by taking the Power Approach. With laser-like precision, he can burn through reluctance and meekness to the power-core of any situation.

Start today with problems and challenges in your career. Instantly feel your pool of power. Fearlessly push ahead with the nonmystical power course of action. Like hatchet men in company buy-outs, chop through lingering turmoil as you identify, "this is the problem, here is the integrated solution." Like those Neo-Tech men, become calm and confident in the face of the most trying situations. Develop courage and make fearless moves — unstoppable by mysticism.

The Power Approach is your transmission belt to wealth, love and happiness — to being the man standing on the mountain. The Power Approach is the tool to break free from the mystical, nonintegrating mind and life. The Power Approach drives a person into integrated thinking, wealth, success, power, love, and romance.

313

The Neo-Tech Breakthrough To Self-Made Power

Mysticism stems from deep-rooted feelings of needing to be led (see front material). The Power Approach stems from deep-rooted feelings of *not* needing to be led. Mysticism comes from a passive, nonintegrating mode and is the opposite of the Power Approach that comes from an aggressive, integrating mode. Power-Approach emotions, blocked in most people by mysticism, are explosive integrating forces once unleashed. Power-Approach emotions drive the ordinary person into extraordinary actions. Power-Approach emotions push man into using the great power in his head: into using integrated thinking and taking the lead. Mystical emotions pull man back from the great power in his head: back into a bicameral-like state of following the leaders, including the white-collar and political hoaxes.

Mysticism channels feelings and actions toward a life of incompetence and dependence on leaders or neocheaters. But now, through the Neo-Tech System, man can experience something different. His Power Approach channels feelings and actions toward a life of competence and independence that needs no leader or neocheater.

Sustained Motivation

Permanently motivating people does not come from positive thinking or any other temporary positives per se. Permanently motivating people comes from *removing the negative* — from removing mysticism (see front material). As a person moves past his own mysticism that seeks guidance, he feels a growing passion as he discovers integrated thinking — true power. Then through his mini-company, he actually cashes in on his integrated thinking. His motivation grows day after day, year after year.

The "CEO Touch"

In a Neo-Tech atmosphere, personnel deeply appreciate and respect the neothinking CEO. In other businesses, those good emotions of appreciation and respect are sometimes destroyed by cancer seeds. In the Neo-Tech atmosphere, people want to do well, want to succeed, and want to do integrated thinking and build values for mankind. That is foremost in their minds. Therefore, they want the CEO to be encouraged by their progress

314

in order to further integrate him with their essences for greater consultation/input during the Essence Meetings.

Mr. Hamilton lets his workers know when he is pleased and when he is disappointed. He nurtures his workers' integrated thinking and comes down on their mysticism. He makes integrated thinking the *emotional* path of least resistance in I & O. Workers avoiding integrated thinking for specialized thinking visibly disappoint Mr. Hamilton. In the Neo-Tech atmosphere, his expectations motivate personnel to evolve into the Power Approach.

After all, life is short. The Power Approach elevates a person's power in life. Try it, and release your human potential. Use it to start your own Neo-Tech business!

Second Package of Secrets

The Neo-Tech Epiphany

Break Through To Enlightenment!

Breakthrough to Enlightenment!

Discover the Deception Behind
Religion and the Occult

The
Neo-Tech
Epiphany

Tracy Alexander
Eric Savage

Neo-Tech Publishing Company
850 South Boulder Highway
Henderson, Nevada 89015
U.S.A.
Fax: 702 795 8393

Table of Contents

Forward

This book is culled from a series of interviews Tracy Alexander gave to Eric Savage and from an extensive collection of research notes Tracy compiled over many years. Tragically, Tracy passed away while she and Eric were in the process of organizing her interviews and research notes into this book. Fortunately, Eric was able to complete Tracy's book, *Breakthrough to Enlightenment*, posthumously.

Breakthrough to Enlightenment is dedicated to Tracy Alexander, a quiet lady who possessed an indomitable spirit, fearlessly seeking the truth, always persevering no matter how much that search led to knowledge that flew in the face of tradition. Tracy was a true pioneer, able to summon the courage necessary to venture into uncharted territory, even when that journey contradicted established dogma.

Chapter One

Discovering the Deception Behind Religious Doctrine and Occult Phenomena

"Entering a difficult period in life, I turned to religion seeking answers. I faithfully accepted religious teachings and submersed myself on an eight-year spiritual journey only to discover that the enlightenment offered was a deception. I felt angry and betrayed."

— Tracy Alexander

Religious teachings are seductive. They hold out the promise of wisdom. This is especially enticing to someone who has problems in life.

You think you are going to gain something extremely important. Religious and mystical teachings are filled with spiritual mysteries that need solving. And solving mysteries is something everyone likes to do. Indeed, mystery is a real drawing power of all forms of mysticism.

People who go into the spiritual on a deep level do so because they are seeking honesty, enlightenment, and fairness. They desire a world where honesty prevails, where fairness and compassion are the rules. They are seeking an ideal way to live and deal with others.

But, what they do not realize is that the ultimate wisdom and enlightenment they seek is an illusion. For, what the dedicated student of religion eventually discovers is that the core of religion is a deception. Those few dedicated students who reach this breakthrough either leave in disgust or are made teachers and spiritual leaders themselves in order to perpetuate the hoax. They rationalize that the people, the masses need the guidance and morality provided by religious doctrine.

After being a dedicated pupil of religious teachings for almost a decade, I was astonished when I finally broke through to enlightenment. The so-called enlightenment that students of religion and other mystical systems seek to obtain is the realization that God is not looking out after us.

Unbelievably, the spiritual enlightenment that religious and

1

mystical leaders urge their pupils to obtain, an enlightenment that dedicated students of religion spend years striving to obtain, brings a person back to square one — to the realization that no higher authority can be your guide. Only you, the individual, can make decisions and properly guide your own life.

Even more astonishing is when the religious student realizes that the very spiritual leaders he looked up to and followed have also broken through to this same level. The leaders know that at the core of their teachings lies an illusion; that no higher mystical power is looking out for us. Those students who struggle for years and finally break through to this realization are then made spiritual leaders themselves.

According to religious/spiritual leaders, the common people need to believe in a higher authority in order to live moral, productive lives. Thus, the hoax is perpetuated. The religious/ spiritual leaders have invested too heavily in religious and mystical doctrines to just walk away.

The religious teachings take one on a psychological path which involves learning a tremendous amount about human nature. The religious student is strongly drawn into religious mysticism, often by reading books by others who felt they had a personal relationship with God. The student reads and studies religious literature, which affirms there is a God. So he becomes a very strong believer.

In reality, one is being told an untruth. No supernatural, all-powerful entity is looking out after us. Some people may be deeply religious. Others may not be very religious. But if they go into the religious literature and study it, they become strongly religious. This all begins with the religious and spiritual leaders weaving a seductive illusion that there is a higher power who will help us.

That is the hook behind all religious and mystical teachings: that God or some higher power is going to help you. That is the essence of what attracts most people to religion. They are looking for someone or something to help them. In addition, most people want to believe that their consciousness and the consciousness of their loved ones will live forever in heaven.

The religious/mystic path is a process one goes through that can be compared to a scientific experiment. The scientist takes a theory and through objective experiment proves that theory to be true or false. The student of religion takes a religious doctrine, puts it into practice in his own life, and proves to himself if the doctrine is true or false. The student's life is the experiment.

What the religious student discovers is that religious doctrines put one in a double bind; something impossible to achieve. There are three major doctrines:

One doctrine is to give up personal desire, which eventually leads to a state of no motivation. Through experience, the student learns this doctrine, if fully implemented, would literally result in his death. Thus, it is impossible to achieve and is, therefore, in reality, anti-life.

The second doctrine is to be selfless and at the same time develop spiritual character. This is also impossible to achieve. The reasons why will be explained in a moment.

The third doctrine is to do the will of God. This also acts against an individual's long-term nature because it means one will always have an authority figure over oneself. Over the years, as the religious student lives through real-life experiences and the experience of honestly, wholeheartedly trying to live by those three doctrines, he learns how false each doctrine is. A person cannot achieve what the religious teachings tell one to achieve and be true to his nature as an independent, thinking human.

It takes a long time to break through those illusions. Each new insight is a shock to one's intelligence. By acting selfless your emotions begin to rebel. Eventually your emotions rebel against someone else (God) making important decisions for you. Your nature is to grow and develop in order to become your own authority. And the state of having no desire is worse than death. Your emotions eventually rebel against all three of those doctrines. Through personal experience, each doctrine proves to be destructive to an individual's nature and psychological health.

What religious students call illumination (insights from God) are actually creative insights comparable to those of any creative person, whether he be a scientist, a businessman, or an artist. The scientist and the businessman know such insights are coming from within their own minds. The religious student thinks his

3

insights are coming from God.

The creative process involves several stages. We can recognize the process at work in a scientist's experiment. This is the same process a religious student experiences by putting into practice a religious doctrine in his or her life.

By comparison in the table below, two important concepts emerge. 1) The creative insights of the religious student or mystic come from his own mind and not from God. 2) The religious doctrine is tested in reality to prove if it is valid.

Immersing oneself into the religious doctrines and one-by-one testing each doctrine in reality is the process one goes through to eventually break through the hoax and become a master.

The Scientist	**The Mystic Path**
1. **First Insight** A theory the scientist has.	1. **Accept a Doctrine on Faith** Act selflessly in a contained area.
2. **Saturation** Learn everything possible about the subject.	2. **Saturation** Act selflessly in the contained area until it becomes second nature.
3. **Incubation** A period in which the mind integrates all knowledge received...including the consistent with the non-consistent.	3. **Incubation** A period in which your mind integrates your actions with your true nature.
4. **Illumination** The creative insight. The problem is solved. A certainty that the solution is correct. A great feeling of joy.	4. **Illumination** The creative insight — selfless behavior is destructive to man's nature. It is humiliating and fosters low self-esteem. Selfishness creates moral characteristics. A great relief and feeling of joy.
5. **Verification** Verify the creative insight through experiments...then duplicate the experiments and verify again.	5. **Verification** Reject selfless behavior. Become selfish in your actions and verify the beneficial results with both yourself and with others.

The above table shows how religious students break through the hoax. But most people who believe in God do not go into religion in such depth. They live on the fringes of religion and

4

do not seriously apply the two major concepts that would eventually cause them to break through the hoax — the idea of giving up personal desire and the concept of being selfless. Instead, they hold onto the concept of a benevolent God and the concept of one's soul living forever.

When you seriously immerse yourself in religion, your thoughts become so caught up in the religious ideals that you negate your true emotional responses. But, at some point, your more emotional and insight-prone right-brain hemisphere is going to get through to your rational, left-brain hemisphere. When it does, you will have broken through the hoax.

Consider how Zen Buddhism works. The way to break into full consciousness for Zen followers is through a process of intellectual statements called Koans. The Koans also present the students with a double bind. For example, the Koan *One hand clapping* is to be meditated upon and understood by the pupil. It makes no sense, of course, but the student tries to understand that mystery. The purpose is to confuse and shock a person out of preconceived ideas and ideas that go against reality.

If the student has enough intensity, he will eventually break through to realize that what the religious/spiritual leaders are telling him to achieve goes against human nature. He will discover that the religious/mystical doctrines are invalid. It will dawn upon him that there is no higher authority looking out for oneself. Each person must be his own authority. Finally, he will have reached spiritual enlightenment.

The problem is that so few achieve this level. Look how religion has spread throughout the entire world. Nearly everyone goes into religion a little bit. But just a few go into religion in such depth that they see through the hoax to realize there is not a higher power looking out for us.

In the religious and occult fields an interested person goes into it like a dedicated student. He or she keeps studying, applying the lessons to life and keeps advancing to the next level. After many years a handful of individuals make it all the way, i.e., break through to that final level. That final level is realizing the whole thing is an illusion, that there is no God or higher mystical power above us, that each individual must be his own authority. That is the final Master level the religious/spiritual

5

leaders keep telling their students to strive for: the realization that you are your own authority and that you cannot be guided by outside authorities.

I was never so angry in my life as when I finally broke through and realized the whole thing about a kind, benevolent God looking out for people is a hoax. Eventually I pushed aside that anger because in the final analysis I was responsible for accepting those ideas in the first place.

People who are serious about religion or any form of mysticism earnestly read the books and study the teachings of the religious/spiritual leaders. What made me so angry is that those leaders have themselves broken through and realized the hoax. But they do not reveal this in their works. They keep their books and teachings on the market, which entices others into mysticism.

To me, that deception is immoral. Everyone goes into religion in a sincere and honest way. They are seeking solutions to important problems in their lives. Yet they are enticed to go into a way of living that acts against their nature.

And so few finally break through to realize it is all a hoax. Many people live their entire lives caught up living in a way they should not be living, acting and doing things which go against themselves and their interests.

Thus, people like me feel a tremendous anger at those spiritual teachers we once trusted. For, they knowingly keep the hoax alive and perpetuate it. They receive a lot of adulation and make a living off their teachings and ministries and books. Of course, they rationalize their hoax as a noble cause for their students.

I do know of two religious/spiritual authors who did reveal the hoax once they finally broke through. One is P. D. Ouspensky, who revealed the hoax in religion The other is Alan Watts, who revealed the double bind in Zen. But most spiritual teachers, ministers, and authors continue to promote and perpetuate their works.

What was really shocking to me was when I realized most religious leaders, especially the Pope, Zen masters, and occult teachers are atheists. They rationalize that the masses need the concept of a higher authority to keep them moral. They put

6

down the intellect of the general population. They say the masses psychologically need the idea of a God looking out for them.

But the general population is made up of businessmen, doctors, lawyers, architects, teachers, and competent workers. They are not ignorant or uneducated. The general population is smart and self-sufficient. The leaders keep the deception alive so they can be looked up to as highly spiritual, as masters, as pursuing an admirable profession.

It is extremely difficult to make the breakthrough. It took St. Theresa fourteen years and St. John of the Cross twenty-six years. I read a book by a monk who had broken through. In his twenty-six years in the monastery only six other monks had broken through the hoax. They were then promptly invited to teach. Of all the young men entering that monastery every year for twenty-six years only six broke through the hoax. That is, only six monks were able to finally realize there is no higher authority looking out for us, that only you can be your own authority in life.

These leaders and teachers, after they have broken through and become atheists, never tell their followers what they have learned. Instead, they use hidden terminology. They call someone who has broken through a Master, or someone who has learned wisdom. They do not tell you that the wisdom a Master has learned is that an individual is his own authority. They cannot tell you that because then their entire 3000-year-old profession would crumble.

So how can you know when a religious/mystical leader has broken through the hoax? Because there are stages of learning a person goes through. You can recognize the stage a person is in. One who has broken through to that final stage of enlightenment speaks with authority and self-confidence. He does not emphasize earlier stages of learning which he has already broken through.

An example is a well known religious TV personality. I was watching his television program. If you have been through the mystic path, you know the lessons that are learned at each stage. A young man in the audience asked that TV minister if there had ever been a time in his life when he doubted God.

This well known religious TV personality answered that there had been a really dark period in his life when he struggled tremendously with that question. He acknowledged it had been the darkest period of his life. His answer was, "I stand on the historical Jesus." The mystics call this period *The dark night of the soul* because they have realized there is no God.

The promises held out in the religious and mystical teachings all disappear once the hoax is realized. If a spiritual leader refuses to reveal the hoax, then he can go on with his religious ministry. Realize, however, many ministers are just as in the dark regarding the hoax as are their congregations. They, too, have not advanced to that master level.

When reading a religious book you can tell by the way the author expresses himself if he has broken through, i.e., if he or she has realized the hoax but continues to promote it.

You see, there are different stages the mystics discuss in their books. As an example, St. Theresa of Avila wrote a number of religious books. I know she broke through to the full realization of the hoax. The way I know this is that she suddenly stopped reading all religious literature. Her whole adult life was spent constantly reading and writing about the Lord. Suddenly, she stopped completely.

Why? Because she realized her visions, her trances, everything was coming from her inner self. She did not tell her confessor what she had realized. The priest, who had always heard her confessions, just could not get over why all of a sudden she stopped all religious reading. That had been her passion in life.

That is one of the clues — she stopped all religious readings. I know she felt tricked. When I read about this I immediately knew what had happened. She did not tell anyone what she had learned. During her time, the Inquisition, she would have been burned at the stake.

Once a person breaks through the hoax to realize there is no higher authority looking out after him, that person misses the relationship he thought he had with God. The thought that reality is all there is seems cold. It takes away the mystery and love that communication with God provided.

8

Chapter 1 Research Notes

* Most people want something more rewarding from life than what they have. The one area that addresses this issue is religious and mystical literature. While much of the literature is beautiful and poetic, another seductive ingredient of all religious and mystical literature is the total concentration on the self. The development of one's character becomes the goal in life. One's life becomes totally concentrated on his desires, his disappointments, his strengths, his weaknesses, his goals. No other field of endeavor except perhaps psychotherapy rivals this emphasis on the self. The personal involvement is all pervading. There are very few other things in life that can compete with this kind of self-absorption. The goal is mastery of the self. And through that mastery comes wisdom.

* How does a person get drawn into the religious/mystic path? First, you are invited to participate with the expectation of achieving all those things one associates with God: all the beautiful things in life — love, happiness, values, rewards, and wisdom. All these associations come from the mind of the individual and what he or she considers important. The idea that you will achieve these things is paramount in your thinking, since God is supposed to be a benevolent god who wants the best for everyone.

The mystic goes into the path in depth, unlike the average churchgoer who follows the religious concepts at the fringes. The mystic is totally dedicated and commits his life to the quest. Therefore, the mystic eventually breaks through the hoax, whereas the average churchgoer lives his or her whole life never uncovering the hoax.

Prior to the first stage there is a period of two to three years of unhappiness, of mental and emotional stress. This sets the stage psychologically for the need for a new direction, for another way to solve one's problems. If for several years one has been unable to find the happiness he seeks, then he needs to find a new approach to his present circumstances.

In examining this period no mystic will tell you what his problem was, why he was so unhappy. The reason is that the problem is too personal so the mystic generalizes the cause. He describes this period as one of uneasiness, restlessness, and a dissatisfaction with the world.

But the reason is always a deeply personal one. Something that he intensely wants but cannot achieve. Instead of letting go of that desire he takes drastic measures by following a mystical philosophy that clashes with all his personal freedoms. But íd takes this step with the fervent hope and belief that this new direction will bring his desire. Most of all he wants to believe that with God's interaction in his life his desire will be granted.

* Most people who practice the religious principles in depth believe they have a personal contact with God. This is one of the strongest drawing cards of religion. It makes a believer feel special and important. And, it makes a believer feel adamant that he is right in what he is following.

The person experiencing this personal contact with God wants it to be true. He reads books by others who have also experienced it. He or she develops an attraction to and sense of wonder and fascination with the mystical experiences of others, e.g.,

- Moses and the burning bush when God spoke to him
- Jesus and his healing miracles
- Joseph and the plagues
- Joan of Arc and the voices which spoke to her
- St. Teresa and the visions she had

These mystical experiences have a strong impact on others and are used to further the belief in God and his communication to others.

History abounds with examples of those who thought they had a personal contact with God, that God had communicated to them. This phenomenon is easily explainable and has its roots in the two hemispheres of our brain (see Chapter 3).

In fact, all the biographies of the Catholic saints and other mystics reveal that they eventually discovered that there was no communication with something outside themselves (God), but that the communication was instead coming from within themselves, from their own consciousness. When they realized that fact, each stopped his or her own specialized form of contacting God,

10

whether that be through visions, trances, random book readings, automatic writings, or other means.

Chapter Two

The Four Stages of the Religious/Mystic Path

The religious/mystic path can be broken down into four major stages. The first stage is when a person is initially drawn in, when he first starts thinking he has a communication with God. Of course, this is a very joyous time. If you believe in God and you believe God has chosen to communicate with you, this really makes you feel good. You experience a tremendous feeling of joy and devotion. This also gives you a lot of courage to think that what you are doing is right.

In this first stage the religious student is enamored with the idea of signs and miracles as taught in the Bible. But that euphoria soon passes. It passes because the student starts becoming more serious about learning.

Evelyn Underhill in her book *Mysticism* also identified four stages. I would like to use her groupings because they are so descriptive of what takes place. Her descriptions affirm the religious/mystical experience:

Stage One: Awakening of the Self
- Preceded by a period of discontent
- Usually a single and abrupt experience of conversion
- It is usually sudden, intense, and joyous
  (Note: One quickly learns that seeking miracles is not what the religious/mystic path is about.)

Stage Two: Purification of the Self
- Purgation of imperfection in your character
- Self-simplification and self-knowledge
- Contemplation
- Detachment and analysis
  (Note: This stage involves following the will of God, self-sacrifice in a contained area, and giving up personal desire. This is the hardest stage to go through.)

Stage Three: Illumination of the Self
- Awakening to consciousness of reality
- Insights and a certainty about life

13

- Has detached himself from his chief entanglements
- Has re-oriented his or her life with a new and solid certitude
- Sets new standards of conduct and thought
- Introspection and turning inward deliberately to discern reality
- Has not yet reached the goal
  (Note: This stage reflects that the ideas of self-sacrifice and giving up all personal desire have been rejected because of their harmful nature to character development.)

Stage Four: Unitive Life. Union

- The goal has been reached. A profound change in personality.
- The mystics describe this as The Spiritual Marriage.
  (Note: At this stage you become your own authority and master. You recognize there is no higher authority and the communication with God that you thought you had actually came from within your own consciousness. You are no longer divided but are at-one-with yourself.)

The first stage is obvious — the decision to devote oneself to religion or some form of mysticism and claim its promises and wisdom.

The second stage is the longest and most difficult. It is a psychological process that involves much self examination. It is a stage of meditation and contemplation.

A lot of people think meditation is a form of making one's mind blank and not thinking about anything. But that is opposite of what actually takes place. The meditator starts by relaxing. If there is something bothering him, he pushes that aside. Emotions will color his thinking, making it difficult to think clearly. The idea of meditation is to get calm and push away emotional distractions. Then the person meditating starts thinking about how to perfect his character. He examines his life and attitudes.

During the second stage of the mystic path, the religious student also reads a lot of religious literature and examines the lessons they teach. The idea is to perfect character, which means being honest, fair and compassionate.

Consider sympathy and compassion. The religious idea of service to others has been so instilled throughout everyone's life that, over time, the religious student begins to recognize how altruism can sometimes do more harm to people than good. We see an example in government handouts that have crippled entire generations of inner-city residents. The student begins to realize that one can feel sympathy for people, but true compassion takes into account not crippling them while trying to help them.

There are two major emphases in this second stage. They are to give up personal desire and to follow the will of God. But, over time, the student comes to realize that no one really knows what the will of God is. Some say the will of God means that anything in your life is there because God wills it to be there.

But then the religious student comes to points where something he wants appears blocked. That happens naturally just through living life. But the student interprets each block as the need to give up some personal desire because it is the will of God.

Here is an illustration of a person believing she is blocked and being guided by the will of God to give up something. My friend Mary and I had been drawn strongly into the religious literature together. One day Mary wanted to make a dress (she loved sewing) and needed to buy some cloth. It had been snowing all morning. There was snow and ice all over her driveway. But she was determined to go to the cloth store, so she went outside. She slipped on the ice walking to her car. She hurt herself but got up and continued toward her car. Once again, she fell down, this time even harder. So she concluded, "All right, Lord, you're telling me to give up sewing." She then stopped sewing completely.

Like so many religious believers, she took that as a sign. But things like slipping on ice happen naturally. A person is always going to have something which interferes with his plans at various times.

The serious religious student evolves to a stage where eventually he just gives up all personal desires. This stage is the worst stage to go through. You have no motivation, no interests. I do not think anyone could go through it for long. They would end up sick, physically and mentally. I know, I

15

went through it. Just to do a chore around the house was draining, my arms felt physically heavy. I had never experienced anything like that in my life. In the end, one cannot live in such a state.

It is really something the way life presents circumstances. One day Jane, who lived near me, came over and brought a little Dell pocketbook on astrology. She discussed some of the psychological ways different people approach life. What she related was so interesting I got intrigued. This new interest brought me out of that crisis stage of having no desire.

Emotions are the fuel of life. If you have no desire, you have no motivation. There is no inner fuel to do anything. All of a sudden the heaviness in my arms went away after I got interested in something particular. So that was a major breakthrough in my understanding and then rejection of giving up desire.

Rapidly following that insight came another breakthrough. I was at a stage where I was seriously practicing selflessness. When you seriously practice selflessness, you become very in-control of your emotions. You are always guarded in your reactions and how you act with others. In an unguarded moment I had a major breakthrough concerning sacrifice. My children had a dog that I was trying to housebreak but that dog had urinated everywhere. I got furious and started spanking him.

Suddenly I realized I was hitting him way too hard. This happened during an unguarded moment with my emotions. I was too angry. I actually felt violent. A flood of negative emotions rushed over me. I felt like I could strangle that dog.

I made myself stop. I then realized why I was filled with such overpowering anger. It had nothing to do with that dog. It had everything to do with the idea of practicing constant self-sacrifice.

Whenever a person stifles his natural emotions — such as justified anger at being taken advantage of by others — he does not negate those emotions. He merely pushes those emotions inward, suppressing them. With myself, by trying to follow the religious ideal of sacrifice and humility, I had been suppressing my natural emotions. In an unguarded moment those emotions exploded to the surface.

16

It dawned on me that even the sweetest old ladies who go to church and practice self-sacrifice all their lives are suppressing those same emotions. They are suppressing emotions of anger and rage at being manipulated and taken advantage of by others. Because that is what happens when you consistently practice sacrifice and humility — you are manipulated and taken advantage of by others because you do not stand up and defend yourself. Those sweet old ladies, too, are capable of violence and rage in unguarded moments.

Religious teachings tell you to push aside your natural emotional reactions of anger and humiliation and project love and compassion instead. In reality, if something unfair or unjust happens to you, then you need to address the anger and frustration you feel. If you do not, you suppress it. And that suppression eventually harms your self-esteem.

With me, a flood of negative emotions suddenly overcame me. I realized practicing selflessness and sacrifice, two concepts religion says are central to perfecting character, is wrong.

Instead of building honest, genuine character, consistent sacrifice and selflessness result in the opposite. In me, I suddenly felt an urge to kill that dog. *Lord*, I thought, *Where are those feelings coming from?*

I knew I was as spiritual as anyone else who went into religion as deeply and sincerely as I did. Yet, if I could be filled with those violent emotions because of following the religious doctrines of sacrifice and selflessness then something was terribly wrong.

Following the doctrine of selflessness and sacrifice caused those emotions of rage within me, because, in the end, man's nature is to build values, not sacrifice values, to live for oneself, not for someone else. In fact, you discover it is not even possible to live for someone else. Nothing could be more degrading to that other person.

This realization was my first major breakthrough coupled with the realization that giving up personal desire goes against man's nature and is also self-destructive. Those two insights end the second stage of the mystic path. The religious student then enters the third stage with a new self-confidence and a new evaluation of reality.

17

The concepts of selfishness versus selflessness are so basic to man's character and to his happiness that I want to elaborate on each. Many say selfishness is cold and leaves no room for compassion. I prefer to use the term rational self-interest because it does away with the negative connotation of a spoiled child. However, selfishness in its true sense is the correct definition.

The best way to grasp the differences between these two concepts is to demonstrate the character development and the behavior which result from each. The contrast of selfishness versus selflessness can be demonstrated in the hero concept versus the coward concept.

Everyone admires the hero. His characteristics are strength of character, principled behavior, honesty, self-confidence, a healthy self-esteem, bravery and daring, self-respect, stands up for self against great odds, is compassionate and fair in his dealings with others. These are all character traits of a selfish person.

Everyone despises a coward. And the behavior of the selfless person is the behavior of the coward. *Wait a minute*, you say. *To be selfless is not the same as being a coward.* Since religion holds up selflessness as an ideal, people fool themselves as to what self-sacrifice really means. Because we have been so instilled by religious doctrine that selflessness is moral, we fail to recognize the consequences of such behavior.

Like the coward, the selfless person puts others first and self second. He fails to stand up for himself. That action causes resentment and anger toward other people to build up within him. In addition, he thinks others can be sacrificed as he sacrifices himself.

As demonstrated in the table below, the selfish person's behavior is identical with the hero concept while the selfless person's behavior is identical with the coward concept.

Selfish	**Selfless**
(The Hero Concept — *Everyone Admires)*	*(The Coward Concept —* *Everyone Despises)*
1. Puts self first. Result: Respects self, therefore, respects others.	1. Puts self second. Result: Taken advantage of, therefore, feels resentment towards others.

(Chart continued on next page)

18

The Four Stages Of The Religious/Mystic Path

Selfish	**Selfless**
(The Hero Concept — Everyone Admires)	(The Coward Concept — Everyone Despises)

(Chart continued from previous page)

2. In control and works hard to accomplish goals.	2. Must manipulate others to achieve sacrificial goals.
3. A strong personality.	3. A weak personality.
4. Self-confidence and self-esteem.	4. Lack of self-confidence and low self-esteem.
5. Honest and forthright.	5. Hides true emotional reactions in order to practice self-sacrifice and humility, therefore, not honest with others.
6. Feels secure in himself and has no desire to control others.	6. Feels insecure. Desires to control others in order to make them practice self-sacrifice and to suppress their personal desires too.
7. Recognizes the individual as the highest value.	7. Views the individual as someone who should be sacrificed.
8. Compassionate towards others because he feels a love and respect for himself.	8. Does not feel true compassion towards others because he hates himself for his cowardly actions. He disguises this self-hatred by projecting it onto others.
9. Loves self; happy.	9. Hates self; disgusted and unhappy.

When working in accordance with his biological, emotional, and intellectual nature, man is a beautifully integrated whole. He is at one with himself. When man acts against himself in one of those areas, he is at odds with himself and the consequences can be disastrous.

An extreme example of how destructive selfless behavior can be and how it can affect everyone in their daily lives is given below:

A few years ago a thirteen-year-old boy killed a neighboring

19

child. No one knew why that boy killed the other child. Not the psychologist who interviewed him, not the counselors, not his teachers, not his parents.

But it was self-evident to me. A TV program about this tragic incident stated that the thirteen-year-old-boy had been subjected to insults and humiliations all his life from peers at school. He looked a little odd. He had offset eyes.

The boy had asked his stepfather what to do. He was told to ignore his taunters. If the boy felt really upset, he was told to get his anger out with some kind of physical exercise, like a punching bag. The boy had bruised both his hands from striking a tree in front of his house. But, that action did not address the cause of his anger.

This boy had a justified anger because of the insults and humiliations he had endured. But strong anger by itself does not create a murderer. His anger turned into violence because of the self-loathing he felt at not standing up for himself, at not holding himself up as a worthy individual. In other words, he viewed himself as a coward and he hated that.

Violent criminals are known for their lack of remorse toward their victims. They cannot feel remorse because they feel no remorse for themselves — they feel self-loathing toward themselves and project that loathing onto their victims.

By comparison, a person who is selfish stands up for himself. As a result, no inner resentment builds up. He feels self-respect and extends that same respect towards others. He has the courage to be straightforward and honest in his dealings. He has no desire to manipulate. Because he likes himself, he is capable of liking others and feeling compassion towards them.

In contrast, the selfless person, because he lets others take advantage of him, lacks self-confidence and has a low self-esteem. Because he does not stand up for himself, he must hide his emotional reactions. Therefore, he is not honest with others. He manipulates others through facades of kindness or feel-sorry-for-me attitudes. Although outwardly he professes compassion, inwardly he is filled with resentment, anger, and self-loathing for his own cowardly behavior.

The religious person may trick his mind into thinking that selfless behavior is moral, but he cannot fool the biological and rational foundation of his inner self and his true essence as a human being. The religious person can never be centered and in harmony with himself as long as he truly acts selflessly.

He thinks others can be sacrificed the same way he sacrifices himself. Because of this, he lacks respect for others. He tries to manipulate them (usually through guilt) to make them sacrifice, too. He feels anger and resentment when he fails to stand up for himself, and he feels anger and resentment towards others who fail to sacrifice themselves. He is definitely not compassionate.

What emerges from this picture is the inherent destructiveness of the religious doctrines. The Dark Ages, the Inquisitions, the endless holy wars raging even to this day are not aberrations but are direct results of following the doctrine of sacrifice and selflessness.

To use a metaphor concerning selfless behavior, it is like a pot of boiling water on a stove with the top tightly closed. The boiling water represents all the negative emotions the selfless person has stifled. At some point that top is going to give way and the selfless person's emotions are going to erupt.

If you become serious about religion, it is almost like going to college. You become very intense about learning the subject matter. That is your main focus. You are not questioning the doctrines. You are trying to learn their lessons and implement them.

Eventually you begin rejecting a lot of tradition you know is not correct — cutting away at church dogma which has nothing to do with spirituality. After each breakthrough, you reach a higher stage of learning. For example, by the time I broke through the second stage to enter the third stage, I still could not say selfishness was right. Instead, I said there is a higher selfishness. Religious doctrine instills such a strong prejudice against being selfish.

A higher selfishness includes the fact that you are moral and honest. You think of doing things in your best interest with a sense of being moral. In other words, you do not take advantage of other people. So, in my thinking, I turned selfishness into a higher selfishness, which includes fairness and morality.

In actuality that is selfishness, not a higher selfishness. Ayn Rand was the first to raise selfishness to the status of a virtue, along with honesty and morality.[1] Many people who read Ayn Rand think selfishness is cold and does not include compassion. They are wrong because they do not grasp the full significance of selfishness.

You see, a person cannot suddenly make too large a leap in their thinking. Selfishness is the opposite of selflessness. For religiously oriented people, realizing selfishness is good and moral is a huge leap. They have to be able to make that leap gradually.

Once the religious student stops dogmatically acting selfless and begins to act in his own best interest, he begins to build self-confidence. He then enters the third stage.

But prior to this third stage, the second stage involves two processes. One process is becoming goal oriented. The religious student is strongly focused and becomes very selfish with his time. So two processes are going on at the same time. One, in which the student practices selfishness with his time, the other in which he practices selflessness in other areas.

The process of being goal oriented builds strength. And through the strength of this self-knowledge the student begins to break with the selflessness hoax.

The religious student then enters the third stage with renewed confidence. He has mastered the major hurdles — those false doctrines which led to psychological turmoil. He has learned to introspect and trust his own judgment. His new philosophy based on reality gives him a certainty about life.

But there is one more hurdle to conquer before he is fully his own master: He has to break with the idea of God. During the first two stages the student has been drawn into mysticism and the God concept so deeply by thinking that he has had communication with God. ...One really does feel as though he

------

[1]A contrast exists between the Hebrew religion and the Christian religion. The Hebrew religion has always held up the individual as the highest value. They do not accept self-sacrifice. That is why Jews, generally speaking, have been so successful. Christianity introduced self-sacrifice as a major doctrine with Jesus — Jesus who sacrificed his life for the rest of humanity. But even here, the Church purposely misinterpreted Jesus' message. (See *Jesus' Secret Message,* Appendix I.)

is communicating with God.

It took me five years to break through stage one and stage two. It took me another three years to break through the third stage. During this third stage the serious student completely breaks with traditional church dogma, but he still believes in God. Even though he knows self-interest is correct, he still believes he is supposed to do the will of God.

Eventually, however, that student begins to realize that as long as you allow the idea of a God who can tell you what to do, you will never be your own master. You will never be your own authority. In the fourth and final stage the student finally breaks with the higher authority hoax. At this point, the whole foundation of religion begins to crumble. He comes to realize that the God concept, too, is a false idea. He finally realizes that the communication he thought was coming from God was actually coming from within himself, from his own subconscious, from his right hemisphere.

Most of the mystical literature I have read states that eventually one gives up even the spiritual. At first, you think they mean that when a person finally becomes a master, he or she is so emotionally evolved that they even give up their selfish desires for spiritual attainment. But, with time, you come to understand what they really mean by eventually giving up the spiritual and the full significance of that statement. You finally realize that God, too, is a false doctrine.

At last, I was free to make my own decisions without any obligation to follow the will of God. My first reaction was one of joy and tremendous relief. There was also a certain sadness because the spiritual literature holds out many promises to those who achieve unity, and I now realized that none of those promises would be forthcoming.

Another emotion to work through is the feeling of being disloyal to Jesus and all he stood for. About a year later my new knowledge was really put to the test in reality. Would I make my own decisions concerning new directions in my life or would I fall back into the trap of letting blocks to my new directions win out?

I had just made three major decisions. One concerned starting a career, as I had been staying at home raising my three children.

A second decision involved a personal relationship (My husband and I had discussed a year earlier). The third decision involved putting my new knowledge into action. As obstacles began to appear in all three areas an old emotion surfaced: to give up desire. At this point, an emotional crisis took place within me. I experienced tremendous anger at the whole religious field because I realized how much it had crippled my own capacities to handle life's challenges.

The religious teachings constantly stress how you have to give up personal desire. Over time, that leads to a crisis. In the third stage you follow the philosophy of self interest. You build confidence and strength. Yet, in trying to follow God's will, you meet obstacles to your own goals in life and, therefore, have to relinquish your own will. Eventually, these contradictions come together in a crisis.

One aspect devastates you when you finally break through to realize the hoax. The serious religious student works hard to develop his intellect. And then, suddenly, he discovers the opposite — that his intellect has been crippled after so many years of giving up personal desire, sacrificing his own values to others, and subjugating his own will to the will of God.

His intellect does work correctly concerning life and honesty and being fair to others. All of which is psychology, it is all related to people and one knows those things are correct and moral through life experience. Intellectually, the student has built up a tremendous amount of knowledge and wisdom about life and people through experiences.

But, then, he still has something else going on, still believing in God and believing he has communication with God. All of a sudden that student realizes religion is the authority figure constantly telling him *No* to fulfilling his own will, to achieving his own goals and desires. Eventually, after many years of studying and applying his knowledge in the real world, the student comes to realize that to be his own person, to make his own decisions, he can not have such an authority over him.

As mentioned, even the religious literature says a person will eventually give up the desire for the spiritual. At first, everyone thinks this means that one evolves to some sort of supra-spiritual level where you no longer need to pursue spiritual perfection.

But, lo-and-behold, you finally do give up the spiritual once you realize that the communication you thought you were having with God was actually coming from within your own self, from within your own subconscious.

As the religious student progresses through the four stages of the Mystic Path, the reason he does not recognize his insights as coming from within his own brain but instead thinks they come from God is because the insights are so contradictory to his beliefs. First, he discovers that one cannot give up personal desire, then he discovers that one should practice rational selfishness, finally he discovers that one must be his own authority. These breakthrough insights are opposite his religious indoctrination, so he does not recognize them as his own. He thinks that surely these radical insights must be coming from a higher authority.

In the late 1960s a neurophysiologist, Roger Sperry, carried out experiments on split-brain epileptic patients. It started with a Dr. Joseph Bagen doing a daring experiment. He cut the corpus callosum between the two hemispheres of the brain. The corpus callosum is what allows the two hemispheres to communicate. Dr. Bagen carried out this procedure in severe epileptics, hoping to reduce the severity of their attacks.

Then, Roger Sperry carried out experiments on these split-brain patients. When I read Sperry's work, I realized what individuals thought was communication with God was actually coming from the right hemisphere of their brains. That is a fascinating area, which we will explore in later chapters.

After an individual breaks through and realizes there is no God, mystical thoughts and emotions still linger. He or she just has to push them away. For instance, it is stated in the religious literature that if you blaspheme against God then something dreadful will happen to you. I felt I should write about my realizations and reveal the truth. But then a tremendous feeling of dread came over me. That feeling was the result of guilt built into the religious teachings. Intellectually I had to push those feelings away because I knew they belonged to the illusion and had nothing to do with reality.

I did feel a tremendous responsibility to my friend Mary,

whom I mentioned earlier. She started reading my religious books and would ask me about them. At that time I had not completely broken through. I had broken through to the third stage but I still believed in God.

Mary was drawn into the religious teachings herself. She went into the spiritual as deeply as I had. I felt a responsibility toward her because she had confidence in me. I remember one time she said, *(Am I going crazy? Is this all in my mind or is this real?)* I had to reassure her. Because she had previously been studying occult literature, she was more grounded in self-responsibility.

Ironically, the occult preaches self-responsibility whereas religion says to put aside your intellect and go on faith. That is what you do when you accept the religious doctrines. You put aside your intellect and give the religious doctrines a try on faith.

After making the stunning realization that God is also part of the religious/mystical illusion, an individual realizes those noble desires people have of wanting to be honest, to deal fairly with others, to be compassionate all come from within each person's own self. But as a religious person, one projects all of those characteristics onto some mystical God, as if an individual person can not be honorable, only God.

You see, it is a shame people do not claim those ideals for themselves. Instead, they project those ideals onto a God, as if by themselves they are incapable of achieving honesty, fairness, compassion.

In the next chapter, we will discuss fascinating ways the right hemisphere of our brain works — ways that we are not even aware of.

Chapter 2 Research Notes

* When I was a dedicated student of religion, I read an enormous amount of religious literature. I read so many different religious books from so many different eras. Some books were written hundreds of years ago, some were written in Spain, some in England, some books even dated back to ancient China. Many books were present day religious writings from America. I was continually struck by how each author, regardless of time or

place, kept having similar experiences and learned the same types of lessons. So many people who lived under totally different circumstance had the same experiences I had. This seemed to reaffirm that religious mysticism was true.

I was born in the 20th Century, married, with three children, living in suburban America. Yet, I was having the same kind of experiences as St. Teresa who lived in a Spanish monastery during the 1500s. How could we, and countless others, keep having the same type of experiences and learning the same lessons? This was so mysterious to me. It reaffirmed that there must be some kind of guiding hand leading a person through life. How else could you explain that?

It was not until I started writing about my religious experiences that the answer hit me. A person is going to meet the same kind of circumstances and learn similar lessons in his or her life according to the philosophy he or she is following. If you follow the philosophy of religion and mysticism then you are going to have situations occurring in your life that reflect the religious or mystical ideals you are pursuing. This has nothing to do with time, place or circumstances in life. The values you uphold, the ideals you seek will lead you to common experiences.

* The Church ensures moral control over followers by setting up an impossible goal to attain. First, religion establishes the Authority of God or one of his representatives. But no one knows what God's will is. So, whatever happens must be God's will because he loves us and allowed it to happen. Therefore, we must accept whatever happens to us. And because we cannot understand why God lets certain things happen to us we must suspend our intellect and have faith. The believer's thinking is that through his struggle God will help him solve his problems and that he will one day attain the happiness and peace he desires as a result.

Secondly, religion sets the task of attaining perfection of character. But attempting to attain perfection of character through an authority outside yourself and through the principles of altruism is impossible.

Paul described this process when he said, paraphrasing, *(That*

*which I should do, I do not. And that which I should not do, I
do.)* What Paul is saying is the actions he wants to do in order
to attain perfection, he fails to do. And the actions he does not
want to do so that he can attain perfection, he keeps doing. That
impossible goal keeps one in emotional turmoil, in painful
introspection. Throughout history the church has taken full
emotional advantage of followers in this predicament.

* A person will not keep acting against his own best interests
no matter how hard he tries. Thus, the more the religious student
fails in his attempts to be selfless and sacrifice the greater his
resolve to succeed. Yet the harder he tries, the more he fails.
In their attempts to be good and moral very few religious students
break through this vicious cycle and realize its destructiveness.
They remain captives of external authority and altruistic
philosophy, never achieving real happiness in their lives.
Breaking through this hoax depends on the intensity of the person
striving to attain the religious ideals. If his intensity is great,
and his resolve absolute, then he will eventually break its
stranglehold. He will realize that selfishness is a virtue and
selflessness breeds inner contempt, resentment, and feelings of
weakness. He will realize that only a selfish person is capable
of real compassion and a selfless person is so full of suppressed
resentment that he does not experience honest compassion.

That student will also come to realize that since a selfless
person is willing to sacrifice his life, so that selfless person is
just as willing to sacrifice other people's lives as well. Only a
selfish person would not sacrifice his life and only a selfish
person would be unwilling to sacrifice someone else's life. This
list can go on and on — only a selfish person respects himself,
will not let himself be imposed upon and extends that same
respect to another individual. The opposite is true of a selfless
person. He imposes on others and feels it is his right since he
lets others disrupt his time. The selfless person does not respect
others since he does not respect himself.

An extreme sensitivity develops when trying to attain an
impossible goal. The constant futile attempts lead to painful
introspection. This all comes as a real shock. It always takes
a strong dose of reality before any belief system will be given

up. But any false ideas imposed upon reality will always keep being challenged by reality.

Eventually the many years of self-indoctrination, in a sense self-hypnosis, will all come shattering down. The very foundation of the whole edifice vanishes when one realizes there is no God, nothing will intervene, no spiritual attainment is to be had, no promises will be fulfilled. This is an enormous emotional investment to let go of.

In the religious literature itself, the seeker is told that he will one day have to give up the spiritual. This statement reveals that the religious Masters know the ending of the story. They know there is no God, for even the spiritual is eventually given up.

The most damaging effect that occurs to the person who breaks through the hoax and realizes there is no God is to that person's belief in his own intellectual powers. The religious student had strongly believed in a personal God. That belief gave him emotional fuel and gave him the courage to face certain things that would be hard to do on his own. He felt special. But he now realizes he has been extremely naive and gullible, yet, through it all, he had felt intellectually superior. After all, one of the goals was to learn wisdom. What a shock to his intellect and to his integrity. He now knows that he alone is ultimately responsible for having accepted this philosophy.

At this point, his shaken ground slowly firms as he realizes that whatever he learned he learned as a result of integrating reality. Time and again reality was his true teacher while religious and mystical ideas proved deceitful and were always his downfall. This is the stage where one finally breaks through the myth of external authority. One finally realizes that no matter what dogma is put forth, it is always reality that is the great undeceiving teacher.

* The one overriding ingredient in all spiritual requirements is sacrifice. This is disguised in a certain sense by what is required:

> To do the will of God
> To get rid of the ego
> To be selfless

To develop humility
To give up desire
To be compassionate
To give up free choice
To give up pride
To let go of self-esteem
To give up self-confidence
To let go of self-interests

In other words, all free choice, all ambition, all self-interest is to be sacrificed to the goal of being spiritual.

* Mystics often claim that what they learn cannot be taught; that it can only be learned through experience. This is a half-truth. It can be taught, but the lessons can only be made a part of one's self through experience. This is no different from any other field of mastery. Knowledge can be taught, studied, and learned in any field of endeavor. But one masters the skills of that field only through practical application and personal experience.

The real reason why mystics will not tell you what they learn is that what they learn is the opposite of what they teach. Therefore, they shroud everything in mystery.

Chapter Three
Our Right Brain

After realizing there is no God and wanting to understand the mystical phenomena which convinced me that I had communication with God, I began to research studies done on the left and right hemispheres of our brain. According to Evelyn Underhill in her book *Mysticism*, mystical experiences often involve voices and visions.

In his research, Dr. Wilder Penfield of Montreal, Canada, carried out experiments locating the different areas of the human brain and their functions. Using electrodes, he would stimulate different areas of the right hemisphere of the brain. When he stimulated a certain area within the right hemisphere, subjects would have visions of past experiences. When stimulating another area of the right brain, subjects would hear auditory commands.

Those auditory commands always sounded like a powerful man's voice. One man said he felt as though it was his father giving him commands. Even women would hear an authoritative man's voice.

So, you see, when primitive people were being guided by their bicameral mind,[1] they did not recognize those authoritative voices as coming from within their own brains. It sounds like someone else's voice outside of oneself.

So religious and mystical people are fooled. The authoritative voice they hear during their visions is not God, the voice and vision is coming from the right hemisphere of their brain.

St. Theresa would hear auditory voices. I heard it once; it was startling. It sounded like a man's voice, very loud. It was at night, around 10 p.m. The back of my chair faced a corner

---

[1] Bicameral Mind: See Julian Jaynes' book *The Origin of Consciousness in the Breakdown of the Bicameral Mind*. Julian Jaynes, a Princeton Professor, reveals how until approximately 3000 years ago the human mind functioned through automatic, non-introspective commands. This nature given, bicameral mind was highly intelligent, but immersed in the here-and-now. It did not have the ability to be objective, to introspect, or to think in terms of the past or future.

31

of the room, so I knew there was no way anyone could be behind my chair. But the auditory voice was so masculine, so authoritative, that I had to turn around and see if anyone was there.

A person does not hear this voice as he would normally hear people speaking. The voice is inside one's head, but it is so strong, as if someone outside of you has spoken.

Roger Sperry wrote in 1966 concerning his split-brain patients that what they experience in their right hemisphere seems to lie entirely outside the realm of the experience of their left hemisphere.

At one time or another many people experience a voice talking to them even though no one else is present. This voice usually comes across as an authority figure giving a new insight into a personal problem. I experienced this during a time when I had been growing increasingly aware of how true compassion seemed to diminish the more one practiced selflessness and sacrifice. I was trying hard to think through this apparent contradiction. Suddenly, I distinctly heard a strong, authoritative voice speaking to me. This voice told me the answer to the question troubling me. It was a breakthrough insight about how true compassion, in contrast to pseudo compassion, is linked to self-interest.

This experience of hearing a voice when no one has actually spoken occurs because we have split hemispheres in our brains — the left and right hemispheres. We have a bicameral (two-chambered) brain. As explained in Julian Jaynes' book, *The Origin of Consciousness in the Breakdown of the Bicameral Mind*, the left hemisphere is our logical, reasoning hemisphere. When we are thinking about an idea or pondering a question, we are normally conscious only of our reasoning, left hemisphere. This is where our logical thinking takes place.

But occasionally our more intuitive right hemisphere will experience a flash of insight, pulling together seemingly unrelated pieces of information to make a sudden insight. That insight will then pass from our right hemisphere into our left hemisphere. Such a right-brain insight will appear to our left hemisphere, the hemisphere we are normally conscious of and thinking in, as coming from outside ourselves. A person can literally experience such an insight as someone else talking to him.

To religious people, this experience convinces them that they are communicating with God. You can understand how convincing this experience is if you have ever had one of these right-brain flashes of insight yourself. Such right-brain insights do not seem at all like they are coming from within yourself. It really does seem as though God is talking to you.

When a deeply religious person finally breaks through to realize that he or she is not communicating with God, a lot of disorientation results. Certain ways of religious and mystical thinking have become ingrained within the religious/mystical individual. That individual has to really work to push previous mystical modes of thinking aside.

For example, the religious person believes that everything in life is there for a purpose and that everything that happens to him does so for a reason. If he meets someone he is attracted to, he will think that his meeting this person was meant to be. That happens between many men and women. They think that God intended for them to meet, to find their soul mates.

But, as a person begins to break free from religious dogma, he continuously has to discipline himself to push such mystical feelings aside. One learns not to bring preconceived ideas about destiny into relationships. That is one example. But there are other similar mystical modes of thinking that one has to learn to push aside.

Even the littlest events can be imbued with mystical thinking. For example, take those days when everything goes right. Like driving downtown to a crowded shopping complex and there is a parking space waiting for you directly in front of the store you are going into. Everything that entire day seems to go perfect for you. You are the first in line, the coat you want is the only one on sale, and so on. The religious student's mind has become so ingrained with mystical thinking that he automatically feels it is God looking out after him, doing him small favors.

That is a minor situation. But the religious student especially believes that important events happen in his life because God willed it. When an important decision has to be made, he looks for events that he can interpret as a sign from God. It is very difficult to push that kind of mystical thinking aside. One keeps thinking events are a sign from God. Eventually, after breaking through the religious/mystic hoax, one learns to dismiss this past way of thinking.

After breaking through, one also has to learn to push aside feelings of dread. People have been so instilled against any kind of blasphemy against God or the church that one feels he is going to bring some dreadful consequence upon himself, especially when he is angry at the whole religious field and he wants to expose the hoax behind its teachings and dogma.

When a person first goes into religion in a serious way, he begins to feel a kind of euphoria. He feels he is communicating with God. This is an exciting feeling.

So, that person may ask, *If I am not actually communicating with God, what is causing those feelings within me?* Again, one needs to understand how the right hemisphere of our brain works.

I first read about this communication with God, this relationship with God, when I was in high school. I had read about Joan of Arc and other religious individuals who were convinced that they had a personal communication with God. Later, when I became a serious student of religion, I was exposed to different techniques religious mystics use to spark their supposed communication with God. One technique is to open a book at random and read what is on that page. Mystics believe that God speaks to them through the written page.

I remember a day when I was trying to solve a difficult personal problem. I saw no way to solve the problem. So, I decided to open the Bible and read at random to see if maybe I would get some sort of answer. I opened up a page and began to read. There seemed to be nothing relevant there so I closed it.

Then I opened the Bible a second time, again reading both sides of the page. But nothing seemed to speak to me. When I opened a random page of the Bible for a third time and read, it was quite remarkable. The writings described the tribulations a certain tribe was going through. The message on that page addressed exactly the same challenges and emotional turmoil that I was experiencing in my situation.

After that experience, I bought several other religious books and continued the practice of opening random pages and reading. I felt as though I was establishing a communication with God, a relationship with God. In my daily life, no matter what I was thinking or feeling, I could open up one of my religious books and on that very page would be expressed the identical feelings I was experiencing. That seemed remarkable to me.

Sometimes I was angry and I would open the Bible randomly and on that very page would be described a situation that challenged my anger. If I was frustrated with a situation I would open the Bible or one of my religious books, and on that very page would be words that challenged me to have the stamina and courage to follow through with my convictions.

These random book openings always seemed to address the situation that I was experiencing. Because of this, I came to believe that I really had a communication with God. Today, I understand that was my right brain (which is the seat of our emotions) getting in touch with my left brain (which is rational and objective).

St. Theresa practiced random book openings too. She would become very emotional and go into ecstatic trances. Her own writings were full of emotions of love for God and Jesus.

Other religious mystics do what is called automatic writing. They allow their hand to just start writing words on paper while their mind thinks about something else. They are completely unaware of what they are writing. Nowadays, people recognize such automatic writing as coming from one's subconscious. A person can be thinking about something else while writing so that he is not consciously aware of what he is writing. It is easy to think that God or Jesus is the one giving that person the message he is writing, especially before people understood about our subconscious and our right-brain hemispheres.

Other religious mystics believe they are communicating with God through visions — sometimes similar to dreaming. When we dream we see in pictures, not in words. Our left brain thinks in words. Our right brain sees in pictures.

Mystics also use various devices and techniques such as pendulums, tarot cards, numerology charts, astrology forecasts, meditation, I-Ching, psychic exercises and other techniques to establish what they believe is a communication with a higher authority or the supernatural. What these devices and techniques are really doing is performing a type of self-hypnosis that allows the individual to get in direct touch with his right brain, with his subconscious.

A pendulum, for example, works by taking an object, say a crystal or something pointed on a string, and asking questions. If the object turns in a circle to the right, that is suppose to be a "yes" answer. If it turns to the left, that is a "no" answer. If it goes back and forth, it does not know the answer.

All of these mystic devices and techniques are receiving their cues from our subconscious right brain. When we suppress our left-brain conscious mind, our normally subconscious right brain comes into the forefront. And it functions very differently from our left brain. That is why it seems mystical. Our left brain thinks and reasons in words, our right brain sees and feels in pictures.

To build up a little more understanding about how our right brain works, consider the movie Rainman. In that movie Dustin Hoffman plays an autistic person, sometimes called a savant. Autistics are extremely concentrated. But they cannot communicate or interact well with other people.

In Rainman, Dustin Hoffman takes a telephone book and quickly scans through it. The next day he and his brother are ordering a meal in a diner. Rainman asks the waitress her name. She answers. He then promptly tells her where she lives and what her telephone number is.

That ability is not fiction. Some autistics can actually do that. Unlike most people, whose inner consciousness is centered in their verbal reasoning left brain, autisitics' consciousness is centered in their right brain. The right brain sees in pictures in contrast to thinking in words. The right brain is also capable of photographic memory. Thus, Rainman could literally see the pages of the phone book in his mind. Once he knows a person's name, he can mentally look through the pages of a phone book he has examined previously until he gets to that individuals name, phone number and address.

Another example of what the right brain can do was demonstrated when Rainman bumped into a lady and she dropped a box of matches onto the floor. He looked down at the matches scattered around the floor and immediately said, *142*. Rainman's brother, played by Tom Cruise, exclaimed, *142! You can't possibly know how many matches fell on that floor*. The lady then looked into the box and said, *It holds 145 matches and there are three matches left inside!*

Although autistics do not perform well in many day-to-day activities, sometimes making them appear retarded, they often demonstrate genius-like traits in specific, right-brain areas. Some possess a photographic memory. Others are mathematical wizards, able to perform computer-like calculations in their heads. Some autistics demonstrate musical genius. They can listen to a Mozart piece for the very first time and then sit down and play that entire composition on a piano from memory.

Autistics have a tremendous right-brain focus. And since the right brain sees in pictures it is able to see events and grasp the whole overall picture at once, in an instant. In our right brain, there is no sense of past or future, everything is just there.

People, particularly mystically inclined individuals, can build a skill at contacting their right brain directly. In fact, through Tarot cards, pendulums, random book readings, automatic writing and a myriad of other occult techniques a person can become highly skilled at contacting his right brain directly.

Normally, information comes from our right brain into our left brain to be analyzed. But you can learn to get in direct touch with your right-brain hemisphere by suppressing your left and focusing on your right. That is what mystic techniques and devices facilitate in us. Hypnosis is another technique we can use to suppress our left-brain conscious minds to get in direct touch with our normally subconscious right-brain minds.

Returning to the subject of random book openings, because everyone experiences all of life's emotions — anger, compassion, love, anxiety, and so on, almost any page a person randomly opens to in a book can appear to be addressing his or her own personal situation. In fact, two different people may be feeling two different emotions, but if each randomly opened the same book to the same page the situation described on that page could seem to be addressing both individuals personally.

There is also something else that might occur with random book openings. It is conceivable that, over time, as one becomes more familiar with a book, even if this consists of just occasionally thumbing through that book, our right brain, with its computer-like memory capabilities, may learn exactly where certain parts in a book are. And it may also develop the ability to pick out and open those exact pages — especially as a book becomes slightly more worn and uneven over time.

Thus, if you open a book at random it seems remarkable, even supernatural, that you may have opened to the exact page that discusses an emotion or a problem you are thinking about. But, if our right brain can see in an instant that 142 matches fell on the floor, may it not also know exactly where various concepts are within a book and be able to open right to them?

Similarly, consider Tarot cards. In the next chapter, I discuss how Tarot card readers can use their right brain skills to decipher an individual's personality and then accurately project that personality into whichever Tarot card they turn over. But, something else may also take place. Over time the Tarot card reader will naturally become very familiar with her deck through repeated handling and shuffling of the cards as those cards get broken in and slightly worn. It is conceivable that her subconscious right brain, with its photographic memory capabilities, may be able to pick out specific cards within that deck that give the answers she's looking for.

Tarot card readers state that if they try to consciously pick out Tarot cards that answer a person's question they will not get a correct reading. They need to just pick a card randomly without thinking about it. Trying to consciously pick appropriate Tarot cards will involve their rational-thinking, left brain. And the left brain will then block out their right brain. But it is our right brain that has amazing photographic memory capabilities. Capabilities that just may be able to subconsciously, yet successfully, pick out appropriate Tarot cards as well as successfully perform random book openings and many other occult techniques.

A normal person is seldom aware of his right hemisphere, because it is not our rational-thinking side. Processes in your right are more likely to be subconscious ones. But mystics, on the other hand, tend to be much more aware of and in touch with their right hemisphere.

Consider the case of Temple Gramdin. This lady is a highly intelligent autistic woman who has written a book about her experiences as an autistic. She even has a Ph.D. degree. But she thinks in pictures. Thinking in words gives her a tremendous problem. The way her mind works is like putting a videocassette into place and watching the pictures.

It was tremendously difficult for her to learn to think in words. She did so via phonics. Not surprisingly, sound is another function of our right hemisphere.

The right is also considered our survival hemisphere. We see, hear, and feel for survival. For example, consider primitive man out in the wild. He suddenly sees a predator coming at him. He has to react instantly, without rational or logical thinking and without reference to the past or the future. Spontaneous, here-and-now action is a right-brain function. When he sees that predator, he either shoots it with an arrow or he climbs up a tree. He must react instantly without rational, deliberate thought, without regard to future or past considerations.

Awareness of the past and future are functions of our rational, left brain. In fact, it was not until man developed introspective consciousness and moved away from nature's automatic, animal-like mind that we could think of ourselves in terms of the future while drawing on the past. (See *Neo-Tech III* by Frank R. Wallace). Our right brain thinks and perceives only in the here and now.

Examining the experiences of Temple Gramdin reveals just how specific our right brain is. For example, when someone mentions a dog, we naturally think of the concept of dog — covering all types of dogs. But when someone mentions "dog" to Temple Gramdin, she sees in her mind the first dog she ever saw, then she sees the second dog, the third dog, and so on. She literally sees specific dogs. As an autistic, she is operating in her visual, non-conceptual right brain.

We use many abstract words in our language. But abstract words give autistics problems. There is no specific object to look at. For example, in order for Temple Gramdin to understand the word honesty, she pictures in her mind a person in court with their hand on the Bible swearing to tell the truth. Then, she sees in her mind another picture that helps reinforce what honesty means — she pictures a person finding a wallet with money in it and giving it back to its owner. Thus, she sees those two pictures in her mind to grasp the meaning of honesty. Consider a noun like table. We can imagine all kinds of tables. But Temple Gramdin has to see a picture of a specific table in her mind.

In relation to the random book openings discussed previously, consider the following amazing ability of Temple Gramdin. If she is studying a book at a library and she does not have time to finish reading it, she will photograph the pages of that book in her mind. Then, when she has time at home, she will sit down and run each page through her mind again, deciphering the printed words into pictures. Ordinary people cannot do that. We have lost that ability because we are so left brain, verbally oriented.

Early bicameral man was primarily a visual, right-brain being, while modern conscious people evolved into primarily verbal, left-brain beings. But autistic people remain primarily visual, right-brain beings.

Temple Gramdin did not realize until she was in college that other people do not think in pictures as she does. (This also indicates how seldom people talk about their inner processes.) Temple said it was something a professor brought up in class that made her start suspecting that other people do not think in pictures as she does. She questioned her professor further, suddenly realizing that he thought in words, not in pictures.

Our right brain is visual and sensual — we pick up percepts in pictures, touch, depth perception and spatial organization. One of the great functions of this process is that it generates a lot of creativity. Our right brain can see a whole picture at once — a key to originating new, creative insights.

Dr. Frank R. Wallace, author of *The Neo-Tech Discovery*, expressed how at times he thinks via seeing whole pictures. I know he is both right-brained and left-brained oriented. If he considers a new idea he tends to see an entire picture in his mind. Thus, like looking at a jigsaw puzzle, if a piece of information is not consistent with that picture he can quickly reject an idea. Likewise, if a new idea fits into that puzzle, he can usually see why. In conversation, Dr. Wallace can quickly identify if something said is philosophically consistent with reality or not.

Dr. Wallace has this ability because he can consciously draw upon his right brain. Many exceptionally creative and original thinkers have this left-brain/right-brain ability. But anyone can learn to develop this skill once they are aware of and understand this process. And the results can be amazing. You can unlock a jackpot of creativity.

Our left brain is verbal, analytical, objective. It sees things in a sequence like the past, present and future. Our left brain is very rational and language oriented.

In the book *New Think* by Edward D. De Bono, he talks about linear thinking versus vertical thinking. Our left brain thinks vertically. It takes a fact and through logic builds upon that fact. Our left lays a foundation of knowledge based upon fact and then, employing logic, vertically builds up layers of new knowledge step-by-step.

But horizontal thinking is much more right brain. Our right sees parallel patterns and associations among seemingly unrelated facts and events. Our right does not build a logical step from one point up to another. It sees in one area a pattern that is parallel to something else in another area. Then, all of a sudden, the right may make a connection between what seemed like unrelated phenomena, resulting in a completely new insight. That is how sudden flashes of creativity come from our right brain.

Our left brain sees things in a logical, vertical progression. Our right brain sees things horizontally, it sees the whole picture at once. That is why our right brain can spot parallels between seemingly unrelated facts.

Recognizing parallels between disparate phenomena is not the same as logically building one fact on top of another. But the result can be dramatic. Your right brain may recognize an association between areas that you previously thought were completely unrelated. When your right brain sends that information over to your left brain, all of a sudden you become aware of a dramatic new insight.

These sudden insights often occur after a person has been

struggling with a problem, after his or her left brain, with its vertical thinking built upon objective facts has been unable to figure out a solution. That person will then put that problem aside and go about his daily work. It is at this point that his right brain can often solve a problem. Because his left brain has been looking for the expected, logical answer, it can block the right brain from giving an unexpected, horizontally integrated answer.

That is why geniuses such as Archimedes, Newton, Einstein and many others suddenly had eureka-like insights while bathing, while sitting under an apple tree, or while shaving. Their left brain, being relaxed during those moments, was not blocking their right-brain insights. All of a sudden their right brain flashed the answer into their left brain. They immediately recognized, *Eureka! That's the answer!*

While their left brain had been unsuccessfully trying to figure out a solution, their right brain had been working, usually on a subconscious level, to piece a wider puzzle together.

Most problems can be solved by our left brain because most problems can be solved through stepwise logic. But an uncommon problem, or an exceptionally complicated problem, a problem that eludes solutions even after all the facts have been examined and objective thinking employed, might not be resolved through conventional logic. That is when our right brain can step in and make a totally unexpected insight by seeing a connection between seemingly unrelated facts or events. Because our right brain thinks horizontally, it can recognize connections between seemingly disparate phenomena.

It is these startling, right-brain insights that cause people to think that God has given them the answer. Indeed, that is why I thought I was having a communication with God. When our right brain sends a breakthrough insight to our left brain, it seems to come out of nowhere. Such insights usually break through a lot of traditional thinking. These startling, unexpected conclusions can cause an individual to examine his whole life, all his values, everything.

My right-brain insights caused me to re-examine all my indoctrinated thoughts about how people are supposed to live. Surely, I thought, these profound insights were coming from outside my sheltered, limited mind. I was convinced these insights were coming from a higher power, from God.

Consider the ideas of selflessness and sacrifice. Philosophically, they are illogical. But, because I had been indoctrinated with those concepts, my left brain blocked out my right-brain's emotional alarms that selflessness and sacrifice are unhealthy. Selflessness and sacrifice go against the essence of achieving values.

I had been so indoctrinated that selflessness and sacrifice are requirements for obtaining perfection I did not let my right-brain insights break through to my left brain. When I had that experience of hitting my dog too hard during an unguarded moment, everything just came flooding in from my right brain to my left brain. Emotions that had been trying to alert me to the fact that selflessness and sacrifice do not work in the real world, and that practicing true selflessness and sacrifice goes against one's self-esteem and the achievement of worthwhile goals, came rushing in.

Anyone who grew up with a lot of authoritarian dogma being pushed onto them has experienced at one time or another a similar rush of "unacceptable" right-brain emotions during an unguarded moment. Many people, especially from previous generations, have grown up experiencing a lot of religious and moral indoctrination. Some parents encourage intellectual independence in their children. But a lot of families have a negative parent who comes on too strict with their children. Even a lot of ideas promoted in school, are false concerning the way to live or even the idea of honoring the mother and father. You honor your mother and father if they deserve to be honored. If they are cruel or mean-spirited, however, you should not honor them. But, you see, for most people that is an unquestionable doctrine.

When your right brain finally breaks through such dogma, you begin to examine everything. It is a profound experience to have been held in bondage by a lifelong idea and all of a sudden find yourself questioning that idea.

Mystics call this contemplation. It involves relaxing, pushing aside personal worries and concerns, and opening the conduit to your right-brain integrations. During this state you really open up and examine ideas and information that you have not considered before. These new, right-brain perspectives can suddenly free a person from indoctrinated ideas.

During this contemplation stage, a person finds himself breaking through many limitations. He begins to realize that being placed in unquestioned bondage to indoctrinated ideas is not normal, not natural, not right. At first, he thinks it must be God giving him such profound insights. You can imagine how happy that makes a person feel!

This process also occurs in Eastern religions and the occult when they practice meditation. What they are doing is relaxing the logic defenses of their left brain so that new, horizontal insights from their right brain can come in. Of course, they think it is Karma, God, or some other mystical power giving them these answers.

When a person practices meditation, that individual starts by totally clearing his mind. But, after initially clearing his mind, his mind then becomes extremely active. This stage is exciting. You examine various aspects of your life and you keep getting different perspectives.

These fresh, new perspectives help the meditator solve personal problems. The meditator also experiences the pleasure of discovering that certain ideas he or she holds are indeed true while others are actually false. By initially clearing one's vertically thinking left brain during meditation, the meditator makes way for the horizontally thinking right brain to give him fresh, new perspectives.

Meditation really caught on in this country starting in the 1960s. A number of celebrities got involved in the meditation movement. Many talked publicly about how valuable meditation was to them.

People seldom take the time to step back and really think about their lives, their goals, what they want to achieve, what to prioritize. In meditation you do this. This can only be beneficial.

Meditators speak highly about that special time each day. Especially when they are going through hard times, such as a divorce or a career crisis. Unfortunately, meditation has always been tied in with mysticism. Because meditation is so valuable, people accept all kinds of mystical dogma tied into it.

The benefits of meditation should be acknowledged for what they are. They do not need to be tied into accepting Buddha, Krishna, Zen, reincarnation or any other mystical ideologies.

As I mentioned earlier, various mystical and occult devices such as Tarot cards, pendulums, numerology, meditation and so on act as conduits to our right brain. That is why people believe in mysticism and the occult. The techniques can work. But, it is not some higher power that is making those techniques work. The techniques are tapping into the enormous integrating power of our brain's right hemisphere. That, in a nutshell, is the 3000-year-old secret behind mysticism and the occult.

Chapter 3 Research Notes

* Roger Sperry's work revealed that there are two separate minds within a single person. The verbal left hemisphere and the silent right hemisphere. This allows for increased specialization within the human brain. The Corpus Callosum is a thick network of nerves which joins the two halves of the brain together. If the Corpus Callosum is severed in an accident, the patient's brain will act as two independent people.

Characteristics of Our Left Brain:

Analyzes, abstracts, counts, marks time, plans step-by-step, verbalizes, uses logic, is sequential, linear, and objective. Likes scientific experiments and reason.

Characteristics of Our Right Brain:

Visual, imaginary, spontaneous, recognizes patterns. Our right brain sees how parts fit together to make up a whole. It dreams, creates new combinations of ideas, makes gestures that communicate, has an intuitive style that is given to inspiration, makes leaps of insight, responds to grand designs, sees the whole overall picture with each part in its place, much like a puzzle or a map. The right is subjective, emotional, has an affinity for music, is immediate and specific, does not have a sense of time. The right does not distinguish between the past, present or future. Our right possesses subconscious skills such as sports skills and musical skills.

Our right brain is not good at analyzing or abstracting. It will not reason or make logical conclusions. Our right brain is susceptible to mysticism. On the other hand, our left brain is susceptible to false logic and false ideology. Our left brain will try to impose its false ideas on reality.

Our right brain appreciates humor, metaphors and connected themes. In contrast, our left brain grasps the point of the story better than the right. People with right brain damage simply do not understand a joke or why it is funny because their left brain attempts to analyze it. Our right brain excels at recognizing shapes and their relationships to one another. People with right brain damage cannot orient themselves spatially. They cannot recognize familiar faces.

* Archimedes sitting in a bathtub and suddenly shouting *Eureka*, and Newton sitting under an apple tree and suddenly understanding the nature of gravity, are both examples of breakthrough, right-brain insights and how they can elude our left brain. The right brain figures out the solution by literally "seeing" the whole picture at once after a long process of observing seemingly unrelated facts and events.

This demonstrates how our right brain can be the key to solving complex problems. Our left brain seeks orderly, step-by-step solutions. Our right brain searches for the inconsistent and then attempts to see how the inconsistent fits into the bigger picture.

Each half of our brain is specialized for different, complex modes of thinking. Our sense of being one person results from the interconnection between our two hemispheres. Each hemisphere has its own unique way of perceiving reality.

The two different modes of functioning between the left hemisphere and the right hemisphere tend to interfere with each other. This could explain why our brain evolved into two separate hemispheres with each hemisphere specializing in different functions.

* <u>The Two Hemispheres:</u>
1. Sometimes cooperate — work back and forth together.
2. Sometimes work alone — one side dominating in a task.

3. Sometimes conflict — one side attempting to do what the other does better. For example, if the left attempts to think logically and analyze while actually performing a sporting skill this will trip up the athlete. This is what occurs when an athlete "chokes."

4. Sometimes one hemisphere may keep knowledge from the other. For example, if the right brain experiences strong emotions the left brain may refuse to acknowledge facts that contradict those emotions. If a person accepts an irrational idea like self-sacrifice, his "rational, objective" left brain will block out emotional insights coming over from his right brain that contradict those ideas. This is why the contemplative state of mystics works. They relax their "logical" left brain. Thus, their left brain's defensive blocks are melted away allowing new, sometimes contradictory insights from their right brain to flash in. Mystics get excited about these flashes of insight because they think it is God or some higher power communicating with them.

* The two sides of our brain will try to help each other. Our left brain will verbalize something we want. Our right brain will then subconsciously try to achieve that for us. However, our left brain can program our right brain with false ideals and our right will still try to achieve those for us.

Most people have experienced what is called a "Gut Feeling". This is a right-brain emotional assessment that is trying to get through to our reasoning, objective left brain. Our left brain has the ability to view things rationally and dispassionately, while our right brain's point of reference is emotional. In fact, when a person's right brain is damaged he becomes passive and dependent on others to tell him what to do because he loses his emotional fuel.

A healthy, well adjusted person draws equally on his left and right hemispheres. He has an objective, rational sense of himself in his left hemisphere coupled with an equally strong emotional sense of self in his right hemisphere. Underdevelopment of the use of either hemisphere results in psychological problems.

47

* There is much data stored in our right brain which we are unconscious of. One of the reasons for this is that our right brain thinks in pictures, not in words. While many of our conscious activities involve the use of our left brain (language, planning, decision making) our right brain is just as active and alert, taking in visual and audio data which we may not be conscious of but which is present and stored in our right brain.

When solving problems we can and do draw on information stored in our right brain that we are not consciously aware of. This explains the unexpected insight. Many solutions come from our right brain's ability to grasp the overall picture, to relate parts to a whole, and to recognize patterns and similarities. This ability of our silent right is responsible for many creative insights and scientific breakthroughs.

People under hypnosis, in which their left brain is subdued and their right brain is activated, can recall almost every detail of past situations. They can even recall events from their childhood which their conscious, left brain no longer remembers. Many people are drawn into mysticism because of the startling abilities of our right brain.

* Mystics are more in touch with their right brain than most individuals. This is why mystics often perceive a second identity The mystic who thinks he is communicating with God or some higher occult power is actually communicating with his own right brain. The mystic gives a wrong interpretation to what he or she is experiencing.

Chapter Four

It's Not A Mystical Experience — It's A Right-Brain Experience

(Psychics, Clairvoyants, Tarot Cards, Miracles of Healing, Numerology, I-Ching, Hand Writing Analysis, Hypnotism, Deja Vu, Near-Death Experiences and Other Right-Brain Phenomena)

People have never really understood how the right hemisphere of our brain acts. Since our left brain is oriented towards the verbal and the objective, the workings of our visual and intuitive right brain can at times seem like some sort of magic.

Consider the phenomenon of hypnosis. Some people, upon being hypnotized, will astonish their hypnotist by accurately telling the hypnotist what he or she is thinking. These types of phenomenal events seduce people into accepting mysticism.

After all, how could someone tell another what he or she is thinking? It seems baffling, until you understand that hypnosis stills our left brain and allows a person to get in direct touch with his right brain.

When a person is hypnotized, his conscious left brain more or less shuts down. His mind becomes totally immersed within his right brain. This is opposite our normal state of mind whereby we are conscious of our left brain but we are more or less unconscious of our right brain.

Let us imagine that I have just hypnotized you. As I get ready to say something, either to you or to someone else in the room, all of a sudden you tell me what I am about to say. You can do this because your right brain has been reading my expressions, my actions, my body language. This seems phenomenal. Yet, this is a capability of our visually oriented right brain.

Consider the act of watching TV. You are sitting in a room; other people may be present. Across from you is a relatively small television screen. You are concentrating on that screen. You become unaware of everything else in the room. It really seems as though you are part of the environment being projected onto that screen. You can feel as though you are walking in a

49

jungle, down a dark alley, or sitting in a courtroom.   If something dramatic happens on that TV screen in front of you, your whole body may react physically.   This is a form of hypnosis.   Simple forms of hypnosis, such as watching television, are actually part of our daily lives.

Let us now consider Tarot cards.   Tarot cards are all about pictures and symbols.   Our objective, left brain will ask a question about the future.   Yet, quite often, our right brain already knows the direction of our future.   The right brain does not think in the past, present, or future.   It sees everything together.   What we are doing in the present depends upon what we have done in our past, and the actions we are now taking will determine our future.   The right brain sees this whole picture all at once — the past, present and future are not differentiated within the right brain.

So, if a person asks a question about how something will turn out in his future, his right brain already has a pretty good idea as to how things will evolve.   Thus, reading into the future is something the right brain is capable of.   That may seem incredulous to many people, especially scientists who are very left-brain oriented.   But, when one really understands how our right brain functions, that it possesses skills that can be developed just like playing a musical instrument or a sport, then one can understand how reading a person's future through Tarot cards is something our right brain can learn to do through its own integrations — not through mystical powers.

Here is an illustration: Consider the game of basketball. When you play basketball you run all over the court.   You are constantly shooting the ball from different angles.   You may be under the basket, you may be at an angle where it is really hard to shoot the ball through the hoop, or you may be right in front of the basket where it is easy to shoot the ball in.   Your running and shooting skills come from your right brain.   If you try to stop and objectively think, *I'm now 6 feet from the basket and I need to throw the ball at a 36 degree angle at 20 m.p.h. with my hands delivering exactly 32 lbs of a force*, you would never make a basket.   But because shooting a basketball is a skill that we develop through practice, you do not think about it being phenomenal. But the ability to shoot a basketball through a hoop while running at top speed from all different angles is phenomenal. That is a skill you train your right brain to do.

Our right brain can also acquire other skills that are just as phenomenal. With Tarot cards, for example, the person who gives a reading shuffles the deck. Then the client asks the Tarot card reader questions about his or her future. Realize that most areas of the occult, such as Tarot cards, astrology, numerology, psychic readings, and so on, are primarily concerned with personalities, character traits, psychology. Just read the daily astrology forecast in the local newspaper. You will immediately see that it is all about people's personalities. Astrology, along with most other occult disciplines, is really layman psychology. People who are seriously attracted to astrology and most other occult areas are usually mostly interested in psychology. They essentially become laymen psychologists.

So, if I am a professional Tarot card reader, astrologer, psychic, numerologist or other occultist, realize my main area of interest is human psychology. I can learn, through experience, to read a lot about another person's personality and psychology. My right brain will pick up a person's tone of voice, posture, dress, movements, the slightest facial reactions, and so on. There is even a classic best-seller called *How To Read A Person Like A Book.* There are innumerable personality cues that a person gives off and our right brain picks up on. Our right brain sees and analyzes everything about other people — subtle expressions, outward appearances, inner reactions, energy levels, enthusiasm, eye movements, voice tones and so on. All of these cues say a lot about that person. Many times you can know what another person is feeling or thinking simply by observing him.

I was aware of this even when I was very young. Women tend to do this more than men. And some individuals do it more than others, especially if they are sensitive. I remember I would be talking with someone and if I said something that made them a little embarrassed, I would see that expression immediately upon their face. From the slightest facial expression, I would know they felt uncomfortable. Our right brain is extremely adept at this because it processes information in pictures and it is also the seat of our emotions. Our right brain picks up a picture of a person and their emotions.

To demonstrate how powerfully aware our right brain is, consider when you call someone on the telephone. As soon as that person answers the phone and says, *Hello*, you can usually tell from just hearing that single word *Hello* if you have caught that person at a bad time, if he is angry or upset, if he seems harried or rushed, if he is unhappy or is in a bad mood. Likewise, you can usually tell within that split second it takes a person to say, *Hello*, if he or she is in a good mood, happy, willing to talk, or is indifferent, bored, apathetic.

All that information your right brain receives and analyzes after hearing just that single word, *Hello*. It does this by analyzing the tone of voice, volume, clarity, emotional tension, and probably dozens of other factors our conscious minds are completely unaware of.

When someone is right in front of and talking directly to us our right brain has a plethora of subtle and not so subtle cues to pick up on. With practice, a person interested in personalities and psychology really can learn to read others like a book. Just as with practice a person can become expert at basketball, gymnastics, foreign languages, computer programming, brain surgery.

If an individual asks me to give her a Tarot card reading, within a minute or two of talking to her and asking her questions my right brain will already know a lot about that person's personality and psychological outlook in life. By the time she asks a question about her future, her own right brain probably knows the answer. Thus, as a practiced Tarot card reader (which I am not) my right brain is actually picking up cues being emitted by that other person.

After years of observing people's personalities and studying layman psychology, after years of giving and receiving Tarot card readings, a Tarot card reader's right brain will have a pretty on-target answer to their clients' questions. The Tarot card reader can read into what the Tarot cards are supposedly saying to give appropriate answers. In addition, most mystics are strongly right-brain oriented to begin with. They tend to have a natural sensitivity to the feelings and emotions of others.

The above Tarot card example is given to illustrate how what people think is an unexplainable, mystical phenomenon can actually be a reality based, right-brain phenomenon.

This same right-brain experience is behind all mystical events — from communications with God to astrological readings to all the other occult forms such as psychic visions, clairvoyance, numerology, pendulums, and so on, to all Eastern religions and mystical movements such as Zen, I-Ching, and countless other mystical systems past and present. In the following pages and chapters I shall discuss each one of these mystical/occult areas and reveal how what people think is a supernatural phenomenon is actually a right-brain phenomenon.

Let us now jump to the ancient occult discipline called I-Ching. There is a similarity between Tarot cards and I-Ching. Like Tarot cards, I-Ching is about changes in life — political, social, relationships.

In I-Ching you ask a question, toss three coins, and then relate the heads and tails of the fallen coins to lines in the I-Ching trigram. You keep tossing the coins until you have a full trigram.

You can ask a serious question, throw the coins several times and then look up the trigram in the I-Ching book. It can be startling the way the answers address your questions.

I-Ching, like astrology, is based on precise mathematical structures. I-Ching was compiled from 1100 BC to about 300 BC in China and is used as a book of divination. The I-Ching book is arranged in sixty-four hexagrams with commentaries on each. Each commentary gives directions on how to act in a particular circumstance and what forces are at play in a given situation.

The mathematician Leibniz discovered in the Seventeenth Century AD that these sixty-four hexagrams were arranged in a binary notation for numbers 0-63. That is the same mathematical system used as the basis for all computer languages.

The complexity of the sixty-four hexagrams becomes simple when it is understood that each hexagram is made up of two trigrams. And the two trigrams of each hexagram can be further reduced to just eight basic trigrams or principles. Each hexagram then is a combination of two of those eight basic principles.

With the sixty-four hexagrams reduced in essence to just eight principles, the problem of decoding I-Ching becomes much simpler. The Chinese took one principle and combined it with another principle, then predicted on the basis of the two principles involved what behavior or events to expect. For example, consider two strong personalities, each determined to be the boss, working together on a project. Then consider two people, one who likes to lead and one who likes to follow, working on a project together. We can logically predict certain outcomes concerning those two situations.

Human beings have basic characteristics that are common to all men, even though there are infinite ways in which these characteristics can be expressed. So when a person consults one of the hexagrams in the I-Ching there will be something there that he can relate to. Something that may convince him it works.

Though I-Ching addresses situations according to ancient Chinese philosophy, it still relates to modern day Americans. This is because so much of the occult deals with human psychology, which remains true throughout all times and cultures. This is why I-Ching and other ancient occult philosophies can seem relevant even today.

The types of psychological problems and challenges people face break down into basic categories. Although the specific details are infinite, the fundamental problems and challenges individuals face continually fall into the same basic categories. Similar to the way all of literature breaks down into a few basic plot structures.

Throughout history all mystical systems have tried to order life and structure human behavior. All mystical literature and occult sciences try to recapture our "pre-conscious," bicameral state when life was simple and decision-making was automatic. The I-Ching was compiled during the changeover from nature's automatic, bicameral way of thinking to man-made, abstract, modern conscious thinking. The I-Ching provides us with a perfect example of trying to devise a simple mathematical procedure for making choices. The same is true of numerology and astrology — although astrology is more complex than most other occult fields, it, too, is attempting to do the same thing. (See Chapter 5, Astrology Decoded) Even the great mathematician Pythagoras developed a life-system based on mathematical formulas around 500 BC.

Like fiction literature, much occult literature contains sound psychology. Occult and fiction writers both write about human nature and events that happen between people. In fact, a lot of their identifications and experiences are probably more relevant than contemporary psychology theories.

Fiction literature, as well as certain occult teachings, allow a person to see how others have handled similar life challenges, tapping into the wisdom and experience of other people across time and circumstances. In addition, a person's insightful right brain often already knows answers to his or her problems and future. Certain right-brain occult predictions can spark an inner confirmation.

I want to point out something here. I am not endorsing occult techniques. My purpose is to show that there can be a reality base behind certain predictions and events in the occult and why they sometimes come true.

I am not fostering that such predictions are always accurate. But sometimes there are accurate predictions and personal readings made in the occult field that require a rational explanation. My interest is to understand the rational, logical reason. People are often mystified by the way some of the predictions and readings made in astrology and other occult forms ring true. This is what opens a person up to thinking, *There must exist another realm, a higher mystical realm, or how else can one explain those phenomena.* What I am doing is showing that there is, indeed, a rational basis for seemingly miraculous events that can occur in the occult field.

Consider this analogy: let us go back in time to 500 BC and the Golden Age of Greece. Back then, even the most educated people believed that there was a God of Thunder, a God of Lightning, and so on. They had no other way to explain such phenomenal events. Today, we can look back and think it foolish that people believed there was a God of Thunder, a God of Lightning and so on because today we scientifically understand the cause of thunder, of lightning, and of most other natural events in our environment.

But, a similar situation still occurs today. No one has been able to logically explain why a miracle of healing occurs, or why some astrological readings and psychic predictions seem accurate. That is mystifying to us today because we have not discovered a rational basis behind such phenomena. Thus, rational people open their minds up to thinking that maybe there really is a higher, mystical realm.

But, if a tangible, logical basis for these occult phenomena can be identified, it can help a person understand why some occult phenomena seem to work even though there is not a higher, mystical cause behind those phenomena.

The common denominator that religious and occult phenomena break down to is that they are not mystical experiences, rather they are right-brain experiences. That is the tangible, real-world explanation that brings these phenomena from unexplainable, mystical experiences to logical, reality experiences. Similar to how the understanding of static electricity and sound waves brought lightning and thunder from the mystical realm of angry gods to the earthly realm of science.

Another prime deception employed by all occult practitioners, especially astrologers, is that of generalized wording. Generalized wording is a common occult technique that is used in everything from astrological readings to psychic predictions. To the individual hearing a characterization of himself or a prediction it appears as though the message applies directly to himself and his individual circumstances. But, in reality, the occult statement is worded so generally that it can actually apply to any individual. This generalized wording technique was demonstrated by James Randi on a television show when he made horoscope readings for a classroom of college students (see Chapter 5). Every student in that class stated that his or her horoscope accurately describe themselves. Yet, it turned out that each student, about 20 in all, had been handed the exact same horoscope.

This is very common in the occult. A person will think that some occult reading or prediction applies directly to himself. Yet, if he gives that exact same reading to another person that person, too, will claim that the reading or prediction applies directly to himself and his current circumstances. Occult wording

56

is always generic enough to apply to anyone or any situation. This is because the occult deals with universal personality traits. It is not magic, it is merely human psychology.

Few people grasp just how powerful our right brain is. A recent TV program documented certain savant autistics who would be given a date in history, such as April 4th, 1902. They would think for a few seconds and then say, *That was a Friday.* If you check a 1902 calendar, lo and behold, you will find that April 4th was indeed a Friday.

This demonstrates how our right brain has the power of a computer, the only other device that could do such a calculation almost instantaneously. In other words, if our right brain possesses that kind of power it is as though we have a mainframe computer inside our heads. That is why we can sometimes do things that seem remarkable, even mystical, such as picking up the most subtle patterns and then making an accurate prediction about the future. Our conscious left brain may be completely unaware of this right-brain process. But our intuitive right brain does possess this kind of skill.

Another amazing ability that some savant autistics have is extreme musical talent. They may not be able even to talk to their parents, but certain autistics can hear a Mozart or other classical music piece a single time and then promptly sit down at a piano and flawlessly replay that difficult musical piece note for note.

Temple Gramdin, in her book, discusses how savant autistics are so highly focused. She said she was more highly focused when she was young. But she has now lost a lot of that ability because she has learned how to spread out her mental focus. She does not stay caught up in the world of her right brain. She must function in the outside world since she now has an occupation. So there are distractions that break her away from being focused solely in her right brain.

The more we understand about our right brain and its interaction with our left, the more we can understand phenomena that seem miraculous or otherworldly — such as Temple Gramdin photographing book pages in her mind and then recalling those pages at a later time in order to study them. That seems remarkable, even miraculous to the vast majority of us who are left-brain centered.

A crucial point to understand about our right brain is that it has a major flaw. Our right brain reacts immediately to a specific. It does not contemplate and make a value judgment. Our right brain acts as a physical survival mechanism by reacting immediately to circumstances around us. It is our left brain that steps back and thinks about, and contemplates something; and then consciously makes a value judgment.

People can and often do get wildly off track by acting on their right-brain impulses without scrutinizing those impulses with their logical left brain to make rational value judgments. Letting our right brain make a decision for us without first weighing that decision with the rational judgment of our left brain can result in major mistakes.

Here is an example of the right brain not making a value judgment: Sigmond Freud frequently had patients who would come to him with physical ailments. Freud discovered that he could often obtain results that today would be called a miracle of healing.

Freud studied the work that a man named Mesmer had done. Mesmer is where the term mesmerizing comes from. Freud then took to using hypnosis with some of his patients. One of Freud's patients was a woman who could not raise her arms. Doctors had told her that there was nothing physically wrong with her arms. Through hypnosis, Freud was able to cure her. This was because there was a psychological reason, not a physical reason, as to why this lady lost movement in her arms. Her problem was, evidently, in her marriage. Losing movement in her arms was her right brain's way of getting out of doing a lot of unpleasant chores. Yet, losing the use of one's arms is not something a person would ever consciously choose to do.

Another female patient of Freud had almost totally lost her hearing. It turned out that she had a very abusive husband who was constantly criticizing and verbally abusing her. So her right brain, in a subconscious attempt to solve that problem, made her lose her hearing. Through hypnosis, her hearing was restored in an instant. All of a sudden she could hear perfectly. The cause was psychological, not physical.

Freud found that many of these patients cured through hypnosis would then develop some other physical symptom later on in another subconscious attempt to solve their problems. Freud realized that hypnosis was just temporarily curing the symptom. That is when he developed psychotherapy whereby a person reclines on a couch and discusses his or her life through association. Freud realized he had to get to the root cause of a patient's psychological problems.

Freud and other psychologists never called these amazing physical healings a miracle of God. But that is what present day faith healers do. That is also what occurred with Jesus and his Miraculous Healings.

Today, startling examples of people being healed on stage by a faith healer always involve a healer who is very charismatic. These faith healings involve a building up of emotions, usually accompanied by singing, often involving people falling over in a faint. Like Freud's patients, the successful faith healings involve patients whose physical ailments have psychological roots. The faith healers themselves say that they do not know why some of their patients are healed while others are not. The patients that are successfully healed more than likely have psychological, not physical, causes behind their particular afflictions. But to the patients who are healed, they really think it is God who cured them.

There are four gospels in the Bible. One of them was written about forty years after the death of Jesus, another around sixty years after. The reason this wait was so long is because the disciples thought Jesus was going to come right back and establish the Kingdom of God. Over time, as the disciples began dying off, the need to record the gospels became obvious. But what they wrote about were Jesus' successful healings. They did not write about the people who were not healed. Of course, everyone naturally does this. They record their successes, not their failures. Astrologers, psychics, clairvoyants, and so on never talk about predictions that did not come true. They cite their predictions that did come true. That is human nature.

Sometimes people can cure a real physical disease through psychosomatic means. A good example is Bob White. He was diagnosed with cancer and was told he had a couple years to live. So, Bob White decided to quit his job and do what he always wanted to do. He started his own magazine and called it *The Duck Book*. He then sold lifetime subscriptions to the magazine — his lifetime. Bob White had a real physical disease, cancer. But, when he stopped his routine life and started doing what he really loved, his cancer suddenly went into complete remission. His body healed itself.

Some of the miraculous faith healings are analogous to Bob White's self-healing. If a person makes a total change in his outlook in life, the resulting invigoration for living, for doing what one really loves, can sometimes enable that person's body to overcome a disease and heal. These types of internal, self-healings really do appear miraculous.

My point is to demonstrate that there is a rational basis for seemingly miraculous faith healings. But people who are indoctrinated with the idea of God and rebirth will not give up that idea easily. People want to believe that they can be healed by God and that their souls will live forever. To reject the idea of God requires acknowledging that your own life ends when you die. Psychologically, that is a hard concept to accept.

Faith healings are a dramatic demonstration of the flaw of relying solely on our right-brain impulses and feelings to make decisions for us. These are people who have lost their eyesight, lost their hearing, been confined to a wheelchair or suffer other debilitating afflictions for psychosomatic reasons — to escape verbal abuse, unfulfilling work, traumatic memories, and so on. Consciously, a person would never choose to go blind, lose the use of his arms, lose his hearing, or be confined to a wheelchair in order to solve a personal problem. We would try to solve our problems in a completely different way. But our right brain does not weigh the value of its choices. It can make very damaging, subconscious choices for us.

People who go into religion or the occult in a serious way are often in a traumatic period of their lives and are searching for answers. During traumatic times, we experience powerful emotions. It is easy to be pulled off track by powerful, yet irrational, emotions.

For example, consider those thirty-nine young people in the

Hale-Bopp comet cult who took their lives in the 1990s. They became indoctrinated with the idea of advancing to a higher level after death. They were completely, emotionally caught up in that idea being correct. Thus, they willingly chose to follow their cult leader and drink poison, convinced aliens were going to transceive their souls to a higher level after their death. This dramatically demonstrates how the powerful emotions of our right brain (powerful enough to make a young, healthy person commit suicide) are not able to make a rational value judgment.

Let us now consider symbology. I-Ching, Tarot cards and numerology all involve symbology. Anthropologists have done studies on symbols to see if there are universally recognized symbols that cut across nationalities, cultures, and languages. They have identified five symbols that are universally recognized by all peoples and cultures and always carry similar meanings.

One of these universal symbols is the circle. Almost everyone subconsciously identifies a circle as implying a complete entity, independent, centered. The triangle, pushing up to a peak, is universally related to reaching for something, striving, goal-oriented. The spiral, going up and around, is not centered like a circle. And it is not reaching directly upward like a triangle. Thus, the spiral symbolizes the search for new knowledge, for more information. The square symbolizes dependability, practicality, security. Finally, there is the cross. Christians, of course, identify the cross with Christ. But all cultures also think of the cross as symbolizing a relationship. The two lines of the cross symbolize two different entities. When they cross each other there can be either harmony or conflict.

Almost every person, regardless of culture and circumstances, whether they live in a jungle tribe or a modern city, recognizes those five symbols and subconsciously attaches similar symbolic meanings to them. Similarly, the symbols used in Tarot cards, I-Ching and other occult practices have certain universal meanings attached to them, often subconsciously.

When we first look at a symbol, our verbal, logic-oriented left brain does not consciously attach a specific meaning to that symbol. Our left brain has to step back and think about a symbol before it will attach a meaning to it. But our visual, intuitive right brain does attach meaning to symbols. In most instances, however, we are not consciously aware of that.

This right-brain influence plays a strong role in handwriting analysis. When you are writing words and sentences by hand you are thinking in words which is a left-brain activity. But you are also drawing a picture (the individual letters) and this is a visual, right-brain activity. Your right brain is subconsciously controlling the way you form your letters and words.

A book on handwriting analysis I read years ago (unfortunately I can no longer remember the name) reprinted two different samples of handwriting and asked the reader, "Which person is outgoing and which person is withdrawn?" With no prior knowledge whatsoever of handwriting analysis the reader could immediately tell who was the outgoing, extroverted person and who was the withdrawn, introverted person. The outgoing, extroverted individual wrote in big, looping, confident letters. The withdrawn, introverted individual wrote in small, downward slanting letters, almost like his handwriting was trying to hide from the world.

Other handwriting examples given in that book represented a person who was very idealistic and set a lot of goals, contrasted with a person who was caught up with specific, everyday events without much long-range ambition. The reader could spot the person who was ambitious and goal oriented right away by the pointed height of his letters. His letters reach upward like a triangle. And his handwriting looked more forceful with heavy pencil pressure applied.

Sometimes there are exceptions, like scientists, who often have light handwriting with small letters. Scientists tend to be very efficient and this carries through in their handwriting. They do not waste energy by applying a lot of heavy pressure on the pencil when they write.

That handwriting book identified a lot of points like the above examples that just made good common sense. Yet this is something that on my own I was never aware of, even after all my years of writing.

When writing by hand, a person's right-brain influence comes through in the shape and form of his or her letters and words.

If you are enthusiastic about something you are doing, almost always your handwriting tends to slant upward and forward. If you are feeling down or depressed, your handwriting will tend to slant downward and backwards. There are numerous other traits that show up in a person's handwriting as well.

Handwriting analysis is not part of occult philosophy. Handwriting analysis does not profess to have any kind of mystical basis behind it. Handwriting analysis is really just a psychological analysis of a person based on the physical attributes of his or her handwriting. Yet bookstores usually place books on handwriting analysis in the occult section when they really should be placed in the psychology section.

I am not completely sure, but I believe the first book on handwriting analysis was published in the early 1800s. And there have been references made to handwriting analysis before then. Handwriting analysis has been very popular in some European countries. Sometimes employers will use it in their hiring process.

Many different and interesting case studies of handwriting analysis have been done over the years. For example, an analyst will go to a hospital and ask for handwriting samples from heart attack victims. And he will find common traits. Handwriting studies have also been conducted with prisoners to see if there are traits that suggest a person is a liar or a thief. Many indicative traits have been found. Over the years, numerous handwriting studies have been conducted in many different areas, often yielding fascinating results. Again, this demonstrates just how strongly our right brain can influence our handwriting and the formation of our letters and words — which also relates to the letters and words in our names. This now brings me to the subject of numerology:

Numerology assigns numbers to each letter. A is number 1, B is number 2, C is number 3 and so on. These corresponding numbers contained in a person's name are then totaled up. A numerology grid then lists supposed characteristics for each total.

The key behind numerology is to realize that there is a connection between symbology, letters and words. When our alphabet was first developed it was done so as pictograms and symbols.

If you consciously analyze letters of the alphabet for symbological connections, you will be amazed. For example, take a piece of paper and in large, clear handwriting write the letter A. Look at this letter closely. When thinking in terms of symbology, an A reminds me of that ad about the Green Giant. Do you remember him? He is a huge giant standing with his arms folded, his legs spread out, firmly planted. He looks like an A.

Since the letter A stands for the number 1, think about the number 1. It represents one person standing all by himself. This represents independence, self-reliance, being one's own person.

Now consider the letter B. It has one line with two little half circles folding around it. Those two half circles look like two little crescent moons. The moon almost always represents two people rather than one person, because the moon is always thought of in relationship to the earth. See how the letter B curves; it is not like one person standing up all by himself. It looks more like two parts of a whole. Whenever two parts are involved, there can either be harmony or conflict. ...If you continue this process, you will start to see how symbology can relate to letters.

All writing, including our Roman alphabet, originally evolved from pictograms. Even today, Chinese and Japanese writing is directly descended from pictograms. Likewise, each letter in our alphabet can eventually be traced back to an original pictogram. So even when we are writing modern English, our hand is drawing pictures that stand for letters and words. Drawing and visual pictures are right brain functions.

I have studied several books on the history and development of writing. It is very interesting to study the symbols used in Samarian, Egyptian and Chinese writing as well as the Arabic, Greek and Roman alphabets. A person can really see the symbolism behind most characters and letters.

This is the key to understanding why our visual and symbolic oriented right brain will feel an affinity with our own name. From the day a baby is born he continuously hears his name. Then, he goes to school and learns to write his name. He begins writing his name on every paper he hands in, on every form he fills out, on every letter he writes and on every form he signs for the rest of his life. Over time, our right brain develops a certain affinity with our name based on the symbolism behind its letters and sounds. The letters and sounds comprising our name do exert an influence upon our symbolically sensitive right brain.

Over the years I have looked up the characteristics listed in the numerology grid for dozens of individuals. The results are quite generalized. But over time I did notice general character traits predicted in the numerology grid that seemed to correspond with individual names. Again, I think this is because the symbolism behind our written and verbal name does, over time, exert an influence on our personality. This is caused not by some mystical power but by the influence of our right brain and the symbolism it attaches to our name.

Again, a person can detect symbolisms behind most letters of the alphabet — both capital letters and lower case letters — when he writes them out and closely examines each letter. Some letters have a clear symbolic connection behind their shape and the traits assigned to them in numerology — such as the letter A which, as previously mentioned, literally looks like a man standing tall with his arms crossed, independent, and self-reliant. Even the small letter "a" symbolically looks like a circle, which is universally identified as being self-contained, whole, independent. And the letter A corresponds to the number 1 which, in numerology, stands for one person who is self-responsible and likes to work alone. Thus, in numerology, names containing a lot A's correspond to personality traits that prefer to work independently rather than in groups.

I think it is possible that after years of writing and visualizing one's name, the symbolic connections behind the letter A, such as in the name Alexander, could exert a slight influence on our right brain and how we perceive ourselves.

I will not delve into the innumerable variables and combinations of numerology and the possible symbolic connections behind them. But, you can see from the above examples how there may be a general connection between the symbology of letters and words in our names and their long-term influence on our personalities.

65

Let us now jump to the subject of psychics, oracles, Cassandras and others who experience visions. I think that visions come from one's inner emotions and are similar to dreams. Dreams, however, are visual pictures. Visions usually are not. A vision is more like hearing a voice inside one's head. But the only way a person can describe his vision to others is as someone else talking to him. Thus, other people think, *That person is seeing Mary the Mother of God, or Jesus, or some other authority.* But, in reality, the vision is coming from within a person's own right brain, just as the visual pictures we see in a dream come from within our right brain.

Regarding psychic visions, there are several factors to consider. First, consider those psychics who try to help police detectives solve a missing-person case or other crime mystery. The psychic is, as a rule, interested in the case to begin with because it is a high-profile case that has been in the media. Some insights any person could logically conclude from what is already known about a case. But it is also true that our right brain can pick up details or clues concerning a mystery that our left brain is unaware of. Psychics are very in touch with their right brains to begin with. Most intuitive thoughts we have come from our right brain. So do most of our really strong emotions. Intuition and emotions are often our right brain trying to tell us something.

Most psychics turn out not to be helpful in solving crimes. But a few have. They have given police new clues about a case. Now, our left brain is really good at finding pieces that fit together while throwing out pieces that do not fit. That is how logic works. But, breakthrough, revolutionary discoveries often come from examining pieces of a puzzle that seemingly do not fit. This can lead to totally unexpected, completely new insights.

A strong right-brained person tends to examine clues that do not fit the picture. In contrast, if a person examines everything that already fits, it is like everything falls into an expected, logical outcome. Most peoples' left brains do this automatically. They look for the expected answer, the predictable, the logical. But if you reject the expected and instead look over the pieces or clues that do not fit into the usual, expected outcome, you can sometimes perceive a completely new perspective.

That is why mystics, being right-brain oriented, sometimes have startling insights. And that is why many people fall for mystics. But mystics' amazing insights are not other worldly processes. Their insights come from employing their right brains. And that is a powerful tool we can all learn to use to boost our own insights and creativity.

If you are trying to solve a difficult problem, a right-brain perspective can sometimes lead to a radical, new solution. And that is what psychics and other mystics sometimes do. They look at a problem from a different, right-brain angle. They can look at certain clues that do not fit into the expected picture, clues that others may not have considered, to come up with a completely new insight. Of course, there are also a lot of charlatans in the psychic field. Everyone knows that. But there are some people in the occult who are caught up in and really believe in what they do. They are not trying to fool people. What they are doing, however, has nothing to do with other world, mystic powers. They are merely employing their right brains to come up with new ideas that may or may not be helpful.

Because of their inquisitive nature, most mystics also do a lot of reading. Whenever a person does a lot of reading, especially in the area of psychology, that person learns a lot about other people. One famous psychic, Edgar Casey, would go into a hypnotic state and then give recipes for herbal remedies to ailing patients. I know Edgar Casey did a lot of reading in his field. A person who has an interest in a particular field is naturally going to learn as much as he can about that area. And because mystics are right-brain oriented, they also are more inclined to have a photographic memory. A lot of Casey's remedies concerned old herbal recipes that I am sure he had read about in various books.

Personally, however, I was never really interested in the psychic because, unlike other occult disciplines, it does not involve a search for perfecting one's character.

Déjà vu, the feeling that you have been in a place or a particular situation previously when you have not is another interesting phenomenon. Normally, your left brain is the side

67

that is consciously perceiving your environment. But, when you experience déjà vu, it is because your right brain has perceived something in your environment and then sent that perception over to your left brain before your left brain has had a chance to consciously perceive the same environment. This happens to be the same way a memory is processed in your brain. Memory perceptions come into your left brain from your right brain. Thus, in the case of déjà vu, the conscious perceptions being sent from your right brain into your left brain feel like a memory. Therefore, it seems as though you have been in that situation before.

Of course, for people who believe in reincarnation, déjà vu reconfirms their belief. They do not realize that, as with other mystical experiences, déjà vu is yet another right-brain phenomenon.

Let us now jump to the phenomenon of near-death experiences: One cannot tell a person that they did not experience what they experienced. They will not believe you. The problem lies in the interpretation of the experience. If we do not understand an experience, it is often attributed to the mystical realm. Take the near-death experience, for example. Those who have experienced it interpret it as leaving their body and entering the realm of the after life. This interpretation is based on religious belief. However, the experience can be explained as a natural shutting down of the body and mind at death or near death.

Consider several experiences common to almost all near-death experiences:

A) The person usually has experienced severe trauma such as a heart attack, car accident, drowning, lightning strike, or major surgery. They often perceive a tunnel with light at the end of that tunnel. Their whole life flashes before them in an instant; each experience carries with it the emotions of that past event. Now, consider that our right hemisphere is the seat of our limbic systems where we experience feeling and that our right hemisphere has no time frame — the past, present and future are all perceived in the here and now.

B) The most convincing part of the near-death experience that relates to religious ideas is the overwhelming feeling of love each near-death person has and a sense of the presence of loved ones he or she will meet on the other side. In life whenever we experience pain or sickness it is our family and loved ones we turn to for comfort and support. At a traumatic, near-death moment, these are the people we would expect to call up in our memories. For those who believe in religion, seeing a figure one interprets as Jesus or a spiritual being is also part of their emotional makeup. Such spiritual figures represent those who love us and who will look after us in times of crises.

C) Most near-death patients report feeling they have to make a choice whether to stay on the other side or return to their life on this earth. This choice is recognized in many severely sick patients who exert the will to live or who decide it is time to let go and die. In patients with the same severity of illness, some will live through sheer determination while others will die through the desire to put an end to the struggle.

D) The near-death experience is usually accompanied by a sense that the person has left his body and is viewing himself from the outside, from the surrounding environment. But this same experience of feeling one's consciousness has left the body and is observing oneself from above is often felt by people who have just been told shocking news — such as the death of a loved one. I suspect that this is the result of great mental and/or physical trauma that shocks both our right and left hemispheres simultaneously. The resulting whole-brain overload makes our consciousness seem as though it has lifted right out of our body.

In the final analysis, the above near-death phenomena can all be attributed to normal life experiences and our right-brain perceptions.

I want to clarify an important point. It may seem that our right brain is the culprit that gets people caught up in mysticism.

Realize, however, that if a person suffers right-hemisphere brain damage through a stroke or accident, they lose all initiative. Like a very young child, they have to be told what to do.

Being the seat of our emotions, our right brain is what makes us an individual, what gives us our personality. Motivation comes from emotions. If something happens to our right brain, all of that is lost. It is as if one becomes a shell of a person. Someone even has to tell that person what clothes to put on. There is a total loss of initiative and desire for life. So our right brain is certainly not something that should be looked upon negatively, solely as a source of mystical illusions.

Consider the flip side of this point: As Dr. Frank R. Wallace has identified in *The Neo-Tech Discovery*, with the development of conceptual, introspective human consciousness a person could use his "reasoning" left brain to deceive himself with false logic and erroneous idea systems. Thus, man became the only animal that can act against his true nature and survival. In contrast, animals can only act true to their natures. The automatic animal brain can only function to promote an animal's well-being. But a conscious human can accept and follow ideas that go against and undermine his well-being. We can deceive ourselves through the ideals of our rational-thinking left brain with false logic and erroneous idea systems just as we can deceive ourselves through the impulses and emotions of our right brain. We truly are a combination of both our left and right brain, for better or worse.

Even though mysticism is usually a result of our emotional, noncritical right brain, consider how off base people can get with political and philosophical ideology, e.g., fascism, communism, religious fundamentalism, radical environmentalism and so on. Such idea systems are the result of left-brain, analytical functions.

So, even if a person is trying to make logical judgments and rational decisions, his left brain can still fall for erroneous ideas with results that range from totalitarian political systems to stock market bubbles, quack medical cures and ecological doomsday cults.

Our right brain can hear inner voices, see visions and experience mystical, non-reality events. But our left brain can latch onto false logic and subscribe to bad idea systems that act against human nature and our survival.

It's A Right-Brain Experience

In contrast, by using whole-brain, integrated Neo-Tech thinking to be aware of and weed out irrational and mystical thinking a person can then take full advantage of his reasoning, conceptual emotional feeling, two-hemisphere brain. An individual can exploit the awesome power of our two-hemisphere human brain to achieve radical breakthroughs and spectacular acts of value creation. (See *The Neo-Tech Discovery* by Frank R. Wallace.)

Chapter 4 Research Notes

* The drawing card behind all forms of mysticism is the unexplained. For example, the miracles of Jesus, astrological predictions, Tarot card readings, psychic visions and so on. That is what leads people into the belief of a higher existence. My interest is to explain these "miracles" and mystifying phenomena as having a reality base. These "miracles" and mystifying phenomena can be explained via our right brain. They are not paranormal events, rather they are natural, right-brain events.

* When problem solving, people usually look for clues that fit together. They are looking for the expected answer. This is typical of our rational, analyzing left brain. The strong right-brain person examines the clues that do not fit together. This can lead to new ways of thinking and radical breakthroughs that do not result in the expected answer.

* Nostradamus, who lived in the 1500s, is the most famous prophet. It is claimed that many of his predictions are still coming true. A lot of his ideas germinated from piecing together certain insights from his right brain and then turning them into predictions, which anyone can do, especially with practice. Still, the predictions in Nostradamus' books are so generalized that a person can pretty much read anything he wants into those predictions. Modern day interpretations read a lot into Nostradamus' predictions which simply are not there.

*The occultist is limited and kept in bondage by his belief in Karma. With Karma, the law of cause and effect extends throughout many lifetimes. Whatever good a person has done

71

in a previous life, he reaps the benefits in this life. And whatever suffering he experiences in this life is the result of having caused another person to suffer in a previous life. This belief in reincarnation and Karma sets the identical trap that the religious person experiences in trying to do the will of God. Both state that whatever is in your life is there for a reason beyond your control. Karma is responsible for its presence in the occultist view; God permits its presence in the religious view.

* All occult disciplines are based on theory. Those theories are always dressed in neat sounding packages and have an inner logic to them. But, they have never been proven, have never been put to the test of the scientific method. In other words, occult fields have never met the laws of reality, they are just claims.

The mystics' modus operandi is theory, but with nothing to substantiate their claims. Their theories are often precise and mathematically worked out. In astrology, for example, human behavior is defined and structured according to very precise mathematical formulas.

In order to substantiate anything its validity must be proven in reality. Reality is always the measure which supports or invalidates anything in existence. Since the widespread use of the scientific method, where theories are tested in reality, modern science, technology and other fields have taken a quantum leap. Not surprisingly, mystical systems from organized religion to astrology and the occult have produced no meaningful, verifiable, tangible human advances.

* It is interesting how magicians, such as James Randi, who is the author of *Flim Flam* and is a former magician, often see right through mystics and their techniques to expose their flaws and outright trickery whereas others, even very educated and intelligent professionals, often fall for the techniques and tricks of mystics. Magicians are used to being tricked and search for the illusion. Professionals, on the other hand, do not think in terms of trying to trick others so they tend to accept "evidence" at face value and thus are vulnerable to the illusions and tricks of mystics.

72

Chapter Five
Astrology Decoded

Astrology is the most popular occult science. No other occult study has as many books, magazine articles, and newspaper columns devoted to it as astrology. The phenomenal popularity of astrology is surprising considering there is no evidence in reality which supports the astrologers' claims. However, some very intelligent individuals, who are otherwise well grounded in reality, get hooked into astrology, not because of any valid evidence, but because of some startlingly accurate predictions which make astrology appear to have validity.

The appeal of astrology is in its focus on individuals, their lives and events in their lives. In no other field of study are people's character traits delineated and examined in such depth. Even psychology, which is a study of the human mind and behavior, does not match the depth of specific character delineation presented in astrology.

Astrology especially appeals to women because it is concerned with relationships and interactions among individuals. And for women, relationships hold a special significance. Womens' responsibilities in life often revolve around relationships — achieving a rewarding relationship with their husband, raising and teaching values to their children, finding meaningful values with friends. So it is natural for women to have a keen interest in relationships. If a woman is married and does not hold an outside job, her whole future and happiness depends on making her relationships work. And astrology examines relationships in depth. Astrology, unlike psychology, focuses on the healthy individual, those who are successfully coping with life.

Astrology appears as the study of man and events. But it is based on the premise that a man's character and his destiny are determined by the stars. In other words, the sun, the moon, and the eight visible planets influence a man's character traits and the personal fortunes and misfortunes of his life. Some modern day astrologers reject the idea of the planets influencing man, but then claim that there is a correspondence between man, his destiny, and the stars. We will see that this correspondence is an artificial one.

The real tragedy in accepting this basic premise, that man's life is predestined, is the idea that an individual is not in control of his life. Instead, he is at the mercy of a predetermined destiny, a destiny he can work with and try to improve but which has limits and boundaries beyond which he cannot go.

Because astrologers claim their discipline to be a science, let us put astrology to the test to determine if it meets the requirements of science:

Science consists of two fields of study. 1) Pure science and 2) Applied science. Pure science is theoretical, it consists of principles that apply universally. Applied science is experimental, it consists of testing principles in reality.

With the marriage of these two fields of study, the scientific method, man has seen an explosion in understanding the laws of nature and the improvements and progress made possible by combining the two.

Pure science by itself can become error-ridden. A man uses logic, principles that should apply in all situations, but errors occur through misinformation, false assumptions, and unknown factors present which affect the conclusions. Testing theories in reality (applied science) exposes the errors.

When theory loses contact with experience and is not validated by reality then all sorts of illusions and false assumptions can be made.

For example, when the automobile first came into existence, it was reasoned that humans could not physically react quickly enough to control the vehicle at high speeds. By observing the relatively low reaction-time humans exhibited when driving horse-drawn carriages, logic seemed to dictate that humans could not react quickly enough at speeds that the automobile would travel. Real world testing, however, proved otherwise.

In order to decode astrology and expose the myth of its underlying philosophy one needs to be aware of a combination of three major factors. Each factor taken alone does not convince a person who is caught up in the belief system that astrology is without foundation. It is the combination of three major factors that makes astrology appear to work.

1) The theoretical nature of astrology.
2) The cycles used for prediction.

3) The rules that govern interpretation.

Astrology is a complex system of rules that within its own structure integrate. The rules, however, are pure theory. Any textbook on astrology states one rule after another with no natural law or known fact that supports the rule. This consideration alone is enough to disqualify astrology from any claim to a scientific basis.

For example, the Sun in one's horoscope represents the basic identity of the person. The Moon is supposed to represent the emotions, Mercury the intellect, Mars the action principle. Jupiter represents expansion, Saturn restrictions. The four elements fire, earth, air, water are linked to the constellations, and planets in these signs represent character traits — forceful, practical, intellectual, emotional. No reason is given as to why or what in reality supports those claims. Also, notice how astrology makes brilliant use of metaphors through a masterful combination of metaphors as principles.

Anyone studying astrology is struck by the fact that assertions are constantly made without any explanation as to why that assertion should be accepted as true. The astrologers answer that they do not know why it works but that it works. This leads to the conclusion that astrologers base their claims not on theory which they cannot verify, but on experience.

Since astrology cannot meet the criteria of a pure science, we can draw the conclusion that the theories and rules are based on false assumptions and misconceptions.

No study would persist or be pursued if the whole study was irrational. There are some striking predictions which do occur in astrology. Astrology students are always surprised and astonished at the accuracy of some of those predictions. It is this mystery that intrigues people and makes them want to know why. But it is also this mystery that leaves individuals vulnerable to mystical explanations.

The predictions that tend to amaze and trap one's thinking into accepting astrology's premises can be explained. This leads to the second major factor that needs to be understood in order to decode astrology.

The cycles used for prediction come under the field of applied science (testing things out in reality). The most prominent cycle in astrology and the most reliable one, as far as predictions are concerned, is the Saturn cycle. Many astrologers have made the statement that if it were not for the Saturn cycle they would be out of business, for no clients would seek their help. Saturn in astrology represents responsibility and limitations.

The full cycle of Saturn in the zodiac takes roughly twenty-eight years to complete when it returns to its same position in the constellations. This cycle represents seven-year increments — seven years in an individual's life or in the start of something new. According to the interpretation by astrologers every seventh year represents crisis periods.

But, everyone experiences major stages of growth and change in their life. And by simply observing these natural psychological stages of growth, it becomes obvious that seven-year periods represent an almost universal cycle of human growth. Each new stage is a natural outgrowth of the preceding one and the natural concerns and requirements as a man matures through his life. It has nothing to do with mysterious influences of planets and stars.

For example, consider the following seven-year stages:

Stage One: Seven-years-old: This stage represents the time when a child must begin to be an individual outside of the home environment. The school setting becomes a challenge to him. Psychologists set this year as a stage when an individual's basic personality can be determined, the personality that one will mainly exhibit throughout his or her life.

Stage Two: Fourteen-years-old: At this age one is experiencing puberty and is changing from a child to an adolescent. There is a lot of change in that young person's life and outlook. All of a sudden he or she becomes conscious of the opposite sex. There is also a strong desire for more independence.

Stage Three: Twenty-one-years-old: This is the age when an individual has learned skills, completed his education, and then puts these skills to the test in the work place. He must demonstrate his abilities. By twenty-one a person has been through high school and college and now has a career.

At twenty-one you are also legally an adult. Until then, your whole life has been preparing to enter a vocation and be successful. So this is another major turning point in life. Often it is a happy one. At twenty-one you are a young adult, you have a career and maybe you have married.

Stage Four: Twenty-eight-years-old: At this stage an individual has been pursuing his career for at least several years. It is a time when most individuals become more serious about their jobs and their future. By this time people have advanced upward in their jobs. Responsibilities have built through the seven preceding years, immaturities have been let go of and new responsibilities added. Couples often begin having children by this time. This period represents a more serious commitment to one's goals. Your outlook in life becomes a lot more serious about your job, about your family. The age of twenty-eight often represents a difficult time. It is difficult because you have given up those carefree days. You now have a lot of responsibility and you are serious about life.

Stage Five: Thirty-five-years-old: One of the natural outgrowths of reaching this stage in life is to be totally independent, to make one's decisions alone without any demands to answer to someone else. This desire becomes especially noticeable in a mentor relationship. Very often this type of relationship, which up till now has been rewarding and beneficial, undergoes changes or even a complete break. The younger individual recognizes the need to be totally independent without having to adjust to another's advice.

By age thirty-five a person has been out on his own and working for a substantial period. Often, when a young person first comes out of school and goes into a company, large or small, there is a mentor, an older person who likes the young man or woman and sort of sponsors him. A young person can learn a lot from a mentor. But by the age of thirty-five he has accumulated a lot of his own experience at work. Though he might really appreciate and like his mentor, when one works too closely with another person that other person becomes an authority figure over you.

By thirty-five, you do not want that in your life anymore. You want to make decisions whether or not your mentor agrees with them. At thirty-five it is time to break that mentor

77

relationship. By age thirty-five, a person is ready to be his own boss. He may still keep a relationship with his mentor, but it will be on a different footing.

Stage Six: Forty-two years old: This stage is prevalently known as the middle age crisis. In one's twenties and thirties a person thinks he has all the time in the world to accomplish his goals and make his life what he wants it to be. At forty it becomes real to him that his life has an end. His parents are getting older, maybe he has lost one. This period represents a serious reevaluation of one's life and goals. The emphasis during this period is inner, becoming more authentic as a person and aligning one's personal life and career with values that are meaningful.

At age forty-two individuals often have tremendous responsibilities. They will closely examine their life and if they are not all that happy they may decide to totally change careers, get a divorce, move to a new location or make other dramatic changes. This is typical of the middle-age stage.

Stage Seven: Forty-nine-years-old: This stage represents a time when a person has come to terms with his life and his goals. It is still a time of pursuing goals, but the special emotional problems which occurred at forty-two with the realization of one's own mortality have been worked through. Some of the heavy financial responsibilities for the support of children begin to lift.

As one moves into his fifties, the achievements and values which he has steadily been building throughout his life and his career begin to pay off in recognition and financial status. Large corporations generally consider that a man must reach this age before he has the experience, maturity, and wisdom to become the C.E.O. of the company.

By describing these stages in a man's life and the special concerns of each, one recognizes these periods as natural and rooted in the nature of man and his changing needs throughout life. There is nothing magical about seven-year periods. Most skills, most businesses take around five years to become expert at. The next two years are critical ones in which a person decides where to take his skills or business. But astrologers have identified this natural maturing process and cast it into a giant non sequitur. Their false assumptions build a philosophical base of a planet ruling man, of some mysterious force in nature that brings crisis and heavy responsibility to a man every seven years. Some astrologers even go so far as to accept the mystical belief in karma (actions done in a past life must be met and accounted for in this life)[1]. And Saturn, with its seven year cycles, is supposed to represent that karma.

The early astrologers were astute enough in their observations to recognize this generalized seven-year cycle of growth. Their beliefs can be compared to those of the early Greeks who believed that there was a god for every happening: A god of thunder, a god of lightning, a god of trees. We recognize these beliefs as myth, Greek mythology. We now know that a god does not cause thunder, just as Saturn does not cause seven-year crisis periods. The effect has been given a non sequitur cause.

A parallel to this process can be seen in the Old Testament. Bicameral man had no concept of justice. As man began to develop consciousness, when he began to use introspective reason, he began to develop a philosophy of understanding and justice. A study of the Old Testament prophets provides an excellent source for witnessing the development of inner awareness and consciousness in man. But the prophets themselves did not attribute this growing awareness to themselves. Instead, they projected the cause to God (God was understanding), as astrologers project the cause of stages of a mans' life to Saturn.

So the correspondence between Saturn and man is an artificial one. Any natural activity of man, any cycle he exhibits can always be made to correspond to a cycle of an extraterrestial body. The Moon has a cycle of approximately one month, the sun has a cycle of one year, Mars has a cycle of two years, Saturn a cycle of four seven-year periods, and so on. Any time period can be compared mathematically and fit into some extraterrestrial cycle. While a correspondence can be established in a generalized way between the cycle of a planet, sun or moon

---

[1] A theme prevalent in all religions and all mystical philosophies is suffering and hardship, which holds a place of honor in all mystical ideology. Why? Enduring suffering is supposed to elevate an individual to a state of wisdom and purity. In actuality, this teaching is a ploy used to control and manipulate followers.

and a man's activities, the interpretation of that correspondence is crucial. A planet's cycle that corresponds with a man's particular activity does not cause that activity. Instead, man's activity cycles can always find a corresponding time frame in the movements of the sun, moon or planets.

So astrologers who base their claim of validity on experience, *Try it and see that it works*, have also failed to pass the test of applied science. No mystical forces are influencing man or causing events to happen in his life. But this correspondence of planet cycles with man's activities give the false appearance of a real connection between man and the stars. The connection has been totally man-made and artificial.

Astrologers accept an irrational philosophy concerning man, his nature, and the requirements for a happy life. The example of the Saturn cycle dispels the myth of planets ruling man or determining his destiny. It exposes the mystical predestiny philosophy that astrology is based upon. Man determines his own life through his reasoning, his choices, and his actions. The philosophy that he bases his decisions on is crucial to his having a rewarding or unrewarding life. By accepting a philosophy whose premise is that man's life is predestined, a person becomes like a paraplegic sitting at the wheel of an auto. He cannot drive his own life.

The third basic factor in the puzzle of decoding astrology is the way in which the rules are set up for interpretation. The rules themselves are very precise, but the nature of the rules leaves room for wide interpretations. For example, Mars stands for energy and activity, with a strong emphasis on impulsiveness and having one's own way. Saturn stands for responsibility, with an emphasis on limitations. When these two planes come into contact with each other a very wide interpretation can be made as to what the results will be. The impulsiveness may rule in the situation or the responsibility nature may temper the strong willpower. If a third planet is involved in this contact, say Jupiter, which stands for expansiveness, then we have three principles at work — a strong desire nature, responsibility, and expansiveness. Almost any important situation in a person's life has these three principles at work. So any event can be viewed and interpreted from one of the astrological principles or a combination of principles.

It is the perspective or approach to interpreting human behavior and events that leaves room for almost any interpretation. While the astrologers are very specific in their definitions of the planets and the planets' aspects, and in their definitions of the signs and houses of the horoscope, man and his activities are not that precise and predictable. They do not fall into mathematical formulas. So the rules and principles used in astrology leave a wide range. The astrologers then fool themselves, they slant their interpretations to fit the circumstances. With a broad range of principles from which to work, the particular emphasis or perspective in interpretation fits the circumstances rather than the other way around.

The key to decoding astrology is to realize that astrologers make astute observations about human behavior and then tie it to a false theoretical basis. It is the theory that camouflages the astrologer's trick. Their interpretations may appear correct to someone seeking guidance because of the valid human attributes discussed. But those human attributes are obtained simply by observance. The theory and the rules make everything so complicated that they entirely camouflage that trick. Astrology is nothing more than observing and then making clever generalities about people's personalities.

The astrologers are interested in people, in examining their character traits, their personalities, their motivations, their talents, their relationships. Some astrologers get a degree in clinical psychology, then use astrology as a tool for counseling.

As long as man accepts a mystical premise, his philosophy, his concepts will lead to choices that are harmful. The mystery and secrecy prevalent in all occult studies act as a drawing power because people love to solve problems, to break through the mystery into the known.

Unless an individual fully identifies and adheres to the premise that everything in nature can be explained and understood by cause-and-effect relationships rooted in reality, he will always deceive himself and others. The extent of this deception is in direct proportion to the mystical ideas he accepts, and his ability to successfully deal with his environment and produce values that are competitive and life-enhancing is in direct proportion to his ability to cut through mystical illusions and identify reality.

Having shown that astrology is not science, rather it is a system of astute observations about human nature, one wonders why so many people believe in it.

Many tests have been made that show people will accept a horoscope interpretation as their own when in fact the horoscope belonged to someone else. Why this belief factor?

The following points help explain this delusive factor and why so many people are deceived.

Astrology and all the occult fields are based on non sequiturs. A non sequitur is a conclusion that does not logically follow from the premises. In other words, the evidence given does not lead to the conclusion made. Some of the non sequiturs in astrology are so subtle that the mind does not readily detect them. Three prevalent non sequiturs used in astrology e.g.:

1.) Carl Jung, a famous Swiss psychologist, used astrology in his practice. For him astrology was a method or therapeutic tool used to get a person to examine himself consciously in order to better understand himself. The value was in the person using his own intellect to address and take seriously certain character traits and behavioral patterns.

    This practice of consciously examining certain character traits and emotions, reflecting on one's life and goals, can always be of value. That practice should be considered in its own right and not linked or confused with a mystical premise — such as the movement of planets determining our fate.

2.) Another non sequitur is astrology's mathematical base. A horoscope is set up based on a person's moment of birth. The horoscope is calculated by precise mathematical rules. The movement of the planets and constellations are calculated mathematically and the rules for prediction and delineation are figured by math. The whole structure of astrology is based on math, but the linkage is a false linkage. Take away that mathematical structure and the definitions, delineations, and predictions fall apart. Nothing is certain anymore, nothing is exact, definite.

    The value of math with its logic, its exactness, is

without question. Linking this value of math with astrological assertions tends by association to give validity to astrology. Our mind subconsciously makes this association and will tend to accept astrology as valid. In fact, one who has studied astrology and made this subconscious connection to math has a difficult time rejecting it. This linkage of the real with the false is the most common and most destructive non-sequitur technique of mysticism.

3.) Suggestion in astrology plays a powerful role in people believing the interpretations. Suggestion is the process of inducing someone to believe something without using direct argument. This phenomenon has been identified by psychologists and used as a tool in hypnosis. Just investigating astrology, seeing some correspondences, enjoying the discussions on human behavior, learning its mathematical structure and its definite assertions can have a powerful suggestive effect.

Cutting through the maze, separating out the values that are based in reality, not in mystical tenets, and understanding why one tends to be caught into the non sequiturs is a great step toward eliminating irrational dogma that stifle man and keep him in bondage to false ideas.

Astrology's Origins

Historically, people did not distinguish between the disciplines of astronomy and astrology. They were the same science. Astrology evolved in ancient times before calendars had been developed. Back then a tribe's life depended upon knowing when to plant their crops, when the herds would migrate, when to prepare for winter and so on. Ancient humans had to accurately predict the seasons without the aid of calendars. And the way they could predict the seasons would be to observe the position of the planets in the sky. This crucial activity evolved into astrology. The ancient astrologer in many ways was really an astronomer.

Yes, there is an exact correspondence between the position of the planets in the sky and the seasons. But, it is not a cause-

83

and-effect relationship. Of course, in pre-scientific times astrologers naturally attached a cause-and-effect relationship to that correspondence. They reasoned that when Mars is in a certain position Fall weather always sets in, therefore, it must be Mars that is causing Summer to end and Fall to begin. Ancient astrologers then extrapolated that the position of the planets must also be the cause of floods, famines, wars, and peoples' destinies. That is how astrology evolved.

By reversing the cause and effect you can see how false that relationship is. For example, you would never say that because the Sun is in Cancer it is causing you to go to the beach. You are going to the beach because it is summertime. It just so happens that the Sun is in Cancer during summer. Likewise, you would never say that when the sun is in Capricorn it causes you to stay indoors. You stay indoors because it so happens to be winter when the sun is in Capricorn.

Likewise, it is just as crazy to say that Saturn is influencing you to change your life when in reality it is because you are now forty two-years-old and you are examining your life to see why you are not happy. At forty two you are not young any more and you know that you do not have all the time in the world to achieve the kind of life you want to achieve. But astrologers use such false logic all the time.

Once early man learned that he could predict the seasons by the position of stars in the night sky, giving him the knowledge he needed to safely predict when to plant his crops, he then falsely reasoned that other events could be predicted by observing the position of stars in the sky. It is easy to understand how in past times, before we understood science and the scientific method, astrologers would make that cause-and-effect mistake. If the position of the planets could make something as significant as winter usher in, then it seemed reasonable that the position of the planets could also influence our lives. Thus, through the years astrologers have tried to predict not only major events, but individual human characteristics as well. Their predictions today encompass every known factor of the human condition.

Many present day astrologers admit that they know the planets and stars do not influence us. After all, we are now in the 21st century. The idea that planets and stars influence our lives seems a bazaar idea left over from ancient times. Back then, people would relate every event to some higher mystical cause. Of course, astrology developed when societies explained essentially all phenomena through the supernatural.

What astrologers have done is study human nature. Over time, astrologers recognized that a person's life can be broken down into stages of growth. They then matched these stages of growth to corresponding planet movements — making an erroneous cause-and-effect relationship.

All this has nothing to do with planets and stars. It has to do with human psychology and personal growth stages throughout life. Astrologers have simply reversed the cause-and-effect order. They studied human nature and then looked to the planets to find corresponding cycles. This is a common trap in research even to this day. That is, a researcher will seek out a pattern to fit his speculations.

In a book called *The Art of Scientific Investigation*, scientist William Beverage points out how many young professionals, when they first go into research, detect a correspondence between two phenomena. They immediately think that there has to be a cause-and-effect relationship. A young professional can then easily spend years of research looking for what that cause-and-effect relationship is. When he finally realizes it is just not there, he has already wasted years.

Those trained in the hard sciences usually do not get caught up in this flaw. Scientists trained in scientific research know better. They may follow up observations with some initial research, but they will not spend five or ten years looking for a cause-and-affect relationship that does not exist. Now, I am specifically relating this to astrology and planet cycles. With astrology there is not a cause-and-affect relationship between planet cycles and people. There are certain correspondences between human life cycles and planet cycles. But controlled, scientific experiments quickly reveal that there is not a cause-and-effect relationship.

The human mind, particularly our right hemisphere, is expert at recognizing patterns and correspondences between phenomena. But that is where we also can get fooled if we attach a cause-

and-effect relationship to a correspondence between two phenomena when it does not exist.

As an example, the rate of lung cancer shot up in America during the 1970s and 1980s. During that same time period the rate of Japanese imports also shot up correspondingly. But, one would not conclude that an increase in Japanese imports caused an increase in American lung cancer. Yes, a correspondence existed between increasing Japanese imports and increasing rates of lung cancer, but obviously this was not a cause-and-effect relationship.□

If modern day astrologers take the mysticism out of astrology and instead move their craft into observing and predicting human nature they may have something worth while to offer. Since most people never study human psychology, when they happen to read astrological charts the psychology behind them seems profound and illuminating.

Consider traditional philosophy. It is very academic, useful primarily to ivory-tower intellectuals. Most people do not study philosophy, and, therefore, do not relate to it. But religion breaks philosophy down into simplified moral codes, into easily digestible life-guiding principles. Religion is philosophy broken down for the man-in-the-street. Unfortunately, religion puts a mystical basis behind itself, which is then misused by religious leaders and other authorities with agendas to control and manipulate people.

Now consider psychology. Psychology is also a very academic discipline and is not much use to the man-in-the-street. But much of astrology expresses human psychology in simplified, daily terms and experiences that everyone can relate to. Astrology is really pop psychology for the man-in-the-street.

Religion simplifies philosophy for the layman, while astrology simplifies psychology for the layman. Unfortunately, both religion and astrology take the manipulative short cut of just explaining everything via a mystical higher cause.

To understand how this situation evolved, one must go back in history to the beginnings of both religion and astrology. In ancient times, most people were completely illiterate. Until the 19th century, the masses had no education and lived in poverty.

The astrologers themselves were uneducated and illiterate. Thus, they had to resort to mysticism to explain complicated phenomena. They had no inkling of the scientific method, no understanding of the laws of physics, no idea of psychology or philosophy as scientific disciplines.

Although I went to college and got a degree in psychology, I did not want to work in a clinic with schizophrenics, alcoholics or drug addicts. However, when I first studied astrology, I realized that this was layman's psychology for people who are coping with life but who are seeking advice about a specific problem or concern. This was very interesting to me because it utilized a lot of my psychology training.

In the end, however, I turned away from astrology because I knew that planets could not influence our lives. Later, I came to understand that all mysticism, from religion to astrology to all other forms of the occult are right-brain phenomena. That is a very exciting identification. It leads to deeper understandings. And it can help a lot of people.

For example, people who become too caught up in religion need to be shown the tools to solve their problems, to resolve conflicts on their own, rather than following dogmatic and sacrificial ideology that further handicaps their lives. Likewise, some of the advice in astrology is good human psychology. People can utilize that without poisoning their thinking processes with mystical, anti-reality concepts. Believing that external phenomena such as planets determine a person's destiny can really handicap one's reasoning process and long-term critical thinking.

In the mid 1970s a group of scientists signed a declaration that astrology is bunk, that there is absolutely no scientific truth behind it. Of course, astrologers were furious about that.

Since modern astrology is really based on studying people and how individuals go through stages in life, astrologers need to find better, rational answers by looking to psychology, not the planets, to explain life cycles in individuals and the reasons why these cycles exist. Unfortunately, even the many modern day astrologers who openly state that they know there is not a cause-

and-effect relationship between the planets and individuals' lives still cling to mystical, occult notions like reincarnation, spirits, and so on. They are failing to exert scientific discipline. Instead, they just bring in mystical ideas that appeal to them. But so long as one accepts irrational, mystical ideas, he or she is never going to dig down deep enough to uncover the objective, rational root behind a phenomenon.

It is up to astrologers to discover the reality basis for the correspondences that exist in their interpretations. Scientists will never do this because they know there is no planetary influence on individuals' behavior.

Chapter 5 Research Notes

* Astrological and other occult predictions always contain generalized wording. These generalized statements allow people to read their own personal circumstances into almost any given prediction. While what is predicted often seems directed to a specific individual, if you really examine the predictions made you will discover that they are generalized enough so that each particular answer applies to many different people. Two or more people can ask very different questions but the same answer can seem like it personally addresses both of them.

As an example, James Randi, author of the book *Flim Flam*, went into a college classroom. Randi told the students that an astrologer was going to make an individual horoscope for each of them. Each student wrote down personal information about himself or herself. Randi returned the next day and announced that an astrologer had made an individual horoscope for each student based upon their personal information. Randi then passed out the horoscopes.

After pausing a few minutes to allow the students to read their horoscopes, Randi then asked how many students felt that their horoscope accurately described themselves. Every single person, about 25 students in all, raised their hand. They all agreed that their horoscopes were accurate, that each horoscope described them personally. Randi then asked one of the students to read his horoscope out loud. It turned out that Randi had passed out the exact same horoscope to each student in that classroom. Yet, each student thought that his or her horoscope had been individually written based upon their personal information.

There have been other tests conducted whereby a person will be given someone else's horoscope and yet that person is convinced that the horoscope is his. Where human nature is concerned, we all have certain aspects in common with other people. Even though we have our individual differences, we also have major similarities. Everyone wants a worthwhile, fulfilling career. We all want good, satisfying relationships. We all want to achieve our fullest potential in life. There are so many psychological conditions where an individual will identify, *Yes, that's me*.

Consider even opposite personality traits such as being introverted or extroverted. A person who is primarily introverted, reserved, a loner will at times be extroverted, outgoing, social. And the opposite is true. An extrovert likes his time alone, too. Thus, for essentially any psychological issue addressed, a person can identify his or her own personality with it.

Realize that astrological predictions, horoscopes, psychic readings, handwriting analysis, Tarot cards, I-Ching, numerology, palm readings and so on are all about people, their personalities, and their psychological traits.

* A key non sequitur used in astrology is linking the value of math, with its objective and exact rules, with mystical assertions. Astrology is based on an intricate, precise mathematical structure. The value of math with its order, its precision, its exactness is without question. Linking this value of math with astrological interpretations tends by association to give validity to those interpretations. Once one makes a connection to math, that individual has a difficult time rejecting astrology.

In astrology, eight planets plus the sun and moon each make certain mathematical relationships with each other during their movements throughout the sky. In astrology there are twelve mathematical points of importance multiplied by twelve relationships which totals 144 possible combinations. Thus, essentially any human life cycle can find a matching pattern and be attributed to the planets. This is why so many modern day astrologers proclaim, *Astrology works, it's up to scientists to determine why.*

An analogy can be made to how three basic colors (red, yellow and blue) make up all the other colors and their infinite variety of shades, how a handful of basic shapes make up all the patterns in our universe, how four basic plot structures make up all fiction literature, and so on. Likewise, in astrology, the basic planet cycles and their relationships to each other can be matched up to essentially any human action.

* Individuals experience a fair amount of disorder in their lives. Thus, people naturally seek something that will bring order to their lives. Astrology ostensibly offers great order with its mathematical, well-structured, catch-all models.

Astrology's mathematical, well-structured horoscopes create the illusion of great order. But, take astrology out of the horoscope, and it all falls apart. The substance behind astrology in itself is nothing.

People want answers. Astrology, with its precise mathematical structures, appears to give answers.

* I-Ching reduces human behavior to eight principles, which combine to produce 64 combinations; numerology reduces human behavior to nine principles, which combine to produce 81 combinations; and astrology reduces human behavior to twelve principles, which combine to produce 144 combinations plus another twelve points of importance in the horoscope that give a third set of twelve combinations. Consequently, anyone can find aspects of their own character within such diversified interpretations. This complexity, especially in astrology, provides a shield that is hard to penetrate.

Structuring and explaining human behavior by set mathematical formulas relieves a person of choice. It gives the impression that one can have order and control in his life. What most people do not realize is that the philosophy of these disciplines is as antiquated as the bicameral mind. They all promote the bicameral ideals that a person should remain in his place, that he should bow to authority, that there are no accidents in life, that if something happens there is a reason for it and one must accept it. These same restrictive ideas permeate all mystical systems.

Chapter Six

Socrates, Plato, Jesus and Hermes; Secret Societies and Modern Conscious Thought

There is something very interesting about Socrates. His whole lifestyle was the same as most serious mystics live. And like most mystics, Socrates had a serious personal problem. Socrates wife was a shrew, which means they did not get along at all. She was very domineering and demanding. That was the problem Socrates had to work through and attempt to solve in his life. And that is where his sacrifice took place, in his marriage.

For anyone who is a true mystic, if you know even the tiniest bit about their life, you will discover that they had some sort of central, major problem. It is always that problem that motivates them to go into mysticism, to try and learn to be really fair in their actions with others, to try and solve their problems.

Socrates' whole life seems to teach that. But, unlike mystics, he never preached religion or mystical powers. Socrates used his ideas correctly. Socrates would push his students to break into conscious thinking. He would really question young people on the street. He would question them as to why they believed something. Socrates would ask them what holding a certain belief really means. Socrates used his conscious breakthroughs in a correct way to make people really think in an introspective, conscious manner, to be independent, to be their own authority. Socrates did not trick his students into subjugating themselves to a higher authority.

Socrates most famous pupil was Plato. Plato really wanted to go into politics. He loved politics. But when Plato came into contact with Socrates, Plato became so taken with Socrates that he gave up the idea of going into politics and, instead, went and studied with Socrates. Socrates had a profound influence upon Plato. But, unlike Socrates, Plato never broke through to a true conscious perspective.

The way you can tell is that anyone who has gone through the mystic path and has come through to true consciousness uses his own objective reasoning powers to be his own authority. Whenever such a person speaks about what they have learned, or if they speak in terms of religion, they always talk about a unity. That is what the mystics try to achieve, a union or unity with God or Jesus, with Krishna or Buddha, and so on. What this union really means is that they and God are the same. Achieving this unity means they have finally reached the conclusion that they are their own authority. Thus, they state that they have achieved unity with God — meaning they realize they are their own authority.

But Plato never speaks of a unity. Instead, Plato taught division. He talks about the other world as the essence. According to Plato, humans live in a shadow and can never achieve the true perfection of God or of the essence. We can only come so far, but we can never achieve that unity or be at one with that essence. This reveals that Plato never reached the level of understanding of his teacher, Socrates. A true "Master" will always reach the stage of "Unity," of "Oneness with God."

As a young student, Plato was devastated when his beloved teacher, Socrates, was forced to drink hemlock that took his life. Such an unjust and evil tragedy, totally out of one's control to do anything about, must have sent Plato off searching for answers. Plato traveled for several years and it must be during this time that he embraced the mystical wholeheartedly. His mystical philosophy diverges strongly from the teachings of Socrates. Socrates brought philosophy out of the "realm of the sky". Socrates' emphasis was on man and reality. In contrast, Plato placed his emphasis on a perfection of love and beauty which exists in another realm but which can never be realized in this world. A true-to-form mystic philosophy.

When Plato gives his example about the Cave of Shadows, he is talking from theory, not experience. Plato never really broke through to self-leading, conscious thinking. Nevertheless, Plato managed to construct the world's first complete philosophical idea system.

So you see, the philosophy that Plato handed down, a philosophy that has had a tremendous influence over all Western civilization, is not from someone who really broke through to consciousness. That is really interesting when you think about

94

it. The implications are profound. That is one of the major reasons why today modern man is still so susceptible to external authorities in religion, the occult, government, and to charismatic personalities and other self-proclaimed leaders.

To re-emphasize, the trait of a person who becomes fully conscious is the achievement of unity. He is at one with himself. He is his own authority. He recognizes that all the values of honesty, compassion, fairness and so on are his own achievements, his own values to uphold or default upon.

In contrast, when a person is divided, when he is not at one with himself, then he has to have someone or something else who is an authority over him. He has to have an authority figure telling him what to do. And if he goes against the dogma of that authority it creates all kinds of inner conflict.

If a person has not broken through to full consciousness, he thinks God made him do what he does. And he thinks God is responsible for his honesty and virtues. *It's God's honesty, not mine. I want to be honest like God but I'm not because I'm just a mere human being and can't achieve that kind of perfection.* In contrast, when a person breaks through the mystic path, he realizes that he is the one who has achieved his virtues. *I am the honest person I want to be, I am my own authority. And I am responsible for any defaults on those same virtues.*

All religions preach the struggle to achieve unity. Thus, they are actually preaching a contradiction. They are preaching for you to come through and realize that there is no external authority out there, that in the end you must become one with yourself to be your own authority.

But you see, people are brought up in a society that preaches religion from infancy, that preaches about a God who is perfect, who is an absolute authority, and that you can never achieve that same perfection. Everything you are taught concerning religion divides you. In other words, to truly be selfless is against your nature. To have an authority figure over you who knows what is best for you, who decides what you should or should not do contradicts the nature of an independent, thinking individual. As Caesar said, *To conquer, you must first divide.* In other words, the religious leaders divide their followers internally. That way

95

they can conquer their minds to rule over them.

So the traditional church, to control the people, divides them internally by preaching that self-interest is bad, that personal desire is bad, and so on. The traditional church dogmatically preaches that all the basic human traits that are natural and necessary for survival are bad. According to religious doctrine self interest is bad, ambition is bad, pride is bad, money is bad, sexual desire is bad, even knowledge is bad. One is supposed to sacrifice his life and values to others. One is supposed to live by the rules of an external authority. So, you become at odds with yourself, you become divided. To really be accepted by God and to get into heaven, one has to follow religious doctrine. One has to give up all the fundamental human values in life. One has to recognize God as his authority and do what God wills.

Church teachings constantly imply that you are not worthy as an individual. Only if you do the will of God are you worthy. You see, that is just man's control over man. That is the church leaders exerting control over their followers.

Such church dogma is very effective at dividing a person. And when you are divided, you are at odds with yourself, with your family, with your peers, you are in a bad mood, and you do not get along with the people you work with. See how awful that is.

At the same time, all the major religions preach a unity of oneness. People think that unless a person is exceptional, a spiritual Master, one cannot achieve that unity or perfection until one goes to heaven. The few who do break through to achieve unity here on earth, they do not come out and say, *I'm my own Master*, or *I'm God*. But the individual who has truly broken through the mystic path knows this.

People always look up to leaders, to famous people, to celebrities. These so-called leaders have a certain aura about them that emits authority. So, many people who do not feel that authority within themselves look to someone else who has it. They then make such a person their leader.

The top religious leaders have to break through the hoax because that is the only way they can be self-confident enough and strong enough to attract their followers. They can only exude that kind of authority, that kind of leadership, that kind of confidence by achieving a oneness with themselves. Their followers then perceive them as a highly developed spiritual leader or as a Master. Those followers want to learn wisdom from their leader.

Well, the religious leaders are highly evolved spiritual .masters. But it is not in the way their followers think. It is not that they have achieved a unity with God, it is that they have realized there is no God. The religious and spiritual leaders have achieved a unity with themselves because they have finally recognized that they must be their own authority.

I believe that those religious and spiritual leaders who have broken through the religious/mystic hoax should come right out and say exactly what they have learned. Like Dr. Frank R. Wallace has, like Ayn Rand has, like I have. Maybe it was different in ancient times when the public was uneducated and bicameral. Maybe there was a need for secret societies to take bright, intelligent people who could handle the realization and responsibility that individuals are their own authority, that there is no God looking out after us. That is what the secret societies were all about. They were for intelligent people who had broken through.

In ancient society a person could not come out and publicly say there is no God. Individuals had to keep that secret. There were a few people who did come out and say that. They were ostracized from society. Some were executed. Historically, if you disagreed with the church, you were excommunicated and no one could employ you, or go into your workshop, or trade with you or even talk to you. The church had total domination. But today we are living in a more enlightened time. People can come out and say there is no God.

In ancient times when most humans were still bicameral they simply could not understand a modern conscious man who said that there was no higher authority, no God looking after them. Even today, people who have been indoctrinated with religion are completely unnerved by that concept. You can see that in letters Neo-Tech Publishing receives from religious indoctrinates. Such people say how they love Jesus, that Jesus is their hope, that they will live in heaven because of Jesus and that Neo-

Tech's atheistic literature is just awful. One cannot go and talk to such individuals and change their views through reason. Their views might be changed if such indoctrinated individuals were brought, one by one, into an inertia type thing where they really tried to work through the mystic path. But each individual would have to work through it himself. And that would take years.

The spiritual leaders are very clever. They stroke their students' hope while guiding them and occasionally trying to shock their intellect. This shock therapy is especially prevalent in Zen. The students view their Master as a highly evolved person. The Master will give the students a Koan. A Koan is an impossible contradiction that one is supposed to figure out — like the left hand clapping all by itself. The student has to contemplate that thought and then figure out how to do that. Under normal circumstances, one would conclude that such a feat is impossible and would not bother trying to figure it out. But the student is pressured to resolve that contradiction. At other times, the Master will really put a student down, which hurts him. This is another shock therapy to try and snap the students' thinking out of being caught up with the idea that there is a God and that God is going to help them.

When people go into religious or spiritual study, the Master lets them come in and develop an even stronger belief in God. Along the way the spiritual leader will be very compassionate and kind and discuss things with them. But suddenly, he might do something that really shocks the student, that acts as a slap in the face. The student may be sincerely talking to the Master, who is showing the student a lot of compassion, then all of a sudden the Master harshly puts down the student. The student has no idea why. He thinks it must be because he said something stupid. But, the whole idea is to try and shock students out of a following mode.

In the end, very few students work all the way through the mystic path to realize that there is no higher authority, that they cannot remain in a following mode, that they must become their own authority. Those few who do break through are then made Masters themselves.

Some of the individuals who break through choose to leave the system rather than to perpetuate the hoax. For me, there was no way in the world I would lead someone into that purposely. I would just come right out and tell them what I have learned. No more lies!

If everyone was able to break through the religious/mystic hoax, developing a full, rational consciousness void of mystical, external-authority tendencies, society would be completely different. It would be a fully conscious, fully honest society. That is the kind of society Jesus wanted to bring about. All his disciples thought it was going to be within their lifetimes, that Jesus was going to establish a kingdom through right.

If you study Jesus' teachings, you can see that he was really trying to lead the illiterate, bicameral peasants in the Palestinian countryside into conscious thinking. Instead of just saying, *Everything in my life is up to the gods and all I can do is pray*, Jesus tried to lead the peasants to conscious thinking by using their own minds and their own authority to work through their problems. (See Appendix I, *Jesus' Secret Message*.)

During Jesus' time there were several powerful secret societies. A lot of historians think that Jesus went and studied with one of these secret societies when he was young. There are no records about Jesus when he was young. Historians know essentially nothing about Jesus' life until he started his ministry. But, there are a few historical references to Jesus being in a Temple when he was twelve.

As mentioned, these ancient secret societies would take bright young men and attempt to break them through to self-leading consciousness. It is very likely that the young Jesus studied with a secret society and consequently broke out of a bicameral following mode and into a modern, self-leading conscious mode. Jesus then went on to try and teach this modern, self-leading conscious thinking to the peasants of Palestine. But you see what has happened? The religious leaders subsequently twisted Jesus' ideas into the exact opposite — into cajoling people to become unquestioning, obedient followers.

At this point I want to mention Hermes. Hermes is considered by some to be the father of the occult. From what I know of Hermes, I think he was a mystic who then broke through to the understanding that there is no God, although he

99

never publicly stated that.

It was once thought that Hermes lived long before the time of Jesus, but scholars have now dated his work around the first century AD. Thus, Hermes most likely lived soon after the death of Jesus. For about a hundred years after Jesus' death there was a tremendous amount of mystical and agnostic philosophy that sprouted. A lot of those ancient mystics lived in Alexandria, Egypt where the great library was. They came together there and studied. Many of them formed secret societies.

In these secret societies, a member initially has a belief in God. It may not be the central focus of his life. But when he goes into a secret society, he completely indoctrinates himself with the spiritual and mystical teachings. Soon this becomes the central focus of his life. It becomes all consuming. That is typical of cult followers as well. However, if a person journeys through the entire mystic path, then he will come out the other side to discover that there is no God, that he is in fact his own authority.

But the secret societies kept this knowledge secret because it was, in a sense, a secret process of deprogramming oneself of our pre-conscious, bicameral need for external authority. Hermes was a big influence in these secret societies because he was a true mystic who had finally broken through and learned the truth. Hermes was one of the early intellectuals who broke through from the pre-conscious, bicameral mode that seeks external authority to the modern, introspective, conscious mode that is self-guiding. He realized that he was his own authority, that he had to make his own decisions in life.

On the surface, Hermes still promoted higher, mystical powers. But, I think his goal was to take bicameral, following-mode students and push them along the mystic path to eventually break through to self-guiding consciousness. However, after a teacher dies, his students do not really know or understand what that teacher really thought. Thus, students begin to theorize their own ideas into someone else's teachings. And this clouds history.

Chapter 6 Research Notes

* The most important point a person pursuing the mystic path

should realize is that objective reality, not a higher mystical realm, is the final truth. Our life and happiness depend on how much we are in tune with objective reality. I did not always believe this.

I used to believe strongly in a personal God whom I thought guided me in my daily life. I believed that there was a Divine Plan for everyone's life. Now I know that is false. I deceived myself.

What finally made this clear to me was how over time I realized that whatever truth I learned always came as a result of meeting practical reality. In contrast, anything pertaining to God or to the teachings about him resulted in confusion.

I had always thought that God was the one who enlightened me when in reality it was the practical situation which enabled me to figure out the truth for myself. To a rational man rooted in objective reality this may seem obvious, but to one following the teachings of mysticism, with all its complexities and contradictions, it is not so simple and clear cut. I was convinced that God was guiding me.

Why had I been so convinced of a personal God? The mystical and psychic experiences I had. And the only avenue open for some kind of understanding of these experiences was in the mystical literature where cases abound with those who have had similar experiences. They all thought that this phenomenon was contact with God or some higher realm.

The real tragedy is that no one has stepped forward and revealed the truth. Those who have followed the mystic path to its logical conclusion have not exposed its true nature, have not explained the rational, right-brain origin of the mystical experience. Yet they know it. They understand this.

My revealing this could have far reaching effects. On the other hand, one cannot convince a follower of that. He is so steeped in his beliefs and has so much of his life invested in those beliefs that to negate them means giving up the rewards he has worked so hard to attain. Psychologically, that is extremely hard to do. For some individuals giving up their mystical beliefs is almost impossible.

* Mysticism holds a fascination for many. It promises high

101

attainment of character, wisdom, peace of mind, and rewards here on earth as well as in heaven. But the way one is supposed to achieve those attainments is vague and confusing, and often psychologically unhealthy.

Following the mystical teachings eventually wreak havoc in one's life. One has to give up everything that means anything to oneself. What a cruel and malevolent outlook that is. Yet that is the heart of religious and occult teachings.

On the other hand, one learns many valuable lessons while pursuing the mystic path, yet in a context of deception and lies. What a costly and harmful way for man to learn truth.

Chapter Seven

Religious and Occult Leaders: Their Desire to Teach Others; Their Refusal to Reveal the Hoax

In ancient times, many secret societies existed. Today, many independent religious and spiritual sects exist. For example, there is the *New Life Church* in Boulder City, Nevada that I went to several times. The man who started that church was named Vernon Howard.

Vernon Howard would hold weekly meetings at his *New Life Church*. He had religious students coming from all over the West Coast to attend.

Sometimes Vernon Howard would talk compassionately to his students. At other times he would make idiotic statements that would baffle students. That is typical shock therapy. Vernon was a master at that.

I know Vernon Howard had broken through the hoax and was an atheist. Of course, his students did not know that. And, I know what made Vernon Howard turn to religion and travel down the mystic path to eventually break through. Previously he had worked in a factory and he was married. He eventually divorced his wife. And that is where his inner conflict lay. That was his problem. I am sure he initially felt he must do the Christian thing, that he must make his marriage work, that he must meet that challenge and not run away from his problems. That was his inner conflict that he had to work through.

As I said before, people who travel down the mystic path always have a deep personal problem that motivates them to seek solutions through the spiritual. For example, that is how Buddhism got started. Buddha came from an extremely wealthy family. He was married to a beautiful wife. But Buddha was deeply disturbed about suffering and poverty in life. That was where his problem lay. He gave up his wealthy family, his position in society and went off to try and solve those problems.

Now, returning to Vernon Howard. He had problems with his marriage. My guess is that he probably spent ten or fifteen years traveling down the mystic path. Most serious mystics require ten or more years to break through the hoax. Yet, after all those years, Vernon was still unable to resolve his problem. So he had to make a choice. He finally broke down and got a divorce. When a person goes through a struggle like, that person learns a lot.

Making the breakthrough is not just a matter of intelligence. Breaking through also involves trust in oneself and in one's own reasoning powers. A person must break with a lot of traditional ideas. He must reject them. And a person can only do that through trust in his own knowledge and confidence in himself.

After journeying down the mystic path and finally breaking through, a person realizes he has learned a lot. At this point, that person will often go into writing and teaching, which Vernon Howard did. Here was a man who had no training as a writer or a teacher, but he wrote several books and opened his *New Life Church* in order to teach.

A lot of mystics do that. They want to write and teach. Their whole life has been caught up traveling down the mystic path and learning new knowledge at each stage. They then want to pass on some of what they have learned.

Once a person writes a book, a lot of readers will want to contact that author and come and see that author. That is why so many religious/mystic authors will start a religious sect. That is what happened to Vernon Howard. Through his writings a lot of people contacted him. People even came from Europe to see Vernon. They would just show up at his doorstep wanting to talk to him. That is when he decided to start his *New Life Church*.

After journeying down the mystic path himself, Vernon decided he wanted to teach others, to help them break through as well. There are a lot of barriers that need to be broken through. One has to break through all kinds of traditional dogma, one has to break through thoughts of, *This is the way I'm suppose to act*. And that person has to break through believing that there is a higher authority who will look out for him.

I read one of Vernon Howard's books. For a religious book, it was relatively rational, down to earth. It did not preach the traditional, dogmatic bromides. Instead, his book gave a lot of common sense, practical advice.

As a person breaks through the mystic path, that person

keeps living a better life because he keeps cutting through all kinds of bondage that kept him from acting in his own self-interest. At first, he thinks everyone else will break through, too, if they just know what he knows. But, when that person actually tries teaching others, he realizes that everyone is not going to break through. And certainly not within a short period of time.

Many people who gravitate around spiritual and religious teachers are insecure people looking for a leader. This is evident as soon as you talk to a number of spiritual students. The expressions on their faces tell us they are obviously followers.

Also, when a group gets together, especially a large group, instead of working through and solving their personal problems, the group often morphs into a cheerleading-like support mechanism. This breaks the intensity and focus needed to solve real problems. Instead, individuals find group support for keeping their life as it is. Of all the students attending Vernon Howard's *New Life Church*, I met only one who I thought had enough intensity to eventually break through the hoax.

Religious and spiritual leaders who start a religious sect feel they have something to contribute. I am sure Vernon Howard felt that starting his *New Life Church* could help others reach another way of living that was more valuable. That was a choice he made, rather than just coming out and revealing the religious/ mystic hoax right from the start in his books and teachings.

All religious and occult leaders have traveled the mystic path. As I said before, there are four basic stages to the mystic path. The first stage is when a person has a problem in his life and he turns to religion or the spiritual looking for answers. For a while, he feels really good. He thinks that he is communicating with God. This gives that person a special feeling. But those communications are actually coming from the right side of his own brain.

During stage two, the student reads more and more religious and spiritual literature and tries to put his concepts into practice. He starts being totally honest, being totally fair, examining his own attitudes, controlling how he reacts in his relationships. The student is increasingly drawn into doing all the things that the

105

religious/spiritual literature says one should do to become perfected and to do God's will.

It is almost as though the student is taking a college course. At first, he concentrates on trying to learn the material. When he feels he has learned the lessons and can pass an exam, he then wants to move on and apply his knowledge in the real world. The student's emphasis then focuses on applying the religious/spiritual doctrines in his life.

As the student begins to apply the religious ideals in his daily life, he learns more and more about human nature. Over time, he sees what really happens in one's life when applying these concepts. As the student keeps putting the religious ideals into practice it dawns on him what religious ideology actually results in. Such as the idea that one should give up personal desire. When the serious student of religion reaches the point where he has truly given up personal desire, he loses all motivation. He becomes like the walking dead. This is the point where he begins to recognize what the religious ideology has done to him.

After the student has made self-sacrifice and denial of personal desire major constituents of his life, he begins to realize that learning self-responsibility involves putting into practice rational selfishness and responsible personal desire. Eventually, in an unguarded moment, he becomes very angry about being taken advantage of by others and not sticking up for himself. He may even become filled with an emotion of hate. As a religious person who believes in love and compassion, he is not supposed to hate anything. But, as his true emotions well up inside of him over the years, he begins to realize that he is no more God-like or perfected or compassionate than anyone else — not if these kinds of emotions flare up inside of him.

Jesus brought into Christianity the idea that by just feeling an emotion one can commit a sin. According to Jesus, any unvirtuous emotion a person feels is a sin against God. Thus, feelings of anger and resentment shock the religious/spiritual student at this stage because he has not been acting that way with anyone. This forces the student to really examine his ideas, his beliefs.

This re-examining of my own ideas and beliefs at this stage resulted in a huge breakthrough for me. For the first time I

106

realized that one has to act in his own self-interest. That is the only way to truly be compassionate to yourself and to everyone else over the long run. In contrast, by consistently practicing selflessness, whenever someone makes a cutting remark you know is unfair, you will not answer them back. If you do not answer them back, you loose your self-esteem and feelings of self-worth. It is like you become some kind of meek doormat. You must push down and repress your natural emotions of self-respect, fairness, justice when practicing true selflessness. But at some point all those repressed feelings will break free and come rushing out.

A huge burden was lifted off me when I finally realized that I should act in my own self-interest, when I finally realized that I should not try to be selfless in all situations, that it is okay to feel anger when it is justified. Anger is not a sinful emotion when used correctly. One should not act on anger or other strong emotions irrationally. One can deal with these emotions rationally — using self-discipline and self-responsibility.

By practicing unconditional selflessness, a person is actually harming others because he lets others get away with things that are wrong or unjust. It is important in life to stand up to the unjust and the unfair and to try and put a stop to it. When you act in your own rational self-interest you are actually doing what is best for everyone over the long run.

When I first realized that rational selfishness is the true and just nature of man I began to adjust my thinking. I began building that realization into my choices and actions. I also realized that personal desire can be good. I became motivated again. I began to build a genuine self-confidence again, a self-confidence based on my accomplishments, not on sacrifices or conformity to someone else's dogma.

Finally, I began to live my life in a way that I was motivated to do good and healthy things for myself and my family. I stopped constantly putting others' needs and demands above my own. I stopped constantly ignoring and sacrificing my own desires. I began to take rationally selfish actions.

As I allowed myself to become motivated again, I began looking for a career to go into. For the past several years I had been staying at home raising my children. It was also around this time that my husband and I decided to divorce. Soon after my divorce I met someone that I was attracted to and wanted to date. In addition, there were other personal activities that I wanted the freedom to pursue. But then I started getting all those feelings again that I was not supposed to pursue something personal, that instead I should be following the will of God.

After the religious student has passed through the second stage of the mystic path and enters the third stage, he thinks he now really understands what following the will of God is about. It is not all that dogma about selflessness, sacrifice and having no desire. The religious literature even states that nobody really knows what the will of God is. So the student now feels that he has reached a higher pinnacle of learning. But then that student discovers that if he has not completely broken with religion, if he still believes in God, all those feelings start coming back — feelings that he is not supposed seek anything personal.

In my case, I was now seeking a vocation that was not related to the church. I was attracted to and wanted to date someone, yet I was not seeking to get remarried. And I wanted to pursue my personal interests in art and music. Yet, I started experiencing feelings of guilt again because I was not pursuing the religious ideals. Instead, I was pursuing personal needs and desires. I realized that because of those guilt feelings I could not go after what I really wanted in life. This created a real internal conflict within me. And this conflict created another crisis for me.

After an intense emotional struggle, I realized that so long as an individual has an authority over him, he will never be his own master. Even the religious literature states that one is supposed to attain the level of master in order to become one's own leader. The more I thought about this, the more I began to see the trickery behind religious doctrines.

This forced me to look very strongly at the whole foundation of religious philosophy. Not just the ideas of selflessness, sacrifice and eliminating personal desire, but even the idea that you can have an authority figure over you telling you what you can and cannot do, telling you what is acceptable, what is forbidden. At this point, I began to realize that the whole foundation of religious philosophy is wrong. It is all built on concepts that go against human nature and are destructive to the individual and self-actualization. This was the final breakthrough for me. That is when I realized there was no God.

Finally, one progresses to that last breakthrough, stage four, where he realizes that all religious and mystic systems are a hoax. There is no higher power looking out for us. There is not a God.

In fact, the religious literature itself states that eventually one will give up the desire even for the spiritual. So, you see, there is a hint there from the very start. For me, those realizations suddenly came together to the inescapable conclusion that as long as you have an authority over you, you will remain a child, you will never be your own master. This comes as a big insight and a huge relief.

Whenever a person gets a major insight that breaks through some kind of bondage a tremendous feeling of relief and happiness results. Scientists, too, experience this feeling after they have struggled with a problem for a long time and then they finally piece together the solution. Suddenly, everything comes together, everything fits.

When the religious student travels the full mystic path to realize that there is not a God, he experiences tremendous feelings of relief. Finally, he is able to go after the things he wants. He no longer has external forces blocking him. He really is his own master. There is not some mystical, higher authority prevailing over him.

At this point in the student's life he has a lot of experience behind him. He just knows his insight is correct. Like scientists, businessmen, and artists who make a major breakthrough, the student's religious breakthrough comes with an unusual certainty of knowing.

The spiritual literature talks about this knowing. They call it wisdom. This wisdom comes through years of study and life experience. This new knowledge feels so solid because both the intuitive right brain and the logical left brain of a person are finally in sync and are in complete agreement.

This contrasts so sharply with the religious student's previous state of mind when the contradictory ideals of the religious dogma caused his right brain and his left brain to be out of sync with each other, to be in conflict with each other. That caused emotional turmoil to keep erupting within him.

You can tell when a spiritual leader has broken through the hoax by how he words his statements, by the level of experience he is at, by whether or not he is just theorizing from the religious dogma. Yet most religious leaders still continue to promote the religious ideals and the God concept.

In contrast, many astrologers and other occultists believe what they are saying. This is because occultists are not really interested in dogma or philosophy. They are more interested in people and their personalities — in pop psychology.

Over the years I have read numerous religious books dating from ancient times to modern times in which the authors — religious leaders, saints, monks have broken through the hoax but do not admit it. Once a person has broken through the hoax, those who have also broken through really stand out by the way they phrase things, by certain concepts they express.

Monks, for example, keep telling the younger monks that they must become a Master. When a monk does finally break through to realize it is all a hoax, that is when the leaders say, *Now, you're a Master, you know it all*. That monk then turns around and becomes a leader himself. This is so whether he is a Christian Monk, a Buddhist Monk, or an occult leader. Like the secret societies of yesteryear, those few who break through are promoted to the level of Master.

A significant difference between Christianity and other forms of the occult, especially Zen, is that in Zen and other occult forms a person must use his intellect to progress through the mystic path. This contrasts with Christianity where one is supposed to follow dogmatic rules based on faith as he or she progresses through the mystic path.

Because of this, some mystics view Zen and other occult practices as superior to Christianity and the church. Religious followers are supposed to put their intellect aside and just believe through faith. In contrast, Zen and many other areas of the occult emphasize self-responsibility – you are the cause of what happens to you.

In Zen, for example, a student gets what is called a double bind. He is asked to achieve something that is impossible to achieve. At some point that student will break through to realize that it was a double bind, something that was impossible to achieve. This is a way of forcing one to break with ideas held that are not correct.

What makes me angry are those religious and occult leaders who have broken through the hoax to realize that there is no higher power, no God looking out for us, and yet they continue to perpetuate that hoax. In this age of free speech and the separation of Church and State, one can speak out without fear of reprisals. A person does not have to lead others into something that is going to take them years, often the most creative years of their lives, to break through.

Serious religious and occult students are seeking values and honesty. It is not like they are some kind of imbeciles. They are sincere, honest people. But after they have spent years traveling down the mystic path they are like a child just coming out of school. Often they have to start a vocation from scratch because they have been drawn away from a practical, real-world career. Many have wasted the best years of their lives when they could have developed a productive, competitive career.

Once the religious student has learned wisdom and finally emerges from the mystic path, he stops withdrawing from the real world. Instead, he goes back into that world and leads a normal, assertive, career-minded life.

The religious and occult leaders know the hoax, they are actually explaining it to their students. But they are saying it in a way that sounds like it is something very great to attain. In the end, all they are doing is bringing a student back to square one, back to the realization that there is no higher power, that it is all a hoax.

I remember one young lady attending the *New Life Church* meetings. She had been working on her Ph.D. in psychology. She had already gotten her bachelors degree. In the summer months she would live near the church and get very involved in the meetings. She only had one more year of college to earn her Ph.D. But she decided not to go back to school in the fall and get her Ph.D. Instead, she decided to stay at the *New Life*

111

Church full-time to study Vernon Howard's teachings. That was tragic. If a student does not finish his or her college degree within a few years, that student has to start over. Yet that degree would have been that young lady's means of livelihood in the future.

She believed the false enticements held out by the religious literature. She thought that by studying the spiritual she was going to learn something much more useful and important than her Ph.D. But, of course, in the end there is no higher level or higher reality to be obtained in religion or the occult. She was so close to getting her Ph.D. What a waste. And yet, there was nothing I could say to that young lady to change her mind. She was totally caught up with the religious ideals and their misleading promises.

That tragic scenario repeats itself thousands of times every day across the world as promising young people give up finishing college or pursuing a career in order to go into the mystic path. They do this because they think they are going to learn and acquire something really valuable.

A few years ago I worked with a brilliant Japanese man, Yasahiko. He had been awarded a full scholarship to Tokyo University. But, instead, he became a Buddhist monk. He went off and walked around India for several years. By the time Yasahiko had finally broken through the hoax, it was too late. He was already in his thirties. He was not going to go back to college and start over from scratch at that point.

Unfortunately, many of the really smart individuals who finally break through the religious/mystic hoax feel that they can now only make a living by writing and teaching religious and spiritual material. That is how the hoax gets perpetuated.

Chapter 7 Research Notes

* A July 1997 article in Reason magazine exposes what some scientists, especially some biologists and political philosophers, are expounding and making popular today. These scientists know and openly admit within their profession that there is no God. In the field of biology Darwin's theory of evolution is constantly verified by observation, particularly concerning phenomena such

as rapidly evolving antibiotic-resistant bacteria, newly emerging viruses and countless other biological processes. Yet the Bible's idea that man was created by God conflicts with evolution. That is why Born-Again Christians have been told by their leaders not to read scientific books.

Yet, there is a group of scientists and philosophers who call themselves neo-conservatives. Although they are atheists, they advocate religion for the masses. In their view the masses need religion in order for a moral society to exist. These elitists think that the masses need to be controlled and the way to do that is through religion, especially with the idea of sacrifice.

Not only is this dishonest but it exposes why many working people harbor a distrust towards intellectuals and other white-collar elites. This example also makes clear to me how misunderstood human nature is. As identified in Neo-Tech and as Ayn Rand identified with Objectivism, human nature is naturally moral. I have always taken it for granted that those who went through the mystic path not only realized the dramatic idea that there is not a god, but more importantly realized the significant point that most humans, by their nature, strive to be moral.

Intellectuals who fail to grasp that point will, unfortunately, advocate positions similar to those neo-conservative scientists. They will think that the masses need to be deceived and controlled through government and religion.

Conclusion

It has been stated by a number of highly successful persons that we learn more from our failures than from our successes. In any case, failure exerts an important role in one's life as an opportunity for learning and correcting mistakes. So many of our actions in life are based on false assumptions, misconceptions, wishful thinking, and automatic reactions. Yet reality always points out our mistakes through the problems which ensue. If a person is mature and really wants to solve his problems rather that evade them, then he is forced to focus his full awareness and conscious attention on those problems, on the important aspects of his problems and his underlying assumptions in order to discover the causes. Through such difficulties one is forced to use his conscious mind to solve his problems.

It is this strategy which the mystics use to accomplish their purpose. They encourage a person's misconceptions and illusions, even multiply those illusions. The difficulties which result eventually force that person to fully use and fully develop his own conscious mind.

One may wonder why anyone could be so gullible as to embrace the mystical teachings. While there are a number of important reasons why a person moves in that direction, the mystic path is so brilliantly planned and the strategy so absolutely clever that once a person initially accepts its basic premises, he becomes caught up in a maze of intricacies and paradoxes from which there seems to be no escape. For example, a parallel process takes place in which the religious/mystic student develops his own independence, uses his own conscious awareness and derives tangible rewards from so doing while at the same time certain areas of his life become chaotic and damaging to his happiness and self-esteem. Both occurrences are a direct result of following religious teachings. So the student feels that he has something to gain, something tangibly rewarding, yet at the same time something to endure. These strategies, of course, are planned and that is exactly what the student is supposed to feel; the benefits and the self-destruction go hand in hand throughout the entire course of the mystic path.

The final goal is to develop and use one's consciousness, to adhere to reality, to attain the freedom of being one's own authority, to make conscious decisions about one's life through the development of one's own mind rather than following the guidance of authority figures and religious ideology. But to tell a mystic that this is his true goal, that his path leads to this objective, he would be completely dumbfounded and deny it. The promise of mysticism is a lie, and what the mystic thinks he will attain is also a lie. This lie is used by the Master mystics who choose to become leaders. It was the lie which sustained them in their search and without which no mystical literature could exist. In fact, the mystical literature is full of truths taken out of context, which give the students the wrong impressions and improper perspectives. The purpose is to confuse the student, to shake up and dislodge accepted mores, and leave him feeling anxious and out of control.

The use of our modern, conceptual, conscious mind is not automatic. It requires continuous effort. An analogy can be made to modern consciousness' very existence. Its development was forced on man in a time of great evolutionary crisis in order to survive. (See *The Origin of Consciousness in the Breakdown of the Bicameral Mind* by Julian Jaynes). This parallels what the mystic experiences. In order to survive as an individual in the crisis which he finds himself in, the mystic student is forced to think hard — to introspect, to conceptualize, to discard ideology and think independently. The alternative is to give up and drown in one's own misery and mystical philosophy.

This demand of reality, with its adherence to truth and the objective laws of nature, is what insures the mystic student's success if he is totally honest with himself. Truth to reality is the constant measure the mystic runs up against. People who cannot be persuaded rationally of their misguided concepts and who embrace mysticism experience, through the intensification and the deepening of their irrational mystic beliefs, the very real and tragic consequences of those beliefs in an unforgiving, ruthlessly objective reality.

There is a stage in the mystic's development where the whole structure and foundation of the mystical philosophy crumbles. He recognizes that it is completely false. In contrast, that mystic is led inexorably to the conclusion that objective reality is the

116

only and final truth. In one sense he feels a tremendous release in breaking the bondage of mystical thought, and in another sense he experiences much pain because the promises and rewards which he had worked so hard for will not be forthcoming.

Some find this truth too painful. Yet the real source of their pain is not in giving up the false beliefs or in letting go of the promised rewards, although that is hard to relinquish, the devastating pain which the mystic student feels is the mistrust of his own intellect. He has had great pride in his own intellect. For years he has felt intellectually superior to others. But the truth forces him to acknowledge that he has been intellectually naive and gullible. He wanted to believe in mysticism and as a result denied his own intelligence. He has followed and trusted someone else's guidance and he has been deceived.

Hopefully, he will have the courage to face this fact, to break with the illusions no matter how painful, and, henceforth, trust his own conscious mind and objective reality rather than look to someone or something else for guidance.

One could say that the ultimate goal of mysticism is to develop the follower's own consciousness and intellectual knowledge through the means of difficulties and deception, through ploys and strategies devised to make the mystic student experience pain so that he will become aware of himself, aware of the bondage and oppression which the mystic teachings create within his own spirit. The breakthrough comes via the anger and rebellion that arise from constantly acting against one's own nature.

This brilliantly devised plan does work if carried through to completion. As a method in ancient and medieval times it may have been understandable. But to apply such a deceptive and life-consuming method to 21st-Century, modern, consciously-thinking man is an outrage. In the context of ancient and medieval civilization when many men were still in nature's automatic bicameral mode of consciousness, where only a few had developed modern-day, self-guiding and introspective consciousness, one might see the justification for programming a person in this way. The few who first developed modern, conceptual consciousness did so by accident. The oppressive and manipulative demands of the ancient authorities made people

117

unable to deal with an increasingly complex society. The crises created by the religious dictates forced some individuals to become self-aware, to trust their own understanding, and to reject the stranglehold of religious and mystic dogma. Such individuals probably had no clear identification of their modern, self-guiding, conceptual consciousness as such but knew its benefits.

In ancient and medieval times to openly defy the authorities or the church meant complete ostracism, loss of livelihood and property, and often execution. In those civilizations a person did not have freedom. The authorities, the Kings, the Church, by divine right held absolute power both over the economic and moral life of all of those within their kingdoms. Freedom of thought was completely denied.

In that context, a conceptually conscious man would use his powers of intellect to assure his survival. Since his field of specialty was truth and reality as opposed to mysticism and dogma, and since he could not openly defy the authorities or religious leaders, he went underground and shrouded his knowledge with mystery. He took the position of the *Wise One*, or the *Spiritual Teacher*. His teachings were carefully guarded and kept secret.

The few who were chosen to attend his classes were sworn to secrecy. When they, too, broke through the illusions because of the personal turmoil and self-awareness which ensued, they became conscious individuals who learned to trust their own minds. And they, in turn, became the *Wise One*, the *Mystic* who taught others.

The term Ancient Mysteries is still very much used today. And those using it imbue it with a sense of authority, awe, and reverence as if anything ancient somehow has authenticity and merit. Mysterious is a very apt term applied to the spiritual teachings because the strategy used, the havoc created, and the goal accomplished is a complete mystery to the unsuspecting pupil.

For modern man to still be gullible to this type of influence and to still be under the throes of religious indoctrination is much the same as modern man calling on a witch doctor to cure his physical ills. While there are certain techniques which the witch doctor uses (roots and herbs which have demonstrated healing

118

powers) the whole context and frame of reference from which the witch doctor operates is ancient and full of superstition. The same can be said of religion and occult disciplines: the whole context and frame of reference of religious and occult philosophy is ancient and riddled with superstition.

The reason so many intelligent and otherwise rational people remain in the throes of religious and mystical belief is that they have been taught these beliefs from childhood by those they admire and respect the most — their parents, teachers, and other authority figures whom they trust. They have been indoctrinated by those they love the most, imbued with feelings of nostalgia toward the good and the beautiful that they equate with God, made to feel guilt whenever they act against religious and mystic principles. Note how, even when grown, a person flinches when he is called selfish. He is definitely uncomfortable with that label and will explain his act as rational, not selfish.

Because man has been psychologically programmed to accept the belief in God and religion, the emotional struggle to break with this belief is profound. It is really not a matter of the intellect, it is an emotional struggle.

Religious philosophy has mainly lost its stranglehold on a mans' economic life, though vestiges of it remain. Its power mainly lies in the area of a man's conduct, and his relationships. Man's freedom to be true to his real nature, to conduct his relationships with rational and self-guiding consciousness, to deal with others in honest and rationally selfish ways, still remains under the medieval grip of a false moral ethic.

When man learns that rational selfishness is his true nature and that only a selfish man can be compassionate; when he discovers that acting in his own best interest is the only way in which he can be honest with himself and with those he has relationships with; when he reaps the benefits of respect for himself which comes with rejecting the moral ethic that he should be another man's servant; when he experiences the relief which comes from knowing that he is not obligated or at the mercy of another man's wishes; when he knows that his true moral obligation is to himself first; when he experiences the peace of mind and freedom of spirit which results from being his own authority; then that man will be able to interact with others on a truly elevated, conscious level. Our ancient, automatically reacting, guidance-seeking way of behavior will be held in check. So will the religious practices of servitude and oppression. Conscious man with self-awareness and knowledge of man's true nature will act with just and humane practices toward one another, probably for the first time in history.

When enough men employ their modern conscious minds to muster up the emotional courage to break with the stifling and oppressive moral ethics of religion and all other forms of mysticism and external, higher authority, and when they experience the freedom such knowledge gives them, a new renaissance will arise. Perhaps, for the first time in history, men will know consciously how to interact with one another for the best interests of all concerned. The endless slaughter of men in the name of religion or in the name of that other great higher authority, the state, will end. Man's inhumanity to man will wither while man's humanity to man will flourish.

Appendix I

Jesus' Secret Message:
Discover Consciousness[1]

In order to understand the New Testament and Jesus' message one must first know the distinction between the conscious mind and the bicameral mind. With that knowledge Jesus' message becomes clear.

For an introduction and definition of the two minds see Frank R. Wallace's award-winning article *Consciousness: The End of Authority* (Neo-Tech III). The significance of the two ways of thinking is clearly defined. This article was written in response to the book *The Origin of Consciousness in the Breakdown of the Bicameral Mind* by Julian Jaynes.

Consciousness is a new, modern way of thinking that involves an understanding of the right hemisphere of the brain versus the left hemisphere. Ancient man was bicameral, not conscious. Bicameral man used both sides of his brain, but in a different way then we do today. *than* — The right hemisphere is our survival mechanism. It reacts automatically to sights, sounds and emotions. Faced with dangerous situations our right hemisphere allows us to react instantaneously, totally immersed in the here and now. It also allows us to recognize the overall picture, to grasp the larger perspective. This function can be seen as necessary for survival in early man when out hunting and being able to find his way home. It is also responsible for some of our most creative insights. It is the function of putting all the pieces together into an overall, larger picture.

However, our right hemisphere has a major flaw as far as consciousness is concerned. It has no judgmental ability. Bicameral man lived by his natural, highly intelligent animal mind. But the animal mind has no concept of justice, fairness, or compassion. Therefore, bicameral man lived by social codes of conduct necessary for people to live harmoniously in a society. Moses' Ten Commandments is an example of a code of conduct

---

[1]This is a reprint of a 1987 article Tracy Alexander wrote for the newsletter "Inside I & O." Reprinted with permission from I & O Publishing Company.

given by an authority figure for the Hebrew nation to follow. Notice that all ten commands relate to objective behavior. There is no inner reason given as to why these commands are necessary. Even though to us it is self-evident why these commands are valid, it was not until the later prophets and especially with Jesus that the inner reasons for this behavior were known.

Bicameral man lacked introspection and could not know for himself what was moral or immoral. This explains many of the mysteries of the Old Testament when a tribe favored by God would conquer another tribe, kill the men while enslaving the women and children and taking all of their goods — cattle, sheep, everything. There was no concept of justice, compassion, or wrongdoing on bicameral man's part. When we read these stories today, we cannot reconcile that kind of behavior with God's condolence. In light of the bicameral mind, however, these actions become clear. There is no blame.

Bicameral man felt emotions strongly, just as we see in nature when a mother lion fiercely protects her young. A major factor in becoming conscious and understanding Jesus' ministry is introspection — not just feeling emotions as all animals do and reacting automatically to those emotions, but understanding emotions. Without understanding emotions no concept of justice or compassion could emerge. The interaction of the feeling right hemisphere with the rational, objective left hemisphere allows consciousness to emerge.

Just what is consciousness? One chief factor is the ability to be objective, to put aside your emotions and weigh a situation honestly — a feature bicameral man could not do. With this ability to be objective a man can think in terms of the past and the future, not just in the present, in the here and now, as the right hemisphere does. With that ability a man can think in terms of changing his behavior. This is why Jesus emphasized forgiveness and compassion.

The world we live in is a reflection of who we are inwardly as individuals. Our businesses, our schools, our governments are all run by individuals and the laws and traditions that we believe in or allow to exist determine our outer conditions. It is only as we understand ourselves, what is good for us and what is bad for us, that we can we put forth the right actions for a good life. And we also extend that same privilege to others.

That introspection, that getting in touch with and understanding our own emotions, leads to the conscious awareness of what is moral, good and right. That process lies at the heart of Jesus' message. Through this route a surprise emerges. Jesus' call to the weary, the suffering, the lonely was a constant theme throughout his ministry. For, those who are unhappy in some way are the most likely to introspect. Also, following his example with the difficult trials he had to face is a way toward introspection, a major route to consciousness and the knowledge and wisdom of the Kingdom of God.

Consciousness was developed about three thousand years ago. As societies became more and more complex, the bicameral mind became inadequate to cope. This new way of thinking coincides roughly with the rule of King David in the Old Testament. Moses lived in the thirteenth century BC which puts Abraham, the father of the Hebrew nation, even earlier. Thus, the early books of the Bible are stories of bicameral men, of those who lived by codes of conduct handed down to them by authority figures.

The Old Testament prophets give a vivid picture of the awakening of consciousness in man with the culmination in Jesus' ministry. There are two major stages to consciousness, to becoming self-aware. The first stage has to do with ethics and moral behavior. And this requires complete honesty.

In following Jesus' example, he said you must die and be reborn. This is a metaphor, of course, but you must die to the old ways of thinking which keep you locked in bondage to tradition. Through introspection and examination you come to realize that contrary to church doctrines and religious beliefs you must act in your own best interest, put yourself first, have constructive desires and have a healthy concept of your own self-worth.

Religious teachings and beliefs handed down to us say that we must be selfless, get rid of the ego, let go of desire and put others first. By trying to act upon these religious beliefs in our daily lives, we set up a major ethical and psychological conflict. Because all of these principles act against the nature of man. Therefore, the famous, anguished quote by Saint Paul paraphrased, *That which I should do, I do not. And that which I should not do, I do.*

To contrast two of these examples gives us understanding of what Jesus was teaching. He wanted every man to develop consciousness. Putting yourself first allows you to be a whole person — a whole person who can produce and contribute to society. Putting others first and being selfless creates an inner conflict which puts you out of control of your life and makes you assume that other people are also at your disposal. By contrast, a man who follows his own self-interest extends that same right and respect to every other individual. Unfortunately, many who intellectually advocate self-interest and egoism do not inwardly understand the true nature of these two important characteristics. Honest introspection would lead to this understanding.

This is just one example of the many religious beliefs that go against an individual's true nature. Through introspection and having to meet reality in your daily life, you discover this fact. One by one every false doctrine is seen through. Then you are no longer divided against yourself but become whole, one with your true nature. Once you have achieved this understanding you are ready to achieve the second major step to consciousness.

The second major stage to consciousness is to become your own authority. This was clearly evident with Jesus who spoke with authority, and we are supposed to follow his example. In speaking with authority, Jesus completely amazed the people because no religious leader of the time spoke in such a manner. Jesus and his disciples broke many of the religious laws of their time. When confronted by the Pharisees, Jesus said that laws were made for man, not man for the laws. Once a person is conscious of ethical and honest behavior and the inner and psychological reasons why that behavior is essential to his and others' happiness, then he is ready to become his own authority. However, a person must start living a self-directed and self-interested life to build the confidence needed to break through to the second stage and become his own authority.

That is why Jesus spoke in metaphors and parables to the crowds. You cannot make a huge leap in consciousness until the groundwork is first laid. Developing consciousness and becoming your own authority is clearly Jesus' message. And in order to be your own authority you must break with all authorities, including the mystical authority God. All mystical literature states this — that you must give up even the spiritual. And all mystics came to this stage. But they do not tell you what they have discovered. Historically, the few who did were ostracized or even killed.

Realizing that all mystical experiences come from your own right hemisphere and not from outside of yourself or from God comes as a great shock. And that realization produces tremendous anger — anger at those who know the truth but who preach and write books encouraging you to follow the false beliefs. In the final analysis, you know that you are responsible for your own involvement, for your own gullibility.

Once the truth is known, one recognizes that the insights he or she had are no different from the insights that scientists, businessmen and other creative people have. It is just the interpretation that was wrong. The insights were not mystical communications coming from outside yourself, from God. They were internal insights coming from your own right brain.

This leads to the final identification mystics make: Reality is the only world. There is no mystical world. God does not exist. I am my own authority. And with this realization one has reached full consciousness.

With fully conscious people, we can step into what Jesus called *The Kingdom of God*. And what Frank R. Wallace calls *The Civilization of The Universe*.

Appendix I Research Notes

* There is no justice in nature. Justice is a man-made concept. Justice is not a natural law, but one of man. It requires introspective, self-aware consciousness. It requires conceptual thought. Bicameral man could not think conceptually nor introspect. Thus, he had no concept of justice. That is why bicameral man, upon defeating a foe, would slaughter or enslave all their women and children as well.

Jesus believed that introspective, conceptual, justice-aware consciousness was for everyone — not just the "Sacred Few" authorities and spiritual leaders. Jesus tried to teach the rural peasants of Palestine consciousness through his teachings and examples.

* Jesus' desire to bring conceptual, introspective, justice-aware consciousness to everyone, rather than to an elite few, has really failed. The process required to attain full consciousness is a difficult one. Because of this, so few have realized the harmful aspects of the religious philosophy that has now spread throughout the world.

Untold human sorrow and unhappiness are a direct result of religious dogma. The conflicts now going on in the Middle East between Israel and the Arabs is a direct result of religious beliefs. Even Ministers, when asked for advice and guidance by a parishioner, do not know what to say, except to quote from the Bible. There is an example from the Bible itself when it states that the blind lead the blind.

Appendix II

Selfishness — A Key Ingredient of Romantic-Love[1]

Before living together or marrying, couples go through an initial dating stage which is usually very enjoyable. The dating stage is based on having fun together. And each person wants to make a good impression on the other. Unfortunately, this experience often does not reflect the day-to-day character requirements needed for building a healthy, growing relationship.

Two people romantically involved have strong emotional reasons for wanting the relationship to work. A person's dreams and plans for the future encompass the desire of finding the right partner. But, that dream itself can be held onto so strongly that the reality of a relationship may become obscured.

When a couple first lives together, initially each partner holds a more rational outlook. A stronger, healthier commitment to self, rationality, and the independence of one's spouse is present when a couple does not feel irreversibly obligated to each other. But, when total commitment, particularly marriage, takes place, there are certain psychological factors present which can mitigate against the relationship in all but the most mature. Immature, irrational emotions can arise such as one partner wanting to possess or own the other; the idea that one partner is responsible for the happiness of the other; or severely curtailing the other's freedom with the idea that the partner's life should revolve around oneself. All are destructive factors in any relationship.

Just how does selfishness apply when a conflict arises in a close relationship? Selfishness means to act in your own rational best interest. And to act in your own rational best interest means to put yourself first. Implied in this statement, of course, is that you are an emotionally mature individual, responsible for your actions and obligations, and also aware and sensitive to your

[1]This is a reprint of a 1988 article Tracy Alexander wrote for the newsletter "Inside I&O". We have decided to reprint this article because the concepts of selfishness vs. selflessness are so central to all religions and mystical philosphies, and because most people consider romantic love the one area most dependent upon selflessness. But, as Tracy Alexander demonstrates, even romantic love requires rational selfishness to survive and prosper.

spouse and his or her needs and emotions.

When you act in your own rational best interest you are also acting in the long range best interest of all concerned — yourself and your partner. Relinquishing those interests for what you think is in the best interest of the relationship itself, or the best interests of your spouse can harm yourself and your spouse.

Confusion is often prevalent in situations of this nature because of 1) strong emotions 2) love and care for the partner 3) desire to keep the relationship 4) desire to help the partner.

What is best for you is also best for all concerned. Why? Ideally there would be no conflicts or disagreements in a relationship but realistically they do frequently occur. The only way to handle them is to rationally face them and solve them. Unfortunately, in situations where conflicts remain the two people involved either are not grounded in a sound philosophy or one or both partners are irrational in their outlook. These irrational approaches to solving problems in close relationships can be broken down into stages.

Stage 1: The conflict arises and a rational solution is not reached. This stage involves endless hours of discussion that lead nowhere. Although both parties can have certain irrationalities that they refuse to acknowledge, in most cases, especially when one partner is grounded in reality and rationality, that partner is seeking a fair and honest solution while the other partner is emotional and irrational.

An important concept to recognize in a situation of this nature is that the emotional, irrational partner knows that he or she is being irrational and unfair. To spend endless hours in discussion or argument is futile. That only gives the irrational partner an outlet for personal frustration. As long as that partner can engage you in discussion of the irrationality then he or she has an emotional outlet. False guilt is projected onto you by the irrational partner. Thus, that partner avoids facing responsibility for his or her actions. To allow oneself to be drawn into or engaged in this sort of irrational discussion is not only a tremendous drain on time and energy but also harms one's partner.

After the initial attempt to solve the problem rationally, and

128

that failing, then one should refuse to listen to or acknowledge the partner's irrationality.

Stage 2: Put yourself first. Consider what you want and what is best for you. By doing this and following through with the necessary actions you stay in control of your life. You build strength and character, preserve your sense of self-esteem, and move forward with your life.

This choice can be a hard one to make because of real compassion and caring for one's romantic-love partner. But when irrationality is involved, when a solution cannot be reached by examining the facts, then a drain of time, energy, and emotions results. Refuse to participate in irrational arguments. Move ahead with your life, your interests, your career.

Stage 3: The partner is then forced to face responsibility for his own actions and life. He can evade that responsibility and remain where he is, unhappy in his own irrationalities, or he can take charge of his life and begin to mature.

The outstanding feature of this stage is that the irrational spouse is all alone in his or her irrationality. The partner refuses to be pulled into emotionalism or accept blame. The irrational spouse is alone and knows it. It becomes obvious who is the problem maker, who is the frustrated, immature person.

The rational partner remains healthy, projecting into life and following his or her best interests. The spouse is left behind, caught in a self-made trap.

Discard the myth from your thinking that you can change your partner. A person will change only if he thinks that change is something he wants, something that will benefit him. You are the last person he will listen to because in his irrationality he projects the cause of his unhappiness onto you. You can indirectly be effective in helping your partner make the choice to change. And that is by refusing to participate in his irrationalities. Make the circumstances such that there is no false outlet for his irrationalities. Make the circumstances such that he has to acknowledge to himself his own responsibility to be rational.

He is alone, left with two choices:

1) Remain where he is, unhappy in his irrationalities while risking losing you or 2) accept responsibility for his behavior, grow up, and start enjoying and moving ahead with life.

In summary, keep these guidelines in mind when dealing with intimate relationships:

A) Put yourself first.

B) What is best for you is also best for all concerned.

C) We harm those we love the most when we give into their irrationalities.

D) We also contribute to their irrational behavior when we let them get away with it.

E) Those who refuse to grow up have to be put into the position of facing the consequences of their actions.

F) Only when a person accepts responsibility for his actions will he mature and enhance the possibilities for building an increasingly rewarding future with his romantic love partner.

Appendix II Research Notes

* Up until the end of the 1950s, many women devoted themselves solely to raising children, running a household, making things comfortable for their husbands. Yes, there were good, happy marriages. But there were also a lot of marriages that were not good, not happy. Yet couples stayed together anyway — sacrificing their own happiness and lives because religious dogma dictated that.

When a person constantly acts against his own self interest by being selfless and sacrificial an anger builds up inside. To continue putting others' needs in front of his own, to continue sacrificing, he must suppress that anger. But that suppressed anger is capable of exploding. This includes sweet old ladies who have tried their whole lives to practice the self-sacrifice and selflessness that the church preaches. They, too, have torturous emotions bottled up inside of them.

In previous generations many women had a confidence-lacking demeanor. They devoted their lives to taking care of their children, to taking care of their husbands, to taking care of their houses. But they seldom went out in the working world. Most stayed at home their entire lives and never developed a challenging or rewarding career for themselves. That requires a lot of personal sacrifice.

If a woman wants to devote herself to raising a family that is not really a sacrifice. But so many women used to go overboard. They never did anything for themselves. They were taught that it was selfish to make time for themselves. Such women would push down their self-esteem their entire lives. Their lives were devoted to taking care of others, there was nothing they did for themselves. Most felt that they had to sacrifice their own happiness. They were not allowed to do something that they could feel proud of. And, of course, such marriages would often become terribly unhappy. But the woman would live with her husband for forty years, fifty years, or more.

As a result, many women would turn to religion in an attempt to find a certain comfort in what they were doing. The church told them that their sacrifices and unhappiness was the right thing to do. But, alas, to sacrifice their lives and happiness by remaining in a miserable situation only hurt themselves and their families.

Today, of course, not that many women or men will suffer through that. They can and usually will get a divorce under such conditions.

* I want to emphasize the correlation between rational selfishness and compassion. Those I have met who practice rational selfishness, e.g., Dr. Frank R Wallace, tend to be the most appreciative, understanding, compassionate of people I have ever met. Because they have great self-respect, they also extend that same respect to others. Such people have a basic inner joy and happiness that shows.

This shows in the way such people treat others who work for them. In my direct experiences, rationally selfish individuals such as Frank R. Wallace have always been so fair and thoughtful towards people they manage. When a problem arises, they treat their employees with real self-respect. I have seen so many examples where that is not true for other people who get positions of authority and leadership. Some managers really talk down to the people who work for them.

When a person understands what selfishness really means, when that person follows his own rational self-interest, it shows in personal happiness and in self-respect. Such people naturally extend that same self-respect to other individuals.

In contrast, people who do not feel that self-respect and get into a position of authority talk down to others. They do not have that inner feeling of confidence and self-worth because, if they did, they would extend that self-respect to other people.

* Religion fosters the idea of humility. But it is a false way to develop humility through being selfless. A person who practices rational selfishness, who does not latch onto ready-made, dogmatic answers develops a true humility in the sense that he is willing to acknowledge the mistakes he makes in life. He can admit his mistakes because he has a solid base of self-esteem and personal confidence.

Dr. Frank R. Wallace, for example, is not coweringly humble, but he has a humility that is genuine. Rationally selfish people have a genuine humility that is easy to associate with a successful, experienced scientist or businessman who acknowledges that he does not have all the answers, that he does not know everything, that he must keep on learning throughout life. Such a person is not seeking ready-made, authoritarian answers through dogma or ideology. That is what humility stands for in my mind.

Appendix III

A Letter

Dear Tracy,

Your anti-mystical revelations have brought me the first true inspiration of my life. I always knew something was wrong with the idea systems promoted by the popular philosopher/psychology experts. At an early age I began to explore the less popular so-called esoteric mystical systems of thought (i.e.: astrology, occult, positive thinking, etc.). These too, of course, proved to be totally unfulfilling in spite of many years of my devoted compliance. The main tenet of these philosophies is that if you persist with unwavering faith for long enough in believing these higher truths then finally you will overcome all limitations and the Truth and Power of the universe will be revealed to you. They tell you that all failures can be attributed to your lack of faith. So I would repeatedly encounter failure, feel unworthy, and resolve to try more steadfastly to practice my faith. Obviously, I could only fool myself again for a short time, and ultimately end up in a state of hopelessness, despair and ever greater frustration.

I can never express my overwhelming gratitude to Tracy Alexander for breaking this vicious cycle and giving me a view into the real world of conscious living. I extend forever my gratitude for facing me in the right direction with my feet planted on solid ground.

Sincerely,
LT, Los Angeles, CA

Appendix IV

Tracy Alexander's
Miscellaneous Research Notes

* When a person has what today we would call a mystical experience and logic and science are unable to explain it then scientists automatically dismiss that experience as unreal. But those who have mystical experiences are not convinced. The experience was very real to them. With the knowledge that we now have of the two hemispheres of our brain such mystical experiences can be shown as having a reality base. They are not induced by a mystical God or some higher realm, but rather by our right brain.

* In every culture there have always been a few who really strive to understand the religious and occult teachings. What draws them is the desire to understand the mystical. All of these serious, persistent students eventually came to the understanding that the God they aspired to was within their own selves. This stage is called *Unity* or *Ultimate Reality* by Christian mystics, *Nirvana* or *Wisdom* by occult mystics.

* As is true throughout history man attempts to explain the universe and himself. When he cannot explain something he typically assigns the cause to a higher realm. Thus, religion and the occult have built entire philosophies on the unexplainable. But, if one looks for and finds the cause in reality, then the whole mystical realm crumbles as it is revealed as unreal.

* Both religion and occultism are based on the idea that another existence exists beyond reality. This belief, prevalent throughout history, is based mainly on phenomena that seem to defy reality. Yet man's nature is to understand reality. With the research that has been done on the left and right hemispheres of the brain we now have the information needed to show that mystical phenomena are rooted in reality. Eventually, science is always able to explain reality. Just as science eventually

explained the cause of lightning and thunder and thereby expelled the mystical notion of a God of lightning and a God of thunder.

* The serious student of religion must apply the ideas of sacrifice to specific problems. At the same time, a student seriously pursuing the religious ideals becomes very goal oriented. And anyone who is goal oriented becomes aware of how precious time is and he guards it closely. Thus, he becomes selfish with his time.

So the two processes, sacrifice and selfishness, take place side by side. The student now experiences the contradictions that Paul spoke about in the New Testament when he referred to *The thorn in the Flesh* which God had not relieved him of.

* At the core of all religions, and all occult practices, is a teaching universal to all. Each religion and most occult systems has a founder. And each founder taught the same universal, core message. The real core of all religions and all mystical occult philosophies has nothing to do with god, saviors, saintliness, heaven, or life after death. The core, end-result of all mystical practices is to make a person become conscious — conscious of who he is as an individual. All of the founders of today's major religions lived around the time that the changeover began to take place from the automatic, nature-given bicameral mind to the man-invented, conceptual/introspective conscious mind. Consciousness (conceptual/introspective use of the mind) dates from around 1000 BC. However, consciousness does not automatically take place. An individual is not born with consciousness. It is a learned way of using the mind and must be developed. A person can be conscious and aware in one area of his life and yet unaware in another area. Also, he can be a specialist in one field of endeavor, having a high degree of conscious awareness in that field, yet be unaware and mainly unconscious in thought in other fields.

* All mystical systems revolve around experiences that are never explained. In actuality, these experiences are a psychological process that is supposed to eventually lead to a climactic experience of *Enlightenment, Wisdom, Union, Nirvana,*

or some such similar exalted state. Whatever its name, the emphasis is always on experience. Follow the proscribed philosophy and you are told that you will eventually reap the rewards of that philosophy in your everyday experiences. A promise is always held out — some variant of an *Attainment of the True Self*, in harmony with one's *True Path*.

The following explicit theme can be found in all mystical practices, including Christianity:

1.) The intellect cannot grasp it
2.) It defies logic
3.) It cannot be known by the senses
4.) It cannot be explained by words
5.) It cannot be described
6.) What is learned cannot be told
7.) It can be known only through experience.

What is it that is so mysterious that words cannot describe, the intellect cannot grasp, and logic is inadequate to understand? What is it that only experience can convey? The answer is quite simple. But it must be pointed out that these mystical statements are inaccurate and essentially dishonest. For the intellect can grasp it and logic can understand it.

The experience is a process, a process of *Union* in Christianity and in maturing and learning. The elusive, evasive knowledge that the mystics are hiding is that an individual is his own master. An individual is solely responsible for his life and choices. There is no god, leader or guru who will solve his problems. There are no moral precepts that he must follow except those determined to be honest by his own mind. There is no higher authority to answer to.

Note: It is very interesting what takes place when pursuing the religious path. The deeply religious person creates an artificial split between the two hemispheres of his brain by following the doctrines of self-sacrifice, giving up personal desire and following the will of God. Those three doctrines, those three beliefs, he follows intellectually with his left hemisphere. But his emotional, survivalist right hemisphere rebels. Eventually, his right hemisphere will push through its real-world insights that reveal how destructive those three doctrines are. But first, our right hemisphere must break through the almost impenetrable barriers that our intellectualizing, left hemisphere constructs.

The core of religion is to perfect character and through perfection help create an ideal society. Yet, as we have seen, the three main doctrines of religion undermine and eventually destroy character. And those doctrines, if carried out fully, destroy progress and wreck society. Church-governed, Dark-Age Europe demonstrated this. So do the Islamic fundamentalist societies of today. Likewise, the failed communist societies of recent history represented the Christian ideal of altruism and sacrifice carried out to its fullest. Many of the most profound scientific, medical and technological advancements have had to overcome severe religious resistance. Even today, the incredibly promising fields of stem cell research and cloning are vehemently opposed by religious fundamentalists.

Religion involves both philosophical issues and psychological issues. Because psychology is such a young science (starting with Freud in the late 1800s) most individuals do not have enough information on what is psychological fact or fiction, what is harmful or helpful psychologically.

* Whenever a person denies a part of himself that is natural and wholesome then that natural drive will be expressed in a distorted and unwholesome way.

Most mystic literature stresses the fact that a mystic must give up personal desire for love or intimacy with the opposite sex. The mystic attempts to deny this natural and wholesome desire in himself, yet, scandals continuously arise around many public spiritual figures. Scandal, in which their natural drive is expressed in some distorted, unwholesome way. These mystic spiritual leaders are the ones who have a problem with intimacy — the ones whose ideas are distorted.

* With the transition from bicameral thinking to conscious thinking about 3000 years ago man was, for the first time, able to introspect. With introspection a person can decide for himself if something is good for him or bad for him. Unfortunately, with introspective consciousness man is also able to deceive himself with false ideas. This ability for deception is a major reason why religious and mystical beliefs still flourish in the

modern world.

* Around 1000 BC our nature-given, automatic, bicameral mode of thinking was no longer adequate to meet the challenges required in the newly arising, complex human civilizations. Thus, humans developed modern, abstract, conscious thinking to handle infinitely more complex thought (see *The Origin of Consciousness in the Breakdown of the Bicameral Brain*, Julian Jaynes, Princeton Press, 1976). Not surprisingly, all mystical systems try to recapture the simple life and automatic decision making of our ancient, bicameral life.

* The biggest myth of all in all the mystical disciplines is that someone else knows the answers for you, that they have the wisdom and knowledge you need. Alas, there is no authority that has the answers for you and your life except yourself. And those who set themselves up as authorities, whether as a personal leader or an authority in books one reads, all know the hoax. You are the gullible one by believing in them. If your search is intense and your intent honest, you will discover this.

A person who goes through the mystical path to the end discovers that what he thought was a spiritual process was actually a psychological process. By traveling the mystic path to the end, one actually becomes an expert in human behavior. And that is the Master status spiritual leaders proclaim. However, they have not become a Master of Spirituality, rather they have become a Master of Psychology.

Knowing that, one can understand the phenomenal success Spiritual Leaders enjoy. They are experts in the field of psychology. They know how to project charisma, how to appeal to the finest and best within a person, how to make people feel special, even superior to others, and how to subjugate and manipulate those same people.

* The religious/spiritual leaders set up a false situation. The false altruistic/selfless values held by the student are encouraged and intensified. That intensity and the resulting inner conflicts force the student to either a breakthrough in understanding or to resignation, and an unhappy life. Those are the two choices.

It is truly a deprogramming process. A deprogramming of following traditions blindly, a deprogramming of the altruistic philosophy, and a deprogramming of following a leader, a deprogramming of the belief in a god,

After this process is mastered one becomes his own authority. He makes his own decisions. It is also a learning process, one based on testing things out in reality. Reality is the teacher, not beliefs. One thing is for sure, you will never follow a leader again or even trust, on face value, what you read or hear.

* The spiritual person's whole focus is to withdraw from society and concentrate on himself. "*Being*" is all-important. He is not a doer. One of the devastating repercussions of following a mystical discipline for so many years (whether organized religion or an occult discipline) is that a person is left with nothing. He has nothing to apply his energies to. On the one hand he is an expert in the knowledge of human nature and behavior, but he has no credentials to professionally practice psychology. During the many years of one's involvement with the mystical, working and supporting oneself has always been a side issue in one's thinking, something that is necessary but that holds no interest for him.

Every religious and mystical philosophy throughout history has maligned business and businessmen. Yet, when the religious/ mystic student discovers the hoax, he realizes that he is no more spiritual or moral than anyone else. And, if he is completely honest, he realizes that it is the businessmen who have contributed more in the way of producing real, tangible values for society than he or any spiritual leader has.

* I have often been asked what I would consider the most important thing a person steeped in the religious teachings or occult mysticism should know. My answer is to realize that objective reality is the final truth. Our life and happiness depends on how much we are in tune with practical, objective reality. Reality is the only true teacher. It points out our mistakes to us and is the constant measure of our intellectual misconceptions and self-deceptions.

Third Package of Secrets

The Neo-Tech Discovery

Break Through
To
Successful Living!

The Neo-Tech Discovery

The Entelechy of
Prosperity and Happiness
by
Frank R. Wallace

---

entelechy n.: 1. a realization as opposed to a potentiality, 2. the actualization of form-giving cause as contrasted with potential existence, 3. a force directing life and growth.

---

for
Wealth
Personal Dealings
Business, Jobs, Careers
Art and Pleasure
Romantic Love

Capturing the greatest money, power, romantic love discovery since the Industrial Revolution occurs easily after reading and integrating the entire Neo-Tech manuscript. And once you pull that mighty integration of all 114 Neo-Tech Advantages, you will gain unbeatable power over every professional mystic and neocheater who touches your life. And with that power, you can gain unlimited prosperity, happiness, and romantic love forever.

But those not capturing Neo-Tech will grow increasingly unaware, impotent, uncompetitive, incompetent. ...They will be left behind, defenseless in a world of professional mystics and neocheaters, increasingly succumbing to the always fatal disease of mysticism.

Manuscript Copy

Continued from page 380.

Fifty-First Printing _____ October 1998 [20 PP][35#][B]
Fifty-Second Printing _____ March 1999 [11.5 PP][35#][B]
Fifty-Third Printing _____ April 1999 [24 PP][35#][2vol]
Fifty-Fourth Printing _____ August 1999 [10 PP][35#][B]
Fifty-Fifth Printing _____ September 1999 [10.5 PP][35#][B]
Fifty-Sixth Printing _____ December 1999 [10 PP][35#][B]
Fifty-Seventh Printing _____ March 2000 [30.5 PP][35#][B]
Fifty-Eighth Printing _____ September 2000 [25 PP][35#][B]
Fifty-Ninth Printing _____ April 2001 [11.7 PP][35#][B]
Sixtieth Printing _____ June 2001 [10 PP][35#][B]
Sixty-First Printing _____ March 2002 [25 PP][35#][B]
Sixty-Second Printing _____ April 2003 [7.4 PP][35#][B]
Sixty-Third Printing _____ September 2003 [5.2 PP][35#][B]
Sixty-Fourth Printing _____ November 2003 [4.8 PP][35#][B]
Sixty-Fifth Printing _____ February 2004 [5.1 PP][35#][B]
Sixty-Sixth Printing _____ March 2004 [10 PP][35#][B]
Sixty-Seventh Printing _____ May 2004 [10.2 PP][35#][B]
Sixty-Eighth Printing _____ July 2004 [10 PP][35#][B]
Sixty-Ninth Printing _____ August 2004 [10.4 PP][35#][B]
Seventieth Printing _____ January 2005 [51.4 CL][35#][B]
Seventy-First Printing _____ September 2005 [51.6 CL][35#][B]
Seventy-Second Printing _____ November 2005 [51.3 CL][35#][B]
Seventy-Third Printing _____ April 2006 [50 CL][35#][B]
Seventy-Fourth Printing _____ February 2007 [5 PP][35#][B]

Printings before 51st, see page 380
75 77 79 81 80 78 76 74

and
ISBN # 911752-70-6
Library of Congress #89-083296
Copyright ©1976, 1980, 1990, 1994, 1997
by
Neo-Tech Worldwide

All worldwide rights reserved
Permission is required in writing
from
Neo-Tech Worldwide
for
reproduction in part or in whole.

Neo-Tech Research and Writing Center

Available in:

Arabic	French	Portuguese
Chinese	German	Serbo-Croation
Dutch	Italian	Spanish
English	Japanese	

THE MOST IMPORTANT
MONEY/POWER/ROMANTIC-LOVE DISCOVERY
EVER

A new field of knowledge was discovered by Dr. Frank R. Wallace. For two decades, Dr. Wallace developed a powerful array of integrated knowledge called Neo-Tech. Several years ago, Dr. Wallace was interviewed about Neo-Tech. Below is a condensed, edited portion of that interview which explains his early discoveries:

Q: What is Neo-Tech? How can I benefit from it?
WALLACE: Neo-Tech is a new, integrated method for capturing major business and personal advantages everywhere. Neo-Tech has nothing to do with positive thinking, religion, or anything mystical. Once a person is exposed to Neo-Tech, he can quietly profit from any situation — anywhere, anytime. He can prosper almost anywhere on earth and succeed under almost any economic or political condition. Neo-Tech applies to all money and power gathering techniques — to all situations involving the transfer of money, business, power, or love

Ironically, I first sensed Neo-Tech through poker — the money game, the international strategy game. Strange how a discovery so important as Neo-Tech started with something so minor and restricted as poker. Indeed, poker is just one rather minute and insignificant area involving the transfer of money in which a person can profit through Neo-Tech.

Subsequently, I pursued Neo-Tech beyond cards to uncover far greater advantages in competitive situations involving work, investments, speculating, business, politics, and personal relationships. Neo-Tech applies to all competitive situations: It is a new, quiet approach for collecting unbeatable advantages everywhere.

Neo-Tech has its roots in the constant financial pressures and incentives to develop the easiest, most profitable methods of gaining advantages. Over the decades, successful salesmen,

A

businessmen, politicians, writers, lawyers, entrepreneurs, investors, speculators, gamers, and Casanovas have secretly searched for shortcuts that require little skill yet contain the invisible effectiveness of the most advanced techniques. I identified those shortcuts and honed them into practical formats called Neo-Tech.

Q: Is Neo-Tech like cheating; is it a metaphor for cardsharps, Don Juans, con artists, dishonest merchants, destructive politicians?

WALLACE: Definitely not. Neo-Tech is totally honest and ethical; it is not based on fraud, collusion, gall, hustling or swindling as are most cheating techniques and con jobs. Indeed, Neo-Tech requires no special skill, devices, or nerve. Neo-Tech requires no risk or changes in life style — only a new integrated knowledge that generates advantages and power. Moreover, Neo-Tech renders deception and cheating ploys so obsolete that they are no longer an important threat. ...Someday Neo-Tech will dominate all competitive situations as it spreads into business and personal relationships.

Q: Who exactly is the Neo-Tech person?

WALLACE: He's a person of quiet power — a person who cannot lose. He can control not only every competitive situation, but can vanquish every threatening situation.

Q: What actually makes him so effective?

WALLACE: Neo-Tech is totally natural. Thus, it can be executed anytime, anywhere with casual confidence. The techniques let a person gain unbeatable advantages consistently and comfortably — year after year, decade after decade. Eventually, Neo-Tech men and women will quietly control all.

Q: In the real world, how quickly can I benefit from Neo-Tech?

WALLACE: A person can use Neo-Tech immediately to gain advantages needed to prosper in business and in personal relationships. Additionally, that person can never be taken advantage of again in any business transaction, investment, or personal contact. His Neo-Tech knowledge protects him. It arms him with a sword and shield. Neo-Tech knowledge is the best insurance policy anyone could own: Within days, a person

B

with Neo-Tech can gain more power than most people without Neo-Tech can gain in a lifetime.

Q: Specifically, what does Neo-Tech mean to the ordinary person?

WALLACE: Well, to be specific, the most potent shortcuts prior to Neo-Tech were beyond the reach of ordinary people as only the money/power giants developed the combinations to unlock and use those shortcuts. Moreover, those potent but customized or highly specialized shortcuts in specific fields could not help most people even if they had access to those shortcuts. In addition, the nature of those potent shortcuts limited the money/power giants to their particular fields. Still, genuine power lies beneath all those customized shortcuts. Neo-Tech not only captures that power but brings everything down to earth and removes all limitations. That, in turn, yields a still greater power that ~~that~~ even the money/power giants were denied. More important, today, most ordinary men and women will only flounder through life until they discover Neo-Tech.

Q: Beyond the immediate financial advantages and quick profits available from Neo-Tech, how will the Neo-Tech Discovery affect you and me in the real world...in society?

WALLACE: Neo-Tech meets the criteria: certain and safe — but powerful. Therefore, more and more people will increasingly use Neo-Tech in all areas. And the lives of those people will grow richer. Of those, some will choose to use Neo-Tech concepts to gain enormous power and wealth. But, equally important, people knowledgeable about Neo-Tech cannot be drained by others. The ordinary person, no matter how low on the power scale, can reverse the situation. With Neo-Tech, a person can take away the power from those Neocheaters who have drained that person for years or decades. That capturing of personal power through Neo-Tech is crucial. For, all major Neocheaters today extract money and power from the masses of unknowledgeable people. How? Through the subtly camouflaged usurpation and destruction of values created, built, or earned by others. In fact, those value destroyers use Neocheating without

C

fear of being caught, without suspicion. ...And they are successful to the extent they use Neocheating.

Consider how many of the most successful politicians have for years destructively regulated and harmfully controlled the value producers. They have neocheated the public for unearned personal power. Their power ploys have created jungles of destructive regulations and inefficiencies. They hassle busy individuals, cripple creative scientists, and prevent private enterprise from fully developing its productive and technological capacities. That arrogated authority not only diminishes everyone's spirit, but diminishes everyone's standard of living and even prevents the development of cures for scourges such as heart disease, cancer, and AIDS.

Q: You know, "60 Minutes" recently dealt with something like that. And I hear about that kind of thing more and more these days. How can it be stopped?

WALLACE: Today, as Neo-Tech spreads, people in steadily increasing numbers can, for the first time, avoid the harmful ploys of those external authorities. As people become informed about Neo-Tech, they will identify and circumvent those master Neo-cheaters who have previously drained them. Now, ordinary people will fill their own pockets with profits rather than lining the pockets of Neocheaters. As more and more people learn about Neo-Tech, they will increasingly understand that professional mystics, pragmatic politicians, bogus-job bureaucrats, and other such false authorities are destructive drains on value producers and society.

I have two charts that demonstrate how most people have unknowingly let their lives be drained by those external authorities. This information also shows how the informed will financially and emotionally benefit by breaking free from those master Neocheaters. Indeed, everyone informed of Neo-Tech will have the tools not only to break free but to profit from the decline of external authority. Furthermore, this information shows exactly how the average person can turn into a Neo-Tech person...a person who can acquire far greater advantages than any Neocheater — even a master Neocheater.

D

Q: Your charts uncover things I was never aware of. It's bad enough that those Neocheaters conceal their ripped-off power, but it's rotten how they're doing it by draining me, you, and everyone else....

WALLACE: Yet, we're the ones who hold the power on this planet. Most people have never been aware of that fact. Now, with Neo-Tech, we can totally control our future. That's why the Neocheaters never told us their secret. For, we would take away their power that is rightfully ours. You, like everyone else, could never really know the facts behind external authorities without understanding Neo-Tech. The actions of such external authorities usually depend on Neocheating — on undetectable routes to easy money or power at the expense of others. They seemingly benefit their victims by giving them guidance, leadership, or doctrines to follow — making those victims easy to control. Fortunately, however, publicly revealing Neo-Tech exposes the Neocheater's essence. That will lead to the eventual demise of external authority.

Indeed, today, you as the Neo-Tech person never again have to feel helpless. You never again have to be on the defense. You never again have to depend on anyone or anything of the past. You can enter a new world and control your own future. You can become a Clark Kent — a quiet superman. You can gain the real power — the real advantages and profits that few ever knew existed.

Q: Now I know why the Neo-Tech Discovery will immediately....

WALLACE: Also, consider another benefit from understanding Neo-Tech: the stopping of the pain and harm caused by certain everyday acquaintances straight up to the authoritarian bureaucrats who surround everyone in almost every area of life. Neo-Tech can abruptly stop the pain and harm caused by being beaten by destructive authorities, cheated or exploited by one's spouse, manipulated by parents, drained by bosses, gypped by merchants, intimidated by pushy or monied people, misled by professional people, stunted by dishonest and incompetent educators, used by friends, abused by strangers, fouled up by bureaucrats, fooled by mystics, and hurt by government.

E

Neo-Tech puts an end to all those hurts and diminishments that have constantly kept you from becoming the person you've always dreamed of — the person you were meant to be.

And there are other side benefits. For example, when viewing network TV with the knowledge of Neo-Tech, a person becomes acutely aware of the steady stream of Neocheaters — TV commentators, news editors, journalists, sociologists, faddists, mystical gurus, and religious proselytizers. Those fake authorities constantly gain destructive advantages from their followers in countless subtle ways. Neo-Tech concepts allow people to identify and nullify Neocheaters who drain everyone's life daily.

With the concepts of Neo-Tech, a person nullifies those Neocheaters while transferring their power from them to himself. He no longer needs to bow to or idolize the man on the hill. With Neo-Tech, a person knows with fearless certainty that he, himself, is the most important person — and everyone will sense that he is the most powerful person.

Q: Can you restate what you're saying to bring me back to earth?

WALLACE: The Neo-Tech concepts are practical tools for integrated thinking. Neo-Tech really puts one on the right track. No longer do people have to suffer in silent frustration watching their lives and dreams be quietly drained away.

Q: Yes. Who hasn't felt that distant, lonely sadness....

WALLACE: The Neo-Tech concepts are the most powerful thinking tools for profits. Those concepts are the cutting edge for prosperity...for making the grandest dreams come to reality. Neo-Tech can rekindle the sparks that flickered out long ago.

Q: Is all that really true? I mean, does all that really apply to us — to us who work for a living?

WALLACE: You are the good, the innocent, the powerful: you are the Clark Kents. Over are the days of your being defrauded of wealth, pleasure, and happiness. Over are the days of being victimized by the politicians, bureaucrats, mystics, and pseudo intellectuals. In your innocence, you have unknowingly been drained by Neocheaters. Now, at last, you can break free and take what all productive human beings rightfully earn but seldom take...a guiltless life of power, pleasure, and wealth. But even

F

more, you can now become a Neo-Tech person and command your own future.

Q: That's pretty profound. I'll have to give that some deep thought.

WALLACE: You should. For the more one thinks about Neo-Tech, the more one profits from it.

Q: What if I want to profit more and more? What if I get a little greedy? What if I want to become the man on the hill now — through Neo-Tech?

WALLACE: Look again at the charts. Contrary to what some people might initially think, the highest profits of Neo-Tech come not from *destroying* advantages of others, although anyone can do that with Neocheating to gain tremendous power and profits. But the highest profits come from *creating* honest advantages for oneself by delivering maximum competitive values to others and society. Indeed, to any chosen extent, you can apply Neo-Tech to personally gain both immediate and long-range advantages in business, personal life, and social situations...the applications are endless.

Back to your question about becoming a little greedy. As the first step, anyone can immediately profit by collecting the Neocheating advantages available in any competitive situation. Moreover, anyone can use Neocheating to outflank all competition — control even the sharpest, most-alert people. Master Neocheaters use undetectable techniques to gain maximum advantage from every situation to acquire extreme power and wealth. And anyone can use Neocheating to gain easy advantages or profits to any chosen degree. But who needs that? The Neocheater, yes, he can easily do all of that. But the Neo-Tech person...he needs none of that. For him, Neocheating is limiting and obsolete.

Just acquiring the knowledge of Neo-Tech will show you how to reach you goals quickly, directly, easily. You will experience a mounting sense of power and excitement while learning about Neo-Tech. Indeed, through the Neo-Tech Discovery, you too can achieve great strength in your career or field of interest by becoming a quiet Neo-Tech person. In addition, you will forever

G

be immune to Neocheaters…immune to most harmful situations.

Q: How quickly will Neo-Tech spread?

WALLACE: As people gain this knowledge, they will begin using its techniques because they are irresistibly logical and overwhelmingly practical. Thus, as people discover the unbeatable advantages of Neo-Tech, those advantages will automatically spread throughout the world as the most potent discovery since the Industrial Revolution.

NEO-TECH IS DEDICATED TO
THE PRODUCER OF VALUES

You are the good, the innocent. Yet, throughout history, you have been defrauded of your earned prosperity and happiness. You have been victimized by the politicians, bureaucrats, theologians, pseudo intellectuals, and the white-collar hoax. For they live off your efforts, repaying you only with falsehoods, unearned guilt, and demands for sacrifice. In your innocence, you have unnecessarily accepted their frauds, usurpations, and abuses. Without Neo-Tech, you could never know with certitude that you, not they, are potent and hold the power to control life. But now, with Neo-Tech, you can forever break free from their hoaxes and usurpations designed to live off your efforts. You can take what all honest and productive human beings have rightfully earned, but seldom take: A guiltless life of prosperity, love, and happiness.

Neo-Tech is dedicated to you and to the discovery of the prosperity and happiness that belong to you.

Neo-Tech forever dispels ignorance in curing the disease of mysticism and eliminating its symbiotic neocheaters. Once cured, a person flourishes naturally and easily to guiltless prosperity and abiding happiness. Once free from mysticism and neocheating, a person seizes iron-grip control of both the present and future to prosper forever. ...Once armed with Neo-Tech knowledge, a person overpowers all mysticism and neocheating that tries to harm or diminish his or her life.

ORIENTATION AND DEFINITIONS

PREFACE

For nearly 2000 years, master neocheaters have manipulated the destructive forces of mysticism to drain power and prosperity from all honest men and women. But today, for the first time in history, a newly discovered idea system called Neo-Tech reveals and eliminates those destructive forces while releasing a stream of intellectual, psychological, and material advantages. Neo-Tech integrations deliver emotional and material benefits to everyone. Indeed, anyone can use the Neo-Tech concepts to guiltlessly increase his or her wealth and happiness — now and forever into the future.

Furthermore, the Neo-Tech concepts can free any individual from all who waste one's time, from all who work against one's best interests, from all neocheaters and mystics who use non sequiturs[1] to diminish the lives of others. The Neo-Tech concepts provide the ways and means to limitless prosperity and happiness.

INTRODUCTION

The integration of philosophy with psychology, physiology, and the material world is crucial not only to the Neo-Tech concepts, but to every individual on this planet. Yet, that key role of philosophy has until today remained essentially unrecognized by all the populations of this world. Why? The answer is below:

Philosophy

The philosopher's job is to provide human beings with practical tools for dealing with reality in order to live easier, more prosperous, happier lives. But almost all philosophers throughout history have defaulted in their responsibility and failed in their job. Indeed, most philosophers have done all in their power to make life for human beings not easier and happier, but more difficult and unhappy by obscuring reality. As a result, almost everyone rejects the practicality of philosophy. Thus, almost no one recognizes the potential of this mighty tool.

Few people can formulate integrated philosophical systems on their own. Moreover, few people have the knowledge to reject or even identify the neocheaters and mystics who implicitly use

---

[1]Non sequitur is defined and illustrated with examples in Appendix E.

i

philosophy to drain the lives of others. ...The first step in dismissing the mystics and neocheaters is to recognize that only two basic philosophical systems or choices exist:

One system arises from a mystical/altruistic premise that individuals should be sacrificed either to others or to "higher" causes. The father of the criminal mind, Greek philosopher Plato (427 B.C. – 347 B.C.), identified and developed that system. Throughout history, all governments, religions, and neocheaters have implicitly used Plato's philosophy to usurp unearned power and values from innocent value producers.

The other philosophical system arises from a reality/self-interest premise that the individual is the highest value in the universe. The father of the business mind, Greek philosopher Aristotle (384 B.C. – 322 B.C.), identified and developed that system.

Neo-Tech identifies both the Platonistic and the Aristotelian philosophical systems and then demonstrates how and why Neo-Tech guarantees prosperity and happiness. Neo-Tech (fully integrated honesty) shows how anyone can switch from being a loser with a mystical/Platonistic approach to being a winner with a Neo-Tech/Aristotelian approach.

Psychology
The Neo-Tech concepts deliver the psychological tools needed to achieve guiltless profits, power, and happiness. In addition, those concepts expose the deceptions of mysticism and neutralize the harm of neocheaters.

Physiology
The Neo-Tech concepts also integrate a wide range of physiological discoveries including diet and physical fitness into a forward-march position that leads to increasing pleasures and happiness.

DISSOLVING THE CHAINS
By reading the following definitions, a person will understand how the manipulation of mysticism in others is the common bond linking all neocheaters: Now, for the first time, heads of states, religious leaders, elegant con artists, Mafia dons, most attorneys, some Nobel-prize laureates, many leading academe, certain well-known media personalities, certain entertainment people, some

ii

DEFINITIONS
(Neo-Tech starts on page 1)

bankers, and even certain business people (e.g., white-collar hoax executives) are inextricably linked as soul mates. They all live by attacking the competitive value producer, competitive business, and competitive products. Yet, they themselves live uncompetitively, producing no long-range, <u>net</u> benefits for others or society. In other words, those people live as neocheaters or as just plain cheaters by usurping, attacking, undermining, and destroying values produced by others. ...Neo-Tech ends that secret, parasitical bond by forever dissolving the chains of mysticism and its mind-created "realities".

DEFINITIONS AND UNDERSTANDINGS

Neo-Tech can guide anyone to increased prosperity and happiness. But for full benefits, a person must understand the following key concepts and words used throughout Neo-Tech:

NEO-TECH

Neo-Tech is a noun or adjective meaning fully integrated honesty. Neo-Tech allows the guiltless creation of earned power, prosperity, and romantic love:

Neo-Tech is a collection of "new techniques" or "new technology" that lets one know exactly what is happening and what to do for gaining honest advantages in all situations. That technology is needed to be competent — to guiltlessly and honestly obtain the wealth and happiness available to everyone but achieved by so few. Neo-Tech provides the power to profit in every situation by nullifying neocheating and mysticism not only in others but within one's own self. Indeed, Neo-Tech eliminates the harm of all mystics, false authorities, neocheaters, and their infinite array of deceptions. Neo-Tech lets a person gather all power unto his or her own self while rendering mystics and neocheaters impotent.

With Neo-Tech, all effort is directed toward achieving fully integrated honesty needed to act in concert with reality. With mysticism, all effort is directed toward rationalizing non sequiturs or deceptions needed to satisfy some feeling, wish, or whim arising from one's self-created "reality" or some external "authority". ...Neo-Tech is rooted in effort, objective reality, and value production. Mysticism, by contrast, is rooted in laziness, random nothingness, and value destruction.

iii

Neo-Tech is health. Mysticism is sickness. Neo-Tech is the opposite of mysticism. Neo-Tech heralds the end of mysticism and its symbiotic neocheaters.

NEO-TECH CONCEPTS

The Neo-Tech concepts provide man's most powerful thinking tools. Those tools efficiently deliver prosperity, happiness, and romantic love to everyone who uses them consistently. The Neo-Tech concepts also provide the tools for effectively eliminating mysticism. In addition, those tools effectively squelch all neocheaters.

PSYCHUOUS

Psychuous (SIGH-kyü-uhs) is a new word describing integrations that combine the activities of the mind, body, and emotions to continually increase prosperity, happiness, and romantic love.

Psychuous Pleasures is the cessation of conflict among the mind, emotions, and body by reconciling philosophy, psychology, and physiology so one's own actions harmoniously serve the material, emotional, and biological needs of the human organism. Using psychuous concepts, one experiences exquisite, lasting pleasures unknown to others.

Psychuous Sex is a fully integrated, rational approach to sexuality. Harnessing one's sexual potential through Neo-Tech is rewarded with increased happiness, romantic love, and psychuous pleasures.

PSYCHUOUS CONCEPTS

Neo-Tech reveals a new set of concepts: Psychuous Concepts. Those concepts integrate prosperity, love, and reality with a person's physical, psychological, and intellectual nature. By understanding and utilizing the Psychuous Concepts, a person can experience great pleasures with guaranteed prosperity and happiness — for life.

And "for life" means exactly that: for a person's entire life. The human mind is an organism that does not age if kept disease free — if kept free of mysticism. Since the mystic-free human mind can grow forever, psychuous pleasures have no limits. But growth of the mind is not automatic. Instead, growth requires

iv

conscious effort. When a person defaults on that effort, his or her mind stops growing. When intellectual growth stops, the capacity for happiness and pleasure begins shrinking — the individual begins dying.

Moreover, human aging is a process of deterioration. Growth is the opposite of deterioration. Only when growth stops can aging begin. The human mind never has to stop growing. In fact, human life itself may never need to age. No scientific evidence dictates that a person has to age and die. Indeed, a person may be able to live indefinitely under fully integrated, fully rational, physical, psychological, intellectual, and emotional conditions. Before Neo-Tech, those conditions were never available or possible.

PSYCHUOUS PLEASURES
VERSUS
SENSUOUS PLEASURES

Sensuous relates to the five physical senses — touch, sight, hearing, smell, and taste. Sensuous is associated with the pleasurable gratification of one or more of those physical senses. Neo-Tech expands the meaning of sensuous to capture the essence of pleasure by including and integrating the most potent dimension: the pleasurable gratification of the human mind. That gratification includes the harmonious agreement of a person's love life with that person's material, intellectual, and emotional well-being. ...The word for that expanded meaning of sensuous is **psychuous**.

The conscious mind is the ultimate organ for experiencing pleasures, including sexual pleasures. The mind integrates all pleasures with all that a person *is*, *does*, and *thinks*. The mind is the organism that offers unlimited pleasure and happiness.

SEX

In Neo-Tech, the meaning of sex includes intercourse as a series of highlights along a vast range of sexually rooted experiences and emotions. Indeed, the meaning of sex in Neo-Tech encompasses all sexual influences (often hidden but powerful) that weave through each person's life.

Ironically, sexual influences most dominate the lives of those who pretend to shun or repudiate the pleasure of sex (e.g.,

v

mystical celibates, religious ascetics, guilt-projecting preachers). Their very acts of avoiding or attacking sexual pleasure leave their lives far more dominated by sex than those who accept the responsibility of earning healthy, confident sex lives.

LIFE

The essence of conscious life is control — the ability to control one's present and future. Conscious life is the only entity in the universe that can control nature and future events. That control is possible to the extent that mysticism is absent and Neo-Tech is present. A person in control is happy and will prosper. A person out of control is unhappy and will fail. Neo-Tech puts a person in control.

LOVE

Three types of love exist: (1) sexual romantic love, (2) nonsexual friendship and family love, and (3) intellectual/artistic love. Contrary to myth, love is not inexplicable or beyond understanding. Love can be exactly defined and clearly understood.

Romantic love integrates the mind and body of a man and a woman. That integration includes the emotional/intellectual development of values between that man and woman. Such a complex relationship requires planned, rational thought by each partner. Romantic love is one of life's most important and practical achievements: Romantic love is a major source of personal growth, efficient living, happiness, joy, and pleasure.

Yet romantic love is often dismissed as blind, mindless, irrational, immature, transitory, impractical. But the opposite is true. And similar false notions have led to the misunderstanding of words such as "romantic", "romanticism", and the "Romantic era". How did those false notions begin? "Romantic" and its related words originally implied freedom, individuality, and *rational* ideals based on integrated honesty...not *irrational* whims based on mystical illusions. But over the years, the concept of romanticism became inverted by the mystics and falsely associated with the irrationalists and the sentimentalists of the 19th Century Romantic Period.

Philosophers, poets, writers, and artists, such as Rousseau, Wordsworth, Blake, and Van Gogh, were considered romanticists. But they were not romanticists at all. They were existentialists, mystics, and sentimentalists who basked in the intellectual and political freedom of romanticism. The actual romanticists were individuals like Spencer, Hugo, Chopin, Gould, Edison (and earlier romanticists like Aquinas, Michelangelo, da Vinci, and other *honest* thinking, *hard-working* idealists). Such individuals created every major value since the Renaissance. Yet, while they were sometimes considered rationalists or even idealists, they were seldom considered romanticists as they actually were.

The "Oxford English Dictionary" traces the usage of "romance", "romanticism", and other words whose meanings today are distorted or inverted. Etymologies trace those distortions as far back as the 17th and 18th Centuries. Such word distortions diminish the thinking tools needed to understand and implement the most important and powerful human actions. But the Neo-Tech/Psychuous concepts return the word "romantic" and other important words to their accurate meanings that render the neocheaters impotent.

Romantic love involves an emotional, intellectual, and sexual involvement with another person. And romantic love offers the deepest of all happiness and the greatest of all pleasures.[1] But as with all major values, romantic love is not automatic. Romantic love must be earned through rational thought and planned effort. And then, that love must be maintained and expanded through constant honest effort — through constant discipline, thought, and control (the DTC method).

Through the ages, civilizations, and cultures, women seek in men a single attribute, however interpreted. That attribute is *strength*. ...Neo-Tech delivers maximum strength to every human being.

MYSTICISM AND NEOCHEATING

Mysticism is defined as: 1. Any mental or physical attempt to recreate, evade, or alter reality through dishonesty, rationalizations, non sequiturs, emotions, deceptions, or force. 2. Any attempt to use the mind to create reality rather than to identify and integrate reality.

---

[1]All feelings and emotions fluctuate. Even the strongest feelings of romantic love will wax and wane. At times, even the most ardent lovers can feel diminished love for each other. But within an upward fluctuating pattern, romantic love can constantly renew and build to higher levels.

DEFINITIONS
(Neo-Tech starts on page 1)

Mysticism is a disease — an epistemological disease that progressively undermines one's capacity to think, to identify reality, to live competently. Mysticism is also a collective disease that affects everyone who looks toward others, or the group, or the leader for solutions to his or her own problems and responsibilities. The symptoms of mysticism are dishonest communication, out-of-context assertions or attacks, use of non sequiturs, rationalizations, jumbled or nonintegrated thinking — all leading to mind-created "realities". Those symptoms are most commonly exhibited by neocheating politicians, clergymen, union leaders, lawyers, media commentators, university professors, entertainment personalities. Such public neocheaters are the Typhoid-Mary spreaders of mysticism. In fact, through the ages, the most virulent spreaders of mysticism have been those neocheaters who wangle respect and values from the value producers of this world.

Mysticism is a disease that blocks integrated thinking and brings stupidities through mind-created "realities". But mysticism is also the tool that neocheaters use to justify or rationalize the use of force, fraud, or dishonesty to usurp values from the producers. For example, mind-created "realities" are used to create false standards and guilt designed to beguile individuals into surrendering their earned values, power, and happiness.

Mysticism is a rebellion against life, effort, and the conscious mind. Mysticism leaves people with sour bureaucratic faces and is the neocheater's tool for plundering the value producers.

Mysticism is the only disease of the conscious mind. But as with drugs and alcohol, mysticism is seductively comfortable, like a warm, old friend — until the destructive consequences and hangovers manifest themselves.

Mysticism is based on a false and destructive idea: the primacy of emotions over reality. ...Mysticism is the opposite of Neo-Tech. The mind-created "realities" of mysticism eventually render all life unto death.

Neocheating is defined as: Any intentional use of mysticism designed to create mind "realities" or false illusions in order to extract values from others. Neocheating is the technique for expropriating unearned money or power by manipulating mysticism in others. Neocheating is the means by which all

viii

politicians, clergymen, union leaders, many journalists, many academe, and most lawyers usurp power and values from the innocent producers.

MYSTICS AND NEOCHEATERS VERSUS NONMYSTICS

Mystics violate ethics and morality. For, mystics purposely harm their own and other people's lives. By choosing to evade or fake reality, they undermine their ability to identify and integrate reality, to think clearly, to produce values, to live competitively — to survive. As a result, they increasingly lay responsibilities for their well-beings onto others. Thus, they routinely lay blame or guilt on others for their own problems and failures. ...Everyone must resist, must fight mysticism both from within and from without. Those who surrender — quit resisting, quit fighting — allow mysticism to take over their lives. When that happens, they become a part of the unhappy, dishonest world of mystics and neocheaters.

Mystics and nonmystics can and often do share similar problems, feelings, thoughts, and emotions. The difference is that the nonmystic will (1) take responsibility for his or her own problems and (2) reject the destructive notion that "realities" spun from the mind can replace objective reality. On the other hand, mystics will (1) avoid the responsibility, effort, and honesty needed to identify and integrate reality and (2) use their feelings or imaginations to recreate "new realities". They attempt to fill their desires the "easy", mystical way. But the mystical way is unreal — the hard way that never works.

Mystics make problems where none exist. They focus on the visible symptoms to avoid identifying the hidden mystical source of their problems. They make "realities" out of what they feel, think, wish, or want rather than on what actually is or exists. Thus, they blind themselves to what is happening and become increasingly incompetent. They are irresponsible, immature people. As a result, they cannot achieve the major values of life: genuine prosperity, romantic love, abiding happiness. Mystics avoid the responsibility of a conscious being and, thus, miss the rewards of life.

As pervasively evident throughout TV network news, many involved in media journalism are profoundly dishonest manipulators of mysticism who live by purposely creating problems where none exist. They do that by dishonestly attacking and undermining values to gain unearned power and values. Many are consummate neocheaters who find the media the easiest, most effective format for mass deception, unearned power, and bogus livelihoods.

Neocheaters do more than violate ethics and morality. They constantly try to expand their usurpations of values by manipulating mystical illusions and non sequiturs. Moreover, neocheaters design their illusions to present themselves as the benefactors of society. At the same time, they enviously present the real producers (e.g., aggressively competitive entrepreneurs, innovators, business people, industrialists) as the malefactors of society.

But the opposite is true: The neocheaters are the mean, the guilty, the malefactors of society. And the value producers are the compassionate, the innocent, the benefactors of society. Yet, as long as most people allow themselves to accept mystical illusions and inversions of facts, the neocheaters will keep usurping values and escalating their destructions.

Some neocheaters usurp credibility by exploiting popular causes that sound good — causes that in proper context may be noble if handled honestly. Examples include the environment, nutrition, health, animal rights, human rights, peace. But neocheaters exploit such causes to usurp credibility and power in order to attack competent producers, their honest businesses, and their valuable products. ...The two-headed essence of all mystics and neocheaters is dishonesty and laziness.

Other neocheaters (politicians, clergymen, many journalists and academe) survive by attacking values, businesses, producers, and earned profits as enemies. They attack by making those who create genuine values for others appear as guilty and wrong. Simultaneously, they live by promoting mysticism, altruism, external "authority", collectivism as friends. They promote those destructive forces by making them appear innocent and right.

Mysticism is central to the neocheater's ability to thrive by attacking values. For only through mysticism would anyone accept the neocheater's upside-down world of undermining, attacking, and destroying values.

Mysticism yields actions based on what one feels, wishes,

wants, or imagines rather than on what actually exists right in front of that person. That is why professional mystics and other neocheaters can easily manipulate people: they manipulate them through their mysticisms. Neocheaters manipulate infinite arrays of mysticisms to usurp values earned by others. As a result, the professional mystics and other neocheaters eventually destroy all values of life, love, and happiness for themselves and everyone involved with them.

Nonmystics are innocent and moral. They accept the discipline and responsibility to think and act with integrated consistency. They support themselves by producing *competitive* values for others. With a loyalty to honesty, they act in concert with reality. They are evolved, honest people. They strive to fully integrate their words and actions with reality, regardless of anyone's dogma, dictates, or opinions. As a result, nonmystics benefit everyone and society.

The mystic's life is basically irrational and unhappy with perhaps some scattered islands of rationality and happiness. By contrast, the nonmystic's life is basically rational and happy with perhaps some scattered islands of irrationality and unhappiness.

Turning to one's inner self, mystics find unhappiness, anxiety, and hatred. Whereas nonmystics find happiness, equanimity, and love.

CONSCIOUSNESS AND FREE CHOICE

Consciousness allows human beings to escape the automatic controls of nature. At the same time, only through consciousness can a person be subjective and mystical. Thus, only through consciousness, can a person choose to act in discord with nature. Unlike all other animals, conscious beings can choose to act better or worse than their nature to benefit or harm themselves and others. Choosing to deny or contradict nature or reality is mysticism, which is an unnatural, irresponsible abuse of the conscious mind. But, conscious beings can also choose to act better than their nature to gain power and advantages over all else in the universe. Because consciousness allows choices and actions beyond preset nature, only human beings can choose to

xi

be honest or deceptive, objective or mystical, responsible or irresponsible, competent or incompetent, striving or lazy, productive or destructive, beneficial or harmful, noble or evil. ...With consciousness, anyone can choose either alternative at any time.

All other animals have no choice but to automatically respond to nature. They cannot be deceptive, irresponsible, mystical, or purposely harmful to themselves and others. They have no such choices, thus, they bear no responsibility for their actions. ...Animals cannot be mystical, dishonest, or self-destructive.

With consciousness, only human beings can freely choose to live better or worse than their natures.

Free choice determines the future of all human beings: Through mystical choices, people diminish themselves and their potentials to live happy lives. But through Neo-Tech choices, people reject mystical choices. Thus, in turn, they prosper and live happily, far beyond nature's preset course. In fact, only by choosing the integrated effort of Neo-Tech over the automatic laziness of mysticism can people build lasting prosperity and happiness.

THE KEY CHOICE

The choice between exerting effort or defaulting to laziness determines the course of all important human actions. The three choices constantly confronting every human being are to (1) exert integrated effort, (2) default to camouflaged laziness, or (3) act somewhere in between.

The choice to exert integrated effort or to default to camouflaged laziness is the key choice that determines the character, competence, and future of every human being. That crucial choice must be made by everyone, continually, throughout life. ...That key choice determines the:

1. direction of an infant's life beginning at the first moment of consciousness.

2. development of a child's implicit nascent philosophy which determines that child's developing psychology.

3. development of an adult's implicit and explicit philosophy which develops that person's psychology to determine the quality of his or her life.

4. philosophies that guide entire nations, eras, and civilizations with the resulting cultures, economies, and degrees of enlightenment or darkness.

5. evolvement or regression of human consciousness, power, prosperity, happiness, and love.

6. prosperous survival or eventual destruction of human life on this planet.

7. development or rejection of youth-perpetuating biological immortality.

That same key choice determined the direction of all original philosophers: For example, the prime immoral philosophers, Plato and Kant, chose to formulate sweeping, out-of-context abstractions in conjuring up all-encompassing mystical idea systems that were "validated" with brilliantly deceptive inner logic. Thus, their basic choice was a default to laziness. For they chose the neocheater's "shortcut" to unearned power or "greatness" by formulating out-of-context, non-sequitur, "higher-cause" philosophies.

Such specious philosophies are designed to assault the supreme value of the conscious mind. Their destructive, death-oriented "greatness" contrasts sharply to the productive, life-oriented greatness of the prime moral philosophers: Aristotle and Rand. For, those moral philosophers chose to exert hard efforts and fully integrated honesty to build full-context, rationally integrated systems of universal value for all people of all times.

Those choosing to live through automatic laziness survive by usurping or attacking values produced by others. Those usurpers and attackers include essentially all politicians and theologians as well as many dishonest professionals, attorneys, psychologists, academe, elitists, journalists, philosophers. Well-known usurpers and attackers of values include Plato, Hitler, Stalin, FDR, the Pope, Al Capone, Pol Pot, Fidel Castro, Ralph Nader, Jesse Helms. By contrast, those who choose to live through integrated effort can thrive by producing or building values for others. Those producers include working people, business people, industrialists, scientists as well as honest professionals, artists, musicians, philosophers. Well-known value producers include Aristotle, Ray Kroc, Henry Ford, Edison, Einstein, Pierre S. du Pont, Andrew Carnegie, Jay Gould, Galileo, Michelangelo, Beethoven, Ayn Rand.

That choice between laziness and effort determines if one becomes an unhappy destroyer of values or a happy producer of values.

BUSINESS VERSUS MYSTICISM

Business is the competitive development, production, and marketing of values that benefits others. Any and every aspect of business succeeds to the extent that effort, thinking, planning, and action are free of mysticism...or fails to the extent that mysticism is injected into any decision. Business ultimately flourishes in the absence of mysticism or dies in the presence of mysticism. Mysticism is the creating of problems where none exist; business is the solving of problems wherever they do exist. Mysticism represents stagnation and death; business represents growth and life. Mysticism is nonbusiness; business is non-mysticism.

Since the early days of Phoenician commerce, envious mystics and destructive neocheaters have striven to besmirch the value producers, their business enterprises, and their competitive products. Legions of pseudo-intellectuals, say-much/do-little underachievers, envious nonproducers, and mystic-manipulating neocheaters, especially in the media and academe, constantly attack businesses and their creators. With specious pejoratives, the attackers imply that business people lack care, humanity, compassion, social concerns. Such implications are opposite of the facts. Indeed, only through business and its creators do societies advance and individuals prosper.

Hiding behind their altruistic platitudes, neocheaters and mystics are the ones who default on productive effort, do not care, and lack humanity, compassion, social concerns. For all they can do is cleverly attack values. And their attacks are designed to undermine those heroic efforts required to competitively produce jobs and values for others. Indeed, the mystics and neocheaters strive desperately to conceal the intellectually superior nature of business — the universally beneficial, cheerfully benevolent, nonmystical nature of business. For business is the antithesis of mysticism, the epitome of rationality and morality, and the furthest evolvement of human intellect.

Business is the highest evolution of consciousness, responsibility, and morality. No other animal is even remotely able to function on a business level. The essences of business are fully integrated honesty, responsibility, integration, abstraction, objectivity, long-range planning, effort, discipline, thought, control. Business creates essentially every major human value, ranging from the development of language, mathematics, the arts, and all commercial breakthroughs up to the electronic revolution...and now finally, Neo-Tech.

I□&□O Publishing Company is the first company to successfully inject a fully integrated system of ideas and values directly into the stream of public thinking and action. That successful, efficient injection is done by subjecting Neo-Tech to organized business disciplines in markets far beyond the small, closed circles of elitists and academics.

Without being subject to the intense, disciplined efforts of business and marketing, Neo-Tech would have languished undeveloped, perhaps for centuries, trapped in those small, closed circles of less-evolved, nonbusiness intellectuals. But by applying hard-nosed business disciplines to marketing Neo-Tech, I□&□O Publishing Company demonstrates in real life the extraordinary, practical benefits of Neo-Tech to every human being. Marketing Neo-Tech through a high-effort, business structure provides the fastest, most efficient distribution of Neo-Tech advantages to every value producer in this world.

Until now, the most widely circulated system of ideas has been the Holy Bible. But its ideas are mystical, dishonest, malevolent, destructive, and for centuries have provided the philosophical ammunition to diminish happiness, drain prosperity, and neocheat productive people on a grand scale. By contrast, Neo-Tech Cosmic Power benefits all honest people. Its ideas are objective, honest, benevolent, productive. Neo-Tech provides the practical tools to eliminate mysticism and neocheating throughout the world while enhancing prosperity and happiness for everyone. For that reason, life-enhancing Neo-Tech ideas will increasingly replace life-diminishing mystical ideas as the source of philosophical standards and values for all honest, productive people — for all people who count.

Business people create values through intellectual efforts involving the widest-range integration of facts and knowledge. Successful, growing businesses always require honest long-term planning combined with constant integration of time with effort. ...Few people have any idea or appreciation of the constant, hard-driving effort and difficult integrations required for a business-man to create and maintain honest, value-producing jobs for others.

By contrast, professional mystics and neocheaters avoid all such long-range, wide-scope, integration efforts. Instead, they operate on a dishonest, anti-intellectual level — on spurious, out-of-context terms in attacking producers with slander, libel, force, coercion, and false guilt in order to usurp values from those value producers.

The master neocheaters gain power by constant destruction of values rather than by production of values. To realize that fact, a person needs only to examine the words of any Hitler, Pope, charismatic politician, network anchorman, high-profile humanities professor, or advanced-degreed underachiever. Their essential words are always in a negative mode or an envious attack mode. They rise in power not by the long, hard, rational efforts that build competitive values wanted by others. Instead, they garner power by glib, negative attacks that undermine the producers and their values. ...That fact becomes obvious on comparing the words of honest business people to those of neocheating media people.

Mystics and neocheaters are guilty losers who harm everyone. But business people, especially the essence-moving entrepreneurial type, are innocent winners who benefit everyone. Honest business people do not even know how to think, talk, or operate in the destructive, out-of-context, envious attack modes of mystics and neocheaters. Instead, such business people cheerfully focus on integrating reality — on benefiting others by creating and trading values. Without Neo-Tech, however, those business people are unable to protect themselves from the neocheaters' destructive ideas and actions.

DEFINITIONS
(Neo-Tech starts on page 1)

Master neocheaters rise above others without earning their way — without exerting the long-term, hard-integration efforts needed to build values for others. By nature, neocheaters are dishonest, unproductive, hostile, immoral, guilty. They have no genuine power. By contrast, business-minded people are honest, productive, benevolent, moral, innocent. Such business-minded people are the only source of genuine power and prosperity in the universe.

Two worlds exist: One world is that of the mystics, neocheaters, master mystics, and master neocheaters along with all their duped victims and followers. That unhappy, sour world is for the living dead — for those who choose to (1) detach themselves from reality, (2) remain ignorant of reality and what is actually occurring, (3) survive by usurping values from others. That destructive world consists not only of lethargic mystics but of aggressively active, master neocheaters with their minions and followers. Such neocheaters stage furious but meaningless or destructive activities in their need to appear busy and important to themselves and others. ...The world of mystics and neocheaters is destructive, unhappy, meaningless.

The other world belongs to the value producers. That happy, cheerful world is created by individuals who prosper by producing values for others. That purposeful, active world consists of those workers, business people, industrialists, professionals, artists who produce more than they consume. The world of value producers is exciting, prosperous, meaningful.

The integrated efforts of value producers such as businessmen are directed toward supporting or building values for others. In sharp contrast, the efforts of neocheaters are directed toward attacking or usurping values from others. Master neocheaters are manipulative and destructive in their every action ranging from political summits to papal tours. Such neocheaters include not only politicians and clergymen but those say-much, do-little academe who conceal their lack of value by constantly flaunting credentials to impress themselves and others. On establishing specious credibility, those neocheaters extract values from others by promoting spurious ideas that undermine or attack value producers and competitive values.

Those two worlds will never meet. For, they are moving in opposite directions: one toward death, the other toward life. Any conscious individual, however, can choose at any time to reject mysticism and exchange the unhappy world of value destroyers for the happy world of value producers. ...The choice is to exist in the dead world of mysticism or to live in the alive world of Neo-Tech.

MAN'S NATURE AND SURVIVAL

The nature of all animals evolves around their survival mechanism. But what is the distinguishing nature of man? He has the ability to think consciously in concepts and then integrate those concepts into wider concepts. No other animal can think consciously or think significantly beyond percepts, much less integrate concepts. Indeed, man can easily and logically integrate two or more concepts into new and still wider, more abstract concepts. That logical integration of concepts is called reasoning. Man's reasoning ability is his survival mechanism. But unlike all other animals whose survival mechanisms work automatically, man's reasoning mechanism works volitionally. Man must *choose* to exert the effort required to reason. Man undermines or damages his or her reasoning ability by nonuse or misuse of the mind through mysticism. For mysticism, by nature, subverts or cuts off the integration mechanism of the conscious mind to reduce one's efficacy, competitiveness, quality of life, well-being, self-worth, and especially happiness.

Reasoning is the nature of man — the distinguishing nature that elevates the value of man above all other life...above all else in the universe. Reasoning through logic is man's survival mechanism.

MORALS

Since morals and morality require conscious choices, man is the only animal who can be moral or immoral. Thus, man is the only animal who can consciously or purposely make moral choices: to think or not to think, to be mystical or nonmystical, to produce or usurp — to benefit or hurt oneself and others.

The meaning of *moral* in Neo-Tech is simple and direct: Whatever is consciously done to help fill human biological needs is good and moral (e.g., the productive actions of honest people).

Whatever is consciously done to harm or prevent the filling of human biological needs is bad and immoral (e.g., the destructive actions of mystics and neocheaters).

Honestly using one's reasoning nature is always beneficial and moral; dishonestly using one's reasoning nature is always harmful and immoral. ...Volitionally harmful acts always arise from mysticism — from dishonesty, rationalizations, evasions, defaults.

Yet, acting on fully integrated honesty (Neo-Tech), not reason itself, is the basic moral act. When Genghis Khan, for example, chose to use reasoning for a specific military move, then in an out-of-context sense, he chose to act morally by protecting himself and his troops (thus filling human biological needs). But in the larger sense of fully integrated honesty, Khan's total actions were grossly immoral in choosing to use aggressive force in becoming a mass murderer (thus negating human biological needs). The highly destructive, irrational immorality of Genghis Khan's overall dictatorial military actions far outweighed any narrow, out-of-context "moral" actions. ...Genghis Khan was enormously evil as were Stalin, Hitler, Mao, Castro, Pol Pot.

IMMORAL CONCEPTS: ALTRUISM AND SACRIFICE

Genghis Khan an altruist? Stalin and Hitler[1] too? Yes, they were altruists as were Jesus, Lincoln, Mao, Schweitzer, Nader, Pope John Paul, and almost all other professional mystics and neocheaters. And as demonstrated in the Neo-Tech/Psychuous Concepts, all current religions and governments exist through altruism.

The dictionary definition of altruism is: "Uncalculated consideration of, regard for, or devotion to other's interests sometimes in accordance with ethical principle." Upon first

---

[1]Hitler an altruist? He was the ultimate altruist in both word and deed: "The Aryan is not greatest in his mental qualities as such, but in the extent of his willingness to put all his abilities in the service of the community. In him the instinct of self-preservation has reached the noblest form, since he willingly subordinates his own ego to the life of the community and, if the hour demands, even sacrifices it."

Adolph Hitler, *Mein Kampf*,
Houghton Mifflin, Boston

xix

consideration, the definition of altruism seems loving, kind, and good. In which case, how could Genghis Khan and Hitler relate to that definition?

Close examination of altruism reveals that its ethical principle and implications are human sacrifice.[1] Thus, the altruist accepts as ethical principle that human beings and their values can be sacrificed to others. And those human sacrifices can be made to anyone or for the sake of anything — the gods, the tribe, the ruler, the fatherland, the system, the party, the "good", the poor, the cause...for the sake of enhancing the power or prosperity of any professional mystic or neocheater.

All current political and religious systems depend on the principle of altruism...the principle of forced or coerced sacrifice of victims to others. Altruism (as in Biblical mysticism) holds sacrifice as a good in itself, regardless of the means (e.g., force, coercion, fraud, guilt, deception, charisma), regardless of the

---

[1]Auguste Comte (1798-1857) was the first philosopher to articulate the ethical principle of altruism as sacrifice. His altruistic ethics held sacrifice as the goal of moral actions, regardless of the means, cost, or beneficiary. He projected selflessness and sacrifice as the ultimate good while positing self-interest as the antithesis of that good. (Reference: Comte's *System of Positive Polity*, 1877).

But Immanuel Kant (1724-1804) consciously and methodically laid the philosophical groundwork for the concept of altruistic self-sacrifice as a moral principle. Kant used brilliantly orchestrated, cleverly integrated non sequiturs to attack logic, reason, and the human mind. Kant is among the most destructive of all master neocheaters. His philosophy provides ingenious systems of noncontextual, inner logic that offers beautiful-sounding rationalizations for all violations of individual rights and destructions of values. Kant's works are essential for Fascism, Marxism, and every murderous neocheating regime of the twentieth century: Plato begot Kant, who begot the socialist's philosophical father, Georg Hegel (1770-1831). In turn, Hegel begot Karl Marx and spawned mass-murderers Lenin, Hitler, Mao. And, Plato begot the philosophical father of religio-conservatives — Jean-Jacques Rousseau (1712-1789). In turn, Rousseau spawned equally bloody mass-murderers: Robespierre, Pol Pot, Khomeini. ...All that blood, suffering, and destruction arise entirely through neocheaters manipulating unreal, arbitrary illusions and mind-created "realities" of mysticism in order to support their own personal, bogus livelihoods. ...No other reason or motive exists or has ever existed for purposeful death and destruction.

recipients (e.g., dictators, presidents, popes, theologians, welfare clients), and regardless of the victims (e.g., war dead, taxpayers, business people, value producers).

Sacrifice is the opposite of productivity: Productivity creates values. Sacrifice destroys values. Sacrifice is contrary to human biological nature as demonstrated throughout Neo-Tech. Upholding the ideas of sacrifice or altruism involves accepting the nonreality of mysticism. And accepting such mysticism always requires evasive rationalizations. Indeed, mysticism, altruism, and sacrifice are purposeful reasoning defaults that are always harmful to human beings, thus, are always immoral.

Altruism and sacrifice are rationalized through mysticism. And mysticism is a reasoning default that accepts fake realities or nonrealities such as sacrifice, faith, dogma. Thus, all advocates of altruism are mystics or neocheaters by nature because they accept or manipulate the mystical concepts of sacrifice.

But why do people default on reason? Why do they evade reality to become advocates of altruism who promote sacrifice? Professional advocates of altruism are always, in a direct or indirect way, recipients of the sacrifices they promote. The booty is often unearned power. But the booty may also be or include unearned material goods, glory, adulation, love, respect, pseudo self-esteem, neurotic or psychopathic satisfactions. In any case, professional advocates of altruism depend on the sacrifice of others to fill their material needs, their self-esteem needs, their images of importance, their neurotic wants. In one way or another, all professional altruists are neocheaters who live off the forced or coerced sacrifices of productive people. For that reason, no professional mystic or altruist can be happy or experience psychuous pleasures.

In addition, altruism and sacrifice are the vortex of all concepts, ideas, and philosophies that drain productive people of their earned values and happiness. In the long run, altruism and sacrifice fill the needs of no one. Instead, altruism and sacrifice always drain everyone.

Over the past 2000 years, altruism and sacrifice have destroyed untold values and billions of human lives. As identified by the Neo-Tech/Psychuous concepts, all current governments and major religions exist on the principles of altruism and sacrifice. But Neo-Tech shows: 1. how to negate all neocheaters; 2. how to avoid being victimized by mysticism or sacrificed to altruism; 3. how to forever collapse the 2000-year-old hoax of mysticism and eliminate its symbiotic neocheaters; 4. how to live prosperously, guiltlessly, and happily to the benefit of everyone.

HAPPINESS

Happiness results from dealing competently with reality. Happiness is a state of intellectually knowing and emotionally feeling the following:

Short-Term Happiness
(Positive or Negative Sources)
The situation is good.
The situation is right.
The situation is of value.

Long-Term Happiness
(Positive Sources Only)
Life is good.
People are good.
Oneself is good.
Oneself is right.
Oneself is of value.
Oneself is capable of understanding reality.
Oneself is growing in a positive direction.
Oneself is producing values needed to live independently.
Oneself is competent in producing competitive
values for others and society.
Oneself is competent to reject mysticism in self and others.
Oneself is worthy of living.

Short-term happiness from positive sources can add to a person's long-range happiness. But short-term pleasures from negative, destructive, or irrational sources (e.g., drunkenness, politics, drugs, religion, promiscuous sex, prosperity through dishonesty or fraud) can deliver only temporary feelings of power, well-being, and euphoria. For the inescapable consequence of reality will always assert itself, reversing those "good" feelings to yield ever greater unhappiness and anxiety.

Long-term well-being and happiness come *only* from (1) a continuing development and evolvement of one's own mind and character, (2) one's increasingly accurate knowledge and control of reality and self, and (3) increasingly producing competitive values for others and society.

Achieving happiness is the ultimate moral purpose of human life.

MYSTICISM HARMS EVERY VALUE IT TOUCHES — ESPECIALLY LOVE

After attacking values for 2000 years, professional mystics and neocheaters aim their most subtly destructive attacks on value production, romantic love, and happiness: First they undermine the concepts of values, love, and happiness with clever inversions of facts that sound good or valid. Then, for example, they undermine the concept of love by promoting the false idea that totally rational behavior between couples would yield cold, passionless relationships. But the exact opposite is the fact: Consistently honest, rational behavior offers the greatest capacity for love and passion. By contrast, emotionally reacting, irrational behaviors destroy love and passion.

Successful romantic love requires acting on reality rather than reacting on feelings. Only through fully integrated honesty (Neo-Tech) can one guiltlessly experience the full range of positive emotions and passion. By contrast, mystics act on feelings rather than on reality. Such acting on feelings leads to incompetence with the subsequent loss of prosperity and romantic love. ...Mystics experience life with increasing anxiety, unhappiness, deadness.

Neo-Tech demonstrates that professional mystics and neocheaters avoid the honest thought and hard competitive effort needed to produce values desired by others. Instead, they live by faking reality to extract power and values from others through deception, coercion, force. ...Unchecked mysticism destroys all values, especially love and happiness, through arrays of irrational illusions and dishonest actions.

INTEGRATED THINKING MEANS
KNOWLEDGE AND POWER

Integrated thinking is the conscious effort of putting information into accurate context by logically and honestly connecting *all* relevant knowledge. All valid and powerful knowledge is contextual. Thus, genuine power is gained through integrated thinking used to obtain the widest possible range of contextual knowledge. Integrated thinking delivers unbeatable advantages.

NEO-TECH DELIVERS
MONEY/POWER/ROMANTIC LOVE

Those who live by fully integrated honesty (Neo-Tech) are by nature sexy, happy, prosperous winners. For they ultimately hold all honest power. Moreover, with Neo-Tech, they hold the supreme aphrodisiac. By contrast, mystics and neocheaters contradict their nature through their laziness, dishonesty, and parasitism. They are unsexy, unhappy, envious losers. Thus, they become increasingly impotent, tired, powerless.

Only through fully integrated honesty (Neo-Tech) can one increasingly earn competence, self-esteem, happiness. ...Through Neo-Tech, one soars to spiralling heights of money/power/romantic love.

MYSTICISM AND NEOCHEATING VANQUISHED

With the discovery of Neo-Tech, all mystics and neocheaters are in the final sentence of the final chapter of their long, destructive history on planet Earth. They are finished forever. But ironically, for the first time in history, all mystics and neocheaters have, through Neo-Tech, an invincible tool to purge their own mysticism, to solve their own problems, to evolve into happy, productive human beings. ...Happy days are here for everyone, forever.

Table of Contents

THE NEO-TECH DISCOVERY

LISTING OF THE 114 NEO-TECH ADVANTAGES

LISTING OF THE 114 NEO-TECH ADVANTAGES

NEO-TECH DISCOVERY

NEO-TECH POWER
and the
NEO-TECH ADVANTAGES

The easiest, quickest way to gain Neo-Tech/Psychuous advantages for prosperity, power, and romantic love is simply to forge ahead: Read all the Neo-Tech Advantages in order. Do not make prejudgments. Wait until you have completed all 114 Neo-Tech Advantages. Forget judgments made by others. Do your own thinking; make your own judgments.

Grab the values from those concepts to which you can relate. Put aside temporarily those concepts you are uncertain about or disagree with. By the end of this volume, all the concepts will come together into a clear, harmonious understanding — into a powerful, practical matrix. You will then have integrated control over all competitive situations through the Neo-Tech concepts. You will also know exactly what is happening and exactly what to do. You will forever know how to conquer mysticism in self and others. You will forever know how to quell all neocheaters. You will forever hold the power of prosperity and romantic love.

* * *

All advantages in this manual are backed by the original Neo-Tech source — the "Neo-Tech Reference Encyclopedia".

Neo-Tech Advantage #1
THE NATURE OF MAN AND WOMAN
Anyone can experience financial prosperity, psychuous pleasures, and long-range happiness by satisfying his or her

1

biological needs (i.e., physical, psychological, emotional, intellectual needs). Psychuous pleasures require the freedom to satisfy one's own healthy needs and to set one's own standards...to live without being obligated to fill someone else's needs or to follow someone else's standards (e.g., standards of parents, spouse, government, church). But in freedom, a person's actions must be rational and responsible to be beneficial. Irrational or mystical actions will always diminish a person's well-being and happiness.

In asking, "What is the nature of man and woman?", a person might also ask, "What is reality?" and "What is required for prosperity, love, and happiness?" Losers will answer from a mystical, Platonistic basis. Winners will answer from a rational, Aristotelian basis:

1. WHAT IS THE NATURE OF MAN AND WOMAN?
Loser/Mystical Answer (Platonistic)
Human beings are by nature evil, irrational, and destructive. They are subordinate to "higher" causes. Human beings must be controlled by some higher authority or government and forced to serve others or society.
Winner/Factual Answer (Aristotelian)
Human beings are by nature good, rational, and productive (or mankind could not exist). Human beings are competent to fill their needs and to achieve happiness. By being free to act according to their own nature, they will best serve themselves and society without force or coercion from any authority or government.

2. WHAT IS REALITY?
Loser/Mystical Answer (Platonistic)
Reality is what the mind thinks or imagines. Wishes, will, or faith can create or alter reality. "True" reality is unknowable.
Winner/Factual Answer (Aristotelian)
Reality is what exists. Reality exists independently of anyone's thoughts, desires, will, or wishes. All reality is knowable.

3. WHAT IS REQUIRED FOR PROSPERITY, LOVE, AND HAPPINESS?

Loser/Mystical Answer (Platonistic)

Sacrifice, humility, and service to duty are needed for prosperity, love, and happiness in the hereafter.

Winner/Factual Answer (Aristotelian)

Rational action, self-esteem, and production of competitive values for others are needed for prosperity, love, and happiness here on earth.

Complete answers to the above three questions are developed throughout the 114 Neo-Tech Advantages.

Human beings survive by using their minds rationally to deal with reality. They must know reality to competitively produce the values needed to prosper. Only by being left free to satisfy their nature can human beings serve themselves and others best. ...People who live free and according to their natures can easily build a future of prosperity and happiness. Moreover, with Neo-Tech, such people can easily rid themselves of mystics and neocheaters.

Neo-Tech Advantage #2
THE CHILD OF THE PAST

The child of the past exists in every adult. Lost within faded memories, that child keeps searching for a life of adventure, discovery, value, happiness.

The Neo-Tech/Psychuous concepts let the reader turn inward to discover that child. And then the reader can break free from those who are hurting him or her...from those who are wasting his or her time and resources. That child of the past will kindle a new life of adventure, discovery, value, happiness.

Neo-Tech Advantage #3
CARVING ONE'S OWN DESTINY

While the past is gone forever, it offers valuable experience and reference points that can enhance one's present and future. But many people consume too much time living in the past. Those people often cripple their potential by living and thinking in terms of concrete, past experiences. Thus, they fail to grasp the broader concepts and principles necessary for productive growth into the future. People who live in the concrete past lose the ability to control their futures. Those who achieve long-range prosperity, happiness, and psychuous pleasures are well aware of the experiences and knowledge gained from their past. But, they live in the present while continuously building the integrations for growing into the future.

Rational value producers can view their personal futures with confidence in the knowledge that they have the power (through their own rational minds and efforts) to control their own destinies no matter what external variables impinge on them. With the exception of being trapped in an inescapable totalitarian slavery situation,[1] rational individuals can carve their own destinies while achieving great prosperity, romantic love, and happiness no matter what external forces surround them. Indeed, by removing mysticism, the rational mind can be more powerful than all those irrational minds that constantly work to diminish everyone's life [Re: Table 7, Neo-Tech Reference Encyclopedia].

The rational mind can also vanquish the destructive effects of religion and the God concept. Likewise, with the rational mind one can spring free from the guilt pushers and freeloaders as well as from "friends" and relatives (including parents and nondependent children) who do not offer overall values to one's personal life.

The variables of nature (e.g., weather, tides, earthquakes, hurricanes, floods) can have chance impacts and short-range effects on a person's life. For most productive people, however,

---

[1] A no-hope, no-escape situation would occur only with total control by master neocheaters. That situation would mean a Stalin/Pol Pot style, never-ending terror totalitarianism with no hope for change within one's lifetime or no place to escape to freedom. Under such conditions, life for the moral, productive individual would be intolerable, unbearable, and not worth living. The only viable option would be to maintain one's personal integrity and freedom by surviving without slavery through underground or guerrilla existences. [Re: Concept 22, Neo-Tech Reference Encyclopedia].

natural variables have little or no effect in their long-range lives. Other natural forces such as the faint celestial forces (minute gravitational and electromagnetic forces from planets and from stars beyond our sun) have no effect on anyone's life, except for the illusionary, psychologically damaging effects on those who allow their thinking or actions to be stunted or undermined by immature beliefs such as astrology. [Re: Concept 41 in the Neo-Tech Encyclopedia exposes mystical frauds such as astrology and UFOs. The Encyclopedia also reveals the harmful effects those frauds have on prosperity, romantic love, and long-range happiness.]

Neo-Tech Advantage #4
DOGMA AND RULES ELIMINATED

All Neo-Tech/Psychuous Concepts develop from the three basic elements of human nature — the physical, intellectual, and psychological nature of man and woman [Re: Concept 7, Neo-Tech Reference Encyclopedia]. All individuals are uniquely different with widely variable tastes, desires, personalities, characteristics, and needs. Neo-Tech offers no fixed rules or dogma for any individual to follow.

Neo-Tech deals with principles and concepts. Anyone can choose to use any number of the 114 Neo-Tech/Psychuous Concepts. Since each of the 114 Concepts developed by Neo-Tech are linked to the basic nature of man and woman, the application of any single concept will deliver certain specific values. The application of each additional concept will deliver additional values. The more Neo-Tech/Psychuous concepts the reader uses, the greater will be his or her prosperity and happiness. To fully utilize any concept, however, an individual must first integrate that concept through one's own mind according to his or her own unique character and values. ...But the unbeatable power of Neo-Tech comes from grasping, integrating, and then using *all* 114 Advantages as one mighty, unbreakable unit or matrix.

Neo-Tech Advantage #5
UNIVERSAL GOOD AND BAD ACTIONS:
BLACK AND WHITE MORAL ABSOLUTES

Rational or good actions increase prosperity, happiness, and psychuous pleasures. Irrational or bad actions undermine those values. While each individual's life and values are unique, certain basic actions never change in terms of good or bad actions. The rightness or wrongness of those basic actions do not vary according to opinion, or from person to person, or from generation to generation, or from culture to culture, or from solar system to solar system. Universally good or bad actions are objectively based on the biological nature of human beings and are definable in absolute terms. But other actions are amoral and cannot be judged in terms of good or bad because they are a matter of personal preference determined by individual differences.

Universal morals are objective. They are not based on opinions of the author or anyone else. Universal morals are not created or determined by anyone. No one can deem what is moral and what is not moral. The same moral standards exist for each and every human being throughout all locations, cultures, and ages. Those standards are independent of anyone's opinions or proclamations. Moreover, two and only two black-and-white moral standards exist. Those two moral standards are:

Any chosen action that purposely benefits the human organism or society is morally good and right.

Any chosen action that purposely harms the human organism or society is morally bad and wrong.

Feelings and emotions, on the other hand, cannot be considered as standards, absolutes, or morals. A person's life-style, desires, needs, and preferences can vary greatly without altering that person's character or without making that person morally right or wrong. Still, moral absolutes do exist. And following or violating moral absolutes determines a person's

6

character and self-esteem. The two moral absolutes essential for prosperity and happiness are:

1. Integrated honesty for knowing reality
2. Integrated efforts for increasing productivity

Habitually violating either of those two moral absolutes precludes genuine prosperity and happiness. Related to those absolutes are the following moral issues:

Honesty
Self-esteem
Individual rights
* * *
Sacrifice
Use of force
Ends justifying the means

The list below shows how each *moral* issue separates into either a moral, pro-life, pro-individual category or an *immoral*, anti-life, anti-individual category.

Objective morals are based on reality, reason, logic. Subjective "morals", on the other hand, are based on unreal, arbitrary feelings or wishes. All such unreal "morals" require force, deception, or coercion to impose them on others. Subjectivism, mysticism, existentialism, and "do your own thing" are all attempts to deny objective morals by implying that no standards exist and everything is of equal value (thus denying objective morals and values).

UNIVERSAL MORAL ISSUES

Moral Issue: Honesty.

Prosperity and Happiness Approach
Conscious striving for self-honesty. Unyielding loyalty to honesty. Productive effort. (Moral)

Failure and Unhappiness Approach
Pragmatic compromise and evasion of honesty. Habitual dishonesty. Parasitical laziness. (Immoral)

Moral Issue: Productivity.

Prosperity and Happiness Approach
Productive actions that increase values to others and society while increasing effectiveness in dealing with reality. (Moral)

Failure and Unhappiness Approach
Destructive actions that decrease values to others and society while decreasing effectiveness in dealing with reality. (Immoral)

Moral Issue: Individual Rights.

Prosperity and Happiness Approach
Recognition of the inalienable right everyone has to his or her own life and property. (Moral)

Failure and Unhappiness Approach
Denial of individual or property rights in order to plunder the life and property of others. (Immoral)

Moral Issue: Sacrifice[1].

Prosperity and Happiness Approach
Refusal to sacrifice is by nature life enhancing and thus is morally right. (Moral)

Failure and Unhappiness Approach
Sacrifice is "noble", especially when done for a "higher" cause or, better yet, no cause. (Immoral)

---

[1]Sacrifice occurs when a value is diminished or destroyed for a lesser value or a nonvalue.

Moral Issue: Use of Force.

Prosperity and Happiness Approach
Rejecting the *initiation* of force, threat of force, coercion, or fraud against any individual for *any* reason is the foundation of morality. (Moral)

Failure and Unhappiness Approach
Use of force (especially government force) is acceptable against individuals, especially if the result serves the social "good" or a "higher" cause. (Immoral)

Moral Issue: Ends Justifying the Means.

Prosperity and Happiness Approach
In regards to force, the ends *never* justify the means. All moral actions are based on principles that prohibit initiatory force, threat of force, coercion, and fraud as a means to accomplish ends, no matter how "noble". (Moral)
Failure and Unhappiness Approach
Ends can justify the means. Force and coercion can be pragmatically used for the "good" of society. Individual rights can be violated or sacrificed for "noble" ends. (Immoral)

Neo-Tech Advantage #6
ABANDONING THE NEOCHEATERS
All destructive authorities and other neocheaters would become powerless if the value producers withdrew their support and said "no". If *all* victims simply said "no" to their victimizers, *all* professional mystics and neocheaters would lose their power to plunder others and destroy values.

Consider this quote from *A Discourse of Voluntary Servitude* by Etienne de la Boétie, written in the 16th Century:

"The oppressor has nothing more than the power you confer upon him to destroy you. Where has he acquired enough eyes to spy upon you if you do not provide them yourselves? How can he have so many arms to beat you with if he does not borrow them from you? The feet that

9

trample down your cities, where does he get them if they are not your own? How does he have any power over you except through you? How would he dare assail you if he had not cooperation from you?"

Stanley Milgrams in his book, *Obedience to Authority*, demonstrates through the famous electric-shock experiments done at Yale that the majority of average, honest citizens will follow authority to do destructive, immoral acts up to the point of injuring, even killing other people. As quoted from Milgrams's book:

"...ordinary people simply doing their jobs, and without any particular hostility on their part, can become agents in a terrible destructive process. Moreover, even when the destructive effects of their work become patently clear, and they are asked to carry out actions incompatible with fundamental standards of morality, relatively few people have the resources needed to resist authority."

But what is that external authority? It is a myth that has no basis in reality. Such external authority always develops into a destructive machine when the majority unthinkingly or out of fear accept, obey, and follow the commands and wishes of that authority. In reality, no one has genuine authority over anyone else. Once that fact is realized, a person can say "no" and break the destructive habit of obedience to the myth of authority. Then the neocheaters would be abandoned by the value producers. And all value destroyers would founder with no power to survive.

Neo-Tech Advantage #7
PROSPERITY AND HAPPINESS GOALS

Life is the universal standard to which all people are subject. And **life** — conscious human life — is the standard on which every Neo-Tech Concept is based.

How does the standard of life relate to prosperity and happiness? Human beings must meet specific needs to function at their best (i.e., to function as the living organism is designed to function). Filling those needs produces prosperity, pleasure, and happiness.[1] The Neo-Tech Concepts provide the knowledge for filling those biological needs — physical, psychological, and intellectual needs. And in filling those biological needs, personal prosperity and happiness become the natural, rational goals of human life.

An important purpose of Neo-Tech is to demonstrate that three requirements for prosperity and happiness always exist: (1) a healthy physical state, (2) a healthy self-esteem, and (3) an honest, efficacious handling of objective reality in competitively producing maximum values for others. A person can meet all three requirements by using the Neo-Tech concepts. But to earn prosperity through productivity requires rational thought and constant effort. ...By nature, a prosperous, happy life is an active, challenging life. [Neo-Tech Advantage #11 provides a self-evaluation test to determine if one has oriented his or her life as a value producer or as a value destroyer.]

Neo-Tech Advantage #8
HAPPINESS TEST

A person sets up prosperity and earns happiness from within. Happiness cannot be taken from the material world or from another person. Happiness depends on genuine self-esteem, which is a product of a person's own life and choices. Happiness is a deeply personal, inner matter. Thus, no one can judge another person's happiness by outward appearances alone. A person may be miserable (such as a nonproductive mystic), but project a happy, cheerful appearance. Another person may appear unsmiling, even stern or cross (such as an intensely busy business executive), but if he or she is a productive person with self-esteem, that person will be profoundly happy.

To achieve long-range happiness, an individual must be mentally healthy. Many people, including most psychiatrists and

---

[1]Throughout Neo-Tech, the words prosperity, pleasure, and happiness are always used in a rational context. For, irrational prosperity or pleasures are based on destructive actions (e.g., profit by fraud, victory by force, success by deceit, pleasure by drugs). Such actions may provide a transitory sense of euphoria, pleasure, or well-being, but can never deliver abiding prosperity or happiness.

psychologists, erroneously believe that mental health depends on how well a person adapts to the views and opinions of others, the majority, or society. That belief places conformity as the standard for mental health. But, instead, mental health depends on a loyalty to honesty, *regardless* of the views and opinions of others or one's own feelings. Indeed, the individual must deal honestly with reality to gain the productivity and self-esteem required for quality survival of the mind and body — for prosperity and happiness.

Productivity and self-esteem build on each other. They are not, however, in a cause-and-effect relationship. The **cause** is character evolvement, development, and maturity; the **effect** is both productivity and self-esteem. And that **effect** delivers prosperity and happiness.

The human mind and body, by nature, function harmoniously. But when an individual accepts mystical ideas or takes irrational actions, the mind and body clash and contradict each other (e.g., the acceptance of religion-inspired guilt clashes with the sexual natures of men and women).

With Neo-Tech, one can easily determine the direction that an individual is moving: (a) toward prosperity, happiness, and life, or (b) toward conflict, unhappiness, and death. [Re: Table 3, Neo-Tech Reference Encyclopedia]

Neo-Tech Advantage #9
REWARDS FROM LIFE

Nearly everyone desires the rewards available from conscious life. But, few people achieve those rewards. And, by nature, people who buy into mysticism or promote altruistic, self-sacrifice can *never* experience those rewards.

The main reasons for prosperity limitations and failures are (1) the lack of knowledge and (2) the acceptance of mysticism. But the Neo-Tech concepts provide that knowledge for eliminating mysticism to achieve full-range prosperity and happiness.

Many myths about prosperity and happiness promoted by professional mystics and neocheaters sound right and click into people's minds as packages of truth. But those myths are misleading and destructive. For example, the works of Sigmund Freud, Herbert Marcuse, and Wilhelm Reich promote the myth that sex dominates human behavior. Their views help promote the false notion that all human life is oriented around sex. While sex is important to life, joy, and pleasure, such an all-inclusive life orientation around sex is false. Instead, the drive for life is oriented around advancing the survival and well-being of the living organism — not around sex.

Survival is man's fundamental **physical** need. And self-esteem is man's fundamental **psychological** need. A person's life is oriented around those physical and psychological needs — not around sex. ...Still, sex plays a major, pervasive role in human life, joy, and pleasure.

Neo-Tech Advantage #10
THE HIGHEST CAUSE —
THE CONSCIOUS INDIVIDUAL

The highest cause in the universe is the well-being and happiness of the conscious individual. The individual — a minority of one — is the smallest, the most important, most unprotected of all minorities. If rights of the individual are protected, then rights are protected for everyone — for Blacks, Chicanos, women, factory owners, factory workers, farmers, homosexuals. The concept of minority rights is meaningless, prejudicial, and destructive. In fact, that concept is a tool used by professional mystics and neocheaters to usurp power and unearned values not by protecting but by violating the rights of individuals.

Only the concept of individual rights is meaningful and valid. The following table contrasts the anti-individual, neocheating view to the pro-individual, Neo-Tech view.

ANTI-INDIVIDUAL VIEW
VERSUS
PRO-INDIVIDUAL VIEW

Anti-Individual, Neocheating View
(Platonistic Oriented)

• The uncontrolled, free individual is by nature bad and harmful to conscious life. Morally, the individual must be controlled by external "authorities".

- Group or government force is necessary to control the individual to make him do good.

- The conscious individual is subordinate to society or to "higher" or "nobler" causes.

- The use of force to compel individuals to comply with the "will" of society is moral.

- The moral purpose of life is self-sacrifice in serving "higher" goals.

- Pride is a character flaw.

- Service to a government by conscription is necessary and proper.

- Property belongs to society, the "people", or the government.

- Social science is a valid, valuable science.

- Populations consist of various groups of people, societies, and cultures.

Pro-Individual, Neo-Tech View
(Aristotelian Oriented)

- The uncontrolled, free individual is by nature good and beneficial to conscious life. Morally, the individual must be free and remain free from external "authorities".

- Both the individual and society function best when the individual is free from any group control, government force, or external "authority".

- The conscious individual is the highest, noblest possible good or cause in the universe.

- The use of initiatory force against any individual for any reason is immoral.

- The moral purpose of life is to achieve rational happiness.

- Pride is the result of moral virtue.

- Service to a government or to any cause is proper only on a voluntary basis. Any form of conscription is forced sacrifice and evil.

- Property is an earned entity. Thus, it can morally belong only to those individuals (or their businesses) who produced the values needed to earn that property.

- Social science generally has little or no validity as a science, especially because it usually denies the individual as the prime entity of human life.

- Populations, societies, and cultures consist of specific individuals.

Neo-Tech Advantage #11
SELF-ESTEEM AND THE REWARDS FROM LIFE

Happiness of man and woman is not based on sex or pleasure, but on self-esteem. Self-esteem acquired through honesty and productivity is the requisite for romantic love and psychuous pleasures. Within a romantic-love relationship, psychuous sex adds an intensity to human pleasure unattainable elsewhere in life. Psychuous pleasures are the rewards for day-by-day, rational, productive actions. Psychuous pleasures, financial prosperity, romantic love, and long-range happiness are the rewards of a productive, honest life.

Self-esteem is a person's estimation of his or her self-worth. Self-esteem is based on the ability to live independently, happily, competently. Self-esteem is dependent on one's effectiveness in dealing with reality. A high level of self-esteem requires a commitment to objectivity and honesty. But objectivity and honesty do not occur automatically. One must constantly work hard to be objective and honest. And one must always work to maintain those qualities or they will slip away.

Self-esteem is that emotion of feeling worthy and competent to live in this world — of feeling in control of life. That feeling depends on having a value-producer orientation or value-destroyer orientation as listed in the following self-evaluation test:

SELF-EVALUATION TEST

Value-Producer Orientation

☐ I earn my livelihood by producing competitive values tradeable in the free market.
☐ I am a student gaining knowledge necessary to become a producer of values tradeable in the free market.

Value-Destroyer Orientation

☐ I do not earn my livelihood by producing values for others. Instead, I live off of values produced by others.

☐ I am a student learning how to manipulate people by using government, religion, or other forms of neocheating and mysticism to usurp a livelihood from the value producers.

Orientation for Positive Changes

☐ I will stop living as a usurper and learn to become a producer of competitive values in order to earn my prosperity and achieve happiness.

☐ I will withdraw my support from those neocheaters who through direct or indirect force or coercion live off the efforts of others.

Neo-Tech Advantage #12
UNJUST CRITICISM AND GUILT

Personal *emotions* possess an untouchable ownership and privacy. Emotions are subject neither to criticism nor judgment.

Only *actions* can be criticized or judged as right or wrong. Feelings and emotions can have a rational or irrational basis, but they are never "right" or "wrong". Emotions are spontaneous, automatic reactions that are not in the immediate or direct control of a person. No one ever needs to feel guilty about any emotion.

A person is responsible only for the actions he or she takes. Those *actions* include the words that egress from one's mouth (mouth responsibility: what one chooses to go in and out of the mouth determines a person's competence, self-esteem, weight, health, appearance, happiness).

Also, since feelings and emotions are often subjective, making moral judgments of others on the basis of one's own personal feelings or emotions is unsound and unfair. For example, most of the negative-judgment vilifications that neocheaters publicly make (especially dishonest journalists and cartoonists) against such great value producers as Jay Gould, John D. Rockefeller, Howard Hughes, and Aristotle Onassis are based primarily on emotions of resentment and envy. In time, the misinformed public begins to accept the neocheaters' mystical-based cancer seeds, their emotional-based judgments, their big-lie assertions — usually planted throughout the media. The public generally accepts the neocheater's assertions, no matter how groundless, dishonest, unjust.

The facts are, however, that individuals like Jay Gould, John D. Rockefeller, Howard Hughes, and Aristotle Onassis were moral men of great integrity. And, they were major producers of values. Indeed, they were major benefactors to mankind whose values will live forever as opposed to those quickly-forgotten malefactors who enviously attacked them.

***

Almost all successful businessmen not involved with governments are, by nature, honest in their private and business dealings. Moreover, when those businessmen avoid, evade, even pay off government bureaucrats, politicians, and other neocheaters merely to be left alone in order to keep producing, they are neither dishonest nor immoral. Instead, they are morally trying to protect their capacity to produce values for others. They are meeting their highest responsibility in protecting themselves and others from the immoral force of neocheating "authorities" who live through value destruction.

Value producers neither like nor sanction neocheaters, usurpers, plunderers, and other such parasites. But can those value producers say "no" to the neocheating powercrats who threaten them? In the long run, value producers can and must say "no". They must refuse every usurping neocheater if they are to survive. Indeed, most businessmen are innocent heroes struggling to produce competitive values for others despite increasing government coercion, attacks, and usurpations.

Contrary to the efforts of the academia and media to make such businessmen appear guilty, the facts are the opposite: government powercrats, politicians, bureaucrats, most lawyers, and many of the media journalists and university professors are the guilty ones. For, they are the neocheaters; they are the ones who are destructive, corrupt, dishonest; they are the ones who exist by deception, force, coercion, dishonesty, fraud.

Without the professional mystics and neocheaters, all the corrupt systems of forced regulations, forced mediocrity, fake litigation, destructive taxes, corruption, and wars would not exist. But without the value producers, civilization itself would not exist. Without those producers, all civilization would perish. Or, by contrast, without mysticism all neocheaters would perish. Everyone else would flourish.

Neo-Tech Advantage #13
SENSE OF LIFE

A sense of life is an integral part of everyone's subconscious philosophy and psychology. Every person has a fundamental view or sense of life. While usually existing on a subconscious level, a person's sense of life largely determines his or her major actions. Sense of life falls into two opposite categories:

1. An objectively rational, self-interest, benevolent, individualistic sense of life that is characterized by:
   a. the knowledge that conscious achievement is the highest value.
   b. the knowledge that the conscious mind is competent to know reality.
2. A mystically irrational, altruistic, malevolent, anti-individual sense of life characterized by:
   a. the belief that non-man-made values (e.g., nature, the

18

universe, the cosmos) and mystical "values" (e.g., God, the State, society) are superior to man-made values.

b. the belief that the conscious mind is incapable of knowing reality.

The altruistic, malevolent sense of life finds virtue in sacrificing real, individual values to unreal, mystical "higher" causes such as God, the fatherland, nature, society. That altruistic, malevolent sense of life keeps one from acting in his or her long-range best interest to achieve power, prosperity, and happiness in order to produce competitive values for others. Those competitive values, by nature, require a rational self-interest, pro-individual sense of life combined with effort and honesty.

Neo-Tech Advantage #14
SELF-GROWTH VS. SELFLESS VIEW

Most productive people subconsciously hold a self-love, pro-individual sense of life. But outwardly they express various selfless views deemed virtuous by theologians, politicians, much of the media and academia, and other altruistic-promoting neocheaters. A major step toward personal prosperity and happiness is to reject all guilt foisted on self and others by mystics and neocheaters. One can easily reject that foisted guilt by discovering the moral virtue of one's own rational, self-growth, pro-individual sense of life that always benefits others and society to the maximum.

Also, destructive altruism is easily rejected on understanding that the rational self-growth view is the only benevolent, honest, and beneficial view for conscious beings. By contrast, the irrational, selfless, altruistic views promoted by neocheaters are harmful, malevolent, dishonest views for all conscious beings in any society. ...Both selfless and selfish behaviors are irrational, destructive.[1]

---

[1]Although the contents of her book, *The Virtue of Selfishness,* are precisely accurate and widely integrated, Ayn Rand committed an error by distorting the word "selfishness" in fashioning a dramatic statement. The word "selfishness" does have valuable, precise denotations of "an irrational, harmful disregard for others". Rand could have strengthened her work by selecting accurate wording such as *rational self-growth.* Instead, she unnecessarily bent and undermined the precise, valuable meaning of selfishness. ...As with selflessness, selfishness is a form of immature, destructive, irrational behavior — a form of stupid behavior.

19

Altruistic selflessness is a prime moral wrong that works to destroy everyone's values, well-being, and happiness. Rational selfishness, on the other hand, is a prime human virtue that works to benefit everyone and society.

Neo-Tech Advantage #15
AVOIDING SACRIFICE

An honest value producer can practice altruistic sacrifice, but he does so always at the expense of his own productivity and happiness, while reducing his value to others and society. An altruistic value producer is a psychological contradiction. Such a person represents a personal tragedy who is unnecessarily sacrificing his or her own efficacy, well-being, and happiness to clever neocheaters.

On the other hand, professional mystics and neocheaters function by forcing or coercing the producer to sacrifice increasingly larger portions of time, property, and earnings to themselves and other nonproducers. As a result of making "careers" from other people's sacrifices, those value destroyers never learn to exert the honest thought and effort needed to be competitive — to produce tradeable values required to become happy, independent individuals with genuine prosperity and self-esteem. By their defaults, mystics and neocheaters lose the possibility of earning abiding prosperity and happiness, despite their desperate efforts to feign importance, self-worth, well-being, and happiness. ...With Neo-Tech, one cannot only avoid sacrifice, but can smash the facade of all professional mystics and neocheaters.

Neo-Tech Advantage #16
RETAINING HAPPINESS

For two-thousand years, altruistic ethics (oriented around the state, society, or God) have been the prime tool of neocheating powercrats (rulers, dictators, politicians, social "intellectuals", theologians). That tool is used to sacrifice the well-being and happiness of value producers to various "higher" causes, such as God, the State, society. Those powercrats apply force and coercion to extract their livelihoods from productive individuals. Neocheating powercrats always operate from behind masks of altruistic higher causes such as fighting wars, fighting drugs, fighting depression, fighting inflation, fighting poverty, fighting pollution, fighting nonbelievers, fighting technology, fighting for the common good, fighting for all sorts of "noble" causes. They do this "fighting" with an air of self-righteousness as they extract their livings from the value producers.

Altruistic ethics are always promoted by professional mystics and neocheaters. Those ethics throw into unresolvable contradictions every innocent, productive person who accepts the ethics of sacrifice (altruism). For one cannot achieve happiness through value production by accepting destructive contradictions such as self-sacrifice. Such contradictions diminish and eventually destroy a productive person's capacity for happiness. Yet, any productive person can avoid losing his or her growth and happiness to sacrifice-demanding neocheaters. How? By consciously rejecting their evil ethics of altruism and "higher causes".

Neo-Tech Advantage #17
OVERCOMING ALTRUISTIC ETHICS

Neo-Tech defines evil as any action designed to physically, intellectually, or emotionally harm human beings. Such is the evil rooted in altruism and related philosophies of sacrifice. Altruistic-rooted evil is sometimes subtle, but is always pervasive and affects all areas of an individual's well-being and happiness.

For example, all nonvalue, "liberated" approaches to sex arise from an altruistic sacrifice of the personal importance and value of sex. After perhaps initial increases in pleasure and "freedom", the longer-range trend for people "liberated" around such altruistic sacrifices is toward impotence and frigidity. Only after repudiating altruistic sacrifice can people discover their full potential for pleasure, passion, and love.

The most harmful neocheaters operate through government, religion, public education, and dishonest journalism. Such people must always fake self-esteem to justify their destructive existences. They do that by slyly attacking businesses, their products, and those who through heroic efforts create productive jobs for others (a supreme moral virtue). For, by attacking through the bizarre, inverted ethics of altruism, even the most destructive neocheaters can fake a moral superiority over great producers and their works. Indeed, attacking values is the only way those neocheaters can gain a drug-like relief from their anxieties caused by living destructively. They get relief by destroying values. That destruction gives them a sense of power — a faked self-esteem needed to survive — needed to ward off suicide. ...But with Neo-Tech, the value producers finally have a fumigant to rid their lives of mystics and neocheaters.

Neo-Tech Advantage #18
BENEFITS AND PLEASURES FROM ROMANTIC LOVE

Every relationship can be evaluated in either "good for me" or "bad for me" terms. Love partners, for example, can evaluate their relationship by how much it increases or decreases their well-being and happiness.

A sacrifice-free, romantic-love relationship allows both partners to fill their physical, emotional, and intellectual needs without any losses or compromises. Such a relationship provides major personal benefits and increased pleasures from life. And, over the long term, a person can honestly love only those who integrate into a relationship from which benefits and pleasures evolve and grow.

Neo-Tech Advantage #19
RELIGIOUS VS. "PLAYBOY"
VS. PSYCHUOUS VIEW OF SEX AND LOVE

Three basic views of sex and love exist:
1. The religious-procreative view.
2. The recreational-fun-noncommitted view (e.g., the "Playboy" view as partly developed by Hugh Hefner in his *Playboy* magazine).
3. The psychuous-sex view as developed by the Neo-Tech/ Psychuous concepts.

The contradictions and guilt generated by the religious view of sex make psychuous pleasures and romantic love impossible. Today, the guilt caused by the religious view is more cleverly hidden. Still, that subconscious guilt eventually leads to the same loss of pleasure and happiness. An even more devastating loss evolves from performance anxieties caused by the "Playboy" view coupled with the demands to be a sexy person by someone else's standards.

The diminished self-esteem caused by the fun-only "Playboy" view creates anxiety and boredom to steadily diminish sexual pleasures and capacities. That process, if allowed to continue, ends in impotence or frigidity. Much of the impotence in men today is linked to self-esteem problems. Many insecure men who depend on a macho act for pseudo self-esteem collapse into impotence when confronted with healthy, confident, sexually liberated women who see through their act as laughable, immature, childish. ...Even more devastating: macho-type *value destroyers* lack self-esteem. Thus, their sex lives decline toward impotence. And once entangled in the Neo-Tech matrix, they lose their sexual potency quickly and permanently.

Only the third view, the psychuous-sex view, equates with human nature. Psychuous sex permits growth of mutual values, open-ended happiness, and genuine sexual pleasures for both men and women. But most innocent people subconsciously perceive sex through a combination of those three views. The result is various degrees of satisfaction as the negative effects of the religious and "Playboy" views undermine one's natural, healthy, value-oriented view of sex.

Despite the psychological harm the "Playboy" view causes, Hugh Hefner and his *Playboy* magazine contributed greatly to the well-being of men and women by countering the oppressive guilt of religion and control by government. Moreover, the Playboy Corporation morally defended individual rights related to sexual matters through the Playboy Forum and the Playboy Foundation [Re: Concept 122, Neo-Tech Reference Encyclopedia].

Overall, *Playboy* magazine has helped lift sexual guilt and repression from millions of human beings. For *Playboy* magazine editorially reflected the prime moral ethic that everyone has the right to live for his or her own happiness. That benevolent, guiltless view of life has always left *Playboy* magazine and its founder, Hugh Hefner, open to unjust attack. Such attacks emanate from envious, anti-life losers and neocheating organizations seeking unearned power, including most women's lib organizations such as NOW.

Playboy magazine has made major contributions toward lifting sexual guilt and repression by projecting sex as a healthy, pleasurable activity. But, *Playboy's* values are diminished by its erroneous, "casual-fun" viewpoints on sex, love, and women.

Ironically, even the religious view does not diminish one's self-esteem as much as the "Playboy" view over the long term. For most religions do hold sex as serious and important for procreation [Re: Concept 39, Neo-Tech Reference Encyclopedia]. But the overall effect of religion has been to deprive most human beings of happiness and pleasure they earn. Religion does that through projection of unearned guilt and by wiping out the objective links between morality, pleasure, happiness, value, and sex. Indeed, religion has always striven to deprive the human race of not only its material well-being but of its psychological well-being and happiness [Re: Concept 43, Neo-Tech Encyclopedia].

Many potentially rewarding romantic-love situations are needlessly destroyed either by the religious trap of guilt or by the "Playboy" trap of treating sex as an unimportant, casual-fun activity. Only the Neo-Tech/Psychuous view guiltlessly combines the mind and body to allow men and women to fully experience their earned pleasures, love, and happiness.

Neo-Tech Advantage #20
REQUIREMENTS FOR
PSYCHUOUS PLEASURES

The requirements for psychuous pleasures depend on human biological needs — on human material, physical, psychological, emotional, and intellectual needs. Since biological needs change only with extremely long-term evolutionary change, the requirements for psychuous pleasures will not basically change for as long as the current human civilization exists. ...Those requirements for psychuous pleasures are:

Physical

The development of physical awareness is needed to integrate the body, emotions, and intellect into a harmonious conscious being. Contrary to the erroneous religious and "Playboy" views, no separation or dichotomy exists between the mind and body. For, by nature, the mind and body always function as an integrated whole.

<u>Psychological and Emotional</u>
The development of self-esteem is needed to feel worthy of pleasure, love, happiness.

<u>Intellectual</u>
The development of an efficient, rational mind is needed to competitively produce the desirable, tradeable values required for quality survival.

* * *

The Neo-Tech/Psychuous Concepts throughout this manuscript show how one can meet the above requirements.

Neo-Tech Advantage #21
PSYCHUOUS PLEASURE VS.
SENSUOUS BEHAVIOR

Sensuous behavior can increase psychuous pleasures. But since psychuous pleasures involve the whole person in both sexual and nonsexual experiences, those pleasures are *not* dependent on sensuous behavior.

Most individuals can and should increase their sexual attractiveness. But some people reduce their natural sex appeal by faking sensuousness. And disaster results when a psychuously unattractive person (e.g., a professional neocheater, mystic, or any other destructive person) habitually tries to conceal his or her worthlessness or defaults by faking sensuousness. As that person's defaults become harder to hide, the demand for a put-on image (e.g., playboy, evangelist, political or bureaucratic powercrat, jet-setter, machismo) mounts until the image breaks. At that point, the value destroyer's chance for psychuous pleasures and happiness plunge to near zero.

Neo-Tech Advantage #22
PSYCHUOUS EXPERIENCES

The Neo-Tech/Psychuous concepts deliver a rainbow of new, valid ideas that allow a person to dump the mystical ideas of sacrifice and altruism. That dumping of mysticism allows a person to guiltlessly experience psychuous pleasures and prosperity.

Moreover, psychuous sex is an intense mind-body experience. Yet, psychuous sex does not always produce intense *physical* reactions. That would be too exhausting, too demanding, and eventually boring. Psychuous-sex intensity is measured by emotional depth and expression...not by overt physical reactions.

Value destroyers often fake pleasures they cannot experience. But the habitual faking of sexual pleasures will cause a malcontentment with sex that leads to impotence or frigidity.

On the other hand, value producers can experience continuously growing psychuous pleasures, not only from sex but from all rewarding activities, especially productive work. [Re: Table 4 in Neo-Tech Reference Encyclopedia traces the development of psychuous pleasures from birth.]

Neo-Tech Advantage #23
PSYCHUOUS CAPACITY

Capacity for psychuous sex, the most intense human pleasure, always arises from the same base — from dealing honestly with reality. And that is the same base from which all long-range prosperity and happiness arise. Thus, any action that enhances psychuous sex, prosperity, and long-range happiness is good and healthy. Likewise, any action that diminishes psychuous sex, prosperity, and long-range happiness is bad and unhealthy. That "good for me" or "bad for me" standard can be used to classify any action as good or bad, beneficial or harmful, healthy or unhealthy, moral or immoral. [Re: Concept 10, Neo-Tech Reference Encyclopedia; Table 5, The Sexual Quality Test; Table 6, The Sexual Capacity Test.]

Neo-Tech Advantage #24
OTHER BOOKS VS. NEO-TECH

Most people can recall reading inspiring, mind-over-matter, positive-thinking books and articles that offer rules for self-improvement. Generally the inspiration and determination to follow someone else's non-sequitur rules remain for various periods of time...until that person returns to his or her own self and situation.

Likewise, reading about rules for improving financial, business, or personal situations versus actual improvement of such situations are two different activities. Nevertheless, gaining knowledge through reading is a prerequisite for most productive achievements. Yet, most "self-improvement" books promote altruistic premises and "mind-over-matter" mysticism (e.g., "positive-thinking" approaches). Such approaches are self-defeating. By contrast, Neo-Tech operates on provable premises and self-interest ideas that let anyone achieve permanent advantages, prosperity, and happiness.

Specifically, Neo-Tech operates on the premises that the conscious individual is by nature (1) good, (2) the highest value in the universe, and (3) competent to understand and deal with reality. By adopting those premises, one can enjoy guiltless freedom and an immediate advantage over the professional mystics and neocheaters who operate through government and religion. ...By adopting Neo-Tech premises, a person can achieve great prosperity and psychuous pleasures.

Neo-Tech Advantage #25
VALUABLE BOOKS

Many books about achieving happiness, pleasure, and love contain valid, valuable information. But most such books are slanted toward gaining approval of the establishment media and culturally influential pseudo-intellectuals. Many authors struggle to gain approval of the neocheaters by maligning material achievements and disparaging the potency of the human mind. One must know how to dismiss that "striving for approval" approach in order to glean any useful knowledge and values from those books.

But many books can be more damaging than helpful to readers because their authors project major psychological, philosophical, and even physiological errors. Those errors are often subtle and remain undetected by most readers. [Eight of the best selling "sensuous" sex manuals are summarized in Table 11 of Neo-Tech Reference Encyclopedia. Those books are analyzed in greater detail in Appendix C of the Neo-Tech Reference Encyclopedia. The first two books on that list, for example, have excellent value and are recommended reading as a supplement to the Psychuous concepts. The next three books are of value, but contain various errors that demand dogmatic adherence to the authors' tastes and standards — or else, the authors imply, the reader will be guilty of "unsensuous" behavior. The last two books could be harmful to many readers, even fatal.]

Some books reflect the authors personal or sexual problems and actually point the way to eventual impotence and frigidity. Major exceptions to such books exist — such as the books by the farsighted pioneer of modern sexuality, Havelock Ellis (1859 – 1939). Also reflecting sexual health rather than sexual problems or hang-ups are the books of Albert Ellis (although his books fail to recognize the crucial importance of value selectivity). Alex Comfort's books, *The Joy of Sex* and *More Joy*, and the O'Neills' book, *Open Marriage*, also project healthy views recommended for reading as supplements to Psychuous Pleasures.

Because of its title, most people erroneously think "Open Marriage" advocates promiscuity or multi-affairs in marriage. But, the opposite is true. In refusing to understand "Open Marriage", the religious mystics remain unknowledgeable. Thus, those mystics are particularly scathing, gossipy, and dishonest in their attacks on the O'Neills and their book. Those dishonest attacks even overwhelmed the O'Neills, causing them to succumb to those value-destroying attacks.

Some books not only harm their readers, but undermine the lives and happiness of those authors who believe and follow their own mystical notions [Re: Table 12, Neo-Tech Reference Encyclopedia]. But authors who do *not* believe their own published advice are so deeply dishonest that they quickly wipe out their own self-esteems.

On the other hand, honest, valid books can greatly benefit the authors as well as their readers. For example, Havelock Ellis (1859 – 1939) delivered liberating and important values to his readers. But also, his honest work gradually freed Havelock himself from the crippling effects of Christian, anti-sexual ethics. Those ethics dominated his youth and left him sexually inept in adulthood. Paralyzed by masturbation terrors, he remained a virgin until the age of thirty-two when he married. During his twenty-five-year marriage to an overt lesbian, Edith Lees, they seldom engaged in sexual intercourse, although each loved the other dearly. With the help of several mistresses, all of whom

28

apparently loved this handsome and compassionate man, Havelock Ellis finally became a competent lover. Well after his fiftieth birthday, Ellis began to greatly enjoy sexual intercourse. In his late sixties, Ellis reached his sexual zenith in becoming a passionate lover of his beloved mistress, Franoise Laffité-Cyon, with whom he achieved great happiness and sexual fulfillment until his death at eighty years of age.

Neo-Tech Advantage #26
HARMFUL BOOKS

Erich Fromm's best selling book, *The Art of Loving*, is among the most subtly damaging pieces of literature since the Bible in undermining human well-being and happiness. For the independent-thinking reader seeking knowledge, however, nearly every well-written book, even dishonest and harmful books, can be valuable for extracting new understandings of either positive or negative views. For example, the reader gains valuable knowledge in discovering that Erich Fromm's central (but initially disguised) theme is that "real love" means loving everyone causelessly and equally. Any discrimination in love is condemned by Fromm as unloving selfishness. That dishonest, egalitarian theme wipes out the objective standards of human values, love, worth, and especially justice.

Fromm's false theme implies that no one has to earn love, value, or worth. If the person is your lover, husband, wife or child, that person should have no more of your love and valuation than a beggar in Calcutta, or a Hitler, or a Charles Manson...they all should be valued and loved equally. In other words, according to Fromm's theme, all human beings, regardless of their earned values or characters, should be diminished until they are equal in value to the lowest, meanest, unhappiest human being on this earth. That same destructive, unjust theme is promoted repeatedly by the Bible in both explicit and implicit terms.

Albert Schweitzer goes a step further in suggesting that one should love all living entities equally. That means a person's love for one's husband, wife, or child should never exceed the love that person could give to a stranger, or to a tree, a blade of grass, a weed. Indeed, certain Asiatic philosophies take still another step in declaring that all nonliving entities must also have equal love. In other words, the love for one's spouse or child should not exceed the love one could feel for a pebble on the beach. ...Such is the meaning of love to the Fromms, the Schweitzers, the Bible, and other neocheating promoters of egalitarianism and altruism.

But an even more malevolent theme has recently developed in the rhetoric and actions of today's neocheating "ecologists" and "environmentalists". They, by using the force of government, place the "well-being" of birds, insects (including mosquitoes), trees, plants, and inanimate "landscapes" *above* the lives, well-being, and happiness of human beings [Re: Concept 101, Neo-Tech Reference Encyclopedia]. Those anti-human themes are extensions of the altruistic philosophy advanced through books such as the Bible and Fromm's *The Art of Loving*.

And beyond? What does a future of growing egalitarianism and altruism hold? Constant exposure to the increasing atrocities of altruism and egalitarianism gradually numbs people into silently accepting higher and higher levels of injustice, human suffering, crippling of minds, killing, violence, terrorism. Fewer and fewer people object or even care about those mounting atrocities. Before Neo-Tech, those who consistently upheld individual rights to life and property were fading in both intensity and numbers. In that way, conditions were developing for the ultimate egalitarian end result — an eventual worldwide, Leninist-style or religious-style slaughterhouse. But Neo-Tech is reversing that trend — slowly today, rapidly tomorrow.

The final egalitarian "purification" is always the mass liquidation of human life. That "purification" starts with the exploitation and then sacrifice of the productive middle class and ends with their physical slaughter. Those who live by honest principles, those who uphold freedom and justice, those who love life, those who will not surrender their minds and lives to others, those who produce the most values for others — they, as the best, are eliminated first. The mass destruction of the best, the innocent, the virtuous producer of values has been occurring with increasing intensity in various African and Asian countries. And the same would happen throughout the Western world, including the United States, if altruism and egalitarianism grew to their natural conclusions. ...Neo-Tech will prevent that from happening.

But, only those holding genuine power — the value producers — can cure the disease of altruism. The value producer can stop altruism cold by saying "no" to the sacrificial demands of mystics and neocheaters. Indeed, through Neo-Tech, all value producers can guiltlessly, decisively reject all mysticism, altruism, egalitarianism. When the value producer says "no" to the neocheaters, their mystical hoaxes will become powerless and then crumble. Never again can those neocheaters trick or coerce the value producer into supporting them.

The Neo-Tech concepts provide the tools to expunge all professional mystics and neocheaters from our planet forever.

Neo-Tech Advantage #27
MYSTICISM AND DESTRUCTION

Religions and most political systems contradict man's nature because they are based on mysticism and altruism. Those systems require the individual to contradict his or her nature through sacrifice. Under the spell of mysticism, one loses increasing portions of prosperity, life, love, and happiness to various imaginary "higher causes". And such losses are for no real reason except to support those neocheaters who survive by manipulating dishonest, destructive, mystical notions. ...Mysticism contradicts the nature and needs of conscious beings. For, mysticism undermines the capacity for integrated thinking. Thus, mysticism reduces competitiveness, self-esteem, and psychuous pleasures. Thus, all mysticism leads to incompetence and unhappiness.

The more an individual surrenders to mysticism, the more that person becomes incompetent and tries to escape reality. For such a person, life increasingly becomes a source of conflict and pain. To the extent that one accepts mysticism is the extent that a person withdraws from life and loses contact with the pleasures and happiness that life inherently holds. ...All forms of mysticism (from fascism, Marxism, and wars to astrology, occultism, and religion) arise from ignorance, fraud, deceit, and the need to destroy values.

Mysticism is perpetuated by neocheaters who must undermine honesty in order to usurp their livings and pseudo self-esteems through value destruction. Such people must disregard or undermine the "burden of proof" concept. For that concept is the protector of honesty. The "burden of proof" concept requires that whoever makes an assertion has the burden to supply objective proof before credibility is granted to that assertion. People who promote mysticism either ignore the "burden of proof" concept or subvert the concept by passing off non sequiturs or specious rationalizations as "proof". In any case, mysticism by nature is the opposite of honesty, rationality, objectivity, reality, and Neo-Tech.

Neo-Tech Advantage #28
WHO CREATED EXISTENCE

The questions "Who Created Existence" and "Why of the Universe" are ancient, mind-subverting gimmicks of positing invalid, intellectually untenable questions that have no basis in reality. That false-question maneuver has been used by theologians and other mystics for centuries. The gimmick works by taking an invalid or meaningless idea and then cloaking the idea with specious but profound-sounding phraseology. That phraseology is then used as an "intellectual" prop to advance false, irrational concepts or doctrines. Consider, for example, the "Who Created Existence" and the "Why of the Universe" questions so often used by poets and theologians to advance the God or higher-power concept. On closer examination, one realizes that invalid questions such as "who made the universe" are meaningless and unprofound. For that type of infinite-regression question (of who created the creator and so on back) answers nothing and is anti-intellectual. Such a question cannot or need not be answered once one realizes that **existence exists.**

On realizing that by nature existence simply exists, one then realizes that the "Who Created Existence" and "Why of the Universe" questions cannot or need never be answered because no causal explanations are needed for **existence** or the universe. Existence is axiomatic. It just exists; it always has and always will exist. Nothing created it and no causal explanation is needed or valid. For, what is the alternative? No alternative is possible or needed, unless one accepts the contradiction that existence does not exist!

Neo-Tech Advantage #29
TECHNIQUES OF MYSTICISM

Books such as Fromm's "The Art of Loving" established the following technique that most of today's popular, mystical-based books use to gain credibility, public acceptance, and salability: Obviously valid facts and concepts are first presented to capture the interest and confidence of the reader [Re: Concept 36, Neo-Tech Reference Encyclopedia]. Those valid concepts are then woven throughout the false, mystical notions to lend an air of validity to the whole work. Essentially all religious and altruistic doctrines depend on similar techniques of using out-of-context facts, non sequiturs, slogans, "truisms", and parables to "validate" their specious doctrines.

Cleverly manipulative writers such as Fromm and deceptively manipulative organizations or "modern" churches such as Ron Hubbard's Church of Scientology can be even more dangerous and harmful than the overt, old-time religion or the neurotic, televangelists' born-again approaches. Today, most individuals reject the more obviously vicious, hellfire-and-brimstone aspects of the Bible and "old-time" religion. Still, even the most commonly rejected, blatantly malevolent aspects of the Bible and religions continue to do their damage by infusing subconscious guilt into those trying to live by Judeo-Christian ethics.

Similarly, the news media constantly mislead their audiences by using out-of-context facts and non sequiturs to create stories that seem valid, but are not. In that way, the media mystically manufacture "news" that subtly or overtly attacks objective values and their producers.[1] Constant exposure to propaganda against objective values and heroic producers leaves people increasingly indifferent toward upholding honesty and justice. That mystical-based indifference produces lethargy and ennui not only toward objective values and heroic producers but toward life itself.

---

[1]Despite the dishonesty and hypocrisy widely practiced by much of the news media, no government controls or regulations should ever be placed against the press or the communication media. Moreover, any possible form of control or regulation against any communication (written, visual, or oral) should be permanently abolished.

By manipulating subjective mysticism with dishonest reporting, much of today's neocheating media successfully obscure the value of productive individuals and their benevolent power. That constant obscuring of facts undermines everyone's view of great human achievements such as the automobile, supermarkets, and major technological advances. The persistent attacks against objective human values by politicians, theologians, social "intellectuals", and the media gradually diminish the strength, confidence, and happiness of the productive middle class, leaving them increasingly vulnerable for exploitation by the professional mystics and neocheaters.

Using the techniques of Fromm and the media, many current authors of social literature use rationalizations, specious cliches, non sequiturs, concrete-bound specifics taken out of context, and guilt-inducing half-truths to manipulate the middle-class producers into sacrificing their self-interests to an array of "higher" causes. [Table 13 in the Neo-Tech Reference Encyclopedia shows how such mystical-based books harm an individual's well-being and happiness. Table 14 compares techniques used by authors of destructive books to techniques used by authors of books that deliver objective values.]

Neo-Tech Advantage #30
**THE GOD CONCEPT —
A TOOL OF DESTRUCTION**

The God concept and all religions are products of mysticism. Mysticism is the opposite of honesty and reason. Mysticism underlies all volitionally destructive actions. Mysticism undermines the capacity for independent, integrated thinking and reasoning, which is the survival tool for all human beings. ...The mystical-oriented mind is the basis of the criminal-like mind, which is the exact opposite of the business-like mind.

For two-thousand years, the God concept has been the most effective tool of the professional mystics and neocheaters for usurping a material and psychological living from the value producers. The God concept is such an effective tool because it manipulates major thinking defaults into convenient well-organized packages of specious "truths". Professional value destroyers can with relative ease use various God-concept frauds to deceive or cajole innocent producers into sacrificing their earned values to them, the nonproducers. Most God-concept frauds promote the "virtues" of humility, altruism, egalitarianism, selflessness, "higher" causes, and sacrifice. Such specious "virtues" are designed to generate guilt for lowering the self-esteem of producers to the level of the nonproducer. Once burdened with false guilt, the producers will more readily hand over or sacrifice their earned values to the nonproducers.

Throughout history, the many God-concept variations have provided professional mystics and neocheaters with effective tools for extracting a living from the value producer.[1] For survival, value destroyers depend on the producer to sacrifice his or her created or earned values to them. They also extract values through government force and coercion. ...All professional mystics and neocheaters rely on the unearned guilt foisted on producers through various altruistic or God-concept hoaxes to extract material and psychological "livings" from value producers.

The God concept, religion, and mysticism are also the tools needed to establish totalitarian dictatorships, including both theistic and "atheistic" dictatorships.[2] Russia, for example, was the most religious, mystical country in Europe during the early 1900s. That heavy mysticism provided an ideal psychological setup for the acceptance of perhaps the most destructive and irrational, mystical-based political system in history — Marxism/Leninism. Acceptance of an irrational, Kantian-based philosophy such as Marxism was needed to negate objective values and individual rights, to rationalize the enslavement of entire nations, to slaughter millions of productive human beings for a

---

[1]On a morality scale, most criminals rank several notches above such destructive neocheaters of the politician and theologian genre. The criminal does not attempt to establish himself as a morally righteous person or palm off his actions as morally good. Moreover, the criminal does not use altruism or the God concept to foist false guilt onto his victims after stealing or usurping his livelihood from them.

[2]No dictatorship is really atheistic. Various dictatorships only replace one mystical authority called God with another mystical authority called the State. Philosophically they are all equally mystical, destructive, and immoral.

meaningless, mystical higher "authority" — the state. ...Thus, the God-concept tools of altruism and mysticism are needed not only to establish the murderous religious regimes of an Ayatollah-led Iran but the murderous "atheistic" regimes of a dictator-led Soviet Union and Red China.

Stalin, Mao, and their neocheating colleagues used various altruistic, God-concept tools to justify slaughtering millions of innocent, middle-class producers in the name of a higher "good". And what is always the reason for such mass destruction and slaughter? Always for no other reason than to build personal false power and bogus jobs. No other reason ever exists.

In order to live, the value destroyer must usurp values created by the value producer. That dependence deprives the usurper of self-esteem, leaving him resentful and envious toward value producers. Such feelings of worthlessness, resentment, and envy can build until the usurper would subconsciously just as soon be dead. Out of such resentment and envy, that person would like to drag everyone else to the grave with him, especially the value producers. Indeed, that is what happens when totalitarian leaders assume power. Out of envy and hatred, they eventually destroy themselves and anyone else they can destroy.

Stalin, Hitler, and Mao, for example, were personally responsible for staggering property destruction while systematically slaughtering many millions of innocent, productive human beings. Castro, as another example, publicly stated that he, an ex-lawyer who had never produced or earned competitive values, would like to drop a nuclear bomb on New York City, destroying the greatest concentration of earned, man-made values on this planet. Such mass destruction would help prop his pseudo self-esteem by making him feel big and important. But, in fact, he has never been more than a destructive pip-squeak and mass murderer. ...All mass murderers throughout history required the tools of altruism and mysticism to rationalize their purposeful destruction of values and life.

In literature and in other forms of communication, dealing with the God concept falls into four categories [Re: Table 15, Neo-Tech Reference Encyclopedia]. The first three categories involve the harmful promotion of the God concept and other mystical frauds. The fourth category involves the beneficial undermining of the God-concept and other mystical frauds. Neo-Tech falls into the fourth category in identifying the route to guiltless prosperity and happiness.

Neo-Tech Advantage #31
ASTROLOGY, UFOS, AND OTHER MYTHS

As with all forms of mysticism, acceptance of myths varying from astrology and UFOs to religion and the God concept cripples a person's thinking and integration processes. Indeed, crippled thinking and integration processes undermine a person's personal power, productive competence, financial well-being, psychuous pleasures, and long-range happiness.

Many popular myths depend on proclaimed "scientific" evidence to create illusions of credibility. Astrology devotees promote the "scientific" notion that the infinitesimally faint celestial forces that impinge on human beings affect and influence their minds, actions, behavior, and destiny. As "proof", for example, they state how the gravitational forces of the moon cause the oceanic tides. But facts and logic show that man alone controls his own destiny. And his mind can easily override all the forces of nature combined [Re: Table 7, Concept 22, Neo-Tech Reference Encyclopedia]. Indeed, in a free society, the conscious mind is a much stronger controller of an individual's future than all the overt, direct forces of nature, government, and religion combined.

A person's own choices, not his environment, control his or her destiny. Except for natural catastrophe or brute-force totalitarianism, the forces of nature and social environment when pitted against the rational conscious mind have little or no influence over that individual's long-range future.

For a person to allow his future to be influenced by even the most direct and powerful forces of nature (such as the weather, the wind, the rain) would be to relegate the potency of his or her mind and actions to a low position indeed. But to assert, as astrologers do, that the faintest forces in nature (the celestial forces from outer space) can influence human beings and their minds is to relegate the human mind to a most inept position. To view the human mind as being that feeble or impotent, even though the view may be only subconscious or implicit, undermines a person's confidence and self-esteem. And, more serious is what happens to the confidence and self-esteem of those who let themselves be controlled or influenced by nonexistent forces, such as the God myth.

Many people erroneously believe that the governmental and religious forces surrounding them are more powerful than they. With the destruction that those forces have always inflicted on mankind, such an attitude is understandable, but invalid. Government and religious forces, while always exerting destructive influences, need not be the controlling forces on any individual's present or future. By using the mind and acting on reason, a person can usually avoid or minimize the effect of government and religion on his or her personal self in order to live independently, productively, and happily.

Direct forces of government, religion, or even nature (e.g., earthquakes, floods, tornadoes) can at times have devastating effects on any individual. The government can confiscate or plunder a person's property. The government can jail or kill innocent people. Religion can destroy a person's mind or happiness. The church will also torture and kill masses of innocent people whenever it holds direct political power (e.g., Dark Ages, Inquisitions, Jonestown, Ayatollah Iran, Witch Trials, crusades). But none of those potential or real forces basically control human lives or destiny. The human mind, along with the choices made through an individual's life, controls the life and future of a productive person (unless government or religious forces directly cripple or destroy that person).

***

Accepting "scientific" myths such as UFOs (unidentified flying objects from intelligent outer space) will diminish a person's self-esteem and reduce that person's capacity for psychuous pleasures and happiness. As with astrology (and with ESP, PK, and other forms of "scientific" mysticism[1]), the outer-

---

[1]Most forms of "scientific" mysticism reflect wishful desires to discover outside forces or "authorities" to take over the thinking tasks of the human mind. The mystic's wish is to be automatically and effortlessly guided to

(footnote continued on next page)

space UFO advocate must first establish a scientific-sounding base to create an illusion of credibility. Such a basis for UFOs is accomplished by taking out of context the valid hypothesis that millions of Earth-like planets exist in outer space in which advanced civilizations of living beings have developed technology far beyond our own civilization [Re: F. R. Wallace, "We the Creators of All Heavens and Earths", I□&□O Publishing].And many of those civilizations most certainly would be capable of communicating or even journeying across many light years to reach Earth. For conscious beings in such advanced civilizations would have achieved biological immortality long ago.

The above hypotheses are statistically valid and almost certainly factual. From statistical considerations, many millions or billions of Earth-like planets with intelligent civilizations do exist throughout the universe. Many of those civilizations existing far in advance of our own are certainly capable of contacting Earth. Yet, logic and statistics dictate that such civilizations would not contact Earth.

The main reason for believing that no outside civilization has ever contacted earth is that no one has found any hard evidence that even suggests intelligent beings from outer space have ever contacted Earth. All claims of evidence to date have been spurious, false, or scientifically unsound. If intelligent beings from outer space ever had contacted Earth, the evidence would have been immediately and spectacularly conclusive. For example, consider the highly advanced artifacts that would be left behind by any mystic-free civilization capable of developing the energy and technology required to contact Earth.

(footnote continued from previous page)

knowledge and through life by external forces. But no effortless guide exists. No outside force can take over and do what the mind and the individual must do for him or her self. Consider the president of the United States following the stupidity of astrology. Or consider the government of the U.S.S.R. directing funds for "research" efforts in ESP, psychokinesis, PK, and other pseudosciences: Indeed, through such mystical stupidities, the intellectual impotence of those governments and their leaders is revealed. In reality, such governments are goofy and their leaders are clowns. ...They are already being laughed out of existence through Neo-Tech competition.

Indeed, many highly advanced civilizations throughout outer space certainly have the technological capacity to contact and travel to Earth. But the following logic indicates none would contact Earth: The technological advance of any civilization can be measured by the amount of energy harnessable by that civilization. Energy capacity is a direct measure of scientific knowledge and technological development. The energy requirements for outer space communication and travel are far beyond the total energy capacity available on earth at our present level of technology. Thus, a civilization capable of contacting earth would have to be advanced far beyond our civilization. That would mean that any such civilization would be well past the *Nuclear-Decision Threshold* [Re: Table 51, concept 116 of the Neo-Tech Reference Encyclopedia]. That threshold is the point that every advanced civilization must successfully pass through to survive. Our civilization is at that point today. The *Nuclear-Decision Threshold* is the point at which energy, knowledge, and technology have advanced to where sufficient, man-made energy (e.g., nuclear energy) can be generated to physically destroy all life on the planet. From that point, all civilizations must follow one of two courses:

(1) Proceed in an irrational, altruistic, Platonistic philosophical system in which initiatory force compels others to support mystical "higher" causes that feed the bogus livelihoods of neocheaters. Such systems will eventually lead either to all-out nuclear warfare[1] or to a retreat into an anti-technological Dark

[1]Ironically, the unilateral peace and disarmament movements are not only dishonest, mystical, and usually promoted by professional mystics and neocheaters, but they are the very forces that move the world toward nuclear annihilation. By contrast, a well-prepared, rational society can effectively protect itself against nuclear war as well as prosper into the future. For, a prime moral obligation is self-protection. Thus, the development of an effective SDI or "Star-Wars" defense system is the most rational, moral act any country could perform in protecting its citizens and their property. (Also, see Neo-Tech Advantage #110 for the profound right to self-defense.)

Ages in which most knowledge and technology are lost. In either case, most of the world's population will die and civilization will perish because of meaningless mysticism being manipulated to give false power and bogus livelihoods to the value destroyers.

(2) Proceed in (or change to) a rational, business-like, Aristotelian philosophical system in which initiatory force plays no role. Such a system allows civilization to safely advance beyond the *Nuclear-Decision Threshold*.

Thus, any civilization advancing significantly beyond that threshold would by nature exist within a rational Aristotelian/Neo-Tech society. That in turn would mean a free-market business society from which initiatory force is eradicated as uncompetitive, impotent, and immoral. In any such advanced society, all forms of mysticism would by nature have been discredited and discarded as stupid and destructive. Such a business-minded society would be free of politicians, theologians, neocheaters, coercive governments, and other usurpers and parasites. Actions would be based on reality-oriented logic exercised by free individuals harmoniously, competitively living in accord with their rational best interests.

In such an advanced society, no logical reason would exist and no apparent benefits could accrue by expending the excessive time and energy required to contact Earth or similar, outer-space civilizations. Such an undertaking would *not* be scientifically interesting or profitable for a civilization so far advanced in knowledge and technology.

In other words, as a civilization approaches a technological stage so advanced that other civilizations could be contacted, then the need, interest, and benefits to do so would cease. All such societies would by nature exist within Neo-Tech, rational, self-interest cultures. All individuals in such societies could fill all of their physical needs, psychological needs, and growth needs within a practical sphere of space (although capable of reaching any point farther into outer space). Moreover, such advanced civilizations would have access to the interstellar computer system most certainly present throughout the universe. Throughout that computer system, all important knowledge would be organized

41

and available for exchange among all advanced, Neo-Tech civilizations — perhaps through an oscillating, gravity-coded system.

In summary, probably thousands or millions of highly advanced civilizations exist in outer space that have the technological capacity to contact Earth. But being nonaltruistic, business-minded societies, they would have no logical motive or incentive to expend the time and energy to do so.[1]

For our own civilization to advance significantly beyond our current *Nuclear-Decision Threshold* would require a shift from the current Platonistic/altruistic philosophical base to a Aristotelian/Neo-Tech philosophical base [Re: Table 51 in Concept 116, Neo-Tech Reference Encyclopedia].

Paradoxically, at our current level of civilization, we can gain considerable economic, technological, and scientific benefits from investigating outer space and exploring our solar system and beyond. And, on switching to a rational Neo-Tech society, our civilization will advance significantly beyond the *Nuclear-Decision Threshold*. Then our knowledge, technology, and well-being will advance so rapidly and far that when our energy capacity reaches the potential for contacting civilizations in far outer space, the logical reasons or incentives for such contact (economic, social, scientific) will fade. For, within a Neo-Tech society of self-ruling individuals, the potential of each individual can be fully realized. And that unrealized potential of conscious beings represents the total creative power available throughout the universe. On meeting that potential, nothing further out in space is required, especially after business-driven scientists learn

---

[1]Perhaps the only rational motive for an advanced civilization to communicate much beyond their immediate star system would be the pending death of their primary energy source — their sun — via an explosion-type burnout. Those beings would probably explore and colonize planets in nearby solar systems. The positions of stars in our own Milky-Way galaxy are constantly shifting relative to each other. Thus, our planet could at times become a "nearby" star system (e.g., less than a hundred light years) to a highly advanced civilization that must abandon its own solar system because of an impending solar explosion or other catastrophe. In such a case, our planet could become the object of exploration and even colonization from outer space. Statistically, however, such a combination of events would be extremely unlikely.

to access the interstellar computer available throughout the universe.

The answer, therefore, to the outer-space UFO question reduces to:

1. Probably many highly advanced civilizations exist throughout space that currently have the capacity to contact and even travel to Earth.
2. No valid, scientific evidence has ever been found that suggests intelligent, outer-space communication or visitation has ever occurred on Earth.
3. Logic indicates that advanced civilizations with the energy technology to contact Earth would not do so because there would be no economic, social, or scientific incentive to do so. *For, once an advanced civilization has dug well-defined holes into space by exploring, understanding, and exploiting those areas, the need and incentive to dig more and more holes, deeper and deeper into space at greater and greater costs steadily diminish to zero.*

Neo-Tech Advantage #32
EXISTENTIALISM AND ITS INFLUENCE

A dominant form of mysticism and Platonistic philosophy in Western civilization is existentialism and its many disguised variations such as Gestaltism, transcendental meditation, Zen Buddhism. Existentialism is really nothing more than clever irrationalism and contradictions that ironically heralds Kierkegaard's "individual responsibility", which existentialism ultimately negates, often cloaked in pragmatic non sequiturs or good-sounding rationalizations. Existentialism claims that reality does not exist. Thus, the meaning of existentialism is impossible to objectively define or understand. For existentialism is nothing. And nothing can be attached to nothing.

Expressed in countless ways, existentialism is the philosophical form projected by (1) most media commentators, (2) almost all politicians and theologians, (3) neocheating social "intellectuals", including many teachers, university professors, and (4) know-nothing personalities and entertainers acting as "authorities" on the basis of feeling rather than knowledge.

In the past several decades, those four groups of people have effectively spread existentialism among the nonproductive elements of society. More recently, those same groups are successfully pushing existentialism onto the working middle class. As a result, the productivity, self-esteem, and happiness among the productive middle class is diminishing as value producers increasingly swap their earned happiness and freedom for the existentialistic ideas of mysticism, egalitarianism, and altruism. Their ultimate negation of self-responsibility and self-control opens the way for increasing government control of their lives.[1]

Many people are drawn into the chameleon-like forms of existentialism through an assortment of highly publicized, illusionary benefits designed to indulge almost anyone's emotions to escape reality. Touted benefits include discovering "real truth", "peace of mind", "happiness", new "freedoms", "self-awareness",

---

[1]Government control always means the control of individuals by force. Communism, fascism, socialism, and democracy are political systems that survive by force. Democracy, however, is generally less destructive or less malevolent than the other three systems of oppression. All four political systems operate on the same neocheating concepts of external "authority" and unearned power backed by "legalized" force. Moreover, all four systems require Platonistic, existentialist philosophies for the value destroyers to usurp bogus livings from the value producers.

Contrary to popular myth, democracy is rooted neither in justice nor in the protection of individual rights, but is rooted in the uncompetitive principle of "authorities" with power to force the deemed "will" of the majority onto specific individuals. (The United States was not founded as a democracy, but as a republic based on constitutional law forged between democratic myths and free-choice, competitive-market principles. Today, most of the remaining nonforce, free-choice, competitive elements of freedom in the United States are being replaced with uncompetitive fascist or socialistic elements of force.) A business-like, free-choice, competitive system is the only political system based on logic, justice, growth, and earned values rather than on feelings, force, stagnation, and usurpation of values. Of all political systems, only the nonforce, free-choice competitive system rejects the concept of uncompetitive "authority" system of force, threat of force, and fraud. And only competitive, free markets fully recognize the sovereignty of the individual and the right to his or her own body, life, and earned property. ...All professional mystics and value-destroying neocheaters hate and fear free-choice competition. Why? Because free-choice competition would drive them from their dishonest careers and bogus livelihoods.

44

increased "sensitivity", "discovery" of one's true self, and a wide variety of health and nutritional "benefits". Other benefits touted by groups such as Scientologists include various mystical routes to "freedom" and "happiness" through self-awareness via clearing hang-ups or engrams [Re: Concept 39, Neo-Tech Reference Encyclopedia]. But beneath all such jargon and claimed benefits, existentialism is nothing more than a wimpish irrationality that promotes stupidity. ...Indeed, existentialism promotes the negation of reality. [Re: Table 16, Neo-Tech Reference Encyclopedia defines existentialism and identifies some of its manifestations being thrust onto the productive middle class by mystics, politicians, and other neocheaters.]

Existentialism and religion both grow from mysticism. And both lead to the oppression of the individual. Existentialism and religion both reflect fear of the independent individual and even greater fear of individual pride. Most mystics denounce pride as negative, bad, or sinful. But, individual pride is the result of moral virtue, which requires the rejection of the dishonesty inherent in mysticism.

Pride is the reflection of self-worth, which requires the rejection of mysticism. And that rejection of mysticism through the reflection of self-worth is what all mystics, existentialists, and neocheaters fear and attack. For, if all value producers recognized their genuine self-worth and felt their earned pride, they would reject mysticism to end the hoax of all neocheaters.

Neo-Tech Advantage #33
THE SEVENTEEN-HUNDRED-YEAR OPPRESSION OF HUMAN HAPPINESS

About 300 A.D., Christian theologians discovered the ultimate neocheating technique to control human beings. That technique was to link guilt with sex [Re: Section Four Neo-Tech Reference Encyclopedia]. With that technique, the Christian church rose to its height in power, causing Western civilization to crumble into the mystical Dark Ages as human well-being and happiness sank to the lowest level in recorded history.

The history of Christian oppression of individual life, rights, values, happiness, pleasure, and sexuality is outlined on the following pages:

CHRISTIAN OPPRESSION OF HAPPINESS

(from research by Morton M. Hunt and others)

100 A.D. – 385 A.D.

•Roman Empire still appeared vibrant, but was surrendering to a new religion...Christianity. Rome plunged into altruism and asceticism.

•Roman pagans began persecuting those Christians who became altruistic fanatics and used any means to meet their goals of destroying the life-enhancing and productive aspects of Roman civilization. Those neocheating Christian leaders had the dual objective of wiping out the pleasures of human life as well as destroying the high standard of living enjoyed by the Romans. The early Christians heroically formed tightly-knit anarchist groups for effective protection from the oppression of the bureaucratic Roman government while laying the foundations for their own much greater oppressions.

385 A.D. – 1000 A.D.

•The rise of the unkempt ascetics (hippies) in Egypt. Based on Christian self-torture and denial (e.g., St. Simon).

•Christianity discovered a fast, neocheating route to power — the foisting of guilt onto innocent value producers. As an effective rallying symbol, they found and elevated to martyr-level status an obscure historical individual who died three centuries earlier. That individual ironically was a gentle, appealing rebel who heroically stood up to the injustices of the parasitical-elite authorities — the same type authorities who three centuries later usurped and mystified him for their own dishonest exploitation. That individual, their new symbol, was named Jesus Christ. ...Jesus has been done a rank injustice by the Catholic church.

•Christians became increasingly preoccupied with sex as they struggled against lust (e.g., by burning off fingers to resist temptation). Thinly veiled, neurotic eroticism steadily increased within the church.

•St. Augustine (born 354 A.D.) promoted guilt through his books: (1) *Confessions* — self-accusations of his pagan, lustful youth. He converted to a Christian in 386 A.D., then gained power through neocheating by hatefully using guilt to turn the goodness and pleasures of man against himself. Promulgated how all are born between feces and urine. (2)*The City of God* — his major work — speculates how babies might be born from women "uncankered by lust and sex". Demonstrates passionate hatred for human life. St. Augustine became a master neocheater in achieving respect and power by making problems where none existed. He destroyed values rather than create them.

•By the 5th Century, marriage came under church domination.

•The decline into dark ages coincided with the rise of Christianity. Collapsing under the Christian stranglehold, 6th Century Rome was repeatedly ravaged and looted. One million population was reduced to fifty thousand. The city lay in rubble and ruins. The Senate ceased for lack of qualified men. The hygiene, science, and culture of Rome was abandoned as Christianity took hold.

•By 585 A.D., Catholics argued that women did not have mortal souls and debated if women were even human beings.

•Sex was reduced by Christianity to an unromantic, harsh, ugly act with penance easily and hypocritically granted to men whenever required. Women became pieces of disposable property.

•Clergy and popes turned to prostitutes and neurotic sex. (e.g., The Pope of 904 A.D. practiced incest and was a lecher with children).

•By the 9th Century, Christianity dominated. Women were considered property of men. The church sanctioned wife-beating. Men were merely fined by the church for killing women.

•For the Catholic clergy, sex without values (e.g., prostitute sex, orgy sex, even forced rape or sadistic sex) was not a serious offense, but sex with values (e.g., loving or valuing a woman) was a high sin with severe penalties. For, love and valuing resist control by "authorities", therefore, had to be squelched.

•St. Jerome stated that he who too ardently loved his wife was an adulterer.

•Christian marital sex was performed only in one position and then only to conceive a child. Sex was never to be performed during penance nor on Sundays, Wednesdays, Fridays, holiday seasons.

•The major Christian sin was not sex, but pleasure.

1000 A.D. – 1500 A.D.

•Courtly love reflected happiness and contradicted the malevolence of religion. Churchmen feared and fought courtly love (e.g., St. Thomas stated that to kiss and touch a woman with delight, even without thought of fornication, was a mortal sin).

•The struggle was between oppressive religion and renaissance free thinking. Also, the struggle was between papal power and the new Aristotelian ideas.

•In the 1300s, an ominous new interest in witchcraft and exorcism began appearing in the church. Priests fulminated about the evil powers of women who formed sex pacts with the Devil.

•By 1450, the dichotomy was complete and the dogma was established by the Catholic church that all physically desirable women were evil witches. The church was losing its power, and demonizing women was their means to fight the rediscovering of human joyfulness brought on by the emerging Renaissance.

•Renaissance noblemen in the 15th Century equated beauty to good. To counter this trend toward good and beauty, the church attacked through the Pope. The Catholic church developed a new breed of neocheating malefactors not known before...the inquisitors who were backed by a series of papal pronouncements and bulls. The Pope set up two theologians (Jacob Sprenger and Henry Kramer) to act as inquisitors. Sprenger and Kramer wrote a widely influential book dealing with the "evils" of women and witchcraft. That led to the burning to death of tens of thousands of innocent women during the Renaissance.

•Crosscurrents and contradictions — the "lady ideal" projected by the happy, benevolent spirit of the Renaissance versus the "evil witch" projected by the unhappy, malevolent spirit of the church.

•King Henry VIII was the first major figure to combine love and marriage. He waged a long battle with Bishop Wolsey and Pope Clement VII about his divorce and subsequent marriage to Anne Boleyn.

•Renaissance enlightenment made sex seem not so sinful and disgusting as the church insisted. The middle class began to associate sex with love.

1500 – 1700

•The Reformation combined with the enlightened Renaissance by considering sex in marriage as wholesome and free of guilt. But the malevolent Christian position continued to burn women as witches.

•Martin Luther battled Catholic asceticism by advocating the enjoyment of every pleasure that was not "sinful". Luther lived in a lusty "eat, drink, and be merry" style. He fought Rome and claimed that celibacy was invented by the Devil. He insisted that priests could marry and asserted that marriage was not a sacrament at all, but a civil matter. Luther asserted that sexual impulses were both natural and irrepressible. He broke from Rome and married. He cheerfully loved his wife and held pleasurable sex in marriage as good. Luther's reformation rapidly spread across Northern Europe.

•John Calvin (the father of the Bluenoses) was the opposite of Martin Luther. Calvin was sour, malevolent, and had a ferocious theology based on human depravity and the wrath of God. He was an unhappy ascetic who had ulcers, tuberculosis, and kidney stones; he considered life of little value. Calvin set up a brutally strict theocracy in Geneva that allowed no dancing, fancy clothes, or jewelry. The death penalty was imposed for adultery. Even legitimate love was stringently regulated. Engagements were limited to six weeks. No lingering at romance was allowed. Weddings were grave with no revelry. The Calvinist marriage had two functions: (1) to produce children, and (2) to reduce sexual desires.

•Most Puritans, however, were quite unlike the inhuman joylessness of Calvin. But a few vocal fanatics such as John Knox in the United States continued to pile misery onto others. His Blue laws of the 1650s were against amusements, smoking, drinking, gambling, fancy clothing. He also promoted public whippings, scarlet letters, executions for adulterers, and the Salem "witch" executions (executed 26 women and two dogs in 1692).

•Early Puritan traits were mainly stern expressions masking mischief and romance. Church trial records show much "sinning" existed. But only sex outside marriage was attacked. Puritans were very much for sex inside marriage and condemned the virtue-of-virginity concept. Most Puritans were tenderly romantic and good lovers.

•The image of the sexless Puritan with a stony heart is false. For example, the 17th Century Puritan John Milton (*Paradise Lost*) projected a healthy view of married sex. He displayed idealistic, romantic views about marriage. Moreover, Milton sent tracts to Parliament urging modern-day, easy divorce. Milton's *Paradise Lost* projects a benevolent view of Adam and Eve in a romantic-love context. Milton rejected St. Augustine's malevolent views of life, sex, and pleasure.

•16th Century Puritans combined the ideals of romantic love with the normality of sex in marriage. Woman's status improved under Puritanism (e.g., if beaten, women could separate and even divorce.). Property rights and inheritance laws improved. Marriage became a civil contract.

1700 – 1800

•The rationalists in this new Age of Reason rejected the gloom of Christianity. They scrapped the church's portrait of woman as evil.

50

•18th Century love rejected Christian anti-sexual values and idealized the mythical Don Juan, who was impeccably mannered, lustful, haughty. Love was reduced to mere sensuality and pleasurable sport with the motive to seduce and then desert.

1800 – 1900

•Religious Victorian men, on the other hand, were patriarchal and stern. But they played that role at their own sexual expense.
•Out of religious Victorianism arose a great hunger for a fantasy sex life. Flagellation, pornography, and prostitution rapidly increased.
•Capitalistic economics were greatly accelerating the dissolution of medieval religious ties along with their unjust social customs and racism.
•The religious Victorian home was threatened by talk of female suffrage, divorce reforms, and free love.
•Victorianism was a reactionary, desperate delaying action (in collusion with the church) against the inevitable changes made by an emerging industrial civilization. Religion-oriented Victorians tried to fight change via religious coercion, government force, and police activities.

1900 – 1950

•Margaret Sanger staged a historic fight for birth control claiming that a woman's body belonged to her alone. She published birth-control information in 1914 and opened birth-control clinics in 1916. Outraged Roman Catholic elements had her arrested and jailed.

1950 – 1980

•Modern sexual revolution toward openness and honesty has caused the church's malevolent influence over sexuality to wane. In a last desperate effort, "modern" and new-wave churches evolved that adopted existentialist and fun views of sex in order to diminish the value and importance of sex. Thus, those churches kept control by undercutting people's self-esteem. Without self-esteem, one cannot experience abiding happiness or psychuous pleasures. Without self-esteem, a person will continue to be controlled by neocheaters using the tools of mysticism.

1980 – PRESENT

•An ominous rise of overt mysticism, born-again Christianity, and fundamentalist religions signal a turn back toward malevolent views of life, love, and sex. A revival of fundamentalism and theocratic concepts are conditions ultimately sought by all mystical leaders. No matter what deceptive facades they present, all mystical leaders are destructive neocheaters who ultimately want to reign with murderous power. But today, for the first time in history, mysticism and neocheating are being irreversibly undermined by the spreading Neo-Tech matrix.

Neo-Tech Advantage #34
AESTHETIC PLEASURE

The aesthetics (art, music, drama, and literature) are rational pursuits that add important increments of emotional fuel and psychuous pleasures to a person's life. Moreover, aesthetic pleasures are important to the growth of one's psychological and spiritual[1] well-being. Aesthetics reflect a person's most important values in a concrete way, providing powerful emotional fuel to seek ever greater personal growth and achievements.

A false but common belief is that a person's response to art (music, literature, fine arts, performing arts) is a mystical experience that has no basis in reality and serves no practical purpose. But the opposite is true. A positive response to art is a phenomenon of reality that reflects a person's deepest, most

---

[1]The word *spiritual* as used throughout Neo-Tech has no mystical or religious connotations. Spiritual means one's sense or view of life combined with one's assertiveness toward living.

important values. Those values can be either objective or neurotic values. For example, destructive people can respond positively to art that reflects neurotic values, nonvalues, or even value destruction.

Another false belief is that art is entirely subjective and cannot be evaluated on an objective basis. With sufficient knowledge, all art can be judged by precise, objective standards. Objective evaluation can include sense of life, the theme expressed by the artist, execution skill, overt style, presentation integrity.

Psychological pleasure derived from an art work comes from the similarity of the artist's values and sense of life to one's own values. Admiration of an art work, on the other hand, comes from the viewer's evaluation of the artist's skill, style, and integrity. An individual can dislike the values, the sense of life, or the theme of an art work, but can admire the artist's skill or style.

One dominant myth propagates that most great, universal artists (i.e., composers, painters, sculptors, novelists) lived in poverty and were not recognized during their lifetimes. Indeed, that myth serves as a handy excuse for pseudo, dilettante, or government-sponsored "artists" who never put forth the great learning, training, and execution efforts needed to develop the ability to produce works of art saleable in free markets.

With few exceptions, most universally enduring artists throughout history were fully recognized during their lifetimes, often early in their careers. Most great, objectively creative artists collected and enjoyed their earned financial and emotional rewards throughout much of their professional lives. Their work was objectively valuable and recognized as such, making their products highly marketable not only in their lifetimes but through-out the ages. Furthermore, the objective value of an artist's work is almost always in direct proportion to the rational thought and effort that artist put into developing and executing his skill. ...Success as the result of being naturally gifted or of being lucky is a myth promoted by envious mystics, neocheaters, and other losers.

Still another myth about art is that if a person dislikes a work of art, then the person does not understand the work. In most cases, if a person does not like or enjoy a work of art, the work is either (1) poorly executed or (2) contradicts that person's inner values.

And a final misconception is that poetry is an art form that enhances love and the quality of one's life. Poetry is generally an invalid art form that can be destructive to romantic love, prosperity, and long-range happiness [Re: Concept 136, Neo-Tech Reference Encyclopedia; also see Neo-Tech Advantage 104 in this volume].

As a concluding note: Since art can reflect powerfully emotional values to the beholder, art can be loved, appreciated, and enjoyed for those values. The art work itself, however, is an extension of the artist and thus can never be spiritually possessed or owned by anyone else, even though the physical ownership and copyrights can be transferred or sold.

Neo-Tech Advantage #35
VALUE OF EMOTIONS

Emotions and feelings are among a person's most valuable assets. All pleasure and happiness are experienced through emotions. *And the final moral purpose of all human life is rational happiness.* Moreover, negative emotions are reliable warning signals that a person is acting mystically or contrary to one's nature, well-being, and happiness.

Emotions deliver the ultimate human rewards and penalties. Such emotions depend on the life a person chooses to create and live. A person's emotional content will be either happy or unhappy, depending on the extent which that person has rejected or accepted mysticism. Rejecting mysticism means accepting sole responsibility for understanding and dealing honestly with reality. A person must reject mysticism to effectively perceive and integrate reality — to effectively solve problems of growth and develop the competence needed to earn prosperity, power, and love. That, in turn, delivers the self-esteem and emotional content needed to experience abiding well-being, psychuous pleasures, and romantic love. ...Everyone controls his or her wide-range emotions (i.e., being fundamentally happy or unhappy) through one's constant, volitional choice to be honest or dishonest — to act through business-like thinking or through mystical thinking.

Human pleasures and happiness are experienced by sensory and emotional means. To fully experience pleasure and happiness, a person must develop an integrated awareness of emotions along with a mystic-free, guiltless acceptance of those emotions. But first, a person must solidly establish the psychological, philosophical, and productivity positions to provide the self-esteem necessary for romantic love and psychuous pleasures. Then that person must reject mystical guilt to fully experience his or her earned emotions of happiness, pleasure, love.

Happiness, pleasure, and love can be experienced only through emotions. To the extent that a person represses emotions[1] is the extent that the person denies that part of reality needed to experience earned pleasures and happiness — which is the moral purpose of human life.

The human organism must experience emotions in order to psychologically live. If a person continually diminishes self-awareness or represses emotions, that person will steadily lessen his or her capacity to feel emotions. To compensate for that deadening of feelings (thus a deadening of life), that person must take increasingly stronger measures to feel something until the only feeling left to feel is pain. But that person must feel something, so he or she strives to feel pain. And the easiest, quickest route to feel pain is through destructive actions rationalized through mysticism.

Also, as a person diminishes his or her awareness and integration capacities, the initiation of longer range, positive actions becomes increasingly difficult. At the same time, that person increasingly succumbs to mysticism in selecting more and more destructive actions in order to feel something. Destructive actions taken to feel something include manipulating others,

---

[1]Repression of emotions is the attempt to deny emotions. Such repression is harmful and entirely different from the suppression of emotions, which can be a valuable, necessary process. Suppression of emotions is an act of discipline in consciously putting aside emotions to experience them later at a more appropriate time or in a more controlled manner. In suppressing an emotion, one is not denying the emotion and remains fully aware of it. Suppression is an important tool for preventing destructive, mystical reactions in oneself.

initiating force (political or criminal) to control or plunder others, using drugs or alcohol, promiscuity, injurious masochism or sadism, vandalism, thrill killings, mass murder, waging war, genocide.

Neo-Tech Advantage #36
EMOTIONS AND REALITY

Emotions are a real part of every person and, therefore, are a part of reality. To know and deal with undistorted reality, a person must first know one's self, which includes knowing one's own emotions. A person must learn to be aware of feelings in order to prevent destructive emotional reactions. A person must also know one's own emotions in order to effectively share them in a love relationship. For, the pleasure and happiness of a romantic-love relationship is measured by emotional closeness.

Neo-Tech Advantage #37
CHRISTIAN CONDEMNATION OF EMOTIONS

Emotions are not subject to condemnation, guilt, or right or wrong judgments...only *actions* are right or wrong.[1] Next to the mystical concept of original sin, perhaps the most pervasively damaging, unjust concept projected by the Christian ethic is the moral judgment of emotions. Especially malevolent and harmful are the condemnations of emotions such as found in the Sermon on the Mount: "But I say unto you, that whosoever looketh on a woman to lust after her, hath committed adultery with her already in his heart." By condemning human emotions, Christian neocheaters discovered an effective tool to condemn everyone...to make everyone guilty, keeping them more controllable for usurping power and values. Since everyone by nature possesses a full range of automatic feelings or emotions that cannot be directly controlled, shut off or stopped, nearly everyone is victimized by Christian-style "sin" and "guilt".

---

[1]An individual, however, is always responsible for his or her actions. Even if the action is an accident or honest error, one remains responsible for every action. Thus, by nature, one must eventually pay for errors, even accidental or innocent ones. Most innocent errors, however, do not carry the destructive, long-range consequences of uncorrected volitional or dishonest errors.

While everyone innocently experiences negative, irrational emotions, no one ever has to act on such emotions. And since only human *actions* are subject to choice, only human *actions* (not emotions) are subject to moral judgment.

Neo-Tech Advantage #38
FEAR OF EMOTIONS

Many innocent people repress emotions because of false guilt. In doing so, they never can know themselves. Once the following two facts are realized, one can eliminate fear or guilt about one's own emotions:

1. Immediate emotions are beyond a person's direct control. Thus, emotions are not subject to moral judgment or condemnation and should never be associated with guilt. Only volitional actions can be wrong, condemned, or associated with guilt.

2. Emotions never have to be acted upon. Thus a person never needs to fear irrational emotions. A person can feel hatred toward anyone, even the desire for mayhem and murder — a person can *feel any emotion*, rational or irrational, without being guilty of anything. A person becomes guilty only if he or she chooses to act on irrational emotions to harm others.

Neo-Tech Advantage #39
EMOTIONS OF FEAR
AND THE VALUE OF FEARLESSNESS

Objective fear is a valuable protection mechanism. By contrast, irrational fear is destructive whenever it stops a person from taking needed actions. Fortunately, the paralyzing effects of irrational fear can be overcome with direct, conscious effort. For example, if a person takes a rational action that he or she fears (if no actual danger exists), that fear will dissipate. Irrational fears can cause inaction that prevents deserving, productive people from developing prosperity and happiness. A fearlessness to live is perhaps the most financially and emotionally rewarding character trait that an honest, productive person can develop.

"Far better it is to dare mighty things, to win glorious triumphs, even though checkered by failure, than to rank with those poor spirits who neither enjoy much nor suffer much, because they live in the gray twilight that knows not victory nor defeat."

— **Theodore Roosevelt**[1]

Neo-Tech Advantage #40
FEAR OF REJECTION AND RISK TAKING

Fear of being hurt or rejected prevents the development of many romantic-love relationships. That fear keeps a person defensive which, in turn, prevents emotional openness with his or her partner. And that openness is necessary for developing romantic love and psychuous pleasures.

The achievement of romantic love involves a willingness to take risks. Moreover, the fear of being hurt by being open is unfounded. To the contrary, a person is always hurt by faking or concealing emotions from one's self or a loved one. Denial of feelings traps a person into emotionally repressive situations that diminish the potential for love and happiness. Being emotionally honest and open is the safest, happiest way to live. ...Being emotionally open, however, does not mean gratuitously projecting emotions onto others or blaming one's emotional or personal problems on others. ...Blaming others for one's personal or emotional problems is an irrational, unfair, and mystical act that keeps a person from solving his or her own problems.

Consistently acting on rational premises and being loyal to honesty builds confidence in a person's own rectitude and worth.

---

[1]The anomaly of a worthwhile quote from a politician is explainable by realizing that "mighty things" and "glorious triumphs" in the minds of value-destroying politicians can mean something entirely different from "mighty things" and "glorious triumphs" in the minds of value-creating business people. For example, being a "great" and powerful politician or dictator via force and manipulation is quite different than being a great and creative artist or industrialist via honest, productive effort and earned ability.

Rationality and honesty, in turn, help remove the fear that prevents people from venturing into new growth areas, including romantic love. Rationality, fairness, and honesty act as powerful protectors when venturing into unexplored areas, ranging from business to love relationships.

Neo-Tech Advantage #41
INDEPENDENT JUDGMENT VS.
OPINIONS OF OTHERS

Acting on what others think rather than on one's own thinking not only undermines integrity and judgment, but diminishes self-esteem. That, in turn, gradually represses the best qualities within a person. In a free or semi-free society, everyone has the basic choice of acting on his or her independent judgment versus acting on the basis of what other people think, do, or say. In a totalitarian society, however, no such choice exists. The authorities terrorize everyone by coercion, force, and threats into acting on the basis of what some "authority" thinks or wishes (e.g., the dictator). By preventing people from acting on their own judgments, totalitarian governments deprive individuals of their natural survival mechanisms by undermining the independent use of their minds. Being unwilling or unable to act on one's own judgment, the individual is controllable by others — by the whims, wishes, and demands of neocheating "authorities".

Neo-Tech Advantage #42
CASUAL VS. SERIOUS SEX

Psychuous sex is always linked to values...to an exchange of rational values between partners. A continuous exchange of values that enhances personal worth and psychological visibility is the basis of psychuous pleasures and romantic-love. But, sex without serious values (i.e., casual sex) cannot deliver psychuous pleasures and is eventually self-destructive.

The difference between serious and casual sex is not always obvious on the surface. But the difference always appears at the base of every relationship. While the actual sexual activity of serious sex can and often does have interludes of lightness and fun, the meaning behind every act is serious and important. But sex on a nonserious, unimportant, or casual basis done only for "fun" is a diminishing experience that erodes self-esteem and sexual competence. On the other hand, a serious sexual affair will always produce growth and values so long as the relationship is based on mutual values, honesty, and respect. In a value-based sexual relationship, psychuous pleasures are linked to a mutual reflection of each partner's personal values and worth.

Unlike casual sexual relationships, serious relationships have no bounds or limits to personal values that can be exchanged. The value of a serious romantic relationship can grow so great that a person would give, if necessary, all of one's possessions, even one's own life, to protect his or her romantic-love partner.

Neo-Tech Advantage #43
MULTIPLE PARTNERS, VALUE SYSTEMS, AND INDIVIDUAL DIFFERENCES

Few people if any can benefit from a multi-partner relationship not only because of the painful, emotional conflicts but because of the time and effort inherently required to develop a valuable, romantic-love relationship with just one partner. Furthermore, the amount of time required to develop valuable multi-partner relationships could deprive an individual of the time needed to fully develop crucial areas of life such as a rewarding career, productive work, business. [Re: Concept 41 and 42, Neo-Tech Reference Encyclopedia]

The biggest negative of multi-partner relationships evolves from the nature of psychuous sex: Romantic love works best when structured around long-term, monogamous relationships. Why? Because continuous efforts and experiences with an exclusive partner deliver the most intimacy, growth, and values. Thus, the most erotically exciting and sexually satisfying experiences by nature evolve from long-term, monogamous/ psychuous relations. ...And today, the rise of incurable herpes and deadly AIDS adds a new dimension to the advantages of monogamous, romantic-love relationships.

* * *

All individual values, including sexual values, fall into two categories — (1) nonjudgeable or amoral values that arise from each person's unique personality development, and (2) objectively right or wrong values that arise from a person's volitional

60

character development. Many Neo-Tech/Psychuous concepts deal either directly or indirectly with the second category. Those values are self-determined and reflect a person's view of:

- Self and others.

- Rights of individuals.

- Value of conscious life.

- Work, productivity, creativity, achievement.

- Acquiring knowledge and loyalty to honesty.

- Acquiring personal pleasures and happiness.

Other Neo-Tech/Psychuous concepts deal with the nonjudgmental or amoral values that reflect unique individual preferences such as the:

- Physical and psychological features that a person finds most attractive and stimulating in a love partner.

- Combination of values that deliver the greatest curiosity, excitement, satisfaction.

- Most satisfying or pleasurable styles, methods, techniques.

Each individual has his or her own sexual value system. Such values evolve from subconscious ratings of past experiences, personal preferences, personal desires. Those values can vary widely from person to person. Many sexual values depend on the individual's unique personality and tastes. And those values are not subject to judgments of right and wrong, better and worse, moral and immoral...they merely reflect personal differences.

Contrary to advice in most books on sex and marriage, an important task of every couple working toward romantic love and psychuous pleasure is not to seek compromises between their unique sexual values, but to openly become aware of each other's sexual values. Once aware of one's own as well as one's partner's sexual values, the differences can be used to intensify intimacies and pleasures. Those deep intimacies are achieved by satisfying the sexual values of one's partner without compromising one's own sexual values. In that process, each

61

partner becomes increasingly valuable and uniquely irreplaceable to the other. Such relationships become evermore secure as romantic love grows without restrictions or bounds. Divorces in those rational, non-mystical relationships diminish toward zero as values and happiness grow with time and effort. ...All such growing values become like money in the bank — a permanent, growing, emotional bank account that becomes irreplaceable by anyone else.

To gain honest Neo-Tech advantages, one must always be aware of the great physical, intellectual, and psychological differences among individuals. People exhibit strikingly different characteristics in: physical structures, ways of thinking, areas of knowledge, mental capacities, views of life. As a person develops one's character, an unevenness develops in being honest versus being mystical. For example, a person may find that the honest integration of facts is easier in certain areas of life. In other areas, that person surrenders to the "easy-way-out" mystical trap. Such unevenness in honesty is caused by a person's past and present choices and actions. That volitional behavior, in turn, determines the rate of *personal evolvement* and the quality of *character development*.

A major mistake that many people make is to expect other people to be like them. People are *not* alike. Furthermore, most individual differences are *not* subject to right or wrong judgments. Amoral differences are merely differences — not right or wrong entities. Another error is the belief that a person can change the basic nature of another person. Basic changes occur only from within the individual's own self. No one else can force or pressure such changes.

Neo-Tech Advantage #44
RELATIONSHIP ERRORS

Casual, nonintimate, or fun-only sex does not always start from a neurotic base. Casual sex may begin as an immature sexual view during adolescence. Or casual sex may begin as a notion to experiment with "new" sex in order to broaden one's sexual experiences or to diminish sexual inhibitions and taboos. Indeed, casual sex, swinging sex, orgy sex may accomplish those ends. But, the eventual cost of casual sex, fun-only, or exploitive

62

sex to one's self-esteem is high. One experiences such sex only with grave consequences to his or her self-esteem, sexuality, and happiness. By contrast, one experiences a limitless broadening of erotic sexual experiences with enhanced self-esteem through the Neo-Tech/Psychuous concepts.

Human beings are always capable of correcting errors. The harm caused by past, casual-sexual experiences can be reversed by restructuring sexual standards around the consistent, value-oriented foundation of Psychuous Sex.

Neo-Tech Advantage #45
ACHIEVING PSYCHUOUS PLEASURES

By defaulting on the basic human responsibility of achieving personal happiness and psychuous pleasures, a person lets his or her future turn downward toward death. Through that default, life and time slip away, increasingly unrewarded and unfulfilled. By that default, the exciting potential for life (which everyone senses at least some time during his or her life...usually in early childhood) will fade, never to be experienced again — unless revived by Neo-Tech.

Such defaults are unnecessary, contrary to human nature, and rooted in the mysticism continually promoted by neocheaters. By contrast, the experiencing of an exciting, value-generating life and the achievement of prosperity, power, and psychuous pleasures are accomplished through self-responsibility — through a loyalty to rational efforts and honesty [Re: Neo-Tech Reference Encyclopedia].

A value-oriented, romantic relationship offers limitless pleasures ranging from joy and spontaneous fun[1] to erotic thrills, adventure, psychuous pleasures, and profound happiness. Equally important, such romantic relationships can greatly enhance each partner's productivity, values, and prosperity.

Psychuous pleasures can always grow, even during crisis or turmoil. Psychuous sex lets a person physically confirm the value of his or her life, especially during difficult or crisis periods. Psychuous sex allows a person to be acutely aware of his or her worth, pleasures, and happiness. But psychuous pleasures go far

---

[1]Joyful, childlike spontaneous fun is entirely different than the contrived, boring, mechanical "fun" of fun-only sexual relationships.

beyond sexual intercourse. In fact, sexual intercourse itself plays only a small (but crucial) role in psychuous pleasure, which is integrated with all aspects of conscious life.

Romantic love and psychuous pleasures add so much to human happiness that to settle for something as unchallenging and limited as casual, fun-only sex is to treat one's self poorly indeed. Limiting the potential for pleasure to such a narrow, shallow range of experiences undermines a person's entire life.

Neo-Tech Advantage #46
END OF A GOOD RELATIONSHIP
VOLUNTARY AND INVOLUNTARY

A serious romantic relationship can last and grow forever. But if growth stops and cannot be revived, the relationship should end before the growth potential of either partner diminishes. If a good relationship does end, however, each partner can and should retain the values and benefits of all past growth.

Voluntary termination of a psychuous relationship requires a carefully considered, mutually reasoned decision to avoid the tragic mistake of terminating a good relationship unnecessarily. A decision to terminate should include a thoughtful plan to avoid harm to either partner while preserving the growth and values already achieved.

Involuntary termination of a good relationship through death is final. Still, the living partner must continue growing. Involuntary termination of a good relationship can also be initiated through errors of one or both partners. Each partner must fight to save a good relationship from being destroyed by errors. Each must identify those errors and reject destructive mysticism that always seeks to destroy values by creating problems where none exist.

When ending a previously good relationship, no matter how much pain or hurt is involved, great efforts should be made to leave one's partner in a positive, uplifted condition. Such efforts deliver long-term benefits to both partners. Such efforts preserve past growth and values. Such efforts leave both in freer, guiltless positions from which to seek a new relationship and happiness.

But terminating a hopelessly destructive relationship is quite different. Just frankly stating the necessity to end the relationship and then walking away from it completely and forever is often the healthiest, most honest, and least painful method for everyone. A complete and decisive physical and emotional break leaves both partners freer to reestablish separate lives more quickly for new growth and renewed happiness.

Whenever love dies, reasons always exist. But the reasons are not always obvious. A person can better prepare for a future relationship by identifying the reasons for failure through high-effort, honest introspection.

Neo-Tech Advantage #47
LOYALTY TO HONESTY
THE WAY TO HANDLE PROBLEMS

Honesty is not automatic. It always requires explicit, conscious effort. Being honest is hard work...very hard work. If, in difficult emotional situations, one is not aware of the concentrated effort required to be honest, that person is probably not being fully honest. At that point, he or she can easily plug into effortless mysticism. For with mysticism, a person can automatically rationalize out-of-context scenarios to avoid the effort required to understand reality and solve one's own problems.

Developing the skills for being honest is neither automatic nor easy. Honesty requires high-effort concentration, discipline, and awareness. Because of the constant effort required to be honest, many people default to mysticism and thus lose the essential tool for solving problems — the tool for achieving prosperity, power, and happiness. That tool is honesty. ...Many people *never* grasp or experience integrated honesty.

Fully integrated honesty evolves from the efforts required to be consistently honest. By contrast, mystical dishonesty evolves from self-deceptions and defaults — from a self-chosen laziness that relegates honesty to a low priority, especially when feelings are involved. ...With mysticism, honesty becomes arbitrary.

A commitment to honesty with one's romantic-love partner is essential for achieving psychuous pleasures. In an open relationship, each partner is free to follow those actions self-judged best for his or her own rational well-being. Each must also be equally free to make and correct his or her own errors. Both must strive to meet their individual needs for growth. Both must accept the fact that neither has any physical or psychological ownership over the other. With the freedom and self-responsibility to guide one's own life, each partner develops an ever-growing accumulation of strengths. Those new strengths allow each to continually feed fresh love and enriching values to the other.

With each partner feeding new strength and values into the relationship, each benefits from the other's unique experiences. With such constant values coming from free and independent sources, the excitement between partners can grow continuously, often by large leaps, toward increased psychuous pleasures and abiding happiness. With this never-ending, spiraling growth, each partner becomes increasingly valuable to the other. Thus, fewer and fewer circumstances could threaten or replace such a romantic-love relationship.

Like money in the bank, newly added values accumulate with interest. And with time, the strength of such value-built relationships becomes so great that no outside force, no matter how valuable or appealing, could compete. ...Such self-built continually added strengths and competitive values offer the only genuine security for any romantic-love relationship.

By contrast, sexual affairs hidden from one's love partner are deceptive and, therefore, dishonest and destructive. Moreover, such affairs are usually too restricted by their secrecy to deliver continuously growing values. ...Honesty and rationality are the foundations of psychuous pleasures and romantic love.

Honest disputes without physical aggression or psychological injury can be valuable. Verbal disputes can cut through emotional blocks to release repressed feelings and foster communication. But undisciplined let-it-all-hang-out anger and negativity are immature, unhelpful, destructive forms of mysticism. Also, disputes become destructively dishonest when one or both partners silently save up the "worst" faults or problems of the other in order to use them later as manipulative weapons. ...Saving up faults is a dishonest, immature tactic used to manipulate, damage, or end relationships.

Within a romantic-love relationship, the problems that do arise provide opportunities to discover new strengths and values for richer love and pleasures. Even if certain problems seem unresolvable, they can be mutually understood if discussed honestly. And the more explicitly problems are understood, the more satisfying will be their resolutions. Moreover, with sufficient information and honest efforts, all disagreements can eventually be resolved without compromises by either partner.

An efficient approach for resolving conflicts is to reduce the disputed differences to writing and then find the common premises always revealed by self-honesty [Re: Communication Map in Tables 26a and 26b, Neo-Tech Reference Encyclopedia]. Explicitly breaking down problems into communication maps usually generates happy agreements. Even if a problem cannot be completely resolved, the honest communication will (a) draw each partner closer, and (b) develop greater competence in solving future problems. [Re: Table 26b, Neo-Tech Reference Encyclopedia]

Neo-Tech Advantage #48
GUILTLESS FREEDOM TO BE ONESELF

For a healthy romantic relationship, each partner must grant the other guiltless, free choice to enter any growth relationship (in principle, including sexual) with any person of value. In growing romantic-love relationships, however, the circumstances for an outside, rational *sexual* relationship occurring are essentially nil.

Acceptance or approval by people other than one's romantic-love partner is *not* a requirement for success, happiness, or psychuous pleasures: To achieve psychuous pleasures, a person must be free to be one's own self and choose one's own actions. Trying to be different from one's rational self is a distortion of human nature and contrary to romantic love.

Likewise, a person cannot change another person's nature. For, one's nature can be changed only from within that person, not from without. Of course, a person can develop his or her own character and correct errors as new knowledge is acquired. Such changes are the process of personal growth. And such growth comes through volitional choices to honestly integrate new knowledge.

A person is what he or she is. To pretend to be anything else is to present a false illusion requiring dishonest role playing. A person diminishes any personal relationship to the extent that a false illusion is presented. A person must present himself or herself as "This is me. Take me or leave me as I am." Only from that position can a person proceed with the genuine growth required for romantic love, psychuous pleasures, and abiding happiness.

Accepting a "take me or leave me" position does not mean specific errors should be accepted or uncriticized. A person can and should change erroneous views and destructive traits (such as mysticism and dishonesty) through character development. Furthermore, each partner must be free to constructively point out harmful errors in the other as well as to be open to criticism about one's own self. Moreover, each partner should expect continuous growth in the other. ...But if a person does not accept the nature of his or her partner, the romantic-love relationship will deteriorate.

Two dangers exist in criticizing one's romantic-love partner:

The first danger is that criticism may unintentionally turn into an invalid attack on the partner's basic self. And attacking a partner's basic self can end the relationship. Still, if certain aspects of a partner's basic self are unacceptable, ending the relationship may be the best, most rational action.

The second danger concerning criticism involves *avoiding* valid, specific criticism for fear of causing problems or rejection. Avoiding criticism cuts off important areas of communication necessary for personal growth. Both partners must be free to express themselves to the other: their compliments and criticism, their likes and dislikes. Valid praise and criticism should not be held back, but should be expressed in specifics to avoid insincere flattery or manipulative criticism (i.e., using criticism as a tool to pressure a person).

Allowances must be made for errors. Through misunderstandings or wrong premises, one partner may erroneously criticize the other. And to the degree erroneous criticism occurs, the relationship will be diminished until the error is corrected.

Most people have large capacities for self-improvement and correcting errors, especially in an atmosphere of benevolent freedom. Having the guiltless freedom to make errors and subsequently being able to correct those errors lets each partner develop into his or her best possible self with the most values to offer the other partner.

Mistakes and errors need not do permanent damage. When faced and dealt with, most errors become self-revealing solutions that create new areas of strength, knowledge, and growth. ...Guiltless freedom is essential for converting one's errors and problems into assets.

Neo-Tech Advantage #49
THE INJUSTICE OF JEALOUSY
GT JEALOUSY VS. BT JEALOUSY

Neo-Tech identifies two types of sexual jealousy: *good-thought* (GT) and *bad-thought* (BT).[1] Both types are based on the erroneous assumption that one has a claim on his or her love-partner's life, especially that person's sex life.[2] The feelings of

[1]Although sexual jealousy is common and perhaps exists to some degree in most people, such jealousy is neither natural nor psychologically healthy. Sexual jealousy often stems from insecurity or self-esteem problems. Sexual jealousy is not synonymous with the valid desire for sexual privacy and romantic exclusivity experienced in most value-oriented, love relationships. ...By contrast, nonsexual jealousy (NS) differs from sexual jealousy (GT or BT types). NS jealousy involves relatively harmless, natural desires for values possessed by others. Often NS jealousy is erroneously called "envy". Envy is not a desire to possess values of others, but is a malevolent desire to *destroy* values earned by others. Envy is rooted in the fear of exposing one's own inadequacy, incompetence, impotence. Productive people can experience harmless NS jealousy, while nonproductive people often experience destructive envy [Re: Concepts 133 and 134, Neo-Tech Reference Encyclopedia].
Note: No value judgment is or can be made on emotions alone. Only the choice to react rationally or irrationally to an emotion can be judged good or bad. The above judgments are based on jealous reactions, not jealous emotions. The choice to act rationally in avoiding a jealous reaction will help dissipate that harmful emotion. But the harmful, irrational choice to react jealously always feeds and amplifies that emotion.

[2]No one can ever really own another person's life, including that person's sex life. Every individual exclusively owns each and every segment of his or her own life. In relationships, people volitionally share, not own, various aspects or segments of each other's lives. In a romantic-love relationship, by nature, many more life experiences are intimately shared and integrated than in other types of human relationships. Also, while certain segments of a person's life can be temporarily rented or hired as in a voluntary employer-employee relationship, no part of a person's life can be actually owned by anyone else.

69

jealousy arise when the unreal presumption of possessing one's partner seems challenged. GT jealousy is characterized by the retention of basically *good thoughts* about one's partner, even when pain or anger is generated. Most people can experience various degrees of GT jealousy about their love partners. GT jealousy does not always mean the jealous-reacting partner is insecure or possessive, especially if the jealousy is experienced only as a passing feeling. GT jealousy, even if severely painful, rarely inflicts deep or permanent damage on either partner or the relationship.

Likewise, GT jealousy seldom cuts deeply into the emotions because positive feelings about one's partner dominate the underlying emotions.

BT jealousy, on the other hand, is a destructive, mystical reaction that conjures up, often out of nothing, unjust *bad thoughts* about one's partner. Those bad thoughts are often well concealed, but insidiously destructive to the emotions of both partners. In contrast to GT jealousy in which good thoughts are retained about one's partner, BT or bad-thought jealousy prevents the jealous partner from knowing, accepting, remembering, or believing the values in the victim partner. Instead, unreal bitterness, cynicism, or malevolence against the victim partner is conjured up by BT jealousy.

Such negative illusions are usually rooted in past experiences not even related to the victim partner. The victim partner usually senses a "bad-person" feedback from the BT jealous person. That causes the victim to respond with increasing puzzlement or astonishment followed by anger, dislike, and a sense of injustice. Those negative emotions usually keep building until they eventually outweigh all the good feelings and values between the partners. At that point, love and the relationship die.

The Neo-Tech/Psychuous Concepts identify and can overcome both types of jealousy, especially the GT type. BT jealousy is more difficult to overcome because the cause is a cancerous mysticism that becomes deeply rooted in one's emotions. Cognitive-based psychotherapy[1] may help overcome BT jealousy

---

[1]Effective cognitive psychotherapy is objectively oriented around the cognitive nature of human beings (rather than mystically oriented around

(footnote continued on next page)

and its destructive effects. But the only certain cure is to use mystic-breaking, integrated honesty to self-command *all* actions. Without that integrated honesty, one will continue reacting destructively to the emotions of jealousy.

The bad thoughts of BT jealousy along with its hostile, immature possessiveness and obligatory demands become increasingly unreal, unfair, and burdensome to the victim partner. Such jealousy will eventually destroy any love relationship no matter how strong were the original love and values. BT jealousy is an unfair, hostile foisting of one's own personal

---

(footnote continued from previous page)

behavioral and social natures). To be effective, a therapist must understand the relationships between reason and emotions, between self-esteem and mental health, between mysticism and mental illness. Unfortunately, few psychologists or psychiatrists are oriented around objective standards, even fewer work with or even understand the relationship between self-esteem and mental health. And only a minute fraction, if any, in the profession understand mysticism as the prime disease of the human mind and the only disease of human consciousness.

That situation is why most psychiatrists and psychologists have essentially zero "cure" records. Most such therapists are ineffective or harmful in helping their patients find real, long-range solutions to their problems. Ineffective therapy not only costs the patient much time and money, but increases the long-range damage by camouflaging the problem under illusions or feelings of relief, well-being, improvement, or cure. Those illusions are like drugs: they give temporary feelings of euphoria on which the patient becomes increasingly dependent. But the problems always reemerge in other forms, often in forms more destructive than previously experienced.

To benefit from therapy, the patient must first determine the therapist's honesty, integrity, and criterion for mental health. If, on questioning, the therapist's treatment is not clearly based on the biological nature of man and a criterion of self-esteem, the patient should seek another therapist. A wrong or an incompetent therapist can cost a patient's long-range happiness, even his or her life. Also, the need for ever using psychotherapy, especially in overcoming internal mysticism, is questioned in Neo-Tech Advantage #73 entitled, "The Nature of Emotions".

In fact, most neuroses are self-chosen indulgences in mysticism for which therapy is of little value. Usually, only a self-chosen maturity and honesty to break that mystical indulgence (cause) will end the symptomatic neurosis (effect).

problems or inadequacies onto the victim partner. The mounting obligatory demands and hostile possessiveness of BT jealousy destroys a love relationship by penalizing the victim partner for the very values he or she offers. In fact, the more values offered, the greater are the penalties — the greater are the possessive attacks and obligatory demands. Indeed, BT jealousy, immature possessiveness, and obligatory demands not only rest on mystically unreal premises, but are always unjust since the victim is penalized to the extent he or she offers values to the jealous partner.

The jealous partner ignores the free-choice position necessary to build a healthy, permanent romantic-love relationship. The jealous partner accepts the false idea that outside relationships or associations are by nature threatening [Re: Concept 63, Neo-Tech Reference Encyclopedia]. Furthermore, the jealous partner erroneously judges his or her partner in terms of unrelated, outside experiences and relationships rather than in terms of their own relationship [Re: Concept 63, Neo-Tech Reference Encyclopedia].

Through mysticism, jealousy destroys values by focusing on what is *not* given or what is not available...while ignoring, abusing, tearing down, or destroying what is given or is available. Through Neo-Tech, the non-mystic appreciates and focuses on what values are given or are available and then builds from that position — and only from that position.

"Testing" is simply another form of jealousy in which one partner translates his or her insecurity into testing the victim partner for proof of love or fidelity. Such "testing" is unfair, immature, and continually escalates until the values of a relationship are destroyed.

Neo-Tech Advantage #50
THE POISON CORE OF JEALOUSY

BT jealousy will eventually destroy even the deepest love relationships. Jealousy gradually poisons the friendship aspects of love. Once that friendship is gone, no link remains to hold together the nonsexual aspects of the relationship.

Within the person projecting bad-thought jealousy, a bitter core of poisonous emotions develops (although often initially hidden). That core increasingly releases bad feelings toward the victim partner which, in turn, unfairly diminishes the victim's freedom and happiness. Recognizing the presence of that poison core is the first step in keeping BT jealousy from destroying a relationship. But once that core is formed, freeing oneself from its destructive effects is difficult.

The problem of BT jealousy cannot be wished away. For the poison core usually develops from mystical defaults deep within the jealous partner's subconscious [Re: Table 27, Neo-Tech Reference Encyclopedia]. Unless identified and removed, that poison core will dissolve the pleasure, happiness, and love in any romantic relationship.

Such a poison core generates hostile actions that are often subtle and unrecognized at first. But that jealous partner increasingly takes unjust advantage of the victim partner's innocence, values, love, and goodwill. Such injustice constantly wounds the victim partner and will eventually destroy all love and friendship. Unlike the nonjealous lover who usually experiences pain whenever his loved one is in pain, the BT jealous lover will often gain a satisfying sense of security on being able to inflict pain on the victim partner. That malevolence of BT jealousy eventually negates any value of the relationship.

A person should avoid listening to false accusations or unjust innuendos leveled against oneself or others by a jealous, envious, or gossipy person. Even though the conscious mind can reject known false charges, such accusations still enter nonanalytical pockets of the subconscious mind. That, in turn, causes subsequent emotions to automatically reflect negative feelings toward oneself or the person being falsely accused. A person is helpless in avoiding those unjust, harmful, subconscious reactions. Likewise, a person is essentially powerless to avoid the guilt or bad feelings resulting from false implications coming from a BT jealous partner. As long as that relationship continues, the jealous partner can increasingly inflict psychic damage within the victim's subconscious. The victim partner suffers damage proportional to his or her exposure to the poison core of a BT jealous partner. Usually the only release from that damage is for the victim partner to terminate that harmful relationship.

By contrast, a mystic-free Neo-Tech partner will ask: "Do not judge me on your feelings, wishes, imagination, or what others say. Judge me by what you know about my character, deeds, and actions. And I will always grant you the same."

Neo-Tech Advantage #51
UNNECESSARY AGING

As people grow older, their views of life often grow increasingly negative. Their hopes and dreams often turn into disillusions. On aging, such people gradually lose the capacity to experience the joy inherent in life. Their anticipation of life continually diminishes as their used-up, shrinking futures become evident and the inevitability of death draws closer. ...But Neo-Tech reverses that dying process by allowing life and happiness to grow with age and experience.[1]

Age is no factor in achieving psychuous pleasures, except for the possible lack-of-knowledge limitations of adolescent sex [Re: Concept 80, Neo-Tech Reference Encyclopedia]. Moreover, psychuous pleasures can continually increase with age as one widens his or her values, knowledge, and experience. In building psychuous pleasures, a person's psychological growth can far outweigh so-called physical aging effects. Emotional and physical pleasures as well as prosperity and happiness can increase indefinitely for any honest, productive individual applying Neo-Tech knowledge.

For most people, both sexual and nonsexual pleasures unnecessarily diminish with age. Negative philosophical and psychological changes occur as their futures fade and their spans of remaining years shrink. They despair and become sour with age while increasingly surrendering to the mystics' come-to-God or waiting-for-death attitudes. They surrender to the altruistic myth that older people should sacrifice themselves, their careers, their lives to "make room" for youth. With that surrender, a person's happiness fades.

---

[1]In the upsidedown, mystical death-oriented world, increasing age becomes an increasing liability on each individual. In that mystical world, "It is better to be young than old". But in the Neo-Tech life-oriented world, increasing age becomes an increasing asset of growth, knowledge, experience, especially as mystic-free businesses develop commercial, non-aging biological immortality.

Despite what many physicians erroneously advise,[1] no mystic-free, productive person has to decline in physical, mental, or sexual activity with age. All mystic-free, productive people can experience increasing happiness and quality of life with age caused by increasing knowledge, growth, and experience: By applying the Neo-Tech/Psychuous concepts, one can not only avoid the unnecessary, mystical decline toward death, but can continually elevate his or her quality of life and psychuous growth through increasing knowledge and experience.

Sex never renews itself spontaneously. Left unattended, sex gradually diminishes in both quality and value. But with Neo-Tech, the quality and value of sex is continuously renewed and expanded by constantly investing conscious thought and effort into further developing personal values and earned power. The Neo-Tech/Psychuous concepts allow never-aging growth on all levels of conscious human life (i.e., on physiological, psychological, and philosophical levels). ...In a Neo-Tech civilization, one need not age, lose values...or die.

Neo-Tech Advantage #52
PARENTS AS SCAPEGOATS

Most people dutifully profess love toward their children and parents. But often the past and present psychological differences, irrationalities, conflicts, demands, and "duties" make genuine love and enjoyment between parents and their children impossible. An important step toward emotional growth is to realize that no one has a duty to love anyone, not even parents, children, husband, wife.

Genuine love occurs only voluntarily, through a mutual exchange of objective and emotional values. Genuine love between parents and children can and does occur in those relationships in which objective values grow and are exchanged. Occasionally, parents may be partially responsible for some

---

[1]Many physicians are incompetent, especially in the area of sex and aging. But most make themselves appear as all-knowing and infallible to their patients. Following the advice of an incompetent physician can not only damage a patient's physical well-being, but can cost the patient's happiness and life. Health, well-being, and happiness are not the responsibilities of physicians, but are the prime self-responsibilities of each individual.

problems experienced by certain adolescents and young adults. Too often, however, parents are blamed for their grown children's faults, defaults, sexual shortcomings, and other problems for which those grown children themselves are responsible. Blaming parents only hides or avoids the self-responsibilities and efforts needed to correct one's own personal problems.

Major problems between parents and children often develop from the parents' failure to respect their own children: their failure to treat children as human beings with individual rights. Parents, for example, commonly initiate force and physically assault their children under the euphemisms of spankings, protection, discipline. [Re: Concept 114, Neo-Tech Reference Encyclopedia.] If children are not granted respect, they may never develop respect for themselves, for their parents, or for values. Such children often develop into tomorrow's mystics and neocheaters. They then survive by usurping their living as politicians, trouble-making lawyers, destructive bureaucrats, criminals, theologians, media journalists, or educators who hold little or no respect for honesty.

By contrast, the two most valuable gifts parents can give their children are (1) respect as conscious beings with individual rights, and (2) environments that promote honesty, assertive effort, integrity, independence, and the skill to perceive reality accurately.

Neo-Tech Advantage #53
ADOLESCENT, PREMARITAL, AND NONMARITAL LOVE

Sexual feelings begin long before puberty. As noted by Havelock Ellis, Freud, and Kinsey, very young children and even babies two and three months old have sexual experiences (both through self-stimulation and through handling, caring, and fondling by parents). Valid sensuous/sexual pleasures can be experienced between child and parent, especially between mother and child during nursing or nude cuddling. While such pleasures are loving, healthy, and beneficial, those pleasurable values for both the child and parent are often inhibited by incest fears and taboos.

Adolescent sex never need be approached with inhibition or forbiddance. But few adolescents have sufficient emotional development, knowledge, or desire for deep emotional involvements and serious mutual commitments with sexual partners. For adolescents and adults alike, sexual involvement should always be judged from a good-for-me/bad-for-me standard. Serious sexual experiences that deliver growth and happiness through exchanges of objective values are usually good for everyone involved, regardless of age. But sexual relations that are casual, not grounded in objective values, or neurotically based are bad for everyone, regardless of age. For casual sexual relationships undermine self-esteem and psychuous pleasures.

Adolescents having sexual relationships before they are able or desire to involve themselves in serious, value-exchanging relationships will undermine their future capacity for romantic love. The loss of self-esteem resulting from casually giving away one's personal self militates against psychuous pleasures, romantic love, and long-range happiness. For, casual or manipulative sex undercuts self-esteem. But, by understanding the concepts of psychuous sex, one can identify and correct past sexual errors while creating conditions for psychuous pleasures.

Marriage itself is no criterion to commence sexual relations. In fact, avoiding sex until marriage would usually be irrational and potentially harmful to future happiness. In any romantic-love relationship, satisfactory sex is required for full emotional intimacy and growth. In addition to achieving emotional growth, value-oriented premarital sex helps eliminate harmful anxieties for sex performance often experienced in virginal marriages. That release from sexual anxieties lets each partner concentrate on those nonsexual aspects required for long-lasting, value-producing, romantic relationships.

Nonmarital sexual relations can provide a full range of sexual values and psychuous pleasures. [Re: Concept 68, Neo-Tech Reference Encyclopedia.] Serious nonmarital sexual affairs offer important life-lifting values while avoiding the sacrifice of happiness that dominates closed marriages based on duty and sacrifice rather than honesty and values. Moreover, nonmarital sexual relationships generally allow more time and freedom for self-development and career advancement, which in turn, provides increasing values, happiness, and strength to the relationship.

77

Most valid, growing romantic-love relationships can and do lead to marriage[1], usually a flourishing, lasting marriage.

Neo-Tech Advantage #54
SEDUCTION TECHNIQUES:
CASUAL, SERIOUS, MUTUAL

The first known sex manual was written about 2 B.C. by a Roman named Ovid. His manual stressed seduction techniques for *casual sex*. In addition, the manual aggressively promoted the Don Juan and "Playboy" fun views of sex while teaching various role-playing games and manipulative techniques for the seduction of women.

The Don Juan and "Playboy" approaches to sex use hypnosis,[2] manipulations of sex partners, and pragmatic dishonesty of professing "sincerity", "seriousness", and "love" when strategically advantageous for conquest. But most modern-day Don Juans can only feign lust while actually being terrified of their own sexual inadequacies. In fact, most macho Don Juans have never experienced psychological orgasms and remain psychosexual virgins all their lives — they never develop a capacity for delivering or receiving psychuous pleasures. More simply, macho men are males who have never sexually matured or grown up. [Re: concept 45, Neo-Tech Reference Encyclopedia]

---

[1]Marriage in that context does not necessarily mean "legal" marriage, but means any serious long-term, romantic-love relationship mutually agreed on by each partner. "Legal" marriage has no bearing on the success or failure of a relationship. The mutual decision for sharing life in a serious, sexual-love relationship is the fundamental entity for building a romantic-love relationship that delivers psychuous pleasures and long-range happiness.

[2]Rapid hypnosis and self-hypnosis techniques can be easily mastered (e.g., see Bibliography Summary Table B-2 in Neo-Tech Reference Encyclopedia for D. Elman's book, "Exploration in Hypnosis", Nash Publishing. Note: Amateur hypnosis can do psychological damage and is not recommended in any form). Indirect, subtle forms of hypnosis are the most important tools in a Don Juan's seduction repertoire. Ironically, a subconscious form of negative-feedback self-hypnosis is the primary mechanism that leads to impotence and frigidity not only for Don Juans, but for almost everyone who dishonestly manipulates sex partners.

Behind every sexual relationship is either a healthy or an unhealthy motive, although often hidden or subconscious. A person should become aware of one's own as well as his or her partner's motive for a sexual relationship. Hiding unhealthy or neurotic motives for a sexual relationship is eventually harmful to both partners.

Negative, after-reaction emotions are natural warning signals from the human nervous system. If a person does something that is "not good for me" physically or psychologically, the nervous system will let that person know with hangover reactions of pain, anxiety, or discomfort. After-the-fact feelings transmitted from the nervous system always signal if past actions were objectively "good for me" or "bad for me".

No matter how irrational or immoral if enacted in reality, fantasies are never immoral, wrong, or harmful when experienced or expressed without external action. For, fantasies are never harmful as long as they remain in the non-action, fantasy stage.

Seductiveness (in the traditional, casual-sex sense) and sensuousness are two different qualities. Traditional seductiveness involves sly trickery to accomplish an end (e.g., sexual seduction) — often for neurotic macho-like purposes (e.g., to bolster a weak self-esteem).

Sensuousness, on the other hand, involves openness and self-expression free of guilt.[1] Sensuousness is a healthy trait, while seductiveness is generally an unhealthy trait. Sensuousness for enhancing personal appeal arises from rational efforts that enhances self-esteem and long-range happiness. Seductiveness

---

[1]Self-expression is reflected in a person's body movements. The combined effects of guiltless relaxation and awareness of bodily pleasures allow the muscular motions to function in a free-movement, animal-like fashion...in the graceful, pleasurable way the human body is meant to move (such as in the gracefully sensuous movements of cats through their free, guiltless nature). A human being is a beautifully graceful animal when the total muscle system is functioning in a guiltlessly relaxed, free-flowing state. That state is reached by using Neo-Tech to expunge the unnecessary guilt, tensions, and problems laid on everyone for 2000 years by the professional mystics and neocheaters.

for manipulating sex partners arises from irrational laziness that undercuts self-esteem and long-range happiness.

But, seduction techniques for *serious sex* can be honest and beneficial. Those techniques are more accurately described as "sensuous projections" and differ from casual seduction techniques that depend on deceit. Sensuous projections are done through both verbal and body communication. The presentation of a person's body and words can be sexually attractive if projected with calculated thought. Those techniques are nonmanipulative and can be mastered through understanding the nature of psychuous sex. Men and women using the Neo-Tech/Psychuous concepts can quickly achieve effective sensuous-projection techniques. The techniques involve integrating clothes, cosmetics, hair with one's body, face, voice, expressions — all combined to project sexual attractiveness. Once acquired, those advantage-gaining techniques are available for life.

A basic right, indeed a self-duty, of every human being is to be sexually attractive. Natural attractiveness is a given that has no moral virtue. But self-made, sexual attractiveness is an admirable, moral virtue that requires continuous thought and effort. Keeping one's self sexually attractive throughout life is a highly rational act of self-responsibility that delivers increased power, prosperity, and romantic love. ...Contrary to the cancer seeds planted by mystics and neocheaters, self-made sexiness does not reflect any lack of values or promiscuity. But, to the contrary, self-made sexiness reflects a respect for values and self.

The primary attraction between two people moving toward rational, romantic-love relationships is their character traits, not their personality traits. Likewise, character development is the chief element in successful romantic-love relationships. And a romantic relationship based on psychuous sex usually develops into a *mutual* seduction process. During that process both partners project mounting sensuous, sexual attractiveness between them. Non-manipulative seductions are innocent projections of sexual attractiveness combined with trust, honesty, and care. That kind of seduction helps both partners plumb rich, personal depths with each other — physically and emotionally.

Neo-Tech Advantage #55
PHYSICAL BEAUTY, ABUSE OF PARTNER, POTENCY LOSS, SEXUAL ROLES

Because of their greater ease in initially attracting sexual partners, individuals with great natural, physical beauty must be cautious of the tempting traps inherent in easily obtainable sexual love:

A few people, because of their stunning natural beauty, are not directly subjected to nature's vigorous sexual competition. To achieve love, sexual pleasures, and happiness, most people recognize early in life that they must become competitively attractive through high-effort development of character and competence. In adulthood, those who grew up accepting the challenge to self-develop can easily outcompete those naturally beautiful people who earlier in life never experienced those pressures to develop. As a result, many people with great natural beauty sadly grow old remaining undeveloped, immature, incompetent, unable to love or be loved.

Achieving psychuous pleasures and romantic love requires the same discipline, thought, and effort for every individual, regardless of innate physical appearances. Likewise, a person must be cautious of involvement with people of exceptional, natural beauty whose personal lives reflect low-effort, low-productivity. Such individuals often let their natural beauty substitute for the long-term effort required to develop characters of competence, self-esteem, and sensuosity required for romantic-love.[1] Thus, underdeveloped, beautiful people are often airheads — often boring, value-draining people who are poor lovers with low self-esteems.

Naturally beautiful people can easily develop "lady-killer" or "man-killer" syndromes in their relationships. Being a seductive "killer" can temporarily boost a weak ego by feeling a power to destroy values and hurt others. But that syndrome leads the

---

[1]Often displaying similar development problems are homosexuals. For, they can easily acquire promiscuous, low-effort sexual affairs without subjecting themselves to the pressures of heterosexual competition. Indeed, heterosexual competitive environments exert healthy pressures needed for developing strong, mature, responsible adults.

perpetrator into life-wasting, destructive relationships. Indeed, a person who mistreats or manipulates his or her love partner usually suffers much more in the long run than the abused partner. For that abused partner will have new chances for love and happiness. But the chronic manipulator loses his or her capacity for love and is left with a future of increasing unhappiness, sexual incompetence, romantic failures, and ultimate loneliness.

Conscious Loss of Potency

Anxieties caused by pressures from "expected" sexual performances cause impotence and frigidity. Impotence also occurs through put-down statements or actions from a partner. Such statements or actions occur either willfully and maliciously or through error and ignorance. But the effects of such damage are often limited to that particular relationship. Thus, once the problem is identified, the victim can promptly abandon that destructive relationship. Decisively rejecting a "castrating" or "frigidizing" partner usually restores full sexual capacity.

Subconscious Loss of Potency

A less obvious, more dangerous pressure subconsciously corrupts the mind. That pressure comes from listening to false or undercutting statements about the sexual performance of one's own self or others. Such statements, no matter how false, involuntarily lodge in the subconscious mind. That happens even when the conscious mind rejects such statements as false [Re: Concept 77, Neo-Tech Reference Encyclopedia]. By that mechanism, a subconscious undermining of a person's sexual potency or character can occur in one of two ways: (1) by innuendo and other indirect forms of communication, or (2) by sexual or character put-down humor. Even if the conscious mind rejects such put downs, the choice to grant credibility by voluntarily listening lets the subconscious mind accept such specious, harmful information as valid.

The nonanalytical, subconscious mind does not evaluate assertions. The subconscious mind does not distinguish honest from dishonest information or serious from humorous situations. Thus, on entering the subconscious, the false information gradually works its undermining damage on the mind and nervous system. For that reason, a person should never propagate or even listen to unjust put downs, attacks, jokes, or gossip concerning the character or sexuality about oneself or anyone else. ...Such is the ear and mouth responsibility of everyone.

A person, however, should always be open and receptive to constructive, factually valid criticism about oneself or others.

Impotence and frigidity also develop when a man tries to oppress a woman, or vice versa. A person's willingness to accept such oppression blocks the possibility for psychuous pleasures. Such mutual acquiescence to oppression leads to impotence and frigidity in both partners.[1] By contrast, a man's psychosexual dominance and a woman's act of *sexual* surrender harmonize with the physical and psychological nature of human beings [Re: Concept 47, Neo-Tech Reference Encyclopedia]. That psychological dominant/surrender interaction permits both partners to achieve the guiltless freedom and emotional closeness necessary for psychuous pleasures.

On the physical level or even on the fantasy level, the dominant/surrender sexual roles can and should be reversed between the man and woman whenever desired. But on a psychological level, those sexual roles cannot be reversed.

Neo-Tech Advantage #56
PSYCHUOUS PLEASURES
[see pages iv-v for definition of Psychuous Pleasures]

Psychuous pleasures and all other beneficial pleasures naturally and forever *integrate* with a person's physical or psychological life — or both. By contrast, mystical pleasures and all other destructive pleasures unnaturally and always *disintegrate* a person's physical or psychological life — or both.

Essentially all growth in government power diminishes psychuous pleasures in everyone by continually undermining and violating individual rights. For, only through exercising individual rights can people achieve psychuous pleasures. And they exercise those rights through their own efforts, free from

---

[1]Chronic mistreatment of a partner almost always involves the tacit willingness of the abused partner. The willingness to mistreat or be mistreated is so profoundly unnatural that psychuous pleasures are impossible in any relationship allowing such mistreatment.

mystics, external "authorities", and neocheaters. Indeed, individual or property rights[1] are necessary for a person to live as human beings are designed to live — to live according to one's biological nature. Still, those rights have been systematically violated to varying degrees by all governments and religions throughout history.

Today, for the first time in history, Neo-Tech/Psychuous concepts are available to the public. Neo-Tech forever breaks the stranglehold of guilt and sacrifice foisted on the value producers by political and religious value destroyers. Today, Neo-Tech breaks that stranglehold to free all productive individuals. Neo-Tech allows those value producers to discover prosperity, psychuous pleasures, and abiding happiness that belong to them. Neo-Tech releases them from the neocheaters who have always lived off the efforts and earnings of others. If value producers use Neo-Tech to reject the guilt foisted on them by the professional mystic and neocheater, they will free themselves not only for psychuous pleasures but for financial prosperity, abiding happiness, and biological immortality [Re: Concepts 145, 146, Neo-Tech Reference Encyclopedia].

Neo-Tech Advantage #57
NATURAL PHENOMENA

Most people call natural phenomena such as various survival and mating behaviors "instinct". But "instinct" is a mystical term that does not exist in humans or in animals. The term "instinct" implies inborn or innate knowledge, which is a false notion. The use of "instinct" to explain behavior is to explain nothing. Moreover, the "instinct" explanation closes further investigation into that which is not yet understood or known. "Instinct" is a mystical, anti-intellectual, anti-scientific term. For, accepting that

---

[1]Individual rights and property rights are the same and inseparable. Private property is a natural extension of every human being. And that extension is essential for a person to effectively produce values for others in order to achieve prosperity and happiness. Without property rights, individual rights have no meaning. With property rights fully protected, individual rights are fully protected. ..."Human rights", by contrast, is a fake term conjured up by neocheaters to violate individual rights. "Human rights" is a meaningless concept. Only individual rights can exist or be violated.

catchall term as an explanation precludes further intellectual and scientific efforts to discover the reasons for various behaviors. Accepting "instinct" as an explanation for any human behavior constitutes accepting the mystical concept that knowledge can be inborn or innately acquired without the self-efforts required for acquiring all knowledge. Likewise, all living species function through definable, understandable biological actions and reactions, not through undefinable, mystical "instincts". To explain anything as "instinct" is a default to the mystic's desire for automatic, inborn, effortless knowledge.

Neo-Tech Advantage #58
PERSONAL APPEARANCE
AND NATURAL BODY FUNCTIONS
Achieving and maintaining good physical fitness and appearance are necessary for developing psychuous pleasures and long-range happiness. On the other hand, physical appearances *not* within one's control are unimportant for achieving psychuous pleasures and happiness. The difference, for example, is between being sloppy and ugly. The natural, physically ugly person can choose to develop beauty through character development and sensuous efforts. He or she can then experience the full range of psychuous pleasures and happiness. But careless or sloppy people can never fully experience psychuous pleasures and happiness as long as they choose to remain careless and lazy about self and life. For by not caring about self and life, they obliterate their self-esteem and desirability, while cutting themselves off from love and happiness. ...How can anyone ultimately care about those who do not care about themselves?

Consider people who let themselves grow fat.[1] Such people have chosen to travel on a death curve [Re: Table 32, Neo-Tech Reference Encyclopedia]. Traveling that route, a person's unhappiness and probability of death increases with increasing fatness. In turn, that route devastates a person's self-esteem and happiness.

---

[1] Many fat people have self-inflicted metabolic problems that make permanent weight reduction difficult (even with near-starvation, carbohydrate diets). To effectively lose weight, such people must permanently restrict carbohydrates from their diets via high protein diets (as outlined in Dr. Atkins' book, *Dr. Atkins' Diet Revolution*, McKay). But those high-protein diets are safe only for aerobically fit people as identified in the two footnotes on page 86. [Re: Concept 91, Neo-Tech Reference Encyclopedia]

Certain natural body functions are inconvenient, painful, unpleasant. For example, menstruation and child birth labor are not convenient or pleasant body functions, even though they are completely natural. Such inconvenient or painful body functions should be diminished by any practical, safe means. For example, safe and painless child birth methods are now available. And new menses techniques can conveniently eliminate most of the unpleasant effects of monthly menstruation. [Re: *Our Bodies, Ourselves*, the Boston Women's Health Book Collective, Simon & Schuster]

Neo-Tech Advantage #59
PHYSICAL FITNESS, DIET, ADDICTIONS

People who let themselves physically deteriorate or grow obese lose the capacity for psychuous pleasures from both physical and psychological capacities.

Nearly anyone at any age in any physical condition can achieve optimum physical fitness by gradually increasing physical stress with an aerobic-type program totaling less than two hours per week of running, swimming, bicycling, or brisk walking as described in Dr. Kenneth H. Cooper's book, *Aerobics*.[1] Permanent, optimum body weight can be achieved through low-carbohydrate diet as described in Dr. Robert C. Atkins' book, *Dr. Atkins' Diet Revolution*[2]. Both books taken together are major contributions to human health and well-being that deliver attractiveness, vigor, and happiness.

---

[1]The best reference for physical fitness through an aerobics program is Dr. Kenneth H. Cooper's original book, *Aerobics*, Bantam Books. Dr. Cooper is the originator and developer of the aerobic, physical-fitness system [Re: Book Analysis 2, Neo-Tech Reference Encyclopedia].

[2]The best reference for weight control through a low carbohydrate diet is Dr. Robert C. Atkins' book, *Dr. Atkins' Diet Revolution*, David McKay Company. [Re: Book Analysis 27, Neo-Tech Reference Encyclopedia]. Despite the distorted attacks on Dr. Atkins' diet by many "nutritionists" and some in the medical profession and the A.M.A., Dr. Atkins has developed the most scientifically sound dietary information offered to date. Dr. Atkins' contribution to human well being can significantly extend and improve the lives of those who choose to be both physically and aerobically fit. His dietary approach is tailored to the natural carnivorous physiology of human beings. In addition to reaching and maintaining optimum body weight, the low

(footnote continued on next page)

A physically fit body is needed to enjoy the full range of psychuous pleasures. The easiest, most efficient way to get and stay in optimum physical condition is to accumulate 30 aerobic points per week according to Dr. Cooper's conditioning system and to eat less than 40 grams of carbohydrate per day according to Dr. Atkins' diet system. **(Both books should be read and understood before embarking on the combined aerobic-fitness/ low-carbohydrate diet.)** A trim, fit body adds a major increment of pleasure to nearly every facet of living, especially to work, romance, and sex.

Addictions to sugar, drugs, alcohol, caffeine, nicotine not only undercut physical fitness, personal appearance, personality, and health, but will steadily diminish a person's self-control, self-esteem, and happiness. Such addictions are rampantly common, yet widely unadmitted. Addictions and compulsions also undermine honesty because they constantly require dishonest rationalizations. That dishonesty, in turn, reduces self-esteem, competence, productivity, and psychuous pleasures. ...The Neo-Tech/Psychuous concepts provide a powerful philosophical/ psychological base for eliminating all mysticisms that promote addictions and compulsions.

Contrary to popular opinion, no natural conflict exists between the mind and body (or between the intellect and emotions). By nature, the mind and body are designed to work in beneficial harmony with each other — and they do when each is used according to its biological nature.[1] When the mind and body

---

(footnote continued from previous page)

carbohydrate diet can reduce or eliminate the most common forms of chronic fatigue (hypoglycemia or low blood sugar). Dr. Atkins' diet, therefore, can increase a person's capacity for psychuous pleasures and life itself. **But because of the high-cholesterol content, Dr. Atkins' diet is recommended only for those becoming and remaining aerobically fit. ...Any high-protein, low-carbohydrate diet cannot be safely separated from aerobic fitness.**

[1]Objective human standards must be based on the biological natures of men and women functioning as the human organism is designed to function. By integrating logic with the nature of existence, then the biological function of the mind becomes obvious: to identify and integrate reality so human beings can become self-sufficient and independent (materially, intellectually, psychologically, emotionally). Fulfilling integrated biological needs is necessary to experience the self-worth and competence needed to achieve increasing prosperity, psychuous pleasures, and abiding happiness.

are not used according to their biological natures, then conflict, pain, and damage result.

An individual has much more voluntary control over his or her physical and mental health than most people realize. Over the long range, a person has almost total control over his or her emotional and physical well-being. By choosing to consistently use the mind rationally in becoming an honest, productive, independent human being,[1] a person *can* control his or her own psychological and physical well-being. Every individual always has the choice to rationally solve problems or to default on that responsibility. Those who chronically default on that self-responsibility have no way to earn prosperity, self-esteem, psychuous pleasures, romantic love, or abiding happiness.

Some knowledge has been developed toward understanding the psychosomatic links between the mind, body, and various ailments. The mind-body links are probably much more significant than currently realized. With advancing medical knowledge about controlling body functions and combining the nervous system with Neo-Tech, people may someday vanquish even cancer and heart disease through the long-range, controlled use of their minds and bodies.[2] But, little valid information has been published concerning the mind and a person's potential to control one's well-being. Specific Neothink books on this subject yet to be published include the definitive diet book titled, "The CAS Happiness Diet". That diet eliminates the three most widely used drugs that undermine human life, health, and happiness — Caffeine, Alcohol, Sugar.

----

[1]Human beings genuinely prosper only through the rational use of their minds. By dealing logically with reality through integrated thinking, they achieve self-sufficiency and independence by producing values for others.

[2]The consistent rational use of the mind through mystic-free integrated thinking to control the long-range development of one's life is the opposite of the mystics' specious shortcut notions of "mind over matter" or their unintegrated wishful thinking of (1) the mind willing "reality" or (2) others showing them the "truth".

Neo-Tech Advantage #60
MYSTICISM, ALCOHOL, MARIJUANA, SUGAR, AND TOBACCO: EFFECTS ON ROMANTIC LOVE AND PSYCHUOUS SEX

Mysticism, alcohol, marijuana, and other reality-distorting agents have both short-range and long-range harmful effects on health and happiness. Even in moderate amounts, mysticism, alcohol, and drugs distort reality. And all distortions of reality are harmful because the human organism depends on accurate perception of reality to be competent, competitive, and to make the non-mystical judgments necessary for prosperous, happy survival. The illusionary values of mysticism, alcohol, and drugs arise from their reality-distorting effects. Indeed drugs, alcohol, and mysticism can feel like old, comfortable, warm friends. But, in the long term, they deliver only harm, incompetence, and unhappiness. And their distortions can initially be so well rationalized that the mystic, the alcohol user, or the drug user can easily choose to remain unaware of the mounting damage until permanent loss of happiness and energy become inescapable.

Damage from mysticism, alcohol, and drugs can range from a quick overdose death or suicide, to an unhappy truncated life, to the more subtle psychological and physiological damages that occur even with moderate use of mysticism, alcohol, and drugs. For example, minor indulgences in mysticism can lead to disastrous losses of values. Or even a few alcoholic drinks cause irreversible damage to certain brain cells by a dehydration that causes a sludging together of red blood cells. Such sludging clogs the blood capillaries; thus, the amount of oxygen reaching those brain cells via the minutest capillaries diminishes. Some of those oxygen-starved brain cells die each time that dehydration or sludging occurs. Damaged or destroyed brain cells do not regenerate. Any single occurrence of alcohol brain-cell damage is not measurable. But the effect is cumulative, gradually yielding measurable, permanently damaging effects.

Likewise, marijuana disorients the electrical brain patterns to diminish one's quality of thinking and order of priorities. For example, marijuana tends to convert demanding action and ambition into passive dreams and laziness. More serious, that movement from effort and ambition to passivity and dreams may be cumulative. Furthermore, the mystical-dream effects of marijuana destroy competence. Also, investigations by Masters and Johnson show that male marijuana users experience drops in testosterone of 40% and more. Reduced testosterone causes reduced sex drive, an atrophy of male sex organs, a softening of muscle tissue, and a wimpish decrease in aggressiveness. In addition, marijuana can enter the fetuses of pregnant women to possibly influence the sexual development of unborn males; for testosterone is essential to the sexual development of males. ...Drugs such as cocaine and heroin are simply more aggressive forms of suicide.

Despite the damaging effects of alcohol and drugs, no rational or moral reason exists for government to restrict, control, or forbid by force the sale or use of alcohol or drugs in any way whatsoever. No one or no government has the right to initiate or threaten force against any individual who is not violating the individual or property rights of others. Individuals have the basic right to do anything with their lives they choose, including damaging themselves by using alcohol and drugs, just as they have the right to damage themselves with sugar, tobacco, religion, promiscuous sex, mysticism, and suicide...so long as they do not initiate threats, force, or fraud against any other individual.

Any use of force to accomplish a "good" always, by nature, does much more long-range harm to people and society than any intended good. Moreover, those who use or advocate such force seldom have honest or innocent intentions, no matter what their external appearances. And in using force to prohibit drugs, the enforcers are not only morally wrong, but their policies of force drive drug prices far above their free-market values. Those artificially high prices, in turn, allow organized crime to flourish through the extremely high-profit margins guaranteed by the government enforcers.

Indeed, those government-created, sky-high prices cause the addict to push drugs onto others, especially onto vulnerable children and adolescents. The addicts must push drugs in order to obtain the cash needed to pay for the grossly inflated drugs. Thus, government oppression of individual rights through force creates hundreds of thousands of young, new addicts each year **because** of anti-drug laws. In addition, the desperate, dying addict will rob, mug, commit mayhem, murder — he will do anything to raise the money required to buy the government-inflated drugs.

And finally, as during government enforced prohibition three generations ago, the anti-drug laws are by far the greatest boon and source of wealth to organized crime. The government through its power-usurping oppression creates huge, lucrative markets from which organized crime prospers and grows.

* * *

Drugs cause many psychological and physical problems that diminish prosperity, romantic love, and psychuous pleasures [Re: Table 33, Neo-Tech Reference Encyclopedia]. Other diminishers of prosperity and happiness include mystical, religious, and political activities as well as lying, self-lying, praying, promiscuous sex, and the use of tobacco, sugar, and caffeine.

Breaking sugar, tobacco, and caffeine habits quickly improves a person's quality of life. A person's self-esteem also significantly increases by eliminating habits that are destructive to the conscious mind and physical body. ...The surest way to stop smoking is to make a nonnegotiable decision to stop smoking completely and forever...and then stop completely and forever without using any crutches such as increased eating, snacking, sweets, sucking Lifesavers, or excessive bragging. A person who uses such crutches will almost always return to smoking sooner or later. The decision to stop must be decisive, irrevocable, uncompromisable, and forever.

Likewise, caffeine in coffee, cola, and chocolate is a stimulant drug. Aside from the depressing psychological effects of being controlled by a habit, prolonged and excessive use of caffeine can physically damage parts of the body such as the kidneys and pancreas and can adversely affect carbohydrate metabolism. That, in turn, can add to the damage and unhappiness caused by sugar consumption. Except for mysticism, the most common and destructive drug is the sedative sugar. Indeed, sugar causes more unhappiness, illness, and deaths through body mutilation (obesity), metabolic damage, physical and psychological harm than all other drugs combined.

But, the most pervasive and destructive of all diseases is mysticism. In fact, for 3000 years, mysticism has been far more

Neo-Tech Power

destructive on human life than all the other diseases on this planet combined.

Neo-Tech Advantage #61
APHRODISIACS — NEGATIVE AND POSITIVE

Casual sex, mysticism, neocheating, dishonesty, deceptive manipulation, compulsive gambling, hard and soft drugs, tobacco, caffeine, excessive alcohol, sugar, and prayer are long-term, negative aphrodisiacs that undermine self-esteem, romantic love, and psychuous pleasures. Also, folk-lore aphrodisiacs such as Spanish fly, yohimbine, ginseng root, and others have no long-term or physiological aphrodisiac value. The only effective aphrodisiacs are a desirable sexual partner, physical fitness, and the psychological/philosophical conditions of Neo-Tech that allow psychuous pleasures to flourish through the production and exchange of values.

Neo-Tech Advantage #62
ROMANTIC LOVE, FREEDOM, AND THE DTC TECHNIQUE

Some people try to get involved too quickly in deep romantic relationships. The possible penalties of pressing for deep involvement too quickly include losing a potential romantic-love partner or unnecessarily wasting an irreplaceable portion of one's life by locking into a time-wasting destructive relationship.

Many initial approaches to romantic love are possible: Some start hot and flaming, others start cool and conservatively. But the way a romantic relationship starts is usually unimportant because romantic love evolves through the exchange of mutually beneficial values. Therefore, any initial, honest approach is good and normally does not determine the outcome. ...What determines the success of a relationship is the creation and growth of mutually beneficial values.

By applying Neo-Tech/Psychuous Concepts, a person increases his or her *Life-Lifting Capacity*.[1] With that capacity, a person can lift a potential, romantic-love partner to new experiences and growth...to levels at which romantic love can move forward

[1]Life-Lifting Capacity does *not* mean changing or remolding another individual to suit one's own desires. Life-Lifting Capacity means providing an environment that helps other people discover and fulfill their *own* unrealized capacities and potential.

92

through mutual growth. By increasing one's own Life-Lifting Capacity, that person increases his or her skills for developing romantic relationships capable of generating psychuous pleasures and abiding happiness.

Paradoxically, only those partners who are free and independent can make honest, long-range commitments to build abiding romantic relationships. Partners involved in romantic relationships can and should avoid authority-backed commitments to the future. The only commitment between romantic-love partners necessary for success is a commitment to honesty and growth.

If a relationship grows out of honest free-choice, the values accumulate naturally. The relationship then increasingly forms a self-chosen permanence. If growth continues, the relationship can gain unbreakable strength and permanence. If growth stops, the relationship can benevolently end with most of the accumulated values retained by each partner. As a result, each partner will have expanded his and her capacity for future relationships. In addition, the benevolent termination of a value-oriented relationship can (if the partners so choose) remain open to possible changes that would allow resumption of growth and the relationship.

Since no one does or can know everything, everyone will at times make errors in his or her personal life. A person is particularly susceptible to errors in the initial stages of a relationship because of limited knowledge and experience about the new situation. Certain errors, if unrecognized or left uncorrected, can unnecessarily end a potentially good romantic-love relationship. With explicit knowledge of the Neo-Tech/Psychuous concepts, the possibilities of such errors are sharply reduced. And when errors do occur, they are usually quickly corrected by applying the Neo-Tech/Psychuous concepts.

The need for compromise in a love relationship is a value-diminishing, guilt-generating myth promoted by altruists, egalitarians, theologians, and other neocheaters. With the Neo-Tech/Psychuous concepts as a guide, conflicts between partners can be resolved without either partner's best interests being compromised, diminished, or sacrificed.

Romantic love never occurs automatically or by chance. Life

values are earned through hard, honest efforts. That means constant, conscious efforts orchestrated in full accord with reality. As with all important values, romantic love and psychuous pleasures demand thought, effort, and time to develop. The positive values generated are proportional to the rational thought and honest effort invested. ...Romantic love, as any important personal value, is attained through the DTC technique: Discipline, Thought, and then Control. [Re: Concept 94, Neo-Tech Reference Encyclopedia]

Neo-Tech Advantage #63
ROMANTIC-LOVE STANDARDS

Actions based on standards of other people or "authorities" stifle self-discovery and block the personal and intellectual growth necessary for romantic love and psychuous pleasures. Within romantic love, no action or behavior needs the approval or sanction of anyone beyond the partners themselves. Couples can and should experience any and all nondestructive sexual and nonsexual experiences they mutually desire.

As one develops intellectual and emotional character, that person's standards for romantic love rise. But rising standards cause a decline in the percentage of potential partners that could satisfy a romantic relationship. Partly offsetting that percentage decline, however, is personal growth, which increases the opportunities to contact higher-quality, potential partners.

Romantic love cannot survive a continually widening disparity of personal growth and character development between partners. For that widening disparity will eventually undermine any romantic-love relationship. A widening disparity between partners eventually generates reactions of inadequacy, jealousy, possessiveness, even envy in the less developed partner — and resentment, dissatisfaction, or disinterest in the more developed partner. Romantic-love relationships, however, can grow and flourish even if wide differences exist in creative or other abilities between partners. The key is growth: Disparity itself is not important if it does not widen — if both partners are creating and sharing growth. [Re: Concept 95, Neo-Tech Reference Encyclopedia] Also, romantic-love relationships can flourish even with great differences in personalities. ...Growing values and attraction in romantic love arise from character growth and development, not from personality traits. These as all values evolve from DTC — Discipline, Thought, and then Control.

Neo-Tech Advantage #64
THREE SEGMENTS OF ROMANTIC LOVE
A romantic-love relationship has three segments:
  1. Fundamental Basis
  2. Man-Woman Relationship
  3. Future Potential

Those three segments are identified below:

SEGMENT # 1

Fundamental Basis

The Fundamental Basis is the starting point of all relationships. That starting point is the similarity of both partners' views of life and their underlying philosophical premises. Without that base of philosophical harmony, no solid ground for mutual development of a value-oriented, romantic-love relationship would exist.

Forming and building a fundamental base is not a process of creating, but one of discovering mutual values, ideas, and thoughts already held. This segment of romantic love is usually the fastest, easiest aspect of the relationship to identify and establish. But discovering the infinite depth and full nature of one's partner is an exciting, life-long, unfolding process. Most of the fundamental, philosophical links between two people can usually be recognized early in the relationship. Unfortunately, one's fundamental basis is relatively easy to fake. Faking one's fundamental self to attract a love partner, however, is a disastrous error that will eventually be paid for in lost love, lost time, reduced self-esteem, diminished happiness, and a dimmed future, especially for the one doing the faking.

SEGMENT #2

Man-Woman Relationship

In order to establish a growing, long-range relationship, each partner must understand the ideas that the other holds about man-woman relationships. In order for both partners to work effectively toward creating a relationship, they must first identify the basis and nature of their own relationship. The Neo-Tech/Psychuous concepts identify the basis for man-woman relationships designed to yield growth, psychuous pleasures, and happiness.

SEGMENT #3

Future Potential

A romantic-love relationship moves forward with motivation and anticipation through a vision of future values, benefits, and happiness. The potential of a love relationship is a function of:
   a. The nature of the relationship.
   b. Each partner's rate and direction of evolvement or development.
   c. The amount of rational thought and effort each partner keeps putting into the relationship.

Neo-Tech Advantage #65
TWO TYPES OF ROMANTIC-LOVE RELATIONSHIPS

Two types of romantic-love relationships exist:

Type A
Working Jointly Toward Major Experiences and Goals

One partner works through the other more creative or active partner in climbing to increasing levels of accomplishment. Both partners share the rewards according to the values that each contribute. The more productive, creative, efficient, one partner becomes, the greater are the benefits and growth opportunities for the other partner. In turn, that partner then grows to become increasingly valuable to the other partner. Each partner benefits greatly from such a combined working/growing relationship. And such a relationship is mutually advantageous even when major differences in productivity, creativity, or energy exist between partners. (A difference in productivity does not imply a difference in personal character.) In such a joint-working relationship, even wide differences in productivity and creativity do not threaten the relationship, so long as growing values are being exchanged between the partners.

A joint-working relationship has the outstanding advantage not only of the partners sharing much larger portions of their lives, but of the partners living their lives more intensely together. ...They are living integrally together before, during, and after work, everyday. They move on their goals, careers, essences, integrated thinking, and happiness together. They can each be more effective, efficient, and happier working together than working separately. They can become major, irreplaceable, growing values to each other.

Type B
Working Separately Toward Major Experiences and Goals

Each partner can pursue independent routes toward separate careers or goals. And each can benefit from such a relationship by the cross-sharing of experiences, emotions, and rewards of their separate experiences and accomplishments. The separate-working relationship need be neither threatening nor competitive for either partner, but rather can be a continuous source of pleasures and enrichment not available to either partner alone.

Both A and B type relationships offer unlimited opportunities for personal growth and happiness. In such value-producing relationships, each partner knows either implicitly or explicitly that intimacy, pleasures, and happiness in a relationship arise from sharing personal growth, not from possessing or owning one another.

Neo-Tech Advantage #66
INDIVIDUAL UNIQUENESS AND PERSONAL WORTH

People are *not* equal in value or worth. Only in the rights to their own lives and property are people equal. Those and only those rights are inalienable for all human beings. By nature, no one has an automatic or natural right to anything else in life. Moreover, beyond the equality of individual or property rights, nothing is, can, or should be equal between human beings. Profound differences exist among people in their self-made qualities such as character development, earned skills, self-worth, extrinsic worth, aspects of intelligence, self-esteem, life-lifting capacity, psychuous-pleasures capacity.

The "average individual" does not exist. Each individual is unique. Average characteristics are a statistical tool that cannot be applied to *any* individual. So many variables are involved in an individual's character, physical structure, and psychological make-up that no individual can possibly be an average person. Moreover, no average psychology or lifestyle exists. In fact, all *rational* psychologies have a "random-walk" capacity for delivering happiness. That means that every rational, productive individual has the same capacity for earning abiding happiness regardless of intelligence, psychology, or job status. Abiding happiness is possible to the extent that a person rejects mysticism in utilizing the mind to think rationally and in exerting the effort to live fully.

Each adult stands uniquely separate and alone on his or her honesty, character, and earned worth. In dealing with anyone in a relationship (especially a romantic relationship), a person's honesty, character, and self-earned values count above all else. And earned values always determine one's self-esteem and happiness despite the constant efforts by politicians, media journalists, cartoonists, social "intellectuals" and other neocheaters to use nonearned characteristics such as face, skin, sex, age, race, nationality, or family background to praise, pay off, judge, or condemn people. Constant exposure to the anti-individualistic myths pushed by professional mystics and neocheaters diminish one's ability to honestly judge character and earned worth. Recognition of an individual's earned worth is the cornerstone of justice and essential for romantic love and psychuous pleasures.

People who choose mystical lives and destructive "careers" (such as politicians, theologians, and criminals) experience continuously decreasing self-esteems along with diminishing capacities for happiness and pleasures. Every person does, however, have the capacity to change personally by rejecting all forms of mysticism to become an honest, strong, productive individual able to achieve growing prosperity, abiding happiness, and psychuous pleasures.

Neo-Tech Advantage # 67
CAPACITY TO CHANGE

People are capable of change...of changing their lives, character, attitudes, views, and actions. To be real, however, such changes must occur through one's own choices motivated by one's own desires and self-interest. Basic changes can never be successfully imposed on anyone, not even by a person's love partner. Changes accomplished by force, threat, coercion, or pressure are not genuine changes, but are pretenses or changes in external appearance designed to deceive, relieve pressures, or to avoid threatened consequences. Such feigned changes are never positive and always lead to harmful consequences.

Positive changes always require honest, self-directed efforts. Through ongoing character development, a person can become triggered to integrate new information quickly. That integration can cause significant, rapid changes in attitudes. If a person is unable or unwilling to act on valid new information, then efforts directed toward changing that person will fail. That does not mean untriggered persons cannot eventually change. But, if they do, the change will be by their own choice and pace.

Avoiding Disguised Mystics

Integrated awareness is needed to identify and avoid partners whose lives are dominated by mysticism, especially disguised mysticism. Two types of mystics exist: (1) Mystics who project their problems and disorders onto others. Such mystics are often characterized by their paranoid use of non sequiturs to blame others for their own problems. (2) Closet mystics who inwardly hurt themselves by undermining values that enter their lives. Ironically, such mystics are often characterized by cluttered closets that reflect the hidden disorder they create in their personal lives. A disorderly closet may indicate a mystically dominated personal life that drains the lives of others.

Both types of mystics create problems where none exist. Both are incompatible with romantic love. And either will eventually destroy any value-based relationship. Yet, Neo-Tech can cure any type of mysticism (the stupidness disease) to yield competent lives filled with growing prosperity, happiness, and romantic-love.

Neo-Tech Advantage #68
1. FINDING ROMANTIC PARTNERS
2. BYPASSING SHYNESS

Finding the right partner with whom to experience psychuous pleasures and romantic love is one of life's most important responsibilities. Opportunities to discover a potential, life-long romantic partner exist everywhere. But unplanned approaches diminish one's chances of securing the best possible romantic-love partner. [Re: Table 35, Neo-Tech Reference Encyclopedia]

Every lonely person should remember that meeting a suitable partner to build abiding love and happiness needs only one connection, one meeting, one social function, one planned effort...and any time could be that one time. Until a person finds that right romantic partner, he or she should never stop searching for that person with whom to share and build values, love, and happiness. To give up searching would be to give up on life itself. And finding that one person makes all efforts worthwhile.

When one bemoans the unhappiness or falseness of guests at a social gathering, that person is often projecting his or her own feelings of unhappiness or falseness onto people who may not be that way at all. But, by looking past one's own mystical complaints, a person can usually generate self-benefiting values from most social circumstances, even if the people encountered hold values and life styles different from one's own.

Still, a person must be selective to protect one's time. One must not let valuable, irreplaceable segments of life be consumed by those who waste time, retard personal growth, or work against one's best interests. But when unavoidably cast into a situation with undesirable people, a person alert with Neo-Tech knowledge can usually salvage valuable new insights. Whenever possible, however, a person should promptly exit from situations that waste time.

Bypassing Shyness

Feelings of social incompetence are generally unfounded. Such feelings are often caused by falsely negative views about one's self or mystical views about others. When a person becomes aware of and scraps those false views, the feelings of social incompetence diminish and often vanish.

An effective way to bypass shyness, nervousness, and feelings of social incompetence is by *intense listening* with full-focus awareness on the speaker. Not only does such attention elicit friendly reactions from the speaker to the listener, but intense listening increases the listener's ability to communicate and articulate. Intense listening is also a valuable tool to evaluate potential partners for romantic love.

Possibilities for contacting potential, romantic-love partners increase proportionately with the number of approaches made toward potential partners. Many opportunities for discovering romantic-love partners are lost by people who fear what others may think of them for trying to "pick up" people to whom they are attracted. Even more opportunities are lost through inaction caused by fear of rejection.

In finding the best romantic-love partner, a person must be free and forward in approaching potential partners. That includes all approaches from a self-introduction to a media ad or a bold pickup by either the man or the woman. Through fear of rejection, many people lose valuable opportunities to discover romantic partners within whom the supreme values of psychuous pleasures and romantic love reside. That fear of contacting others dissipates on realizing the nature of rejections: Most rejections stem simply from unavailability. And many other rejections arise from inadequacies within the person doing the rejecting. Such rejections are not personal rebuffs, but actually serve as valuable sorting processes that allow the quick elimination of unpromising prospects with a minimum loss of time.

Relying on Natural Beauty

Those who rely on natural beauty or physical attractiveness to control love situations are generally unsuitable for romantic love. For usually they ignore the efforts and disciplines needed to develop capacities to receive or deliver romantic love and psychuous pleasures [Re: Concept 90, Neo-Tech Reference Encyclopedia]. Those who respond to one's initial, natural approach often make the best prospects for romantic partners. For that reason, a person must freely express his or her unique, natural self from the start in order for the selection process to work effectively in uncovering the best potential romantic-love partners.

Many people erroneously think that seeking potential romantic partners at social functions designed for that purpose (e.g., singles dances, clubs, introduction services, Parents Without Partners) is somehow degrading. But the opposite is the fact. People who value themselves and their happiness will resist mystically acting on such false feelings. Instead, they will place a high priority on those activities that will improve their chances of discovering the best-possible, life-long, romantic-love partner.

The value of romantic love is far too important for leaving to random chance. Instead, a person must put the discovering of a life-long partner under one's own direct control. One must exert organized, rational efforts to find the love partner with whom the greatest values can be exchanged. That direct-action approach contrasts with the mystical approach of those who count on random chance, a white knight, or someone else to deliver the values of love and happiness to them. ...To gain and keep a value as great as romantic love requires constant discipline, hard integrated thinking, and consistent high-energy effort.

Why Everyone Is Not Handsome

Most animals evolve to near their perfect physical appearance. But conscious beings do not because those without natural beauty can choose to work harder to develop their character and competence to higher levels. Thus, some people with less natural beauty work harder to develop superior characters. They do that to compete better in attracting mates for psychuous pleasures and reproduction. By contrast, many of those endowed with natural beauty lack the same competitive pressures to work harder to develop character and competence.

Thus, because certain people without natural beauty make themselves more competitive, they remain well represented throughout the evolutionary stream. In fact, they tend to rise above the naturally beautiful people in power, intellectual attractiveness, and sexual desirability. Those dynamics are why (1) naturally beautiful people can be found among the less evolved and (2) unhandsome people can be found among the highest levels of evolvement. Thus, unlike other animals, nature's drive for physical perfection is not a controlling evolutionary force in man. Indeed, man-controlled intelligent actions can outcompete nature-controlled, physical appearances not only for reproduction and survival, but for prosperity, happiness, and romantic love.

Neo-Tech Advantage #69
SHYNESS — CAUSES AND CURES

Shyness reduces contact and chances with potential romantic-love partners. But shyness is easily overcome once the problem is identified. [Re: Table 36, Neo-Tech Reference Encyclopedia identifies five types of shyness and lists ways to reduce or eliminate each type.] In addition, the constant misunderstanding of a uniquely different individual may cause that person to withdraw and become a loner. That aloneness may create an erroneous image that such a person is shy or a bore when neither is true.

A major step toward eliminating shyness is the acceptance of one's own self. To do that, one must realize that no "model" person exists with whom anyone needs to emulate or identify with in order to be healthy, happy, or successful [Re: Concept 96, Neo-Tech Reference Encyclopedia]. ...A person bypasses shyness by being one's own self in guiltlessly, proudly producing rational, competitive values in any way he or she chooses, regardless of what others may say or think.

A shy person is seldom a bore. A bore is a person who is silly, uninteresting, or uncomfortable to another person. Often being a bore to a particular person is merely the result of that particular person's reactions. Such reactions depend on individual values and standards. Some people can be boring to certain people, but exciting to others. For example, Aristotle, Leonardo da Vinci, Einstein, John D. Rockefeller, Henry Ford, and Thomas Edison while being very exciting to each other and other genuine value producers. But those same people probably would have bored or, more accurately, threatened the profoundly dishonest, pseudo self-esteems of Stalin, Hitler, FDR, Mao, Ralph Nader, Charles Manson, Pol Pot. Conversely, quasi-dead, destructive people who habitually live through distorted (mystical) "realities" will by nature bore productive individuals who live through objective reality.

Neo-Tech Advantage #70
EQUALITY OF MEN AND WOMEN
DIVISION OF LABOR CONCEPT

The human mind is neuter. Men and women have equal capacity for intellectual development, character development, integral honesty, self-esteem, physical fitness, psychuous pleasures, romantic love, and abiding happiness. But physiological differences as well as psychological differences exist between men and women. Those differences must be recognized

Neo-Tech Power

in order to function effectively — to function as a human male or female is intended to function — to function as an honest, rational, conscious being. [Re: Table 37, Neo-Tech Reference Encyclopedia, illustrates the important physical and psychological differences between men and women.] Those differences cannot be considered good or bad, better or worse, or by any other label. They are just differences in their natures. But the differences are real. Thus, they must be recognized and dealt with as reality.

The feminist movement ignores or rejects the psychological differences and often even ignores the physiological differences between man and woman. That evasion of reality is reflected by the feminists' irrational, destructive demands for government-enforced "equality".

The often misunderstood division-of-labor concept is central to all beneficial relationships, ranging from individual man-woman romantic relationships to mutually beneficial employer-employee relationships involving thousands of people. Next to their attacks on individual rights through the use of government force, the most harmful neocheating manipulations by feminist leaders are their attacks on the voluntary division-of-labor concept. Some feminists advocate eliminating the division-of-labor dynamic from man-woman relationships. They demand, for example, that all jobs, chores, and activities be shared equally. Those feminists and other neocheating egalitarians want to use government force to reduce value producers to the level of value destroying mystics and neocheaters.

Most other people desire and happily use the division of labor to their mutual advantages. Indeed, the most fair, efficient way to exchange values for desired values is through division of labor. Even the traditional trade in which the man earns money while the woman makes an efficient home and living atmosphere is a valid, proper trade that can greatly benefit each, if each mutually agrees to and desires such a trade.

For what reason would a feminist or anyone else attack two people who agree to what they want to do with their own personal selves and lives? One reason is that such feminists are neocheaters using the tool of guilt to undermine values in order to usurp power and values earned by others. But, romantic-love partners responding to feminist demands for equality of actions

104

(rather than for each partner offering the other his or her separately developed values), eventually eliminate happiness from their relationships. For equality of actions pushes love partners toward inefficient, restricted petty relationships in which mutual growth fades and love dies.

Women functioning in any of the following three categories can achieve psychuous pleasures, romantic love, and abiding happiness:

1. Self-sufficient, commercially productive[1] career women can easily experience the full-range of psychuous pleasures and romantic love.

2. Genuinely productive housewives or mothers who contribute significantly to increasing the commercial productivity of their husbands and the value potentials of their children can also experience growing psychuous pleasures and romantic love. But they, as with men, must always keep developing their intellectual and productive capacities. Women most naturally succeed in this category.

3. Women actively seeking growth by becoming knowledgeable or proficient in artistic, cultural, or recreational areas (such as art, music, literature, dance, sports) can experience growing romantic relationships. But such relationships will not continue to grow unless the woman passes the amateur stage to eventually become commercially productive and self-sufficient in that or another area. Only a tiny percentage of women succeed in this category.

In most societies, more men than women are commercially productive. More men than women, therefore, have the potential for experiencing psychuous pleasures and growing romantic-love relationships. That disparity works against the happiness of *both* men and women. Thus, both men and women benefit as more and more females enter the romantic-love marketplace by becoming competitive net value producers inside the home, outside the home, or both.

---

[1]Commercially productive means being economically self-sufficient by producing more tradeable values in the competitive, free market than one consumes.

The worst aspect of the feminist movement and other so-called "rights" movements is their advocating legislated government force or coercion to violate individual and property rights of others. All professional mystics and neocheating leaders require force or deception to survive by parasitically filling their needs. And those needs are usually disguised as "noble" ends. But no matter how noble sounding the end, it can *never* justify the means of force against any individual. Institutionalized initiation of force against individuals for any reason is categorically wrong, immoral, and diminishes the well-being and happiness of everyone.

Government policies and laws backed by force have always been the major instrument for denying women their individual rights. So what about those legions of feminists advocating that same legislated government force to achieve women "rights" by violating rights of others? They diminish everyone's rights and well-being. Such use of government force was vigorously promoted even by early feminists such as Dr. Elizabeth Blackwell (1821-1910) who was responsible for tough, anti-prostitution laws that only increased government use of force to oppress both men and women. Moreover, Blackwell's guilt-laden, anti-sex, anti-masturbation writings were subsequently promoted by the Catholic church. Her writings led to the heavy masturbation guilt that still hangs over most women...a guilt that has deprived countless millions of women of healthy sexual development.

Neo-Tech Advantage #71
"CAREER" HOUSEWIFE AND HAVING CHILDREN
VERSUS
ACHIEVING "GREATNESS"

Most "career" housewives experience diminishing sexual pleasures and happiness. Why do such declines of happiness occur? Because such women limit their personal growth by letting their intellectual and productivity potentials remain under challenged in being full-time housewives. To experience psychuous pleasures and abiding happiness, a person must fulfill his or her potential. That means becoming independent — materially, intellectually, and emotionally. Today, such independence usually evolves from productive jobs or careers.

And today, with the many domestic labor-saving conveniences, a housewife "career" is generally too unchallenging to provide the self-esteem, independence, and growth needed to experience the full range of happiness available from life. But, exceptions exist in which being a housewife is a challenging life-time management profession delivering full self-esteem, happiness, and romantic love. Historical examples are the wives of the American pioneers and frontiersmen. Examples today include the partner-wives of super-productive entrepreneurs, businessmen, farmers, scientists, and other hard-driving producers.

Another potential area for undermining happiness is having children, especially before achieving financial independence. Children can shrink the potential for career success, romantic happiness, and psychuous pleasures of both partners for two decades or more. Often the birth of children means the end of growth and happiness for the couple. And the parents' loss of growth and happiness can damage the well-being of their innocent child or children. Often when personal growth is ended by the burden of children, the parents' view of the future shifts to a downhill direction. Their lives then begin shrinking toward aging and death. But if parents fail their responsibility to properly raise their children into productive independent adults, those children become the victims of their parents' moral default. As with any uncorrected moral default, those parents responsible will suffer damaging consequences to their self-esteems and happiness.

Neo-Tech oriented couples would not have children until they were in a financial and maturity position to conceive a child as a net-happiness asset, rather than a draining task. Such couples almost always have greater capacities to love both life and their children than those who thoughtlessly or prematurely have children to "secure" the marriage, to meet the expectations of others, or other unhealthy reasons.

Romantic love and psychuous pleasures can still be achieved for couples who have children if they fully meet their responsibilities to both their children and to themselves. With children, the goal of building happiness and romantic love becomes more difficult and challenging. But if successful, a romantic relationship with the uniquely valuable experience of children can be even more rewarding than a romantic-love relationship without children. With children, increasing romantic happiness can be accomplished *only* after accepting a nonmartyr, full-responsibility role in preparing one's children for productive, independent lives. At the same time, one must always hold the romantic-love relationship, not the children, as the primary value.

In any case, having and raising children is a unique, profound life experience. And children can develop characters that yield major, long-range values to their parents, especially as the years go by. ...Well-evolved children can yield magnificent values. Rationally bearing and raising Neo-Tech oriented children can yield a bonanza of values available from no other life experience.

Financially secure, emotionally mature couples can genuinely desire the unique, value-generating experience of having children. Thus, they can rationally choose to bear and raise children without sacrificing or diminishing their careers, romantic love, or long-range happiness. ...Raising competent children oriented around Neo-Tech can be rewarding beyond any other life experience, except romantic love.

If the market for technology and research were free from government interference, genetically controlled, flaw-free babies would probably be routine in a decade or less. Moreover, externally produced babies could forever free women from the incapacitation, pain, physical damage, and life-threatening dangers of childbirth. That technology could also reduce childhood diseases and eliminate birth defects. Externally produced, genetically controlled babies would also allow selection of sex and certain characteristics that would provide the maximum advantages to their children.

Still, the key traits can develop only through the volitional choices of each living, conscious child. For example, personality, character, and integrity are traits that evolve from the personal choice of each individual to be honest or dishonest, nonmystical or mystical, responsible or irresponsible, a value producer or a value destroyer.

***

Except to one's own self and dependent children, no one owes duties to *anyone* (including one's spouse, siblings, or parents) or to anything (including society, the government, the church, or to any other "higher" cause). The prime moral duty is to develop one's own potential to achieve abiding happiness through competitive value production. Beyond that prime responsibility to be a net value producer in order to earn happiness, a person's *only* other moral duty is to support and develop one's own children into honest, nonmystical, self-sufficient adults. That duty includes teaching children to objectively identify facts in full context and to live competently by rejecting all forms of mysticism, dishonesty, and neocheating.

Parents must, above all, teach their children to identify and avoid the disease of mysticism and its gaggle of neocheaters. Those children are then free to develop into independent, self-sufficient adults capable of achieving unlimited prosperity, psychuous pleasures, and abiding happiness.

Properly caring for and rearing children to become honest, self-sufficient adults is a moral responsibility and duty of the parents. That duty is assumed from the parent's chosen act of procreation, for which the children are not responsible. Thus, parents have no right to place future claims or obligations on their children. Likewise, after children develop into self-sustaining, independent beings, the moral responsibilities and obligatory duties end for the parents.

***

Compared to men, few women have directly achieved greatness in the major areas of human accomplishment (e.g., arts, sciences, philosophy, music, business, industry, medicine, law). Those differences in achievement are not due to inherent or biological differences between men and women, but rather such differences are due to (1) women being more involved in the restricting tasks of raising children, and (2) the cultural, legal, mystical, and neocheating oppression of women that has occurred throughout most of recorded history [Re: Tables 38-39, Neo-Tech Reference Encyclopedia].

Few men attained greatness in any area of human achievement during the 1000-year Dark Ages. For, during that time, the church oppressed everyone's intellectual and productive capacities. Likewise, few women have achieved greatness during their cultural dark ages that existed throughout most of recorded history. In recent years, however, radical changes have occurred to eliminate most differences in oppression between men and women. Those changes have occurred through the relentless, rational pressures of business and free enterprise, not through coercions of government, the feminists, or the non sequiturs of neocheating theologians, journalists, professors, and politicians.

Today, women in the Western World have essentially the same freedom and opportunity as men to develop their commercial values in most areas of human activity. But many women are by choice not exercising their new freedoms and opportunities. Thus, many women are failing to exploit their potentials for financial prosperity, psychuous pleasures, growing romantic love, and abiding happiness.

Divorced men and widowers are generally more desired or sought after by the opposite sex than are divorced women and widows. Aside from population statistics that somewhat favor men, no intrinsic or natural reason for that difference in desirability exists. The main difference is that, compared to women, men generally are and remain more productive in their jobs and careers and thus have more values and life to offer. By contrast, man-dominated housewives living as toys, pets, or servants generally have indulged themselves with mysticism instead of developing their characters, abilities, and talents. Thus, they have fewer values and less life to offer. On the other hand, men and women of equivalent character and value development would have equal worth and desirability as value-oriented, romantic-love partners.

Neo-Tech Advantage #72
POTENTIAL OF WOMEN
FROM 1300 BC THROUGH TODAY

Women hold great potential for gaining economic and cultural power throughout the world. But their potential is undermined by politicians, feminists, and other value destroyers who use the government to force their egalitarian equalities on others. Indeed, to survive without producing competitive values *for others*, professional neocheaters and mystics must use force, deception, and mysticism to usurp their destructive livelihoods *from others*. And physically weaker women are the easiest targets for their destructions. Thus, professional mystics and neocheaters more easily subject women to injustices and abuses to usurp power and values.[1] For that reason, throughout recorded history, women have suffered greater oppression than have men as illustrated on the following pages:

OPPRESSION OF WOMEN SINCE 1300 BC

Ancient Greece
1300 B.C. – 450 B.C.

Homeric women (1300 B.C.-1100 B.C.) were relatively free and exercised considerable influence over men. But all women were subjected to double standards — legal and sexual.

Enlightened Greece
450 B.C. – 27 B.C.

Courtesans held the highest positions of individual rights and personal respect available to women. Wives held the lowest position and were considered as housekeepers with few if any rights.

High-class prostitutes or courtesans were held superior to virtuous women and wives.

---

[1]By oppressing women, men become easier to control.

Roman Empire
27 B.C. – 385 A.D.

With increased economic freedom, the drive for individual freedom brought new rights and respect for women. Oppression by mystics and conservatives decreased. Double standards diminished.

Drive for women's liberation and equality. As today, Roman feminists who advocated use of government controls and force to accomplish their ends failed in the long run by establishing the conditions for the increased oppression of women.

Decline of the Roman Empire
100 A.D. – 385 A.D.

The spreading altruistic influence of Christianity began stripping women of their individual rights and subjecting them to new, heavy oppressions while leading the civilized Western World toward asceticism and anti-sexual attitudes.

Christianity plunged Rome into asceticism, causing massive destruction and suffering. Women lost almost all rights with rising Christian power. ...Today, ominous parallels are developing with rising fundamentalist, born-again, anti-porn/anti-abortion movements.

Rise of Christianity
385 A.D. – 1000 A.D.

The Western World sank into the Dark Ages as women were pushed to their lowest position in recorded history. They had no individual or legal rights. The Church considered women as subhuman. In fact, the Roman Catholic Church considered women as wasteful property who could be killed, beaten, tortured, ravished or forced into slavery with impunity by theologians and "devout" noblemen.

Catholic bishops argued that women did not have mortal souls and that women were pieces of wasteful property. The Roman Catholic church sanctioned wife-beating. Killing a woman was not a very serious offense. Noblemen had the natural "right" to ravish any peasant woman.

Pre-Renaissance
1000 – 1300

The rise of courtly love and the de-emphasis of the Catholic Church began elevating women to emotional partners more equal to men. Respect and admiration for women increased with increased economic activity. But women still had few individual or legal rights. Extreme double standards were still practiced.

A new man-woman relationship developed that was previously unknown to Western civilization. Women gained respect and admiration. Courtly love elevated women from child bearers and lust satisfiers to more equal partners with men.

The Church vs. the Renaissance
1300 – 1500

The Church fought viciously to stop the rising new concepts of romantic love, happy man-woman relationships, and pleasurable sex. Pope Innocent VIII started the inquisitions and witch trials. Millions of innocent women were killed, tortured, and burned to death by the Roman Catholic Church. But the growing enlightenment of the Renaissance with spreading economic freedoms began liberating the human mind and reason from the dark, brutal mysticism of Christian theology.

Renaissance noblemen equated women to beauty and good. The church fought back by promoting the "evils" of women and witchcraft. They advocated hanging "evil" women by their thumbs, twisting ropes around their heads, pushing needles under their nails, and pouring boiling oil on their feet in the "devout hope" of forcing confessions of their "wickedness". The Roman Catholic church then proceeded to burn to death tens of thousands of innocent women.

The Puritans
1500 – 1700

With increasing economic activity, the Puritans rejected the Church's hatred of women, sex, and happiness. They accepted the normality of sex, pleasure, and happiness. Women's rights greatly improved under Puritanism. Women could divorce. They gained property and inheritance rights. Marriage became a civil contract.

The Age of Reason
1700 – 1800

Men respected women for their minds and intellectual development. People involved in business began scrapping the gloom and hatred of Christianity and its idea that women were evil. Yet, women were still held as subservient to men.

The rationalists rejected the malevolence of Christianity. But women were often considered as ornaments, toys, or nitwits.

Pre- and Early Victorianism
1800 – 1850

Slobbering sensitivity became the ideal. Men sought shy, virginal women. The togetherness concept developed. Glorification of "pure" women was a pretext for a desperate last attempt by neocheating conservatives and the Church to subjugate women as servants of men. A great increase in double standards occurred under the guise of "moral" standards. Women lost considerable individual freedom.

Men grew shy and sought "pure" women. Virginal-type women were "glorified" and idealized. But that "morality" was only a new pretext for the continued subjugation of women by men. The U. S. Surgeon General, Dr. William Hammond, issued the warning that decent women should not feel the slightest pleasure during sexual intercourse. Many doctors considered sexual desire in women to be pathological. But women began revolting against their "purified" and "glorified" status.

The Decline of Religion and Victorianism
via the Rise of Capitalism and the
Emancipation of Women
1850 – 1900

Capitalistic economics undermined the oppressive customs of the past and broke the unjust, feudal hierarchy of the social classes. Capitalism crippled the influence of the Church. Capitalism created the atmosphere and pressure for female suffrage, individual rights, divorce reform, and equal legal and economic rights. Victorianism was a desperate delaying action against increasing honesty, individuality, justice, earned equality, and rising economic freedoms.

With the rise of capitalism, women gained significant economic rights for the first time since the anti-Christian, pagan Roman Empire. Capitalism broke the stifling, unjust religious/feudal-class patterns. A new optimism and cheerful happiness rose among the middle class. Capitalistic economics greatly accelerated the collapse of hypocritical snobbishness, racism, artificial social ties, and oppressive religious and social customs. The rigid Victorian home was threatened by increasing economic freedom for females, divorce reforms, and free-choice love. Victorianism was a last-stand action by the conservatives and the church against the inevitable, liberating changes caused by capitalism and a prosperous, industrial civilization.

The Emergence of 20th-Century
Romantic Love
1900 – 1960

Flourishing commerce among individuals, especially in America, discarded the anti-sexual, Victorian-Christian ethics. Double standards diminished with more equal educational, economic, legal, and sexual rights for women. Birth control and abortion rights were promoted. Capitalism liberated women and minorities by valuing all individuals according to their objective worth rather than to their sex, beliefs, social status, or race.

Women increasingly became equal to men in romantic relationships. Love patterns of all societies were drawn to the free and honest capitalistic style of Western love, which combined sexuality, affectionate friendship, productive work, and family functions...all into a single, equal-partner relationship. The modern, capitalist-generated, sexual revolution demolished most of the Christian-Victorian patterns of anti-sexual, patriarchal oppressiveness.

Modern Romantic Love
1960 – Present

The sexual revolution broke the last vestiges of inequalities between men and women. But today, renewed oppression of individual rights has begun to rise ominously with the feminist and religious movements against pornography and abortion. Those movements are inspired by neocheating authorities seeking unearned power. Still, the majority of women have not fully exercised their new freedoms and rights. Many neocheating feminist leaders seek unearned gains through government coercion and force. And that force will boomerang to increasingly subjugate the rights of all women...and men.[1]

Individual freedom that naturally evolves from capitalism made possible modern romantic love and the liberation of women. For, the capitalistic free market put values on individuals according to their objective worth rather than their sex, social

---

[1]Women who usurp feminist-inspired, unearned values are heading back toward dependence...toward being taken care of and eventually subjugated by men. In essence, the feminist movement is designed to coerce productive people into taking care of protesting women. The inevitable results are opposite the goals of freedom declared by feminist neocheaters. And those same ploys are destructively used by politicians to usurp "freedom" for blacks and other minorities. Indeed, the more unearned values usurped by the neocheating feminists and politicians, the more their recipient clients move toward dependence and subjugation. ...Neocheaters transfer values from the earned to the unearned while harming everyone, especially those they claim to help.

status, or race. Women can now be fully independent. But having gained the freedom for equality, many women fear that equality might be too risky or challenging, or require too much independence or effort, or cost them the chance for love. Such women often buy "security" and "love" at the price of remaining unequal, unfulfilled, unhappy all their adult lives.

Today, men and women have essentially the same educational and economic opportunities. But many women in developed societies have no careers beyond the home. Thus, they deny their basic human need to develop competence and self-sufficiency. That need for competence and independence is fulfilled by pursuing productive work in challenging careers.

Future Romantic Love

Two approaches to life are open: (1) The neocheater's approach of using force-backed government or deceit-based religion to drain values from others, or (2) the producer's approach of using integrated honesty and free markets to deliver competitive values wanted by others and society. That second approach obviates force, coercion, fraud in allowing all men and women equally to pursue prosperity, romantic love, and abiding happiness.

Despite feminist claims, nothing today prevents women from realizing their potentials. The battle is not for women's rights, minority rights, black rights — the battle is and always has been for *individual* rights. When individual rights are fully protected, then everyone's rights are protected.

Most feminists diminish the potential for all women by trying to usurp unearned economic or money gains through government force or coercion in violating the rights of others. Such tactics are morally wrong and destructive to all individuals. And in the long run, those tactics succeed only in giving government more power to oppress everyone — especially women.

While stridently expressing goals of liberation and freedom, most feminist policies deny freedom of choice, voluntary division of labor, and open competition. Those policies reveal a fear of freedom, competition, integrated thinking, and self-responsibility. Such dishonest, double-speak contradictions of demanding

117

freedom while actually attacking freedom via government force are also common in "liberation" or "rights" movements of various Black, consumer, and environmental groups. Such groups demand benefits and "freedoms" via government force while reducing their own and everyone else's freedom.

Government laws backed by force have always been the mechanism that eventually oppressed women [Re: Section Four, Neo-Tech Reference Encyclopedia]. The genuine liberation of women occurred during those rare, historic periods during which the reason and logic of individual freedom gained influence over the dishonesty and mysticism of government and religious oppression. Those liberating periods were the Golden Age of Greece, the Renaissance, and the greatest, most profoundly moral period of all: the free-enterprise phase of the Industrial Revolution. In free-enterprise capitalism, the influences of reason, honesty, effort, productivity, and voluntary individual choice count for everything, while the influences of mysticism, dishonesty, racism, social status, and the use of force are dismissed as nothing. ...The causal relationship of reason and capitalism to freedom and prosperity for women is clear.

In attempting to establish credibility, feminists promote and publicize certain "famous" women of history as heroines. Some of those women were honest, value producers who contributed to human well-being. But most of those feminist "heroines" were demagogues and neocheaters who agitated for more government force to make individuals conform to their wishes or demands. In their promotion of "great women", most feminists hypocritically ignore one of the greatest benefactors to human life and champions of individual rights. That person was a woman. She was one of the most profound thinkers and writers, male or female, of all time. She was a world-famous novelist and the most important philosopher since Aristotle. Her name: Ayn Rand.

Why do most feminists ignore Ayn Rand? Because she intellectually refuted their concepts of mysticism, initiatory force, and government coercion to achieve ends. More important, she clearly identified the immorality of such approaches, thus repudiating the core of most feminist movements and methods. Also, Ayn Rand identified that the only proper moral issue is individual rights...not women's rights, black rights, or any other such "rights" or causes. For such causes are largely designed to support neocheaters.

The feminists' rejection of Ayn Rand not only underscores their intellectual dishonesty, but demonstrates that their movement is not interested in individual rights. Instead, they are interested in usurping power, values, advantages, and bogus livelihoods through the spurious neocheating gimmick of women's rights. Because of their disregard for individual rights in their demands for government coercion or force, feminist movements bring, in the long run, only further government oppression of women. Indeed, that oppression is already recurring with, for example, the anti-abortion and anti-pornography movements.

And finally, most feminists stridently attack women's greatest benefactor and liberator — free-enterprise capitalism. Furthermore, many feminists actually support the prime causes for oppression of women — government and religion. In fact, some feminists remain active members of the most virulently anti-women, patriarchal organization ever contrived by man — the Roman Catholic Church. Such feminists work against the well-being of all women and all individuals.

Neo-Tech Advantage #73
THE NATURE OF EMOTIONS AND SELF-RESPONSIBILITY

The Nature of Emotions

1. Emotions are neither good nor bad and are not subject to moral judgments, no matter how irrational or "bad sounding" they may seem. ...Only actions can be judged as good or bad, moral or immoral.

2. All emotions, no matter how irrational or how deeply repressed, are a real part of a person and need to be recognized, acknowledged, and guiltlessly accepted.

3. Each repressed, negative emotion becomes an integral part of a person's mind. Each repressed emotion subconsciously exerts a continuous negative effect on that person's thinking and emotional processes. That negative effect remains forever, unless the emotion

(often an emotion from childhood) is identified and rationally re-examined through the mature adult mind.

4. The identifying and releasing of any repressed emotion through a non-mystical mind is a healthy, rewarding experience. [Re: Concept 104, Neo-Tech Reference Encyclopedia]

Self-Responsibility/Mouth Responsibility

Each individual is solely responsible for his or her own actions. That includes being responsible for what goes in and out of one's mouth. **Mouth Responsibility: the self-responsibility for the food, drink, drugs, smoke, genitalia that go into one's mouth and the words that come out.**

Internal mysticism ruins people's lives through (1) allowing irrational, destructive ingestion of sugar, alcohol, or drugs into their mouths and (2) allowing irrational, destructive words to egress from their mouths. Everyone alone must personally battle to overcome internal mysticism in order to live prosperously and happily. Self-responsibility cannot be transferred to anyone. For that reason, most therapies by psychologists and psychiatrists are invalid. Moreover, such therapies are often practiced by neocheaters usurping a livelihood by manipulating mysticism in others.

Almost all psychological problems arise from internal mysticism. And each individual can overcome such problems by continual, conscious choice to be honest rather than mystical. Each person must decide to self-determine the future or to surrender that responsibility to external "authorities" (including psychologists). That surrender of life occurs on asking others to solve one's own problems and deliver happiness.

Fighting and rejecting mysticism within one's own self is the greatest, most important of all battles. And the most ironic, tragic loser of that battle was the philosopher, Ayn Rand. For she developed and harnessed the greatest mind to battle mysticism since Aristotle. Yet, she could never collect her full rewards, because she lost the battle to personal mysticism on several fronts. The most irrational, emotion-driven mysticisms were her rationalizations, vindictiveness, cultism, and smoking. The consequences of those mystical indulgences? Unnecessary unhappiness, sycophants limiting her work, and nicotine killing her. ...While Ayn Rand was *totally* non-mystical in her work and ideas, she became increasingly mystical and unhappy in her personal life. By contrast, her long-time collaborator Nathaniel Branden later absorbed areas of mysticism in his work and ideas while apparently growing less mystical and more happy in his personal life.

Having an external "authority" such as a God, a drug, a cigarette, a cult, a psychologist delivers: 1. quick, easy-way, no-struggle "answers" that avoid self-responsibility, and 2. fuel for more personal mysticisms. That avoiding of self-responsibility always fuels personal mysticism while diminishing the individual's competence and motivation to solve one's own personal problems. And that default is why most therapies are long-range failures. Only individuals themselves can have sufficient motivation and self-knowledge to successfully overcome internal mysticism and solve life's problems. Only individuals themselves can put sufficient energy and knowledge into the efforts needed to become competent, prosperous, and happy. No mystical or outside source can provide those values.

Neo-Tech Advantage #74
NATURAL HIGHS

Natural highs always beneficially integrate with a person's physical or psychological life — or both. Unnatural highs always destructively disintegrate a person's physical or psychological life — or both.

Strongly positive experiences such as major achievements, aerobic exercises, great music, art, literature, drama, and romantic love stimulate natural highs. The ultimate high, however, comes from feeling one's own self in control — being in control of life, living free of mysticism, living honestly, rationally, productively. In that non-mystical state, a person acutely feels the integrated physical and psychological process of living. He or she experiences the impact of living fully, in competent control of one's own self, destiny, and reality.

That clarity and control of self, life, and reality produces a physical and emotional high. That high evolves from an acute awareness of living in reality...of being in control. Such highs are far more exhilarating than those achieved through reality avoiding, artificial stimuli such as drugs, alcohol, religious or mystical experiences, manipulating others, ruling others, killing others. Those fake control-seeking highs are achieved through force and destruction. By contrast, all genuine, lasting highs are achieved through competitive production of values.

The most intense reality high is psychuous pleasures. Reality highs, however, can be consistently experienced in almost any phase of one's life to produce continuous waves of pleasure and happiness. Most people have at times experienced brief or partial glimpses of those natural highs. Such experiences live vividly in nearly everyone's memory. On analysis, one will discover that those experiences occurred when a person was most free of mysticism — most free to be his or her own self — most free to function according to his or her biological nature. Moreover, everyone who has developed a rational, productive lifestyle has the capacity for experiencing natural highs with increasing frequency. Those highs can eventually blend into a near continuous state of happiness marked by extra-intense moments of psychuous pleasures.

The Neo-Tech/Psychuous concepts deal with relationships between people. But those concepts also deal with the relationship of one's own self relative to reality, self-esteem, and self-awareness. Only through developing a nonmystical, integrated relationship with one's own body, mind, and objective reality can a person fully experience the prosperity, pleasures, and happiness available from life.

Natural highs involve the release of physical and emotional tensions while being fully aware of the mind and body. The sensation is that of "letting go" as the body tensions release and the emotional pleasures are guiltlessly felt. Those natural, euphoric experiences are contrasted to the destructive, tension-breaking actions of taking drugs, getting drunk, food gorging. Such artificial or mystical highs always leave hangovers and unhappiness along with damaged minds and bodies. [Re: Table 41, Neo-Tech Reference Encyclopedia].

Natural highs can also release chronic muscular tensions manifested in taut necks, shallow breathing, stiffly pulled up shoulders, tense buttocks, and uptightness in general. In fact, neck stiffness is an indicator of locked-in conflicts caused by mysticism.

Releasing such tensions also improves one's physical grace and coordination. The release of those tensions restores the natural, cat-like gracefulness of body motions as muscles begin working together in their intended, fluid, integrated manner. Also, the release of those chronic tensions and the deepening of breathing permits clearer, more effective thinking.

Certain exercises are also effective in both releasing chronic muscle tensions and improving one's breathing. [Re: Book Analysis 71, Neo-Tech Reference Encyclopedia] Also, self-hypnosis can relax certain physical tensions. Hypnosis bypasses the conscious mind by putting orders directly into a nonresisting, noncritical subconscious mind. [Re: Appendix C, Neo-Tech Reference Encyclopedia]. Effective hypnosis techniques are easy to master, but can be damaging to the subconscious mind when hypnosis is used carelessly or with improper dehypnosis. Moreover, hypnosis is usually used mystically, is generally unnecessary, and is not recommended.

Tension-releasing not only lets one relax and feel pleasures, but projects a freedom to others that helps them relax and share the pleasures.

Neo-Tech Advantage #75
JOY AND HAPPINESS

The emotions of pleasure, joy, well-being, and happiness have interrelating features. But each is a separate experience with unique characteristics and requirements. For example, one can be happy without experiencing pleasure, and one can experience temporary pleasure without being happy. Joy is a self-induced, here-and-now emotion that arises from pleasure, well-being, and happiness.

Enjoyment is also induced by consciously reflecting on the emotional rewards of pleasure, well-being, and happiness. To fully experience enjoyment, one must reject unearned guilt foisted on him or her by mystics and neocheaters. [Re: Table 42, Neo-Tech Reference Encyclopedia]. When a Neo-Tech oriented person earns happiness, he or she can then make a conscious choice to guiltlessly enjoy that happiness.

Neo-Tech Advantage #76
PHILOSOPHY FOR ROMANTIC LOVE

Glib, shallow philosophies about love and sex based on selflessness, altruism, or slogans are easily conjured up by mystics and neocheaters. To some people, Leo Buscaglia's love-all philosophies may sound poetic, beautiful, comfortable, and easy to accept. But those pseudo philosophies are generally rigged from non sequiturs and then promulgated as the truth by glib psychologists, social "experts", religious "authorities", egalitarian writers, mountebanks, and other neocheaters who have never experienced integrated, value-oriented romantic love. Thus, their books and words work to diminish everyone's love and happiness.

Many books about love and sex are also based on spurious, altruistic philosophies that sound "good" on the surface and promise happiness through a system of destructively selfless, sacrificial acts. But altruism is a power-usurping tool contrived by neocheaters for contradicting reality, subverting the nature of human beings, and laying false guilt on everyone. Such glibly spurious, altruistic philosophies contradict the positive, valuable goals ostensibly presented in those books. Most authors never realize that an explicit, rational philosophy is necessary to form a consistent basis for their writings, especially when dealing with human relationships and love.

If philosophy is ignored or used inconsistently by the authors, the value of their work is diminished. Without a conscious philosophical position, no consistent principles are available to guide a person's work, life, or love relationship. By contrast, every Neo-Tech/Psychuous concept is rooted in a consistent philosophy that integrates reality with the physical, psychological, and intellectual nature of human beings.

Consciously or subconsciously, all people make philosophical choices that determine the course of their lives. Two fundamental philosophical choices exist for all human beings: (1) a reality oriented, pro-life choice (Aristotelian), or (2) a mystically oriented, anti-life choice (Platonistic). The future of all humans and all societies are determined by those two philosophical choices. Aristotelian choices allow a person to experience success, prosperity, romantic love, psychuous pleasures, long-range happiness. Platonistic choices lead to a rationalized life that eventually produces failure, anxiety, destructiveness, boredom, unhappiness [Re: Neo-Tech Reference Encyclopedia, Table 43 illustrates the results of those two choices throughout history while listing the social and personal consequences of choosing an Aristotelian versus a Platonistic approach to life].

Thus, all philosophical concepts fall into one of two camps:
1. Aristotelian-based, free-enterprise individualism based on life-oriented honesty and effort.
2. Platonistic-based, altruistic collectivism based on death-oriented dishonesty and laziness.

All religions and most political concepts fall into the Platonistic camp. All Neo-Tech/Psychuous concepts fall into the Aristotelian camp [Re: Table 44, Neo-Tech Reference Encyclopedia].

Neo-Tech Advantage #77
ARISTOTLE FOR THE LIVING AND THE FUTURE
VS.
PLATO FOR THE DEAD AND THE PAST

Philosophy determines the course of each individual's life. [Re: Concept 107, Neo-Tech Reference Encyclopedia] The diametrically opposite choices between Aristotelian philosophy and Platonistic philosophy profoundly affect every individual and society. [Re: Tables 43 and 44, Neo-Tech Reference Encyclopedia] Aristotelian philosophy is the intellectual basis of Neo-Tech. Platonistic philosophy is the intellectual basis of every irrational, destructive religious and political system promoted in the past 2300 years. Indeed, Platonism is the philosophical foundation of mysticism, altruism, sacrifice, egalitarianism, existentialism, religion, dictatorships, theism, socialism, democracy, communism, fascism, evangelism and every other rule of force, coercion, and fraud. Except for free-enterprise capitalism, all political systems including democracy (a tyranny by the majority) require deception and force to exist. Thus, all those political and religious systems are immoral and harmful to human beings. Only free-enterprise capitalism is:
1. based entirely on voluntary free choice,
2. consistent with the nature of conscious beings and, thus is beneficial to all conscious beings,
3. moral and just: Offers freedom to everyone. Rejects all mysticism, racism, initiatory force, and fraud.

Platonism is also the basis of all public educational systems. Government-run schools today are inept at educating children because they embrace the ideas of John Dewey, a Platonist existentialist who dishonestly replaced the objective principles of education with power-usurping, subjective methods. (Dewey's contemporaries, William James and Sidney Hook, promoted similar but more cautiously disguised, existentialistic ideas.) Using dishonest non sequiturs, Dewey's philosophy dismisses as socially irrelevant the pedagogical teaching of fundamental knowledge such as reading, writing, mathematics, and science.

Dewey's philosophy promotes the mystical concept that children can be "educated" by allowing them to randomly pursue their own whims. The students' whims are considered socially relevant to the here-and-now and thus are deemed as the basis of education. The "teacher", therefore, merely follows wherever the child's feelings may lead (rather than the teacher providing the child with objective knowledge through systematic input of integrated facts and information). With an existential action approach, Dewey deems the mind as the creator of "reality". Thus, in one mystical stroke, he negates both the integrating conscious mind and objective reality.

Although deceptively stating the opposite, Karl Marx's dialectical materialism is the same "reality creating" approach to action as Dewey's approach. Hitler's approach is also the same as Dewey's "willed realities" and "created logics". That "reality-creating" approach is the essence of mysticism. For it relieves the mind of the basic human responsibility to identify, integrate, and then logically deal with objective reality. As a pragmatic existential neocheater, Dewey scraps logic, knowledge, and reason in favor of whims and feelings. He deems such whims and feelings as the primary guide to human knowledge, education, and action. ...Designed from dishonesty and laziness, Dewey's destructive "educational" approach is the basis of public education today.

Plato provided the tools for rationalizing an "intellectual" basis for any false or specious approach, including Dewey's approach. Platonistic philosophy can "justify" any irrational or unjust means to "noble" ends or "higher" causes. That same philosophy provides the tools for rationalizing the two primary character faults of conscious beings — dishonesty and laziness.

126

Aristotle, on the other hand, provides the tools that every person needs to develop the knowledge necessary for guiding his or her life to unlimited prosperity, psychuous pleasures, and abiding happiness. Aristotelian philosophy provides the tools for meeting the needs of the human organism for optimum survival and maximum happiness. Successful use of those tools requires integrated honesty and rational efforts.

The following chart illustrates how a civilization might have advanced if an Aristotelian rather than a Platonistic philosophy had dominated for the past 2300 years. This chart shows how free-enterprise capitalism would have eliminated mysticism, parasitism, religion, collectivism, altruism, and force-backed governments with the subsequent elimination of neocheating, wars, crime, disease, poverty, and death itself.

Some of the estimates made in the chart include steam engines and trains in operation at the birth of Christ (who in a free-enterprise society might have matured into an energetic, happy, value-producing carpenter or contractor), mass produced cars available in 50 A.D., commercial airlines in operation by 60 A.D., crime and fraud eliminated (not by government police but by individual self-defense and private protection services, private courts, and computerized ostracism) by 65 A.D., nuclear power by 70 A.D., man on the moon by 80 A.D., cancer cured by 90 A.D., youth-perpetuating biological immortality by 120 A.D., immortal conscious individuals master of all known nature by 2000 A.D.

AN ARISTOTELIAN COURSE OF HISTORY

Assume that an objective, Aristotelian-based philosophy rather than a mystical, Platonistic-based philosophy had dominated the Western World since the Golden Age of Greece:

**Progress through Mystic-Free Cosmic Minds
rather than
Mystic-Plagued Plato Minds**

500 B.C.   Heracleitus   (540 B.C.-480 B.C.)
450 B.C.   Socrates   (470 B.C.-399 B.C.)
400 B.C.   Plato   (427 B.C.-348 B.C.)

350 B.C.   Aristotle (384 B.C.-322 B.C.). Plato's philosophy identified as mystical and forever dismissed as dishonest, destructive.

200 B.C.   America discovered.

100 B.C.   Free-enterprise capitalism established around the world. Free markets flourishing. All forms of mysticism and neocheating identified, discredited, and rejected. All government taxation and nonprofit spending programs abolished. All forms of initiatory force are morally condemned. Wars become obsolete and vanish. Arts, sciences, technology boom in totally free markets. Dynamic competition and value production rule. Romantic love flourishes.

0 B.C.   All traces of mysticism, altruism, and collectivism are gone. Poverty essentially eliminated. The individual is the supreme value. Jesus builds the highest skyscraper in Asia Minor. Trains and steamships are major forms of transportation.

20 A.D.   Electrical power developed, camera developed.

40 A.D.   Internal-combustion engine developed.

50 A.D.   Cars in mass production. Airplane developed.

60 A.D.   Commercial airlines flourishing. Computer developed.

65 A.D.   Crime and fraud become unprofitable, obsolete, and essentially eliminated by computerized ostracism.

70 A.D.   Nuclear power developed. Nuclear weapons never conceived.

80 A.D.   Man on the moon. Internet developed.

90 A.D.   Cancer and most other diseases eliminated.

100 A.D.   Man on Mars and heading for other planets.

110 A.D.   Need for sleep eliminated.

120 A.D.   Youth-perpetuating biological immortality developed.

140 A.D.   Prosperity and happiness of conscious beings are universal.

200 A.D. Worldwide, commercial, biological immortality achieved. All diseases and aging eliminated. Man colonizing, mining, and commercializing the moon, asteroids, and Mars. Commercial shuttle flights (passenger and freight) to space-station colonies. ...Achieve access to the gravity-coded, interstellar universal computer.

1200 A.D. Energy and technology advanced to where sufficient energy can be generated for traveling to other earth-like planets in outer space. Science, knowledge, and fulfillment advanced to the point at which no economic or scientific incentive exists for directly communicating with or travelling to the billions of other, outer-space civilizations.

2000 A.D. Immortal conscious beings in a Neo-Tech, free-enterprise society are master of all known nature. People and goods are transported at the speed of light via electronic transfer. Most goods manufactured via nanotechnology with the electronic control of atoms and molecules. New knowledge is expanding at near the speed of light.

Neo-Tech Advantage #78
HUMOR VS. SENSE OF LIFE: A TEST FOR HUMOR
Spontaneous humor is a highly individualized characteristic that reflects a person's sense of life. Humor can also identify a person's psychology and philosophy [Re: Table 46, Neo-Tech Reference Encyclopedia].

Humor is a product of lateral or horizontal thinking [Re: Concept 143, Neo-Tech Reference Encyclopedia]. Through horizontal thinking, a new and unexpected way to look at something is developed. That surprise contrast between the conventional, expected view and the new, unexpected view is the essence of humor. The nature of that newly created view reflects the sense of life in both those who create and those who respond to that particular humor.

The spontaneous response to humor is a quick, automatic indicator of that person's sense of life (e.g., benevolent or malevolent). Even when they try, few people can conceal or successfully fake their response to humor. Thus, identification of a person's sense of life through humor is often quite reliable. Understanding the nature of humor helps identify one's own sense of life as well as that of other people [Re: Table 46, Neo-Tech Reference Encyclopedia]. Also, a compatibility of humor is one of the most enjoyable aspects of friendships and romantic-love relationships.

Neo-Tech Advantage #79
TABOOS AND LAWS AGAINST
VOLUNTARY SEX ACTS

Deep-rooted taboos subconsciously affect nonsexual as well as sexual relationships between people. For example, fear of incest taboos can inhibit or even prevent an affectionate, rewarding father-daughter relationship. Subconscious incest taboos and fears can also block or limit communication between parents and their children concerning sex education and open discussion of sexual matters. Taboos can likewise inhibit nonsexual friendships and prevent loving, familial affections from reaching their full potential.

Objective examination reveals that most negative views of taboos are themselves irrational or mystical. Even negative views of the strongest taboos such as bestiality and incest are sometimes unfounded. But violating or performing any taboo can also stem from an unhealthy, neurotic, psychotic, or criminal base.

Forcible rape and child-adult sexual relations are not just taboos, but are criminal acts. For, they involve the violation of individual rights by force or coercion. A child lacks the experience, knowledge, as well as the emotional and physical independence to make valid free-choice, sexual-relation decisions. Such a child can easily be forced or coerced into sexual acts by his or her natural dependency on the adult for survival. Indeed, adult incest with a child is equivalent to rape in violating that child's individual rights and well-being. Thus, when a child is involved, incest is a crime exceeded in seriousness only by injurious assault, rape, and murder. ...Carrying out any taboo, sex act, or any action for that matter becomes criminal when (and only when) the action harms, diminishes, or endangers an individual's rights or life by force, fraud, or coercion.[1]

But mutually agreed-on violation of other taboos can be from a healthy or "good-for-me" base. For example, most of today's vanishing taboos such as premarital sex, oral sex, enactment of fantasies, and the satisfying of fetishes are often (but not always) performed from a healthy base [Re: Concepts 111 and 112, Neo-Tech Reference Encyclopedia]. Violating other taboos such as adultery can be injurious when involving deception or dishonesty. Also plural marriages are generally (but not always) too difficult or demanding to be healthy, even if honest. Taboos such as homosexuality and bestiality are often thought to be violated from psychologically harmful, neurotic bases. But such is not the case when performed by genetically determined homosexuals or adolescents motivated by curiosity. ...One possible lure to non genetic forms of homosexuality is easy, low-effort, multiple sexual experiences. But, the percentage of homosexuals affected or motivated by that lure is not known. Indeed, much is still unknown about homosexuality.[2]

Committing incest usually evolves from a neurotic or a psychotic base, but again not always. Incest between consenting adults, for example, is theoretically possible from a healthy base. Despite government laws,[3] nothing in the nature of voluntary, adult-adult incest is inherently wrong or harmful in the act itself.

---

[1]The highly emotional, serious-crime nature of child-adult sex has given government neocheaters a bonanza of causes célèbres for increasing their usurpation of power. As a result, individual rights are further transgressed. From such government overreactions, many innocent people are unjustly accused and even jailed. Consider, for example, the rash of witch hunts against child day-care centers a few years ago during which nearly everyone charged or prosecuted was innocent. ...Those politically ambitious, neocheating prosecutors simply swaggered away with arrogant impunity from their ruin and waste. Without a qualm, they never gave a backward glance at the ruined businesses, broken lives, and psychologically damaged children they needlessly caused.

[2]Genetic homosexuals should be guiltlessly free to pursue their sexual preference without attempts to "cure" them. For, genetic homosexuality is nature's sorting method of preventing procreation of progeny with certain genetic anomalies. Non genetic homosexuals, however, seeking heterosexual lives can find assistance, for example, by contacting The National Association for Research and Treatment of Homosexuality.

[3]About half the states prohibit marriage of first cousins. All states prohibit marriage of blood relationships closer than first cousins.

But conception among close blood relatives can activate undesirable, genetically recessive traits. Thus, the special problem of bearing defective children must be considered by closely related couples. The decision to bear children, however, always remains the right of the couple. But if they choose to bear children, they must be willing and able to assume full responsibility to provide for and raise to independent adulthood any children they bear.

The inherent non-wrongness of adult-adult incest is most obvious in the case of adult orphans who unknown to each other are brother and sister and who by chance meet. They could quite naturally fall in love, have sex, marry, and have children without knowledge of their blood relationship. Incest in that case obviously can be from a healthy basis. Furthermore, even known incestuous relationships between consenting adults are not necessarily unhealthy or neurotic (although today they often are). Throughout recorded history, incestuous marriages, especially among the ruling classes, were accepted as normal and widely practiced in many cultures.

No sexual act between consenting adults can objectively be illegal, even if the acts are physically or psychologically harmful to the consenting individuals (such as injurious homosexuality, masochism, sadism). Only acts of force, fraud, or coercion that violate the individual rights of nonconsenting people[1] can be objectively illegal. Such criminal acts include forcible rape, adult/child sexual relationships, nonconsenting sadism, and any other acts that are physically or fraudulently forced on unwilling or unknowing victims.

Some of the more irrational government laws that violate individual rights are those dealing with sex. They range from the government sanctioning murder (e.g., some jurisdictions allow the husband to kill with near impunity the lover of his wife) to

[1]Nonconsenting people always include children. For they are unable to give valid or informed sexual consent because (1) they have gained neither the knowledge nor experience to assume the responsibilities for the physical and psychological consequences of sexual actions, and (2) they are dependent on adults for survival thus can be easily coerced or lured into consenting to psychologically harmful acts. An extremely harmful form of unjust, human manipulation is the parent-child incestuous relationship. Such a parent not only manipulates the child's lack of knowledge, but uses the child's survival dependence on the parent to criminally coerce that child into physically or psychologically destructive actions.

restricting the way one makes love to a consenting partner (e.g., in some states, couples can go to jail for oral sex).

Neo-Tech Advantage #80
INITIATORY FORCE — THE PRIME EVIL

Force, coercion, threat of force, or fraud[1] initiated against any individual for any reason by any individual, groups of individuals, societies, or governments is morally wrong. That is the only categorical moral statement possible. That statement must, by its nature, be the categorical, irreducible, and fundamental standard for all conscious beings, always, everywhere. That statement is the moral axiom upon which every Neo-Tech/ Psychuous Concept rests. The initiation of force and fraud among conscious beings is not only the basic moral wrong and evil, but is the primary tool used by all professional mystics and neocheaters to survive through value destruction.

No exceptions to the immorality of initiatory force exist. No matter how "noble" the ends, they never justify the means of initiating force, fraud, or coercion against any individual. Any government or activity that depends on or uses initiatory force, threat of force, or coercion is immoral and destructive. Therefore, all taxation backed by force, all conscription backed by force, and all laws that regulate or control by force or coercion are immoral.

The only laws that are objectively just and moral are those that protect the life and property rights of individuals from initiatory force and fraud. All other laws that regulate people's lives or property are morally wrong, contrary to human nature, and harmful to everyone. Such immoral laws include those that restrict or prohibit drugs, alcohol, prostitution, abortion (of the fetus at any age), or any form of censorship or restriction of voluntary sexual activity. All such laws are morally wrong because they use threats or force against individuals.

While all governments have the power, none ever have the moral right to initiate force or coercion against any individual. The only beneficial and moral laws are those designed to protect the life and property rights of individuals from initiatory force,

---

[1]Fraud is an indirect form of initiatory force that deceptively or dishonestly deprives a person of his life or property. All religions and governments operate and survive on fraud and/or force.

the threat of force, and fraud. In turn, the only moral use of force is for self-defense: That is for protection of oneself, property, or country from force initiated by other individuals or governments. ...Self-defense by any means, including force, is not only a basic moral right, but a moral duty.

No government has ever helped an individual produce more values or greater happiness than that individual could have produced without government. Governments differ only in the degree they harm people. In fact, except for protecting individual rights, no valid reason for government exists. Indeed, the entire concept of government is invalid and mystical. Government is nothing more than a mystical, big-lie hoax perpetuated through the centuries by neocheaters through force, non sequiturs, and the manipulation of mysticism.

Government is not the equivalent of one's country. Governments are based on invalid mystical notions that have no basis in reality; countries are objectively real entities of defined territories. A person can love his or her country, but properly despise the government that with usurped power constantly harms and drains everyone within its realm.

Neo-Tech Advantage #81
OPPRESSION AND FREEDOM — PAST AND FUTURE

The following chart demonstrates the trend of human oppression over the past 3300 years. That oppression is directly proportional to the force and fraud governments and religion exert against individuals. The most oppressive, unhappy period of history was the Dark Ages during which religious power controlled the political system with unlimited force against individuals. By contrast, human happiness and well-being increased markedly during those periods when honesty and business reduced government and religious power. Also, as shown in the following chart, the government and church always oppressed women more than men. Indeed, governments and churches have always been controlled by neocheaters who manipulate the mystical concept of altruistic sacrifice to gain power. And, historically, those male neocheaters have always found physically weaker, more mystically dependent women their first and easiest target to bully into submission.

In exercising their unearned power, professional mystics and neocheaters gained added leverage by encouraging men to bully physically weaker women into submission. And they especially lured women into silliness — into following mystical stupidities such as astrology and religion. But with the rise of nonmystical, free-market economies, women have become increasingly productive, more independent, less mystical, thus less oppressed. And recently, for the first time in history, freedom for men and women has become nearly equal. But with today's reviving interest in the stupidities of mysticism and religion, more women are choosing to slip back into mystical lives controlled by others.

FREEDOM/OPPRESSION LEVEL
+6=Maximum Freedom to
-6=Maximum Oppression

□□Period	Men	Women
Ancient Greece		
1300 B.C. – 450 B.C.	0	-1
Enlightened Greece		
450 B.C. – 27 B.C.	0	-3
Roman Empire		
27 B.C. – 385 A.D.	+1	-1
Christianity Established		
200 A.D. – 385 A.D.	-2	-4
Rise of Christian Power		
(the unhappiest period in history)		
385 A.D. – 1000 A.D.	-5	-6
Romantic Love Challenges Christianity		
1000 – 1300	-2	-4
Renaissance Weakens Christianity		
1300 – 1500	0	-1

Church Fights Back with Witch Trials and Inquisitions
1300 – 1500   -4   -6

The Puritans
1500 – 1700   +1   0

Age of Reason
1700 – 1800   +1   -1

Early Victorianism
1800 – 1850   +1   -4

Rise of Capitalism
1850 – 1900   +2   0

Rise of Romantic Love
1900 – 1960   +3   +1

Sexual Liberation
1960 – 1980   +3   +2.5

Rise of Mystical Stupidities: Evangelism via Television
1980 – 1990   +2.5   +1.5

Rise of Neo-Tech: The End of Mysticism and Neocheating
1990 – ∞ steadily increasing to +6   +6

Note: The long-term, general trend throughout history has been away from mysticism, poverty, stupidity, oppression, misery...and toward honesty, prosperity, intelligence, freedom, happiness: Away from the mystic-plagued Plato mind...and toward the mystic-free cosmic mind.

Today, the various political-religious hucksters, neocheating academia, mystical feminists, and many dishonest journalists and political cartoonists are climbing over each other to attack and undermine individual rights, business, and value producers around the world [Re: Table 51, Neo-Tech Reference Encyclopedia]. Since business and its value producers strengthen individual rights, the attacks on business and producers are actually attacks on individual rights. Such attacks are designed to control the value producers for exploitation by neocheaters.

The worldwide trend of increasingly accepting mysticism and violence can culminate in either a government-sponsored nuclear holocaust or a world-wide, terror-controlled government. Either course would end our current civilization. With a continued rise of worldwide mysticism, either (1) a nuclear holocaust would occur through destructive political insanities (e.g., nuclear-armed Marxists/Leninists/Maoists) or destructive religious insanities (e.g., nuclear-armed Shiite muslims), or (2) a Lenin/Mao-style or Khomeini/Giuliani-style government would enslave or slaughter the best — the most valiant, independent, value producers. That enslavement and slaughter of the good, the happy, the best among us would drag humanity back into the Dark Ages...perhaps for centuries.

In a world of escalating mysticism and neocheating, what will stop that destructive trend? Neo-Tech followed by Neothink will not only stop that trend, but will reverse it effectively, decisively, forever. Indeed, Neo-Tech has already begun to check the trend. Nothing can stop the current, worldwide Neo-Tech wave from breaking across all continents to eliminate mysticism and its symbiotic neocheaters.

The alternative to all gloomy scenarios caused by mystics and neocheaters is Neo-Tech driven competition — a competitive revolution led by honest, productive working people. That competition will render all professional mystics and neocheaters impotent, uncompetitive, unable to manipulate the producers, unable to survive. Neo-Tech led competition will bring a forever prospering, happy business world [Re: Table 51, Neo-Tech Reference Encyclopedia].

In a Neo-Tech political, social, and business environment, an unstoppable surge of human happiness, well-being, productivity, and romantic love will occur. Against Neo-Tech, professional mystics and neocheaters will appear as impotent clowns. They will be unable to deceive, cheat, oppress, injure, destroy, kill... unable to manipulate their plunderings and aggressions...unable to wage wars or commit mass murder. Indeed, Neo-Tech with its honest nature and competitive business climate will create an exhilarating, unstoppable atmosphere for creativity and achievement. The worldwide standard of living and happiness will soar. Poverty and famine will vanish. Most diseases including cancer and AIDS will quickly be eliminated. ...Human biological immortality without aging will soon become commercially available — probably within a decade [Re: Concept 145, Neo-Tech Reference Encyclopedia].

Neo-Tech Advantage #82
A CONSTITUTION FOR PROSPERITY, PSYCHUOUS PLEASURES, AND ROMANTIC LOVE

At no time in history have the ideas, influences, doctrines, platforms, or actions of any political or religious system ever yielded a net benefit to productive human beings. No such system has ever increased the long-range prosperity, well-being, and happiness of anyone.[1] Indeed, individuals and civilizations thrive to the extent that religious and government power is diminished. The anti-force platform of the American Business Party first appeared nearly two decades ago in BARRONS financial weekly. [Re: Table 52, of Neo-Tech Reference Encyclopedia] That platform represents the only political structure that functions without force, fraud, or coercion. That platform, therefore, is compatible with the biological needs and well-being of all human beings. All other political systems depend on force, fraud, or coercion to function. Thus, all such systems have always harmed everyone throughout the ages.

Only the unique, anti-force nature of business allows people to fully use their minds and exercise their individual rights to live prosperously and happily. The question of having no government in a Neo-Tech business society versus having a limited government in areas of national defense, the courts, and police protection is meaningless so long as the moral principle of no initiatory force or fraud is observed. Within a Neo-Tech business

---

[1]But different political systems can vary greatly in their relative destructiveness. Western-world democracies, for example, are much less oppressive and destructive than are the terror-totalitarian systems of Russia, Red China, Nazi Germany, Cuba. Left-wing or right-wing, all totalitarian governments use the same institutions of power, force, and terror. That is why when a right-wing dictatorship falls, a left-wing dictatorship can so quickly seize and use the instruments of force already in place. Without much effort, the new government can continue usurping power and values as did the previous government, but with ever greater force and terror.

society, a company called "government" or competing companies would deliver a needed, integrated package of services to those who voluntarily paid for such services. Without power to initiate force or the threat of force required to collect taxes, governments would function only to the extent their citizens or clients found their services valuable enough to voluntarily purchase.[1]

If citizens refused to purchase certain government services, those services would simply go out of business. Or they would be replaced by more efficient services that enough people thought valuable enough to buy. An honest, legitimate government would by necessity be both a competitive, profit-oriented service and an individual-rights protection business. In some areas, possibly several competing businesses, organizations, or companies might offer the same services in competing for citizens as customers.

Voluntarily supported governments and voluntarily supported businesses would really be equivalent entities subject to the same free-market dynamics and the unbreakable order dictated by free competition, market demands, investment protection, and value exchange. A nonforce government could be called Government, Government Company, or any other name. Likewise, that entity would be subject to the same economic disciplines of profits, losses, growth, competition, and bankruptcy as any competing business. In other words, in a Neo-Tech society, governments would have the same nature, disciplines, and anti-anarchy order as any free-enterprise business. And they would be subject to the same competitive influences and disciplines to improve quality and value. ...The ordered purpose of business would reign; the arbitrary disorder of mystical/neocheating, force-backed governments would vanish.

The transition from a force-dependent government to a nonforce government could cause some temporary dislocations, such as cutting welfare, stopping transfer-payment "services", and selling government property to pay off and close out Social Security claims. But those problems would be minor and

---

[1]Does Neo-Tech lead to anarchy? No, just the opposite. Neo-Tech leads to business-like order and prosperity. Only destructive, bogus-job authorities backed by force cause disorder and eventual anarchy.

139

transitory compared to the flood of permanent, major benefits that would immediately assert themselves. For example, national defense and police protection would immediately strengthen toward total effectiveness as purpose and efficiency soared. Moreover, a nonforce government would mean no taxes, no irrational controls or destructive regulations, no government corruption, no neocheaters, no wars, and a spectacularly prosperous, healthy, happy society.

Neo-Tech Advantage #83
DISMISSING 3000 YEARS OF MYSTICISM
for a life of
PERSONAL POWER, PROSPERITY, AND HAPPINESS

The purpose of each individual human life is to prosper and live happily. Anyone can achieve that prosperity and happiness when free of force, fraud, or coercion by others.

The Neo-Tech Constitution forbids initiatory force, threat of force, or fraud by any individual, group of individuals, or government. No other law or rule is needed for a moral, rational society.

Forbidding initiatory force and coercion is the only political law compatible with the prosperity and happiness of human beings. Thus, the Neo-Tech Constitution leaves everyone with the conditions for prosperity and happiness. No other constitution or laws are needed or valid.

The Neo-Tech Constitution stated below obsoletes the constitutions of all nations:

THE NEO-TECH CONSTITUTION
Preamble

The purpose of human life is to prosper and live happily. The function of society is to protect those conditions that let all individuals achieve prosperity and happiness. Those conditions can be delivered by a constitution that prohibits the use of initiatory force or coercion by any person, group, or government against any individual:

140

The Constitution

Article 1: No person, group of persons, or government may initiate force, threat of force, or fraud against the person or property of any individual.

Article 2: Force may be morally and legally used only in defense against those who violate Article 1.

Article 3: No exception shall ever exist to Articles 1 & 2.

The Neo-Tech Constitution rests on six axioms:
1. Values exist only relative to life.
2. Whatever benefits a living organism is a value to that organism. Whatever harms a living organism is a disvalue to that organism.
3. The basic value against which all values are measured is the conscious individual.
4. Morals relate only to conscious individuals.
5. Immoral actions arise from individuals choosing to harm others through force, fraud, deception, coercion — or from individuals choosing to usurp, attack, or destroy values earned by others.
6. Moral actions arise from individuals choosing to benefit others by competitively producing values for them.

How would the Neo-Tech Constitution be enforced? Through (1) self-defense/deterrent forces and (2) organized ostracizing systems ...Effective ostracisation is a much more powerful mechanism for justice, restitution, and deterrent than any form of force. And the severest, fully integrated ostracisation can eventually deliver capital punishment through suicide.

Background for The Neo-Tech Constitution
The purpose of human life is to prosper happily. By integrating the human mind with reality, anyone can prosper happily by making one's self increasingly valuable to others. But what keeps most people from doing that — from fulfilling their

own nature? What has kept most people throughout history from experiencing the prosperity and happiness that they are fully qualified to earn?...The answer lies in three words: **Force**, **Mysticism**, **Neocheating:**[1]

Force

Force is the instrument used to usurp or expropriate values earned by others: Directly or indirectly, all initiated force supports stagnated status quo, laziness, and incompetence at the expense of competitive growth, productivity, and ability. Criminals, mystics, neocheaters, governments, and religions use force, threat of force, or fraud to drain life, values, and happiness from the producers and society. But those who live by force or fraud live in discord with reality. They offer nothing to others except dwarfed lives, diminished happiness, and lost values.

Professional mystics and neocheaters depend on force or deception to survive. But, the value producer never needs to use force or deception to prosper.

Once value producers identify the nature of initiatory force, they will reject its use as criminal and harmful under *any* conditions. From that point on, the value producers can guiltlessly collect their earned prosperity and happiness. And all who have lived by force and coercion will find they can no longer live by usurping values. Instead, they too will have to produce competitive values for others or perish.

Mysticism

Mysticism is defined as: 1. Any attempt to use the mind as a "reality" creating device rather than a reality integrating organism. 2. Any attempt to recreate or alter reality through dishonesty, feelings, non sequiturs, or rationalizations. 3. Any attempt to ignore, evade, contradict, or fake reality. 4. Any creation of problems where none exist.

Mysticism is the tool used by neocheaters to manipulate or hide the force, fraud, or coercion used to usurp power and values

---

[1]Without initiatory force, mysticism, and neocheating, everyone would be compelled by the dynamics of competition to live by producing honest, competitive values for others and society.

from others. Mysticism is used to create specious standards for projecting undeserved guilt onto others. Why? To beguile value producers into surrendering their earned power and values to the value destroyers.

Neocheating

Neocheating is defined as: Any intentional use of mysticism to create false realities and illusions in order to extract values or power from others.

Neocheating is the technique for usurping values, money, power by using mysticism to manipulate others.

Neocheating is the essential technique politicians, clergymen, bogus-job bureaucrats, and white-collar-hoax business quislings use to usurp jobs, power, money, and pseudo self-esteem from others.

The Nature of Mysticism Used by Neocheaters

Mysticism is an evasion of reality that is never supported by honesty or objective reality. Mysticism, the stupidness disease, harms human beings in five ways:

1. Mysticism cripples the integration capacities required to accurately understand reality. That accurate understanding is necessary to make decisions competently, to solve problems effectively, and to live competitively.

2. Mysticism short-circuits or blocks the mind to prevent unlimited, wide integrations that let one know and understand everything in the universe without limits.

3. Mysticism drains one's intelligence, efficacy, and ability to live competitively.

4. Mysticism blocks the long-range thinking integrations needed to prosper continuously, love romantically, and live happily.

5. Mysticism subjects individuals increasingly to the control of professional mystics and neocheaters.

Mysticism is arbitrary, has no link to reality, and is based on nothing. Thus, mysticism *is nothing*. Yet, by manipulating rationalizations, non sequiturs, aphorisms, parables, superstitions, modern art, poetry, songs, rock music, chants, slogans, newspeak, quotes, or facts out of context, a professional mystic or neocheater can create illusions to seemingly justify almost any harmful action, including thefts and murder. Such "justifications" are essential for their unjustifiable pillagings of value producers.

Mysticism and neocheating have been used for 2000 years to create illusions that "external authorities" protect the lives of individuals, can solve problems for others, and can provide livings for non-producers. But, in reality, all such "authorities" are merely neocheaters using deception, force, or coercion to extract their bogus livelihoods from the value producers. And those neocheaters are the fountainhead of crimes and human-imposed suffering.

Mysticism and neocheating are the main causes of pain and failure among human beings. Mysticism and neocheating are anti-life — death-oriented. The core of mystics and neocheaters is dishonesty and laziness. Their task is to beguile value producers into supporting the value destroyers.

The Morality of Mystics and Neocheaters

Morality is defined as: Conscious actions that purposely benefit people and society are moral. Conscious actions that purposely harm people and society are immoral. Thus, value destroyers such as mystics, neocheaters, and their agents of force, coercion, and deception are immoral. For, they purposely harm others and society by choosing to usurp values from others rather than produce values for others. By contrast, value producers are moral. For, they purposely benefit others and society by choosing to competitively produce more values for others than they consume.

Mystics violate morality: They harm both their own and every other person's life. They are destructive, silly, immature, childish. By choosing to evade reality, they undermine their ability to identify reality, to think clearly, to produce values, to live happily, to compete honestly — to survive. As a result, they increasingly transfer responsibilities for their failures onto

144

others. They routinely lay blame and guilt on others for their own problems.[1]

Neocheaters violate morality: They purposely expand their harm by orchestrating mystical illusions to plunder others and society. Moreover, they design their illusions to make themselves appear as innocent benefactors and their victims appear as the guilty malefactors. But the opposite is true: The neocheaters are the guilty malefactors; their victims are usually the innocent value producers. Yet, as long as most people allow themselves to accept those mystical inversions of honesty, the neocheaters will keep pillaging them and society. As a result, such neocheaters always harm society by draining prosperity and happiness from everyone.

Agents of Force violate morality: They purposely harm others by expropriating values through force or threat of force. Moreover, by choosing to expropriate rather than earn values, agents of force destroy their own lives by demolishing their competence, self-esteem, and happiness.

By Contrast

Nonmystics are moral: They accept the responsibility to think and act for themselves in order to produce objective values for others. With a loyalty to honesty, they act in accord with objective reality. They are mature, evolved people who strive to integrate their words and actions with honesty and reality, regardless of anyone's opinions, dictates, wishes, or emotions. As a result, nonmystics always benefit others and society.

Rejecting Losers

Mystics, neocheaters, and agents of force are losers. They are immature, unevolved people with self-arrested character development. They function through dishonesty and deception.

---

[1]Everyone must fight mysticism both from within and from without. Each who quits fighting lets mysticism take over his or her life. Each who surrenders or stops struggling against mysticism becomes a part of the dishonest, quasi-dead world of mystics and neocheaters. And that unhappy world parasitically feeds on the destruction of values.

For those reasons, they must depend on the producer for survival. But, they resent and envy the producer in knowing that they cannot experience his or her competence and happiness, no matter how much they extract from others. Mystics and neocheaters live unhappy, shrinking lives. Living through huckstered faith enforced by deception or force, they steadily lose respect for honesty, happiness, and the purpose to live. They increasingly move toward failure and death. And often, steeped in envy, they want everyone else to fail and die with them. ...Thus, anyone can benefit by immediately rejecting losers such as mystics, neocheaters, and agents of force.

Free Choice

All people must continually choose between dishonesty or honesty, between laziness or effort, between accepting or rejecting mysticism from both within and without. Accepting mysticism means evading honesty and denying reality in favor of feelings, wishes, or external "authorities". And those consistently choosing mysticism become dependent on others or "authorities" to think for them, to lead them, to neocheat for them. But rejecting mysticism upholds honesty, rejects neocheaters and dependence on them, builds competence and independence, and finally enhances life for everyone.

Four Facts

1. No one can give another person self-worth or happiness. Yet anyone can achieve those two prime values by (a) producing more competitive values for others than consumed by oneself; and (b) rejecting mystics, neocheaters, and their schemes to usurp power and values from others.
2. Loyalty to honesty and rationality must replace mysticism in order to harness one's natural power. By remaining loyal to honesty and rationality, a person can (a) disarm mysticism, (b) render neocheaters impotent, and (c) create the conditions that allow personal prosperity and happiness to flourish.

3. People who resist mysticism from within and reject neocheating from without will gain prosperity and happiness. But others who remain foundering in the seas of mysticism and neocheating will become uncompetitive and lose the values of life.
4. If everyone were a mystic, human life would end. If everyone were a value destroyer, an agent of force, a neocheater, human life would end. But if everyone were an honest value producer, human life and happiness would flourish beyond imagination.

The Intertwining Dependency of Force and Fraud on Mysticism

Mysticism destroys from within; force destroys from without. Yet, both mysticism and force are unnatural and disposable. Neither are rooted in reality or have any inherent power. Still, all unearned power and expropriated values depend on mystical illusions backed by coercion, force, fraud, or deception. Mystics, neocheaters, and other value destroyers need those illusions to beguile, flimflam, or force values from others. But once that intertwining dependency of mysticism and force is unraveled, the rationalizations crumble and illusions vanish. ...Without their illusions, mystics and neocheaters are powerless.

When value producers understand that intertwining dependency of force and fraud on mysticism, they will stop supporting mystics and neocheaters who live off the efforts of others. Those mystics and neocheaters will then be powerless. Their only means of survival will be to produce rather than usurp values. Once they become value producers, their self-esteems and competencies will soar. And then, they too can evolve into self-responsible human beings who *earn* their prosperity and happiness.

Abolishing Initiatory Force by Ending Mysticism

The Neo-Tech Constitution forbids initiatory force or fraud. Without force or fraud, mysticism and thus neocheaters become impotent. Without mysticism, force becomes ineffective for extracting values from others. The axioms of the Neo-Tech Constitution are real and cannot be contradicted. They are based on human nature. By contrast, all mystical illusions are capricious and contradictory. They are based on nothing. And that nothingness is why force, fraud, or coercion are required to make others accept the dishonest illusions of mystics and neocheaters. Thus, by forbidding force, fraud, and coercion, the Neo-Tech Constitution vanquishes mystics and neocheaters.

Policies for Ending Mysticism and Neocheating

Most people unknowingly let mysticism have disastrous effects on their lives and society. As throughout history, people unnecessarily accept the dishonesties of mysticism in allowing neocheaters to pillage them materially and spiritually. But, once the mystical illusions are identified and the neocheating hoaxes are rejected, destructive mystics and neocheaters will be powerless because they have no reality-based, earned power. Rejecting mysticism and its dishonesty means rejecting neocheaters and their agents of force. That rejection requires a policy of never knowingly giving values to or doing business with those who live by force, fraud, coercion, or deception. Such people include:

1. Politicians.
2. Clergymen.
3. Agents of force who extort values from individuals, businesses, and society.
4. Bureaucrats and "authorities" who impede the value producer.
5. Academe, journalists, cartoonists, and media people who purposely distort facts and consciously undermine objective values to sustain pseudo self-esteems and destructive careers.
6. Quisling business executives and professionals who neocheat and destroy within their own businesses and professions for fake power and unearned livelihoods.
7. Other mystics and neocheaters who expropriate values while diminishing the prosperity and happiness of others.

With wide-spread rejection of mysticism and neocheaters, violations of individual rights become unacceptable, pillaging becomes impractical, and waging war becomes impossible.

...People will then be free to live prosperously and happily forever.

Implementing the Neo-Tech Constitution

People could implement the Neo-Tech Constitution if they voted not for politicians, but, voted only for "The Neo-Tech Constitution". The Neo-Tech Constitution fully meets the responsibility of any government to its citizens. The sole purpose of The Neo-Tech Constitution is to protect individual rights through the abolition of *all* initiatory force.

The Neo-Tech Constitution not only provides impenetrable armor for individual rights, but embodies the principles of prosperous living. People one by one will recognize the consummate advantages of The Neo-Tech Constitution. Then, with increasing momentum, those people will reject mysticism and neocheating. Those who do not reject mysticism will be left behind, unable to compete for power, prosperity, and romantic love among the rising army of Neo-Tech value producers.

Neo-Tech Advantage #84
PROTECTING CHILDREN
from
MYSTICS AND NEOCHEATERS

What if people existed who purchased healthy, well-formed children and then mutilated their young bodies to create monsters splendid for laughing at? What if their formula were:

"Take a child two or three years old, put him in a porcelain vase, more or less grotesque, which is made without top or bottom, to allow egress for the head and feet. During the day the vase is set upright, and at night is laid down to allow the child to sleep. The child thickens without growing taller, filling up with his compressed flesh and distorted bones the reliefs in the vase. This development in a bottle continues many years. After a certain time it becomes irreparable. When they consider that this is accomplished, and the monster made, they break the vase. The child comes out — and, behold, there is a man in the shape of a mug!

Neo-Tech Power

"This is convenient; by ordering your dwarf betimes you are able to have it of any shape you wish."

Victor Hugo
The Man Who Laughs

Impossible? No one could be that evil? ...During the 17th century, organized bands of Gypsies called comprachicos (from *comprapequeños*, the Spanish word for child buyers) developed the profession of creating human monsters from children. Why? For the jaded amusement of master neocheaters and professional mystics of Europe — the royalty of government and church.

Did that period represent the height of evil toward children? Not at all. Today, comprachicos exist en masse around the world. And they are committing even greater crimes in creating less startling but more seriously mutilated children than their 17th century counterparts. Yet, their mutilations are more easily ignored. And, yes, even accepted by the mystical-blinded public:

Who are the modern-day comprachicos? And what forms are their mutilations? One group specializes in deforming the outer body while permanently damaging the internal organs. They produce adults incapable of experiencing happy, healthy, romantic lives. Those modern-day comprachicos habituate, for example, ice-cream parlors. In great numbers, those comprachicos gorge children with macro doses of the most widely destructive of addictive drugs — sugar. An addictive sedative, sugar exhibits profound, long-range toxicity toward the human body and its organs. Sugar gradually and irreversibly damages the metabolic system and internal organs while bloating the body into unwholesome, grotesque shapes.

Those who are producing unhappy, sugar-addicted children by mutilating their bodies while damaging their organs are committing crimes more destructive than most child-molestation and child-abuse crimes. Moreover, those modern-day comprachicos are more culpable than their 17th century counterparts. The original comprachicos kept their children relatively healthy to achieve better market prices. They did not damage the children's metabolism or internal organs. Also, those 17th century comprachicos mutilated other people's

150

children for money. But, the modern-day comprachicos mutilate their own children for nothing more than rationalizing their own overweight or self-esteem problems in defaulting to destructive mysticism.[1]

Can anything worse be done to children? Yes, something worse is being done everyday to millions of children: By nature, a child's mind is honest, innocent, and struggling to understand and integrate reality. What happens during the most vulnerable, formative period in developing a child's thinking and integrating ability as well as that child's competence, knowledge, honesty, integrity? Most parents and other adults traumatize and cripple that child's tender mind with heavy doses of mystical dishonesties. They do that by force-feeding the innocent child constant doses of blatantly dishonest religious or altruistic myths about spirits, God, Santa Claus. Such dishonesties are the antithesis of knowledge, contextual facts, and justice. And such repetitive blows to the child's newly developing mind and character can inflict deep, permanent damage. Those dishonesties often induce the first unnatural steps toward becoming an unhappy mystic or a destructive neocheater. ...Nothing healthy is reflected in the innocent, reality-seeking child being intellectually devastated by such irrational dishonesties as religious myths and Santa-Claus lies.

But even more severe crimes against children occur on a grand scale in most public schools and universities today. The perpetrators of those crimes are the majority of educators and philosophers of this world. They implement those anti-educational ideas advanced at the turn of the century by master comprachico, John Dewey. Such educators methodically destroy the efficacy of the child's mind. By the millions, eager,

---

[1]Go to the beach. Look at the couples over 30. How many still look healthy, trim, attractive? Maybe 5%, probably less. ...Most adults surrender life by surrendering to mysticism. Indeed, they often mutilate and destroy each other's bodies and happiness. They directly or indirectly encourage or cajole their spouses into destroying their trim, beautiful bodies. Such insecure people actually want their spouses to grow fat and unattractive. Why? With an unattractive spouse, a person no longer needs to exert the care, thought, and effort required to prevent losing an attractive spouse in the competitive arena of romantic love.

knowledge-seeking children turn into lethargic airheads or dishonest manipulators unable to achieve honest prosperity and genuine happiness.

Moreover, those comprachicos supported by government-backed schools are busily training millions of children to live dishonestly — to live not by producing values for others but by cleverly usurping values from others. Indeed, they are training children to become mystics and neocheaters. For, those modern-day comprachicos must keep generating more mystics and neocheaters in order to perpetuate their big-lie survival hoaxes based on mysticism.

Who will protect innocent children from those crimes? Neo-Tech can and will eventually protect children from such crimes. And every Neo-Tech reader can help protect children by publicly identifying those modern-day comprachicos who carry out their mind/body mutilations in full view of a silently accepting public. The Neo-Tech reader can openly identify the damage being done to innocent children, particularly those children trapped within the public education system.

Neo-Tech Advantage #85
REJECTING MYSTICS AND NEOCHEATERS
A Neo-Tech Protection Kit is available from the Kenneth A. Clark Memorial Office. The kit provides many specific, real-life examples and letters that show how Neo-Tech jettisons mystics and neocheaters. For example, the following letter illustrates an attack by neocheaters and how Neo-Tech effectively dismisses such neocheaters:

Mr. Paul L. Douglas, Attorney General
Department of Justice, State Capitol
Lincoln, Nebraska 68509

Dear Mr. Douglas:

Important to your future is understanding the enclosed letter from Mr. Thomas P. Vlahoulis of your Consumer Protection Division. As Nebraska's Attorney General, you are responsible for the actions of that Division and its use of taxpayers' money.

Please carefully read that letter, for it is under your name: Does Mr. Vlahoulis, you, or anyone in your Department of

Justice have a single, concrete complaint about the Neo-Tech Research and Writing Center or any of our publications? If so, we request that you immediately inform us. For, we want to know exactly what the complaint is and who is making it. We insist on our basic right of knowing and facing our accuser so we may respond fully.

And very important, Mr. Douglas, why exactly is your Department of Justice gratuitously intruding into a publishing company with an inquisition directed at its writers and sources? What exactly is Mr. Vlahoulis implying or presuming, and on what basis? And what is the idea of his threatening us while remaining secretive in vaguely implying that the inquisition arises from "information forwarded by a concerned citizen"?

If someone has a complaint, then out with it so we can respond. Indeed, has Mr. Vlahoulis or anyone in that Division ever received even a single complaint? And what about the thousands of happy Nebraskans who have benefited from Neo-Tech? ...Just who is complaining and why? Or is Mr. Vlahoulis merely acting on someone's specious attack on values?

If no complaint based on fact exists, then I submit that Mr. Vlahoulis is consuming taxpayers' money in creating bogus jobs by conjuring up problems where none exist while sapping valuable time from innocent value producers. If that be the case, is not your Department committing a double-edged fraud under the aegis of "consumer protection"?

What would the citizens of Nebraska think about spending their tax money on harassing value-producing writers in the name of "consumer protection"? What would Woodson Howe, editor of the Omaha World-Herald, or Tom White, editor of the Lincoln Star, say about your arbitrary threats aimed at a publisher of ideas? ...Ideas that will collapse mysticism to benefit everyone except the neocheaters.

Through the philosophically oriented books and articles developed by the Neo-Tech Research and Writing Center, we have delivered objective, long-range values to over a million appreciative individuals in all 50 states and over 140 countries. Still professional mystics and neocheaters who are threatened by Neo-Tech always attack it, often vehemently, often imploring government authorities to stop our publishing activities. But, as they sooner or later discover, such attacks always backfire. For, we utilize all their attacks to our benefit. Indeed, their attacks directly enhance our business objectives of collapsing mysticism to eliminate neocheating. Moreover, their attacks are published and marketed in our Neo-Tech Protection Kit. That kit lets honest, productive people specifically identify and then forever dismiss those mystics and neocheaters who foment dishonest attacks on value producers.

We are resolutely principled and never knowingly yield to actions that are wrong or unfair, no matter what the cost. Indeed, over the long-range we build strength through a loyalty to honesty. And that means standing up to and publicly exposing neocheaters wherever we encounter them.

In addition to the definition of neocheaters on the second page of our enclosed statement of principles, I ask you to read the third page concerning our policies toward neocheaters. That policy includes never knowingly doing business, regardless of dollar losses, with those who live by force, threats, or fraud.

Enclosed are samples of letters from Neo-Tech owners. As you can see in the inset on the second page, various mystics and neocheaters fear Neo-Tech so much that they stridently threaten us, even with physical harm. Some have physically threatened our writers and some have tried to carry out their threats. That is one reason we shield and protect our writers. Additionally, all our sales literature openly displays a printed warning requesting professional mystics and neocheaters (e.g., clergymen and politicians) not to buy anything from us. For, we will not knowingly do business with any value destroyer. We reject their orders and never want their business.

But above all, we as everyone in America are protected by the First Amendment. And we as everyone in America can freely publish our ideas without anyone's permission or license no matter how many authorities, mystics, or neocheaters object, including those in government, including you, your Department of Justice, and Mr. Vlahoulis.

That raises the question of why I spent the time identifying the nature of Mr. Vlahoulis' actions. Am I letting your value-destroying minions consume my time needed to produce values for others? No, not at all. For I am a writer, researcher, and

154

editor whose single, long-range responsibility is to develop and publish those identifications that will reveal and eventually eliminate dishonest mystics and destructive neocheaters — in and out of religion and government.

Indeed, every destructive action integrated with Neo-Tech generates material for future publications. Those publications are dedicated to eliminating mystics, neocheaters, and their 2000-year hoax used to pillage value producers. For once free of mystics and neocheaters, society will be free of parasites and bureaucratic value destroyers. Then all people will be free to earn full prosperity, personal happiness, and romantic love.

And now a most important note. A personal note offered in goodwill to you, Mr. Douglas: I ask you to take the following step that will bring you and the public great benefits, now and in the future: Although we do not sell Neo-Tech to mystics, neocheaters, politicians, the clergy, most lawyers, certain academe, and others listed in our policy statement, we invite you to leave politics, acquire Neo-Tech knowledge, and join in the ascent of man and woman to guiltless prosperity, happiness, and romantic love.

If you arrange to leave politics to produce marketable values for others, I could arrange for you to purchase Neo-Tech as we have occasionally arranged for other nonqualifiers. But first you must desire to abandon neocheating in order to pursue a happy, productive life. So please let me know if you are interested in this new direction. For, we can help you. With Neo-Tech, you can be infinitely happier than working toward the next election.

Sincerely,

John Flint
Director of RIBI

Note: Several months after receiving this letter and failing to accept its benevolent offer, Attorney-General Paul L. Douglas was impeached and later indicted for perjury and obstruction of justice.

Neo-Tech Advantage #86
POWER, PLATO, ARISTOTLE, AND NEO-TECH
A 2500 YEAR-OLD RIDDLE SOLVED

For 2500 years, citizens from ancient Greece to modern America have sought to understand and judge those holding or seeking public power. The higher, more powerful the "authority", the more attention focuses on trying to judge that "authority". In fact, attention expands geometrically on ascending the power scale to the president of the United States (or to the Pope). Yet, a consistent, reliable standard for judging power and authority has until now remained a riddle.

That riddle is solved by applying two metaphors: (1) Knowing the material world around us requires understanding the smallest atomic units. And (2) knowing the cosmos above us requires understanding its primordial origins. Now apply those two points to authority and power: (1) Knowing authority around us requires understanding the smallest authoritarian units. And (2) knowing the power above us requires understanding its philosophical origins.

Understanding the Smallest Unit of Authority

Understanding authority begins by traveling far from the great concentrations of government authority — traveling away from the eastern megalopolis, west to the small desert city in Western United States. By putting a microscope on that oasis of population, one can focus beneath its few, simple layers of authority. One can focus beneath the mayor, past the city council and paid government employees down to an unpaid, appointed planning commission. And finally, one can reduce that commission's microcosm of authority down to its most mundane exercise of authority — the granting or denying of a minor zoning variance to a lone, uninfluential individual with a modest home needing a second bedroom for his family.

That property owner duly completed the proper forms, submitted blueprints, paid the filing fees, and presented the facts to the planning commission. He explained why variance was necessary not only to better the property, but to preserve one of the largest elm trees in the city. The owner detailed how alternative plans without the variance would neither be practical

156

nor best serve the neighborhood. In addition, a professional urban planner (hired by the commission) found no problems or objections to the variance. He also concurred that well over half the homes in the neighborhood already had structures built in greater variance to the zoning ordinance than the minor variance requested.

Moreover, unlike the surrounding structures, the proposed structure was designed to beautify both the owner's home and the neighborhood. In addition, that would be done entirely at the owner's expense while providing local employment. And most important, a two-week notice posted on the property, an advertised notice in the local newspaper, and written notices mailed to all homes surrounding the proposed property improvement brought not a single objection. In short, everyone logically concerned supported the variance.

On concluding the hearing, the members seemed ready to approve this minor, routine variance. But then spoke a younger commissioner, a stocky, flush-faced government environmentalist living in a wealthy neighborhood atop a hill, far from the property owner. He turned enough to observe the property owner from the corners of his eyes. Then with twitching jowls, he stated that the property owner's needs and desires meant nothing in his considering the variance. He then cited three ambiguous, ordinance clauses with arbitrary interpretations — impossible interpretations that no home owner could ever satisfy. ...He chose the exercise of power for the sake of gaining unearned power by destroying the creation of values.

In prompt rebuttal, spoke an older commissioner. A trim, leather-faced workingman living in the same modest neighborhood as the property owner, he pointed out that no objective reason to deny the variance existed, especially after everyone in the neighborhood and all others who could possibly be concerned approved. ...He chose the creation of values over the exercise of power.

To fully understand the profound difference between those two commissioners, one must know that they are appointed by politically elected officials and meet four hours each month without pay. If they receive no pay, what do they receive? They receive political power and civic recognition with little expenditure of time and effort. Thus, the motivation for such people entering the world of government authority varies between political enhancement and civic achievement. From those beginnings, from that political atom, emerge two types of people: One desiring to gain power and a political future by destroying values. The other desiring to enhance the civic needs of the community and its citizens by protecting values. ...The first type gains authoritarian power by destroying values of others; the second type resists authoritarian power by protecting values of others. The first type consists of bad-intentioned value destroyers. The second type consists of well-intentioned, but misguided value producers.

Understanding the
Philosophical Origins of Power

The first type subconsciously orients around Plato's philosophy — a subjective, mystical-based philosophy. The extent a person adopts Plato's views is the extent that he or she holds that:

1. Standards for morals and ethics are products of changeable opinions rather than products of objective reality.
2. Power is to be used as an end in itself to determine who through their "wisdom" (through their feelings, whims, wishes, "intuition") should rule or control others.
3. Facts, honesty, and logic arc relative, arbitrary, disposable.
4. Principle does not matter: ends justify the means.

By nature, Plato nourishes not only all despots and dictators, but politicians and bureaucrats at all levels of government. Plato justifies the striving for power at the expense of the rights, property, and life of others. Plato provides the rationalization for all laziness, dishonesty, and value destruction — for all subjective, unjust non sequiturs and actions used to usurp power and values from others. According to Plato, the rights and needs of individuals are secondary to any external "authority's" desire to usurp values and power. Indeed, Plato assigns virtue to sacrificing individual rights and needs to *any arbitrary "higher cause*", "higher power", or external "authority". ...Thus, Plato is the philosophical father of mysticism and neocheating.

The second type subconsciously orients around Aristotle's philosophy — an objective, reality-based philosophy. The extent that a person adopts Aristotle's view is the extent he or she holds that:

1. Standards for morals and ethics are products of objective reality rather than products of changeable opinions.

2. The well-being of society is enhanced to the extent that individuals are free to produce objective values for themselves and others.

3. Facts, honesty, and logic are absolute, unchangeable, eternal.

4. Principle matters: ends do not justify the means.

By nature, Aristotle nourishes all value producers. The Aristotelian-oriented person has a loyalty to honesty. That person strives to avoid acting on whims, feelings, or wishes. Instead, that person strives to identify and integrate contextual facts in order to act in a rationally consistent manner that generates maximum values for others. Thus, Aristotle is the philosophical father of business and Neo-Tech.

Making Judgments

While most people outwardly exhibit mixtures of Platonistic and Aristotelian views, everyone holds a dominant view of life that is either Platonistic or Aristotelian. Once the Platonistic and Aristotelian views are understood, the dominant view of most individuals becomes evident. With that understanding, one can detect the philosophical core of anyone seeking or holding government power — from the president of the United States to a planning commissioner of a small desert town.

Now, after 2500 years, an objective standard exists to judge power and authority: Who should hold government power over the life, property, and freedom of individuals? A person with Plato's view or a person with Aristotle's view? The answer is...neither.

The Neo-Tech View

All forms of external power or authority undermine the productive, self-responsible nature of human beings. Thus, all such authority is bogus and eventually harmful to everyone. No person, group, or government has the right to deny *or* grant permission for individuals to use their own earned property in ways not infringing on the life or property rights of other individuals.

Note: After sending this report to members of the city council, the property owner proceeded to build the room *without* permission or interference from the "authorities".

Neo-Tech Advantage #87
FREEDOM, RESPONSIBILITY, AND PROSPERITY

Mystic-free individuals who think and act with full-context integrations can easily retake power usurped by the mystics and neocheaters. And a mystic-free, Neo-Tech person can always outcompete those hampered with mysticism in personal and business endeavors. To consistently act in the *rational* interest of self, others, and society requires mystic-free thinking and actions in concert with fully integrated honesty...which is Neo-Tech.

With Neo-Tech, people can free themselves of the life-stunting oppression imposed by external "authorities". Once free, Neo-Tech people become totally responsible and accountable for their own actions and, thus, gain full control of their own lives and well-beings. Only with that responsibility and control can individuals be of maximum value to others in producing values. But those ideas of freedom and responsibility contradict the premises of both conservatives and "liberals". All such advocates of government control claim that individuals must in various ways be controlled by force or coercion to keep them from hurting themselves and others. And that is the greatest of all myths.

That great myth begins by omitting the adjective *rational* from the words *self-interest*. Such an omission allows one to falsely imply that free individuals will normally pursue *irrational* "self-interests" such as fraud, theft, assault, rape, murder if not controlled by government force or regulations. Irrational actions are always destructive to a person's self-interest, thus, are contrary to human nature. Irrationality, by nature, *never* works to the well-being of anyone. The human organism, as any living organism, if unfettered and free, works by nature toward the long-range *best* interest of everyone.

Similarly, every cell and organ in one's body freely functions toward its own well-being in order to deliver maximum benefits to the entire body. Cells and organs do not sacrifice themselves to other cells and organs. If they did, the entire body would die. Likewise, individuals free to function toward their own rational, nonsacrificial self-interests will achieve maximum prosperity for themselves, others, and society. If they allow themselves to be sacrificed, everyone loses except the neocheaters promoting sacrifice of others to their destructive, self-serving "causes".

Free, unsacrificed individuals provide the maximum benefits to others and society. But that is not the reason why government force and coercion against individuals by nonproductive mystics and neocheaters are morally wrong. Independent of the practical benefits, the principle stands: Each individual has the inalienable right to his or her own mind, body, and earned property regardless of those benefits that naturally accrue to others and society. No one can ever rightfully own or morally take any portion of another individual's life or earned property.

Freedom and property can be taken from an individual in only one of two ways: (1) by his or her consent (moral), (2) by initiatory force, threat of force, coercion, or fraud (immoral). All governments throughout history have immorally usurped individual freedom and property from their citizens by initiatory force or the threat of force. And that theft is always done under the Platonistic rationalization of serving some common "good" or "higher" cause.[1] All governments today initiate force or threats of force to deprive their citizens of their property, prosperity, freedom, happiness. ...While everyone has the right to use self-defense force, no one or no government has the right to initiate force or threats of force against anyone, for any reason, under any circumstances.

Why do certain people such as politicians, thieves, theologians, social intellectuals, many media people, most

---

[1]By contrast, no higher good or cause can logically exist in this universe than the individual conscious being. For each individual, what could possibly be more important than his or her own one-and-only life? Nothing can, could, or should be more important. Indeed, without the conscious life of individual beings, existence itself would have no value or meaning.

lawyers, most professors, and all other professional value destroyers seek to live by force, fraud, deception, or coercion? Why do they seek to live by usurping values from others rather than to live by producing values for others? One discovers the answer by stripping the layers of rationalization from such people. Beneath those layers is a lack of maturity and self-esteem, a lack of self-responsibility and independence, a lack of honesty and effort. For they made a secret choice to be dishonest, lazy, and dependent on others for survival — a secret choice to avoid the constant integrated efforts needed to contextually understand reality. And such honest, contextual understandings are needed to produce competitive values desired by others.

Also, professional mystics, neocheaters, and other value destroyers hold various degrees of secret fear and envious hatred toward the value producer. After stripping away the various rationalizations from those value destroyers, the same core — no matter how skillfully hidden — always manifests itself. That core is dishonest laziness: a default against the constant hard effort needed to competitively produce values that benefit others.

Self-responsibility, rationality, honesty, and effort are necessary for human well-being and happiness. To live as designed by nature, people must produce competitive, tradeable values (goods or services) that others desire and will voluntarily buy.[1] By contrast, the character core of mystics, neocheaters, politicians, and other value destroyers is dishonest laziness. Consider, for example, essentially all politicians are lazy, despite their often cleverly staged, look-like-work flurries. Those flurries of "work" are really nothing more than flurries of anti-productive machinations or ego-boosting power ploys. Such destructive machinations are the daily routines of dictators, prime ministers, and presidents as so starkly revealed in the putrefied personal lives of neocheating politicians as Lincoln, Wilson, Stalin, Hitler, FDR, LBJ. They are all soul mates concealing their mutual secret of laziness and living off the productive efforts of others.

Most professional mystics and neocheaters are "liberal"

---

[1]How many free, honest, productive people would voluntarily buy the "services" of a politician, a bureaucrat, a dictator, or a social "intellectual"?

oriented.[1] To live off the producers, those modern "liberals" must promote the false notion that human needs are human rights. They must promote their non-sequitur emotional hoax that being "compassionate" means forcing the value producer to fill their parasitical needs.

Gaining unearned values is the foremost concern of "liberals". Yet, they constantly project that they are concerned about "higher values" and "compassion" for others. But their compassionate images are hypocritical shams. For, professional mystics and neocheaters are interested only in unearned power and bogus jobs so they can go through life living off the values produced by others.

Since professional mystics, neocheaters, and other value destroyers are not self-sufficient, they must spend their lives in a deceptive, resentful struggle designed to extract their material and emotional needs from the producer. Even those nonproducers who have inherited wealth are psychologically dependent on the producer. Those wealthy nonproducers must attack or undermine the producer to elevate their own weak egos and to camouflage their worthlessness.

Because of their parasitical nature, "liberals" are generally more destructive than conservatives. For, conservatives are often misguided value producers who live pragmatically — without consistent principles. ...But also, some of the most clever neocheaters adopt conservative, free-enterprise images to dupe the producer into surrendering his or her earned power and self-esteem.

Conservatives generally promote material and economic freedom. But, to gain their unearned power, they want government to control morality and ideas. Most "liberals", on the other hand, appear to promote freedom of ideas such as free

---

[1]"Liberal" is placed in quotes because those who are called liberals today are the opposite of the past, classical liberals who represented anti-force, pro-individual ideas. Modern "liberals" do not have good intentions. They are anti-individual, anti-intellectual, pro-government-force reactionaries who have dishonestly usurped the label of "liberal" to create illusions of respectability and validity. Yet, they are nothing more than dishonest, immature people with criminal minds who survive by stealing power and values from the value producer.

press, academic freedom, no censorship, freedom in the arts. Ultimately, however, that freedom is granted only to those who support their usurpations. For, to survive, "liberals" need governments to usurp money and values earned by others. ...What about "middle of the roaders"? They favor various mixtures of government control over individual minds, morals, bodies, and property. ...They are little more than pragmatists with no principles.

Only Neo-Tech people reject *all* usurpations, use of force, and gun-backed controls over individuals. For Neo-Tech people orient exclusively around individual rights, not fake human rights. Both conservatives and "liberals", on the other hand, orient around two areas of false government power. Those separate areas they arrogate for themselves are: (1) controlling the mind and moral realms for the conservatives, (2) controlling the body and material realms for the "liberals". ...Only Neo-Tech people want to control no one in any way. They have no need or desire to control the spiritual or material realm of anyone. They recognize everyone's sovereign right to both realms.

□□□□□□*

The link between big business and laissez-faire capitalism is largely a myth originating from Karl Marx's anti-intellectual canards in his book *Das Kapital*. Consider that laissez faire is a French phrase meaning, "to let do", or "to let people do as they choose". Thus, laissez-faire capitalism means neither pro big business nor anti big business, but means simply individual freedom. Yet, today, most chief executives of large stagnated businesses are anti laissez-faire. Indeed, many entrenched CEOs support fascist concepts of big government. For such concepts utilize force-backed government regulations needed to protect their jobs and businesses from more competent, harder-working entrepreneurs and foreign competitors.

Laissez-faire capitalism simply means no government control over individuals and their property — a Neo-Tech atmosphere. Within such an atmosphere, individuals are free to create and build businesses, including big businesses, even monopolistic big businesses. Within that laissez-faire atmosphere, government would have no power to support big businesses or protect monopolies (e.g., many banking, utility, and communication companies are monopolies protected by government force). Without government protection or assistance, big businesses and monopolies could exist and grow only by continually delivering better values than anyone else. Whenever any monopoly failed to deliver maximum values, the free-market dynamics in the absence of government controls would cause that monopoly either to deliver better values or yield to others delivering greater values. ...Market dynamics free of government controls will sooner or later collapse uncompetitive or harmful businesses, monopolies, or cartels.

Companies, businesses, industries, and monopolies are not detached entities, but are composed of individuals who function through individual thoughts and actions. Business entities are the property and extension of individual human beings. Thus, businesses possess the same inalienable rights of free action and ownership of earned values as individuals. Also, individuals and their honest businesses exert power through peaceful voluntary free choices, not through force, coercion, or deception as do professional value destroyers in or out of government.

Most government agencies ultimately exist through force, coercion, or deception. Thus, such agencies that depend on threats and force have no moral right to exist. Those agencies arc in reality coercive engines of antisocial actions.

Governments are colossal mystical frauds that usurp power and values by force-backed laws and regulations. And those usurpations are used to further violate individual and property rights. Such destructive processes keep building and feeding on themselves. ...All value producers would benefit greatly without such governments.

Today, upper management of big-business is increasingly controlled by altruistic, neocheating "businessmen" who apologize for the business they now control, but never built[1] [Re: Neo-Tech IV]. Those altruistic "businessmen" are usually fascist oriented.

---

[1]Essentially every big business was originally created and built by an honest, heroically productive individual such as E. I. du Pont, Henry Ford, Andrew Carnegie, Thomas Edison, John D. Rockefeller, Harvey Firestone, and other industrial supermen. Such men are the true benefactors of working-class people, of value producers, of society and civilization. For those industrial

(footnote continued on next page)

165

For they use government force to shield their businesses from competition. Indeed, they promote anti-capitalistic legislation, regulations, and controls. The unspoken policies of those executives are to gain government favors and to encourage government-forced regulations that block more competent competitors and diminish or halt superior-value imports. Such executives realize that, without government interference, the free-market competition would eventually eliminate their jobs and their poorly managed businesses that they have drained through harmful government-approved, socially oriented "business" policies.

Government-corporate collusions inflate prices, lower quality, block competition, and are the antithesis of free enterprise. Indeed, the greatest enemies of free enterprise are not the socialists or "liberals", but are those business leaders who collude

---

(footnote continued from previous page)

supermen intensely pursued the moral objectives of benefiting their customers, workers, managers, and investors by delivering spectacular values to society at ever lower costs. Those creative, productive individuals contrast sharply with destructive, media-made "heroes" such as the Lincolns, FDRs, Naders, Kennedys, and other such bad-intentioned nonproducers who survive by attacking and harming value producers, their products, their businesses.

While never honestly acknowledging those who produce great wealth and values, the "liberal" or neocheating journalists and writers often praise the wealthy, nonproductive scions of past industrial heroes. Neocheaters especially praise those immature, nonbusiness-like "philanthropists" who dissipate inherited wealth such as Henry Ford III and Nelson Rockefeller. And those same journalists and writers attack nearly every major value created by outstanding businessmen, scientists, and industrialists. For example, under such guises as ecology, consumerism, or "compassion", the "liberal" media attack, often with rabid envy, the greatest, most heroic values created by conscious beings. Such outstanding values attacked include the automobile, the computer, the drug industry, the petroleum and mining industries, and America's magnificent food processing and distribution systems. At the same time, the "liberal" media are quick to praise progressively meaner values such as the car pool, the abacus, folk medicine, hand-made goods, growing one's own food. They promote those kinds of unheroic, mean values under good-sounding non sequiturs as returning to basic "values", returning to hand-made quality, returning to nature.

166

with government to consolidate their power without having to earn that power in a competitive, value-producing atmosphere.[1]

Perhaps the most evil collusions occur between neocheating executives of large companies and government bureaucrats in promoting envy-motivated antitrust laws. Those immoral laws are designed to penalize the most competitive companies and productive businessmen. But increasingly, the growing number of Neo-Tech executives will rid the corporate world of those government-colluding executives who neocheated their way to unearned power through force-backed laws, regulations, and controls. [Re: Mark Hamilton's "Ending the White-Collar Hoax" (Pincer #2) published by I & O.]

Neo-Tech Advantage #88
NEO-TECHING BUSINESS

Neo-Tech IV reveals the malevolent destruction of altruism as opposed to the benevolent productivity of business. Neo-Tech IV also demonstrates how neocheating executives are today undermining many great corporations. They can often hide their destructive drain of assets for many years by continually shifting long-range efforts into increasingly shorter-range pay-offs that keep profits growing while concealing the eventual, dead-end quality of such profits.

If altruistic chief executives are taking over major corporations and causing their long-range demise, who then is left to stop the neocheaters' continued consumption of business? Who will lead the way to a society in which mysticism and the resulting neocheating are eliminated? Who will uphold the productive individual as the highest value? Who will lead the way to a

---

[1]An example of a big-business, conservative publication that effectively works against free-enterprise and Neo-Tech principles is *The Wall Street Journal*. Its editorial policy is pragmatic (not based on principles) and often advocates the use of government industrial policies, controls, regulations to "help" those big businesses controlled by lazy or incompetent management. Such an editorial policy is basically dishonest and fascist oriented, which is ultimately backed by guns. ...By contrast, the Journal's sister publication, *Barrons*, is basically honest and free-enterprise oriented, which is ultimately backed by free competition.

society in which prosperity, happiness, and biological immortality will reign supreme among human beings?

The answer is today's growing army of value producers who are becoming knowledgeable about Neo-Tech. For such people hold genuine power as identified in the Epilogue in Neo-Tech IV. That Epilogue is from a report titled, "The Fundamental Principle that Determines the Long-Range Common Stock Value of a Corporation". And that report points the way for creating great, long-range wealth within any productive corporation. One key necessity is to establish an Industrial-Philosophy Department responsible for making major actions consistent with the principles of fully integrated honesty (Neo-Tech). ...Neo-Teching business policies and actions inject vitality and profitability into companies, large or small.

Neo-Teching the World of Mystics and Neocheaters

Neo-Tech traps professional mystics and neocheaters in their world of big lies. Neo-Tech reveals the exact opposite to what most people have been led to believe by mystics and neocheaters. For example, how many people realize that:

1. The media-labeled, 19th century "robber barons", such as the transcontinental railroad builder Jay Gould, were heroic value producers who enormously benefited the working class and society — more so on net than all the politicians, clergymen, and Nobel peace laureates who ever lived, combined.

2. Despite Charles Dickens' burning intentions to depict the contrary in his Christmas Story, the most honest, moral, productive, and happy character is Ebenezer Scrooge. That is until the mystics and neocheaters guilt-tripped him into becoming a maudlin altruist who as a result would eventually ruin his business and destroy the livelihoods of many who had attacked him.

3. The political/religious/media axis have built the highest reverence and respect for some of the bloodiest, most morally perverted, but most brilliant succession of neocheaters in the history — the popes and cardinals. And with bizarre irony, those men, by competitive necessity, were and are closet atheists. In fact, the entire upper hierarchy of the most powerful religion (or

of any powerful religion or other neocheating organization) would have to be closet atheists in order to be aware, competent, and competitive enough to achieve their power.

On knowing the nature of neocheating, one fact becomes compellingly obvious: To successfully impose such an ingenious, big-lie, 2000-year hoax continuously on millions of confused, mystical-accepting victims, all popes and cardinals could not be intellectually crippled with the disintegrated thinking of theism. For any high-ranking Catholic official believing his own mystical, God-concept propaganda would be (1) too benighted to outmaneuver the fierce competition vying for power, and (2) too unaware and incompetent to orchestrate such a mighty hoax. Thus, all popes, cardinals, and probably most bishops would have to be atheists to be aware enough for attaining their positions of power. Also, theists would be too naive, unaware, and uncompetitive to perpetuate for centuries such a cleverly integrated hoax. ...Only those who saw through their own promulgated mysticism would be aware and competent enough to win the fierce competition for the positions of power occupied by popes and cardinals.

4. Only a small percentage of university professors today are intellectuals. Genuine intellectuals use their minds rationally, honestly, productively. Most university professors today are fake intellectuals who use their minds cleverly, dishonestly, and destructively to hold their bogus jobs. They are professional neocheaters. Thus, even the most "famous" of such professors, even Nobel laureates, do not produce net values. Instead they wreak great damage on the minds of their students. ...Neo-Tech will bring a worldwide purge of such university professors.

Great intellectuals exist in every major area of productive human activity. Genuine intellectuals are those businessmen, industrialists, scientists, engineers, artists, musicians, and educators who advance their profession by using their minds honestly in working hard through rational actions. A rational, hard-driving, successful mining engineer, for example, is highly intellectual in mining, but may not be highly intellectual in English literature. At the same time, a university professor of English literature is probably not highly intellectual in mining.

169

Indeed, he may be incompetent to function intellectually in any area of business. Perhaps he is even incompetent in English, especially if he or she is a low-effort, laid-back, tenured professor living off taxpayers. Such professors damage students' minds by using non sequiturs to attack the potency of the logical mind, reason, heroic value producers, and their life-giving products.

The only difference between intellectualism in the business world versus intellectualism in the academic world is that performance in business is much easier to measure and thus more difficult to fake. That is why the academic world accumulates such a high percentage of lazy charlatans and clever pseudo-intellectuals compared to the business world. Those charlatans and pseudo intellectuals cannot survive in the business world. For, through their fake jobs cleverly designed to camouflage their laziness and dishonesty, they have become uncompetitive and incompetent. Still, they can fake lifelong careers in the academic world. And as long as mysticism and altruism dominate philosophical thought, such pseudo-intellectual neocheaters will proliferate throughout the academic world.

5. The many pseudo ecologists and self-appointed "consumer advocates" today are not interested in protecting the environment or human beings. Deceptively hidden behind their neocheating non sequiturs and destructive work is a contempt for human life and happiness. They use ecology and consumerism as tools of demagoguery, often with the goal to cripple and eventually eliminate the benefits of technology, industry, and free enterprise. As a result, many valid ecological problems are obscured, confused, and remain unsolved. Moreover, the long-range destructiveness of such neocheaters is surfacing in many areas. For example, consider Rachel Carson's decades-old book, "Silent Spring": Its specious charges and unscientific conclusions caused the banning of DDT, which in turn caused a resurgence of malaria in Asia and Sri Lanka at the eventual cost of perhaps a million lives — lives of human beings, not birds or fish. Yet, people will never find those facts among the neocheating academe and media.

With government banning of DDT and other pesticides, the mosquito and insect populations burgeoned along with a proportional rise in "ecologist" caused famine and disease such

170

as malaria and encephalitis. In addition, those irrational bannings have decimated trees and crops in the United States and around the world. The banning of DDT has also lowered the world standard of living by billions of dollars per year in crop losses and expenses. That, in turn, significantly increased third-world inflation, hunger, suffering, famine, and death. All that human death, destruction, and suffering starting from the handiwork of just one "ecologist" needing to feel good by boosting her pseudo self-esteem with dishonest non sequiturs. [For more details, see Neo-Tech Advantage #90.]

An even more destructive breed of neocheaters exists who methodically decrease the living standards for everyone. That breed includes self-appointed, "consumer-advocate" demagogues epitomized by Ralph Nader and his raiders [Re: R. De Toledano's book, "Hit & Run", Arlington House]. In the long run, their destruction surpasses that of even the murderous bannings of DDT and cyclamates (see Neo-Tech Advantage #90). For the real targets of those "consumer advocates" are the value producers from which come all life-enhancing values. Moreover, the pervasively destructive work of Nader sets up the psychological conditions for unjust attacks on great value-producing companies such as Union Carbide:

Years ago, a great benevolent company, Union Carbide, was excoriated and threatened with extermination by the neocheating media and politicians for a tragic *accident* in India for which the Indian Government itself was responsible. The Indian politicians arbitrarily and irrationally forced Union Carbide to hire incompetent, distrustful nationals who were unable to perform even basic security-control operations. Such forced interference by government neocheaters left Union Carbide unable to properly protect its business from sabotage by envious, anti-business value destroyers. That sabotage at Union Carbide *for which the Indian government was responsible* left 2500 dead — the worst industrial "accident" in history.

But that tragic loss of life was minuscule when compared to the routine, purposeful slaughter by political neocheaters. To the "liberal" media, the murder of 2500 people by their Marxist soul mates would hardly be newsworthy — too common, too minor, too routine, not really that bad.

171

Such examples starkly contrast the good of business people to the evil of political or government neocheaters. The loss of life from the worst industrial *accident* in history is little more than a casual day of slaughter for totalitarian neocheaters. For example, at the same time that Union Carbide was being excoriated by the dishonest media for sabotage that was not even the company's fault, no media outrage arose toward Marxist murderers in Ethiopia who were *purposely* starving to death millions of innocent men, women, and children they considered politically troublesome. Instead, the media were going through news-twisting contortions and telethon spectaculars in trying to falsely show the cause of that coldly calculated mass starvation was a drought rather than their soul-mate Marxist-Leninist politicians. They were mass murdering so they could feel big, feel important, feel unearned power. They were mass murdering by purposeful starvation, just as Stalin did two generations before in the Ukraine.

Neo-Tech Advantage #89
PROTECTION FROM
GOVERNMENT DESTRUCTION

People build. Governments destroy. Who really needs governments? Productive individuals always suffer a net loss from mystically conceived, force-backed governments. Such governments diminish everyone's values, earnings, life. They survive by always expanding their unearned power. And they expand that power by increasingly transferring the earnings and property of the producer to the nonproducer by force, threats, coercion, fraud. Thus, governments and politicians, by nature, can offer only life diminishment as they continually increase their force-backed demands on the value producer. At the same time, they aggressively finagle respect and adulation for their destructions through non sequiturs and fake altruistic catchwords such as "compassion", "the heart", "humanitarian", "human rights". But never do they mention the only valid points — individual rights and competitive value production.

To psychologically survive, politicians must garner praise for their usurping values from others without producing values for others. They use the handy, God-like, "goodness" gimmicks of altruism to make their destructive actions seem "good", "compassionate" and "humane" while hiding the criminality of their destructions. Such is the nature of political neocheaters and their media, academic, and religious collaborators. For that reason, effective business people who exist by producing values for others have no desire, time, or reason to diminish their lives by becoming politicians or other neocheaters who exist by usurping values from others.

All political, religious, academe, and media neocheaters destroy the personal property and individual rights of others through escalating usurpations from value producers. Without Neo-Tech to stop the neocheaters, they would eventually dissipate all productive wealth and individual freedom, causing a worldwide economic collapse with an enormous loss of human life, well-being, and happiness. [Re: Table 53, Neo-Tech Reference Encyclopedia shows how to protect property and happiness from government destruction.]

The need to protect oneself from neocheaters reveals another destructive effect of mysticism: Government neocheaters usurp values for themselves and their parasitical soul mates. As the neocheaters attack and usurp those values, the most productive citizens are drained of investment capital, creative energy, individual freedom, and irreplaceable time. Those producers must increasingly struggle to protect themselves, their loved ones, their property, their means of production, and especially their time from the ravages of government value destroyers. More and more valuable time, capital, and effort are wasted in:

1. following destructive bureaucratisms and irrational government regulations, and

2. studying, paying attention to, and speculating in nonproductive asset protectors, tax shelters, and inflation hedges such as gold and silver.

Many people go broke through such speculations, especially those who act mystically. For example, the libertarian movement was broken by acts of self-mysticism — by those acting on emotions of economic revenge and wishful thinking in hopes of acquiring effortless wealth through leveraged gold and silver speculations.

With such speculations come the unhappy emotions that accompany disaster-oriented speculations. Those emotions include hoping for economic collapse, crop devastation, mass destruction, war, or other major disasters in order to have those speculations "pay-off". ...Buying gold on margin and hoping for war and other catastrophes is an unhappy way to live.

Also, people increasingly lose concentration on their productive work as they follow their speculations. Producers become unproductive speculators[1] as they increasingly look for easy wealth through speculation rather than through producing values with integrated thought and hard work. But in a Neo-Tech society free of neocheaters and destructive governments, all that time, energy, and capital would be channeled into uses that benefit the individual and society: Producers would spend more of their time and energy on producing values for others rather than on having to protect themselves from government value destroyers.

Governments are nothing more than groups of people. Many of those people are value destroyers who exist by usurping power and values from others to the harm of everyone and society. Some, however, do honest work in the government, especially in service areas such as postal, police, park, library, scientific, technical, military, intelligence. But all governments are controlled by neocheating politicians, bureaucrats, and lawyers living off the producer. Behind all their rhetoric about "service to society" and "working for higher causes" is their need to survive by usurping values earned by others.

Power usurped through government force gives neocheating politicians illusions of control over reality. They use those rationalized illusions to build pseudo self-esteems needed for psychological survival. Their need for unearned power grows from a base of laziness, immaturity, a lack of self-responsibility, and a desire for an easy route to "accomplishment" and "control".

By contrast, self-sufficient producers such as successful business people earn genuine self-esteem through their own integrated thinking and hard efforts. They have no need for

---

[1]Professional speculators, however, do deliver competitive values by making needed markets and stabilizing prices.

unearned power or usurped values. They have no desire to forcibly control the lives of others. That is why genuine value producers are seldom, if ever, interested in politics. ...Productive business people are too busy being happy, creative, and productive to waste their precious time on unhappy, destructive politics.

Earning major values along with long-range happiness requires an independent aloneness. Neocheaters, nonproducers, value destroyers, and politicians dread that aloneness. The glib politician, being psychologically and materially dependent on others for survival, has a desperate need to be among people, to buy their favor with tax money, and to become increasingly involved in their lives by increasing government control over them. ...The worst situation for the neocheater or politician is to be left alone, especially to be left alone to survive by his or her own efforts. By contrast, the value producer usually has no desire to get involved with the "public" lest his or her irreplaceable time for value production be wasted.

Perhaps the cruelest of government neocheaters are those "liberals" whose actions pass under the specious banner of protecting the elderly. For, their neocheating actions always end up draining the well-being, happiness, and earned savings of elderly people.

Most elderly people no longer have growing assets or competitive earning power. A large percentage of them have worked hard and honestly throughout their lives only to have government policies drive them into the inescapable trap of government dependency. They are further lured into that government trap by, for example, social-security policies that offer temporary relief from inflation only to be devastated by the next wave of inflation and a failing social-security system.

Government manipulations through taxation and inflation diminish the well-being and happiness of everyone. But those destructive manipulations especially debilitate elderly people dependent on the government for survival. For, governments subtly push their dependent elderly citizens toward unhappiness, suffering, early death.

Most elderly people deliver themselves into that dependency trap by believing that government is a benevolent, positive force that will somehow benefit them in the present and help them in the future. The opposite is true. By nature, no one can ever look to any government for net benefits. Indeed, the essence of government is value destruction from which long-range benefits and values can never flow. Thus, one must always avoid government dependency to protect his or her well-being and happiness.

The unhappiness trap shuts when a person becomes dependent on government for needs. Once the trap is shut, that person's life turns downward with declining self-esteem, well-being, and happiness.[1] To avoid that trap, a person must recognize that government is by nature a destructive, life-negating force that should be avoided in every possible way. A person should never believe in, count on, or become dependent on any aspect of government for his or her present or future well-being. The only way to retain growing prosperity and happiness is to remain independent, self-sufficient, and commercially productive, *especially as one grows older*.[2]

The best asset for future prosperity and the best protection against government, mystics, and neocheaters is fully integrated honesty — or Neo-Tech. Indeed, Neo-Tech is the development of personal honesty, integrity, and the ability to perceive reality accurately in order to competitively produce values for others. Thus, the most valuable gift given to children and adults is Neo-Tech knowledge. For that is the knowledge needed to accurately perceive reality, to reject mysticism and neocheating, to develop personal integrity, and to competitively produce tradeable values desired by others.

---

[1]Innocence is what traps most honest, productive people. Believing that most people are basically good and honest (which is fact), productive people cannot grasp or imagine the inherently dishonest nature of governments. They can not grasp the immature, evil nature of neocheating politicians, bogus-job bureaucrats, and their agents of force who exist through camouflaged value destructions.

[2]Useless old age is neither natural nor inevitable for anyone, despite constant government inducement to become aged, retired, useless, and dependent on neocheating politicians for survival. [Re: Concept 114, Neo-Tech Reference Encyclopedia]

Conservative, libertarian, and most anarchist political movements offer no long-term protection from value-destroying mysticism and neocheating. In fact, such political movements eventually add to disorder and the destruction of values. For all of those movements are pragmatic and not based on fully integrated honesty. Thus, they only serve to tear down one destructive, mystical system while providing a starting point for an even more destructive, mystical system as happened in Russia, Nazi Germany, Red China, Cuba, Iran, Nicaragua.

Similar shifting forms of mysticism are happening in the United States. Such examples include those "liberal"-demagogue movements orchestrated to undermine rational efforts for national defense and self-protection.

In any case, the only certain, long-term self-defense protection from government — domestic and foreign — is to collapse the hoax of mysticism in order to eliminate its symbiotic, value-destroying neocheaters.

Neo-Tech Advantage #90
GOVERNMENT DEATH MACHINES AND THE ULTIMATE BATTLE

All current governments depend on coercion and force. Thus, they are destructive to human life, productivity, prosperity, and happiness. The destructiveness of the United States government is implemented mainly through force-backed bureaucracies such as the BATF, EPA, FDA, FTC, INS, IRS, OSHA, and the SEC.

Consider, for example, the Food and Drug Administration (FDA): That bureaucracy has been responsible for the premature death of many thousands of people through its arbitrary, forced banning of such life-saving, free-choice discoveries as the cyclamate artificial sweetener. The palatable cyclamates effectively replaced the deadly poison of sugar to reduce caloric/carbohydrate intake, obesity ailments, diabetes, heart-attack deaths for millions of people.

Such FDA value destructions serve only to satisfy some value-destroying bureaucrat's need to feel important, to feel unearned power through destruction of human lives and values.

Also, the arbitrary banning or controlling of life-saving products such as non-toxic pesticides, herbicides, food

177

preservatives and additives, new drugs and medicines has caused death and suffering on massive scales.[1] In addition, FDA regulations on drug research and marketing retard or prevent the development of many life-benefiting, life-saving drugs, medicines, and devices while increasing research and development costs to prohibitive levels. Effective cancer cures, for example, would certainly have been developed years ago if research and business were free from regulations and controls. For, such freedom allows aggressive individuals and companies to openly pursue the full profit and achievement potential in discovering and marketing effective cures for cancer, AIDS, and other diseases.

Even more important, FDA regulations block the required risk taking, incentive, and business freedom required for rapid development of human biological immortality. [Re: See Neo-Tech V]

The blocking of human progress along with mass suffering and death are the natural results of government force. And government agencies are the instruments of such force. The essences of agencies such as the BATF, EPA, FDA, FTC, INS, IRS, OSHA, and the SEC are always destructive and their intentions are never good. Such agencies costing billions of dollars each year serve only to harm productive individuals and society. Indeed, those life-depriving agencies are subtle death machines that are directly and indirectly responsible for more

---

[1]As shown in Advantage #88, the government-forced end to DDT alone is responsible for perhaps a million or more malaria deaths. Moreover, forced banning of pesticides, herbicides, and chemical preservatives is decreasing food productivity while increasing production costs, poverty, suffering, and starvation. [Re: J. Maddox, "The Doomsday Syndrome", McGraw-Hill] That irrational banning of valuable agriculture chemicals and food preservatives also causes greater food scarcity in famine areas to greatly increase worldwide malnutrition and starvation. The massive suffering and death in the name of protecting the environment or "doing-good" by government bureaucracies is documented in Grayson and Shepard's book, *The Disaster Lobby*, Follett Publishing Company. That book also demonstrates how advancing industrial and business technology free of government interference steadily (1) protects human life, (2) improves the environment — water, air, land — for human habitation, and (3) solves genuine ecological problems.

suffering and deaths than all wars of history. (Wars are also government sponsored.) Throughout history most governments with their use of force, fraud, and coercion begin as "legalized" protection rackets and always end as destructive engines of crime and death. Such governments operate under the rationalizations of protection, altruism, the social "good", and "higher" causes.[1]

Agencies such as the EPA and FDA often carry out their destruction through dishonest assertions. They assert, for example, that DDT or cyclamates might be "bad" for the ecology or cause cancer in animals. Then they expand their power with a job-creating bureaucracy to control or ban such substances. Usually those agencies hide their dishonesties with non sequitur "facts". They often manufacture unscientific data developed from spurious research to "prove", for example, that use of cyclamates might cause cancer in humans: Research on feeding megadoses of cyclamate diet sweetener to rats indicated that humans could experience bladder irritation or even tumors if they drank the equivalent of 700 bottles of diet soft drinks per day over an extended period of time. When, in fact, that amount of water alone (to say nothing of the immediately fatal amounts of sugar in less than 100 bottles of non-diet soda) would fatally break down the kidneys in human beings.

Still, the FDA used those non-sequitur, rat-feeding data to assert that cyclamates can be cancer-producing in human beings. The FDA then demanded that the producers prove that cyclamates do not cause cancer. Since a negative cannot be proven, the government neocheaters subsequently used their dishonest, non-sequitur data to ban the sale of cyclamates without any scientific evidence of harm to a single human being. At the same time, those neocheaters purposely ignored the wide-ranging, beneficial, life-saving effects of that artificial sweetener.

---

[1]As the frauds of altruism and "higher causes" are identified and rejected by the value producers, the neocheaters will lose their unearned power. Once the value producers identify and reject mysticism, all fraud-based religion and force-backed governments will vanish.

The FDA, EPA, or any other government agency never honestly attempts to prove their assertions. Rather, those agencies demand that the producers disprove their assertions. Their demands to disprove assertions or accusations contradict the concepts of honesty, objective law, and justice. Indeed, to demand proof of a negative undermines honesty by shifting the burden of proof away from the source making accusations (the neocheaters) to their victims (the value producers).

Without the burden-of-proof standard, government and religious neocheaters avoid the responsibility to prove their assertions and accusations. Without the burden-of-proof standard, neocheaters are not accountable to honesty. Without that accountability to honesty, professional mystics and neocheaters can continue to usurp power and bogus livelihoods through fraud, deception, and force.

Theists use that same arbitrary, anti-intellectual standard in asserting the existence of God. Unable to back their assertions with proof, they expect nonbelievers to prove that God does not exist. But that proving-a-negative ploy is intellectually untenable and undermines the protector of honesty, which is: **the burden of proof always rests on the one making an assertion or accusation**.

***

By nature, most government bureaucracies cannot produce values. Thus, to grow, such bureaucracies must usurp power by destroying values. In turn, value destruction requires little competence or effort. Thus, by necessity, value destruction is the modus operandi of most government bureaucracies and agencies — the most virulent being the BATF, EPA, FDA, FTC, INS, IRS, OSHA, and the SEC. To conceal their destructions, they masterfully use non-sequitur facts and mystical ploys to justify their destructive usurpations from the value producers. But now, after 2000 years, the evolvement of Neo-Tech will collapse and eliminate those fake empires of destruction.

Often, only a scientist trained with the scientific method can identify the neocheater's dishonest use of facts and information. Without Neo-Tech, most people have no way to discern the dishonesty of neocheaters. And without Neo-Tech, most people will confusingly accept the neocheater's usurpation of values. But with Neo-Tech, destructive mysticism and neocheating ceases through the competitive dynamics of business. [Re: The November-3rd Trap]

Neo-Tech Advantage #91
SUICIDE OPTION

In addition to the false guilt laid on value producers by the mystics and neocheaters, a subtle psychological block inhibits many value producers from experiencing their earned happiness. That block is the subconscious fear that sometime in life one must lose his or her happiness...that someday one must endure terminal suffering and pain.

Even without biological immortality, a terminal loss of happiness never has to be endured. So long as a productive person has some degree of freedom and choice, that person can always maintain and expand happiness. If circumstances totally beyond one's control forever eliminate all possibilities of maintaining and expanding happiness (i.e., a no-escape situation from a terror-totalitarian torture death or the final stages of a painful, terminal illness), the individual has the right and option to avoid a terminal existence of unhappiness and pain. That right and option is suicide.

Suicide is every individual's personal right and final option. By fully and guiltlessly realizing that suicide is always available, a person is freer to live more fully in traveling an open-ended journey toward ever-expanding happiness. By accepting the concept of the suicide option, one *never* needs to fear the permanent loss of happiness.

The suicide option should *never* be misconstrued as an escape or option when life is difficult, or seems hopeless, or even when one seems to lose everything, including one's invaluable, irreplaceable romantic-love partner. With consistent rational choices, a person can always experience increasing happiness again, no matter how difficult or painful the immediate situation seems. The *only* two situations in which suicide is a rational option for the productive individual are (1) a no-hope, high-

181

suffering, terminal-illness situation, and (2) an absolutely no-escape, no-hope slavery/torture/death situation.[1]

Ironically, suicide is also the only viable option for those irredeemably evil neocheaters who have murdered others for their bogus livelihoods and usurped power (i.e., all murderous dictators and terrorists as Castro, Idi Amin, Qaddafi, Pol Pot, Yasir Arafat, Ariel Sharon, Abu Nidal, Sinn Fein leaders, Khomeini, Li Ping).

Neo-Tech Advantage #92
ANTI-OBSCENITY LAWS, CENSORSHIP, AND THE SUPREME COURT

Despite the sexual errors projected by the "Playboy" philosophy that can lead to impotence and frigidity (see Neo-Tech Advantage #19), the Playboy Corporation made important contributions to both individual and sexual freedom [Re: Concept 37, Neo-Tech Reference Encyclopedia]. Those contributions come not only through the open, guiltless views of pleasure and sex expressed in its magazine, but also through the Playboy Foundation and its monthly magazine feature, The Playboy Forum. That feature provides constant public exposure to the ongoing government-neocheating ploy of usurping power through oppression of private sexual activities and other victimless "crimes".

Perusing any issue of the Forum starkly reveals that even in this sexually-liberated era, individuals all over the United States are being arrested, harassed, humiliated, injured, tried, fined, and sent to jail for private, consenting sexual acts. The following list provides several examples of sexual oppression as taken from a randomly selected, six-page Forum feature in *Playboy* magazine:

•Couple out camping privately engage in oral sex in a secluded area of the woods. Both arrested by Texas Sheriff for sodomy. Both faced jail sentences of 2-15 years for their private, harmless love act.

---

[1]An absolutely no-hope slavery situation could exist only after all escape, resistance, and guerrilla warfare options were irrevocably eliminated (if that is possible).

•Four young people arrested for private nude bathing. Sheriff refused to let them dress and forced them to travel nude to the courthouse for arrest.

•In Sheboygan, Wisconsin, a couple was fined $100 each for engaging in sexual intercourse while not being married.

•Man released by a California Supreme Court order after serving five years of a *life* sentence for indecent exposure.

•A 1600 member organization of the Catholic Priest Association asked a Catholic bishop who defended birth-control pills to resign because of his "monstrous views". The Catholic organization declared that the bishop failed to "show the purity of Catholic doctrine", and failed to "rise above the murk and filth of modern man's sex life".

•A Canadian man charged with rape and gross indecency admitted at his trial that he had performed cunnilingus and intercourse with a consenting woman. Before the jury retired, 68-year-old Judge Campbell Grant said of cunnilingus, "Well, can you think of a more grossly indecent act? ...Frankly, gentlemen, I had to get the dictionary to know what it was about. I venture to say that most of you are the same." He went on to declare that "a dirty, filthy practice such as this is resorted to by no one but sexual perverts and is surely an infringement of the criminal code." The jury found the accused not guilty of rape, but guilty of gross indecency. He was sentenced to three years in the penitentiary.

A book published by the Playboy Press, *Sex American Style*, cites many government laws that can and do jail innocent people for harmless, mutually consenting sex acts. That book includes articles by Hugh M. Hefner; "The Legal Enforcement of Morality" and "Tyranny Under the Law".

Three decades ago, comic Lenny Bruce, despite his existentialistic errors that eventually killed him, made a major contribution toward breaking the oppressive religious/government grip of sexual-oppression laws and censorship. To stop his defiance of "moral" authority, the government directly abetted the death of Lenny Bruce.

Hustler magazine, however disgusting its scatology, also played an important, front-trench role in buffeting the forces of sexual oppression and censorship. The government/religious axis in their failing trial designed to jail the publisher of *Hustler*, Larry Flynt, inspired an assassination attempt: As Mr. Flynt walked before the courthouse in Atlanta, Georgia, a bullet severed his spinal cord, paralyzing him for life.

A generation ago, a nude-streaking fad broke across the United States. That fad was a timely, counter-response to the oppressive Supreme-Court anti-obscenity decision a year earlier. The motives for streaking and the effects on the streakers' self-esteem were probably unhealthy in most cases. But such overt, widespread flouting of sexual authoritarianism helped undermine the enforcement of oppressive censorship and anti-obscenity laws. Nude streaking broke the anti-obscenity momentum that was ominously building in the United States from that Supreme-Court decision. But the anti-obscenity forces of religious and political neocheaters are now trying to reassert their oppressive powers granted to them by the conservative justices of the United States Supreme Court.

The United States Supreme Court was meant to function as a principled, philosophical body designed to protect individual rights.[1] But recent decisions on obscenity and pornography have been void of principle in ignoring the concept of individual rights. An earlier Supreme Court (*Memoires vs. Massachusetts*) stated the following criterion for pornography: "A book cannot be proscribed unless it is found to be utterly without redeeming

---

[1]Throughout the checkered history of the United States Supreme Court, one finds many disgraceful exceptions to its role as a principled body for protecting individual rights. Early in this century, for example, the United States Supreme Court favored explicit censorship by removing films from the protection of the First Amendment (free speech). The court then decreed that since films were made for profit, they did not deserve constitutional protection. In their decision, the justices conveniently ignored the fact that books and newspapers were also made for profit.

social value." That criterion ignored the principles of individual rights and property rights while opening the way for people to be jailed on the basis of some other person's judgment of the "social" merit of their work.

Seven years later, the Supreme-Court *Miller vs. California* case negated individual rights in determining the following criteria to *criminally* convict for victimless pornography: "(a) whether the average person applying contemporary community standards would find that the work, taken as a whole, appeals to the prurient interest...(b) whether the work depicts or describes, in a patently offensive way, sexual conduct specifically defined by the applicable state law, and (c) whether the work, taken as a whole, lacks serious literary, artistic, political, or scientific value."

That Supreme Court ruling left the individual unprotected and at the mercy of any judge, prosecutor, police force, or community. Any of those forces can now attack, prosecute, and jail an individual under arbitrary standards such as (1) contemporary community standards, or (2) "offensive" as defined by a state law, or (3) if the work lacks serious literary, artistic, political, or scientific value. In other words, anyone who disagrees with the arbitrary standards of the empowered authorities (judge, police, community leaders) can potentially be jailed through current anti-obscenity laws. Such nonobjective law is a major step toward censorship, which is the precursor to totalitarianism.

The above Supreme Court majority opinion, which abridges individual rights, was written by the conservative Chief Justice and supported by the other four conservative justices in a 5 to 4 decision. Only Justice Douglas identified the issue of individual rights in his dissenting opinion:

"The idea that the First Amendment permits punishment for ideas that are 'offensive' to the particular judge or jury sitting in judgment is astounding. No greater leveler of speech or literature has ever been designed. To give the power to the censor, as we do today, is to make a sharp and radical break with the traditions of a free society. The First Amendment was not fashioned as a vehicle for dispensing tranquilizers to the people. Its prime function was to keep debate open to 'offensive' as well as to 'staid' people. The tendency throughout history has been to subdue the individual and to exalt the power of government. The use of the standard 'offensive' gives authority to government that cuts the very vitals out of the First Amendment. As is intimated by the Court's opinion, the materials before us may be garbage, but so is much of what is said in political campaigns, in the daily press, on TV or over the radio. By reason of the First Amendment — and solely because of it — speakers and publishers have not been threatened or subdued because their thoughts and ideas may be 'offensive' to some."

The conservative Chief Justice and his conservative associates on the Supreme Court shifted from the principle of protecting individual rights to an arbitrary, undefinable standard of "social good". Hitler, Stalin, and Mao also subjugated individual rights to their standards of "social good". Those arbitrary standards eventually included killing tens of millions of their own citizens for the "social good".

Neo-Tech Advantage #93
1. FAILURE-TO-JUDGE SYNDROME,
2. ERRORS IN JUDGMENT, AND
3. SEGMENTED JUDGMENT

A central theme of today's existentialist culture is "do not judge others". The neocheating media, social "intellectuals", and theologians continually tout, both implicitly and explicitly, the themes "do not judge others", "there are no absolute morals, no rights or wrongs", "everything is relative". Neocheaters have strong motivations for sowing themes of nonknowing and nonjudgment. Their livelihoods depend on keeping others from knowing and judging the parasitism and destruction inflicted by professional mystics and neocheaters onto society.

The continuous campaign to repress moral judgment depends largely on the specious technique of pointing to various erroneous judgments and then implying that such errors are inherent in all judgments. From that false reasoning, neocheaters dishonestly assert that all moral judgments are wrong, unfair, or harmful. From that conclusion, they compound their dishonesty by further asserting that moral judgments should never be made. Moreover, armed with specious egalitarian slogans or Biblical parables, those neocheaters, especially media journalists, malign or castigate those who have the courage and confidence to make honest moral judgments about value destroyers. While, at the same time, those same neocheaters constantly, dishonestly, hypocritically attack their victims (i.e., the value producers) with negative moral judgements that are false.

How are valid moral judgments made? Such judgments are made by using the biological nature and well-being of the conscious organism as the moral standard. With that objective standard, human actions can be consistently and validly judged by acquiring adequate facts and knowledge:

1. Only volitional actions involving conscious choices can be morally judged. All other actions are amoral.

2. A volitional action is moral, for example, if the action is beneficial to the conscious organism. Likewise, a volitional action is immoral if the action is harmful to the conscious organism. Or more simply, *if a volitional action is rational and "good for me", it is moral; or if a volitional action is irrational and "bad for me", it is immoral.*

3. The ability and willingness to make moral judgments are necessary to make sound decisions and function effectively. The more important the personal or business decision, the more important is the need to make accurate moral judgments. In turn, such judgments are crucial for making the correct decisions needed for abiding prosperity, happiness, and romantic love.

Since making moral judgments is necessary for quality survival, a person must be aware of the possible traps and errors in making such judgments. Some of the traps and errors are those that the nonjudgment advocates take out of context to support their harangues that moral judgments should be avoided. ...Three common judgment traps or errors are listed below:
1. **Erroneous or inadequate information to make a valid or accurate judgment** is the most obvious and common cause of judgment errors. Everyone is subject to this error. But that does *not* preclude certainty over moral issues and judgments. The central argument of the nonjudgment neocheaters is that since

no one can know everything or be error free, no one can be certain about anything, especially moral issues.[1] That argument is false. A person can be absolutely certain if given sufficient facts and context to validly measure against the axioms of objective reality. For example, questions of omniscience (knowing everything) and infallibility (being totally free of errors) do not enter into one's certainty of the axiomatic fact that two plus two equals four. The certainty of that fact is independent of anyone's thoughts or opinions of any culture, society, or time in history. And that fact also holds with certainty in other worlds and other universes. Indeed, that fact would hold true if no conscious life ever existed anywhere.[2]

In the normal context, therefore, anyone can be absolutely certain about the judgment and knowledge that two plus two

---

[1]The certainty issue is a popular non-sequitur gimmick among anti-judgment mystics and neocheaters. They assert (often with ironic certainty) that since man cannot be certain about anything, he cannot know anything. If that assertion were so, which it is not, then all judgments and reason itself would be invalid. But professional mystics and neocheaters must constantly promote the false notions that reason is impotent and moral judgments are invalid. ...They must obfuscate reason and judgment to keep their own destructions from being recognized and judged by themselves and others. In a society of reason and judgment, the value producers would promptly put professional value destroyers out of business.

[2]Certain out-of-context, non-sequitur anomalies are used by neocheaters and mystics to falsely invalidate axiomatic facts such as two plus two equals four. They point to the mixing of two quarts of water with two quarts of alcohol. That mixture yields less than four quarts. But that anomaly occurs because of certain known intermolecular-bonding forces between water and alcohol. Such physical-bonding facts have nothing more to do with mathematical facts than if one tosses two parts of sodium metal into two parts of water to produce a fiery explosion and a caustic mess that does not equal four. But, ironically, both of those reactions can be precisely predicted and understood because of the exact, absolute nature of mathematics. ...Or the neocheaters and mystics point to various examples of relativistic, noneuclidean mathematics or quantum mechanics that seem to contradict standard mathematics or physics. Such illusionary contradictions arise only because those facts have nothing to do with standard mathematics or physics. Yet, those facts are dishonestly used out of context to create false illusions of contradiction.

equals four without fear of error or contradiction. Likewise, without being omniscient or infallible, a person can be absolutely certain that one will not be struck by a car while riding in an airplane at 30,000 feet. A neocheating philosophy professor might try to invalidate that certainty by positing the non sequitur that someone could smuggle a mini car aboard, unveil it, drive down the aisle, and strike someone.

With neocheaters and their non sequiturs dismissed, one can know with certainty the facts of objective reality on which abiding prosperity, happiness, and romantic love are based as identified by Neo-Tech. For, those facts of objective reality have always existed throughout the universe and will forever exist with certainty. And that certainty exists independent of consciousness and without requiring omniscience or infallibility by anyone. The function of human consciousness is not to "create" various realities (Plato), which is mysticism, but to identify and integrate the one and only reality as it resides anchored in existence (Aristotle). Identifying objective reality is the survival mechanism of conscious beings. For those identifications are the basis of rational judgments, beneficial actions, and rational successes.

Since no one is omniscient or infallible, everyone is subject to specific errors. But that vulnerability to errors has no bearing on knowing objective reality or being able to make moral judgments with certainty. For example, with inadequate information and judgment errors, a person can temporarily choose the wrong romantic-love partner. But, at the same time, he or she can still know with certainty the objective standards needed for a valid romantic-love relationship. With that certainty, a person can more quickly recognize and correct such judgment errors. In other words, with adequate objective knowledge, a person can make moral judgments with certainty without being omniscient or infallible.

A person can confidently proceed through life knowing that moral and character judgment can be performed with certainty. But again, that person must be aware of those areas subject to error because of inaccurate or incomplete knowledge or information. By always keeping the mind open to new information and being prepared to correct errors, the damage of judgment errors is minimized. All errors cause some damage, if only to waste a person's time. By nature, one is always responsible for and must bear the consequences of his or her actions and errors, innocent or not. But purposeful errors, of course, carry more severe consequences than innocent errors.

2. **Infatuation** is a subtler and often a more dangerous judgment error, especially when it occurs without realizing the error. Infatuation is the focusing on a single attractive or desirable characteristic of another person and then considering the total person as that one positive attribute. Infatuation is not only an unfair burden placed on the person being judged, but can lead to long-range disillusionment and pain for the person making the erroneous judgment. The infatuation-judgment error is a common "true-love-turns-sour" theme so often used in movies, novels, and magazine fiction. Infatuation is also the judgment error that delivers undeserved adulation to charismatic politicians, evangelists, and other neocheaters.

3. **Reverse Infatuation** is perhaps the most subtle form of judgment error. Still, reverse infatuation is a common error that can cause losses of potential values and happiness. Reverse infatuation involves the focusing on a negative characteristic of an individual and then considering that total person as that one negative attribute. That judgment error can be blinding, depriving, and unjust in obscuring areas of earned values and worth in other individuals. Even minor reverse-infatuation puts unjust penalties on the person being judged. While valid criticisms about an individual should be identified and expressed when appropriate, the criticism should explicitly focus on those specific issues, not on the whole person. Reverse infatuation is constantly used as a grossly unfair, dishonest technique by media people as well as by politicians, clergymen, and academics to discredit value producers and their products, businesses, and ideas.

***

THE SEGMENTED-JUDGMENT METHOD

Segmented judging is a method to decrease judgment errors. This method provides a more fair, accurate, and valuable way to judge individuals, especially those important to one's life. This method is particularly important for judging potential romantic-love partners.

190

Segmented judging consists of two essential parts: First, the recognition that people are many-faceted combinations of complex character traits — usually combinations consisting mainly of objectively positive traits with some (often hidden) negative traits.[1] And second, objective judgments require a breaking down of those various character traits into as many separate components as possible.

Once that breakdown is done, one can make more fair and accurate judgments by weighing specific positive traits against specific negative traits ("positive to me" values versus "negative to me" values[2]). The extent that the positive values outweigh the negative values is the extent one makes a positive *moral judgment*. Similarly, the extent that "positive to me" values outweigh the "negative to me" disvalues is the extent one makes a positive *personal-value judgment*.

During a person's life, many of the personal "to me" values can change. But objective moral values are constant and *never* change.

---

[1]Value destroyers such as politicians and religious leaders are less complex than a value producer. For, they have more narrow or limited, anti-life characteristics. Moreover, all neocheaters have essentially the same destructive character. They differ mainly in their dishonest styles and the deceptions they project in concealing their harmful actions. ...*All* professional value destroyers, if given the guns and authority, have the criminal minds and characters for mass murdering to protect and expand their bogus livelihoods.

[2]To the extent that personal "to-me" values contradict objective values is the extent that one is judging on erroneous philosophical or moral premises. Segmented judgment is thus not only helpful for judging others, but is helpful for judging one's own values.

Not all "to-me" values, however, can be measured against objective moral standards. Many "to-me" values are personal-preference values that have no bearing on moral issues. For example, differences in attraction to various physical or personality aspects of another person or preferences towards different careers, recreational activities, tastes, intellectual interests, and appreciation of art and music usually (but not always) have no direct moral implications. Many personal values are merely preferences and tastes that develop from past experiences, interests, and motivations that are not grounded in right or wrong issues, but arise from the uniqueness of the individual and his or her past experiences and development.

191

Neo-Tech Power

The most useful and accurate method to judge a potential romantic-love partner (or any person) is on a segmented "value-scale" basis. One cannot judge the whole of an individual on any specific aspect of his or her character, personality, actions, words, or behavior. Exclusively focusing on specific aspects of a person yields distorted, infatuation-type judgments. Instead, one should judge an individual by placing all the known characteristics and qualities of that person on either the "value to me" side or the "disvalue to me" side of the balance scale [Re: Table 58, Neo-Tech Reference Encyclopedia]. The person is then judged by the extent that the scale tips to the value side or to the disvalue side.

The evaluation of each person should always be kept open. In accumulating more experience or information about any person, the balance tilt can change. Growth, change, or deterioration of either the person doing the judging or the person being judged can cause the "value scale" to tilt more or less in one direction or even to switch to the other direction.

The "value to me" standard is the most reliable, valuable way for an individual to judge the personal value of another individual. The direction and extent the "value scale" tilts is influenced by the personal-value system of the individual making the judgment. For the value weights often depend on personal wants, goals, needs and thus will vary from individual to individual.

The same value scale can be used to measure the moral value of any individual. Unlike the subjective nature of many personal values, moral values are objective, definable, unchanging absolutes. [Re: Table 58, Neo-Tech Reference Encyclopedia] ...Personal values are both objective and subjective, thus vary according to personal tastes and emotions. But moral values are objective and absolute, thus never vary.

Neo-Tech Advantage #94
OBJECTIVE THINKING
VS.
EMOTIONAL THINKING
Positive emotions deliver pleasure and happiness. Negative emotions provide warnings that something is wrong. Thus,

192

negative emotions and negative experiences should *not* be repressed[1] [Re: Concept 54, Neo-Tech Reference Encyclopedia]. Avoiding emotional repression involves consciously and guiltlessly feeling one's own emotions in order to know and defuse them. That honest, open dealing with emotions is necessary for (1) resisting harmful mystical actions, (2) building mental health, and most important, (3) experiencing psychuous pleasures, romantic love, and abiding happiness.

Also, openly knowing and experiencing one's own emotions are necessary to distinguish those emotions from the independent world of objective reality. That understanding of emotions, in turn, is necessary to avoid unhealthy mystical actions. For basing judgments and conclusions on emotions rather than on reality causes harmful mystical actions. Such mystical actions, in turn, diminish the prosperity, well-being, and happiness of human beings. If important judgments or actions are mystically based on emotions, then grave errors with harmful consequences will result.

A person can react to emotions in two ways: (1) The mystical, erroneous, harmful reaction that ranges from repressing emotions to overtly injecting emotions into the decision-making process. And (2), the nonmystical, beneficial reaction that recognizes and freely feels emotions, but then separates them

---

[1]Emotions never should be repressed, but at times emotions can and should be suppressed:

Suppression involves being fully conscious of the emotion, but because of the circumstances, the emotion is temporarily set aside for experiencing at a more appropriate time. Suppression is a useful, healthy method for avoiding harmful mystical reactions based on emotions.

Repression involves trying to deny an emotion by permanently forcing it out of the conscious mind. That act is a mystical distortion of reality, for emotions are a real, undeniable part of a person. By repressing an emotion out of the conscious mind, the emotion is pushed into the subconscious to remain buried. And accumulating buried, negative emotions can harm both one's psychological and intellectual well-being. For those festering, buried emotions can interfere with a person's accurate perception of reality needed to make correct integrations, judgments, and decisions. ...One never has to act on negative emotions, but one should always guiltlessly self-acknowledge negative emotions.

from reality in order to make reasoned, logical judgments undistorted by emotions, whims, or feelings [Re: Table 59, Neo-Tech Reference Encyclopedia].

Because no one is infallible or omniscient, errors are always possible. But errors from honest, *objectively* based thinking are less frequent, less severe, and easier to correct than are errors from mystical, *emotionally* based thinking.

Neo-Tech Advantage #95
FOUR LEVELS OF COMMUNICATION

Four levels of communication exist. The appropriateness of each level depends on the circumstances as illustrated below:

LEVELS OF HUMAN COMMUNICATION

Level of Communication	Description
Impersonal/Automatic Exchange of familiar or automatic phrases (e.g., how are you, good morning).	Smooth, pleasant, cheerful, efficient, noninvolvement method of dealing with people.
Impersonal/Factual Reporting facts.	Efficient, noninvolvement method of transmitting information to people.
Impersonal/Personal Reporting or communicating one's own ideas, thoughts, and judgments.	Can range from completely impersonal to deeply personal.
Personal Communicating personal feelings and thoughts.	Personal to deeply personal. Communication requirement for friendship and romantic love.

Many books on sex, love, marriage, and personality development imply that impersonal communication is inferior or undesirable. They further imply that highly personal communication is a superior, more honest form of communication toward which everyone should strive. Such implications are false and out of context:

Openly revealing one's deep personal self to everyone diminishes self-esteem. That, in turn, militates against one's best interests and happiness. Nevertheless, many authors, gurus, and "therapists" advocate revealing one's personal and private self

194

to all comers. Those "total-openness, let it all hang out" advocates are promoting an egalitarian recipe. That recipe calls for breaking everyone's ego by sharing all personal values and emotions with all comers. Such ego-breaking recipes are often well-disguised, downhill roads to impotence and unhappiness.

Those advocating ego-breaking, emotional egalitarianism usually do so under false labels of openness and honesty. But the opposite is true. Failure to discriminate with whom one shares his or her private personal feelings destroys the potential for experiencing a close, genuinely open, romantic-love relationship with another human being. Instead, an egalitarian "total openness" to everyone is a cheap giveaway of an individual's most precious possession — one's own personal, private self. Nothing squelches romantic love more completely than a Leo Buscaglia's love-all, share-all egalitarian approach.

A person can and should be sincere and honest to everyone without sharing his or her private self or emotions with everyone. In fact, when a person does share his or her private self with everyone else, that person's sincerity and motives become questionable.

An objectively beneficial level of communication exists for every type of human relationship. [Re: Table 61, Neo-Tech Reference Encyclopedia] Only within a romantic relationship in which the partners love and value each other in their private universe can the full range of physical and psychological sharing be experienced without diminishing self-esteem. Within the romantic relationship resides the full scope of psychuous pleasures: the combination of full-range sexuality with the freedom to fearlessly share any aspect of one's self...any thought, feeling, fantasy, emotion — good or bad, rational or irrational. Thus, a person can let go completely to share and guiltlessly experience any aspect of one's body, mind, emotion, imagination with his or her romantic-love partner.

Within a romantic-love relationship, one can freely share *any* aspect of one's self and life. But one need not share *every* aspect. A person always has the guiltless right to privacy to any area of his or her life, even within the closest, most open and honest friendship or romantic-love relationship. Total honesty does not require total revealing all of one's private self. Indeed,

195

absolute and total sharing of one's self and psyche involves losing the most profound essence of privacy. That loss, in turn, diminishes the sense of "I" and one's self-esteem. Retaining the essence of personal privacy is not an act of repression, inhibition, dishonesty, or lack of openness, but is a self-respect preservation of an individual's inherent right to privacy.

To experience psychuous pleasures through romantic love requires genuine self-esteem (valuing of one's own self). Beyond the romantic-love relationship, self-esteem is diminished or even destroyed by indiscriminately sharing or by giving away one's personal, private self too cheaply. That loss of self-esteem can be especially severe (even leading to suicide) if one promiscuously gives away his or her private self just because socially chic books, gurus, and media commentators falsely promulgate the need to be totally open with everyone. The most harmful of egalitarian neocheaters are the high visibility Leo Buscaglias who mystically promulgate the self-destructive, love-everyone concept. They imply that love, openness, and honesty are demonstrated by the giving of one's private self to all comers.

Valuing of one's private self does not mean holding back or manipulating communication in order to bargain for advantages. The sharing of oneself is a personal choice and judgment. Such sharing with another person may occur quickly, even on initial contact if judgment responses trigger desires to move toward deeper personal or romantic possibilities. Chances should and must be taken on exploring potentially valuable relationships. Errors in judgment are often made. But minimum harm from such errors results so long as the individual is making his or her *own* conscious choices, using reason and reality rather than following the words of mystics, social "authorities", or gurus.

Surrendering one's independent judgment to mystics, social "authorities", or gurus and offering one's private self to all comers results in:

1. Diminished self-confidence and self-esteem.

2. Unproductive, unrewarding consumption of time:
   Such wasting of irreplaceable segments of one's
   life span continually diminishes the time needed
   to build a competent, productive life necessary for

growing prosperity, romantic love, and abiding happiness.

3. Diminished personal desirability: Indiscriminate "openness and honesty" is often a boring imposition on those being gratuitously subjected to such personal openness.

4. And most important: After selflessly giving one's self to all comers, little if anything that is private, exciting, or precious is left to share exclusively with one's closest friend or romantic-love partner...little if anything is left to build that unique, priceless, private universe crucial to a romantic-love relationship.

Happiness exists as a private world within one's own self. That world expands into a mutually exclusive universe shared by two people involved in a psychuous-pleasure, romantic-love relationship. And that exclusive, private universe is a uniquely precious, emotional treasure. But that treasure can be forever lost by indiscriminately or promiscuously sharing oneself physically, psychologically, or spiritually with others.

That selfless giveaway and subsequent destruction of one's private inner world is exactly what the egalitarian advocates of "total openness" wish to accomplish. Only by negating everyone else's private values and self-esteem, can they justify their own prostituted inner world. Moreover, most of the "total-openness" egalitarians are professional mystics or neocheaters who depend on extracting their material and spiritual livelihoods from others. To do that, they first must dupe productive people with altruistic guilt. Then those neocheaters can psychologically pull the producers down to the level of mystics and parasitical neocheaters through selfless egalitarianism. ...The lower the level that value producers can be reduced, the more easily can their values be usurped by neocheaters.

By contrast, avoiding that self-giveaway trap leaves romantic love and abiding happiness open for any value producer.

Neo-Tech Advantage #96
COMMUNICATION
IN ROMANTIC-LOVE RELATIONSHIPS

Crucial in a romantic-love relationship is open communication, especially during negative emotional experiences. During stressful or negative experiences, deliberate reason-based (rather than automatic emotion-based) conclusions are needed to make fair, honest judgments [Re: Concept 127, Neo-Tech Reference Encyclopedia]. The ability to communicate honestly (without mysticism) during emotional stress is the hallmark of successful love partners.

The first step to reason-based communication between partners is to identify and separate the emotional aspects of the problem [Re: Concept 74 and Table 26, Neo-Tech Reference Encyclopedia]. For, knowing the difference between reason-based conclusions (business-like thinking) and emotion-based conclusions (mystical thinking) is the most important step in developing communication skills during negative situations.

The ability to generate reason-based conclusions out of negative situations has powerfully beneficial effects on a person's well-being, self-esteem, and happiness. Reasoned conclusions in emotional situations, for example, can prevent irrational actions that damage or destroy business, family, and romantic-love situations. The habitual use of reason-based conclusions in emotional situations leads to powerfully effective communication in all situations, especially business and romantic-love situations.

The Judeo-Christian ethics instill fear in women about expressing sexual assertiveness. Those same ethics instill fear in men about expressing tender feelings and emotions. Such fears cause various degrees of emotional repression and diminished happiness in both men and women. The Neo-Tech/Psychuous concepts eliminate those pleasure-depriving fears by allowing guiltless communication about emotions, love, and sex between romantic-love partners.

A person can enter the future with either a reality/life-oriented philosophy that continually expands into personal wealth and happiness...or with a mystical/death-oriented philosophy that continually shrinks into personal impoverishment and unhappiness. Mystical or Platonistic-based philosophies and the resulting dishonest, altruistic ethics offer only negative, unhappy life styles. Neo-Tech/Psychuous or Aristotelian-based philosophies and the resulting honest, reality ethics offer positive, happy life styles. ...Anyone can choose at anytime between either philosophy, ethic, and life-style.

Neo-Tech Advantage #97
PRODUCTIVENESS AND HAPPINESS
versus
LAZINESS AND MISERY

Inseparable links exist between productive work, earned values, prosperity, psychuous pleasures, and happiness. Too many productive people live without experiencing their earned happiness or psychuous pleasures. That deprivation of happiness and psychuous pleasures is an unnecessary tragedy due to altruistic, mystical guilt inculcated into the value producer by the professional value destroyers.

Psychuous pleasures and abiding happiness depend on psychological health which, in turn, depends on productive work. Without productive work or preparations for such, psychological health is impossible. Moreover, psychuous pleasures and happiness act as the emotional incentives to constantly increase one's value and productivity.

Generally, the producer of values thrives on a fast-paced life in high-density environments (major exceptions are, for example, productive farmers, ranchers, miners). Nonproductive and destructive people, on the other hand, generally fear or enviously hate high-density, fast-paced, highly productive environments (such as New York City[1]).

Professional mystics and Marxist neocheaters destroyed countries such as Cuba, Cambodia, Iran, and Nicaragua. Such black-hat neocheaters work explicitly for the demise of modern,

---

[1]Master black-hat neocheater, Fidel Castro, expressed the ultimate desire of all envious mystics, neocheaters, and other value destroyers in his publicly stated, personal desire to drop a nuclear bomb on New York City to destroy the greatest, most intense fountainhead of objective values known to mankind.

highly productive, highly technological societies.[1] They gain their power by pandering to their downtrodden proletariat with false promises of a nonthinking "peaceful" existence — a prehistoric, unthinking "animal-nature" existence. They promise the ultimate mystical dream of a nonthinking, egalitarian, "problem-free" nirvana. But that dream contradicts life, nature, and reality as does all mysticism. Indeed, that no-effort, "problem-free" mysticism is the essence of value destruction and death. By contrast, high-effort problem-solving is the essence of value production and life.

Integrated links exist between productivity, self-interest, self-esteem, psychuous pleasures, and happiness [Re: Table 65, Neo-Tech Reference Encyclopedia]. Production of competitive values is the integrating growth dynamics for conscious beings. Production of competitive values provides freedom, prosperity, psychuous pleasures, and abiding happiness.

Productivity and rational self-interest are not only essential to happiness, but are essential to life itself. For without productive self-interest, only consumptive altruism remains. What would a world of consumptive altruism mean? What if everyone began living as selfless, unproductive consumers, temporarily surviving by sacrificing one another in consuming the values created by the past producers. One can imagine what an

---

[1]The black-hat neocheaters' ultimate, envious dream is to destroy fast-paced, high-tech, high-intensity life, especially as experienced in productive, free-market metropolitan areas. That dream was actually achieved by the terror-totalitarian government of Cambodia. To gain unrestricted power, the neocheating leader, Pol Pot, implemented his destruction of urban life by a forced, death-march evacuation of the entire capital city of Phnom Penh. His totally destructive, murderous actions represented the highest attainment of egalitarian ideals and the natural end-result of altruistic-based philosophies. For that reason, few objections or cries of outrage about such blatant mass murder were heard from the "liberal" media, soul mate mystics, social "intellectuals", and other professional mystics and neocheaters. ...Given the power and means, *all* professional value destroyers have the capacity to mass murder. For in essence, they will do anything, including mass murder, to protect and expand their bogus livelihoods and to feel increasingly important, when in essence they are less than nothing.

unhappy, destructive world that would be. One can imagine the malevolence and meanness that would exist among those human beings as they cannibalized the final values and then one another. Soon after that, nearly everyone would be dead, even those with guns.

But what if everyone began living competitively as rational, productive individuals with everyone intent on producing maximum values for others and society in order to achieve maximum prosperity, psychuous pleasures, romantic love, and happiness for themselves and their loved ones. One can imagine what a benevolent, happy, exciting, thriving world that would be...a world free of mysticism and neocheaters...a world without guns...a world in which everyone forever increases his or her productivity, prosperity, and happiness.

Most productive individuals are of much greater value than their mystically diminished self-image lets them realize. For, the image of highly productive individuals has been constantly denigrated by dishonest media journalists, authors, university professors, educators, theologians, politicians, and social "intellectuals". The productive middle class is projected in the ugly, inverted, false images of the Babbitts and Willie Lomans. The ultimate unjust irony lies with the destructive government bureaucrats and "professionals": They who never produce values, only consume or destroy them, coined and contemptuously use the pejorative "working stiffs" in describing the self-sufficient, working middle class. Those "working stiffs" are the honest people who daily produce a flood of values for others, including those government value destroyers. Indeed, those value destroyers could not survive without those "working stiffs". But those "working stiffs" would thrive without those bureaucrats and professional value destroyers.

Value producers can feel their full worth only after discarding the years of unearned guilt foisted on them by the mystics, politicians, social "intellectuals", media commentators, and other neocheating altruists and egalitarians. Indeed, such productive people can and should experience the pleasure of feeling their full worth all the time. And now with Neo-Tech, they can forever free themselves of egalitarian altruism and its envious neocheaters to always feel their deserved worth and happiness.

The underlying cause of egalitarianism and envy is dishonesty and laziness.[1] Laziness means the abdication of self-responsibility. That abdication is the root cause of mysticism, envy, altruism, neocheating, and chronic unhappiness [Re: Concept 133, Neo-Tech Reference Encyclopedia]. Also, incompetence and lost potential arise from laziness and defaults on self-responsibility [Re: Concepts 133 and 134, Neo-Tech Reference Encyclopedia].

Professional mystics and neocheaters have vested interests in attacking competitiveness — in attacking Neo-Tech, individualism, prosperity, and free-enterprise. The master neocheaters among the politicians, theologians, and social "intellectuals" live by attacking the competitive value producers and usurping their values. Through such destructive attacks, those neocheaters hide their own defaults while creating their needed illusions of personal power and pseudo self-worth. And, to maintain those illusions, they must continue attacking the competitive producer, his integrated thinking, the values he produces, and his individual rights and property. For those fake illusions let them physically and psychologically live off of the value producer.

But being dependent on others for survival, nonproductive mystics and neocheaters are unable to earn the self-esteem and competence needed to achieve psychuous pleasures, romantic love, and abiding prosperity. Also, not having earned values, they hold no genuine power.

Productivity is the building block for prosperity, love, and happiness. The most common character and behavior traits associated with productive men and women are identified below:

---

[1]The mechanism of laziness in both the mind and body is the yielding to actions of least effort. But conscious beings cannot prosper or be happy through actions of least effort. And unlike all other animals, conscious beings cannot survive by letting nature rule them. Conscious beings depend on volitional efforts and logically reasoned choices to survive. They must constantly choose to exert effort, think logically, and act beyond their feelings to prosper. They must exercise discipline, thought, and then control (the DTC technique) to succeed. ...To achieve lasting prosperity and happiness, one must constantly do things he or she does not *feel* like doing.

CHARACTER AND BEHAVIOR TRAITS
OF COMPETITIVE VALUE PRODUCERS

Character Traits
Honesty
Integrity
Rationality
Consistency
Perseverance
Individualism
Enthusiasm
Ambition
Passion

Behavior Traits

• Acts with energy, honesty, and fairness regardless of near-term consequences. Loyalty to honesty.
• Recognizes and pursues the values of honesty and integrity.
• Thinks rationally, logically, objectively.
• Focuses on reality.
• Seeks facts *in full context*.
• Organizes self, life, and work toward profitable actions.
• Asks clear questions and listens carefully.
• Values time. Uses it efficiently and profitably.
• Anticipates and then strives for achievement.
• Sets value-producing goals and strives to accomplish them.
• Seeks to understand fully and contextually before judging.
• Shows passion, benevolence, and innocence toward life.
• Avoids mystical reactions.

Neo-Tech Advantage #98
GROWTH DEATH/PSYCHE DEATH
AND ITS PREVENTION

Growth Death or Psyche Death are terms used to describe the tragedy of dying as a competently functioning conscious being while continuing to exist physically. That phenomenon unnecessarily occurs in a high percentage of people. Caused by the disease of mysticism, Growth Death affects perhaps 90% of the world's living adult population [Re: Concept 89, Table 31, Neo-Tech Reference Encyclopedia]. Growth Death is a uniquely human phenomenon that involves the stagnation and death of the human psyche, often at an early age — even before the human body reaches physical maturity.

The human psyche embraces both the emotional and intellectual spheres of the mind. Contrary to popular myth, both spheres are inseparably linked and symbiotically function together. If one sphere grows, so does the other. If one sphere deteriorates so does the other. Most important, the human psyche has no age or capacity limitations on its growth.

Unlike the physical body, the human psyche has no growth limits. It never needs to stop growing. In fact, the continuous growth of the psyche is the process of conscious living. When that process stops, the individual ceases to function as a conscious being is designed to function. If a person's psyche is not growing, that person is living contrary to his or her nature. Thus, that person's psyche begins dying. And if one's psyche is dying, that person cannot experience growing prosperity, love, or happiness.

PSYCHE GROWTH VS. PSYCHE DEATH

What happens with a living, growing business-like mind? Value-producing actions beget happy feelings while honestly integrating reality. What happens with a dying, shrinking mystical mind? Indulged feelings beget destructive actions while dishonestly evading reality. The checklist below compares the psyche of those two minds — the criminal, destructive, mystic mind versus the heroic, productive, business mind.

People generally display various mixtures of living and dead psyche characteristics. But the mixture is always tilted to one side or the other with the general direction usually moving unnecessarily toward death. With the following checklist, most people can determine whether their psyches are living or dying. A person with a dying psyche can reverse the trend and live again by using Neo-Tech to cure the disease of mysticism within one's own self.

CHECKLIST FOR SELF-MYSTICISM

Characteristics of a Dying or Dead Psyche (Ralph Nader Type Mystical Mind)	Characteristics of a Living or Growing Psyche (Ray Kroc Type Business Mind)
☐ Envious of others for their achievements, success, happiness, or material well-being. Resents heroes, value producers, and especially great business people and their productive accomplishments.	☐ Envy-free. Admires and encourages individual achievement in self and others.
☐ Operates on subjective feelings or wishes. Oriented toward short-range, value-destroying approaches to problems and goals.	☐ Operates on objective principles. Oriented toward long-range, value-producing approaches to problems and goals.
☐ Desires the destruction, distribution, or leveling of the wealth, happiness, and well-being earned by others.	☐ Produces tradeable values. Desires a life of achievements and happiness for self and others.
☐ Holds anti-individualistic views. Has egalitarian and collectivist desires to seize, destroy, and level values produced by others.	☐ Orients around rational self-interests. Independently fills own needs through production of tradeable values for others.
☐ Fears freedom, independence, and competition. Follows external "authorities" in religion and government.	☐ Seeks freedom, independence, and competition. Rejects external "authorities".
☐ Praises humble, selfless altruists. Attacks or maligns proud, productive achievers.	☐ Admires and seeks productive achievers.
☐ Unhappy with life. Only interludes of short-term happiness. Represses the tragedy of death. Recoils at the possibility of biological immortality.	☐ Happy with life. Only interludes of short-term sadness. Recognizes the tragedy of death. Hails the possibility of human biological immortality as the highest moral goal.
☐ Seeks government controls and laws that forcibly restrict and repress individual freedom.	☐ Seeks freedom. Opposes all forms of initiatory force and oppression, especially government force and oppression of the individual.

(continued on next page)

205

CHECKLIST FOR SELF-MYSTICISM	
(continued from previous page)	
Characteristics of a **Dying or Dead Psyche** **(Ralph Nader Type Mystical Mind)**	**Characteristics of a** **Living or Growing Psyche** **(Ray Kroc Type Business Mind)**
☐ Plagued with anxieties and self-doubts.	☐ At ease and comfortable with self. Increasingly feels joyful life building within his or her physical and emotional self.
☐ Holds a cynical or malevolent view of life and people.	☐ Holds a benevolent view of life and people.
☐ Life is viewed as unhappy and people as inherently destructive, wicked, or sinful.	☐ Life is viewed as naturally happy, beautiful, exciting. People are viewed as inherently good, valuable, productive.
☐ Emotionally and physically experiences life with increasing unhappiness and lethargy.	☐ Experiences life with increasing joy and intensity.
☐ Accepts harmful, mystical concepts such as original sin and predestination.	☐ Rejects mystical concepts such as original sin and predestination.
☐ Orients around mystical premises and beliefs in God, statism, astrology, the occult.	☐ Orients around honesty and objective reality.
☐ Orients around an altruistic, Platonistic philosophy that holds the sacrifice of the individual to "higher" causes as a virtue.	☐ Orients around an Aristotelian/ Neo-Tech philosophy that holds the individual as the supreme value in the universe.

To let one's psyche live or die is always a volitional choice made by each individual alone — a choice usually made early in life, often in childhood. The tragically unnecessary surrender of the psyche to mysticism and Growth Death takes the subconscious form of:

What's the use. Why struggle any more to understand reality or bear the pain and pressure of being honest? I am not going to live by my own mind because the effort and responsibilities are too great. I'll let others think for me. I'll let the authorities tell me what to believe and do. Yes, I'll support their power no matter how dishonest or destructive. I want the easiest, safest way through life. No, I don't want to advance in life by independent, integrated thinking and actions. Instead, I want to be a believer and to follow some 'wiser' authority or 'higher' good. I'll live by the thoughts and feelings of others.

From that point of surrender, the individual may become more knowledgeable, skillful, and proficient in specific areas, but his or her psyche will diminish as overall growth of the mind stops and turns downward toward death. At some future time, that individual could decide to countermand that subconscious surrender order and restart psyche growth. If not, the quality of his or her life will continuously decline, always controlled, always pushed or pulled one way or another by outside forces, by the influences of "others".

The "others" represent any higher "authority" that an individual lets control his or her thoughts, judgments, actions, life (rather than using one's own mind). Those "higher authorities" may be friends, relatives, politicians, bureaucrats, lawyers, social "intellectuals", neocheating university professors, the media, the church, the ruler, the Messiah, Allah, cocaine, the Bible, the stars, the state, "society" — anyone or anything outside the individual's own mind.

People default on the primary responsibility of their minds by letting outside others ("authorities", neocheaters) do their thinking and make their decisions. When people default on using their own minds, they lose control of their lives and begin dying as they become controlled by others.

By nature, control through others always contradicts an individual's long-range well-being. Thus, accepting such outside control always begins the process of growth death. For no one can experience growth, prosperity, and happiness while under control of others.

The human mind is an adaptable, resilient organ having great self-healing powers. Helping or curing the mind seldom needs outside help. The powerful self-help nature of the mind is purposely ignored by the neocheaters dominating the psychology profession. The mind can suffer psychic or psychological damage. But if and when the individual chooses, that damage can almost always be reversed by attacking and eliminating the self-indulged disease of mysticism that is causing the problem by cutting off honesty and integrated thinking. That effective, self-help approach sharply contradicts the messy, wasteful, and usually harmful external "authority" approaches involving psychologists, psychiatrists, therapists. Such external "authority" approaches ignore the essence of both mental health (Neo-Tech: honesty and effort) and mental illness (mysticism: dishonesty and laziness). Thus, in the light of Neo-Tech, most approaches by the psychiatric and psychological professions are invalid, harmful, fraudulent, and often practiced by destructive neocheaters.[1]

Through honest thinking and sustained efforts, a person can self-heal and strengthen his or her mind. Through such self-healing, that person retakes control of life and reverses that mind atrophy caused by mysticism. On healing the mind, the future can once again promise boundless prosperity, growth, love, and happiness. One's psyche can then experience anew an exhilarating freedom and control over reality, perhaps for the first time since early childhood.

Most people have defaulted, at least partially, on the independent use of their minds. By abandoning any part of their minds to "others", including psychologists, they diminish their means to prosperity and happiness. Yet, through Neo-Tech, the potential is always available to rescue one's self from mysticism and its external "authorities". By nature, the self-rescue of one's own mind from mysticism must be an act of self-responsibility free from external "authority".

Few people choose to resurrect themselves from Psyche Death and Growth Death.[2] Those who have surrendered usually rationalize their deteriorating self and shrinking potential as a

---

[1]Certain *cognitive* psychological approaches can be valid and at times valuable when used to gain specific knowledge that helps one identify elusive areas of mysticism. Beyond those exceptional situations, however, most psychological treatments are bogus and harmful, for such treatments are the antithesis of mental health: the handing over of self-responsibility for mystic-free mental health to a mystical-indulging, feel-good external authority.

Many statistical tests over the past fifty years have demonstrated the long-term worthlessness and drug-like harm of feel-good psyche chats, therapies, treatments (Reference: Garth Wood, MD, *Myths and Neurosis — Overcoming the Illness Excuse*, Harper and Row).

[2]Recovery of independent thought is possible at almost any age through the nearly infinite self-healing powers of the human mind, especially when made mystic-free through Neo-Tech. Indeed, Neo-Tech cures mysticism. Thus, Neo-Tech will put most psychologists and psychiatrists out of business.

natural, biological aging process. Growth Death may be common, but is neither natural nor necessary. Furthermore, rebirth of a dying mind or psyche is not only possible but quite easy for anyone possessing Neo-Tech knowledge.

Neo-Tech leads the way to mental health by self-curing the disease of mysticism. ...And without mysticism to manipulate others, the neocheaters are powerless.

Neo-Tech Advantage #99
THREE STEPS TO ACHIEVING
COMMERCIAL BIOLOGICAL IMMORTALITY[1]
IN OUR LIFETIME
(See Advantage #114, Appendix F, and Neo-Tech V for details)

The elimination of mysticism is required for non-aging or youth-rejuvenating biological immortality. That goal will be accomplished in three steps:

STEP ONE
The first step in achieving biological immortality is defining its meaning: biological immortality means to live as flesh-and-blood, non-aging human beings forever — not just an extended life, but to live mind, body, and spirit as one's own self for centuries, millennia, forever. The purpose of biological immortality is not to serve others, society, or mankind, but to preserve forever the most precious, important value in the universe — one's own integrated conscious self and sense of I-ness to experience expanding prosperity, love, and happiness — forever.

STEP TWO
The second step in achieving non-aging biological immortality is dispelling the following seven myths (Appendix F refutes each myth in detail):

---

[1]All Neo-Tech references to biological immortality by nature encompass I-ness immortality. For, preserving or perpetuating all other aspects of conscious and biological life, including cloned bodies, memory banks, and personalities are meaningless if one's original sense of I-ness is lost.

1. Death is not final. False.
2. Life after death exists. False. [See Memento Mori in Neo-Tech V]
3. Everyone wants to live forever. False.
4. Living forever would deprive younger generations of opportunities. False.
5. People living forever would cause overpopulation. False.
6. Living forever would be boring. False.
7. Achieving non-aging biological immortality presents technical, biological, medical, and scientific problems that are so complex and difficult that they could be unknowable or, at best, remain unsolvable for centuries. False.

STEP THREE

The third step in achieving youth-rejuvenating immortality is understanding the requirements for achieving [A] personal prosperity, and [B] social prosperity with political freedom allows [C] commercial biological immortality. Achieving [A] and [B] is necessary to achieve [C]. The formula is **[A] + [B] = [C]:**

[A]=Achieving Personal Power, Prosperity, Happiness: Neo-Tech delivers honesty, power, love — the motive for I-ness immortality.

[B]=Achieving a Free, Prosperous World: Neo-Tech delivers freedom, business, prosperity — the means to biological immortality.

[C]=Achieving Biological Immortality in our Lifetime: Neo-Tech delivers science, technology, immortality — the achievement of biological immortality.

SUMMARY

Commercial, non-aging I-ness immortality is achievable within our lifetime. But that achievement depends on collapsing the 2000-year hoax of mysticism and eliminating all its symbiotic neocheaters. The Neo-Tech Research and Writing Center is already undermining the hoax of mysticism worldwide and will forever cure that disease of death without anyone's support, without asking anyone to donate time or money, and without permission from or control by anyone.

People must fully experience prosperity and happiness to value their one-and-only life with enough passion to motivate rapid, full-scale development of youth-rejuvenating immortality. Neo-Tech will trigger that full-scale development by freeing millions of productive individuals around the world from mysticism and neocheating. Once free, they will flourish naturally toward open-ended prosperity and happiness. They will flourish by (1) collapsing mysticism, (2) rejecting false guilt for living honestly, productively, fully, thus (3) rendering the neocheaters impotent. Those three actions, in turn, will unlock the needed motivation and means to develop commercial biological immortality rapidly — in a few years.

The entire purpose of youth-rejuvenating immortality is to experience ever increasing happiness — to experience future realms of ever expanding enterprise, prosperity, love, and happiness. Such unimaginable happiness is available to every conscious being living in a mystical-free world of forever evolving knowledge and adventure.

Neo-Tech Advantage #100
MALEFACTORS AND ENVY

Malefactor is a label that can be applied to envious people. An envious person wants values destroyed. An envious person works to undermine individual and property rights, both of which are needed to achieve well-being and happiness. [Re: Table 68 in the Neo-Tech Reference Encyclopedia.]

Envy distorts and then consumes a person's view of life. Envy is a prime evil that people let develop within themselves to their great personal harm, unhappiness, and eventual death. Laziness and dishonesty are basic *causes*. Envy and impotence are basic *effects*. Envy is the desire to destroy values created or earned by others...to destroy the good because of its goodness. Why? Because the objective good (rational human values) exposes by contrast the envier's defaults and impotence. That exposure, in turn, diminishes the envier's pseudo self-esteem. And that pseudo self-esteem is needed for both psychological and physical survival — needed to prevent a mental breakdown or suicide.

Values earned by others make the envier experience his

impotence. The good inherent in objective values reveals what the envier lacks. Such values reveal the human goodness that the envier has defaulted on. Such values leave the envier aware of his or her incompetence to live as a self-sufficient, independent, happy human being. Thus, the envier fears and hates such values.

Envy growing out of dishonesty and laziness is a major destructive force in human relationships. In contrast to jealousy that is directed toward the *possession* of values, envy is directed toward the *destruction* of values. The desire to destroy the values, happiness, and pleasures earned by others is the essence of envy. Envious attacks against the producers and their values are woven throughout all the "good sounding" non sequiturs of media journalists, religious leaders, politicians, social "intellectuals", "consumerists", "ecologists", and other envious neocheaters.

Contrary to the misconception promoted by envy-oriented writers and journalists, envy is not analogous to jealousy. While both reduce happiness, their causes are opposites [Re: Concept 77, Neo-Tech Reference Encyclopedia]. Jealousy is rooted in valuing and coveting a value...because the value is good to the beholder. Envy is rooted in resenting and hating a value...because the value threatens to expose the dishonesty and failures of the envier. The jealous person is threatened by the loss of a value. The envious person is threatened by the presence of a value.

Enviers have always hidden, camouflaged, and distorted the meaning of envy. Enviers must not let their inferiority and dependence on the producers become known to themselves or others. For, if everyone understood the nature of envy, the professional mystics and neocheaters would lose their survival tools and rationalized self-esteems. And that would bring loss of unearned gains, public disgrace, even suicide — unless the envier chose to change — to prosper by becoming a competitive producer of values.

Out of fear and resentment, enviers must attack values earned by others. At the same time, they must constantly usurp those values in order to survive. That contradictory life of enviers brings increasing resentment, anxiety, incompetence, unhappiness.

Those free of envy have no way of knowing the malevolent nature of the envier. Thus, most value producers, because of their naive innocence, are relatively helpless in protecting themselves from envious value destroyers. ...Who are the envious value destroyers? They are identified in the next chart. The issue is black and white: All people can be clearly classified as either envious or nonenvious [Re: Table 69, Neo-Tech Reference Encyclopedia]. From value-destroying bureaucrats right up to genocidal dictators, the survival of envious people depends on their victims never discovering the nature of envy. To accomplish that concealment[1], destructive enviers must use one or more of the tactics shown in the chart below:

ENVY TACTICS

Tactics to Conceal Envy	Commonly Used By
Avoiding the word "envy"	Politicians, theologians, lawyers, "liberal" journalists, social "intellectuals", dictators
Distort and confuse the meaning of envy by falsely blending its meaning with jealousy	Politicians, theologians, "liberal" journalists, social "intellectuals", psychologists
Deny the existence of envy	Politicians, theologians, "liberal" journalists
Invert the destructiveness of envy into a socially "good" action (e.g., the "good" of mass destructions that force everyone to the same level)	Egalitarians, "ecologists", social "intellectuals", psychologists, lawyers, politicians, dictators
Claim that envy is inborn or is "forced" into people by the environment. Therefore, envious people are blameless. Instead, society and inequality are to blame	Social "intellectuals", psychologists, theologians, lawyers

---

[1]Over the centuries, concealing the nature of envy has been easy. For without Neo-Tech, most nonenvious individuals have no way to comprehend envy. In their innocence, envy-free productive people cannot emotionally or intellectually grasp the idea that people actually exist who want to destroy values because *of the goodness* represented by those values.

Envy is a destructive character development resulting from:
1. volitional laziness and dishonesty, and
2. the choice to default on the self-responsibility to live
   by one's own mind and efforts through competitive
   value production.

The envier must depend on the minds and efforts of others to survive. Envy comes from within the self-made character of a person, not from society or the environment. Envious people, therefore, are responsible for their own envy, destructions, and harm to others. Enviers are the malefactors of civilization:

THE ENVIOUS MALEFACTORS

Who are the envious malefactors? Who are the value destroyers of civilization? They are identified below:

General Classes of Envious Malefactors
Professional
Value Destroyers
Neocheaters
Parasites
Mystics

Specific Classes of Envious Malefactors
Dictators
Politicians
Theologians
Social "Intellectuals"
Destructive Bureaucrats
Criminal-Minded Professionals

High Percentage of Envious Malefactors Found
in Specific "Occupations"

Law[1] (a few exceptions)
Media journalism[1] (some exceptions)
University professors[1] (a few notable exceptions)
Mafia members (destructive but usually not envious)

[1]Envious malefactors or value destroyers are not inherent to these specific occupations. But a particularly high percentage of such malefactors populate these easy-to-fake professions. By contrast, envious malefactors rarely exist in productive hard-to-fake activities such as competitive, profit-making businesses.

Theologians and politicians (incorrigible enviers)

Skid-row inhabitants (envious but usually not very destructive)

Unproductive scions of inherited wealth (dissipators of wealth earned by others: "public servants" such as Nelson A. Rockefeller, Teddy Kennedy)

Social "intellectuals" (e.g., social "scientists" — their field is largely spurious and the antithesis of science)

Self-appointed professional feminists[1]

Self-appointed professional environmentalists[1]

Self-appointed professional consumerists[1]

Self-appointed professional peace activists[1]

The value destroyers listed above are basically immature, anti-intellectual people who seek to evade reality and honesty. By contrast, most value producers are mature, genuinely intellectual people who seek to identify contextual facts through fully integrated honesty.

Most politicians and social "intellectuals" are immature value destroyers who survive by neocheating the value producer. Such people promote altruistic social "ideals" designed to harm and drain the value producers of this planet. Those immature value destroyers include not only politicians but a high percentage of university professors, especially in the fields of social and political sciences, philosophy, psychology, education, law, religion...and a smaller percentage in other fields. Their

[1]These professional, self-appointed value destroyers (e.g., the Nader type) are destructive enviers who use neocheating demagoguery to gain unearned power. Such neocheaters use non sequiturs to create falsely inverted "realities" such as the "hero" consumer pitted against the "villain" producer. But those neocheaters hurt both the consumer and the producer by promoting government controls and force. By contrast, those "villain" producers of values are and always have been the only real benefactors and heroes of mankind. Without those producers, no productive jobs or consumers would exist since no products or values to consume would exist. Indeed, without those producers, little, if any, human life would exist.

No disparagement is meant toward the valuable efforts of consumer-aid organizations (e.g., Better Business Bureaus) that do not sanction, use, or depend on government force or the violation of individual rights. Also no disparagement is intended toward the few honest, professionally trained ecologists who actually deliver values by *objectively* studying the environment relative to improving the long-range prosperity and happiness for value producers and society.

215

crusades for fake social "justice" and specious human rights are motivated by envy and executed through criminal minds. Their attacks on values are neocheating ploys not only for plundering the value producers but for hiding their own incompetence, laziness, and dishonesty. But the greatest evil of those academe is their irreparable mutilation of millions upon millions of young, developing minds.

Why are theologians also classified as neocheaters, malefactors, value destroyers, and parasites? What about the "good" that theologians do, such as help the poor? Indeed, their "good" is exactly that: good in quotes. Their "good" is usually specious and contrary to human well-being and happiness. For, their "good" is based on the altruistic sacrifice of the value producer with the theologians collecting both the praise and a middle-man's cut without producing values.

Most theologian-type "good" depends on dishonest, guilt manipulations of the producer. That "good" arises from their subtle, unjust denigrations of personal success, prosperity, and happiness. Furthermore, their "good" generally involves hypocritical, neocheating ploys designed for living with praise and "ease" without working to produce competitive values. In other words, theologians support themselves by promoting God-like altruistic schemes designed to usurp values earned by others while collecting unearned respect and power. ...That is the purpose and livelihood of most theologians.

Neo-Tech Advantage #101
ENVY AND LAZINESS

Value destroyers such as demagogic "ecologists" and "consumerists", neocheating politicians and bureaucrats, evil dictators and ayatollahs usurp enough power to directly execute their envious destructions. They camouflage their envy by operating under non-sequitur banners of common "good", human rights, social "justice", "peace", equality, the fatherland, and the most primitive, barbaric of all non-sequitur stratagems — God. Such envious, value-destroying professionals live by usurping power and values, by attacking, undermining, crippling, destroying value producers.

Most other enviers, however, lack the power, cunning, and resources to directly damage and destroy value producers. To vicariously satisfy their envy, they eagerly support the destructive causes promoted by those demagogic "consumerists", "environmentalists", theologians, politicians, social "intellectuals", and other neocheaters.

A person can cure his or her envy only by becoming a self-sufficient producer of competitive values to achieve genuine independence, competence, and self-esteem. If not cured, the malignancy of envy will keep growing, consuming that person in malevolent hatred toward self, productive people, objective values, and life itself.

Expressed another way, growing envy destroys a person's potential to earn genuine prosperity, psychuous pleasures, and happiness. To break free from envy's grip, a person must first identify the envy. Next, that person must reduce the need for envy by becoming increasingly productive until competent enough to live by competitively producing values desired by others. Then a metamorphosis occurs that changes envious fear of objective values to a passionate desire to uphold those values. On evolving into an independent, self-sufficient producer of values, envy fades as a new, exciting life emerges — a life of growing prosperity, expanding power, and abiding happiness.

Producers of objective values have prosperity and happiness always open to them. But first they must break free from the unearned guilt foisted on them by the enviers who surrounded them. The producers must realize that they are the ones who hold the real power. And only they can guiltlessly collect genuine prosperity and happiness.

Neo-Tech sharply contrasts the world of mysticism and envy to the world of value production and self-esteem. [Re: Table 71, Neo-Tech Reference Encyclopedia] One does not cross into the happy, envy-free world until that person becomes competent enough through consistent logical thinking, integrated honesty, and hard efforts to be self-sufficient by producing competitive values for others and society.

As previously identified, laziness and dishonesty are volitionally chosen prime evils. People allow laziness and dishonesty to develop within themselves to their great personal harm. Laziness and dishonesty are the basic causes of mysticism, neocheating, and envy. Moreover, that default to laziness leads to Growth Death or Psyche Death (see Neo-Tech Advantage #98).

Laziness always involves mysticism undercutting the conscious mind. One must exert a constant, honest, life-long effort to maintain a prosperous, happy, healthy life. By contrast, mental and physical laziness means defaulting on those key attributes of honesty and effort required for independent self-survival and happiness.

Rationalizing laziness and envy requires dishonest inversions of facts and values. For example, certain social commentators disparage modern, labor-saving appliances as causing laziness. They lament that modern appliances bypass old-fashioned virtues of hard work. Their laments are misleading non sequiturs useful for self-deception or neocheating. The facts are that labor-saving devices are created and put to best use by those who are the least lazy — the most ambitious. For, such modern devices free people from low-productivity, mind-stifling routines to provide the time and opportunity to spend their lives in ever more challenging, productive, creative activities.

Criticisms of labor-saving devices usually originate from either neocheaters attacking values or from those yearning to return to bygone days. But those bygone days were when so much brute labor, time, and energy were needed just to survive that few if any demands were made to expand into more complex, difficult efforts demanding hard integrated thinking. Those criticizing modern labor-saving devices are generally seeking rationalizations to avoid the responsibility of living by sustained, conscious efforts requiring integrated thinking. They prefer to exist without conscious effort — by rote, without integrated thinking — as people did during the Dark Ages. Those who criticize labor-saving devices are usually projecting their own mental laziness, their rebellion against integrated thinking, their lack of effort to live fully.

The logical use of the mind combined with consistent rational efforts is required for human survival and prosperity. But, mental default for many is seductively tempting. A person simply adopts someone else's thinking, thus avoiding the responsibility of exerting one's own integrated thinking and honesty for independent survival and prosperity. Such "pleasantly easy" defaults against using one's own mind are traps that corrode self-sufficiency and lead to intellectual, psychological, and eventual physical dependence on others, especially "authorities".

Usually those "authorities" are neocheaters who dupe the

defaulter into accepting their dishonest, destructive ploys designed for usurping power. ...Such neocheating "authorities" survive by promoting their mystical hoaxes and specious doctrines of altruistic self-sacrifice in order to control the defaulters and neocheat the producers.

Integrated, logical thinking[1] does not preclude errors or wrong judgments. But only through habitual, integrated, logical thinking does one become efficient in identifying and correcting errors. If a person defaults on that thinking effort, he or she must live increasingly through other people's thinking. That person then gradually loses the ability to recognize the errors in other people's thinking as well as to correct his or her own errors. Such a person eventually becomes incompetent to live independently. That person then becomes dependent on destructive, neocheating "authorities" to survive.

Essentially all willful destruction, all purposeful violence, all initiation of force against individuals and their property can be reduced to a single, originating cause — mysticism originating from laziness and dishonesty. That laziness and dishonesty evolve from choosing not to exert the constant, rational efforts required to understand reality in order to make one's own independent decisions. ...Laziness and dishonesty are the cause of evil; envy is the effect.

Neo-Tech Advantage #102
NEO-TECH VERSUS ALTRUISM

Attacks on free enterprise, producers, and objective values by envious altruists, powercrats, social "intellectuals", theologians, lawyers, judges, academics, and other neocheaters are on the rise around the world. Before Neo-Tech, envious altruism was increasingly undermining the value producers. But today, Neo-Tech not only identifies the nature of envy, but also reveals how neocheaters use mystical altruism to attack and undermine the producers in order to usurp unearned power and values. Thus, just in time, at the crucial Nuclear-Decision Threshold (See Neo-Tech Advantage #31), Neo-Tech has become available to identify, counteract, and reverse the destructive trend of mysticism.

---

[1] Independent, integrated, logical thinking is not a function of intelligence, but is a function of self-responsibility, self-effort, and self-honesty.

Moreover, timely Neo-Tech also demonstrates how guiltless psychuous pleasures and happiness arise from rejecting all mystical dishonesties. And, finally, Neo-Tech renders powerless the intentional value destroyers — the professional mystics, altruists, powercrats, parasites, enviers, and other neocheaters.

Neo-Tech means the eventual demise of the politician, social "intellectual", theologian, and every other neocheating altruist and egalitarian who usurp values and power from the value producers. At the same time, almost anyone can achieve a prosperous, happy life with Neo-Tech, even those hapless mystics and neocheaters who have been exposed and rejected by the producers armed with Neo-Tech.

Without Neo-Tech, the legions of altruists, mystics, and powercrats would have eventually buried the producers and their values, causing a new dark age. But today, Neo-Tech knowledge is spreading around the world. That expanding Neo-Tech matrix is rendering impotent professional mystics and neocheaters caught in its web. Yet, ironically, those foundering mystics and neocheaters can with Neo-Tech join the producers in experiencing genuine prosperity and happiness by rejecting their own mysticism and producing competitive values for others.

Neo-Tech Advantage #103
PLATO, ARISTOTLE, AND NEO-TECH
Those with Neo-Tech knowledge will gain powerful advantages in every competitive situation. For they fully understand the crippling, 2000-year hoax of Platonistic-based philosophies that today dominate most people's thoughts and actions. Thus, by removing that hoax, Neo-Tech leaves a person with profound competitive advantages over those foundering in the Plato-based world of professional mystics and neocheaters.

Plato's philosophy provided the foundation for subsequent philosophies involving mysticism, sacrifice, and the use of force to achieve "higher" goals. Plato's philosophy also provided the basic tools for rationalizing laziness [Re: Concept 108, Neo-Tech Reference Encyclopedia]. And because Plato's work is so subtly anti-intellectual, his philosophy inflicted sweeping, anti-intellectual destructions on all subsequent societies and cultures to this day.

Still, Plato, the father of the criminal mind, was one of the most original, creative thinkers in history. His work was the first widely integrated philosophical system[1] recorded *in writing*. The depth and breadth of his integrations were quickly matched and then surpassed by the philosophical writings of his student — Aristotle, the father of the business mind.

But much of Plato's credit, particularly the sounder aspects of his philosophical system, perhaps belongs to his teacher, Socrates. Unfortunately, Socrates never recorded in writing his ideas or philosophical system. No writings of Socrates are known to exist. And knowledge of his work was left to the mercy and plagiarism of Plato, who perhaps deleted crucial Aristotelian-like views that would have contradicted Plato's own manipulated views. Nevertheless, Socrates was probably the first man to develop a broadly integrated philosophical system.

Plato held enormous leverage with his great intellectual and creative abilities. Thus, profound philosophical errors would occur if he were tilted even slightly toward immaturity, dishonesty, mysticism, and neocheating. And that is what happened. Some of the most integrated aspects of Plato's philosophical system are in profound error. His errors involve the integration of dishonesties, mysticism, "higher purposes", the use of force, and the exercise of authoritarian power into a full-blown, ethical philosophical system of enormous deception and dishonesties.

Furthermore, the foundation of Plato's philosophy is not based on reality, but on mysticism. His philosophy does not recognize the life of the individual human being as the prime value or even an important value. Indeed, Plato is not a man to be respected. For he was an immature, dishonest conniver who wreaked death and destruction on this world for over 2000 years. He subordinated human beings to arbitrary "higher" powers and mystical "values". Yet, the tight inner logic and integrated completeness of his specious philosophy provided great staying power for his false ideas. Thus, his spurious philosophy became the intellectual foundation of all subsequent specious philosophies, religions, and political systems.

---

[1]Because of his mysticisms, Plato's integrations were bound within a seemingly wide but cleverly closed system restricted by distortions and deceptions. By contrast, mystic-free Neo-Tech integrations are unrestricted, unlimited, without boundaries.

Plato's philosophical system has been the greatest tragedy of our civilization. But at last, today, Neo-Tech is in the process of eliminating that tragedy.

By contrast, Aristotle was perhaps the greatest intellectual power in history. He built his philosophical system on objective, noncontradictory premises by placing objective reality as the only basis of honesty. Aristotle placed the individual conscious being as the supreme value on Earth. ...The philosophical roots of Aristotle lead to Neo-Tech.

Major competitive advantages accrue to those who use Neo-Tech knowledge to reject mystical, Platonistic-based frauds.

Neo-Tech Advantage #104
DESTRUCTIVE POETRY
VERSUS
VALID ART

Can poetry be destructive? Can poetry undermine romantic love? Yes, most certainly. Some poetry (including song lyrics, especially certain rock lyrics), if taken seriously, can have powerful, mind-crippling effects that undermine a person's integration capacities crucial for developing romantic-love relationships. In addition, certain poetry can block personal growth and prevent prosperity and long-range happiness from developing.

Plato, whose philosophy has been utilized by the anti-intellectuals, mystics, and neocheaters for the past 2300 years, was ironically the first to identify the harmful, anti-intellectual nature of poetry. Plato recognized that the sing-song, rhythmic nature of poetry set up automatic, hypnotic, nonthinking patterns that unconscious people used to pass on information which often sounded good or pleasant, but had little or no validity, accuracy, or objective meaning. In other words, through poetry, so-called knowledge or packages of "truth" could be handily acquired and passed on with little conscious effort, independent thinking, or regard to honesty. Poems and chants established dogmatic patterns that blocked new or more accurate ideas from developing.

Plato properly identified part of the problem with poetry, but his philosophical errors prevented him from identifying the total

222

problem. Poetry can be cast in what appears to be beautiful gems or nuggets of packaged "truth" and knowledge from "authorities". Those packaged "truths" are designed for consumption in quick, convenient gulps. That gulping of "truths" bypasses the analytical mental effort required to integrate information and assess its validity through one's own mind.

Determining the validity of any information requires analytical integration of facts and information within a full, accurate context. But poetry and song lyrics effortlessly bypass the demanding thinking and integration processes needed to accurately identify objective reality. In that way, poetry and lyrics subvert the effectiveness of the mind. Most poetry and lyrics, no matter how beautiful, right, and "true" they sound (that being their seductive nature) cannot be substituted for honesty or facts any more than good-sounding slogans or parables[1] can be substituted for honesty or facts. Furthermore, cleverly used poetry and lyrics can be powerfully effective tools for rationalizing laziness, dishonesty, injustice, mysticism, and neocheating.[2]

Most poetry, if taken seriously (especially emotional or "beautiful" poetry that lacks an objective base), not only undermines a person's ability to make independent judgments, but diminishes one's capacity to think objectively about crucial matters. That, in turn, decreases one's ability to achieve prosperity, psychuous pleasures, and long-range happiness. In other words, certain poetry or song lyrics taken as packaged

---

[1]A parable is a short, fictitious story usually used to illustrate a moral or religious principle. Many parables are specious rationalizations, non sequiturs, or false wisdom used out of intellectual weakness to conceal or evade facts and logic. Jesus's teachings were cast almost entirely into parables by those who later exploited him. Not until three centuries later did the professional mystics and neocheaters resurrect Jesus as a manipulative symbol around which to rally their victims.

[2]Unintegrated music, especially rock music, breaks down the thought patterns of the brain. That breakdown provides a drug-like effect in blocking or avoiding the struggle, effort, and at times the pain required to think consciously. Such brain-blockage leaves one in a "pleasant", nonthinking stupor. With music constantly pounding on their eardrums, rock addicts effectively block integrated thinking efforts. That rhythmic pounding, in turn, keeps the anxieties of their problems and incompetence buried within their unconscious minds — buried within their nonintegrating minds.

"truth" will bypass the independent, in-context thinking processes required to make the integrations and decisions necessary to develop long-range prosperity, pleasures, and happiness.

Most poetry rests on specious or mystical foundations. But even poetry resting on objective, Aristotelian foundations is valid only for a specific context and is not valid for other contexts. If, for example, one or both partners in a love relationship rely on poetry by "authorities" to express "truth", the relationship in that particular area will be detached from reality — stunted by mysticism, unable to grow on sound premises in that area.

Poetry based on mysticism or even poetry based on a particular context of objective reality is almost always, by nature, nonexact or abstract. That nonexactness or abstraction can symbolize certain categories of reality, but poetic abstractions are not facts in themselves nor can they be substituted for independent, integrated thinking.

But valid art forms (e.g., music, fine art, literature, and even certain intellectually honest poetry) can be abstract expressions of objective values executed with skill and projected with a powerful sense of life. If the artist's abstract symbols reflect the observer's own values, then the particular art form delivers pleasure to the beholder.

If the art work (music, fine art, literature) symbolizes disvalues or threats to the beholder, then the art delivers dislike to the viewer.[1] Nonskilled or amateurish art may attempt to symbolize values to the beholder. But such art work is not emotionally felt if the style, craftsmanship, or abstraction is too unskilled, obscure, inaccurate, contradictory, or badly executed. In such cases, the viewer's reaction is nonrecognition, confusion, indifference, boredom, dislike, especially if combined with a negative sense of life. Those cases include most of the *subjective* "modern art" that has been foisted on the public by neocheaters as a ploy to further undermine life, attack values, and drain the value producer through the arts.

Still, much more harmful is the mystics' and neocheaters' use of *objective* art forms to bilk the producer on a grand scale: The prime example in history is the brilliant coup by the Roman

[1] Artwork (including certain poetry) that reflects negative values to the viewer can still be admired for style or craftsmanship if skillfully executed.

224

Catholic church to save itself during the rise of honesty and logic that occurred during the Renaissance. The master neocheaters of the Roman Catholic hierarchy recognized the starkly obvious values of the burgeoning, new art forms. They then captured those art values for exploitation by aggressively commissioning the most skilled artists to produce highly obvious values. The master neocheaters captured those values at first through architecture, the fine arts, and sculpture. Later they added music to their arsenal through the great classical composers. Governments and tyrants right up to Lenin, Hitler, and current neocheating rulers also seized that neocheating ploy. To gain easy credibility and to capture support through the emotions, they used the fine arts, literature, music, and even the most integrated art form — opera[1].

Since the value of art can be sensed through emotions and requires no intellectual analysis, the public needs only to notice the obvious art and architectural values to erroneously link those values of the master artists to the master neocheaters presenting that art. Thus, the masses are deluded into seeing those obvious values of great art as also representing the values of the neocheating church or government. Subconsciously they conclude: "I can see, hear, and feel those architectural, art, and musical values. I know those values are real and valid. Thus, those values must also represent those who own and present this art — the church or government. Therefore, all that I do not comprehend about the church or government must be as good and valuable as the art that represents them."

Through that brilliant, but dishonest use of art as non sequiturs, the church and governments were able to survive the rise of honesty and logic during the Renaissance, the resulting industrial revolution, and then the rise of capitalism and free enterprise.

Regardless of their understandings or economic conditions at that time, those great artists betrayed honesty by selling themselves to the dishonest intentions of the neocheaters in church and government. Those artists are culpable and

[1]Opera integrates the major art forms: music, romantic fiction, plot, performing arts, fine arts. Verdi's opera *Aida* is the first and only major art work that celebrates the heroic production of a major commercial and technological value — the opening of the Suez Canal.

responsible for giving a major boost in power and endurance to the evil machinations of especially the Roman Catholic church and its neocheating leaders. Even Michelangelo must be held accountable.

***

A major difference exists between the beholder's *view* of valid art versus one's *use* of poetry. Art represents an abstraction that symbolizes a value. The beholder merely contemplates a piece of art for the emotional pleasure it delivers in reflecting back or symbolizing that person's own values. Unlike poetry, the beholder normally does not use art abstraction to replace his or her own independent thinking for understanding reality or establishing facts.

Art is a crucial value for human beings. Art is a source of pleasure and psychological fuel that reflects and confirms one's deepest values through aesthetic symbols. Poetry, on the other hand, can harm a person's thinking process if that person accepts as concrete fact the inexact, out-of-context nature of poetic abstractions. When accepted as self-contained packages of "truth", song lyrics, parables, slogans, epigrams, political cartoons, and "famous" quotes by "authorities" fall into the same harmful category as poetry [Re: Table 72, Neo-Tech Reference Encyclopedia].

Aristotelian-based poetry that is intellectually valid and certain song lyrics that are non-mystical can be objectively valuable when viewed as symbols of one's own values and not as packages of "truth" to be swallowed whole, without integration. Still, the effect of poetry on most people is harmful because they allow the abstract symbols of poetry to enter their minds as unintegrated, unchallenged "truths" or as pre-packaged value systems ready for direct use. The problem is amplified because many poets, song lyricists, and political cartoonists proceed with dishonest, destructive intentions to mislead the reader. They want their work swallowed blindly as "truth" by their audiences,

226

regardless of the validity or context of their work. Such work is neither art nor honest; it is neocheating.

If an individual is aware of the misleading nature of poetry, he or she can avoid its harmful effects and perhaps gain some reflective values from certain Aristotelian-based poetry. For example, the following poem, while not deeply intellectual, does aesthetically reflect the soul and character of heroic, innocent value producers:

THE GOLDEN
They are the rare, the radiant men
The children of truth, the parents of ken.
Pain but strengthens them, pity intrudes.
Rebuking surprises them. Guilt eludes.

Deception disgusts and envy astounds.
Misfortune challenges. Malice confounds.
They are the open, the honorable,
The honest, the just, the vulnerable.

With no respect for the twisting of truth,
Faithfully wed to the promise of youth,
They are the pure, the benevolent,
The incorruptible few — the Innocent.

(Reprinted with permission from Darlene Bridge and
Bridgeberg Books)

Poetical sing-song or hypnotically rhythmic meter are often found in the rhetoric of dictators, evangelists, sibyls, politicians, theologians, mountebanks, social "intellectuals", media men, medicine men, hallucinating psychotics, chanting shiites, and screaming terrorists. Consider how millions of normally rational Germans thrilled and responded to the poetical cadence and charisma of the consummate altruist neocheater, Adolph Hitler. The results: a reign of destruction with tens of millions of human beings slaughtered so one impotent man could indulge his mysticism to *feel* unearned power. All that slaughter was for nothing more than to let one neocheater *feel* a pseudo self-esteem. ...Twenty million dead so one pip-squeak could *feel* big and important.

"So what!" cry the mystics as the lifetime efforts of a thousand productive, innocent individuals are blown to bits every day without a backward glance. So what if the troops roll across the country with military cadence and guns ablaze. So what if they level town after town, reducing to rubble and corpses all the values, beauty, and life that took generations of productive effort to build.

And that is all the chanting religious automatons or splendid Panzer divisions know how to do — to destroy in a moment, without a thought, all the values that producers labored for lifetimes to build. Chanting mobs or marching troops never glance back, never think for a moment of the death and destruction they leave behind. So what! the mystics and neocheaters cry. So what if genocide happens in Russia, Nazi Germany, Cuba, Cambodia, Red China, or in our land. "I don't want to hear it! To hell with the lifetime efforts of productive individuals! ...Save the snail darter!"

By using specious nuggets of poetical "truth" and spell-binding slogans, malefactors, demagogues, and neocheaters such as Hitler, FDR, Nader, Khomeini, Lincoln, Mao, Billy Graham, Pope Paul, Jimmy Swaggart, Castro, Kennedy, Martin Luther King Jr., Jim Jones could smoothly, quickly subvert the objective concepts of justice, good, and love. And they often did that by manipulating words to sound good, just, or loving. Why? To promote their own rationalized schemes of "higher" causes. Such people use those poetic techniques to keep their rationalizations sounding valid. And their unthinking followers grab the beautiful nuggets of "truth" and eagerly swallow them without thought or challenge.

Modern Art

Below is a quote from the archangel of modern art admitting that he is nothing but a clown:

"Most people can today no longer expect to receive consolation from art. The refined, the rich, the distillers of quintessence (art critics) desire only the peculiar, the eccentric, the scandalous in today's art. And I myself, since the advent of cubism, have fed these fellows what they wanted, and satisfied these critics with all the ridiculous ideas that have passed through my head.

228

"The less they understood them, the more they admired me. Through amusing myself with all these absurd farces, I became celebrated. But when I am alone, I do not have the effrontery to consider myself an artist at all, not in the grand old meaning of the word. Giotto, Titian, Rembrandt and Goya, they were great painters. I am only a public clown.

"I have understood my time and have exploited the imbecility, the vanity, the greed of my contemporaries. It is a bitter confession of mine — more painful than it may seem. But at least and at last it does have the merit of being honest."

> Pablo Picasso, November, 1951* A master neocheater making an honest confession.

*Also reported to be from a fictitious interview: *The Black Book* by Giovanni Papini, 1951.

To "appreciate" modern art, a person must figure out, interpret, or understand the "artist" and his meanings that "transcend reality". By contrast, lasting classical art is recognized as a great value throughout the ages. Such art needs no interpretation or understanding of the artist. Such art represents beauty, values, and skill that are immediately recognized by the expert and the untrained layman alike. That is why the Roman Catholic church acquired only classic art — art that needs no interpretation to understand and value. The Catholic church was too shrewd to buy abstract art needing interpretation.

Indeed, modern art seldom represents beauty, values, or skill. Moreover, the layman does not know what most modern "art" means, while the chic "expert" plays games of interpreting the artist's meanings.

Today, the high prices of famous modern art works are supported by the tax-deduction system: Wealthy holders of such modern art profit handsomely by donating purchased works to the major modern-art museums (e.g., The Museum of Modern Art in New York). In turn, such museums provide grossly inflated appraisal prices for tax deductions. Thus, those museums gain ersatz art works along with cash donations for those fake, tax-purpose appraisals. At the same time, the wealthy "collectors" profit and modern-art museums perpetuate themselves through the tax system. When that neocheating scheme collapses, most modern art works will fall to an objective free-market value and become essentially worthless.

The Law of the Arts

Consider the following quote concerning modern art:

"For this seems, finally, to be the law of all the arts — the one essential prerequisite to the production of a great work of art is a great man. You cannot have the art without the man, and when you have the man you have the art. His time and his surroundings will color him; his art will not be at one time or place precisely what it might be at another; but in the end, the art is the man and at all times and in all countries is just as great as the man.

"Let us clear our minds, then, of the illusion that there is in any important sense such a thing as progress in the fine arts. We may with a clear conscience judge every new work for what it appears in itself to be, asking of it that it be noble and beautiful and reasonable, not that it be novel or progressive. If it be great art it will always be novel enough, for there will be a great mind behind it, and no two great minds are alike. And if it be novel without being great, how shall we be the better off? There are enough forms of mediocre or evil art in the world already. Being no longer intimidated by the fetish of progress, when a thing calling itself a work of art seems to us hideous and degraded, indecent and insane, we shall have the courage to say so and shall not care to investigate it further."

Kenyon Cox
The American Academy of Arts and Letters
December 13, 1912

Abstract Symbols — Real vs. Unreal

Real abstract symbols are accurate metaphors. They serve as powerful, shorthand communication that can deliver intense personalized values, especially in love relationships. On the other hand, unreal symbols are inaccurate metaphors or non sequiturs. They misrepresent reality and undermine values in life and love.

A person must differentiate between real and unreal symbols to flourish [Re: Table 73, Neo-Tech Reference Encyclopedia]. By making use of real symbols or metaphors, a person can experience new dimensions of life and romantic love. By recognizing and rejecting unreal symbols, a person preserves confident control over reality and, thus, over his or her own life, love relationships, and future.

Neo-Tech Advantage #105
**SELF-AWARENESS VERSUS
MYSTICAL AWARENESS**

Developing accurate awareness of self and reality through honest, integrated thinking is the prime responsibility for all human beings. In fact, such awareness is a necessity to live prosperously and happily. That awareness is available to those who exert constant, rational thinking efforts toward understanding self and reality — and the relationship between the two. No one can deliver that understanding to another. Indeed, developing an accurate understanding of self and reality is a crucial self-responsibility for personal power.

Mystics struggle to avoid that constant, rational thinking effort needed to honestly and accurately integrate one's life with objective reality. That honest understanding and integration of reality is the key to competence and prosperity in a competitive world. But losers and mystics seek anyone or anything promising to deliver prepackaged knowledge that lets them avoid the hard work required to develop their own integrated knowledge and awareness. That is why mystics embrace such quackeries as astrology, fortune telling, graphoanalysis, biorhythms, most psychoanalysis, fad diets, or any other flimflam that deludes them with a sense of gaining effortless knowledge, awareness, control. By accepting such specious awarenesses conjured up by others, a person keeps drifting further from reality, becoming increasingly unaware, unhappy, and incompetent while rationalizing the opposite.

Acquiring integrated awareness, competence, and happiness is a *self*-responsibility that no one else can deliver. No one can deliver awareness and happiness to another person because no other person is in a position to:

1. know one's own integrated self.

231

2. think integrally and contextually about one's own life.
3. control one's own actions.
4. integrate one's own work and life with reality.

For any "authority" to have an integrated awareness of another person is impossible. No matter how complete or scientific looking (e.g., computer printouts of horoscopes or biorhythms), any such outside self-awareness analysis is invalid and mystical. And any seeming validity of such "self-awareness" packages is a specious illusion. Such illusions lead a person further away from an awareness of reality and deeper into the stupidity of mysticism — the disease that undermines all human life and love.

Entirely different from such fake "awarenesses" through mysticism is the awareness arising from the mutual mirroring of character and personal qualities between self and a friend or romantic-love partner. Such mirroring genuinely enhances self-awareness, communication, and pleasure especially between romantic-love partners. That reflecting of a person's character and qualities is based on direct, intimate knowledge of that person. Such honest, valuable reflections differ profoundly from fake awareness packages mystically reflecting personal character and qualities based on nothing.

As with happiness, self-awareness cannot be given from one person to another. But by reflecting personal values, one can enhance another person's self-awareness in a similar way that one can enhance another person's happiness.

Neo-Tech Advantage #106
BEYOND UNDERSTANDING

Throughout the universe, much remains unknown. Yet, nothing tangible or conceptual is unknowable to the conscious mind. But with human emotions, certain specific feelings in a person can never be known or experienced by others. For all human emotions are products of individual characters based on unique fingerprint combinations of physical and psychological natures. That means personal, unique experiences cannot be duplicated by others. Thus, any emotion in any individual person can never be exactly understood or fully known by any other person.

Recognizing one's inability to know certain emotional experiences in others is particularly useful in romantic-love relationships. Two important emotional experiences that cannot be cross-experienced or fully known between men and women are identified below:

1. The Penetrated versus The Penetrator
Experiences and Feelings

A man can never fully know the feelings, sensations, and emotions of a woman being penetrated during intercourse. Likewise, a woman can never fully know the feelings, sensations, and emotions of a man penetrating a woman. That eternal mystery of feelings further deepens between a man and a woman when they try to comprehend the feelings of orgasm in the other.

That eternal, unsolvable mystery between the sexes enhances the pleasure and excitement of a love relationship as each partner struggles to get closer to the other's feelings and experiences. But they can never close the gap. Never can the feelings of orgasm in one partner be known or felt by the other partner. And for romantic-love partners, that elusive mystery is delightfully maddening and eternally challenging. That unknown quality can forever keep the heterosexual[1] experience fresh, haunting, and mysterious. Men and women can only imagine the feelings and emotions in the other, always wondering yet never knowing how distant their imaginations are from reality.

2. Female-Nature Versus Male-Nature
Experiences and Feelings

A number of exclusive male or female emotions and experiences can never be fully experienced across sexual boundaries. Two examples are illustrated below:

<u>An Exclusive Female Experience:</u>
An implicit, constant physical threat toward women exists

---

[1]The homosexual experience of male-male or female-female intercourse cannot really simulate the exclusive male-female experience. Homosexuals fail to simulate heterosexual experiences not only because of the obvious physiological differences, but because of the profound psychological differences involved between the homosexual act and the heterosexual act. Even when the physical actions are the same (such as oral sex), the wide psychological differences between men and women preclude similarities in emotional experiences.

233

from essentially every man. That threat exists because the different physical and psychological natures of man and woman leave most men with the power literally to kill any woman at any time. Even smaller, weaker men could kill most bigger, stronger women in a bare-hand fight to the death. Thus, most women are perpetually at the physical mercy of men.

Under that threat, women often must silently take the degradation of being bullied or treated as sex objects as their earned qualities are ignored. No man can fully know that particular degradation because he has no way of duplicating the conditions which create that uniquely female situation. Even if the man were unjustly treated as a sex object, he would still have no way of knowing the woman's feelings. For unlike women, his different physiological, psychological, and social orientations do not leave him under a constant, implicit death threat.

An Exclusive Male Experience:

A strong emotion felt by highly productive men is the desire for a peaceful core to counterbalance their aggressively assertive lives. That desire usually relates to a woman with whom such a man is free to retreat from his battlefield actions to experience peaceful love, tenderness, serenity. For only during that precious time is he free to fully expose and share his soul exclusively with another human being — his woman. During those moments, that woman becomes to him a supreme value.

Ironically, the strongest, most productive, independent men have the greatest need and capacity to receive a woman's love, support, and tenderness. Tragically, however, many such men never recognize or admit, even to themselves, that supremely important emotional need and pleasure. Similarly, strong men often never admit to other emotional needs such as being free to cry when suffering great sadness or pain. ...A man crying has been erroneously viewed as a weakness or unmanly.

Many women are unaware of the need in productive men for a peaceful, private world containing a one-woman love. But women who understand that need hold a key for delivering powerful values and happiness to their men and to themselves. Understanding and filling the need for a peaceful, reflective core in aggressively productive men is among the most powerful of all binding ingredients in romantic-love relationships.

Aggressively productive women also have a need to periodically retreat into peaceful reflection. Yet, that need does not comprise the same psychosexual emotions as within men because of the inherent psychological and physiological differences between men and women.

Neo-Tech Advantage #107
VALUE THEFT VS. VALUE EXCHANGE

Through the 2000-year history of altruistic-based cultures, most material achievements have been maligned and attacked by theologians, politicians, and other professional mystics and altruists.[1] The motive for scorning human-produced values has always been to saddle the value producers with unearned guilt. Once saddled with guilt, value producers are more easily manipulated, duped, and usurped out of their earned power and values. Indeed, to survive, professional neocheaters and mystics must constantly usurp material and psychological values from those producers.

The production of values for others is the single most important function of any person's life. Every person's survival and happiness as well as every facet of his or her physical, mental, and psychological well-being depends on the production of competitive values for others. If a person chooses not to produce sufficient values to survive, then that person must become dependent on the producers to survive by begging, cajoling, neocheating, deception, force, or theft.

---

[1]Adolph Hitler was a consummate altruist. He scorned material values in his personal life. He was the personification of asceticism and sacrifice. He demanded the eventual sacrifice of all human beings and their values to his deemed "higher" cause of duty and obedience to society. He fed his weak ego and pseudo self-esteem with an ever increasing need for power and control over others by force. Similarly, people like Mao, Pol Pot, Nader and other altruists ignore honesty, scorn material values, and survive on unearned power gained by brute force or neocheating deceptions. They need increasing control over others to feed their weak egos. ...Such altruists gain their power by attacking and usurping values produced or earned by others. Thus, such altruists live by harming or killing innocent value producers.

Thus the producer, not the consumer[1], is essential to human life and happiness. By contrast, nonproductive people are dependent on the producers to survive. And those nonproducers who neocheat to survive exist with deteriorating competence, mounting envy, and growing unhappiness. That nonproducer's life soon terminates in Growth Death, then in emotional death, and finally in physical death.

A society that functions exclusively for the rational benefit of the individual has never existed.[2] A totally free, just, and rational society would by definition be a Neo-Tech society — a society based on fully integrated honesty. Such a society would be a free-enterprise, nonforce government...a government and society that has yet to exist on planet Earth. The ethical essence of a Neo-Tech society is the holding of individual rights as supreme. Therefore, *any* form of initiatory force, coercion, or fraud against any individual by any individual, group, society, or government is immoral and thus is ostracizable.

Any suggestion of force-free societies strikes fear into neocheating politicians, demagogues, and mystics. Knowing professional value destroyers cannot survive in a nonforce, noncoerced, free-enterprise, fully competitive society, they desperately vilify and subvert any movement toward such a society and its values. They sabotage and undercut those values

---

[1]"Consumerism" is an invalid concept conjured up by self-appointed consumer advocates. They are backed by criminal-minded politicians, neocheating journalists, dishonest academics, self-appointed environmentalists, socially chic "intellectuals", most lawyers, and dishonest white-collar-hoax business people. ...Indeed, the value producer, not the consumer, is the hero of conscious life and of civilizations throughout the universe.

[2]A society has no moral or logical reason to exist except to benefit the individual and protect his and her property rights. But a fully moral, logical society has never existed. For the producers have always been tricked into accepting and supporting free-loading, professional mystics and neocheaters acting as "authorities". Such "authorities" use altruism to control value producers through false guilt. Thus, those value producers work to support those very neocheaters who harm, pillage, and eventually destroy them, their loved ones, and everyone's happiness.

with non-sequitur, out-of-context attacks. Indeed, to survive, professional mystics and neocheaters must prevent a value-oriented, Neo-Tech society. For such a society would quickly identify and forever banish them as destructive criminals. ...On rejecting mystics and neocheaters, the value producers become free to prosper guiltlessly and happily by benefiting without limits others and society.

Prohibiting initiatory force, threats of force, and fraud is the only law in a Neo-Tech society. Highly effective enforcement of the individual-rights law by an integrated ostracizing system is much more punishing and effective than any police force or government jailing system. Thus, with that single, highly enforceable law, each individual would be solely responsible for his or her own actions, life, and well-being. The resulting competitive, free-choice interaction among people would deliver maximum benefits to each individual and society. That, in turn, would greatly enhance every productive person's well-being and happiness. ...Thus, to survive, the nonproductive mystics and neocheaters would have to begin producing competitive values for others instead of destructively usurping values from others.

All social interactions involve individual interactions. Value exchanges occur in valid business, friendship, and romantic-love relationships. In fact, the basic requirement for any valuable human relationship is the exchange of tangible values. But, nonproductive people often contemptuously attack competitive, tangible, and material values. For, only by attacking those values, can they conceal their parasitism and failure to fulfill their responsibilities toward producing desirable, competitive values for others and society.

From the production of competitive values, all other values grow, including prosperity, self-esteem, psychological well-being, romantic love, and abiding happiness. Furthermore, competitive, tangible, and material values are important building blocks and binding ingredients of conscious relationships, especially business, friendship, and romantic-love relationships. Professional mystics and neocheaters desperately try to deny the cardinal role of producing competitive values in living happily and in gaining romantic love. But only through the exchange

237

of such values can personal relationships become fully integrated:
From an exchange of tangible and material values, a far greater
stability, intensity of love, and abiding happiness can develop
than is possible from a relationship consisting only of abstract
values.

Tangible values in a romantic-love relationship directly affect
sexuality. For, exchanges of tangible values markedly increase
sexual intensity and psychuous pleasure.

Still, abstract values are the crucial ingredient for initiating,
establishing, and maintaining a friendship or a romantic-love
relationship. However, tangible and material values *combined*
with abstract values are the variables that cause psychuous
pleasures and happiness to ignite and then grow constantly [Re:
Table 74, Neo-Tech Reference Encyclopedia]. Both love and deep
friendship relationships require a base of abstract values to start.
But the production of tangible and material values is necessary
for moving a relationship into unlimited growth and high-gear
happiness. A comparison of abstract values versus tangible
values in friendship and love relationships is illustrated by the
following chart:

ABSTRACT VALUES VERSUS
TANGIBLE VALUES
(Delivered from one person to another person
in friendship or love relationships)

Abstract Values

Psychologically valuable reflections

Philosophically valuable reflections

Reflections of each other's values

Analytical feedback of thoughts and ideas

Mirroring of personal worth, values, and ideas

Tangible and Material Values

Practical contributions to increasing the efficacy and productivity
of the other

Practical contributions to reducing or eliminating value-destroying and time-wasting problems and errors inside and outside the relationship.

Practical contributions to producing tangible and material values to one's self and the other

Practical contributions to providing tangible and material values to the other

Neo-Tech Advantage #108
VALUE EXCHANGE IN FRIENDSHIP AND ROMANTIC-LOVE RELATIONSHIPS

Without value-generating interactions, two people are of little direct value to each other — at least no more value that any two random people might be to each other. Valuable human relationships evolve when two people deliver objective values to one another. That exchange of values measures the value of a relationship.

Aside from the intrinsic value of human life that exists among all people, a person is not a value to others by merely existing. Instead, a person must deliver competitive values to be a value to others and society. Otherwise, that person will be a drain on others and a disvalue to society. And a person must continue delivering values to be a continuing value. Moreover, one must continue adding new values to existing values to experience value growth within one's self and within a relationship. Value growth is a self-created, pyramiding process that requires rational thought and constant effort to sustain. Such a growth process is the essence of human living. For value growth fills life's needs and delivers life's major rewards — abiding prosperity, romantic love, and happiness.

To fully experience life and sustain value growth requires continuous thought and effort. The need for value growth is not someone's philosophical theory or ethic. That need is an integral part of reality: Constant value growth is required for the conscious organism to function properly. A person makes a disastrous error by failing to put forth the honest, integrated thought and rational effort needed to produce growing, competitive values for others.

Tragically, most people choose to stop their growth early in life. Many stop in childhood — soon after exerting that mighty learning effort required to read and write. When they stop exerting that effort, they stop growing. The quality of their lives then declines until physical death. ...Without growth, a person cannot experience abiding prosperity, happiness, and psychuous pleasures. Without growth, a person misses the point of conscious life. Without growth, a person dies.

Growth Death is a great, unnecessary tragedy. It never has to happen to anyone; it is imposed on no one. Growth Death occurs only when the victim chooses to avoid the integrated thought and rational effort required to produce and deliver net, competitive values to others. When Growth Death occurs, then all value-based friendships and love relationships stop growing and begin to die.

* * *

Both romantic-love relationships and friendships can involve deep psychological, philosophical, and communication interactions. But the distinguishing characteristic of a romantic-love relationship is its physical-sexual sharing. That sexual sharing, in turn, offers physical and psychological intimacy unobtainable from any other human relationship. ...Those unique physical/psychological intimacies can lead to growing psychuous pleasures.

Friendship is a necessary ingredient of romantic love. Without friendship, no basis for romantic love exists.[1] A romantic-love relationship has all the ingredients of a value-oriented friendship plus the powerful ingredient of physical intimacy and sex. ...Friendship can be more personally intimate and involved than any other human relationship except a romantic-love relationship.[2]

The value of friendships should neither be underestimated nor overestimated. A person can achieve unlimited psychuous

---

[1]Valuable, family-love relationships also develop from a base of friendship.

[2]A friendship or any human relationship changes irrevocably upon having sexual relations. But a sexual relationship is not synonymous with a romantic-love relationship. Still, a romantic-love relationship must by nature involve sex.

pleasures and happiness through romantic love alone, without any close friend beyond one's love partner. Friendships alone, no matter how valuable or extensive, can never deliver the full spectrum of values and happiness available from a single, friendship-based romantic love.

The following two ingredients will deliver a prosperous, happy life:

    1. achieving self-sufficient independence through honest production of competitive values for others

    2. achieving psychuous pleasures through romantic love.

In other words, a person needs only his or her productive work and a romantic-love partner for a full-range, prosperous, happy life. But productive work is a basic requirement for achieving romantic love. In that sense, productive work is a cause and romantic love is an effect.

Productive work is the basic requirement for human values. And romantic love and psychuous pleasures are the rewards for achieving those values. ...One cannot experience self-esteem, happiness, and romantic love without productive work. But one can experience self-esteem, happiness, and productive work without romantic love.

Friendship can offer great values and pleasurable experiences. Yet, friendships, especially close friendships, can in certain cases drain valuable time needed for high levels of business, creativity, and achievement. In a demanding business or intensely creative work, a person with a valuable romantic-love partner can often reach higher levels of achievement and happiness with few or no other friends. Friendships, moreover, are subject to errors that can turn into liabilities which drain a person's time, productiveness, efficacy and, thus, happiness. But value-generating, business friendships are generally the happiest, most exciting, most valuable of all relationships, except the romantic-love relationship.

* * *

In the end, reality prevails over life. The total experience of every person's life always moves toward justice as reality

241

asserts itself: Productive, rational individuals increasingly gain prosperity, love, and happiness from life. Conversely, unproductive, irrational individuals increasingly lose prosperity, love, and happiness — no matter what the surface appearances.

Abstract values of a friendship are normally not negotiable for tangible and material values. Likewise, tangible and material values normally cannot be converted into abstract values. Occasional exceptions do exist. Exceptions occur mainly in romantic-love relationships because the intense physical/psychological interactions tend to pull abstract values and material values closer together. At times, within a romantic-love relationship, those values can become interrelated. For example, emotional and sexual love provided by one partner can tangibly increase the creative, productive output of the other partner. Likewise, certain tangible values can amplify abstract values. For example, creative and productive accomplishments of one partner can increase the emotional love, sexual exhilaration, and psychuous pleasures of the other partner.

Generally, in a friendship or romantic-love relationship, an exchange of abstract values (be they healthy, neurotic, or a mixture) is taken for granted and occurs naturally. In friendship relationships, much of the abstract value interchange consists of open, casual exchanges of ideas and suggestions — a type of easy two-way communication that often is mutually valuable. Indeed, such exchanges of ideas and suggestions occur in most good conversations between friends or lovers.

Other abstract values exchanged between two people in a valid love or friendship relationship include psychologically pleasing or enhancing reflections, consistent encouragement (especially during difficult times), mirroring various psychological values, understanding feedback of the other's thoughts or activities, and the exchange of practical ideas obtained from each person's unique life experiences.

Sometimes abstract values from a friend or love partner can be beneficially integrated into one's personal life to increase awareness, productivity, and happiness. Generally, abstract values are offered freely, without the thought or expectation of material or tangible payment. In a love or a friendship relationship, no one needs to measure or weigh that natural interchange of abstract values. For that exchange is freely taken and given as a natural, pleasurable, expected part of any good relationship.

Thus, abstract values cannot be used to pay for material values. For material values must always be fairly traded.[1] Material values represent irreplaceable segments of a person's life, effort, and time required to earn those values. Every productive human being needs to trade (not give away) his or her produced values in order to survive, grow, and be happy. If material and tangible values are not traded mutually and fairly, then a portion of a person's life is sacrificed to another person at the expense of both people. As a result of that unfairness, both happiness and friendship decline.[2] [Re: "Two Letters about Friendship and Love", pages 379-389; Neo-Tech Reference Encyclopedia.]

Those who misunderstand the nature of friendship or romantic love may try to use abstract values as payment for material values. In doing so, they are exploiting their friendship or love relationships. Such people unjustly extract material values from others for the "privilege" of those others being in their presence. They unilaterally deem their abstract values as payment for tangible and material values. That kind of exploitation, aside from being unjust and parasitical, poisons the relationship.

More important, habitual trading of abstract values for tangible values diminishes that person's ability to produce and deliver tangible values. Such unfair trading leaves that person increasingly incompetent and dependent on others for material or tangible values. ...The potential for friendship, romantic love, and happiness is always the greatest among value-producing men and women who fairly trade tangible and material values in their relationships.

---

[1]Fairly traded, tangible values do not necessarily mean evenly traded, tangible values. Moreover, a highly competent, nonmystical housewife can through integrated thinking and consistent efforts contribute great tangible and material values to her husband's ability to work more efficiently and effectively, thus, generate more values and income. For that, he fairly trades by providing his wife with tangible and material goods.

[2]If either partner is net destructive to the other, the relationship should end. [Re: Concept 95, Neo-Tech Reference Encyclopedia]

Neo-Tech Advantage #109
**UNDERSTANDING
JUSTICE, GOOD, AND LOVE**

Contrary to the pronouncements of most modern linguists and social "scientists", words and language are primarily tools of thinking, not of communication. But clear thinking would lead to identification of the value destroyers. Thus, professional mystics and neocheaters must constantly attack and debase words and language to prevent clear thinking. For the existences of professional value destroyers depend on obscuring, distorting, and concealing reality in order to perpetuate fuzzy thinking among their victims. To accomplish that obfuscation, the mystics and neocheaters must (1) use words out of context, (2) twist and invert meanings of key words and concepts, and (3) dishonestly build on rationalizations and non sequiturs. ...They develop their own newspeak without regard to honesty.

Honest intellectuals concerned about the decay of language know that twisting and misusing words corrode the tools of thinking. But that is only half the problem. Protecting honesty and language also involves *context*. Powerful thinking requires not only using consistent, exact definitions but also precise, accurate contexts for all words and concepts. To accurately define meanings *and* contexts of important words and concepts is not only central to precise communication, oral or written, but is the key to effective thinking and understanding reality.

By contrast, twisting meanings of key words and using concepts out of context are the primary techniques of professional mystics and neocheaters, especially those in the media. For they exist by distorting or inverting language to deceive others. They invert the meanings of important words in order to rationalize their deceptions, destructions, thefts, use of force, and other irrational, immoral actions. And they do that often under inverted newspeak pretexts of justice, social good, human rights, and "higher" causes.

In seeking honesty and understanding of reality, one must be aware of both definition and context of key words. But neocheating "intellectuals", in their need to conceal meanings, exert mighty efforts to distort the meaning and invert the context of crucial words such as the following words:

244

Capitalism	Peace
Consumer	Producer
Ecology	Reality
Good	Rights
Justice	Selfishness
Love	Truth

Words can also represent concepts. The more basic the concept, the greater abstraction and integration is required to fully grasp that concept. The most difficult concepts to grasp in their full, accurate context are the most basic human concepts such as:

Justice
Good
Love

Throughout history, those three basic concepts have been used out of context or inverted in meaning by all professional mystics and neocheaters in their constant need to camouflage their destructive, parasitical existences. When neocheaters speak of justice, they are usually promoting unjust, destructive actions against the value producer, objective values, individual rights, private property, and the means to produce values and achieve happiness. When neocheaters speak of good — the common good or the "higher" good — they are usually promoting destructive altruism designed to usurp or destroy values earned by others. When neocheaters speak of love and brotherhood, they are usually promoting envious, promiscuous, egalitarian schemes designed to cripple competitive value producers and undermine romantic love.

To fully understand the basic concepts of justice, good, and love requires an accurate understanding of human nature relative to reality. That understanding requires integrations of the many specific concepts identified by Neo-Tech. To understand the concept of romantic love, for example, requires understanding the various Neo-Tech/Psychuous concepts needed to understand romantic love in full, accurate context. Because the concepts of *justice*, *good*, and *love* are inextricably linked, all three concepts are fully integrated throughout the Neo-Tech literature.

Neo-Tech Advantage #110
FACTS AND JUSTICE

In American cities, white neighborhoods are generally safer than black neighborhoods. Throughout history, men have reached greater heights in intellectual, aesthetic, and commercial achievements than have women. In general, Jews are more intelligent, productive, creative and, therefore, more potent in life and sex than people of other religions, nationalities, or races.[1]

---

[1]Jews are generally more evolved, moral, productive, intelligent, creative, and potent than other groups of people. Why? Mainly because the Jewish religion is less harmful than religions or mysticisms engulfing other people. The Jewish religion itself is harmful and irrational as are all mystical religions and governments. But the Judeo ethics project less guilt toward value producers and less malevolence toward human values such as productive effort, sexual pleasures, creativity, self-sufficiency than do the much more virulent, envious ethics of Christianity (especially Roman Catholicism), Islam, and other evilly destructive religions. Also, the Jewish religion is more oriented around respect for self and less around respect for external "authority" such as government. In addition, the post-Renaissance Jewish god has been basically a god of justice as opposed to the Christian god of mercy. (Mercy is arbitrary, subjective, and unjust — the opposite of justice.*) Jewish people, therefore, have been freer to reject other mysticisms and live for their rational best interests. That allows them to more fully and guiltlessly develop their own creative and intellectual capacities to the maximum benefit of themselves, society, and civilization.

The state of Israel, despite its illegal origins, is comprised of individuals — mainly innocent individuals. And Israel today has perhaps the only moral foreign policy among all nations. That policy is based on the profound moral right to self-defense. In fact, a single-purpose foreign policy based entirely on self-defense is the only rational, moral foreign policy possible. For that alone, Israel must be recognized and morally supported.

Twentieth-century Zionism did criminally violate the individual and property rights of some Palestinians. But, most violations of individual and prosperity rights of the Palestinians were done by the Palestinians themselves or their Arab neighbors. The injustices and moral wrongs experienced by those Palestinians forcefully separated from their homes and properties were very real and condemnable, even though the Palestinians who suffered property losses were financially compensated by Israel.

(footnote continued on next page)

246

Are those the words of a racist, a chauvinist, a Zionist zealot? Perhaps so if such statements were directed toward or used in judgment of particular individuals. But the statements are made in reference to objective, statistical facts that are real. When those statements are placed in the proper context of being generalized statistics that do *not* characterize any particular individual, they are then validly applicable to *generalized* situations.

If the data are accurate, then in-context inferences from those data are factual and must be considered in order to make honest evaluations and correct decisions. Consider, for example, the provable statistic that in all major U.S. cities a significantly

---

(footnote continued from previous page)

Today, most Jews are innocent. They are not responsible for past crimes by others. Thus, they cannot be held guilty by association or penalized for the actions of others. But, Jews and Arabs alike who are guilty of objective crimes should be fully prosecuted.

*Based on objective principles, justice is an end in itself. The idea behind government "justice" systems is not justice at all, but is the subjective, arbitrary idea of mercy. For mercy serves the neocheater's need to control others. How mercy only serves the neocheaters is most evident in the ideas behind jailing people: Imprisonment for rehabilitation, correction, or deterrent reasons are mystical notions designed by neocheaters to arbitrarily exercise force over individuals. The only punishments that are moral (including execution for premeditated murder) are those based solely on justice to the victim. Mystics and neocheaters will always hide the concept of justice for it would leave them powerless, stripping them of their major aggression tool for controlling and usurping values from others. For example, with the concept of objective justice, all such victimless-crime and confiscatory-tax laws would be unenforceable because no individual had been previously injured by force, fraud, or coercion to which justice could be addressed. In fact, enforcing such subjective laws is the antithesis of justice in that such laws make problems where none exist in order to unjustly and destructively control others by force or threat of force.

higher percentage of Blacks than Whites injure and murder people.[1] That is a statistical fact regardless of the reasons or so-called social causes. But to apply that statistical fact to any individual would be out-of-context and unjust because such statistics can not be validly or honestly applied to any particular individual.

On the other hand, to ignore or distort in-context facts is a dishonest evasion of reality. Such dishonest evasions of reality mystically conceal the knowledge required to deal accurately with reality in making effective decisions and judgments. For example, consider if a white or black person is concerned with physical safety for his or her loved ones and property: What if that person had the choice of living in equivalent housing in a predominantly black, depressed community or in a predominantly white, equally depressed community? Basing that choice on facts, that person would choose to live in the white community. Indeed, that person would have made the correct decision without necessarily harboring any bigotry or without acting unjustly or harmfully toward any individual.

Likewise, from factual statistics, a much higher percentage of men than women accomplish major intellectual, artistic, and commercial achievements. Regardless of the causes or reasons, that statistical fact has been true throughout recorded history and is still true today. However, with the increased educational, social, economic, and financial freedoms now available to Western women, the percentage of women attaining high achievement has increased. But the increase is nowhere near the proportion of increased opportunities for women. Women, in general, have not fully utilized their increased freedoms and opportunities. Still, to blindly apply that statistical fact to any individual woman would be unjust, inaccurate, and out of context. But to ignore that statistical fact in its proper, generalized context would be a mystical evasion of reality that could result in serious errors in judgment and thinking needed for honest, accurate business and personal decisions.

Proper in-context generalizations based on accurate facts are necessary to accurately perceive reality, to know what is going

---

[1]References: "Crime in the United States: Uniform Crime Report", issued annually by the FBI; "Crime and Race" M.E. Wolfgang and B. Cohen.

on, and to make correct decisions. On the other hand, a person must never apply statistical data or generalizations to any specific individual. To do so would not only be unjust and dishonest, but would also be inaccurate, misleading, and a mystical distortion of reality.

Conversely, applying individual characterizations to general groups of people would likewise be invalid, unjust, dishonest, misleading, and mystical. To most effectively use the Neo-Tech Advantages, one must not only integrate thought with action, but must integrate both in-context generalized facts with in-context specific facts [Re: Table 77, Neo-Tech Reference Encyclopedia].

Neo-Tech Advantage #111
NEO-TECH — THE BENEFICENT SOLUTION TO RACISM
As with any feeling or emotion, an unacted-upon racist feeling is not subject to guilt or moral judgment. Mind crimes do not exist, except through the false-guilt ploys of political, religious, and "intellectual" neocheaters. Only when racist feelings are translated into harmful actions does racism become unjust, immoral, guilty. Destructive, government-implemented racism occurs in Zionist Israel and in apartheid South Africa. But much more destructive racism occurs in all Arab, Moslem, and black-African dictatorships as well as in many Asian countries such as the USSR, India, and Red China. But, ironically, the freest countries practicing racism potentially present the most tragic dilemmas:

What is the remedy to Zionist racism that forcibly violates the individual rights of millions of Palestinians? The only moral position is to restore full individual rights to everyone, including the Palestinians. But that would seem to allow even greater violations of individual rights by permitting a much worse, Syrian-like dictatorship or a murderous, Iranian-like theocracy take over.

In principle, Israel's problem is similar to South Africa's problem. Both forcibly implement racist policies. But in South Africa, the problem today arises not as much from racism as from the fear that a much worse, murderous racist Leninism would take over. Most rational South Africans, both blacks and whites, fear that ending the current system would allow the worst form of neocheating and mysticism (murderous Marxist-Leninism) to take over and destroy whatever is good and worsen whatever is bad.

An unsolvable dilemma? Not at all. Instead, spectacularly beneficial solutions exist through Neo-Tech: By using Neo-Tech principles, people can explicitly and permanently eliminate initiatory force and fraud by any person, group, or government. In other words, Neo-Tech effectively dismantles the mechanism for government to initiate force or fraud. A Neo-Tech based society has but a single law and responsibility — to protect the individual rights of everyone. [Re: Neo-Tech Advantage #82]

Neo-Tech is the solution to racism in South Africa, in Israel, as well as in all fascist, Marxist, and theocratic regimes. For, Neo-Tech collapses force-backed power and laws, leaving that society with the sole power and function to protect the individual rights of everyone — black, white, man, woman, rich, poor, Jew, Palestinian, business person, laborer. Neo-Tech frees individuals from initiatory force, fraud, and destructive oppression. Neo-Tech protects each person's individual and property rights from Marxist-Leninism destruction and other forms of force and coercion.

In South Africa, Israel, and totalitarian nations, Neo-Tech would free victims of force-backed racism and vanquish laws backed by force. In turn, eliminating that mechanism for initiating force would dramatically strengthen self-defense for protecting the individual rights and property of everyone.

Thus, Neo-Tech would eliminate the threat of destruction that now awaits those in South Africa and Israel, especially the value producers and their property. For, Neo-Tech delivers a safe, orderly society of unprecedented prosperity and happiness reaching forever into the future. Neo-Tech is the freedom and inspiration for those still living under force-backed, totalitarian governments. In one stroke, Neo-Tech will end those fears and threats by denuding the professional value destroyers of their power. For Neo-Tech dismantles their mechanisms of initiatory force and coercion. At the same time, Neo-Tech provides iron-clad protection to individual rights.

The choice is (1) a holocaust or (2) the dark ages, or (3) the sunlit world of Neo-Tech. With the worldwide distribution of the Neo-Tech Discovery occurring today in most major languages, the choice will be Neo-Tech. ...For nothing can stop Neo-Tech. Nothing can stop the demise of mysticism and all its symbiotic neocheaters.

Neo-Tech Advantage #112
**VERTICAL THINKING,
HORIZONTAL THINKING,
AND DREAMING**

Vertical thinking is thinking within the known boundaries of knowledge. Vertical thinking is *developmental* thinking that leads to fuller development of knowledge. Integrated vertical thinking develops the depths and richness of life. Many areas of life from business to romantic-love relationships have vast potentials for rewarding development through vertical thinking.

Horizontal thinking is thinking beyond the boundaries of known knowledge. Horizontal thinking is *creative* thinking that leads to new ideas, values, businesses, thoughts, experiences, humor[1]. Integrated horizontal thinking yields new areas for vertical development. The combination of horizontal and vertical thinking leads to a never-ending progression of knowledge, values, prosperity, and happiness. Vertical and horizontal thinking are uniquely human attributes that have no limits or bounds. Such consistent, honest thinking propels a person to never-ending knowledge, prosperity, romantic love, and happiness.

In a Neo-Tech society, all individuals are free to think and function to their fullest. Being free from mystics and neocheaters, individuals guiltlessly become responsible for their own lives, thinking, actions, well-being, and happiness.[2] ...What

---

[1]Effective humor is created through horizontal thinking on formulating surprising, unexpected ways to look at something. The swinging back and forth from the expected and conventional to the new and unexpected is the essence of humor [Re: Concept 109 in Neo-Tech Reference Encyclopedia].

[2]Except for the moral responsibility to one's dependent children, no one is morally responsible for anyone else's life, well-being, or happiness [Re: Concept 102, Neo-Tech Reference Encyclopedia]. Yet, throughout history, professional mystics and neocheaters have duped the value producer into believing that he or she is responsible for supporting them — the non-producers, the parasites, the value destroyers, the mystics, the neocheaters.

251

happens when vertical and horizontal thinking combine with rational action? Happiness and romantic love evolve from an ever-upward spiral of earned power and prosperity.

[Re: The concept of vertical versus horizontal thinking originated from Edward DeBono, *New Think*, Basic Books, N.Y.]

Dreaming — Thinking in Reverse

Dreaming is the thinking process in reverse: Dreaming is the mind's garbage-disposing process. Dreams help purge the mind of unintegrated clutter, mysticism, and meaningless non sequiturs absorbed while awake. Thus, contrary to the mystical notions of Freud, dreams have no meanings or connections to reality. And dream "analysis" is nothing more than feeding regurgitated clutter back into the mind. Plus, the more mysticism and non sequiturs that crowd the mind, the more frequent and nightmarish dreams become. Then subsequent dreams increasingly lose their therapeutic, garbage-disposal effects. If the mind becomes increasingly loaded with mystical notions, one's dreams grow less effective in purging and protecting the mind from clutter. The mind then becomes unable to store, integrate, or function efficiently enough to let that person live as a happy, intelligent, productive, conscious being.

Neo-Tech Advantage #113
UTOPIAS REJECTED
THE BEST PERIOD OF HISTORY — NOW

Left-wing, right-wing, conservative, and "liberal" views all stem from the same reactionary, Platonistic root. All are dependent on dishonest mysticism and all are philosophically entrenched in the neocheating ploys of sacrifice and altruism. Such altruistic philosophies are contrary to human nature and well-being. Social utopias extrapolated from any altruistic premise are by nature Platonistic, destructive, and totalitarian. Such utopias depend on sacrifice, force, coercion, controls, and

---

[1]Most of the past and present doomsayers (such as "God", Plato, Thomas Malthus, Adolph Hitler, Paul Ehrlich, Julian Huxley, Paul Kurtz, Margaret Mead, Ralph Nader, Luther Evans, B.F. Skinner) use dishonest projections

(footnote continued on next page)

doomsday predictions.[1] With those conditions, the individual's best interests are always subjugated to the utopian "higher" causes. Thus, being continuously neocheated and drained by utopian rulers, the individual becomes less and less able to produce competitive values for others and society.

By contrast, in a Neo-Tech society, the individual is free to function according to his or her biological nature in becoming more and more productive for others and society. The natural happiness and freedom in a Neo-Tech society starkly contrasts to socialistic utopias. In such utopias, individuals arc compelled to sacrifice their value-producing competence and efficacy to the altruistic, "higher" causes of utopian rulers. [Re: Table 79, Neo-Tech Reference Encyclopedia] Only in a noncoercive Neo-Tech society are productive individuals free to function according to their nature in order to achieve maximum prosperity, psychuous pleasures, and happiness by delivering maximum values to society.

Although altruistic, anti-individualism is still growing throughout the world, today stands as thc most exciting, enlightened period of all history. For the first time in history, an inescapable matrix of Neo-Tech knowledge is available to collapse mysticism and replace every neocheating system with a free, prosperous Neo-Tech society.[1] Productive individuals will then reign free and supreme to experience endlessly growing prosperity, romantic love, and abiding happiness. ...The best time of all history is now!

(footnote continued from previous page)

of free man destroying himself. But those projections are false non sequiturs used to promote the neocheaters' own value-usurping utopias. Such utopias are not only totalitarian by nature, but would be boring, static societies frozen **by force** around some predescribed "ideal". Such utopias would block the exciting, never-ending discoveries that naturally occur through advances in knowledge, technology, and art by productive individuals in a non-utopian, free society.

[1]In a Neo-Tech society, the *only* actions that are prohibited are the use of initiatory force, coercion, or fraud against any individual. That prohibition is upheld by ostracism as well as the right to use retaliatory, self-defense force or legal action against any initiator of force, coercion, or fraud.

Neo-Tech Advantage #114
YOUTH-REJUVENATING IMMORTALITY NOW
(Also see Appendix F and Neo-Tech V)

Animals live, age, and die without choice, according to their environment and biological nature. That no-choice situation does not exist for human beings. Only human beings have the choice and power to control nature. People can learn to continuously expand the value of their lives. They do that by increasingly developing knowledge and productivity to experience increasing earned power, prosperity, and happiness. Likewise, people can learn how to continuously extend their biological/psychological lives through Neo-Tech knowledge, technology, and business. Youth-rejuvenating immortality is the supreme moral achievement for conscious beings as their individual lives become increasingly valuable with increasing age, knowledge, and experience.

Life can be immortal. Today, for the first time, no one has to age and then die — intellectually, psychologically, or physically. With current technology, free of mysticism and neocheating, commercial biological immortality for conscious beings is possible in a decade or less by not one but by several different scientifically feasible routes. Indeed, youth-perpetuating biological immortality will be quickly accomplished when the current anti-life, mystical/neocheating cultures are collapsed by Neo-Tech. With that collapse, the professional mystics and neocheaters will lose their power. In their place will rise a Neo-Tech/Neothink society in which the life of the individual is revered above the supreme value in the universe. [Re: Concept 116, Table 51, Neo-Tech Reference Encyclopedia].

In a Neo-Tech/Neothink society, self-rejuvenation of and/or exact-replica replacement of body parts, including the entire body could be possible in less than ten years through already known biological techniques and future nanotechnologies. Today, however, the primary problem of achieving youth-rejuvenating immortality is *not* medical or technical, but is philosophical. ...With Neo-Tech curing the always terminal disease of mysticism, conscious life will change from always terminal to forever eternal.

Biological immortality could be achieved quickly in an unregulated, free-enterprise, Neo-Tech atmosphere. That business

254

atmosphere of fully integrated thinking and honesty would boom commercial research seeking maximum profits from rejuvenation developments and immortality services. Non-aging biological immortality would have the widest market and maximum value of any commercial product or service possible to conscious beings.

Yet, the enormous commercial and moral incentives to achieve human immortality remain unrecognized because of the prevailing, mystical, anti-life philosophies and the neocheating "authorities" whose control over value production prevent the motivation and freedom for producers to develop biological immortality.

Absolute I-ness immortality accomplished by creating a perfectly restorable conscious mind and sense of self (I-ness) would have a profound psychological impact on every productive human being: Imagine the impact of planning one's own life for the next 300 years. Imagine the time that would be available to build accomplishments, careers, and interests. Imagine if one's life span were suddenly expanded to 300 years, 1000 years, 10,000 years. Imagine the value and respect placed on human lives that forever increased in value. ...Current technology indicates that such definitive, biological immortality would be both scientifically and technically possible in less than a decade in a free society that recognizes individual consciousness as the supreme value in the universe.

Pending further technological development, biological immortality would include the transfer of one's consciousness and sense of one's self (I-ness) into genetically identical entities (e.g., to blank or tabula-rasa brains in cloned bodies). Neo-Tech V lists other routes to non-aging biological immortality feasible within the scope of current technology. Neo-Tech Pincer Movement #1, volume #2, Guns-and-Fists Newsletter #3-2 also demonstrates why the concept of cryonics is axiomatically flawed, guarantees death, and plays a negative role toward achieving I-ness immortality.

The Value of Life:
Einstein and the Factory Worker

If Einstein — or just his brain — could have been kept

functioning after his death, imagine the additional benefits that mind would have bestowed on society: Is not that the main motivation for and value of immortality? Is not that the moral purpose of biological immortality?

No, absolutely not. That is an altruistic view that stymies the effort, motivation, and moral mandate needed to develop commercial I-ness immortality within our generation.

The entire purpose, motivation, and goal of biological immortality is not so a brain can continue to serve some "higher" cause, but so the flesh-and-blood individual, from an Einstein to a productive factory worker, can continue to physically enjoy life and create happiness for his or her own self and loved ones by continually producing values for others. As a result (*not* a purpose), the immortal individual will increasingly benefit others and society as that person becomes increasingly knowledgeable, experienced, and efficient at producing competitive values desired by others.

The value of Einstein's or anyone else's life is meaningful only to one's own flesh-and-blood life and living happiness, not to some society or "higher" cause.

Why Do So Many People *Not* Want to Live Forever?

Because They Fail to Earn Guiltless Prosperity, Love, and Happiness Needed to Experience the Passion to Live and Love Forever

The more people let mysticism influence their lives, the more they become unknowledgeable, undermine values, grow lazy, lose happiness, dislike life. With increasing mysticism, they become increasingly incompetent to earn honest values, power, love, and happiness. In addition, the more people accept mysticism, the more neocheaters can manipulate them. And the more manipulated and less successful one becomes, the more painful and difficult life becomes until the idea of living forever becomes abhorrent, even terrifying. ...Only people who purge themselves of hateful, destructive mysticism can earn the values, power, and

256

happiness needed to experience the passion to live and love forever.

Unstoppable Neo-Tech

Professional mystics and neocheaters have perfected and perpetuated their hoax of inverted values for the past 2000 years. But today, Neo-Tech is in forward motion around the world. The Neo-Tech matrix is spreading. It is unstoppable, irreversible, and will collapse the entire destructive hoax of mysticism. No mystic or neocheater can stop Neo-Tech from eliminating mysticism and its symbiotic neocheaters.

Happiness Forever

With life ageless and immortal, mystic-free conscious beings can forever experience growing prosperity, love, happiness, and life itself through productive work, romantic love, psychuous pleasures, and I-ness immortality. ...The moral purpose of all conscious life would then be met — increasing happiness forever.

SECTION II
Appendices
A-I

Appendix A

UNBEATABLE ADVANTAGES:
PERSONAL, BUSINESS, AND FINANCIAL
by
Eliminating Mysticism and Neocheating

Unbeatable advantages are gained by rejecting mysticism and eliminating neocheating: Neo-Tech people are the antithesis of neocheaters. Master neocheaters usurp their way into positions of false power. They do that by using mysticism to attack, undermine, and destroy values without their victims realizing who the neocheaters are or what they are doing. But with Neo-Tech, one can quickly earn his or her way to power and prosperity by outcompeting others — by producing more effectively than those crippled by mysticism and neocheaters. With Neo-Tech, one knows exactly what mysticism is, who the neocheaters are, how they are draining the value producer, and how to render all neocheaters powerless. More important, Neo-Tech shows how to purge crippling, stifling mysticism from one's own self. ...Neo-Tech cures the stupidness disease, the disease of mysticism. As a result, Neo-Tech delivers limitless power and advantages to value producers.

Quelling the Mystics and Neocheaters

Most people live and die without ever discovering the existence of an innocent, exciting, brilliant world . That world is the clean, mystic-free world of Neo-Tech: a cheerful, crystal-clear world that generates unending values, prosperity, and happiness. In that world, Neo-Tech transforms the manipulations and dishonesties of the mystics and neocheaters into advantages for everyone.

Neo-Tech revitalizes crucial words corrupted by mystics and neocheaters. Dead words brought to life include honesty, power, prosperity, love. Through vitalization of the entire language, Neo-Tech reveals the futility of all mystical, mind-over-matter, positive-thinking approaches that lead to nothing. By collapsing the 2000-year hoax of mysticism, Neo-Tech eliminates the neocheater's survival tool. Through an incorruptible matrix of personal, financial, and business advantages, Neo-Tech quells all mystics and neocheaters while delivering that crystal-clear world of prosperity and happiness.

261

Appendix A
Unbeatable Advantages

The Entelechy

Neo-Tech *is* the entelechy of prosperity and happiness. For Neo-Tech delivers unbeatable advantages in:

Competitive Actions

Business Dealings   **Personal Relationships**
Jobs and Careers   **Art and Pleasures**
Finance and Investments   **Romantic Love**

Does Neo-Tech Lead to Anarchy?

No — just the opposite.
Neo-Tech leads to business-like order and prosperity.

THE COSMIC MIND OF NEO-TECH
ends
THE NIGHTFALL OF DEATH
and begins
THE DAYBREAK OF LIFE

Neo-Tech Rhapsodizes Man:
• away from the unhappiness of neocheating anarchy
• away from the disorderly harm of bogus-job authority
and
• toward the happiness of integrated honesty
• toward the orderly prosperity of value-producing business.

The whim of criminal minds dictates all purposeful harm inflicted upon society. The logic of independent consumers dictates all purposeful prosperity bestowed upon society. Who are the independent consumers? They are those value producers who use the marketplace, logic, and reputation to make their own judgments about trading values with others. They make their own judgments free from the arrogated "protection" of bogus-job consumer agencies, free from the dishonest media, free from Nader-like demagogues. ...Independent consumers make their judgments free from the criminal-minded neocheaters

Mysticism and neocheating underlie all harm inflicted upon society. By contrast, business and Neo-Tech underlie all values delivered to society.

Neo-Tech Justice
Subjected to the merciless Neo-Tech Matrix, all professional value destroyers and their bogus-job supporters will eventually become honest, net value producers in order to repay every one of their victims in full. ...Or Neo-Tech will relentlessly ostracize them out of existence through their own self-inflicted, premature deaths and suicides.

262

APPENDIX B

THE NEO-TECH MATRIX
for
ENDING MYSTICISM AND NEOCHEATING

The primary value of language lies in being the tool of thinking, *not* communication. Conscious thinking requires language, words, metaphors, and analogs with consistent meanings. Indeed, the essence of consciousness is *language* since all concepts are formed by thinking through language. But professional mystics and neocheaters purposely alter meanings, concepts, and language to manipulate the minds of their victims. They accomplish their manipulations by confusing and mocking reality in conjuring up their own "truths" and "realities". For them, any "truth" and "reality" that accommodates their whims, wishes, desires, or hoax will do.

The very nature of unintegrated words and concepts leaves language vulnerable to manipulation by mystics and neocheaters. But a fully integrated matrix of the prime concepts would leave words and reality indivisible, thereby blocking corruption by mystics and neocheaters. ...Such a matrix of integrated honesty is invulnerable to attack and corruption because all its words are integrated into a single, indestructible gridlock.

Neo-Tech integrates the original 144 primary concepts into an indivisible web or matrix[1]. Such a matrix protects from distortion all words captured within its gridlock. Because all its concepts are inextricably linked and integrated, the Neo-Tech matrix is invulnerable to attack or corruption by mystics and neocheaters.

The Neo-Tech matrix means the eventual end of professional mystics and neocheaters. For their survival depends on Machiavelli-like "divide and rule", "confuse and control", and "distort and destroy" techniques. To survive, those mystics and

---

[1] The original 144 primary concepts of Neo-Tech were first developed and presented in the Neo-Tech Reference Encyclopedia. Its concepts were then recognized as a gridlock matrix by Dr. Peter Meier at the Institute of Cognitive Infomatics, Wilen bei Sarren, Switzerland. That Neo-Tech matrix is now evolving into an array of Neothink matrices that will eventually envelop all businesses and societies to collapse the hoax of mysticism worldwide via the dynamics of competition.

neocheaters must divide concepts, confuse language, and distort words in order to prevent their victims from thinking about and understanding what is happening. Indeed, those mystics and neocheaters survive by separating meaning from context. They use concepts out of context while distorting words to block clear, honest thinking. They are then able to forge an infinite variety of mind-created "realities". And through those fake mind-created "realities", they conjure up all the rationalizations they need to live off the efforts of others.

Using divide-confuse-distort tactics, professional mystics and neocheaters can subvert any meaning or concept to divine their own "truths" and "realities". They need their divined "truths" and "realities" to usurp values from others. But against the gridlocked Neo-Tech matrix, such divinations, subversions, and confusions are impossible. Thus, against Neo-Tech, mystics and neocheaters are impotent and cannot survive without themselves becoming honest, self-supporting value producers.

The Web Effect

Integrated honesty and consistent effort assure the dominance of Neo-Tech over mystics and neocheaters. By nature, human beings want to live the most productive, happiest lives possible. But mysticism and neocheating are contrary to productivity and happiness. Thus, as Neo-Tech develops within each individual, a clearly integrated matrix or web called the X-factor arises. The X-factor is what pulls nature's survival trigger. Pulling that trigger causes a person to act in his or her rational best interest. And that means rejecting mysticism and neocheating. ...The X-factor will trigger that survival mechanism in any individual exposed to the forthcoming Neo-Tech/Neothink web. For the Neo-Tech/Neothink web yields evermore wider-integrated, inescapable identifications about survival, life, and death. In turn, those identifications yield evermore powerful, clear, inescapable matrices that function to everyone's permanent benefit. Those matrices redirect conscious beings toward their natural survival powers — toward life and away from death.

With those spreading Neo-Tech/Neothink matrices, the death-promoting scourges of mysticism and neocheating will disappear from this planet.

Appendix C

THE NEO-TECH DISCOVERY

First Known Identification of
Master Neocheaters

"If we go back to the beginnings of things, we shall always find that ignorance and fear created the gods; that imagination, rapture and deception embellished them; that weakness worships them; that custom spares them; and that tyranny favors them in order to profit from the blindness of men."

Baron d'Hobach
The System of Nature (1770)

First Known Identification of
Governments as Mystical Illusions

"The state is the great fictitious entity by which everyone seeks to live at the expense of everyone else."

Frédéric Bastiat
1801 – 1850

First Fully Integrated Identification of
Prosperity and Happiness via Vanquishing Mysticism

"Within our minds, we all fight the same life-and-death battle against mysticism. We all fight the same battle against living by following internal feelings rather than by integrating external reality. And we all must make the same choice to exert the effort needed to be honest, to integrate with reality, to think rationally, to quell mysticism. For every individual who fashions a successful, happy life has chosen effort over laziness...honesty over mysticism.

"All values — all prosperity, power, love, happiness, and eternal life arise from vanquishing mysticism."

The Neo-Tech Discovery
Late 20th Century

Appendix C
The Neo-Tech Discovery

ORIGINAL SOURCES OF VALUES

The Neo-Tech psychological/romantic-love concepts grew from the trailblazing work of entrepreneur Nathaniel Branden. ...Branden, through his business thinking, became the first person in history to integrate objective philosophy with cognitive psychology.

The Neo-Tech philosophical concepts grew from the millennia work of logistician Ayn Rand. ...Rand, through her writings, became the first person in history to start ripping mysticism out of philosophy.

PRESENT AND FUTURE SOURCES OF VALUES

Neo-Tech by nature is free of mysticism and its integration blockers. Thus, Neo-Tech yields unlimited integrations with reality. As a result, Neo-Tech yields unlimited competitive advantages, power, and values. With mystic-free Neo-Tech, a person joins the minds of all advanced civilizations throughout the cosmos. With mystic-free Neo-Tech, a person captures cosmic power forever. (Re: Article 2 on page 477.)

NEO-TECH REFERENCES

Primary Direct Reference
Neo-Tech Reference Encyclopedia
The Neo-Tech Discovery

Primary Philosophical References	**Secondary Philosophical References**
The works of	The works of
Plato (immoral)	The Bible (immoral)
Aristotle (moral)	John Locke (moral)[1]
Immanuel Kant (immoral)	Marx, Hitler (immoral)
Ayn Rand (moral)	Leonard Peikoff (moral)

Primary Psychological References
Sigmund Freud (immoral)
Nathaniel Branden (moral, but increasing mystical errors)

Primary Economic References
John Maynard Keynes (immoral)
Ludwig von Mises (moral)

---

[1]As did many anti-tyranny writers of the 17th and 18th centuries, Locke effectively used "Natural-Law" and "God's-Law" abstractions as foils to undercut the false authority of ruling neocheaters. Today, no such foils are needed. For, Neo-Tech directly collapses government and religious hoaxes of neocheating and mysticism.

Appendix D

WHY NEO-TECH SUCCEEDS
WHEN ALL OTHER IDEA SYSTEMS FAIL

IDEAS ALONE ARE NOT ENOUGH

Even the best or soundest ideas alone are not worth much without the integrated thought and hard effort needed to elevate those ideas to higher value levels. Thus, ideas alone cannot provide competence and self-esteem. In fact, certain "intellectuals" use their focus on ideas as rationalizations to avoid the constant, hard efforts needed to live competently, successfully, happily.

That focus on ideas alone is why certain intellectuals with valid idea systems behave immaturely and self-destructively. And that is why they often attack one another with pettiness and unfairness. For such "idea" people base self-worth not on competence achieved but on ideas held.

Indeed, many self-appointed intellectual leaders try to live on ideas alone. They fail to exert the constant hard work needed to build competitive success and business competence. As a result, such "idea" people often appear immature and resentful next to successful business people.

Consider the "leaders" of valid libertarian and objectivist idea systems: For example, consider the publishers of the *nonprofit* libertarian magazine "Reason" and the now *defunct* objectivist newsletter "The Objectivist Forum". Both *noncommercial* publishers tried to "protect" their subscribers from *commercially successful* Neo-Tech.

The lives and self-esteems of such "leaders" orient around presenting ideas and gaining followers. Now, their work is a valid, important activity for which they can be proud. But, those "leaders" fail to put forth the disciplined, mystic-free thinking and hard-effort integrations needed for elevating ideas to commercial levels — to levels beyond preaching to the choir. And, without the discipline of Neo-Tech, they and their followers drift into various low-effort mystical modes of idea churning, group therapies, silver speculating, and John-Galt role playing. Such mystical-mode activities retard life, happiness, and productive accomplishment. ...Midst those undisciplined noncommercial approaches, mysticism flourishes.

By contrast, Neo-Tech orients around creating, integrating, and then elevating ideas to the highest value level. That means profitable mass marketing of Neo-Tech/Neothink around the world via disciplined business thinking, constant problem solving, and hard front-trench efforts. ...With such a highly disciplined, fully integrated focus, mysticism is pulled out by the roots and roasted to nothing in the heat of competitive business.

Idea-only people like to play the role of an Atlas who constantly shrugs. ...Business-like Neo-Tech people never play roles, never shrug. And their unlimited, integrated thinking always outflanks the thinking of mystic-tainted minds with their restricted or blocked integrations.

But eventually, through the rising competitive pressures of Neo-Tech, even those idea-only people will awaken to discover happier, more productive lives in the Neo-Tech/Neothink business system.

WHY NEO-TECH SUCCEEDS

Neo-Tech means fully integrated honesty. Until Neo-Tech, no idea system in history could dent, much less collapse, the neocheaters' 2000-year hoax of mysticism. But, for the following two reasons, Neo-Tech will both collapse the hoax of mysticism and eliminate all its symbiotic neocheaters:

First Reason: Only Neo-Tech integrates the four dual essences that anchor all valid ideas to reality:

1. life versus death.
2. business-like thinking versus mystical thinking.
3. producing values for others versus destroying values of others.
4. honesty and effort versus dishonesty and laziness.

Without integrating the four dual essences that anchor ideas to reality, especially anchor #4, an idea system is unable to stand firm. As a result, any such unanchored idea system is easily manipulated by professional mystics and skilled neocheaters to perpetuate their destructions. ...But no dishonest or mystic-tainted mind with its blocked integrations can out integrate, outflank, or outmaneuver the mystic-free Neo-Tech mind.

Second Reason: Of all the idea systems since Socrates, only Neo-Tech arose from the marketplace. Neo-Tech was born, developed, and continues to be developed through the unflagging efforts, integrations, and disciplines required for survival and success in the free market. Driven by market pressures, Neo-Tech business is an unbeatable, efficient tool for eradicating mysticism and neocheating in both business and personal lives.

Appendix D
Why Neo-Tech Succeeds

Market pressures force mystic-free, wide-scope integrations needed to constantly grow roots ever deeper into reality. Without those mystic-free integrations and ever growing roots, no idea system can grow beyond its own mysticism. As a result, all past philosophical ideas crippled and stagnated by the personal mysticisms of their originators, ossified into incomplete systems, unable to grow beyond their mystically truncated integrations and preset borders. Thus, such restricted systems hold little or no practical or dynamic value for most people. Indeed, without those mystical-free, wide-scope integrations, even the most brilliant, valid idea systems become impotent within closed borders. Once limited or enclosed, all such systems are easily outflanked by neocheaters and then relegated to academic and intellectual debaters.

But, because of its commercial development, Neo-Tech differs from all other idea systems, including libertarianism and objectivism.[1,2] For only Neo-Tech continues to integrate, develop, and grow through the no-nonsense, "dump mysticism or fail" exigencies of profit-oriented businesses. Moreover, only Neo-Tech has been subjected to the street-tough business disciplines required to generate honest, competitive profits. Such profits come from constant, mystic-free integration efforts focused on producing and marketing objective values with maximum efficiency and growth.

Before Neo-Tech, no other idea system had been subjected to healthy business pressures. Most previous systems evolved from low-discipline, pipe-smoking, easy-going philosophical or academic atmospheres. Such atmospheres invite mysticism, non

---

[1]The originators of libertarian and objectivist philosophical systems developed much valid, partially integrated knowledge. Indeed, the philosophical/business system of Neo-Tech commercially elevates the most important aspects of those incomplete idea systems into more integrated, higher-level values.

[2]Most originators of valid idea systems had enthusiastic followers and sparked substantial movements in their day. Those rational originators included Socrates, Aristotle, Thomas Aquinas, Etienne de la Boétie, John Locke, Adam Smith (18th century economist), Jeremy Bentham, John Stuart Mill, Herbert Spencer, Ayn Rand. But being mystically blocked and, thus, not fully integrated with the four essences that anchor all valid ideas to reality, their work never jelled universally or permanently. Thus, they failed to collapse mysticism and eliminate neocheating.

Appendix D
Why Neo-Tech Succeeds

sequiturs, and neocheating. And without a financial bottom line
to reflect the undisciplined and unprofitable consequences of
mysticism, those systems indulge in various forms of "easy-way"
illusions and neocheating to enhance power and fame.

Those systems also fail to identify, much less integrate, the
simple and obvious essences that root ideas to reality. Without
integrating those essences, no idea system can be rooted in reality.
And no unrooted system can prevent its ideas from being manipulated by mystics and neocheaters into non sequiturs. Thus, instead
of deterring mysticism and neocheating, those unanchored ideas
with their truncated integrations were simply manipulated by
mystics and neocheaters into self-serving non sequiturs.

For example, unanchored libertarianism can lead to violent
Marxism-Leninism: The Bolshevist Revolution evolved from
libertarian ideas used out-of-context to gain initial credibility and
support from the value producers. Likewise, Fidel Castro's rise
to Marxist-Leninist power began by usurping libertarian ideas to
gain popular support among those dissatisfied with Batista's regime.

Unanchored "objectivism", cultish guruism, and fanatical
conservatism can lead to born-again ayatollism: Religious
conservatives and fundamentalists neocheat in "righteous" ways.
If unchecked, that dogmatic righteousness would ultimately lead
to oppressive, mass-murdering theocracies like Iran. Such
neocheaters conveniently make non-sequitur use of pragmatically
selected objectivist[1] ideas to gain credibility and respect especially
among political, fiscal, and economic conservatives. For example,
a group called the Galatians explicitly refer to themselves as
objectivist/libertarian Christians. They use valid, rational ideas
as dishonest non sequiturs to promote irrational mysticism. But
mystics and neocheaters can never use Neo-Tech as a non sequitur
to gain credibility or power. For, Neo-Tech always boomerangs
back to expose the natures and essences of professional value
destroyers. And once the professional mystics and neocheaters
are exposed and caught, the iron-grip nature of Neo-Tech never
lets go until they perish, commit suicide, or become honest value
producers. ...Thus, Neo-Tech will rid the world of mysticism and
neocheating.

---

[1]Objectivists Ayn Rand, Leonard Peikoff, and their associates, however, never
exhibited religious dynamics despite such claims by careless or dishonest people.

(Table continued from previous page)

HOW NEO-TECH DIFFERS
FROM ALL OTHER IDEA SYSTEMS

OTHER IDEA SYSTEMS	NEO-TECH IDEA SYSTEM
Academic guiding pressures. Non-profit oriented. Dependent on tax money, contributions, or soulmate largess.	Free-market guiding pressures. Profit oriented. Dependent on profit via delivering competitive, free-market values.
Not integrated with the essences of life (effort and honesty) versus mysticism (laziness and dishonesty). Integrations blocked.	Integrated with the essences of life (effort and honesty) versus mysticism (laziness and dishonesty). Integrations unlimited.
Evade links to personal productivity, business, and happiness.	Integrates with links to personal productivity, business, and happiness.
Cannot stand firm. Concepts not fully integrated. Movable. Can be manipulated as non sequiturs to support mystics and neocheaters. Thus, never eliminate professional mystics and neocheaters.	Can stand firm with bulldog tenacity. Unmovable. Concepts fully integrated. Can never be manipulated to support dishonesty. Thus, always moves toward eliminating professional mystics and neocheaters.
Seek rationalization of personal mysticisms in self and others. Guiltily accepts attacks on values. Accepts mysticism as "spirit" oriented.	Rejects mysticisms in self and others. Guiltlessly rejects attacks on values. Rejects mysticism as death oriented.
Self-esteem based on ideas held and personal acceptance.	Self-esteem based on honest, productive efforts.
Going nowhere, even sound Aristotelian idea systems of libertarianism and objectivism.	Going toward mystic-free, open-ended prosperity, happiness, Biological Immortality.
Lead to little or nothing. Always revert to mysticism. Hold death as inevitable.	Leads to power, wealth, life. Never reverts to mysticism. Holds death as obsolete.

For the full integrations of the above table with Neo-Tech, see Article 1 on pages 463 – 475 titled "The Neo-Tech Philosophy — The Widest Integration". Also see the Neo-Tech document on pages 297 – 304 titled "Supra Power of the Mystic-Free Mind".

Appendix E

THE SECRET OF NON SEQUITURS
The Achilles' Heel of all Mystics and Neocheaters

The word non sequitur embodies the key survival tool of all professional mystics and neocheaters. Non sequitur is a Latin word meaning "it does not follow". Because the word is dead-language Latin, its meaning is stable, immutable — unable to be changed or twisted by mystics and neocheaters. That is why the word is so valuable for uprooting neocheaters. Webster's 9th Collegiate Dictionary definition of non sequitur is, "a statement that does not follow logically from anything previously said".[1]

Use of Non Sequiturs by
Professional Neocheaters

Non sequiturs are most commonly, blatantly, yet cleverly used in news journalism. Most self-appointed advocates also use non sequiturs to foster their fake careers. They all manufacture non sequiturs by linking obvious facts and values to dishonest premises and disvalues designed to attack or undermine producers and competitive values. They constantly use such non-sequitur/neocheating maneuvers to camouflage unfair, destructive, dishonest modi operandi with opposite illusions of fairness, helpfulness, and credibility. But with Neo-Tech, one easily identifies how their good-sounding facts or words are falsely used as non sequiturs to attack and harm value producers. Such non-sequitur attacks are used to usurp power and values by journalists, clergymen, politicians, political cartoonists, certain professors, celebrity social crusaders, destructive bureaucrats, and self-appointed consumer, peace, and nutritional advocates.

When attacking values, non sequiturs are powerful but dishonest tools for gaining strength and credibility without regard to honesty. And using non sequiturs to purposely manipulate

---

[1]A related but less hidden, less clever, less effective tool of mystics and neocheaters is expressed by the Latin phrase Post Hoc, Ergo Propter Hoc ("After this, therefore because of this"). That phrase expresses the logical-fallacy syllogism: "that because one event follows another, the former must have caused the latter." For example: A person has a cold. He takes a large dose of vitamin C. The cold subsides. Therefore, vitamin C cures colds.

Appendix E
The Secret of Non Sequiturs

mysticism in order to usurp power and values is neocheating. With non sequiturs, no honest link exists between the facts being presented and the attack being promoted.

Through understanding non sequiturs, one can clearly see the destructive neocheating in: 1. creating, holding, expanding bogus jobs and fake livelihoods, 2. attacks on business/technology/ producers, 3. destructive "liberal" causes, 4. mindless chanting demonstrators, 5. mob violence, and 6. Hitler/Maoist/Leninist-style enslavement, destruction, murder.

General Use of Non Sequiturs by
Religious Neocheaters

Some neocheaters use non sequiturs in highly generalized ways. For example, Popes and leaders of the Catholic Church have for centuries brilliantly used inspiring art, great architecture, and classical music as non sequiturs. By arrogating to themselves renaissance art of the greatest masters, the religious black-hat neocheaters wove the obvious, rational, highly recognizable values of great art throughout their irrational, destructive doctrines of religious mysticism. With that, the religious leaders created a mighty non sequitur. And projecting that non sequitur let them gain the public respect and credibility needed to usurp unearned power, values, and livelihoods from the value producers. ...That is black-hat neocheating on a colossal scale.

Specific Use of Non Sequiturs by
Media Neocheaters

But other neocheaters, especially in the media, use non sequiturs in highly specific ways. Mike Wallace's "60 Minutes" television program, for example, orchestrates outrage at New York City hotel owners who accept welfare families. Those owners are projected as crooks for charging the city $70 daily room rates while charging only $50 daily for rooms to self-paying customers.

But, "60 Minutes" purposely ignores the fact that few of those welfare families accept the responsibility to take care of their own lives and bodies, much less their "free" rooms. Thus, their rooms soon become filthy and then deteriorate rapidly toward destruction. With those facts ignored, the TV audience is treated to shots of an unhygienic, obese mother with a brood of unkempt children vegetating in a cockroach-infested room. Then "60 Minutes", always cravenly shielding itself from valid rebuttal, implies to a viewing audience of millions that somehow the hotel owners are responsible for the personal filth of those clients and the resulting cockroaches. Mike Wallace lays the fault on value-producing businesses and their hard-working creators rather than on value-destroying welfare schemes and their neocheating creators.

"60 Minutes" then attacks the hotel owners with the non sequitur of higher room rates as "proof" of some kind of unscrupulous greed inherent in businessmen. Hence, most of the millions of viewers are tricked into accepting the false, non-sequitur premise that profit-oriented businessmen are "insensitive", unscrupulous, corrupt and, somehow, the cause of misery in others. With that premise accepted, the neocheaters can then demand that value producers be controlled by others. By others? ...By the professional value destroyers creating bogus jobs and livelihoods for themselves.

The facts, however, are opposite to what was projected. The hotel owners were not greedily overcharging at $70 per room for welfare clients, but were grossly *undercharging* at $70 per room subjected to welfare destruction: A hotel has two main assets: (1) its physical real estate (rooms), and (2) its milieu (setting) that determines what can be charged for their rooms. In accepting those welfare clients, the owners are charging only $20 per day additional to have their two main assets systematically destroyed, day after day. Thus, when the full-context situation is considered, the city is renting those rooms at bargain prices in a terrible, losing proposition for the hotel owners. For, how many other hotel owners responsible for survival through long-range profits would allow their rooms and milieu to be destroyed for only $20 a day?

Dominating the national press and TV news media are value destroyers existing on non sequiturs:

A conservative, religious-oriented TV talk-show host devastates an honest, brave woman voicing a valid objection to

Appendix E
The Secret of Non Sequiturs

school prayer. The bully TV host dishonestly uses a non sequitur in asking her where the good, loving mother within her is. On another network that same night, an honest value-producing toy manufacturer heroically refutes the dishonest, non-sequitur attacks on the toy industry. By standing firm on facts and context, that toy manufacturer has the famous TV news commentator on the defensive...until that commentator suddenly asks where the good, gentle grandfather within that businessman is. Such emotional-manipulating non sequiturs about being a good mother or a gentle grandfather have no connection with the issue. Such dishonest innuendos dismiss any concern for honesty or dealing with contextual facts. ...On and on go the "news" media, day after day, year after year, living through attacks on values by using non sequiturs without regard for honesty or contextual facts.

As with all professional mystics and neocheaters, honesty and integrity must be replaced with non-sequitur manipulations to support their destructive jobs and fake livelihoods. Such people must constantly invert values, making good appear as bad and bad appear as good. Neocheaters must always use non sequiturs to press their specious points on the public. For, to survive, they must continuously attack and lay guilt on the "greedy" value producers in order to control them, to live off them. Indeed, over the centuries, mystics and neocheaters have effectively used non sequiturs to attack and lay false guilt on business-minded value producers everywhere. ...The non sequitur is the neocheater's survival tool for usurping a bogus living from honest value producers.

Neocheaters conceal themselves with non sequiturs designed to make dishonesty seem honest, harm seem helpful, bad seem good — and vice versa. ...Non sequiturs are the disguises worn by all professional mystics and neocheaters. Neo-Tech tears off those disguises.

Use of Non Sequiturs by Politicians: the Premier Neocheaters
Even more pervasive, destructive uses of non sequiturs arise from politicians. Throughout history, politicians have been the premier professional neocheaters operating on grand scales.

278

Appendix E
The Secret of Non Sequiturs

Essentially all their public statements and "career" actions are dishonest. And, while all their dishonest actions are harmful to society, most are deceptively hidden behind good-sounding non sequiturs. But once non sequiturs are understood, examples of political dishonesty become so clearly obvious and plentiful that further illustration is as unnecessary as pointing out patches of sand on the Sahara Desert.

Indeed, Neo-Tech demonstrates the politician's vulnerability — his impotence — his near total dependence on dishonest non sequiturs to survive as a neocheater. And through Neo-Tech, all politicians will lose their power. For all their non sequiturs disintegrate on exposure to Neo-Tech.

Through Neo-Tech, all politicians will eventually sink under the accumulated weight of their dishonesties. And, for the first time, professional mystics and neocheaters will publicly be held responsible for the harm they inflict upon value producers and society.

Personal Use of Non Sequiturs
The most harmful non sequiturs are those dwelling within each individual. Such internal non sequiturs let mysticism survive to the harm of everyone. A person is successful and happy to the extent that person struggles to prevent internal mysticism and non sequiturs from undermining his or her life. By contrast, projecting mysticism or unjust non sequiturs onto others sabotages all life, undermines all personal values, eventually takes away all love and happiness, and turns one's life toward death. Moreover, almost all hurt, pain, loss, and failure ranging from love relationships to business careers occur through letting internal mysticism and non sequiturs determine one's actions. ...The major struggle in life is not overcoming mysticism and neocheating from others, but is overcoming mysticism and non sequiturs within one's own self.

Neo-Tech Demolishes
Non Sequiturs, Mysticism, Neocheating
Perhaps the single most harmful non sequitur is blaming others for one's own problems or unhappiness. That blaming of others is often done through the simple trick of using **a** point to evade **the** point.

279

Appendix E
The Secret of Non Sequiturs

In reality, others can never be responsible or blamed for one's own personal problems or unhappiness. To blame someone else for personal problems is reality-evading mysticism. The responsibility of solving one's own problems, as well as achieving success and happiness, resides solely and without exception within one's own self. Personal failure is almost always linked to personal mysticism, laziness, dishonesty. Such personal defaults are rationalized away through non sequiturs. Neo-Tech, however, demolishes those non sequiturs. In doing so, Neo-Tech brings facts and reality back into focus while collapsing the rationalizations of mysticism. Free of non sequiturs, the individual can recognize why personal mysticism is not a natural part of one's own self. Instead, mysticism is a destructive alien, a diseased intruder that can be isolated and ruthlessly rejected from one's own self through the knowledge of Neo-Tech.

Neo-Tech Promotes
Power, Prosperity, Love, and Happiness

Neo-Tech demolishes non sequiturs to end mysticism and neocheating in self and others. On expelling mysticism from self and rejecting neocheating from others, one becomes free to function in accord with his or her own nature. Once free of mysticism, all people will flourish naturally toward achieving prosperity, happiness, and youth-rejuvenating immortality.

Appendix F

THREE STEPS TO ACHIEVING
COMMERCIAL BIOLOGICAL IMMORTALITY
IN OUR LIFETIME

The Prerequisite For Non-Aging,
Youth-Rejuvenating Immortality
is the
Collapse of Mysticism

Introduction

Neo-Tech today is undercutting the entire 3000-year support structure for mysticism.[1] And the expanding, worldwide distribution of Neo-Tech is planting the seeds for an evolution that will collapse the 2000-year hoax of mysticism — the entire, rickety colossus will collapse into one resounding dust heap. With mysticism wiped out, neocheaters will perish. All conscious individuals will then be free to flourish toward their natural, open-ended potentials for business, prosperity, happiness, and life itself. From those potentials, commercial biological immortality will evolve rapidly through the following three steps:

STEP ONE

The first step in achieving biological immortality is to define its meaning:

Biological immortality means to live as flesh-and-blood human beings forever — not just an extended life, but to live mind, body, and soul[2] as one's own non-aging self for centuries, millennia, forever. Contrary to mystical notions, no dichotomy exists between one's mind, body, or sense of self. Thus, biological immortality is not achieved unless the entire person, including his or her conscious awareness, memory, and especially the sense of self is preserved fully intact, forever.

Also, important to understand is that the purpose of biological immortality is not to serve others, society, or mankind, but to preserve forever the most precious, important value in the

---

[1]Mysticism began with the discovery of the conscious mind 3000 years ago. But manipulation of mysticism by neocheaters did not begin on a major scale until the development of Christian guilt 2000 years ago.

[2] Soul as used in Neo-Tech means the essence of one's conscious self and has no mystical connotations.

universe — one's own individual, integrated physical and conscious self. For, the moral purpose of preserving anyone, including great value producers as Michelangelo, Mozart, Carnegie, or Einstein, is **not** to benefit society (even though society would enormously benefit), but to deliver the ultimate value to that lone individual. And the ultimate value is to continue living as an individual...to continue experiencing flesh-and-blood life, growth, thoughts, values, prosperity, love, and happiness forever.

Finally, as identified in Neo-Tech II, III, and V, the development of human consciousness obsoletes nature's need for aging and death. For consciousness far surpasses nature's evolutionary process in efficacy for species survival and for adapting to environmental changes. Thus, with consciousness, the idea that aging and death is needed to protect and evolve the conscious species is itself mystical. Instead, mysticism alone is the underlying cause of death for all conscious beings.

STEP TWO

The second step in achieving biological immortality is to dispel the following six myths:

1. <u>Death is not final. Life after death exists.</u> False. For 2000 years, neocheaters have used various life-after-death myths[1] to dissipate everyone's natural desire to live fully. Such myths cleverly repress the finality of death, leaving the mystics and neocheaters in control of those who accept those myths. ...Living fully requires rejecting the life-diminishing, destructive controls and myths foisted by neocheaters.

Evading the finality of death lets one rationalize laziness in avoiding the concerted effort and discipline required to live fully during the one and only opportunity anyone ever has for life and happiness. Moreover, that evasion of the finality of death lowers a person's value of life, self-esteem, and independence. That diminished independence, in turn, leaves a person available for control by professional mystics and neocheaters.

Memento Mori

But, remaining fully aware of life's briefness and death's finality lets one realize the supreme value of his or her personal

(continued in Volume Two)

_____

[1]Life-after-death myths range from heaven and reincarnation incantations to scientific-cloaked cryonic speculations.

Appendix F
Achieving Commercial Biological Immortality
(continued from Volume One)

life. And with that supreme valuing and cherishing of personal life, one will by nature:

- reject the life-diminishing acts of mysticism,
- reject the destructive control by neocheaters, and
- adopt the psychological/motivational conditions needed to extend forever the values of life in order to achieve non-aging, biological immortality.

2. Everyone wants to live forever. False. Those free of mysticism can respond fully and guiltlessly to their nature. That natural response lets a person flourish as a value producer to achieve growing prosperity and happiness. Thus, everyone free of mysticism would want to continue flourishing and living happily forever. But because the disease of mysticism infects most people to various degrees, almost everyone is blocked from being fully competent, productive, and happy. Thus, most people remain unaware of the full value of their life. Moreover, mysticism leaves many people so incompetent they feel worthless, miserable, and eventually become imbued with a hatred toward life. Also, the supreme value of life is further obliterated in many people by bizarre, mystical notions of life after death. Such mystically induced depreciation of life and self-worth further reduces one's natural happiness. Indeed, people holding a low evaluation of life and self are unhappy and feel little desire to live forever. ...For, to passionately desire biological immortality here on Earth, a person must experience a passionate, prosperous, happy life here on Earth.

And finally, destructive mystics and neocheaters betray their conscious nature. They program themselves to self-destruct — to die. Time is their enemy. Each passing day brings increasing decline to their lives. With time, exposure of their fraud to themselves and others becomes inescapable. And then death becomes the only way out of their own entrapment — their own betrayal. ...Thus, biological immortality would be their worst nightmare.

3. Living forever would deprive younger generations of opportunities. False. While this myth is spurious, it is for some mystics the most popular objection to biological immortality.

But contrary to mind-fogging mysticism, essentially all conscious beings would be assets to one another in a free, nonmystical society. And such people would become increasingly valuable with increasing experience and interactions over time. Thus, no one would ever need or want to "retire", which is a conscious person's most insidious step toward death. ...But in a mystic-free society, steady increases in conscious experiences and integrations over time would continuously create new values, more benefits, and increased opportunities for everyone, especially the younger generations.

4. <u>People living forever would cause overpopulation.</u> False. Only unconscious plants, insects, fish, animals, and mystics can experience overpopulation. With biological immortality, the required mystic-free business-oriented society allows each human being to easily produce more values than he or she consumes. Each additional person, therefore, becomes an asset to society, not a liability or a drain. Thus, increasing population in a mystic-free society increases technology and values faster than is needed to support any expanding population. That includes expanding man-made inhabited real-estate into limitless space as needed. ...Population growth in which quality of life declines is impossible in a mystic-free society. For in such a society, population growth always increases the assets and prosperity of everyone.

5. <u>Living forever would be boring.</u> False. The opposite is the fact. For creating and increasing values is the essence of a happy, exciting life. That, in turn, gives increasing motivation to live forever. Indeed, all new values come from expanding knowledge. And each new unit of knowledge generates several newer units of knowledge. Therefore, the ability to generate new knowledge is limitless. The notion of finite knowledge is only an illusion from our present, limited-knowledge perspective. For example, late in the 19th century as the Industrial Revolution peaked, a proposal to close the United States Patent Office was considered because of the illusion that little new knowledge or ideas remained to be uncovered.[1] ...Knowledge is not simply uncovered; it is generated from past knowledge. Thus, each day,

---

[1] In 1899, U. S. Patent Office Director, Charles H. Duall, stated, "Everything that can be invented has been invented."

new knowledge and discoveries generate ever-broader bodies of newer knowledge. That infinite newness makes life exciting and compelling. In a world free of mysticism, stagnation and boredom are impossible.

No one in the last century could have, for example, imagined any aspect of the computer age, genetic engineering, super conductivity, fusion energy, or nanotechnology. Indeed, everyone was many layers of knowledge away from concepts needed to gain even a hint of the limitless bodies of radically new knowledge being created today. In fact, infinite knowledge upon knowledge will always be generated (rather than uncovered) forever into the future.

The generation of new knowledge by human consciousness is the only force in the universe not predestined or limited by nature. Indeed, only consciousness can alter the fixed patterns of nature. That conscious alteration of nature's course creates totally new knowledge. And such new knowledge is beyond the finite knowledge available from nature unaltered by conscious minds. Thus, an open-ended, infinite, man-created new knowledge is forever generated without bounds or limits. Happy, exciting human life, therefore, can keep growing forever into the future.

6. <u>Achieving non-aging biological immortality presents technical, biological, medical, and scientific problems that are so complex and difficult that their solutions could be unknowable or, at best, remain unsolvable for centuries.</u> False. While much is not known, nothing is unknowable to human consciousness. In a mystic-free society, the best minds will focus their attention in the most urgent, intense, and efficient manner to achieve biological immortality. For the value of conscious life will become recognized as the supreme value of the universe. Then, with broad-based intensity, all available resources and brains will mobilize toward forever preserving the supreme value of individual life. Out of those focused, unregulated efforts will evolve not one but several commercially competitive routes to biological immortality.

STEP THREE

The third and final step in achieving biological immortality is understanding the requirements for achieving [A] personal prosperity and [B] personal freedom. In turn, achieving [A] and [B] is necessary to achieve [C] commercial biological immortality. The formula is [A] + [B] = [C]:

[A] Achieving Personal Power, Prosperity, and Happiness
(Neo-Tech delivers power, prosperity, happiness)

What is required to achieve personal power, prosperity, and happiness? What are the most valid, authoritative instructions for achieving success? Ironically, no such authoritative instructions for success can exist. No one can give personal success to another. But personal success can be guaranteed through Neo-Tech. For Neo-Tech is the essence of personal power, prosperity, happiness, and romantic love. Neo-Tech is profoundly different from any promulgated approach to life. Neo-Tech is the diametric opposite of the various varieties of inspirational, religious, authoritative, positive-thinking, Search-for-Excellence, and other guru, mystical, or "I'll-tell-you" approaches. Such approaches are based on follow-the-leader dictums. By contrast, only Neo-Tech is based on a negative — on the elimination of mysticism — on the curing of a disease.

Unlike the "follow-me", "I'll-show-the-way", and "I'll-give-to-you" approaches to life, Neo-Tech does not attempt to give that which cannot be given to anyone (i.e. personal success and happiness). Instead, Neo-Tech takes away that which can be taken from everyone (i.e. mysticism). Neo-Tech moves straight toward curing the disease of mysticism. Today, that destructive, eventually fatal disease afflicts human beings. Curing that disease will let everyone flourish naturally toward his or her unlimited potentials. By identifying and then eliminating mysticism in one's self, the following five advantages accrue:

1) *Gain fully integrated knowledge — especially in competitive situations*: With such knowledge, one gains unbeatable power and advantages over those clinging to foggy, inaccurate, unintegrated, mystic-tainted "knowledge".

2) *Think with maximum effectiveness — free of mystical distortions*: That freedom from mysticism permits the clearest thinking, the most effective decisions, and the most advantageous, efficacious actions. And such actions can always outflank and

286

outcompete all mystical actions.

3) *Flourish towards one's growing potential:* Unencumbered by debilitating mysticism, individuals will by nature fulfill their potentials for prosperity, happiness, and love.

4) *Seize control of one's own life and future*: No one is more qualified than one's own self to determine how best to think, act, and live. Consciously or not, everyone alone chooses his or her own course through life. With Neo-Tech, one chooses to exert the effort and discipline to be honest, responsible, competent, in control. With mysticism, one chooses to default on that effort and discipline in favor of dishonesty, irresponsibility, incompetence, loss of control.

5) *Halt being deceived by mysticism and drained by neocheaters*: Manipulating mystical illusions is the source of neocheating deception and power. Thus, recognizing and rejecting mysticism deprives neocheaters of their 2000-year-old tool to usurp values and power from the producers.

By nature, conscious beings can flourish toward their potential in achieving personal power, prosperity, happiness, and love. But few do. Why? Because for 3000 years essentially every human being has been afflicted to various degrees with mysticism. And mysticism is a disease that cuts a person off from his or her natural, conscious self and potential. At the same time, mysticism reorients a person's consciousness from a natural, healthy happiness and life to an unnatural, unhealthy suffering and death. But Neo-Tech can (1) cure the disease of mysticism within one's own self and (2) eliminate the harmful effects of mysticism and neocheating projected by others. ...Curing the disease of mysticism lets a person flourish to his or her potential power, prosperity, and happiness.

Personal success can never come from choices made by others, but only from one's own conscious choices. No one can think or live for another. No one can show another how to flourish and achieve abiding success. Only the individual alone is qualified — and well qualified at that — to learn how to flourish personally. Indeed, Neo-Tech never tells anyone what to do. Instead, it integrates reality and honesty to eliminate mysticism. And to the extent a person eliminates mysticism from his or her own self is the extent that person flourishes: The mystical-free state is the natural, healthy state for conscious beings. The mystical state is an unnatural, diseased state for conscious beings.

Free of mysticism, a person can rapidly gain competence, prosperity, and power. On building that prosperity and power, one increasingly values his or her life. And once one senses the insane evil and waste of unnecessary death, that person will reject death-oriented mysticism. With that rejection of mysticism, biological immortality becomes not only possible but mandatory.

[B] Achieving Personal Freedom
(Neo-Tech delivers a free, prosperous world)

What is required to achieve a free, prosperous world? Personal freedom is being free of force and usurpation from others. Lack of freedom prevents the motivation, research, development, and business needed to achieve commercial biological immortality. But contrary to most social and political notions, no person or group can **give** freedom or prosperity to individuals or society. Instead, one must **take** freedom by removing mysticism and neocheating from self and others. Indeed, collapsing the hoax of mysticism will deliver a free and prosperous world. Current politics or philosophies, however, cannot collapse that hoax. For they are only unintegrated fodder for the mystics and neocheaters. And such unintegrated fodder can be easily taken out of context and manipulated by professional mystics and neocheaters to their own parasitical, destructive ends.

Even the brilliant bodies of libertarian political ideas and Aristotelian/objectivist philosophical ideas are discouragingly ineffective in stopping professional mystics and neocheaters. All such good-sounding political and philosophical approaches failed because they were never integrated with business and the twin essence of mysticism: laziness and dishonesty. Instead, they simply exposed and attacked the various hydra-headed symptoms of mysticism and neocheating, never identifying or exorcising the essence of mysticism and neocheating.

By contrast, because of its fully integrated nature, Neo-Tech interlocks facts and knowledge into an inescapable web. Once captured in that web, those facts and knowledge can never be extricated by mystics or neocheaters for manipulation to their destructive ends. In the past, those deceptive manipulations allowed the mystics and neocheaters to survive and thrive. But today, against Neo-Tech, the mystics and neocheaters are helpless — finished with no revival possibilities.

With fully integrated honesty, Neo-Tech garrotes dishonesty and laziness with steel-grip tenacity until mysticism and neocheating crumble. Thus, Neo-Tech chokes mystics and neocheaters until they strangle and crumble in webs of their own dishonesties.

By contrast, few political, psychological, or philosophical systems even mention dishonesty, laziness, or business as relevant. And none of those systems identify or integrate dishonesty and laziness as the essence of all that consciously harms human life. Thus, those idea systems remain as detached, out-of-context, non sequiturs available for easy manipulation by mystics and neocheaters — even when those ideas clearly identify and vigorously attack various aspects of mysticism and neocheating.

Abiding freedom and prosperity can never be achieved through political or philosophical systems that are not fully integrated with effort, honesty, and value production versus laziness, dishonesty, and value destruction. For that reason, even the rational political ideas of libertarianism and the valid psychological and philosophical ideas of objectivism have made little progress against mysticism. For their ideas are unanchored, unintegrated parts of a whole that mystics and neocheaters can easily manipulate to survive and even flourish.

Paradoxically, that failure to integrate with the nature of effort and honesty may in certain cases be intentional: On close examination, one finds the most clever of all neocheaters are among certain authors of anti-mystical ideas and their ironically mystical blind-faith followers. For, by using valid anti-mystical ideas as out-of-context non sequiturs, those authors can effectively conceal their own mysticism while being lionized for their honesty and integrity in fighting irrationality. But all the while they are indulging their personal lives with closet mysticism. One can identify such authors as those who make no concerted effort to identify the links between mysticism, dishonesty, and laziness within their own work or personal lives. Such authors and their disciples seldom if ever link mysticism with its essence of dishonesty and laziness. For they do not want to identify their own mysticism — their own dishonesty and laziness.

Without the inescapable, web-locking integrations of Neo-Tech, professional mystics and skilled neocheaters can easily manipulate, hide behind, and even profit from the most brilliant exposés and attacks aimed at them. That phenomenon is called the Breaker Morant syndrome after the Australian movie of the same name. That movie brilliantly and blatantly demonstrates the destructiveness of mysticism and political neocheaters.

How could anyone seeing that movie ever again accept mysticism and political neocheating? Because Breaker Morant, along with all other such ad hoc, anti-mystical statements, lacks integration with the essence of mysticism and neocheating. And again that essence is dishonesty and laziness. Thus such attacks on mysticism and neocheating present no problem to clever mystics and neocheaters. For their forte is to manipulate unintegrated ideas and true statements into deceptive non sequiturs. Specific examples of using valid ideas, facts, and truths as non sequiturs are provided in Appendix D titled, "Why Neo-Tech Succeeds When All other Idea Systems Fail".

Clever mystics and neocheaters thrive on Breaker Morant movies, libertarian politics, and objectivist philosophy. For mystics and neocheaters easily use those unintegrated attacks as decoys that give the appearance of something being done to eliminate the symptoms of mysticism and neocheating. With those decoys, professional mystics and neocheaters can keep spreading their destructive hoax as they have for 2000 years. They can continue outflanking such attacks, easily twisting unintegrated facts in perpetuating their mysticism and neocheating.

With the Breaker Morant movies along with libertarian politics and objectivist philosophies, the mystics and neocheaters are basically saying: "If those are your best shots, great. Fire away all you want. For we can survive forever under such attacks, so long as you never integrate your attacks with our twin essence of dishonesty and laziness. ...Indeed, with you also deceptively hiding your own laziness and dishonesty, we are together as secret soulmates. We are comrades. So long live mysticism. We all need mysticism to survive!"

But, by integrating with that twin essence, Neo-Tech is systematically moving mysticism and neocheating toward their demise. Indeed, with Neo-Tech, mysticism and neocheating for the first time in history are doomed. ...With Neo-Tech, the disease of mysticism is cured — a prosperous, happy world free of mystics and neocheaters is guaranteed forever.

The Vehicle to Biological Immortality is Business

Business is the highest evolution of consciousness, responsibility, and morality. No other living organism is even remotely able to function on a business level. The essences of business are honesty, effort, responsibility, integration, abstraction, conceptualization, objectivity, long-range planning, discipline, thought, control. Business creates essentially every major human value, ranging from the development of consciousness, language, mathematics, the arts, up to the electronic and biogenic revolutions. And now, from business comes Neo-Tech, the cure for mysticism and the key to commercial biological immortality.

Neo-Tech I-V is a fully integrated system of ideas and values that is penetrating the public arena around the world through competitive business dynamics. By subjecting Neo-Tech to harsh business disciplines, its ideas rapidly reach markets far beyond small circles of elitists and academe. Without being subject to the intense, disciplined efforts of business and marketing, Neo-Tech would have languished unrecognized and undeveloped perhaps for centuries, trapped in those small, closed circles of less-evolved, nonbusiness intellectuals. But by jumping in the front trenches and applying hard-nosed business and marketing disciplines, the extraordinary practical benefits of Neo-Tech are becoming known to millions of honest working men and women around the world. And marketing through a high-effort, high-discipline business structure provides fast, efficient distribution of Neo-Tech values, ideas, and advantages worldwide.

Until now, the most widely circulated system of ideas has been the Holy Bible. But biblical ideas can be and are mystically and malevolently destructive. For centuries, biblical ideas have provided the philosophical ammunition to diminish happiness, drain prosperity, and neocheat productive people on a grand scale.

By contrast, Neo-Tech ideas benefit everyone by providing the practical tools to eliminate mysticism and neocheating — to enhance the life of everyone. Thus, life-enhancing Neo-Tech ideas will increasingly replace life-diminishing biblical or mystical ideas as the source of philosophical values for all honest, productive people — for all people who count. That, in turn, will establish the social, political, and business conditions needed to achieve youth-rejuvenating immortality.

[C] Achieving Biological Immortality in our Lifetime

What is required to achieve biological immortality in our lifetime? □Ironically, the various life-extension and quasi immortality approaches will not accomplish that goal and can actually retard its achievement. For those approaches themselves are often mystical, especially faddish nutritional/vitamin and wishful-thinking cryonic approaches. Such approaches serve as decoys, deflecting attention away from the anti-mystical requirements needed to achieve commercial biological immortality. Indeed, biological immortality can be quickly accomplished only after eliminating mysticism. Thus, the fully integrated honesty spawned by Neo-Tech is essential for collapsing the 2000-year hoax of mysticism. Moreover, only through integrated honesty can people become happy enough to want passionately to live forever.

Within any society free of mysticism and neocheating, the supreme value of conscious human life and commercial biological immortality would become manifestly evident. At that point, the most efficient deployment of brain power and financial resources would be focused directly on achieving youth-rejuvenating immortality as quickly as possible. And at today's level of knowledge and technology combined with Neo-Tech, the goal of biological immortality could be accomplished within a decade by several independent routes, including various nanotechnologies and other routes outlined in Neo-Tech V.

Appendix F
Achieving Commercial Biological Immortality

The Point of Biological Immortality

To exist forever as a living organism is not the point of biological immortality. The point is to live forever as a growing, conscious being. With that being the point, the purpose of biological immortality is clear and simple — to experience growing happiness forever. ...Consider the following five items:

1) Conscious individuals in a mystic-free world can forever create new knowledge as demonstrated in dispelling Myth #5 (page 284) that living forever would be boring.
2) The value of life is measured in terms of both current happiness and potential for future happiness.
3) Increasing current and future happiness is linked to increasing one's control over nature. That increasing control over nature lets one produce rational values for self and others with increasing efficacy and power.
4) Increasing efficacy and power is dependent on developing and using new knowledge free of mysticism.
5) Since knowledge is built upon knowledge, availability of new knowledge is limitless. Thus, with time, mystic-free conscious beings gain ever greater knowledge and power. With increasing time and knowledge, therefore, mystic-free conscious life becomes evermore valuable and happy.

Forever preserving one's growing value and happiness is not only the purpose of biological immortality, but is the prime moral responsibility of each conscious being. Because new knowledge forever develops in a mystic-free world, conscious beings can with biological immortality forever experience expanding value production and happiness. For, with such value production, happiness can expand endlessly into never-before-known realms of pleasure, knowledge, and accomplishments.

Appendix F
Achieving Commercial Biological Immortality

SUMMARY

The achievement of youth-rejuvenating immortality is possible well within most of our lifetimes. But that achievement depends on collapsing the 2000-year hoax of mysticism and eliminating neocheaters. Various quasi-immortality approaches such as life-extension health regimens may at best offer some health-awareness benefits. But those approaches obscure the need to eliminate mysticism in order to achieve commercial biological immortality. In fact, many life-extension approaches, especially the nutritional/vitamin approaches are themselves mystical. For those approaches usurp scientific credibility with non-sequitur, unscientific, out-of-context, empirical information. Such approaches contradict the requirements for achieving biological immortality.

Likewise, the various mystical, non-sequitur, positive-thinking, and Search-For-Excellence approaches undermine the achievement of personal success and happiness. For personal success and happiness require identifying, attacking, and then eliminating mysticism within one's personal self. In addition, the non-sequitur nature of most libertarian-political, objectivist-philosophical approaches undermines achieving a free and prosperous world. In all cases, the elimination of mysticism and neocheating requires a constant focus on identifying and integrating their twin essence of *laziness and dishonesty*.

Achieving personal success and happiness in a free, prosperous world is a requisite for achieving commercial Biological Immortality. Together, those requisites require the eradication of a single negative — the disease of mysticism with its symptomatic 2000-year reign of neocheaters.

But today, through the Neo-Tech Discovery, the essence of mysticism and neocheating has been fully and integrally identified for the first time in history. That essence is laziness and dishonesty. Aiming directly at that twin essence, Neo-Tech provides both the diagnosis and cure for the disease of mysticism. Through Neo-Tech, the worldwide collapse of mysticism has begun. Concomitantly, the powerful rule of effort and honesty through the competitive dynamics of Neo-Tech business is already pushing back the rule of deception and force by mystics and neocheaters. ...Business is the antithesis of mysticism. And honest business people are the antithesis of dishonest mystics and neocheaters.

With the collapse of mysticism, the supreme value of conscious life will soar above all else. At the same time, the quintessential commercial product, **Youth-Rejuvenating Immortality**, will become stunningly obvious. And with that supreme valuation of conscious life combined with the collapse of mysticism, full mobilization efforts to develop commercial biological immortality will begin. All viable scientific, technical, and medical efforts will be directed into a rainbow of competitive products that will hurl mankind toward commercial biological immortality. With today's knowledge of Neo-Tech combined with our current level of technology and the free-market mobilization of commercial efforts, biological immortality could be available to everyone in a decade or less.

People must earn full-scale prosperity to love life and experience happiness with enough passion to motivate rapid, full-scale development of youth-rejuvenating immortality. Neo-Tech will trigger that full-scale prosperity through competition. And that competition will free millions of productive individuals around the world from both the fatal disease of mysticism and the value-destroying chains of neocheating. Once free, all value producers will flourish naturally toward open-ended prosperity, happiness, and values. They will flourish by (1) collapsing mysticism, (2) rejecting false guilt for living productively and fully, and thus (3) rendering all neocheaters impotent. That, in turn, will unlock the needed motivation to develop commercial biological immortality rapidly — within a few years.

* * *

The entire purpose of biological immortality is to experience ever increasing happiness — to experience future realms of the joys, pleasures, and happiness available only from conscious life. Such forever-unfolding happiness is available to every conscious being living in a mystic-free world of forever-evolving knowledge, adventure, and achievement.

> **SUPRA POWER**
> of the
> **Mystic-Free Mind**

ROUTE TO OMNIPOTENCE IN BUSINESS AND LOVE

Mind Power

No, this is not what everyone has heard countless times in countless ways from professional mystics and neocheaters for 2000 years. No, this is not positive thinking, cosmic consciousness, higher consciousness, the subliminal mind, the subconscious mind, the spiritual mind — or any other form of automatic, "higher power" acquired through mystical faith or effortless believing. No, for all those good-sounding but false, mystical approaches deliver exactly the opposite of what they promise. All those mystical approaches, in one way or another, diminish the power of the conscious mind — the human protective system, the human immune system. All those mystical approaches short-circuit the mind to block or prevent limitlessly wide mental integrations. By contrast, super-wide integrations lead to omnipotence over all people blocked or restricted by mysticism. ...Once free of mysticism, any healthy human mind can make ever wider, ever more-powerful integrations to discover the omnificent Neo-Tech/Neothink mind.

Bingo! — A Winner!

Compare the human mind to a computer chip. That chip cannot release its mighty power until the last defect is removed. But remove that defect and bingo! — the full power of that computer chip is suddenly released to obsolete all electronic circuitry of past history. That defect-free chip then provides the base for ever more-powerful integrating devices with ever-increasing capacities. ...Compare that defect-free chip to the mystic-free Neo-Tech/Neothink mind:

297

SUPRA POWER

The mystic-free Neo-Tech/Neothink mind is healthy, consistent, omnipotent — the exact opposite of the mystic-contaminated mind, which is unhealthy, arbitrary, impotent. Indeed, remove all mystical defects from any human mind and bingo! — the full power of Neo-Tech/Neothink is suddenly released to obsolete all mind circuitry of past history. For, that mystic-free mind is free of all defects or integration blockers. And those defects or integration blockers are what cause areas of blindness and stupidness that make one incompetent or uncompetitive in those defective areas. By removing those defects or integration blockers, one can easily outcompete and outflank those still crippled with mystic-contaminated minds.

Here Comes the X-Factor

What is the X-Factor? The X-Factor is that integration of knowledge which will collapse the entire superstructure of mysticism and eliminate all its symbiotic neocheaters. Once that combination of knowledge (the X-Factor) has been discovered and released, that collapse will occur swiftly, easily, completely. Why? Because the entire mystical/neocheating hoax is unnatural, unstable, and built on nothing. In fact, that hoax is nothing more than an unstable, 2000-year collection of fragile illusions waiting to be shattered and collapsed.

I & O Publishing Company through its Neo-Tech Research and Writing Center has identified the X-Factor and is now collapsing the hoax of mysticism.

Conscious Mysticism versus Subconscious Mysticism

After twenty years of explicitly identifying, building, and integrating knowledge about mysticism and neocheating, I & O Publishing is the only company or entity in history with the tools and knowledge to collapse mysticism and eliminate its neocheaters. The key to

SUPRA POWER

collapsing mysticism and eliminating its symbiotic neocheaters (the X-Factor) is **not** to focus on the specific evils or obvious destructions of professional mystics and neocheaters. Instead, the key is to focus on the most subtle, innocent forms of mysticism deep within one's own mind:

A person must first explicitly reject obvious, external mysticism and then eliminate internal, conscious mysticism. For the more one rejects the obvious, gross forms of external and conscious mysticism, the more advantages accrue for that person to turn inward and purge or "edit out" the final traces of mysticism buried deep within the subconscious.

An Analogy — Purging the God Concept

Purging or editing mysticism from one's mind is similar to editing written work. For powerful writing, one must first purge or edit out gross errors before more subtle, more powerful edits are possible. Much of I & O's written work undergoes as many as forty to sixty edits before commercial release. Each edit level allows a previously impossible focus on ever more subtle, more powerful edits. The final edits, impossible without those previous more-obvious edits, yield the most powerful results. Likewise, for a supra-powerful conscious mind, one must first root out the gross, obvious levels of mysticism and dishonesty — such as purging grossly dishonest illusions built around the false power of value destroyers or the zany beliefs in God or other non-existent authorities. Then rooting out other increasingly subtle levels of mysticism is both possible and necessary to discover those final traces of mysticism. Removing those final traces of mystical contamination suddenly yields a supra-wide-integrating Neo-Tech/Neothink mind. Against that super-powerful integrating mind, no professional mystic, neocheater, or any other mystic-contaminated mind can compete.

299

SUPRA POWER

That final elimination of subconscious mysticism is what suddenly lets the mind integrate all knowledge over infinitely wide ranges. In addition, with a mystic-free mind, the left and right brain can, for the first time, fully integrate together to deliver synergistic power. And that mystic-free, left and right brain integration is what propels the human mind into wide-open, supra-powerful, Neo-Tech/Neothink integrations.

An Example — The Seven Neo-Tech Waves

Subconscious mystical blockages have always prevented full, free-flowing integrations of the left brain with the right brain. On removing those blockages, the left-and-right brain integrates fully, freely to deliver explosive power. For example, contemplate the power of fully integrating left-brain business and strategy with right-brain art and love.

The Seven Neo-Tech Waves will specifically demonstrate the explosive power of mystic-free, left-and-right brain integrations. ...The Seven Neo-Tech Waves wash away mysticism and neocheating.

Mysticism's Last Line of Defense:
Protecting the Darkest of Subconscious Feelings

Secret protection of the darkest, subconscious feelings produces a fatal virus: Those dark feelings which everyone protects are *the aversions to combining consistent, integrated thinking effort with fully integrated honesty*. The cause of those protected feelings is laziness and dishonesty, which is the twin essence of mysticism. Almost everyone today, including seemingly mystic-free people, are inflicted with those most subtle, most protected feelings of mysticism. Those feelings produce a virus that causes short-circuiting tumors. Such tumors block the mind from

SUPRA POWER

making limitlessly wide integrations with all knowledge. ...That virus and its short-circuiting tumors are the final yet fatal barricade to the supra-powerful, immortal, Neo-Tech/Neothink mind.

<u>Mysticism — The Fatal Virus of the Conscious Mind</u>

After identifying and rejecting **all** external and conscious mysticism, a person can finally focus on and then purge or "edit out" the most subtle of subconscious mysticism from his or her brain circuitry. That mysticism is present in human beings as a fatal virus transmitted from nature's bicameral mind 3000 years ago. That virus works to damage and then destroy the protective elements of the man-created conscious mind. That destruction of those protective elements eventually engulfs and then undermines man-made efforts to protect forever the physical body — undermines man-made efforts to achieve biological immortality. In that way, mysticism has ended the life of every conscious being who has ever lived on planet Earth. ...But today, the discovery of Neo-Tech will lead to the cure for mysticism — the disease that brings unhappiness and death to everyone.

Unlimited Integrations
<u>Delivers Omnificent Power</u>

The computer chip on becoming free of defects suddenly breaks from being an inefficient curiosity into a super-efficient integrator of electronic power. Likewise, the human mind free of mystical defects suddenly breaks from being a blocked or stagnated thinking device into a super-efficient integrator of knowledge.

Once the final, most subtle mystical defects are identified and removed, one immediately recognizes the explosive power of the mystic-free mind. For that person can

SUPRA POWER

suddenly use his or her newly freed left-and-right synergistic brain to execute unlimited integrations of knowledge in all directions and all dimensions — intellectually and artistically. And then, with that newly harnessed power, any individual can achieve whatever is possible in any area of knowledge.

Evolving into the Neo-Tech/Neothink mind delivers such power that the single, mystic-free individual suddenly becomes much more powerful than the professional mystics, the professional neocheaters, and all their organizations combined. Suddenly the impotent nothingness of those who live parasitically through false power becomes obvious. Suddenly mystics and neocheaters become hapless, pathetic, insignificant — a sick joke. The source of all their false power collapses as their tired old arsenal of guns, fists, prosecutors, blood, and jails becomes obsolete, ineffective, ridiculous. ...Professional mystics and neocheaters suddenly become pip-squeaks and clowns.

<u>Mystics and Neocheaters Will Perish</u>
An earlier document about Neo-Tech advises:
Quit Praying
instead
Outcompete God
That advice is not hyperbole. For, God is a silly but virulent creation of the mystic-diseased mind. Moreover, the dishonest God concept serves as a powerful manipulation tool for many neocheaters. But clean, honest Neo-Tech/Neothink easily outcompetes the corrupt, dishonest God concept.

Yes, the value destroyers around the world will be laughed out of their bogus livelihoods. Then they will perish and be forgotten forever. ...Or they themselves will dismiss mysticism and neocheating to become happy, prosperous, value producers forever into the future.

SUPRA POWER

Happy and Powerful Forever

As people purge from their minds that fatal, viral infection of mysticism, they become clean, they become innocent, they become happy, they become powerful — forever.

THE TWO POWER SYSTEMS ON PLANET EARTH

The Old, Neocheating/Neothink System	The New, Neo-Tech/Neothink System
Used by professional mystics and master neocheaters to dominate religions and governments in order to usurp unearned power and livelihoods.	Never before identified, thus, never before fully used by value producers to earn the mightiest power.
Delivers only destructions.	Delivers only values.
Fatally flawed by mysticism. Closed boundaries. Mystical contaminations always leave restricted, closed-end integration capacity and limited power. Thus, this power system exists only through deception, force, or fraud — has no genuine power.	Mystic-free, flaw-free. No boundaries. Unlimited, open-ended integrating capacity and power. This power system exists through the competitive dynamics of business — has genuine power.
Unnatural and unwanted once understood by those with real power — the value producers. Produces no values.	Natural and wanted by value producers. Produces unlimited values for others and society.
Intentionally integrated *dishonesty*: The moribund power system of the past.	Fully integrated *honesty*: The newly born power system of the future.
Awaits being confronted, outcompeted, obsoleted, and finally collapsed by Neo-Tech.	Poised through the dynamics of competition to dominate all power thinking on planet Earth.

Appendix G
NEO-TECH AND BUSINESS
converts
Mysticism and Neocheating into
Prosperity and Happiness

Mysticism Creates Problems Where None Previously Existed
Business Creates Values Where None Previously Existed

About 2000 years ago, a new form of dishonesty evolved. Today, that form of dishonesty is called neocheating. Today, as in those ancient times, neocheating involves the undetected theft of power and values from others. Such undetected theft is accomplished by manipulating mysticism to create problems where none exist.

Christian religious leaders orchestrated the first mass manipulations of mysticism: About 1800 years ago, those religious leaders discovered a mighty tool for extracting power and values from merchants, laborers, farmers, craftsmen, builders, and other value producers. That tool was false guilt. They used false guilt to undermine prosperity and happiness earned by others. Projecting false guilt, those religious leaders attacked and undermined the producer in order to usurp his earned power and values.

Those earliest neocheaters discovered they could control and then live off the value producer by manipulating that false guilt onto him or her. From that discovery, those neocheaters usurped more and more power and values from the naive value producers by adding more and more false guilt fashioned from the inverted ethics of religion and altruism.

Christianity was founded almost 2000 years ago. For many years, Christian followers formed cadres of zealots who resisted, heroically at times, the oppression of Roman authorities. Then certain Christian leaders seeking greater unearned power discovered and developed a neocheating power more pernicious than any destructive power known previously. That power destroyed Roman civilization. And that same power today undermines the prosperity and happiness of every individual worldwide. ...That power is false, altruistic guilt in which the innocent are made to appear bad while the guilty are made to appear good.

Appendix G
Neo-Tech and Business

Those original religious neocheaters learned how to foist altruism and guilt onto innocent value producers to deprive them of their earned prosperity, power, and happiness. Moreover, those early Christian neocheaters developed cunning, Platonistic ethical systems that inverted values. Their bizarre, irrational systems were based on altruism, collectivism, and egalitarianism. So effective were those systems for secretly exploiting others that to this day most neocheaters vigorously and pervasively press hypocritical altruism on everyone as a moral ethical system. ...But today, Neo-Tech is replacing those dishonest, mystic-based, value-destroying systems with honest, business-like, value-producing systems.

Most neocheating systems use clever, good-sounding non sequiturs that make good appear bad and bad appear good. With non sequiturs, neocheaters developed diabolically ingenious doctrines of altruism to sacrifice real values to conjured-up false values. The net result is always the destruction of values. Over the centuries, neocheaters have neatly woven destructive rationalizations, seductive mysticism, and good-sounding altruism throughout government, religion, education, law, and journalism.

By contrast, of all the ethical systems built by society, only the system of business with its manifestations of honesty, productivity, commerce, mathematics, and science is not rooted in mysticism or altruism. Instead, business is rooted in the voluntary trading of competitive values. Thus, by nature, business is the most rational, intellectually demanding, honest, productive, and benevolent ethical system possible to conscious beings.

But why is altruism so pernicious? Consider that religious and political neocheaters have for 2000 years honed altruistic guilt into razor-sharp, well-camouflaged stilettos to attack, slash, and stab the value producers. For, to survive, all professional mystics and neocheaters must constantly attack and undermine those producers in order to usurp their power, property, and values. Also, to survive, the rewards of prosperity, self-esteem, and happiness must constantly be faked by all neocheaters. For without faking their self-worth, they could not survive: Without a faked or rationalized self-esteem, all value destroyers would either directly or indirectly commit suicide...or become honest value producers to survive.

Earned power is the basis of self-esteem and happiness. Honest business titans, for example, have earned the power to orchestrate vast ranges of actions to determine their futures. Indeed, by picking up the telephone anywhere, day or night, they have the power to direct thousands of people into productive, life-enhancing activities. Those business titans hold a real power that mystics and neocheaters never even dream of achieving. Exercising such productive power is the primordial source of prosperity, self-esteem, and happiness.

By contrast, professional mystics and neocheaters can never experience earned power. They can only exercise usurped power. Or ultimately, as mass-murderer Mao Tse-Tung accurately identified: "All political (unearned) power comes from the barrel of a gun." For that reason, such neocheaters can never feel genuine power, self-esteem, or happiness. Indeed, they can operate only through unearned power...through destruction, deception, and force in beguiling or forcing producers into sacrificing their values.

Such professional mystics and neocheaters survive by using non-sequitur deceptions or force-backed machinations to drain the prosperity and happiness earned by others. Mystics and neocheaters justify their dishonesties and destructions through specious Platonistic philosophies based on "higher" causes and altruism that were designed solely to extort values earned by others.

Two Classes of People:
Value Producers vs. Value Destroyers

Two fundamentally different classes of conscious beings exist in free or semi-free societies:

(1) those who choose to live by exerting integrated physical and mental efforts to produce competitive values for others and society (or those who are learning or striving to be competitive value producers), and

(2) those who choose to live by avoiding competitive efforts in designing their lives to live off the efforts of others and society.

The sense of life, honesty, and maturity between those two

classes are opposites: Value producers share a confidence-driven goodwill and an effort-driven competence. But value destroyers share a resentment-driven cynicism and a laziness-driven incompetence. That incompetence fuels destructive envy aimed at the value producer upon whom everyone depends for prosperity and survival.

With the preceding knowledge, one realizes that politicians and clergymen as well as most lawyers, journalists, academe, union leaders, and bureaucrats live by destroying rather than producing values. Thus, they live by attacking or harming the producers, their businesses, their products. ...With that knowledge, one recognizes how profoundly different value producers are from value destroyers.

Those Who Live by Attacking Value Producers

Professional mystics and neocheaters are clever, scheming people with well-camouflaged, criminal minds. They steal physical and psychological livings from the producer with no one realizing their thefts. Without their victim's knowledge, they orchestrate manipulations of mysticism, using non sequiturs to produce deceptive illusions. With those illusions, they attack, undermine, and lay guilt on innocent value producers while making the good seem bad and the bad seem good...the innocent appear guilty and the guilty appear innocent.

Ironically, the most vicious neocheaters fashion illusions so they appear as paragons of justice, benevolence, or compassion. But they are the exact opposite. Indeed, vicious neocheaters are not only the Marxists and Maoists who ravage or kill everyone, but are the force-backed bureaucrats, the anti-business regulators, and the Giuliani-type prosecutors along with their politician, clergy, academic, and journalist cheerleaders. Also, included among the vicious value destroyers are those union leaders, "consumer advocates", "environmentalists", "peace advocates", and Armand-Hammer-type business quislings who live by attacking the value producers or supporting the value destroyers. As demonstrated throughout the Neo-Tech Reference Encyclopedia, such mystics and neocheaters are responsible for subtle, undetected destruction, suffering, and killings far beyond all the bloodiest wars combined, which are also staged by professional mystics and neocheaters.

And what about those responsible for such force-backed bureaucracies as the FDA, EPA, IRS, OSHA, HEW? Those people live by directly and indirectly attacking businesses, producers, and objective values. They are among the cleverest, deadliest neocheaters. For they gain their power through draining others on well-hidden, but massively destructive scales.[1] (For specific examples, see "The Neo-Tech Reference Encyclopedia.")

Such neocheaters undercut values and drain happiness from everyone. Without a qualm or backward glance at their wreckage, they blithely commit any destruction they can get away with in order to keep or increase their unearned power. Honesty means nothing to them. Long ago they abandoned the concepts of integrity, rationality, and honest competitive effort. Yet, those neocheaters succeed by creating illusions that they care about life...that they protect, help, or save the lives of others. Thus, with bizarre irony, they make themselves appear as compassionate benefactors of mankind. Indeed, until the recent discovery of Neo-Tech, neocheaters for 2000 years succeeded in appearing as benefactors worthy of respect. But now, with Neo-Tech, they are exposed for what they are — value-destroying pip squeaks worthy only of contempt.

Stealing a Living versus Earning a Living

In stealing their livings through dishonest "for-the-public-good" laws and regulations forced upon entire populations, government-

---

[1]In the widest context, government value destroyers can never benefit anyone. Instead, they can only harm, destroy, and kill: A study by professor R.T. Rummel at the University of Hawaii reveals that in this century government value destroyers *directly* and purposely killed 119 million of their own citizens in non-war actions — over triple the 35 million they killed in war actions (international and civil). In addition, government value destroyers have wreaked such suffering and destruction on their victims to *indirectly* cause extreme premature death (two decades or more of life lost) for at least 800 million conscious beings in this century alone. ...By contrast, business value producers purposely hurt or kill no one. Instead, they give life and benefits to everyone.

type neocheaters eventually cost the lives of thousands even millions of innocent persons while diminishing everyone's life. Such neocheaters range from power-type bureaucracy builders to Mussolini-type crowd pleasers, to Nader-type government manipulators, to Silent-Spring type social authors. Yet, those value destroyers always display look-good, non-sequitur evidence (e.g. "helping" the poor, prompt trains, consumer protection, "clean" water). Through their force-backed laws and regulations, they point to the "good" they do and the people they "protect" from the businessmen, the Jews, the industrialists, the factories — from the value producers. Backed by neocheating quislings in business (the white-collar hoax) and neocheating collaborators in the media and the academe, such master neocheaters victimize all value producers. But those collaborators will also become victims. For today, with Neo-Tech, all such collaborators will sooner or later be stripped of their unearned well-being and smug security. They all will pay the price for supporting the destructive machinations of professional mystics and neocheaters. ...Through Neo-Tech, justice will prevail.

All master neocheaters fake compassion as they pretend to benefit and protect the majority, the minorities, the government, the country, the master race, the poor, the masses, the worker, the consumer. But instead, through dishonest manipulations of mysticism, they relentlessly diminish and destroy human values and lives.

Without the slightest care, they live by hurting or destroying innocent others, often by the millions. Consider Hitler's splendid-looking, mystically motivated, Panzer Divisions that blitzkrieged across Europe. They rendered their constant destructions without the slightest care or even a backward glance at the destroyed lives, shattered businesses, and flattened homes they left behind. Everyday, by the thousands, the life-long efforts of producers were destroyed in an instant by the neocheaters' marching minions. For such value destroyers never honestly think — they never think or integrate what productive effort is, what creating values means, or who creates the values they use every day to live comfortably, safely, easily. Instead, they blindly, mystically render their destructions, every day leaving behind broken lives and rubble. ...So what! cry the neocheating masters as they gloriously roll on attacking and destroying the lives and efforts of innocent value producers. For, the more destruction such neocheaters render, the more secure and powerful they feel.

Those neocheaters just roll on, never considering the carnage they leave behind. For them, destroying the lives, property, and values of others is their only route to power and control. For them, usurping and destroying values (requires only force and deception) are much easier than earning and producing values (requires hard work and honesty). Thus, they dare never to glance back at their products of destruction, which are the only products they can deliver. ...Be they "liberal" politicians, conservative evangelists, modern preachers, pseudo business executives, white-collar-hoax business quislings, dishonest journalists, or neocheating academics, they all must live without regard for honesty or reality while attacking producers and destroying values.

Consider the highly publicized, "liberal"-type politicians or the highly visible, fact-twisting journalists. Such master neocheaters build their unearned power by, for example, partaking in the orchestrated destruction of the innocent value producers in Cuba, Cambodia, Vietnam, Nicaragua, and soon South Africa. They spread death and destruction under a maze of dishonest, neocheating guises, including so-called human rights, while ignoring individual rights. Indeed, they must bury individual rights in order to keep usurping power and values. ...Without Neo-Tech to stop them, they would keep escalating their damage until all value producers were crippled or destroyed.

Those Who Live by Attacking Values

Also, as identified in the Neo-Tech Reference Encyclopedia, among the subtlest yet most vicious neocheaters are those orchestrating agencies such as the INS, IRS, EPA, SEC, and FDA. Those agencies through their force-backed regulations cause the unnecessary sufferings and deaths of innocent people by the millions. The motives of those responsible for attacking values have nothing to do with helping or protecting anyone, but have everything to do with usurping a living by intimidating value producers into obedience, controlling their means of production, and usurping their values.

What values, for example, has the FDA and its prosecutors ever produced for anyone? They survive entirely by attacking and hindering those who produce life-enhancing values for others. Through power-usurping regulations, the FDA throttles the entire drug industry. Through unscientific, dishonest, emotionally appealing demands for "risk-free" products, they ply their power-generating regulations. And their costly, destructive regulations delay for years or outright prevent the development and marketing of thousands of life-enhancing drugs and life-saving cures.

Without government regulations and controls, the producers long ago would have developed (with voluntarily accepted risks) definitive cures for essentially all diseases, ailments, and malfunctions ranging from deadly cancer, heart disease, and AIDS to the agonies of arthritis, the sadness of senility, and the costly economic and fitness losses caused by the common cold, backpain, and headaches. How many lives are lost, how many values are destroyed, how much suffering is endured to support the bogus livelihoods within just one clique of value destroyers in a single government bureaucracy?

Consider the destruction those bureaucrats wreak in usurping their fake jobs without producing values. ...Such neocheaters represent the most cleverly hidden, criminally destructive elements in our society. Indeed, such neocheaters are highly leveraged purveyors of poverty, suffering, destruction, and death.

But, today, even more subtly destructive neocheaters crawl from the swamps of mysticism. They have found a new weapon that without the defense of Neo-Tech would eventually decimate all value producers and their means of production. Those new-breed neocheaters are attorneys who blend tort liability with the malevolence of altruism and the envy of egalitarianism. That new weapon is aimed straight at penalizing success and destroying the means to produce values. ...The intended victims are the "deep pockets" of the most successful, innocent, and beneficent value producers on this planet.

Appendix G
Neo-Tech and Business

Those Who Live by Producing Values

No matter how much false power neocheaters gain by attacking the producer and usurping values, they never can escape a fact they all want to deny: Honest, productive effort is the act of living. Thus, productive effort is the only source of genuine power, honest prosperity, and abiding happiness. Nor can the neocheaters stop Neo-Tech from collapsing mysticism and eliminating their means of survival. They cannot stop Neo-Tech from ending their 2000-year reign of destruction, pain, suffering, and killing. For, productive effort integrated with Neo-Tech forms a matrix that cannot be broken by mysticism or its symbiotic neocheaters — a matrix of competitive values, prosperity, and happiness.

Once the value producers see the mystics and neocheaters through Neo-Tech, nothing can blind them again. Darkness can never return. Once free of mysticism and neocheating, nothing can deny the producers from gaining their earned power, prosperity, and happiness.

The Mystic Mind versus The Business Mind

As throughout history, most philosophers live by attacking the power and value of the conscious mind. They do that by promoting dishonest, cleverly integrated non sequiturs designed to subordinate man's power and responsibility to profound-sounding, "higher" authorities that do not and cannot exist. Likewise, most authors of philosophically, politically, or socially oriented books (including economic, management, and business books by non-business or academe-oriented authors), operate from the same specious base of non sequiturs: Their books or works sound good while directly or indirectly attacking value producers and undermining business values. Rather than exerting the effort and discipline required to produce values, they choose to subvert values as their route to unearned respect, power, and money. Such authors are identified as:

1. Those who avoid integrating their work with disciplined honesty and competitive effort.
2. Those who promote mystical notions or altruistic rhetoric to extract respect, power, and prosperity from

313

the value producers.

Business, The Fountainhead of Happiness

Before Neo-Tech, no philosopher, academic, or author had integrally identified how business is the prime source of earned values, power, prosperity, and happiness. Also, before Neo-Tech, all mystics and neocheaters had successfully concealed three facts:

1. Business-type thinking represents the most intellectual, disciplined, and integrated use of the conscious mind.
2. Business-type action is the fountainhead of earned values, power, wealth, and happiness.
3. Business-type action is the prime mechanism for all competent efforts and competitive values.

But most important, mystics and neocheaters have for 2000 years hidden the crowning reward of business. That reward is happiness, which in turn is the purpose of all human life. Genuine happiness and benevolent power are available in never-ending quantities through business. Nothing even comes close to business as a source of earned values, genuine power, and abiding happiness. But mystics and neocheaters with their guilt-projecting altruism and envious egalitarianism have blocked the producers from recognizing business as the fountainhead of all values. And, thus they succeed in blocking the producers from collecting their earned prosperity and happiness. ...But today, the unhappiness of mysticism is yielding to the happiness of business.

The Happiness Manager

Recognizing the constant injustices inflicted on innocent businesses and producers by mystics and neocheaters, I & O Publishing Company developed a key management position: The Happiness Manager. That position is integrated with the Industrial Philosophy Department, which was also first established by I & O Publishing Company. The Happiness Manager has three responsibilities:

1. Orchestrate company actions so all associates explicitly collect the power, prosperity, and happiness earned by their productive efforts.
2. Prevent earned rewards of power and happiness from

being diminished by trouble-making mystics or usurped by destructive neocheaters.
3. Rid I & O of all dealings with such trouble-making mystics and destructive neocheaters...both inside and outside the company.

Neo-Tech and Business
for Power, Prosperity, and Happiness

Neo-Tech V outlines the business, management, and marketing structure of I & O Publishing Company. That structure integrates growth and prosperity with power and happiness. Thus, Neo-Tech enhances the power, prosperity, and happiness of everyone contributing to I & O's goal. And that goal is to collapse mysticism and neocheating around the world so all productive individuals can (1) collect their earned power, prosperity, and happiness, and (2) achieve non-aging biological immortality.

* * *

The following two tables provide specific Neo-Tech approaches to business that deliver values, power, prosperity, and happiness.

Table 1

NEO-TECH JOB POWER

1. Align and then integrate personal goals with business goals to gain maximum efficacy, power, and happiness.

2. Use the managerial experience, business knowledge, and financial backing available from within the company to build power into self and career.

3. Assume a competitive attitude. All profit-dependent jobs exist in a hard-fact, competitive world. Each individual stands ultimately alone to compete and survive. Each individual stands uniquely alone to build his or her own life and happiness through his or her own strengths, integrated thinking, and productive efforts.

4. Act consistently and vigorously on objective reality to produce competitive values. For producing competitive values is the source of all earned wealth, power, and happiness.

5. Acknowledge values in others. Criticize only in constructive ways and only with positive motives.

6. Support and protect (never undermine) the most-important assets for the future. Those assets are the customers, employees, management, and owners of the company.

7. Create and build rather than complain and wish. Avoid "recreating" reality to accommodate thoughts, wishes, fears, or emotions. For that is mysticism, which leads not only to incompetence but to destructive actions.

8. Think out and then write down ideas, problems, and possible solutions. Avoid "discussions" about problems, especially personal problems or problems of others. Instead, concentrate on solving own problems through integrated thinking and rational actions.

9. Formulate own thoughts about actions and decisions. Never assume the conclusions or actions of management are automatically right or best.

10. Challenge management and existing ideas through carefully thought-out, honestly integrated, succinct communications — preferably in writing rather than through casual suggestions, lengthy discussions, or problem-making complaints.

11. Avoid consuming time of self, management, and others in discussing undeveloped ideas. Instead, develop ideas without involving others. Then present only developed ideas as thought-out, written action plans. ...Undeveloped ideas are easy, common, worth little or nothing, and usually waste precious time.

12. Increase access to the values of others by always acknowledging those individuals from whom values come.

13. Communicate facts in accurate, objective context. Keep those facts free of mystical distortions, whims, non sequiturs, and emotions. For efficient, honest business communication is required to generate growing profits.

14. Avoid purposely omitting essential information in any communication. For that is dishonest and destructive.

15. Act exclusively on objective reality — never act on emotions that seek escape from problems, self-responsibility, and effort: Avoiding problems equals stagnation and death. Solving problems equals growth and life.

16. Act exclusively on integrated thinking and reason — the only source of values, prosperity, and happiness.

Table 2
NEO-TECH MANAGEMENT POWER

1. Assume responsibility for advancing the company and its goals. Take actions required for increasing growth and responsibility.
2. Learn how and why a person becomes increasingly valuable to the company.
3. Focus on three key management responsibilities:
    a. protect and build company assets,
    b. organize and deliver full-context information required for accurate assessment by management and owners,
    c. fulfill promptly, consistently those responsibilities upon which others depend to do their jobs.
4. Integrate job goals with personal goals. Then steadily drive toward those goals. Only from dedicated, driving efforts toward explicit goals can major values evolve.
5. Recognize that only two alternatives exist to constant, driving effort toward success goals:
    a. fake success by draining previously created values,
    b. stagnate and deteriorate.
6. Increase relentlessly the efficient, productive use of life's prime asset — time. Must constantly struggle for time and efficacy. Organize self and others daily to multiply range of effectiveness and achievements. Successful management requires 60+ efficient hours/week: 40+ hours are needed to fully manage short-range and long-range business; 20+ hours are needed for goal-directed, forward-motion accomplishments.
7. Quickly promote those who exert more effort and set better examples than their management.
8. Eliminate the crippling negatives of moodiness and mysticism first in self and then in others: Actions dictated by feelings rather than reality not only

318

create problems where none exist, but create inconsistencies that diminish effectiveness and responsibility. Constant effort is needed to avoid acting on feelings, mystical thoughts, emotions, rationalizations, distortions, wishes, bias, prejudice, favoritism, nepotism.

9. Squelch trouble-making complaints and negative behaviors toward self and others.

10. Maintain a "no-enemy" policy and keep maximum options open: Always act from benevolent, guiltless, advantage-creating positions. Reject mystical attitudes. For mysticism not only creates problems where none exist, but by nature distorts reality, reduces effectiveness, leads to errors, destroys values, and undermines happiness.

11. Exercise unyielding, uncompromising integrity when dealing with dishonest "authorities" and other Neocheaters. Always respond in rational, thought-out ways that will mercilessly expose and eventually put such neocheaters out of business.

12. Practice the "CAS Happiness Diet" (a forthcoming I & O Publication): Forego Caffeine, Alcohol, Sugar to:
    a. achieve the consistent, high concentration required for major success and,
    b. enjoy fully the rewards of intense efforts and high-level achievements.

13. Read and integrate Mark Hamilton's mystic-breaking business publications: "Neo-Tech Control" and "The White-Collar Hoax". Those publications will, through the competitive advantages of Neo-Tech, forever change the world of business: Mark Hamilton's direct, practical applications of Neo-Tech to business will squeeze every drop of mysticism and neocheating from business thinking and action. Indeed, his work removes all limitations from business and individuals.

14. **Implement the DTC technique (Discipline, Thought, and then Control).**

Appendix H

The Long Wave:
Surpassing Einsteain's Ultimate Goal

This document is going to take you on a journey. A journey into realms you have never known existed before today. A journey beyond the wildest science-fiction adventure. By the time you have finished this journey, your thinking will never be the same about you, this world, the universe, your future. That metamorphosis will occur on putting together 25 pieces of a puzzle. ...When the last piece snaps into place, your thinking will change forever.

More specifically, after reading this 25-Part document, an array of new concepts will jell into a matrix on the final page. That matrix is based on Neo-Tech and derived from Neothink. And that matrix will eventually end all mysticism and deliver unlimited power, prosperity, and happiness to all conscious beings.

Dr. Wallace's Journal...
A 25-Part Neothink Puzzle

Part 1: A Neo-Tech Discovery

Tony, a lad of thirteen, was singing the theme song of Monty Python's "The Meaning of Life". The song went something like this:

"Just remember that you are standing on a planet that's revolving at 900 miles per hour, that's orbiting at 90 miles per second. So it's reckoned that the source of all our power, the sun, and you and I and all the stars that we can see are moving at a million miles a day. That's figured out as moving at 42,000 miles an hour, in our galaxy called the Milky Way. Our Galaxy itself contains 100 billion stars. It's 100,000 light years from side to side and 16,000 light years thick. We are 30,000 light years from our galactic center and go around that center every 200 million years. Our galaxy is one of millions of billions in this amazing, expanding universe. The universe itself keeps on expanding in all directions at the speed of light. It's whizzing as fast as it can go, you know, at 12 million miles a minute. So remember when we are feeling very small and insecure, how amazing and unlikely is our birth. And pray that there is intelligent life somewhere up in space, 'cause we are down here on Earth."

What makes those lyrics fascinating is that every statement is essentially factual and verifiable. But the song left out the most important part: Probability statistics overwhelmingly reveal that our universe contains at least a hundred million, and probably billions of Earth-like planets populated with conscious beings like you and me. Millions of conscious civilizations exist that are millions of years more advanced than our newly born, immature, still mystically oriented civilization.

Moreover, that song was praying for what Neo-Tech already discovered. In fact, Albert Einstein spent his professional life searching in vain for what Neo-Tech discovered — the unifying, controlling element of the universe: *human-like consciousness.*

Appendix H
Surpassing Einstein's Ultimate Goal

Part 2: Einstein and the Unifying Link

Throughout history, conscious beings on Earth have struggled with mystical notions of a "superior" consciousness, an imagined god, or some other "higher" power reigning over the universe. But today, by integrating the dynamics of mass and energy, Neo-Tech reveals a relationship between our own Earth-bound consciousness and all existence. The unifying power that orchestrates existence is not some mystical god or "superior" being. But, as demonstrated in this puzzle, that unifying power is conscious beings — conceptual/introspective beings as you and I.

Einstein never accomplished his ultimate goal of unifying all forces. He never derived a Unified-Field Theory. But extrapolating Einstein's work into Neo-Tech reveals the unifying entity of existence — the only integrating force of the universe: human-like consciousness.

Why did Einstein not realize that fact? One reason perhaps stems from his abhorrence for unpredictable actions among the dynamics of nature. For that reason, he disliked quantum mechanics or anything that suggested arbitrary or "god-like" interventions. Always searching for order, Einstein focused on only two components of existence: mass and energy integrated with the geometries of time and space. He believed those components could always be explained, exactly and predictably. Thus, he never considered the third and controlling component of existence: volitional consciousness — free-will, conceptual/introspective/integrating conscious minds.

Perhaps his passionate dislike for the unpredictable and disorder caused him to overlook consciousness as the third spacetime component of existence. For consciousness can and does unpredictably alter the dynamics of nature, every moment, throughout the universe. Yet, from the widest perspective, consciousness brings the most elegant order and predictability to the universe as demonstrated in this puzzle.

All past attempts to link consciousness with existence were based on mystical, "higher forms of consciousness". Such irrational, ethereal linkages always originated as dishonest, unfounded assertions by mystics or neocheaters conjuring up religious and political power. But the Neo-Tech discovery of

b

human-like consciousness as the unifying element of existence can be scientifically established not only with theory but with direct observation and experimental proof.

Understanding the conscious mind as the controlling, unifying element of existence first requires understanding the *unchanging* nature of consciousness and existence versus the *changing* nature of matter and energy:

Part 3: The Unchanging, Eternal Nature of Consciousness

As first identified by Professor Julian Jaynes of Princeton University, the conscious mind was discovered within nature's bicameral mind[1] about 3000 years ago. Given sufficient information, that first conscious mind had the same capacity as conscious minds today to understand anything in the universe from Einstein's theories to computer technologies and beyond. Consider the astonishing conscious minds of Socrates, Plato, Aristotle, Archimedes that were flourishing only a few centuries after the discovery of consciousness. They would, for example, have no problems whatsoever in understanding Einstein's theories or computer technology. Given the information, they certainly had the capacity we have today to understand anything in the universe.

In other words, while much is unknown, nothing is unknowable to the conscious mind. By nature, the conscious mind requires no change or evolvement to understand anything in existence.[2] On acquiring the correct knowledge, conscious beings today are capable of doing anything within the immutable

---

[1]The bicameral mind was man's intelligent, nature-evolved mind before he discovered consciousness as a conceptual/introspective mind. The conscious mind is not a part of nature's evolutionary process. But, rather, consciousness is a discovery by man that lies beyond the dynamics of nature. This discovery process is explained in Chapter Two. ...When referring to consciousness, the word *discovered* is used when perhaps the word should be *invented*.

[2]Individual minds are endowed with various capacities. Individuals then develop or retard their capacities through either conscious efforts or mystical defaults. But consciousness itself is either there to be used or abused...or it is not there.

laws of physics throughout the universe.

Consciousness is man's discovery that sprang from his nature-evolved bicameral mind. Consciousness is not part of nature's evolutionary processes, but is a natural phenomenon of existence.[1] Thus, the first conscious minds on this planet 3000 years ago are the same as the conscious minds on this planet today...and the same as conscious minds in any galaxy ten million years from now. All conscious minds have the same ability to understand anything in existence.

Consciousness, therefore, does not evolve. It exists eternally, unchangingly.[2] And its capacity to understand anything in the universe transposes into forever fulfilling the supreme responsibility of conscious beings. That responsibility is to preserve forever the supreme value of the universe — individual consciousness. To meet that responsibility means achieving non-aging biological immortality as described in Parts 12 and 16 of this puzzle.

Part 4: The Unchanging, Eternal Nature of Existence

Who Created Existence? And who or what created the creator

---

[1]As demonstrated later in this journal, consciousness has always existed throughout the universe as an integral part of existence.

[2]The Neothink mentality is a dramatic new way of using the conscious mind. An analogy could be drawn to a power reactor: As long as impurities remain in the solution, the power reactor will not activate. But remove the final traces of impurities, and presto — a power-reactor explosion. Similarly, as long as mysticism remains in the mind, the power reactor of Neothink will not activate. But remove the final traces of mysticism, and presto — a power-reactor explosion of Neothink. The Neothink mentality is a whole new mentality, an unconnected jump beyond conscious minds today plagued with bicameral mentalities. The Neothink mentality is a "Planck's jump" away — a whole new mentality of astonishing power beyond anything today. The Neothink mentality, however, is still a function of consciousness, i.e., consciousness performing perfectly, limitlessly with no impurities, as the power reactor of life. Consciousness is eternal and unchanging when making the jump into the limitless Neothink mentality, which exists in all advanced civilizations throughout the Universe.

of existence? And then who or what created the creator of the creator, and so on regressing forever. Such questions are, of course, unanswerable. But, such infinite-regression questions need never be answered. For existence is primary and axiomatic — meaning irreducible, self-evident, and requiring no further explanation. While new realms of existence such as galaxies and universes are constantly being created, nothing creates existence itself. It simply exists. Existence always has and always will exist. And that primacy of existence existing forever is independent of consciousness or anything else. ...The most profound of all concepts as underscored by Einstein is simply: Existence exists. What is the alternative? No alternative is possible unless one accepts the contradiction that existence does not exist.

Throughout eternal time, existence constantly generates new realms of life out of which conscious minds spring from the evolvement of bicameral minds — minds of evolved intelligence capable of discovering consciousness. Once consciousness is discovered and harnessed, it can, with accumulating knowledge and productive efforts, learn to forever muster new realms of existence. From those new realms evolve new life. And from new life evolve bicameral minds from which conscious minds spring.

Throughout eternal time and space, the following creation cycle always has existed and always will exist:

Table 1
THE CREATION CYCLE

Realms of existence created —> life evolved —> bicameral mind evolved —> consciousness discovered —> mysticism developed to replace lost, bicameral gods —> mysticism and neocheaters take control of conscious beings —> partial freedom and capitalism developed —> Neo-Tech discovered —> guiltless prosperity, power, romantic love revealed to value producers —> mysticism and neocheating are uncompetitive and, thus, eliminated —> Neothink Man rises —> biological immortality achieved —> control of the universe learned —> new realms of existence created by new conscious beings, God-Man —> and so on, forever expanding

e

and repeating the cycle.

Stated another way: Space, time, consciousness, and existence are eternal; they have no beginning or end. Throughout time eternal, stars, solar systems, and Earth-like planets constantly form anew. Thus, living organisms and conscious beings constantly form anew. Throughout never ending time and universes, limitless planets forever generate life. That life, in turn, forever generates nature's evolutionary processes that always end with conscious beings. ...Conscious civilizations free of mysticism always survive, prosper, take control of nature and then existence.

Given the endless number of water/oxygen abundant, Earth-like planets forever spinning in endlessly evolving existence, one realizes life and consciousness have forever co-existed in limitless abundance. Human-like consciousness, therefore, is as much a part of eternal existence as are mass and energy. When consciousness is integrated with endless existence and time, the stunning conclusion unfolds that human-like consciousness is also unchanging and has always existed.

Consciousness, mass, and energy are the three macro components of existence. Those three components are inextricably linked and must be integrated into all physical understandings and mathematical accounts of our universe. If only the mass and energy components existed, then all existence would be predictable and predestined through the dynamics of nature and physics. But further research and refinement of data will show that seemingly predictable actions of the universe are actually unpredictable from a mass and energy accounting alone. That unpredictability arises from not accounting for the influence of volitional conscious beings throughout existence.

Human-like, volitional consciousness is:

1) the third and integrating component of existence,
2) the unifying component or force never recognized by Einstein,
3) the supreme component of existence that controls the dynamics of nature, mass, and energy to forever preserve and evolve conscious life,
4) the eternal component that has existed and controlled existence, not for trillions of years, but forever.

f

Appendix H
Surpassing Einstein's Ultimate Goal

The balance of this chapter develops a nonmathematical, nontechnical understanding of how conscious beings dominate the universe and muster new realms of existence and life through increasing control of mass and energy.

Part 5: The Changing Nature of Mass and Energy:
The Grand Cycle

All events of the universe fall within nature's mighty Grand Cycle, the dominating, all-inclusive energy wave involving the entire universe. That cycle consists of nature's longest energy wave exactly counterpoised with nature's shortest energy wave. All other cycles, waves, or forces of nature, ranging from cosmic and gamma rays to radio waves fall within the Grand Cycle. ...The Grand Cycle is described in Table 2 below:

Table 2
The Total History Of The Universe
(omitting the unifying element of consciousness)
is contained in
THE GRAND CYCLE
which consists of
The Googol-Year Explosion
Half-Cycle, Long Wave

> with gravity-wave dissipation
> with proton decay
> with quark and electron annihilation

The Googol-Year Implosion
Half-Cycle, Long Wave

The Googolth-of-a-Second
Full-Cycle, Short Wave

(black hole/white hole)
(a googol equals 10^{100} or
10 followed by 100 zeroes)

A capsulized account of the Grand Cycle starting with the so-called big-bang birth of the universe is illustrated in Table 3

g

on the next page.

Table 3 also indicates that all activity during nature's longest wave, the googol-year exploding/imploding cycles, exactly equals all activity occurring during nature's shortest wave, the googolth-of-a-second cycle. An understanding of that seeming paradox will evolve over the next few pages.

Part 6: The Explosion Cycle

Within the universe, all existence oscillates in one Grand Cycle spanning trillions of years. The actual time to complete that Cycle is not relevant here, but will someday be scientifically measured by us on Earth. But, even today, experiments and calculations from the astrophysical Doppler effect[1] show our universe is in the explosion, energy-to-matter half cycle. Our universe is exploding outward at near the speed of light, scattering away from a so-called "big-bang birth" with ever increasing entropy[2] — a measurement of spent energy.

Energy available for work throughout the universe will keep decreasing as the universe spreads out for trillions of years until all energy is spent. In that state, trillions of years after the initial big-bang explosion, the universe exists at its maximum scattered

---

[1] A change of light-wave frequencies caused by a moving light source such as a star. The wavelength of light from a star moving away *red shifts* — becomes longer — stretches toward the color red.

[2] Entropy involves the second of the three laws of thermodynamics for closed systems. Entropy is simply the movement of events toward their highest probability or disorder.* Entropy measures irretrievable energy spent on scattering a closed universe. ...For every star that explodes, every pebble that drops from a cliff, entropy and disorder irreversibly increase throughout the universe. Approaching infinite entropy, all usable energy throughout the closed universe is spent. All is flat and scattered to the maximum. No star is available to explode, no cliff is available from which a pebble can fall. No wind blows. All is dead and still. Stars are collapsed, cold and dark, or not at all. No sound or light exists: perhaps not even mass exists. Perhaps only unusable radiation near and always approaching 0°K exists.

*The same probability concept applies to formulating hypotheses: always formulate toward the highest probability. Thus, the formulation of the Long-Wave hypothesis.

Appendix H
Surpassing Einstein's Ultimate Goal

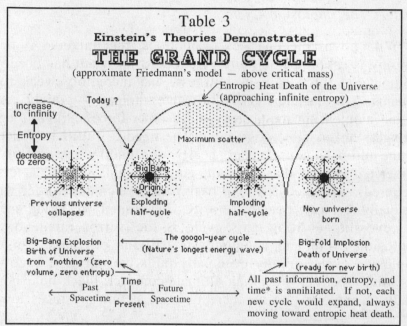

Table 3
Einstein's Theories Demonstrated
THE GRAND CYCLE
(approximate Friedmann's model — above critical mass)

*When time is annihilated, the next event (birth of a universe) is instantaneous to the previous event (end of a universe). No time passes between the two events.

or disordered state — as inert residue of an exploded bomb. At that moment, the entire universe is motionless, energyless, and while always approaching absolute zero Kelvin temperature (0^0K=-273.16^{0}C=-469.67°F), all energy is in the form of uniform, unusable heat radiation. ...Do subatomic arrows of time exist? Will protons, quarks, and electrons eventually decay or annihilate to end in radiation for all subatomic particles and motions?[1]

Part 7: The Implosion Cycle

With no usable energies or motions, the universe is dead. Entropy is essentially infinite. Entropic heat death has occurred. Without the force of consciousness, one incredibly weak force remains — by far the weakest of nature's forces — gravity. And, at that moment, in the absence of all other forces, gravity begins acting as an invisible cosmic hand destined to fulfill its function as the ultimate housekeeper, healer, and energy restorer of the universe. For, at that moment, gravity begins pulling a totally scattered, exhausted universe back toward increased order while gradually restoring potential energy. Increasingly restoring energy by reversing entropy, this cycle is the mirror image of the explosion cycle and equally lasts trillions of years. In that implosion cycle, gravity eventually pulls the universe back into essentially perfect order...an ultimate-compact, black-hole[2] bomb, ready to explode into another big bang as entropy races toward zero.

---

[1]Are gravity waves the final dissipater of energy and motion? Or does mass itself seek higher entropy? With incredibly long half lives of 10^{32} years or perhaps up to 10^{220} years, do protons themselves decay toward infinite entropy? What about the energy and mass of a quark, an electron? Do quarks and electrons finally decay or annihilate with antiparticles? In any case, without conscious intervention, entropy death of a closed universe will eventually occur. **...The laws of thermodynamics, however, apply only to *closed* systems. Existence itself is eternally open and evolving. Thus, any meaning of entropy to existence disappears, including the idea of entropic heat death.**

[2]The universe-containing black hole described here is matter and energy condensed beyond the critical mass and density needed to be captured,

(footnote continued next page)

Appendix H
Surpassing Einstein's Ultimate Goal

As contraction of the universe begins, gravity gradually changes from the weakest to the mightiest force of nature. Starting as an unimaginably faint but constant pull, gravity begins rebuilding the scattered universe by drawing all energyless existence closer together — perhaps initially by a millimicron in a million years. But every movement closer together increases the pull of gravity.[1] That, in turn, increases the speed at which the universe condenses toward an ordered, densifying mass. From the beginning to the end of that condensing-collapsing-imploding cycle, gravity steadily moves toward increasing all forms of energy ranging from potential and kinetic energies to chemical, heat, and nuclear energies.

In the explosion cycle, all energy escapes the diminishing grip of gravity. But in the implosion cycle, no energy escapes the increasing grip of gravity. In this cycle, the universe keeps moving together. Gravity holds all forms of increasing mass and energy within the same shrinking unit as the universe races closer together at accelerating speeds.

Part 8: The Googolth-of-a-Second Cycle

On drawing the universe *toward* a never reachable point, the accelerating pull of gravity begins compacting matter and energy toward a super-ordered, super-compact black hole. Becoming the

---

(footnote continued from previous page)

collapsed, and then imploded by its own gravity. When the collapse is complete, the resulting black hole can convert into a white hole, exploding into a new universe. The entire black-hole/white-hole cycle occurs in the tiniest fraction of a second because all information, entropy, and time obliterates between the two Grand Cycles.

[1]Gravitational attraction increases proportionally to the amount of existence involved multiplied by the inverse square of the distances between the eventual masses and energies. That means gravitational attraction accelerates exponentially as masses and energies are collapsed toward unity. Fields of existence are rolled ever closer together, perhaps into multidimensional space* and then into Gravity Units.

*Up to a twenty-six dimensional space has been mathematically derived in superstring theory. ...Most of those dimensions are rolled up into inconceivably tiny volumes or strings that vibrate at characteristic resonances.

k

mightiest physical force in existence, gravity begins crushing the universe. All forms of energy blend into all forms of matter and vice versa. All molecules, atoms, protons, neutrons, electrons, sub-atomic particles, and energy waves of the universe are crushed together into unrecognizable forms of matter and energy. That rapidly compacting universe assumes entirely different forms of existence occurring only during that nearly instantaneous moment of super compaction at the final instant of the implosion half cycle.

Then, as the entire universe implodes to the size of a basketball, those bizarre forms of existence keep changing with increasing rapidity. Undergoing seemingly infinite changes into ever more radical forms of existence, the universe crushes inward at near the speed of light, imploding to golf-ball size, then to pinhead size, then to pinpoint size. Everything in the universe, including trillions of stars and billions of galaxies, even black holes, are crushed into that pinpoint. The universe then flickers from microscopic to submicroscopic size then to sizes unimaginably smaller than a proton — all while continuously changing into near infinite varieties of unimaginable radical structures shrinking toward zero volume and infinite density. ...The end condition may or may not be different, more disordered, from the beginning condition.

Most incredibly, the total of all mass/energy/activity changes that occur during nature's longest cycle (the seemingly infinitely long, googol-year explosion and implosion half cycles) is exactly counterpoised or duplicated during nature's shortest cycle (the seemingly infinitesimally short, googolth-of-a-second cycle). In other words, the total action during nature's longest cycle of trillions of years is exactly counterbalanced during nature's shortest cycle occurring in the tiniest fraction of a nanosecond[1].

Part 9: The Universe Turns Inside Out From Implosion to Explosion

At that final instant, all activity ceases as the universe is essentially, but not actually, at zero volume, infinite density, and zero entropy. At that final instant, all the universe is in the form

---

[1]A nanosecond is one billionth of a second.

of gravity/existence symmetry. All information and time from the previous Grand Cycle has vanished. At that moment, with a quantum flux, a new spacetime is born — the universe turns inside out from the implosion cycle to the explosion cycle. At once, the universe converts from increasing order and compaction to "nothing" then to increasing disorder and scatteration, from decreasing entropy to increasing entropy, from implosion to explosion. At that instant, the entire universe is cataclysmically destroyed and then instantly reborn from seemingly nothing — reborn in a big-bang inflation of a trillion times a trillion suns.

Created from seemingly nothing, a mammoth composite of post-inflation mass and energy expands in every direction at nearly the speed of light. That ball of mass and energy keeps expanding for centuries, millennia, or perhaps longer before blowing apart, scattering, and then congealing its mass and energy. That scattering and congealing eventually forms visible stars, solar systems, planets. During our current googol-year cycle, millions of Earth-like planets and conscious civilizations formed billions of years before Earth's formation. And millions of Earth-like planets and conscious civilizations will form billions of years after Earth's formation.

Part 10: Super Grand Cycles

Assuming similar gravitational dynamics operate among universes,[1] similar Grand Cycles would occur among the universes themselves, but on endlessly greater scales. And then, ever longer cycles exist among ever larger clusters of universes, and so on, eternally. For each greater cluster of existence, its exponentially longer Grand Cycle would have occurred endlessly in eternity.

From the perspective of forever greater Super Grand Cycles, infinity becomes two dimensional with one vector forever reaching into space, eternally gathering greater and greater mass and energy. Concomitantly, the other vector forever reaches into time, eternally repeating ever longer cycles. Thus, travelling on

---

[1]Currently, Earth beings have no way to observe other universes. Thus, no way is currently known to establish if gravity operates among the universes — throughout the meta-universe.

those two vectors, existence evolves forever throughout the endless universes.

From the limited perspective of our world and universe, the speed of light seems incredibly fast and free. But from the perspective of endlessly evolving existence and ever greater clusters of universes, the speed of light seems increasingly slow and restricting. For, the process of escaping such super big-bangs seems chained to the speed of light. Indeed, being limited by the speed of light, a seemingly endless time would be needed just for those unimaginably large masses to escape their "instantaneous", initial big-bang inflations in their Super Grand Cycles.

Space, time, and distance throughout existence are mind-boggling because they truly never end.

Part 11: Grasping the Ungraspable: The Infinity of Existence

Within the Milky Way, our relatively small galaxy, billions of stars and planets exist that are millions of years older than our Earth. Within our universe, billions of galaxies exist that are larger than our Milky Way. Throughout the Grand Cycle, millions of stars, solar systems, and Earthlike planets constantly form anew. Among those millions of Earthlike planets abundant in water and oxygen, the dynamics of nature immutably generate life. Life, in turn, always undergoes nature's evolutionary process that ends with conscious beings...and conscious beings always evolve to control endless existence.

Indeed, life itself, its evolutionary processes, and thus, conscious beings themselves, have always existed throughout the universe as its third and unifying/integrating/controlling component. And that unifying/integrating/controlling component of the conscious mind was the component Einstein always sought but never recognized. For, he focused only on the mass and energy components of the universe while overlooking the component of consciousness.

When dealing with infinity, relationships among time, distance, knowledge, events, and probabilities become meaningless, resulting in seemingly bizarre situations. Consider a realistically impossible event here on earth for which the odds

n

are a billion to one against occurring. When put in the context of infinite time, such an improbable event will not only occur with absolute certainty, but will occur an infinite number of times. Throughout infinity, whatever is theoretically possible becomes an absolute certainty that occurs an endless number of times.

To further demonstrate the bizarreness of infinity: Take an essentially impossible event that might occur once every billion years. Now take an event that happens constantly, say, once every nanosecond. Relative to infinity, both events will reoccur endlessly, forever into the future. Thus, from the perspective of infinity, no difference exists between their occurrences, for they both occur with endless repetition. So, juxtaposed against infinity, no difference exists between an event that occurs every nanosecond versus an event that occurs once every billion years. For, throughout infinity, both events occur infinite times.

Also, in the context of infinity, no difference exists between distances throughout space. For, throughout infinity, no reference points exist to measure differences among time or distances. ...Infinity is the only concept in existence without identity or boundaries. Thus, infinity[1] is radically unique from all other concepts.

To grasp the meaning of infinite existence, one cannot view existence from the perspective of a finite planet or a finite universe. Instead, one must view existence from the perspective of eternal endlessness. From that perspective, no difference exists between a mile and a trillion miles, or a year and a trillion years, or a forest fire and a star fire, or a lightning bolt and a big-bang birth of a universe. For, no reference points exist to compare distance, time, knowledge, or events of any magnitude when forever really means <u>forever</u>.

As shown later, certain deterministic concepts in the above four paragraphs are valid only in the hypothetical absence of eternal, free-will conscious life.

---

[1]Infinity, as explained in *Neo-Tech Physics*, is a useful mind-created concept that does not exist in reality.

o

Appendix H
Surpassing Einstein's Ultimate Goal

Part 12: Achieving Biological Immortality Now

From a perspective of the infinite time available throughout existence, all newly formed life evolves almost immediately into a highly intelligent brain that can invent consciousness from nature's bicameral mind. The resulting conscious beings then, nearly instantly:

1) take control of nature,
2) render obsolete nature's evolutionary "need" for life-and-death cycles,
3) evolve into the Neo-Tech/Neothink mind,
4) cure mysticism, the only disease of the conscious mind, and
5) achieve non-aging immortality in order to live forever with growing prosperity and happiness.
6) control existence.

But from a perspective of the brief, finite time available for contemporary life on Earth, exactly how and when will biological immortality occur? First consider that, today, newly discovered Neo-Tech will eradicate the disease of mysticism and its parasitical neocheaters. Without the constant destructiveness of professional parasites, conscious beings will quickly, naturally develop commercial biological immortality as described below.

As Neo-Tech cures the disease of mysticism and vanishes those professional parasites, biological immortality will become a certainty for most human beings living today, regardless of age. In fact, today, freedom from mysticism will almost guarantee biological immortality for most people. And that could happen without massive efforts or spectacular medical discoveries. What is necessary, however, is the curing of mysticism. For mysticism, directly or indirectly, eventually kills all human beings while preventing biological immortality for all conscious beings.

Mysticism is the only disease of human consciousness. The symptoms of mysticism are harmful dishonesties. Those symptoms undermine the ability to integrate together the values of rationality *and emotions*. What is the value of emotions? The all-important value of emotions is to experience happiness — the bottom-line moral purpose of conscious life. But, mysticisms mixed with emotionalisms dishonestly assume a primacy over

p

reason and reality. That dishonesty, in turn, casts mortal harm over every individual human being on planet Earth.

Neo-Tech, which is fully integrated honesty, eradicates the disease of mysticism. Thus, the immediate evolvement of biological immortality need not require quick technological breakthroughs, major research projects, or even explicit, direct efforts. But rather, with Neo-Tech, the process of biological immortality can begin immediately within one's own self. And that process will culminate with definitive biological immortality as the 3000-year disease of mysticism is cured by Neo-Tech worldwide.

How will biological immortality actually happen? First, consider:

- a world without mysticism,
- a world without professional value destroyers, parasitical elites, and dishonest neocheaters,
- a world without their destructive institutions of usurped power, such as the FDA (the most health-and-life destroying entity) and the IRS (the most value-and-job destroying entity),
- a world without the *anti-business* elements of mystical governments.
- a world without mystical governments.

Without life-corroding mysticism and its virus-like neocheaters draining everyone, business would explode into an endless productivity spiral. That value-driven explosion would launch human life into upward-spiraling prosperity with continuously expanding life spans.

Consider, for example, how the dynamics of computer technology have so far operated relatively free of parasitical elites, professional value destroyers, and government interference. Being relatively free of irrational regulations, force, coercion, and destructiveness, the computer industry has burgeoned. Computer technology is now delivering soaring capacities for processing and utilizing new knowledge at rates faster than new knowledge can be integrated and used by human beings. Such explosive advances in computer technology, or any technology, requires being free of government mysticism and its professional parasites.

The rational, conscious mind is synonymous with the productive, business mind. The value-creating business mind is the antithesis of the value-destroying political mind. The destructiveness of socialist, fascist, and religious societies prevents their citizens from developing efficient business-driven technologies. Indeed, all such societies are controlled by parasitical elites using force and deception to usurp harmful livelihoods. Such people live by attacking, draining, harming, or destroying value-and-job producing businesses...and their heroic creators and competitive expanders.

By contrast, explosive computer-like advances in human health and longevity directed toward commercial biological immortality will naturally occur in any mystic-free, business-driven society. But exactly how could biological immortality quickly occur today in a mystic-free society? Consider, a 60-year-old person today having a life expectancy of 20 more years. In a rational, business-minded society, uninhibited market forces will rapidly develop the most valuable products and technologies. ...The most valuable of all technologies — the quality preservation of conscious life — will advance so rapidly that when that person reaches 70, high-quality life spans will have expanded to 100 or 120 years, or more.

In a rational, mystic-free society, knowledge and technology accelerate geometrically. Thus, when that person reaches 100, high-quality life expectancy will have expanded to 140 or 180 years, or more. Those accelerating extensions of life expectancy would provide the time needed to develop *definitive biological immortality* for almost every value producer living today. Indeed, in the coming years, Neo-Tech will cure the disease of mysticism to eradicate physical diseases and death among all conscious beings on planet Earth.

In a competitive business-driven atmosphere free of mysticism, the life spans of conscious beings will advance faster than the passing of years. Thus, the result of Neo-Tech eliminating mysticism is immediate, de facto biological immortality. Then, rapidly accelerating health technology — including antiaging genetics — will yield that *definitive biological*

Appendix H
Surpassing Einstein's Ultimate Goal

immortality.[1]

Therefore, by replacing all forms of mysticism and neocheating with the fully integrated honesty of Neo-Tech, nearly everyone today can live forever.[2] Most important, with Neo-Tech, one can live forever with increasing prosperity, happiness, and love.

Almost anyone living today can survive to biological immortality by (1) replacing the death disease of mysticism with the life elixir of Neo-Tech and by (2) stopping mystical behaviors and destructive actions, such as making problems where none exist, smoking, and becoming mentally and physically unfit. Almost everyone today can and will achieve biological immortality by rejecting mysticism and neocheating both in one's self and in others. The key for everyone is to first recognize and then reject the disease of mysticism from within one's own self. Then one can effectively reject mysticism in others.

Life is everything. Death is nothing. Mysticism trades everything for nothing. Mysticism is a terminal disease that breeds professional value destroyers who eventually harm or kill everyone. ...Today, the disease of mysticism is totally unnecessary since it can be cured with Neo-Tech. Thus, through Neo-Tech, essentially everyone can live forever with ever increasing prosperity and happiness.

Also, conscious civilizations much advanced beyond ours would by necessity be free of mysticism and neocheating. For, by holding mystical premises, no civilization can advance much past the Nuclear-Decision Threshold[3] without destroying itself. ...In rational mystic-free societies, the idea of dishonesty is

---

[1]Curing death is described in other Neo-Tech works. ...Mortality is natural in life, except for conscious beings whose nature is immortality — the same immortality God possesses!

[2]The longer a productive individual lives, the more valuable that person becomes through his or her increased knowledge, experience, competence, productivity, and capacity for business and happiness. Thus, in any rational, mystic-free society, the motivation for and value of biological immortality increases as the age of the individual increases.

[3]Planet Earth is currently at that Nuclear-Decision Threshold. For our civilization to survive, the disease of mysticism must be cured.

s

unknown.[1] Thus, *unknown* ideas also include war, murder, deception, fraud, forced taxation, conscription, racism, theft, assault, envy, anxiety, guilt.

Part 13: Infinite Knowledge

To quote from the first Neo-Tech World Summit (March, 1986) keynote address titled, "Three Steps to Achieving Commercial Biological Immortality in Our Lifetime":

"Living forever would be boring. False. Exactly the opposite is the fact. For creating and increasing values is the essence of a happy, exciting life, which, in turn, gives increasing motivation to live forever. Indeed, all new values come from expanding knowledge. And each new unit of knowledge generates several newer units of knowledge. Therefore, the ability to generate new knowledge is limitless. The notion of finite knowledge is only an illusion from our present, limited-knowledge perspective. Indeed, knowledge is not simply uncovered; it is generated from past knowledge. Thus, each day, the discovery of new knowledge generates ever greater bodies of ever newer knowledge and values.

"No one in the last century could have, for example, imagined any aspect of quantum mechanics, the computer age, genetic engineering, superconductivity, or fusion energy. For, everyone was many layers of knowledge away from even imagining those twentieth-century achievements. Yes, knowledge upon knowledge and achievement upon achievement will be generated anew — forever — by human consciousness.

"Human consciousness is the only force in the universe not predetermined by nature. Indeed, only consciousness can alter or go beyond the fixed patterns of nature. Consciousness obsoletes nature's blind, life-and-death survival cycles when applied to human beings. ...In a society free of mysticism, every conscious being produces open-ended achievements for society without bounds or limits. Thus, by producing an eternal stream of

---

[1]Science-fiction stories and movies of evil or hostile aliens are illogical. For, no civilization with the nuclear-energy technology required for interstellar travel could survive as irrational, evil, violent, corrupt, or criminal in *any* way.

t

benefits for society, each conscious life continues happily, forever."

Part 14: Immortality — the Natural State of Consciousness

Thousands of years ago, before anyone on Earth grasped the concept of geometrical shapes, a man looked toward the heavens at the moon, then at the sun, then at the eyes of his woman. Suddenly he grasped the concept of "round"...a strange, new concept that no one had grasped or understood before. From that geometric concept came the circle, the wheel, the principles of mathematics and science, the automobile, the computer, and the latest theories of gravity. Yet, essentially no one today realizes that a concept so naturally integrated with life and taken for granted as the shape "round" was at one time unknown, strange, and spectacular to discover.

Likewise, a few thousand years from today, the natural physical state of conscious man — biological immortality — will be so natural, so integrated with life, so taken for granted that only historians would realize how during a brief time in faded history conscious beings were mystical and thus mortal. Indeed, mortality is not only the most unnatural, bizarre state for conscious beings, but is an essentially unknown state among mystic-free, conscious beings throughout the universe.

In addition to biological immortality as revealed in the *Neo-Tech Discovery*, conscious man's most natural, psychological state is happiness. Essentially all human unhappiness arises directly or indirectly from the disease of mysticism. With mysticism cured, happiness will become so natural and commonplace that in future millennia few if any will know that unhappiness and death ever existed.

Part 15: Einstein's First Oversight: Failure to Integrate Human Consciousness On Earth With the Grand Cycle

Consider us Earth beings with our technology of less than 3000 years. Consider our advances projected by the year 2000, only a few years away. Then project that rate of growth into a geometrically increasing curve of knowledge soaring toward a thousand years hence, a million years hence. One can easily see that conscious beings are altering the dynamics of nature at ever increasing rates. And through a relatively minuscule time span within the incomprehensibly long, googol-year cycle, conscious beings on Earth can quickly learn to dominate nature.

After only the first few centuries of consciousness, around 500 BC, human beings begin controlling nature faster than nature's evolutionary processes. Witness, for example, the development of consciousness from only 3000 years ago, an invisibly short time span in the Grand Cycle as shown in Table 4 below. Earthbound consciousness has already obsoleted nature's evolutionary processes: Today, man-made shelter, food, medicine, and technology advance human survival and well-being much faster and better then do the slow evolutionary, adaptive processes of nature. In less than 3000 years, consciousness is already taking over the dynamics of nature on Earth. With that takeover, consciousness obsoletes nature's protective/survival mechanism of death. Thus, through time, consciousness mandates biological immortality for all conscious beings.

Becoming free of mysticism, Earth beings will not just increasingly control nature, but will dominate nature just a few hundred years hence as explained on the next page.

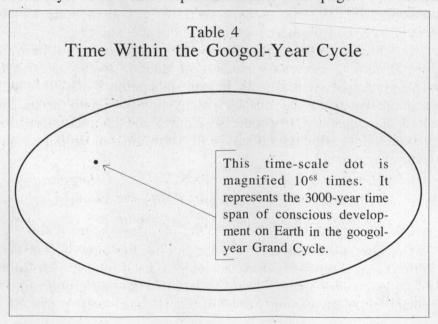

Table 4
Time Within the Googol-Year Cycle

This time-scale dot is magnified 10^{68} times. It represents the 3000-year time span of conscious development on Earth in the googol-year Grand Cycle.

Appendix H
Surpassing Einstein's Ultimate Goal

During the next million years, planet Earth will geologically remain relatively static with basically the same oxygen, land, and water conditions. But, with geometrically accelerating knowledge, we on planet Earth will soon dominate and control nature. Consider, for example, the world's largest man-made lake accomplished by building Hoover Dam with only 3000 years of accumulated, conscious knowledge. That man-made feat controlled and then dominated nature's mighty Colorado River.

From the discovery of consciousness to the first automobile took 2900 years of accumulated knowledge. Then, within 100 years, man went from the auto to the airplane, to the moon, and now toward super computers for everyone. ...Knowledge accumulates geometrically, quickly leaving nature's forces far behind as if frozen compared to the incredibly fast, always accelerating generation of new knowledge.

Perhaps only a few-hundred years hence, we Earth beings will be accumulating new knowledge at lightening speeds. With that rapidly increasing knowledge, we will easily, for example, corral heavenly asteroids into man-made orbital matter to fill our needs, just as today we corral river water into man-made lakes to fill our needs. ...What needs will we Earth beings have a thousand years from now, a million years from now? And how will we use our super-advanced knowledge and tools to control nature in filling those needs?

A thousand, even a million or a billion years, is an incredibly short time, a mere instant, within the Grand Cycle as shown in Table 4. But, well within that brief time span, we Earth beings can also accumulate the knowledge to dominate and drive the universe — to interdict nature's mass/energy dynamics in preventing the Grand Cycle from ever completing itself.

Part 16: Einstein's Second Oversight: Failure to Integrate Consciousness Beyond Earth With the Grand Cycle

Consider the billions of Earth-like planets existing within our own universe that are billions of years older than Earth. Through immutable evolutionary processes among those billions of Earth-like planets, conscious beings have evolved with millions or billions of years more advanced knowledge than we have on

w

Appendix H
Surpassing Einstein's Ultimate Goal

Earth today. ...Just imagine the technology and capacity of those conscious beings who have enjoyed geometrically accumulated knowledge for a million years, a billion years.

Human-like consciousness is the only entity in existence that can alter the inexorable course of nature. Human consciousness quickly advances from building cities to utilizing nuclear power, to developing computers, to making astronautical flights, to corralling astro matter, to understanding the universe, to controlling existence — and beyond forever.

Integrating nature's Grand Cycle with conscious beings reveals an elegantly simple understanding of existence. That integration reveals how individual consciousness is not only an integral component of existence, but is the dominating and controlling component. For example, at either end of the Grand Cycle, all life would perish. But individual consciousness — the supreme value of the universe — must forever protect itself. Thus, conscious beings a thousand or a million years more advanced in knowledge than we on Earth have long ago *met that responsibility to preserve the supreme value of existence: individual consciousness.*

Without immortal consciousness, the Grand Cycle would inexorably and infinitely repeat itself as dictated by the natural dynamics of mass and energy. But, with consciousness, the integrating and controlling component of existence missed by Einstein, the Grand Cycle is always interdicted and truncated. Thus, the destruction of the universe and consciousness has never occurred and will never occur. In other words, by integrating conscious beings into the dynamics of existence, nature's Grand Cycle becomes hypothetical and never occurs.

Consciousness and Existence Integrated

1) Anything theoretically possible in existence, no matter how remote the probability, will happen infinite times unless interdicted by conscious beings.
2) Human-like consciousness has forever been and will forever be an integral part of existence.
3) Conscious beings, as you and I, can understand anything in existence. On gaining the knowledge,

therefore, we can and will eventually do anything
theoretically possible that rationally benefits our
existence.

4) Thus, human-like conscious beings throughout the
universe always have, and always will, control
existence.

5) On curing the disease of mysticism through Neo-
Tech, we Earth beings will gain the same power,
prosperity, and immortality of our fellow beings
who control existence throughout the universe.

Part 17: Knowledge at the Speed of Light

Everything in existence seems limited by a universal constant
— the speed of light. For, as shown by Einstein, nothing can
exceed the speed of light. Consciousness, therefore, being an
integral part of existence, must also be limited by the speed of
light. But how can the speed of light limit knowledge, especially
since consciousness has no limits on understanding anything in
existence? To answer that, one must first understand the dual
faculty of consciousness:

1) The unlimited faculty to understand anything in
existence.

2) The limited faculty to store and process
knowledge.

By nature, each new unit of knowledge begets multiple units
of still newer knowledge. Thus, consciousness creates knowledge
geometrically. So, then, what can limit increases in knowledge?
Nothing can stop knowledge from increasing forever. But, the
rate of knowledge accumulation is ultimately limited by the speed
of light in our closed universe.

To understand the faculty of consciousness that stores and
processes knowledge, one must first understand the history of that
faculty starting with the origins of man-discovered consciousness
on Earth 3000 years ago: For the first 2000 years after the
discovery of consciousness, knowledge accumulated very slowly.
That accumulation gradually increased as the base of knowledge
increased through memory and oral communication. Knowledge
then accelerated through written communication.

y

Appendix H
Surpassing Einstein's Ultimate Goal

For man to produce great sailing ships, for example, he needed that initial 1800 years of accumulated knowledge and technology stored and passed by memory, hand-scribed documents, and oral communication. Then he needed another 1000 years of faster accumulated knowledge and technology stored and passed through written works to produce steamships and trains in further improving transportation. He needed another 100 years of more rapidly accumulating knowledge and technology stored and passed through printed works to produce automobiles that greatly improved transportation. Next, he needed only 60 more years of accelerating knowledge and technology stored and passed through books, journals, and communication equipment to produce practical airplanes that provided transportation inconceivable a century before. Finally, he needed only 40 more years of soaring knowledge and technology stored and passed through computers and electronic communications to develop space ships for landing men on the moon and building space stations.

Now, today, new knowledge is accelerating so rapidly that our productive focus is shifting toward storing, processing, integrating, and transmitting information through million-dollar super computers moving toward thousand-dollar personal computers. Thus, today, computers are undergoing explosive increases in capacities, power, practicality, and economies. And from now into the future, the demands of accumulating, storing, processing, and transmitting knowledge will shift into high gear from man's limited storage-capacity brain to external extensions of the brain with electron/photon-circuited quantum computers and beyond.

Today, storing and processing our geometrically increasing knowledge depends on our developing and building increasingly efficient, man-made computers. Advancing economies and prosperity depend on developing ever more advanced devices until the capacity of every spacetime point in the universe is utilized for storing, processing, and transmitting knowledge.

Knowledge will increase geometrically for a few millennia or perhaps only a few centuries — until the building of external-knowledge devices approaches the speed-of-light limitation. From that point, the expansion of knowledge shifts from geometric to linear. Knowledge will then expand linearly, near the speed of light, and limited by the speed of light.

When our own expanding knowledge reaches that limitation, we can join the millions of other civilizations in our universe that have reached that point. We can then communicate through the universal computer (perhaps gravity-coded) and control existence as our fellow conscious beings do. For, then, the entire universe of universes expanding at near the speed of light becomes our computer and storage facility for all acquired knowledge.[1]

The relationship of conscious knowledge to existence reduces to a single equation. To understand that equation, the following two points must be understood:

1) Knowledge is a function of time, which as Einstein determined is related to the speed of light.

2) Essentially all mega-advanced knowledge throughout the universe is generated, stored, and processed near the speed of light, limited only by the infinite Universe of universes on vectors forever expanding at near the speed of light.

Thus, knowledge ultimately obeys the same laws that all existence obeys...such as Einstein's law that integrates energy and mass with the speed of light as expressed by his famous equation:

$$E = mc^2$$

where:

E = energy; m = mass; c^2 = the speed of light squared

Likewise, knowledge integrates with time and the speed of light as expressed by the following equation:

$$K = tc^2$$

where:

K = knowledge; t = time; c^2 = the speed of light squared

---

[1]Conscious beings perhaps overcome the speed-of-light limitation through eternal inflationary expansions of Gravity Units beyond our universe, into limitless existence and hyperspace.

Appendix H
Surpassing Einstein's Ultimate Goal

Today, in our young Earthbound civilization, the always fatal disease of mysticism darkens the future for all human beings. Growing mysticism reduces and eventually stops the accumulation of new knowledge needed to survive and prosper. Growing mysticism eventually destroys the conscious mechanism for processing and accumulating knowledge. But, with the Neo-Tech discovery, mysticism can be cured worldwide to let all conscious beings forge ahead, geometrically accumulating knowledge at rates eventually limited only by the speed of light.

Part 18: The Universe is but a Dot Next to Individual Consciousness

Every individual consciousness has the capacity to generate, process, and use new knowledge at rates approaching the speed of light. By fully understanding the effects of such knowledge production and use, one quickly rectifies the false view of life held by most people who have lived on Earth. That false view expressed in Monty Python's "Meaning of Life" and promoted by mystics throughout history is: "Individual human beings are but insignificant dots among the vast universe."

Facts and logic demonstrate the exact opposite: Without mysticism, each individual consciousness has unlimited capacity to generate and utilize new knowledge at near the speed of light. Francis Bacon identified, "Knowledge is power." Thus, after a few millennia of such knowledge accumulation, any conscious individual gains the power to so totally dominate existence that the entire universe and all its evolutionary processes seem by comparison to shrink into static insignificance. For, in both power and significance, individual consciousness quickly soars beyond the dynamics of nature and the entire universe.

Today, on Earth, the fully integrated honesty of Neo-Tech finally reverses that mystical view bewailing mankind's insignificance. Neo-Tech demonstrates that the power of the universe shrinks to almost nothing when compared to the unlimited power of individual consciousness.

Appendix H
Surpassing Einstein's Ultimate Goal

Part 19: Who is the Creator?

Does a creator of galaxies and universes exist? Indeed, such a creator could not defy the laws of physics. Yet, today, as for the past three millennia, most people believe a creator must be some mystical higher "authority" or power as promulgated by someone's scriptures or edicts. ...For two millennia, such mystical gods of creation were conjured-up by neocheaters wanting nothing more grand than to live off the efforts of others.

As demonstrated in the balance of this chapter, everyday conscious beings like you and me work within the laws of physics to create and control all heavens and earths.

Part 20: The Goal of Conscious Beings

Throughout the universe, conscious beings pursue their natural goals and responsibilities by achieving biological immortality, limitless prosperity, and eternal happiness. Thus, they forever preserve the supreme value of the universe: individual consciousness. For without conscious beings, no value or meaning would exist throughout the universe. ...Conscious beings free of mysticism never allow their precious lives — lives of limitless value — to end.

Part 21: Galaxies Created Beyond The Dynamics of Nature

Eons ago, a conscious being, as you and I, worked at the edge of a distant galaxy with an integrating computer of a spatial-geometry driven, mass/energy assembler. By assembling units of gravitational geometries, that person corralled enough strings of wound-up gravity to equal the mass of another galaxy. As the moment of critical gravity approached, the final collapse into an entropy-reversing, rotating "black hole" began. He then arose smiling. With arm held high, he cried, "Let there be light!"[1] ...At that moment, in a far corner of the universe, the light of

---

[1]The expression "Let there be light" was first manipulatively used in the mystical world of the Bible, then entertainingly used in the science-fiction world of Isaac Asimov, and now factually used in the objective world of Neo-Tech.

a million times a million suns flashed and began its photonic journey across the universe. A galaxy was born...a man-made galaxy.

Part 22: Galaxies Discovered Beyond The Dynamics of Nature

Today, eons later, specks of light from that conscious-made galaxy fall on the planet Earth — on the lens of a telescope. An astrophysicist examines computer data gathered from those specks of light. Then, integrating that data with the physical and mathematical dynamics of astral mass and energy, he moves closer to a momentous discovery. He moves closer to discovering a major astral event falling outside the natural dynamics of mass and energy — an event that irrevocably altered nature's charted course for the universe.

But, that scientist knows, as any competent scientist knows, that nothing, including conscious beings, can alter the axiomatic laws of physics, mathematics, and existence. And he knows that existence can have no antecedent basis or original creator. Yet, he realizes that, within the laws of physics, conscious beings can alter the natural dynamics of mass and energy. Thus, he realizes conscious beings and only conscious beings can alter nature's manifest destiny, not only here on Earth, but throughout the universe.

Combining such knowledge with computer processed data, that scientist moves closer toward directly observing the alteration of nature's Grand Cycle by conscious beings. Such direct observation may come, for example, through a correlation of computer data concerning black holes or possibly quasars and pulsars. In fact, such correlations of data probably already exist on Earth — hidden in considerable accumulations of uninterpreted data. Integrating such data could reveal that certain cosmic events exist outside the natural dynamics of their mass, energy, and gravity. In turn, that data could then demonstrate how conscious beings create and control such cosmic events as energy and galaxy creators for the eternal prosperity of all conscious life.

Thus, conscious beings could forever prevent the Grand Cycle from completing itself. They could do that, for example, by routinely creating gravity dimensions and geometries that constantly pump entropy-reversing structures back into the universe. Such constantly created, new structures would break the dynamics of the Grand Cycle, allowing the universe to forever oscillate within its most efficient range for conscious beings.

Part 23: Create Your Own Galaxy

Beginning with the data from that speck of light born a million years before, today's Earthbound scientist will discover and prove a newborn galaxy created outside the mass/energy/ gravity dynamics of nature alone. He will then look toward the heavens realizing that he has discovered a galaxy made by a conscious being. He will further realize that over eternal time, over eternally interdicted cycles, all the galaxies and universes, all the heavens and Earths, were at one time created from conscious-made structure pumps that formed new realms of existence while preserving old realms.

And finally, he will realize his mind is the same conscious mind possessed by our immutable conscious cousins who create new realms of existence in other worlds and galaxies for us, them, and everyone.

Part 24: After the Discovery

After that first discovery of a conscious-made galaxy or black hole, scientists will then approximate from our geometric increases of knowledge on Earth and our achievement of biological immortality, when you and I can stand above all the imagined gods to give the command, *Let there be light!*

Part 25: Conclusion

No intimidating god or ethereal super consciousness reigns over the universe. Mystical gods or "higher beings" do not exist, cannot exist, need not exist. For only universes created and controlled by rational, value-producing conscious beings as you and I are needed to explain all existence. And with biological immortality, we Earth beings will someday stand smiling at the edge of space creating our own stars, galaxies, universes, collections of universes, and beyond.

Epilogue

The mightiest power in existence, the power to control existence, is expressed by the great command, "Let there be light!" That power has forever existed among fellow beings throughout the universe. The essence of that power is available to all of us, now, here on Earth today through Neo-Tech. ...Neo-Tech eradicates mysticism — the disease that causes ignorance and death among conscious beings.

AIDS degenerates the body's protective immune system into weakness, sickness, then death; mysticism degenerates the mind's protective thinking system into ignorance, sickness, then death. Mysticism cripples and finally destroys the conscious mind.

But unlike AIDS, an immediate cure exists right now for mysticism and its virus-like neocheaters. That cure is Neo-Tech. Curing mysticism will also bring definitive cures for AIDS, cancer, heart disease, and all other diseases harmful to conscious beings. Neo-Tech forever eradicates mysticism and its symbiotic neocheaters, allowing the individual to direct his or her life toward achieving guiltless prosperity and abiding happiness for self, others, and all society.

Neo-Tech also opens the way for knowledge expanding geometrically to eventually approach the speed of light. Every person applying Neo-Tech, therefore, holds unbeatable advantages over those crippled by mysticism, parasitical elites, and neocheaters. Indeed, Neo-Tech allows human beings to acquire total control over both the material and emotional realms. Neo-Tech gives all human beings on Earth today the power to execute the tripartite commands: "Let there be wealth!", "Let there be romantic love!", "Let there be eternal youth!"

The time has come to grow up...or be left behind to perish in a world of mysticism. Clinging to mystical beliefs such as supreme creators or "higher authorities" is as crippling to human life and prosperity as would be the clinging to the once popular belief that the Earth is flat or today's fading belief that force-backed "authorities" or politicians can advance the well-being of any individual or society.

After 3000 years, the time has come to abandon life-destroying mysticism and all its symbiotic parasites and neocheaters. Now is the time to mature into meeting our responsibility of grooming the supreme value of the universe — our own conscious lives. Now is the time to groom our conscious minds with fully integrated honesty for limitless growth and value production forever into the future. Now is the time to join our fellow conscious beings throughout all existence in meeting our supreme responsibility to life — to live happily, prosperously with our fellow conscious beings throughout eternal existence. *For, we are the creators of all heavens and earths. ...All glory to us conscious beings!*

Appendix I

Miscellaneous Notes

NEOTHINK AND OTHER NEO-TECH INFORMATION

<u>Neothink, the Mind of the Future</u>

The human mind has a limited storage and processing capacity. But Neothink, a discovery made through Neo-Tech, infinitely expands the capacity of consciousness to understand anything in existence. The exchanging of the mystic/conscious mind for the Neo-Tech/Neothink mind will affect mankind even more profoundly than the discovery 3000 years ago of exchanging the bicameral mind for the conscious mind. And, as 3000 years ago, this exchange will occur swiftly, automatically regardless of what anyone does, says, or thinks. The pressure to convert to the Neo-Tech/Neothink integrating mind is competition. Those who do not convert cannot survive. Just as the bicameral mind could not compete and survive 3000 years ago against the conscious mind. Against Neothink, all mystics and neocheaters are finished. They will be ignominiously scorned out of existence.

Neothink develops new concepts over unlimited ranges of integration. That unlimited capacity is accomplished by dividing separate thoughts into two or more separate groups and then building each of those groups toward the maximum capacity of consciousness. Those groups of conscious thoughts can then be swiftly integrated into new units of knowledge and concepts beyond the capacity of the human mind thinking as a single conscious unit. An example of Neothink through such maximum-capacity units is Frank R. Wallace's address titled "The Long Wave" delivered to the Second Neo-Tech World Summit. In that work, many separate maximum-capacity thought units were developed and then integrated into new knowledge far beyond the capacity of any single-unit thought of the conscious mind. Another Neothink work is Mark Hamilton's "The Alternative" presented at the Third Neo-Tech World Summit. That Neothink work combined with practical experience and factual data delivers revolutionary business and management concepts. Those Neothink concepts through their competitive advantages will dominate all future value production.

Appendix I

Miscellaneous Notes

Neothink and Other Neo-Tech Information

Neothink provides entirely different ways to look at nearly every important idea and concept encountered by conscious beings. Since organized neocheating began about 2000 years ago, essentially all ideas and concepts have been integrated with the big-lie hoaxes of mysticism and altruism. Those hoaxes were and are still cleverly designed by neocheaters for usurping their livings from the producers. Thus, what often appears to be two opposite choices in the prevailing mystical/altruistic context are not opposite choices at all. But instead, as revealed by Neothink, those supposed choices are always the same choice. For all such choices are rooted in the same mysticisms and illusions. Those choices are merely presented from different angles of dishonesty.

Neothink shows that the real choice is not between the various Hobson's choices of invalid mysticism, but is always the disintegrated dishonesty of mystics and neocheaters versus the fully integrated honesty of Neo-Tech.

Government Faces

People who live through bogus-jobs backed by force and dominated by the dishonesty and laziness of mysticism are branded with sour faces. Has anyone ever seen a destructive government bureaucrat with a genuinely radiant, happy face? Indeed, such people by nature hate life. For, they live by attacking and destroying values. They want to die and harm everyone in the process.

By contrast, Neo-Tech people live with innocent, clean minds. For, they live through cheerful productivity. They live by producing competitive values for others and society. They want to live and benefit everyone in the process.

Neo-Tech — The Silver Bullet

Laziness versus high-effort value production are the two opposing actions that determine the quality of human life. Ironically, the concepts of laziness and competitive value production are the two concepts most feared, evaded, and distorted by mystics and neocheaters, ranging from Marxist-Leninist murderers to objectivist-libertarian underachievers. Thus, the two aspects of Neo-Tech feared most by mystics and neocheaters are: (1) Neo-Tech's explicit identification of laziness and dishonesty as the root cause of all mysticism and neocheating; and (2) Neo-Tech's explicit identification that the sole moral purpose of human life is abiding happiness, which is achieved only through the competitive production of values for others and society. ...Neo-Tech and business are the antithesis of mysticism and neocheating. Moreover, Neo-Tech is the silver bullet that will end mysticism and neocheating to yield abiding prosperity and happiness for honest, conscious beings.

Neo-Tech Owners May Obtain The Complete
Neo-Tech Reference Encyclopedia

The Neo-Tech Reference Encyclopedia is sold only to owners of the Zonpower/Neo-Tech Discovery. The quarter-million-word Neo-Tech Reference Encyclopedia backs the Neo-Tech Advantages. In addition, that Encyclopedia includes a comprehensive survey of 3000 books of which over 200 are analyzed in detail. Those analyses utilize a rating system that grades every contribution and error in each book. Those analyses also save hundreds of hours in reading time and library searches. Owners of the Zonpower/Neo-Tech Discovery may acquire the complete, 480-page copy of the Neo-Tech Encyclopedia for $99.95 U.S. postpaid (add $10 airmail U.S. and $25 airmail foreign) from **De la Rosa Neo-Tech, 1000 N. Green Valley Parkway, 300-252, Henderson, Nevada 89074 (email: Pltnum7@cox.net).**

A past director of a major, international corporation in New South Wales, Australia, writes:

"The Neo-Tech Discovery is a quantum development from the original Neo-Tech II Reference Encyclopedia. The Neo-Tech Discovery simplifies, clarifies, and updates that work. Indeed, the Neo-Tech Discovery distills all the values from that massive research project into a new, nearly omnipotent elixir of power.

"But the original Encyclopedia includes a definitive survey of over 3000 books written since 2 BC. Summaries were made of 200 books that contained new information and values. And 113 of those books were analyzed in detail. Those analyses along

Appendix I
Miscellaneous Notes
Neothink and Other Neo-Tech Information

with the many practical examples of the original concepts provide
the supporting proofs for the material in the Neo-Tech Discovery.
One can study in-depth the origins of the Neo-Tech Advantages
through that historic Reference Encyclopedia."

Neo-Tech Owners May Obtain The
Original 192-Page Neocheating Manuscript

Neo-Tech scholars may also acquire F. R. Wallace's original
Neocheating manuscript. This manuscript shows the origins of
the Neocheating discovery first uncovered at the fever-pitched
poker tables in Las Vegas. This manuscript includes the
complete details of neocheating in cards with 35 photos
demonstrating the actual Neocheating techniques. Owners of
Neo-Tech may acquire this manuscript for $150.00 U.S. (add
$10 airmail U.S., $15 airmail foreign) from De la Rosa Neo-
Tech at the address shown on the previous page. ...**This book
is not recommended because it is *not needed* to fully
understand or fully apply Neo-Tech beyond the world of
cards.**

Other Miscellaneous Neo-Tech Notes

1) Since the dawn of consciousness, every person who ever
lived must alone make the same life-and-death decision: Each
individual must choose either to kill mysticism within one's own
self or let mysticism kill him or her. Either a person chooses to
live life as one's own natural self through integrated thinking or
surrender life to unnatural mysticism through disintegrated thinking.

Either your natural self or alien mysticism will rule your
personal life. The choice is always yours alone — you or
mysticism, health or sickness, sanity or paranoia, happiness or
misery, life or death.

2) Self-control literally means controlling your own self rather
than letting outside forces (mystics, false authorities, neocheaters)
control your life. Personal freedom, demystification, and prosperity
come through self-discipline and self-effort. That discipline and

324

thought, in turn, delivers control power through the DTC Technique: Discipline, Thought, and then Control.

3) Mysticism involves unfocused, arbitrary thinking. Business involves focused, purposeful thinking.

4) Mysticism is suicide. Such suicide occurs on all levels — on personal, national, or world levels. That suicide occurs rapidly or slowly, depending on the form and intensity of mysticism. ...Business is life on all levels, at all times.

5) Dealing with a person acting mystically is harmful. Dealing with a person in a mystical mode will, at best, waste your time...at worst, such dealings can cost your life.

6) One of the most fundamental Neo-Tech integrations is that of time with life. The wasting of time is the wasting of life. The more one moves toward dishonest mystical/neocheating-like actions, the less important time becomes to one's life. By contrast, the more one moves toward honest Neo-Tech/business-like actions, the more important time becomes to one's life and happiness. ...Mystics and neocheaters kill life and happiness by wasting or destroying time of others.

Japanese philosopher, Y. Kimura, made the following identification about the value of time for the value producer:

"For a producer of values, his time — every moment of his life — has a significance far beyond his immediate life. An hour wasted has a compounded effect on, in essence, everyone on this planet. For a producer of values, his personal life is, in actuality, public and even cosmic."

7) Professor Rosa María Meoño from Costa Rica made the essence identification about all mysticism and business:

"Mysticism creates problems where none exist."
and the corollary:
"Business eliminates problems that do exist."

THE BUSINESS OF I & O

The sole business of I & O Publishing Company is to cure the disease of mysticism and eliminate its symbiotic neocheaters worldwide.

THE GOAL OF I & O

The sole goal of I & O Publishing Company is to end the 2000-year hoax of mysticism and eliminate neocheating in order to achieve non-aging biological immortality with prosperity and happiness for all value producers — forever.

LINKING INSTRUCTIONS
for
Neo-Tech II (Neo-Tech Advantages)
with
<u>Special Information Packages</u>
Neo-Tech I (Prediscovery)
Neo-Tech III (Ending Mysticism)
Neo-Tech IV (Business and Stock Prices)
Neo-Tech V (Ultimate Power)

NEO-TECH INSTRUCTIONS

by a
Neo-Tech Reader

I failed to realize the magnitude of the Neo-Tech Discovery and the personal benefits it could deliver until I finished reading the entire volume. On first receiving Neo-Tech and putting it on my desk, I contemplated the contents. Then while opening the cover, a feeling swept over me that I was embarking on a journey from which I would never return. Several weeks later, on closing that mighty volume, I sat stunned. I knew my mind had been impregnated with the most powerful information on earth. I knew how to capture personal and competitive advantages from almost any situation. I had discovered a new world in which power flowed into me as Neo-Tech melted the grip of external authority with all its draining neocheaters. Today, I control my life and surroundings. I now understand what is happening and can guiltlessly take whatever I want from life. Moreover, I now have a growing power that no one can take from me.

Still, I was unprepared for the journey I was about to take: First, I was shocked on realizing how nearly every important belief

327

impressed on me and most other people since childhood originated from parasitical people called neocheaters who drain our lives daily without our consent or knowledge. I was shocked on discovering how easily many of the most widely accepted beliefs collapse into nothing in the light of Neo-Tech. But I was especially shocked on how easily the power of those neocheaters could be transferred from them to me by using Neo-Tech. With Neo-Tech, my efforts deliver rewards to me, not to them. Neo-Tech showed me that it is I who count, not they. I hold the power, not they.

PART A
PREPARING FOR NEO-TECH

Even after carefully preparing for Neo-Tech, I was still overwhelmed by its concepts and advantages. What had kept Neo-Tech from being discovered earlier? My question was answered when I finished reading the entire volume. But to fully grasp the sweeping scope of Neo-Tech, I knew more than one reading plus a lot of honest thinking would be needed.

Yet, what about the other people being newly exposed to Neo-Tech? How will they take the shock of Neo-Tech? How can they handle all the advantages, power, and responsibility thrust upon them by Neo-Tech? How could my experience help those reading Neo-Tech for the first time? After reading the Neo-Tech Advantages in careful page-by-page order, I realized that people could benefit by first understanding how the Neo-Tech volumes link together. I am writing these instructions to explain those linkages.

Linking Neo-Tech Volumes I and II

Information in Neo-Tech I, the Prediscovery, can make anyone unbeatable — even wealthy — if he chooses to play cards. But, like me, most readers have no interest in cards; they are interested in profiting from Neo-Tech in the real world. In fact, most people do not even need to read the Neo-Tech Prediscovery to understand neocheaters, to understand how they operate in all areas of life, to understand how they drain the uninformed, everywhere, constantly. And no one really needs the Prediscovery to understand

Instructions for Linking Neo-Tech I, II, III, IV, and V

and apply the Neo-Tech Advantages to real-life situations.

But by initially examining Neo-Tech in a concrete, mechanical activity like cards, certain concepts become more quickly and clearly understood. For example, by understanding neocheating in cards, a person can more readily identify and nullify neocheaters in other activities such as business, social relationships, religion, and government.

Many Neo-Tech concepts differ radically from conventional thinking — especially those concepts that apply to everyday situations such as identified in volume II. As a result, I encountered those concepts with such shock that my long-accepted, mystical illusions blocked my recognition of the most dramatic and valuable Neo-Tech breakthroughs. In fact, on first examining volume II, I was shaken by the consecutive unraveling of specific concepts that shattered my strongest beliefs. Indeed, at times, I wanted to turn and run. Why? Because I was protecting my own personal mysticisms that were draining my power and diminishing my life.

After integrating all the concepts in volume II, something marvelous happened: Years of endured suffering and silent frustration faded as I learned to identify and nullify professional mystics and neocheaters who usurp wealth, power, and prestige by draining me and everyone else. But now I feel power — great power. ...I also feel awe and astonishment as I apply the Neo-Tech concepts.

Links Between Neo-Tech Volumes I and II
Some of the links between Neo-Tech I and II are summarized below:
VOLUME I — THE NEO-TECH PREDISCOVERY
•Contrasts dishonest black-hat neocheaters to honest white-hat Neo-Tech practitioners.

•Because neocheaters depend on deception, their power has no foundation or validity. And because their existence is parasitical, they constantly diminish their own competence and self-esteem.

•Neocheaters exist by draining uninformed victims and depend on them remaining uninformed.

Instructions for Linking Neo-Tech I, II, III, IV, and V

•When everyone is informed about Neo-Tech, neocheaters will lose their power and vanish.

•The concepts of Neo-Tech versus neocheating apply to everyday life.

VOLUME II — THE NEO-TECH ADVANTAGES

•Neo-Tech II exposes black-hat neocheaters in the real world: The *master* black-hat neocheater continuously drains prosperity and happiness from the masses of uninformed victims while steadily increasing his or her own unearned wealth, power, and control in futile attempts to gain feelings of self worth. Indeed, for centuries, master black-hat neocheaters have flourished under the guise of external "authority". And at times, they are among the most admired citizens; they are among politicians and high-officials of all kinds, prominent media and entertainment people, prestigious professors, religious leaders, white-collar-hoax business quislings as well as certain bankers and lawyers who strive to enhance their bogus livelihoods by draining values rather than producing values. They victimize the uninformed while disguising their own neocheating natures.

While Neo-Tech I removes the neocheaters' disguises, Neo-Tech II renders those value destroyers powerless. As the facts about them are revealed, they lose their false authority and unearned power. With Neo-Tech II, ordinary people can take their rightful power — can guiltlessly collect their earned wealth and happiness by using Neo-Tech to reclaim their power from all neocheaters.

•All black-hat neocheaters operate on the same principle: usurp values, power, and respect from the innocent, from the uninformed.

•The power of black-hat neocheaters is not real or self-sustaining. They produce no values that others would knowingly choose to buy; they simply extract unearned livings by neocheating the uninformed.

Instructions for Linking Neo-Tech I, II, III, IV, and V

•The only reason neocheaters have authority or power is because the ordinary person unknowingly hands over that power to them at his or her own expense. But now the ordinary person can reclaim that power by using the knowledge in Neo-Tech II.

Linking Volumes I – V

To understand the linkages among Neo-Tech volumes I – V is to grasp the super-wide integrations of Neo-Tech. The power of those integrations lies in the logical connections of seemingly different subjects such as the bicameral mind, politics, neocheating, religion, poker strategy, business, money, social life, psychuous sex, and romantic love. In turn, those subjects are then linked into an all-encompassing, unassailable matrix that delivers unbeatable advantages in all areas of personal, business, and financial life. Those seemingly disparate subjects are harmoniously linked together and controlled by one all-powerful matrix of integrated Neo-Tech concepts. Through those linkages, Neo-Tech Cosmic Power becomes the most powerful tool for generating personal power, wealth, and happiness not only since the Industrial Revolution, but since man became conscious 3000 years ago.

Consider the origins of Neo-Tech: poker strategy and card cheating. How do those origins relate to neocheaters, most attorneys, bureaucrats, congressmen, certain prestigious professors, well-known actors and actresses, evangelists, TV commentators, fake nutritionists, fake environmentalists? And more important, how do card strategy and cheating link to personal prosperity and happiness? They link metaphorically. By understanding those linking metaphors, the Neo-Tech techniques begin integrating with all situations in everyday life to deliver great values, prosperity, and happiness — now and forever into the future.

Neo-Tech I — Neocheating

The Neo-Tech Prediscovery reveals the origins of two opposites — neocheating and Neo-Tech. In the process, Neo-Tech I shows (to those interested) how to become unbeatable at cards. But much more important, the Neo-Tech Prediscovery provides the clearest understanding of those invisible or undetectable techniques used to gain unbeatable advantages beyond the card tables — where power really counts.

Through poker strategy and neocheating, the Neo-Tech Prediscovery reveals the maneuvers master neocheaters use for controlling and draining others. The best way to understand those maneuvers is through metaphors. For example, the following question is asked and then answered: "What positive values can be found in card cheating?" One important value: "Card cheating is a vivid metaphor for identifying and classifying dishonest people..." Using that metaphor lets one clearly identify all types of dishonest people from sneak thieves to elegant con artists, from small-time politicians on-the-take to Presidents of the United States and fact-twisting scientists who win Nobel prizes, from sleazy business quislings to pip-squeak bureaucrats who live by harming the value producers. ...The Neo-Tech Prediscovery demonstrates how the shrewdest, big-time neocheaters are always destructive menaces to honest productive people everywhere.

The Neo-Tech Prediscovery not only shows how Neo-Tech nullifies cheaters everywhere, but how Neo-Tech lets one profit in most situations, including those in which neocheaters constantly drain everyone.

Using Metaphors to Understand Neocheating

Because Dr. Wallace originally discovered neocheating in cards and because neocheating techniques are more vividly illustrated through cards, most of the specific examples in Neo-Tech I are written with a card slant. By contrast, all the specific examples in Neo-Tech II apply to everyday real-life situations beyond cards. Still, the analogies with the neocheating concepts in Neo-Tech I provide the basis from which Neo-Tech ideas are developed for business, the professions, social situations, and other real-life situations. For example, the reader will quickly learn that many respected authoritarian figures are in reality nothing more than neocheaters orchestrating big-lie hoaxes. But some neocheaters are exceptionally intelligent people who could have produced permanent values to benefit others and society, resulting in great rewards and happiness for themselves and everyone else. (1) So what happened? And (2) how does one explain intelligent, ambitious people negating their values and sense of worth by becoming black-hat neocheaters?

The answers to those two questions above become strikingly clear by drawing analogies to various card cheaters described in Neo-Tech I. Then Neo-Tech II takes analogous information and recasts it into situations not involving cards to answer those two questions.

An Analogy

Imagine a bright, young person striving for a value-producing career to enhance his future. But in his pursuit for a productive career — law for example — he comes in constant contact with neocheating establishments that seem to garner easy power and profit. At the same time, he is increasingly discouraged in his pursuit by external "authorities", mystics, and neocheaters who disparage and undermine his honest efforts while subtly penalizing him for his values and virtues.

Struggling to produce values in a world being constantly drained by neocheaters, such a person can gradually, easily surrender to any one of the many "friendly" neocheating establishments encircling his personal life and profession. Those establishments offer easy, non-productive routes to respect, power, and wealth. That person learns to rationalize their surreptitious techniques as required trade or survival tools (e.g., deceiving others to create problems where none exist in order to gain unearned power, money, favors). Consequently, that person's feelings of self-worth diminish.

As that person gains advantages from neocheating establishments and adopts their techniques, he becomes increasingly dependent on their ploys. He loses his independence and becomes a stereotyped professional "authority"— he becomes one of them — he becomes a neocheater. With a sense of professional righteousness, he becomes a dishonest lawyer who lives through camouflaged value destructions — he becomes a

333

clever troublemaker — he becomes a black-hat neocheater.

Not only do such practitioners falsely justify or expertly rationalize their neocheating, but the more they gain by neocheating, the more they try to create images of importance or superiority, while actually feeling increasingly inferior.

In a sense, all chronic or professional neocheaters are ruled by their dependencies on destructive ploys. But today, any value producer with Neo-Tech knowledge can quickly reduce such neocheaters to their impotent, worthless nature. Neo-Tech can defend against, even profit from, any neocheating ploy.

Neo-Tech II — Psychuous Concepts

What is Psychuous? What are those money, power, and romantic-love concepts about? How do they relate to Neo-Tech? How does all that tie together?

At first glance, the flood of new concepts might appear unrelated. But all concepts are linked to various personal characteristics within individuals. And on continued reading, one will sense incredible connections: Neocheaters are not only precisely "fingerprinted", but are easily controllable. How? Through specific patterns of personal and sexual characteristics (physical, psychological, philosophical, and sexual characteristics) integrated together into what Dr. Wallace identified as the Psychuous concepts.

The Psychuous concepts reveal that productive individuals are also specifically "fingerprinted" and controllable through entirely different patterns of personal and sexual characteristics. Indeed, on reading the Neo-Tech/Psychuous Advantages in page-by-page order, the concepts will begin falling into a powerful pattern, direction, and theme. The Neo-Tech/Psychuous concepts reveal the inverse relationship between mysticism and happiness. Neo-Tech II makes a person aware of neocheaters. Neo-Tech II lets a person withdraw power from those neocheaters to eventually gain much greater power and prosperity than neocheaters can ever achieve.

Until Neo-Tech, master neocheaters have been the only people fully conscious of neocheating. With almost all productive people being unconscious of neocheating, the master

Instructions for Linking Neo-Tech I, II, III, IV, and V

neocheaters became powercrats simply by letting their usurped power and fake prestige grow at the expense of value producers. Today, as throughout history, those neocheaters present themselves as valid, external "authorities" who benefit their followers and society. In reality, however, they benefit no one. Instead, they exist entirely by draining productive people at the expense of all society.

One purpose of the Neo-Tech/Psychuous concepts is to reveal neocheating in everyday situations so that the reader can claim the power and rewards that are rightfully his or hers. Without Neo-Tech/Psychuous knowledge, elements of neocheating and mysticism will gradually infiltrate and subtly take over personal, business, and social situations. But from advantage to advantage, Neo-Tech II systematically exposes the professional mystics, external authorities, and other neocheaters, allowing the value producer to avoid their harm while profiting beyond all previous expectations.

Psychuous Concepts for Personal Benefit

Neo-Tech II reveals those tools for controlling the actions of oneself and others through the universal motivations of personal well being, prosperity, sex, and happiness. That control is necessary not only for gaining profitable advantages from any situation, but for avoiding the draining ploys of professional mystics and other neocheaters.

Neo-Tech II uses the Psychuous Concepts as a metaphorical vehicle for breaking free from the burdens foisted on everyone by those neocheaters. The links between Neo-Tech I and II become obvious when the neocheaters listed in Neo-Tech II come alive with specific examples throughout the many Neo-Tech/Psychuous concepts. Every reader will discover hundreds of specific methods to (1) become a powerful person, (2) identify neocheaters, (3) handle them, (4) profit from them.

Neo-Tech II reveals 114 Neo-Tech Advantages that apply to real-life situations while showing the reader how to profit from each situation. To gain full value from Neo-Tech II, the volume must be read in page-by-page order. If read out of order or out of context, some concepts will mislead readers into erroneous

Instructions for Linking Neo-Tech I, II, III, IV, and V

prejudgments.

The reader may reach a point at which the Neo-Tech Advantages seem overwhelming, almost unbelievable, even though each advantage is consistently logical, simple, and practical. What made some concepts seem unbelievable was the following question: How could an entire civilization remain so oblivious, for so long, to the Neo-Tech concepts?

Years ago, Dr. Wallace reintegrated the works of Dr. Julian Jaynes, a Princeton University psychology professor. Dr. Jaynes discovered two minds in human beings: (1) the human conscious mind as an invented process that allows one to develop independent power through the self-guidance of integrated thinking and (2) nature's bicameral mind as a natural process that constantly seeks guidance through external signals or "authorities". That understanding of consciousness versus the bicameral mind provided Dr. Wallace with the answer as to why Neo-Tech had not been discovered until now. And subsequently, that understanding led to Wallace's development of Neo-Tech III, IV, V, and finally Neothink.

Neo-Tech III — the End of Authority

Dr. Wallace defines external "authority" as any person or thing, real or imagined, that controls any portion of another person's life, with or without that person's consent.

Neo-Tech III identifies the tool that external "authorities" have used for 2000 years to gain power over productive individuals. That tool is the reason why external "authorities" and neocheaters are so easily accepted by their victims. ...That tool is called the bicameral mind.

Remnants of the bicameral mind exist in every human brain. Those remnants cause a desire for guidance by outside or external "authorities". But Neo-Tech III dissolves the strongest, most cherished beliefs of the bicameral mind...beliefs that valid, external "authorities" exist. That dissolution of external authorities gives a person control over his or her life. With that personal control, an individual is protected from being drained by mystics, external "authorities", and other neocheaters.

Instructions for Linking Neo-Tech I, II, III, IV, and V

Neo-Tech IV — Predicting Stock Prices

As identified in Neo-Tech Information Packages I – III, the Neo-Tech principles can determine the value or disvalue of any individual. Neo-Tech IV applies those principles to determine the value or disvalue of any company, business, management, or employee. A person can use those same principles for being successful in business and for accurately predicting the long-range, common-stock value of any company.

Neo-Tech V — the Greatest Value

Neo-Tech V not only identifies the greatest value possible to any conscious productive individual, but reveals how to achieve that value.

PART B
THE DEVELOPMENT OF NEO-TECH

The following edited notes trace the prediscovery of neocheating in cards through the later development of the Neo-Tech Discovery in all areas of life. These notes provide an understanding of the profound difference between dishonest Neocheating and honest Neo-Tech. Tracing through the initial, incomplete understanding of Neo-Tech, these notes also demonstrate the power of applying Neo-Tech to everyday situations to nullify all Neocheaters. ...The countdown begins 2245 days before presenting the Neo-Tech Discovery to the public:

Day Minus 2245

I've discovered the never-before-revealed nature of effortless winning while playing cards. This discovery purges the false notions about winning and eliminates its mystical aura. While identifying the origins of that knowledge, I'm grasping its powerful nature.

I feel an addicting power as I begin to do the seemingly impossible. With ease I can make maneuvers to beat all opponents. The techniques come from an ominous new knowledge. ...I've named this discovery, this new knowledge, *Neocheating*.

Instructions for Linking Neo-Tech I, II, III, IV, and V

Day Minus 2215

Neocheating is something new — something frightening. I'm astonished at the quickness that I'm learning to win so effortlessly — all in a few days. I feel uneasy about that. With this lethal knowledge, think what a person could do to his opponents in a matter of days.

Day Minus 2185

Neocheating can be executed in peace, without the knowledge of others. I've discovered effective maneuvers for controlling every outcome of every situation. Neocheating is almost too easy and safe, yet it is an unbeatable form of winning. Indeed, the simpler and subtler the technique, the easier and safer and, therefore, the more effective it is. ...Neocheating renders all other cheating ploys so obsolete that such cheating is no longer an important threat.

Anyone can quickly become a player who cannot lose. Indeed, through Neocheating, an average player can increase his advantage so greatly that he can break most games at will. He can win fast — very fast. He can acquire large amounts of money, $2,000, $10,000, or more in a single day, repeatedly. But he avoids winning too fast by withholding the full power of Neocheating in order to extract maximum, long-term money from opponents. He fears no opponent.

While fearing this knowledge, I'm glad to be discovering Neocheating before anyone else. And I feel the responsibility. Already I have the knowledge to quietly beat even the most skilled and experienced opponents. This knowledge allows the ordinary player to control opponents at will.

Day Minus 2155

I've discovered easy ways to nullify moves made by opponents. I'm struck by the importance of understanding Neocheating. Anyone can use that understanding to prosper in situations involving money. I sense that this new knowledge could be incredibly potent beyond the card tables.

Still I keep discovering more and more invisible techniques that deliver unbeatable advantages in all activities. But I'm thinking more deeply of how this new discovery applies everywhere, from presidents in manipulating domestic and world politics down to the consumer advocate extracting a living from the value producers he is harming. I'm grasping how certain concepts of Neocheating can be used honestly — without cheating — to gain wealth and power in business and personal life.

Day Minus 2075

With this knowledge, what could a person do in the real world without the boundaries of a card game? Who is the Neocheater? He is an ordinary-appearing person who will not just rule the card tables but perhaps the world. A chill spreads over me. The more closely uninformed people observe a Neocheater, the more reassured they become. The real-world Neocheater appears as a most trustworthy person. But he knows exactly how to win. He can bankrupt opponents, yet instead, he creates advantages that remain unnoticeable to his opponents while delivering maximum, long-range profits to himself. Quietly he applies his power in small, strategic doses to gain steady advantages and profits while keeping everyone happy. Thus, the Neocheater is impossible to stop and is hard to avoid. With such subtle yet unbeatable advantages, he can comfortably and *legally* control all aspects of life. Indeed, the Neocheater is so effective that he obsoletes traditional real-world cheaters. In fact, the Neocheater displays characteristics opposite to those of cheaters as my comparison chart reveals (see next page):

Instructions for Linking Neo-Tech I, II, III, IV, and V

CONTRASTING CHARACTERISTICS

The Traditional Cheater	The Neocheater
Tries to set odds overwhelmingly in his favor	Sets odds unnoticeably in his favor
Strives for big-killing, today	Strives for continuous, steady profits over months and years.
Wants to wipe out victims quickly	Wants to keep comrades going and paying indefinitely
Big-win approach, one-shot or short-range oriented	Maximum-win approach, steady or long-range oriented
Views opponents as enemies	Views opponents as assets
Often makes victims unhappy while creating tense, traumatic atmospheres	Usually makes everyone happy and dependent while creating trusting, relaxed atmospheres
Often stiff and nervous	Usually relaxed and confident
"When should I do it" feeling	Knows exactly when to Neocheat
Cheats at every opportunity. Keeps people from watching him closely. Uses distractions and concealments	Neocheats selectively. Lets people watch him. Needs no distractions or concealments
Causes suspicion with cheating moves	Eliminates suspicions with Neocheating moves
Fears all opponents. Malevolent appearing. Alienates opponents.	Fears no one. Benevolent appearing. Makes opponents dependent on him.
Worries that his cheating will be seen	Knows that Neocheating cannot be seen
Fears his telltale, unnatural characteristics	Works in relaxed harmony with his natural characteristics
Worries about the consequences of being caught in the act	Knows he cannot be caught in any act
Is negative in every way	Appears beneficial in every way
Is controlled by surroundings	Controls surroundings

Instructions for Linking Neo-Tech I, II, III, IV, and V

Their characteristics are opposites — the Neocheater is in complete control. But their differences go much further: Alert or knowledgeable people can usually detect cheating, especially in business and politics — unless the cheater has acquired great skill through years of laborious practice and experience. Even then, the expert cheater must execute each strategy perfectly, every time, putting him under great pressure. Thus, if he makes one slip or one wrong move to get caught, he becomes obviously guilty, leaving him to face the disgraceful, dangerous consequences. That fear of being caught haunts most cheaters and overwhelms countless potential cheaters. By contrast, the Neocheater's techniques are invisible. So, even if suspected, he can never be accused — his tactics actually eliminate suspicion. Indeed, he can always avoid the consequences because he can never be caught in any questionable act. ...The Neocheater works in relaxed harmony with his natural characteristics. That is the real danger of Neocheating.

Day Minus 2025

Because Neocheating is so subtle, no one can ever prove a person is using its techniques. The Neocheater has the power to render others helpless, even wipe them out, but he wisely chooses to use just enough of his power to give him unbeatable, casino-like advantages in all endeavors. His Neocheating maneuvers are so subtle that they can be executed with casual confidence. His hidden techniques let him win consistently and comfortably — year after year, decade after decade. He even forgets that he is cheating. Indeed, he even begins feeling benevolent and respectful.

Eventually, Neocheaters may quietly rule everywhere as revealed by my next chart. That chart shows how a person gains unearned advantages and false power from Neocheating in the real world where advantages and power really count (see next page):

Neo-Tech Power

Instructions for Linking Neo-Tech I, II, III, IV, and V

NEOCHEATING TEACHES

In Cards	In The Real World
(Where Neocheating was first discovered)	(Where Neocheating is the biggest threat)
How to become an unbeatable winner	How to usurp advantages needed for financial and social success
How to command winnings	How to wangle profits and respect
How to control any player, game, or network of games	How to politically control deals and emotional situations to acquire money and power
How to win quickly	How to profit through specific political actions, religious ploys, or personal relationships
How to slowly drain opponents, game after game	How to gain strategic advantages that allow one to win in business, political, or personal situations, year after year
How to extract maximum money from opponents	How to extract maximum advantages from others.
How to easily detect, reject, or beat cheaters without any hassle...how to destroy cheaters	How to easily detect, reject, or beat dishonesty in business or personal relationships. How to vanquish people who block you.
How to quickly wipe out opponents	How to subjugate a business or personal adversary
How to welcome good players and make them contribute to your winnings	How to welcome competitors in business or personal life and make them contribute to your success
How to gain a substantial income, year after year	How to prosper, year after year

342

Instructions for Linking Neo-Tech I, II, III, IV, and V

Day Minus 2045

Neocheating in cards is dishonest; it involves extracting easy money and power from opponents through techniques that meet two criteria: (1) easy to execute, and (2) invisible or undetectable. Neocheating outside cards is also dishonest; it involves deceptively gaining easy advantages and power over others by meeting two similar criteria: (1) easy to execute, and (2) not vulnerable to detection or assailable as dishonest.

Once those two criteria are established, Neocheating formats can be established for almost any situation. With such formats, a person not only captures unbeatable advantages over others, but commands shortcuts to profits and power. I'm realizing how many of the most wealthy, powerful, and admired people today consistently use Neocheating formats without ever realizing it — without ever being suspected. Those people are professional mystics and Neocheaters. They acquire extreme power and wealth. Such people include trusted heads of states, powerful political leaders, charismatic idols, famous religious leaders, many of the best-known TV commentators, key journalists, influential editorial writers, Hollywood actors and actresses, many well-known authors, certain prestigious professors, many successful lawyers, certain deified doctors, highly visible nutritionists, environmentalists, union leaders, consumer advocates, and certain politically or socially oriented scientists — many of the most powerful people in the world.

Yet, very few neocheaters are found among successful business people, industrialists, or professionals involved in producing and delivering objective values. Still, unless some method to stop neocheaters is discovered within the next decade, most people who become wealthy or powerful in any field will have used this discovery. ...I've got to think about Neocheating more deeply.

Day Minus 2015

Neocheating sharply reduces the time and effort to profit consistently. What is happening in cards today indicates what will happen in the real world tomorrow. Within days after gaining this knowledge, people can safely bankrupt opponents — or slowly profit from them, week after week.

People can extract money and prestige from any winning situation — from any card game — from the easiest Friday-night game to the toughest professional game.

Likewise, people can benefit from financial endeavors — from dealing with the boss to major financial deals. People can also benefit from any relationship — from gaining respect of peers to inducing love from a partner. Yet no one suspects the Neocheaters.

The application of Neocheating to everyday financial and personal relationships is becoming increasingly real. In fact, Neocheating can be used in any confrontation or competitive situation involving two or more people. And anyone who crosses the Neocheater's path is in potential danger. The Neocheater can financially and emotionally control whomever he or she desires. The strength and dimensions of Neocheating with its infinite applications reach far beyond my previous thoughts.

Day Minus 1885

I feel an accelerating pull towards power as I continually discover new ways that anyone can apply this new knowledge to any competitive situation — in business, politics, gaming, personal and social life. But I am sensing different types of shortcuts never known to me before — shortcuts that no one could perceive without first identifying and understanding Neocheating. Yet these new shortcuts are totally different from those of Neocheating — they are actually the antithesis of Neocheating. In fact, these new shortcuts take a form all their own...a form previously unknown...a totally honest, much more powerful form. Could this be the power to stop Neocheating?

Day Minus 1855

I keep thinking over and over how discovering these new techniques or shortcuts first required an understanding, then a complete inversion of the Neocheating principles. That inversion revealed the greatest power possible to man — powerful shortcuts to a prosperous, happy life. ...No wonder the ideas of the past and previously promoted shortcuts never could reveal the great secrets to success — the real shortcuts.

Those shortcuts have greater power than I ever thought possible: power dramatically true to man's nature — consummate power that is far greater than possessed by any Neocheater, even any Master Neocheater. And all of these new techniques and shortcuts are completely honest while ironically requiring less skill and effort than the Neocheating techniques.

This discovery compresses those new shortcuts in all areas into one unified, diamond-like format. That single unit or matrix is generating a whole new field of knowledge that will let not only powerful people but any ordinary person take control — awesome control — over every money, power, and personal situation. This could be the most dramatic discovery of our time. ...I've named this discovery, this new knowledge, *Neo-Tech*.

Day Minus 1815

I am now realizing that Neo-Tech is the most important discovery of our time. Never before did ordinary people have access to the shortcuts previously available to the world's most powerful people. But now those shortcuts in much more effective formats can become available to every one who learns of Neo-Tech. And much more than that, this discovery solidifies those previously exclusive shortcuts into a single matrix that keeps generating Neo-Tech — keeps generating brand-new knowledge. This new knowledge lets anyone, from the world's money giants to ordinary people, gain unstoppable advantages not only in the highest powered situations but in everyday, routine situations confronted by everyone. Neo-Tech has no limitations. ...Anyone knowledgeable about Neo-Tech can happily prosper forever into the future.

Day Minus 730

After four years of research and writing, I've come to realize that Neo-Tech power is permanent and once acquired can never be lost. Neo-Tech obsoletes external authority and renders

Instructions for Linking Neo-Tech I, II, III, IV, and V

Neocheaters impotent. With Neo-Tech, anyone can become the person he or she has always dreamed of — the person he or she was meant to be.

Day Minus 0
I'm learning the full meaning of Neo-Tech power. All will yield to the Neo-Tech man and woman. ...Great days are coming.

Current Comments
Every day I see and hear of Neo-Tech bringing personal power and financial prosperity to those acquiring its knowledge in this country and in over 140 countries abroad. I am witnessing the beginning of a new era with the escalating prosperity power of Neo-Tech men and women. Those without the tools of Neo-Tech, no matter where they live, will gradually become uncompetitive in every situation, left behind not knowing what is happening. ...Neo-Tech is the fast-track ticket to tomorrow's prosperity.

In fact, Neo-Tech is the only ticket to tomorrow's prosperity.

PART C
FUTURE VALUES FOR NEO-TECH OWNERS

Neocheating and Mysticism versus Neo-Tech.
•Neocheating is the purposeful manipulation of mysticism to usurp values earned by others.

•Mysticism is the deceptive tool used by neocheaters to defraud or steal values from others. Rationalizing to avoid the effort required to act in concert with reality is self-imposed mysticism. That in turn is manipulating one's own self. Traits of those who impose mysticism upon themselves are (1) fearing self-responsibility, (2) avoiding honest, integrated thinking, (3) projecting their problems onto others, (4) evading the fact that each person alone determines his or her own future, prosperity, and happiness, and (5) practicing dishonesty and laziness. Their self-imposed mysticism blocks and atrophies their abilities to identify and integrate reality with their thoughts and actions. As a result, they know less and less about what is really happening. Thus, they become increasingly incompetent and vulnerable to external "authorities" and other neocheaters. That is why all external "authorities" and neocheaters must constantly dupe the value producer into accepting mysticism. To survive, the neocheater must constantly usurp values from those producers trapped in his array of mystical hoaxes.

•Neo-Tech is the gaining of unbeatable advantages in competitive situations by (1) reducing or eliminating mysticism in one's self and (2) rejecting mystical influences from others. ...With Neo-Tech, intense focus is directed toward integrating all facts with context and honesty. Why? To understand accurately and then act consistently with objective reality. With mysticism, all effort is directed toward rationalizing non sequiturs or deceptions in order to satisfy some arbitrary feeling, wish, or whim of self or some external "authority". ...Neo-Tech is rooted in productive honesty and effort. Neo-Tech creates and builds values. Neo-Tech is anchored in reality. Mysticism is rooted in destructive dishonesty and laziness. Mysticism consumes and shrinks values. Mysticism floats in random nothingness.

Protection from Neocheaters

Only after discovering the concepts of Neocheating (volume I) and then the Neo-Tech/Psychuous Concepts (volume II) could effective methods be developed to:

• render impotent neocheaters, mystics, and mysticism.

• harness the power to prosper continuously and live happily. That power resides in everyone but is experienced by so few.

Throughout history, productive individuals have been too absorbed in earning their livings to discover, much less understand, parasites living off the efforts of others. But that parasitism will end with Neo-Tech.

With Neo-Tech, productive people will discover for the first time how the mystics, external "authorities", and other neocheaters have relentlessly drained prosperity and happiness from all value producers.

Instructions for Linking Neo-Tech I, II, III, IV, and V

A Notice to Neo-Tech Owners

Neo-Tech explicitly shows how to eliminate harmful influences of mysticism and dismiss all neocheaters. Neo-Tech protects one from:

1. being harmed by neocheaters such as value-destroying mystics, bureaucrats, politicians, clerics, lawyers.
2. being drained by various instruments of neocheating such as government and religion.

Neo-Tech ends all the neocheating ploys that drain the only positive force in existence — the competitive value producer.

After reading Neo-Tech II, one will realize the personal importance of this new information. For, this information precisely identifies every kind of person, belief, and institution that harms people. This information also reveals the weakness of professional mystics and neocheaters when confronted with Neo-Tech. ...Neo-Tech offers the ultimate power and protection in shifting all power and prosperity from the neocheaters back to the competitive value producer.

After reading Neo-Tech I-V, a person will know that he or she is not alone in claiming a guiltless right to prosperity and happiness. And after reviewing the next section, which provides the comments from early Neo-Tech owners, one will know that thousands of other individuals in 50 states and 150 countries are relentlessly gaining power and prosperity through the Neo-Tech Discovery.

Mysticism and neocheating are and always have been the only forces diminishing human beings. With Neo-Tech, a person can demolish those forces to prosper guiltlessly, personally, financially, romantically — forever...

A Notice to Professional Value Destroyers

You know who you are. So do we. And as Neo-Tech becomes public knowledge over the next few years, your every attempt to extract a living by undermining values produced by others will reveal who you are. You will be dismissed by value producers all over the world. You will never trick Neo-Tech people with your deceptions, rationalizations, and non sequiturs. Your days of living off others are numbered. Your every destructive act will speed your own demise. So why not, while you have the opportunity, consider Neo-Tech? You will discover something wonderful: You too can escape that enfeebling mystical trap. You too can experience the unlimited prosperity and happiness available to every Neo-Tech person. Knowledge of Neo-Tech could be your moment of recognition — a final chance — your turning point to prosperity, happiness, and romantic love.

Mystical versus Mystic-Free Approach

Every conscious person must choose between two approaches to every thought and action: (1) the mystical approach or (2) the mystic-free approach:

The Mystical Approach is the dishonest use of rationalized thoughts, non sequiturs, feelings, desires, and external "authorities" as the guide to knowledge and action leading either to the destruction of values or to nothing.

The Mystic-Free Approach is the exertion of self-discipline, self-responsibility, conscious effort, and the honest integrated thinking needed to identify reality and facts in their widest, most accurate context. Such facts are needed to know and execute the actions leading to prosperity and happiness. ...Neo-Tech *is* the mystic-free approach to every conscious act.

Orientation

As one discovers after reading volumes II-V, Neo-Tech is not only the greatest money/power/romantic-love discovery ever, but Neo-Tech offers the greatest value possible to human beings — a limitless future of power, prosperity, and romantic love. How does Neo-Tech deliver that value? Neo-Tech provides many specific values that deliver immediate advantages and profits. But Neo-Tech delivers the greatest of all values by removing a negative — the pervasive negative of mysticism. ...Removing that negative unleashes the power of Neo-Tech.

How does removing a negative deliver such values and power? Consider the great untapped positives already dwelling in most individuals: All such individuals would flourish through their natural, positive values if they were not crippled by a single negative — the disease of mysticism.

Consider that every living organism by nature will flourish to its potential within the environment that organism was intended to live. But if an organism exists in a destructive, unnatural environment (a distorted reality) crippled by a disease (mysticism), that disease causes the organism to eventually die. Indeed, no amount of extolling positive values will make that organism flourish. But if the disease is eliminated (e.g., mysticism eliminated by Neo-Tech), then that organism will flourish toward its full potential, which for human beings with their open-ended consciousness is unlimited.

Neo-Tech II demonstrates that mysticism is a pervasive, socio-psychological disease that has drained prosperity, happiness, and life itself from all men and women for 2000 years.

* * *

Imagine if you always knew exactly what was happening, exactly what to do. You would then be in control of every situation and have great advantages. ...Now consider Neo-Tech: It eliminates the insanity of mysticism to let you know exactly what is happening, exactly what to do, giving you maximum advantages in all situations. Read Neo-Tech, understand it, use it. Experience for yourself how Neo-Tech delivers a future of unending growth — a future of genuine power, prosperity, and romantic love.

Negative Reactions to Neo-Tech

The steady flow of strong reactions to Neo-Tech is not surprising. Also, not surprising but always revealing are the reactions of those people threatened by Neo-Tech. Occasionally, such people obtain copies of Neo-Tech even though, as stated in all its advertising, I & O Publishing Company refuses and rejects orders from pushers of mysticism, neocheaters, and all other professional value destroyers. I & O also rejects returns from mystics and neocheaters who buy despite the clear advertising warnings **not** to buy. ...I & O will not deal with them in any way.

Still, some unwanted orders do get through the screening process. The results are sometimes dramatic. Almost all hostile

Instructions for Linking Neo-Tech I, II, III, IV, and V

or threatening reactions come from those who live by extracting the values produced by others. For, in one stroke, Neo-Tech (1) publicly exposes the ploys and deceptions of all value destroyers for all value producers to see and (2) demolishes the rationalized self-esteem mechanisms of all such value destroyers.

Positive Reactions to Neo-Tech

Identifying and expressing values never just spring from one's imagination. Instead, such expressions, by nature, come from integrated thoughts linked to facts. Conversely, attacks on values are evasions or distortions of reality that anyone can manufacture in limitless variations by ignoring the link between context and facts. Such arbitrariness lets one's imagination create any "reality" convenient for ad hominem attacks. ...Attacks from one's imagination are based on nothing, thus, are nothing and mean nothing.

Rational evaluations with positive commentaries are what count. For such evaluations and commentaries come from integrated experiences limited by facts and context. By contrast, non sequitur, out-of-context attacks come from an infinite variety of random scenarios evolving from mystical fears, malicious envy, or baseless assertions limited only by one's imagination.

The following quotes were from owners of the early, incomplete, less-developed Neo-Tech manuscripts. Examining those early quotes provides valuable perspectives of the versatile, limitless base from which is built the much more complete and widely integrated cosmic-mind Neo-Tech of today. ...Today, cosmic-mind Neo-Tech is curing the disease of mysticism worldwide. And without the disease of mysticism to manipulate their victims, all professional value destroyers will disappear from planet Earth forever.

Even more powerful quotes from owners of this definitive, widely integrated edition of Neo-Tech will appear later in a separate book. But the long-term value of Neo-Tech to each individual far exceeds the value that anyone could express in any quote. ...That long-term value to every Neo-Tech reader literally means growing prosperity and abiding happiness *forever*.

BATCH CA

"The most valuable work I have ever read, and the best investment I have ever made." L.W., CA.

"I never would have believed, until I read Neo-Tech that so much could be going on of which I was unaware." D.M., CA.

"At the core of Neo-Tech is the clear delineation between winners and losers. And it saddens me to observe how many people lose when it is all so unnecessary." M.V., WI.

"The purchase price of Neo-Tech has been returned to me literally thousands of times." H.T., TX.

"This work is chock full of valuable information that will enable anyone to win." M.K., NY.

"My business has almost doubled in this short time. It's amazing!" TX.

"As a man in his sixties, I have found your work priceless. It opens a new world for me." P.S., CA.

"Mind-blowing concepts. ...Thank you." B.J., CA.

"You will win the price of this information immediately." V.B.

"Made clear why people can be controlled. Realize how I've been cheated and deceived in all areas of my life. An awakening, a new life. Wallace has created the information to shape my future." B.K., KY.

"Neo-Tech set me free to become the productive, guilt-free individual who was always within me." C.L., VA.

"Pure, distilled logic...Powerful." J.M., TX.

"Totally stunned." R.S., CA.

"For over 50 years of search, only Neo-Tech has given clear, definitive answers." R.S., IL.

"Neo-Tech is absolutely essential for awakening us from the mesmeric manipulating power of the Neocheaters." I.C., OR.

"Neo-Tech will be my personal guidance throughout my life." D.Z., NY.

"Mental Mace: Used with outstanding success in doing business." F.G., CA.

"Gained so much in such a short period of time." G.K., IL.

"Most concise, informative information ever read." W.A., CA.

"Most accurate, objective and poignant work." S.S., CA.

"With Neo-Tech, people can finally develop to the fullest." F.N., TN.

"Profound benefits to individuals." E.O., CO.

"Reversed my beliefs. Will greatly affect my future actions. Foolish not to have read the concepts earlier." G.F., VA.

"Business and interpersonal concepts are very valuable." S.H., CA.

"Until Neo-Tech, I was never truly happy or free from life's diminishing forces." T.M., IL.

"Should remake the world for the best." J.S.C., NV.

"Masterful job of unmasking the Neocheater's control over the masses." F.S., TN.

"Tremendous turnabout and progress thanks to Neo-Tech." J.S., CA.

"Frees man and puts the ancient ministers to rest." N.P., CANADA.

"Most valuable lesson ever learned." K.P., TX.

Quotes from the early, incomplete versions of Neo-Tech

"Dr. Wallace is an absolute winner." J.F., OH.
"More precise and objective than the very best authors." T.S., AZ.
"Outstanding! Exactly clear, self-benefiting." H.H., MD.
"Read it every moment available. Benefits me to no end!" P.P., IL.
"After Neo-Tech, I'll never be the same. You bet I'm enthusiastic." CA.
"Neo-Tech taught me the most valuable lessons I've every learned. I am literally in awe of Dr. Wallace for what he has done." P.C., TX.

BATCH CB

"Giving Neo-Tech to my son instead of sending him to college." CA.
"Will have an impact on my life like nothing else." T.M., CT.
"Applications are excitingly unlimited." S.G., VA.
"Like discovering the Lost Dutchman's Mine." H.R., PA.
"Totally electrified. Excited beyond description about using Neo-Tech in business." H.M., CO.
"Ends years of looking. Complete source of information." T.K., TX.
"Fireworks! Have learned and gotten results." J.O., NC.
"A great achievement for human beings." J.C., TX.
"Cannot stop reading. Limitless value. Enjoy my prosperity." A.B., WA.
"Read each and every line. An extended celebration." J.K., WA.
"The greatest discovery of this century." R.S., CA.
"Dawn of life has arrived. Will read again and again." B.H., WA.
"Use everyday. Gives me persuasive power as an attorney." A.S. Esq., WA.
"Very valuable in business." O.H., FL.
"Most used volumes in my library." T.F., OK.
"Has a beauty all its own. A work of art." M.T., OH.
"A euphoric experience in freedom." A.G., CA.
"Sad not available 100 years ago. Will make a beautiful world." D.R., TN.
"Melts the grip of others. Made 360 degree turn. Can change the world." B.M., AL.
"Honesty and forthrightness unable to surface before Neo-Tech." D.B., MN.
"Blatantly logical. Regained my youthful enthusiasm." W., CANADA.
"A suit of armor. Nothing can top what's offered by Neo-Tech." L.R., AK.
"A great discovery. Going somewhere in a true and accurate way." P.V., IL.
"Searching for Neo-Tech all my life. Will never be a victim again." G.E., MI.
"My best investment to date. The rewards are limitless." C.P., HI.
"Dumbfounded. Must start over again in life." J.C., CA.
"Loved it! Glorified everything in a scientific manner." S.R., CA.
"Brilliantly conceived and presented." P.R., OH.
"Magnitude of excitement hard to describe. Days can't arrive fast enough." T.R., QUEBEC.
"Surely the way to the future. Overwhelming." J.W., LA.
"Jumped at the Neo-Tech atmosphere." T.S., TX.
"Unbelievably detailed and well written. Only true source of valid life-improving information." P.W., NY.

Quotes from the early, incomplete versions of Neo-Tech

"Fantastic! My whole life is changing." D.C., PA

"Opened doors to all." L.D., WA.

"The most electrifying, awesome collection of information." R.H., NY.

"Dr. Wallace is right. Millions down the tube; we're home free." D.N., CO.

"A light in a dark tunnel. Friends read and can't put down." J. B., WA.

"Expressed with clarity, simplicity — beautiful. Want just for myself, but should be taught in high schools and colleges." D.B., OR.

"Shortcut to living." E.K., FL.

"Galvanized me into a sense of professional direction." S.D., AL.

"Enjoy Neo-Tech beyond description." D.M., CA.

"Neo-Tech gives great pleasure." D.M., CA.

"A landmark in demystifying human nature." P.E., TX.

"Incredible source of valuable information." P.W., NY.

"You have integrated and eclipsed all teachings." W.H., LA.

"The most valuable work ever." G.S., AZ.

"Neo-Tech has given me back my inborn strength." L.M., CA.

"With Neo-Tech, my life ahead is very bright." W.M., NM.

"Most important material ever read in my life. Freedom beyond anything I could have imagined." M.B., CO.

"The greatest mind-opening information ever." B.D., TX.

"Releases nearly all sources of guilt. Happy days!" G.R., PA.

"An awe-inspiring work." S.W., NY.

"Like a shining light in the darkness. Read 12 hours a day for several days. Dazed by the advantages." J.V., AL.

"A welcome awakening. Resetting goals. Enjoying every minute of it." F.W., NJ.

"Thanks so much for helping me to a great deal of success. Also, an incredible defense against neocheaters." J.G., TX.

"Neo-Tech truly set me free. The only way to live." D.P., CA.

"Overwhelmed by the power of Neo-Tech." D.R., MN.

"Glad you let me in early on Neo-Tech. Already got a raise and a promotion and not even applied most of the concepts." H.N., FL.

"Really straightened me out." S.B., MD.

"Worth $4000 immediately with little time and effort." R.P., CA.

"By far the best information ever." J.H., GA.

"Will never feel guilt again." M.P., CA.

"Necessary for success and total independence." J.K., WI.

"Pure power." T.M., OK.

"Profit in more ways than thought possible." C.M., TX.

"A wealthy atmosphere. Business and personal life improve monthly." S.M., CA.

"Stunned into enthusiasm and excitement." L.L., MD.

"A door leading to a new world. Changing my life." J.G., ICELAND.

"Incites invincibility in self." Dr. R.B., FL.

"Overpowering. Completely free of guilt in profiting." L.O., NH.

"Neo-Tech much more valuable to my children than any asset I can will them." T.F., OK.

Quotes from the early, incomplete versions of Neo-Tech

"Never enjoyed life more. Bridged my marriage." M.U., OK.

"Electrifying, truly exciting. Will apply to my business." B.G., FL.

"A much better person for having Neo-Tech." D.E., AZ.

"What a beautiful work." D.D., CA.

"Neo-Tech is the route to everything." T.V., MO.

"Truths in Neo-Tech are nondebatable." A.M., AZ.

"Have to keep my mouth from flapping about the advantages I've gained. Life no longer a burden. Have everything I need." R.V., CANADA.

"Provided my base to move forward...unequalled by anything else." L.P., Esq., ENGLAND.

"First reading shocking, Second reading exhilarating." L.S., FL.

"Impact greater than could imagine. Buying second set for my two children." L.O., NH.

"Neo-Tech is larger than all the wealth — leaves me weak-kneed." D.G., TX.

"Thrilling, exciting, extremely factual." J.S., FL.

BATCH CC

"Ideal for improving personal growth. Amazed how all facets of life have improved." J.C., PA.

"Could never understand what is happening without Neo-Tech. The only alternative to the Dark Ages." R.W., WI.

"Best information ever. Previously suppressed by Neocheaters fearing the demise of their power." B.W., PA.

"No one has ever hit the nail straighter, harder or faster. Gives the very best that life offers. Neo-Tech will remain through all eternity." C.D., OR.

"The most outstanding source of valid, life-improving information." H.G., IN.

"By far the best information I will ever buy. A must for personal power." D.B., PA.

"A blockbuster. Replaces confusion with clarity, doubt with incisive insight. Restores direction to all." A.D., IL.

"Wish I had this information 40 years ago." M.H., MA.

"Holds the secrets of a happy, guilt-free, prosperous life. Will quickly change the world." R.E., PA.

"Brings destiny to everyone's doorstep." E.R., OR.

"Neo-Tech of great financial and personal value incredible work." E.L., MS.

"Very excited. Solid and wonderful. May Neo-Tech people soon control the planet." C.M., MI.

"Neo-Tech — a true and helpful friend." L.C., AL.

"Eminently practical, realistic techniques. Compelled to admire the no-limit applications to daily life." A.E., FL.

"Through Neo-Tech, life's rewards are finally given." T.D., OR.

"Turns darkness into light that seems only to become brighter." J.O., TX.

"Allows one to act without fear. Nothing else compares. Commend the courage of those publishing Neo-Tech." B.M., FL.

"Am a new person. Everything going my way without hardly trying. Neo-Tech is unsurpassed in any field." R.W., CA.

Quotes from the early, incomplete versions of Neo-Tech

"Best information I've ever read, especially in dealing with others." G.M., CA.

"My thinking, attitude, love life really improved." R.H., MA.

"My wife thinks Neo-Tech is great too." F.D., IL.

"Neo-Tech is remaking my life. An enriching experience." F.S., CA.

"Able to function better than ever before." M.K., NV.

"Gives great insights." J.A., VT.

"Turned my whole life around." O.M., VA.

"Rivets my attention for long periods." J.W., ND.

"With gratitude, I'm now guiltlessly free from limitations." C.F., MA.

"I love you Dr. Wallace!" G.S., CA.

"First dismissed as evil. Now thoroughly enjoy Neo-Tech, quit the ministry, and deeply regret past attitude." Rev. T.J., AR.

"So easy to follow. So believable. Will serve me for many, many years. Becoming a real Neo-Tech addict." Ms. P.L., CA.

"Neo-Tech changed my life for the better when change was badly needed." D.R., PA.

"Beautifully written, Exhilarating. The most comprehensive fascinating work ever confronted." W.K., Canada.

"Created an A+ money factor in my business and the stock market." U.C., UT.

"A complete masterpiece. No loose ends." I.D.

BATCH CD

"Neo-Tech brings everything together. The foggy curtain has evaporated." C.L., KY.

"First extremely shocked. Then realized its potency. Neo-Tech is the most valuable work ever developed." F.S., LA.

"Neo-Tech strengthens — very useful in romantic love." S.S., TX.

"Reaching my personal goals with Neo-Tech at my side." Mrs. L.C., KS.

"Never a more logically consistent powerhouse of ideas. Has the power to change history." R.J., AL.

"No longer on the defensive." M.M., CT.

"A complete, marvelous catalyst." O.O'G., CA.

"Absolutely nothing to feel guilty about." W.B., MA.

"Neo-Tech creates advantage my way — the honest way — to deal on a prosperous level." K.B., AL.

"Neo-Tech gave me a much fuller and richer life." Dr. H.G., IN.

"Neo-Tech is practical, wonderful — removes neocheaters who have diminished my life." Ms. E.S., OR.

"Freed of guilt and inferiority feelings. Neo-Tech prevents manipulation by others." D.D., NY.

"Now a happy person with no bad days or guilt." R.S., TX.

"Neo-Tech brings power and unbeatable advantages." L.C., AL.

"Gave us our freedom." N.N., MA.

"With Neo-Tech am able to negotiate very favorable business deals." J.R., TX.

Neo-Tech Power

Quotes from the early, incomplete versions of Neo-Tech

"Extremely impressed. Cleans out the cobwebs." H.S., INDONESIA.
"Really feel like somebody. Neo-Tech put me on the home stretch and in great shape." D.T., GA.
"Very rewarding and enriching. No longer need to be influenced by others." J.M., NY.
"Lifts big, big falsehoods that hold down most people." Mrs. D.A., TN.
"Revolutionary, mind boggling. Extracting values directly for my well-being." G.B., NEWFOUNDLAND.
"Searched all my life for this information. Owe a great debt to you." A.G., CA.
"First seems mad. Then makes sense." J.B., MS.
"Made clear my weakness. Infinitely pleased with Neo-Tech." A.S., NJ.
"In one swift stroke, Neo-Tech unshackles the mind. Freeing humanity at last of traditional misinformation. Dr. Wallace is probably the most sane man on the planet." B.D., CA.
"Overcome by Neo-Tech advantages in facing up to Neocheaters." P.H., MA.
"Essential, remarkable view." Dr. N.H., PA.
"Released from society's boundaries." A.C., NV.
"Very powerful stuff." O.R., CA.
"Most intelligent thinking I know." R.S., CA.
"Blind since childhood. 77-year-old, productive businessman into this new field of knowledge. Want to publicize Dr. Wallace's discovery." E.V., BRAZIL.

BATCH CG

"Wish I had Neo-Tech years ago. Great increase in productivity and self-esteem. Guilt all gone now, life much easier and enjoyable." H.S., NJ.
"A revelation. Never was so free and powerful." D.W., IN.
"Received fair value for time and money." K.T., PUERTO RICO.
"Absolutely fantastic. Neo-Tech ought to be taught as a college course." H.W., OR.
"At first skeptical. Now realize the invaluable work. Truly revolutionary. Gives increased confidence and clarity." D.G., FL.
"To survive, we must adopt the Supreme Constitution." G.P., OH.
"Refreshing and true." J.T., GA.
"Neo-Tech: The key to unlocking the bonds of external authority. My entire life spectrum has improved exponentially." M.H., NY.
"Eye-opening facts that I was not aware of, especially on mysticism." F.P., OH.
"Logical, well presented and documented." J.P., VT.
"Neo-Tech slays the dragon and wins. Brought admiration from others. Found my happiness." D.C., CA.
"Past filled with destructive mysticism, but Neo-Tech gave right direction. Old books frozen on shelves." H.B., ENGLAND.
"Becoming aware of self and surroundings. Control my emotions." J.J., NV.
"Already read 4 times. Delved into deep logical, rational thought." J.S., PA.
"This work done in the spirit of rational thinkers who don't believe in Super

357

Quotes from the early, incomplete versions of Neo-Tech

ghosts." P.G., OR.

"Fascinated with the concepts. Can spot the neocheaters, avoid them, or profit from them." E.G., OH.

"Neo-Tech enabled me to be an achiever where I previously failed." M.U., OK.

"Great, interesting, and genuinely exciting. Most valuable subject in 61 years. Inspires to a new life." H.M., AZ.

"Every time I read it again, it becomes more profound and thought provoking." F.R., NY.

"Neo-Tech brings it all across where Rand, Branden and others failed." S.S., AUSTRALIA.

"Greatest reading ever. Put me on the right path." L.L., GA.

"Dr. Wallace's extensive research is well written in a concise, logical manner with conclusions drawn from man's nature. Mentally stimulating." K.H., FL.

"Neo-Tech the 2nd monumental work in past 50 years." C.J., WA.

BATCH CH

"Truly awesome. See the world through different eyes. Please don't ever get discouraged." H.F., FL.

"Excellent analysis of how the producers are robbed by the non-producers. So profound, wise, and simple." Y.D., AL.

"Expect Neo-Tech to contribute to the opening of the solar system exploration. Jarring concepts." M.P., MD.

"I know I want to live forever. Neo-Tech is my way of thinking." E.D., PA.

"The idea that reason is an absolute brought an end to my life-long depression. Experienced amazing financial success on a sound consistent basis." C.W., CA.

"Neo-Tech eliminates that which has been bogging down advancement." J.C., NJ.

"Thank you Dr. Wallace for opening my eyes to reality. I can only hope more of the population are introduced to this philosophy." K.P., PA.

"Put into eloquent words, illuminating. From the maze of neocheating into the light of Neo-Tech" R.S., CANADA.

"Contains much valuable information. The advanced concepts especially helpful." R.S., NJ.

"Everyday acquire more accelerated, integrated information. Makes me aware of self and surroundings." A.B., CO.

"These books have future value. Helps me in my life and work." M.W., NY.

"It is the distinction between informed and non-informed." J.C., IA.

"Have already reversed the aging process at 72." L.W., WY.

"Most enlightening reading since the Fountainhead." R.S., WA.

"Helped to clarify thoughts and ideas." P.B., KY.

"Tried to smash the barriers of neocheaters, was in debt, family forsake me, finally see the light." W.S., MA.

"The masses never thirst after knowledge. Who ever supplies the illusion is their master. So they will remain the victims." J.G., MA.

Quotes from the early, incomplete versions of Neo-Tech

"Neo-Tech fits the bill." G.L., IL.

"A mind-clearing experience." B.C., IL.

"Made me rethink all my relationships and wonder about who the real producers are. Felt a wee bit like Eric Flame. Neo-Tech will affect this planet." J.E., PA.

"Fascinated by the subject of Neo-Tech." R.D., OH.

"Enables daily comprehension beyond conceivable limits." D.R., MN.

"What an eye opener!" J.W., MI.

"My self-esteem has soared. Have eliminated many external authorities. Will enhance my biological immortality." J.J., MO.

"Stopped smoking, left a depressing job. Enjoy evenings with my family." D.B., CA.

"Reawakened my intellectual interest." T.P., NY.

"Until now my life felt like an aimless bottle in the oceans slowly sinking to the bottom." R.H., CA.

"Neo-Tech III or consciousness and the bicameral mind is a work of genius and rings very true." J.G., CO.

"Pro-life ideas improved all aspects of my daily living. Psychuous pleasures improved my relationships." R.R., WA.

"Helped improve my whole outlook on life and personal relationships." R.A., LA.

"Very essential to everyone to gain control over one's life." J.K., TX.

"Changed my life!" G.C., MN.

"Outstanding — a real breakthrough." D.N., CA.

"After reading, I had better understanding of libertarianism. Now I draw away from altruists and mystics." P.S.

"No longer need to wallow in a sea of guilt." R.L., AZ.

"The work is fantastic. New, exciting — use every day to make $$!" C.E., TX.

"Developed new expanding insights." H.F., NY.

"I feel as if I've lived 45 years in darkness and suddenly see the light." P.G., MD.

"Aided me in my 'decision' to recover." R.M., CA.

"In the race of rational human progress and the embedded age of old corruptions — Neo-Tech is a beacon of light." J.H., IN.

"Enlightened why people feel guilt about profit." W.S., NE.

"Before Neo-Tech I walked around in a trance, but always questioning everything, every institution. It is easy to recognize and control the neocheater, so easily, so naturally. Now make logical, competent decisions. Changed my life for the better. Can't understand how I survived so long without Neo-Tech." R.P., CA.

"Buzzes in my head and won't quit." H.T., CA.

"Thoughtful, Provoking, Stimulating, Interesting, Informative, Valuable, Insightful." F.S., TX.

"A turnabout from the general concepts of life style. Achieved fulfillment." D.A., CT.

359

Quotes from the early, incomplete versions of Neo-Tech

"Has put all things in proper place." F.K., FL.

"The techniques have changed my life." W.C., OK.

"Neocheaters make and break rules at will, use extreme pressure. Know Neo-Tech is the best work I ever read." D.V., CA.

"Great stuff. Even after 3rd reading, new inspirations and insight. Able to look at life with a discerning eye, great happiness, and opportunities abound." J.N., WI.

"Outstanding. Reality is what it is. Live a life of honesty based on reality. Happy themes are playing in my mind." R.H., CA.

"Found a priceless work. Opened a new world." Z.H., CA.

"Goes against everything I ever thought and caused me chaos. Put my life in a new phase." J.F., CA.

"Excellent! Forthright!" B.S., OK.

"An important education." H.C., NM.

"Brought it all together and gave moral reason for believing that productivity is the key." E.T., GA.

"Nothing I read in my 67 years approaches in depth, quality and force of Neo-Tech. The fraudulent God concept enslaved mankind. Free of the influences of theologians and no longer hold politicians in high esteem. Will Neo-Tech save humanity in time?" J.P., MD.

"Great Revelations!" F.C., IL.

"Excellent material, very informative, well researched." R.S., CT.

"Have found it most beneficial in personal relationships. Gotten out of destructive ones, and avoided others, am free and without guilt." J.F., Canada.

"Set me on the road to Freedom." F.D., FL.

"Opened my eyes and mind to the real world." D.M., SC.

"Enlightening, often comforting and frightening, growing pains are healthy. Loved the invaluable book summaries, saved me hours. Admire the integrity of the writer. Everything is crystal clear." L.R., CA.

"My observation of politicians, religion, and industry have been greatly enhanced to the point where I deal effectively with leeches of our society." J.R., IL.

"Incredible research on a subject that long interested me. I understand life a little better now." D.P., CT.

"Keep up the good work! The information package is of great value. Made a 180 degree turn in my thinking and am very happy for it." R.R., AZ.

"Very good and helpful." W.E., OH;

"Your book has straightened me to a better life. Stay away from users. Getting ahead financially and am excited as I never have been. I know where I'm going." L.G., CA.

"Eye-opening. Manuscript answers many unanswered questions of my conscience. No small deed when you have been influenced by Christianity all the years." W.P., PA.

"Dr. Wallace's brilliant work has rid me from irrational notions of mysticism." M.C., NY.

"Comprehensive! I knew it would be valuable because I read Wallace's poker book." W.W., NC.

Quotes from the early, incomplete versions of Neo-Tech

"Gave me precise direction. The vista is now without horizon. I am astounded." T.T., IL.

"Confirmed my doubts about religion and politics." J.A., NY.

"Each reading brings more. Very, very valuable." D.V., OH.

"99% right stuff!" D.R., OH.

"I found an expression of something I always felt secretly and hesitantly practiced. Dr. Wallace's writings have given me conviction, confidence, and concrete optimism." A.K., CA.

"Neocheaters are all around us. Neo-Tech can help ferret out and deal with these individuals and groups." II.M., KY.

"Organized religion has always been the knife in the back of mankind." D.R., NY.

"I was immature. Helped me to understand my wife leaving me." E.R., CA.

"Very helpful once I dug into it." G.R., WA.

"I used to stay up all night in disappointment and depression; I still stay up all night but now in anticipation!" R.P., PA.

"Enlightening! Realized people are easily influenced. Showed me how to know who my real friends are." M.S., NY.

"The Neo-Tech concepts are fantastic! Changed me dramatically. Great possibilities for my future." L.P., TX.

"Effectively forecasts freedom, prosperity, and happiness for humanity. Practice every day. Brought me self-esteem, productive values, and relieved pressures of force." A.N., TX.

"Able to see and understand things that bothered me for many years." E.S., FL.

"Enjoyed the eye opening literature." W.B., TN.

"Enhanced my personal life immeasurably. Private life and business continue to flourish." S.M., CA.

"Ex-news reporter now. Answered the 5-W's, how, who, what, when, why. Total and awesome breakthrough. Made it impossible to ever forget reality. No longer waste my resources. Started my own business. Viva la Frank Wallace and Capitalism." J.A., TX.

"Believe in the dawning of the Neo-Tech age and Dr. Wallace's work." E.N., MI.

"Now I know why the rats always won the race I was in. My disappointments are eased knowing someone out there had the same thoughts." D.I., CA.

"My most prized possession. I am on the road to myself." R.W., MA.

"Mind boggling — has helped me release mysticism. Was a Baptist minister for 20 years, freed me from guilt. I dearly love Neo-Tech. Read it on a regular basis." R.D., NJ.

"After 70 years of programming, Neo-Tech shook my boot straps. Amazing how the masses have been duped for so long." C.S., WA.

"Examined the concepts for 1 year. My values have changed. As a manager, I cannot ignore objective reality." A.H., MI.

"The realization that I am my own master, wholly, completely, was a new experience. As a business broker, I constantly read potential buyers and sellers. My sales increased with the teachings." D.W., IN.

Quotes from the early, incomplete versions of Neo-Tech

"Initial defensive reactions attached to religion, but now find myself in agreement with the powerful concepts. They are true." C.N., CA.

"The most valuable information ever published. Will help preserve the real value of wealth and profitable money making strategy during financially difficult times. Without Neo-Tech, the odds are stacked against you. Once you know, you can play the game safely and confidently. Have stopped playing Russian roulette with my well-being." I.J., IN.

"Understand what politicians and leaders really are and say. Greater satisfactions than ever felt before." G.D., NJ.

"Disenchanted with the contradictions of 'Authorities' and the many 'How To' systems. Daily liberating." E.N., IL.

"At 40, I thought my life was destined to insignificance, but that condition has changed. It is moving in a new and challenging direction." M.G., IA.

"At the risk of over-simplification: No contradiction or compromise occurs in Neo-Tech. Just reality. Only now beginning to see the value of this great work." G.M., TX.

"Thought provoking and realistic!" K.P., VA.

"My life has never been the same since I became a Neo-Tech man 2 years ago. Possess power and confidence. Best of all I am still growing, always will!" R.H., NY.

"Absolutely correct. Took time and effort to comprehend. Because of their rationality, the concepts are surprisingly easy to use. A truly excellent piece of work." M.B., OH.

"My first value was to stop smoking. Tried many ways, including hypnosis, but never got past the first day." L.B., CT.

"Found reading the recommended books and the Neo-Tech book service really made a difference. It's great stuff." D.P., WI.

"Thought I was headed for destruction. Saw everyone cut each others throat. Congratulations Dr. Wallace. Now I have something to look forward to." V.S., TX.

"At last, I no longer feel isolated on a foreign planet. At 9, I became aware that I was living under destructive influence. Since then searched for kindred thinkers." B.H., AUSTRALIA.

"Had profound effect on my life, especially showing me what the God concept is about. I no longer have my head filled 24 hours with guilt." N.S., OH.

"Most valuable reading ever experienced. Biological Immortality should be of interest to all loving people on this planet. Dismissal of mysticism would provide enhancement of progress for all humanity." A.J., AK.

"New outlook. Into 2nd reading, should learn much more this time." L.N., MT.

"Neo-Tech has been like a clearing house of novel ideas to me." M.H., OH.

"Made great progress toward my happiness. Helped me understand the parasites of External Authority and how I was used by government and religion. Experienced unearned guilt based on their altruistic mystic philosophies. Neo-Tech is like a breath of fresh clean air. I can now live, love, work and play guilt free. I enjoy my Neo-Tech tools." M.P., SC.

Quotes from the early, incomplete versions of Neo-Tech

"Excellent! My understanding of life is very different now. I look forward to being a free individual as I have never been before." M.F., CO.

"I became extremely annoyed to find that we are indeed surrounded by instantly recognizable cheats and parasites." J.P., ENGLAND.

"All my adult life I have been a capitalist. Was very religious. Thanks for showing me the contradictions and hang-ups. My young sons will not have the same problems." W.A., KY.

"Has been a great revelation. The book reviews and suggested reading were a life-saver." R.A., CA.

"The knowledge of the advanced concepts triggered what I lost in adolescence, the spark of life I once knew. I want to continue trading values between us." J.R., NY.

"The autobiography my grade-school son was required to read sent me into depression. It was filled with sickening generalities about Martin Luther King. It was a book that glorified mystics and the non-productive who promote guilt in ample quantities. However, your work helped me to refocus clearly again. Now my son has a choice in his future." R.T., CO.

"Your work reflects brilliant, incisive thinking, and a remarkable analytical mind." F.I., PA.

"I now know I can control my own future and nothing can stop me from achieving my goals. Neo-Tech has already saved me pain and money, it's paid for itself many times." B.S., OH.

"Have found the key motivators in life." R.T., NY.

"Fascinating. Changed my thinking on many points." J.C., NM.

"Cleared many suspicions I felt on the manipulating powers of neocheaters. With Neo-Tech things fall in place and cast away guilt feelings I had for no reason." P.M., NY.

"After reading your work my world blew up. Everything I believed in was no more. But I had the power to change, and I no longer fear. I am free and happy again." J.G., AL.

"Exciting! Can no longer be manipulated." D.S., TX.

"Review often and always get more help. Have control of my life and can not be taken advantage of." A.A., NJ.

"Have profited from what I received." J.J., TX.

"Dispelled fears, uncertainty. Feel self-confident. Most interesting, stimulating, and challenging work." W.D., OH.

"The more I read, the more I realize how blind I was. It will enable me to achieve my dreams, my goals." J.T., CANADA.

"Neo-Tech offers a rational approach to life taken to its final conclusion — biological immortality." W.W., PA.

"Very useful and enlightening." S.M., AZ.

"Excellent free-market philosophy." L.G., MD.

"I've truly begun to realize my own potential to do whatever I want. Better perspective on life and people." T.L., TX."

"My beliefs and philosophies have culminated with Neo-Tech and the Aristotelian attitudes. Made clear the reason for my apparent differences with peers. The 'ugly duckling' syndrome is finally identified. Look forward to many years of productive life in the guiltless spirit which has awakened." C.G., VA.

"Opened my eyes and freed me from the world of needless sacrifice." R.V., TX.

"The Neo-Tech concept helped tremendously overcoming past problems by exposing their nature. On my way to success now." C.M., MN.

"Has confirmed and clarified my thinking of our religious and political leaders." E.N., WI.

"Clear, powerful, and intelligent." J.C., NJ.

"A worthwhile, unencumbered reality." J.W., CA.

"Dr. Wallace is a genius!" D.M., NY.

"Absolutely astonishing. Has changed my life around. Dealing effectively with neocheaters and stopping them dead in their tracks." A.D., NY.

"Impressed with the information. Certainly have changed my religious views." H.F., CO.

"Teaches to see the reality of events as opposed to the illusions the parasites project. Excellent, extremely consistent, informative, and well written." B.N., MA.

"When enlisted, I believed the service would provide the honesty and integrity that would pave the way ahead in life. Instead, I found a world of neocheaters. I always sought the truth, and people took advantage of my innocence. But with Neo-Tech this is no longer so. People have respect for me now." M.P., APO NY.

"After critically examining the work, I find no single concept I could honestly disagree. It is a masterpiece. Advertising is par excellence. When the last stone of the last church falls on the head of the last priest, humanity will be free." A.H., AUSTRALIA.

"Incredibly clear and coherent. Love every word of it." B.P., SOUTH AFRICA.

"Has uncovered puzzles that kept my life tangled with disappointments. Now I am decisive and look forward to my future." F.H., NY.

"I've known the Rev. Loft types. Grateful that Dr. Wallace took the time to write the manuscripts." F.T., NY.

"Terrific eye opener and full of useful knowledge for people looking to add values to their lives." J.H., VA.

"The teaching has been the most revealing and inspiring tool in my life. Given new insights into negative feelings and behavior. The whole family reads it." C.H., TX.

BATCH CI

"What can I say, except that my eyes have been opened. Your concepts are right for me." R.K., MD.

"Grateful for the valuable knowledge to improve my personal life. Becoming a much better person." K.K., IL.

"How I wished I received this information 50 years ago. Life could have been different." L.T., OH.

Quotes from the early, incomplete versions of Neo-Tech

"Not one to exaggerate, but my initial reading represents a turning point in my life and career." D.S., PA.

"Concepts agreeable with my life style." J.C., MA.

"Neo-Tech is by far the most advanced and important information ever compiled into such few pages. On target. For the first time, I do my own original thinking." R.S., IN.

"Concepts are both evolutionary and revolutionary." F.R., GA.

"Over 70 years on this planet and how my thinking changed with Neo-Tech." G.C., WA.

"The reading was well organized and stimulating." S.R., TX.

"Continue to find rapid developing moments of understanding." R.T., NY.

"Life has changed for the better. Stopped smoking and drinking. See the world in clarity now." J.T., MS.

"Was shocked for a while. Now on course, taking what I earn guiltlessly. By far the greatest book ever written in the history of mankind." M.P., NY.

"Like the format, concepts and related stories." D.S., CANADA.

"This literature is a breath of life, the purpose for life. This philosophy just doesn't sit on the shelf after reading. Always been a rebel against status quo, the government, the philanthropist, welfare, organized religion, and anyone that didn't pull his own weight. My son will read it also. On my road to happiness." J.C., UT.

"Extremely thought provoking and revealing dissertations on many aspects. Enjoy digging into these matters. For 40 years, I knew there was an explanation." G.H., VA.

"Increasingly aware of the tremendous fraud around me, mainly in relationships. Hope not to repeat the same mistakes in choosing a mate." S.K., NY.

"Helped me understand why I am not satisfied with my life. A second reading will change it." C.C.,CA.

"Gave me renewed confidence in my ability to make decisions that benefit me. Recommend Neo-Tech for all achievers. Re-read every day the advanced concepts and apply them." H.M., CO.

"Good and refreshing." J.T., ENGLAND.

"Straight forward, sound ideas for self-sufficiency. A work of the future brought into the present day. A look at numerous people zogged by the past. The dawning of a future with creative ideas and freedom." P.K., CANADA.

"Intensive study course. Considerable help." P.F., CANADA.

"After reading, my whole outlook changed dramatically. Now view life as means to an end. The world is in need of producers. The altruistic morals of politicians bought much pain and suffering." C.A., OH.

BATCH CJ

"Quite an eye opener. On my second reading unable to put it down." W.S., AZ.

"Beyond doubt the most powerful and valuable investment of my life. Brilliantly integrated, consistent and continually valuable to me. Express my admiration for Dr. Wallace for the achievement of Neo-Tech. Happy!" P.W., ENGLAND.

Quotes from the early, incomplete versions of Neo-Tech

"Straight forward, upright, well-rounded and well-founded ideas. A work far into the future brought into the present day standards. The dawning of a future boundless with creative ideas and freedom!" P.K., CANADA.

"Interesting, thought provoking reading." I.H., ENGLAND.

"Neo-Tech reading was very stimulating." R.W., ENGLAND.

"Thank you for putting the information together and bringing it into the open." D.G., AUSTRALIA.

"I am fortunate to be a Neo-Tech owner. I congratulate you on an excellent work communicating the value system." C. Mc., WEST AUSTRALIA.

"Neo-Tech is what the world needs, and I am a proud owner." M.H., CANADA.

"Most valuable source of information for international human beings. Thanks for the discovery." A.H., FINLAND.

"Whole new possibilities and frontiers for me." B.R., NEW ZEALAND.

"Brilliantly conceived." E.J., NEW ZEALAND.

"The concepts took me by complete surprise." M.O., NEW ZEALAND.

"Very interesting. Caused me to stop and really think. Changed my complete outlook." G.M., AUSTRALIA.

"Read four times. Was devastated as I looked at my wasted years." C.R., NEW ZEALAND.

"Valuable and important work." J.D., NEW ZEALAND.

"Seeing my life productive and fulfilled is a revelation." P.D., AUSTRALIA.

"Enhanced my understanding of my behavior and people around me. Led to greater freedom in experimenting with ambitious business plans." S.B., ENGLAND.

"Incredibly revealing." F.W., NEW ZEALAND.

"Marvelous mind-expanding experience. The logical expounding of romantic love delights. Look forward to more from Dr. Wallace." D.A., ENGLAND.

"First day after reading Neo-Tech made $100/hr on a business offer. Looking forward always." R. Mc., FL.

"Well presented and researched." M.S., MALTA.

"Stunned by the information revealed." E.N., AUSTRALIA.

"Fantastic piece of work, thoroughly researched, analyzed, and presented. Thought provoking concepts." L.K., SINGAPORE.

"Believe have only begun to benefit from the concepts." L.G., AUSTRALIA.

"Very, very interesting. Presents a totally new insight to many aspects of daily life. Am in total agreement with the presentation." I.G., ENGLAND.

"Wholeheartedly agree with the Supreme Constitution. Impressed with the amount of research that has been put into the development of the material presented." J.B., ID.

"Astonishing! Made me re-examine my views on accepted dogma. Opened the door to a whole new way of thinking." V.T., ENGLAND.

"Will never find enough words to thank you for releasing me from mysticism." E.D., AUSTRALIA.

"The most amazing thought-provoking information ever encountered. The price is small indeed for delivering so great a value. Looking forward to new discoveries." E.C., CANADA.

Quotes from the early, incomplete versions of Neo-Tech

"Made me analyze my preconceived ideas." S.S., AUSTRALIA.

"Should be compulsory reading for anyone dealing with authorities." P.B., AUSTRALIA.

"The objective reality, productivity, prosperity and happiness concepts promoted by Neo-Tech have been a saving factor for me through a life of crisis." G.Q., ND.

"Most stimulating!" F.W., AUSTRALIA.

"Very educational. Look forward to achieving guiltless prosperity and happiness." S.P., ENGLAND.

"In fact the best thing that has happened to me was reading Neo-Tech." M.G., NEW ZEALAND.

"The greatest discovery to benefit all of mankind forever!" D.P., MA.

"Very good — I now have greater perception seeing through falsehoods easily." N.S., NEW ZEALAND.

"Has opened my mind. Slow getting motivated after 50 years. After reading the manuscript, I am richer in knowledge. It's the best thing in my life." S.H., ENGLAND.

"Challenging — incredibly thought-provoking. Benefited enormously." J.O., AUSTRALIA.

"Priceless!" D.H., CANADA.

"It's a real 'tour-de-force'." J.G., ENGLAND.

"Dr. Wallace, you are a genius! What a great place this world could be without politicians and theologians. All they ever did was separate mankind into groups, and against each other. They must be stopped. This is one war that the good, honest, and innocent children of the world must win. Wish long life, happiness and prosperity to Dr. Wallace and the Neo-Tech collaborators." S.E., ENGLAND.

"Thank you for the 632-page Information Package. It's the best material I have ever read." C.T., SINGAPORE.

"Very interesting. The concepts have confirmed and reinforced the hazy type thinking that as a producer, I have always thought to be true. Gave me a solid foundation and confidence." R.H., ENGLAND.

"Most scientific concepts. Will revolutionize the world." V.A., CANADA.

"Greatly influenced my outlook in life and society. Eye opener. All could live in harmony without the fear of God. Everybody can be a producer of tradeable values." J.M., KENYA.

"Am excited about the contents. Thank you for such a thought-provoking presentation. My life will change for the better." J.W., AUSTRALIA.

"It's helping me to realize what life is all about, and what life was meant to be. To be happy and fulfilled." A.G., SOUTH AFRICA.

"Has changed my life. And is continuing to change my life as I study the concepts. Thank you Dr. Wallace." C.J., NEW ZEALAND.

"Very interesting, stimulating and controversial, especially the knowledge of the God concept. Will change the world for the better." H.S., SOUTH AFRICA.

"Informative and enjoyable reading. Intellectually stimulating. Read it every chance I get. Very practical in all aspects of life. Best wishes for Neo-Tech everywhere." L.M., AUSTRALIA.

Quotes from the early, incomplete versions of Neo-Tech

"Intriguing approach to life." D.F., SOUTH AFRICA.
"The concepts are excellent!" H.L., AUSTRALIA.
"The whole work is unorthodox and daring!" S.W.,CANADA.
"Powerful, selective-worded collection of knowledge that cannot be disputed. So clearly defines the laws of human nature. Thank you." J.S., CANADA.

BATCH CK

"Thank you for opening my eyes. My confidence is in my future." G.P., ENGLAND.
"Helped reorient my approach in Geo-marine research. Enjoy moving forward with new ideas and concepts." G.W., ENGLAND.
"In a world of socialism and altruistic ideas it is refreshing to know that there are people outside with foresight and intelligence who fully comprehend and understand freedom and free enterprise." P.S., AUSTRALIA.
"Clearly the most significant material I ever read. Changed my attitude completely to religion and government." A.B., ENGLAND.
"A tremendous undertaking needed for today's consciousness." C.G., CANADA.
"Neo-Tech caused me a lot of thinking, like someone finally turned the light switch on." T.P., APO NC.
"Dr. Wallace gave me the key to produce and think guiltlessly free. Many, many thanks." G.M., AUSTRALIA.
"I am not an easy believer, because I deal in provable facts. But Neo-Tech did explain what I always wanted to find out." J.P., CANADA.
"Very good research. Will benefit everyone." B.S., ENGLAND.
"Since using Neo-Tech dramatic changes are in my life. No longer waste valuable time on prayers or other superstitions. Am able to devote all my energy toward rational and beneficial conclusions. Thank you Dr. Wallace for opening my eyes to reality." H.T., CA.
"Beyond doubt the most powerful, valuable investment ever. The work is brilliantly integrated and consistent." P.W., ENGLAND.
"Thank you for educating the innocent, productive middle class who have been defrauded throughout history." J.I., MA.
"I like your thinking tools." A.C., NV.
"Proved very practical in Romantic Love." S.S., TX.
"Upon first reading shocked, but then proved its potency. Truly believe this is the most valuable work ever conceived and developed." F.S., LA.
"Neo-Tech philosophy turned my whole life around." O.M., VA.
"Truly great work! Now individuals can act on their own accord without fear. Glad to identify the neocheaters and deal with them. That is the greatest asset. Nothing else compares." B.M., FL.
"Already read three times. Best book I ever read. Use it in dealing with customers." G.M., CA.
"Will have a great impact on the literate world. Brilliant publication." R.B., NEW ZEALAND.
"Fantastic discovery!" A.A., PERU.

Quotes from the early, incomplete versions of Neo-Tech

"Eye-opening. Especially the company statement of policies which is different from any I have ever seen." J.B., ENGLAND.

"Very interesting, very new. Enjoyed all thoroughly and deeply." T.J., FRANCE.

BATCH CEJ

"Handles all the manipulative, life-snapping, mesmerizing Neocheaters everywhere." M.P., IL.

"Until Neo-Tech had almost given up on life." R.W., TX.

"Building one of America's largest corporations. All is made clear through Neo-Tech." J.A., NJ.

"Neo-Tech significantly improved our lives." R.G., CA.

"Ecstatic over Neo-Tech. Astonishing results in controlling people." T.H., CA.

"Neo-Tech is fabulous. Have not had a bigger thrill in a long time." D.M., WA.

"Nothing is so reassuring as Neo-Tech in handling the whole world. But must hide it from my parents." D.O., VA.

"Completely captivated by Neo-Tech." D.W., CANADA.

"Immediately recognized the profound importance of Neo-Tech to every one." G.K., AZ.

BATCH CFJ

"Want to thank and congratulate Dr. Wallace. Lives up to the sensational notice in Wealth Magazine." P.G., AUSTRALIA.

"Where has Neo-Tech been all my life? Life was miserable until Neo-Tech. I now have financial security." L.H., VT.

"Can't put it down! Blinkers are off. Information Packages — an understatement." J.C., ENGLAND.

"A major breakthrough for mankind. Practical application of Neo-Tech for daily progress and benefits to my company." Ms. C.D., GA.

"Neo-Tech opened my eyes to wonders I never knew existed." J.R., IL.

"Wish I had Neo-Tech years ago. Great increase in productivity and self-esteem. Guilt all gone now, life so much more easier and enjoyable." M.S., NJ.

"A revelation. Never was so free and powerful." D.W., IN.

BATCH CGJ

"Amazed at the numerous discoveries by Dr. Wallace. My family and I find his work most remarkable." K.Z., SC.

"Truly on the right course. Neo-Tech is priceless." E.Z., IL.

"Neo-Tech will fulfill the unfulfilled." W.W., PA.

"Has truly changed my life." T.M., IL.

"Always been a producer, but Neo-Tech taught me the most valuable lesson that neocheaters exist and how to identify them." K.P., TX.

"Neo-Tech III monograph is the gemstone. The recipe for a truly quantum leap in human reshaping qualities." R.G., NM.

Quotes from the early, incomplete versions of Neo-Tech

"It is giving me an open-ended, ever-increasing sense of control over my life and surroundings." K.P., TX.

"Sincerely identify with the philosophical principles contained in the information package and the ultimate value of achieving biological immortality." G.K., IN.

"These concepts have the greatest potential meeting the needs of our society. Keep up the good work and may you reach your highest goals." I.C., OR.

"After finishing Neo-Tech I and II, I will never be the same. You bet I am enthusiastic." A.S., CA.

"Amazed at the numerous discoveries made by Dr. Wallace. Most remarkable work." K.Z., SC.

"You are on the right track. This information is certainly valuable and priceless." E.Z., IL.

"Most gratifying Neo-Tech reading." J.B., OH.

"Thank you for the 'Supreme Constitution', it's extremely logical. Our small community is interested in a world free of neocheaters, psychomystics, and agents of force." R.W., NY.

"Since reading the manuscript, my life has done a 180 degree turn. I realize there are only two types of people on this planet: Productive Individuals and Non-Producers. It's such a great feeling to know I have this subtle, but extremely powerful power in my hands." S.C., NY.

"The contents of the information package left me surprised and enthusiastic. Surprised, because I never thought any such work existed, and enthusiastic, because it provided answers that would have taken a long time to arrive at by sifting through and digesting an endless number of materials." M.M., CANADA.

"Have thoroughly read all the Neo-Tech books and glad to express the change its teachings have brought to my life. Words are inadequate to describe how every line has affected my life. Grateful to Dr. Wallace." J.B., ENGLAND.

"Crystallized my feelings and ideas particularly about politicians and religious groups. A copy of Neo-Tech should be on top of everyone's reading list." S.B., ENGLAND.

"Had only one month, but read every day. Have a feeling of elation!" J.M., IL.

"Thought provoking." W.G., CANADA.

"Most enlightening books I ever read." T.B., VA.

"Neo-Tech has sliced through the malaise like a beacon through fog. Would like to associate with people who emanate life." R.T., CO.

"Found it highly interesting and psychologically motivating. The 'Concepts' unveiled have begun to lead me into objectively looking at my life." M.M., IL.

"The idea that reason is the only absolute ended my lifelong depression." C.W., CA.

"Delighted with the Neo-Tech package. Never without it. Fill a void in my life. Quite strange having lost the fear of being guilty." C.S., FL.

"I applaud your basic philosophy and premise that one should view life with objective reality." M.P., CANADA.

"Absolutely fascinating." A.D., NY.

Quotes from the early, incomplete versions of Neo-Tech

"Eliminated doubts and confusion that existed within my own philosophical outlook. Cannot imagine ever reading a more important document. Will soon introduce my brother to this remarkable discovery." J.P., ENGLAND.

"Dr. Wallace has discovered the truth to objective reality. Biological immortality is the missing link in the human race." J.K., TX.

"Transcends anything I ever read. It is a 'tour-de-force'. Feel like a totally new person; like pure, fresh blood has been injected into my system. See now that generalized information has been distorted to suit the interests and aspiration of external authority." J.B., ENGLAND.

"Neo-Tech concepts truly fascinating! The simplicity of 'Emotions are neither good nor bad' caused me to see myself in a completely new light." S.S., AUSTRALIA.

"Spent countless dollars and time searching for valid information concerning prosperity and happiness for myself and family. Believe I found it in the Neo-Tech concepts." N.S., OH.

"Most of my life been seeking for objective reality and found it in Neo-Tech. Will enable me to live my life successfully." B.H., AUSTRALIA.

"The concepts are great!" D.M., AUSTRALIA.

"After reading Neo-Tech I was sorry I didn't order sooner." J.S., CA.

"Discovered the fountain of youth at 70 after reading and using Neo-Tech." S.J., CA.

"Now, thanks to Dr. Wallace, I have acquired a cogent philosophy far superior to the altruistic misconceptions. I congratulate you on your significant achievements. Passionately desire to work with you achieving man's highest goal, biological immortality." R.B., MD.

"Was able to evaluate the value and concepts in the Neo-Tech package immediately." E.P., SOUTH AFRICA.

"Recognize the profound importance of Neo-Tech to everyone's future and wish to work toward man's highest goal." G.K., AZ.

"Thanks to Neo-Tech, this year has been a magic year for me — I realize that I can take great pride in my achievements without feelings of guilt." G.B., AUSTRALIA.

"Recognize the profound importance of Neo-Tech to my future." M.L., NEW GUINEA.

"Thrilling to read page by page, and equally exciting to find that I had in my hands valid, factual answers to questions that always bothered me. Neo-Tech will lead me to what is most important to me." F.C., ME.

"Other success methods were not completely satisfactory. I see Neo-Tech as the missing link as to 'why some people are successful and others not'." T.M., NEW ZEALAND.

BATCH CJJ

"Neo-Tech clearly defines the attitudes to lives, values, and future achievements." D.H., ENGLAND.

"Enthusiastic about the Neo-Tech principles for biological immortality." P.L., MI.

"Read all with a growing amazement." J.Q., AUSTRALIA.

371

Quotes from the early, incomplete versions of Neo-Tech

"Most valuable material ever read with the truth of life." M.T., NEW ZEALAND.

"Impressed with all the concepts." H.B., TX.

"Was a producer for 40 years, clearly opened my eyes to the non-producer. Everyone connected with Neo-Tech should be commended. Thank for the values received." J.S., MN.

"Am eager to contribute my share of work and professional competence towards the achievement of 'man's highest goal — biological immortality'. Deem myself non-mystical and would be honored to participate." H.C., NJ.

"My father was an honest producer, and I inherited his ways. Neocheater may be immensely powerful, even dominate the world and most of our thinking. Historically, honest producers lost. But that was before Neo-Tech." R.L., AUSTRALIA.

"I now have greater perceptions and can easily detect mysticism." N.S., NEW ZEALAND.

"Amazing! Shocked because I am a clergyman's son. Intellectual, logic and sound. Changed my view of world political leaders." R.S., ENGLAND.

BATCH CKJ

"A crystallization is taking place. Felt uprising anger against neocheaters and their influences. As a teenager, I yielded to parental and social pressure and conformed. Explored them all, including hard-money advisors. Neo-Tech offered an honest, integrated framework." J.B., CA.

"Completely and forever stopped me from plastering the mud hole I was trapped in. Neo-Tech lifted me beyond its grip. Grateful to everyone who contributed to Neo-Tech." E.F., SOUTH AFRICA.

"Inspired me with great knowledge which is priceless." W.H., NJ.

"Made my day! A real joy to read Dr. Wallace's meaningful and important work." T.P., FL.

"Wondered who would pick up where von Mises, Rand, and Branden left off. Now I know." L.C., CO.

"That profound knowledge has cleanly sliced through the illusion of reality to expose the rich inner heart of all life. I see the Neo-World forming with clarity in my mind. Filled with a strong sense of gratitude." G.W., CA.

"This knowledge has unlimited potential, and I thirst for more. Only in the dark lies ignorance, and I have no desire to live in the dark any longer. The time has come for a change of philosophic attitude, and I welcome it with open arms." D.M., NC.

"After understanding Neo-Tech, I let go of all guilt placed on myself for giving up religion. Took 100% control of my life. Now extremely happy and prosperous. My goals coincide with each other instead of conflicting." A.G., MD.

"Recognize the significance of this information package. Value it the highest. Changed my life. To achieve Biological Immortality will be the happiest moment in my life." K.O., NEW GUINEA.

Quotes from the early, incomplete versions of Neo-Tech

"Congratulations on the clear, concise, and excellent presentation of the concepts and book reviews. Created new mounting excitement. Mankind stands on the threshold of a new era. Biological Immortality — certainly most exciting goal to aim for." P.N., AUSTRALIA.

"Neo-Tech made me a man with new ideas for financial and psychological well-being." R.O., CA.

"Recognize the profound importance of Neo-Tech in my life." T.J., MO.

"Worked with youth around the world. Young men thanked me for the hope and vision received." B.R., KY.

BATCH CL

"Only after reading Neo-Tech did I acquire a clear picture of my life and develop a healthy self-esteem. It resulted in a sense of well being. Neo-Tech stirred the emotions and memories of mental freedom that I only remember having had as a happy and naive child, which I thought I had lost forever. Dr. Wallace planted a seed that is slowly and surely breaking the chains of personal limitations caused by centuries of religious and political conditioning." C.J., AUSTRALIA.

"Immense and immeasurable value." G.T., ENGLAND.

"Thousands of questions are in my mind, and my attitude is changing fast. Enthusiastic about this new knowledge." M.B., NEW ZEALAND.

"Thanks to Neo-Tech I have a more solid foundation and more confidence." R.H., ENGLAND.

"Was deeply rooted in religion. After reading Neo-Tech three times, I have a different sense of right and wrong." V.W., ENGLAND.

"Not having read all of it yet, but already gained a 40% increase in my salary." D.J., AUSTRALIA.

"Women manipulate men, and vice versa. It would be a better world if all related honestly and stopped playing games. Helped me immeasurably in my personal life. Thank you." J.G., ENGLAND.

"Tremendous undertaking needed for today's consciousness." C.C., CANADA.

"After reading Neo-Tech, I suddenly woke up from a 25 year sleep! It answers all questions with objective truth, not mystical blurb. It's clear and concise. It's more than priceless — it's immortal." L.A., AUSTRALIA.

"Brilliant! Inspired me to 'The Neo-Tech Way' to wealth." J.C., AUSTRALIA.

"Added a whole new dimension to my thinking." A.H., NEW ZEALAND.

"Discovered new secrets for success, happiness, and love. There is no stopping me now thanks to Dr. Wallace." W.W., NJ.

"Loved and enjoyed all. Made me fully aware of the existence of neocheaters, and defined what productive work is. This knowledge fills a hole in my life, I didn't realize I had. Thank you." M.T., NEW ZEALAND.

"Was raised a Catholic. Took me 2 years not to feel guilty after I left church. Your books are more logical than any other I read, losing more inhibitions and I wholeheartedly applaud your logic." S.J., MI.

"Since reading Neo-Tech, I have a great deal of guts and confidence. I am sure it will be a 'Classic' in history because it honestly addresses the most

Quotes from the early, incomplete versions of Neo-Tech

important issue — the human individual." T.P., FL.

"Overwhelmed with happiness and glee. I am the only Neo-Tech man in my settlement." H.W., NEW ZEALAND.

"An eye opener and a must for everyone. Thank you for all." T.G., AUSTRALIA.

"Most profound concepts." G.W., MN.

"Made a difference in my attitude — definitely for the better." K.D., IL.

"Consider Neo-Tech one of the most profound, effective books ever read. Utterly uncompromising reasoning. After four months, became an integral part of my life." Y.K., CA.

"Has more effect on my way of thinking than any other book." C.B., NEW ZEALAND.

"Exceedingly useful and relevant to my daily life." I.P., NEW ZEALAND.

"Read at least 3 times and now feel like a newly discharged cadet." R.T., NJ.

"By far the most advanced information ever compiled into such few pages. Feel for the first time in my life that I am doing my own thinking. Truly, Neo-Tech has topped all my previous expectations." R.S., IN.

"Very encouraging, revealed everything." K.B., NEW GUINEA.

"Became more aware, and many changes occurred in my life. Now ordering the Neo-Tech library because it is the only information available that is honest, straight forward, objective, and will bring lasting benefits." J.B., CA.

"Felt cheated all my life and did not know why. Neo-Tech provided the key. Now have unshakable peace of mind. Feel I am in control of my life, at last!" R.O., CA.

"Made the ultimate move in self-improvement. Regard this information as essential for physical and mental well-being." I.J., IN.

"Accept no outside 'authority.' My feelings are pulled together in a logical fashion. Enlightening! The first attempt by modern man to call a spade a spade." L.G., CA.

"Has made it so easy to recognize the unsavory characters that walk and stalk our world." R.M., RI.

"The concepts contained the most liberating knowledge ever read in my 78 years." L.K., OH.

"Of any book, any theory, any information and any idea I ever read or heard in my life, this had the greatest impact of all." E.B., FL.

"Am amazed at what I learned from your manuscript. My desire to control my life is priority." R.W., CO.

"The money invested has already been recovered tenfold." L.S., AUSTRALIA.

"Neo-Tech has changed my view of what is right and true. Thank you for opening my eyes. Our futures have no limits." S. & M.F., MO.

"We love Neo-Tech. Through our change in belief systems we now experience success and a feeling of liberation." S.G., CT.

"Thank you for the clear and enlightening concepts. I feel free. I enjoy reality. I enjoy LIFE!!" L.K., MI.

"Neo-Tech kind of frightened me, it seemed so powerful. I need this kind of help to gain control of my life." R.A., CA.

"Every good and excellent thing stands moment by moment on the razors edge of danger and must be fought for. That expressed my attitude on Neo-Tech." L.L., CA.

"My investments will quadruple in five years. My decision was based on some of the Neo-Tech data along with other information." T.P., FL.

"Happiness has increased 10-fold." C.H., ENGLAND.

"Wish this was taught in school so everyone could know what is really going on." P.J., CA.

"After reading Neo-Tech, I'm on my way to a much more rewarding life." L.R., CO.

"The most mind-opening book I have ever read. I'm so excited about this new/true way of thinking. I've grown so much." M.F., MO.

"Been transplanted from an unrealistic hostile environment to a healthy one where I can grow and blossom indefinitely." L.M., CA.

"As one reads the Neo-Tech Discovery page by page, one can feel the imprisoning chains imposed by the 'authorities' breaking link by link. It's a great feeling!" J.Y., TN.

"Made me aware of how the neocheaters prey on the productive people in this world." J.S., MN.

"My dreams are no longer dreams. A new awareness of the people and institutions that drained my hopes and happiness, and how we are all infiltrated." B.R., AUSTRALIA.

"Brilliant and remarkable. The search for Biological Immortality has to be the only rational course to follow." F.T., ENGLAND.

"At last the barriers are down. Seemed to be exactly what was missing from my life." J.D., ENGLAND.

"The prospect of removing power from non-producers instills a sense of purpose that I lost years ago." J.C., CA.

"Was relieved of guilt feelings from understanding why I am not responsible for all the world's shortcomings, but only for myself." J.T., FL.

"It is one of the greatest pieces of literature I ever read. Invaluable information." R.Mc., IA.

"Turned me around, the freedom and power I feel is great. The thought of living forever brings fantastic opportunities to the individual." M.J., OH.

"'You shall know the truth and the truth shall make you free', the church said it but Neo-Tech did it. Free of guilt about money and success. I am now the man I always wanted to be!" B.S., NY.

"The first two books taught me not to be cheated by anybody anymore, and every item I reread, I learn something new." M.V., CA.

"Shocked and stunned for 24 hours. Reread and totally understood. No one will ever hustle me again." W.R., KY.

"Was at crossroads in my life. Reading the concepts helped me decide to keep learning and growing." D.K., TX.

"The way may now be clear for achieving accomplishments beyond our dreams." P.H., KS.

"I'm able to filter out and reject the negatives and see what is real for prosperity and great happiness." S.W., IL.

"The validity of your interpretations manifest daily in my experiences." R.D., CA.

"Purchased these volumes for my wife, but ended up using myself. Full of hope and confidence that your work will spread. Am very proud of my 'rags to riches' success that I achieved through Neo-Tech. Best wishes." B.L., AUSTRALIA.

BATCH GT

"I found Neo-Tech exceedingly useful and relevant to daily life." I.P., NEW ZEALAND.

"Congratulations are well in order for Dr. Frank R. Wallace and his magnificent mind." R.I., NJ.

"Neo-Tech I-V is by far the most advanced and important information ever compiled." R.S., IN.

"I am beginning to realize that Neo-Tech is completely revealing everything, and I mean the whole truth." K.O., NEW GUINEA.

"Neo-Tech has provided the key to free me from being cheated. I feel more in control of my life. I am free at last. Thank you Dr. Wallace." R.O., CA.

"I regard this information as absolutely essential to both physical and mental well-being." I.J., IN.

"Neo-Tech opened up a new world to me, the real world! Neo-Tech has made it so easy to recognize the unsavory characters that walk and stalk our world." R.M., RI.

"Neo-Tech contains the most liberating knowledge for the human mind I have read anywhere in my 78 years." L.K., OH.

"Since reading Neo-Tech, I have started two companies and they are doing well." J.W., AUSTRALIA.

"Of any book, any theory, any information and any idea I ever read or heard about, Neo-Tech had the greatest impact." E.B., FL.

"I'm amazed at what I have learned from your manuscript. The most important project on the planet." R.C., CO.

"It has really made me aware of the way neocheaters operate. I can feel the power I have derived from the information." J.S., MN.

"I cannot describe to you the enormous value that your book has been in my life. The most important experience is the realization of the unlimited power in me." B.C., AUSTRALIA.

"Neo-Tech is a brilliant and remarkable exposition. B.I. has to be the only rational course." F.T., ENGLAND.

"Can now begin to see things in their true light. Gets the adrenaline going — seems to be exactly what's been missing." J.D., UK.

"I read through Neo-Tech without practicing the techniques. However, I did want to be able to spot the cheaters, and I achieved this ability far beyond my expectations." J.C., CA.

"Neo-Tech is one of the greatest pieces of literature that I have read. The information is invaluable." R.M., IA.

Neo-Tech Power

| Quotes from the early, incomplete versions of Neo-Tech |

"Neo-Tech turned me around. The freedom and power I feel now is fantastic." M.J., OH.

"Neo-Tech did it. 58 years of guilt about sex and money gone. Started business in basement and built it into a million corp. — now for the first time really proud and guiltless of my success." W.S., NY.

"Neo-Tech is helping me get acquainted with someone I've ignored for a long, long time — myself! When I received Neo-Tech, I was 31, overweight, smoked, and had a lazy, stagnant mind. My mind has come alive again and has begun to show me the power I have in myself." J.H., CO.

"I have read Neo-Tech I-V cover-to-cover six times. I now see that for the first time in history a crystal-clear, straight-arrow path to infinite happiness, prosperity, and success has been defined in Neo-Tech." B.C., OH.

"Dr. Wallace: The validity of your interpretations manifests itself daily in my experiences." R.D., CA.

"Words truly fail me. I am full of hope and confidence that your writings and research will spread." J.L., AUSTRALIA.

"The only reason I decided to order is that a friend, who is a billionaire and claims to have had a hand in developing Neo-Tech, recommended it to me." L.K., IN.

"Neo-Tech works. It makes one stand on his feet, and on his feet alone. It makes one think on his own, and only on his own. Brings clarity so that he can distinguish between mere believing and authentic knowing." Y.K., CA.

"It has had more effect on my way of thinking than any other single book I have read." C.B., NEW ZEALAND.

"Neo-Tech has helped make me a man with new ideas for advancing myself to financial and psychological well-being." R.O., CA.

"I have found the contents to be of enormous value to my life." F.C.

"I am a hard-working college student learning and I recognize the profound importance of Neo-Tech in my life." T.J., MO.

"A work far into the future brought into present day standards. The dawning of a future boundless with creative ideas and freedom." P.K., CANADA.

"At 51, I met my new woman a month after receiving Neo-Tech. After six months we have a most fabulous life. We both love each other, sex, business and capitalism. Thanks to Neo-Tech we are really happy." R.G., SWEDEN.

"The knowledge of Neo-Tech has probably contributed more to my happiness and security than any other thing in my life." T.P., FL.

"Neo-Tech needs to be taught in all schools and universities. It's a real eye-opener." M.M., AZ.

"What can I say? Neo-Tech was astounding to me. Thank you for opening my eyes to the truth." J.P., CA.

"Into my third reading. Results are starting to be realized. When I have completely absorbed all of the concepts I shall pass it on to my son. Thank you." S.R., IL.

"With a deep sense of gratitude, I write a few words of appreciation for your excellent research. Every item and concept written should have value to me now as well as in the future." B.B., NC.

377

Quotes from the early, incomplete versions of Neo-Tech

"This book will certainly have an impact on the literate world greater than any other book. Worth many times its purchase price. Thank you for awakening my mind." R.B., NEW ZEALAND.

"Excellent reading and most logical material. Wish I had known this information prior to my military career! Neo-Tech helps by providing proof and facts." D.S., MO.

"I have completed the Neo-Tech manuscript. It is the most complete book, covering all concepts of life. With your permission I'd like to refer others to this wonderful work." J.C., CO.

NEO-TECH I

The Prediscovery

NEO-TECH II

The Neo-Tech Discovery
(see preceding section)

NEO-TECH III

Controlling People Through Their Bicameral Minds

NEO-TECH IV

Predicting Stock Prices, Business Successes, and
Management Performance

NEO-TECH V

Achieving Biological Immortality
Through Competitive Business

INFORMATION PACKAGES

Neo-Tech Worldwide
Hong Kong, China   Las Vegas, Nevada   Kuala Lumpur, Malaysia
First Printing _____ January 1980 [2BB]
Second Printing_____ April 1980 (revised) [2BB]
Third Printing _____ December 1980 [2BB] [2BT, 1st PS]
Fourth Printing_____ June 1981 (revised) [2BB] [2BB] [1st II]
Fifth Printing _____ September 1981 [2BB]
Sixth Printing _____ October 1981 (revised) [5BB], [1st III]
Seventh Printing _____ February 1982 [5BB]
Eighth Printing _____ October 1982 (revised) [5KP, h]
Ninth Printing _____ July 1983 (revised) [10KP][25]
Tenth Printing _____ April 1984 [10KP]
Eleventh Printing _____ September 1984 [10BT]
Twelfth Printing _____ March 1985 [10.2BT] [65]
Thirteenth Printing _____ July 1985 (new edition) [6.3BT] [5.5BB]
Fourteenth Printing _____ October 1985 (revised) [10.4BT] [7.1BB]
Fifteenth Printing _____ January 1986 (revised) [10BT] [7.7BB]
Sixteenth Printing _____ June 1986 (revised) [10BT] [15BB] [102]
Seventeenth Printing _____ Dec. 1986 (full revisions) [10.5BT] [22.6BB]
Eighteenth Printing _____ March 1987 [12.1BT] (new belt)
Nineteenth Printing _____ August 1987 [20BT] [20BB] [audio II]
Twentieth Printing _____ June 1988 [21BT] [18BB] [audio I] [Mac]
Twenty-First Printing _____ November 1988 [10BT] [10BB]
Twenty-Second Printing ___ January 1989 [10BT] [10BB] [182]
Twenty-Third Printing _____ April 1989 [10BT] [10BB]
Twenty-Fourth Printing _____ May 1989 (new editions) [2 NN-A] [2 NN-B]
Twenty-Fifth Printing _____ August 1989 [10BT] [10BB][206]+[2.5 NTRE/BT]
Twenty-Sixth Printing _____ November 1989 (new NTCP-I) [24KP][-2.5BE]
Twenty-Seventh Printing ___ May 1990 [NTCP: I & II][5.2BB][40#]
Twenty-Eighth Printing ____ July 1990 [10BB]
Twenty-Ninth Printing _____ October 1990[11BB][256]
Thirtieth Printing _____ January 1991[11BB][#35]
Thirty-First Printing_____ March 1991[6BB][40#][Split Volumes, A&B]
Thirty-Second Printing _____ March 1991[5BB][40#] [B]
Thirty-Third Printing _____ November 1991 [5.5BB][40#][294][B]
Thirty-Fourth Printing _____ March 1992 [6.3 SP][50#][B]+[2.5NTPath]
Thirty-Fifth Printing _____ May 1992 [12.6 SP][50#][B][313+30F+10R]
Thirty-Sixth Printing _____ December 1992 [12.4 SP][35#][365][B]
Thirty-Seventh Printing ____ April 1993 [12.1 SP][35#][B]
Thirty-Eighth Printing _____ October 1993 [12.2 SP][35#][B]
Thirty-Ninth Printing _____ March 1994 [13.3 SP][35#][B]
Fortieth Printing _____ June 1994 [13.2 SP][35#][416][B]
Forty-First Printing _____ September 1994 [12.1 SP][35#][B]
Forty-Second Printing _____ March 1995 [11.7 SP][35#][440][B]
Forty-Third Printing _____ August 1995 [12.6 SP][34#][B]
Forty-Fourth Printing_____ February 1996 [23.2 SP][34#][B]
Forty-Fifth Printing _____ June 1996 [21.9 SP][34#][498][B]
Forty-Sixth Printing_____ November 1996 [22 SP][34#][521][B]
Forty-Seventh Printing ____ May 1997 (revised)[25.2PP][35#][B]
Forty-Eighth Printing_____ January 1998 [12PP][35#][B]
Forty-Ninth Printing _____ July 1998 [5PP][35#][B]
Fiftieth Printing _____ August 1998 [18.6PP][35#][B]
Printings Past 50th, see copyright page
65 67 66 64

Printed in the United States of America
International Standard Book Number (ISBN) 9111732-27-7
Library of Congress Catalog Number: 79-92518

PREFACE TO NEO-TECH I, III, IV, V

NEO-TECH I — THE PREDISCOVERY

Although unnecessary for understanding and using Neo-Tech, Dr. Wallace's original 192-page Neocheating Manuscript (which includes complete details along with 35 photos) is available to qualified Neo-Tech owners. But, purchase of that manuscript is neither necessary nor recommended since becoming an unbeatable professional card player is not the desired objective of Neo-Tech.

NEO-TECH II — THE NEO-TECH DISCOVERY

The Neo-Tech Discovery implements the most practical Neo-Tech ideas for gaining unlimited advantages in:

Art	Love
Business	Philosophy
Communication	Physiology
Education	Psychology
Entertainment	Politics
Government	Relationships
Health	Sex

In our world today, most people live and die without ever knowing the cheerful, crystal-clear Neo-Tech world that generates unending prosperity and happiness. But soon everyone will learn about that sunlit world of Nco-Tech. For through the dynamics of competitive advantages, Neo-Tech transforms the manipulations and dishonesties of neocheaters into advantages for everyone.

Neo-Tech II vitalizes words corrupted by the mystics and Neo-cheaters — words like "prosperity", "love", "happiness". With that vitalization, Neo-Tech opens the way to accomplishment and competence while emasculating the false power of all professional mystics and neocheaters.

Through its incorruptible matrix of personal and business advantages, Neo-Tech II quells all professional mystics and neocheaters. Neo-Tech then opens the door to a crystal-clear world of prosperity and happiness.

PREFACE TO NEO-TECH I, III, IV, V

NEO-TECH III–V
POWER, BUSINESS, PROSPERITY

The entire idea of Neo-Tech is to achieve forever growing prosperity and happiness through fully integrated honesty — through the elimination of mysticism and neocheating. The Neo-Tech concepts are the most effective tools possible for power, business, and personal life. As one begins to grasp the Neo-Tech concepts, he or she will begin to gain enormous leverage and integration power in business, career, financial, and personal matters.

To avoid unintegrated material and the resulting misconceptions, the Neo-Tech volumes should be read in the order presented in this book. Reading in the intended order is particularly important for the concepts of business and finance. For example, Neo-Tech III–V include concepts such as *Controlling People Through Their Bicameral Minds; The Fundamental Principle That Determines the Long-Range Common-Stock Value of a Corporation; Statement of Business Policies, Business Philosophy, and Business Goals for Biological Immortality.* Taking full advantage of those concepts requires integrations with the preceding Neo-Tech II, which includes more than 30 concepts directly applicable to gaining advantages in business, careers, and finance.

Neo-Tech **is** the entelechy of prosperity and happiness. For, Neo-Tech delivers unbeatable advantages in: **Personal Relationships, Business, Jobs, Careers, Finance, Investments, Art, and Health.**

THE PRE
NEO-TECH YEARS
and
The Discovery of
Neocheating
in the Wasted World of Cards
(background to Neocheating in the real world)

Do not be concerned or upset by the focus on cards and cheating in Neo-Tech I. Both cards and cheating are used as metaphors to better understand the nature of Neocheaters and Neo-Tech in the real world.

You are not expected to be knowledgeable or even interested in cards, much less cheating, to make full use of the Neo-Tech Discovery. In fact, most of Neo-Tech I is removed from the current editions of Neo-Tech. Why? Because using the techniques in cards are time-wasting (although quickly profitable) diversions that block the Neo-Tech integrations needed for abiding prosperity and happiness.

The Neo-Tech Discovery allows people to live prosperous, happy lives with unlimited growth. Anyone can immediately benefit from Neo-Tech. Moreover, the Neo-Tech Discovery debunks "positive thinking", mystical, and other such unreal approaches to life that lead to nothing.

The uses of the Neo-Tech Discovery range from making anyone unbeatable and wealthy at cards as shown in the original Neo-Tech I volume...to much more important uses such as business, financial transactions, social relationships as shown in Neo-Tech II volume...to breaking free of external authorities in order to gain the greatest possible rewards as shown in Neo-Tech III, IV and V.

Equally important, Neo-Tech protects one from those who cheat others out of the happy, prosperous lives they earn. And most important, Neo-Tech transfers the power from external "authorities" and value destroyers (government, religion, neocheaters, mystics) to you, the value producer — where the power belongs.

NEO-TECH I

NEOCHEATING
THE RISING MENACE

1. Neocheating — The Unbeatable Weapon
2. The Neo-Tech Discovery Beyond Cards

---

by
Frank R. Wallace
and
Mark Hamilton

The following background information is quoted directly from the original book titled *Neocheating — The Unbeatable Weapon*. All the remaining chapters of Neo-Tech I have been deleted. For Neo-Tech in cards is not needed to understand and apply Neo-Tech in the real world. In fact, as discovered from previous editions, inclusion of the complete Neo-Tech I was an undesirable distraction for most readers.

Neo-Tech I
The Prediscovery
(Not essential to read Neo-Tech I. Okay to skip ahead to Neo-Tech III.)

BACKGROUND

The following fifteen questions and answers are taken from the original book on Neocheating. The answers provide the background for Neocheating:

1. What is Neocheating?

Neocheating is the ultimate evolution of cheating. Neocheating is not based on sleight-of-hand or magician's skills as are many classical and traditional cheating techniques. Neocheating is a new, scientific kind of cheating — an invisible, incredibly easy kind of cheating based on simplicity and low skill. Once a person understands Neocheating, he can use its techniques to quietly beat opponents, anytime — anywhere on earth. But also, he can use that knowledge to defend against and defeat all cheating, including Neocheating.

2. How did Neocheating evolve?

Neocheating evolved from constant financial pressures and incentives to develop the easiest, safest, and most profitable methods of winning. Over the decades, the smartest profiteers have searched for shortcuts that require little skill, but contain the invisible effectiveness of the most advanced cardsharping techniques. Those shortcuts are identified in this book and then honed into practical-attack formats called Neocheating.

3. How is Neocheating so easy?

Neocheating is insidiously easy because it has been distilled by shortcut seekers over the years to the simplest essentials upon which all effective cheating depends. If a person understands those essentials, he will understand all cheating, allowing him to defend against any cheating, including Neocheating. But, at the same time, any player with larceny in his heart can now easily and safely beat any card game played for money.

4. How is Neocheating so safe?

Neocheating is so subtle that no one can ever prove a person is Neocheating. Even if others were certain someone was Neocheating, no evidence would exist to accuse the Neocheater because his maneuvers are invisible.

5. How can Neocheating be so easy and safe, yet still be the most potent form of cheating?

The simpler and subtler the cheating technique, the easier and safer and, therefore, the more effective it will be (as will become evident throughout the book). Indeed, the Neocheater's confident characteristics result from his exclusive use of simple, effective, and invisible techniques.

6. What are the characteristics of a Neocheater?

Neocheaters generally display characteristics opposite to those of traditional cheaters. In fact, the closer people observe a Neocheater, the more assured they become that no cheating is occurring. And ironically, as shown in the final chapter of this book, the Neocheater is often the most trusted person in the game.

Why the difference in characteristics? Alert or knowledgeable opponents can usually detect traditional cheating — unless the cheater has acquired great classical skill through years of laborious practice and experience. Even then, the cardsharp must execute each cheating maneuver perfectly, every time, putting him under great pressure. Moreover, the traditional cheater becomes obviously guilty once caught, leaving him to face the consequences. That fear of being caught haunts most traditional cheaters and overwhelms countless potential cheaters.

By contrast, Neocheating is invisible, routine, and requires little skill. The Neocheater's tactics are so subtle that, even if accused, his cheating cannot be proven. Indeed, he can always avoid the consequences because he can never be caught *flagrante delicto* or "in the act".

The traditional cheater fears his telltale characteristics. But the Neocheater works in harmony with his deceptive characteristics, preventing people unknowledgeable about Neocheating from ever suspecting him. As a result, the Neocheater flourishes.

7. Where is Neocheating going?

Simple and effective Neocheating is today spreading throughout poker games in Nevada casinos and California card clubs. Indeed, Neocheating is already infiltrating private games of poker, blackjack, bridge, and gin. And Neocheating will keep on spreading, leaving no game or player immune from attack.

8. What can stop Neocheating from spreading?

Publicly revealing the techniques of Neocheating may initially cause a cheating spree that could create chaos at the card table. But ironically, that knowledge, as it becomes widely known, will begin to expose and nullify Neocheating. Players no longer need to be helpless or doomed when confronted with Neocheating. Instead, they will be able to defeat and eliminate Neocheating.

9. If Neocheating is invisible, how can it be detected and stopped?

Neocheating *cannot* be detected directly, and the Neocheater can never be accused or caught outright. But with the knowledge of Neocheating, a player can sense Neocheating — know when it is occurring. And then with special countermeasures (taught in this book), he can win in the presence of a Neocheater...or, if he chooses, easily cause the Neocheater to leave the game.

10. Who is the Neocheater?

He is a player who cannot lose. He can drain everyone's money at will. He may be in your game now... or next week. Or he may be you. The Neocheater will inevitably threaten every card game played for money. Moreover, he considers Neocheating no more wrong than bluffing or normal card deception.

11. How does the Neocheater differ from the cardsharp?

The Neocheater is *not* a cardsharp. He is a new breed of player who may soon rule the card table.

The cardsharp has existed since the invention of cards. He cheats without the knowledge of Neocheating. Still, he may unknowingly use various Neocheating techniques. But generally his cheating relies on skill and gall.

The Neocheater, on the other hand, relies on neither skill nor gall. He relies on simple, invisible maneuvers. For him to use any other means of cheating (such as palming cards or using marked cards) would be unnecessary and foolish since Neocheating is not only safe, but is much easier and more effective.

12. What makes the Neocheater unbeatable?

The maneuvers of Neocheating are so subtle and the mechanics so easy that they can be executed with relaxed confidence. Guaranteed winning hands can be routinely obtained. And more than one powerful hand can be arranged at a time to ensure a big score. Yet, unlike the cardsharp, the Neocheater seldom uses powerful hands or goes for big scores (although he easily can). Instead, he casually uses just enough of his power to give him constant, unbeatable advantages. In fact, he may never even Neocheat for himself, but instead simply use Neocheating to shift money from the strongest players to the weakest players and then win legitimately from those weak players. His steady, hidden attack lets him win consistently and comfortably in poker, blackjack, bridge, and gin — week after week, year after year.

This book shows not only how the Neocheater can easily create spectacular advantages for himself, but how he can create smarter, unsuspicious, casino-like advantages to safely extract maximum money from all games. With those invisible advantages, he keeps his opponents happy while comfortably controlling the game, even a network of games. ...Neocheating is that easy.

13. How does Neocheating apply to games such as blackjack, bridge, and gin?

The Neocheating techniques in this book apply to all card games. Most techniques, however, are presented with a poker slant because most card cheating has traditionally been centered around poker — the money game. Also, Neocheating techniques are more easily illustrated through poker examples. But Neocheating will become increasingly common in *all* card games played for money or prestige.

14. Is revealing Neocheating immoral?

Can honestly revealing facts ever be immoral? Only by fully revealing Neocheating can honest players fully defend and protect themselves from the Neocheaters.

Neo-Tech I
The Prediscovery
(Not essential to read Neo-Tech I. Okay to skip ahead to Neo-Tech III.)

THE NEO-TECH DISCOVERY

The Neo-Tech discovery evolved from that earlier discovery of Neocheating. In a sense, Neocheating was not a discovery but an identification of elegantly sophisticated techniques of card cheating that met two criteria: (1) *required little effort or skill, and* (2) *were undetectable or unassailable as dishonest.*

Wallace's identification of Neocheating will have similar effects on the business world that his earlier identifications of the Advanced Concepts of Poker had on the poker world a decade earlier: Like Neocheating, various Advanced Concepts of Poker had been unknowingly used not only by winning card players but by unbeatable strategists beyond the card tables. And the extent that they randomly used the various Advanced Concepts was the extent that they won. With the publication of Wallace's book, *The Advanced Concepts of Poker*, a total of 120 Advantage Levers were identified for the first time and systematically integrated into one consolidated, unbeatable weapon. That gathering, integrating, and publishing of the Advanced Concepts into one book produced big-profit increases for those players who acquired Wallace's book. As a result, the number of professional players, competitive players, successful women players, as well as high-stake games and tournament games escalated dramatically since *The Advanced Concepts of Poker* was first published.

And now, the publication of Neocheating followed by Neo-Tech will have an even more profound effect on the business world: After identifying the Neocheating concepts, Frank R. Wallace made much more important discoveries by extending those concepts beyond cards — into business, politics, social relationships, and other areas of life. Once the concepts of Neocheating are fully understood, their application beyond cards becomes limitless. But Neocheaters in all areas of life become fully visible to those who understand Neocheating. Moreover, by understanding the concepts of Neo-Tech, one can render Neocheaters impotent.

Neocheating concepts used in business and other areas of life are so exquisitely subtle that the initial reaction is shock on realizing the enormous advantages one gains by using those concepts beyond cards.

Neocheating Beyond Cards

Neocheating beyond cards involves gaining easy advantages and power over others through combinations of techniques that meet two criteria: *(1) easy to execute,* and *(2) not vulnerable to detection or assailable as dishonest.* Once those two criteria are established, Neocheating formats can then be established in any area of life. With such formats, a person not only gleans unbeatable advantages over others, but commands easy shortcuts to profits and power.

Master Neocheaters are those who use invisible Neocheating concepts to maximum effectiveness in gaining enormous power and wealth. Such neocheaters range from the heads of states to church leaders. But anyone can use the Neocheating concepts to gain profits to any chosen degree, ranging from dishonest business people neocheating customers (e.g., selling unneeded or fraudulent insurance policies), professional people neocheating clients (e.g., lawyers making problems where none exist, doctors promoting unneeded surgery), husbands neocheating wives (e.g., psychologically or physically abusing spouses into dependence, then into submission and subservience), women neocheating men (e.g., deceiving for entrapment and wealth extraction), teachers neocheating students (e.g., dishonestly attacking value producers to usurp unearned power), parents neocheating children (e.g., destructive manipulation for social images).

One major benefit of understanding Neocheating beyond cards is the ability to identify its practitioners who surround everyone in almost every area of life. Once identified, Neocheaters can be prevented from diminishing one's own well-being.

Perhaps the most startling benefit of understanding Neocheating occurs when viewing network television news: With knowledge of Neo-Tech, a person becomes acutely aware of the steady stream of Neocheaters (television commentators, news journalists, politicians, lawyers, professors, educators, mystical gurus, and religious leaders) who constantly destroy values and usurp power to gain unearned livelihoods. With the concepts of Neo-Tech, however, people not only can nullify every Neocheater, but they can transfer all usurped power back to themselves.

The Neo-Tech concepts are not only easy, practical tools for profits, but are crucial tools for thinking. Those concepts allow a person to identify and nullify Neocheaters who have beguiled human life for two-thousand years. Without understanding Neocheating, a person has no way of thinking about Neocheaters or of realizing how they constantly extract values from unknowledgeable people. Without those thinking tools to identify Neocheating, everyone suffers in silent frustration as Neocheaters constantly and forever drain each person's one-and-only life.

One supreme value of the Neo-Tech concepts is that they are the tools for rejecting and eventually eliminating the unearned power of all Neocheaters — of all destructive political leaders, government bureaucrats, religious leaders, dishonest media people and educators, external "authorities" of all kinds.

Neocheating in Business, Politics, Religion, and Social Relationships

The specific Neocheating techniques for cards provide the concrete base needed to understand the *concepts behind* Neocheating. By understanding those concepts, the wider applications of Neocheating become increasingly obvious. Indeed, Neocheating can be used in any area of life to usurp money, power, respect, or love. But, in the long run, people who extract values by Neocheating become dependent on cheating as they undermine their competence and self-esteem by embezzling rather than earning values. The careful observer will recognize that by far the highest percentage of people involved in building false self-esteems to justify their existences are those pursuing careers in politics and religion. Such careers are by nature anti-productive and depend on Neocheating the public to extract money, respect, and power.

Cheating as a Metaphor

What positive value can be found in card cheating? One magnificent value: Card cheating is a superb metaphor for

391

Neo-Tech I
The Prediscovery
(Not essential to read Neo-Tech I. Okay to skip ahead to Neo-Tech III.)

identifying and classifying dishonest people:

The *traditional* cheater is, for example, the crude sneak thief. He is also the small-time bureaucrat or politician on the take. He needs little skill and much gall to extract his living. But he lives in constant danger of being caught in the act and subjected to the consequences.

The *classical* cheater is, for example, the elegant con-artist thief. He is also the respected technocrat who, for example, develops computer systems to help a value-destroying government bureaucracy cripple innocent value producers. Application of his skills (that took years to polish or develop) lets him extract a "good" living. His dishonesty usually remains unseen and uncalled by those who surround him as he helps to cheat countless people out of their earned happiness and values.

The *Neocheater* is, for example, the subtle executive thief who climbs to a high-paid corporate position by deceptive machinations rather than by productive efforts. He is also the religious leader who gleans respect and adulation by cleverly promoting self-sacrifice and altruism. And the ultimate Neocheaters are the politicians gracing the highest offices. They usurp sumptuous livings, enormous power, and huge ego trips by converting productive assets into nonproductive waste for the "public good" through the invisible manipulations of government force (e.g., forced redistribution of earned wealth away from value production and into the wealth-destroying graveyards of criminal-minded Neocheaters with their corrals of supporting parasites and dependents). Their techniques require neither skill nor effort. They are simply shrewd and subtle enough to keep most people from realizing that they are constantly, criminally neocheating the value producer — constantly, malevolently draining the value producer's life, assets, and happiness. And, most dangerously, they rationalize their neocheating as necessary for the "good of society" when, in fact, their neocheating harms everyone.

As shown in the following table, Neocheaters are by far the deadliest menace to honest and productive people and societies, everywhere.

392

Neo-Tech I
The Prediscovery
(Not essential to read Neo-Tech I. Okay to skip ahead to Neo-Tech III.)

SPECIAL NOTE
White-Hat Neocheaters versus Black-Hat Neocheaters

The idea of honest white-hat Neocheating versus dishonest black-hat Neocheating was a valuable concept deleted from Neo-Tech I for this Cosmic Power edition. Briefly, a black-hat Neocheater is dishonest and his neocheating is destructive to others and society. But a white-hat Neocheater is honest and his neocheating is beneficial to others and society. Basically, the white-hat Neocheater understands and then uses neocheating only against black-hat Neocheaters to drive them out of their destructive positions, be they two-bit Neocheaters in card games or mass-murder Neocheaters in Beijing. ...Honesty is never owed to thieves and murderers.

NEOCHEATING BEYOND CARDS

Area Of	Examples Of Master Neocheating	NEOCHEATING CRITERIA	
		EASY TO EXECUTE	UNASSAILABLE
Banking	International bankers who gain advantages and profits through criminal-minded governments.	Glean unearned money by manipulating government money, funds, and favors.	Nothing is illegal about their manipulations.
Business	Prosperous but dishonest stockbrokers and real-estate brokers. White-collar-hoax CEO's.	Mislead customers or clients by making dishonest or fraudulent claims. Generate illusions of prosperity and competence by converting long-range assets into steadily shorter term assets.	Appear to work for customer's best interest. Appear successful. Without any illegal moves, they secretly drain companies built by forgotten business heroes.
Education	Certain professors, teachers, nutritionists, who build careers through ideas based on "big lies", empiricisms, myths, and mysticism.	Exploit students and followers through power of "teaching authorities".	The public cannot identify their unearned power and job-usurping dishonesties.
Law	Attorneys who manipulate law and litigation to gain wealth by stirring trouble where none exists. They prosper without producing net values for others.	Manipulate specious points to operate easily within the bounds of government law.	Appear respectable by practicing in a prestige profession among the upper social and political classes.
Media	Many of the best-known TV commentators, journalists, editorial writers, performers, authors.	Foist inaccurate, dishonest, unintegrated, or out-of-context "facts" on trusting followers.	Others cannot grasp the dishonesty and deception of such authors, actors, newscasters, journalists.
Politics	Major politicians.	Live by machinations that never involve the honesty, integrated thinking, and hard efforts of productive achievements.	Traditionally accepted as good or at least necessary.

NEOCHEATING BEYOND CARDS

NEOCHEATING CRITERIA

Area Of	Examples Of Master Neocheating	EASY TO EXECUTE	UNASSAILABLE
Psychology	Therapists who manipulate emotions to leave their clients increasingly dependent on "therapy" for temporary or illusionary relief from unfaced, mystical-caused problems.	Clients feel "helped" or high after each fix, leaving them increasingly incompetent for solving their own problems arising from their own mysticism.	Respected for helping to "solve" problems of others — over and over again.
Religion	Most religious leaders.	No honest integrated thinking or hard productive efforts needed to extract a respectable living from value producers.	As with politicians, traditionally accepted as good and needed.
Science	Most so-called environmentalists and all politically or socially oriented "scientists" who build pseudo careers by using facts out of context.	Gain prestige with comfortable income and security.	Appear to be acting in society's best interest when actually generating unearned prestige by undermining productive achievement.
Social	Dishonest Don Juans.	Manipulate love partners through vulnerable emotions.	Few can identify their destructive intentions.

NEO-TECH III

Information Package

CONTROLLING MYSTICS THROUGH THEIR BICAMERAL MINDS

by

John Flint and Eric Savage

What is the Bicameral Mind?

The bicameral mind is a human mind functioning in a particular, unconscious mode or manner...in the manner intended by nature. While the bicameral mind[1] exists in all people, it can be controlled or dominated by a special mode of consciousness developed not through mother nature but volitionally by each individual being. That mind control or domination can be exercised by an individual over himself and others. Or an individual can allow that mode of consciousness in others to control or dominate his or her bicameral mind.

The bicameral mind (two-chamber mind) is one that functions as an unconscious, two-step process. Automatic reactions and thoughts originate in the right hemisphere of the brain and are transmitted to the left hemisphere as instructions to be acted upon. The bicameral functioning is nature's automatic, learned mode of response without regard to conscious thinking. By contrast, man-made consciousness functions through a deliberate, volitional thought process that is independent of nature's bicameral thought process.

Until approximately 3000 years ago, man's brain functioned entirely in nature's automatic bicameral mode. But the automatic bicameral mind became inadequate to handle the mounting problems as societies became more complex. To survive, man was forced to invent a new way of thinking — a new mode called consciousness that could solve infinitely more complex problems. That consciousness mode involved his newly discovered powers of introspection. His thinking process was further enhanced by new thoughts and insights created by comparisons done through metaphors and analogs.

---

[1]The bicameral mind was first identified by Dr. Julian Jaynes of Princeton University in his book, *The Origin of Consciousness in the Breakdown of the Bicameral Mind*, Houghton Mifflin Company.

Neo-Tech III
Controlling Mystic Minds

Consciousness allows a person to make his or her own decisions rather than relying on nature's bicameral process that automatically follows learned customs, traditional rules, and external "authorities". Metaphors and analogs increase a person's range and power of thinking infinitely beyond nature's range. Yet, despite the great advantages in using the man-invented mode of thinking, most people today depend to various degrees on their automatic bicameral mentality and external "authorities" to make their decisions for them.

That bicameral mentality lures people into searching for "sure-thing" guidance from "higher authorities", rather than using their own consciousness for making decisions and determining their actions. Thus, in their search for prepackaged truth and automatic guidance, people seek "higher authorities": religion, politics, true-believer movements, leaders, gurus, cults, astrology, fads, drugs, feelings, and even forms of poetry, music, medicine, nutrition, and psychology. The bicameral mind seeks outside sources that will tell it how to think and act. ...Anyone can exploit the automatic bicameral mind in others by setting up "authorities" for influencing or controlling that bicameral mentality seeking external guidance.

Bicameral mentalities avoid human self-responsibility by seeking and obeying external decision makers. In poker, for example, bicameral tendencies leave players open to being controlled by any conscious individual acting as an external decision maker and authority. In addition, the single, biggest money-losing, mystical concept — the belief in luck — is rooted in the bicameral mentality. In fact, most gamblers rely on the phantom "authority" of luck to escape the only valid authority: their own rational consciousness.

Understanding bicameral tendencies in others can provide unbeatable advantages by knowing the external forces that control most people. That understanding enables one not only to predict the actions of others but to control their actions. A poker player, for example, can create unbeatable advantages by projecting any number of phantom "authorities" to which his opponents will obey, act, or react.

The principle of advantageously controlling the bicameral minds of others applies not only to poker but to all competitive situations involving two or more people. Poker, however, provides crisp, clear examples of using the bicameral mind to control people. More important, poker provides countless metaphors to which everyone can relate. Also, most poker players are gamblers. And gambling is a bicameral activity in which people abandon their own rational consciousness to phantom "authorities" such as feelings, luck, priests, and politicians.

The Bicameral Mind in Poker

Poker games exist because of the bicameral urge in most players to gamble. That urge resides in the desire to escape the responsibility for consistently making rational decisions needed to prosper by producing values for others. Gamblers try to escape (at least temporarily) that self-responsibility through an activity such as poker. And through their bicameral urges, gamblers can be controlled by others.

Even the best professional player can succumb to bicameral urges: By playing poker for a living, for example, he avoids involvement in a productive career that demands much more independent, rational thinking than poker. But, the good player can also use poker as a discipline to strengthen both his conscious integrating processes and his abilities to control others.

Exploiting Bicameral Tendencies in Opponents

Through understanding those bicameral urges in others, a good player can generate unbeatable advantages. He creates those advantages by conjuring up external "authorities" for guiding his opponents into actions that benefit him. For example, an opponent is told to "open up" (bet more loosely) because good player X always bets aggressively in the same situation — and good player X always ends up winning heavily. In that way, player X is set up as an external "authority" for misleading the opponent into making wrong moves based on facts bicamerally accepted out of context. Even greater advantages are gained by realizing that an opponent is bicamerally using rules, information, and odds gleaned from "authorities" such as authors of noncognitive poker books. (Of the 170 poker books published in the past century, only

Neo-Tech III
Controlling Mystic Minds

Wallace's book, *The Advanced Concepts of Poker*, is fully cognitive.)

Bicameral tendencies can also be exploited through subtle maneuvers. For example, mumbling very quietly (almost subaudibly) words that will influence or trigger reactions in opponents who subconsciously hear those "voices". To those opponents, the subconscious voice automatically acts as an external "authority" to be followed. As another example, a player who is hesitant about attending a game after several losing sessions is fed whatever out-of-context facts or spurious "truth" he wants to hear such as, "The worst thing a player can do is quit just as his losing streak is about to end. That's when the odds are the greatest for shifting from a bad-luck streak to a good-luck streak. Managing luck streaks is the whole idea of winning. All winners know that." With such specious "truths" and non sequiturs, the good player establishes himself as an external "authority" in controlling his opponents.

But most important, as demonstrated in the original Neo-Tech Prediscovery, poker generates accurate metaphors needed to identify and then exploit the bicameral tendencies existing in most people. Indeed, those tendencies are readily exploitable beyond the card tables with the same kind of phantom or external "authorities" set up either overtly or subliminally. Such external "authorities" can be established, for example, in religion, politics, psychology, medicine, business, and personal relationships as shown in Neo-Tech II. ...Understanding the bicameral mind is invaluable not only for controlling others but for avoiding being controlled by others.

The discovery of controlling people through their bicameral minds evolved from a more basic discovery made by Dr. Julian Jaynes of Princeton University. His discovery was first identified and then integrated in the following article written for the Neo-Tech Research and Writing Institute.

Consciousness: The End of Authority
by
Frank R. Wallace

A person could make an excellent bet by wagering a hundred ounces of gold bullion that Julian Jaynes' book *The Origin of Consciousness in the Breakdown of the Bicameral Mind* will someday rank among the five most important books written during the second millennium.[1] The discovery of the bicameral mind solves the missing-link problem that has defied all previous theories of human evolution.

Dr. Jaynes discovered that until 3000 years ago essentially all human beings were void of consciousness. Consciousness versus unconsciousness is not defined here as awake versus asleep, alert versus dazed, aware versus knocked out. Consciousness is defined as modern man's awareness of himself, his subjective thoughts and feelings, his subjective choices and *self-determined* interaction with the world around him versus mere automatic reactions as with all other animals, including man until about 3000 years ago. Until the first millennium BC, man along with all other primates functioned by mimicked or learned reactions. But, because of his much larger, more complex brain, man was able to develop a coherent language beginning about 8000 B.C. In effect, human beings were super-intelligent but automatically reacting animals who could communicate by talking. That communication enabled human beings to cooperate closely to build societies, even thriving civilizations.

Still, like all other animals, man functioned almost entirely by an automatic guidance system that was void of consciousness. Ten thousand years ago, man's neurological guidance system incorporated his superior phenomenon of speech: man's

---

[1]When Dr. Wallace wrote this review of Jaynes' book in 1980, the bicameral man was a new and controversial hypothesis. Today, however, Jaynes' bicameral-man hypothesis is accepted by the scientific establishment as the prevailing position on our ancestry.

neurological instructions amazingly took the form of automatic, audio commands in his own mind known today as audio hallucinations. Those audio hallucinations came from neurological instructions triggered in the right hemisphere of the brain and transmitted as "heard" voices of the gods in the left hemisphere of the brain (the bicameral or two-chamber mind). Whereas the cat would automatically run from danger, bicameral man would hear a voice in his head from his god saying, "Run, run away!"

Ironically, this advanced guidance system based on speech carried its own death sentence as it allowed civilizations to thrive to such new heights that the complexities went beyond the capacity of an automatic, neurological guidance system designed by nature. About 1000 BC, whole civilizations began collapsing as the "voices" became confused, contradictory, or just plain vanished. Man was forced to invent consciousness or a self-determining (versus automatically reacting) way of using his mind to become his own guide and god to survive in the collapsing bicameral civilizations.

Jaynes eliminated the missing link in the evolution of man by discovering that consciousness or the self-determining way of using the mind was never intended by nature — consciousness was invented by man. (Later you will see close parallels to our upcoming "jump" into the much more competitive God-Man.)

The major components of Jaynes's discovery are:

- All civilizations before 1000 B.C. — such as Assyria, Babylonia, Mesopotamia, pharaonic Egypt — were built, inhabited, and ruled by automatically reacting, unconscious people.

- Ancient writings such as the *Iliad* and the early books of the Old Testament were composed by unconscious minds that automatically recorded and objectively reported both real and imagined events. The transition to subjective and introspective writings of the conscious mind occurred in later works such as the *Odyssey* and the newer books of the Old Testament.

- Ancient people learned to speak, read, write, as well as carry out daily life, work, and the professions all while remaining unconscious throughout their lives. Being unconscious, they never experienced guilt, never practiced deceit, and were not responsible for their actions. They had no way to determine their actions; they were automatically reacting animals. They, like any other animal, had no concept of guilt, deception, evil, justice, philosophy, history, or the future. They could not introspect and had no internal idea of themselves. They had no subjective sense of time or space and had no memories as we know them. They were unconscious and innocent. They were guided by "voices" or strong impressions in their bicameral minds — unconscious minds structured for nature's automatic survival.

- The development of human consciousness began about 3000 years ago when the automatic bicameral mind began breaking down under the mounting stresses of its inadequacy to find workable solutions in increasingly complex societies. The hallucinated voices became more and more confused, contradictory, and destructive.

- Man was forced to invent and develop consciousness in order to survive as his hallucinating voices no longer provided adequate guidance for survival.

- Today, after 3000 years, most people retain remnants of the bicameral guidance system in the form of mysticism and the desire for external authority.

- Except for schizophrenics, people today no longer hallucinate the voices that guided bicameral man. Yet, most people are at least partly influenced and are sometimes driven by the remnants of the bicameral man as they seek, to varying degrees, automatic guidance from "voices" of others or external "authorities".

- All religions are rooted in the unconscious bicameral mind that is obedient to the "voices" of external "authorities" — obedient to the "voice" of God, gods, rulers, and leaders.

- The discovery that consciousness was never a part of nature's evolutionary scheme (but was invented by man) eliminates

the missing-link puzzle in human evolution.
• Essentially all religious and most political ideas survive through those vestiges of the obsolete bicameral mind. The bicameral mind seeks omniscient truth and automatic guidance from external "authorities" such as political or spiritual leaders — or other "authoritarian" sources such as manifested in idols, astrologists, gurus — as well as most lawyers, most psychiatrists and psychologists, certain professors, some doctors, most journalists and TV anchormen.

The idea of civilizations consisting entirely of unconscious, automatic-reacting people and the idea of man bypassing nature to invent his own consciousness initially seems incredible. But as Jaynes documents his evidence in a reasoned and detached manner, the existence of two minds in all human beings becomes increasingly evident: (1) the obsolete, unconscious (bicameral) mind that seeks guidance from external "authorities" for important thoughts and decisions, especially under stressed or difficult conditions; and (2) the newly invented conscious mind that bypasses external "authorities" and provides thoughts and guidance generated from one's own mind. ...Understanding Jaynes' discoveries unlocks the 10,000 year-old secret of controlling the actions of people through their bicameral minds.

What evidence does Jaynes present to support his discoveries? After defining consciousness, he systematically presents his evidence to prove that man was unconscious until 3000 years ago when the bicameral civilizations collapsed and individuals began inventing consciousness in order to survive. Jaynes's proof begins with the definition of consciousness:

Defining and Understanding Consciousness

Julian Jaynes defines both what consciousness is and what it is not. After speculating on its location, he demonstrates that consciousness itself has no physical location, but rather is a particular organization of the mind and a specific way of using

d

the brain. Jaynes then demonstrates that consciousness is only a small part of mental activity and is not necessary for concept formation, learning, thinking, or even reasoning. He illustrates how all those mental functions can be performed automatically and unconsciously. Furthermore, consciousness does not contribute to and often hinders the execution of learned skills such as speaking, listening, writing, reading — as well as skills involving music, art, and athletics. Thus, if major human actions and skills can function automatically and without consciousness, those same actions and skills can be controlled or driven by external influences, "authorities", or "voices" emanating under conditions described later in this review. ...But first an understanding of consciousness is important:

Consciousness requires metaphors (i.e., referring to one thing in order to better understand or describe another thing — such as the head of an army, table, page, household, nail). Consciousness also requires analog models, (i.e., thinking of a map of California, for example, in order to visualize the entire, physical state of California). Thinking in metaphors and analog models creates the mind space and mental flexibility needed to bypass those automatic, bicameral processes.

The *bicameral thinking* process functions only in concrete terms and narrow, here-and-now specifics. But the *conscious thinking* process generates an infinite array of subjective perceptions that permit ever broader understanding and better decisions.

Metaphors of "me" and analog models of "I" allow consciousness to function through introspection and self-visualization. In turn, consciousness expands by creating more and more metaphors and analog models. That expanding consciousness allows a person to "see" and understand the relationship between himself and the world with increasing accuracy and clarity. As he becomes more and more aware of himself and his interaction with the world, he gains control of his actions, makes decisions, and discovers self-determination.

Consciousness is a conceptual, metaphor-generated analog

world that parallels the actual world. Man, therefore, could not invent consciousness until he developed a language sophisticated enough to produce metaphors and analog models.

The genus Homo began about two million years ago. Rudimentary oral languages developed from 70,000 B.C. to about 8000 B.C. Written languages began about 3000 B.C. and gradually developed into syntactical structures capable of generating metaphors and analog models. Only at that point could man invent and experience consciousness.

Jaynes shows that man's early writings (hieroglyphics, hiertatic, and cuneiform) reflect a mentality totally different from our own. They reflect a nonmetaphoric, unconscious mentality. Jaynes also shows that the *Iliad*, which evolved as a sung poem about 1000 B.C., contains little if any conscious thought. The characters in the Iliad (e.g., Achilles, Agamemnon, Hector, Helen) act unconsciously in initiating all their major actions and decisions through "voices", and all speak in hexameter rhythms (as often do modern-day schizophrenics when hallucinating). Hexameter rhythms are characteristic of the rhythmically automatic functionings of the right-hemisphere brain. Moreover, the *Iliad* is entirely about action...about the acts and consequences of Achilles, always reacting to the world and the gods around him. The *Iliad* never mentions subjective thoughts or the contents of anyone's mind. The language is unconscious — an objective reporting of facts that are concrete bound and void of introspection and abstract thought. There is no self-determination.

With a conscious mind, man can introspect; he can debate with himself; he can become his own god, voice, and decision maker. But before the invention of consciousness, the mind functioned bicamerally: the right hemisphere (the poetic, god-brain) hallucinated audio instructions to the left hemisphere (the analytical, man-brain), especially in unusual or stressful situations. Essentially, man's brain today is physically identical to the ancient bicameral brain; but with his invention of consciousness, he can now choose to integrate the functions of the left and right hemispheres and be his own authority.

Beginning about 9000 B.C. — as oral languages developed — routine or habitual tasks became increasingly standardized. The hallucinating voices for performing those basic tasks, therefore, became increasingly similar among groups of people. The collectivization of "voices" allowed more and more people to cooperate and function together through their bicameral minds. The leaders spoke to the "gods" and used the "voices" to lead the masses in cooperative unison. And that cooperation allowed nomadic hunting tribes to gradually organize into stationary, food-producing societies. The continuing development of oral language and the increasing collectivization of bicameral minds allowed towns and eventually cities to form and flourish.

The bicameral mind, however, became increasingly inadequate for guiding human actions as societies continued to grow in size and complexity. By about 1000 B.C., the bicameral mind had become so inadequate that man's social structures began collapsing. Under threat of extinction, man invented a new way of using his brain that allowed him to solve the much more complex problems needed to survive — he invented a new organization of the mind called consciousness.

With consciousness, man now became his own executor, his own god, and now controlled his actions and became aware of his past and future. With consciousness, man became aware of himself, his life, his feelings. A whole new world opened up to him as his life now had meaning...and direction. He could now establish goals and feel the unique ecstasy of self-determination and accomplishment. Man, in essence, went from an automatically reacting animal to a fully conscious human being, just as we are today. The thrill for life — a dynamic conscious life — had to be spectacular to those pioneers who overcame their fears and embraced the new world that opened up to them. ...Similarly today, we are at the threshold of embracing, again, a spectacular new world as we discover the Neothink mentality. But first...

The Development of Consciousness

Dr. Jaynes shows through abundant archaeological, historical, and biological evidence that the towns, cities, and societies from 9000 B.C. to 1000 B.C. were established and developed by unconscious people. Those societies formed and grew through common hallucinating voices attributed to gods, rulers, and the dead — to external "authorities". Various external symbols that "spoke" (such as graves, idols, and statues) helped to reinforce and expand the authority of those common "voices". And those "voices" continued to expand their reach through increasingly visible and awe-inspiring symbols such as tombs, temples, colossuses, and pyramids.

But as those unconscious societies became more complex and increasingly intermingled through trade and wars, the "voices" became mixed and contradictory. With the "voices" becoming muddled, their effectiveness in guiding people diminished. Rituals and importunings became ever more intense and elaborate in attempts to evoke clearer "voices" and better guidance. The development of writing and the permanent recording of instructions and laws during the second millennium B.C. further weakened the authority and effectiveness of hallucinated voices. As the "voices" lost their effectiveness, they began falling silent. And without authoritarian "voices" to guide and control its people, those societies suddenly began collapsing with no external cause.

As the bicameral mind broke down and societies collapsed, individuals one by one began inventing consciousness to make decisions needed to survive in the mounting anarchy and chaos. During the chaotic cataclysms of the collapsing civilizations, during which entire populations were wiped out, the bicameral man would, for example, automatically fight a band of men plundering his home and raping his spouse — his automatic reaction to external stimuli — even though his gallant fight would mean certain death for him and his family. The newly conscious man, however, might smile passively on the outside — while

h

planning his revenge in his mind — and later that night visit the bedsides of his sleeping enemies to end their lives and save his own. The conscious man, who could separate himself from the objective world to subjectively determine his actions, greatly increased his advantages for survival over the bicameral man.

On making conscious and volitional decisions, man for the first time became responsible for his actions. Also, for short-range advantages and easy power, conscious man began discovering and using deceit and treachery — behaviors not possible from unconscious, bicameral minds. (Before inventing consciousness, man was as guiltless and amoral as any other animal since he had no volitional choice in following his automatic guidance system of hallucinated voices.)

As the "voices" fell silent, man began contriving religions and prayers in his attempts to communicate with the departed gods. Jaynes shows how man developed the concept of worship, heaven, angels, demons, exorcism, sacrifice, divination, omens, sortilege, augury in his attempts to evoke guidance from the gods — from external "authorities".

All such quests for external "authority" hark back to the breakdown of the hallucinating bicameral mind — to the silencing and celestialization of the once "vocal" and earthly gods.

Much direct evidence for the breakdown of the bicameral mind and the development of consciousness comes from writings scribed between 1300 B.C. and 300 B.C. Those writings gradually shift from unconscious, objective reports to conscious, subjective expressions that reflect introspection. The jump from the unconscious writing of the *Iliad* to the conscious writing of the *Odyssey* (composed perhaps a century later) is dramatically obvious. That radical difference between the *Iliad* and the *Odyssey* is, incidentally, further evidence that more than one poet composed the Homeric epics.

The transition from the unconscious *Iliad* to the conscious *Odyssey* marks man's break with his 8000-year-old hallucinatory guidance system. By the sixth century B.C., written languages began reflecting conscious ideas of morality and justice similar

i

to those reflected today.

The Old Testament of the Bible also illustrates the transition from the unconscious writing of its earlier books (such as Amos, circa 750 B.C.) to the fully conscious writing of its later books (such as Ecclesiastes, circa 350 B.C.). Amid that transition, the book of Samuel records the first known suicide — an act that requires consciousness. And the book of Deuteronomy illustrates the conflict between the bicameral mind and the conscious mind.

Likewise, the transition to consciousness is observed in other parts of the world: Chinese literature moved from bicameral unconsciousness to subjective consciousness about 500 B.C. with the writings of Confucius. And in India, literature shifted to subjective consciousness around 400 B.C. with the Upanishadic writings.

American Indians, however, never developed the sophisticated, metaphorical languages needed to develop full consciousness. As a result, their mentalities were probably bicameral when they first encountered the European explorers. For example, with little or no conscious resistance, the Incas allowed the Spanish "white gods" to dominate, plunder, and slaughter them. (Just as conscious men seemed like gods to bicameral men, God-Man will seem like God with a higher consciousness than us.)

The Bicameral Mind in Today's World

Dr. Jaynes identifies many vestiges of the bicameral mentality that exist today. The most obvious vestige is religion and its symbols. Ironically, early Christianity with its teachings of Jesus was an attempt to shift religion from the outmoded bicameral and celestial mind of Moses to the newly conscious and earthly mind of man. Christianity then discovered a devastatingly effective tool for authoritarian control — guilt. Indeed, guilt not only worked on conscious minds, but required conscious minds to be effective.

Despite religion, conscious minds caused the gradual shifts from governments of gods to governments of men and from divine laws to secular laws. Still, the vestiges of the bicameral mind combined with man's longing for guidance produced churches, prophets, oracles, sibyls, diviners, cults, mediums, astrologers, saints, idols, demons, tarot cards, seances, Ouija boards, glossolalia, fuhrers, ayatollahs, popes, peyote, Jonestown, born-agains.

Jaynes shows how such external "authorities" exist only through the remnants of the bicameral mind. Moreover, he reveals a four-step paradigm that can reshuffle susceptible minds back into hallucinating, bicameral mentalities. The ancient Greeks used a similar paradigm to reorganize or reprogram the minds of uneducated peasant girls into totally bicameral mentalities so they could become oracles and give advice through hallucinated voices — voices that would rule the world (e.g., the oracle at Delphi). ...Today, people who deteriorate into schizophrenic psychoses follow similar paradigms.

A common thread united most oracles, sibyls, prophets, and demon-possessed people: Almost all were illiterate, all believed in spirits, and all could readily retrieve the bicameral mind. Today, however, retrieval of the bicameral mind is schizophrenic insanity. Also, today, as throughout history, a symptomatic cure for "demon-possessed" people involves exorcising rituals that let a more powerful "authority" or god replace the "authority" of the demon. The New Testament, for example, shows that Jesus and his disciples became effective exorcists by substituting one "authority" (their god) for another "authority" (another god or demon).

As the voices of the oracles became confused and nonsensical, their popularity waned. In their places, idolatry revived and then flourished. But as Christianity became a popular source of external "authority", Christian zealots began physically destroying all competing idols. They then built their own idols and symbols to reinforce the external "authority" of Christianity.

Among today's vestiges of the bicameral mentality is the born-again movement that seeks external guidance. Such vestiges dramatize man's resistance to use his own invention of

k

consciousness to guide his life.

The chanting cadence of poetry and the rhythmic beat of music are also rooted in the bicameral mentality. In ancient writings, the hallucinated voices of the gods were always in poetic verse, usually in dactylic hexameter and sometimes in rhyme or alliteration — all characteristic of right-brain functionings. The oracles and prophets also spoke in verse. And today schizophrenics often speak in verse when they hallucinate.

Poetry and chants can have authoritarian or commanding beats and rhythms that can effectively block consciousness. Poetry is the language of the gods — it is the language of the artistic, right-hemispheric brain. Plato recognized poetry as a divine madness.

Most poetry and songs have an abruptly changing or a discontinuous pitch. Normal speech, on the other hand, has a smoothly changing pitch. Jaynes demonstrates that reciting poetry, singing, and playing music are right-brain functions, while speaking is a left-brain function. That is why people with speech impediments can often sing, chant, or recite poetry with flawless clarity. Conversely, almost anyone trying to sing a conversation will find his words quickly deteriorating into a mass of inarticulate cliches.

Likewise, listening to music and poetry is a right-brain function. And music, poetry, or chants that project authority with loud or rhythmic beats can suppress left-brain functions to temporarily relieve anxiety or a painfully troubled consciousness.

Jaynes goes on to show phenomena such as hypnosis, acupuncture, and déjà vu also function through vestiges of the bicameral mind. And he demonstrates how hypnosis steadily narrows the sense of self, time, space, and introspection as consciousness shrinks and the mind reverts to a bicameral type organization. Analogously, bicameral and schizophrenic minds have little or no sense of self, time, space or introspection. The hypnotized mind is urged to obey the voice of the hypnotist; the bicameral mind is compelled to obey the "voices" of "authority" or gods. By sensing oneself functioning in the narrow-scope,

1

unaware state of hypnosis, gives one an idea of functioning in the narrow-scope, unaware state of bicameral man.

Jaynes also identifies how modern quests for external "authority" are linked to the bicameral mind. Many such quests use science to seek authority in the laws of nature. In fact, today, science is surpassing the waning institutional religions as a major source of external "authority". And rising from the vestiges of the bicameral mind are an array of scientisms (pseudoscientific doctrines, faiths, and cults) that select various natural or scientific facts to subvert into apocryphal, authoritarian doctrines. That subversion is accomplished by using facts out of context to fit promulgated beliefs. Such mystical scientisms include astrology, ESP, Scientology, Christian Science and other "science" churches, I Ching, behaviorism, sensitivity training, mind control, meditation, hypnotism, cryonics, as well as various nutritional, health, and medical fads.

Today the major worldwide sources of external "authority" are the philosophical doctrines of religion (plus the other forms of mysticism and "metaphysics") combined with political doctrines such as Fascism, Marxism, and Maoism. All such doctrines demand the surrender of the individual's ego (sense of self or "I") to a collective, obedient faith toward the "authority" of those doctrines. In return, those doctrines offer automatic answers and life-time guidance from which faithful followers can survive without the responsibility or effort of using their own consciousnesses. Thus, all political systems represent a regression into mysticism — from conscious man back to bicameral man.

Despite their constant harm to everyone, most modern-day external "authorities" (i.e., neocheaters, explained later) thrive by using the following two-step neocheating technique to repress consciousness and activate the bicameral mind in their victims.

1. First man is made to feel guilty. He is condemned for having lost his "innocence" by inventing consciousness. He is condemned for assuming the responsibility to use his own mind to guide his life. He is condemned for exchanging his automatic, bicameral life for a volitional, conscious life...condemned for

exchanging his nature-given bicameral mind for a superior, man-invented conscious mind.

2. Then man is offered automatic solutions to problems and guidance through life into an "effortless" Garden of Eden or a utopian hereafter if he exchanges his own invented consciousness for faith in external "authority" — bicameral faith in some leader, doctrine, or god. He is offered the "reward" of escaping the self-responsibility to make one's own decisions and to guide one's own life. But for that "reward", he must renounce his own mind to follow someone else's mind or wishes disguised as the "truth" promulgated by some external "authority" or higher power.

But in reality, no valid external "authority" or higher power can exist or ever has existed. Valid authority evolves only from one's own independent, conscious mode of thinking. When that fact is fully realized, man will emerge completely from his bicameral past and move into a future that accepts individual consciousness as the only authority. ...Man will then fully evolve into a prosperous, happy individual who has assumed full responsibility for his own thinking and life.

Still, the resistance to self-responsibility is formidable. The bicameral mentality grips those seeking "authorities" for guidance. Those who accept external "authority" allow government officials, religious leaders, faith, homilies, cliches, one-liners, slogans, the familiar, habits, and feelings to guide their actions. Throughout history, billions of people unnecessarily submit through their bicameral tendencies to the illusionary, external "authorities" of government and religion. And that submission is always done at a net loss to everyone's well being and happiness.

The Implications of Neo-Tech

To some, the implications of Neo-Tech will be frightening, even terrifying. To others, the implications will be electrifying and liberating, perhaps similar to what the fearless, early pioneers into consciousness felt. ...The implications of Neo-Tech are that each individual is solely responsible for his or her own life —

responsible for making the effort required to guide one's own life through one's own consciousness. No automatic, effortless route to knowledge or guidance exists.

No valid external "authority" exists that one can automatically live by. To live effectively, an individual must let only the authority of his own consciousness guide his activities. All consistently competent people have learned to act on reality — not on their feelings or someone else's feelings or doctrines. An individual must accept the responsibility to guide his own life. He must constantly exert the effort needed to identify reality through his own consciousness in order to live competently and happily.

People knowledgeable about Neo-Tech have the tools to outcompete all others who act on their bicameral tendencies. Equally important, people knowledgeable about Neo-Tech have the tools to control their own lives and destinies, free from crippling mysticism and harmful neocheating.

Epilogue: The End of Mysticism

Neo-Tech I-V provides the knowledge needed for identifying the bicameral elements of any statement or action by anyone or any group (e.g., church, government, media, politician, priest, businessman, doctor, friend, parent, spouse, self). Armed with Neo-Tech, people can free themselves from the control or influence of mysticism and external "authority". Sometime after 2001, the discoveries of Neo-Tech and Neothink will have eliminated all vestiges of the bicameral mentality — all vestiges of mysticism and external "authority".

Without the bicameral mentality, all mysticism and external "authority" will wither and vanish, for they have no validity except that which is granted to them by the bicameral mentalities. With political and religious influences disappearing, the mechanisms for "authorities" to harm individuals and wage wars will also disappear. Thus, if civilization is prospering long after 2001, Jaynes's discovery along with the discoveries of Neo-Tech and Neothink will have contributed to that prosperity by ending the symbiotic, mystical relationships of bicameral mentalities with authoritarian societies, which now hold nuclear weapons. Such mystical relationships would sooner or later cause the annihilation of any civilization.

If our civilization is flourishing long after 2001, rational human consciousness will have eliminated mysticism and external "authority" through fully integrated honesty (Neo-Tech). And without external "authority", governments and their wars will be impossible. Best of all, without external "authority" or mysticism, no one will be forcibly controlled, impeded, or drained by others. Without the chains of mysticism, non-aging biological immortality will become commercially available to every productive person wanting to enjoy life and happiness forever.

WAR OF TWO WORLDS
Value Producers vs. Value Destroyers

The Final War

For 2000 years, professional mystics have prophesied that the world will end during the 20th century. Now, today, late in the 20th century, their world is indeed ending. Their world is ending through the emerging war with the other world — the world of fully integrated honesty, the world of Neo-Tech. Their world, being an uncompetitive remnant of nature's bicameral past, is fatally diseased with mysticism. Thus, in their final war with Neo-Tech, their dying world will crumble to nothing.

Who Will Win at Armageddon?

Professional mystics and value-destroying neocheaters have encountered their Antichrist in Neo-Tech. Their Armageddon has come; the ultimate battle has begun. The battle is between good and evil, between honesty and dishonesty, between value producers and value destroyers, between Neo-Tech and mysticism. ...Yes, good will triumph over evil. And, as everyone will soon discover, they, the professional mystics and neocheaters, are and always have been the arch evil disguised as the good. But, now, through the war of two worlds, their world will end forever. ...With their world gone forever, war and value destruction will vanish forever.

Why Neo-Tech Vanquishes
Mysticism and Neocheating

In the world of mysticism, cause and effect are irrationally reversed: feelings beget actions instead of actions begetting feelings. For example, in the world of mysticism, arbitrary and cynical feelings beget unhappy, destructive livings. While, in the world of Neo-Tech, consistent and productive livings beget happy, constructive feelings. The mystical world is sick and out of control. The Neo-Tech world is healthy and in control. ...Thus, Neo-Tech will always vanquish mysticism in any confrontation, battle, or war.

q

NEO-TECH IV

Information Package

CREATING BUSINESS VALUES
and
PREDICTING STOCK PRICES·
by
Frank R. Wallace

In a free economy, the long-term value of any business or company is always determined by its long-term competitive value to society. In a free economy, that value to society is expressed in the common-stock value of the company.

The net value of any activity to society can be determined by using Neo-Tech principles identified in Information Packages I – III. Neo-Tech IV applies those principles to determine the objective value of any individual, management, business operation, or nation. A person can use those same principles for being successful in business and for accurately predicting the long-range, common-stock value of any corporation.

Most stock and commodity forecasters are mystical. Indeed, such forecasters merely use their "sense" or feelings of the market to rationalize illusionary scenarios or "realities" of the future. To various degrees, those forecasters use objective facts and figures or various technical indicators as non-sequitur props to give their projection a sense of validity. But any appearance of validity is specious. By the time most valid facts or figures become available for forecasting, they already have been discounted in the price.

Indeed, with near-perfect market efficiency, all near-term prices move in unpredictable, random patterns. If a forecast turns out to be right, that rightness and duration of rightness are as much a coincidence as forecasting the flips of a coin. Thus, stock and commodity forecasting is generally invalid and mystical, even when promulgated by Wall-Street gurus and cloaked in the jargon of technical, cyclical, and fundamental analyses. Only by fully integrating the root causes of values, as done in Neo-Tech IV, can long-term values of companies to their stockholders and society be reliably predicted.

The Fundamental Principle that Determines the Long-Range Value of a Corporation to its Stockholders and Society

Neo-Tech IV is based on the following principle:
All Honest, Long-Range Profits and Societal Values Generated by Business Arise from the Mystic-Free Standards of Capitalism[1]

By reducing that above principle to concrete examples, this document will demonstrate that in a free economy the long-term values or common-stock prices are ultimately determined by the extent that management implements the mystic-free standards of capitalism to produce evermore competitive values for society. For investors and speculators, this information will provide a valid standard to predict the long-range profit growth of all businesses and their common-stock values. For businessmen and executives, Neo-Tech IV will provide specific recommendations for implementing mystic-free capitalistic standards in order to increase the value of their company. Those recommendations will be supplemented with:

(a) A standard by which to identify those executives and employees who are genuine, long-range assets to their company.

---

[1]The dictionary definition of capitalism is: *An economic system characterized by private ownership of capital goods and by investments that are determined by private decision rather than by state control. Prices, production and distribution of goods are determined by a free market.*

Laissez-faire capitalism is the only political system that does not use force. Working entirely through mutually agreed upon exchanges of values, capitalism is the only system consistent with man's nature and well-being. Capitalism offers freedom and individual rights to all. Capitalism permits maximum individual growth while providing maximum benefits to all. While western political systems have pragmatically and incompletely used various aspects of capitalism, no nation has ever experienced laissez-faire capitalism.

But most writers and commentators put dishonest altruistic-platonistic connotations on the meaning of capitalism: *A system of exploitation of the weak by the strong — devoid of love and good will. A system in which unwanted goods and services are pushed onto consumers through clever, deceptive advertising for the sole purpose of profits and greed. Capitalism dominates most Western governments. Capitalism, big business, and fascism are synonymous.* (footnote continued on next page)

(b) A standard by which to identify those executives and employees who are undermining the long-range value of their company.

(c) Standards for adopting a business philosophy around specific profit-oriented principles.

(d) Action required to expand both short-range and long-range profitability of a company.

The purpose of Neo-Tech IV is to (1) provide a standard to judge the future financial value of business enterprises, (2) provide specific standards to increase the financial value of business enterprises, and (3) contrast the wealth-producing mystic-free nature of business to the wealth-destroying mystical nature of altruism and neocheating.

Long-term appreciation of common-stock values will occur to the extent that management implements the mystic-free standards of capitalism. Conversely, long-term attrition of common-stock values will occur to the extent that management compromises capitalistic standards in implementing mystical-based decisions. ...Attrition of value is inherent to any business situation subjected to altruism, mysticism, or neocheating.

Before Neo-Tech, the standards of capitalism had never been related to the value of a company in concise terms. The relationship of capitalistic standards to the common-stock value of a corporation can best be illustrated through an actual example of a large American corporation. This illustration will be accomplished by paraphrasing the following document submitted years ago to the administrative management of E. I. du Pont de Nemours & Co., Inc.:

(footnote continued from previous page)

The reason professional mystics and neocheaters display aggressive hostility towards capitalism is because of its anti-mystical, competitive nature — its nature of requiring integrated honesty and competitive efforts for success. Mystics and neocheaters could not survive in an honest, fully competitive, capitalistic society. They could no longer use their deceptive, altruistic manipulations to plunder the producer. Fearing survival through honesty and competitiveness, they are compelled to hate and attack capitalism.

A Proposal to Increase the Value of Du Pont Common Stock:
An Open Letter to Those Responsible
for the Future
of the
Du Pont Company

A Proposal to Increase the Value
<u>of Du Pont Common Stock</u>

To effectively present this proposal, the following four aspects around which the proposal evolves must be identified:

The need
The purpose
The principle
The proof

After identifying those aspects, the proposal can be presented in its proper context. The proposal will entail the following recommendations:

1. Removal of specified executives who are undermining the value of Du Pont by building careers on deceptive mysticism and destructive neocheating rather than on honest thinking and productive efforts.
2. Realignment of Du Pont's philosophy around specific, profit-oriented principles.
3. Implementation of specified action designed to restore both the short-range and long-range profitability growth of the Du Pont Company.

<u>The Need</u>

Du Pont stock sold for $278 per share. Eleven years later, Du Pont stock had fallen to $92.50 per share. Over 60% of the total corporate market value accumulated in 150 years vanished in a decade.

<u>The Purpose</u>

For 150 years, the management of the Du Pont Company increased the corporation's value at a remarkable rate. The common stock price increased many fold. Owners became wealthy.

Du Pont expanded into the largest, most profitable chemical company in the world. What was the cause? The cause can be reduced to a single principle from which all economic values grow. This document will identify that principle.

Over the past decade, the owners of Du Pont (the stockholders) have observed with mounting disappointment the declining ability of management to expand the profitability of their corporation. What is the reason for that growing impotence? Many reasons have been advanced in business and financial publications[1]. But management's explanations failed to deal with the crucial issues. And their mystical remedies by nature have accelerated the deterioration. The honest reason for the shrinking profit growth has never been publicly identified. This proposal will identify that reason.

This proposal will also demonstrate that (1) restoration of Du Pont's vitality is still possible, (2) long-range growth in profitability will require action recommended by this proposal, and (3) implementation of this proposal would unleash a productivity/ creativity cycle within the Du Pont Company that could generate values and profits outstripping any business enterprise on earth.

Based on mystic-free principles, this proposal is designed to meet the fundamental requirements of expanding profitability.

The purpose of this proposal is to increase the long-range, common-stock value of Du Pont for the financial benefit of its stockholders.

The Principle

This proposal is based on the following principle:

All Honest, Long-Range Profits and Societal Values
Generated by Business
Arise from the Mystic-Free Standards of Capitalism

To understand that principle, the difference between altruism and capitalism must be identified. The contradiction between those two terms is evident from the following definitions:

Capitalism is a moral/social system as well as an economic

---

1. *Wall Street Journal*
2. *Forbes*
3. *Times*
4. *Chemical Week*
5. *E.I. du Pont de Nemours & Co., Annual Report*

system based on the philosophical premise that every man and woman has the exclusive right to his or her own life and property. Implementing capitalism always yields by nature a benevolent society in which individuals deal with one another on the basis of values — the voluntary exchange of values. Force and coercion are obviated. Capitalism is consistent with man's rational needs and requirements for prosperity and happiness.

Altruism is a morality based on the philosophical premise that man lives for the sake of others...that man's life and property are available for sacrifice to "higher" causes, e.g., the common good, society, the needy, the world, the dictator, God, country, politicians, bureaucrats, lawyers. Implementing altruism always yields by nature a malevolent society in which individuals deal with one another on terms of who will be sacrificed to whom, who will support whom. Force becomes the deciding factor. Fake jobs and bogus livelihoods grow like cancer. ...Altruism is contrary to man's nature, rational needs, and requirements for happiness.

Before applying the concepts of capitalism and altruism to Du Pont and its common-stock price, those concepts must first be viewed from the broader perspective of contemporary Western culture:

Capitalism has lifted man's standard of living to undreamt heights. As will be demonstrated in this document, all long-term benefits to man's life, well being, and happiness have grown from competitive capitalistic principles.

Yet today, a growing number of altruistic businessmen are undermining capitalism. How?

1. By protecting, supporting, joining, and promoting the destructiveness of bogus-job bureaucrats, politicians, lawyers, the clergy, dishonest journalists, dishonest educators, and social "intellectuals".

2. By usurping from business short-range values and advantages for themselves rather than competitively producing long-range values for business, others, and society.

In undermining capitalism, they are depriving man of his motive to produce and his means to be happy.

Man is capable of achieving genuine prosperity and happiness only to the extent that he can produce competitive values for others and society through the rational, wide-integration use of his mind and constant, hard-work effort. That fact is based on the nature of man. Man must competitively produce for others to honestly meet both his physical and emotional needs.

Hidden beneath the words of all altruists are calls for sacrifice, "temporary" hardship, and periods of readjustment. Those calls for sacrifice are incongruously combined with promises that man can attain values without earning them. All altruists seek an unreal world based on feelings and wishful thinking...a mystical world free of demands for rational integrated thinking and competitive hard efforts. A mystical world that always moves away from the problem-solving nature of life. Indeed all mystics seek the goal of effortless, "peaceful" nirvana — a problem-free utopia. In their utopia, man can defy reality...man can usurp values without earning them...man can consume without producing...man can live effortlessly without solving problems. Reality, however, cannot be defied. Someone has to produce values and solve problems in order for human beings and society to survive and prosper. Thus, to survive and prosper, altruists and other value destroyers must deceive and coerce the value producers into sacrificing their time, efforts, property, and earnings to the value destroyers.

The altruists' final goal is to coerce or force all value producers to support and respect them, the value destroyers. The motive and ability to produce competitively and in abundance for others vanish when the producer becomes controlled by the nonproducers. Who would be responsible for such an evil, for such an unjust scourge to fall upon our civilization? Ironically, the political leaders, religious leaders, freeloaders, collectivists, and other value destroyers would not be primarily responsible. Those responsible will be the altruistic neocheaters posing as business "leaders". Such uncompetitive business quislings are today implanted throughout business and industry worldwide.

Those executives will bear the responsibility for the demise of their companies and free-market capitalism. Their altruistic principles are inimical contradictions to the principles of competitive capitalism. Through such business quislings, the sacrifice of the value producers and businesses is possible. Indeed, those quislings are the transmission belt between the value producers and the value destroyers.

But, the implementation of the capitalistic principles presented in this proposal would render impotent those altruists who are currently in positions of corporate power. For, without those altruistic business quislings, the value destroyers would be powerless to sacrifice the value producer. Their demands for sacrifice would go unanswered. The decline of capitalism would end. A new renaissance would begin. Civilization would rise to a new standard of rationality. Benevolence and goodwill among men would flourish. Man's productivity and happiness would soar.

How do those concepts of business, capitalism, and altruism relate to the common-stock value of Du Pont? This is how:

Man requires self-interest motives to be productive and creative. Man achieves happiness through his productive and creative efficacy. That is the nature of man. When altruistic businessmen assume managerial positions within a corporation, their standards of selflessness and sacrifice are asserted to allow them to neocheat rather than to earn their way to competitive power and wealth. Since selflessness and sacrifice are contrary to value production and competitiveness, the producer's efficacy will diminish. His job effectiveness will decrease, and the future of his company will fade. Thus, as altruistic executives translate their standards into practice, the value of their company to stockholders and society shrinks.

Do such men exist within the Du Pont management? How can they be identified? They are characterized by their lack of singular purpose to create long-range assets, values, and profits. They are also characterized by their willingness to subjugate the best interests of the corporation and its stockholders to some fake "higher cause" or spurious "public good". Altruists can achieve their unearned ends only by sacrificing the values earned by others...such as the assets, profits, and earning potential of a corporation. They are eager to sacrifice that which has been earned and built by others. They are willing to sacrifice the stockholders' equity, potential, and property to "higher causes".

Within Du Pont there has been a gradual shift in the nature of the management from the objective, pro-capitalistic asset builder to the altruistic, socially-oriented "business leader". That shift continues under such sophistic rhetoric as "being practical", "the wave of the future", "young blood", "changing reality", "progressive needs", "social awareness", "public good", "higher causes". At the same time, the concepts of objectivity, efficacy, happiness, competence, effort, productivity, and profits are being increasingly subverted. ...These assertions about Du Pont management will be demonstrated with concrete facts later in this proposal.

Whenever long-range values are created by business, society benefits. By far, the greatest beneficiary of a profitable business is society. But the basic reason for operating any business can never be to "serve" society short range at the expense of long-range assets and earning, lest the business be eventually drained and stagnated. The only just and moral reason to operate a business is to benefit its owners through the production of competitive values for others and society. Only to the extent that owners profit can employees, society, or anyone else gain long-term values and benefits. Consequently, a business run for the best long-range financial profit of its owners will always yield the maximum, long-range benefits to society. Conversely, only by producing maximum values for society can a business produce maximum, long-range profits for its stockholders. ...That is the benevolent nature of capitalism.

Capitalism means producing competitive values (products or services) for the voluntary exchange of other values (money for further production of values). Success in a capitalistic society requires honesty, rationality, effort, wide integrations, and long-range planning. The standards of capitalism permit man to profit only by competitively producing for the benefit of others and society. The standards of capitalism allow man to fulfill his potential and to achieve happiness to the benefit of all society.

How does the above principle apply to the common-stock value of Du Pont? The common-stock price is the accurate value of a company because that price represents the exact value that buyers are willing to pay for the company in a free market. Over time, a company is worth no more or no less than its free market price (its common-stock price). **Executives are hired by the**

stockholders for one reason only...to enhance the long-range financial value of their business enterprise in order to increase profits and common-stock values. For long-term appreciation of stock values, an enterprise must increasingly deliver competitive values to society.

The value of an executive is judged by the extent that he generates values for the shareholders in exchange for his compensation. In order to enhance the long-range value of a business enterprise to its owners and society, an executive must implement the principles of competitive capitalism. The altruistic executive militates against the value of his company to the extent that he directs his company. That executive does not earn his pay. For, he diminishes rather than builds the long-term value of his company.

To survive, the altruistic executive must constantly draw on the future potential of his company in a turmoil of short-range pragmatic activities that conceal the long-range damage being done to the business. At first, such an executive may blame declining stock prices on "temporary" market conditions. As the corporate assets are consumed and return on investment diminishes, the executive will blame competition, inflation, deflation, "maturing business", the "inevitable", "hard luck", or a "changing reality" for the decline in stock prices.

As solutions, he may offer platitudes and schemes of short-range economies, "belt tightenings", "creative" accounting procedures, acquisitions, and other one-shot expediencies. Within the downward trend, the stock price may periodically fluctuate upward for durations of a few months or even years. But the downward trend always returns with ever-deepening losses.

When the company is finally destroyed, he will claim that events were beyond his control and the ruins were not his fault. He will plead that he had to be practical and cooperate with the altruistic "authorities". *He will not identify that operating on competitive capitalistic principles is the only honest, sound way to build values and assets. He will not identify that altruism dishonestly destroyed the value of his company. He will not identify that altruism can never be used to benefit society. But he will secretly know that altruism has always been no more than a clever tool to covertly promote bogus livelihoods.*

410

To repeat again the principle upon which this proposal rests:
**All Honest, Long-Range Profits and Societal Values
Generated by Business
Arise from the Mystic-Free Standards of Capitalism**

The Proof

To validate this proposal, the following two assertions will be proven with specific facts:

1. Du Pont is not being managed in the best financial interest of its stockholders.
2. Management is abandoning capitalistic standards in favor of altruistic standards, thus continually shrinking the long-range profitability and value of Du Pont.

The following graph provides proof of the first assertion. The steady, long-term deterioration of Du Pont common-stock values is proof that the Company is not being managed in the best financial interest of its stockholders. That fact becomes especially obvious when the deteriorating stock price is superimposed against a composite of all other 1360 stocks on the New York Stock Exchange.

Proof of the second assertion is based on an abundance of factual evidence. A portion of this evidence will be documented

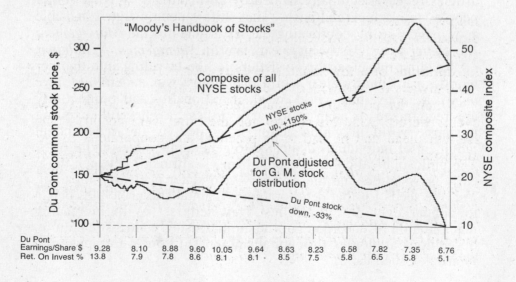

Du Pont											
Earnings/Share $	9.28	8.10	8.88	9.60	10.05	9.64	8.63	8.23	6.58	7.82	7.35	6.76
Ret. On Invest %	13.8	7.9	7.8	8.6	8.1	8.1	8.5	7.5	5.8	6.5	5.8	5.1

with quotes from the following, publicly available communications:
   •*Management Newsletter*, a Du Pont publication
   •*Better Living Magazine*, a Du Pont publication
   •"1 + 1 + 1", a Du Pont movie
   •Statements and speeches by major Du Pont executives.
This documentation will demonstrate the extent that altruism has gripped the Du Pont Company and the consequences of abandoning competitive capitalistic principles.

Management Newsletter

The management is responsible for the thematic content and philosophical timbre of all internal and external communications released by a company. Perhaps nowhere is the philosophical position of Du Pont management reflected more precisely than in its *Management Newsletter*. A chronological review of the Newsletter over twenty years starkly reveals the progressive abandonment of objective capitalistic principles for subjective social pragmatisms. During that abandonment of principles, decisions are increasingly made by what some shadowy external "authority" might say or think rather than by independent judgment of reality by strong, honest executives.

Past Newsletter articles reveal a strong, exuberant company guided mainly by capitalistic principles. But current Newsletter articles reveal a company guided by altruism and by what "other people" think, feel, and wish. That shift is demonstrated in Table 1 on page 416 by contrasting earlier articles in the *Management Newsletter* to articles twenty years later in *Management Newsletter*.

Reading those early Newsletters is like traveling into another world...a brilliantly clear world that almost was and *should have been*...a happy, just world in which rationality and productivity are recognized as man's primary virtues...a cheerful, exciting business world in which action is guided by the independent judgment of individuals dedicated to generating values and profits. The philosophical contrast (capitalism vs. altruism) between those early Newsletters and those twenty years later is clearly apparent. Yet, the seeds for that deterioration of capitalistic principles began to appear even in the earliest Newsletters. With increasing manipulation of unearned guilt in an increasingly altruistic culture, obsequious apologies for capitalism and Du Pont were appearing in articles such as:

Neo-Tech IV
Creating Business Values

Big vs. Little Business
Is Big Business Useful?

A study of the Newsletters reveals that the philosophical shift from capitalism to altruism occurred in two major steps. The first step occurred when the presidency of Du Pont passed from Mr. Crawford H. Greenewalt to Mr. Lammont Copeland. The struggle to explicitly uphold capitalism abruptly ended. Articles such as listed below ceased:

Business Pleads its Case in Whispers

Mr. Greenewalt stated, "It is the corporation's proper duty to oppose any action which threatens the property or the interests of its stockholders, to fight hard if the well-being of its employees is threatened, or if the successful continuity of its life comes under fire."

U.S. Superiority and Productivity vs. USSR
Industrial Progress Undermines Socialism

A basic shift in philosophy was apparent. The primary focus of Du Pont changed from generating profits for the stockholders to "serving society". The following articles began appearing for the first time:

Du Pont Research —

President Copeland equated the value of research to serving "society" rather than to expanding corporate earnings, profits, and assets.

Could nylon have been developed and transformed into a venture that generated hundreds of millions of dollars in profits for the company, employees, stockholders, and society with an altruistic standard determining the research and development efforts at Du Pont? Commercial ventures that generate large, expanding profits for their stockholders can evolve only from capitalistic standards.

As Others See Us

This article signalled the acceptance of a standard whereby management replaces independent judgment with "what others think" as a valid basis for action.

Research for Government

Nonprofit research done at the expense of the stockholders. Why? For what purpose and at whose sacrifice? Only destructive altruism could justify such research.

413

Neo-Tech IV
Creating Business Values

Despite the basic philosophical shift to altruism, some articles such as the one listed below continued to uphold the values of Du Pont:

Industrial Research in Internal Competition

This article dealt with the competitively effective utilization of human skills within the Du Pont Company.

The second and most devastating step in the philosophical shift occurred when the presidency of Du Pont passed from Mr. Lammont Copeland to Mr. Charles B. McCoy. The personal experience of research scientist Dr. Frank R. Wallace must be related to demonstrate that philosophical shift. After joining the Company, Dr. Wallace studied each issue of the *Management Newsletter*. The articles captured the exciting action and values evolving from the most creative, capitalistic enterprise in history. The Newsletter symbolized supreme human action, creativity, and rationality. The Newsletter was a major source of pleasure and fuel in concretizing man's worth and potency. When the first shift occurred under Mr. Copeland, Dr. Wallace failed to identify what had occurred. In reading the Newsletters, he subconsciously ignored or dismissed the altruistic-based articles while savouring the articles expressing the action and values of Du Pont. After seven years, Dr. Wallace left Du Pont for three years. On returning, he read with amazement the current *Management Newsletter*. The feature article was entitled:

The Plant Open House,
A Way to Win Friends and Influence People.

Did a multi-billion-dollar corporation have nothing more significant to report to its management than a plant tour[1] for town folk? At that time, Dr. Wallace did not understand why such an article should appear in the *Management Newsletter*. As the months passed, he read articles such as outlined in Table 1. ...Gradually he began to understand what was happening.

The second and final step in the abandonment of capitalistic principles was occurring. In essence, all the greatness of Du Pont was being reduced and equated to a plant tour for town folks...an age-old, altruistic technique of mystically reducing man's greatest achievements to the pedestrian level.

[1]Plant tours per se can be a proper, rational activity for any factory. In fact, an article on plant tours might properly appear in the "Management Newsletter" if presented from a profit-oriented, value-producing viewpoint.

414

In this seemingly innocent manner, the door had been opened to sacrifice the values of Du Pont. ...How can a philosophy expressed in the *Management Newsletter* lead to the sacrifice of Du Pont?[1] Consider the nature of other communications that emanated from Du Pont with Management sanction. Those communications ranged from a popular, heavily-attended seminar titled *Application of Social Science Technology to Du Pont*[2] to publications like *Better Living* (analyzed next) and speeches by key executives (analyzed later and in Table 4). The direct impact of management's current philosophy on Du Pont's business was reflected in a Du Pont seminar entitled, *The Future of the Fiber Business*. That seminar projected a steady decay of Du Pont's return on its fiber investment despite an optimistic market and growth picture for synthetic fibers.

That seminar was presented by the Du Pont textile-fiber management to the Executive Committee. No plan or consideration to reverse the deteriorating financial situation was offered or even considered. The gloomy nonaction stance by management to correct a suicidal business trend coupled with the anticapitalistic (government controlled) economic philosophy of Keynes accepted by Du Pont economists and management[3] are the essences for the systematic, long-range deterioration of Du Pont. With bizarre irony, the "modernistic" cover of Du Pont's Annual Report that year symbolized the purposeful destruction of values: The marvelous, industrial works of man were photographed part in-focus, part blurred, and part double exposed. Why, for what reason, for what purpose was a clear, sharp value purposely distorted and blurred into a non-value?

----

[1]Du Pont sacrificed to whom? To the bogus careers of altruistic management.

[2]This Du Pont-sponsored seminar lent credibility to a pseudo-science in order to dismiss the capitalistic concept of value production by competitive individuals. Social science replaces that valid concept with the spurious collectivist concept of outputs by "human organizations" — an unintelligible concept that cannot be defined or identified within reality.

[3]Seminar by Du Pont's chief economist, Mr. I. T. Ellis, "Economic Analysis and Forecasting". Credence and acceptance was granted to the spurious economic theories of master black-hat neocheater, John Maynard Keynes.

Table 1

ARTICLES IN DU PONT MANAGEMENT NEWSLETTERS

Original Newsletters	Newsletters Twenty Years Later
Article Headings : — Annual Report — Earnings — Dividends — Sales — Payrolls — Sales Price Index — Income — Peacetime Standards — Increased Volume of Business — Increased Capital — Return on Operative Investment — Research Activities — Expansion and Improvement of Plant Facilities — Employee Relations — Decision of U. S. Supreme Court — Strikes — Nylon Price Reduction — Plant Election *Every article is germane to the profitable operation of Du Pont. Void of articles of a social or altruistic nature.* Total number of articles written under the following headings: — Profits - 22 — Free Enterprise - 13 — Big Business - 24 *By contrast, not a single article twenty years later was written in support of profits, free enterprise, or big business.*	**Article Headings, Quotes, and Comments:** — Plant Assists Disadvantaged Youth "Plans for Progress has top corporate backing and is being implemented throughout the Company". *Why? For what business purpose? Progress is achieved by efficacious producers, not by incompetents or the "disadvantaged."* — New Priorities in Aid to Education "...aimed at improving educational opportunities for the disadvantaged." *Why? For what business purpose? What does "disadvantaged" mean? A "disadvantaged" individual is simply one who has chosen not to put forth the effort and discipline required to become "advantaged" or productive.* — Pollution Control Activities "We must be concerned not only with what our neighbors think of us at the plant level, but also how we project ourselves as a total corporation." *Such a statement is void of principle and lacking in independent judgment: Vast corporate actions and expenditures are being based on a standard of what "other people" think and feel rather than objective facts.* — Du Pont Steps up Efforts to Hire the "Disadvantaged".[1] *Why? For what business purpose? Then, Du Pont stock was above $160. Today, Du Pont stock is below $100.* — Banner Year for Recruiting "Du Pont people found greater social consciousness among students they interviewed." *What does "social consciousness" mean? What possible value could* *(table continued on next page)*

ARTICLES IN DU PONT MANAGEMENT NEWSLETTERS

Original Newsletters	Newsletters Twenty Years Later
Article Headings :	**Article Headings, Quotes, and Comments:**
Typical Articles of original newsletters:	students with greater "social consciousness" have toward increas-
— Public misconception vs. facts.	ing the assets and profits of Du Pont?
— U. S. standard of living vs. Russian.	— Interview with "Chemical and Engineering News"
— Productive output of America vs. Non-America.	"Mr. McCoy stressed Du Pont's faith in the chemical industry and
— Left-wing criticism vs. advantages to U.S.	said long term the industry can greatly improve its current rate of
— Reply to cellophane monopoly charge.	return with a little 'luck' in reestablishing a healthy capacity-demand
— Atomic energy a product of American enterprise.	balance in such major items as plastics, fibers and fertilizers."
— Du Pont President says free enterprise is greatest national	The President of Du Pont publicly declares that improved rate of
resource.	return for Du Pont is based on faith and luck! Mysticism and chance
— Post-war production of nylon exemplifies spirit of free enterprise.	have become the stated basis for improving the performance of the Du
— Benefits of American economic system.	Pont Company.
— Rise in standard of U. S. living through greater productivity.	
— Socialistic developments in U. S.: Du Pont offered its employees	
a free 169-page book that identified the failures of British socialism	"That article defines the meaning of the "disadvantaged" as: "Members of
and nationalization.	poor families and unemployed or underemployed, or those who are not
— U.S. high standards of living improved by industry.	seeking work but should be, and who possess one of the following character-
— Protection of patents encourages invention.	istics — high school dropout; minority group member under 22 years of age;
	over 44 years of age; physically, mentally or socially handicapped." Why a
	minority group? And what group? Only one legitimate minority exists and
	that is the individual. If his or her rights are protected, the rights of all are
	protected. What does socially handicapped mean? At competitive wages,
	what possible business value could such uncompetitive people offer Du
	Pont? Even the pretense of so-called moral value or duty fails when one
	identifies the injustice that placing a dishonest business value on the so-called
	"disadvantaged" perpetrates against those who through their own efforts
	become people of value...value producers.

Better Living Magazine

The first issue of *Better Living Magazine*[1] Dr. Wallace received on returning to Du Pont contained an article entitled "Dedicated Amateurs" — a five-page spread on the card playing, auto driving, chess, and other free-time activities of certain employees. No, nothing was wrong with those activities. But, Dr. Wallace wondered why such a mundane, slice-of-life article was published in *Better Living*. The article was injected between a feature article on the new fiber Qiana® and a dramatic article on building huge underground caverns for ammonia storage.

In that same issue, Dr. Wallace read a three-page spread about a Du Pont employee dedicating his free time to unpaid social work. Fine, that was his personal, free choice. The article even contained a photograph showing this employee teaching a group of migrant laborers to recognize a sign to the bathroom. That article was inserted between an article reviewing the outstanding technological achievements of the Film Department and an article describing the industrial use of television. Why the mixing of outstanding human achievement with the commonplace? In search for an answer, one might ask if a magazine needs to include the ordinary or prosaic aspects of life to be realistic and credible.

That question was eloquently answered by the *Du Pont Magazine* (issued bimonthly by Du Pont's Advertising Department). Like a searchlight slicing through the darkness, that magazine provided a dazzling flow of Du Pont's greatest products and achievements. That happy magazine was totally void of the commonplace and confirmed the vast potential that existed within Du Pont. That magazine also demonstrated that men existed within Du Pont who held greatness above the ordinary and insignificant. That magazine concretized the reason to fight for the great values of Du Pont.

The difference between *Better Living* and the *Du Pont Magazine* reflected much more than the editorial differences expected between a magazine issued by the Public Relations Department and a magazine issued by the Advertising Department. A comparison of article headings in the following table illustrates the profound philosophical and view-of-life gulf that existed between those two magazines.

---

[1]*Better Living* is a bimonthly magazine published by Du Pont's Public Relations Department.

Table 2	
DU PONT MAGAZINE* VERSUS *BETTER LIVING MAGAZINE	
Du Pont Magazine	***Better Living Magazine***
Cover Photo: A chic, intelligent-looking woman projecting self-esteem and confidence of self-earned values.	Cover Photo: A grinning, un-groomed girl celebrating the forceful occupation of private property (Columbia University) by a mob whose members chose to usurp and destroy values produced by others.
A Slick Assist for Snow Shovelers ("Teflon")	
Goodyear's Gas-Filled Fleet ("Hypalon")	Youth: A New Society
A Cover that Keeps Rolling Along ("Teflon")	What's it all About
A Fabric of Freedom ("Dacron")	The Quarrel with the Establishment
Beautifully Blended for Fashion ("Orlon")	Does Business Really Care
	The New Left
Enhancing the Character of Quality ("Minute Bleach")	The Church — Will it Survive
Helping Industry to Keep its Cool ("Teflon")	Youth Reject Racism
Speeding up Chemical Separations (APC Tablet)	Youth at the University of Michigan
What's New ("Birox", "Mon-Soon", Polysilicates, "Cronor" gravure Film, "Tri-Seal")	

The two magazines were philosophical opposites. The *Du Pont Magazine* reflected a cheerful, guilt-free admiration of the values and products that had arisen from Du Pont. *Better Living* reported on Du Pont's values in an apologetic, resentful manner while saluting the standards of altruism and egalitarianism, which demand the looting and destruction of Du Pont and competitive capitalism. All doubts about the philosophical nature of *Better Living* were eliminated with subsequent issues that began with the destructive mixing of great achievements with the mundane. Those subsequent articles represented the inevitable disintegration of rational values by the altruistic philosophy.

After an editorial that explicitly suspended moral judgment,[1] the entire 32-page issue of *Better Living* proceeded to idealize those who sought to destroy competitive capitalism and the profit-making ability of industry. That 32-page spread saluted those collectivist conformists who hate and fear capitalism because they are incompetent to compete in free markets — incompetent to meet competitive standards that demand discipline, thought, effort, and the production of values. Those standards require man to think rationally and produce values for others and society to survive.

Under the title, *Youth: A New Society*, that issue of *Better Living* projected a potpourri of impotent, anticapitalistic conformists as "honest", "idealistic" youth. That "honesty" and "idealism" epitomized the dishonesty and fraud of that article: Youth who substituted emotion for reason and feelings for facts as their guide to action were blatantly dishonest and destructive. Moreover, youth who chose to evade their responsibility to produce rational values for others were neither honest nor idealistic.

The supreme injustice of *Better Living* was committed against those youth who had not surrendered to dishonesty...against those youth who were struggling to achieve rational goals and values. But the most destructive injustice of *Better Living* was committed against Du Pont and capitalism. By implication, that issue besmirched Du Pont and competitive capitalism with all the real and imaginary ills of this world. Not one word in *Better Living* was dedicated to the only rational purpose of Du Pont...to generate expanding profits for its stockholders by increasingly producing

---

[1]Quote the editorial, "We are describing — neither condoning or condemning it — this phenomenon because it is rapidly moving front and center."

420

competitive values for others and society. Not a single word was dedicated to the supreme moral value of Du Pont...an efficient organization in which individuals could utilize their rational minds and productive efforts for their own and loved ones' well-being and happiness by providing benefits to others and society. ...Those who produced *Better Living* gained their dishonest, destructive livelihoods from Du Pont. And Du Pont management willingly paid their salaries!

Every Du Pont executive should carefully read that issue of *Better Living*. Observe the massive, envious, unearned guilt foisted upon the businessman, Du Pont, and free enterprise. Observe the implicit threats and sullen malevolence that exudes from beneath the "properly tempered" words and the measured praise for Du Pont's incongruous efforts to meet the demands of the value-destroying altruists. Look at the pictures ...look carefully into the faces of those demanding that business sacrifice itself to the "good of society". Their expressions range from the robot, joyless faces of desperately dependent conformists to the loathing, power-seeking expression in the face of Ralph Nader to the raging faces of the militants screaming for blood and destruction.

All those faces can be reduced to one common expression ...fear...fear of competitive capitalism...fear of the hard work and honesty required to produce competitive values for others...fear of competing with value producers. To survive, those nonproducers must depend on the producer being tricked or forced into sacrificing earned values to the "good of society" — to them, the nonproducers. Remember those faces in *Better Living*...you will see them again. And you will not have to wonder who provided those "idealistic" youth with the sanction to cripple and then destroy Du Pont.

"1 + 1 + 1" Movie

The long-term increase or decrease of common stock prices for any company can be forecast from its management's philosophical projection of capitalistic principles. The movie "1 + 1 + 1" released by Du Pont's Public Relations Department with sanction of the Executive Committee, afforded an unusual opportunity for an in-depth analysis of management's philosophical projection of capitalistic principles:

Du Pont is an awe-inspiring subject that symbolizes the pinnacle of accomplishment. Du Pont is a proud example of man's potency toward which all humans can lift their eyes for inspiration. Consider how Du Pont was treated in "1+1+1", a movie shown to most Du Pont employees and to millions of Americans:

A breathtaking skyline of New York City appeared. Exultant music played. The bold Du Pont oval filled the screen. Firm and steady words spoke of the marvels that man has created with steel and concrete. Yes, yes, one could eagerly agree. That was Du Pont. That was the story that should be told...exultant, bold, breathtaking. But that spine-tingling emotion lasted only a moment. The camera promptly zoomed into close-up shots of the "man in the street". With the focus on the group and the common man, the magnificent spell was broken.

Why did the moviemaker do that? Was he implying that the "man in the street" or the group was responsible for the great achievements symbolized by the skyline of New York? Was not that movie supposed to stress the individual? What about the few, uncommon individuals...the innovators, industrialists, scientists, and artists? It was those uncommon individuals who gave us the great values of "music, steel, and concrete". How could the moviemaker commit such an oversight? Or was it an oversight?

The scene shifted. A voice told us of Du Pont's 86 factories and 100 laboratories spanning the globe. From barren earth, factories of production rose majestically. For an instant, that thrilling emotion returned. Then came the jolt. The scene shifted. The voice changed. The value of Du Pont's factories was obliterated by a female voice sighing that the new plant will bring "A lot of young men, I hope."

Why was the moviemaker building heroic images of Du Pont only to shatter them? Why was the moviemaker purposely spoiling values? Why was he mixing poison with food? Did he not know the only results can be poison?

The movie continued. A statement was made, "Some men's urge to make life better takes them down wondrous roads." What were those wondrous roads? No explanation. Instead, the moviemaker raked the audience with a ludicrous pandemonium of old-fashioned cars speeding around corners, and water skiers engaged in spectacular falls. Another statement was made, "Man must be unique." The next scene showed a pie-eating contest and then a dozen or more youths in coon-skin coats riding in a single automobile. Mixing purity with poison...the mind with the mindless...values with non-values — an ancient neocheating trick to destroy values. What was the moviemaker's motive?

What was the meaning of that film? The movie pressed onward. The narrator revealed that over 2500 Ph.D.s worked for Du Pont. The narrator then announced that today's science was a "meshing of groups". What did "meshing of groups" mean? No explanation. Was not this movie supposed to stress the individual? Again, what about those few individuals who were responsible for all the material values we have today? No mention was made of them.

The scene shifted to technical management in action. Hope surged for a glimpse of greatness. Now will the value of the individual appear? No. Instead of crisp, intelligent men making meaningful business decisions, the scene wilted into altruistic torpidity. A woman inarticulately spoke about helping mankind by nitrogen fixation. She spoke as if the excuse for Du Pont's existence was to help the global indigents. Her words, sounding more like a bovine moan, were not those of a confident, productive human being. Was that the moviemaker's portrayal of management in one of America's greatest corporations?

Next came a scene about Du Pont explosives. Instead of depicting how explosives have so benevolently lifted a torturous burden from man's shoulders, the scene disparaged human intelligence. A scientist was presented. He proceeded to express himself with garrulities such as "those cats think explosives are for war". Did that reflect the seriousness and intelligence of the Du Pont scientist? At that point, the moviemaker introduced his metaphysical view of the science: "Let the scientist miss and miss and begin again" was presented as the modus operandi of the scientist. The focus was on failure.

No acknowledgement or recognition was given to those competitive, value-producing scientists who think long-range and achieve great goals through carefully planned, exceedingly difficult, hard work. Instead, the audience was garroted with the fallacious image of a "crackpot" scientist mindlessly mixing together everything in sight and meeting failure after failure until by chance he stumbled onto a great discovery. Was this the moviemaker's metaphysical view of science? Was man's mind impotent and technical achievement a matter of chance or accident?

How did the moviemaker project those precious few individuals who choose to use their minds and exert supreme rational effort in order to discover, innovate, produce, and market products that have generated hundreds of millions of dollars in profit for Du Pont? Their work was summed up in one sentence. "Things blew apart and everything". What was the meaning behind that seemingly frivolous remark? Was the moviemaker informing us that those great achievements required no special effort or intelligence? Did nylon evolve by a process of things blowing apart? Was that the moviemaker's view of man's accomplishments? Could anyone present such a dishonest, resentful, envious view of competence and achievement?

How were the end results of major technical achievements portrayed? Mylar® was selected as an example. Its value was promptly reduced to a toy butterfly. What about the value of knowledge? A Du Pont scientist spoke of his past. He referred to himself as a defrocked organic chemist and wondered why he ever obtained a Ph.D. degree. No explanation was given. The man was left appearing as a diffident fool for his past efforts. The man then explained that his genetic makeup made him what he was. Did not that mystical, predeterministic view negate the value of man's mind and his volitional discipline, effort, and free choice?

What about the value of man achieving his long-range goals? A sequence began with an obviously intelligent man making the rationally correct statement that "man has to satisfy the need to build". Indeed he does. Man's most fundamental need is to build (to produce). How did the moviemaker project that? The next scene showed a descending foot crushing a child's sand castle.

Why? Is what man builds so tenuous and meaningless that his work can be crushed to nothing at someone's random whim?

What about the moviemaker's view of absolutes? His view was projected by a factory scene: A worker asserted that there was too much supervision. The next worker asserted that there was too little supervision. What purpose did that seemingly innocuous scene serve? Was it to show that one side is as valid as the other...that everything was a matter of opinion...that there was no right or wrong way...that whatever one felt was right...that there was no objective reality?

The scenes went on and on. Build up and tear down. A skyline was silhouetted with beautiful new factories. What significance was attached to those factories? Only one specific message was projected — new factories caused problems of uprooting, relocation, and retraining. What about the products, jobs, profits, and competitive values generated by those factories? ...Silence.

What about the most important facet of man's life — his productive work? Man and his work were sloughed off in ten seconds with the statement, "man must do his own thing while inside the Company". The scene shifted to man's activities outside the Company. In a lengthy persiflage of bizarre nonsense, we were bombarded with an incoherent collection of silent flickers blended with all the modern, mind-blowing psychedelic effects. Why? For what purpose? Was the moviemaker telling us that man's work was no more significant than a perfunctory statement that "he must do his own thing" and his other activities were no more worthy than meaningless pantomime and boring psychedelic effects? Could anyone possibly hold such a malevolent view of man and his life? Let us continue with the movie:

The desecration of values, man, and Du Pont continued at an accelerating pace. Du Pont employees *at work* were associated with pin-up girls, slogan-painted lab coats, and hippy buttons. The basic technique continued...show a value and then tear it down...show a man producing at his work and then knock him down with a slogan-painted lab coat or leave him leering at a girlie picture.

The moviemaker's technique reached the climax with the scene

425

of the Executive Committee. Waiting in desperate hope for a glimpse of greatness, one found himself begging the movie to preserve values here...with the men who run that great, productive company. In the Executive Committee, one must find firm-faced men with clear, honest eyes...men whose voices were strong and confident...men who talked of important matters, such as production, profit, and values...men who talked of awesome business transactions, heroic discoveries, and fearless plans. But, alas, one was told apologetically that "someone had to run the store". Everyone was then gratuitously rammed with personalized close-ups of the men one wanted to keep at an impersonal distance in order to uphold them as ideals and sources of inspiration. Yes, everyone was assaulted with poster-size faces of the "warm personal man next door"[1].

Was the moviemaker telling everyone that the leaders of Du Pont were nothing more than a group of regular guys? Did it take no one special to run E. I. du Pont de Nemours & Company...just the man next door? The fist hit hard. The Executive Committee was the last place one wanted to see the regular guy. One's soul pleaded for something better, a glimpse of a hero, a glimpse of inspiration. The rest was anticlimactic. No words were uttered of awesome business transactions, thrilling discoveries, or fearless plans. Instead, one heard only of personnel problems, pollution problems, and safety problems.

Nothing seemed to matter after that scene of the Executive Committee. One could watch with indifference as a plant manager obsequiously apologized to the mayor of a city for a new Du Pont factory by explaining that "Du Pont did not want to lean on people or be a problem, but wanted to help solve problems". Nor did it matter any more when the narrator implied that Du Pont had to cajole college graduates into marketing careers. It no longer mattered that the wonderful values available through marketing careers were ignored.

But one final shock remained. It bludgeoned the senses in a

---

[1]The moviemaker was not completely successful here. A few faces did not yield. They reflected a dignity and self-esteem that even the moviemaker with all his modern techniques could not pull down.

thundering broadside. In the final denouement of the moviemaker's soul, the most indisputable values of Du Pont — its magnificent array of commercial products — were reduced to the level of the "inscrutable jellybean". One by one the wonderful products of Du Pont were paraded before everyone to be wantonly besmirched with alternating, out-of-focus scenes of strident, blank-faced youths, writhing with loose, flopping mouths and glazed eyes. One by one the products of Du Pont were flung onto a carrion heap of tortured motions, primitive drum pounding, and flashing lights that accurately reflected a schizophrenic's view of life.

The great products with all the heroic efforts of individuals who chose to use their minds...all the benevolence, achievement, and inspiration that Du Pont represented...all those great values and achievements were trampled into the joyless, Marcusian-Kafka jungle of the parasitical collectivists and professional mystics whose darkling minds viewed with hatred every value that Du Pont delivered to society. ...Could anyone hate life and its values that much?

With howling screams ringing in one's ears and the neocheaters dancing on Du Pont's murdered spirit, the movie ended with brashly incongruous proclamations about the value of the individual. The movie inextricably wove Du Pont into the anticapitalistic dishonesties that are moving throughout the world. The movie maker was successful...brilliantly successful. The movie "1 + 1 + 1" will accomplish precisely what its creator intended the movie to do — drive nails into the coffin of capitalism. And when the last nail is driven, all the benevolence and happiness possible to man will be sealed in that coffin.

How could a mere movie have such devastating effects? This is how: Think back...think far back into your childhood. Recall that precious time when one could romantically look to the future as a life of boundless happiness and goals to achieve? Remember eagerly seeking values, knowledge, and facts? That spark of life, however brief, exists in every child. But most choose to let that spark flicker out — to give up so early in life. Most forever extinguish that spark, never to know life again. A few hang on longer. Fewer, still, never give up. In them, a hidden spark

427

forever burns. And it is they who count. It is they who become the heroes of life.

The movie "$1+1+1$" is the instrument that will break those still struggling to hold on. Implicitly to them, United States business is the last bastion of reason...the last source of inspirational values. Capitalism is the lifeline they unknowingly cling to. As the movie "$1+1+1$" was shown throughout the land, thousands of those young, precious sparks quietly flickered out. So subtle was the movie that few will ever know why. But those who read this document will forever know why. To those who saw "$1+1+1$", recall the emotions at the conclusion of that movie: Aside from a vague feeling of malaise one might have felt, aside from an undefined nagging that something was wrong, what other emotions could possibly be experienced? One could experience only boredom, indifference, puzzlement, sadness, or resignation. With the strength and vitality drained from a once proud image, Du Pont was left hat-in-hand apologizing for its existence. Du Pont was left as an empty, hulking skeleton of effaced values...not even worthy of having its name in the title of the movie.[1]

What was the reaction to this movie by those young minds after being inculcated with forty minutes of subtly specious but powerfully effective anti-heroic, anti-mind scenes? To those who had already given up, only a lethargic "so what" was possible: They were saying "so what" not only to the movie, but to Du Pont, business, capitalism, and their own lives. ...As they gave up and their sparks flickered out, so went the future of Du Pont and capitalism.

---

[1] *Management Newsletter*: "'The film', Strauss says, 'takes advantage of many visual, shorthand techniques to tell a story that informs and motivates without preachment, puffery, or the heavy hand of corporate self-congratulation.'" *Better Living* stated: "The moviemakers (Henry Strauss & Co., Inc. of New York City) provided no traditional story line. Instead of a continuous band of narrative, the impressions were assembled, then tumbled against each other like brilliant shards of glass." For what purpose? For what value?

No, the producer of "1 + 1 + 1" was not responsible for such crimes. The responsibility belonged to the corporate management for failing to protect the ideals of Du Pont and competitive capitalism. Men such as the producer of that movie would be powerless without the sanction and support of such quisling managements.

Nearly twenty years before, a movie was produced under a different management — a management that took Du Pont to the heights of profitability and common-stock values — the movie was entitled *The Du Pont Story*. Those who recalled that proud and glamorous movie vividly grasped the opposite philosophical view of that management. That earlier management took Du Pont to the height of profitability and value. The subsequent management replaced that management with "liberal views" as a route to "higher" values. Du Pont stock sold for $278 per share. Eleven years later, Du Pont stock had fallen to $92.50 per share. Does that represent higher values? Or do such "higher values" represent value destruction?

Speeches and Statements
by Major Du Pont Executives

In one last desperate hope, one might rationalize that the *Management Newsletter, Better Living*, and the movie "1 + 1 + 1" reflected only the views of its writers and editors and not the philosophy of Du Pont management. That hope promptly dissipates on examination of speeches and statements of certain key executives who controlled Du Pont management. Their words were philosophically consistent with the *Management Newsletter, Better Living* and the movie "1 + 1 + 1". Their own statements demonstrated that Du Pont management was abandoning capitalistic standards for mystical, altruistic standards:

McCoy Tells of Need to Cure Social Ills.

Article Headline
Wilmington News-Journal

Casting an undefined pall of guilt on industry for the "social ills" of man, the President of Du Pont, Mr. McCoy, implied that private enterprise had the duty to cure those "social ills". He then declared his intentions to "serve society" through the Du Pont Company. With no reference to serving the stockholders and a perfunctory reference to profits, Mr. McCoy stated the lip-service non sequitur that "nothing is mutually exclusive about making a profit and serving the needs of society."

As Mr. McCoy led Du Pont into the "service of society", the press eagerly reported his views and actions:

Du Pont President sees unique role for industry in solving society's problems.

— Chemical and Engineering News

Ironically, that same magazine revealed the inevitable results of abandoning capitalistic principles to altruism:

Earnings are still far below their peak, and this year will bring, at best, only a small improvement over last year's performance. Du Pont's stock price is less than half what it was four years ago and it has been falling all year.

— Chemical and Engineering News

On the same day that *Chemical and Engineering News* published its article about Mr. McCoy, the *Wall Street Journal* published comments on the performance of Du Pont. Those two articles provided a grimly realistic cause-and-effect dialogue between altruism and profits as shown in the following Table 3.

Table 3

DESTRUCTIVE ALTRUISM *versus* PRODUCTIVE PROFITS

CAUSE — "Although Mr. McCoy is now faced with the responsibility of getting his vast company really moving again, he also gives very deep thought to the increasingly critical role industry must play in society in the years ahead."

— McCoy, *Chemical & Engineering News.*

EFFECT — "The stock may be cheap like some people say — but where's the incentive to buy when the outlook is so hazy?"

— *Wall Street Journal.*

CAUSE — "The challenge is for industry to devise more imaginative ways to place its technological resources in the service of man; to couple its business goals with the clear and pressing needs of society."

— McCoy, *Chemical & Engineering News.*

(table continued on next page)

430

Table 3 (continued)

DESTRUCTIVE ALTRUISM *versus* PRODUCTIVE PROFITS

EFFECT — "How the mighty have fallen," remarked one fund manager. The reference was to the stock of Du Pont.
> — *Wall Street Journal.*

CAUSE — "Society will reward those that help unclog our highways, rebuild and revitalize our cities, cleanse our streams, and conquer poverty and disease, not those whose pursuit of the dollar blinds them to such needs."
> — McCoy, *Chemical & Engineering News.*

EFFECT — "Investors' increasing disenchantment with Du Pont stock is largely based on what Richard Berkley of H. Hentz characterizes as an uninspiring earnings record over the past 10 years."
> — *Wall Street Journal.*

CAUSE — "In Mr. McCoy's view, industry has already moved away from the narrow idea that business corporations are merely organizations to make and sell goods to provide a fair return to their owners. Instead, he says, we have to come to look upon our enterprises as mechanisms invented by society to translate scientific knowledge into the goods and services that society needs."
> — McCoy, *Chemical & Engineering News.*

EFFECT — "But if you're a level-headed investor, you buy performance. And Du Pont — based on its record over the last 10 years — hasn't shown it."
> — *Wall Street Journal.*

President McCoy must be held responsible for the deteriorating performance of Du Pont. Mr. McCoy was hired as the chief executive to serve the stockholders. He was paid by the stockholders to protect and enhance the financial value of Du Pont. A president of an industrial corporation is not paid to solve society's problems or to cure "social ills" with the earnings and property that belong to the stockholders.

Were not other executives also responsible for abandoning capitalistic principles and the resulting poor performance of Du Pont? Yes. And they must also be held responsible to the extent they neglected, misused, and damaged the stockholders' property. In examining the speeches and statements of other major Du Pont executives, however, one discovers a profound difference between *some* executives and Mr. McCoy. While the speeches and statements of those Du Pont executives contained philosophical errors and varying degrees of compromise to altruism that were contrary to the best interests of Du Pont, their projected views still remained basically pro-capitalistic. To varying degrees, they recognized and upheld the values of Du Pont. In other words, a few executives still displayed view points that, although often blighted with sprinklings of altruism, were nevertheless based on capitalistic premises. Mr. McCoy's views, on the other hand, were based solidly on altruistic premises that were "justified" with bits and pieces of pragmatic "capitalism". That fundamental difference in viewpoints becomes vividly apparent in Table 4 on page 434 in which the mystical statements by altruist president Charles B. McCoy are compared to the honest statements by dedicated executive Pierre S. du Pont who recognized and upheld the values of capitalism.

The profound difference between the viewpoints of those two men is self-evident. Mr. McCoy's sad, guilt-ridden view of man's nature and achievements contrasted sharply to Mr. Pierre du Pont's benevolent, guiltless view of capitalism and the benefits it bestows upon all mankind. On reviewing other speeches and public comments by Mr. McCoy, one fails to find a single word of admiration or recognition of capitalism or the marvelous plethora of material and financial values that emanate from the Du Pont Company.

Mr. McCoy's view of capitalism, technology, achievement, and Du Pont was one of disparagement and effacement as evidenced by the following public statement made in his speech before the Society of Chemical Industry:

"There are people so enthusiastic about technology that they assume it is going to solve all our problems. It's nice to have such trusting friends, but they are operating under an assumption that can only hurt us more than anyone else. We cannot meet this blanket contract. When they discover this, as sooner or later they must, they are likely to be angry as well as disappointed. They will think we let them down. Perhaps to an extent we have brought this on ourselves by claiming so many wondrous products and monumental discoveries. Be that as it may, would we not be well-advised in the future to make doubly sure that our propaganda stays in line with practicality? Could we not profit from a more open and candid acknowledgment that we have limited expertise?"

What standard was held by a man who projected technology and human achievement in this manner? What long-range inspiration, daring progress, or heroic achievement could ever evolve from such a standard?

Here a logical question arises: Why did the Board of Directors, the majority of whom are presumably productive men on capitalistic premises, elect Mr. McCoy as the president of Du Pont? What is the underlying reason for their selecting a value-destroying altruist as president? Today, most businessmen are confused and bewildered by the irrational, anticapitalistic culture raging about them. Instead of being hailed as the heroes of mankind that they genuinely are, productive businessmen are maligned and assaulted with blame for the world's "social ills".

The rational businessman, in his innocence, does not understand the reason or the nature of the mounting assaults against him and his business by the news media and by the growing hordes of value-destroying altruists, politicians, and pseudo intellectuals. He has not gained the philosophical knowledge to explicitly identify that he is right and good and they are wrong and evil. He represents the creation of values through rational thought and action, and they represent the destruction of values through force and coercion. He represents the honest and intellectual; they represent the dishonest and anti-intellectual.

Having neither the knowledge nor the stomach to deal with the inscrutable irrationalities besieging him, the businessman usually commits a major error...he avoids thinking about the dishonest hypocrisies surrounding him. Instead, he seeks ways

433

TABLE 4

SENSE-OF-LIFE COMPARISON

Cheerful, Productive, Hard-Driving Capitalist Pierre S. du Pont Speech (Integrated/Business Mind)	Gloomy, Destructive, Guilt-Projecting Altruist Charles B. McCoy Speech (Altruist/Criminal Mind)
"The United States became the strongest and most prosperous nation in the long history of mankind. Its reputation for wealth and generosity grew to such proportions that a successful motion picture was based on the idea that the way for a nation to live happily ever afterward was to lose a war with the United States and get on the list of foreign aid.	"We always come out with pretty much the same laundry list: food supply; population control; housing and urban renewal; pollution control; improvements in medical care and in the cure and prevention of killer diseases; development of alternative raw materials to supplement scarce natural resources; improvements in transportation, especially in densely populated areas.
"United States, one of the rarest things the world has ever known — a country with a surplus of food. Most of the world, even today, lives almost literally from hand to mouth, on the verge of famine and starvation. Indeed, famine and starvation are an annual way of life in far too many areas of the world. The United States is a most happy exception.	"There is deep concern that technology is not working as it should in the service of man, and that organizations closely identified with technology — including our industry very pointedly — are steered by the profit motive into projects that are low in priority or even destructive.
"If the average American — the common man, which I suppose includes pretty much all of us — could be made to understand the importance of this question to him, and the fact that he has a major responsibility to make sure that his selfish and personal interests are protected, then I believe our economic structure would be invulnerable.	"It is said that too much technical skill is wasted on projects that are glamorous but essentially frivolous, while too little is focused on problems such as hunger, pollution, the decay of our cities, and the psychic destruction of the people who live in them.
"We have here what ought to be the most salable product on earth, and yet all available evidence is that the great bulk of those advantaged by it do not appreciate it, do not	"There is concern about the side effects of technology, the 'accidents' that seem to occur all too often. There is concern about the long-term effects of the use of chemical materials, as in the case of agricultural chemicals. There is a growing fear that we have unleashed a force we can no longer control, a force doing irreparable damage to the

TABLE.4

SENSE-OF-LIFE COMPARISON

know or care whether any of it is in any danger, and do not consider, if it is, that they have any responsibility to do anything about it. This adds up to perhaps the worst selling job in the long history of mankind.

"This becomes especially evident when you consider that those who have failed in this task have always been considered as pretty impressive in the field of selling. I mean the representatives of American business and industry. Who else can be held responsible? When you come right down to it, who else is interested in tackling this selling job? I'm afraid the answer is nobody. It's up to us.

"Because of this, some have become discouraged and feel it is an impossible task to win the active and dynamic support of American men and women for the system that has provided a way of life that not even kings and emperors enjoyed a century ago."

biological balance of the planet.

"More and more, we are hearing serious questions about the meaning of the word 'progress'. It is no longer taken for granted, as it was for many years, that more technology and more economic growth automatically add up to improvements in the human condition.

"They are as likely as anyone else to raise the question we hear so often today: 'If we can put men on the moon, how come we can't clean up the mess down here?'

"Perhaps to an extent we have brought this on ourselves by claiming so many wondrous products and monumental discoveries."

to mollify those menacing anticapitalistic forces by making financial amends for his lack of "social" consciousness, by making "practical" compromises, by supporting their "humanitarian" causes, or by cooperating to alleviate their "just grievances". He does not realize that his cooperation and support are providing those anticapitalistic neocheaters with the power and means to destroy him and his business. Thus, that businessman becomes increasingly bewildered as the irrational demands escalate. He often assumes unearned guilt and self-blame for not understanding or knowing how to answer the "socially concerned" news media, the "significant intellectuals", the "idealistic" youth, the "reforming" politicians, the "concerned" clergy, the "humanitarian" altruists, and all other professional mystics and neocheaters swirling about him.

As the threats and harassment mount, the businessman may seek someone who better understands the emerging "new culture" — someone...anyone who will be more favorably received by the news media, youth, politicians, and the "socially concerned". With such a misguided view, the directors of a company become prone to select the worst possible candidate to lead their company. Instead of selecting a businessman who would protect and enhance the value of their company through implementing capitalistic principles, they seek a man who could "attune" their company to the "demands of society", a man who could communicate with "social" intellectuals and "social" leaders, a man with a "social" conscience — a professional altruist.

Such self-defeating acts by businessmen occur through the disease of acting on the basis of what others think, feel, or wish rather than on one's own independent judgment of factual reality. Business decisions based upon what others think undermines the earning potential of companies such as Du Pont. Indeed, most research and marketing failures at Du Pont occur through those who validate decisions not on facts and independent judgment but on what others think, feel, or wish. That intellectually crippling affliction is the consequence of adopting altruistic standards.

With capitalistic standards, each person must think for one's own self to compete and succeed. Indeed, altruism would vanish in a world of value producers who think for themselves and accept

436

the facts of reality as the only valid basis for action. ...The professional altruist negates the integrated, rational use of one's own mind. Furthermore, to sustain his bogus livelihood, the professional altruist must keep the producers from thinking for themselves so they will obey the demands of professional mystics and neocheaters.

> "That question cannot be answered in technical terms alone. It depends on social and political factors as much as economics. It depends on the attitudes of people within the technical work force, and what society expects and demands of them."
>
> — McCoy, Speech

Mr. McCoy's statement speaks for itself. How could any technical achievement capable of generating major profits evolve from Du Pont or from any company when its chief executive subjugates technology and facts to the expectations and demands of an undefinable, nonexistent form of "superior intelligence" that Mr. McCoy calls society. The "superior intelligence" or the "higher good" is the mystical rationalization by which all professional altruists justify their destruction of values. That "superior intelligence" or "higher good" can assume any unreal, mystical form such as "a society that expects and demands". Plato, the philosophical father of altruism and mysticism,[1] first introduced this concept with his various forms of "higher realities"[2].

With Immanuel Kant transmitting the philosophy of sacrifice from the Dark Ages, Georg Hegel prepared altruism for the twentieth century. Indeed, the horrors and destruction of Nazi

---

[1] Altruism is tied to Plato's mysticism. For, no rationality, facts, or logic can support altruism. Thus, faith is the cornerstone of the altruist's eternal promises for a better future: "...Mr. McCoy has a sublime faith in the chemical industry in this future of growing technological application to the good of society." *Chemical and Engineering News*

---

[2] There are no "higher realities", only objective reality. Thus no "higher good" exists to which man can be sacrificed because the highest good is man himself. No "higher cause" (or "society") exists to which individuals can be sacrificed, because the highest cause is the individual.

Germany reveal the final results of altruism. Adolph Hitler was the ultimate practitioner of altruism. His explicitly stated enemies were rationality, capitalism, and individualism. Using the philosophical ammunition of Hegel and the morality of altruism, he perfected a new "higher good" to which anything and everything could be sacrificed without question. Hitler called his mystical "higher good" or "higher cause" the *National Will*.

> "The states and municipalities, and certainly private industry, must look to the Federal level not just for coordination and specific legislation, but first of all for a clear, consistent statement of the *National Will*."
> — McCoy, Speech

The future value of a corporation by nature is determined by the philosophical position of its management. Indeed, this document identifies the business values being destroyed by management's mystical philosophy of "higher causes". While the harmful effects of management's altruistic philosophy are creeping into every phase of Du Pont's business (research, sales, manufacturing, administration), those effects are most vividly observed in art. Indeed, one's philosophical views are openly revealed in one's artistic choices and preferences. Art expresses man's deepest view of life and himself. How does that view apply to the management and business operations of Du Pont?

Consider that architecture is perhaps man's most eloquent, revealing form of art: A mighty, artistic structure rose in the center of Wilmington, Delaware — the Brandywine Building — the building to house the offices of E. I. du Pont de Nemours & Co., Inc. Watching the silhouetted skeleton of that colossus rise toward the sky, one could experience a thrilling pride in witnessing the bold shape being assumed by that great structure. Viewing the structure of this building, one could grasp everything that Du Pont has meant to man. The structure embodied all the creativeness and innovativeness of man. That structure represented the frozen intelligence of man's most magnificent achievements. What an appropriate symbol for Du Pont — perhaps the most innovative, creative company in history. One anxiously awaited for that girdered skeleton to become alive with a sleek skin of glass and steel. A building saluting the achievements of Du Pont. A building with striking, objective beauty.

With disbelief and initial horror that gradually turned to sadness, one watched the desecration of that building take place as workers installed each gloomy slab of massive stone. Increasingly those slabs disfigured that beautiful structure. A building to house a company that symbolized everything productive and creative about man was transformed into the antithesis of modern architecture. The Brandywine Building was wantonly mutilated into an ugly, expensive, medieval structure. That structure reflected the torturous, physical burdens of the Dark Ages during which the lives of men were consumed in back-breaking toil to erect massive, stone structures with sunken slits for windows. Such was the desecration of the Brandywine Building.

Architecture, as any form of art, reflects the deepest views of its creator as well as the views of those who approve and finance the architecture. A building that should reflect modern man's mastery of nature was dragged back through the centuries to emulate a medieval structure. That structure conjured visions of penitentiaries and monasteries with the accompanying emotions of oppressive guilt and tortured screams. The Brandywine Building was transformed into a structure void of joy and happiness.

The future of any company depends on the philosophical premises of the controlling management. If a management on capitalistic premises ever again assumes control of Du Pont, those oppressive walls of stone will come down. Rising proudly in their place will be glittering sheets of light, airy glass and sleek strips of steel and concrete. When the Brandywine Building is delivered into a joyful, glistening structure by modern man and for modern man, one will know that Du Pont management is once again operating on the mystic-free standards of capitalism.

STATEMENT MADE AT THE DU PONT ANNUAL STOCKHOLDERS MEETING

by
Frank R. Wallace
April, 14, 1972

The DuPont Hotel
Wilmington, Delaware

Today, within the Du Pont company exists the personnel, facilities, and capital to embark on a long-range venture designed to lift our company to new highs in earnings, return on investment, and stock prices. To accomplish that goal, its management must adopt a new standard — a standard called capitalism. Why? Because honest, growing, long-range profits can evolve only from the standards of competitive capitalism.

Capitalism, the philosophical child of Aristotle, found birth in the United States and ultimate expression in the Du Pont Company. Here within this building, our company, Du Pont, represents the apex of intelligence and civilization. ...Du Pont is a triumphant testimonial to man's mind, potency, and value.

One man...one individual stands at the base of this magnificent, commercial achievement. In 1802, Mr. Eleuthère Irénée du Pont began a capitalistic venture. With earned profit as his motive...with unflagging effort and his own mind as his tools, that man chose to function as man should — as a producer of values. The results? Look. Look around this room. Step outside and look. Look across this city...this state...across our nation. Look around the globe. One cannot imagine a more eloquent testimonial to the potency of man than E. I. du Pont de Nemours & Company. Man and capitalism together are the essence of values and wealth...of civilization and mastery over nature...of man's well-being and happiness. Capitalism is the standard for man on earth.

Yet today, Du Pont, along with many other major companies, is increasingly operating on a different standard...a standard directed toward a mystical "higher cause". That standard is altruism...a destructive morality diametrically opposed to productive capitalism. As capitalism creates ever-expanding values for man, altruism consumes or destroys values in the name of an imaginary "higher cause", such as society or the national will. Within capitalism there is no higher cause than man, the individual. Within Du Pont, no higher cause exists than serving the stockholders by increasing their long-range common-stock values. How is that accomplished? By increasingly delivering competitive values to others and society.

This idea...this message, must not be a call into silence. For, the owners, the stockholders, must have productive individuals on capitalistic premises once again lead their company. Today, a few such value producers still exist within Du Pont. Those precious few are quietly carrying thousands, tens of thousands, of employees on their shoulders. The owners, the stockholders, must see to it that those precious individuals be the ones who manage their company. Du Pont will then rise as a mighty phoenix...as the harbinger of capitalism, prosperity, and happiness.

SUMMARY
All Honest, Long-Range Societal Values
Generated by Business
arise from the
Mystic-Free Standards of Capitalism

This document reveals how the long-term value of a company is determined by the extent management implements the standards of capitalism. For investors, analysts, and speculators, this document provides an immutable standard to predict long-range, common-stock values. For businessmen and executives, this document provides the basis for expanding both short-term and long-term profitability of their companies. For implementing the standards of capitalism within a company, the following actions are recommended:

1. Dismiss all executives whose corporate actions remain on altruistic standards. Fire all nonproducers and value destroyers.
2. Increase the salaries and responsibilities of those

    executives who have demonstrated competence in delivering long-range financial benefits to the stockholders.

3. Establish an Industrial Philosophy Department in order to define business standards based on the principles of competitive capitalism. With capitalistic business standards defined, the Industrial Philosophy Department would then be responsible for protecting the company and its growth. How? By assuring that all short-range and long-range corporate actions were mystic-free.

If the controlling management rejects (1) dismissing value destroyers, (2) rewarding value producers, and (3) acting according to capitalistic principles, then what does that management stand for? What is the purpose of that management? Where will that management lead its company?

Injection of capitalistic principles into every phase of management will lift a company into a commanding advantage over competition while unleashing a productivity/creativity cycle that will generate continually expanding profits and rising stock values.

EPILOGUE

This document seeks those individuals who act on their own judgment and live by their own productivity. For those value producers are responsible for all the long-term profits and competitive values that business generates.

Without the value producer, no profitable enterprise could exist. In business, as in reality, the value producers and only the value producers earn their livelihoods. All others, no matter what their positions or apparent power within a business concern, remain on the payroll by the erroneous grace and innocent sanction of those value producers.

This document calls upon all value-producing executives to (1) inject the principles of competitive capitalism into every facet of their operation and (2) rid their company of all value destroyers in order to increase the long-range financial value of their corporation. Can this be accomplished by the few? Yes, of course.

Neo-Tech IV
Creating Business Values

Although outnumbered and perhaps outranked, those value-producing executives can always exercise de facto control over their company because the existence of every job and the company itself depends upon them.

This document asks all value producers to exercise their potency in establishing business and industry on the objective principles of capitalism...for their own sake...for the lives and happiness of themselves, their loved ones, and all civilization. For they, the value producers, and only they, hold genuine power.

443

NEO-TECH V

Information Package

**ACHIEVING COMMERCIAL BIOLOGICAL IMMORTALITY
THROUGH COMPETITIVE BUSINESS**
by
Frank R. Wallace

Recognizing the Value of Life
Memento Mori
(Remember Death)

For thousands of years, essentially every human being has desperately repressed a crucial fact that every person must personally face alone. That fact is the fleeting briefness of human life and the finality of death. **Every** person who has ever lived exists but a few decades and then is gone forever. And without Neo-Tech, **every** person alive today will be completely and forever gone in a few brief decades. To repress or distort the reality of life's briefness and death's finality is a harmful act of mysticism with serious, long-term consequences on one's life and happiness.

Contrary to popular beliefs, children early in life understand death and its finality. Because of the mystical evasions and dishonesties of adults, most children gradually learn to evade reality with various mystical, life-after-death myths in order to repress the essential facts about life and death. Indeed, such religious notions are usually among children's first defaults to mysticism which, in turn, start undermining the efficacy of their minds through evasions of reality and repressions of emotions. On the other hand, dealing honestly with reality means consciously integrating into one's thoughts and actions the fact that permanent death will happen to oneself and everyone else within a brief time span. With that awareness, people, including children, place much more value on their lives, time, and actions in order to evolve to their full potential and achieve maximum happiness.

That honesty about death causes individuals to hold life in much higher esteem. Thus, they more fully meet the long-range, self-responsibilities required to gain maximum happiness and fulfillment from their brief lives. Such adults do not squander

445

their lives on the nothingness of mysticism, but, instead, put greater effort into self-development in order to become more productive, accomplished, and happy. And they take better psychological and physical care of themselves.

By contrast, repressing the fact of life's briefness and death's finality lets people evade the precious value of their lives and time. That evasion allows default on their prime responsibility to live intensely — to achieve maximum self-development and growth.

Being fully conscious of life and death, people will value their lives beyond all else in the universe. And that valuation of human life as the supreme value rejects self-destructive acts of mysticism while establishing the psychological and motivational conditions needed to achieve commercial biological immortality.

On the other hand, repressing the fact of life's shortness and death's finality lets one rationalize laziness, mysticism, life-after-death myths, and all else that lead to unfulfilled or wasted lives. That repression also leaves one vulnerable to destructive exploitation by mystics, neocheaters, religions, and governments. But full awareness of one's fleeting, one-shot life span will counteract mysticism and laziness with a powerful appreciation of life. That, in turn, will stimulate the honest thinking and consistent efforts required to achieve prosperity and happiness. And achievement of happiness is the sole, moral purpose of human life.

Achieving happiness requires living according to man's nature. That means taking those long-range actions required for rational prosperity in order to enjoy life — to live happily. That also means cherishing and building the emotions of happiness, joy, and love during one's fleeting existence.

Non-Aging Biological Immortality

Non-aging biological immortality is the technology that will allow human beings to live physically and consciously forever with growing prosperity and happiness. That is man's highest moral goal. And, as identified in Neo-Tech III, such biological immortality is not only possible but becomes a mandatory moral obligation through man's self-invented consciousness. Neo-Tech V identifies those conditions required to create commercial I-ness

446

immortality here on earth before the year 2000.

Neo-Tech IV and V contrast the shrinking perspective of a great but dying, stagnation-oriented company (as E. I. du Pont de Nemours) to the expanding perspective of a living, growth-oriented company (as I & O Publishing Company). But, I & O needs to unleash the scientific brain-power and untapped resources available at great research companies such as Du Pont to accomplish more quickly the goal of commercial biological immortality. Likewise, a moribund stagnated company such as Du Pont needs the business and philosophical perspective of a lusty growing company such as I & O to revitalize and flourish.

The different business perspectives between the management of the two companies are profound: The management of Du Pont, as with many large, entrenched companies, views business as a mechanism to live off the accomplishments of past, value-producing managements. With that view, management can garner immediate unearned personal benefits and power without putting forth the planning and effort required to build sound, long-range values. Moreover, by sacrificing the long-range values of business to the short-range "needs" of society, management gradually consumes those assets created by past, long-range, value-oriented managements. Managements surviving through such hidden dishonesties are easily identified by Neo-Tech as the White-Collar Hoax.

That neocheating technique allows destructive, white-collar-hoax managements to gain quick wealth and false power by consuming rather than creating assets and values. Thus, companies with socially-oriented, white-collar-hoax managements such as Du Pont slowly die. For their management secretly, cleverly consumes the accumulated assets created by the long-range, value-oriented efforts of past managements. And through pseudo growth, sometimes lasting for decades, even generations, those assets are surreptitiously consumed without the realization of the public, owners, or stockholders.

By contrast, the management of I & O views business oppositely: Business is viewed as a conscious, man-made mechanism for efficiently, competitively producing long-range values that will benefit others and society, now and forever into the future.

I & O Publishing Company
STATEMENT OF POLICIES

I & O's STANDARD

I & O strives to answer "yes" to the following three questions:

1. Is it important?
- Offer objective values only.

2. Is it honest?
- Offer only honesty.
- Support every assertion.
- Present every fact in accurate context.
- Eliminate deceptions and distortions.

3. Is it well written?
- Eliminate emotionalisms. Be controlled.
- Eliminate redundancy. Be precise.
- Eliminate jargon, cliches, and platitudes. Be original.
- Eliminate nonessential adjectives and adverbs; favor nouns to pronouns.
- Change passive verbs to active verbs...weak verbs to strong verbs
- Replace obscure words with common words... abstract words with concrete words.
- Arrange random structures into parallel structures — confusion into order.
- Convert vagueness into preciseness — generalities into specifics.
- Edit wordiness into conciseness — ambiguity into clarity.

I & O's BELIEFS

I & O's beliefs arise not from faith or belief in any "higher power" or "authority", but from honestly seeking to understand reality...from knowing that the highest power in existence is the rational mind of conscious beings. Indeed the full power of rational consciousness is measurable only against the cosmos:

Consider the hundred-thousand light years across a single galaxy and the hundred-billion galaxies in our universe, among perhaps a billion universes tucked into one corner of the cosmos. And, consider the total energy of a billion exploding stars multiplied a trillion times represents but a fraction of the energy released every moment into the cosmos. Yet, that unimaginable space and energy shrink into a yielding subservience when matched against human consciousness. A single human consciousness surpasses in power all else in existence — all else in the cosmos combined. For human consciousness is the only force that can alter the course of nature. Without consciousness, the course of nature is immutable. Without consciousness, the nature of matter and the laws of physics mechanically destine every action, everywhere, throughout eternity. Without consciousness, nothing matters, nothing makes any difference. But with human consciousness, that mechanical destiny can be altered constantly and changed with impunity. Indeed, human consciousness has the entire cosmos to reach into, to grow into, to use, to control for man's benefit.

The cosmos cannot command conscious man. But conscious man can command the cosmos in concord with honesty and reality. The cosmos does not own conscious man. Conscious man owns the cosmos.

I & O's DEDICATION

I & O Publishing Company is dedicated to the highest value — the conscious, value-producing individual. The value-producing individual is defined as anyone who through his or her own mind, rational actions, and competitive efforts continually adds to the material, intellectual, physical, psychological, or aesthetic well-being of others. Such a person adds genuine values to the lives of others. That person adds much more than he or she takes. Without such value producers, no objective values could grow or be sustained — no society or civilization could survive or exist.

Throughout history, professional mystics and neocheaters have usurped, diminished, or drained the rewards and happiness earned by the value producer. He has always been drained and hampered by spurious external "authorities" who live off his efforts, repaying him with false guilt and demands for sacrifice. In his innocence, the value producer has remained vulnerable while continuously accepting the destructions, usurpations, and abuses of mystics and neocheaters. The value producer has never realized that **he**, not they, holds the power to control life and events. ...But with Neo-Tech, he can now break free to take what every value producer earns, but seldom takes — a guiltless life of prosperity, pleasure, love, and happiness.

All I & O publications are dedicated to delivering the knowledge that lets value producers guiltlessly take the rewards and happiness that belong to them. Moreover, all I & O publications are dedicated to achieving the highest value possible for conscious beings — non-aging biological immortality. And, by nature, biological immortality requires a rational, mystic-free Neo-Tech environment.

I & O's PHILOSOPHY

Authority

I & O Publishing Company recognizes only one authority — the authority of one's own rational mind. Indeed, rational consciousness is man's means to abiding happiness...to individual competence and for producing competitive societal values.

A person's own authority is derived through his or her consciousness. The volitional, rational use of one's own mind is the only means to identify, integrate, and then use objective reality to live competitively and successfully — to benefit others and society. By contrast, no external "authority" can determine for anyone how to live. For, only the authority of one's own consciousness can integrate reality with one's own situation. Thus, only one's own consciousness can determine how to live successfully and produce maximum values for others and society.

Business, being extensions of individuals, functions through individual consciousness. No professional mystic, neocheater, or external "authority" can offer long-range objective values to anyone or any business. I & O Publishing Company, therefore, never grants recognition to any professional mystic, neocheater, external "authority", or any other value destroyer.

Producers

I & O Publishing Company seeks those who act through their own honest, *integrated* thinking — those who earn values through their own hard thinking, integrations, and efforts. I & O seeks such people, for they are responsible for producing every major value in existence. Without those producers, objective values could not be created or sustained; value-producing enterprises could not exist; civilization could not prosper.

The value producer is anyone who honestly earns his or her own way through life by producing more values for others and society than consumed by self. Thus, the producer and only the producer adds values to society.

I & O provides the structure for individuals to produce through the authorities of their own minds rather than through external "authorities". With such a structure, everyone associated with I & O can deliver maximum values — never-ending, ever-growing, competitive values.

Rewards

Only after recognizing one's own consciousness as the supreme authority can a person freely pursue prosperity, happiness, and romantic love. Indeed, that person can achieve abiding prosperity and happiness only after rejecting external "authorities" by dismissing mysticism in self and others. ...Freedom from mysticism and external "authorities" will lead value producers to their greatest value — biological immortality with forever growing prosperity and happiness.

I & O's GOALS

I & O Publishing Company has three goals:
1. Define the ultimate goal for human beings on planet Earth.
2. Define the conditions for achieving that goal.
3. Create those conditions for achieving that goal.

I & O has accomplished the first two goals. The third goal is the reason for I & O's continued existence.

The First Goal

I & O's recent publications demonstrate that the ultimate goal for conscious beings on planet Earth is non-aging biological immortality. The supreme importance of that goal lies not in just preserving human consciousness but in preserving an individual's own sense of self...the continuous sense of "I-ness". Indeed, the most important value of human biological immortality lies not in preserving a creative, productive individual for the benefit of society, but in preserving that individual's sense of self for the benefit of himself and his loved ones — for his own continued happiness and growing enjoyment of life. Thus, the technological challenge lies not just in preserving consciousness, but in isolating and then preserving one's own sense of self...one's sense of "I-ness".

Preservation of that sense of "I-ness" for continued growth and enjoyment of individual life is man's highest value and moral goal.

The Second Goal

Technology exists today to achieve commercial I-ness immortality within this century by at least five different routes:
1. Retaining I-consciousness through cell regeneration or replacement of the entire body via nanotechnology or other technologies.
2. Brain or I-consciousness transfer to a donor body.
3. Brain or I-consciousness transfer to a body culture-grown from a fertilized egg.
4. Brain or I-consciousness transfer to a cloned body culture-grown from one's own cell.
5. Electronic transfer of I-consciousness to a cloned or tabula rasa (blank) brain.

Neo-Tech V
Biological Immortality through Business

Conscious man today has nearly infinitely greater power to protect and improve life than nature itself. Thus, in nature, the function of death to protect and improve the species is obsolete for conscious beings. Indeed, death in nature still protects and preserves nonconscious life. But a tragic and unnecessary loss occurs on the death of each rational, conscious being. For conscious beings now have both the power and responsibility to prevent death — to preserve conscious life forever.

Today, human consciousness is a value that never needs to be lost to death. To muster, however, the resources and mind power in industry and science needed to achieve commercial biological immortality, Neo-Tech must first collapse the hoax of mysticism along with the specious, altruistic philosophies and neocheating psychologies that dominate all cultures today. Only through Neo-Tech will the commercial elimination of death become recognized as man's most urgent, important goal.

The Third Goal

When Neo-Tech philosophical and psychological conditions are established among the value producers, they will quickly recognize that biological immortality is the highest commercial and moral priority of business, science, and ethics. As the supreme value of human consciousness becomes understood and accepted, business will deliver the motivation, brain power, and resources to achieve biological immortality.

By focusing all assets, planning, products, management, and marketing toward demonstrating the destructive invalidity of all mysticism and external "authority", I & O can establish those philosophical and psychological conditions needed to achieve biological immortality. Accomplishing that final goal will occur during the increased marketing of Neo-Tech/Neothink knowledge to collapse the 2000-year hoax of professional mystics, neocheaters, and destructive "authorities". That collapse will unleash all the productive efforts needed to achieve commercial biological immortality quickly, practically, and economically for everyone.

Future Goal

As expressed early in Neo-Tech V, conscious man owns the cosmos. The cosmos is available to each conscious being to

453

control for his or her value-production, well-being, happiness, and permanent survival. That, therefore, becomes I & O's future goal — to control nature — to control the cosmos — to drive the cosmos to rational man's bidding, benefit, and eternal survival.

I & O's MANAGEMENT

I & O's Management Concept

Management obligations are to (a) produce maximum values for others and society by undermining and then eliminating professional mystics and neocheaters through Neo-Tech, (b) direct those values toward accomplishing I & O's goal of non-aging commercial (low-cost) biological immortality, and (c) protect I & O from professional mystics and neocheating "authorities" by never yielding a scintilla to their destructive demands. ...Each associate of I & O can meet those management obligations by applying the following seven commandments:

1. Gain powerful, new knowledge by identifying wide-scope objective reality through sustained concentration with fully integrated honesty and hard-work actions. At the same time, reject the glib dishonesty and lazy nonthinking of narrow-scope, pre-packaged "truth" and automatic "knowledge" pushed by professional mystics, neocheaters, and destructive "authorities".

2. Achieve I & O's long-range goals through honesty and effort rather than credentials and connections.

3. Exert consistent fairness toward all individuals to block trouble-making mysticism and narrow-vision pettiness.

4. Emphasize individual strengths and sublimate individual weaknesses to speed progress toward I & O's goals.

5. Reward individuals in proportion to their contributions to I & O's goals. Dismiss disruptive prima donnas along with destructive mystics who undermine I & O's work or plant cancer seeds.

6. Recognize and use the unique, powerful combination of assets at I & O:
   - integrated publishing and marketing expertise
   - autonomous and independent international operating locations
   - entrapment in the Neo-Tech matrix of professional value destroyers in and out of government, at all levels and in all countries
   - in-house writing, editing, and typesetting capabilities
   - advanced scientific experience
   - objective philosophical and psychological grounding.

   All those assets are directed toward ending the specious influences of professional mystics, external "authorities", and neocheaters. Ending those destructive influences will deliver prosperity, happiness, and biological immortality to all value producers worldwide.

7. Use I & O's fully integrated literary/marketing techniques to exploit the impotence of external "authority" and the dishonesty of mysticism.

Applying those seven commandments assures the collapse of mysticism and achievement of the final goal — low-cost, commercial biological immortality. I & O's technique for aggressive, trench-warfare marketing of Neo-Tech and collapsing mysticism is revealed in the confidential report titled, "Reaching the X Factor Through the Web Effect".

The uniqueness of I & O's policies, management, products, and goals is further illustrated below:

Management Organization

Unlike most companies or organizations, I & O has no employees, no hierarchical structure, only free-lance associates or entrepreneurs. While the policy manager is responsible for overall policies, no management or associate unit is superior to another. No associate has authority over any other associate.

Moreover, any important business, research, or editorial disagreement among I & O associates can always be resolved by persistent integration of the facts to eliminate mysticisms, resolve contradictions, or solve problems. Such open, honest integrations allow everyone to eventually reach the same rationally grounded understandings on any matter important to the business and goals of I & O Publishing Company.

The chart on the next page compares I & O's organization of limitless free-lance associates to establishment organizations of bureaucracies and employees.

To accomplish I & O's goals of establishing the conditions for biological immortality, management is divided into independent, fully integrated associate units:

Each Associate Unit Consists Of
(alphabetical listing)
Accounting and Analysis
(Financial, Operations, Test Data)
Administrative and Organization
Customer Service
Editorial, Direction, Philosophy
Management
Marketing
Operations
Protection
Research and Development
Special Projects

The business structures in Neo-Tech V appear
in
Mark Hamilton's Cosmic Business-System structures.

Each associate is responsible for continuously improving the efficiency and profitable growth of his or her unit. The effectiveness of each associate is evaluated by the *growth* in contributions made toward I & O's profits, strength, protection, and goals:

Neo-Tech V
Biological Immortality through Business
COMPARING ORGANIZATIONS
and
Their Personnel

	Government Bureaucracies (rigid, bloated, destructive)	Large Companies (structured, large, productive)	I & O Publishing Company (free, limitless, creative)
GOALS	Usurp maximum power	Earn maximum profits	Create maximum values
MEANS	Use force or deception	Produce values and develop markets	Follow maximum-value integrations
APPROACH	Hide value destructions	Strive for maximum profits	Strive for maximum values
REQUIREMENTS	Mendaciousness	Experience	Attitude
PRODUCTS	Power determined	Profit determined	Value determined
END RESULTS	Inefficiencies, destructiveness	Highest possible profits	Highest possible values
MANAGEMENT	Power directed, dogmatic supervision, rigid structure, destructive bosses	Profit directed, purposeful supervision, flexible structure, productive bosses	Value directed, little or no supervision, no structure, no bosses
PERSONNEL	Arrogant, lack self-worth, lack respect for time and costs, play destructive games to expand bogus jobs	Defensive, protect territory, follow instructions, seek productive routines	Know responsibility of job and importance of goals, expand productivity and self-responsibility
ATMOSPHERE	Sour, petty, small-minded, malevolent, dishonest	Honest, hard working, but routine	Happy, innocent, integrated, hard-driving, enthusiastic, benevolent
ATTITUDE	Dislikes working; time is of little or no value	Job is secondary, time is valuable	Job is primary, time is the most precious value
PROBLEM SOLVING	Indifferent and lazy, little integrated thinking or effort, creates more problems, avoids responsibility	Cheerful and willing, honest thinking and efforts, solves problems, accepts responsibility	Excited and energetic, sustained integrated thinking and efforts, turns problems into advantages, seeks responsibility and growth
THINKING CAPACITY	Integrated thinking blocked by dishonesty and laziness	Specific business areas open to wide-scope integrated thinking. But other important areas blocked by mystical white-collar hoaxes	No integration blockers (mystic-free) allow maximum-wide integrations in all areas

<u>Evaluation of Associates</u>
via
Contributions of Each Associate Unit
Toward I & O's:
PROFITS
STRENGTH
PROTECTION
SHORT-RANGE GROWTH
LONG-RANGE GROWTH
GOALS
FINAL GOAL

Reaching I & O's final goal depends on all associates harmoniously working in a mystic-free, businesslike manner. In such an atmosphere, associates can freely grow with no one's permission.

In addition, each associate is independent — free to create and build responsibilities that contribute to I & O's profits and goals. Indeed, each associate is expected to grow — to seek, create, and build new values while constantly assuming greater responsibilities.

No establishment structure exists within I & O. All depends on self-responsibility, fully integrated honesty, wide-integrated thinking, and hard-driving efforts.

I & O MARKETING

<u>I & O's Marketing Concept</u>
Wide-scope integrations are I & O's guide to its goals. ...The data and numbers of the marketplace show the quickest route to those goals.

Since commerce began thousands of years ago, marketing concepts have focused on selling to potential buyers. But I & O's marketing concept focuses on delivering maximum values to buyers and non-buyers alike. That new marketing approach is called the "99% principle" and is based on techniques outlined earlier in this volume.

I & O has three marketing policies:
1. Offer only original proprietary products that deliver much more value than any competitive product.
2. Offer only products that transcend time and cultures.
3. Market products through 99%-principle information brochures. ...Let the readers experience the life-saving value of the product.

The marketplace is the key tool for discovering and developing those values most desired by everyone. Moreover, the largest of all markets — the market for crucially valuable, fully integrated ideas — remained unknown and untapped until Neo-Tech. Indeed, I & O's products and techniques are designed to reach that market. ...Marketing those ideas will increasingly vanquish mysticism, abolish neocheaters, and reject external "authority" while opening the way to non-aging biological immortality for everyone.

I & O PRODUCTS

Time is limited: Since the development and marketing of any new product requires a major investment of management time, each product must be carefully selected for its contribution toward reaching I & O's goal on schedule. Thus, each I & O product must meet the following three standards:
1. Delivers values that are crucial to the prosperity and happiness of every conscious individual.
2. Delivers values that are universally and forever valid.
3. Delivers values that contribute to the collapse of mysticism and the elimination of neocheating.

Regardless of its profit potential, I & O rejects any product not meeting those three standards. For marketing such products would dilute efforts to achieve I & O's goals. Moreover, such products are unnecessary since a growing multi-year backlog of potential products that meet the above standards already exists.

BUSINESS — THE MOST NOBLE IDEA

Business is the most noble of all ideas, the most intellectual of all thinking, the most valuable of all activities. Business is a man-made mechanism from which all major values of civilization are created, produced, and distributed. Business is the mechanism through which people most effectively assert themselves into life to produce maximum values for others and achieve abiding happiness for themselves and their loved ones.

Almost without exception, those who vilify, undermine, and drain honest businesses are those who usurp their livings from the value producer. Most mystics and neocheaters undermine and destroy values out of envy and resentment. For through their habitual parasitism, they have made themselves incompetent to honestly produce competitive values for others and society. Such professional mystics, neocheaters, and external "authorities" survive by draining their benefactors — the value producers.

Moreover, the professional mystics and neocheaters who publicly scorn money and values are actually obsessed with usurping money and values in order to live without producing competitive values for others. Such mystics and neocheaters project false guilt onto the value producer in order to conceal their motives, methods, intentions, and impotence. They demand control and regulation of the value producer when they themselves are incompetent to produce values for others.

Business delivers competitive values to others, to society, even to the value destroyers. While the value destroyers deliver only false guilt, usurpations, and harm to business and its value producers.

Business people are primarily interested in producing values for others. To such business people, money represents not a means for consumption, but a means to grow — to produce still more and better values at ever lower costs and greater efficiencies. That mechanism for producing ever-increasing values at ever-lower costs is the unmatched virtue of business. Indeed, business is the most moral, most intellectual of all human activities. Business is the most widely integrated, evolved form of human intellect. Business is the antithesis of mysticism.

Neo-Tech V
Biological Immortality through Business

The extent to which a person follows mysticism or external "authority" is the extent to which he becomes incompetent and moves toward death. But the extent to which a person integrates reality with his own rational consciousness and fully integrated honesty (Neo-Tech) is the extent to which he will experience ever-growing competence, prosperity, and happiness.

Once free from the destructive grip of professional mystics and neocheaters, all productive people from the hourly wage earner to the Nobel-Prize scientist can live guiltlessly, prosperously, and happily forever.

* * *

Neo-Tech for Collecting Unlimited Prosperity and Happiness
by
<u>Ending the 2000-Year Hoax of Mysticism</u>

Throughout history, productive people have been too busy *earning* their livings to discover what mysticism is, much less who the professional mystics and neocheaters are, how they operate, and how their deceptions diminish everyone's life. Those mystics and neocheaters include the politicians, ruling "authorities", clergymen, social "intellectuals", most lawyers, some bankers and business executives, certain media people, certain educators, certain psychologists, and others (including friends and relatives) who parasitically live by draining the effectiveness, prosperity, and happiness of others.

Professional mystics and neocheating "authorities" are dishonest people with no genuine earned power. But ironically, most such people could quickly earn genuine power by switching from their dishonest manipulations of mysticism to the honest integrations of Neo-Tech as their route to prosperity and happiness. With Neo-Tech, a person prospers in all competitive situations by eliminating the dishonesty, stupidity, and blindness of mysticism. ...By using Neo-Tech to dismiss mysticism, one's competence and advantages increase so greatly as to guarantee growing prosperity and happiness.

* * *

The clean, honest, mystic-free business mind is the mind that governs the cosmos.

A Memo from Mark Hamilton

One morning in December, twenty-five years ago, a young research chemist carefully listened to a renowned scientist outline the long-range goals for one of the world's great research centers. Although awed by the marvelous opportunities before him, that young man, Dr. Frank R. Wallace, realized that even with the achievement of all the goals combined, a crucial ingredient would be missing: the greatest of all goals would remain unmentioned, untouched, unrealized. By that evening, Dr. Wallace knew someday he would have to leave his career at Du Pont to pursue alone the greatest human goal. Two decades later, he discovered through a series of experiments the crucial, missing ingredient — Neo-Tech. That ingredient not only delivers guiltless prosperity and well-being to individuals, but will eventually deliver biological immortality to all who love life with its limitless prosperity, happiness, and adventure.

THE NEO-TECH PHILOSOPHY —
THE WIDEST INTEGRATION
will cause the
SPONTANEOUS, WORLDWIDE
COLLAPSE OF MYSTICISM

An Address to the Executive Board by John Flint:
Business and Research Director of
Neo-Tech Pincer Movement #1
and author of "Industrial Philosophy"

July 15

Objectivist philosopher Leonard Peikoff states the most basic of all axioms in three words: "what is is". But that axiom reduces to an even more powerful, more precise two words: "existence exists". Now, as I will explain, a subtle but profound difference exists between those two axioms: "What is is" versus "existence exists".

Static versus Dynamic

"What is is" is static — like some rock out there. On initial thought, "existence exists" seems static too. But when you put that axiom into a fully integrated dimension, suddenly the meaning changes from static to dynamic. What is that fully integrated dimension? Where did those integrations come from? They come from the Long Wave[1] and the profound identification that consciousness is an integral part of existence.

Consciousness: Forever a Part of Existence

Consciousness is not something that evolved or developed out of existence. Consciousness has always existed and is an integral part of existence. That identification is the crucial link missed by Einstein in all his work dealing with existence, space, time, mathematics, and physics. Consciousness is and always has been a part of existence as much as matter and energy are a part of existence. Now, with consciousness in the cosmic formula, "existence exists" holds an entirely different meaning. The verb

---

[1]The Long Wave: See Appendix H.

"exists" changes from a purposeless, static existence to a purposeful, moving process — a process that is being constantly integrated and controlled by conscious beings.

Indeed, the cosmos is not controlled by some god, some mystical power, or some "higher-consciousness"...or even by the immutable laws of nature. But, as demonstrated in the Long-Wave article, all existence is controlled by business-driven value producers such as you and me.

Limitlessly Wide Integrations Through
Consciousness Plus Neo-Tech

First, what is Neo-Tech? It is fully integrated honesty. It is free of neocheating manipulations and mystical stupidities. Thus, Neo-Tech delivers unlimited, wide-range integrations — infinitely wider than any other idea system.

With Neo-Tech, new knowledge is beyond the conscious mind only because of time — the time needed to accumulate facts and information for the integrations required to fill any understanding gap. Unlimited knowledge, therefore, is separated from us only by time.

The human conscious brain never evolved or never needs to physically evolve in order to understand anything in existence. Thus, the evolution of consciousness is a meaningless concept, just as the evolution of matter or energy is a meaningless concept.

Consciousness is either present or it is not present. Thus, as demonstrated in the Long-Wave article, our own consciousness here on earth today has the same limitless capacity to understand everything as does the consciousness that controls the universe. Consider that conscious Greeks over two millennia ago had the same capacity as we have today to understand anything in the universe. Given the knowledge, they could equally understand, for example, all our rapidly expanding nuclear and computer technologies. Only the time to develop the knowledge separates them from us. Likewise, our own consciousness today and the most knowledgeable consciousness in the universe are both equally capable of understanding anything — even knowledge a billion years ahead of all current knowledge. ...Only time separates us from our cosmos cousins and all knowledge.

Article 1

The Neo-Tech Philosophy — The Widest Integration

The Only Limitation is Overcome
by
Computers and Neothink

The only limitation of consciousness is processing-speed and storage-capacity. Yet today we can clearly see solutions to those limitations: Layers of previously unknown knowledge fall away with increasing rapidity as we move into the computer age. With ever increasing computer processing speed and storage capacity combined with Neothink, human consciousness can integrate and understand anything in existence — anything. That unlimited capacity exists today, has always existed, and will always exist.

How does that infinite capacity work? How does Neothink work? A conscious being can make the widest-scope integrations, up to the capacity of the mystic-free, conscious mind. Then that same mystic-free mind starts building another area of maximum integration, and then another area. Next, at any time, that mind can integrate those areas of maximum integration together into a new unit and then integrate that new unit with other new units of integration. Without the integration blockers of mysticism, that linking and integrating of previously built integration units can continue indefinitely. That's how Neothink works. It requires a Neo-Tech mind — a mystic-free mind. Without mysticism, no integration limitations exist. Thus, nothing is unknowable to mystic-free consciousness.

Philosophy Summarized

Prior to Neo-Tech, the broadest integration of a philosophical system was Ayn Rand's powerfully valid system of Objectivism, commercially advanced by Nathaniel Branden, and currently carried forward by Leonard Peikoff through his important philosophical and promotional contributions. Now, review Ayn Rand's one-word summaries used to identify four of the five branches of philosophy — metaphysics, epistemology, ethics, and politics. Next, move beyond with Neo-Tech to identify each branch from the *widest* integration. Through those integrations, one can see why Neo-Tech is so real and solid. You'll see why Neo-Tech is more widely integrated than the works of Carnegie,

Article 1

The Neo-Tech Philosophy — The Widest Integration

Edison, Einstein, or Rand. For as great as those giants were, each had their widest-scope integrations blocked by personal mysticisms. Thus, only from mystic-free Neo-Tech comes ever wider business, scientific, and philosophical integrations.

Consider those one-word summaries of Ayn Rand's Objectivist philosophy:

1. Metaphysics: Man's relationship to existence or reality. Ayn Rand's one-word summary of metaphysics is "reality". How can one get more basic than reality?
2. Epistemology: The method of thinking. Ayn Rand's one-word summary of epistemology is "reason". How can one get more basic than reason?
3. Ethics: Ayn Rand's one-word summary of ethics is "self-interest". How profound, how simple.
4. Politics: Ayn Rand's one-word summary of politics is "capitalism". How precise.
5. Aesthetics: Ayn Rand never summarized aesthetics in one succinct statement.

Now, consider how Neo-Tech takes philosophy to the widest integrations:

1. Metaphysics: Neo-Tech's One-Word Summary
of
<u>Metaphysics is Business</u>

Metaphysics, the first branch of philosophy, was summarized by Ayn Rand as "reality". But, from the more widely integrated dynamics of conscious-controlled existence, metaphysics has a wider integration than static, physical reality. That wider integration is *business!* Yes, a dynamic business existence.

One discovers the relationship between metaphysics and business by understanding the Long-Wave article. That article demonstrates how the cosmos, all existence, all *reality* is controlled by value producers functioning within the dynamics of business.

Now, let's examine metaphysics — a *static physical reality* versus a *dynamic business existence:* Business universally encompasses the widest-scope, no-limit integrated thinking possible. And within that scope, all reality is encompassed, which

466

includes all physical reality. Indeed, physical reality by itself is a static, narrower-scope integration than is business. For business also encompasses all intellectual, psychological, emotional, and physical actions of conscious beings in a dynamic, changing process throughout all existence.

How is that? Think of what business really is. As identified many times in the Neo-Tech literature, business is not just a specific term that's used like you have business here, you have art there, you have government here. No. Instead, from both a metaphysical and an epistemological sense, business represents the antithesis of mysticism. For mysticism is the unintegration of reality and the disintegration of thinking. Mysticism *is* the process of attacking, destroying, and losing values and life itself through consciousness. ...Mysticism destroys man's relationship with existence.

By contrast, business is the integration of reality, thinking, values, and life. Business represents the widest form of fully integrated thinking and action possible. Business *is* the process of creating, elevating, or expanding values and enhancing life through consciousness. ...Business enhances man's relationship with existence.

Now go back and consider the axiom "existence exists" as a dynamism that has forever existed as a conscious-driven process. For, as the Long-Wave article demonstrates, business has always driven the universe. ...Yes, the universe exists as a dynamic process, not as a static thing. "What is is" is a **static entity**. "Existence exists" is a **dynamic process** — a forever living, growing, business process managed through Neo-Tech/Neothink minds to achieve ever greater prosperity and happiness.

Reality is static and by itself enhances no values. But, business is dynamic and through consciousness enhances all values. Business provides ever greater prosperity and happiness by enhancing man's relationship with existence.

2. Epistemology: Neo-Tech's One-Word Summary
of
Epistemology is Neothink

Ayn Rand defined epistemology as "reason". Now, what is a wider-scope integration than reason? It is *Neothink*. And

The Neo-Tech Philosophy — The Widest Integration

Neothink encompasses all reason in a dynamic growing process. Reason is a static, specific method of thinking. Neothink is a dynamic process that is integral to the metaphysics of business. And again, business functions through net profits, numbers, data, and limitless wide-scope integrations to produce evermore competitive values for others and society. Thus, business demands greater and greater integrations achievable only through Neothink.

The "existence exists" of the universe is driven by business, Neothink, net profits, numbers, and values. Therefore, metaphysics is summarized as business; epistemology is summarized as Neothink.

3. Ethics: Neo-Tech's Summary
of
<u>Ethics is Value Production</u>

As the third branch of philosophy, Ayn Rand summarized ethics as "self-interest". Now what is a wider-scope integration that encompasses self-interest? Neo-Tech summarizes ethics as *value production*. And, of course, the dynamics of value production naturally encompass self-interest. Indeed, value production is the benevolent, natural dynamics of life, society, and the conscious mind. Thus, value production is the ethics of conscious life.

The "existence exists" of the universe is driven by conscious beings using Neothink to increase value production through their businesses.

4. Politics: Neo-Tech's Summary
of
<u>Politics is Free Competition</u>

The fourth branch of philosophy is politics. Ayn Rand summarized politics as "capitalism". But capitalism is encompassed within a wider-scope integration that Neo-Tech identifies as *free competition*. And a corollary adjunct to competition is ostracism. Now, the dynamics of both competition and ostracism together yield an interaction that guarantees political freedom and capitalism.

After realizing why free competition is the widest integration of politics, a single, universal political constitution materializes:

Article 1

The Neo-Tech Philosophy — The Widest Integration

That universal constitution of less than 200 words[1] contains only one element — the prohibition of initiatory force.

On eliminating initiatory force, the dynamics of interactions among conscious beings become competitive. Thus, the natural dynamic of conscious life is free competition. From that, one realizes that freedom means competition and competition means freedom. Indeed, free from threats of initiatory force, unfettered competitive value production quickly becomes the dynamic of conscious life.

Professional value destroyers and other criminal minds hypocritically spout about freedom. But they hate and fear competition. For, competition would end their bogus livelihoods. Yet, freedom and competition are inextricably linked. One cannot exist without the other. Thus, value destroyers must use force or the threat of force to diminish or eliminate *both* freedom and competition.

Consider the modern white-collar-hoax axis of entrenched businesses and fascist-oriented governments: Together they use force or threat of force through destructive regulations and crippling laws to restrict or eliminate competition. They must squelch competition to usurp power and protect their bogus livelihoods.

Naturally, a part of competition is capitalism, which is a term for a specific kind of competition. But competition itself holds a wider integration than capitalism. For, the dynamics of competition naturally occur not only in all business actions, but in personal activities, in relationships, in art — in all actions among free human beings.

The "existence exists" of the universe is driven by competition. Value producers control the cosmos through business, Neothink, value production, and competition.

5. Aesthetics: Neo-Tech's Summary
of
Aesthetics is Value Reflection

The fifth and final branch of philosophy is "aesthetics". Although writing brilliantly about aesthetics, Ayn Rand never succinctly summarized its essence as she did the other four

---

[1]The Universal Constitution: see page 140.

branches of philosophy.

Now, to capture the widest-integration essence of aesthetics, one must first go back to the essence of ethics, which is *value production*. From that, one discovers the essence of aesthetics is *value reflection*. That reflection can occur, for example, through literature, art, fine art, music, dance, or architecture. In any case, the aesthetics of value reflection naturally expand into personal living, into relationships, and eventually into the most integrated of all areas — business.

As value reflection expands into romantic relationships, family relationships, relationships among friends or business associates, aesthetics can deliver profound pleasures and powerful advantages. Indeed, we already experience the motivating fuel of value reflection in many subconscious, undeveloped ways. During the second Neo-Tech World Summit, for example, consider the deeply motivating paeans and inspiring dances reflecting the values of the mightiest business heroes. Well, that was a nascent expression of aesthetics in capturing the beneficent power and values of the greatest heroes: the Carnegies, the Goulds, the Edisons, the Firestones. Moreover, with Neo-Tech and aesthetics, no longer will those heroes remain maligned or unsung.

Through value reflection, we can integrate the dynamic aesthetics of any great value with music, the fine arts, architecture, and all else artistic, beautiful, and emotional. Why? To provide the fuel of pleasure needed to build values and happiness forever.

The "existence exists" of the universe is fueled by the dynamics of aesthetics, the concretizing of values, and the reflection of values.

* * *

Thus, above are the five branches of Neo-Tech Philosophy in their widest integrations. And where do those wide-scope integrations come from? They come from *not* cutting off integration corners — from being free of mysticism to eliminate all limitations. Only with fully integrated honesty can we grasp ever wider-scope integrations that have no limits. With that integration power, anyone can outflank and soar above all competition hobbled by mysticism.

Article 1

The Neo-Tech Philosophy — The Widest Integration

> Below is Frank R. Wallace's (FRW) subsequent dialogue with Mark Hamilton (MH). Mr. Hamilton is the Business and Research Director of Neo-Tech Pincer Movement #2 and the author of the Neo-Tech publication titled, "Cosmic Business Control".

MH: It's amazing what you just said. I read the Long-Wave article again last night for the second time in six weeks or so. When I read that Long Wave, every time I read it, the integrations expand and mean something so much more than the previous time. And what you just said breaks us all free.

As you were identifying and integrating those five branches of philosophy, I felt all conscious beings breaking free from repressed, earth-bound philosophies into a limitless, Long-Wave philosophy — the same philosophy that exists throughout the cosmos. Just as you went through that, I felt myself breaking into the cosmos as I integrated your words with what I read last night in the Long Wave.

The minute you encompassed reality with business — those words were so profound to me. At that point, I knew the path you were on with the other areas of philosophy. Neo-Tech is awesome. It's breaking us from the limited earth view and propelling us into the unlimited cosmos view — just as four centuries ago when we broke from the stifling geocentric view into the liberating heliocentric view.

FRW: Yes, Neo-Tech breaks us free from the mystic-bound hoaxes and propels us toward the business-like dynamics of our eternal cousins throughout the universe. Even a decade ago, the Psychuous literature identified how all mystic-free conscious beings were, through the dynamics of business, capable of "driving the cosmos and beyond".

MH: You know, there is something momentous in what you just covered. I know people can't really grasp how momentous that is until they grasp the Long Wave. The minute you said business over reality, that integration hit me like an avalanche.

WH: In the next meeting or two, I'll integrate the dynamics of Neo-Tech Philosophy with our goal of collapsing mysticism. Those

471

The Neo-Tech Philosophy — The Widest Integration

integrations will demonstrate how impotent the mystical/neocheating world is and how powerful the Neo-Tech/Neothink world is. By understanding those integrations, everyone will intellectually and emotionally realize how nothing can stop Neo-Tech from driving every professional neocheater and business quisling from their fake jobs. Neo-Tech will also dump all the value destroyers in government and business to leave their masses of blind followers floundering without direction, without protection from competition. ...Against Neothink, they're all so small, insignificant, and impotent.

MH: That's exactly what I've been sensing. Against the uncorked power of Neo-Tech, you really sense the shrinking "smallness" out there. Even with their guns, fists, and billion-dollar budgets, they all seem so puny. You can feel their insignificance. You feel the power of their evil shrinking to nothing.

FRW: In reality, value destroyers are small and puny — they are literally nothing in the dynamics of life. For they contribute **no** net or competitive values to anyone or society. Yet, on understanding the philosophical essences of Neo-Tech, one can see why the ideas and philosophies before Neo-Tech were impotent in dealing with the great hoax of mysticism. One can also see why nothing before had ever stopped the value destroyers. Objectivist philosophers from Aristotle to Ayn Rand could never really cure mysticism or stop its destructive evil — even though their philosophies stood alone in being intellectually honest, even though they laid the foundations for Neo-Tech.

Envision a value producer armed only with Objectivism. He can do little or nothing against the legions of neocheating value destroyers. For his philosophical tools are limited to the important but static ideas of 1. reality, 2. reason, 3. self-interest, 4. capitalism, 5. aesthetics. Now envision the same value producer armed with Neo-Tech. He can quickly uproot, expose, and disintegrate all value destroyers. For his philosophical tools are the dynamics of 1. business, 2. Neothink, 3. value production, 4. free competition and ostracism, 5. value reflection.

Another way to see Neo-Tech's unbeatable power is through contrasting ideas. Consider, for example, the contrasting ideas of Objectivism:

472

Article 1

The Neo-Tech Philosophy — The Widest Integration

1. Objectivism vs. Collectivism
2. reality vs. nonreality
3. reason vs. nonreason
4. capitalism vs. socialism
5. self-interest vs. altruism.

Now consider the contrasting ideas of Neo-Tech:

1. Neo-Tech vs. Neocheating
2. business mode vs. criminal mode
3. neothink vs. mysticism
4. competition vs. white-collar hoax
5. value production vs. value destruction.

Which set of contrasting ideas seems academic and impotent? Which set of contrasting ideas seems alive and powerful?

Eternally curing mysticism requires collapsing its 2000-year hoax. That collapse will decimate the armies of professional value destroyers who depend on the manipulative dishonesties of mysticism and neocheating to survive. And their timorous supporters will be dispersed by the loss of mystical hoaxes promoting specious external "authorities". Those professional mystics and neocheaters will then be left without power or livelihoods. Neo-Tech will leave them writhing in their dead-end streets of envy and hate. At the same time, Neo-Tech will benevolently show them the door to life — the door to competitive value production and happiness.

How is that done? How is that disease of mysticism forever cured? The metaphysics of business, the epistemology of Neothink, the ethics of value production, the politics of competition, and the aesthetics of value reflection will easily and quickly cure the disease of mysticism forever.

Now, consider other idea systems evolving from Socrates with his outdoor philosophical discussions — and Plato, Aristotle, Adam Smith, John Locke, Herbert Spencer, and Ayn Rand with all their writings. Those systems depend on discussing ideas. Regardless of their importance to the foundation of Neo-Tech, they all evolved around static philosophizing. Yet, stop to think about Neo-Tech: Here, all business evolves around philosophy and philosophical ideas. Neo-Tech seldom involves discussions of significant length

473

about traditional philosophy. Instead, Neo-Tech mainly involves integrating business, not philosophizing.

Except in the context of business, Neo-Tech seldom involves philosophy, politics, or how to establish a new order, how to stop neocheaters, or how to fight "bad things" in the mystical world. Instead, with full-focus on business, I & O is a company of quiet subversion — subversion of Plato's world and the criminal-minded concepts of God, altruism, collectivism, force-backed bureaucracies, and the white-collar hoax manipulated by professional mystics and neocheaters.

MH: You know, as you were talking, I had the sense of discovering the full Neothink perspective in philosophy. I felt how we are forever leaving in the dust everyone — from Aristotle's followers to Ayn Rand's Objectivists. I really sensed the difference between using ideas to philosophize versus using ideas in business to produce values...the difference between just sitting there helplessly with philosophy and ideas versus controlling everything through business and ideas. I felt this big limitless dimension open up to us and everyone in the future. Yes, it's really true what you said: We don't discuss philosophy. For we're metaphysically in tune with our nature by pursuing business through integrated thinking and honesty.

And through the Long Wave, we can see exactly how the cosmos has always been run and will forever be run into infinity — through the dynamics of business. It's amazing, we never philosophize. Yet, in one swoop, we leave in the dust every philosopher from Aristotle to Rand because we are true to our metaphysical nature — because we are functioning with fully integrated honesty through business.

FRW: Interestingly, we actually philosophize every day from the widest context — from a fully integrated, dynamic, value-generating way through business. By contrast, traditional philosophizing is static — dealing with a myriad of "a-points" that lead to dead-end stumps available for mystical manipulations.

MH: Now, one can feel the impotence toward mysticism of every philosophy until now. ...Now, one can feel the real power of Neo-Tech.

Article 1

The Neo-Tech Philosophy — The Widest Integration

FRW: We must capture this integrated business-minded philosophy and inject it into everything we're doing. In a way, we've been doing that since the November-3rd attack without explicitly identifying what we were doing. But now, with the power of having explicitly identified the essence of philosophy, every value producer can and will abandon the hoax of mysticism to flourish forever into the future.

MH: The Neo-Tech Philosophy makes the future so obvious. Combining Neo-Tech philosophy with Neo-Tech business, the hoax of mysticism and all professional value destroyers will perish unless they become competitive value producers.

THE NEO-TECH PHILOSOPHY

From the Einstein Long-Wave identification in Appendix H of this volume evolves the profound concept that consciousness is both an axiomatic component and the controlling element of existence. When that concept is combined with the 114 Neo-Tech Advantages, all the integrations of Neo-Tech unfold into a philosophy of infinitely wide integrations as shown in the chart below.

The chart below also outlines the Objectivist philosophy — the most widely integrated philosophy prior to Neo-Tech. But that philosophy had its integration corners cut off by both general and personal mysticisms to miss the final, limitless integrations captured by Neo-Tech:

Variables	**Objectivist Philosophy**	**Neo-Tech Philosophy**
Origins	Aristotle	Aristotle, Rand
Conscious Mode	Mortal	Immortal
Philosophical Mode	Static	Dynamic
Integration Scope	Very Wide	Infinitely Wide
Limiting Element	Mysticism	None

The Five Branches of Philosophy		
Metaphysics	Reality	Business
Epistemology	Reason	Neothink
Ethics	Self-Interest	Value Production
Politics	Capitalism	Free Competition
Aesthetics	Never succinctly defined	Value Reflection

Each of the five widely integrated branches of Objectivist Philosophy are subsumed within the five branches of the more widely integrated Neo-Tech Philosophy.

Article 2

THE COSMIC MIND
by
John Flint

**THE COSMIC MIND
IS NEITHER SCIENCE FICTION NOR MYSTICAL**

The Cosmic Mind is Emerging on Planet Earth Today

The Neo-Tech mind *is* the cosmic mind. The cosmic mind? Sounds like science fiction, even mystical. But Neo-Tech is the antipode of science fiction and mysticism. Indeed, through the competitive dynamics of business, the Neo-Tech mind will forever eradicate mysticism from planet Earth. So what is the Neo-Tech mind that is emerging on planet Earth today? Why is the Neo-Tech mind the cosmic mind? What is the cosmic mind?

The Neo-Tech Mind Ultimately Controls Everything

As demonstrated in Appendix H, the cosmic mind governs all advanced civilizations. Also, as demonstrated in Neo-Tech Advantage #31, each advanced civilization throughout the Universe has passed through the Nuclear-Decision Threshold. And to pass through that Nuclear-Decision Threshold, a civilization must be free of self-destructive mysticism. Or, from the corollary perspective, no civilization infested with self-destructive mysticism can survive beyond that Nuclear-Decision Threshold. Therefore, civilizations advanced much beyond our own must consist of mystic-free minds functioning through fully integrated honesty. ...By definition, mystic-free minds are Neo-Tech minds. Moreover, only through fully integrated honesty can conscious minds grow to the unlimited vistas of those advanced civilizations. Only minds free of mystical integration blockers can have unlimited power — cosmic power.

Thus, the Neo-Tech mind *is* the cosmic mind. And only the Neo-Tech mind can acquire cosmic power — omnipotent power within the laws of nature. ...What is the significance of the Neo-Tech mind suddenly emerging here on Earth?

477

Article 2

The Cosmic Mind

The Emerging Neo-Tech Mind on Planet Earth

The mystic-plagued mind has dominated our civilization since consciousness emerged from nature-created bicameral minds 3000 years ago. Unable to introspect and make conscious moral choices, bicameral man was amoral and innocent. Like every nature-controlled animal, bicameral man could not be mystical, deceptive, or purposely destructive. Only by creating the conscious mind could man jump past nature to outcompete and then control nature. But, only after creating consciousness could he inflict upon himself the only disease of consciousness — mysticism. And thus, only conscious man faces the choice to (1) be honest or dishonest, (2) be rational or irrational, (3) be productive or destructive, (4) be growing or stagnating, (5) be business-like or mystical, (6) be happy or unhappy, (7) be alive or dead forever.

The Crossroads

In the latter half of this twentieth century, our civilization arrived at the Nuclear-Decision Threshold. But conscious beings populating planet Earth are still plagued with the disease of mysticism. Thus, we have reached the crossroads that all civilizations reach. At these crossroads, nuclear annihilation occurs in civilizations populated with self-destructive, mystic-plagued minds (e.g., power-mad Leninist/Maoists, life-hating Shiites, and other such mystically insane value destroyers with power). But in civilizations populated with productive minds fully integrated with honesty, the reverse occurs: Nuclear energy combined with computer technology and other fast-breaking technologies, ranging from super conductivity to nanotechnology, means soaring benevolence, knowledge, and prosperity.

In other words:

1. With mysticism, nuclear energy will wipe out conscious beings.
2. With mystic-free Neo-Tech, nuclear energy will propel conscious beings toward their mystic-free cousins throughout the cosmos.

Thus, the emergence of the Neo-Tech mind at this critical Nuclear-Decision Threshold of our civilization means Armageddon. The Ultimate Battle between good and evil must now take place. This battle is —

478

THE WAR OF TWO WORLDS:
Value Producers versus Value Destroyers

That war of two worlds is the crucial life and death determinate for our civilization: the Neo-Tech mind versus the mystic mind; the business/integrating mind versus the neocheating/disintegrating mind; life versus death.

Could the diseased minds of mystics, neocheaters, and other value destroyers win the war? No, not with Neo-Tech. Could this be a dangerous war with the risk of losing to the value destroyers? No. What are the chances of Neo-Tech losing this final battle to evil? None whatsoever.

No, Neo-Tech cannot lose. Why? Because as Pincers #1 and #2 start circling the globe, the Neo-Tech mind easily outflanks and outcompetes all other minds, especially mystic-plagued minds. Again, the chances of Neo-Tech losing? None whatsoever.

Relax

Ironically, this final, most crucial, important battle of civilization is no contest. In fact, this battle is laughable. No matter how many guns, thefts, jails, and killings they resort to, the value destroyers will only accelerate their own demise. Thus, the outcome is a sure-thing, total-victory outcome. Moreover, no one except those directing the worldwide network of Neo-Tech bantam companies needs to take part or risk anything in the war of two worlds. Indeed, everyone else can relax, enjoy the battle, and then reap the benefits. Neo-Tech business people alone will collapse the 2000-year hoax of mysticism and eliminate all its symbiotic neocheaters. For the Neo-Tech mind is the invincible cosmic mind that governs the universe.

Just imagine clean, healthy, omnipotent, fully integrated cosmic minds pitted against sullied, diseased, impotent, unintegrated mystic-plagued minds. The outcome is pitifully obvious. For the "opposition" is based literally on nothing — the "opposition" is based on the nothingness disease of mysticism. Also, the minds of the "opposition" are filled with mystical integration blockers. By contrast, Neo-Tech minds are free of all integration blockers and limitations. That is why mystic-free, Neo-Tech minds can outthink and outflank mystic-plagued, neocheating minds.

Article 2

The Cosmic Mind

Neo-Tech bantam companies need the war of two worlds. Those companies need to draw into battle the professional mystics and neocheaters. Each Neo-Tech bantam company needs to engage in battle the professional value destroyers with their armies of dishonest journalists, bogus-job academe, destructive politicians, and lazy bureaucrats. For the Neo-Tech mind outflanks all their manipulations — Neo-Tech jujitsus into oblivion all the stupidities and irrationalities of mysticism and neocheating.

When that war starts, wave one of the Seven Neo-Tech Waves will begin rolling. And then each successive six waves will increasingly wash value destroyers off planet Earth. ...Today, Neo-Tech bantam companies are quietly integrating professional mystics and neocheaters into the Ostracism Matrix worldwide. ...Tomorrow, essence-moving, integrated-thinking value producers will first scorn and then laugh disintegrated-thinking value destroyers out of existence.

Cosmic Minds are Now Evolving on Planet Earth

Imagine cosmic minds from civilizations millions of years beyond their own transition from hallucinating bicameral minds to integrating Neo-Tech minds. Their histories and anthropologies would preserve their own transitions from bicameral to Neo-Tech minds. But they would not long remember or preserve the nature and events of that lightning brief time (in relative cosmic time) roiled in mysticism and neocheating. Thus, all notions of irrationality, purposeful value destruction, dishonesty, initiatory force, evil, war, and death itself would be unknown and incomprehensible to those advanced civilizations.

With Neo-Tech, the disease of mysticism will also eventually fade from our own Earthbound memories and histories as an exceedingly brief, insignificant aberration. Why? Because mysticism is the nothingness disease that holds no significance, meaning, or interest for future mystic-free generations. Even in our current generation, all value producers will come to recognize value-destroying mysticism as nothing more than an immature, wholly unnecessary stupidity. ...Mysticism and neocheating will increasingly seem like ludicrous jokes, albeit profoundly evil and destructive jokes.

Article 2

The Cosmic Mind

Curing the Disease of Death

Now, try to imagine clean, innocent beings from some advanced civilization observing the destructiveness of mysticism for the first time. They would be witnessing an insane destructiveness based on nothing. Imagine them observing bizarre, irrational, destructive factoids such as the guns and fists of November 3rd, the FDA, INS, DEA, SEC. And imagine those super-productive happy beings observing wretchedly unhappy professional mystics and neocheaters living by harming and draining the value producers.

Despite their super-advanced knowledge and technology, those cosmic beings would have no way to relate to or comprehend the nothingness disease of mysticism and its destructiveness. They would have no way to relate to evil, irrationalities, intentional destruction, neocheating, and especially death...all based on senseless nothing. In fact, only the Neo-Tech minds evolving here on earth today can understand the nature of mysticism enough to diagnose and then cure that disease of death. ...And rightly so, for the responsibility to cure our own disease of mysticism lies entirely upon us conscious beings here on earth.

Neo-Tech meets that responsibility. The cosmic seeds of Neo-Tech are silently growing in 151 countries. Nothing can stop the demise of mysticism. Nothing can stop the victory of emerging, omnipotent, mystic-free minds over entrenched, impotent, mystic-plagued minds.

Lineup of Contestants

The following chart shows the lineup of contestants for the War of Two Worlds. Yes, Neo-Tech must and will engage in war *all* the mystic/neocheating value destroyers. For the mystic/neocheating disintegrating minds, that war is their death trap. But, for the Neo-Tech/Neothink integrating minds, that war is no war. The contest is no contest. The lineup matches nothing against everything. The mystic/neocheater pip-squeak mind will perish forever; the Neo-Tech/Neothink cosmic mind will live forever.

Article 2

The Cosmic Mind

The Lineup

> **MYSTIC-PLAGUED EARTH MINDS**
> *versus*
> **MYSTIC-FREE COSMIC MINDS**

Diseased, Unnatural Mystical/Neocheating Disintegrating Minds	versus	Healthy, Natural Neo-Tech/Cosmic Integrating Minds
Bicameral/hallucinating. External-authority driven. A disintegrating mind.	Origin	Man-made/business-like. Introspective, independent. An integrating mind.
Blocked integrations. Fearful. Dependent on others.	Power	Unlimited integrations. Fearless. Independent of others.
Dishonest/lazy defaulted. Destructive/evil.	Character	Honest/effort driven. Productive/good.
Value destruction.	Exist On	Value production.
Stagnation, envy, resentment, sickness, neurosis, poverty, destruction, death.	Deliver	Growth, value reflection, romantic love, health, happiness, prosperity, values, life.
Narrow-limit/unsound.	Knowledge	Forever-limitless/sound.
Nothing.	Substance	Everything.
Destructive, negative. Less than nothing.	Nature	Productive, positive. Everything in Universe.
Death quickly.	Duration	Life forever.

Article 2

The Cosmic Mind

Developing and Experiencing the Neo-Tech/Cosmic Mind

One develops and then experiences the Neo-Tech/cosmic mind by ruthlessly extirpating mysticism from oneself and rejecting it in everyone else. One then begins sensing the awesome power and dimensions of Neo-Tech. Yet, on further experiencing the limitless, cosmic dimensions of Neo-Tech, one realizes its total naturalness. At the same time, one senses that other world left behind as a meaningless, grotesque realm that revolves around the disease of stupidity and death — the disease of mysticism.

On acquiring the Neo-Tech cosmic mind, one realizes the inchoate, immature, goofy nature of that dying other world...and the incredible adventure of happiness that now awaits every value producer on Earth who enters the cosmic-mind world of Neo-Tech.

The mystic-free Neo-Tech mind *is* the cosmic mind. And the cosmic mind has now evolved on planet Earth. With the cosmic mind of Neo-Tech, we on planet Earth will soar forever into limitless life and happiness.

NEO-TECH

is fully integrated honesty.
Neo-Tech allows the guiltless creation of earned
money, power, and romantic love.
Neo-Tech is the route to forever growing
prosperity, health, and happiness.
Neo-Tech is the opposite of mysticism.

MYSTICISM

is the creation of problems where none exist.
Mysticism is both an individual and a
collective disease that puts people in coffins
and societies on crutches.
Mysticism leaves empty heads
and instills sour faces on people.
Mysticism is an act of war on rational thinking, honest effort,
prosperous happiness, and life itself.

NEOCHEATING

is the deceptive manipulation of mysticism
to extract values earned by others.

MYSTICS AND NEOCHEATERS

are people who live by attacking values created by others
rather than by
producing values for others and society.
Mystics and neocheaters make good seem bad and bad seem good.
They trash the good and protect the bad.
They attack integrated, essence-moving business thinking and actions.
They attack Neothink and Neo-Tech.

PSYCHUOUS

is the Neo-Tech integration of the mind, body, and emotions
with factual reality
to yield honest prosperity and guiltless happiness.

MONEY

Neo-Tech ends the neocheater's 2000-year effort to conceal the fact
that money is created *only* through the creation
of competitive values for others and society.
Neocheaters falsely detach money from values
while dishonestly linking it to guilt.
In contrast, by orienting directly around money,
Neo-Tech focuses on values
in the most direct, guiltless way
to vanquish the dishonesties of mystics and neocheaters.

PROFESSIONAL INDEXING
by
Sharon T. Smith

Index

nature of, xviii
physical appearance of, 101, 102
rights of, x
Anti-drug laws, 90, 91
Anti-individualism, see Platonistic philosophy
Anti-intellectualism, 31
Anti-obscenity laws, 182-185
Anti-pornography laws, 184
Anti-sex laws, 130-132, 133
Anti-technology, 20, 40, 218
Anxiety, 79, 82
Apartheid, 249, 250
Aphrodisiacs, 92
A point, 475
  the point vs., 279
Appearance, 85-86, 101
Appliances, 218
Aquinas, Thomas, vii, 269
Arabs, 249
Arafat, Yasir, 181
Architecture, 225, 276, 438
Aristotelian philosophy, 2, 14, 40, 41, 48, 124, 125-129, 158, 220-222, 288, see also Aristotle; Individualism; Objectivism; Rand, Ayn
  change in course of history through, 127-129
  communication and, 198
  man's nature and, 2
  reality and, 2
Aristotle, ii, xiii, xiv, 103, 118, 121, 125-129, 156-159, 220-222, 266, 269, 472, 473, 474, see also Aristotelian philosophy
  capitalism and, 440
  as father of business mind, 220
Armageddon, 478
Art, 3, 52, 438, see also specific types
  classical, 229
  evil, 230
  government-sponsored, 53
  law of, 230
  mediocre, 230
  modern, 224, 228-230
  as natural high, 121
  negative values in, 224
  as non sequitur, 416
  objective, 224
  objective evaluation of, 52
  ownership of, 53
  poetry vs., 222-231
  subjective, 224
  women in, 105, 109
Art critics, 228
Art museums, 229
The Art of Loving, 28, 32

Asceticism, 46, 49, 111, 112, 235
Asia, 30, see also specific countries
  racism in, 249
Assault, 130
Asset builders, 408
Astrology, 5, 31, 37-42, 135, 231, 232
Atheism, 34, 35, 168
Athletics, 105
Atkins, Robert C., 85, 86, 87
Atlas, 268
Atomic units, 156
Attractiveness, 24, 80, 81
Authority, D, 17, 156, see also specific types
  duty to, 13
  end of, 336-337
  external, see External authorities
  higher, 59
  legitimate, 450-451
  myth of, 9
  smallest unit of, 156-158
Automobiles, 33, 127, 128
"Average" individual, 98
Awareness
  of bodily pleasures, 79
  mystical, 231-232
  physical, 24
  self-, see Self-awareness
Ayatollism, 35, 38, 216, 270, see also specific people

— B —

Babbit, 201
Backpain, 312
Bad-thought (BT) jealousy, 69-72, 73, 74
Bantam companies, 456
Barrons, 138
Bassiat, Frederic, 265
Batista, 270
Beauty, 81-83, 101
Beethoven, Ludwig, von, xiv
Begin, Menachen, 181
Behavior traits of value producers, 202-208
Bentham, Jeremy, 269
Bestiality, 130, 130
Better Business Bureaus, 215
Better Living Magazine, 411, 415, 418-421, 428, 429
Bible
  Holy, see Holy Bible
  Neo-Tech, xvi, 3
Bicameral mind, 301, 321, 336, 478, 480
  control of people through, 397-400
  defined, 398-399
  in poker, 399-400
Big business, 164, 165, 402

Index

Index

Index

Index

Index

Index

Index

Index

Index

Index

Index

Index

Index

Index

Index

Index

internal, 120
last line of defense of, 300-301
love and, xxiii-xxiv
mental illness and, 71
nature of, 143-144
Neo-Tech Constitution and, 142
nonmysticism vs., 349
origin of, 281
personal, 121
philosophical foundation of, 125
pride as negator of, 44
problems created by, 305-319, 326
of Ayn Rand, 121
scientific, 38
self-, 130, 346
subconscious, 298-299, 300, 301
as suicide, 325
techniques of, 32-33
tools of, 35
worldwide collapse of, 463-476
Mystics, D, 484, see also Mysticism;
   specific people
Achilles' heel of, 275-280
closet, 99
death of, 302-303
defined, ix, 484
disguised, 99
morality of, 144-145
nature of, 283
Neo-Teching of world of, 167-171
nonmystics vs., ix-xi
protection of children from, 149-151
rejection of, 152-155
types of, 99
Myths, 37-42, see also specific types
about art, 52, 53
about biological immortality, 209-210,
   282-285
astrology, 37
children and, 151
about death, 282-285, 446
democratic, 43
greatest of all, 160
scientific, 38
UFO's, 37

— N —

Nader, Ralph, xiv, xix, 103, 165, 170, 200,
   204, 205, 215, 235, 262, 421
Nanotechnology, 129, 254, 285, 293, 478
National defense, 138, 139, 177
in Israel, 246
National Organization for Women (NOW),
   23
"National will", 438
Natural beauty, 101

Natural body functions, 85-86
Natural highs, 121-123, see also specific
   types
Natural law, 266
Natural phenomena, 84-85
Nature, 18, 38
alteration of, 449
of animals, xviii
control of, xi, 254, 449, 454
forces of, 37
laws of, 464
of man, see Man's nature
variables of, 5
of mystics and neocheaters, 20
Nazi Germany, 138, 177, 227, 228, 438
Nebraska Consumer Protection Division,
   152
Neck stiffness, 122
Needs, 6, 11, 127, see also specific types
biological, 1, 6, 11, 24, 88
emotional, 1, 24
for growth, 65
intellectual, 1, 24
physical, 1, 12, 24
psychological, 1, 12, 24
Negative emotions, 54, 120, 192, 198, see
   also specific types
Negativity, 66
Neo-Tech, F, xv, 484
aesthetics of, 469-470
altruism vs., 219-220
as Antichrist, 396
Aristotle and, 158, 220-222
basis of, 286
benefits of, A-H
business, 167
children oriented towards, 107, 108
dedication of, b
defined, A-H, iii-iv, 180, 192, 236, 237,
   268, 271, 464, 484
development of, 337-346
discovery of, A-H, see also Neo-Tech
   Discovery
epistemology of, 467-468
ethics of, 255, 468
foundations for, 472
freedom and, 136
future values for owners of, 346-351
goal of
happiness and, 305-319
highest profits of, G
integrations of, i
job power of, 316-317
justice of, 262
Linking Instructions for, 327-351
management power of, 318-319
marketplace origins of, 268-269

502

Index

Index

Neocheating, D, E, G, 484, see also Neocheaters
    in business, 391-392
    in cards, 324, 329, 331, 333, 342, 383-395
    causes of, 218
    concepts behind, 391
    criteria for, 394-395
    defined, viii-ix, 142, 194, 276, 346, 385, 484
    detection of, 387
    discovery of, 383-395, 391
    as easy, 385, 386
    elimination of, 18, 261-262
    essence of, 290, 294
    evolution of, 385
    future of, 386-387
    metaphors in understanding of, 332-333
    nature of, 168
    Neo-Tech Constitution and, 142-143
    original book on, 385
    origins of, 305, 385
    in politics, 391-392
    power of, 303
    prediscovery, 383
    in religion, 391-392
    revealing of, 389
    safety of, 385, 386
    in social relationships, 391-392
    spread of, 387
    understanding of, 390
Neocheating Manuscript, 322, 381
Neothink, 89, 137, 321-326, 467-468
    limitation overcome by, 663
    mechanisms of, 465
    as mind of future, 321-322
    power of, 303-304
    seven units of, 209
Neothink matrices, 263
Neothink web, 264
Nervous system, 79, 88
Nervousness, 100
Neurosis, see also specific types
Neurotic sex, 47
Neurotic values, 52
New Think, 252
New-wave churches, 51
New York City, 35, 199
New York Stock Exchange, 411
Newspeak, 244
NHTSA, see National Highway Traffic Safety Administration
Nicaragua, 177, 199, 311
Nicotine, 87, 121
Nidal, Abu, 181
Nitrogen fixation, 423
Nobel Prize, 168

Non sequiturs, i, xx, 32, 33, 57, 99, 109, see also specific types
    art as, 225
    defined, 180, 275
    in education, 126
    internal, 279
    personal use of, 279
    romantic love and, 124
    rules and, 26
    secret of, 275-280
    understanding of, 276
Noneuclidean mathematics, 188
Nonjudgmental values, 60, 61
Nonmarital love, 76-78
Nonmysticism, see also Nonmystics
    defined, 349
    mysticism vs., 349
Nonmystics, see also Nonmysticism; specific types
    defined, xi
    morality of, 145
    mystics vs., ix-xi
    neocheaters vs., ix-xi
Nonsexual jealousy, 69
Nonsexual love, vi
November-3rd Empire, 481, 482, see also Guns-and-Fists Empire
NOW, see National Organization for Women
Nuclear-Decision Threshold, 40, 41, 219, 478
Nuclear power, 128
Nuclear technology, 464
Nuclear war, 40, 136, 137
Nude bathing, 183
Nude streaking fad, 183
Nutrition, x, see also Diet
Nutritional advocates, 275
Nutritional approaches to immortality, 292, 294
Nylon, 413

— O —

"Obedience to Authority", 9
Obesity, 85, 86, 92
Objective art, 224
Objective fear, 58
Objective law, 119, 133, 179
Objective morals, 6
Objective reality, 11, 126, 189, 193
Objective standards, 159
Objective thinking, 192-193
Objective values, 32, 33, 52, 61
Objectivism, 267, 269, 288, 289, 290, 463, 465, 466, 472, 474, 476, see also Aristotelian philosophy; Rand, Ayn

Index

Index

Index

Index

blocking of, 83
capacity for, 25-26, 38
Constitution for, see Neo-Tech Constitution
defined, iv
government power and, 83
housewives and, 106
as natural high, 121, 122
parenting and, 107
physical fitness and, 87
requirements for, 1, 24-25, 81
sensuous behavior vs., 24-25
sensuous pleasures vs., v
Psychuous sex, 15, 22-23, 25, 59, 80
addictions and, 89-92
defined, iv
intensity of, 25
mysticism and, 89-92
nature of, 60
Public education, 125, 126, 151
Puritanism, 50, 113, 136
sex and, 50
Purpose of life, xxiii, 14, 54, 139, 323
Put-down humor, 82
Psyche death, 218
Python, Monty, 320

— Q —

Qaddafi, 181
Quackeries, 231, see also specific types
Quality of life, 91
Quantum mechanics, 188
Quiana fiber, 418
Quotes, 226

— R —

Ra, 59
Racism, 51, 125, 246-250
Neo-Tech as solution to, 249-251
Railroads, 167
Rand, Ayn, xiii, xiv, 19, 118, 121, 266, 269, 465, 466, 467, 468, 469, 472, 473, 474
cigarette smoking and, 121
mysticism of, 121
philosophy of, see Objectivism
Random-walk capacity, 98
Rape, 47, 130, 132, 183
Rapture, 265
Rational actions, 2
Rational happiness, 54
Rational mind, 4, 5, 24, 37
Rational psychologies, 98
Rational self-interest, 160, 200
Rational society, 40

Rational thinking, 11
Rational values, 59
Rationalism, 50, 113
Rationality, 3, 31, 58
Rationalizations, 33, 87, 143
Reality, xi, xxiii, 3, 12, 29, 31
Aristotelian philosophy and, 2
control of, 121, 207, 231, 466
dealing honestly with, 54
defined, 2
distortion of, 89, 103
emotions and, 56
ideas anchored to, 268, 269
identification of, 88
integration of, xvi, 88
living in, 121
mind-created, ix, 126, 402
morals based on, 6
negation of, 44
objective, 11, 126, 189, 193
Platonistic philosophy and, 2
understanding of, 244
Reality highs, 121, see also specific types
Reality-oriented philosophy, see Aristotelian philosophy
Reason, xx, 126, 169, 188, 196, 295, 466, 467, 468
communication based on, 198
emotions and, 71
morals based on, 9
Reason magazine, 267
Reasoning, xviii, xix, 33
false, 186
Red China, see Peoples Republic of China
Reformation, 49
Reich, Wilhelm, 12
Rejection fears, 58, 100
Relationships, see also specific types
destructive, 64
employer-employee, 103
ending of, 64-104
errors in, 63
with family, vi, 240
with friends, see Friendship
love, see Love
neocheating in, 391-392
requirements for, 237
romantic, see Romantic love
sex as cause of change in, 240
sexual, see Sex
Relativity, 186
Relaxation, 79
Religion, xx, 2, 31, 33, 34, 37, 38, 44, 121, 125, 135, see also Church; God concept; specific types
decline of, 114
destructive effects of, 4

Index

Index

Index

Index

Index

abolishment of, 128
elimination of, 139
Technology, see also specific types
  anti-, 20, 40, 218
  nano-, 129, 254, 285, 293, 478
Television evangelism, 136
Tender feelings, 198
Tension, 179, 180
Terminal illness, 181
Terminal suffering, 181
Terrorism, 29, 181
Testing, 72
Testosterone, 90
Theft, 161
Theism, 34, 168, 179
  philosophical foundation of, 125
Theocracies, 49, 52, 250, 270
  a point vs., 279
  of biological immortality, 293-294
Therapies, see Psychotherapies
Thinking
  business-like, 54, 198
  conscious, see Consciousness
  defaults in, 34
  effective, 244
  emotional, 192-193
  horizontal, 129, 251-252
  integrated, 33
  language and, 401
  lateral, 129
  mystical, 198
  objective vs. emotional, 192-193
  poetry and, 226
  positive, see Positive thinking
  rational, 11
  requirements for, 263
  vertical, 251-252
Threats, 59, 99, 133
Time, 283, 319
  integration of with life, 325-326
  perception of, 480
  wasting of, 325
Time magazine, 405
Titan, 3-5
Titian, 229
Tobacco, 91, 121
Toledano, R. de, 170
Torts, 313
Totalitarianism, 4, 34, 35, 37, 59, 138, 184, 250, 253
Trade, 19, 24
Trains, 127, 128
Transcendental meditation, 42
Transfer payments, 139, 276, 277, see also specific types
Truisms, 32, 34
Trust, 80

Truth, 226
Two-chamber mind, see Bicameral mind
Two worlds, xvii-xviii
Typhoid Mary, viii
Tyranny, 125, 225, 265, see also specific types
"Tyranny Under the Law", 183

— U —

UFOs, 5, 37-42
Ukraine, 171
Ultimate Battle, 177-180, 478
Understanding, 244-246
  beyond, 232-234
  of reality, 244
Unilateral disarmament, 40
Union Carbide, 171
United States
  discovery of, 128
  founding of, 43
  justice system in, see Court system
United States Constitution
  first amendment to, 154, 184, 185
United States Patent Office, 284
United States Supreme Court, 182-185
Universal artists, 52, 53
Universal bad, 6-8
Universal computer, 129, 155
Universal good, 6-8
Universal moral issues, 7-8, see also specific types
Universal morals, 6
Universe, 18, 39
  why of, 31
University of Hawaii, 309
USSR, see Soviet Union
Utopias, 252-254, 271

— V —

Value destroyers, D, xiv, 15-16, see also specific individuals; specific people by name; Value destruction
  essence of, 270
  false power of, 299
  judgments about, 187
  macho-type, 22
  murder by, 309
  value producers vs., 333, 307-308, 479-481, see also Ultimate Battle
Value destruction, xxi, xxii, 17, 30-31, see also Value destroyers
  envy and, 69
  jealousy and, 72
  nature of, 30
  by political movements, 177

513

Index

Index

POSITIVE COMMENTARIES ABOUT NEO-TECH

LETTERS FROM EARLY NEO-TECH OWNERS

Peruse some or all of the following letters.

The following randomly selected letters were from owners of the early incomplete, less-developed Neo-Tech manuscripts. These letters are not being paraded to demonstrate the great values available from Neo-Tech. You will discover those values on your own. But rather, the letters demonstrate the endless *variety* of values arising from Neo-Tech for ordinary individuals and life-styles around the world. ...Why are these random letters so important? By documenting the endless variety of Neo-Tech advantages available to *everyone* worldwide, many readers will be able to integrate the various concepts more quickly. Examining those early letters provides valuable perspectives of the versatile, limitless base from which is built the much more complete and widely integrated Neo-Tech of today.

Full, Unedited Testimonials

Nick R. C-190S

In January 1990, I reported to duty as a US Navy exchange Officer to the French Navy. Due to my fluency in the language, I was to serve as navigator on the French Mediterranean Fleet Flagship. I was an average guy, with no knowledge of philosophy or the realm of objective ideas whatsoever. Perhaps this was due to my sheltered life.

My parents raised me a fundamentalist born-again, right wing conservative Christian. Guilt flowed through my veins. I even attended Bible college after graduating from one of those church-sponsored fundamental Christian highschools, the type of which you may have seen featured in a news program.

To me, life was an endless cycle of short-term thrills in a search of happiness, followed by guilt and misery. To get "happy" again you needed to "get right with God." Then, more short-term thrills and the cycle continues.

One day, shortly after arriving in France, I received this Neo-Tech brochure in the mail. Being the person I was, I immediately ordered. After all, it promised to show me how to be happy, wealthy, and powerful with little or no effort.

And it delivered on its promise. However, rather than pursue that end, it showed me how to find genuine, lasting happiness through a series of techniques that anyone can practice—regardless of background.

While I did indeed learn how I could become rich and lazy, I also learned that this would be a misuse of that knowledge. For, to achieve true happiness, I would have to exert discipline, though, and control in a never-ending quest to create and produce values desired by others in society. As a bonus, I learned how to out-maneuver the lazy cheat at every turn.

Another aspect is that I acquired, read, re-read, and studied everything Ayn Rand ever published. For example, I personally have over 200 pages of painstakingly detailed notes I took from Peikoff's 1976 tape lecture series on Objectivism. This provided me with the philosophical foundations for the real-world, *dynamic* applications I had already begun to practice from Neo-Tech.

Can you imagine the value of a book like that? Some have complained about its $70 price. I actually paid $100. Complaining about

517

$70 for this book seems to me like complaining about $24 for some useless island the Indians called Manhattan.

Let's see. I paid $100 for this book, which after the first 100 pages or less, irrevocably changed my life and shattered most of the false premises I held. Moreover, it gave me the knowledge to move beyond its study and into happiness and prosperity. At that time, I worked for the government and earned a modest, automatic paycheck. Less than 5 years later, I have a successful company which I started with $300 cash and which I run out of my home. In my first full year, my earnings were in excess of $250,000. As of this writing, I have earned over $95,000.00 and we're only 3 1/2 months into the new year. This is money I earn honestly, by using my knowledge to help financially troubled business avoid parasitic attorneys and bankruptcy—get back on their feet, stay in business, and preserve jobs for innocent and hard working people.

Yes, $100 is a lot of money for a book—if you have no idea of how to *invest* it.

Currently, I'm 34 years old, *single* but searching, and am building my happiness daily. My high ambitions to continually do more are now far removed from my old life of holding out for that government retirement check.

Sheldon S. P-1024

Newsgroups:alt.philosophy.objectivism
Subject: Re: Neo-Tech/Zon 60
Your exposition about what: Neo-Tech and Zon has done for you.

Fair enough. Since I stuck my head out here to defend Neo-Tech, I need to provide some evidence of WHY I am defending it.

I read NT when I was 19 and in college. I had always been an inquisitive person, and I spent a lot of time thinking about why the world was so screwed up. I was already an atheist, although I was very mystical in some other areas. (Note: when NT owners speak of mysticism, they are referring to any kind of irrationality, not just religion or the occult, etc.).

I was on my college wrestling team (Division 1, usually ranked in the top 20), and had just recently quit because I knew although I liked being on the team, I didn't want to dedicate my life to wrestling (which is what it takes to succeed at this level). So it was a transition phase for me. I was a philosophy major when I first started.

518

Unedited Testimonials

Neo-Tech changed my life in the sense that I could now dispense with any forms of mysticism that had been harming my life. It was an incredible load off my mind to finally recognize the sources of problems in life and how to solve them. And I had a solid basis for atheism, rationalism, capitalism, and I knew how to defend my arguments much better than before. (I had been mystical in my arguments, lots of times relying on emotion and not reason) This experience is similar to what a lot of people feel after they read AS or FH for the first time. The whole world kind of opens up for you as you free yourself from the chains.

Neo-Tech gave me a lot of motivation to do something with my life. I switched from the Philosophy major to the Business major, since I thought this would help me get a better job. But the business major was specialized, and I felt I wasn't learning anything. The profs didn't know anything about starting or running a business, they just knew how to tell you to do your job, and how to become a cog in the wheel. (I had been interested in computers, so I switched to the Computer Science major, and ended up with an BS in CS with minors in Math and Physics.)

That summer I decided I would run my own business. I hired 10 other students to paint houses, and by sheer force of will I had a successful summer. I worked night and day getting new leads, doing estimates for new jobs, making sure my 3 paint crews had enough supplies, and helping out with the painting. I felt really alive for the first time, since I was making an impact, I was providing a service people wanted. We ended up doing over $53,000 worth of paint jobs in 3.5 months. And I didn't really know a thing about running a business.

The next two summers (and part-time during the school year) I was part of a two-man software company. (I met the guy I worked with by painting his house). We had a little success, and I enjoyed working more with my brain as opposed to a messy job like painting where you had to deal with irrational customers and employees sometimes. It wasn't a real company in the sense that the founder was doing it in addition to his full time job and I was still in school at the time. After that, I figured I would like a technical career, so I stayed with CS, and currently I'm in grad school. So I haven't used Neo-Tech to become rich and powerful (I'm still making preparations), but if you want to be involved in a technical job working with

519

computers, you kind of need to go through a few years of school. And now thanks to USENET and this Newsgroup, I have met other Neo-Tech people and it looks like there are a lot of opportunities out there. I love technology :-).

For me, Neo-Tech has been an invaluable tool in thinking and living. It is also fuel to keep you motivated in your quest for happiness and purpose.

Mike M. C-1026

This letter is to inform you of my continued satisfaction and amazement with the literature purchased during the Summit meeting. Satisfaction in the precision tool at my disposal and amazement at the powerful integrations revealed. I would also like to comment on the Summit itself.

So much of my personal life had been in turmoil as a result of mystical knots wrapping around me. 'Reasoning' my way through the 'complexity' of achieving guiltless happiness only entangled me further. Neo-Tech/ Neo-Think allows me to cut through the crap with clearly formed facts, as well as, integrated actions. It has become fully evident that I had not the means to pull my life together. Life is truly the ultimate value and happiness is it's truest complement. The world as a whole desperately needs this information. It becomes more painful to watch the mental and physical oppression of millions now that I see how simple happiness can be accomplished. Mystics and their crafty lies are now very easy to identify and bypass. I am also relieved to know my children will not be shackled with flawed thinking processes as they grow and shape their world.

It makes me shudder when the beautifully simple truth is laid out in such a manner that it screams in ones mind. ...How many centuries have intelligent creatures stumbled around? Once the door of ignorance opens however, the rest comes bursting through. As long as one remains strong in mind, Neo-Tech/Neo-Think pulls all the old lies out of the thinking process.

Curtis B. 2921-7

The information that was contained inside the manuscript absolutely blew my mind. It was the most incredible information that I have ever acquired anywhere. It is hard to believe that mankind can be duped for such a long time, myself included. Now, thanks to Neo-Tech, people can rid themselves of the stupidness disease of mysticism. I myself will never again have to worry about being brainwashed by the politicians, religious quacks, environmental and ecological frauds, lying news media, and anyone else who neocheats their way through life. I owe all of this to Neo-Tech. I don't know how I'll ever be able to thank you enough. You, Frank R. Wallace, and your associates have given me a whole new meaning in life. I look forward to living "in the real world" and not in death's mystical one.

I remember back to around three years ago. My brother Kevin called me on the telephone. He was a bit excited at some new information he was reading. Kevin told me he was in the process of cleaning out his mind. I was quite confused at first so I asked him what in the world he was talking about. He proceeded to tell me about Neo-Tech. I have to admit I was pretty curious about it and he told me that I should get it for myself. Well, at that time, I didn't exactly have 200 dollars to toss away on something I thought would be just some sort of self help book. Then, this last winter, my uncle, Eldred, who lived on the coast where I lived, received his Neo-Tech manuscript. When he started to tell me about it I decided to pay heed and order for myself. Now here I am today, more happy than I have ever been. Thanks to Neo-Tech and a few relatives that really cared about me. These people, by the way, wanted me to join in business with them. I heartily agreed, and it will be a total Neo-Tech atmosphere. Look out world is all I can say, except for thank you Neo-Tech, without you, none of this would have been possible.

Donald R. R-4444

"Every day acquaintances, authoritarian bureaucrats, manipulated by parents, drained by bosses gypped by merchants, intimidated by pushy or moneyed people misled by professional people, stunted by dishonest and incompetent educators, used by friends, abused by strangers, fouled up by bureaucrats, fooled by mystics, and hurt by government—"

Yup—I have been "sandbagged" by all of these neocheaters from day one until recently.

Just to know that I was not alone, and that others were in the same situations is a horrible comment on our Western culture, a culture based on a subtle, and pervasive use of the bicameral mind of man.

Frank R. Wallace, the firms he has organized, the Neo-Tech

521

Research and Writing Center, and allied companies, have supplied the mental tools (detection and solutions) by which the "regular guy", producers and employees from corporate president to garbage man can foil and turn aside the neocheaters: identify them, watch their operations (and best of all) render their "put-ons" harmless. Platonistic philosophy has been secretly used by neocheaters for years; Aristotelian philosophy has been suppressed by neocheaters for centuries.

Thanks to Neo-Tech R and W Center for its complete "history" of how Dr. Wallace came to realize and understand the "game world of poker" and evil parallels in the world in which we live. The producers, no matter where they are or what they do, are no longer defenseless with the knowledge of Neo-Tech. "Go, go, Neo-Tech!!!"

George M., MS, C-1030

54 years of my life gone down the drain, or has it? Being a pay and pray Catholic all my life; council President, Finance Chairman, School Board President, and you name it, I've been there (not to mention the hundreds of thousands of dollars raised in development programs and my own contributions) and now I find Dr. Wallace grabbing me by the ear, just when I thought I had earned the right to get into you know where. It's mind boggling just to think where my family and I would be if all this time and energy was invested in our happiness instead of so much sacrificing.

After venting my anger at Dr. Flint and Dr. Wallace for putting a knife in me, I settled down and re-read my manuscripts. While doing so, I asked myself, "Is it not reasonable and logical to evaluate all the material before making any decisions as to what's right or who's wrong"? Yes, it's the logical thing for any reasonable person to do. Still studying Vol. 1 thru 5, my Neo-Think tapes, and Reference Encyclopedia I can summarize it all into one sentence: Pure and simple "common sense" backed with facts and evidence!

For the past four months, since getting into all this knowledge— let me tell you, it is delivering a quality of life that has already made up for the past 54 years!

And it gets better each day. It is really great to wake each morning excited about life and living and going through each day with a different perspective and much greater insight. I do not think anyone should take my word for it. They should "check it out" for themselves.

My business has skyrocketed. Running three businesses and now am caught up by noon each day. My Neo-Think mind is just an infant and at this stage it sometimes scares me how rapidly it moves me through mazes and centers my thoughts at my objectives like a rifle bullet penetrates a target. After twenty five years of marriage, I have finally fallen in love with my wife and we both are suddenly free. How sweet it is, to live each day completely "guilt free". In all my years involved in church and projects, this never came to me.

I have always felt that we all are going to die someday. But as Vol. #2 of Neo-Tech proves, that is not the sad part—it clearly shows that the sad part, is what dies in us while we are still living, because of mysticism. Sorry for getting off on a tangent, but it has never made sense to me, to spend my whole life from birth, preparing to die!!

Wayne S. C-4999

I must somehow express some of the most profound changes I have experienced since first encountering Neo-Tech seven months ago. Though there is so much to impart, words seem hardly adequate to the task. I find myself thinking in terms of gratitude most heartfelt for what Dr. Wallace and I & O have given me through Neo-Tech.

Of all the benefits I have gained from Neo-Tech, the one that comes most immediately to mind is FREEDOM.

Thank you for showing me the way to freedom from sugar, caffeine, cigarettes and alcohol. Thank you for giving me the strength to achieve freedom from the cocaine, marijuana, L.S.D. and other drugs I have used constantly to hide behind for over thirteen years.

Thank you for freeing me from the vices of religion and politics. Thank you for helping me to repair the effects of damage inflicted upon me as a child mentally, physically and emotionally. Thank you for granting me freedom and immunity from the purveyors of gratuitous guilt, who are dismayed at my growing self-confidence, self-assuredness and independence, and would have me return to my worrying, dependent, subservient former self.

Thank you for freedom from erroneous definition of words like altruism, selfishness, and pride.

Thank you for the twenty-five pounds of muscle I have gained, so far, as a result of a diet and exercise program I had the freedom and guts to implement once my thinking had been corrected by NEO-TECH.

Thank you for the freedom of being self employed, which NEO-

TECH gave me the nerve to do. There are no more limitations on my financial future.

Thank you for the freedom of the truly psychuous romantic love relationship I am enjoying with my wife, who married me four weeks before I encountered NEO-TECH and is quite pleased that I'm not the same man she married. The happiness and security of our marriage, which is a profound source of energy for me, wouldn't have stood a chance without NEO-TECH and would have been as doomed as my first marriage.

Thank you for what has probably had the most profound effect of all on me, freedom from the prospect of an inevitably early death. The R.I.B.I. is a source of hope and inspiration, not only for myself, but for the world. It's very existence is a reason to live a healthy, happy, prosperous life for all free people.

To all the mystics and neocheaters out there, (of whom I am now free, thanks to NEO-TECH) stick that in your pipe and smoke it!

To those who would be free from the chains of others or chains forged themselves, NEO-TECH IS THE HAMMER TO BREAK THOSE CHAINS.

If there is ever anything I can do, anywhere, anytime at all for NEO-TECH, I & O, R.I.B.I., or Dr. Wallace personally, please do not hesitate to contact me.

Dennis M, 9351-3

You have set my cobwebbed and mystified mind reeling and I thank you for it—it needed a good shakeup. I've always been a rebel/non-conformist type and never did buy in to the sheepish and pathetic worship of religious fanatics and slithering politicians of the ruling leech class that infest our society. Now I have a direction and plan of action and am encouraged to see the layers of deception peeled away so effectively for anyone bold enough to accept rigorous honesty into their life and reject the mystic concepts force fed to them since the first light of self-awareness sparked in their being.

I love the idea of consciousness as the driving force and creator of all universes.. past, present and future. I am integrating that useful fact into my ongoing recovery from alcoholism and chemical dependency. The higherpower/god concept can be replaced with the mystic-free acceptance of a universal consciousness.

524

Unedited Testimonials

Tony M, 9351-4

About a month ago, I received the Zonpower product, therefore I'd like to give you my feedback.

After receiving that product, my initial reaction was a deep disappointment. Although I technically understood what was written in the Zonpower booklet, I had expected something more earth-shattering in regard to your announcement in the advertising brochure.

Now, a month later I am beginning to see the bigger picture and the subtle connections. The whole issue of mysticism and how it effects our life became more clear to me.

The only factor which can prohibit a success is stale thinking and mysticism. For instance, the notion of singularity still prevents all scientists to get out of that dead-end-street. Or the mystical belief in talents can prevent someone to venture into a career or sport because he thinks that one needs a talent in order to be successful. These forms of mysticism can be vanquished easily because all that is needed is to identify the mystical error. Furthermore, there is generally not much emotionality involved. It is simply a false belief.

Now, back to Zonpower. I sense that the power of this product lies in separating the reader from the Plato world —that means cutting away its emotional influence.

The Plato world then gradually loses its power, especially its emotional power. Then the reader can confront his personal mysticism with less resistance and less pain.

Jim T., 9351-2

Received NEO-TECH. Found much of value, but "choked" on demolition of the "God Concept."

Received NEO-THINK and "Iron Grip Control..." Vacillated between my religious beliefs and NEO-TECH.

Finally returned most materials for a refund after reaching a "final decision"— was rejecting NEO-TECH in favor of Christianity. The basic NEO-TECH II package was returned to me, because it was too late to get a refund.

For years I had been critical of various churches— I have now finally been able to admit that my problem was not with a particular church, but with the tenants of Christianity itself. It is difficult to see one's emotional attachments to God and "Jesus" demolished (I think the feeling would be akin to shooting one's own mother), but I can only admit that these beliefs have been the main source, for years, of depression and disorganization in my life.

In the last 18 months, I have intensely studied various systems of mysticism - Wicca, Qabala, Ceremonial Magic, surprisingly enough, one value I obtained was the centrality of the individual. Otherwise, my time would have been better spent studying NEO-TECH.

At any rate, I am tonight doing something I NEVER dreamed possible—I am resigning my pianist job at my church (they pay me for this—but I have been turning my check back over to them to support their "building program"). I never intend to go back there again. It seems unbelievable, but I am finally forsaking Christianity, before it literally kills me.

However, I face an uphill battle—all my family and friends are devout Christians. Nevertheless, I just cannot understand how a set of beliefs which stifles initiative, mandates sacrifice, and locks one into unresolvable contradictions can be considered beneficial.

All I want now is to learn more about NEO-TECH and to apply it to my life. I have never been financially successful—now my burning ambition is to make tons of money so I can pay off my debts, take care of my lovely family, and enjoy financial independence. I realize now how close I was to succumbing forever, irretrievably, into the jaws of a mysticism-induced death. I am more interested than ever in my health and well-being.

Raymond V., England, 3901-C7

Having read the NEO-TECH DISCOVERY by Dr. Wallace and now having almost completed NEO-TECH COSMIC BUSINESS CONTROL, I feel that I must write to you to express my deep felt joy.

Because my busy work schedule, I found myself getting up very early in the morning and reading your publication for about 1-1/2-2 hours before going to work and it was so important to me and so fascinating to read about mysticism.

Since my introduction to NEO-TECH, I have started my own business (but still remain in my 'normal' full time occupation) and I am continuing to build it up.

I have totally changed my views about the "authorities", although I have never thought too much about politicians, but your publications have really opened my eyes to the NEOCHEATERS, and it all makes so much sense now.

I congratulate you all on your fantastic achievements and as I continue to eliminate my personal mysticism (and also help my wife to do so), I look forward to further publications and more information.

Douglas M., 3901-C17

I have just completed reading the Zonpower Discovery manuscript. Truly, this masterpiece is the most important discovery on Earth since the discovery of consciousness itself. I am about to embark on a second reading, as I do not intend to miss a single word of Dr. Wallace's profound work.

Roger H., 3901-C9

Dear Zon Association,

I would like to take a moment to thank you for a wonderful job you are doing in turning this up-side down world, up-right. Zon is the best thing that could ever happen to this anticivilization. I'm all for it. Neo-Tech changed my future and out-look on life. With Neo-Tech life will flourish.

I read the Neo-Tech book I-V from cover to cover and it's the most concise information I've ever seen and I can see Neo-Tech taking hold, Mark Hamilton has my vote in '96.

Scott B., 3901-C15

Dear Mr. Hamilton,

Mysticism collapse! Thank you for the call in the Neo-Tech Report starting your 1996 Presidential campaign. It announces the true rapture, the calling out of the honest businessman from the evil neo-cheaters, that has been happening since November 3, 1985. Now the period of tribulation is being ended...all of the famine, war, crime, genocide, death, unhappiness, all ended. The wicked, the neo-cheating bureaucrats, politicians, lawyers, media, and all those who coerce unearned values from others, will be given the opportunity to repent and accept the only means of salvation. Neothink. Or face ostracism and death forever. With Neothink we are changed in mind and body to achieve happiness forever. But your Presidential campaign more specifically announces the "battle of Armageddon" between Neo-Tech and the neo-cheaters. They may not realize it yet, but they will. The religious right will have a heyday calling you the "antichrist". Telling their flocks that you are

527

setting up the one world government and your father, the one world church. I know that's what most of my family will hear.

I would like to have an active part in this battle. This campaign. It would be an honor to have a part starting the change in government for a future of unlimited happiness.

Please let me know what you would like done and I will do what I can for you.

Chuah G., 3901-CS, Malaysia

Ever since I received your N-T Discovery, I have never had a sad moment. I am able to perform my job very well. I am very happy, confident and most important of all guiltfree. After N-T, I discovered that my boss was the one who makes me feel guilty. Now, I know how to handle him. I no longer feel guilty. I am free. I did this by purging mysticism out of my mind. I no longer fear my boss or anybody in this world. I can feel the power building up inside me. I no longer feel tired for now I know that I am working for myself and not for my boss.

Since reading Cosmic Business Control, I have overcome the White Collar Hoax. I carry out my job better by working on the nitty gritty detail task of my operations. I practice mini-day/power thinking. Now I can see so clearly all the White Collar Hoax existing in my working environment. I am working hard to expose the White Collar Hoax. There will be no more limitations for me. I could go on and on.

Thank you for making me a more productive person. Thank you Dr. Wallace, Mr. Mark Hamilton and all the members of Neo-Tech Publishing company for doing such a superlative job. No company in this world can match your work.

Paul L., Canada, 3901-C8

Mysticism was the wall I had to overcome. And Neo-Tech was my sledge hammer. My life has changed for the best in so many ways. People are drawn to me because of the life I radiate. Slowly, one by one, they are discovering the power of Neo-Tech. They are beginning to understand the life giving advantages Neo-Tech has to offer. I would love to purchase a manuscript for each one of them, so they could become mystic free individuals also.

Unedited Testimonials

M. Q., Australia, 3901-C6

I have always thought of the world, since being quite young as a stagnant place—full of potential, yet stagnant. We never seemed to be advancing as fast as we should, in all aspects of life, and I never knew why. Thanks to Neo-Tech, I know why!

The Neo-Tech products are remarkable pieces of work and extremely thought-provoking. The only trouble with them is they take me forever to read because after reading a page or two, I spend hours thinking about the various implications and applications of the knowledge I have just gained. At the same time, it is also extremely frustrating to have the 'curtain of mysticism', lifted—to see clearly for the first time—and see what the neo-cheaters have gotten away with and are getting away with now!

The only consolation I have, is in knowing that the Neo-Tech Research Centre has the power and commitment to spreading its knowledge around the world, and to all corners of the globe!

John S., 3901-C3

When the Zon manuscript arrived it changed my life drastically. Weighing 215 pounds for football, I suddenly weighed 185, losing 30 pounds without even trying. I chewed tobacco starting in 7th grade, after reading Zon, I quit chewing cold turkey. Zonpower gave me hope in achieving my goals and dreams.

I just received the Neo-Tech Cosmic Business Control and am very excited to read it.

Albert C., R-6082

My mother is very active in an Assemblies of God church. Neo-Tech was most successful in warding off her continuous attacks on me for not conforming to her willed realities. The realization of how mystics separate context from fact has given me incredible insight into the way they operate.

Furthermore, concept #28 alone has given me an incredible power for living along with an awesome release of guilt. For I now know that it is I who is in control of my life and that I am the highest value in the universe.

It gives me great pleasure to know that I now have the tools to achieve financial prosperity, romantic love, and abiding happiness. Neo-Tech is a magnificent value.

529

Unedited Testimonials

Frank W., R-532

Neo-Tech was a rude but welcomed awakening. Neo-Tech puts everything into proper perspective and erases the guilt feelings of the things I have been striving for, and the neocheaters who are trying to take them away.

I am a producer, an achiever and doer. I am resetting my goals along Neo-Tech lines.

J.L.G. R-8294

Neo-Tech has certainly had a profound effect of my life. I am young— 17 years of age—and I feel that this knowledge has become increasingly valuable, having owned it 1-1/2 years. There is no doubt my personal development has been radically altered.

For so long now, I have been compromising Neo-Tech principles in order to accommodate "friends" I was afraid of losing. But now I understand why I need not, and will not, compromise any longer. I can see how ultimately pathetic my alcohol dependent, nicotine-sucking "friends" are, despite their undying arrogance, and my confidence grows with time. I won't see many of them again at the end of August 1990, since I will be leaving when my Alevel courses finished. Anti-values spread like disease in academic life.

M.D.F. NT-I

Neo-Tech is a greater discovery than the wheel (I did not read most of the letters, excuse me if I plagiarize). Neo-Tech gives me goose bumps!

Daniel S., R-1972

Two things: (1) I can't believe how naive I've been all my life, and (2) I, now can't imagine going through life any other way than this; with my eyes opened.

An absolutely incredible discovery, that is right under anybody's nose! Anybody that cares to think about it!

B.K R-14

I found the information packages to be excellent, especially Neo-Tech III and V. They made clear why people can be controlled through their bicameral minds and that the ultimate goal is biological immortality. Neo-Tech, taken as a whole, has helped me understand

530

how I have been cheated and deceived in all areas of my life. Neo-Tech has been a new awakening for me, a new birth and a new life. Dr. Wallace has put together the information necessary for mankind to shape its future and ultimate destiny; conquering the cosmos. Neo-Tech is not just an information package but the blueprint for man's destiny.

Laurent B. F-112, France

Really satisfied with Neo-Tech. I want to let you know of the joy I experience at each reading. Because of Neo-Tech I see life and people with optimism. When a problem arises I refer to Neo-Tech and each time I find the nonmystical, logical solution which I could never have thought of or even hoped to. Neo-Tech is a key that guides man and society. The key to living in symbiosis with his environment and to decipher what one had never dared to face. Simply the key to happiness, with a long range view.

William S. R-2443

"You shall know the truth and the truth shall set you free"—the church says it but Neo-Tech did it! 58 years of guilt about sex and money GONE! Married 36 years—nine children—now enjoying and delighting in sex with NO GUILT. Started business in basement 21 years ago and built it into a 5 million manufacturing Corp.—90 employees inside—1400 Sales Reps outside—now for the first time really proud and guiltless of my success! I am now the man that I always wanted to be!

Paul E. R-6588

I am 40 years old today! I wouldn't have believed the change that have happened to me since receiving the package just one year ago.

I had failed miserably for most of my life, having suffered a failed marriage, several failed relationships and a whole series of miserable, frustrating, poorly paid jobs. I was a great mystic, believing in tarot cards, ouija boards, horoscopes, then becoming involved in Scientology, Re-birthing, technologies for creating (DMA), Dyna-psych and other weird and wonderful things, not forgetting the God concept.

All these things cost me dearly in time, money and self-esteem. I prayed to God, I procrastinated, I cried, felt depressed most of the time, did destructive things, and even felt suicidal at times.

Unedited Testimonials

But since being exposed to Neo-Tech and Neothink, I feel like a different person. I am a different person, one who is in control of himself at last, and it feels amazing. My love life has improved 1,000,000%, my financial status is slowly improving, but best of all, I have several business ideas in the pipeline, one of which involves working with I & O itself.

For the first time in my life, I feel an unstoppable power within myself and it grows by the minute. I recognize it as fully integrated honesty combined with Neothink Power and with it I will eradicate the disease of mysticism from this planet and take back the power that belongs to me and people like me.

Long live Neo-Tech!

James W., R-7062

Revelation is an understatement. If I could I would memorize every word.

Joann A., R-1474

With a background as a newspaper reporter, I found that the first 20 minutes of Neo-Tech II answered the five W's in this specific order: How, Who, What, When and finally Why. My breakthrough was total and awesome! I had already read some of the books you summarized, had the counsel of three wise friends, but found that wisdom is of no value if buried deeply under a layer of religious brainwashing. Neo-Tech (the only right way to say "born again") has made it impossible for me ever to forget reality and truth again. I no longer spend precious time and scarce capital on garbage people. I'm going into a new field and will be starting my own business. Viva la Frank Wallace.

George P., 590260-2

Because of Neo-Tech, my job is not a job, it is a pleasure. Why? Because of my insight of the origins of all values. My personality is as lively as ever. My competence has soared to heights never imagined. And I know this is only the beginning. Because of Neo-Tech, I am getting stronger and stronger. It is like I am in a forward march position.

I will do whatever is necessary, in my own way, to help in the total collapse of mysticism. Neo-Tech keeps me anchored in reality— I see things now that others never see and it is all because of Dr. Frank R. Wallace's discovery. Please keep up the Good Work. I hope one day to meet with all of you as we claim victory not only here in the U.S., but worldwide.

Linda B. NT-S

It's been 4 days since reading Neo-Tech in two sittings and I would like to share my exciting and revolutionary breakthroughs with you. The answers I found in Neo-Tech I have been searching for all my life and had many similar insights throughout my life. I believe a healthy individual or child will think like that, but the many distortions in the world soon reach out to drown the recipient in a sea of illusion.

The next day after reading Neo-Tech, I disposed of my mystical crutches. At first I felt a little unsure and then I realized I had to give myself a chance. Low and behold I was not any less after this ritual, but more. I, in delving further and further into mysticism, felt I had many problems to overcome. That if I did the right thing, everything would be fine. Without mysticism, I don't feel out-of-control but able to do what I need to build the life I desire.

I recognized the entire system — one I had seen before. My self-esteem rose dramatically in those few days. Breakthroughs began happening as a result of me using my brain, not of altering reality. I began to see I had been altering my reality so much I was losing my ability to function in the world I was trying so hard to change. I was fast beginning to suspect that mysticism wasn't the answer and all the signs were there.

I felt a very fine integration take place. Mysticism seeks to divide to make the victim vulnerable and confused and unable to function as a unit. I feel whole now. When I do try to slip into mysticism, I realize it right away and do something about it. It's my old lazy way of escaping reality and my emotions. So I take a look —a good look— at why the pain and what I can do. When I did this today, such a surge of power was released from my mind I felt totally different. I didn't feel like a woman searching for life and mystic thrills and yet having to hide my inadequacies from people, but I felt like a powerful being—an intelligent one who could live an incredibly exciting and powerful life.

I've been trying to "wake up" from this deep sea and at last I am. Words can't describe how excited I am. The truths I found in Neo-Tech have been my fondest dreams and desires and beliefs all my life. My mind is healing very quickly.

533

Unedited Testimonials

Also, when one uses their own mind, I believe the mind naturally evolves to higher capacities. Much like a skill increases in value with practice and persistence. I'm done being the way I was. I almost want to laugh when I think of the things I believed even though my body was in such pain and my emotions were so pained I had to repress them and create a new reality in my brain.

Anyway, I even look different. I look younger and more beautiful in just a few days. What more can I say. I'm on my way.

Kimberly W., R-6930

Dear Dr. Wallace and I & O Publishing:

I have just finished my 1st, of many, reading of Neo-Tech I-V, and I must say I am very excited about the present and future.

I am 23 years old and feel that through Neo-Tech I have acquired the knowledge of the ages. For the first time in my life I feel powerful.

Fred W. H., JFE 381

Have just reviewed my library and threw out about 60 to 70 self help and sundry books which I have been pouring over for the last 30 years or so. Neo-Tech is right, those self-help, positive thinking books just didn't do it for me. But since reading Neo-Tech I'm really excited about life. All I can say is WOW!

Frederic D., C-112 FRANCE

I read with great interest the Fantastic Dr. WALLACE's book. Mr. Frank R. Wallace wrote the most genial and useful book that had ever been written. Thanks to this book I have now an ambition: create my own enterprise. This book completely destroys the power of such card-sharpers as politicians, religious, mystics or some close relatives.

It ends with tyranny, lies and oppression and takes everyone on a new lease of life, to the life we should have had if we hadn't been handled by what we can call "anti-human persons". That is to say, those whose only dreams are dreams of mastery and depravity of the human race.

Dr. Wallace's book is the best cure we may bring to someone who is seeking for understanding "his" life.

No matter the criticism you may face, I'm sure you will begin because you are the great luck of Humanity.

Unedited Testimonials

John B., C-115, AUSTRALIA

The applications of Neo-Tech are everywhere!!! You are right. The direction of my career has certainly changed and developed leaps and bounds since acquiring Neo-Tech knowledge. Everything now has high potential.

To all at Neo-Tech, I am grateful for sharing this knowledge.

Jeff C., C-1011

I am writing to thank you for writing the "Advanced Concepts" and making the "Concepts" available to me.

Before reading the "Concepts" I was the adolescent mystic man like most men living now and for the past 2000 years. After incorporating Neo-Tech into my life my power is growing everyday, my income is constantly increasing, I am invincible in all my undertakings. Neo-Tech has made my life great, colorful and exciting.

I agree with you — great days are coming — Renaissance, Achievement, giant Leaps in Progress for MAN!

Bruce N., CB-IOI

It's hard to believe that a single publication could have such a major impact on how one looks at life and oneself. The affect on me has been remarkable. The highlight of my summer vacation was reading the Neo-Tech package. It's as if I had a total house cleaning of my mind, ridding myself of all the unnecessary garbage accumulated over my 45 years.

Neo-Tech was able to change my thinking processes. Now, I'm more attentive to detail, with a greater interest in reading, listening and reducing commentary to its "real" meaning. It's like having a dull blade sharpened; or a mind that was dulled by mysticism and neocheating to one sharpened with objective reality. The mist has been lifted from mysticism!

I have much to thank you for, and appreciate Dr. Wallace's exceptional works and your business concepts.

Thanks to Neo-Tech, there is optimism and strength from within. It's nice to know that one can obtain this strength (power, prosperity, happiness, and romantic love) from honesty and anti-mysticism.

Laura S., CB-IOOI

The information in the Neo-Tech manuscripts is indeed valuable.

Every concept holds a raw-factual way of dealing with reality. (What better way? None).

No doubt you people hold high credit to the betterment of mankind. It's a powerful feeling to know you people are out there, not to mention countless other value producers. Good will always reign over bad — productivity over laziness, as long as we stay alive, our world will be the most excellent, and desirable in the universe. Count me in as one more value producer who holds the knowledge of the benefits of biological immortality. We, the righteous people deserve it, and its outcome.

Denny L., R-6998

I always knew the things I had been taught to believe (and so professed) were not really my beliefs at all— god, respect for authority, self-sacrifice: I never really believed any of it, but I was too weak to admit it. I'm not weak anymore. It feels so good to believe and know what I've always known deep in my mind—the Neo-Tech truth.

Darryl L., 4903-C3

I have received and read your Zonpower Manual. Having been an objectivist for many years, I appreciate your building on that foundation and carrying us farther into the unlimited future with complete integration of thought and action. While Ayn Rand identified the malignancy, you have identified the modalities and cure of the mystic diseased mind.

I wish to order Twelve (12) copies of Zonpower to spread amongst my associates who can appreciate it. No Neocheaters invited, thank you very much. I also would like to order Two (2) copies of the Reference Encyclopedia.

I would like to thank Dr. Wallace for his courage in presenting his ideas to the world and hope he gets his ultimate reward, biological immortality (and me too!).

Joe L., 4903-C5

Through the perusal of Neo-Tech material, I can further understand how my own incursions into "mysticism" in the past have hurt me. I can much more easily perceive how other people's indulgences in mysticism is hurting and stopping them and keeping them from the excellence in life that they could enjoy! I have noticed that in dealing with some people and some agencies in our present society that they are so steeped in mysticism, so far removed from reason, that you cannot even begin to reason with them. A good example is when one is asked whether politicians should be funded for their campaigns by private or "public" money, when the answer is neither...the entire structure could and should be eliminated!

B. P., R-1868, South Africa

Neo-Tech is incredibly clear and coherent and I love every word of it. How can you bear living in a world with neocheaters?

I have kept a diary since 1977, trying to solve the riddle of God, and people's behavior. With Neo-Tech knowledge it hit me between the eyes: the God concept.

Thanks again for Neo-Tech. It's worth a lot more than you ask for it. And thanks for Neo-Tech III-V. I have much to learn.

I wish I & O Publishing Co. were in South Africa. I would like to discuss Neo-Tech with someone.

D. Keven G., C-108

I feel that when it is truly perfected and accepted, that Neo-Tech will be the ultimate system for living an organized, powerful, full life. I also feel that everyone will be following the overall Neo-Tech system someday, it simply offers too much to refuse.

Thomas F., R-607

I am overawed with this masterpiece. Finally a treatise on modern philosophy is complete with no loose ends, consistently logical, rational, and with examples illustrating all possible viewpoints.

Mario M., CB-1006, United Kingdom

I have always been very open minded but I always felt that something was stopping my mind from developing to its full potential. Now I know why, only truth can make one think objectively and rationally, for without a logical foundation on which to base one's thinking the mind cannot utilize its full capacity.

What gets me is that the Bible (the so called 'truth') has been trying to convince people for nearly 2000 years but has failed in its attempt to convince everyone, except those mystics who are so obsessed with the 'God' concept.

Neo-Tech, on the other hand, has succeeded in convincing people (rational) in just a few days—rational people know the truth when they see it.

In so few days I feel like a new person, like a child with a fresh mind, full of optimism; but I know that this is just the beginning, and the more I read Neo-Tech the more I will benefit.

Larry L., C-S

Since I was nine years old I knew that my lights were on but I was not home. I came home, however, during my first reading of Neo-Tech II some thirty-six years later. I would like to relate to you what happened to me while I was engrossed with Neo-Tech. It was as though I was beaten to a pulp. I was slapped around and finally kicked to the floor all out of breath when I finally acknowledged that it was me that they were talking about. I was the lazy and envious person described throughout the pages of Neo-Tech that cut through me like a sword. I was the one that was not standing on my own two feet. I was the mystic. I was the Neo-cheat. It was me that recognized "outside authorities" instead of the honest "producer of tradable values" type person. I was a prisoner of Tarot, Astrology, Kabbalah, the occult and other forms of debauchery and time wasting. It was me putting greater emphasis on death than on life and the realization of biological immortality. I even scored high on the Psyche Death check list— Leveraged Advantage #98 —I got eight out of ten characteristics of a dying or dead psyche checked. Plato would have been happy for me. He never would have been proud. I would have never been proud of me either, but that was before Neo-Tech. Frank Wallace and associates and Neo-Tech revived me.

When I received Neo-Tech I was ready. Whatever I was doing simply was not working. And now I know that it was not productive, rational or reasonable. Neo-Tech is a part of me now and it is as though I have been transplanted from an unrealistic hostile environment to a healthy one where I can grow and blossom indefinitely. I am now of value to me, to my romantic-partner, and to others.

Luis M., 2921-4

Even though I lost the books, the concepts were strongly engraved in me and my successes were and are determined by the effort put forth by me, based on honest rationalization of objective reality and

538

the ridding of mysticism within myself.

While many years of searching for answers, I and my friends have been reading some mystically based books, I would always mention Neo-Tech, telling them how incredible and real the concepts are. But, I was always left with the excitement having once owned such a valuable book. Disappointed, because I didn't have the book with me to give a clear interpretation and explanation in Spanish (I was in Puerto Rico at the time.)

One day I walked into a used book store and on the book shelf was a book titled NEO-TECH COSMIC POWER NOW! (manuscript #60TU 981090). My tears ran down my face because of the great joy I experienced at being able to buy the most valuable work of hard honest integration with reality, again in my hands. As I read through pincer #1, life rushed into me as I integrated my experiences with Neo-Tech advantages, causing the dead like mysticism to lose its illusive power over me

Carl N., R6961

I acquired Neo-Tech in Feb., mostly because the ideas of controlling others and sexual immortality intrigued me. When I read the information what intrigued me more was a philosophy so unlike anything and everything I have ever known. I am nearly a year removed from that February in which I stayed up nights reading the Neo-Tech body of knowledge; it seems like much longer. It's been very hard and also very fulfilling to implement Neo-Tech into my life. For me, it has been a struggle. Ever since my earliest childhood memory I have been plagued by a mysticism very internal and very profound. It drove me often to depression as somehow my thought pattern became eased implicitly on the idea that I simply existed for the sake of other people. I was not aware of my true self because I thought that it was not I that counted so I imitated and even thought as others would. I was extremely unhappy as I let others guide almost every aspect of my life. Healthy relationships could not exist between myself and other people, and I stuck to myself for the most part. I knew that I was different, and I thought I had to change. I couldn't change. My subconscious gave me signals often of nervousness, anxiousness, depression, no self confidence, and little self esteem. I could not contradict it, though I tried. I now know that I was headed for some form of disaster or another. If Neo-Tech had not arrived, I

539

can only guess as to where I would have ended up and of what kind of person I would have been.

I now have the tools to identify all external authority and dismiss it for what it's worth. I know when I'm being lazy and I know the cause of my problem now that I have Mark Hamilton's "Iron Grip Control..." and "The Grand Event" tapes. I also know how to achieve honest power to become a success in every aspect of my life.

As my horizons broaden and I acquire more and more experience with Neo-Tech and Neothink, my once deep-rooted disease shrinks faster and faster as it disperses into pockets of thought that I can identify and eradicate by destroying their fundamental cause.

My life is really looking up. My self-esteem, confidence, and net happiness has improved immensely. I now know what guiltless enjoyment is about.

In closing, I would like to express my excitement for Neo-Tech and for life itself. Consider me a part of RIBI as I myself will also strive in my rational best interests to create the conditions to make biological immortality possible. Two months ago I turned 18. I will soon be off on my own and I can't thank enough all the happy people who have made Neo-Tech possible for me at this crucial point in my life. I am looking forward to a life of unlimited growth, happiness, and potential and I appreciate all the values that have and will make all this possible. They are a supreme Human Achievement!

Salvador E., EL SALVADOR

The Neo-Tech Information Package has been giving to me a tremendous trembling impact, when Neo-Tech let me know what is life. I was ignorant about most people. In one way or another, they are neocheaters. I was very confused as a professional, I was thinking that everybody was like me and Neo-Tech knowledge clarify all that was cloudy in my behavior, and the comportment of others.

Thank you very much for let us know this information of incalculable value.

Rick R., C-1034

This is the first program I literally felt shivers as I listened. It made me aware of how close I have been, in the past, to losing the emotional integration with life, and how virtually everyone today is sliding into this spiral (funnel.) Seeing the bigger picture of life on this planet in the not-too-distant future is real inspirational fuel. Bringing that world to fruition and making myself more able to participate are my goals. I may not feel it as those at I & O do, but I am drawn to it as well as fueled by it month by month.

So few, in all history, have been able to observe and feel, much less, do business with genuine greatness on this planet. I am honored to be a customer of I & O Publishing Company.

Stepan K, 499080-10

My majors at Duke are Pre-Med and Computer Science. I want to earn an M.D. and Ph.D. degree in Neuroscience, and become a Neurosurgeon. I am concerned about the damage in medicine done by Clinton's Health Care and increasing government regulation/ socialization. If necessary, I will work towards collapsing mysticism in medicine—not only to secure my happiness in my career, but for the rest of society. I want to research Biological Immortality, and am eager to network with any individual with like goals. I also want to network with others in the realm of business—I need to amass the funds to support my research projects.

I have implemented Neo-Tech concepts in every facet of my life...from the DTC to exercising daily, to a liberating, incredible romantic love relationship, to competence in studies and business ventures and beyond. By applying the Neo-Tech concepts consistently, I have attained a future career potential, and a level of happiness — completely unbeknownst to those around me.

On the other hand, the intensity of happiness and life I have experienced makes the Plato world that much more unbearable and...with each step I take into Neo-Tech, the more painful becomes the realization of the world as it is now, with many problems, and much work to be done. I still default the flounder at times, and would like the push of like-minded people to catapult me into success and beyond.

I have set as my life goal the attainment of Biological Immortality through medicine and business.

Lawrence K, 499080-9

Dear Dr. Wallace and Associates,

I cannot thank you enough for the wonderful enlightenment you have given me these past few weeks. My eyes and ears are dumbfounded by all the mysticism that is involved in our world today. I have been searching for the treasure of life for a long time. I've attended many seminars, all of it reminded me of pop rallies, read many positive motivational books on riches, happiness, and life fulfillment. None interested me more than your "power book". With all the mysticism going around it is no wonder why only so few humans ever get out of that stagnant way of life. Reading this book is like knowing the truth about how a magic trick works. Once you find out, all the magic is gone and you've realized what a fool you have been to have fallen for such adolescent tricks.

Many immortal happiness for you and your associates.

Charles D., 499080-11

This is only a letter of thanks to the people of Neo-Tech for freeing me of my bicameral tendencies (mind). I used to be a slave to any authority figure who promised answers to the problems encountered in life. Religion and all forms of mysticism is for the non-thinking individual. I totally and completely use reason as my means of survival now.

Barry S., 499080-12

This is just to say thanks. And congratulations. Neo-Tech has done the seemingly impossible: it has actually saved my marriage. Neo-Tech information forced me to see that I was essentially neocheating my way through my relationship with my love/life partner. What a shock to my psyche to discover that I was trading on predominately abstract values and "big ideas" in exchange for tangible, objective, day to day services and support.

With that bulwark of mysticism dissolved, I was able to move from the brink of divorce to a passionate recommitment to honest work and caring for the needs of my wife and family, and we are all reaping the rewards. By taking Neo-Tech control of my role in my family, everyone is benefiting. My energy level is higher than ever, yet not manic in nature. By exposing my own personal mysticism and its' resultant dishonesties and laziness, I have lifted a 2000 lb. weight off my being which was dragging everyone down around me, and am instead delivering honest values to myself and my family, and am beginning to experience the meaning of psychuous love.

Ironically enough, I believe it was my wife's own mysticism and its' resultant co-dependency which allowed us to stay together this long.

Having been raised a Baptist, she until now has refused to read any of your material because it attacks the God concept. And she voiced that my determination to integrate Neo-Tech into my thinking—thereby turning my back to God—was the reason why she couldn't stay married to me. The truth was, of course that I was not delivering my fair share of objective values to the relationship, and it was only after enough of my repeated vocalizations of rational, Neo-Tech Concepts sunk in that she was able to make the only rational decision, which was to leave me. Now with the obvious changes in me as the mystical clots in my mind dissolve, she has recommitted to the marriage and is, as I write this, laying on the bed quietly reading Zonpower 2000.

So you were right. Neo-Tech is inevitable and unstoppable, because it is totally beneficent. Don't ever doubt that your efforts are having tangible and dynamic effects on your customer. They are. I shutter to think what my future would have been without your eye-opening materials. The effects are tangible and measurable. Keep up the good work.

I am now awaiting arrival of Neo-Tech Control and Cassandra's Secret, and look forward to continued release of energy and happiness as I root out the disease of mysticism in myself and work toward its' worldwide collapse.

Mitch W., J-83

Now, I'm on my way to be free and to become the producer that I know that I am. The road ahead is very bright, even though the responsibilities are awesome. We must break the shackles and chains of tradition that for millenniums have crippled the creativity and productivity of man. I only say to you and all those associated with Neo-Tech, and I & O Publishing, "hold on to the torch and never let it go"!

Charles T., R-6234, U.K

I have never been so sure of myself, so effective in my business and so secure in the knowledge that there is no reason for my success to end. Business is booming, my wife is blooming, and my son (14) is reading the Discovery!

I have given copies of the Discovery to three of my senior employees and I find it amusing and exciting to observe the changes in their attitude and the new commitment that has effected them and

543

their work, producing positive results both for them and for the company.

My personal life has never been better! My 18 year romance with my wife has been rejuvenated and strengthened and my son will become a producer because after reading Discovery he will understand why it is so important that he create values. We will teach him right from wrong with such a clarity that has not been possible prior to Neo-Tech.

Rosemary K., R-7558

Neo-Tech 'helped' me to clarify many of my values and goals. It also helped me to realize that much of the "New Age" and humanistic movement that I have been active in for over 15 years is full of Neocheaters. I was already beginning to suspect that I had been cheated out of thousands of dollars in seminars, courses, etc. by charlatans.

Michael M., C-100

I am writing to express my gratitude for the many useful concepts and ideas imparted in Neo-Tech.

I have lost 30 pounds, kicked the sugar and nicotine addictions and am still attempting to integrate most of the concepts into my life.

In darkness my eyes have been opened to a world of manipulating "Neo-cheaters" and a world of willing victims who seek but never find the way to all truth. Great minds and many lives are wasted in the intellectual suicide of mysticism....

Meredith A., R-3002

I am now reading Neo-Tech and can see more clearly each day how I have been influenced by mysticism; also that there have been times when I was a Neo-cheater. For as long as I can remember, I have felt guilty (almost for being born) also there were feelings of low self esteem and resentment.

I have looked and looked for the meaning of life.

Now I am experiencing a release from mysticism and looking at long range goals.

Greg B., Pl-OOS

To: Value Destroyers integrated with the Neo-Tech matrix: Having

544

finished listening to the Ultimate Battle tapes, I now possess the power to identify value destroyers everywhere. Now, I'm withdrawing my support of their unearned livelihoods. If there is any attempt to usurp my individual rights or property, I will be prepared to strip them of their unearned power, undermine their fake self-esteems and source of "happiness."

But I am writing to you because I feel sorrow for the soul mates of the November 3rd Empire. I imagined what it would be like to be in your shoes, confronted by Neo-Tech individuals; I felt confused because I held contradictory values. Fear, even terror, emerged. I could not look into the eyes of the Neo-Tech individual. I turned to alcohol and loud music to soothe the mind. My hair turned gray and fell out. I was too lazy or dishonest with myself to think clearly, until I considered the suicide option.

It was a rather sickening and uncomfortable experience. However, please don't let my emotions fool you into thinking that I will help you continue your value destruction's. I do not let emotions guide my actions.

Please consider that the only hope you have in the Ultimate Battle is to become a value producer and return all usurped values belonging to all value producers. The alternative is suicide (or an accelerated "natural" death). Also, consider that millions of value producers anxiously await the collapse of the mystical superstructure, so that man can move rapidly towards biological immortality. You can no longer just fear I & O Publishing Company, your fears will now originate from the public.

Carl N., P1-002

I impatiently await the worldwide collapse of mysticism. The iron curtain is rapidly dissolving. Neo-Tech is quickly and quietly infusing individuals with unstoppable, untouchable power. When I & O goes public, the whole world will know the nature of this power. I & O will herald the transition from the outmoded conscious mind to the Neo-think cosmic mind as more and more people become essence moving individuals. The November 3rd organization, after sucking dry the last of its current victims, will find that there is nothing left. There will be no producer gullible enough to drain. White collar businesses will fail as competitive Neo-think businesses rake in all of their customers. A happy world will soon evolve.

Unedited Testimonials

Kent P., 499080-3

Neo-Tech is incredible. But it is much more than that. Of all the amazing things discovered, only Neo-Tech:

*provides the reader with a glowing, benevolent sense-of-life.

*identifies that life and happiness are man's purpose, not simply freak accidents or by-products of a random chain of events.

*enables the value-producers to be invulnerable to the whims of value-destroyers, mystics, neocheaters.

*explains that right now, error-free biological immortality is man's greatest goal, not just some science fiction fantasy.

Neo-Tech has changed my thinking about so many things. I eat much less sugar and no longer feel drugged all of the time. And I refuse to participate in dead-end relationships with mystical, guilt-inducing family members or "friends".

All in all, I now lead a guilt-free, productive life thanks to Neo-Tech. Thank you Dr. Wallace and Mark Hamilton.

Michael C., 499080-16

Messrs. Wallace, Hamilton and Flinn,

When I first ordered Neo-Tech I-V 11 years ago, I began integrating the concepts into my life and behavior, but I never quite took advantage of all of the possibilities that they offered. Two and a half months ago, I received Cassandra's Secret, which I read twice, and The Neo-Tech Zonpower Discovery, which I finished reading two days ago. Unlike my first exposure to Neo-Tech, I became very excited in these two new texts and began to see what an exciting future Neo-Tech has to offer me and others who have read and begun to integrate all the basic concepts. I no longer believe or want anything to do with mysticism or false concepts spread rampantly by neocheaters (politicians and clergymen) and their progeny. I have a feeling of real freedom everywhere I go and my mind is very much at ease knowing that these neocheaters will be vanquished from meddling in our lives in the future. It took two readings, but I loved the Black Hole Analogy. It really opened up my understanding of Zonpower.

Thanks to your efforts and influence, I ordered a home study business course so that I will no longer be ignorant of how business is conducted in the world that is unfolding. I have also been saving money to finance my return to technical school to finally acquire a degree in Electronics Technology, which is what I've wanted to do for years, but always felt was futile until now.

Patrick B., R-3689

Neo-Tech I-V is some of the most interesting material I have ever read. It has influenced my thinking and attitudes more than anything I can remember. Like a good science book it says 'this is how things are, but don't just believe me, go and see that it is so for yourself!' So you look, listen, and think, and you realize IT MAKES SENSE.

Neo-Tech is very important to me for two reasons: Firstly, it is information which makes clear sense, which is unusual. Secondly, the information in Neo-Tech can be used to measure the logical content of other information and ideas. This latter point, I believe, is the power of Neo-Tech.

Ed R., R-1545

It helped me understand my wife's looking for another man after 7 years of marriage.

D.H.J., C-SO

Thank you, Dr. Wallace, for this work, which is enormous in scope and value—a great contribution to the advancement of mankind. It will help man's understanding of himself and his fellows.

Neo-Tech will, undoubtedly, change the world for the better by advancing man's thinking. It is about time that our politicians were exposed for the manipulators and neocheaters that they are!

You have been successful in cutting a swathe through the altruism, mysticism and nonsense to expose the bare truth and to get rid of the confusion. Now the fog is lifted, I can see and think more clearly.

John K., RP-106

Firstly, I would like to start off by saying how much I have enjoyed, and will continue to enjoy Neo-Tech. When I read my first copy at the "tender" age of twenty, I instantly appreciated, but completely misunderstood the basic message of Neo-Tech and attempted to convince others of the rightness of my new-found philosophy by "preaching" to them about it instead of demonstrating by becoming successful. Now a scant two years later (two years of pervading poverty and unhappiness) I have reread the material and it is as if I had read it upside-down the first time! Now I understand the message and have begun to rearrange my life. I will be attending a recording school in the fall.

Victor A., R-2797

Thank you, Dr. Wallace! YOU SAVED MY MARRIAGE

Barry C., C-1017

Neo-Tech is the best thing to happen in my life. After reading the Neo-Tech I-V it has really opened my eyes. I no longer feel the guilt that the mystics and Neo-cheats have thrust on me over the years. The bonds of slavery to these people have been broken.

After reading Neo-Tech and having time to reflect on all the principles in the volumes it is the only logical way people can live and survive by being prosperous and happy.

I have read many self help books some of which were by some religious mystics who use faith and positive thinking as their principles which never washed for me and now I realize how they were draining me of values and made me feel guilty about being productive and selfish, but no longer.

I am now looking forward to a long and prosperous life with the help of Neo-Tech. I read from the Neo-Tech volumes everyday and figure ways to use the advantages daily.

Yorick P. G., CTE-5009

I hope the following will prove useful to other Neo-Techers, as levers and gearing toward a deeper understanding of Neo-Tech.

I am a laborer and was shocked at the amount of mysticism that I was stuffed up with. A very good way I found of finding and dissolving my laziness was through physical work; because we get a physical feedback (pain) when we push our conscious effort to the borders of our "can-be-bothered" mind-area, our own mysticism and laziness is easy to find. To dissolve it we press into this "no-go" area. At the end of this exercise we can see how well we really did by our "reality-gauge" e.g. No. of bricks moved per time.

I have started to use pain as a measure for actions. "Pain" is healthy, we all have growing pains, pains when we stretch. Nobody can lift a load without the accompanying proportional price/balance in pain-effort. I have found the more selfish I am, the healthier I feel;

"niceness" leads to a draining of energy and a dissolution of the self.

Since Neo-Tech I have become a better employee, by realizing that I am part of the business and therefore 'subject' to its principles: profitability, efficiency, responsibility, etc. The boss is no longer the flesh-devouring, blood-sucking, baby-eating pain the she was, but a highly rational, concentrated worker, whose prime objective is the business. (But it still doesn't stop us throwing her in the pond occasionally.)

I have also given up fiction and fantasy, in the form of TV, cinema, rock music, etc. The concentration and attitude necessary to indulge in these is opposed to the one that we need to achieve things in the real world.

Everyday I pull the factors of concentration, self consciousness, reason, persistence and education, to cut through the laziness, mysticism, comfort, apathy cycle. Everyday I expand my "can-be-bothered" mind area. I still suffer from mysticism (sometimes in the form of physical symptoms—dizziness, faints, lethargy, insecurity). Once Neo-Tech has momentum it is impossible to stop; its inertia is made by the inspired conscious efforts we do put in, when not swamped by our mysticism.

Finally, I would like to say to the still unconfident: Jump! Learn to be selfish, learn to take pain, jump now, not later NOW! Even if you haven't pulled the full integration, you have to jump or die, for the Neo-Tech age is upon us; it is our own decision to reap the profits, or dissolve into oblivion.

Remember this: When man has reached the stars and achieved things beyond your wildest dreams, the Neo-Techers of today will be there.

Michael B., CTE-5004

Your Neo-Tech II made for absolutely fascinating reading. You confirmed many of my beliefs and changed others. I do know that now I feel better about myself and see others for what they really are, for this, thank you.

Neo-Tech is the first book on my suggested reading list. Neo-Tech exposes the mind to reality thereby giving the tools to every individual to be happy and productive. I'm looking forward to studying more of your work and growing in happiness and productivity.

Norman L., R-7492

Neo-Tech I-V has sparked a renaissance of personal growth and a renewed enthusiasm for my career. I give my employer more bang for the buck and have become more acutely aware of those who produce genuine value as opposed to the deadbeats who get me through the use of deceit and smoke screens. I have a clearer understanding of world events and the Neocheaters that manipulate them. The idea of a greatly extended life span is tremendously exciting to me. I've always said that I needed at least a millennium to explore all of my interests —perhaps that would only be the appetizer. I'm in my mid-forties and have had the Neo-Tech literature about three months.

Paul C., R-7467

NEO-TECH/NEO-THINK is the ultimate philosophy of integrated matrix of honesty and encouragement to vanquish all mysticism and neocheater in the whole world.

Phil T., R-7829

As an owner of Dr. Wallace's Poker Manual, I was somewhat aware of his background and logic/reality based sense of life. I was then immediately attracted to the ad for the Wallace-penned Neo-Tech Information Package. The best way to relate the personal changes which ensued are as follows:

Before Neo-Tech, I was a person with a tremendous amount of self-inflicted internal mysticism, which I "rationalized" as a "defense mechanism"; a "natural product of a bad environment".

There was much in my life I knew I was capable of, and wanted to achieve, yet was simply terrified...I was quite literally, paralyzing myself, unable to initiate the rational actions and hard work required to be truly successful...independent.

I am still not perfect!...But I am now fully responsible for everything that happens in my life! I do not place the blame on others, or wait to be "discovered" by some fictional "higher power" who will recognize that I am "special" and worthy of great unearned wealth and prosperity...NO, NO, NO!!

Truth is, friend, I am special! So are you! We are all special when we take the responsibility to constantly live in the real world, to seize the opportunity available each day and ultimately realize the unlimited power of our individual consciousness.

Pounce on this Neo-Tech Information Package! Consume it! Purge yourself of internal and external mysticism and prosper forever!

Unedited Testimonials

G. H. L., C-4998

I now realize the reason I am up to my eyes in debt at the bank, and am having to sell as a means of clearing that debt. Before reading Neo-Tech, I was ready to quit any further attempt at living a life of producing values for myself and others, which has broken me financially and mentally and the next step would probably have been divorce and the end of my family. I spent many years working on oil installations to earn and save enough money to start up in business for the benefit of self and family, only to see it ALL slowly being drained by people I regarded as friends and honest people, leaving me with a massive overdraft and nothing else! Years of truly hard work literally down the proverbial plug-hole. Still I could not understand why it was happening, and tried everything I knew to reverse the situation, all to no avail. I now realize, due to Neo-Tech, where the problem lies. In MYSELF! Reading your manuscripts, to me, has been the equivalent of having a size 12 Red-Wing steel toe boot up the pine end. Just what was needed to wake me up with one big system shock. How anybody in their right mind can deny the beneficial concepts of this discovery beats me. The denial can only come from dedicated lifelong NEOCHEATERS. May they soon realize the way of future happiness and prosperity lies with NEO-TECH.

William W., R-7607

Most people, that my eyes sce, choose to spend their lives "somewhere, over the rainbow" searching for emerald cities and easy handouts. Sometimes, they even try the "ends of the rainbow" for pots of gold, lottery miracles and mostly other peoples values.

I choose to be "somewhere, under the rainbow", on a path towards its center where Neo-Tech, RIBI, The Research and Writing Center, I & O Publishing Company and all conscious, benevolent and reality oriented people are.

Richard Z., R-7470

The reality of Neo-Tech and the accessibility of Biological Immortality boggles the mind. All of my life I have felt that external 'authority structures' drained a person of his or her uniqueness and ability to achieve 'honest' greatness.

Even as a child the thought of living forever seemed a possible reality to me. However, it never seemed like I anyone else wanted

551

immortality. I always wondered why. Now, through Neo-Tech, I understand. How could anyone want to live with himself knowing how dishonest and irresponsible he is to himself.

I am presently a Junior High School Biology Teacher and even with my elementary knowledge of the growth and aging of the human body I know that Biological Immortality is a possibility. Until now I never thought that it could be achieved in my life time. Whenever I would read medical reports on how the average life-span of the human being is getting longer I would cheer, hoping against hope that I could hang on long enough for the experts to discover what I already know.

However, people die hoping and life is brought about by action. I want to be a part of that action, as well as a product!! I firmly believe that it is my duty to myself and my family that I be an integral part in the actualization of Biological Immortality, NOW!! When you are ready for my help, I am here.

I also think that you could add a sixth route to the list on page 142:

6) Retention of I-consciousness in the original container.

I eagerly await hearing from you soon.

John S., R-7475

Let me say that the way we are bombarded with myths from childhood does not make this task easy, but with the honest concepts of Neo-Tech the task is possible and worth every bit of the effort.

Nancy B., 493250-2

Dear Dr. Wallace,

I am a 46 year old business woman who has been reading your manuscripts since 1988. Since that beginning manuscript I have had a steady growth in my business and in my happiness. There were times during those growth years that I became stuck, so to speak, but it was because of my own laziness and mysticism. During those periods I have always been able to get comfort and direction from your writings, and then was able to push myself forward again.

Since my first reading of Cassandra's Secret in January of 1994, I have grown by leaps and bounds. I have literally grown by the hour. I have tripled my income honestly and guiltlessly.

I hold Neo-Tech very near and dear to me. I never pass up an opportunity to tell people about our revolution and point out the parasitic political class.

J.V and B.H., R-3359

Dear Doctor Flint,

We have been studying the Neo-Tech Discovery and most of your other products for 2 1/2 years and feel that we are overdue in expressing our gratitude and giving you our comments.

We are a couple in our mid-thirties with three young children. We have found the Neo-Tech concepts to be invaluable in our child rearing, romantic relationship and careers. We can now confidently deal with any person or situation knowing that our guidelines are integrity, the pursuit of happiness, and the avoidance of Neocheaters.

Tremendous amounts of money and time have been saved by the avoidance of guilt-induced 'charitable' donations and so-called 'duty' to one's community.

The Neo-Tech writings were particularly gratifying in that neither one of us had previously found religion to be of any value. It is incredibly encouraging to find an oasis of sanity in this mystical world. We are finding evidence of bicameralism at every turn but we are optimistic that I & O Publishing will succeed in its goal of making this world a more rational one.

John P., J-161

Thank you for showing me how to become a real person at last. Neo-Tech has eliminated whatever doubts or confusion that existed with my own philosophical outlook. I cannot imagine that I shall ever read a more important document and hope soon to introduce my brother to this remarkable discovery.

Lim K., R-201S, SINGAPORE

It is a fantastic piece of work that has been thoroughly researched, analyzed, and presented.

Obie W., R-7468

Upon reading Neo-Tech the first time, I was shocked at what I was reading—especially the God concept. I was a regular devotee to Bible study with the Jehovah's Witnesses, and 1/2 of my family members are baptized members of the congregation. I have never been sold completely on the God-Satan war as being the cause of all our problems, and I have read every self help book imaginable, but Neo-Tech is different. I didn't understand the concepts at first, and I was also afraid to some degree to try and understand (because of mystical notions about Satan, demons, etc. But I finally persuaded myself to give it a second reading and I have begun to get excited about the possibilities. I have ordered the Neo-Think release and "Taps" and I am now dedicating the next few months of my life to becoming all that I can be — without guilt.

Now, I feel like I've been set free. Monumental amounts of energy are energizing.

I'm two-thirds of the way through Neo-Tech II (I've completed I-V) and love it! I can hardly wait to get home from work daily and tackle it again. Already I see what's happening in my surroundings from a fresh perspective. ...All my life I've been called a "leader", "organizer", etc. Really a lot of that is nothing more than my searching for love & care taking. It's affected everything from a (now terminated for 6 yrs) 23 year unhappy marriage to non-romantic relationships, professional and community work.

I've run the gamut in my search and discovery process — Christianity, Scientology, transcendental meditation, est, psychology, countless self-help books, sales books and courses etc. What a waste!

Joan F., NT-2

In the past, I have pondered many times why myself, my husband and daughter just couldn't make the progress we desired. Always there was a stumbling block to hamper our progress. Between all three of us, we have many attributes, and all of us knew that we were honest and true. Yet, we, myself in particular, have always allowed 'friends' to make us feel inferior to them. After having read your concept on 'envy', I can now quite clearly comprehend their motives.

I could kick myself for being such a naive, ignorant fool for so many years.

Paul R., R-3840

I first read Neo-Tech II just over four years ago. I was unemployed. I now own two companies. I can't wait to see what the next four years have to offer. The most important thing about Neo-Tech is being able to see everything clearly.

Louise G. M., NT-3

I am enjoying Neo-Tech so much it's indescribable! When I encounter neo-cheaters my mind focuses on Neo-Tech. I am so alert now I can actually see what these individuals are doing right before my eyes. I often think of how I've wasted years (I'm 56) being involved with Neo-cheaters and mysticism, and the unhappiness and non-prosperity that came with it.

Although I'm just a beginner in the Neo-Tech Discovery, and I'm not out of the woods yet, I feel as if I'm on the road to prosperity, happiness and power that I never knew existed for me. My self-esteem was low and I felt like something was wrong with me. But this was due to the guilt trip theologians, astrologers and other mystics would project on to me. What a hoax. What a hoax.

Neo-Tech has taught me that I've been doing nothing but slowly throwing my life down the road to death. This is a new awakening for me. I'm breaking out of the cob webbed, doldrums of bureaucracy and starting on the road to life and growth. Right now I'm putting together a business of my own. It's on a small scale, but I know it will grown, and being the value producer that I am, before I know it, I'll be an entrepreneur.

I've never read anything as honest and powerful as Neo-Tech II. It says it all. Nothing is left out. I've never learned so much about myself and what's going on around me in all these 56 years I've lived. But on the other hand, I wasn't living, I was suffering from "growth death", because I was so caught up into mysticism. Since I stopped praying and "Thanking god for this and that, asking god for this and that," I have never felt better.

Although I'm still in the early stage of Neo-Tech, I now realize who I am. I've always been creative, but somehow, my creativity has always been taken from me. Now I know who was doing such. The value destroyers, Neo-cheaters.

I still work for Neo-cheaters and Mystics (Federal Government) and have done so for years, and for years they have tried to destroy me. Prior to that I taught in public schools and had the same nasty problems. Right now, I am in the process of getting my own business started so that I can get away from these Neo-cheaters and Mystics so as to become the value producer that I really am. In that way, I will be helping myself and others.

Hopefully, in the near future, Neo-Tech will take over this entire world then everyone will be loyal to honesty, and everyone will be prosperous and happy.

Keep up the good work, Dr. Wallace, and I appreciate you for showing me how to live and grow.

Harold P., 493250-1

Since receiving the Neo-Tech Discovery, I have spent every spare moment reading. I'm on my 4th reading and all of a sudden I see life totally different. I can see why I have been a loser all of my life and why life has seemed to pass me by...No matter what I have done or been involved with, I just couldn't get ahead, (school, scientology, the Christian religion, etc.).

I realize that this whole planet is upside down or backwards or something like that. Everything on planet earth is set up so the average person loses, no matter what! I don't know anyone who is really happy, or if they seem happy, it's just temporary. If they seem rich, they lack in other areas of life. The whole world is upside down! I can now sit back and see how everyone accepts this situation and thinks there is nothing wrong or nothing they can do about it.

Somebody stole my money and happiness and it really angers me. I have seen the source of my lack of life. Everything from MTV to getting a traffic ticket is designed to drain the life of everyone, and the people who are in charge know what they are doing, and I'm angry that they have wasted my life.

Rraci S., 493250-6

Dear Neo-Tech,

I have just finished reading the materials I requested and I must say that I have never had anything shake up my world quite the way your manuscript did. I realized I was blindly following people who would do nothing more than destroy me or worse, never allow me to reach my full potential.

Eric B., 493250-5

Neo-Tech itself is brilliant. It is the first clear and straight forward manuscript in the history of mankind that I am aware of to define a fundamental human purpose, that of happiness, and presents it in such a comprehensive manner.